Praise for Radi~~~~ ~

"Hundreds of books about the history and contemporary experiences of Mexican Americans in the United States have been published since the 1960s. Until now, however, a book on the role of the Mexican American working class in the development of the US Left has remained largely missing. *Radicals in the Barrio* is a remarkable book that fills the gap. In particular, the author has done an excellent job documenting the role of Mexican men and women on both sides of the US–Mexico border who played a significant role in Left organizations beginning with the Industrial Workers of the World (IWW) in the early 1900s to the Socialist and Communist parties, unions, and other Left organizations up to the 1950s. The author also details the reasons for both the emergence of those organizations and their decline. In short, the book is a valuable contribution on the lessons of the past that can be useful for the emergence of new Left organizations in the twenty-first century."

—Dr. Carlos Muñoz, Jr., author of *Youth, Identity, Power*

"Justin Akers Chacón's *Radicals in the Barrio* is a broad, transnational history of the working men and women of greater Mexico. This well-documented book offers a gripping narrative of more than half a century of radical ideologies and organizing among Mexican Americans, ranging from anarchist traditions that predated Mexico's 1910 revolution to Cold War struggles among farm, mine, and other workers across a broad borderland. Two essential takeaways of this excellent book are that US immigration policies and racism structured the economic exploitation of Mexican Americans, and that their transnational labor and struggles were essential to the making of both nations."

—John Lear, author of *Picturing the Proletariat*

"*Radicals in the Barrio* is truly an impressive book. Justin Akers Chacón's study is the rigorous recording of a historical process that propelled social development in the United States and Mexico. The transformation of these countries is analyzed from the social struggles undertaken by men and women located at the very base of American and Mexican societies. To understand the dimension of this research, which covers a wide period until the 1950s, it is sufficient to traverse the bibliography used. It is exhaustive, supported by impressive documentation that includes archival sources, periodicals, testimonials, and iconography that allow Akers Chacón a critical perspective and an undeniable contribution to social history. It is therefore advisable to take a deep breath and carefully and attentively read this exceptional book, and be prepared to better understand our past and our present."

—Javier Torres Parés, professor of history at the Universidad Autónoma de México and author of *La revolución sin frontera*

"Justin Akers Chacón's *Radicals In the Barrio* gives the most comprehensive account we have of the making of the Mexican working class in the United States. From its origins in the transnational experience of extractive and industrial labor in both Mexico and the United States, through the period of the Mexican Revolution and the intense class warfare of the US West in the 1910s, to the organization of agricultural and industrial workers in the 1930s, and through the McCarthy period and the civil rights movement, Akers Chacón focuses on the political experience of Mexican workers. He does all of this within a Marxist framework, and with particular attention to the role of women workers. A formidable book in every way, it will be of interest to labor activists, Latino communities, and scholars. I highly recommend it."

—Dan La Botz, author of *What Went Wrong? The Nicaraguan Revolution*

"It is impossible to overestimate the importance of Mexican workers in the US working class, yet their story is little known outside academia. Justin Akers Chacón has set out to change this, with a thorough, detailed, and well-told recounting of their history. What a history it is—miners fighting a US boss and starting the Mexican Revolution, taking on the Rockefellers in Colorado's coal wars, providing the backbone for Communist- and Socialist-led strikes in the California fields, or organizing the unemployed and homeless to build a base for the historic pecan strike in San Antonio.

Akers Chacón pays attention to the radical ideology that drove the social struggles of Mexican people in the United States, not just their actions and tactics. He profiles the activists who developed that ideology, from Texas Communist strike leader Emma Tenayuca and "The Mexican Question" to Bert Corona, father of the modern immigrant rights movement, and to Luisa Moreno who led the CIO in California in its most radical years. Their desire to change society fundamentally is a contribution that still resounds among workers and in unions today.

Akers Chacón shows that linking working-class struggles in the United States and Mexico isn't just a product of NAFTA, or the recent decades of deportations. Emma Tenayuca went to the "Workers University" organized by labor leaders in Mexico City. Radicals in the Workers Alliance fought deportations throughout the Southwest eighty years ago.

It's not just that this history belongs to working people today. Akers Chacón describes in detail the importance Mexican workers gave to left-wing politics and organizing. This is rich material for understanding their value to winning the same fights today. Akers Chacón's book is at the same time exciting history and a resource with real meaning for Trump-era struggles for social justice."

—David Bacon, author of *Illegal People* and *The Right to Stay Home*

Radicals in the Barrio

Magonistas, Socialists, Wobblies, and Communists in the Mexican American Working Class

Justin Akers Chácon

Haymarket Books
Chicago, IL

© 2018 Justin Akers Chacón

Published in 2018 by
Haymarket Books
P.O. Box 180165
Chicago, IL 60618
www.haymarketbooks.org

ISBN: 978-1-60846-775-4

Trade distribution:
In the US, Consortium Book Sales and Distribution, www.cbsd.com
In Canada, Publishers Group Canada, www.pgcbooks.ca
In the UK, Turnaround Publisher Services, www.turnaround-uk.com
All other countries, Ingram Publisher Services International,
IPS_Intlsales@ingramcontent.com

This book was published with the generous support of
Lannan Foundation and Wallace Action Fund.

Cover design by Eric Kerl.

Printed in Canada by union labor.

Library of Congress Cataloging-in-Publication data is available.

10 9 8 7 6 5 4 3 2 1

Dedicated to the memory of Guadalupe Chacón Mena y Magaña

Contents

Part 4

Introduction

"The United States can intervene in Mexico with men and it can intervene
with money. It can intervene with guns and it can intervene with gold.
The means differ but the purpose and the effect are the same. The cause of
liberty can be shot to death by long-range guns from Washington, Berlin,
and London just as readily as by rapid firing guns at Mexico City."
—**Pancho Villa**

The Mexican working class has a long and deeply rooted history in the United States, one that is intimately interwoven into the experience of the labor movement as a whole, and one in which Mexican workers have played a pivotal or leading role at its most critical junctures. Alongside epochs of rising class struggle has co-evolved a rich tradition of Mexican labor radicalism, referring to the formation of left-wing political ideologies that have informed collective action. Anticapitalist political doctrine entered into Mexico with European immigrants and co-evolved with indigenous and organic expressions of Mexican radicalism. While the Mexican working-class experience has been intrinsically interconnected with other segments of the working class in the United States, Mexican workers, and especially those who migrated after the turn of the century, brought with them a radical and revolutionary tradition emanating from their collective experiences in Mexico.

US Imperialism in Mexico

An historical analysis that links the experiences of the working class in Mexico, Mexican migrants to the US, and the Mexican American working class must begin with a discussion of US-Mexican relations at the turn of the twentieth century. The nexus of US imperialist domination of Mexico, class conflict, radical ideological formation, revolutionary struggle, transnational migration, and political cross-fertilization infuse the character of Mexican labor radicalism in the United States. The Mexican laboring classes, while not triumphal, were instrumental in shaping the course of events and outcomes of the revolutionary process in Mexico. As transnational workers, they took their organizations, traditions, and doctrines with them into the United States. There, this outlook and their experiences cross-fertilized with radical organizations and the dynamics of class struggle north of the border. As an integral part of this working class, Mexican workers also influenced the trajectory of the labor movement in the United States.

Between 1876 and 1910, Mexico underwent a tumultuous period of uneven and combined capitalist development.[1] This was driven externally by the imperialism of the United States and the European powers, who scrambled to extend their empires into the rich soil of Mexico. Three factors influenced US capitalists to stake out a claim over

1

Mexico's natural resources, markets, and labor. Corporations were legislated into existence to serve as the progenitors of capital accumulation, reinvestment, and profiteering on an international scale.[2] Secondly, the international banking crises of 1871, 1893, and 1907 led the US and European nations to expand their investments into Latin American and Caribbean markets, "looking for political stability and monetary mechanisms that would permit them the most favorable conditions for their business operations."[3]

The third impulse was driven by international competition. As US investors began to enter foreign markets, they found Europeans were already afoot in extending their own economic spheres of influence in the same terrain. The first US intervention into the world-imperialist system began with the acquisition of Caribbean and Asian colonies after the defeat of decaying regional rival Spain in 1898. As international competition increased in contested places such as Mexico, each country's diplomatic corps and military attachés became the arbiters of their nation's capitalist interests there, contributing to Mexico becoming one of the staging grounds for World War I.

For instance, despite allusions to the peaceful nature of international commercial expansion, US capitalist investment in Mexico came up against the threat of both European competition and popular revolt. Military power served as the scaffolding for projecting and protecting US investments, and so the development of an armed force to fulfill foreign policy objectives occurred in tandem with economic expansion beyond US borders. As Frederick Howe observed:

> This is the immediate background of war and preparations of war, of preparedness, navalism, and the overseas interests of the great powers. Earlier foreign policies were bent on the maintenance of national boundaries and the preservation of the balance of power. The new imperialism is interested in loans, concessions, protectorates, spheres of influence, the closed door, and other privileges arising from the financial interests of the ruling classes, which have become world-wide in their extent.[4]

After the Mexicans ejected the French colonial regime in 1867 and repudiated the emperor's debts, European capitalists colluded to lock Mexico out of international capital markets as punishment.[5] They were not interested in seeing Mexico develop as a potential rival, but rather as a large store of untapped resources for their own enrichment. When international capitalists entered Mexico, they were not seeking "free markets" for which to compete, but rather they wanted to extend internationally their existing monopolies or create new ones.

Vladimir Lenin described this as a tendency for foreign capitalists to be a corrupting influence in the dominated markets, making corruption itself an institutional form of doing business.[6] For this reason, the alliances formed between international capitalists and their local partners were saturated with payoffs, bribes, collusion, palace intrigues, and other techniques aimed at advancing their own interests against rivals and competing cliques.[7] Oil baron Edward Doheny pithily summarized the American formula this way: "You first try to win a man over, and failing this, you buy him."[8]

In their pursuits, foreign capitalists cultivated junior partners in the Mexican bourgeoisie. These cliques were geographically represented, with the most established group being a collection of prominent, old-money landowners and merchants known derisively as "Los Científicos" (the "scientific ones"). These men were typically *capitalinos* who were gathered around the self-styled dictatorship of Porfirio Díaz (1876–1910). A second group was clustered in the far north of the country and had more recently built their fortunes as a result of Díaz's pro-capitalist policies and through partnerships with foreign capital.

Lacking large stores of capital and infrastructure, they saw attracting foreign investment from established, liberal-minded capitalist nations as a key to accelerating modernization. Científico thought envisaged the development of a native bourgeoisie through partnership with foreign capital, which, in theory, had a direct interest in supporting the rise of a like-minded liberal capitalist state along its southern border. Admiring their northern neighbors, the Científicos envisioned this as a spiritual "liberal front" with American Republicans, whose surplus capital could be deposited in Mexico, ensuring US investors profit while helping to foster a neighboring state in their own image.

Central to their project was the privatization of indigenous and communal land and unrestricted foreign capital investment, which necessitated the suppression of resistance movements that challenged rapid capitalist "modernization." According to Justo Sierra, a leading light of this school, Mexico's working majority had to be compliant, wages had to be suppressed, and unions had to prohibited in order to make Mexico stable for capitalist development, leading him to call for a "social dictatorship" in Mexico.[9] As Jorge Basurto explains, the liberal state under Porfirio Díaz

> assumed its role as regulator of the new relations of production; but with Mexican capitalism developing from a backwards and dependent position and having to manage the development of the country, the most important aspect was to impede any form of defensive action by the proletariat: in the relations between the national bourgeoisie and the proletariat to encourage capital accumulation, and between the international bourgeoisie and the proletariat in order to create the ideal conditions to attract foreign capital.[10]

Part of the allure of investing in Mexico was the abundance of exploitable labor. US owners willfully adapted to and embraced existing local coercive labor practices. This started with purchasing the services of labor contractors, local *jefes políticos* (state-aligned political bosses) or relying on the federal rural police (*Rurales*) to keep workers in line through constant surveillance and draconian punishment. In the oil camps, for instance, disobedient workers could be subjected to various forms of corporal punishment, put in stocks overnight, forced to work against their will, or arrested and expelled from the camp without any form of due process.[11] State-sanctioned repression became even more urgent when workers began to rebel against their conditions.

British, French, and other European capital had entered Mexico as early as the 1830s. By 1896, the Díaz government had abolished all barriers to foreign investment and offered monopoly privileges, tax exclusions, tariff exemptions, and concessions to exploit natural resources, clearing the way for foreign corporate ascendancy within the Mexican economy.[12] This opened the floodgates for US capital, as regional cabals of investment bankers and speculative combinations in the US jockeyed for position to finance the exploitation of Mexico's wealth and make their fortunes.[13]

In 1902, investment bankers such as Goldman Sachs, & Company, Lehman Brothers, J.P. Morgan and Company, and others opened up a branch of the International Banking Company in Mexico City, becoming the first multinational bank, which soon operated on a global scale.[14] Through its Mexican operations, it distributed some 250 loans totaling $1 billion between 1900 and 1913, with the largest amount earmarked for Mexico.

These loans financed the activities of US-based companies seeking to extend their operations into Mexico, or speculators pursuing quick fortunes. Between the years 1890 and 1910, over forty stock companies were organized to direct investment in Mexico in the cattle-production and farming industries alone.[15] The massive infusion of foreign capital, led by the US, increased exponentially. As early as 1900, foreigners owned outright 172 of 212 commercial establishments in the Federal District.[16] By 1906, 943 North American–owned businesses had been established throughout Mexico, and total US investment increased from $200 million in 1897 to nearly $1.1 billion in 1911.[17]

In the scramble for Mexico, US capital competed with European rivals Great Britain, France, and Germany. In his study of economic imperialism in Mexico, José Luis Ceseña looked at the prominence of foreign capital in Mexico's seven largest industries in 1910 and 1911. Foreign capital arranged through investment companies controlled 100 percent of Mexico's oil (US share: 40 percent); 97.5 percent of mining and metallurgy (US share: 81 percent); 96 percent of agricultural production (US share: 67 percent); 85 percent of manufacturing (US share: 15 percent); 77 percent of the banking system (US share: 18 percent); 87 percent of electricity production (US share: 8 percent); and 27 percent of railroads (US share: 9 percent; although US investors controlled a 50 percent share in the "national" rail system).[18] By 1912, an estimated 62 percent of total foreign direct investment came from the US, which surpassed the investment of its rivals and the total Mexican national investment. Mexico was seen as an extension of the US for economic purposes.[19]

Key to the integration of the Mexican economy's strategic sectors into US and international markets was the development of a national railroad system. Railroads reduced transportation costs and connected regional, national, and international markets, and drove up the market value of land, fueling rampant speculation. The Díaz regime granted extensive land concessions to British and US railroad interests and in some cases paid them from the Mexican treasury to lay track. This could range between $6,000 and $15,000 per mile depending on the terrain, and sometimes investors were granted additional land-use rights, tax exemptions, and other blandishments.[20]

Between the years 1877 and 1910 the railroads expanded from 400 miles to nearly 12,000, with US capital accounting for 61 percent ($644 million) of the total investment.[21] The impetus for the explosive growth was given by the passage of a federal law in 1882 that allowed for the expropriation of all lands required for public works. This was one of the various mechanisms used to radically shift the social balance of power and privilege toward the primacy of foreign investment. As historian Teresa M. Van Hoy concludes:

> The law was intended to force railroad development on rural and provincial communities of late 19th-century Mexico, as is indicated in the ministry's instructions to the first federal agent hired to implement it. The instructions stated that the expropriation law gave ample grounds so that an "intelligent person can wield successfully the weapons which it [the law] offers" in order to gain access quickly and cheaply to the land necessary for railroad development.[22]

The expansion of the railroads was essential for linking Mexico's nodes of production and transporting goods and people, with oil production and export being the greatest prize.

The foreign colonization of Mexico's rich oil deposits took shape in a similar manner. The Díaz regime passed a law in 1901 that designated its right to grant concessions to foreign investors on public land and excluded oil deposits from public domain claims. Oil companies, investors, and speculators poured into the country in search of quick profits. By 1907, a single American oil speculator, Edward Doheny, controlled half of all oil production in Mexico, making an estimated $10 million in profit each year through 1925 (in today's currency, about $230 million yearly).[23] By 1916 around 400 oil companies were known to be in operation; 75 percent were American owned.[24] An estimated 2,500 American personnel and 4,000 total foreign nationals were living and working in Mexico's oil zones during this time. All told, by 1917 Mexican oil fields were churning out 55 million barrels annually, of which 97 percent was controlled by foreign (mostly American) interests.[25] Other sectors, such as the vast textile industry centered in the state of Veracruz, were dominated by French capital.[26]

US and European capitalist interests also had a significant foothold in agriculture, land speculation, energy, and banking. Effective control extended not only over the export of oil, precious metals, and minerals, but also beef and cowhides, cotton, chickpeas, rubber, vanilla, sugar, guayule, henequen, chicle, and ixtle.[27] British bankers set up the first commercial bank in Mexico, the Banco de Londres y México (Bank of London and Mexico) in 1864. French merchant capitalists and US investors joined efforts to counter the British by funding the Banco Nacional de Mexico in 1884. By 1910, these two banks controlled 75 percent of the nation's deposits.[28] Furthermore, in 1902, US investors set up the International Banking Corporation as a "conduit for US investments in government bonds and securities, mining, oil companies, agriculture, timber and ranching," qualifying it as the first US-based multinational bank.[29] Most foreign banks operated outside of the direct supervision of the Mexican government, and were typically capitalized at a rate three times higher than their Mexican counterparts.[30]

Empire and Racism

As an extension of class relations in the United States, racism was instrumental in the functioning of US imperialism in Mexico. US intervention into Mexico evoked a racist paternalism in the discourse of the investor class, national political circles, and in the media; contextualizing the plunder of economically subjugated people as a "civilizing mission" on behalf of a self-proclaimed superior people. As an anteced-ent of the contemporary notion of "humanitarian military intervention," disruptive foreign investment, military invasion and occupation, and the imposition of colo-nial-like relationships became couched in such language so as to reaffirm national-istic and chauvinistic sentiment among the general populace.

Clarence W. Barron, the owner of Dow Jones & Company, manager of the *Wall Street Journal*, and founder of *Barron's* magazine, was one of the most influential fi-nancial thinkers of the era. In his widely read 1917 book, *The Mexican Problem*, he pro-moted a paternalistic racism and heavy-handed imperative for imposing economic imperialism, stating that "[t]he redemption of Mexico must be from the invasion of business, forcing upon the natives—the good people of Mexico—technical training, higher wages, bank accounts, financial independence, and the rights of citizenship and accumulation."[31]

Another intellectual proponent of US expansionism affirmed in *Harper's New Monthly Magazine* in 1881:

> It is doubtful if any equal area on the face of the globe possesses larger deposits of the precious metals. . . . Now it is evident that any rapid progress in Mex-ico must come through the colonization of some higher and more progressive race, or by the introduction of capital in large amounts to develop her natural resources by the aid of native races, who are peaceable and industrious.[32]

From the boardrooms of the leading investment houses in New York, Jim Crow racial stratification was required to maximize profits, and maintained from the fields of California to the mines of Arizona. This practice was reproduced within US-controlled zones in Mexico. As Gilbert Gonzalez describes it,

> Blacks brought from the United States served as cooks and porters while whites were the managers and administrative personnel. Chinese immigrants cooked, cleaned, and washed in the American oil camps. More than just segregation marked the distinction between the American foreigner and the Mexican; the for-mer dominated the town and often the region both economically and politically.[33]

The importation and vertical integration of foreign labor within Mexican industry was most notable in the railroads, where "[r]egional operating managers, train engineers, brakemen, clerks, telegraph operators, line men, and track foremen were Americans."[34]

US personnel in Mexico were often housed in finer dwellings, given the better jobs, and paid more for the same work. They were also more likely to enjoy upward mobility, as English was used as the official language of business operations above manual labor. Racial divides reinforced social distance between European Americans and Mexicans that retarded skill transfer and local development. Often, indigenous workers were employed and treated with disdain. As Jonathon Brown describes racial divides in the Mexican oil fields: "Back in the States, these men willingly taught the oil field business to their white brothers who had come off the farms. They did not teach the skills of modernization, however, to those whom they considered racially or ethnically inferior."[35] Even skilled Mexican workers were often shunned and disallowed from sharing in profits, growth, or development. In one recorded case, a journeyman Mexican miner named Luis Canizeros helped a group of American investors locate several million-dollar veins of gold. Despite his efforts, he was denied a share of the wealth, and later offered testimony that the American managers didn't "think a Mexican could do anything but carry ore."[36]

Brown further concludes that the social structure of imperialism reproduced a new form of the colonial-era caste system:

> Foreign [US] personnel occupied the ranks of the privileged, exactly as had the Spaniards in the colonial period. Native-born mestizos occupied the ranks of the semiskilled. Itinerant *campesinos*, many of them Indian, entered the work force at the lowest rank as peons ... [This] new social hierarchy had many similarities to past models—except that the non-Spanish speaking, non-Catholic foreign workers were not immigrants and could not be absorbed.[37]

For their part, the Mexican bourgeoisie also promoted racial ideology. Two prominent and influential liberal academics who informed Científico thought, philologist Francisco Pimentel and demographer Antonio García Cubas, wrote in the 1860s that the indigenous population (about 40 percent of the 10 million Mexicans in 1875, and a substantial component of the agricultural proletariat) could not be integrated into a modern Mexico, but had to either be dispensed with or forcibly dismantled and gradually intermixed with European immigrants.[38] Through the characterization of their own population as intrinsically backward, the liberals embarked on a project that gave foreign capitalist speculators priority over national economic development.[39]

Empire and Migration

Through imperial arrangements, foreign capital sources and their Mexican partners profited enormously, with little or no intention to develop internal markets, share technical expertise, or reinvest in Mexican social development. The massive transfer of wealth, coupled with the dispossession of millions from the land and the integration of Mexican regional markets into the United States through the railroads, induced the beginning of Mexican mass emigration to the United States, especially the southwestern states of Texas, New Mexico, Colorado, Arizona, and California. With the expanding railroad complex linking regional Mexican cities to the US Southwest, capitalist "modernization" induced contradictory circumstances in which foreign investment led to economic immiseration for the laboring classes, while simultaneously providing the means to escape it.

It was commonly circulated information among the foreign business community that the average annual rate of profit was 10 percent to 15 percent of investment during the era of the Díaz regime (known in Spanish as the *Porfiriato*), while in the peak years of 1895–1900, return on investment reached 20 to 25 percent.[40] In mining the rate of return for investors reached astronomical levels. Mexican historian Gastón García Cantú cites some shocking examples: between the years 1899 and 1909 two of the largest US-owned mining companies, Los Peñoles and Dos Estrellas, returned dividends to their investors at the rate of 2,876 percent and 2,520 percent respectively.[41]

As a result, a new class of American multimillionaires cropped up from profits derived from investments in Mexico. Oil magnates like Edward Doheny, William Buckley, Henry Clay Pierce, and others amassed personal fortunes amounting to the hundreds of millions.[42] Not only did wealth accrue in the hands of speculators, but the benefits of transferring Mexico's national resources at relatively low costs were a boon for US economic development as a whole. Between 1911 and 1919, for instance, crude oil export to the United States increased from 1 percent to 80 percent of total Mexican production.[43]

The patterns of investment led to substantial transfers of wealth and natural resources from Mexico to the United States. For instance, the pattern of railroad construction linked Mexico's resource-rich regions directly to major economic hubs north of the border. By 1910, for example, 77 percent of Mexico's mineral exports were shipped directly to US markets.[44] At the same time, foreign-owned railroads charged up to 50 percent less to transport agricultural products for export to US markets than they charged to deliver to domestic markets within Mexico.[45] This monopoly over the movement of goods stymied the development of domestic industries, limited circulation of commodities within internal markets, and inhibited Mexican trade with Europe.[46]

Substantial wealth transfers also took place in other industries. Between 1900 and 1910, for instance, US-owned mines in Mexico paid investors $95 million in dividends, an amount that surpassed by 24 percent the combined net earnings of all the banks based solely in the United States over the same period. Standard Oil's Mexican subsidiaries paid yearly dividends amounting to 600 percent of its capitalization annually in the first six years of the twentieth century, reflecting profits that ranged between $2 and $3 million per year.[47] According to Raymond Vernon, companies that had negotiated oil concessions during the Porfiriato received on average a mere 10 percent tax levy on their profits, an arrangement unheard of anywhere in the oil-producing world ever since.[48] The value of Mexico's exports not only enriched US investors and speculators in Mexico, it also benefitted US consumers and stimulated economic development in secondary ways in the United States. By 1918 total Mexican exports amounted to $183.6 million, of which $175 million was destined for US markets.[49]

As wealth derived from Mexican land, resources, and labor flowed north, so too did a growing number of Mexican laborers as they became displaced from within the Mexican economy. The export of wealth through its extraction and repatriation to the United States, as opposed to its local development, more equitable distribution through sustainable wages and tax redistribution, and reinvestment; meant that localized economies were disrupted and destroyed in foreign-investment-heavy regions of Mexico and access to land or sustainable employment declined in relation to the existing populations. This forced growing pools of redundant rural labor to migrate elsewhere for sustenance.

By 1910, it is estimated that 80 percent of the 15 million people in Mexico lived in rural regions (where agriculture and mining were prominent economic activities), and an estimated 98 percent of this population was landless.[50] While difficult to gauge out-migration to the United States among such a large and transient population, national estimates of out-migration to other parts of Mexico or to the United States range from 4 to 17 percent of the total population leaving their respective states to find work elsewhere, numbering in the hundreds of thousands. Economic displacement, coupled with the outbreak of revolution, resulting inflation and rising prices, starvation, oversaturation of diminished labor markets, high unemployment, declining working conditions, and violence led an estimated one million people to move to the United States by 1920.[51] By 1930, over 1.5 million Mexicans lived in the United States, with the great majority settling in Texas, California, Arizona, and New Mexico.[52] This sparked a mass population shift northward from within the heartland of Mexico that continued as US capitalism became structurally dependent on Mexican labor for its accumulation, sustenance, and growth. Between 1900 and 1940, for instance, the total population of the US and Mexican border states increased from 6 million to 14.5 million, with most of the growth coming from central and southern Mexico.[53]

The depletion of the Mexican rural population coincides with the growth of the Mexican population in the United States and the expansion of capitalist production based on their labor in the Southwest. According to Arthur F. Corwin and Lawrence A. Cardoso:

> The economic development of the American Southwest coincided with the northward drift of Mexico's population. Railroads, using Mexican and other immigrant labor, integrated the Southwest into the nation's industrial economy. Mining shifted from precious metals to industrial minerals such as copper and coal, as in New Mexico, Arizona, Colorado, Utah, and Oklahoma. Copper mines in the West increased from three in 1869 to 180 in 1909, and coal mining, heavily using Mexican labor, boomed in those states. Citrus and cotton cultivation in California, Arizona, and the lower Rio Grande Valley of Texas flourished because of rail facilities, cheap labor, and desert irrigation projects encouraged by the federal Newlands Act of 1902.[54]

While emigrants poured out of Mexico, others joined revolutionary uprisings. The scale of US investment, ownership, and influence within Mexico reached a point that alarmed even the most sycophantic admirers of US capital in the Mexican bourgeoisie. In an effort to prevent the singular domination of US capital over the national economy, sections of the Mexican bourgeoisie, including Díaz himself, expedited partnership with German, French, British, and Japanese capital to serve as a counterweight.[55] Some contingents of Mexican capitalists that had profited from these arrangements, including northern landowning capitalists such as Francisco Madero and Venustiano Carranza, began to turn against the Díaz regime after popular uprisings against imperialist exploitation threatened to undermine the existing capitalist system as a whole.

Empire, Class Struggle, and the Mexican Revolution

Imperialism in Mexico contributed to rapid economic development, but in a way that accelerated an extreme inequality and polarization between social classes, eventually producing the revolutionary uprisings of the early twentieth century. American capitalists carved out for themselves large swaths of Mexican territory and natural resources and, in the process, created an asymmetric industrial base that subordinated Mexican national and social development to the needs of US and international accumulation and consumption. The patterns of development created a "simultaneous process of integration and marginalization," where foreign-controlled markets within Mexico were linked by railroad to international markets, while large segments of the national economy were neglected and reduced to marginal backwaters.[56]

Foreign interests formed relationships with Mexican *políticos* and used their money and influence to shape economic policy as well as draw on the repressive forces of the state to police local populations. Racism was also a mechanism of imperialist implantation and control, as European Americans carried with them their homegrown notions of white superiority into Mexico. Taken together, the forms in which US imperialism operated in Mexico retarded its development by siphoning wealth out of the country, precluding skill and technology transfer as well as local social development, and displacing millions of people, creating a vast and volatile landless proletariat.

Furthermore, despite the rapid growth of foreign investment in the Mexican economy during the Porfiriato, the wealth generated was distributed unevenly. Between 1850 and 1910, real wages in the industries remained relatively constant while worker productivity increased substantially.[57] Between 1900 and 1910, the general price indices for the majority of consumer goods increased 32 percent.[58] Furthermore, economic historian Aurora Gómez-Galvarri observed that the value of real wages actually declined 18 percent between 1907 and 1910.[59]

The Porfirian alliance broke down by the first decade of the twentieth century, cracked by the rise of class struggle as capitalist crisis and pent-up opposition to existing arrangements came out into the open. The first manifestation of revolutionary agitation occurred from within a reinvigorated liberal opposition, in the form of the Partido Liberal Mexicano (Mexican Liberal Party; referred to by its Spanish-language acronym PLM and *magonistas* throughout the text). The radical middle-class left wing of the party, led by Ricardo Flores Magón, took direct action to topple the dictatorship in 1906. The development and progress of this movement, which evolved into a transnational, anticapitalist, and revolutionary organization with a working-class orientation by 1908, will be the subject of in-depth analysis in this work.

Several factors contributed to the overthrow of Porfirio Díaz after nearly forty years in power. First and foremost was a profound economic crisis that rattled the national economy in 1907 and 1908, intensifying the regional and political fracturing of the bourgeoisie that was by then already at an advanced stage. The high level of integration into the US economy made Mexico more vulnerable to economic convulsions in the United States, itself under stress from the 1907 world financial crisis. During the crisis, the cost of basic food necessities skyrocketed, while the banks raised interest rates and cut credit, and the government fell deeper into debt. Mining and agricultural production collapsed and numerous banks failed, cutting off lines of credit and throwing thousands of workers into unemployment. Reflecting a rapidly growing imbalance of payments, the country's external debt increased fivefold, from $127 million in 1890 to $578 million US dollars on the eve of the revolution.[60] The crisis coincided with a substantial drought and crop failure in the north, and the first major spasms of revolt among the industrial working class as their standard of living plummeted. These strikes broke out in predominantly foreign-controlled industrial sectors, shaking the confidence of foreign investors in Díaz's ability to continue his reign with more significant convulsion.

While the US government and capitalist class had long favored the continuity and stability of Díaz, the breakdown of the dictatorship led them to abandon the flagging leader. This was accelerated as the Mexican government began to curry favor with European capital to counter US control. In 1905, Díaz terminated the "free-trade zone" established in the border region in 1885, which gave primacy to US investors, granted oil concessions to the British, and began to aggressively nationalize the majority of national railroads.[61] The rise of the wealthy Coahuila-based landowner Francisco Madero presented a palatable alternative to US investors, who were wary about the looming threat of destabilization of the Díaz government, and the regime's shift in favor given to European capital. The US-educated Madero had partnership ties to US capital, was from one of the richest families in Mexico, firmly opposed land redistribution to the poor, and focused on moderate electoral reform.[62] In a 1908 book entitled *La Sucesión Presidencial en 1910* (The Presidential Succession of 1910), he presented himself to both the Mexican elite and foreign investors as the best hope to contain the agrarian and labor radicalism unleashed by the crumbling Díaz regime. In it, he proposed a liberal democratic system with universal suffrage, the right for workers to organize unions, public education, and an end to the costly and violent wars against the Indians.[63] Writing the book amid a series of national strikes, he communicated a subtle warning to his class that the repression and impoverishment of *porfirismo* was stirring the laboring classes into revolt:

> With such motive, and with legitimate right, the workers have organized themselves aggressively, constituting a powerful league. They began by organizing their forces to engage the fight, and following the example of workers all over the world, they unite in order to not succumb in the incessant struggle between labor and capital.[64]

Madero was the product of the aspiring northern bourgeoisie, itself a product of porfirismo, that now attributed some of the main obstacles of effective government to foreign economic domination and its attendant corruption and social underdevelopment perpetuated by Díaz.[65] Despite his conservative economic positions, his 1910 electoral campaign for president was violently repressed by Díaz.[66] After escaping arrest, he fled to San Antonio, Texas, where he was allowed by the US government to arrange his government in exile and proclaim his Plan de San Luis Potosí. With the tacit support of President William Howard Taft, Madero's plan called for an armed revolution to begin on November 20, 1910, which temporarily united his supporters, with the radical magonistas into the *maderista* army.

In a show of support for Madero, leading bankers in the United States cut off credit to the weakening regime, signaling their decision that Díaz's time had come.[67] The US government then sent warships to the Gulf of Mexico and troops to the Texas border four months after the initiation of the revolution. The US also intended for the show of force to serve as a warning to Germany and Great Britain, which had their own interest in the outcomes of the conflict, as well as to the radical wing of the of the revolutionary movement, which began to articulate its own actions and demands. After the maderistas captured Ciudad Juárez, the revolutionary forces began to seize territory across the nation, and concurrent popular uprisings in Mexico City against the dictatorship threatened to topple the whole regime, the porfirista oligarchy withdrew its support from Díaz. As a result, Díaz capitulated and went into exile on May 31, 1911.[68]

Hastily organized elections officially brought Madero into the presidency in October of 1911, and he quickly affirmed the continuation of the Díaz military and state bureaucracy, albeit under his authority. The federal army, the repressive arm of the Porfirian state, was understood as the essential guarantor of the land tenure system, and was left intact. At the same time, the campaign significantly raised expectations among the laboring classes for radical change. First and foremost was the desire for land redistribution, a demand first espoused by the magonistas and the PLM, followed by radical agrarian campaigns led by Emiliano Zapata in Morelos and Francisco "Pancho" Villa in Chihuahua. The ability to contain radicalism of this sort was critical for continued US support.

In response to his legalization of unions, socialists and anarchists in Mexico formed the Casa del Obrero Mundial (International Workers' Center; COM), which began to organize the working class along militant and industrial lines with an orientation toward class struggle in the foreign-owned industries. Madero then turned against the nascent radicalism after worker self-activity grew beyond the limited scope he was willing to tolerate. (The experience of the COM, representing the most significant development of working-class radicalism and self-organization in the revolutionary period, will also be discussed in this work.) In the countryside, he unleashed the federal army to suppress the zapatistas. The federal army failed in its efforts to squash agrarian land seizures, which began to spread to other parts of the country.

By 1913, domestic and foreign capital was reeling from the threat of radical land expropriations as revolutionary armies began to take shape. Squeezed between radicalizing labor and revolutionary agrarians on one side, and anxious oligarchs, investors, and landowners on the other, the base of support for Madero collapsed. The imperial representatives from different nations, previously in a state of low-intensity competition, now closed ranks against Madero as they began to sense revolution. Led by the United States, they conspired with Porfirian military officials to carry out a coup.

From the very top of the US government, the orders were given. President Taft, his secretary of state, Philander Knox, and appointed ambassador to Mexico Henry Lane

Wilson, engineered a coup led by porfirista general Victoriano Huerta to topple and murder Madero. The coup, orchestrated in February of 1913, brought together disparate elements who put aside their differences to unite against an existential threat in the form of a popular insurrection and to maintain the rule of capital over labor. Even on the eve of World War I, foreign powers, US and European investors and corporate representatives, the old porfirian-aligned oligarchy and Catholic Church, the Científicos, and the reactionary military hierarchy all supported the effort to bury the revolution.

Within one year, in April of 1914, the US invaded Mexican territory once again. While the previous administration had helped to topple Madero, the incoming government of Woodrow Wilson withheld recognition of Huerta's regime as the revolution raged on, and refused to sell his administration arms. Reminiscent of Díaz and Maderos's concerns over US imperial predominance, Huerta began favoring British over US oil interests and staking out diplomatic recognition and backing from European governments, purchasing arms and munitions from them as a means to consolidate his power.

This became a source of contention after Wilson publicly announced his opposition to Huerta, telling British diplomat Sir William Tyrell that he aimed "not merely to force Huerta from power, but also to exert every influence [the United States] can to secure Mexico a better government under which all contracts and business concessions will be safer than they have ever been."[69] Historian Alan Knight contends that Wilson believed that Huerta's incompetency and brutal dictatorship fueled destabilization and a more unpredictable outcome for the revolution.[70] Under manufactured pretenses, Wilson ordered a naval invasion and occupation of the Gulf port city of Veracruz.[71] Of concern was the security of the US-controlled oil fields in the region, which was threatened by the advance of popular revolutionary armies. The occupation did not end until the United States received assurances from the dominant faction of Venustiano Carranza, who became president in 1914, that US interests would be protected.[72] The threat of US intervention remained constant during the course of the revolution.[73]

Bowing to US threats and beset by increasing military defeats from revolutionary armies in the north, Huerta resigned and fled shortly thereafter. The defeat of the counterrevolution transitioned to the second, social phase of the revolution. Between 1914 and 1920, revolutionary forces composed of different class forces fought it out militarily, in the factories and workshops, and over the control of land and natural resources.[74] While the proletarian leadership elements were unable to cohere an independent, class-based party and political program capable of uniting the urban and rural working class, they shaped, and were shaped by, every stage of the process.

Through their participation in the Mexican Revolution, a "bourgeois democratic" revolution, sectors of the laboring classes developed and refined their own class-conscious ideologies, grounded in anticapitalism, anti-imperialism, and various manifestations of socialist thought. The Mexican migrants carried these traditions with them into the barrios of the Southwest, where they came into contact and conflict, and in some cases converged with US working-class ideologies. The first and most dominant representative of these ideologies was the business unionism and racial exclusionism of the American Federation of Labor.

Empire and the American Federation of Labor (AFL)

The boosters of empire within the major political parties in the United States found an ally in the emerging conservative leadership of the American Federation of Labor (AFL) by the turn of the twentieth century. The AFL, the primary labor federation in the United States, had become a mostly white, craft-based, national labor body that had shed the Socialist pretenses of its early days and aligned itself politically with the aims of the US capitalist class on the questions of empire. The US territorial acquisition of Cuba, Puerto Rico, and the Philippines after the Spanish-American War raised a fundamental question of empire-building at the turn of the century: Would the US engage in old-style colonial administration or endeavor to control foreign economies without the enormous costs and conflicts associated with direct military occupation? The capitalist class within both major parties fragmented into rival camps over the issue, which became known as the "Imperialists" and the misnamed "Anti-Imperialist League."

While majorities within both camps served the burgeoning capitalist appetite for international expansion under the framework of American exceptionalism, they differed on the specific methods of empire-building. Imperialists generally embraced annexation or direct rule along the lines of the European systems. The anti-imperialists promoted a vision of free markets, where the US could dominate from the outside by wielding its preponderant economic power and control the markets, exchange, resources, and trade policies of other countries. The inherent instability of this arrangement necessitated military buildup and geo-strategic positioning of US naval forces to maximize armed intervention and protect investments and aligned client regimes when necessary.[75]

The craft unions of the AFL denounced "old-style colonialism" because it opened up the possibility for capitalists to export capital and production to captive labor at the expense of craft workers. They also opposed annexation as it would create a pathway of citizenship—and thus the right to migrate—for colonized people. This, they believed, enabled capitalists to encourage an influx of foreign workers into US labor markets to weaken union leverage. They supported the nonterritorial imperial expansion of US capitalism through the creation of free markets, as these endeavors opened up new territories and markets for manufactured goods and created access to cheaply attained raw materials. To facilitate expansion, they favored a buildup of the military, support for a US-created transoceanic canal, and the Open Door policy in China under the claim of "equal trade rights . . . for all nations."[76] At the same time, they opposed the idea that the US was obligated to invest in industrial development abroad, as that would create international competition with US-based production and undermine their advantage. Through these positions, the AFL became more explicitly aligned with the Democratic wing of the ruling capitalist cliques.

As part of its imperial orientation, the AFL leadership became enthusiastically pro-war and increasingly receptive to white supremacist doctrine. The leadership supported the Spanish-American War, pledging 250,000 union volunteers to carry the fight to the decaying Spanish empire. In the aftermath, they opposed the annexation of Cuba and the Philippines based on the fear of an influx of "semi-barbaric" Filipino workers and black Cubans who lacked the "Caucasian" values of "patriotism, sympathy, [and] sacrifice" that made "the modern trade union possible."[77] The AFL became supportive of military actions abroad, even while the military was being used to break industrial strikes at home. In fact, the military was used to break 328 strikes in 49 states and territories between 1886 and 1895.[78]

By 1910, economic expansion without direct colonization proved more successful and lucrative in the Caribbean basin (with the exception of Puerto Rico). "Dollar Diplomacy," as capitalist expansion euphemistically became known, allowed for a gradual convergence of interests between the leadership of the AFL and the most ardent imperialists within the capitalist camp. In its coevolution with imperialism, AFL president Samuel Gompers and his loyalists in the leadership even began to support and promote the inherently racist and chauvinistic ideology being borne out of the structures of imperial conflict. This was inverted inward, as the labor federation became increasingly hostile to nonwhite workers, immigrants, and the "unskilled" workforce in general. As defenders of empire abroad, and increasingly insular, exclusive, and conservative at home, capitalists saw collaboration with AFL unions as a worthwhile trade-off to ensure stability and profitability. As labor historian Jack Scott explains:

> Once convinced of the fact that the craftsmen were content to operate within the context of the established order, and satisfied that their profits would not diminish appreciably as a result of trades organization, employers showed a willingness to cooperate with the business unionists.[79]

This relationship was also cemented by the AFL's disinterest in organizing industrial workers, whom it perceived as a marginal and powerless segment of the workforce. Together, both groups fought vehemently against industrial unionism.

This arrangement served as a conservatizing force within labor, leading the crafts to pursue more aggressively the narrow interests of its skilled, primarily white European male workers and bureaucratic structures. While strikes did periodically occur in craft locals, they became decreasingly effective as industrial factories replaced workshops and mass production created an enlarging, differentiated, "unskilled," and unorganized workforce that dwarfed the craft workers and diminished their leverage within the changing workplace. When industrial workers organized radical alternatives, the AFL leadership positioned themselves as conservative opponents to radical and anticapitalist labor, thereby gaining a position of privilege with employers. When radical labor movements involved nonwhite or immigrant labor, employers and the AFL worked together to promote, support, or defend racial and immigration restrictions to maintain a system of racial and national stratification and division within labor. This collaboration provided a bulwark against the formation of a radical or revolutionary left within the industries.

The control of foreign markets, export of capital, and control over foreign labor and natural resources did benefit craft labor in the short run. Nevertheless, craft labor

was weakened by its own internal contradictions as the workforce expanded and differentiated, and as imperial relations led to the deindustrialization and destabilization
of foreign economies that fueled out-migration from places like Mexico and the Philippines. For its part, capital came to rely increasingly on importing immigrant labor to
expand the non-union workforce, but simultaneously decried excessive immigration
as a means to align with AFL calls for immigration restrictions. The immigration policies that emerged further aligned the AFL and capital as they tended not to block
entrance, but to restrict mobility and citizenship for various groups once inside the
country. While employers benefitted from unorganized and segregated labor filing
into the industries, the AFL crafts were content with the discriminatory outcomes
that limited direct competition from these "unskilled" workers and fortified the stratification of the working classes.

Despite its inability to relate to the growing ranks of the industrial working
classes, the AFL was periodically rehabilitated and promoted by the state and capital
as an instrument of opposition to radical alternatives at home or as a way to export its
brand of business unionism abroad, where US capital investments were sometimes
threatened by anti-imperialist labor movements. Alliances of convenience with capital
became a recurring feature of "pure and simple" craft unionism, as it was confronted
from within its own radicalized sections or other external forces being created by class
struggle and the periodic structural crises of capitalism.

Collusion between labor and capital toward shared goals of economic expansion
became complete by the turn of the century. As Jack Scott explains,

> The imperialist aim of economic domination, in place of territorial acquisition,
> with all its intendant problems gained the united support of the unions, includ-
> ing the minority "anti-imperialist" wing. Of course, the unionists were prepared
> to lend support to military intervention in the event of American investments,
> and "American rights," being violated by some foreign power unappreciative of
> the blessings of American civilization. From 1898 on, it had been the . . . often
> articulated policy of the AFL not to "oppose the development of our industry,
> the expansion of our commerce, nor the power and influence which the United
> States may exert upon the destinies of the nations of the world."[80]

Once the leadership of the craft unions lined up with the general trajectory of empire, they were brought closer into collaboration with the governing administrations
of the Democratic Party. AFL labor leaders would be called upon repeatedly to assist
in efforts to rationalize production during war, to follow the flag of empire in establishing compliant labor group allies abroad, and to oppose the radical Left within its
own ranks, which arose periodically to challenge the dominant arrangements. Radical
Left minorities did develop within the craft unions (and later the industrial unions)
as well as from within imperial holdings. Sometimes, these radical groupings were
able to wield enough influence to challenge existing leadership and policies, especially
during an upsurge of class struggle or, in the case of Mexico, a binational revolutionary
movement.

Jim Crow in the Southwest

The deeply rooted and historic role of state-sanctioned racism as a legal, political, and social mechanism to subjugate, separate, and marginalize African Americans in the period after the Civil War directly framed the experience of Mexicans in the United States as "nonwhite" labor.[81] In the opening up of the Southwest to economic exploitation and colonization after the Civil War, waves of white migrants from Jim Crow states poured into the region, bringing with them established racial notions:

> Throughout the 1800s, white southerners flowed west . . . pushing into Missouri, Kansas, Colorado, and New Mexico, joining the California gold rush and every subsequent rush that filled the golden state. White out-migration grew especially heavy in the two decades after the Civil War . . . many [white migrants] supported a lively network of southern heritage clubs and Confederate veterans' organizations. Altogether, census-takers at the end of the century counted over 1 million southern-born whites living outside their birth region . . . [increasing] in 1930 [to] more than 4 million.[82]

Southern migratory expansion coincided with the appearance of the Ku Klux Klan across the Southwest. By the mid-1920s, chapters of the organization sprang up across Texas, New Mexico, Arizona, Colorado, and California, incorporating Mexicans alongside its traditional targets for committing racial terror.[83]

Furthermore, US imperial machinations toward Mexico, from territorial conquest in 1848 to military intervention and occupation during the revolution, produced an outpouring of racist ideological froth aimed at dehumanizing the Mexican population as savage, incompetent, and inferior.[84] These factors influenced the racialization of Mexican labor and created the infrastructure of segregation that isolated Mexican workers within larger society. During the period of rapid Western industrialization (1866–1913), racism intertwined with the class system in its formative development.[85] Mexicans were subjugated within the industries for which their labor was essential, and paid less than other groups for the same work; especially in physically demanding occupations on the railroads, within agriculture, and in mining. The normalization of such practices was such that "Mexican work" and the "Mexican wage" became synonymous with the hardest type of work and the lowest paid wage.

Despite the historic presence of Mexicans in the Southwest, and the important role that their labor played in the incipient stages of industrial development, their political identity was erased and reconstructed as "alien" even as their labor was in demand. While racism was present in earlier forms of capitalism, its use evolved in the context of industrial development, where the formation of a mass working class drawing from different ethnicities and nationalities provided useful opportunities for capitalists to stratify and segment the labor force to keep it divided so as to thwart unionization. Racial subdivisions within labor were elaborated into "immigration policy," which, under the pretext of exclusion from entry, determined which sections of labor already within the country could not exercise citizenship rights. While applied to different ethnic and national groups over time, these exclusionary statutes have been used most consistently against Mexican workers. The resulting stratified racial, ethnic, and national labor matrix has been further subdivided by sex and gender, with Mexican women drawn into separate and even more subjugated compartments of the labor force.

The primary mechanism for racializing and denationalizing Mexican labor resulted from the machinations of Anglo employers within the process of capitalist development. As a strategy for social marginalization, racist law was established to introduce rigid social divisions in all spheres of life. This was enforced through the elaboration of a state apparatus that used violence as the primary method of separation and control. The elaboration of a racist citizenship regime within the architecture of law further widened the space between immigrant and citizen worker. To further fragment the working class politically, capitalist strategists used Mexican labor (and other forms of nonwhite labor) as strikebreakers or divided them into distinct workgroups within industries, both horizontally and vertically, to inhibit communication, collaboration, and the emergence of a collective class consciousness that could transcend the immediate barriers. The success of preexisting forms of racism carried over into the industrial period in such ways that existing and subsequently formed labor organizations were incapable or unwilling to challenge the emerging racial and national class system.

The condition of Mexican workers was also undermined by their isolation from the rest of the working class, as they were generally neglected by organized labor and the early radical Left, which, to varying degrees, accepted and incorporated racial discrimination and exclusion into their practice. Given these conditions, Mexican workers in the United States have had to overcome significant obstacles in order to form unions and organize political resistance to racial segregation and systematic underdevelopment of their communities within the United States. Disenfranchisement and state-sanctioned policies of exclusion closed the door to electoral politics for most Mexicans and Mexican Americans well into the 1960s. Political marginalization left only their power as workers to collectively disrupt capitalist industry as a means to fight for economic justice and political equality. Racist attitudes and discriminatory practices also pervaded established US unions, severely handicapping solidarity and limiting the resources available to sustain struggle. Organized labor's general neglect for Mexican workers left them to their own devices, although minority voices and factions within the labor movement challenged this trend. In this vacuum they created their own self-defense organizations, often against tremendous odds.

Class Organization and Radical Ideology

Despite these great odds, Mexican workers drew from their own experiences and formed their own class organizations from the ground up. In some cases, they brought their politics and organizations with them across the border, constructing *mutualistas*, or self-help organizations. In other cases, they developed incipient or hybrid unions to promote their interests through class struggle. Interaction with left-wing labor activists aided their efforts. When they could form alliances with the broader Left or existing labor movement, support was often ephemeral or short-lived, contributing to the demise of radical working-class formations forged in the heat of the class struggle. Nevertheless, Mexican workers were present in many of the great labor upheavals of the twentieth century, even if their presence is seen only as a footnote or confined to the background in contemporary narratives.

The formation of a generation of Mexican working-class militants from Texas to Los Angeles laid the foundation for the rise of a radical Left, especially as the organizers of the revolutionary Mexican Liberal Party (referred to throughout the text as the PLM). The PLM crossed the border and moved into the barrios of the Southwest, providing the first cohesive leadership, a radical press, and an organizational infrastructure for Mexicans across the region. The radicalization of Mexican workers coincided with the rise of new political organizations that challenged the exclusionary practices of traditional unions, which proved incapable of resisting the adverse effects of industrialization and whose racial policies rendered them meaningless to a growing proletariat comprised of Mexican workers. Influenced by Mexican radicalism and the PLM, the Industrial Workers of the World (IWW) and southwestern branches of the Socialist Party launched the inaugural effort to organize the first generation of Mexican radicals north of the border.

Even after the first wave of twentieth-century radicalism receded in the aftermath of World War I and massive state repression of the Left, these radical traditions were carried on by individual militants in the different Mexican communities in the Southwest. The Bolshevik Revolution, the first successful workers' revolution, encouraged an international regroupment of radicals into the Communist Party, including many Mexican veterans of the PLM, the IWW, and the Socialist Party. The Communist Party built its organization among Mexican farmworkers, packinghouse and cannery workers, miners, and others, facilitated by the extant radical traditions that led Mexican workers to see class organization and class struggle as the traditional way to improve their condition.

The history of Mexican labor radicalism in the United States is the story of a people who have been at the forefront of grassroots labor unionism in this country. It is also essential for understanding the working-class roots of civil rights activism. Class struggle for equal rights, from the point of production, to schools, communities, and halls of government, cannot be truly understood without understanding the historic role of magonistas, Socialists, Wobblies (members of the IWW), and Communists organizing among their *compañeros*, *compatriotas*, and *camaradas* in the working-class barrios across the Southwest. This will be the central focus of this work, which is also motivated by the idea that the current generation of those engaged in class struggle can greatly benefit from understanding past experience.

Class Struggle and the Contours of Mexican American Labor Historiography

Accompanying the repression of Mexican labor radicalism in practice has been the suppression of Mexican working-class history. Prior to the 1970s, this rich history of

Mexican labor radicalism in the United States has been captured only in fragments. An aggressive and reactionary antisocialism, deeply implanted in ruling-class institutions, politics, and media, wages constant war in the arena of historical narrative.[86] Neverthe-less, the periods of class struggle in the twentieth century produced their own documen-tation, giving some authentic glimpses of this history. Radical organizations focused on in this work, from the PLM to the Communist Party, used their press to document and analyze the struggles of the Mexican working class. These primary sources provide useful and rich snapshots of the strikes and political activities within the barrios, as well as counternarratives to the pro-capitalist media. The latter only typically reported on Mexican laborers in the context of denouncing their union or radical activities.

The first great breakthroughs in Mexican radical historiography emerged in the context of the Chicano movement. As Mario García explained, "Militant Chicano his-torians . . . looked to a radical past to legitimize the emergence of a contemporary Chi-cano protest movement."[87] These Chicana/o historians gained access to the academy as a result of class struggle, which became embedded in their scholarship. They began producing knowledge that could intellectually arm the movement, beginning by ex-cavating, studying, and extolling the antecedent radical forerunners of the Chicana/o movement. In doing so, they consciously rejected the conventional anticommunism of McCarthyism that sterilized academia over the previous generation and salted the soil to inoculate against independent and radical academic endeavors not in line with prevailing Cold War conventions.

It fell upon Chicana/o historians to revive their radical forebears and tell the story from the perspective of the Mexican working class. With some exceptions, labor history in general in the United States has reflected prevailing social attitudes that have largely ignored Mexicans' contribution to the labor movement.[88] There-fore, both Mexican labor history and the history of Mexican labor radicalism are relatively recent developments as part of the larger narrative of US labor history, and these histories have mostly been established by Chicano and Chicana histori-ans and others influenced by the period. This includes the works of Mario García, Juan Gómez-Quiñones, Zaragosa Vargas, Gilbert González, Raul Fernández, Car-los Muñoz, Jr., Vicki Ruiz, Emilio Zamora, Tomás Almaguer, Mario Barrera, Doug-las Monroy, Camille Guerin-Gonzales, Frank Barajas, Jeffrey Marcos Garcilazo, and Elizabeth R. Escobedo. Others that have produced invaluable historical work on Mexican labor and radicalism include Devra Weber, Ward Albro, Julia Kirk Black-welder, Clete Daniel, and James Lorence.

There has also been substantial production by Chicana and Chicano historians who focus on regional studies, in many cases their own hometowns, especially as part of a wave of dissertations over the last decade. Aside from that there has been some-what scant but important research conducted by others who have been sympathetic to the radical labor struggle within the Mexican community, sharing interest or even affiliation with one of the tendencies described in this book.

A third element that has proved essential in understanding the political traditions of Mexican workers and radicals begins with Mexican labor history. There is a vast body of research on labor history in Mexico, and significant exploration of radical labor traditions. Some of this important research has been produced by veteran labor activists Rosendo Salazar and Jacinto Huitrón, and by sympathetic intellectuals like Paco Ignacio Taibo, Armando Bartra, Jorge Basurto, Gaston García Cantú, Daniela Spenser, Gerardo Peláez Ramos, Anna Ribera Carbó, and Enrique Condés Lara, to name a few. US-based contributors to the literature include Friedrich Katz, John Mason Hart, James D. Cockcroft, W. Dirk Raat, Donald Hodges, John Lear, and Dan La Botz.

A more recent field of historical research that fits within the category of transnational labor history has followed the patterns of labor migration, militancy, and political action across borders. Mexican and US scholars have also paid significant attention to the question of Mexican workers and radical traditions crossing borders, and how this has affected the international character of Mexican labor activism on both sides of the border. These scholars include Javier Torres Parés, Marco Antonio Samaniego López, Sonia Hernández, Arturo Santamaría Gómez, David Bacon, and Paul Buhle. The groundbreaking work of these scholars helps to frame the background of this study, and their works are cited throughout the text.

Current events inform its contemporary relevance. Since the 1980s, a new immigrant-led workers' movement has emerged. Immigrant and migrant workers from Mexico, Central America, and the Caribbean have been at the forefront of rebuilding a union movement that had been in decline since the 1970s. Since the early 2000s, immigrant workers and their US-born children have been at the forefront of a new civil rights movement, confronting yet another cycle of anti-immigrant laws designed to divide and weaken working-class resistance to the imperatives of capital. The mass strikes, boycott, and marches that took place across the country in 2006 revived International Workers Day, "May Day," in the United States, and will hopefully serve as a catalyst for a new generation of literature centered on the role and power of Mexican labor in US history. Additionally, these efforts will likely inform a new generation of radicals rising from the ranks of the transnational working class in the twenty-first century.

Part 1

Chapter 1
The Mexican Working Classes

*"[T]he Mexican peon prefers to rebel rather than to work . . .
This condition will make the task of the pacification of Mexico a
difficult one, either for the Mexican chief who finally obtains power,
or for this country in case we are obliged to intervene."*
—US newspaper editorial, 1913

Historian Rodney Anderson has argued that Mexican working-class politics were influenced more by the liberal political traditions of the native bourgeoisie than by what he refers to as "militantly, class-conscious European ideologies." Only during the Mexican Revolution of 1910, he implies, did workers rally behind these doctrines as the national bourgeoisie closed ranks against radical land and labor reform.[1] While it is may seem intuitive to say that workers only *consciously* embraced revolutionary doctrine while participating in the revolution, this argument overlooks the dynamics of class struggle and the history of radicalism before the Mexican Revolution.

The incorporation of Mexico into the US sphere of imperial influence and the dislocations and despoliation that followed informed labor radicalization that transcended the framework of liberal, democratic capitalism. Furthermore, this argument misunderstands how revolutionary organizations influenced by anarchist and Marxist doctrine crystallized consciousness among the most militant workers in the years preceding the revolution, especially in those strategic sectors of the economy dominated by foreign capital.

As John Mason Hart explains, the tendency to ignore, dismiss, or underestimate the role of the working classes in the Mexican Revolution is the continuation of a "traditional-conservative historiography and fictional literature which denied a radical working-class tradition, revolutionary working-class consciousness or even a comprehension by workers of contemporary revolutionary events."[2] In fact, radical political movements rooted in anticapitalist ideologies began to germinate in the interstices of class struggle in the second half of the nineteenth century.

Due to the particular characteristics of Mexico, radical philosophies first entered into the country through European and continental American immigrants, which resonated with the local traditions of collective indigenous resistance. The two major radical schools of thought, anarchism and Marxism, entered and took root in Mexico, adapting, mixing, and informing the organization of the working classes. As Anna Ribera Carbó observes, "even though their recently created organizations lacked defined objectives, the Mexican working class embraced syndicalist, socialist, and anarchist doctrine."[3] These organizational expressions gestated during the Porfiriato and flowered through the period of the revolution.

The growth of the industrial working class and proletarianization of the peasantry occurred within the matrix of imperialist intervention and domination. Class conflict pitted Mexican workers and peasants not only against domestic, landowning oligarchs and the Porfirian state, but also against foreign capitalists backed by their respective states. By 1910, US and foreign capital established their presence in the Mexican political system in order to conform it to their interests. The working class came to resent the ubiquitous political corruption that sprang from economic colonization. They also resented the government's willingness to repress the laboring classes who refused to accept their role as a commodity for capitalist accumulation and foreign profiteering.

For this reason, working-class consciousness gravitated toward anti-imperialism and anticapitalist political ideologies. As historians Jaime Tamayo and Patricia Valles explain: "It is important to pay attention to the specificities of this influence on the development of the Mexican working class, that although in an embryonic state—as a class—anarchist and socialist postulates were integrated into its practice."[4]

While the Mexican working class was not politically cohesive on a national level at the time of the opening shots of the revolution, their participation was instrumental in undermining the Porfirian regime. Strikes led by industrial workers shut down capitalist nerve centers of the economy, while large numbers of radicalized agricultural laborers, the bulwark of the villista and zapatista armies, brought the seemingly omnipotent landowning oligarchy to its knees. These episodes of class struggle brought about the Díaz regime's demise. The revolution's momentum then shifted to the urban centers, where a radical workers' movement emerged as an independent force amid the revolutionary factions vying for power. These experiences, radical political ideals, and incipient forms of organization were ingrained in class memory. They were carried across the border with the waves of migration that brought Mexican workers into the United States.

Urban Workers

Mexican working-class formation and the character of class struggle have been shaped by the combined and uneven development of capitalism resulting from a history of colonial and imperialist domination. In Mexico's complex colonial history, wage labor emerged alongside slave and indentured labor and peasant agrarian communalism. The homogenization of the workforce developed slowly over the colonial period through independence, accelerating rapidly during the period of the Porfiriato. By the turn of the twentieth century, Mexico's class structure was highly stratified. A tiny but extremely wealthy and powerful landowning oligarchy and assortment of foreign capitalist classes controlled the countryside. Production was incorporated into international markets, depending on a vast population of agricultural laborers and small and subsistence farmers to till the soil, as well as large clusters of industrial workers to work in the mines, oil fields, and along the railroad lines. In the urban centers, a rising commercial and industrial bourgeoisie (both domestic and foreign) developed alongside a middle class composed of small business people, professionals, and government functionaries; while working-class barrios expanded rapidly in proximity to the burgeoning factory districts as displaced rural populations poured into city centers.[5] Urban industrial workers soon eclipsed in size the artisanal workforce engaged in handicraft production in small workshops.[6] In analyzing this social panorama, historian W. Dirk Raat concludes that by 1900, 91 percent of Mexico's population of 13.5 million comprised the "popular classes," including agricultural laborers, sharecroppers, industrial workers, soldiers, beggars, and other unemployed urban and rural poor.[7]

Between 1877 and 1910, the population of Mexico grew 61 percent, with the most rapid expansion taking place in emerging, urban industrial zones. For instance, by 1910, 30 percent of the population lived in the cities, with twenty-two urban zones containing a population of twenty to fifty thousand inhabitants.[8] According to John Mason Hart, an urban craft-based working-class movement began to take collective action on a national scale as early as the late 1860s.

> By 1871, the tailors of Mexico City, the vendors, the carpenters, street lighters, beauty shop workers, candlestick makers, alcoholic beverage deliverymen, schoolteachers, carriage makers, typesetters, musicians, weavers, button makers, and tobacco and textile workers had organized. In 1871, they sent representatives to a labor congress that met in the capital with delegates from worker groups from the cities of Durango, Guadalajara, Oaxaca, San Luis Potosí, and Veracruz, and many smaller towns. They created the nation's first workers' council, the Círculo de Obreros de México, whose purpose was to coordinate union business such as negotiations and strikes over broad areas.[9]

Alongside the craft industries, a discernible industrial workforce developed in the mine, railroad, textile, and oil industries, especially in relation to the massive influx of foreign capital. As foreign investment increased in these industrial operations, the proportion of industrial workers grew as a result. For example, by the turn of the twentieth century there were about 90,000 to 100,000 factory workers (31,000 employed in 150 textile mills), 23,000 working on the national railroads, and an estimated 100,000 working in the mines.[10] By 1910, nearly 750,000 people (of a total population of 15 million) had come to work in modern industry, accounting for 16 percent of the workforce.[11] Alongside this grew an attendant urban workforce servicing the needs of an economy connected to the arteries and causeways of the world economy: warehouse workers, port workers, bank personnel, teachers, public employees, etc.[12]

The industrial proletariat began to grow and assert itself within Mexico's largest cities. For instance, the cotton textile industry was heavily concentrated in four distinct zones in close proximity: Mexico City, Puebla, Atlixco, and Orizaba. Within this region, thousands of workers at hundreds of different mills established close communication, formed and spread unions, and participated in political affairs.[13] While numerically small and regionally concentrated, the developing industrial working class wielded power disproportionate to its size and played a significant role in shaping the course of events during the revolution.

Women workers formed a portion of both the urban and rural workforce, albeit concentrated in certain economic spheres and regions. In 1895 there were 275,000 registered domestic servants, mostly women, working in near slave-like conditions. By 1902, they comprised 17 percent of the textile industrial workforce.[14] Women workers were also distributed across artisanal occupations, as seamstresses, cigar-makers, needle-workers (*empuntadoras*), weavers, food service employees, laundry workers, midwives, primary school teachers, stenographers, and across a wide array of other occupations.[15] In Mexico City, Mexican women comprised 35 percent of the paid workforce in 1910, while comprising a majority of sex workers as well as unpaid labor as servants.[16] According to statistical records, women comprised only 14 percent of the economically active population nationally in 1910.[17] But historian Anna Macias refutes the low percentage through deeper analysis of the construction and devaluation of socially feminized work:

> What the directors of the 1910 census did was to imagine that a clear-cut division of labor between the sexes existed in Mexico, that men were the providers and women the homemakers . . . The 1910 census ignored the fact that in rural areas women spent most of their time outside the home, raising animals, fruits, vegetables, and flowers for sale in the town and village markets when they could, or working as peons alongside the men when they were landless. The . . . census takers also ignored the women living in the vicinity of railroad stations who spent a large part of the day preparing food to sell passengers . . . Others . . . were artisans, pieceworkers, [and] street vendors.[18]

This was also the case in the border region; the transnational capitalist development proletarianized and incorporated women workers at the industrial margins. While men were drawn into the mining, railroad, smelting, and oil extraction and refining sectors, women formed the ranks of labor in cigar, textile, and garment factories.

Mexican textile workers (obreras textiles) during the Porfiriato

Agricultural Workers

While the country remained predominantly rural by the turn of the twentieth century, capitalist relations of production in the countryside had reduced the land holdings of the traditional peasantry and small-holding class, creating a substantial population of landless campesinos drawn into wage labor on export-oriented capitalist farms and processing plants, into the mining complexes, or into debt peonage on the traditional hacienda. Indigenous communal land holdings and village commons (*ejidos*) were enclosed by haciendas and capitalist speculators, and small and subsistence farmers liquidated as they were drawn into regional market competition.

Railroad expansion linked hacienda agricultural zones to US markets and ports that further circulated commodities to global markets. Increasing profitability through integration of the agricultural economy into the world market sparked an impulse to expand the haciendas to produce on even grander economies of scale. Peasant displacement coupled with the growing need for agricultural and industrial workers in the export sector contributed to the formation of an agricultural proletariat.

Between the 1850s and 1870s, successive liberal regimes embarked on an economic project of capitalist modernization. During the presidency of Ignacio Comonfort, his finance minister, Miguel Lerdo de Tejada, passed what became known as the Ley Lerdo. The law was passed with the intention of privatizing communally held indigenous lands as well as undesignated Catholic Church–held lands to be sold for more productive use. In practice, little Church land was touched, while indigenous populations saw substantial swaths of their communal land sold off in a frenzy. One newspaper, *El Constitucional*, denounced the wholesale land theft, claiming the Indians were being left without "an inch of land for which to stand." Another prominent liberal congressman, Ignacio Ramírez, criticized the rampant corruption greasing the process, claiming that "usurpation of the communal properties has occurred in a variety of ways . . . judges have been paid off with complicity of the higher authorities."[19] Nevertheless the practice continued.

Comonfort also authorized the disbursement of substantial land concessions to European and American economic interests. This practice continued under Benito Juárez, who in 1864 ceded the greater part of Baja California to a single US-based company (as well as awarding ten years of tax exemptions and other inducements), with the hope that such colonization projects would become engines of economic growth.[20] Later, in 1875, liberals in Mexico's Congress passed a law granting foreign companies concessions of land along with the right to import migrant labor. Land was made available on the cheap to would-be skilled migrants, who were expected to repay these generous offerings by becoming Mexican citizens. This opened the door to the pattern of economic colonization that became normalized during the Porfiriato: labor importation in place of developing and training local workforces, rapacious extraction done cheaply, only to be marked up on the world market, and expansion and encroachment that created regional displacement.

Díaz and his Científico cohorts then introduced a novel way to accelerate land transfer to capitalists beginning in 1883. So-called "vacant lands" (*terrenos baldios*), which included large repositories of commonly used lands, pastures, and forests that sustained small villages throughout the country, were declared the property of the state. The state took a direct role in distributing land into the hands of capitalists and giving the green light for haciendas and foreign investors to lay claim to the best communal farms, village plots, and other small holdings in their paths. For their part, capitalist *hacendados* geared toward increased production for export ended the practice of tenant farming and sharecropping in order to more effectively exploit former peasants as laborers.

Already by 1883, an estimated 3 million landless agricultural workers lived in the countryside; a population which grew precipitously thereafter.[21] By 1910, it is estimated that 9.5 million out of a rural population of 11.6 million were agricultural wage workers or hacienda workers (*peones*), in a country with a total population of 15 million.[22] The proletarian segment of the rural workforce was mobile, subjected to unstable employment due to market fluctuations, and susceptible to radical plans or doctrines calling for restitution. As such, they became a key combustible element and the determining factor of the revolutionary upsurge. This was especially the case in regions with a previous history of struggle, or where existing organizations were capable of giving expression to manifesting anger.

The Porfirian land grabs increased profitability of export-led hacienda production for the world market. For example, the value of one hacienda in Durango called Santa Catalina del Alamo y Anexas had a growth rate of about 10 percent annually in net profits for each year between 1903 and 1911, providing a 54 percent return on capital investment.[23] By 1908, the seventeen largest sugarcane haciendas in the state of Morelos controlled 25 percent of the total land surface of the state, including the most fertile regions.[24] Of the 118 villages in Morelos, many saw their holdings shrink and their populations dwindle. Eighteen pueblos had disappeared altogether, expropriated by the sugar haciendas.[25]

Indigenous communal lands were liquidated outright. For instance, in the far north of the country, the Yaqui peoples were forcibly removed from their ancestral lands in the state of Sonora to make way for substantial land transfers to US investors. According to John Kenneth Turner, the Porfirista governor of Sonora provoked a war with the Yaqui in order to justify their expulsion: "The Yaqui country is rich in both mining and agricultural possibilities. American capitalists bought the lands while the Yaquis were still on them, then stimulated the war of extermination and finally instigated the scheme to deport them into slavery in Yucatan."[26]

Concentration and displacement also took on other forms. In different regions of the country, intensified capitalist production created similar, identifiable patterns. According to historian David Walker:

> Hacienda managers . . . increased productivity by reducing wages, eliminating surplus employees, charging higher rents to tenants, extracting maximum advantage from sharecroppers, and enclosing hacienda land and collecting fees from local residents for the use of water, wood, pastures, and other resources.[27]

The number of haciendas grew at the expense of smallholders, and multiple haciendas became concentrated in fewer hands. Between 1854 and 1910 the number of haciendas increased from 6,092 to 8,245, while the census that year counted only 840 hacendados, showing that few owners controlled multiple haciendas.[28] Individual land holdings became so immense that one owner, Luis Terrazas, controlled a surface area larger than the entire country of Costa Rica. The next eight largest estates amassed over 56 million acres, and another fifteen hacendados controlled estates around 247,000 acres each.[29] Meanwhile, foreign economic interests also partook in the land grab. About fifty US companies received some 21.2 million hectares between the years 1878 and 1908, acquiring one of every three hectares they surveyed on behalf of the Mexican government.[30] Between 1883 and 1910, over 27 percent of the total land area of the republic was transferred to private companies, representing a small handful of foreign investors with immense holdings.[31] By 1912, the Díaz regime had transferred almost 58 million acres of public lands to foreign capitalists.[32]

By 1910 it is estimated that over 90 percent of the total Mexican population owned no land, while 68 percent of the rural population was landless.[33] Land confiscations not only enlarged the haciendas, but also expanded the workforce as displaced farm-ers entered the ranks of the agricultural proletariat. For instance, in 1854 there were an estimated 5,021 ejidos, or recognized communal land holdings. By 1910, these had all but disappeared, with the displaced *ejidatarios* filing into the ranks of a swelling landless proletariat. This included women, who joined the ranks of *jornaleros* (day laborers) and made up the plurality of wage workers and sorters in ixtle (rubber), *pi-loncillo* (sugar), coffee, and tobacco-producing haciendas and workshops.[34] Those not proletarianized were part of an estimated four hundred thousand small landowners with land holdings of twelve acres or less, becoming "*minifundistas* on the margins of the expanding haciendas."[35] Food production was disrupted as small and subsistence farming gave way to large-scale production for export, leading to declining consump-tion rates before 1890. While food production and consumption increased after that year, it was because the government increased food imports.[36]

To protect haciendas and foreign properties from disgruntled peasants, rootless workers, and the growing ranks of bandits, and to smother the recurring revolts of indigenous groups, a special gendarme was created. As early as 1861, Benito Juárez developed the prototype of a rural police force that comprised ranchers and former bandits called the Resguardo del Comercio (roughly "Protectors of Commerce").[37] Rural armed groups (referred to by then as *rurales*) were expanded greatly and cen-tralized under Díaz, and transformed into a de facto arm of the military apparatus in the countryside. The function of repression became an urgent necessity as the rural displaced population expanded and became more unstable. The total displaced rural population—untold millions of mostly indigenous and mestizo peasants—reached a critical mass by 1910, forming the ranks of the revolutionary armies that took up arms against the Porfirian state.[38]

Friedrich Katz identifies the regional forms of marginalization experienced in the countryside, illustrating the ways in which workers were drawn into the revolu-tionary movements. In the northern region, where ancestral communal land-holding traditions were the weakest, the revolutionary armies were composed of semi-agricul-tural, semi-industrial workers facing unstable employment on the haciendas and in the mines.[39] In central and southern Mexico, these armies comprised former commu-nal landowners, increasingly expropriated and reduced to tenant sharecroppers and temporary laborers on what was often the least favorable and productive land. Tenant farmers, especially in the southern states with the larger indigenous populations, were drawn into debt peonage and other more direct forms of forced labor.[40]

Agrarian Rebellion
The forceful expropriation of the small and subsistence farmers that accompanied the liberal modernization project did not occur without resistance. The Mexican agrarian population has a long history of resistance to the foreign capital and the domestic landowning oligarchy. The early resistance to the US invasion and occupation of Mex-ico in 1847, according to historian John Coatesworth, "had mobilized and armed tens of thousands of peasants in the center of the country, and left the surviving veterans to

return to their villages and farms to lead the innumerable movements . . . that wracked the Mexican countryside from the 1840s to 1880s."[41] Furthermore, states William K. Meyers, "[i]n the years 1888, 1890–94, and 1898–1900, violence erupted repeatedly, pushing the countryside to the edge of social revolt and instilling in the propertied class the fear of a mass uprising."[42] The traditions of armed resistance carried over into an erstwhile class struggle that graduated into revolution by 1910.[43]

Resistance among rural workers during the Porfiriato intertwined recent historical memory and accumulated experience in opposing foreign occupation with new threats created by economic imperialism abetted by the authoritarian Mexican national government. While rural participation in the intervals of the revolutionary period was uneven, geographically dispersed, and heterogeneous in character, the most conflictive and decisive class struggle raged in the countryside, reaching a crescendo after 1910 and involving tens of thousands of agrarian workers and campesinos directly in land occupations, strikes, guerrilla attacks, and eventually full-blown war. The mobilization of the rural proletariat was the inexorable physical force that brought down the Díaz dictatorship and laid the basis for the expropriation of the Porfirian oligarchy.

From those states with existing radical organizations and recent traditions of resistance emerged the most formidable revolutionaries in those years. Consciousness was also heightened among northern agricultural workers as an "increasing awareness on the part of the peon of the better wages and living conditions of both the Mexican urban worker and the agricultural worker in the United States increased his restlessness making him more receptive to ideologies of protest and political action."[44]

In the state of Chihuahua, the bastion of the feared Division del Norte—the rough and tumble army of Pancho Villa that brought down the Díaz regime—was forged from two decades of episodic revolts grounded in bitter disaffection and hostility to the policies of the Porfiriato. Rural-based movements in that state had taken up arms against the Díaz regime in the Tomóchic from 1891 to 1892 and in Cruces in 1893. Also in 1893, a statewide guerrilla insurgency led by popular leader Santana Pérez took to the field. In response to the rebellions, the federal army was sent in to repress the pueblos in revolt, and cut off popular support for the guerrilla efforts through raids, occupations, and summary punishments. The brutal repression "left a painful imprint in the collective memory of the people, and resistance to those actions provided a clear precedent for popular struggle."[45] Other antecedents contributed to the radicalization of Chihuahua's peasantry. According to Rubén Osorio:

> The construction of railroads to connect Chihuahua with the southwestern United States and the interior of Mexico precipitated a social disequilibrium within the peasantry. In combination, railroad construction and capitalist development engendered an export-oriented economy, provoked a sudden increase in property values along the border and the railroad lines, and led to underhanded dealings such as those of Limantour in the Guerrero district to expropriate land from the Chihuahuan peasantry and indígenas.[46]

The economic crisis of 1907 exacerbated problems as the US mining industry in the border region contracted severely, closing off a crucial economic outlet used by many proletarianized peasants who relied on seasonal mining income to supplement diminished farm-work income. Thousands of Mexican miners laid off during the near collapse of copper prices in Arizona and New Mexico returned to their pueblos, joining the ranks of the landless proletariat. These zones of conflict became ripe for the growth of antigovernment politics. In the years 1905 through 1909, they became fertile grounds for organizing opposition, "marking a qualitative change in the level of dissension in the towns, from latent resistance to open antagonism toward the state and foreign landlords." From this material, the Partido Liberal Mexicano drew participants into several failed attempts at orchestrating an armed uprising, until a critical mass was reached in 1911.[47]

Agrarian militancy grew into insurrectionary struggle, especially as the Porfirian state unraveled. In various parts of the country agricultural workers began to surge in rebellion against local haciendas. For instance, peons and sharecroppers in eastern Durango began to stage numerous strikes and land occupations in 1912. On one hacienda in Cruces, Durango, the sharecroppers organized a general strike, "demanding $0.75 for a six-hour workday, an increase in hacienda payments for their corn and cotton, and reimbursement by the hacienda for harvesting costs." Strikes then spread to several other haciendas in the region. On another hacienda in Cuencamé, Durango, workers and sharecroppers took possession of the hacienda's lands, buildings, equipment, supplies, and livestock.[48] Others were also sacked. The insurrectionary spirit of the farmworkers, animated by the revolution, led one embattled hacendado to lament:

> There is an animosity against the hacienda that I cannot explain and it would seem to me to be incredible, and not only because it is occurring every moment. Many of the servants whom we believed faithful have deceived us; and that is because of the promises made by the revolutionaries that they will divide the land . . . and now [the workers] do not think of anything more than to see realized that beautiful dream. Some of those who owe the hacienda the most for the services rendered to them are those that show the most desire for the division [of the hacienda].[49]

In the southern Mexican state of Morelos, a rebellion against Porfirista landholders had begun in earnest well before 1910. Under Díaz, profit-minded landowners aggressively expanded sugar production by confiscating small and communal land holdings and enlarging their haciendas, having shifted to capitalist production for world markets. Morelos became a hotbed of revolutionary action as the peasantry had been expropriated and proletarianized through this process. Furthermore, the sugar plantations now employing the displaced peasants intensified class polarization by suppressing wages. As Roger Bartra explains, this was done as a means to generate enough surplus labor value to profit two bourgeoisies: the domestic producers of raw materials and the foreign capitalists in imperialist countries that refined the product and delivered it to international markets.[50]

Encouraged by the maderista uprising against Díaz in 1910, Morelos peasants widened their campaign to expropriate land from the Porfirista hacendados. When

Madero opposed their efforts, they proclaimed against him, with the intention of continuing the agrarian revolution. This crystallized in the Plan de Ayala in 1911. The plan rejected Madero and called for the restoration of lands taken from the pueblos by haciendas and foreign capital. This regional revolt, which came to be led by Emiliano Zapata, soon constituted itself into a popular army that defeated and expelled first the Porfirian state from its environs, along with any semblance of Maderista authority, by 1913. In the aftermath of Madero's overthrow, Zapata issued a decree in September 1914 declaring that the lands of the Porfirista oligarchy and aligned foreign capital would be seized. Their experience in successfully resisting the federal forces under Madero and later helping to topple Victoriano Huerta further radicalized their outlook. Urban radicals and intellectuals, including anarchists and magonistas, who flocked to zapatista banners as the legitimate continuation of the revolution and performed various roles in the zapatista movement, emerged as a highly skilled and experienced guerrilla army of armed villagers with a leadership that was politically rooted in "old communal traditions and in the traditional social Indian structures which had always been an instrument of struggle and resistance."[51] These traditions carried into the larger political arena during the short-lived 1914–1915 Pact of Xochimilco, which saw villista-zapatista armies collaborate to capture Mexico City after the break with the conservative landowner Carranza, who refused to concede radical land redistribution as part of his vision for reconstructing Mexico. After the Zapata-Villa armies captured Mexico City, the "Conventionalist" government began the process of expropriating the landowning oligarchy through the development of land commissions instructed to reclaim and restore village and communal lands. The attempt was most thoroughgoing in Morelos, where the armed zapatistas in control of the region could impose the rulings of the commissions on landlords and foreign capitalists.[52]

Through this process, the zapatista army proceeded to dismantle the large haciendas and nationalize without compensation the sugar mills and distilleries. By 1915, Morelos had been transformed into what Adolfo Gilly refers to as the "Morelos Commune." As he explains, though the radical agrarianism of the zapatistas could not transcend its rural and agrarian roots and offer a national vision, it did

> set forth a full-scale transformation of the country, with a revolutionary dictatorship based upon liquidation of the latifundia and land distribution under the control of the peasants' local organs of power. It was not a socialist, but a radical-Jacobin program. Yet it established a dynamic that corresponded to the anticapitalist thrust of the Mexican peasant war—*a petty bourgeois dictatorship from above*, wedded to mass initiative from below and an onslaught on the enemy involving *expropriation without compensation*. This combination had set up a Socialist dynamic which, above all in 1915, magnified the original revolutionary import of the Ayala Plan.[53]

During the period of the Morelos Commune, which endured from 1913 to 1917, the zapatista leadership engaged in the development of radical and popular structures to strengthen its position within the state against its encroaching enemies. This included the creation of village councils to administer newly liberated territories and to assert the will of the common people, to direct investment in universal education and literacy, and to arrange the military organization of the villages and their incorporation into the zapatista army. While the commune was ultimately encircled and defeated by the Constitutionalists, the experience left an indelible mark and instilled a radical self-identity within hundreds of thousands of agricultural workers and small farmers who lived through the experience.

Labor Organization—from Mutualistas to Unions

The historical development of labor unions and the emergence of strike actions by workers was a slow process that accelerated rapidly after the turn of the twentieth century. The character of working-class formation mirrored Mexico's uneven process of capitalist development, which combined pre-capitalist agricultural communalism, small-scale, pre-industrial artisanship, and large-scale industrial production. These factors impeded the development of a homogenous, concentrated, or unified working class. Furthermore, the Díaz regime outlawed unions and repressed strikes as a barrier to capitalist development, and persecuted the exponents of radical ideologies that challenged the existing order.

The prototypes of modern working-class organization first developed from within the mutualistas and workers' cooperatives. These organizations, formed at the twilight of the pre-industrial period, expressed the defensive posture of the artisans facing displacement by the emerging factory system. They were tolerated so long as they confined their operations to "self-help activities."

Mutualistas gradually became mixed in character as economic change and competing external political influences induced changes in composition and structure. As radical doctrines circulated within Mexico in the 1860s, for instance, disciples of Proudhonist anarchist thought posited within the mutualistas that workers should reject the destructive forces of industrial capitalism by forming self-sufficient communes and cooperatives. They envisioned horizontal expansion and integration based on socialist collaboration and exchange that could undercut the disarticulation and commoditization of labor under industrial capitalism. In other cases, industrialization led to the arrangement of "labor mutualistas," which were more closely associated with workers within a particular trade or industry.[54] Concurrently, more conservative mutualista variants were created through the aegis of the Catholic Church as a result of the 1891 papal encyclical Rerum Novarum. These were officially sanctioned by the Porfirian ruling class, as they offered an antiradical and church-administered alternative to the growth of socialist- and anarchist-influenced unions and mutualistas.[55]

The first expressions of class-based worker solidarity, mutualistas in Mexico developed in alignment with the ascendant liberal regimes by the mid-1850s. The liberals formed alliances with the urban working classes as a way of maintaining their support against the forces of reaction, offering various privileges and blandishments to maintain their loyalty. Mutualistas were even given legal protections by the Civil Code of 1871, although this same piece of legislation also proscribed work stoppages.

For this reason, the mutualistas eschewed class struggle in favor of harmonious relations between capital and labor. Instead of critiquing the failure of capitalism to meet the basic needs of workers, they substituted self-help doctrine for this deficiency, communalizing funds for health care, education, insurance, burials, loans, and other forms of aid for their members.[56] Nevertheless, they formed out of the necessity to respond—even in a limited capacity—to the apparent deficiencies of capitalism. By 1870, over a hundred mutualistas of this nature were formed with an estimated membership of 125,000.[57] The first effort to unify the mutualistas into a national organization took place in 1872, with the creation of the Gran Círculo de Obreros de México. The effort was propelled forward by the rise of the Paris Commune, the first workers' uprising to create a semblance of socialism and workers' control of the means of production.

By 1876 the Círculo had thirty-five sections spread across the country, concentrated in the central states of México, Puebla, and Hidalgo.[58] The Gran Círculo also formed the Congreso Obrero (Workers' Congress) in order to articulate class positions and to insert an organized workers' voice into liberal electoral politics.[59] Despite internal alignments mirroring the factionalization within the liberal establishment, the leadership of the Gran Círculo pulled together a consensus to form linkages and mobilize worker support for Porfirio Díaz after his usurpation of the presidency in 1876. Despite this alignment, the growing frequency of labor strikes during the Porfiriato—technically illegal, but increasingly deployed—put organized labor and the Díaz regime at odds.

The acceleration of investment-led industrial capitalism transformed the economic landscape. Small-scale handicrafts were replaced with factories, and large armies of labor were assembled to work on railroads, textiles, and mines. With deskilling, scientific management, and market pressures came increased labor exploitation and atomization. Under these conditions, traditional mutual aid societies organized away from the point of production became increasingly impotent as a form of resistance. According to Juan Felipe Leal, with the "disintegration of the artisan-worker movement, the accentuated differences that previously existed between its different components [of the working class] . . . so starkly defined in the previous decade, had ceased to exist as such."[60]

The development of national industries created a larger and more homogenous workforce that began to form regional and national linkages. As class consciousness deepened, demands for standardized wages and working conditions within an industry became more common. Workers began to utilize strikes more frequently as they became aware of their collective power, especially through the creation of explicitly "labor" mutualistas. By 1902, for instance, sixty-two mutualistas existed in Mexico City alone.[61] These quasi–trade unions grouped together workers along class and industrial lines, elevated demands for higher wages and better working conditions over other concerns, and began to serve as the first vehicles for conducting strikes. As Leal observes, the interval of 1906–1910 witnessed the "[g]rowing systematization and uniformity of their social-economic demands within the different branches of industrial activity, and an unprecedented intensification and multiplication of labor conflict."[62]

The qualitative shift toward industrial-based organization was facilitated by the entrance of radical doctrines grounded in anarcho-syndicalism, which began to penetrate the working-class mutualistas by the 1880s. As Marjorie Ruth Clark asserts, "socialist doctrines began to infiltrate the country. . . . A small group of intellectuals composed of probably no more than 100 people in the entire Republic, started to diffuse new social doctrines among the masses."[63] Anarcho-syndicalists rejected collaboration with the liberal bourgeoisie as a failed project, and instead advanced the necessity of class struggle through direct action. Since class struggle embodied the irreconcilability of the proletariat and bourgeoisie, they agitated for the creation of revolutionary unions, taking a confrontational approach with capital and the state, using labor strikes as the primary weapon.

Anarchist ideas took hold among newer generations of workers shaped by the realities of industrial capitalism. These workers were grouped in larger concentrations under working conditions that configured them as more or less equal; and through their collective labor—and the ability to withdraw it—they became conscious of their power as a class. This experience induced workers to create forms of organizations that facilitated class struggle at the point of production. As historian John Lear explains, labor mutualistas became "societies of resistance during moments of [class] conflict... that had outgrown mutualist forms and in their demands and actions resembled trade and industrial unions in all but name."[64] Labor mutualistas were gradually transcended by the *sindicato* (labor union), which moved class-based organization to the point of production for the purpose of the *huelga* (strike). Between 1906 and 1908, for instance, it is estimated that eighty thousand workers in Mexico were organized into some form of labor mutualista, compared to the sixteen thousand workers who belonged to craft unions, of which ten thousand were railroad workers.[65]

Class-Struggle Unionism

Manifestations of militant class-struggle unionism erupted within the major industrial sectors after the turn of the twentieth century. Despite being outlawed during the period of the Porfiriato, 250 strikes occurred between 1881 and 1911, with twenty-five major shutdowns in 1907 alone.[66] Mexican labor historians disagree on the historical birthplace of syndicalism, but most pinpoint strikes of railroad workers, miners, and textile workers beginning in 1906 and 1907.[67] These strikes were the first significant confrontations between the working classes and the Mexican state, opening up a revolutionary process that culminated in the fall of the regime in 1910.

Industrial class conflict first escalated in the far north of the country beginning in 1904, becoming a major cause for concern for the Díaz government, especially as some strikes began to take on a political character. As one report to the regime cautioned, "conflicts between capital and labor have already begun . . . in manufacturing and [were] frequent and dangerous."[68] As Sonia Hernández elaborates: "the convulsion that shook the far northern borderlands began to manifest itself in the factories, expansive haciendas, oil fields, and smelters. Mexicans demanded safer working conditions, called for an end to debt peonage and physical abuse on the haciendas, and insisted foreigners leave the country."[69]

These strikes began to take on an industrywide character after 1906. Concurrent with economic objectives, the mass mobilizations also served to crystallize nation-wide political opposition to the Díaz regime and to give an amplified voice to popular sentiment against foreign domination.

Three factors converged to produce the potent and even quasi-insurrectionary strikes in that induced a seismic shift in the balance of class forces in that period: the economic crisis of 1906–1908, the growth of industrial workforces' relative power in these foreign-dominated industries, and union-organizing efforts led primarily by anticapitalist radicals. As labor historian Jorge Basurto concludes, these "second-generation unions made clear, socio-economic demands and began to utilize new methods of struggle . . . especially the strike."[70]

One of the first examples of militancy and modern strike action occurred among railroad workers. Workers in the railroad industry had begun to develop unions in their respective sectors between 1884 and 1903, modeled on those developed in the United States.[71] The character of the railroad unions began to take on more militant and industrial forms, as workers began to organize work stoppages, later consolidating their units in order to take more coordinated industrywide strike action against powerful foreign companies.

A universal grievance of the railroad workers had to do with their unequal treatment compared to US workers. By the turn of the twentieth century, up to thirteen hundred US workers staffed the Mexican railroads, occupying the top jobs as dispatchers and full railroad crews and receiving twice the pay for comparable work.[72] In 1906, a strike by three thousand members of the Unión de Mecánicos Mexicanos was initiated to demand equal pay with US mechanics. The first significant strike on the railroads, it demonstrated the workers' capacity to shut down an essential conduit of the national economy—especially the export sector—crippling key arterial routes of the national rail system in the northern states of San Luis Potosí, Nuevo León, Aguascalientes, and Chihuahua.[73]

By 1908, several smaller craft-oriented unions merged into the Gran Liga Mexicana de Empleados de Ferrocarril, the first prototype of an industrial union, which claimed a membership of ten thousand. Growing resentment toward abusive US supervisors—now intensified by economic crisis—and other complaints led to a general rail strike that year. According to James D. Cockcroft, "The strike brought traffic to a standstill for six days and 'tied up every foot of the Mexican National Railroad, consisting of nearly 1,000 miles of road running from Laredo, Texas, to Mexico City.'"[74] While the railroad strikes did not succeed in achieving their demands, and faced mostly setbacks prior to the revolution, they signaled the rise of a new militant unionism spreading across the industrial workforce.

Workers across the textile industry also went on strike in 1906 and 1907. Centered at the modern industrial textile plant at Río Blanco (on the outskirts of Orizaba, Veracruz), a local strike turned into a regional battle that spread across several states.

By 1906, workers at Río Blanco had formed a mutualista called the Gran Círculo de Obreros Libres (GCOL). What made this effort unique was that members the leadership were committed anticapitalists. This group coalesced through a shared history of previous struggle in the factories and had consolidated through their alignment with the 1906 plan of the Partido Liberal Mexicano. The plan contained the first call for comprehensive labor reform, akin to the calls for radical reform in the United States in the 1880s, then advocated by anarchists and Marxists. While reformist in nature, the plan contained radical ideas for its historical context and represented an early and evolving phase of a later revolutionary position. This included the call for the eight-hour workday, six-day workweek, a minimum wage, restrictions on child labor, safe and sanitary working conditions, accident and sickness benefits, cash wages, abolition of company stores, and the right to strike.[75]

At Río Blanco, local worker leaders like Manuel Ávila, Genaro and Arturo Guerrero, and José Neira were veterans of previous struggles in the factories and were avid readers and followers of the PLM newspaper *Regeneración*. Precipitating the strike, this group had formed the nucleus of a PLM-linked revolutionary organization to promote socialist ideas among the workers, support union organizing, and advocate for the toppling of the Díaz government.[76] They developed a radical newspaper, *Revolución Social*, which stoked class consciousness and hammered home the idea that the strike was the only means for workers to defend their interests.[77] The new group sent out worker-organizers steeped in the radical politics of Magonismo throughout central and eastern Mexico to agitate among textile workers. Within the first five months of its existence, the GCOL formed eighty branches throughout the region from Veracruz to Mexico City.[78]

Numerous complaints by textile works poured out of the pages of *Revolución Social*. Workers endured fifteen-hour workdays with few breaks, and faced arbitrary fines, penalties, and punishments. Pay was abysmally low. While textile workers had a history of militancy—there were at least thirty strikes between 1881 and 1895—existing worker organization within the industry was limited to mutual aid societies.[79] Despite wage increases of 15 percent between the years 1877 and 1898 as a result of the strikes, after 1900 they slipped back to pre-1877 levels.[80] Furthermore, child labor was common, company towns lacked schools for the workers' children, and there were strict rules regulating housing. By 1906, there was a growing militant mood among the workers. The program of the GCOL attests to this, stating that in response to the abysmal working conditions, the workers planned to take direct action. "In case of difficulty with the firms we will use the strike, if the strike does not accomplish anything we will resort to dynamite or revolution."[81] According to Karl Koth, "There were good reasons for this militancy. A price inflation caused by the decline in the price of silver, the introduction of machinery, which caused a reduction in the work force, and the 1907 Wall Street crisis, which lowered the prices of henequen, cotton and minerals, led to violent strikes in the last five years of the Porfiriato."[82]

In textiles, Mexican labor historian Moisés Gonzalez Navarro identifies seventy-five strikes in the textile industry during the Porfiriato, with several smaller textile strikes precipitating the eruption of class conflict in 1906.[83]

The fear of more strikes led by the nascent union worried the textile bosses, who took preemptive action. They formed a bosses' syndicate, the Centro Industria Mexicana (CIM), and decreed a series of new work rules designed to break the back of the new union organization. The CIM lengthened the workday and imposed a seven-day workweek, along with other demands designed to humiliate workers.[84] According to the CIM's calculations, a heavy-handed approach would break the fledgling organization, and in failure the workers would become demoralized and turn against the union.

Instead of backing down, sixty-eight hundred workers went on strike in December of 1906, shutting down thirty-four textile factories in the states of Puebla and Tlaxcala.[85] Their list of demands included the right to join unions, a pay raise, an end to fines for broken tools or defective materials, that workers have the right to access reading materials on the job, the abolition of company stores, and disability compensation, among others.[86] The GCOL had organized other groups of textile workers to donate a part of their income to support their striking brethren. With the Díaz regime's tacit approval, the CIM members declared a lockout at all textile factories, dismissing another twenty-two thousand workers in Veracruz, Puebla, and Tlaxcala in a concerted demonstration of their class power. In response, other groups of textile workers walked out on strike so that an estimated thirty thousand textile workers total, from ninety-three factories spread over twenty-two states, were affected by the strike/lockout by January 1907.[87] Militant workers organized to keep the factories from reopening. In Río Blanco, the workers formed "combat brigades," creating an elaborate organizational model designed to do everything from keeping scabs out of the factories to collecting and distributing food. One brigade of women, led by textile worker Lucretia Toriz, gained national attention for being at the forefront of self-defense efforts when the strike was threatened by military repression in the early stages.[88] This brigade then provided key logistical support and frontline fighters against company guards and scabs:

> At Río Blanco, a group of women [Anselma Sierra, Carmen Cruz, Margarita Martínez, María L. de Pensamiento] . . . formed a combat brigade that was in charge of collecting chunks of stale bread and hard tortillas that they hid in their *rebozos* [to sneak into the guarded company compound] and very early in the morning they would stand guard at the door of the factory waiting to see if anyone dared try to break the protest movement, at which point they would cruelly stone them with the symbolic remains.[89]

With the industry paralyzed and with no sign of collapse in the resolve of the workers, the Díaz regime sent federal troops into the textile zones and intervened to arbitrate, albeit as a dishonest broker seeking to strengthen the position of the textile investors.

During a "cooling-off period" in the negotiations on January 7, a skirmish broke out between striking workers and factory foremen at the large textile factory at Río Blanco. After the killing of a worker by a foreman, a large and angry body of workers surged through the town, razing the company store, freeing prisoners from the town jail, cutting the electricity to the factory, and seizing upon homes and buildings associated with the more oppressive aspects of daily life. The following day, as protests continued, a detachment of federal troops arrived and took up positions against the unarmed protesters. To the horror of those present, the troops opened fire on the crowd of hundreds, killing seventeen outright and wounding eighty. In the aftermath of the shooting, workers scattered and three days of street battles ensued, as some workers organized resistance. Others fled but were hunted down and shot. Over the course of three days, the official death toll states that 200 workers were killed along with 25 soldiers (while other estimates state as many as 700 workers were killed); with 118 workers facing prison sentences of varying lengths.[90] Many of those killed and jailed were key leaders of the GCOL.

While the strike collapsed as a result of the preponderance of forces aligned against it, which effectively smashed the GCOL as a regional union, it did not signal the end of the labor movement, nor did it stifle worker militancy, even in textiles.[91] In fact, it showed how the Díaz regime perceived the growing threat of an independent workers' movement and its power to challenge the capitalist class on a regional and potentially national level. According to Carmen Ramos-Escandón, "The decision to violently suppress the [textile] workers can be interpreted as a desperate gesture on behalf of the authorities as they realized that the workers were gaining in strength and organization."[92] The textile strikes of 1906–1908 signaled a new willingness of workers to confront capital directly through strikes, organizing themselves on a larger and more militant scale. Even in defeat, they dealt a fatal blow to the Díaz regime. The illusion of invulnerability was shattered, as the regime had to rely on brutal force to maintain its grip on power. The Mexican working class's forcible entrance onto the political stage weakened the Díaz regime and widened social polarization, creating the conditions for radical ideology to gain a wider audience within the laboring classes.

Chapter 2

Mexican Workers: From Liberalism to Anticapitalism

"Mutual-aid societies as a form of association did not offer the means of self-defense for the working class, but they had already been organized in the industries [across the country]. In order to defend themselves against General Díaz, they needed revolutionary socialism to understand how to come together into one giant fist."
—Rosendo Salazar, a leading working-class revolutionary and participant in the Mexican Revolution

Early bourgeois liberalism carried with it high ideals that appealed to the working class in relation to the previous epochal struggles against feudal conservatism and reactionary clericalism (known as the Wars of La Reforma between 1854 and 1857). The working class was a small and dispersed segment of the population during this conflict, incapable of articulating an independent political strategy. Because of this, the liberal worldview united a cross section of social classes aspiring to break the chains of colonialism and underdevelopment. The historic victory of the liberal bourgeois forces carried with it the immediate aspirations of a nascent working class: the prospect of economic and political modernization. More specifically, an end to forced labor and the introduction of democratic reforms such as universal education, expansion of suffrage, and freedom of assembly were liberal ideals that initially bound working-class loyalty.

Despite high hopes, the realization of meaningful and substantive reform remained elusive for several reasons: conservatives continued to actively oppose the liberal project, even allying with the French during their occupation of Mexico from 1862 to 1867. More significantly, rather than lead to the social development of all classes in Mexican society, the liberal project of capitalist modernization relied on opening Mexico to unfettered foreign investment and exploitation of natural resources, dispossession in the countryside through the privatization of communal village lands, and increased exploitation of a proletarianized peasantry and urban and industrial labor. As liberals increased integration into the world economy, the exigencies of capital accumulation changed the idealism of the previous generation into a crushing reality for the next.

While the Constitution of 1857 did guarantee "free labor" and "freedom of association," it did not prescribe specific rights for workers. In fact, labor was viewed by bourgeois policymakers as an essential commodity to be exploited in the interests of capital accumulation.

Ricardo Pozas Horcasitas described factory working conditions in the 1850s this way:

> The working hours ranged from 12–16 hours a day . . . workers were not compen-
> sated for religious holidays or frequent temporary closures. The factory owners
> operated in a paternalistic fashion, much like the owners of the haciendas, hav-
> ing control over the administration of justice. There was also the use of prisons
> and torture, if that was deemed necessary to maintain control.[1]

The growth of the industrial working class and its efforts to create its own organizations raised the specter of unions and strikes. To prevent this, the liberals
introduced the Penal Code of 1872, which imposed up to three months in jail and
monetary fines for any effort to raise wages or impede the "free exercise of industry
or labor."[2] Despite these measures, worker organization sprouted across the country,
with a budding proletarian press appearing in the cities by the early 1870s. A workers'
rights counternarrative began to provoke reaction among the liberal ideologues. For
instance, wealthy banker, liberal Científico, and member of Congress Pablo Macedo
illustrated this by raging against the idea of such a thing as "workers' rights," and by
decrying policies that attempted to protect the working class from the vagaries of the
"free market." Using liberal rhetoric, he condemned "this doctrine of tutelage, of the
protection of the weak and unfortunate citizen . . . [this is what has] killed freedom of
industry, freedom of labor, and freedom of thought."[3]

In practice, the imperatives of capitalist accumulation led to governmental practices that increasingly subordinated or repressed workers. The liberal state developed
three mechanisms to achieve this:

> A judicial apparatus that permits the legal exploitation and oppression of one
> class over another; the state as an instrument of [direct] domination over the
> laboring classes; and the application of both in combination. This combination
> of factors is what impeded the struggles undertaken by the workers growing into
> a threat to the interests of the capitalist class, making it difficult for the workers
> to see the state as an enemy of their class, and retarding the development of
> genuine and broad class consciousness.[4]

While a personal and political rupture took place between Juárez and Díaz in the
years of the "restored republic" (1867–1876), a primary focus on capitalist development remained intact once Díaz assumed total power in 1876.[5] Díaz and his bourgeois
cohort only broke with the previous generation of liberals in that they made their
peace with the Catholic hierarchy by ceasing their church land confiscations and restoring previous rights and privileges. They were also more willing to concede to the
demands of US investors, who were irritated by the juaristas' nationalist impulses that
attempted to contain the extent of foreign control within the economy.[6]

In power Díaz pursued a unique form of coalition building that propelled the
liberal goal of peasant dispossession, free markets, and economic modernization in a
more strategic way. While suppressing labor, the porfiristas co-opted their conservative adversaries, ameliorated banditry in the countryside by converting bandit gangs

into a well-paid rural police force, and opened the sluice gates to foreign investors.

Meanwhile the policy of peasant displacement could continue as the catalyst of economic modernization. This included not only the goal of land transfer to the hacendado and capitalist speculators, but the creation of a workforce from the growing ranks of displaced farmers that would have to sell their labor to survive. As Raymond Vernon described it:

> From Díaz's point of view, there were very few risks and many advantages in continuing the process which Juárez had unintentionally began—the process of separating the peasant from his land. The Díaz political machine would be strengthened by helping the landowners extend their holdings, and by satisfying the needs of the haciendas which were short of labor. At the same time, foreign investors would be given better conditions for investment because labor would be made available for the mines in the north and the plantations of the Gulf Coast.[7]

The Porfirian model produced a point of convergence for rival bourgeois factions—that the subordination of labor served the common interest of national development, even if factions still quibbled over the details. As William D. Raat summarized, "[b]y the time of the Porfiriato, the traditional distinctions between liberalism and conservatism were meaningless."[8]

The cross-class popularity of nineteenth-century liberalism reflected a shared but temporal opposition to the backward institutions linked to the conservative old guard. This alliance fractured as the internal reactionary threat receded, the French were expelled, and the turn toward foreign-investment-led development gained steam. During the early phase of this transition, liberals maintained their influence over the working class by granting privileges and blandishments.

This included providing loyal working-class organizations with printing presses, building space, and night schools, and allowing subservient labor leaders to obtain lower-level positions in the government bureaucracy.[9] Efforts to control and retard labor militancy became even more developed during the years of the Porfiriato. According to David W. Walker, "The Díaz government developed a flexible and sophisticated array of labor policy instruments" that fluctuated between the dispensing of patronage and the occasional mediation of labor conflicts, to brutal, heavy-handed repression.[10] During the waning years of his government, Díaz's ability to contain labor began to slip.

As previously mentioned, a growing militancy and the increased frequency of strikes among industrial workers began to change the internal dynamics of labor organization. Sections of the working class began to break with liberalism, forming an audience for radical doctrines to make sense of changing social realities. In fact, John Mason Hart argues that cross-class liberal alliances began to fracture along class lines "with the advent of strikes and modern class conflict during the 1860s, [and] the factory owners soon became the primary enemies and took their place alongside the . . . conservative oligarchy."[11]

Therefore, the trajectory of liberal policies from Juárez to Porfirio Díaz fragmented the capital-labor alliance by the late nineteenth century. The rise of industry, the implementation of coercive labor rationalization, increased exploitation and market-driven instability, and imperialist impositions induced quick growth spurts of class consciousness among the workers. In the ideological cracks of liberalism, radical philosophies began to fill up space. Gaston García Cantú describes how the imperatives of capitalism rendered the possibility of harmony between workers and owners farcical:

> What the [liberal labor leaders] wanted was an equilibrium between capital and labor by means of a fair wage . . . [but] the owners avoided the demands of the workers by asserting that if they don't like the wages or hours of work that they are free to find work elsewhere. But that response—the workers would say—was a joke: the owners crusaded together against the workers for that which they had no alternative: accept the conditions that they imposed by way of slavery, or die of hunger. Against this infamy, socialist doctrine arose . . . [along with the idea that] only the strike can stop the abuses of the capitalists.[12]

The complicity of the state in abetting labor exploitation also alienated the workers. Liberal politicians took the side of business and industry with recurring frequency, feigning neutrality when it came to "private" affairs between capital and labor.[13] In this atmosphere, the vanguard elements of the Mexican industrial working class became receptive to radical and anticapitalist doctrines and direct action at the point of production as a means to combat capitalist exploitation, state complicity, and foreign domination. A small but significant segment of women also looked to radical doctrines to help construct a feminist challenge to the deeply rooted sexism that pervaded liberal notions of a "woman's place" in the late nineteenth century.

Early Anarchist Movements in Mexico

According to John Mason Hart, anarchism was the principal ideological expression of Mexican working-class radicalism between 1865 and the Revolution of 1910, with anarchists providing the mind and muscle behind the formation of mutual aid societies, cooperatives, industrial unions, and regional and national workers' councils.[14] Anarchist ideas entered into Mexico as early as the 1860s, as European immigrants brought with them the doctrines of incipient anticapitalism from their home countries. Greek proto-anarchist Plotino Rhodakanaty arrived in Mexico after participating in the failed Hungarian uprising of 1848, and settling in Paris, France, where he became immersed in the study of emerging anarchist thought. Inspired by the ideas of Charles Fourier and Pierre-Joseph Proudhon (as well as Protestant Christian doctrine), he set out for Mexico in 1861 after learning of the existence of large and semiautonomous agricultural regions with enduring traditions of collective peasant farming, the ideal setting for the establishment of agrarian socialist communes. After the rise of the Paris Commune in 1871, which created an international shockwave as it showed the potential power of the working class to replace capitalism with their own form of self-government, Rhodakanaty and his followers shifted their attention to urban workers. This set into motion the Mexican anarchist tradition as the foundational root of proletarian radicalism.

In 1861, Rhodakanaty produced and distributed the first known appeal for socialism in Mexico with his pamphlet *Cartilla Socialista*. In it, he applied Fourier's utopian notions to conditions in Mexico, asserting that society could be perfected if cooperative communes were established among Mexico's peasants based on socialist principles. He explained the possibility for socialist transformation in spiritual terms, stating, "I firmly believe that within the scope of man and through the act of realizing his terrestrial destiny, he replaces a world of misery, deceit, oppression, war, devastation; in a word of *evil*; with a kingdom of abundance, truth, justice, peace, and of work; in a word, of *goodness*."[15]

In 1863 Rhodakanaty established an anarchist Escuela Libre (Free School) in the pueblo of Chalco, on the outskirts of Mexico City. Influenced by similar incipient anarchist movements in France, Italy, and Spain, he believed that Mexicans would be predisposed to adopt a formal anarchist project because the peasants already had a tradition of communal-based forms of radicalism in their resistance to the encroachment of capitalist-oriented haciendas. His early educational efforts attempted to politicize local artisans and small farmers around the Proudhonist idea that ascribes "the right of a man to effective control over his dwelling and the land and tools he needed to work and live."[16]

Through his writings over the next two decades Rhodakanaty challenged and refuted the "positivist" theories emanating from the prominent bourgeois academic institutions of the period that were publicly extolled by the Porfirian Científicos. He directed a fusillade of polemics against the ideological arm of porfirismo, publicly discrediting the pronouncements that added a pseudoscientific veneer to characterizations of indigenous and agrarian communalism as anachronistic, symptomatic of cultural inferiority, and an irreconcilable obstacle to the fruits of capitalist modernization.[17]

Through these efforts he cultivated an audience and intellectual following from within the youthful circles of the educated artisanry and declassed peasantry. This coterie of followers took up his vision to organize peasants and artisans into egalitarian agrarian communes in the countryside.

When Rhodakanaty's idealistic efforts failed to attract significant popular participation through moral persuasion, one of his closest followers named Julio López Chávez broke with his methods. López Chávez tried to force the question by calling for armed struggle against the landowning oligarchy. Between 1867 and 1869 he led a guerrilla peasant campaign with a force of up to fifteen hundred campesino followers against the large landowners in Chalco, proclaiming "war against the rich and the redistribution of the hacienda land to the indigenous."[18] The uprising occurred after a land speculator drained Lake Chalco, which local campesinos depended on for their livelihood. The campaign quickly spread through the states of Mexico, Tlaxcala, Puebla, and Veracruz before being violently suppressed by federal troops under orders from Juárez, who had López Chávez killed by firing squad. Before being shot, he allegedly proclaimed, "¡Viva el socialismo!" ("Long live socialism!")[19] Other agrarian revolts inspired by utopian socialist ideals continued to flare up into the early 1880s.[20]

International events inspired a significant shift in the orientation of anarchists in Mexico at that time. In 1864, European radicals created continental linkages to lay the basis for the creation of the International Workingmen's Association, a political party committed to the foundation of international socialism. Also known as the First International, the IWA became the midwife for the rise and dissemination of the two great anticapitalist political traditions with an orientation against private property, the bourgeois state, and the collective, revolutionary potential of the urban working class: anarchism and Marxist socialism.

After 1868, the First International began to impact Mexican anarchists, especially the current associated with Mikhail Bakunin. Bakunismo located the social revolution as one in which the workers' movement creates an alternative to capitalism by forming its own egalitarian exchange cooperatives, rejecting all forms of hierarchy in favor of direct democracy, thereby effectively undermining the basis by which bourgeois political economy could continue. The first modern uprising of an urban workers' movement that appeared to follow this trajectory, the Paris Commune of 1871, sent shock waves around the world as it testified to the potential for workers to shepherd historical progress forward by toppling capitalism and implementing socialism.[21] The Paris Commune sparked a flourishing of radical thought and inspired the first efforts at organizing workers on a national level.

Anarchist politics in Mexico soon absorbed the lessons of the Commune. In 1871, Plotino Rhodakanaty and his band of disciples directed their efforts toward urban workers, beginning with the publication of the newspaper *La Internacional*. The paper preached the values of "the mutualista, the necessity of establishing collective contracts for work, the efficiency of cooperatives for production and consumption, and the use of the strike as the ultimate recourse for worker self-defense against the abuses of capital."[22] Through these efforts, a new generation of young intellectuals became devoted to the cause of organizing workers along anarchist principles. They also became the first coterie of anarchist organizers to make inroads into the working class and to challenge the dominance of liberalism. As Hart explains,

> The group included the future leaders of Mexican socialism: Francisco Zala-costa, a young [Spanish émigré and] zealot who took the lead in future agrarian struggles; Santiago Villanueva, the organizer of Mexico's original labor movement; and Hermengildo Villavicencio, who worked with Villanueva . . . They all became artisans after leaving school and began their organizing activities among Mexico City's handicraftsmen, who expressed increasing disgruntlement with the growing factory system of commodity production.[23]

As Mexican workers began to organize on a larger scale in the 1860s, many groups within the workers' movement, especially in central Mexico, began to incorporate anarchist agendas.[24] By the late 1860s, anarchist organizers began to openly criticize the liberal ideology and mutualist orientation of existing workers' groups, indicating the first class-based rift within the liberal alliance and the first articulation of independent working-class political ideology.

A significant step toward a national orientation for labor occurred with the launch of the Gran Círculo de Obreros de México in 1870. In its earliest manifestation, the Círculo developed as a national federation of mutualistas, but rapid industrialization began to change its character within a short span of time. The formation of a national workers' organization brought to the fore the question of political orientation, especially in light of rapid industrialization and foreign capital's increasingly strong grip over the economy.

Since the triumph of liberals, the presidential administrations of Benito Juárez and Miguel Lerdo de Tejada (and into the first years of Díaz) sought to suppress the development of working-class politics or at least constrain it within their framework for liberal capitalist development. Strikes were forbidden as a bane to national development, so allegiance was maintained as long as the threat of the reactionary power of the Church and the conservative oligarchy reared its head. The fresh memories of the revolutionary gains of La Reforma remained a part of working-class consciousness well into the late nineteenth century, that of the consolidation of the liberal Mexican bourgeoisie. Coinciding with the diminishing threat of foreign intervention, the defensive nationalism that subordinated independent working-class development to the larger goal of national liberation began to lose meaning.[25] For the nascent prophets of anticapitalism, this became especially apparent as "national interests" became indistinguishable from "bourgeois interests." They observed how the national imperative was being redefined as a singular urgency to entice foreign investment and to accumulate domestic capital at the expense of Mexico's working classes, who were being forced to shoulder the costs of capitalist modernization through the exploitation of their labor.

As cross-class unity waned, liberal regime brokers created patronage systems to maintain loyalty and labor peace, offering monetary contributions, direct channels of communication, and other blandishments to co-opt labor leaders. This created divided loyalties within the Gran Círculo, compelling anarchist ideologues to create an independent and radical alternative to the leadership of liberal labor lieutenants.[26] This became even more urgent when the liberal leadership in the Gran Círculo joined efforts with the liberal governor of the Federal District in breaking textile factory strikes in the mid-1870s, as they were an open affront to the liberal labor code of 1871.[27]

In larger cities across the country, the anarchists developed their own organizations within the Círculo called Sociedades de Resistencia (Resistance Societies). These focused on propagating explicitly anarchist ideology toward the larger working class and advocating for the formation of cooperatives and strikes as a means to challenge capital. These groups spread across Mexico and came to wield considerable influence within the base of the organization, even as they remained a minority. These anarchist groups also began to propagate the first explicitly anticapitalist tracts through working-class and anarchist-leaning newspapers that began to emerge in the major urban centers, like El Obrero Socialista (Socialist Worker), Obrero Internacional (International Worker), El Hijo del Trabajo (The Son of Labor), and La Huelga (The Strike). An 1874 edition of Obrero Internacional exemplified the radical tone of the papers, stating, "All of the workers of the world, tired of being slaves and victims of the unbridled ambition of the capitalists, work tirelessly for their liberation; the two weapons that should help them achieve it: the cooperative society and the strike."[28]

Nineteenth century anticapitalist newspapers in Mexico

The outbreak of class conflict between workers and the new capitalist landlords, as well as growing opposition to foreign capital's hegemonic influence, laid the basis for rupture in the old liberal alliance. In the cracks of the old, new political realignments embracing different variations of anarchism developed. While liberalism remained the dominant ideology of the working class into the 1870s, these anarchist factions cohered in the larger urban centers and gradually formed the nucleus of a national, left-wing opposition advocating for a more radical trajectory.

One of these groups was led by Rhodakanaty and his collaborators, who were joined by militant anarchist émigrés from Spain. Together, they formed the anarchist collective called La Social, which viewed itself as a vanguard organization to contend for leadership against the liberals in labor formations like the Círculo. The anarchists criticized the inherent weaknesses of mutualism, since it did not "provide a comprehensive program for the transition of society away from capitalism . . . [and because it] made no attempt to ameliorate the differences between the rich and the poor, the powerful and the weak."[29] Through their newspapers, the anarchists took aim at the liberal bourgeoisie and their labor sycophants, whom they criticized for corrupting and conservatizing politics with money and cronyism.[30]

Amid this period of political fermentation, another group, led by utopian socialist and associate of Rhodakanaty Juan de Mata Rivera, made their first attempt to establish a workers' congress that could transcend the limits of traditional mutualism. In 1876, they launched the Congreso General Obrero de la Republica Mexicana, with the hopes that it could create a vehicle that could win over and lead the ranks of the Círculo toward a more explicitly socialist program. Through its manifesto, the Congreso called for the spread of "libertarian socialist" ideology, "social guarantees," cooperatives to begin "emancipating the workers from the capitalist yoke," and "independence from individual and capitalist interest, in order to put an end to misery and its accompanying ills."[31] La Social also entered into the Congreso as well, intending to provide a Left revolutionary leadership in the ensuing class struggle. By 1881, they became the strongest political force within the Congreso and the Mexican working class as a whole, claiming over a hundred sections and fifty thousand members after reorganizing as the Mexican section of the anarchist International Workingmen's Association.[32]

The anarchist wing of the workers' movement began to gain a large following and exercise national leadership in relation to the increased frequency of strikes. According to Jorge Basurto,

> It is without a doubt that [anarchist] propaganda had an effect on worker action in the second half of the nineteenth century judging by the broadening scope of activity during that period, however underprepared at first or repressed after. The strike, the classic instrument of struggle for the proletariat, was utilized in effect, with more or less frequency but with few successes and diverse outcomes; but, of course, with the invariable opposition and persecution of the authorities.[33]

Despite these developments, the anarchist movement remained largely artisanal in character, with a political outlook that could not transcend utopian socialist fantasies as a defense against the atomization of industrial capitalism. A second wave of radical ideas then entered into Mexico by the turn of the century, brought in by anarchist and Marxist migrants versed in the gospel of class struggle at the point of production. These revolutionaries found a new audience in the industrial working class, especially amid a strike wave in key industries between 1906 and 1908. As Basurto explains, rising class conflict "opened up space for the flourishing of anarchist, Socialist, and progressive ideas, beginning to transform the traditional mutualistas and resulting in new forms of organization committed to action."[34]

Class Struggle Doctrines Enter Mexico

A second wave of radical movements emanating from Europe found their way into Mexico with exiles fleeing their homeland ahead of fierce repression, or revolutionists seeking to spread their doctrines internationally. The events that created and circulated the revolutionaries internationally were the great upheavals and revolts of the nineteenth century, and the reactionary waves of repression that typically followed. These included the revolutionary waves that washed over Europe in 1830 and 1848, the Paris Commune in 1871, the Spanish uprisings of 1854, 1856, and again in 1873 and 1874, to identify those most relevant for Mexico. By the turn of the century, a significant population of international anarchists, Anarcho-syndicalists, and Marxist Socialists followed revolutionary developments through the Caribbean, South America, and into Mexico.

A wider dissemination of socialist philosophies took place between 1880 and 1914, mirroring the deepening of imperialist conflict, industrial development spreading within the contours of the global economy, and the radicalization of the working-class resistance of the period. For instance, strikes increased in frequency during this period, reaching a total of over 250 of diverse magnitude and character by the end of the Porfiriato.[35] A second generation of Anarchist ideas generally referred to as "anarcho-syndicalism" were diffused through the production, translation, and circulation of radical books and tracts, the transoceanic and international mobility of revolutionary migrants and political exiles, the linkages of international political networks, and then coincided with the cultivation of home-grown adherents. As Carl Levy describes,

The anarchists played a prominent part in the generic internationalist syndicalism, in which antimilitarism and industrial trade unionism were disseminated
by a new mobile proletariat of laborers, transportation workers, and some
skilled artisans, most notably Italians, Spaniards, Russians, Scandinavians, Brit-
ons, Irish, and Yiddish-speaking Jews of various nationalities. They were part of
the vast labor migration between Europe, the Americas, and the so-called White
Dominions of the British Empire.[36]

The entry of international anarchists into Mexico also occurred specifically vis-à-vis
the Caribbean, especially Cuba. In the late nineteenth century Spanish anarchists
had amassed in Cuba, where many participated in that nation's independence movement and hoped to shape the postcolonial outcomes. In Cuba, according to historian Julie Greene,

> anarchism became the dominant ideology among workers during the late
> nineteenth and early twentieth centuries . . . Anarchists in Cuba built effective
> unions, led strike movements, created schools and workers' associations, and
> published newspapers. They strove to build unity between workers in different
> industries and of different levels of skill, and they were unusually supportive of
> women's struggles. They also made antiracism into an important part of their
> movement, taking an unprecedented stand for solidarity between *peninsulares*,
> creoles, and people of color.[37]

From Cuba, anarchist internationalists fanned out through the Caribbean Basin,
with groups forming in Florida, Puerto Rico, Panama, and the Gulf Coast of Mexico,
especially Veracruz, where a large Spanish émigré population was concentrated. The
radical ideas later spread along with migrant workers and exiled radicals to New York
and Chicago, to the north and west, and from Colombia to Chile to the south.

The revolutionary ferment in Cuba and the subsequent entrance of foreign-born
radicals into Mexico's Gulf Coast did not go unnoticed by the Díaz regime. A successful revolutionary movement just off the coast of Mexico, especially one in which
a radical workers' movement played a prominent role, could undermine imperialist
labor arrangements in Mexico. Internationalist anarchists and Marxists would undoubtedly seek to replicate their efforts in Mexico. In response, the Díaz government
imposed strict neutrality in the conflict and closely policed the Gulf States, detaining
and searching all Spanish ships to display its fealty to US imperial aims.[38] The suppression of radicalism became a central tenet of the last and repressive phase of the
Porfiriato. In exchange for its loyalty, the United States agreed to observe strict neutrality in kind. This accord became an important mechanism for the Díaz regime (and
subsequent heads of state) to coordinate with the US government to arrest, detain,
and even deport Mexican radical exiles who moved north of the border to continue
their revolutionary efforts.

The diffusion of anarchist, and later syndicalist and Marxist, ideas occurred in conjunction with the accelerating transnational capital flows, political maneuvering, and
military interventions of the United States throughout the region.[39] In 1898, the United

States government intervened in the Cuban independence struggle, declaring war on Spain and announcing support for Cuban self-determination. After defeating the small and decrepit Spanish military, the United States then denied Cuban independence and occupied the island with the intention of converting it into a neo-colonial asset.

While the US government declared Cuba independent in 1898, this "independence" was contingent on the acceptance of a constitution that included stipulations that granted the United States unfettered access within the economy and the right to militarily intervene to protect its interests. The Platt Amendment, as this set of guarantees came to be known, allowed for nominal political independence in exchange for the forfeiture of economic sovereignty. The arrangement was contingent upon the cultivation of a new ruling elite willing to administer US policy, while the anti-imperialist movement regrouped and reentered the stage of opposition.

As US capital quickly established ownership across the economy, both foreign and native-born radicals turned their attention to organizing the working class. The growth of Anarcho-syndicalist and Marxist thought viewed the formation of labor unions as new frontlines of struggle against US imperialism. In Cuba, they challenged US-based industrial capital invested in the newly established sugar and tobacco export sectors. They also

> attacked the emergence of US-styled representative democracy that they saw as deceptive: the masses supposedly had a voice, but the elite ran these places to advance their own interests and the interests of the US overlords . . . they [also] criticized Caribbean governments' collusion with the US, decried US military interventions and militarism in general, and challenged US concepts of Pan-Americanism. As a result, regional anarchists confronted not only "national" governments, companies and the Catholic Church, but also the imperial reach of US economics and politics in the Caribbean.[40]

In response to the advent of worker radicalism within their newly acquired domain, US administrators worked through their Cuban subordinates to suppress the first threat to their economic interests. In 1902, they approved the selection of pro-US presidential candidate Gerardo Machado in tightly controlled elections. With the full support of the US government (and with backing from the military), one of Machado's first endeavors was to crush the nascent labor movement. As Steven Hirsch and Lucién Van der Walt note:

> Shortly after his assumption of power, the repression against anarchists and Marxists ensued. The government labelled both as "pernicious foreigners" and jailed, disappeared, assassinated, deported, or forced dozens of anarchists and other radicals into exile. The "machadato," as the era of Machado's rule is remembered, marked the end of the anarchist movement as an effective element for radical social change in Cuba.[41]

The fledgling anarchist and Marxist networks witnessed these events with a wary eye, and began to identify US imperialism as an existential threat throughout the region.

Many radicals regrouped in Mexico.

Once in Mexico, anarchist philosophies stirred intellectuals and workers into revolutionary action as they were applied to the particular national characteristics. As John Lear observes, many urban workers

> were now a generation removed from the rural backgrounds of their parents and had been exposed to radical worker ideologies from abroad through contact with foreign workers in Mexico, such as Spanish craftworkers in Veracruz or Mexico City, and with U.S. railroad, mining, and oil workers on both sides of the Rio Grande.[42]

Anarchist intellectual and agitator Ricardo Flores Magón, along with the Organizing Junta of the Mexican Liberal Party, was the first to attempt a coordinated insurrection against the regime of Porfirio Díaz as early as 1906. By the height of the revolutionary period, veterans of the magonista movement and other radicals had formed the first nationwide and transnational revolutionary organization in the contours of the unfolding revolution. The Anarcho-syndicalist Casa del Obrero Mundial/ International Workers' Center was the first manifestation of independent working-class thought and action within the revolution. While anarchist ideas continued to find resonance and organizational expression within the workers' movement well into the 1920s, the success of the Bolshevik Revolution in Russia inspired a seismic shift in orientation toward Marxism after 1917.

International Workers' Day commemoration Mexico City 1913

Chapter 3
Los Caballeros de Labor

"They [politicians and the rich] want the working people to starve to death
while hoarding wealth through monopoly and lowering the wages of the
working class, who are the only producers of wealth and true industry;
unlike bankers, usurers, and speculators that produce nothing and take
all, the Caballeros de Labor aspire to nothing more than that the workers
are well paid so that they can also enjoy the comforts of life."
—Juan José Herrera, organizer of the Caballeros de Labor
(Knights of Labor) in the Territory of New Mexico

The US invasion and military occupation of Mexico between 1846 and 1848 precipitated the forceful acquisition and absorption of Mexico's frontier region into the expanding North American economy, replete with its people, their cultures, and their traditions. The subsequent victory of the Republican-led Union forces in the Civil War further consolidated the hegemony of industrial capitalism as the singular economic model to be imposed on the newly acquired territories to the west. The opening of the Southwest to a flood of capital, speculators, and settlers seeking quick fortunes produced direct conflict with the people and their existing social order. Backed by federal and state forces, the capitalist class was given free rein to disrupt the existing state of affairs throughout the region in order to redistribute the land, natural resources, and labor power of the native people to serve their own interests. In New Mexico, with the largest and most historically established Mexican population in the region, the penetration of capital came into direct conflict with the existing land tenure system.

Between 1850 and 1880, most of the Mexican people living on the colonial-era land grant of Las Vegas, New Mexico, had lost access to the pasture and farming land they had previously held or used in common. The once pastoral and farming community had been transformed by the new industrial relations of production. The previously sedentary population had become displaced, having to now find itinerant work on the railroads intersecting their pueblos or in the mining complexes springing up throughout the region. They entered into the developing migrant channels that took them to industrial centers as far away as Denver and Chicago. Here, they came into contact with labor unions and radical political ideologies that could both explain the injustice of their condition and provide an organizational and ideological framework for how to resist.

This defines the experience of Juan José Herrera, a displaced *nuevomexicano* whose interactions with socialists and the Knights of Labor informed the creation

of the Cabelleros de Labor. The class-struggle approach of the Caballeros, which included mass direct action by a subgroup of adherents called Las Gorras Blancas (The
White Caps), temporarily defeated the march of Anglo capitalism through northern
New Mexico in the late nineteenth century. The case of Las Gorras Blancas provides
the first significant demonstration of Mexican class struggle in the industrial Southwest, a recurring phenomenon situated at those historical junctures where rising labor
struggle and the flourishing of left-wing ideology has given tangible expression to the
notion of working-class solidarity.

The Knights of Labor in the Southwest

The veterans of the First International Workingmen's Association that maintained a
principled commitment against racism and sexism were instrumental in the formation
of the Holy and Noble Order of the Knights of Labor. Established in Philadelphia by
garment workers in 1869, this secret fraternal order was dedicated to the organization
of all workers regardless of race and gender into one national federation.[1] The founders believed that capital had been concentrated at such a scale as to attain a preponderance of power over individual trade unions, which were like "a bundle of sticks when
unbound, weak and powerless to resist combination."[2] They observed that the bosses
made good use of the racial, gender, and skill stratification of the working class, playing
groups against each other to prevent unity. Through the organization of "all branches
of honorable toil" and political education, the first Knights discouraged strikes and
class conflict as harmful to the "common good," and instead believed they could use
the ballot to abolish capitalism. The path forward toward this goal included registering electoral victories for the eight-hour workday, an end to child labor, equal pay for
women and workers of color, the abolition of prison labor, and the legal right to join
a union. Since the organization lacked a defined national doctrine, local branches and
assemblies developed their own local character and strategies over time.

The political orientation of the Knights of Labor led to significant growth of the
organization by 1886, including the formation of Mexican worker-led lodges in the
state of New Mexico. This organizational model of the Knights was similar to the traditional Mexican mutualista, seventeen of which were formed throughout the territory
of New Mexico between 1885 and 1912.[3] This may explain why so many Mexican railroad workers and miners were willing to join the national labor union, especially in a
period when the first big industrial labor conflicts were taking place. The Caballeros
de Labor, as they were called in Spanish, organized one of the most significant popular
rebellions in New Mexican history.

The organizational model originally chosen was that of a secretive and semiautonomous fraternal lodge as the base unit within a national structure that convened
delegated national conventions, or assemblies. The lodge model emphasized association and formal unity as the primary pole of attraction and the active participation of
members in local worker assemblies, which founder Uriah Stephens considered the
primary school for educating and preparing labor to assert its own interests.[4] Since the
founders believed that the growth of class consciousness had been stunted as a result

of the concentration, combination, and preponderant influence of capital, this model would facilitate the educational development and class consciousness of the working class. Inevitably, it was postulated, class power could then be wielded at the ballot box to wrest control from the capitalists.

The strategy for electoral ascendancy proved an abysmal failure as only small numbers flocked to Knights of Labor assemblies. For some observers within the group, the organization only seemed to grow when it helped organize strikes and functioned more like a labor union. By 1883, a rift emerged within the group over the question, foreshadowing its decline.[5] At the same time, the Knights were committed to organizing workers of color, although they were commonly organized into separate locals, reflecting accommodation to the existing patterns of racial segregation in the workforce. In the railroads, for instance, where the Knights had the most success in this endeavor, black workers organized locals in Texas and Louisiana, and Mexican workers formed locals in New Mexico.[6] By 1886, the Knights claimed sixty thousand of its seven hundred thousand members were black, organized into four hundred locals.[7]

The growth and spread of the Knights of Labor was slow and tenuous following the "common good" electoral model. The rapid rise of corporations in the Southwest and their concentration into vast trusts altered the political landscape, giving this form of capital preponderant influence and control within the electoral arena by the 1880s.[8] The first twelve years of the organization witnessed modest growth of the Knights, with an estimated twenty-eight thousand members joining lodges.

By the early 1880s differing opinions emerged within the loose-knit organization, with some groupings retooling themselves to function as trade unions. This transition proved fruitful for the rapid growth of the organization. Between 1880 and 1885 the membership spiked to 100,000, and then exploded to 12,000 local assemblies with 750,000 by 1886.[9] The dramatic growth coincided with shifts away from the fraternal lodge model toward the trade union organization necessitated by intense employer opposition, and in particular the rise in Knight-led strikes.

In the early 1880s, worker militancy began to increase. The movement for the eight-hour day, spearheaded by radical labor leaders in Chicago, began to gain traction on a national scale. The campaign was launched at the national convention of the Federation of Organized Trades and Labor Unions (forerunner to the AFL), calling for labor associations around the nation to join in coordinated strike action on May 1, 1886. Over the course of the month of May, over two hundred thousand workers went out on strike, making it the largest strike in US history up to that point.[10] Significant victories inspired the strikes to spread. According to the US commissioner of labor, between 1881 and 1890 workers won concessions in 62 percent of the struck establishments, including higher wages and shorter work hours.[11] By mid-1886 workers were flocking into the Knights of Labor, as many of its local assemblies led or participated in the strikes around the country.[12]

Two strikes that helped to fuel the growth of the Knights and to connect to Mexican workers were the southwestern railroad strikes of 1885 and 1886. The expansion of Jay Gould's rail lines made him the single largest employer in the Southwest;

employees laid 14,085 miles of track between 1880 and 1885, extending from New Orleans to South Texas and all the way to the Pacific Coast.[13] The railroad strikes had their roots in the economic downturn of 1884, when the railroad magnates pushed wage cuts, first in September 1884 and then in March 1885. Shop mechanics on the Missouri Pacific system—most of whom were Knights—went out first, with others following suit all the way from St. Louis, Missouri, to Laredo, Texas. At its height, eleven thousand railroad workers were out on strike, led by those sectors of workers excluded by the "skilled" craft unions, as well as those whose work experience put them in direct contact with the work crews that handled all of the support operations. At the ground level of train operations, the workers tended to be Knights of Labor militants, more oriented toward solidarity and collective action. As historian Theresa Case observes:

> Not coincidentally, these workers played a leading role in the 1885–86 strikes and identified strongly with the more [racially] inclusive Knights, in contrast to conductors, engineers, and firemen, who generally belonged to the craft-based, racially exclusive, conservative brotherhoods. Switchmen and brakemen also played a prominent role in the strikes. Due to their frequent contact with men in the yards of other railroads, the running trades, meatpacking, and freight handling, these semiskilled railroaders traditionally acted as a "natural bridge between workers employed on different roads" and were particularly inclined to engage in sympathy strikes.[14]

Since the Knights had organized separate black assemblies throughout Texas, both groups of workers unified to make the strike a success. As such, the group expanded into the black community. "In the aftermath of the March 1885 [strike] victory," Case continues, "the Knights of Labor 'sprung up overnight' and 'took like wildfire' among black and white workers in towns along the Gould system, particularly among railroaders."[15]

The spread of the Knights of Labor westward into industrial centers such as Chicago and Denver converged with existing radical left-wing labor traditions, press, and organization. The increase in class struggle in the region in the 1880s saw the further projection of radical doctrine, especially through the mining camps and along railroad junctions throughout the region. The radical left wing of the Knights, which included professed Marxists and anarchists, proselytized their doctrines to the growing ranks of migrant and itinerant workers moving through the region. Radical ideas and union organization filtered through the Knights of Labor and were adapted to the ongoing class struggle of nuevomexicanos defending themselves and their historical lands from capitalist dispossession and exploitation.

Capitalist Dispossession in New Mexico

After the Mexican-American War, speculators worked aggressively through political channels in the US capital to open up the newly acquired Mexican territories for American capital. Justification for the expropriation of Native and Mexican territories was framed in the pervasive imperialist and racist narrative dominating national discourse. This conceptualized expansion as a preordained, Anglo-Saxon-led conquest of the vast expanses of western "wilderness"; expelling or subsuming its inhabitants that were perceived as innately inferior for lack of capitalist development. Senator Lewis Cass from Michigan, a prominent national politician, conveyed this preference for colonization of Mexico without Mexicans, stating, "We do not want the people of Mexico, either as citizens or subjects. All we want is a portion of territory which they nominally hold, generally uninhabited, or, where habited at all, sparsely so, and with a population which would soon recede, or identify itself with ours."[16]

Since *mexicano* possession of land grants had been firmly established through tradition and local law, they proved the only substantial barrier to land transfer and capitalist development. Through the careful design of the Treaty of Guadalupe of 1848, President James K. Polk and a congressional majority crafted language that prevented mexicanos from directly retaining their lands de jure. Instead, they were compelled to go through a lengthy and costly legal process, through which fraud, corruption, and other forms of malfeasance facilitated rapid dispossession.

Conflicts also played out along legal and extralegal planes. Anglo capitalists and settlers entered into Mexican-majority communities where long-standing political traditions and customary practices were established. The Anglo population asserted their interests aggressively against the local population, counterbalancing their political connections to state and federal entities to the New Mexicans' local networks. As Charles Montgomery has observed about the aftermath of the Mexican-American War in New Mexico:

> Here a Spanish-speaking elite, backed by New Mexico's majority population of "Mexican" voters, shared power with an outnumbered but well-organized and growing Anglo minority. Wary of the potential power of its adversary and fearful of broaching the "race issue," each side moved cautiously to broaden its base of support.[17]

San Miguel County was primarily a rural region, with many families earning a living through farming on substantial land grants dating back to the Mexican and Spanish periods.[18] These land grants became prized by international capitalist speculators, especially after military conquest brought the territories under US control. Between 1865 and 1900 nearly half a billion dollars of British venture capital poured into western states, with increasing focus on New Mexico's mining, commercial farming, and railroad development after 1886.[19] To entice investment and skilled workers, the New Mexico Bureau of Immigration specifically promoted San Miguel County "as possessing the greatest and most varied natural resources [in the territory]."[20] The flood of speculative investments "overwhelmed common property relations, supplanted subsistence production, and integrated places like Las Vegas into a network of global financial markets."[21]

The elite *ricos* (rich Mexicans) were gradually incorporated into the new ruling class through economic partnerships, intermarriage, and political alliance within the two Anglo capitalist parties, the Democrats and Republicans. For the marginalized Mexican middle class and vast majority of laborers and small ranchers, maintenance of their way of life, including preservation of their land grants, became paramount to sustaining their livelihood and identity amid the powerful forces at play around them. The working classes' indigenous and mestizo racial identity and class position prevented them from being absorbed as easily into the new Anglo capitalist reality, other than as dispossessed proletarians.[22]

Behind the scenes of this process in New Mexico, competing groups of capitalists jockeyed for access to and control of the legally exposed land grants. By 1880, at least nineteen mining corporations had set up operations in the region, working with and against each other through the competing political factions of the Democratic and Republican parties.[23] The most successful of the groups was a secretive cabal of speculators known as the Santa Fe Ring, which formed a united front against the mexicanos and indigenous landholders. Led by Thomas Catron, the largest landowner in the country, this group included prominent Anglo lawyers, judges, speculators, and journalists. The Ring was closely linked to state governors in office between the years 1860 and 1885, regardless of their party affiliation.[24] Already by the late 1880s the government-appointed surveyor general had rejected 22 of 35 land grant claims with an area covering over 2 million acres.[25] Between 1870 and 1890, forty-six banks opened their doors, fueling rampant speculation through easy access to credit, the perceived abundance of land, and the availability of cheap native labor.[26] By 1889, the mexicano inhabitants of the Las Vegas land grant in San Miguel County knew what they were up against.

The Las Vegas grant comprised half a million acres of prime pasture and woodland, as well as being located in a region geographically significant for transcontinental railroad expansion. After the Mexican-American War, these farming communities found themselves gradually besieged by encroaching capitalist enterprise, led by the Atchison, Topeka, and Santa Fe Railway expanding its network throughout the region. As railroads linked New Mexico to markets back east, the local economy was transformed. An influx of goods and people began to stream into the region. New Mexico's mineral wealth and other natural resources were very attractive to speculators, merchants, ranchers, and others seeking to make a quick profit. About thirty-five hundred Anglos linked to capitalist expansion settled among San Miguel County's nineteen thousand mexicanos during the 1880s; with over twenty thousand more Anglos pouring into the area over the course of the 1890s.[27] Mexicans outside the expanding city center were already poor, but an estimated two-thirds of household heads owned small parcels of land and relied on common lands within the grant areas for collective needs.[28] An influx of corporate ranchers, railroad interests, speculators, and other prospectors began usurping the land, water, and timber that the local community had come to rely on for decades.[29]

Despite being a communal grant, some mexicano farmers within the community sold their plots while others found their lands fenced off and sold without their consent; they found no recourse by complaining to local authorities. Many displaced farming families joined the growing industrial workforce, with some going into mining while others began working on the same railroads that now traversed the landscape. The pattern of land expropriation did not respect boundaries between existing grants, with speculators and thieves parceling off cross sections of multiple grants simultaneously. The rapid and haphazard nature of the process aligned the different *mercedarios* (grant-holders), creating the basis for larger-scale opposition and mutual collaboration in resisting the colonizing entities.

As segments of the community were becoming proletarianized or pauperized through displacement, the persistent memory of their ancestral lands and a desire to retain what remained fueled resentment. Therefore, resistance contained a contradictory element for the leaders of Las Gorras Blancas: proletarianized, industrial, and agricultural workers resisting capitalist privatization and further industrialization that threatened a pastoral way of life already at an advanced stage of decline. The organizing skills, the experience of worker struggle, and support from a national organization enabled the leaders of Los Caballeros de Labor to form Las Gorras Blancas, even if the nature of the struggle would only allow the group a short, transitional existence.

Juan José Herrera and Las Gorras Blancas

The figure of Juan José Herrera figures prominently into the history of Los Caballeros de Labor and the uprising at Las Vegas. Herrera's ancestors had been responsible for establishing the pueblo at Las Vegas. His father had been a soldier throughout the Mexican and postwar territorial periods, and maintained a military garrison charged with protecting the zone. Juan had left the area to fight with the Union army during the Civil War, when he attained the rank of captain. He continued to work for the federal government as an Indian agent, learning English, French, and several Indian languages along the way. He returned to Las Vegas in the 1870s and remained working on the land amid the first phase of Anglo settlement in the region. In 1880, he left once more to look for more lucrative work in the booming industrial railroad, mining, and lumber zones in adjacent states.

Herrera became an itinerant worker who migrated across New Mexico, Utah, Wyoming, Colorado, and the Midwest working on railroads, as a miner, and as a lumberjack. Herrera was drawn into the industrial labor movement, where he came into contact with various lodges of the Knights of Labor, radical organizers, and anticapitalist doctrine. He witnessed (and possibly participated in) the great railroad strikes of 1885 and 1886. He also observed firsthand the efforts of agrarian radicals to form a national political party, the People's Party (also known as the Populists), to represent the interests of agricultural laborers and smallholders.

At some point along the way he met and joined the Knights of Labor and became an active member. According to David Brundage, Herrera joined the Knights in Denver, Colorado, where the local chapters of the group were influenced by the socialism and labor radicalism of a district organizer named Joseph Buchanan.[30] Aside from being affiliated with the Knights, Buchanan also established a local International Workingmen's Association chapter. He was a labor newspaper editor committed to incorporating Marxist revolutionary ideas into the Knights of Labor and steering it in a direction toward class-struggle unionism.

By 1884, there were eight Knight assemblies based in Denver, Colorado, seven for men and one all-female group. The Denver group was considered within the organization to be the most ardently socialist and radical, due to the large number of militant miners and railroad workers in their ranks. Buchanan explained the political outlook of the group, aligning its political outlook and activities with the radical groups organizing in Chicago in the lead-up to the Haymarket massacre:

> In Denver the labor movement was in better condition than in almost any other city of the country . . . We were having our share of strikes—several small strikes during the time of the miners' trouble—and were occasionally scoring a triumph [and] . . . we were internationalists, and kept our eyes upon the movement throughout the world . . . Anarchists, as well as socialists and Communists, were supporters of the labor movement, and their principal agitation was directed against the existing industrial system because of the injustice to the workingmen it embodied . . . There were no anarchists in Denver . . . but there was a strong socialistic element in the assemblies and unions and it was composed of the most active and influential members.[31]

Under the tutelage of Buchanan, Herrera had received a commission as a Knights of Labor district organizer in 1888 with orders to return to his hometown of Las Vegas, New Mexico, to organize chapters among mexicanos. Las Vegas was located in the northeast corner of the state, which served as a regional junction for the Atchison, Topeka, and Santa Fe. Las Vegas contained the largest population in the state, with mexicanos comprising 80 percent of the twenty-four thousand residents.[32] Three English-speaking chapters existed but none among the Mexican population, which comprised the majority of the working class in the region. Herrera returned to Las Vegas to organize, applying his acquired skills, his aversion to Anglo speculators, and later his military skills to organizing mass resistance to the forces of capitalist displacement.

The national organization of the Knights of Labor supported the efforts of the mexicano community to protect their land. Within their platform they opposed land speculation, asserting that public lands be used to satisfy local needs and that ancestral occupancy was the equivalent of title.[33] In 1887 the national organization provided resources to launch the Las Vegas Land Grant Association, which waged a quixotic struggle against powerful corporations through the courts. While the court battles raged on for months, the companies and squatters quietly expanded their settlements throughout the land grant with impunity, establishing de facto claim through occupation. Even when court rulings went in the Mexican community's favor, local and state authorities did nothing to enforce them.

By 1890 Herrera and his brothers Pablo and Nicanor had formed at least twenty Spanish-speaking Knights assemblies in the northeast region of the state, with eleven assemblies in San Miguel County.[34] The local assemblies were "mixed," representing the diversity of occupations of the Mexican workers, including miners, railroad workers, teamsters, agricultural workers, and others.

These chapters became the recruiting ground for a more militant submovement that formed as a result of the blatant land grab happening under the nose of the state.

In 1889, the Herrera brothers went on to form Las Gorras Blancas, a secretive organization within the Caballero lodges that carried out coordinated raids and attacks against those illegally occupying their lands. They chose to conceal their identities behind masks, understanding that Anglo repression would be swift and merciless if the participants could be identified. They applied the organizing skills they had acquired through membership in the Knights toward resolving land disputes with Anglo capitalists raging throughout the region. While most New Mexicans had been displaced from their traditional land grants by the late 1880s, the tenacious defense of remaining lands defined a collective, historical, and generational experience that shaped a common identity of the Mexican people in the region. Popular memory and a historical claim to the land now coexisted and merged with proletarian consciousness, collective power, and union organization. While the lodges of the Caballeros organized workers on the railroads to strike for higher wages, Las Gorras Blancas carried out other actions against the capitalists after nightfall.

The Knights provided an organizational vehicle to give expression to the frustration of thousands of *pobres* in New Mexico, as rapid industrialization, land expropriation, and proletarianization transformed the previous way of life. Las Gorras Blancas provided a means to directly resist through organized and collective action. Within the first year of its existence, an estimated seven hundred Mexican Caballeros had formed the ranks of Las Gorras Blancas, and the number doubled shortly thereafter with broad approval within the Mexican pueblos.[35]

Claiming a membership of fifteen hundred, they rode out at night in large groups, armed and on horseback, laying waste to the buildings, machinery, and materials that encroached on their lands. In groups sometimes numbering in the hundreds, they roamed the land grant zone cutting down fencing, burning railroad bridges, tearing up railroad tracks, and toppling electrical lines serving the construction. Over the course of eighteen months beginning in 1889, the White Caps carried out at least eighty actions against encroachers.[36] Initially, the national organization defended their actions. Knights of Labor leader Terrence Powderly claimed "'the mass of the poor people" had been "systematically robbed by means of the courts and legal process" and so the "clandestine and violent resistance" of the people was therefore an understandable response to the wholesale corruption in New Mexico.[37]

By 1890 their actions became more explicitly class conscious. In their efforts to inform and mobilize popular sentiment behind their actions, the group published communiqués and distributed them widely among the pobres. Speaking on behalf of all members of the "helpless class," they condemned the condition of workers within the capitalist system and the corruption and cronyism it brought into the political system. This included calling for better pay and job security for Mexican workers, and an end to uneven wage scales between Anglos and Mexicans. They also appealed to Mexican workers to go out on strike against Anglo companies.[38] These pronouncements informed their actions.

Las Gorras Blancas were broadly popular among the masses of workers and poor mexicanos and were despised by regional elites. When hostile press would condemn them, an independent and sympathetic Spanish-language Mexican press provided support and a platform for the group. *La Voz del Pueblo*, a Mexican-owned paper run by middle-class Mexican intellectual and journalist Felix Martínez, captured the sentiments of those sectors of the Mexican population losing out politically and economically to the corrupting influences of Anglo capitalism. As A. Gabriel Meléndez explains:

> Martínez openly supported las Gorras Blancas . . . As populist movements the base of support for [this group] was in the poorest sectors of *Nuevomexicano* society and among those directly impacted by Anglo-American encroachment on the land grants, anti-*Mexicano* bias in the legal system, a dual wage system for Anglos and Mexicanos, and the unequal living standards between an Anglo East Las Vegas and mexicano West Las Vegas.[39]

Martínez used *La Voz del Pueblo* to champion the cause of the White Caps. While the ricos and conservative middle-class nuevomexicanos sought partnership or local entry into the Democratic and Republican parties, Martínez threw in his lot with the poorer classes, seeing it as aligned with their own interests to arrest the consolidation of Anglo power. The paper became a mouthpiece for the group, defending their actions, countering the narrative of the Anglo press, publishing their communiqués, and otherwise echoing their condemnation of Anglo speculators and land grabbers. The paper proved essential for reaching the vast working-class base that supported the group and aligning it with the popular demands of the group. This popular support factored into the group's capacity to resist and thwart attempts to repress their actions.

When San Miguel County district attorney Miguel Salazar spearheaded a campaign of repression against Las Gorras Blancas on behalf of railroad investors, commercial speculators, and ranchers, the strategy backfired as corruption of local government by "land-grabber" money was a well-known fact at the time.[40] Demonstrating their popularity, Las Gorras Blancas began to stage mass parades and processions up to a thousand strong through the center of town. Sometimes these were silent and somber torchlit affairs, other times they included marching bands, with banners reflecting their demands.[41] The scale of the movement, and its willingness to confront the local government, rendered law enforcement impotent to stop or detain participants. The Catholic Church published a series of denunciations of Las Gorras Blancas in their press, frequently citing biblical scripture in Spanish to condemn their actions. The local Anglo-owned newspaper, the *Las Vegas Daily Optic*, incredulously decried the brazen oppositional activities of the group and the threat they posed to Anglo property, while also claiming to be unaware of the motivation:

> Bands of masked men have overrun cities and villages on horseback . . . Private individuals have been the recipients of threatening letters, warning them to leave their homes, or their improvements, or their ranches . . . various persons have been attacked by those masked men . . . [and] railroad bridges have been seen burning without any seeming explanation of the origin of the fire, other than the

perverse desire to do wrong and destroy . . . It is safe to affirm that the dominant idea in all these depredations is exactly this—to destroy property.[42]

When the Anglo commissioners tried to rally vigilante actions against individual members or perceived leaders of the group, the Gorras Blancas hit back quickly.

During round-ups and detentions of suspected members, Gorras Blancas staged demonstrations that showed their power and mass popular support. For example, in protest against the detention of twenty-three suspected members, sixty-three Gorras Blancas surrounded Salazar's home at midnight to demonstrate their power and reach and his vulnerability. In another case, the county sheriff who was complicit in the fencing schemes was forced to uproot his own crops and tear down his own fencing after receiving similar threats. When local officials tried to prosecute those suspected of being Gorras Blancas, witnesses would not take the stand against them and no jury would convict them. When the men were released, a crowd of several hundred supporters would meet them. As a strategy of repression faltered, paranoia overtook local officials who came to see White Caps behind any act of resistance or discord, no matter how small or apparently unrelated.

Their actions led to a halt of all railroad and cattle operations by the summer of 1890, as new groups of Las Gorras Blancas were organized and began carrying out similar actions in neighboring counties. Local business linked to railroad construction and other enterprises also shut down, sending ripple effects across the state. This undermined the goal of the capitalist class in the state to leverage economic development to attain statehood for New Mexico, thus giving them more power in national politics. As Robert Rosenbaum explains, "Not only were the White Caps braking the wheels of Commerce, but, as the *Albuquerque Democrat* complained, they were destroying New Mexico's chances for immediate statehood. Secretary of the Interior John Noble began to exert extreme pressure on Governor [L. Bradford] Prince to quiet the situation."[43] Reeling from the rupture of power produced by the insurgent mexicanos, internal divisions emerged within the Anglo population, with factions turning against each other and laying blame for their own impotence at each other's doorstep. After a failed attempt to get federal troops sent into San Miguel County to crush the insurgency, the governor chose to do nothing further to inflame the situation, effectively conceding temporary defeat.[44]

The Rise and Fall of El Partido del Pueblo

The temporary victory of Las Gorras Blancas and divisions between the Knights of Labor and the Caballeros de Labor led the group to disband. The tactics of the Gorras Blancas, which included property damage and threatening both Mexicans and Anglos who worked on illegally obtained grant-land, perturbed the Anglo Knight locals who perceived this as an affront to their right to work. In practice, their conception of "broad working-class unity" ignored the role of racial oppression against the Mexicans in the context of the land struggle and how systematic discrimination denied the Mexican population equal protection before the law. Furthermore, pervasive racism among skilled Anglo workers undermined the possibility for genuine solidarity. In ultimately siding with the state against Las Gorras Blancas, as the Knights of Labor did after 1890, the group cut itself off from the mexicano community, which was left isolated and more vulnerable to repression.

In the vacuum created by the absence of a common enemy of "land grabbers" and increased federal attention, the group could not maintain the same strategy. While the governor continued to appeal for federal intervention, the leaders of Las Gorras Blancas became drawn into local electoral politics. By 1886, local middle-class Mexican and Anglo farmers and políticos had formed a local version of the Populist Party, which in Spanish became known as El Partido del Pueblo. While the party fared poorly in its first few electoral forays, it found an opening during the uprising period of Las Gorras Blancas. Inspired by the group's victory over powerful Anglo interests, local Mexican políticos saw the potential for an electoral alliance with the Caballeros del Labor/Gorras Blancas that could challenge the Anglo political establishment. These men recruited the leadership of Las Gorras Blancas into the party, which gave it an immediate mass-base.

With the White Cap leadership now running for elected office, the Republican Party went on the offensive. On the eve of the 1890 election, the *Las Vegas Daily Optic* warned voters:

> Property in San Miguel will depreciate fully fifty percent, if the white-cap ticket shall be elected. The outrages of that element have already caused a heavy decline in nearly all classes of property—especially such as is located in the country and in small villages. Insurance companies have called in their risks; and this is only an indication of the timidity of capital. Men who had money in the county have withdrawn it. Men who contemplated investments have changed their minds . . . But what has been suffered will not be a drop in the bucket compared to the consequences of electing the white cap ticket.[45]

For its part, *La Voz del Pueblo* rallied around the Caballero de Labor-Partido del Pueblo cause.[46] The election went overwhelmingly to what their opponents called the "white-cap ticket."

The candidates of El Partido del Pueblo were swept into power across the county, including Juan José Herrera, who was sworn in as the county's probate judge. His brother Pablo was elected as the county's representative to the territorial legislature. Despite these victories, the party faltered as it brought together mexicanos of different social classes with very different aims and objectives. The party became paralyzed politically, as its dominant middle-class leadership leveraged its electoral influence to form alliances with Anglo business interests. An editorial in the Anglo press noted with satisfaction that the leadership of the party would restrain its newly elected officers and focus on "maintaining order and in protecting life and property."[47] The active leadership drawn from the ranks of the Caballeros de Labor became frustrated with the inability to unify the party around a common platform that represented the interests of workers and the poor. They also came in direct contact with the deep corruption that followed moneyed interests into the state government apparatus. Both Juan and Pablo resigned their positions and left the party within one year. According to David Correia,

> Pablo Herrera resigned from the legislature and left the party in disgust. One session convinced him that neither the legislature nor the Partido could be a vehicle for radical political and economic changes. "The time I spent in the penitentiary was more enjoyable than the time I spent [in the legislature] . . . There is more honesty in the halls of the Territorial prison than in the halls of the legislature."[48]

The party gradually fragmented and ceased to exist, with the middle-class leadership merging into the Democratic Party.

While collectively they were able to keep forces of capitalist displacement at bay for a year, the victory of Los Caballeros de Labor/Las Gorras Blancas could not be sustained for long by electoral means. They did not wield similar power in government, where even the best intentions proved fruitless so long as the same capitalists and speculators exercised complete capitalist control over the economy. The height of their power coincided with the fragmentation and decline of the Knights of Labor nationally, increasing the isolation of the Mexican workers from the labor movement. The militant resistance of the White Caps forced the US Congress to expedite the land grant issue, specifically creating the United States Court of Private Land Claims to adjudicate the New Mexican land question in 1891. The apparent success of Las Gorras in forcing the federal government's hand contributed to the demobilization of the groups' activity and eventual disbandment. Under the drawn-out terms of federal arbitration, conditions changed rapidly. With the Knights gone and the Gorras Blancas demobilized by the mid-1890s, reaction and backlash against the mexicano community surged from within the state. By the turn of the twentieth century, 94 percent of land grant claims covering 33,439,493 acres were rejected, with the land quickly passing into the hands of Anglo capitalists and speculators.[49]

Chapter 4
The Japanese Mexican Labor Association

"I cannot avoid the conclusion, forced on me by my contact with the Japanese and Mexicans in California—where they have of their own volition been organizing— that a social revolution is as possible among these people as any in the world."
—John Murray, socialist, AFL labor organizer, and supporter of the 1903 strike in Oxnard, California

The labor caste system established through the Southwest relegated most Mexican workers in California to agriculture. Beginning in 1850, large-scale mob violence was orchestrated to drive thousands of Mexicans, Chinese, South Americans, and other nonwhites from the mines. Racial animus was exacerbated by the California legislature, which passed a series of laws that targeted nonwhites for exclusion or persecution, including the Foreign Miners Tax Acts of 1850 and 1852 and the notoriously anti-Mexican "Greaser Act" of 1855.[1]

During the first two decades of the twentieth century, Mexican workers became the majority of the agricultural workforce, while others found work on the railroads. Mexican communities had long existed in urban California coastal cities like San Diego, Los Angeles, and San Francisco; and they expanded after the turn of the century. Mexican families could also be found throughout rural farm towns across a patchwork of farming communities in central and Southern California. One of these was the town of Oxnard, California, founded as a sugar-refining operation by capitalist investor Henry Oxnard, who was eagerly following favorable federal tariff policy to create a state-of-the-art production facility that was the second largest in the nation in 1898.[2]

The rapid expansion of agriculture into the far southwestern states was aided by several factors: large-scale, corporate capital investment in agricultural machinery; mass migration and Anglo resettlement; protectionism; and heavy government land and water subsidies and the expansion of the transcontinental railroad and refrigerated car.[3] By the turn of the twentieth century, agriculture was becoming industrialized, transitioning from smaller diversified plots heavily dependent on skilled human labor and animal power to large-scale, monocrop, corporate industrial farms that relied on substantial numbers of migrant laborers. These economies of scale displaced small and family farms, increased productivity, and came to rely on vast armies of migratory labor.

In 1903, a workforce that comprised Japanese and Mexican farm laborers united to form one of the first known agricultural unions. The Japanese-Mexican Labor Association (JMLA) won an unprecedented strike against one of the largest industrial sugar corporations in the country, and a league of growers intent on creating and maintaining a subjugated workforce through the use of racism and armed violence. The strike victory, supported by Los Angeles Socialists affiliated with the American Federation of Labor (AFL), ran aground when the national federation refused to issue a charter to any union with Japanese workers. While the rebuke sounded the death knell for the small union, it served as a powerful example of how radicals and class-conscious workers came together and built a militant, interethnic union capable of defeating the most powerful capitalists of the period.

The Making of a Sugar Beet Industry

The sugar beet industry in Oxnard was the result of state-directed and subsidized capitalist development and the forcible displacement of the local Mexican population.

The Federal Land Act of 1851 was the first postwar effort to expropriate and redistribute indigenous and Mexican lands to Anglo speculators and settlers. The Board of Land Commissions was created to oversee the validation of Spanish and Mexican grants, but in practice it systematically displaced Mexican *ranchos* and common lands through its authority to invalidate land claims. By the 1860s, pre-Oxnard Mexican inhabitants lost 40 percent of their land due to "the strain of a declining cattle economy, debt, and the cost of litigation, [and] the increasing presence of Euro American squatters."[4]

Anglo investors poured into the region, buying up the expropriated lands. By 1868, the largest tracts of land had passed from a class of Mexican rancheros to eastern capitalist speculators who had also founded the Philadelphia and California Petroleum Company and the San Buenaventura Mining Company on former land grants.[5] Thomas Bard, a speculator who also joined the rush to profit from the newly opened regions in Southern California, was later appointed land commissioner to distribute the land of Ventura County after serving as a commissioner in nearby Santa Barbara County. Between 1868 and 1888, sixteen thousand acres were sold off cheaply to Anglo settlers and speculators from the Midwest and eastern United States to encourage commercial farming.[6] European American workers often followed suit, moving into commercial agricultural or industrial settlements in the hopes of working enough to acquire their own land and fortunes.

This acquired land cut through historic Mexican land grants situated near the Spanish-era Mission San Buenaventura, including the Rancho el Río de Santa Clara o la Colonia, a pre–Mexican-American War, forty-four-thousand-acre grant that was gradually expropriated and parceled out for capitalist investment. As a result of this expropriation, the Mexican population was dispossessed and the traditional cattle-ranching industry was decimated in favor of privatization, capital investment, and white resettlement for commercial farming. The long-standing Mexican population was proletarianized and gradually confined to the Mexican barrio of La Colonia, which, along with incoming migrants, provided the workforce in expanding capitalist agriculture, especially sugar beet production.[7] In 1901, workers in La Colonia formed the first known mutualista, the Mexican junta, which likely served as a proto-organization for the *betabeleros* (beet workers) and facilitated coordinated labor action in the years that followed.[8]

Investors in beet sugar production and refinement enjoyed their first successful commercial ventures in 1870 in Alvarado, California (Alameda County), and then spread quickly through central and Southern California and ultimately across twenty-one states. The Oxnard brothers were prominent New York sugar barons looking to expand their empire through beet sugar refinement. The Oxnards had founded six sugar refineries in Nebraska, Colorado, and California (San Bernardino County) before seeking a seventh in Ventura County. In 1897, the Oxnards purchased a hundred acres in a rural area north of Los Angeles that became their namesake in 1900. This growth was leveraged under the auspices of pro-grower government legislation. In 1890 the McKinley Tariff gave direct disbursements of cash to growers to entice beet production. In 1897, the federal government passed the Dingley Act, raising tariffs on foreign sugar imports. Capitalists like the Oxnards poured investment into domestic sugar beet production, which was further abetted by the passage of the 1934 Jones-Costigan Amendment to the Agricultural Adjustment Act, which reclassified sugar as a protected commodity.[9]

While commercial farming was taking root across the state, industrial beet sugar production in Ventura County accelerated the transition toward beets in the surrounding environs. By 1900, many local farmers had transitioned to growing beets to feed refinery production, which in turn necessitated more migrant labor. Following and replicating established racial patterns in other parts of the country, the Oxnards reserved management positions and jobs in the refining factory for the local white workforce. For agricultural work, they relied on the availability of local Mexicans, Japanese, and Chinese workers; and in proportion to the industry's growth they used labor contractors to bring itinerant groups into the region during key stages of production. These industrial needs coincided at first with increased migration from Asia, especially China and Japan. By the turn of the twentieth century, this changed with the onset of immigration restrictions resulting from virulent anti-Chinese and Japanese campaigns. From 1905 to 1930, a succession of state and federal measures were enacted to drive the Japanese out of California agriculture. As Juan Gómez-Quiñones describes this transition:

> In the period 1900–1920, they were one of several ethnic and social groups consigned to the fields. Only gradually did they gain predominance. With the construction of the Spreckles sugar beet operation in Watsonville, Monterey County, California, in 1899, and the organizing of the Sugar Trust in 1902, the sugar beet increased in importance and, with it, Chicano labor. For the sugar beet crop, labor was seasonal, employment was on a contract basis and mostly migratory. The labor force was approximately one-fifth (1/5) Japanese, four-fifths (4/5) Chicano.[10]

With the enticement of favorable federal legislation, cheaply acquired land, and access to immigrant labor, a "sugar boom" took place with the founding of Oxnard, California, where Henry Oxnard and his brothers, Benjamin, James, and Robert, established the American Beet Sugar Company (ABSC) in 1897. They also founded the

Bank of Oxnard, which financed the burgeoning class of beet farmers that directed their product to the refinery. With the establishment of the refinery, land was commoditized, parceled off, and sold to Anglo investors and settlers moving into the area.

Their efforts were given a supportive boost by the government-subsidized rail line, which linked Oxnard on a north–south axis between Los Angeles and San Francisco. Anglo farmers in the regions surrounding Oxnard turned to sugar production in droves, leading to growth of the town. By 1902, the Oxnard brothers' sugar operations were one of the largest in the word, producing upward of 160,000 tons of refined product.[11] By the turn of the century, labor needs of the beet-sugar industry attracted groups of Chinese, Japanese, and Mexican agricultural workers who came to form the ranks of the betabeleros.

Beet sugar production was divided between three primary stages: local farmers purchased land and increased the beet harvest to meet rising demand; farmworkers migrated into the region to maintain, prepare, and harvest the crop; and the ABSC factory purchased the beet harvests for refining into sugar. Due to persistent labor shortages and the lack of a local working-class base, growers relied on the workers themselves to spread the word among the migrant farm workforce and attract labor from other regions.

Labor contractors emerged from within the predominant Japanese and Mexican groups, utilizing linguistic and kinship networks to recruit and then negotiate fees with the growers. In time, these contractors became intermediaries, detached from fieldwork and pursuing new sources of labor full time. Some even became shareholders in the companies they served, pushing them to benefit from conditions of exploitation. While many labor contractors became notorious for manipulating and exploiting vulnerable workers, charging exorbitant fees, or even aligning with growers to discipline rebellious workers, some developed into quasi–union leaders.

Class Conflict and the Intensification of Racism

Oxnard's class structure was preconfigured by existing patterns of wealth accumulation, in which Anglo American capitalists had amassed great quantities of wealth and sought to reinvest it at the expense of disinherited and dispossessed peoples in other regions. The dividing lines of class between the two groups ran parallel with distinctions of race, ethnicity, and culture. While the Oxnard brothers were enabled by their accumulated wealth and favorable government policy, their profits depended on the creation and subordination of a permanent, seasonal workforce. This workforce was constructed from the populations of disinherited people, in which historical memory and collective traditions carried into the reconfigured class divisions.

It was at the point of agricultural production where these class and ethnic distinctions were intensified by class conflict, as Japanese, Mexican, and Chinese migratory workers resisted the conditions of exploitation. The outbreak of class struggles along racial lines, conversely, led the newly consolidating ruling class of Oxnard to deploy racial animus and structured segregation as a means to divide and weaken class consciousness and interethnic organization.

By early 1903, about seven hundred Japanese, Mexicans, and Chinese worked side by side in the beet fields but lived in racially segregated ethnic enclaves clumped together in the eastern section of the town close to the sugar factory.[12] They also found themselves in the lowest rungs of a racially stratified hierarchy in which they were relegated to the hardest labor, received the lowest wages, and encountered the least opportunity for advancement.

In the initial phase of labor, growers and the ABSC relied on the Japanese and Mexican contractors to furnish sufficient field labor. As the conditions of work became more industrialized, i.e. more standardized, more labor intensive, and on a greater scale, and as the growers tried to suppress wages to increase profit, the distinct class of labor contractors began to differentiate as a result of pressures emanating from disaffected workers. A fissure developed within the intermediate strata of Japanese contractors, with a subgroup that began to identify with and give expression to the demands of the workers. Under this system, this group gradually took on the characteristics of a representative leadership, seeing greater potential to leverage collective class power to yield concessions over individual gain at the expense of the collective. Two historians, O'Brien and Fugita, identify the cultural roots of this early form of class solidarity in the following manner:

> The labor contractor-worker relationship was . . . supported by the traditional Japanese principle of *iemoto* . . . which emphasized the obligations of superiors toward subordinates . . . This principle of organization . . . in effect created a quasi-kin relationship between Japanese of different ranks of hierarchical organization.[13]

Perhaps even more significant, many Japanese workers had labor organizing experience after having spent time working on Hawaiian plantations prior to coming into California. In Hawaii, Japanese workers were one group among many, with agricultural interests purposefully maintaining polyglot workforces of different nationalities imported onto the island to work on the massive sugar and pineapple plantations. Within the racial hierarchy imposed on the workers to impede collaboration and union agitation, the Japanese workers proved instrumental in overcoming racial divides. They successfully aligned with other nationalities to coordinate five of the forty-nine strikes that took place on the island during the first decade of the twentieth century.[14] This recent history was present in the minds of workers when they encountered similar divide-and-conquer strategies in the beet fields of Oxnard.

The role of these contractors gradually morphed into that of a hybridized union leader, as they became aware of their ability to leverage labor power to wring concessions from the growers. They formed mutually beneficial relationships with the workers, coordinating strikes, slowdowns, and other disruptive actions at pivotal points in the harvest cycle in order to negotiate higher contracting fees and wages for the workers.[15] John Murray, a Socialist labor organizer from Los Angeles who assisted the JMLA, claimed that the Japanese contractors who organized the workers were themselves socialists:

[T]he Japanese have proven themselves to be apt students of the international working-class movement that believes in a common ownership of the means of production and distribution. Their leaders in California—I speak of those whom I have met and talked with—one and all regard Socialism to be the logical conclusion of the trades union movement.[16]

The success of these militant contractors outraged the bosses at the ABSC, who aspired to regulate and stabilize sugar beet production. They were eager to keep farmworker wages artificially low in order to maintain high farmer profits, thus encouraging the farmers to maintain and expand production. Since farmworker militancy threatened to disrupt this arrangement, they counseled the growers on how to undercut the contractors. The local ABSC-aligned newspaper, the *Oxnard Courier*, noted, "As ... our beet fields will spring into life very rapidly ... there will be an urgent need for thinning. It then will be simply a question of whether the Japanese-Mexican labor classes will control labor or whether it will be managed by conservative business men."[17]

By 1902, the ABSC and local capitalist interests tied to the sugar industry developed a scheme to break the independent labor contracting system. In league with the two newly incorporated Oxnard banks and sugar beet farmers, they formed the Western Agricultural Contracting Company (WACC).[18] Underwritten by the banks, money was provided to fund the incorporation of loyal contractors as "managers," under the direct control of the ABSC. Instead of paying contractors, all workers were required to pay a direct fee to the WACC. The growers then agreed to collectively refuse to negotiate with independent contractors and required all farmworkers to register through the WACC.

The newly consolidating ruling group of industrialists, bankers, and growers crafted and introduced racial divisions into the developing structures of production in an attempt to fragment and weaken the independent contracting system and to suppress wages. Through the pages of the weekly *Oxnard Courier*, the editors tried to cultivate support among the town's white working, middle, and professional classes. Residential segregation, the introduction of a racial hierarchy into production, and anti-Japanese and anti-immigrant sentiment at the state level (and federal level) served these aims. Over the course of the 1903 strike, the paper whipped up racial resentment against the strikers, characterizing their efforts at unionization as a cultural anomaly, inimical to "white" society and alien to the methods of "white" labor. In the immediate aftermath of the strike, the paper further added to the climate of racist polarization, by "warning" the white population of the potential for "thousands of negroes" to migrate to Oxnard, "bringing a class that we could better do without."[19]

The WACC structure purposefully promoted white contractors into the strata of management, using employment stratification as the first wedge between whites and the other workers. They also employed a handful of company-loyal Japanese and Mexican contractors to campaign among their own respective ethnic groups, promising in the vernacular of the workers more contracts and better pay if they broke from the popular independent leaders. Furthermore, the WACC also formed partnerships with local merchants and growers to create company stores. Through this ploy,

workers could be paid in company scrip to be used only at designated stores where
workers were charged exorbitant prices for basic goods. By February 1903 the WACC
controlled 90 percent of labor contracts, effectively eliminating the independent contracting system.[20] The *Oxnard Courier*, which also served as the mouthpiece for the
WACC, promoted the arrangement in crude, racialized terms, distinguishing between
loyal "American" contractors and foreign, plebian elements: "The farmers of this valley
have too much confidence in American contractors to throw them over for the lowest
class of Japanese and Cholo labor that has ever come into the valley headed by one or
two labor agitators, some of whom do not know what a contract is."[21]

With the WACC in control of labor contracting, workers experienced a significant reduction in their wages. This resulted from having to pay fees to work, and as
growers depressed wage scales as they were now less vulnerable to work stoppages
since they no longer dealt directly with the workers. In response to the beet growers' attempts to cut wages, Japanese and Mexican agricultural workers held various
mass meetings to discuss the new situation. Meetings were conducted in Japanese and
Spanish concurrently. Understanding the potential for the sugar bosses and growers
to divide the workers against each other with the advent of protest, they took an unprecedented step and merged efforts to form the Japanese-Mexican Labor Association (JMLA), an independent union that was the first in the state to unite different
ethnic groups together in common cause. The primary goal of the new organization
was to disband the WACC and return to the previous system. On February 11, 1903,
the JMLA was officially launched with the support of about 800 workers (about 500
Japanese, 200 Mexicans, and 100 others, mostly Chinese).[22] When appeals to negotiate failed, JMLA workers stopped working through the WACC, effectively going on
strike on February 28, 1903.

By the second week of March, the JMLA grew to include 1,000 Japanese, 200
Mexicans, and 100 Chinese workers, making this the first significant effort to build an
interethnic labor union, and the first strike against a major capitalist agricultural enterprise in the state.[23] The JMLA came to represent 90 percent of all sugar beet workers, unifying the majority of the working class in the town, while the sugar bosses,
local law enforcement, and growers closed ranks against them. In a demonstration of
their unity and solidarity in the face of coordinated opposition between local capitalists and government officials, the JMLA staged a parade and mass rally on March
6 through the center of town. The show of power startled the local power structure.
The *Oxnard Courier* illustrated the local elite's racial disdain and class fear in its description of the event.

> Dusky-skinned Japanese and Mexicans marched through the streets headed
> by one or two contractors and beet laborers four abreast and several hundred
> strong. They are a silent grim band of fellows, most of them young and belong-
> ing to the lower class of Japanese and Mexicans.[24]

Over the course of the strike the police tried various tactics to intimidate the
workers. This included the arrest of strike leaders on trumped-up charges, and

increasing patrols and staging "crackdowns" within the Mexican and Japanese quarters. Despite the repression, new leaders stepped up and the workers adapted their tactics. The JMLA set up pickets and squads around town to turn back strikebreakers. In one instance, a group of fifty Mexican betabeleros raided a strikebreaker camp set up on one grower's property, cutting their tent ropes and sending the eighteen men on a direct path out of town. They set up a restaurant for the strikers, covered medical expenses, shared funds, and provided other forms of mutual assistance.[25]

The unity of the strikers in keeping away from the fields rattled the farmers. Their strike occurred during the crucial stage of "beet thinning," in which underdeveloped seedlings were removed to prevent root damage among those ideal for harvesting. By March 2, only four thousand of the sixteen thousand acres of sugar beets had been thinned.[26] The *Oxnard Courier* further attempted to inflame racist sentiment against the Japanese, Mexicans, and Chinese, claiming the independent contractors used their shared cultural traits to manipulate the workers through their ability "to write and talk hieroglyphics," which "convinced the little brown men that they were being [wronged]." Furthermore, the editors attempted to exploit racial differences in their characterization of the efficacy of unions:

> The character of [Japanese and Mexican] labor is against enlightened management; and therefore also a union, which in the hands of intelligent white men is made an instrument for their mental and moral uplifting and material advancement, in the hands of a people whose experience has been to obey a master, rather than to think and manage for themselves, it becomes merely a tool for a few crafty schemers to work their own ends.[27]

Appeals to turn general public sentiment against the JMLA had little effect on the resolve of the strikers. In the face of such a well-organized strike operation, the farmers attempted to negotiate, offering to sit down with both the WACC and the newly constituted union, eventually making offers to split representation. When the union held strong on its demand to represent all sugar beet workers, the sugar bosses and law enforcement turned to armed violence. Under the leadership of the ABSC/WACC, the growers ramped up their scabbing operation. On March 21, they formed a rival union called the Independent Agricultural Labor Union. In practice, this "union" was an armed group of growers and contractors that attempted to physically break through picket lines. To enable scabs to be brought in, the sheriff deputized growers and their foremen to allow them to directly escort strikebreakers to their farms.

By deputizing and arming the growers, local law enforcement gave them license to use violence to break through roving and fixed pickets set up by the strikers. They began armed incursions on March 23, when they escorted a caravan of wagons full of scabs to the fields. A group of roving, unarmed picketers approached the wagons, unfurling the JMLA flag (which showed Mexican and Japanese hands shaking against a backdrop of the rising sun) in an effort to discourage the strikebreakers. Within moments of the confrontation, shots rang out from the caravan. One "deputized" grower named Charles Arnold approached a striker and shot him point blank in the back of the neck. Before the enraged strikers managed to disarm the group, five JMLA members—three Mexican and two Japanese workers—had been shot and wounded. Luis Vásquez, the Mexican unionist shot in the neck, died shortly thereafter. For the rest of the day, the strikers effectively took over the town, setting up checkpoints and roving patrols to look for and arrest any strikebreakers who had fled from the scene of the shooting earlier in the day.[28]

In response to the violence, the Mexican and Japanese secretaries of the JMLA issued a joint statement decrying the collusion between the WACC-affiliated growers and the local sheriff's department. In the communiqué, they defended their strike and called on the police to "no longer neglect their duty but arrest those persons who plainly participated in the fatal shooting."[29] Since the local ruling clique wanted to eliminate the union, their appeals fell on deaf ears. Despite over fifty eyewitnesses testifying at the inquest into the death of Vásquez, including over a dozen who identified Charles Arnold by name and description, the company-friendly all-white male jury refused to indict the killer, proclaiming in their verdict, "We find the deceased came to his death as the result of a gunshot wound received at the hands of some party unknown to us, said wound having been received during a labor riot at Oxnard, Ventura Co., Monday, March 23, 1903."[30] News coverage of the event across Southern California repeated in exasperated and racially paranoid histrionics the patently false claim that the union members fired upon the strikebreakers and somehow managed to shoot their own.[31]

Despite the repression, the JMLA continued to win over Japanese and Mexican beet workers. John Murray reported over the following week that at least two more subsequent caravans failed when the JMLA convinced the incoming Japanese and Mexican workers to join the union on the spot. On March 30, the company conceded defeat, restoring wages and removing the WACC from the beet fields.[32] The victory was significant, as it signaled the first major strike victory against an industrial agricultural giant in California history. It also signified a major ideological challenge to the labor movement, rejecting the notions that Mexican and immigrant workers were passive, lacked class consciousness, were unwilling to be organized, or were somehow incapable of self-organization.

It also was a major blow to the efficacy of white supremacy as an organizing tool. The Los Angeles Council of Labor passed a resolution in the aftermath of the strike victory, calling for all "Asiatics" in California to be organized into unions.[33] The support from Los Angeles labor riled the virulently anti-union editors of the *Los Angeles Times*. In an editorial they intertwined racial contempt with their standard anti-union rant:

> Rioting and bloodshed was indorsed [sic] last night [by] the council of labor. A discussion of the recent rioting, bloodshed, and murder at Oxnard by newly unionized Jap and peon laborers, provoked the [Labor Council leadership] into "resoluting." The substance of the unanimously adopted resolutions was that all labor should be unionized (willy-nilly;) that no matter what might be the social

status or racial degradation of people that work with their hands, they should be rounded up and branded with the union [label], so that if their incompetence or general unworthiness proved a bar to their obtaining high wages they could resort to the strike to enforce big pay.[34]

Racial and class disdain for the strikers and the socialists who supported them was soon shared and amplified by landowners, capitalist speculators, and their media outlets across the region. The pending question at this critical juncture was whether or not the JMLA unionists would get the backing and support of the American Federation of the Labor.

A Failure of Historic Proportions: The AFL Rejects the Japanese

The events surrounding the formation of the JMLA and the Oxnard strike were watched closely by both state business interests and the AFL leadership. By 1903, the national union federation, led by Samuel Gompers, had strategically abandoned agriculture in favor of skilled white workers in the urban trades. Furthermore, the conservatizing turn toward business unionism and labor-capital partnership saw the right wing of the union leadership accommodate more seamlessly the racist and anti-immigrant campaigns increasingly underwritten by sections of the capitalist class. Wealthy landowners and investors like the Oxnards began to equate labor radicalism with the nonwhite and foreign-born sections of the working class, promoting white supremacy, racially dividing their workforces, and advocating for racial exclusions.[35] The American Federation of Labor accommodated this line of thinking, despite its own stated mission that all workers, regardless of race, color, religion, or nationality, were welcome in the American Federation of Labor. By 1904, the AFL convention officially called for Japanese exclusion, outlining the "inherent" differences between white and Japanese workers in their official organ *The American Federationist*:

> Their God is not his God. Their hopes, their ambitions, their love of this country are nothing to him. It is a question of making some money which he cannot get in his own country . . . He will come, stay, and leave us a stranger. Herein lies the greatest danger. I can say that our interest can never become his. He cannot be unionized. He cannot be Americanized.[36]

While the national leadership of the AFL moved into alignment with the general precepts of white nationalism, Socialists in positions of local leadership challenged this trend by providing material support for the organization and inclusion of all workers into the federation. The Socialist Party, formed in 1900, had made some inroads into AFL unions with the intention of building a national party as well as a more militant and inclusive brand of unionism. In some regions of the country, Socialists wielded influence within local labor councils. In Los Angeles, a Socialist labor caucus even won leadership in the Council of Labor in 1902, after ousting a conservative, Gompers-aligned faction.[37]

Under the influence of two prominent Socialist Party members and labor leaders, Southern California AFL organizer Fred C. Wheeler and Typographical Workers'

Union member and editor of the Los Angeles-based *Socialist* newspaper John Murray, the Los Angeles Council of Labor made contact with the JMLA. Both men counseled the workers during strike negotiations, passed resolutions of support through council, and published articles in the Socialist press explaining the strike and appealing for support. In a 1903 edition of the *International Socialist Review*, Murray challenged the exclusionist notions in the AFL and appealed to Socialists to see the significance of the strike in racial terms:

> For Socialists, it is needless to point out that to whip a capitalist today means nothing more than that you must fight him again tomorrow, but the significance of this particular skirmish, in the great class war, lies in the fact that workers from the Occident and Orient, strangers in tongues, manners and customs, gathered together in a little western village, should so clearly see their class interest rise above the racial feeling of distrust.[38]

Murray asserted that in his experience he perceived the Japanese workers to be inclined toward socialism and unions, and mistakenly believed that unions would reverse course and welcome them into their ranks once they saw this in practice in Oxnard.

While the workers won the strike and the union continued to grow quickly as a result, the victory was short-lived. The sugar bosses at the ABSC, bankers and landowners, and local government closed ranks to try to drive the union out of the fields at any cost. Although the company couldn't defeat the JMLA at that juncture, it negotiated to bide its time until more favorable conditions presented themselves to break the union. According to John Murray, the factory manager confidently stated to the JMLA representatives at the conclusion of the first union contract negotiation: "[W]e will have to take steps to drive you out of the country and secure help from the outside—even if we have to spend $100,000 in doing it."[39] Under these circumstances, the leaders of the JMLA understood the necessity of building outside support to avoid isolation and the costs of fighting a long-term war of attrition with an enemy that had unlimited resources at its disposal. Shortly after the strike, the newly named Sugar Beet Farm Laborers Union applied for an American Federation of Labor charter, which could provide resources and national support for its efforts to institutionalize itself in California agriculture.

The national office of Samuel Gompers promptly responded to the application, offering approval for the charter only in the event that the Japanese were expelled, as they were not welcome in the organization. Enraged, the president of the union, Jesús María Lizarras, replied,

> Your letter . . . in which you say the admission with us of the Japanese Sugar Beet and Farm Laborers into the American Federation of Labor cannot be considered, is received. We beg to say in reply that our Japanese brothers here were the first to recognize the importance of cooperating and uniting in demanding a fair wage scale . . . They were not only just with us, but they were generous when one of our men was murdered by hired assassins of the oppressor of labor, they gave expression to their sympathy in a very substantial form. In the past we have counseled, fought and lived on very short rations with our Japanese

brothers, and toiled with them in the fields, and they have been uniformly kind and considerate. We would be false to them and to ourselves and to the cause of unionism if we now accepted privileges for ourselves which are not accorded to them. We are going to stand by men who stood by us in the long, hard fight which ended in a victory over the enemy. We therefore respectfully petition the A.F. of L. to grant us a charter under which we can unite all the sugar beet and field laborers in Oxnard, without regard to their color or race. We will refuse any other kind of charter, except one which will wipe out race prejudices and recognize our fellow workers as being as good as ourselves. I am ordered by the Mexican union to write this letter to you and they fully approve its words.[40]

In rejecting Gompers's condition, the Mexicans stood their ground. As Lizarras concluded at a mass meeting where the decision was made: "Better to go to hell with your family than to heaven by yourself."[41] While the Los Angeles Socialists tried to sway the national leadership, their appeals were ignored. The *Los Angeles Times* gleefully proclaimed that "Gompers action . . . will kill the young union."[42] They were correct. Ultimately, the charter was rejected, and the union soon disappeared, along with any other sincere attempts by the AFL to try to organize farmworkers in California for the next three decades.[43]

Chapter 5

Mexican Miners in Arizona

"The Strike of 1903 was an uprising, a massive threat to 'American' arrangements of power. It had not begun that way, but that is how it ended. The mines, mills, and smelters stopped, a heart attack shutting down Clifton-Morenci's supply of blood and oxygen."
—**Linda Gordon, *The Great Arizona Orphan Abduction***

Beginning in the 1870s substantial copper ore deposits were discovered across Arizona, opening up the territory to a massive and rapid influx of capital and people. With the electrification of industrializing nations and the need for ever-expanding grids, global demand for copper increased exponentially, attracting international flows of speculative capital investment to Arizona. By 1903, US mines produced 52 percent of all copper globally, with Arizona mines contributing about one-third of total US output.[1]

By the turn of the century three major corporations dominated copper production: the Arizona Copper Company, the Detroit Copper Mining Company, and the Shannon Consolidated Copper Company. Representing US and Scottish finance capitalist interests, these companies formed the organizational models that came to dominate mining production in the Southwest for the first three decades of the twentieth century.

Mining towns were created by the companies, with each aspect of production, commerce, and transportation controlled by a single group or conglomerate of investors. Mining had become immensely profitable, attracting capital and migrants from across the globe. Mining and affiliated activities turned massive profits for stockholders. For instance, by 1912, the Phelps-Dodge Mining Company "earned 23 percent on its capital of 45 million dollars, and its principal property, the Detroit Company, paid a dividend of 146 percent on a capitalization of 1 million dollars that year."[2] According to Arizona mining historian Eldrid D. Wilson, copper extraction amounted to $3.2 billion between 1858 and 1945 (in 1945 dollars).[3]

Arizona mining development was aided by the federal government, which distributed land grants to railroad companies and homesteaders, and made significant investments in dams to assist in agricultural production. In short order the launch of large-scale mining operations coincided with the expansion of an arterial network of railroads and energy infrastructure. The Southern Pacific railway, for instance, linked Tucson to Los Angeles all the way to the west; to El Paso to the east, and then continued all the way to Chicago. By the turn of the century, the southern Arizona mining region was effectively linked into the world economy by a patchwork of intersecting railroads.[4]

It was at this critical nerve center of global copper production, a conductive metal essential for the expansion of capitalist industrialization on a national and international scale, that Mexican miners opposing racial discrimination in pay and working conditions organized one of the first and most comprehensive shutdowns of all mining operations in the towns of Clifton, Morenci, and Metcalf in 1903.

Arizona: Jim Crow and Industrial Copper

Land tenure had already begun to change after the Mexican-American War and annexation, greatly accelerating with the "copper boom." The lands of Arizona once inhabited by at least ten Native American groups, and a patchwork of parcels informally claimed by Mexican ranchers and miners, were gradually consumed by incoming colonists and speculators assisted by the federal government. Anglo migrant settler groups comprised of veterans of the 1850s California and Nevada gold and mineral rushes, as well as waves of post-Confederate Southerners, moved into southern Arizona, bringing with them white supremacist notions that informed the settlement process. Patterns of racial segregation and discrimination were seized upon by the copper companies, who utilized these divides to keep unions out of the camps and to maintain the lowest copper-mining wages in the nation.

While Mexicans were displaced in the advance of the new industrial order, they continued to comprise a large segment of the mining workforce, although as second-class workers who were systematically paid less than white workers and concentrated in the most difficult and dangerous jobs. Because of their precarious and exploitative conditions, Mexican miners were at the forefront of labor actions in the later nineteenth century, even though their efforts were severely hampered by the rigidly structured racial caste system. Furthermore, they were excluded from the organizing efforts of the Western Federation of Miners, the only industrial union actively trying to organize the miners in Arizona at the time.

In 1903, Mexican miners developed their own organizing strategies to unite with other groups of miners to launch a massive strike against the major mining companies in the districts of Clifton and Morenci. Influenced by socialist ideas, the miners countered the operators with a strategy of solidarity and mass direct action. Over the course of the strike, thirty-five hundred mostly Mexican and Italian workers not only shut down all operations in Clifton-Morenci but dispersed the sheriff's deputies and Arizona Rangers, effectively taking armed control of the whole mining district. Only after a large military force was assembled and sent into the area, and after a devastating flood, was the strike ultimately broken. Nevertheless, the strike showed how the powerful industrial copper corporations could be defeated when the miners overcame racial divides and organized militant action to bring the forces of production to a halt. The copper discoveries attracted international capital investments as well as an influx of miners from other regions. As Thomas Sheridan describes, "an aggressive community of miners, merchants, and territorial officials sprang up in the middle of Yavapai and Apache country and one bonanza generated ripples of exploration that led to other bonanzas."[5] Many of these miners brought with them residual anti-Mexican sentiment from their participation in or support for the campaigns to drive Mexican, Native American, Chinese, and foreign-born miners out of the gold camps in the 1850s.

In the post-conquest period, this influx of Anglo migrants and settlers sought to wrest control of the land, mines, and other resources from Mexicans. In 1859, for instance, during the Sonoita Massacre, a white settler named George Mercer along with seven other armed men vowed to drive all Mexicans from the region, rounding them up for "deportation." In one incident, they shot and killed four Mexicans and one Yaqui at a mescal distillery. As word spread of the attack, almost a hundred Mexican mine workers and their families fled the Heintzelman mine and smelter in Arivaca, Arizona, to Sonora, Mexico.[6]

The gold rush was one of the first large-scale efforts of white miners to assert their economic primacy, based on the racial notions of superiority, especially as skilled miners from Sonora proved to be more successful in the mines.[7] Ken Gonzales-Day has documented the lynching of 132 Mexicans and South Americans in the wave of racial violence during this time.[8] Hubert Bancroft identified the high point of the violence as 1855, when there were 535 murders, 7 state-sanctioned executions, and 49 lynchings.[9] Anti-Mexican sentiment in Arizona was further enhanced by attempts at Confederate colonization.

In 1862, the Confederacy claimed Arizona as a Southern territory, after slave-owning interests from Texas invaded Arizona in efforts to preempt Union forces and establish a foothold. The presence of slave-owning Texans created tensions early on with antislavery sentiments in the small Mexican settlements that ultimately sided with the North in the Civil War. After small skirmishes, Union forces vanquished Confederate forces prior to the war's conclusion. Nevertheless, a Southern-aligned population took root and established Arizona as a base for the Democratic Party.

Like in Texas, the Democratic Party ruled the Arizona Territory as a virtual monopoly, which served as the vehicle for spreading Jim Crow segregationist policy and customs into the Southwest. This sentiment informed patterns in the 1870s, during which time white miners established "white man's camps," which prioritized US-born and northern European miners within a racial hierarchy that relegated Mexicans, Native Americans, and other "nonwhite" groups to the lower rungs.

During and after the end of the Civil War came the first waves of white colonization. In a 1908 book, *The White Conquest of Arizona*, Orick Jackson blithely recounts the ghastly tale of a campaign of annihilation against Arizona's original indigenous inhabitants, known as Woolsey's First Expedition. King S. Woolsey was an ex-Confederate soldier and scalp-bounty hunter who earned a reputation for brutality in wars of extermination against indigenous peoples in Alabama. He later moved to Arizona with a crew of fellow mercenaries to ply his trade, slaughtering bands of Apaches in south Arizona to clear the land for white settlement. After arranging a meeting with Apache chiefs in 1864 under peaceful pretenses, he and his posse served the men poisoned *piñole*, a sweetened mashed corn drink laced with strychnine. Jackson describes the massacre with delight:

[W]hile the food was being devoured, Indians began to groan piteously and fall into the circle in front. At this juncture Woolsey gave the signal to begin operations, at the same time whipping out his six-shooter and shooting the two chiefs dead in their tracks. What the bullet did not hit, the pinole did.[10]

As many as 150 men, women, and children were killed in Woolsey's first expedition; his second was even bloodier. In 1865, the US War Department encouraged and funded private mercenary regiments in the mold of Woolsey to clear out the Native peoples. By the end of the Civil War, five such hunting parties were in operation throughout in the state. Woolsey himself went on to become a member of Arizona's first legislature, which also proposed a scalp bounty of a hundred dollars for each indigenous inhabitant murdered by "white pioneers." Woolsey himself was rewarded for his efforts by being chosen to preside over the state's first senate.

In the aftermath of the war, there was strong resistance to the Constitutional amendments that theoretically established racial equality between all males regardless of race. In efforts to resist the integration of blacks and Mexicans in the territory, white settlers adapted Jim Crow laws to Arizona, extending them into the mining camps developed in the early 1870s.[11] The majority Mexican population was subject to a growing list of racial restrictions that penetrated deep into the social fabric. For example, Mexican miners were prohibited from making independent claims, required to pay a prohibitive miners' tax, and were subject to "lynch law" as a way to impose their racial subordination.[12] Later, after the significant 1903 strikes in Clifton-Morenci and Metcalf, in which Mexicans played a leading role, further restrictions were elaborated. In 1909, for instance, the state implemented a literacy test for polling and in 1914 passed an anti-immigrant labor law that restricted immigrant workers to 20 percent of the mining workforce.

Mexican Miners

Mexicans and indigenous peoples were the majority of the mining workforce in US-owned and operated mines in southern Arizona as early as 1860, coming from Arizona and Sonoran pueblos.[13] Mexican miners from Sonora are credited with helping to launch the US copper-mining industry in the 1870s, as Anglo speculators depended on their technical skills to found and develop the first major sites that later produced the copper boomtowns. Mining in Sonora developed as an industry in the late 1600s, and miners from the region were some of the world's most advanced at the time. Prior to the US occupation and acquisition of modern-day Arizona with the Gadsden Purchase in 1853, Mexican miners had established and worked in silver mines for decades. They returned to work in the 1850s and '60s, albeit now as workers in US-owned mines. Mexican migration and settlement accelerated with the advent of a series of booms, starting with silver and then copper, and Anglos quickly came to depend on their labor. By the early 1870s, Mexican labor migration and settlement into the copper-mining region led them to once again become the majority of the population.[14] An 1876 census, for instance, identified that 94 of the 100 residents of the Clifton-Morenci-Metcalf region were of Mexican origin.[15]

Due to the geographical isolation of the copper region and its natural topographic barriers, there was little historic settlement in the region aside from the different Apache groups taking refuge from US military campaigns of forced removal that took place until 1886. Sonora provided the most accessible labor for the mining speculators, as it already had a long mining history. The first copper speculators staked their claims, and then relied on Mexican workers to break ground. One of the first groups of investors in the Clifton region, the Lesinsky brothers, hired Mexican workers with the understanding that the knowledge of the land and time-tested techniques were essential to their success.

Knowing that "Mexicans had a traditional knowledge of smelting, Henry Lesinsky recruited a small force with experience in copper mining, deciding to leave it to them to build and operate the first smelters at Clifton . . . built entirely by Mexican labor."[16] The significant role of Mexicans in the early foundation of the state's mining industry was buried in the soil of Arizona history, especially as the doctrine of white supremacy was elevated to state policy by the 1890s. When the mining complexes were in full operation, further migrant labor was enticed from Mexico as well as Chinese migrant laborers fleeing persecution from California's coastal cities.

Despite the reliance on their knowledge and expertise, Mexicans were gradually relegated to the lowest class of mine labor. In the aftermath of the bloody war of 1846, US capitalists perceived Mexicans as a conquered people, thereby exploitable as manual labor and deserving of less pay at the outset. Anti-Mexican sentiment, still percolating in the postwar period, was seized upon early on by Anglo speculators to establish the foundations of a racial class system, especially as labor importation of untested US miners from back east proved costly, and migration was slow and inconsistent.

In the short term, Mexican labor was preferred since it was cheaper, due to proximity and availability. Nevertheless, as more Anglo settlers migrated into the region, the mine operators quickly established a racial hierarchy as a means to keep the workers separate—segregated—and to establish an artificial low-wage threshold to anchor down all wages. For example, one early observer noted at the Rosemont copper mine in southern Arizona,

> Mexican workmen at the furnace received $1 per day for twelve hours; able-bodied miners $15 per month; and other Mexican laborers $12. In addition to these wages, each man had weekly a ration of sixteen pounds of flour. At the same time, American workmen received from $30 to $70 per month and board.[17]

The rapid influx of capital into the remote mining regions necessitated more labor, leading mine operators to rely on the mass importation of immigrant labor, which was met initially by intensive recruitment of Mexican workers. Miners from Sonora had historically ventured into Arizona on mining expeditions, accumulating knowledge of the terrain and becoming adept at the various stages of copper extraction and production. Migration in significant numbers was accelerated with the rapid privatization of village and communal lands under Mexican dictator Porfirio Díaz beginning in the late nineteenth century. To encourage migration north, mining companies sent recruiters into mining towns with the promise of jobs and pay. Chinese workers were also brought into the region, and later an assortment of European immigrants.

Late nineteenth-century immigration policy and practice co-evolved with the labor needs of capital investments in the Southwest, even when it was necessary to accommodate to the growing chorus of white supremacists within the two national political parties. Racial exclusionists, from the Southern Democratic planter class who were given a new lease on life after the end of Reconstruction, to California growers leery of competition from Japanese farmers and the threat of labor militancy, clamored for Asian exclusion and segregation. Anti-immigrant and racist ideologues were then given an elevated platform by the 1896 Supreme Court ruling *Plessy v. Ferguson*, which sanctioned racial segregation on a national scale.

For instance, the Immigration Act of 1891 revised the 1882 Chinese Exclusion Act by extending "illegality" and a provision for deportation to any worker that entered the country "without inspection." Mexicans were required to enter only after inspection, but only two inspection sites were situated along the nearly two-thousand-mile border by 1894, making it extremely difficult and therefore virtually impossible (and effectively undesirable) for most Mexican miners to enter "legally."[18] The precarious legal state of Mexican workers was used opportunistically by the mine operators, who recruited them into their mines, while socially separating them and treating them as expendable and even deportable immigrants when they tried to unionize, collectively bargain, or withhold their labor.

As a result of these efforts, an estimated sixteen thousand more Mexican workers moved into Arizona between 1900 and 1910, building up the ranks of the mining workforce.[19] By 1910, Mexican workers composed 70 percent of the Arizona mining workforce, another 30 percent was composed of later-arriving European immigrants and US migrants from the east, as well as a small number of Yaqui Indians crossing the Mexican border to escape state repression.[20] The patterns of migration, employment, and racial discrimination determined a racial separation that led to the formation of majority white camps and majority Mexican camps scattered throughout the state. The mining camps in Globe and Bisbee, for instance, became majority white; while those in the Clifton-Morenci-Metcalf region were majority Mexican.

The Racial Camp System

As early as 1863, "White Man's Camps" were established in the mining districts of Globe, Jerome, Bisbee, and Miami, Arizona. These designated and prescribed mining rights, occupational rights, and other privileges to US-born Anglos and northwestern European immigrants. In these camps, whites comprised a majority and were concentrated in the most preferred, best-paid, and most secure occupations. This typically meant working in the above ground stages of production in management, in the mills, concentrators, and smelters; as well as working in craft production and processing as carpenters, boiler-makers, machinists, pipe-fitters, welders, blacksmiths, railroad workers, etc. While whites also worked in the more dangerous underground jobs alongside Mexicans, southern and eastern European immigrants, and other "nonwhites," they were fewer in number, and were paid more for the same work.[21] White man's camps were founded near later copper discoveries, in regions where Mexican mining traditions did not already exist and where economic integration to the regional Sonoran economy was least established.[22]

In the white camps, Chinese workers were excluded from employment and residency while the Mexican population could take up residency, but separately from white families. Mexicans sometimes worked underground, or more commonly in "unskilled" aboveground work in construction, railroads, and maintenance, or did secondary refinement work in smelters and mills. Only in Clifton-Morenci, where Mexicans were the large majority and had the deepest roots, did they work at all levels of the mining economy, even though they were paid less in every category than whites in the white man's camps. After 1885, wages were standardized throughout Arizona mines and defined in racial terms as "white wages" and "Mexican wages." This dual-wage system established that whites customarily received from one-half to one-third more in pay than Mexicans across the board.[23]

From the operators' point of view, this racial separation was a foil against unionization, so long as the Anglo miners themselves accepted and enforced it. In 1884, white miners in Globe established the first union, which was designated as "white only." The notion that their racial identity was equated with primacy within a capitalist system dominated by whites, and that this "racial solidarity" somehow guaranteed them a job and good wages, gained traction among the miners, but proved ephemeral. Andrea Yvette Hugginie observed,

> [T]his was a paradox for Anglo American copper workers: their racial and cultural backgrounds and notions of Anglo American superiority bound them to the copper owners, but divisive class interests made Anglo workers and Anglo bosses, at best, superficial allies.[24]

While in times of stability or growth, white miners could cherish their access to better jobs, nicer company housing, shared ethnic identity with their wealthy and powerful employers, and the illusion of cross-class unity, these benefits melted away at other times. Fluctuations in international copper prices, economic downturn, or increased competition between producers compelled employers to lay off employees, depress wages, cut benefits, or reduce spending on safety infrastructure for white miners as much as other groups. Furthermore, it didn't prevent them from virulently opposing unions and replacing white strikers with Mexicans and vice versa. Local sheriffs, Arizona Rangers, and federal troops used physical violence or its threat to prevent, curtail, or squash strikes regardless of strikers' skin color.[25]

Applying white supremacist politics to their advantage, Arizona's copper operators publicly derided the presence of nonwhite labor in "white" labor markets. At the same time, employers hired Mexicans on a consistent basis, using their presence to their advantage. The copper mine operators learned early on the value of dividing miners into racially separate groups in hiring, housing, and occupation. While pseudoscientific racial thought attempted to underpin this practice as a "natural order," the routinized practice of racism proved to be a profitable enterprise. This differentiation was based on employers' accumulated observation and experience of using workforce segmentation as leverage to keep wages as suppressed as possible. According to a study of the function of the "white" camps,

> Segmentation of the labor market allowed employers to transform individual prejudice and discrimination into a system for locating workers into a racist hierarchy. Employers exploited these divisions . . . repeatedly trying to introduce low-wage immigrants who were desperate for quick incomes as a way to drive down wages and break strikes among existing workers.[26]

While the European American copper miners made more than their Mexican counterparts, the suppressed "Mexican wage" also kept white wages lower than those of their counterparts in the north and midwest of the country, while retarding the potential for unionization in the region.[27]

In the other camps, employers favored the use of Mexican labor and immigrant labor for parallel reasons. Mexicans were preferred because of proximity to the border, and the isolation of the mines gave the growers more control of their workers. Politically normalized racial discrimination rendered Mexican workers vulnerable, especially as the local state apparatus denied them equal protection under the law. This gave the growers the ability to quickly dispatch Mexican workers if they contested wages and working conditions. Law enforcement, deputized vigilante squads, and a legal apparatus designed and maintained by the companies served at the ready to threaten, arrest, or deport unwanted workers.[28] Similar forces were at play with "racialized" Italian immigrants who worked in the mines.

Italians comprised the largest group of European migrants in Arizona, gravitating toward the southern mining complexes after Chinese exclusion fueled labor shortages in the border region. Due to the segregation of camp life, Italians tended to be concentrated alongside Mexicans. As Phyllis Cancilla Martinelli explains,

> Upon entry into the United States, Italians were subject to numerous categories, mostly negative. Concepts of race and nationality over-lapped, so that . . . Italians might be lumped with other southern Europeans, noted for their Mediterranean origin, or with the Latin race, which was seen as not quite white. This meant that in the West, Italians and Mexicans were often close in status.[29]

Ironically, the racialized class system that developed in Arizona copper mines relegated skilled Mexican and Italian miners to the lowest-paid "unskilled" work, especially after northern and western European American migrants arrived and as mechanization replaced many of the skilled tasks previously performed by the Mexican workers. Mine operators suppressed Mexican wages to maintain a low wage floor, and then used this stratification to exert downward pressure on the wages of the other workers. They also placed other burdens on Mexican miners, such as allowing shift bosses to extort bribes from the miners as a means of maintaining their jobs. Along with pay differentials, these daily abuses and indignities imposed on Mexicans conveyed the perception of privilege among white workers, which fostered more loyalty to the mine bosses under normal conditions.

Furthermore, the employers provided little in the way of safety equipment or preventative measures, with no insurance or injury compensation programs, instead deducting health care and insurance fees from workers' paychecks. Mexican and immigrant workers were concentrated in the most difficult and dangerous occupations, making them more susceptible to injury. Aside from high death rates from silicosis and lead poisoning, working conditions were abysmal. According to Linda Gordon:

> If we could add to the deaths and accidental injuries the mine-, mill-, and smelter-induced illnesses, the proportion of men hurt by the copper industry may well be over 75 percent in a camp with as young a population as Clifton-Morenci. Exposure to acids, chlorine, cyanide, mercury, arsenic dust, and a variety of other chemicals, often unrecognized, ate away at skin and internal organs, despite the workers' resourcefulness in devising protective clothing.[30]

During a period of labor conflict and negotiations with white workers, the mine owners in the predominantly white camp would oppose wage increases using the racial divide in their favor. They would first blame Mexicans for their "willingness" to work for low wages, and would threaten to replace disgruntled or striking white workers with Mexican workers. What's more, mine operators purposefully used Mexican workers as strikebreakers in mine camps where white workers predominated; and white workers in the camps where Mexicans predominated.[31] This divide-and-rule strategy worked as long as the racism against the Mexican workers could be successfully stoked. As José Amaro Hernandez explains: "[T]he idea to blame foreign laborers for depressing wages and causing unemployment served no useful purpose; instead, it only aggravated the problem of the working people and increased the already [racist] sentiments in Southern Arizona."[32]

The systematic degradation of Mexican labor was further established through restrictive legislation, championed primarily by the Democratic Party. This included a 1909 law that instituted a literacy test for voting, and a 1910 proposition that prohibited non-English speakers from underground mining and craft work under the pretext of safety, denying these jobs to 90 percent of the Mexican workforce.[33] Another law, passed by referendum in 1914, required all businesses in the state to employ no more than 20 percent noncitizens, even though this was only selectively enforced in the mining camps.[34] Through legal restrictions; overt racial discrimination, from the local police down to the mine foreman; and the rhetoric of white supremacy that permeated state politics, many white workers came to see the apparatus of the state as the "defender" of their labor. Andrés Jiménez summarized how this broad pattern of racial oppression induced Mexicans to unite into mutualistas.

> As a result of this common identification as Mexicans, rights of formal US citizenship were effectively denied to those people of Mexican descent who held citizenship. From the point of view of the larger society, their subordinate status as Mexicans took precedence. In turn, this outgroup identification of Mexicans by the Anglo-American community reinforced the self-identification of the

Mexican community as being "Mexican" and encouraged the development of community-oriented defense strategies based on ethnic solidarity and cutting across class distinctions within the group.[35]

The company town was also a source of frustration for the workers as the corporations established monopolies over local commerce. The companies extracted significant profits not only by keeping wages artificially low, but also by charging exorbitant prices for basic necessities through stores run by affiliated merchants. As James Kluger explained the extent of control:

> More than just employers, these three companies controlled almost every aspect of the workers' lives. Merchandise was brought into the district on the railroad owned by the Arizona Company and sold in company stores—the Arizona Copper Company Store Department in Clifton or the Phelps Dodge Mercantile Store in Morenci. Men lived in either company-owned houses, or in houses built on company property. These homes were lighted by company power plants and furnished with water from company reservoirs.[36]

While prices were significantly inflated, the company stores were often liberal with credit, so much that workers "might become shackled by debt to the store in much the same way as the peon south of the border was, and is, bound to the *tienda de raya*."[37] These conditions made mine work volatile and primed for class conflict; but the absence of unions worked to favor the dominance of the mine operators, that is, until the Mexicans began to organize.

Efforts to organize mineworkers were undercut by the employers, who used various tactics to break efforts including wage decreases, lockouts, blacklists and other means. In response to growing miner militancy, the corporations formed their own organization called the Mine Operators Association. Through corporate alliance the capitalists leveraged greater influence over the levers of local, state, and federal government; and they could rely on a sympathetic media to promote their cause. Even when labor could unite enough popular sentiment to change local law, higher institutions of government would overrule the efforts. Furthermore, in some cases, like with the passage of the Arizona eight-hour work law in 1903, the employers ignored or complied only on terms favorable to them. As James Byrkit explains, "legislation, as in so many other situations involving the cause of the common man during this period, did not mean much change in practice by mining companies. Backed by the higher courts, the companies expressed their independence of the law with impunity."[38]

In a landscape where capital's power grew to form the very structures of government, legal and electoral routes to workers' rights and independence were choked closed through autocratic veto power or noncompliance. Even against these lopsided odds, miners had the power to weaken capital and the state apparatus through the strike, as halts in production disrupted capital accumulation and sent larger shockwaves through the industrial economy, whose growth depended on precious metals. Since effective unionization depended on unity, more significant than the bosses' political power was the effect of racial ideology. The racial divides within the working class prevented unionization efforts more conclusively than could physical repression.

Formed in 1893, the Western Federation of Miners (WFM) launched the first effort to organize the south Arizona mining region. The WFM quickly developed a militant tradition, leading miners in strikes against corporate mining behemoths throughout Michigan, Colorado, and Idaho, and sought to expand throughout the West. The strikes became warlike, as the battle for control of the West between capital and labor would be fought in brutal and often deadly class struggle. The WFM briefly affiliated with the American Federation of Labor in 1896 but broke with the AFL a year later and went its own way. It rejected the conservative craft focus of the AFL and its failure to actively support the WFM miner's strikes. By 1897 the WFM began to embrace industrial unionism, socialist politics, and more radical class-struggle tactics. For example:

> At the federation's 1897 convention [union president Ed Boyce] at least implied syndicalism—control of the means of production by workers' syndicates—in recommending that the union purchase mining properties to operate. He also suggested the possibility of direct action, urging federation locals to form "rifle clubs"; not for the locals' defense, but: "so that in two years we can hear the inspiring music of the martial tread of 25,000 armed men in the ranks of labor."[39]

Despite this radical turn, the WFM did not initially see the importance of organizing Mexican workers and instead concentrated its efforts in the white camps. In its first attempt to organize Anglo miners, it claimed support for the exclusion laws favored in the mine camps that were majority Anglo. It launched Local 60 in Globe in 1897, establishing a white-only membership, but the local foundered and failed to attract significant numbers or be recognized by the mine companies.

The failure in Globe led the WFM to divide internally on the question. A radical minority of WFM organizers began to see the futility of racial exclusion and in breaking with this strategy began to organize Mexicans and whites together at the mining camps of Jerome and Kofa. When the debate spread into Local 60, the membership divided over the question of including Mexicans. When the debate became public, the mine operators and business community perceived the threat of a unified workforce and quickly threw their weight behind the "exclusionists" against the "radicals," trumpeting the urgency for maintaining Globe as a white man's town.

Reinforcing the position of the exclusionists, the companies effectively split the union by relinquishing their opposition to recognition of the WFM but agreeing to negotiate only with the exclusionist wing of the Local. The radicals were soundly defeated, and in the aftermath, many left the Local and some were driven out of town altogether. Despite their victory, the ultimate failure of the exclusionist wing's strategy revealed itself swiftly. With the threat of a broad, united workforce removed and the union divided and weakened, the companies turned the tables on the WFM Local by refusing any concessions in contract negotiations. Wages remained frozen, working conditions remained the same, and the blacklist stayed in place.[40] Soon the divide-and-rule strategy was replicated in the other mining camps, and the radicals favoring inclusion found themselves marginalized.

The Clifton-Morenci-Metcalf Strike of 1903

Mexican miners were at the forefront of labor action in the Arizona mines. Between 1885 and 1889, they led three strikes, two of which won concessions. Between 1896 and 1915, Mexican miners led four of the five major strikes in the state.[41] Wildcat strikes led by Mexicans and Mexican Americans occurred in Ray, Arizona, in February of 1901. They halted operations in the mines, demanding an eight-hour shift and a wage increase to three dollars per day, on par with white miners. Influenced by anarchist thought deeply rooted in Mexican labor traditions, which was grounded in universalist notions of equality and mutuality, they bristled at the idea of being paid less or treated differently for reasons of race.[42] The mine operators fired over twenty Mexican leaders and closed down the mine until the workforce could be repopulated with other groups of workers unsympathetic to labor action or from different ethnic or linguistic groups.[43] The lack of support and preparation, as well as their exclusion by the Western Federation of Miners, led the miners to take a different organizing approach two years later at Clifton-Morenci.

Continuing the tradition from their homeland, Mexican workers in Arizona formed mutualistas as self-help and self-defense organizations. A prominent mutualista that played a significant role was La Alianza Hispano Americana. Formed in 1894, it began as a cross-class organization led by established middle-class Arizona mexicanos, who perceived the need to unite and defend the community against the rising tide of white supremacy resulting from the rapid influx of Anglo migrants. The organization spread across Arizona, claiming three thousand members by 1910, with the overwhelming majority of the members drawn from the working class, including large numbers of miners.[44] The class nature of the Alianza shifted in the mining regions, where local branches came to function as a labor union as class conflict intensified at the turn of the century. The growth and spread of the Alianza among Mexicans in the southern Arizona mining camps was revealed in the Clifton-Morenci strike of 1903. Upward of 80 percent of the workforce was Mexican, and had collectively reached a boiling point of frustration with lower "Mexican" wages and more dangerous working conditions.

Italian working-class immigrants in the United States shared another feature with their Mexican co-workers: experience with mutualistas. By 1895, there were 6,725 mutual aid societies spread across Italy, providing the largely poor and working-class membership with a "spirit of comradeship and class solidarity."[45] This experience converged with that of the Mexicans, who invited the Italians to join the mutualistas in Clifton, Morenci, and Metcalf. Italian workers also brought with them vibrant anarchist and socialist traditions. The Marxist-inspired Italian Socialist Party, for instance, was formed in 1892 and boasted a national membership of 131,000 within its first year, with 446 workers' organizations and mutual aid societies affiliated by 1895. By 1901, there were 661,478 members of unions and labor organizations, of which 23 percent were agricultural workers.[46] Many of the eight hundred thousand Italian migrants who had arrived to the United States by 1900 had labor organizing experience.

The spark for the second strike occurred with the passage by the territorial government of an eight-hour workday rule, a WFM-supported ploy that had a thinly veiled, secondary intention. Despite the progressive veneer of reducing work hours for miners, the law was intended to reduce the employment of Mexicans and other nonwhite workers. It was already common practice for Mexican miners (and some Italian immigrants) to be concentrated in jobs requiring the hardest grunt work deep below the ground, extracting the ore at the face through tedious and exhausting methods. While they worked in conjunction with small numbers of other European and native-born workers carrying out other stages of production above ground, their pay and work rules were different. European American miners at white camps in Jerome and Bisbee, for instance, and in the aboveground work at Clifton-Morenci, already worked eight-hour days and were paid on average 20 percent more per hour. In the Clifton, Morenci, and Metcalf mines, Mexicans, Italians, and other nonwhites commonly worked ten-hour shifts for $2.50 a day, so the hourly cut was also a wage cut that affected them alone.

The supporters of the law asserted that some mine operators were increasing the ranks of Mexican workers in the camps at the expense of white workers, especially in the Clifton-Morenci region. By capping all shifts at eight hours, it was reasoned, the law would compel employers to reduce the employment of Mexicans and other nonwhite workers. By requiring standardization of work rules, mine operators would lose incentive to employ more "exploitable" Mexican labor that could be worked for longer hours and less pay. Rather than achieving the desired effect, the mine operators at Clifton-Morenci used the law to their advantage, by now paying the Mexican and Italians for only eight hours of the ten-hour workload. They also removed allowances for the Mexicans to be paid for time spent descending and ascending to and from the underground mines. This was too much for the Mexican and Italian mineworkers, who pursued collective action. When the workers declared their intention to strike, an emergency meeting of the three corporations led to the announcement of an eleventh-hour proposal to pay nine hours for eight hours' work. The strikers held strong with the demand that they be paid for ten hours, like before. When the companies balked, the strike was on.

On Monday, June 1, 1903, the same day the new eight-hour law was to go into effect, about two hundred miners walked out of the Metcalf mine, which was almost completely Mexican in composition.[47] From there, delegations of striking miners then marched to the other mining complexes in the area to call out their counterparts.[48] By the end of the week, an estimated thirty-five hundred miners, mostly Mexican, with the support of Italian and some Anglo workers, shut down the Clifton-Morenci mines, mills, and smelters in southeastern Arizona, leaving all other non-striking workers idle.[49] Eventually, all labor operations of the Arizona, Detroit, and Shannon Companies in Graham County came to a halt for a period of three weeks. As the *Bisbee Daily*

Review reported, "At Metcalf, where practically all the men employed are Mexicans, the tie up of operations was complete from the start . . . The men prevented the loading of any ore in the cars which haul it to the Arizona reduction works at Clifton."[50]

The initial organization was provided by the mutualistas, with at least two months of planning and networking before the strike was called.[51] La Alianza Hispano Americana, operated in Morenci, and La Sociedad Juárez Protectora, whose membership was concentrated in the Metcalf mine, were among the organizations that provided support and leadership for the strike. While Italian workers had their own mutual aid society in Clifton (Societa Fratellanza Italiano di Mutuo Soccorso), they were also part of the elected officer core and membership of the Clifton branch of La Alianza Hispano Americana.[52] Abrán Salcido, who became president of La Alianza Hispano Americana, was also elected president of the strike committee. He was a recent arrival to the area and had political connections with the revolutionary movement in Mexico. Alongside him was Wenceslao Loustaunau (nicknamed "Three-fingered Jack"), a Romanian Mexican blacksmith chosen as vice-president. A third leader was Cornelio Chacón. All three were mutualista presidents. The committee also included Mexican miners Francisco Figueroa, Manuel Flores, smelter worker Juan Bautista de la O, and an Italian miner named Frank Colombo.[53] One witness to the strike claimed that the miners had sent for a representative from a miners union in Nacozari, Sonora, in the days before the strike.[54]

In immediate response to the strike, the mine operators stonewalled the possibility of negotiations, claiming that an increase in wages would lead costs to supersede the thin margin of profitability of the low-grade copper in that region. Perhaps more practically, the mine operators believed that any concessions would strengthen the hand of the Western Federation of Miners by raising the low-wage threshold.[55] Instead of concessions, they set out to bust the strike. They initially tried to do this by dividing the Anglo and Mexican miners and deflating white support for the strike. Ironically, they were aided in this effort by the Western Federation of Miners, which had decided to ignore the strike so as to not upset its base of support among white miners who supported Mexican exclusion. As a result of the racial divisions and the lack of support, those Anglo miners who had walked out in solidarity gradually left the area to find work elsewhere, leading one hostile observer to comment that the remaining strikers were "mostly Mexicans but a lot of Dagoes, Bohunks, and foreigners of different kinds . . . no whites at all."[56] This division allowed the operators and their media allies to paint the strike in racial terms and to try to inflame white reaction.

The remaining organized strikers, two thousand mostly Mexican miners along with a smaller number of Italians, formed a strike committee and held regular mass meetings in Morenci to develop their demands and debate strike strategy. The initial demands focused on restoring the cut pay for the underground workers. As the strike gained momentum, the miners also demanded a closed shop, which meant only mutualista members would be hired; price controls in the company store; job protections; and company-provided health care.[57]

Lacking a union hall, they gathered at an abandoned lime quarry to hold daily mass meetings, debating strike strategy and tactics. They placed pickets on rotating shifts at all of the struck mines, and organized regular marches from mine to mine, to demonstrate their unity and resolve.[58] According to eyewitness Jennie Parks Ringgold, the workers waved red flags during their marches, rallies, and mass meetings, revealing an affiliation or identification with the burgeoning Socialist movement.[59] In their marches and rallies, the workers armed themselves with rifles and dynamite, and their pickets effectively occupied and idled all of the arteries of production throughout the district, including mines and smelters, tramways, and company stores; creating the impression that the miners were in control. As the *Bisbee Daily Review* reported on strike organization:

> The strike is now composed of almost entirely Mexicans. Quite a number of Americans have left the camp. These men are taking no part with the Mexicans . . . . At Metcalf, where practically all the men employed are Mexicans, the tie up of operations was complete from the start. The men prevented the loading of any ore in the cars which haul it to the Arizona [Copper Company] reduction works at Clifton. . . . It seems that the Mexicans are being led by one or two prominent leaders; they gather two or three times a day in Morenci and listen to speeches from the leaders who are very industrious [and] have used harsh language concerning the "gringos". This morning at 5 o'clock, more than two hundred Mexicans were already gathered at the mouth of the Humboldt tunnel, listening to the harangues by the leaders and music by the band. . . . It is not believed the strike will last long, and . . . will probably be the end of Mexican labor in the district.[60]

When Morenci general manager C. E. Mills refused to even meet the striking miners, they sent out armed patrols to capture and arrest him, compelling the frightened copper boss to flee the town on horseback through back roads. Shortly thereafter, other mining company executives left the area.[61] At one point, the miners surrounded the company store in Morenci and threatened to blow it up with dynamite. In response, the local sheriff deputized sixty white men, including ranchers, cowboys, and shopkeepers, but they proved insufficient to contain or disarm the miners. When they tried to assert control over any group of striking miners occupying company property, they were quickly surrounded by roving pickets and disarmed, a scene that replayed several times, with the sheriff's deputies retreating each time.

The miners were in full control, and in their resolve to win the strike they had carried out what appeared to the frightened ruling class of copper mine operators to be an armed uprising. Military-like detachments of armed miners were stationed at all vantage points overlooking the town and mines. They cut telegraph and telephone lines to prevent calls for reinforcements and "threatened prominent citizens, most of whom are officers of or managers of departments of the copper company."[62] Rather than concede their demands, they fled to nearby towns and called in state and federal armed forces to put down the strike by force of arms. This sense of alarm was aided by the local pro-capitalist press, which ran their stories verbatim from the mouths of the mine operators, with headlines such as "Morenci at Mercy of Armed Foreigners."[63]

The response from the mine operators was to make urgent appeals to the acting governor of the territory, Isaac Taft Stoddard, and to the federal government. In response, the governor sent in the Arizona Rangers. The Arizona Rangers was an Anglo paramilitary force set up by the territorial government in 1901 to suppress strikes and investigate crimes against property.[64] Like their counterparts in Texas, they were notorious for their mistreatment of Mexicans. They were more trusted by the operators, as the sheriff's deputies had roots in the community and some personal connections to the miners. The Rangers operated as a semi-clandestine force whose identities were kept secret; and they were empowered to deputize at will and commandeer local law enforcement when required. In this way, they could function as the shock troops for the mine operators.[65] Together with the deputies, their ranks grew to about 125.

Their calls for the workers to disarm and relinquish control of company property fell on deaf ears. In direct defiance of the sheriff and Rangers, two thousand armed workers paraded through the center of Morenci in the pouring rain on June 9 with the sheriff's deputies and Rangers looking on helplessly.[66] When they tried to disarm the miners, they were surrounded by the miners and later dispersed from the area. The strikers focused their efforts on keeping production halted until the mine owners conceded.

Incapable of disarming and dismantling the strike alone, the governor brought in all six companies of the Arizona Territorial Militia, and the president himself, Theodore Roosevelt, ordered in troops from the US Calvary, from nearby military forts in Arizona and from as far away as Colorado and Texas.[67] Together with the deputies, and with the whole force of Arizona Rangers, the number of armed government troops reached nearly a thousand by June 10.[68] Since the federal troops were transported in by rail, the sheriff's deputies and Rangers retreated to guard the railroad-bearing bridges that would be used to transport the troops into the towns, especially as workers allegedly threatened to blow the tracks up with dynamite. Meanwhile, the Mexican consul to Arizona, Arturo Elías, alongside the local Catholic priest, was brought in to plead with the workers, but to no avail. State and federal forces took up strategic military positions around the town, while the miners also prepared for battle. The stage was being set for a bloody war on a scale unseen since the US wars against the Apache.

Along with the substantial show of repressive military force, a massive torrential storm conspired against the strike on June 12, pummeling and flooding the region in what turned out to be the greatest storm in the district's history. Thirty-nine people perished, mostly the wives and children of the miners, as the raging floodwaters laid waste to whole residential sections of Clifton where many of the families lived and took refuge.[69] The organized body of miners declined in number, desperately returning to their homes to deal with the emergency situation. Under the chaotic conditions, martial law was declared as a means for the government forces to begin physically clearing the more sparsely occupied company properties. Despite the odds against them, the strike persisted for another month, even as the workers abandoned the mines and company properties, and strike leaders went into hiding to avoid arrest. In the interim, the strike committee sent out an appeal to the Western Federation of Miners (WFM) to join their efforts, provide relief for the miners, organize a local, and use the current situation to negotiate a meaningful contract.

News of the strike emboldened the radicals in the WFM to push for direct support for the strikers and to change the policy toward the inclusion of Mexicans, immigrants, and others previously excluded. At the national convention of the WFM, happening while the strike was taking place, delegates voted to reject the "white man's camp" policy and to actively organize Mexican miners. Registering the shift, the president of the union, Charles Moyer, sent a message that "the men at Morenci have the full support of the Western Federation of Miners," and that cooperation rather than exclusion was a better course.[70]

Nevertheless, active support for the miners was not forthcoming, and the strike was broken in July of 1903. Lacking resources and allies in the face of coordinated local, state, and federal repression, the miners relinquished control of the mine properties, surrendered, and gave up their arms. In the aftermath, company reprisals were meted out against the strikers. The Rangers and sheriffs conducted house-by-house searches for strike leaders, strikers' arms were confiscated, blacklists were used to exclude militants, and ultimately fourteen men identified as strike organizers were given two-year jail sentences. Millions of dollars in state and federally financed human resources were spent to crush the strike, so that the mine operators would not have to pay the Mexicans and Italian immigrant workers the same as whites. The local newspaper, the *Copper Era and Morenci Leader*, used the opportunity to run an editorial that called on mine operators to expel "foreign labor" and make the area a "white man's camp":

> Mexican and Italian Labor have found a refuge at Morenci and Clifton, and have been given preference to the American miner in large numbers. This foreign labor has returned thanks to their employers by inaugurating a vicious strike, and threats of violence to the property of the company are a daily occurrence . . . If before the present trouble is ended, Morenci is the scene of rapine and murder, carried on by these same foreigners, the recollection will long be in their memories . . . The present difficulty . . . should put a stop to the employment of foreign labor . . . Now is the time to be rid of a continual menace, get rid of the foreigners.[71]

Abrán Salcido, a leader of the 1903 strike at Clifton-Morenci and Metcalf, Arizona

At the strikers' trials, not a single member of the jury was Mexican or Italian. Among the incarcerated were the mutualista presidents, including Abrán Salcido and Wenceslao Loustaunau, and Italian leader Frank Colombo. The rest of the arrested strike committee leadership, revealing its Mexican and Italian composition, included: A. C. Cruz, Manuel Flores, Francisco Gonzales, Gaetano Parriani, F. E. Montoya, Francisco Figueroa, Juan de la O, José Porepe, Frank Serlini, Rafael Murrillo, and Severo Montez.[72] After serving two years in the Yuma prison, Salcido returned to Clifton-Morenci. Sometime in early 1906, he began to actively organize local chapters of the revolutionary group Partido Liberal Mexicano in the mining camps of south-eastern Arizona to build support for their planned uprising that year. He later left the area to help organize a miners' strike in Cananea, Sonora, alongside other magonistas. Upon his return, he was arrested and deported by direct order of the secretary of commerce and labor for being an "undesirable foreigner."[73] Once in Mexico, he was turned over to Mexican agents. He was immediately arrested and sent to the prison San Juan de Ulúa, where he languished until the overthrow of Díaz in 1911.[74]

As a condition of their return to work, the company agreed to pay the miners nine hours of pay for eight hours of work. Despite the otherwise crushing defeat, the strike of the Mexican miners had changed the equations in western class politics. Mexican miners went on to spearhead waves of union organizing again in 1907, 1911, 1915, and 1917, helping to defeat white supremacy within emerging labor unions and giving shape to a new version of radical politics that embraced the need for uniting the whole working class against capital, regardless of race and nationality.[75]

Chapter 6
Early Mexican Labor Radicalism in Texas

"From the time that the worker first conceived of the sacred and liberating strike, there has been no peace in the consciousness of the tyrant."
—*El Defensor del Obrero*, **April 1907**

Mexicano resistance to Anglo occupation, dispossession, and the institutionalization of racial violence and segregation has been a constant feature of borderland existence since the Mexican-American War. Long-standing Mexican ranching and agricultural pueblos situated along the South Texas border faced an influx of speculators and settlers imbued with a sense of superiority and entitlement to the land, who could not enjoy the fruits of their conquest without the forced removal, dispossession, and subjugation of the region's mexicano and indigenous inhabitants. In essence, the land as the basis for wealth accumulation had to change hands. This occurred through a legal strategy through the state when possible, and through systems of direct violence when not. As historian Richard Griswold del Castillo summarized:

> In the first half century after ratification of the Treaty of Guadalupe Hidalgo, hundreds of state, territorial, and federal legal bodies produced a complex tapestry of conflicting opinions and decisions. The citizenship seemingly guaranteed in Articles VIII and IX was not all it seemed. The property rights for former Mexican citizens in California, New Mexico, and Texas proved to be fragile. Within a generation, the Mexican Americans who had been under the ostensible protection of the treaty became a disenfranchised, poverty stricken minority.[1]

In the interregnum between the Mexican-American War and industrial expansion, the first acts of resistance began to manifest. Displaced ranchers, village pueblos, and Native American groups revolted against deteriorating conditions and racial discrimination, including events known as the Cortina Wars of 1859, the El Paso Salt War of 1877, the Apache uprising of 1879, and the Garcista uprising of 1891.[2] While these popular rebellions and guerrilla wars slowed the progress of capitalist displacement and racial subordination in South Texas, they were inevitably suppressed by state and federal forces with superior arms and resources.

While rebellions and acts of insurgency were passively supported by many in the community, they could not be sustained in the face of overwhelming repression. Large-scale military operations were employed to crush revolt, and vigilante terror became widespread throughout the Southwest as a means to demoralize the mexicano population and discourage further resistance. Furthermore, mob violence and extrajudicial killing involving public and private Anglo citizens within contested zones were techniques used to displace and consolidate control over land and assert newly established "sovereignty." The lynching of those resisting subjugation was widespread. For instance, between 1848 and 1928 a documented 597 mexicanos and Mexican Americans were lynched by white vigilantes, while some historians estimate that thousands were killed by Texas Rangers in extrajudicial operations over the same period.[3] While systematic violence blunted the rebellious eruptions over time, institutionalized forms of racial segregation throughout the Southwest served as the control mechanism to integrate mexicanos into their prescribed role as disenfranchised labor.

The internal containment, marginalization, and subjugation of the conquered mexicano population did not prevent new forms of resistance and organized opposition. Rather, the locus of resistance shifted within the terrain of industrialization. Within the matrix of segregated labor, Mexican ranchers and small and subsistence farmers were transformed into a proletariat that reached deep into the mines, railroads, construction zones, and agriculture throughout the Southwest and into the Midwest. This arterial network expanded as migration swelled the barrios north of the border and distributed mexicano workers through the economy. In an industrial setting, mexicanos interfaced for the first time with other groups of workers and came into contact with new political ideas and forms of class-based organization. Miners, farmworkers, and railroad workers crisscrossed the border on a regular basis. Through the nexus of migration and exile, the mexicano and Mexican American worked together north of the border, and radicals from Mexico and the United States intermixed, shared ideas, and merged efforts.

By the turn of the century, Mexican workers began to realize their collective power as a class to join or form unions, organize strikes, and take other actions. Border realities aided the movement of people and ideas. Furthermore, Mexicans and Mexican Americans regularly crossed the border to live and work, creating strong transnational linkages based on kinship, land usage, trade and economic interdependency, and shared culture and customs. The incipient challenge to racialized Jim Crow capitalism was given ideological expression when waves of migration from Mexico infused local communities with radical political doctrines that had been forged in the class struggles of Mexico. This process further intensified in the years preceding the outbreak of the Mexican Revolution. Alongside rising labor unrest in Mexico in the first decade of the twentieth century, so too did Mexican Americans and mexicanos in the Southwest begin to assert their collective power as a class.

The Making of a Mexican Proletariat in Texas

Eastern US and British capital penetrated the Panhandle and southern border region after the war, with local operations reporting back to home offices in New York or London. According to Texas historian David Montejano, the influx of outside capital investment accelerated differentiation among the early Anglo settlers into "cattle kings" and "cow hands."[4] Their small numbers and their relative ignorance of the land, people, and economy led this first generation of Anglo and European speculators and settlers in the South Texas border region to be absorbed into the existing Mexican ranchero culture. Nevertheless, the commodification of the land led to an enclosure movement with which large swaths of common pastures were enclosed and privatized.

Barbed wire fencing, for instance, was first developed and patented by producers in the Northeast. It was introduced into Texas in the mid-1870s and legalized by the state government in 1879.[5] Smaller and less competitive ranchers were gradually pushed out of markets by the more capitalized and connected. A non-landowning class of Anglos was incorporated as foremen, ranch-hands, and cowboys. They formed political, economic, and even familial relationships that retained the pastoral and cultural character of the pueblos, albeit as the new elite.

The opening up of South Texas to capitalist market forces occurred in earnest during the 1880s when investment patterns shifted from ranching to the financing of large-scale cotton production. The construction of the railroads linked southern Texas cotton to world markets, opening up the region to a flood of investors, real estate speculators, banking and merchant interests, engineers, fortune seekers, and other settlers over the course of the decade. Through state and federal political connections, larger stocks of capital, rapid accumulation of the land, and direct influence over the construction of local government, they transplanted their social and economic structures on the people of the region.

David Montejano states that this model of "North Atlantic capitalism" destroyed existing "unproductive" societies, breaking apart communal ties and replacing them with "new material and social structures, with new social relations, new solidarities, and new metaphors."[6] This was not carried out without class conflict, as witnessed by a "cowboy" strike for higher wages. These ranch workers halted production on five of the largest capitalist ranches in South Texas for nearly three months in 1883.[7] By the turn of the century, the earlier established population of Anglo cowboys, foremen, and displaced ranchers was gradually transformed into a class of sharecroppers and laborers. They entered the ranks of a rural proletariat alongside Mexicans, who were affected by the same forces, albeit further subjugated by racial stratification through the implementation of Jim Crow laws.

To maintain an expanding rural workforce that was divided and docile, Anglo and European capitalists maintained or implemented racial segregation laws that had already been established throughout the South, with Mexicans designated as a "racially inferior" people genetically akin to African and Native Americans.[8] For Mexicans, racial oppression coincided with proletarianization, laying the basis for a century of labor suppression through state agents and extralegal, vigilante violence.

The Mexican ranchero economy was even more decimated, especially throughout the fertile area between the Nueces and Río Grande Rivers known as the Nueces Strip. While some ranchers made the transition to farming, a larger share became sharecroppers and laborers. This reconfiguration also carried within it the racialization of Anglo capitalist relations of production. While Mexicans lost their lands through taxes, mortgage debts, legal battles, market fluctuations, and buyouts; they more systematically experienced fraud, institutional discrimination, and occasional spasms of state and vigilante violence.[9]

Anglo settlers that moved into South Texas viewed the local population as not only racially inferior, but also a conquered people without sovereign claim to their own lands. The racial attitudes of the more recent Anglo arrivals did not distinguish between the aristocratic hacendados and the landless campesino, or whether one was native-born *tejano* or immigrant. For Mexicans, patterns of racial segregation were structured into daily life, although most intensively imposed and enforced along racial and class lines. Dispossessed, landless, and later migrant workers from the Mexican border region comprised the growing ranks of a disenfranchised agricultural proletariat by the turn of the century.

With settlement and capitalist redevelopment came the creation of armed enforcement groups, both official and vigilante, to police a large population of displaced Mexicans and suppress oppositional activity. The Texas Rangers were officially constituted in 1835 after US filibusterers led by Sam Houston engineered an overthrow of the regional Mexican government in Tejas and proclaimed a Southern-aligned slave-owners republic the following year. The Rangers became the first legally sanctioned, armed enforcers of the Anglo-centric new order. Composed of and funded by the landowning class, they were tasked with fugitive slave recovery, Mexican and Indian removal, and suppressing agricultural labor organizing.[10] After the outbreak of the Mexican Revolution, they became the advance guard of counterrevolution, violently and systematically repressing Mexicans in South Texas in the context of stanching the spread of agrarian radicalism.

By 1892, many Mexican farmers and ranchers had systematically lost their lands across the border region. The situation in Cameron County, in the Río Grande Valley at the southern edge of Texas, illustrates the extreme of this phenomenon. While census figures calculated that over 95 percent of the fourteen thousand residents were Mexican, the wealthiest forty-six Anglos in the county controlled 1.2 million acres, about four times the total territory owned by the Mexican population.[11] This pattern was replicated (on a smaller scale) in the other southern border counties of Hidalgo and Starr, where a small white minority controlled most of the land while most of the Mexican population became tenant farmers, or agricultural or industrial laborers. Land ownership further eroded for Mexicans after the turn of the century. Between 1900 and 1910, Mexican-surnamed landowners lost more than 187,000 acres of land in Cameron and Hidalgo Counties.[12]

Like the rest of the South after the end of Reconstruction, Texas became a bastion of the white supremacist Democratic Party and functioned as a one-party state. Jim Crow laws were institutionalized within state and local government, as new ruling groups consolidated power and worked to deprive blacks and Mexicans of any electoral means to challenge the new arrangements. The Texas state government implemented a racially restrictive poll tax in 1902, and in 1903 it passed the Terrell Law, which established requirements for primary elections while allowing the Democratic Party to determine its own criteria for how to conduct them at the county level. This devolution of decision-making power allowed the Democratic Party leadership to devise a "white-only primary" system in 1904, ensuring all candidates were white and effectively vetted by party leaders. This gave full power to the grower establishment in the South to exclude blacks, indigenous, and Mexicans from local and statewide political office, and limited their participation where it still existed to validating preselected, white-supremacist candidates.[13]

While wealthier and whiter Mexicans could find niches within local political and economic structures, Mexican communities in general became impoverished and politically inert. This was the structure in place when migration from Mexico began to increase significantly after the turn of the century, driven by similar economic factors occurring simultaneously south of the border. The suppression of the indigenous, black, and Mexican populations and the rapid advancement of capitalist development into the border region changed the tenor of further US expansion, especially as the Díaz regime became more amenable to US economic interests within the territories of Mexico. As the *Galveston Daily News* editors observed in an article written in 1880, there was "the dawning of a new era of domestic peace and healthy progress" in Mexico and candidly advocated "seeking the commercial, not political, annexation of that country."[14]

Facilitated by the favorable policies of the Díaz regime, US investors sank great quantities of cash into railroads, mines, and land farther into the Mexican border region. Often backed by large investment companies based in New York and Boston, Texan land speculators bought up huge tracts of land across northern Mexico, in some cases in partnership with Mexican capitalists. One speculator, Josiah F. Crosby, bought a half million acres in Chihuahua that included some of the richest silver mines in the region. Another, named John Millet, purchased the entirety of the Kickapoo tribal region, three hundred thousand acres in the state of Coahuila.[15] Handfuls of wealthy speculators backed by financial capital syndicates bought up large swaths of northern Mexico in such a manner. The Díaz-sanctioned growth of a class of US and European speculators and colonists consumed communal lands and encroached upon smaller ranching and farming operations in the pueblos.

The establishment of the Mexican Central Railroad linked El Paso to Mexico City, integrating markets along the way and encouraging a massive influx of foreign capital and technology, and creating a direct link back to northern markets for the mining and agricultural enterprises now under US control. In Chihuahua, the "capitalist invasion" from the north further concentrated land in the hands of a few companies between 1870 and 1920, bolstered by the growth of banks and other creditors, which financed the rise of large enterprise at the expense of local economies.[16]

Between 1880 and 1910 another significant migration of labor took place from the central states of Zacatecas, San Luis Potosí, and Coahuila to the border region looking for work in the railroads and other foreign-owned or controlled industries.[17] Along with the displaced farmers, these groups together constituted a forty-thousand-strong "floating" proletariat, which crisscrossed the border working in railroads, mines, and seasonal agriculture.[18] Migration into Texas increased, accelerated by the railroads, which moved people more easily and rapidly between border towns by the turn of the century. Between 1902 and 1908, an estimated sixty thousand Mexicans crossed into El Paso alone, significantly increasing the ranks of the South Texas working class.[19]

Migration and Mutualismo

Mexican labor migration into the United States followed the character of regional economic integration more than the abstract demarcation of national boundaries. For instance, Mexican migration into Texas was facilitated by the development of a vast cotton-producing region spanning from the economically vital agricultural zone of La Comarca Lagunera in northern Mexico to the Río Grande Valley in South Texas. Beginning in the 1880s, campesinos displaced by the land privatization policies of Porfirio Díaz began to migrate north from the interior to La Comarca Lagunera, a cotton- and guayule-growing region intersecting the states of Coahuila and Durango, and then followed the harvest corridor north into the East Texas cotton belt. This coincided with the expansion of the railroads into the Southwest, accelerating the rapid growth of capitalist agriculture. As production outpaced migration from the East Coast, Anglo rail companies and landowners began to coax Mexican workers northward to meet labor needs.

As previously mentioned, mass migration moved nearly a million workers into the United States over the first two decades of the twentieth century, with the largest share entering into South Texas. By 1910, three of the four largest Mexican barrios in the United States were in Texas: San Antonio, Laredo, and El Paso.[20] Urban and rural workers merged and mixed together in the barrios and even in the same households, as labor migration became a feature of daily life for most workers who could not find yearlong or steady employment in the cities. Women and children also formed into the working class. By 1910, for instance, 15 percent of Mexican migrant women were wage workers in South Texas.[21]

Growers and railroad companies recruited large numbers of these mexicanos through the establishment of employment agencies in these towns. El Paso, Texas, for instance, had six employment agencies operating within the city eager to recruit northward-moving migrants. As a result of intensive recruitment, Mexican workers became the majority of rail workers in the western United States, concentrated heavily in "low-status" work such as maintenance, construction, repair work, and loading. As Juan L. Gonzalez, Jr. describes,

> Mexican laborers were considered indispensable for the development of the extensive railway system of the Southwest. As early as 1880 Mexican laborers made up approximately 70 percent of the section crews, and 90 percent of the extra gangs. During an eight-month period in 1908, the railroad companies of the Southwest brought in 16,471 laborers from Mexico . . . The railroad industry's heavy reliance upon Mexican laborers as the chief source of manpower continued into the 1960s.[22]

As the Mexican workforce expanded, it did so within the rigid occupational hierarchy of Jim Crow racism. The enforcement of segregation and the dual wage structure was even more rigid in South Texas, where a spectrum of organizations from the Ku Klux Klan to the AFL adjoined with Texas Rangers, police, and immigration enforcement agents to control Mexican labor. In some cases, Texas AFL locals even spearheaded campaigns to discourage the hiring of Mexicans in government or public works. Under these circumstances of exclusion, Mexicans formed their own organizations, transporting and adapting the traditional mutualista (mutual aid society) organization from Mexico to conditions in Texas. As Emilio Zamora describes,

> As a result of immigration, racial conflict, and estrangement from Anglo institutions, Mexican workers' organizations looked southward to Mexico for support and inspiration. The work of exiled groups in Texas and binational interactions involving labor groups constituted important unionist influences during the early 1900s. Mexican workers and their organizations . . . continued to operate in a relatively independent manner and ultimately fended for themselves.[23]

The mutualista tradition, especially the variant comprised of a working-class membership that could function as a quasi–labor union, was first established in Laredo, Texas, where at least thirteen mutualistas were established between 1880 and 1900. Six of these were wholly working-class associations and four were comprised of all women.[24] The advanced level of Mexican and working-class organization in Laredo was influenced by several factors. Among these was the fact that Laredo was one of the first US centers linked to the interior of Mexico by railroad, and consequently it became an entry point and refuge for radical political exiles fleeing the Díaz regime.

This is illustrated by the experience of Silvino Rodríguez, a railroad worker from Chihuahua who migrated to San Antonio after the Mexican railroad reached Texas in 1881. While there he helped organize a mutualista called La Sociedad Ignacio Zaragoza, as an alternative to the Anglo craft union brotherhoods that excluded mexicanos. In 1898, Rodríguez returned to Mexico and formed the Unión de Mecánicos Mexicanos, considered the first industrial union in that country, whose worker militancy and strike action in 1906 is considered one of the key factors leading to the fall of Díaz.

Situated on the border, Laredo was linked by rail to the large-scale, capitalist, export-oriented agricultural complex known as La Comarca Lagunera. La Comarca Lagunera was a volatile region, with a history of intense class struggle going back several decades. The region, like other major commodity export zones, had previously been the site of intensive capitalization and the conversion of much of the land to produce cotton and guayule for export to US and European markets. Investments in railroads and access to world markets via Texas facilitated the growth of foreign- and Mexican-owed seasonal megafarms, and also spurred the development or reactivation of mining complexes in proximity to the lines. Sharecropping, tenant farming, and more traditional forms of hacienda production persisted alongside a massive and mobile landless agricultural proletariat. Between 1885 and 1910, for instance, as many as twenty thousand agricultural workers migrated into the region, as Torreón became a central hub connecting Mexico City in the south up to El Paso and Laredo.[25]

The volatile nature of the economy made the region susceptible to periodic out-breaks of protest, strikes, and revolt. Radical doctrines also found welcome reception; in the first decade of the twentieth century, socialist doctrine and union ideas spread among railroad workers in tandem with the sprawling transnational and intersecting railroad lines. Periodic fluctuations in world cotton prices, ecological constraints pro-duced by perennial water shortages, and the seasonal nature of the work made for a precarious existence for many laguneros. Unemployment was high in the off-season, while large waves of migrants were brought in during peak harvest time and moved out with its conclusion, ensuring a consistent flow of workers into Texas.[26] With these mi-grant flows came political doctrines, organizational memory, and class consciousness that gradually informed labor organization throughout Texas and beyond.

Between 1900 and 1920, for instance, mexicanos in other parts of Texas formed sev-enteen mutualistas.[27] In some cases these fraternal associations evolved into defense or-ganizations, providing the nuclei for both civil rights agitation and union organizing and strikes, especially as radical doctrines with an orientation toward class struggle began to filter into the region via revolutionaries moving into the area from Mexico.[28] Some mutu-alistas even functioned or saw themselves as branches of organizations based in Mexico. For example, an Austin-based group called itself El Gran Círculo de Obreros, an exten-sion of another mutualista of the same name just over the border in Monterrey, Nuevo Leon. El Gran Círculo began as the first national labor movement in the late nineteenth century, and its branches spread throughout Mexico and into the US Southwest.

Radical Ideas Enter South Texas

Radical politics first entered into Texas through the Partido Liberal Mexicano (PLM). The PLM was a political party that formed in opposition to the dictatorship of Porfirio Díaz, and it actively sought to topple his regime after 1901. After 1901, exiles aligned with the anti-Díaz movement begin pouring into Laredo as a result of state repression. By 1904, the PLM leadership, led by Ricardo Flores Magón, moved their base of operations across the border into Texas to escape jail or assassination. After a short stay in Laredo, they then moved to San Antonio, where they began to organize for revolution in Mex-ico. Along their journey, which involved a nearly two-decade odyssey to organize a rev-olutionary party while facing constant arrest, a network of radicals and revolutionaries (magonistas) was formed throughout the Mexican barrios of the Southwest.

A core of exiles aligned with the PLM had been established in Laredo early on among local mexicano intelligentsia, some of whom had gone into exile years before. Radical journalists such as Sara Estela Ramírez, Juana B. Gutiérrez, and Elisa Acuña y Rosete worked tirelessly to promote the magonista project through their newspapers, which carried significant weight among the city's Mexican working class and circulated across the border as well.[29] Furthermore, magonista railroad workers and supporters moved into the booming railroad industry north of the border and played a key role in agitation among mexicanos and Mexican Americans. Railroad workers were among the earliest Mexican workers in the north of the country to embrace socialist ideas, which informed the basis of their commitment to unions and labor solidarity.

Laredo and San Antonio, Texas, were significant juncture points for migration, labor organizing, and the spread of radical ideas, as seasonal migrations through the cotton region facilitated strike experience, cross-border contact, and the circulation of radical politics. In a Mexican-majority town like Laredo, where an older, organized, Mexican capitalist class exerted its class interests alongside whites, there weren't the rigid, socially defined class divisions between Anglos and mexicanos that were commonplace in other South Texas border towns. This has led one historian to conclude that mexicano workers articulated their opposition to racial divisions on the railroads in class terms and not exclusively racial or national ones; even as racism became the defining barrier to improving their conditions.[30] Alongside the agitational efforts of radicals from both sides of the border in the Mexican barrios, this can help explain why so many workers rallied to the socialist cause. Emilio Zamora summarized how large numbers of mexicano workers embraced socialist ideas, especially in the context of cross-border migration and increased class struggle on both sides of the border:

> Chicano socialist labor activity occurred during and was a result of this period of intense socio-economic conflict and changes. It also was influenced by radical ideological expressions in both Mexico and the United States. These socialist influences were generated by El Partido Liberal Mexicano, the Western Federation of Miners, the American Labor Union, the Industrial Workers of the World (IWW) and individual socialists from Mexico and the United States. Influenced by prevalent notions of the class struggle, many Chicano workers in Texas opted for the socialist position in the resolution of their problems.[31]

The formation of a transnational, industrial working class; the spread of socialist ideas, and the consolidation of labor mutualistas laid the basis for industrial unionism in South Texas and the US-Mexico border region. An early expression of this socialist labor agitation was expressed among Mexican railroad workers in Laredo, Texas, and the American Federation of Labor, Federal Labor Union 11953.

Federal Labor Union 11953

In 1905, Mexican railroad workers formed their first independent union in Laredo, Texas, continuing a trend toward unionization that had been developing along the rail lines in central and northern Mexico. Granted an independent "federal" charter by the American Federation of Labor, the union was called the Federal Labor Union 11953 (FLU) and operated with significant autonomy from the national union hierarchy. "Federal" charters were those granted to industrial (deemed "unskilled") workers in the early twentieth century when the AFL leadership still had an ambivalent attitude toward the inclusion of non-craft workers. Since the federation did not technically support the foundation of industrial unions, federal unions tended to have a marginal and short-lived existence. This was especially the case for self-organized charters with significant nonwhite and "unskilled" workers, who were deprioritized and routinely neglected by the national federation.[32] The level of attention and support tended to increase in periods when there was rising class struggle, and when the AFL federal model was posited as a safe and controllable alternative to radical IWW industrial unionism and later Communist Party-controlled unions.[33]

Despite its isolation, the union developed in coordination with the mutualistas and fraternal organizations, growing a membership among the working-class elements within these organizations and giving it a broad base of support. Under the leadership of socialists Rafael Guevara and Luis Alvarado, the president and secretary of the Federal Labor Union 11953 respectively, the local began organizing rail workers but expanding to include Mexican workers from all of the local trades, many of which were linked to the railroad directly or indirectly, such as boiler workers, painters, carpenters, miners, metal workers, and teamsters.[34]

Influenced by Marxist ideas, the socialist leadership established a newspaper, *El Defensor del Obrero* (Labor Defender), as a means to disseminate radical ideas emphasizing unity between all workers regardless of race, nationality, or gender; and promoting class struggle as the means to defeat the bosses and overturn capitalism. The July 1906 issues exemplified this, stating:

> As socialists we demand that all of the wealth that has been produced be distributed collectively between the class that created it. . . . Comrades, the time is now that the parasitic class, that we call the bourgeoisie, disappears; the time is now that each person is given the total product (socially speaking) of their labor.[35]

In a later edition, they continued:

> When we achieve socialism, we will truly achieve brotherhood. We will not have this as long as we compete with each other for work; we will not have it when we are victims of speculation, profiteering, or usury; but only when we control the means of production and work toward the same common interest, because this is how we can produce the best results.

An issue from that September declared, "With capitalism, we can only hope for more hunger and misery; slavery and servility; yokes and chains for us and our children."[36] The editors of *El Defensor del Obrero* used a socialist analysis to challenge machismo and appeal for unity between working-class men and women:

> What does it mean to be humanitarian, if it doesn't pain you to know that 2 million poor women bend over the bathtub every week to do your laundry? Under socialism, this hard work will be done in public laundries, equipped with the best scientific-mechanical means, and difficult work that used to take ten hours will be easily completed in one. If you truly value your wives and daughters, which system would you prefer?[37]

They called on men to see women workers as their allies and for women to join the union alongside the men, criticizing backward men and inverting sexist stereotypes of femininity: "And you, lovely fighters in the class struggle, you should not pay attention to those who tell you that you shouldn't join the union. How does it serve you to be beautiful, attractive, admired, and smart . . . if you waste all of this working from sun-up to sun-down?" [38]

As part of their views towards socialist education, they fervently stressed the power of the working class as builders of all, yet people who could not enjoy the fruits of their labor: "We workers build up the tallest palaces, yet we live in shacks . . . we build the temples but have to pay the clergy to intervene on our behalf . . . we produce all of the food, but go hungry."[39] They exhorted workers in all industries to join the proto-industrial union, proclaiming,

> the capitalist forms their own associations to exploit the industries to their satis-
> faction . . . they have the right to "value" the labor of workers as they see fit . . . in
> sum, they have all the "rights" . . . while the worker has no right to object to the
> bad treatment by the bourgeoisie . . . unionism offers us a wide field to develop
> our efforts and energies and to form workers organizations . . . into a common
> federation.[40]

Each issue of the paper, which was published for two years, contained articles explaining socialism, debating and polemicizing with other newspapers, advertising community cultural events and news, and promoting the daily goings-on of the union.

Local radicals with ties to the revolutionary movement in Mexico joined the efforts to build the union. One example was Sara Estela Ramírez, a well-known journalist and Partido Liberal Mexicano sympathizer. Ramírez "encouraged Mexicans in skilled positions such as the railroad workers to unionize along the border. Ramírez spoke often in the mutualistas (mutual aid societies) and helped establish one of the earliest unions organized by Mexicans in the Southwest."[41]

By 1906, the socialist-led union had organized 300 railroad workers, and by the following year, at its height, it had branched out and expanded to 1,000 members in Laredo (and another 300 in mining districts outside of town organized into the Unión de Mineros 12340), comprising 21 percent of the population when including households.[42] Like their counterparts inside Mexico, one of the most pressing grievances was the practice of reserving the prime, skilled jobs for Anglos, and paying Mexicans in the less-skilled labor jobs less than whites received for the same work, notoriously referred to as the "Mexican wage."

Using Marxist formulation, the Socialist leadership of the union declared that workers should be "compensated based on the full product of their labor."[43] Several articles criticized the racial hypocrisy of Anglo-owned companies, where Mexican labor was systematically devalued. For instance, the editors of *El Defensor* criticized the owner of the Mexican National Railroad, who claimed to "sympathize" with his Mexican workers because they worked harder than the gringos but vehemently opposed their petition for an equal pay raise.[44]

Opposition to racial segregation in rail employment and wages was a factor for workers on both sides of the border. Strike actions were already underway in different parts of Mexico by the time the FLU was formed. For instance, as early as 1902, railroad strikes that included the demand for higher wages for Mexican workers broke out among different work crews in Orizaba, Veracruz; among station and shunting yard workers, and later among mechanics on the Ferrocarril Internacional in Torreón, Coahuila; among brakemen on the Ferrocarril Interoceánico in 1903; among signalmen and porters on the Ferrocarril Mexicano in 1905; among mechanics in Chihuahua in 1906 (which spread to the Ferrocarril Central, the central hub linking north and south); and in 1908 among various groups of workers on the Ferrocarriles Nacionales de México. While the results of the individual strikes were mixed, they pressured the government to begin racial desegregation of the rail lines (referred to as Mexicanization) in 1909.[45]

The union was less than a year old when it organized a strike against the US investor-controlled Mexican National Railroad, a rail line connecting Laredo to the interior of Mexico.[46] Anglo machinists in Laredo had struck one year earlier and won their demands for a twenty-five-cent hourly wage increase. When the Mexicans followed suit in calling for similar wage increases, they were stonewalled by the company. In November 1906, all of the mexicano workers in FLU 11953 walked off the job, producing a virtual general strike in the city. In response to the mass strike, the company shuttered all of its operations and shifted them across the border to Nuevo Laredo. In essence, the strike for wage parity threatened the racial labor caste system. A company representative explained that "he would have found the demands just and reasonable if they had been submitted by Anglo workers. But since they [Chicano strikers] were indios, the demands were unacceptable."[47]

When the *Laredo Times* characterized the strikers as "peons," a racially derogatory term used to characterize Mexican workers as ignorant, skill-less, and uncultured, *El Defensor* angrily retorted:

> Can we call the ironworkers that raise the rails from their forges, all of whom are Mexican, and who are paid pennies, "peons"? Are they peons, the coppersmiths that construct the boilers? Are the wood-workers that raise the foundations from their workshops "peons"? Are the carpenters that are in charge of building the service and passenger cars for the [Mexican] National "peons"?[48]

The workers maintained high levels of strike organization and enjoyed broad support from the community against the Mexican National. Messages of support and solidarity were published in their paper, including a statement of support from a socialist grouping in Mexico City called Socialismo Mexicano.[49] They also received solidarity greetings from the Gran Liga Mexicana de Empleados de Ferrocarril, who invited them to send a delegate to their 1907 convention.[50]

After two months, the company conceded the wage demands, in February 1907. A second strike was launched and won a month later when the company kept scab workers from the first strike on the payroll. The success of the strikes led to a boom in union organizing throughout the region, as the FLU helped launch a miners' union local and supported the formation of several craft unions outside the railroads. Despite the victories, the capitalists behind the Mexican National won out against the union. Within a few months after the second strike, they reconfigured operations in order to close down all of the workshops and rail yards in Laredo and relocate them permanently across the border in Nuevo Laredo.[51] Within a short time, the FLU dissolved as most of its members relocated to other towns to find work.

El Primer Congreso Mexicanista

Despite the decline of the FLU, socialists continued to organize in Laredo. The outbreak of the Mexican Revolution in November of 1910 revived radical sentiments and aspirations among mexicanos in the US, as the maderista uprising toppled the dictatorship of Porfirio Díaz six months later. For mexicanos in South Texas, the revolution provided the context for drawing together the Mexican communities into a regional organization that could develop a plan to address their own grievances. These efforts culminated in El Primer Congreso Mexicanista, a regional, delegated congress of mexicano organizations and individuals.[52] Convened in Laredo, from September 14 to 22, 1911, the organizers aimed to "express and act upon a variety of social grievances which were the culmination of an encroaching Anglo-American domination of Texas-Mexicans during the latter half of the nineteenth century and into the early twentieth. This period was marked by the transfer of almost all Texas-Mexican land into Anglo-Texan hands through various legal and illegal means."[53]

The *congreso* reflected two ideological strains among the mexicano communities in South Texas at the time: socialism and liberal Mexican nationalism. The systematic oppression experienced by mexicanos through the intensification of racial violence across the Southwest and economic marginalization drew together the socialist union activists of the FLU and the sections of the middle class; the latter also being squeezed by Anglo migration, competition, and economic displacement. The latter group was represented through the leadership of Nicasio Idar, a former railroad worker who had gone on to become a prominent journalist, then owner and editor of the Laredo daily newspaper *La Crónica* in 1910. Through the pages of *La Crónica*, Idar had become a leading critic of the rising tide of state and vigilante violence against mexicanos and the intensification of segregation. The paper became a tribune for community members to tell their stories and a record for publicizing and documenting instances of racial abuse and state violence. For instance, *La Crónica* documented killings of Mexicans by police officials and Texas Rangers, and "had noted the general climate of racial discrimination particularly in Central Texas where signs such as 'No Lots sold to Mexicans' and 'No Mexicans admitted' were prevalent, and where, in Austin, [the only Mexican] State Representative J. T. Canales was called 'the greaser from Brownsville' during the session of the legislature."[54]

By 1910, Idar began to use the paper as an organizer, supporting Mexican merchant-led boycotts against Anglo businesses, and advocating for educational reform, and regional collaboration between Mexican organizations. The efforts culminated in the convocation for a *mexicanista* congress in September of 1911, in which those seeking fundamental change could develop a plan of action. Unlike the socialists of the FLU, who attacked the capitalist system, the middle-class reformers sought significant structural changes within the framework of capitalism. For instance, during the 1906–1907 strike, representatives of the Mexican merchant middle class criticized the socialists for their class-struggle unionism. As was reflected in a newspaper article expressing this viewpoint, they argued that while they supported the "aspirations" of the workers, they denounced the "anarchic" leaders that were "prejudiced against capital and non-union workers" and opposed their militant picket lines as against the "freedom to work" and tantamount to exercising a "monopoly" over labor.[55]

While class differences emerged between the socialists and liberal nationalists on some issues, on others they agreed. The *congresistas* criticized the assimilationist model underpinned by anti-Mexican racism, which promoted the idea that social advancement could occur only by teaching Mexican children to reject their own culture and by limiting political participation to the narrow confines prescribed by Anglo-controlled, Jim Crow political structures. Given that assimilationism existed to perpetuate mexicano marginalization, the congresistas openly espoused local control over education and curriculum, with an emphasis on raising cultural awareness and promoting bilingualism. They called for unified mexicano action against the "oppressor," but ambiguous and diverging plans of action emerged for how to achieve this beyond the creation of bilingual mexicanista schools.[56]

Socialists present at the congress echoed the call for unity and resistance to oppression, but drew different conclusions for how to achieve these goals. José María Mora, a socialist and activist who had previously been a member of the Federal Labor Union and a contributor to *El Defensor del Obrero*, attended as a representative of the working-class mutualista La Sociedad de Obreros Igualdad y Progreso. He appealed to congreso participants to seek solutions in terms of class struggle. Reminding them of the accomplishments of the FLU, he pointed out that Mexican workers at the point of production could exert considerable power that doesn't exist in the social or political sphere.

> Not long ago there used to exist a great organization, and we saw how capital treated the workers, to the point of working them to death. Capital, like the politicians, sees unity of the workers as a dangerous threat to their interests. I urge you to focus on the organization of the working class, and principally those mexicanos on this side of the border.[57]

Ultimately, the congreso did not meet again, perhaps owing to several factors. Many mexicano activists and partisans were drawn into the revolutionary events, crossing the border to participate or to focus their work on building support for different factions. Another plausible factor was that activism was suppressed due to increased militarization of the border and incidents of state violence against Mexican radicals in border communities as the US government sought to suppress revolutionary sympathizers, real or imagined. Nevertheless, the socialist ideals and organizational memory of the Federal Union 11953 and the Laredo strikes of 1906–1907, as well as the civil rights advocacy of the Congreso Mexicanista, would reemerge in the barrios of South Texas soon thereafter.

Part 2

Chapter 7
Ricardo Flores Magón and the Rise of the PLM

"No liberal party in the world has our anticapitalist
tendencies, which are about to launch a revolution."
—**Ricardo Flores Magón**

The legacy of Ricardo Flores Magón and the Partido Liberal Mexicano has been consigned by historians as "precursory" and subsequently eclipsed by figures of greater significance, such as Francisco Madero, Venustiano Carranza, Francisco Pancho Villa, and Emiliano Zapata.[1] Furthermore, the role of the radical evolution of the group and their cross-border internationalist influence has been significantly understudied. As historian Claudio Lomnitz points out:

> Ricardo [Flores Magón] and his closest collaborators . . . would be referred to reverentially as "Precursors of the Mexican Revolution," despite the fact that they were its contemporaries. Along with this displacement in time—the denial of this group's contemporaneity—the radical group's binational makeup was played down . . . while in the United States the group is but the vaguely recalled fringe of a dimly remembered margin.[2]

Although Magonismo is not characterized as a progenitor of the revolution it deserves much more credit as both a catalyst and a shaping force of the revolutionary process than it has received. As the expression of an evolving revolutionary doctrine and activist and intellectual core of adherents most closely aligned with the laboring classes throughout the course of the revolution, it shaped all phases of the revolutionary period: the origins, tempo of events, the outcome, and aftermath. It also provided the first tangible expression of revolutionary internationalism, informing the US Left in its articulation of anti-imperialism and solidarity and providing a catalyst for the first generation of Mexican American labor radicalism on a regional scale. In this way, Magonismo is stamped in the DNA of the Mexican and Mexican American Left from the first waves of migrants to the Chicano/a generation, and offers contemporary generations a doctrine as relevant today as it was in 1910.

The Mexican Revolution of 1910 is a defining event of the twentieth century and also the starting point for understanding the trajectory of Mexican radicalism in the United States. A popular revolutionary energy upsurge toppled the dictatorship of Porfirio Díaz, and a series of revolutionary and counterrevolutionary battles that raged for over a decade resulted in the defeat of the landed oligarchy and the Catholic Church, and landed a blow against imperialism. In the revolutionary process, two significant developments occurred. Throughout the era, millions of small and sub-sistence farmers, agricultural workers, and urban industrial workers were radicalized and indelibly influenced by their participation in revolutionary battles, strikes, occu-pations, and other activities. Many of these campesinos and workers later migrated to the United States, taking their lived experiences and memory of these events along with them.

Second, an anticapitalist and anti-imperialist current developed among the Mex-ican revolutionary leadership, which articulated a broader vision for social transfor-mation that evolved from liberal restructuring to social revolution. This current came to be identified with the political writings, agitation, and ideological leadership of Ri-cardo Flores Magón and the Partido Liberal Mexicano (PLM). The Mexican liberal movement was initially a cross-class alliance of intellectuals that opposed the dictator-ship of Porfirio Díaz and promoted a reform project within the liberal political tradi-tion associated with Benito Juárez, or Juarismo; but fissures developed in the convul-sions of revolutionary events that produced more radical manifestations of the group.

Magonismo, to describe the far-left, anticapitalist current of the PLM, became an ideology that inspired the radical movements on both sides of the border, especially as it evolved into a doctrine of class struggle. Three factors led the magonistas to break with the liberal paradigm. The first was the rising militancy of Mexican workers, es-pecially during the insurrectionary strikes at Cananea in 1906 and Río Blanco in 1907. The second factor was a hardening of opposition to the imperialist interventions and the domination of foreign capital in Mexico, especially capital from the United States. Lastly, in the course of crossing the border, the magonistas encountered aspects of the US that further shaped their outlook: a Mexican American population racially sub-jugated and relegated into the margins of society, and a combative US working class with potent radical doctrines also engaged in class struggle. After 1908, the magonis-tas openly espoused an anticapitalist and internationalist position.[3] They committed themselves to the revolutionary project, infusing their radical politics into the DNA of the workers' movement on both sides of the border, and creating the foundation for generations of radicals to come.

The Early Foundations of Magonismo

Ricardo Flores Magón's ideological formation was shaped by several key turning points in his political activism, beginning with his move from the state of Oaxaca to Mexico City in the early years of his youth. As Oaxaqueños, the Flores Magón broth-ers, Jesús, Ricardo, and Enrique, were initially influenced by the political traditions of their family and region. Flores Magón's father, Teodoro Flores, was a Mazatec indig-enous cacique and defender of the traditional collectivism that was deeply rooted in the Oaxacan highlands from the pre-Hispanic era. He was a teenaged veteran of the war of resistance to the American invasion of 1846, later a partisan on the side of the liberals in the Wars of the Reform (Juarismo had its roots in Oaxaca), and later took up arms once again to expel the French colonial occupation of the "Second Empire" in the years 1862–1867.[4] He later served as a partisan of then liberal Porfirio Díaz during the Tuxtepec Rebellion, the military coup that brought the future dictator to power, achieving the rank of lieutenant colonel. After his years of military service, he returned to his birthplace and to life as a farmer.

Jesús, Ricardo, and Enrique Flores Magón

For his loyal service to the liberal cause, he was awarded land in the district of Teotitlán del Camino in the state of Oaxaca, where he reintegrated into rural life and local traditions of communal reciprocity.[5] Through participation in the wars against foreign invasion and colonization, Teodoro developed a liberal, nationalistic outlook that combined with a distrust of an authoritarian and centralized conservative government that imposed burdensome taxes and denied the formation of local government.[6] As Paul Friedrich describes Teodoro's influence on his sons:

> Their father had come from a Oaxacan Mazatec Indian village and allegedly instilled in them a keen appreciation of "communal ownership of water, of woodlands, and of pastures, the collective work of seeding and harvests, the religious traditions in which the indigenous conserve a breath of paganism," all conceptually intertwined with egalitarian and republican ideals.[7]

As the Porfiriato diverged from its liberal ideals, Flores saw his fortunes fade over time. There was pressure to privatize communal lands, encroachment by large haciendas and foreign investors tied to the export model, and rising taxes. By the time of his death in 1893, the family income had declined precipitously. Over half of their land had been lost, and the family faced bankruptcy.

The mother of the Flores Magón brothers, Margarita Magón, was also a significant influence. She is attributed as being a person of firm principles rooted in a sense of justice, especially for the rural populations in her environs losing out or being threatened by Porfirian land policies. She envisioned her sons becoming leaders who could advocate for the marginalized. She took her sons to Mexico City at a young age to seek out quality education, with the intention that they would ultimately become lawyers who could defend the rights of the pueblo (common people).[8] By 1892, Jesús had graduated from the National School of Jurisprudence, Ricardo was close to finishing, and the youngest son, Enrique, was enrolled in the National Preparatory School on the path to follow his brothers. After the death of their parents and the loss of financial support, they had to take on jobs to support themselves.

Margarita Magón is believed to have been a big influence in the early political development of her sons, especially Ricardo, who inherited her unwavering sense of commitment to ideals. For example, her sons were arrested by Díaz for their antigovernment activities as she lay on her deathbed. Díaz offered her their freedom and the chance to spend their last moments together if she could persuade them to renounce their efforts. She is said to have replied: "Tell General Díaz that I would rather die without seeing my sons, and what's more, I would prefer to see them hanging from a tree or a tall pole than have them retract or repent for anything that they have done against you."[9]

The fundaments of magonista radicalism were instilled in them from their youth and called forth in the articulation of resistance, first to dictatorship and then capitalism. According to Genaro Amezcua, the Flores Magón brothers "re-affirmed the traditions of their tribe as their political, social, and economic credo, when they discovered that these contained the basic principles of autochthonous libertarian socialism—simple, just, and egalitarian—without impositions or tyranny."[10] Magonismo took shape in the context of an organic political evolution; an interaction between in-depth study of doctrine, constant observation and analysis of world events and their implications through newspaper media, and the agitation for the organization of direct action. Distilled in the laboratory of revolution, Magonismo articulated the foundations of radical thought: anti-imperialism, indigenous socialism, and nascent anticapitalism. These politics crossed borders in the minds, memories, and experiences of Mexican migrants; they also resonated with Mexican American workers, for whom Magonismo breathed life to radicalism north of the border.

Rise of the Partido Liberal Mexicano (PLM)

While their initial aspirations as students were high, the Flores Magón brothers were drawn away from comfortable careers in the civil bureaucracy and toward radical politics. Declining family fortunes, the deaths of their destitute parents, and the deterioration of rural conditions contributed to an anti-Díaz feeling among the Flores Magón brothers. They were attracted to the *antireelecionista* (anti-reelection) movement against Díaz that began to take shape during the staged elections of 1892.[11] As the Díaz machine engineered rigged elections to ensure his continuation in power, a student movement arose in protest.

The Flores Magón brothers helped organize a student movement against the Díaz regime composed of middle-class students coming of age as the Porfirian regime had consolidated a political machine fueled by corruption, patronage, and repression. The layer of aspiring civil servants, bureaucrats, and reform-oriented jurists who lacked ties to the ruling cliques that formed the architecture of the Porfirian state did not have access to pathways of upward mobility. There was an acute decline for the rural-origin middle class, like the brothers Flores Magón, who had the least clout and connections in the capital. By the mid-1890s, for instance, Ricardo Flores Magón had to take manual labor jobs to make ends meet.

As the privileged of this group expressed their discontent in discreet forms, the more marginalized of these elements channeled their discontent in the form of protests against the central figure of Díaz. The political ferment first expressed itself on the campuses, where disenchanted and declining middle-class students like the Flores Magón brothers connected with other politicized students. This "generation of 1892," as it came to be known, began to analyze and question social and political realities, as a way of finding meaning in the social stagnation they perceived all around them. Ricardo Flores Magón began to examine the class nature of the discontent and to see himself as a representative of the most oppressed. According to historian José Valadés,

> he began to see himself as part of the lowest classes; he believed this because his lovers belonged to those classes, because his friends were from those classes. In terms of class analysis, we can say that at that phase in his life, Ricardo Flores Magón was "proletarianized" in his thinking and his feeling.[12]

The students organized rallies against the dictator and founded their own press as a mouthpiece for their movement. Through the press, the Flores Magón brothers began to emerge as the ideologues of the movement, while also braving police batons and mass arrests and detention. The dominant idea that formed the basis of their criticism against the metastasizing dictatorship of Díaz was *juarista* liberalism, which was reinvigorated after the defeat and expulsion of the French (1867) and their conservative allies.

In the eyes of the student radicals, the Díaz regime had abandoned the sacrosanct tenets of the liberal 1857 Constitution, rehabilitated the reactionary Catholic Church, and sold out the national economy to foreign economic interests. The Flores Magón brothers formed the Gran Comité Nacional de Estudiantes (The Central National Committee of Students) in 1895, now joined by future PLM militant Lázaro Gutiérrez de Lara. Standing out within this milieu, Ricardo Flores Magón emerged as a nationally recognized student protest leader, whose prowess for acerbic, uncompromising, and rhetorically unmatched denunciations of the regime and its crimes won him a mass following and propelled him into the national leadership of the emerging opposition.[13] Through the leadership of the Flores Magón brothers, the student movement made links to other nuclei of opposition taking shape in different parts of the country. After student protests swept Mexico City and threatened to spread to the provincial capitals, the Díaz regime unleashed the police with unrestrained ferocity, signaling an intention to strangle the reinvigorated liberal movement in its infancy. Ricardo Flores Magón was arrested, doing his first stint in prison at the age of nineteen. As a result of the repression, elements of this generation were radicalized, left the campus, and joined efforts to unite the disaffected cross sections of society into a national movement.

After the election of 1892, it became apparent that Díaz intended to perpetually rig the political system to extend his rule indefinitely. This occurred against a backdrop of over a decade of systematic dispossession and rural crisis, foreign domination over much of the economy, and rampant corruption and authoritarianism subverting any semblance of democracy. As a result, the significant first stirrings against Díaz and the Científicos began to take place across the country: workers, peasants, and urban intellectuals began to express opposition to Díaz in different forms.

From his experience in law school, which he never completed, Flores Magón devoted all of his energy, and the greater part of his adult life, to bringing an end to the Porfiriato. When the juridical path to reform proved intractable in the face of repression and the resiliency of the traditional liberal opposition acquiesced, the politics of Magonismo developed a more radical bent. Jean-Pierre Bastian characterizes this radicalizing segment of the Mexican petty bourgeoisie as "Jacobin", which is historically described as:

> A social grouping that formed into a political organization in France in the second half of the 18th century. This organizational form represented a rupture within the corporate structures of the old regime, based on collective action and a new political culture focused on the abstract individual and their democratic potential that consisted of the general will as the basis for the establishment of law.[14]

The intrinsic conservatism and vacillation within the late-developing bourgeoisie, in the face of an ossified dictatorship determined to squash all opposition, led the more radical elements in the Mexican middle class to look to more urgent and expedient means to dispose of the Díaz regime.

The Manifesto of 1903 of the Club Liberal Ponciano Arriagawhich served as the first nerve center of the revitalized liberal movement, expressed the voice of the distressed middle class:

> Is there equality in our country? No. The capitalist, the priest, and the high-placed civil servant, whether in civil or military service, are not treated the same way as the humble worker or the common people, hidden in society, but brilliant in their historic deeds in service of the nation. The common civil servants lead a life of humiliation and misery. Privilege and jurisdictional rights have created a useless and depraved elite, that can be identified as social parasites. The predominance of virtue has disappeared; now gold, power, the priest, and the foreign [capitalist] predominate and nothing more.[15]

By the turn of the century, clusters of anti-Díaz groups around the country began converging into regional and national associations. The mechanisms by which porfirismo held together a broad base of support of the previous decades—especially among the liberal ranks forged out of the juarista period—began to break down with time. As Florencio Barrera Fuentes explains this process, a new generation of liberals came of age after the wars of La Reforma, and was shaped by a new set of harsh economic realities and limited political horizons that eclipsed the old loyalties and arrangements:

> General Díaz forgot that after his generation came another that had not lived through . . . the civil conflicts and wars against foreign occupation. This

generation came of age at the same time that the founders of the original Liberal tradition were disappearing, and in their decline had been incapable of halting the rise of those who had betrayed their principles . . . This generation saw the need to revolutionize the consciousness of the urban masses and to awaken it from 20 years of dormancy.[16]

The first efforts at organizing discontent into a national political program developed internally within the ranks of the liberal petty bourgeoisie, led by the lower strata of professionals whose pathways to upward mobility were stymied by the Díaz political machine. In 1900, a group of liberals led by Camilo Arriaga, an engineer from a prominent San Luis Potosí family, established the Club Liberal Ponciano Arriaga. This grouping also included future PLM radicals Juan and Manuel Sarabia, Librado Rivera, and Antonio Díaz Soto y Gama within its ranks. The club was conceptualized as the nucleus of a new anti-Díaz political party, named after a populist liberal lawyer who was the chief architect of the liberal 1857 Constitution.

In draping themselves in the colors of the juarista liberal reform movement, the anti-Díaz campaigners imagined themselves as the new standard-bearers of the liberal cause betrayed by Díaz and the Científicos. In 1900, the club issued a public call for the organization of similar anti-reelectionist clubs across the nation, the convening of a national congress, and ultimately the formation of a political party. Through these efforts different groups and social forces opposed to the Porfirian status quo flocked to their banners. They issued their first manifesto in 1903, loyal to the tenets of liberal nationalism. They criticized the Porfirian state as a fetter to national capitalist development, individual liberty, and prosperity that could uplift all social classes in Mexico rather than the foreigner and autocrat. They also identified the underdevelopment of the rural economy and super-exploitation of indigenous peoples as inhibiting more productive and prosperous agriculture.[17] While their ideology was confined to bourgeois liberal notions, the declarations of the Club Liberal Ponciano Arriaga can be understood as the opening act of the Mexican revolutionary process, and the inauguration of Ricardo Flores Magón as its leader.

The participation of Ricardo Flores Magón as a delegate represented his leadership in the student wing of the movement, which was a key to building a national organization. In the formative stages of the revitalized liberal movement, he and his brothers shared the desire to see a restoration of past ideals and launched a newspaper named *Regeneración* in 1900 that captured the essence of their class aspirations at the time. Through the paper, efforts were made to unify and solidify a base of opposition, culminating in the convening of the First National Congress of Liberal Clubs in February of 1901. The convocation of the Congress was officially initiated to bring clubs and the oppositional press together to counter the growing power of the Catholic Church, which had been greatly weakened in the wars of La Reforma. Despite the putative restrictions on its power enshrined in the 1857 Constitution—the forfeiture of lands, the abolition of religious communities, restricted participation in public affairs, etc.—it had reemerged as a pillar of the Porfirian state. The regime had ignored the Constitution and allowed the Church to rebuild its economic empire, assert itself in politics, and be elevated to state partner in exchange for throwing its moral support behind for the regime, especially as it served to assuage the growing ranks of disgruntled peasants. Coming out of the Congress, the Mexican Liberal Party was born, with *Regeneración* as its most recognized progenitor.

In the first editions of *Regeneración*, Ricardo Flores Magón and his co-thinkers were concerned with the restoration of the ideals of juarismo. The pages of *Regeneración* labeled porfirismo as an aberration, a barrier to the fuller development of capitalism and democracy, and promoted juridical solutions to the problems of dictatorship.[18] Despite the modest political aims, the language and tone of the periodical gradually took a more militant stance, as growing numbers of disaffected Mexicans, especially from the working classes, rallied to the anti-Díaz banner.

The liberal movement gathered disparate groups of regime opponents under one umbrella. In fact, Diego Abad de Santillan asserts:

> All of the discontents of Porfirian despotism are collectively labeled liberals; under this denomination existed diverse tendencies in Mexico, convictions varying in intensity, contradictory ideological currents, but temporarily united against Díaz, the predominant interest at the moment.[19]

Early financial backers included sections of the bourgeoisie, such as Francisco Madero, representing northern capitalist interests that resented the centralization of political power through patronage systems, the primacy and privileges awarded foreign capital within the economy, and their limited influence in national politics. Madero helped found the Club Benito Juárez in Coahuila and invited Flores Magón to help him write a liberal manifesto that could be distributed to the people of his home state.[20]

Over the course of its first six years, the liberal party grew to include patchworks of industrial workers, urban artisans, and proletarianized peasants, especially after the leftward-moving Jacobin wing consolidating around Ricardo Flores Magón began to criticize the conditions of labor under Díaz. Working-class activists influenced by the thought and writings of the magonistas also embarked on union-organizing campaigns in strategic sectors of the industrial economy. As a result, a large popular base expanded within the cross-class alliance, ultimately pushing the left wing of the PLM on a trajectory toward radicalization, especially as class struggle intensified in the years leading up to the outbreak of the revolution.

After facing harassment, collective arrest, and the threat of being disappeared into the dreaded Porfirian prison complex, the now-cohesive Jacobin wing of the liberal leadership was then driven out of the country and into underground exile in the US. Both governments embarked on a campaign of elimination of the magonista movement, as US economic interests were bound up with the perpetuation of the Porfiriato. By 1906, PLM radicals had redefined and repurposed their movement as revolutionary; committed to the toppling of Porfirio Díaz through direct action. In crossing the border, Magonismo became a transnational movement that further broadened in scope, evolving an internationalist and revolutionary proletarian framework.

The First Divisions Emerge

The PLM was a collection of contradictory elements from its inception. The party temporarily coalesced as a cross section of forces whose scope and depth of opposition varied along class lines. This included wealthy bourgeois backers with a singular focus on replacing Díaz, to middle-class radicals seeking more profound structural changes consistent with their class interests, and militant workers and artisans organizing unions and conducting the first significant strikes of the early twentieth century. The unifying principle was the reaffirmation of the laws of La Reforma in light of Díaz's transgressions, including freedom of the press, effective suffrage, political decentralization, labor reforms, and the abolition of rural peonage.[21] Beneath this unity, deeper cleavages emerged around social and economic questions. For instance, as early as 1901, the Club Liberal Ponciano Arriaga, which became the standard-bearer of the Liberal Party nationally, organized study groups that included the works of nineteenth-century revolutionary thinkers and anarchist and socialist ideologues such as Joseph Proudhon, Peter Kropotkin, Élisée Reclus, Max Stirner, and Karl Marx.[22] The members of the group that later coalesced around Ricardo Flores Magón had immersed themselves in engagement with revolutionary doctrine, which informed the fault lines of the class fractures that gradually emerged in the group. The first ruptures surfaced over the very basic question of what was to be done to get rid of the Díaz regime, and what should replace it.

Symptomatic of the limited aims of the bourgeois and conservative middle-class elements that dominated the inaugural Congress, the question of Díaz and the state was completely sidestepped by the prominent liberals. Instead, their fire was trained on the Catholic Church, which had maintained itself as a center of conservative power and one of the largest landlords in the country. The Díaz government had formed an alliance with the Church and ceased enforcement of the 1857 Constitution's provisions invoking the expropriation of Church land and negation of its political power. The Church had become the focus of liberal derision—instead of Díaz himself—as it was a safer target than the regime.[23] The Congress was in effect reduced to a restatement of sanded-down platitudes invoking the spirit of 1857 Constitution, devoid of any substance or call to action. That is, until Ricardo Flores Magón took the floor.

When Ricardo Flores Magón had his chance to speak, he pulled no punches. In a speech that reverberated throughout the Congress hall and across the nation in the days that followed, he appealed for the delegates to openly declare themselves in opposition to Díaz, boldly denouncing his administration as a "den of thieves" and referring to the Constitution as a dead issue, and raising the question of revolution as the only means to dislodge Díaz.[24] Within several months of the Congress, Magonismo was taking shape as the articulation of an action plan to topple Díaz. "The reforms contained in the resolutions of the first Liberal Congress," he wrote later in 1901, "are impractical and utopian because the power to freely express opposition [under Díaz] remains a myth."[25]

La Constitución ha muerto - The Constitution is dead

In taking this very public stand in an atmosphere of heavy-handed repression, Flores Magón galvanized the opposition and planted the flag of revolt as the only viable means to bring down the dictatorship. From very early on he was closest to the pulse of common Mexicans, and his analyses and proclamations shepherded into existence the first significant prerevolutionary radical current throughout the country; one that pushed forward the first wave of revolutionary struggle. From that point on, the magonistas emerged as the first national leaders of the revolution, even though it would take several more years before political divides within the party fully matured and fragmented into separate and distinct bourgeois and proletarian camps.

In the gradual clarification of positions within the new movement, Ricardo Flores Magón and his allies established themselves as the radical wing of the revitalized liberal movement, developing a more thoroughgoing vision for reform through the pages of *Regeneración*.[26] Originally founded by Ricardo's older brother Jesús as a legal journal taking positions on points of legal reform, under the emerging leadership of Ricardo it transformed into "an anti-Díaz propaganda organ that . . . boldly publicized the shortcomings of all branches and levels of Mexican government."[27] Indeed, to avoid ambiguity around the specific role of the newspaper, either as a tepid voice of restrained criticism, or one linked to merely promoting a rival faction within the liberal apparatus, Ricardo Flores Magón declared *Regeneración* an "independent newspaper of combat" in 1901. In this phase, the paper also began to critique economic exploitation and foreign control. This allowed the party the means to broaden its social base of support and call for the formation of aligned groupings throughout the country.[28]

With this, the advance toward open confrontation with the Porfirian state took a radical turn, widening the space between traditional and revolutionary "liberals." Nevertheless, until 1906, the PLM still envisioned itself as a broad, popular alliance of all "patriotic" social groups united against dictatorship. While shifting the focus toward the laboring classes, Ricardo Flores Magón restated the aim of attracting sincere liberals "not put off by the militancy of the majority" of working-class adherents.[29] As another circular in October 1906 stated, "Our party is well-organized throughout the country and involves all social classes showing its truly popular character, which is what makes it most effective."[30]

The growth and combative rhetoric of the PLM was not lost on the regime. Over fifty clubs were established in thirteen states at the time of the first congress, and the circulation of *Regeneración* grew to twenty-six thousand nationally.[31] Key to the first phase of growth were the radicalizing sectors of artisans and marginalized middle-class discontents across the country that launched liberal clubs or affiliated their mutualistas to the cause. The middle-class character was symptomatic of the internal economic and political structures of porfirismo which developed into rigid hierarchies of power based on corruption and centralization. During this time, the middle class grew but ran up against a closed system that hindered social mobility.[32]

As Pedro Anaya Ibarra succinctly describes this stage of magonista radicalism, "the magonistas participated [in the National Congress of Liberal Clubs] in order to deepen its anticlerical, Jacobin character, giving it a social content more modern, real, and profound."[33] Budding políticos of the radical middle class across Mexico looked to *Regeneración* for guidance and analysis; many of them became significant participants in the revolutionary period. This included (future president) Plutarco Elías Calles, José María Maytorena (constitutionalist general), Adolfo de la Huerta (governor of Sonora and future president), and Salvador Alvarado (future governor of Yucatán), to name a few. They helped to constitute a national movement with two specific objectives: politicizing discontent along their line of march, and forming an organizational base at the local, regional, and state level that could be mobilized to take some form of action.[34]

Feminists Align with Flores Magón

A significant intellectual current within the radicalizing middle class was a group of feminists who aligned themselves with the PLM. This layer of pioneering feminists saw in the emerging liberal movement a vehicle to advance their own interests alongside the broader goals of the convention. Feminist thought repudiating the oppression of women emerged in the early Porfirian period, appearing in the pages of the radical press in 1876. In *El Hijo del Trabajo*, a writer under the pseudonym Juana La Progresista boldly defended the equality of women against the presumed dominance of males,

> arguing that sexism had no basis in science since men and women were physiologically the same, and above all in intelligence . . . [the writer] lashed out against the unfair treatment of women, arguing that the man always has preeminence in all: in education, in job opportunities and social treatment, which allows them to convert the women into slaves.[35]

Radical women played a prominent role in the opposition to the dictatorship, which brought many women into the fold of the magonista movement. One early supporter of the PLM, Juana Belén Gutiérrez de Mendoza, was a socialist and feminist editor of the newspaper *Vésper*, which launched only a few months after *Regeneración*. As early as 1901 the pages of *Vésper* were calling for "anticapitalist revolution by Mexico's peasants and workers against the Díaz regime."

> Angered by the foreign domination of Mexico's banks, insurance companies, mines, textile mills, and railroads; aroused by the increasing impoverishment, exploitation, and debasement of the country's landless peasants and workers; and disturbed by the resurgence of the Catholic Church in Mexico . . . [she] established [the] newspaper . . . in the extremely traditionalist provincial capital of Guanajuato.[36]

According to historian Angeles Mendieta Alatorre, her journalistic campaigns against the tyranny of the Díaz regime, condemnations of the clergy, and support for worker struggle earned her the great admiration of Flores Magón, as well as jail time in the same prison after the Díaz regime clamped down in 1902.[37] Gutiérrez de Mendoza is also credited with being the first to publish tracts from the works of anarchist thinker Peter Kropotkin. His *Conquest of Bread* is thought to be one of the texts that most influenced Flores Magón's radical thinking.[38]

Women were among the first delegates to the convention and went on to form several of the clubs in different regions of the country, resulting in several being jailed, beaten, and even killed for their efforts. For instance, liberal activists Concepción Valdés, sisters Otilia and Eulalia Martínez Núñez, Josefa Arjona de Pinelo, and Josefa Tolentino helped launch the PLM-aligned clubs Benito Juárez, Sebastián Lerdo de Tejada, Gutiérrez Zamora, and Valentín Gómez Frias, as well as the Gran Círculo Liberal Veracruzano in the environs of the capital city of Veracruz. These groupings would later play a key role in supporting the PLM-led efforts in that state, including the abortive armed uprising of 1906 and the great textile strike of 1907.[39] After the repression of the 1907 textile strike, several PLM-aligned radical women in Mexico City formed the group La Sociedad de Socialistas Mexicanos (The Mexican Socialist Society) and launched the paper *Anáhuac*. They dedicated themselves to organizing workers and artisans in the capital and building support for various anti-Díaz efforts in the months leading up to his downfall in 1910.[40]

The combativeness of the radical feminists further influenced the PLM. As early as 1901, Flores Magón wrote in the pages of *Regeneración* with a searing tone:

> Now as many men weaken and through cowardice withdraw from the struggle without putting up a fight for the vindication of our freedoms; now as many men without vigor retreat afraid in front of the phantom of tyranny, and filled with terror abandon the liberal banner in order to avoid the fatigue of a noble and rising fight, there appears the woman, spirited and courageous, ready to fight for our principles which the weakness of many men has permitted to be trampled and spat upon.[41]

While in their theoretical formulations the PLM had advocated for full equality for women, equality was conceptualized within a gendered framework. In the 1907 article "El Deber de la Mujer" (The Duty of the Woman), female supporters of the PLM were encouraged to "inspire their men not to be meek, to be real men that take up arms to fight for liberty."[42] This simplistic and patriarchal notion relegated the role of women to supporting cast, serving as mediators, messengers, and clerical staff. While the PLM also understood women as part of the working class, and therefore vested in the revolutionary process, their primary function was to be "stronger" than the weaker men:

> For this reason, though women work more than men, they are paid less, and misery, mistreatment, and insult are today as yesterday the bitter harvest for a whole existence of sacrifice . . . Demand that your husbands, brothers, fathers, sons and friends pick up the gun. Spit in the face of those who refuse to pick up a weapon against oppression.[43]

Women continued to be leaders of the revolutionary movement, and radical socialist feminists were instrumental in shaping the further theoretical development of Magonismo. By 1911 a corps of female leaders took up leadership positions within the organization, including polemicists and writers such as Francisca Mendoza and Concha Rivera, who wrote articles for *Regeneración* and became public speakers in the plazas and labor halls. The elevation of women into the leadership allowed for critical voices to emerge capable of articulating an in-depth critique of the oppression of women under capitalism.

Revolt and Exile

The radical middle class that coalesced behind the ideological leadership of *Regeneración* set itself apart from Díaz's bourgeois liberal critics. Northern capitalists, urban professionals, and the educated, idealist, and politically restive offspring of ruling-class families avoided direct confrontation with the regime, and had no interest in mobilizing the laboring classes behind their banners. State repression prevented a second convention of the Liberal Congress, during which time the movement fragmented as various leaders including the magonistas fled into exile. The crackdown only temporarily concealed the tensions between the emerging camps, which soon developed into full-blown rupture and political reorganization in the years that followed.

By 1907, the magonistas were openly criticizing the bourgeois liberals within the anti-Díaz movement, characterizing them as opportunists who wanted to limit reform to political and not economic democracy; who wanted to merely exchange one exploiter for another. Early bourgeois supporters such as Francisco Madero severed affiliation. By 1910, magonistas asserted that the politics of Maderismo did not propose a profound alteration of the social structure, and that the limited reforms proposed by Madero were designed to facilitate a rapprochement with the Porfirista state without Díaz.[44] In these iterations of distinction from the liberals, the magonistas defined and refined their differences in practice and in theory.

Bourgeois liberals saw salvation dawning from within their own class leadership, marshaling a cross-class alliance in hopes a reconstituted Liberal Party could regroup and reclaim the lost mantel of Juarismo by inserting itself against Díaz in the electoral realm. When the path to their electoral conquest to power was closed by an intransigent regime, they vacillated and recoiled in the face of repression. Later, in an interview with a US journalist in 1908, when Díaz publicly announced his intention to not seek reelection, the bourgeois liberals rejoiced and retreated politically to their erroneous assumption that their time had finally come.

For the Jacobins drawn into the gravitational pull of Ricardo Flores Magón, there had to be a revolutionary reckoning to rid Mexico of the regime. Confronting the dictatorship of Díaz, therefore, begged the question of which social forces could and would carry out a revolution to its conclusion. When their bourgeois allies offered no direction, they took the initiative, calling the amorphous "masses" of Mexico into direct action to topple the regime. By 1906, this meant the call for armed struggle in the aftermath of the Cananea strike.[45] After the second PLM-led armed uprising was launched amid a devastating economic crisis in 1908, Francisco Madero was spurred into action. He convened the Democratic Party that year, a new political party of the ascendant northern bourgeoisie, which aimed to provide a stable transition away from porfirismo as well as a moderate alternative to the radical magonistas.[46]

Throughout their odyssey of repression, incarceration, and ultimately exile, the social forces that rose to the occasion with the courage and force to confront the Mexican state were distilled down to the laboring classes: the urban workers and indigenous agrarian campesinos. Drawing from anticapitalist ideological currents at each juncture of their revolutionary trajectory, the PLM gradually combined elements of anarchism, Marxism, and indigenous communalism to conclude that the laboring classes would have to take the factories and land directly into their own possession and in their own interests.

In taking the preliminary steps toward active revolt, the nascent movement was quickly set upon by the Díaz regime's extensive machinery of repression. The Porfirista state set out to extinguish the threat by first arresting its leadership. Ricardo Flores Magón and others were imprisoned in 1902, and their printing presses shuttered. They then relocated to Mexico City to establish a new center for the movement, a new press, and a new offensive. Constant harassment and the threat of long-term incarceration prevented this.

Porfirista governors and generals then followed suit across the nation, prosecuting and arresting partisans of the revived liberal movement, eliminating the possibility for an active and cohesive opposition to operate within national boundaries.

By 1904, the core of a new leadership of the Partido Liberal Mexicano decided to go into exile in the United States to escape the prospect of indefinite incarceration or worse. Shortly after crossing the border, the magonistas reconstituted themselves as the Organizing Junta of the Mexican Liberal Party and declared their intention to organize the overthrow of Porfirio Díaz.

After entering into Laredo, Texas, in 1904 on the first leg of their exile, they encountered former collaborator Camilo Arriaga. During this reunion, the first rupture
was formalized. In 1905, the reformists in the PLM, led by Arriaga and bourgeois supporters like Francisco Madero, began to express their distaste for the firming critique
of capitalism in the group and the embrace of direct action by the working classes,
followed by their exit en masse.[47] For their part the magonistas relocated to St. Louis,
Missouri, where they had established contact with a group of anarchists based in that
city. As the Socialist, fellow exile, and Flores Magón ally Juana B. Gutiérrez de Mendoza described:

> Since leaving Mexico . . . there is a sharpening of disagreement amongst us here
> and I am happy that we can finally clarify these gray areas [. . .] I have not
> come here to invent or falsify my principles. My [bourgeois] friends believe that
> Mexico would be better off if they governed, but I don't agree. I don't believe the
> happiness of the people will come with just a change of personnel.[48]

In publicly declaring their intention to overthrow Díaz, the magonistas immediately found themselves targeted for suppression by the US government for violating
existing "neutrality laws." The Roosevelt administration allowed the Díaz regime to deploy its own agents alongside a motley assortment of US-based private detectives, guns
for hire, and spies to track down and return the men to Mexico.[49] Eventually, various
US agents also joined in the pursuit of this small handful of rebels across North America. For three years, the magonistas were hounded and pursued throughout the country, leading the group to frequently relocate their base of operations. Their odyssey
began after crossing the border into Laredo, Texas, in 1904. After eluding arrest, they
fled to San Antonio and then to St. Louis, followed by a stint in Toronto, Canada; and
then on to San Francisco. They ultimately ended up in Los Angeles, California in 1907.
The US government's relentless drive to capture and debilitate this small handful of
fugitives indicates the perceived threat they posed, from their first steps in the country.

Not only was Díaz an ally of the US, but economic stability was paramount for
the broad array of capitalist investors moving vast stocks of capital into Mexico. The
repression of the PLM intensified as it grew in size and influence on both sides of the
border, as their followers conducted armed uprisings in Mexico, and as they began organizing Mexican workers alongside the Left in the United States. By 1908 the magonista press had multiplied throughout the Southwest. Revealing a further radicalization
of the group, the pages of Regeneración began to articulate a binational perspective that
included a criticism of US capitalism, advocacy for social revolution, including calls
for the expropriation of foreign wealth, and calls for their Mexican followers north of
the border to join US unions and revolutionary parties. By 1911, the PLM had merged
with the revolutionary Industrial Workers of the World, which included a short-lived
joint takeover of several Mexican border towns after the onset of the Mexican Revolution. As the US government began its own campaign against radicalism during the
period of the Mexican Revolution and World War I, the PLM was also marked for its
capacity to influence the actions of thousands of Mexican workers in the Southwest.

Over the course of their exiled existence north of the border, the radicals broadened their revolutionary outlook. Not only did they face state repression, dispelling their once-held admiration for the high ideals of US democracy, they were also directly immersed into the experience of the Mexican working class in the United States. As self-imposed exiles crossing the border, they joined the ranks of the Mexican working class in the United States, both as workers and as organizers. In the barrios of the Southwest, they experienced and witnessed the functioning of Jim Crow capitalism. They also formed relations with the US Left, which introduced them to other revolutionary doctrines that helped further shape their internationalist and anticapitalist orientation.

Chapter 8
The PLM Turns to the Working Classes

"The most genuine proletarian ideological current of the bourgeois democratic revolution in Mexico was represented by magonismo and Ricardo Flores Magón."
—José Revueltas, **Ensayo Sobre un Proletariado sin Cabeza**

The second stage of development of Magonismo involved the elaboration of an economic critique of porfirismo, taking aim at capitalism and imperialism and recentering the locus of revolutionary transformation in the working-class and indigenous populations. The evolutionary leap was influenced by three factors: a shifting orientation toward the working class in the realization of revolutionary objectives, especially as growing worker militancy culminated in the insurrectionary strikes that shook porfirian Mexico in 1906–1908. Industrial workers began to demonstrate power, disproportionate to their size and political influence, and were inherently antagonistic to capitalism and foreign ownership. Second, after crossing the border into the United States in 1904 they came into contact with a combative US working class, giving a cross-border dimension to the crystallization of their class consciousness. They included a large number of Mexican immigrants, living under conditions of Jim Crow racial segregation, and US revolutionaries who shared a common outlook. A third factor was the influence of collective indigenous resistance movements, which demonstrated in practice the capacity to resist and prevent capital-driven land expropriations in the countryside.

As Flores Magón first observed as a student activist in 1893, groups of artisans had independently formed an anti-Díaz group called the Club de Obreros Antireeleccionista alongside the other elements taking shape in the nascent movement. When he and others began to organize protests against Díaz in Mexico City, Flores Magón observed that only the common workers were willing to stand their ground and fight back against the police sent in to disperse them. According to John M. Hart, Mexico's labor movement has had an independent character, with episodic explosions of militancy. Charting the development of working-class traditions under corrupt and repressive local regimes and weak or unstable national governments, he states that these conditions "encouraged a radical-revolutionary bent . . . and distrust of formal political institutions."[1]

As a radical student leader Ricardo Flores Magón developed an appreciation for the militancy of the working class

While the mutualistas of the late nineteenth century were incorporated into the patronage structures of the liberal governments and the early Díaz regime, the channels of control and negotiation closed with the turn toward imperialist-led capitalist development. Workers frustrated by increased exploitation, underdevelopment, and overt complicity of the government began to turn against the Díaz regime by the early 1890s. These incipient forms of independent combativeness multiplied in the final decade of the Porfiriato and resonated with the political radicals that came together as the revamped leadership of the PLM in exile.

After the turn of the twentieth century, a newly defined proletariat in the form of an industrial workforce emerged, imbued with the power to shut down the major arteries of industrial capitalism. As revolutionaries seeking a motor to drive the revolution forward, the magonistas gravitated toward the industrial proletariat as it began to act in its own self-interest, confront the Porfirian state, and demonstrate the capacity to bring the great capitalist trusts to their knees. Furthermore, this occurred in parallel with a rise in working-class struggle in other countries, and Flores Magón and his collaborators carefully studied international developments in a scientific manner in an attempt to translate and apply their lessons and meaning to the Mexican landscape.

One significant development that intervened in this time period was the Russian Revolution of 1905 (and again in 1917), which, according to Ellen Myers, profoundly affected Flores Magón's thinking about the revolutionary road.[2] The Russian Revolution of 1905 nearly brought down the Russian Czar after a workers' revolt, general strike, and the first appearance of the "soviet," or workers' governing council, as an alternative to both czarism and bourgeois parliamentarianism. Given the growth of the industrial workforce, the rise of left-wing political parties with a proletarian orientation and composition, and demonstrations of the potential power of the working class to topple authoritarian regimes, revolutionaries in different parts of the world, including Mexico, began to rethink the nature of revolution, now looking to the Russian example.[3]

While the PLM leadership began to turn their sights toward the working classes as the motor of social revolution after 1905, they diverged from the trajectory of the Russian Bolshevik model and instead remained loyal to an eclectic set of principles rooted in idealistic and utopian conceptions of class struggle. This divergence was especially defined in their assessment of revolutionary consciousness in the proletariat, and by extension, the necessary form of organization needed to advance consciousness into action.

Unlike their Russian counterparts, the magonistas did not view labor unionism as the essential vehicle for organizing collective power at the point of production; and wielding that power as a battering ram on the economic foundations of the regime. Instead they believed that revolution would spring from a spontaneous mass uprising in which workers would play a vanguard role, activated by a revolutionary leadership. Unlike the Leninist conception of a vanguard workers' party, a national organization composed of the most class-conscious and organized sectors of the working class capable of providing revolutionary leadership for the urban and rural proletariat in its war of positioning against the bourgeoisie, the magonistas located the guiding force in themselves. The *junta* conceived of revolutionary leadership as coming from a correct political line of march disseminated through their press, and acted upon by underground PLM cadres whose individual direct action heroics could inspire the oppressed classes into revolt.

The Rise of the Mexican Working Class

The magonistas were also inspired by the rising working-class movement in the United States. Citing the data of research scholar William Willoughby, Ángeles Mendieta Alatorre asserts that the estimated 22,793 strikes throughout the United States during the years 1890–1900 conveyed to the PLM leaders the transformative power of working-class struggle.[4] In Mexico, state governors began to introduce labor reforms in the aftermath of strikes in 1904–1906, demonstrating the capacity for collective labor action to compel a previously intransigent state to concede to its demands.[5] These observable patterns also became the basis for emerging magonista proletarian internationalism. As Ricardo wrote in 1911,

> There is logic in the progress of my ideas; there is nothing strange or false about them. In the past I believed in the political system. I had believed that the law contained the necessary force to bring about justice and liberty. But then I saw that what is happening in Mexico is occurring across the world; that the people of Mexico are not the only unfortunate ones. When I looked for the cause of the suffering of all of the poor people across these lands, I found it: *Capital*.[6]

Direct interaction with radical workers initiated the magonistas' gradual divorce from liberalism, as their militancy and fortitude contrasted sharply with the tepidity, vacillation, and passivity of the liberals in confronting the Díaz dictatorship in years prior. By 1906, the now-distinct magonista-led PLM was making its first coordinated efforts to extend its base within the working class. Magonistas around the country made headway in building party nuclei within key sectors of industry, especially in those situated at the nexus of the international economy: mining, textiles, and railroads. This occurred in the context of rising class struggle. According to Zebadúa, et al.,

> Another strike wave began in 1905 and spread in 1906 and 1907. Half of all of the conflicts took place in Mexico City . . . but also included Veracruz, Puebla, Nuevo León, Tamaulipas, Chihuahua, San Luis Potosí, Jalisco, Querétaro, and throughout other parts of the country. The strike wave extended all the way to 1909.[7]

The potential of the working class and its inherently irreconcilable relation to the corporate trusts perceived to be plundering Mexico was accelerated by the outbreak of nationwide labor struggle during the years 1906–1908. According to James D. Cockcroft, three massive labor strikes rocked Mexico in these crucial years, precipitating the outbreak of revolution. In these years, thousands of miners shut down the country's largest mining complex at Cananea, Sonora. This was followed by a nationwide textile workers' strike that spread from Río Blanco, Veracruz, to other states. A third outbreak in the strike wave shut down the nation's primary rail lines, from the mining regions of San Luis Potosí to the northern borderlands.[8]

Between 1906 and 1907 there were 128 strikes, propelling the PLM leadership's class consciousness and fanning its revolutionary fervor.[9] These strikes widened the class differences emerging between the middle class and bourgeois sectors of the liberal movement and the more radical elements now developing a working-class orientation. According to Ward Albro, "[t]he growing concern for worker and peasant causes reflected in the writings of Flores Magón and the plans for revolution eventually drove away most of the upper class or 'high status' liberals and intellectuals, such as Arriaga and Madero."[10] As the workers' struggle was the force pulling them left, the PLM responded in kind—reconstituting itself after 1906 as an explicitly revolutionary party that saw the working class as the leading force.[11] As Flores Magón synthesized his understanding (and disavowal) of "revolution from above" in favor of class revolt from below:

> The Mexican Revolution did not develop from the desks of lawyers, the offices of the bankers, or the army barracks; the revolution emerged from the cradle of human suffering: in those depositories of pain called factories, in those tortuous abysses called mines, in the dank dungeons called workshops, and in the prison-houses called haciendas.[12]

Concurrent with the surge in workers' struggle, the PLM began drafting a program for revolution in 1906. Revealing their desire to engage the proletariat in their project, the readership was invited to discuss and debate the tenets within the pages of *Regeneración*. Through this process, the PLM established and maintained a connection with its networks of supporters and larger readership, with an estimated twenty to thirty thousand copies of each edition of *Regeneración* in circulation in the year 1906.[13] In fact, it was within the PLM-affiliated clubs throughout the country that workers participated in discussions to formulate the demands that filtered into the elaboration of the program.

1906 Program of the PLM

Their plan was not an appeal to workers and peasants to take action, but a reflection of the action already being taken; with the PLM seeking to promote their political framework as a way for workers to generalize their experience, form unions around the stated demands, and connect workers' struggle to the battle against Díaz. The final product, which became known as the Plan of the Mexican Liberal Party (1906), was published in September of that year and circulated broadly at the crest of the strike wave. Somewhere between a quarter and three-quarters of a million copies were circulated throughout Mexico as well as across the US Southwest.[14]

The substance of radical labor and land reform embedded in the Mexican Liberal Party's Plan of 1906 has been described as the "foundation of the social revolution in Mexico" and the basis for the content of the 1917 Constitution.[15] Within its pages, it contained the call for the eight-hour workday, a minimum wage, protections for domestic workers, the abolition of child labor, workplace safety regulations, and workers' compensation. Land reform was envisioned through the redistribution of idle land not in cultivation on the big estates, to be redistributed to the landless, while those haciendas under cultivation were to pay higher, fixed wages. To support a new small-farmer class, the plan called for the creation of an agricultural bank to provide low-interest credit. Lastly, ancestral indigenous ejidos were to be expropriated from the oligarchy and foreign capital and restored to indigenous communities.

Through the dissemination of the plan and increased circulation of *Regeneración*, the radical wing of the party grew in large numbers, as workers across the country formed their own PLM-affiliated clubs in the urban and industrial zones or followed PLM militants in their workplaces.[16] Worker-leaders were tasked with forming clubs, propagandizing among the workers, distributing and discussing the newspaper, and agitating for the formation of unions.[17] In effect, the PLM provided the first vehicle for radical workers to act in their own interests on a national scale.[18]

The actual number of worker adherents to the PLM is unclear. Based on the estimates of a private investigator monitoring the PLM for the Mexican government at the time, the party had an active membership of over a thousand militants across the country with strong bases of support in the industrial zones.[19] The two most significant centers of PLM-led worker organization occurred in the mining camps at Cananea, Sonora, in 1906 and in the textile factories in Veracruz in 1907.[20] The location of Cananea on the US-Mexico border is significant and warrants special focus. Several factors exemplify the way in which internationalism developed in practical terms as a result of the strike: the cross-border movements of workers, revolutionaries, and their ideas and organizations; and the collaboration between capitalists, governments, and law enforcement agencies in attempting to suppress them.

Striking Miners gather at Cananea (1906)

Cananea

By 1906, the magonistas had begun to appeal directly to workers, through the pages of *Regeneración* and through efforts to launch PLM clubs and union organizations in mining camps. The strike that year at the US-owned mining camp just south of the

US-Mexico border at Cananea was a watershed event that jolted their efforts forward; the first powerful show of force by workers against both the state and foreign capital. While the PLM had made efforts to align the miners to their broader cause, the force of the strike wave shook Mexico to its foundations during the years 1906–1908 and induced an evolutionary leap in the proletarian orientation of the party.

The mine camps at Cananea were part of a large, US-controlled copper mining complex that spread from the state of Sonora in Mexico across the border through Arizona, New Mexico, Utah, Colorado, and all the way to Montana. The Díaz regime had actively encouraged US investments in the northern Sonora mining region, with well-placed porfirista políticos buying into cross-border, speculative arrangements and partnerships with an Arizona-based capitalist by the name of William C. Greene in Cananea. In turn, they rewarded themselves and the other investors with tax breaks and other financial incentives. For instance, profits made by the Cananea Consolidated Copper Company that were reinvested back into the corporation, to build smelters, railroads, and telegraph lines were exempted from state and municipal taxation for its first twenty years. Numerous other business transactions were exempted from taxation, and the company was even given the right to expropriate adjacent lands if current owners refused to sell.[21] Greene ultimately attained land concessions to mine, raise livestock, and produce timber on a landmass that spanned four and a half million acres spreading across several states.[22]

By the turn of the twentieth century, investment in mining already amounted to $27 million, fronted in large part by Wall Street investment houses and prominent Los Angeles–based speculators, making it a strategically important mining center for the US economy.[23] Copper was needed in mass quantities to develop the arterial conduits for electrical power in the rapidly industrializing US in the second half of the nineteenth century. Unlike other precious metals, copper was only profitable in mass quantities, necessitating economies of scale. According to historian Philip Mellinger, the process for large-scale copper extraction:

> meant massive blasting, hauling and loading, using complex road and rail systems and huge factory extraction operations. The newly created western copper-mining and processing operations had physical presence and economic power sufficient to dominate counties and entire subregions of the southwest and intermountain West.[24]

These operations required an industrial army of twenty-five thousand miners and support workers that spread across the region.[25] With regional integration, mine workers moved between mining camps across the border and came into contact with radical doctrine, especially the anticapitalist outlook of the Western Federation of Miners, whose partisans co-mingled and supported the efforts of the PLM in Mexico.[26] This paralleled capitalist integration, shaping the world view of the miner. As Brayer points out, "the close association between the Arizona companies and the Cananea corporations made it inevitable that labor activities would not recognize either the international line or the Mexican law forbidding labor unions not sanctioned by the government."[27] Juan Quiñones asserts that this was how PLM partisans diffused their connections and influence.[28]

By the early 1900s Mexican and Mexican American workers were organizing or participating in strikes against wage reductions, racial discrimination in pay, and anti-union blacklists.[29] For instance, Mellinger described the 1903 Clifton-Morenci copper strike as the "first really large Mexican or Hispanic strike anywhere in the United States."[30] The two-week strike of up to three thousand miners ultimately failed, following a pattern of savage state repression that usually accompanied strikes in the early twentieth century. Nevertheless, it was the opening shot of a much longer struggle that witnessed rising wages and unionization rates among Mexican American workers.[31] These class struggles in mining also provided the PLM with a receptive audience to their calls for radical change.

PLM activists attempted to develop a following and organizational base at the copper mining camps in the US-Mexico border region. The newspaper as organizer and agitator was essential to understanding the initial success of the PLM. Armando Bartra compares the role of *Regeneración* (and similar PLM-aligned papers in other parts of the country) to that of the Bolshevik newspaper *Iskra* and the role it played in shepherding the Russian revolutionary movement:

> The clandestine diffusion [of the paper] helped consolidate the secret nuclei of party militants and around them the "branches" or "clubs" that then forged the broader organizations with a mass character, capable of raising the immediate, concrete demands of the workers and linking them together through the revolutionary press . . . The Leninist tactic described in the book *What is to be Done?* with its specific features of a "national press," "party organization" and "mass organizations" were developed in almost identical terms by the Junta Organizadora del Partido Liberal.[32]

By 1906, PLM activists had formed auxiliary groups at mining camps at Santa Barbara, Chihuahua, Cananea, Sonora, and across the border at Douglas, Arizona, and Clifton-Morenci, Arizona. While the overthrow of Díaz was the primary focus for the groups on both sides of the border, PLM activists also became involved in and drawn from localized class conflicts. One of the most significant of the strikes of this period was the Cananea strike of 1906.

Cananea was the largest of the mining camps, employing over eight thousand Mexican miners and twenty-three hundred US personnel. The mine was owned and operated by William C. Greene, while Díaz's vice president, Ramón Corral, was listed as a junior partner and co-owner in the arrangement. Given the prominent ownership, the governor of the state and Díaz crony Rafael Yzabal allowed Greene to run the mining town like an autocrat, setting up mining operations as if he were operating on US soil. Greene's style of management became a focal point for the simmering resentment felt by Mexicans toward the imperialist economic arrangements of the time. For instance, American workers brought across the border from Arizona were given the higher paid and favored positions, placed in management positions over Mexicans, paid in dollars, paid two to four times more for the same work, and were provided superior housing in white-only enclaves within the camp.[33] Other forms of racial discrimination were rampant in the camps, as the conditions of American racial discrimination were imposed on camp life *within* the territory of Mexico. Miner and PLM adherent Esteban Calderón explained the frustration of the workers in the camp:

> Foreign racial hegemony was imposed on us throughout the company, in our own country, at the expense of national interests, at the expense of the Mexican worker, of national dignity, and of the basic elements of justice and decorum.[34]

While this was common operating procedure, and ignored in the press, the PLM's *Regeneración* took note.

According to a 1905 issue, "the Cananea Consolidated Copper Corporation, a Yankee Corporation, is committing a civic and repeated infraction of the law in order to take advantage of the Mexican laborer."[35] Through the pages of *Regeneración*, the PLM raised the demand of "equal pay for equal work" in response to this two-tier system in the foreign-dominated industries.[36] As a result of the steady reporting and incisive political analysis of *Regeneración* about the specific issues facing workers at Cananea, PLM-aligned activist workers in the mining camps found a receptive audience among their co-workers and were able to distribute the newspaper widely throughout the mining camps.

Historian Devra Weber also identifies a wide subterranean network of PLM radicals on the US side that coordinated with Cananea miners. Fernando Palomares, for example, was a Mayo indigenous worker from Sinaloa who organized Yaquis and Mayos in Cananea mining camps on behalf of the PLM as early as 1903.[37] Three other PLM militants, Manuel M. Diéguez, Esteban Baca Calderón, and Francisco Ibarra, had been the transmitters between the workers and the PLM leadership in 1905–1906. As Calderón explained his preliminary experiences in organizing among the miners:

> Ibarra and I then began the work of convincing others to join the PLM, beginning with those that we considered the most conscious and most capable of understanding the risks involved with being the first organizers of a rebellion . . . based on the popularity of *Regeneración*, there were many supporters [of the PLM] in the mining camps.[38]

By mid-January 1906 these three, along with Plácido Ríos and Lázaro Gutiérrez de Lara, were instrumental in organizing mineworkers into the PLM-affiliated club Union Liberal Humanidad in the environs of the mining camps.[39] The club originally restricted its operations to disseminate anti-Díaz communiqués and resolutions, but was then drawn into supporting the miners' specific grievances against the company. After further recruitment of a core of radical miners by April, the Club Liberal de Cananea was created as a vehicle to organize an industrial union of mine workers, starting with Cananea and eventually extending out to the other camps, merging into the envisioned Liga Minera de los Estados Mexicanos. Historian León Díaz Cárdenas describes this attempt (which was ultimately unsuccessful) as the prototype of the first industrial miners' union in Mexico.[40]

PLM organizer Lázaro Gutiérrez de Lara

Through this legwork, a significant readership developed, and over a short period PLM leaders developed a following among the most combative workers. According to the historian Salvador Hernández Padilla, Magonismo took root among the miners "because the mining camps created the optimal conditions for radicalization: frequent unemployment, discrimination, overcrowding, inflated living expenses."[41] In late May, a delegation of the PLM that comprised Juan Sarabia, Librado Rivera, and Lázaro Gutíerrez de Lara met clandestinely with representatives of the miners union after it became known that the workers intended to walk out on strike. The magonistas counseled patience, to allow for further organizing in the different mines to assure strike unity. The organizing efforts were still in an incipient stage when workers walked out on strike in June 1906. On May 31, the workers produced a list of demands, and the following day they began the strike. The walkout began when four hundred miners walked out of Cananea's "Oversight" mine, led by a militant core affiliated with the Unión Liberal Humanidad. Historian Ramón Ruiz claims that all of the actual leaders of the 1906 strike were affiliated in some way to the PLM.[42]

Several factors converged to lead the workers to take action: the daily humiliation of Jim Crow racism within the camp, a recent peso devaluation undercutting the purchasing power of miners, and growing frustration with the Díaz regime's complicity with foreign capitalists like Greene.[43] By the second morning of the strike, two thousand workers had walked out of mines and workshops and gathered in front of the company store, with homemade flags that read "5 pesos" on one side and "8 hours" on the other. Fourteen delegates were chosen from the body to present the demands, which included: the dismissal of hated company foremen, a minimum wage of five pesos per day for all workers, regardless of race; and a maximum of eight hours per day. They also demanded that 75 percent of jobs be reserved for Mexicans, who should have equal access to "skilled" positions; and that honest men be selected from the group as foremen and shift leaders.[44] An anonymously produced flyer was circulated among the crowd, which proclaimed for the overthrow of Díaz as part of the strike:

> Mexican people: rise up! Learn what has been forgotten. Organize yourselves and determine your rights. Demand the respect you deserve. Each of us Mexicans are despised by the foreigners, but we can be equal to them if we unite and demand our rights. We are detested as less than the white, black, or Chinese, on our own Mexican soil. This is because this dreadful government gives advantages to mercenaries while harming the true owners of this unfortunate land.[45]

When Anglo foremen tried to disperse the gathered strikers with high-powered fire hoses, the crowd responded with a barrage of rocks. In the ensuing melee, a section of the crowd tried to open a gate to the main office and was met by a volley of gunfire from company guards taking potshots from the window balconies. Three were killed and an untold number were wounded. The enraged crowd then overpowered the guards with the hoses while others proceeded to burn down several buildings, killing four of the company guards in the process. Running battles then proceeded for the rest of the afternoon, including an ambush of strikers leaving the area by armed Anglos, which killed six. While most workers fled to hide out from the bloodshed, others regrouped to seek out guns and repel the company guards. By the end of the day, at least two more strikers and two guards were killed in the battle, while the strikers and Anglo guards fortified their positions.[46]

In response to the strike, Greene sent word immediately to the governor's office as well as to the headquarters of the Arizona Rangers. Federal troops and rurales (Díaz's "rural police") were dispatched to the region, while a train was arranged to bring armed Rangers from the border, who eventually crossed the border "individually as civilians" and were designated by Governor Izábal as "Mexican volunteers" to avoid international controversy.[47] Fernando Palomares, writing about the strike two years later, noted that while Ricardo Flores Magón sat in a US jail for violating "Neutrality Laws," Porfirio Díaz "tolerated outlaw foreigners violating neutrality laws in order to exterminate Mexican miners."[48]

It took a combined multinational force of Mexican rural police, infantry, Arizona Rangers, company guards, and a detachment of armed Anglo volunteers from Bisbee to suppress the strike. Reprisals followed the disarming of the striking miners, as untold numbers "stood against an adobe wall . . . and [were] shot."[49] But the swiftness of the outcome belied its repercussions. According to Hernandez Padilla, the PLM's orientation on the Cananea strike revealed a strategic understanding of its political and economic significance. While the strike originated from the miners themselves, the influence of PLM supporters has led historian Ward Albro to declare it a result of a wider magonista movement:[50]

> The political undertones of the struggle go much deeper than just the primary demand of "5 pesos & an 8 hour workday" and the organization inserted itself with a broader and more complex intention: to link, influence, and lead the developing industrial working class of Mexico.[51]

In the aftermath of Cananea strikes spread through textiles and the railroads, beginning a wave of revolt that ultimately toppled the Díaz dictatorship. For the PLM leadership the strike wave was a confirmation of the revolutionary potential of the industrial proletariat, a sentiment that continued to evolve in relation to the rising workers' role within the revolution. The growing influence of Magonismo was not lost on Díaz, who posted a $20,000 bounty for the capture of Ricardo Flores Magón in the aftermath of the Cananea strike. When the porfirista governor of Sonora, Rafael Izábal, petitioned for the right to execute the strike leadership, including three magonistas, the vice president under Díaz, Ramón Corral, responded in the negative, stating that execution would cause a "national scandal."[52] They were charged with rebellion and sent to the notoriously dreadful prison at San Juan de Ulúa, facing fifteen-year terms (although they were released by the Madero government in 1911).

Despite the violence and repression, the strike was broadly supported by the Mexican population, whose sympathies lay with the miners and simmering resentment against Díaz and the foreign capitalists. This caused great consternation among the backers of the regime, cracking open what had been referred to as the Pax Porfiriana. Conversely, the strike gave great hope and confidence to its detractors and combatants. Over the next four years the party grew, becoming the first political vehicle for revolutionary action for thousands of working-class partisans. By 1910, for instance, it is estimated that between 200 and 350 liberal clubs had formed throughout Mexico, with a substantial proletarian base.[53]

The PLM clubs embedded within the working class in Mexico were instrumental in the insurrectionary strikes during the revolution. During the Madero-led uprising, strikes were pivotal to the collapse of porfirismo. By December of 1911, thirty thousand textile workers, virtually the whole workforce, walked out. According to Jeffrey Bortz, "the textile strikes reverberated throughout the country in which the old mechanisms of political control were collapsing."[54] Inspired by the textile strikers, rural workers carried out their own strikes against haciendas in various parts of the country, raising demands for higher wages and shorter work hours. By early 1913, strikes also spread to the mines, the railroads, the communication and transportation sectors, as well as the electrical industries.[55]

Not only did the textile strikes secure the first industrywide labor agreements, they signified the crystallization of a class-conscious working class beginning to assert its own objectives in a revolutionary context. The potency of the strike wave, combined with the weakened state, led to a series of concessions enacted first at the state level, later enshrined in the labor code of Article 123 of the Constitution of 1917.[56] Jeffrey Bortz asserts the growth and forcefulness of the workers' movement produced examples of workers control in the factories. While great strikes in these sectors helped bring down Díaz, radical workers' organizations had to be rapidly built in the vacuum, and they were neither sufficiently organized nor ideologically prepared to chart an independent path.[57]

Indigenous Resistance

By the time he crossed the border, Ricardo Flores Magón and his collaborators had already developed an incipient criticism of capitalism, a process influenced by the writings of radical nineteenth-century European thinkers theorizing the intrinsic failings of capitalism and bearing witness to the first international stirrings of class struggle. The intellectual material now circulating internationally was bolstered by world events. The forceful entrance of the working class onto the stage of history in the second half of the nineteenth century, from the Paris Commune to the Russian Revolution of 1905, fired the imagination of radicals the world over, giving blood, flesh, and bone to the idea of Socialist revolution. For the magonistas, emerging anticapitalist doctrine also refracted through a distinctly Mexican historical lens. Aside from the assimilation of foreign radical doctrine, radical tradition was also distilled from the generational cycles of indigenous resistance and rebellion that framed the great epochs of Mexican history since Spanish colonization.[58] The PLM's anticapitalism grew within the womb of its liberal structures, pushing forth gradual changes, conflicts, and splits until it took its final shape as an instrument of anticapitalist insurrection.

According to various historians and biographers, it was widely believed that Flores Magón and the other leaders of the PLM were well versed in the writings and thought of the leading thinkers of the nineteenth century, such as Karl Marx, Mikhail Bakunin, and Peter Kropotkin.[59] The works of Kropotkin were especially influential, as the self-styled PLM modeled their programmatic views on his conception of "anarchist communism" after 1910.[60] Their influences began to reflect in the pages of the magonista press. Even more influential was the entry of the workers' movement into the theater of Mexican revolutionary politics, which demonstrated a powerful force that could strike potent blows against the seemingly impervious dictatorship of Díaz.

The third root can be identified in the organic expression of primordial Mexican socialism that lies in the experience of indigenous collective communalism. As early as the First Liberal Congress of 1901, the profound poverty and marginalization of the indigenous population was factored in as another failing of the period. Orthodox liberal thinking toward the plight of the indigenous population was explained in terms of their relation to the capitalist system vis-à-vis the "Spenserian positivism" associated with the liberal Científicos. Only through their incorporation into the economy as productive farmers or wage labor, and through aggressive state-run instruction in modern, European thought, could their "backward-looking" culture and collectivist consciousness be dismantled.[61] "Indians" could only fit into modern society through aggressive assimilation and market incorporation, something prevented by the Church's dominion over indigenous populations. This modus vivendi was tolerated by the formerly liberal regime of Díaz, according to bourgeois liberal critics, creating bulwarks against modernization and democratization.

The radicals regrouping around *Regeneración* gradually moved away from this philosophy, based on an evaluation of their capacity for resistance to colonization, self-preservation, and episodic revolts. During their college days, Ricardo and Enrique Flores Magón were already beginning to question the dominant anti-indigenous notions embedded in bourgeois liberalism. Their sentiments crystallized against the backdrop of the uprising of Tomochic in 1892. Indigenous Tomochitecos and other Serrano communities in the state of Chihuahua rose up against central authority after seeing their lands encroached upon and privatized as a result of federal policy. They began to reframe their own history as one rooted in the indigenous experience. By extension, they contextualized their own rebellious spirit and antigovernment feelings as part of the larger historical backdrop of indigenous resistance to centralized and corrupted colonial authority that degraded their lives.[62]

By 1908, they came to understand the indigenous campesinos and rural workers as "primitive Communists" who had occupied the front lines in the struggle against Díaz through ongoing resistance to the atomization of their ancestral lands. They, in effect, were the most intransigent opponents of capitalist expansion and natural allies within the revolutionary camp. This framed the foundational thinking for Ricardo Flores Magón, who drew from familial heritage, remote memory, and contemporary rebellions taking place. As Ricardo Flores Magón explained his admiration for indigenous socialism in the pages of *Regeneración* in 1911:

> Some four or five million Indians live in Mexico who until twenty or twenty-five years ago lived in communal villages. Mutual support was the rule in those communities . . . in those communities there were no judges, mayors, jailers . . . Everyone had a right to the land, water for irrigation, to firewood from the forest, and lumber to build their homes. The plows were passed from hand to hand, as well as the teams of oxen. Each family worked their own plots of land to produce what they needed, and then worked together on common lands, sharing the harvests and preparing for the following season, and then pulling together as a community to help others in need to build their homes.[63]

An indigenous framework was also inspired due to resistance. The privatization of common-use lands (*baldíos*) and the encroachment of large landholdings onto ancestral holdings put the project of the liberals and later porfiristas at odds with indigenous communities, whose "concept of property was neither private nor individual but social and communal."[64] Chassen-López has described this tension developing between liberal capitalists and the Zapotec communities in the Oaxaca Valley in the years preceding the revolution, quoting a representative of the Científico clique and owner of Oaxaca's largest hacienda, who concluded that the "love of private property" would have to be fostered among the Indians before the "imperfect and absurd socialism of their villages would disappear."[65] Recent studies have shown that the scale of resistance to dispossession in indigenous Oaxaca greatly impeded the forces of state-led capitalist privatization, allowing for the perseverance of indigenous cultures. Indigenous resistance to dispossession took various forms, including episodic armed revolts.[66] The vigorous defense of land was the nexus to the preservation of culture and identity, where the contemporaneous dividing lines between extinction, *mestizaje*, or assimilation, or the perseverance of indigenous self-determination, were defined historically by the scale of resistance waged by the people against the colonizing state.

Historian Moisés González Navarro generalizes this experience. While the indigenous generally lost out through innumerous *despojos*, displacement was the least successful where organized resistance was the strongest. Resistance of the indigenous pueblos to the alienation from their land was most successful in the center of the country, where an estimated 2082 indigenous pueblos, or 41 percent of the total, were successful in conserving at least some of their ancestral lands.[67] Conversely, revolt was more likely to occur after the outbreak of revolution in those regions where displacement had been the most thorough.[68] It is through observation of widescale indigenous communal resistance to capitalist dispossession that the Flores Magón brothers first understood the possibility of defeating it.

The Organizing Junta of the PLM applied their understanding of indigenous revolutionary agency in the form of direct solidarity, alliance, and co-organization with indigenous groups, especially those already in a state of resistance or rebellion. As Juan Carlos Beas, Manuel Ballesteros, and Benjamín Maldonado observe:

> In their proclamations, circulars, articles, programs, mobilizations, the indigenous claim to the land and also defense of the communal lifestyle was always present as an alternative organizational model of a new Mexican society. The Socialist ideal of the magonistas identified inclusive representation, collective labor, and the enjoyment of the land in common, like in the Indian villages of the past, as representative of a revolutionary alternative.[69]

This reflected in the prominence of the indigenous land struggle their Program of 1906 which called for the return of all expropriated lands to the indigenous communities, and the appeal for legal defense of indigenous communities facing dispossession. By the time of the manifesto's release, several PLM militants were already in some way working with indigenous rebels.

Lázaro Gutiérrez de Lara, for instance, had provided legal aid to Yaqui pueblos facing dispossession of their lands by the Cananea Copper Company.[70] Based on his observations of Yaqui resistance and interactions with those working in the mines, Sonora-based PLM leader Esteban Baca Calderón wrote of the need "to declare for the return of the lands that had been plundered from the Yaqui and Mayo tribes and all of the indigenous groups in general scattered throughout the country."[71] Magonistas like Baca Calderón and Gutiérrez de Lara also understood the correlation between US capitalist investment in the mining zones of Sonora and the urgency for the suppression of both the Yaqui and miner revolts. They both threatened economic stability, and thus the flow of profits. Linking workers' rights to the return of original peoples' lands was a logical conclusion for the revolutionaries.

The significance of this land proclamation in 1906 cannot be understated for understanding the course of the revolution. For example, it influenced and enjoined the thinking of the zapatista revolutionaries in Morelos, who put the substance of the plan into practice after 1911 with their Plan de Ayala. Zapata, by 1911, had numerous former magonistas as part of his general staff, even adopting the PLM slogan of ¡Tierra y Libertad! (Land and Liberty!) as his own. Later, during the 1913 Huertista coup to restore the primacy of the landed oligarchy, hundreds of thousands of indigenous campesinos and landless workers joined the armies of Pancho Villa and Emiliano Zapata. The armies coalesced against Huerta with the 1914 Pact of Torreón, which contained the first radical articulations of Villismo and Zapatismo calling for land expropriation and redistribution on a national scale. The centrality of the land question in Magonismo explains why some of the most dedicated magonistas and PLM stalwarts were of indigenous descent, especially in the border regions where the wars of removal against indigenous groups such as the Yaqui were still fresh in the collective memory.

> In preparation for their insurrections, the PLM junta divided Mexico into military jurisdictions and assigned party leaders to each in order to agitate, form alliances, and oversee the building up of a revolutionary network. In 1906, for instance, PLM militants Fernando Palomares, a Mayo, and José María Leyva, a Yaqui named after the famous leader, were sent to foster an alliance with Yaqui *guerrilleros* holding out against the regime. They spoke the Yoeme language, spoken by both Mayo and Yaqui in the region, and understood the people. In their later uprising to capture northern Baja California in 1911, a troop of five hundred Yaquis joined in on the assault of the regional military headquarters of the federal army in Pitahaya, Sonora, revealing the fruits of those efforts. After the combined group captured the base, they raised a red flag with the inscription "Tierra y Libertad" on the flagpole.[72]

It is in this context that magonistas not only took up the claims of indigenous communities in their press and programs but attempted to join ranks and unite efforts. Their principled efforts led layers of indigenous working-class militants into the ranks of the PLM. Indigenous partisans rallied to the banner of the PLM, becoming key regional organizers and in some cases mass leaders in their own right. This included

Hilario Salas (Mixtec) in Veracruz, Fernando Palomares (Mayo), and Javier Buitamea (Yaqui) in Sonora, Camilo Jiménez (Tarahumara) in Chihuahua, and Primo Tapia (Naranjo) in Michoacán.[73] Indigenous magonistas recruited among migratory workers or in the cities, and became important liaisons to indigenous pueblos in the countryside. They formed networks to support against land grabs or to coordinate as part of the PLM-led uprisings.

For example, Hilario Salas was named as the PLM's attaché to the regions of Veracruz and Tabasco. In 1905 he began to organize among the Popoluca people living in various pueblos in the district of Acayucan, in southern Veracruz. Over the previous several years, the people had seen their lands confiscated by foreign and domestic capitalist interests with connections to the Díaz government:

> Romero Rubio, the father-in-law of Porfirio Díaz, acquired some 149,404 hectares of land in the districts of Acayucan . . . including most of the communal lands of Soteapan and Mecayapan. These lands were later sold to [British oil baron] Lord Cowdray, becoming part of a land empire totaling 177,110 hectares held by various companies such as the Veracruz Land and Cattle Company, Mexican Real Estate Company, and El Aguila, the petroleum company.[74]

In September of 1906, Salas led a PLM-inspired uprising with a force of up to a thousand indigenous followers to retake the land. After capturing several small towns, they attempted to take the city of Acayucan. The uprising was defeated on the second day, and the collective reprisals against the associated communities conducted by the federal army were barbaric.[75] Despite the failed uprising, Veracruz continued to be a pivotal theater of class struggle up to and beyond the overthrow of Díaz.

Magonista-indigenous convergence also took place in other regions around the country in the revolutionary period. Between 1906 and 1910, Maya-speaking magonistas disseminated *Regeneración* and organized PLM clubs in the Yucatán Peninsula. An armed insurrection was attempted in Valladolid in 1910, led by PLM adherents Maximiliano Ramírez Bonilla, José Expectación Kantun, and Atilano Albertos. While the uprising was defeated, Maya-speaking veterans of Magonismo continued to be at the epicenter of political developments in the region throughout the revolutionary period. Magonistas launched revolts with indigenous support across other parts of the country between 1906 and 1911. In the borderlands of Baja California in 1911, for instance, they captured several border towns with support from the indigenous Diegueño, the Paipai, and Kiliwa peoples.[76]

While these efforts failed in their stated aims, they propelled the revolutionary process forward. Furthermore, they elevated indigenous demands as campesinos and workers to the forefront of the demands taking shape as part of the national revolutionary "plans." They also showed how indigenous people comprised the bulk of the agricultural proletariat situated at the frontlines of the class struggle.

Chapter 9
The PLM and Borderland Internationalism

---

*"[Práxedis] Guerrero had much contact with the workers during his time
as a lumberjack, in the mines, on the railroads, and other industries, and
under these circumstances he had crystallized the ideas ... of forming
an ... 'International Worker League' with the object of fraternally
uniting workers of all countries in order to defend themselves against
the abuses and injustices of the capitalists and entrepreneurs."*
—**La Vida Heroica De Práxedis G. Guerrero**

When the PLM leadership crossed the border, they entered into the ranks of a
Mexican population that had migrated in waves as a result of displacement
due to the Porfiriato. Once in the US, their sensibilities were shocked by the
experience of racial discrimination and labor exploitation, state and vigilante violence
against Mexicans, and their own incessant persecution by both the US and Mexican governments. The exiled leadership of the PLM entered into the United States
through the same corridor used by thousands of their *paisanos* and ended up living
in and navigating through the same racially segregated barrios, *colonias*, and camps.
It was from among this population that the magonistas identified the raw material for
their cross-border insurrectional plans.

Through organizing and recruiting through mutualistas, the widespread dissemination of their radical press, the active creation of a US-based network of clubs, and through
affiliation and collaboration with US radicals, the PLM built an impressive network of
organizers and adherents. As Devra Weber describes, they built an "organizational base
in motion," in which "labor and revolutionary foci thus moved across the transnational
space, facilitating the spread of ideas, organizing strikes, and revolutionary forays."[1]

In doing so, they attracted the most class-conscious elements of the mexicano and
Mexican American working class, including a second generation of magonista cadre
whose leadership emerged from the unique conditions and struggles of the Mexicans
in the United States. Through these efforts the PLM and the Mexican working class in
the US were able to congregate power and mobilize resources toward struggles in their
own barrios in tandem with their antigovernment forays into Mexico.[2] These changing circumstances of operation contributed to the political evolution of the PLM toward an explicitly internationalist orientation.

In conducting their international revolutionary activity as unwelcome guests
north of the border, they faced a transnational response from their enemies. The
US and Mexican governments, along with a host of police, spies, and detectives,

conducted an incessant campaign to isolate and eliminate the threat to capitalism and the imperial project posed by the PLM. Concurrently, the PLM also began to find common cause with the US left, especially the Socialist Party and the Industrial Workers of the World (Wobblies). The alliance with the radical Left in the US coincided with a series of political splits in the PLM, as the magonistas began to draw anticapitalist and proletarian conclusions about the class character of the coming revolution.

Mexican Migration into the Barrios

Earlier waves of Mexican migrants had entered the US in the decade preceding the arrival of the PLM fugitives. The displacement of Mexican people and their migration coincided with a growing US economy and labor shortages, especially throughout the sparsely populated Southwest. Mexican workers were absorbed into the US economy, but under conditions of racial segregation and labor segmentation. Through the formation of a labor caste system that combined a Jim Crow legal framework and employer collusion, Mexican workers were primarily channeled into the various stages of agricultural production, railroad construction and maintenance, mining, and domestic work; becoming the majority of workers in many of these sectors by 1910.[3]

Mexicans were confined to segregated communities and heavily policed to keep them isolated from other working-class populations. Employers also segregated them within these industries and paid them less, and they generally worked in substandard and dangerous conditions. Furthermore, Mario Barrera describes the structural disenfranchisement of Mexican labor that served to maintain a reserve army of labor providing two functions that increased profitability for capitalists north of the border. Firstly it could:

> give elasticity to the labor force, so that as the demand for labor increases the workforce can be expanded, without having to compete for labor and thus drive up wages. Secondly, a group of unemployed workers can be used by employers to leverage in bargaining with or controlling their workers. If workers can be easily replaced, as in a strike situation, their power is greatly reduced.[4]

This population became a substantial substratum of the southwestern US working class facing another form of underdevelopment distinct—but indirectly linked—to what was happening in Mexico. Many moved back and forth across the border for work or maintained direct connections to Mexico and events taking place in that country. It is among this population that the magonistas recruited to launch their revolutionary activities in Mexico, but in the process, they were drawn into the class struggle north of the border. Compelled by poverty, many of the émigré leaders themselves had to take jobs on the side of their activism in what was designated "Mexican work," giving them a firsthand experience of the oppressive conditions of mexicanos in the US.[5]

In the course of organizing support for revolutionary efforts in Mexico, they came into contact with the US Left and the Mexican American working class, whose experiences with the American brand of Jim Crow capitalism drew the cadres of the PLM into local struggles and to incorporate analysis and criticism of US politics into its press and activism. It is in this context that Magonismo evolved into the first effort to organize Mexican workers on both sides of the border with a common anticapitalist objective.

Over the span of eighteen years, the PLM and Ricardo Flores Magón built a substantial following among Mexican American workers and formed comradely associations with radicals north of the border. According to Chicano historian Carlos Larralde:

> [B]y [1904], Chicanos along the American border were already following magonista beliefs . . . [and] many Chicanos carried his philosophy throughout the Southwest, especially in Arizona, California, and Texas. Other Chicanos with the magonista gospel followed the "Wobblies" to Washington, Idaho, and other regions.[6]

In their short history in Mexico (between 1900 and 1903) the Mexican liberals had already launched a national organization. As Mexican exiles in the United States, especially after reconstituting themselves as the Organizing Junta of the PLM, they again played a key leadership role as the first significant Mexican leadership body to organize a mass base in the Mexican and Mexican American working classes north of the border. This was achieved through the recruitment of an organic leadership, with organizing experience and knowledge of the people and terrain, the reconstitution of their press, and its mass dissemination to a US readership.

Being Mexican and immigrant in the US immersed them into an ecosystem in which Anglo-Saxon racism intertwined within the class structure to shape all aspects of social reality: where they could work and live, and how they were viewed and treated by the state (the police, the courts, etc.). Racial oppression gave them insights into the functioning of American capitalism, which sharpened their critique.

International Repression

From the commanding heights of both the Mexican and United States governments, massive human and material resources were deployed to destroy the magonistas on both sides of the border. Already arrested and jailed three times in Mexico, Ricardo Flores Magón and other PLM leaders encountered repression across the border. The reconfiguration of the PLM in the United States allowed the group a momentary reprieve, but not for long. The US government applied the Neutrality Acts and a host of other legal maneuvers to selectively repress the Mexican exile community in the US as part of protecting its economic interests in Mexico.[7] When kidnapping and assassination attempts by Díaz's henchmen and well-paid hirelings failed to silence the exiles, the US government proved more successful using its legal system. By incarcerating the leadership, suppressing the production and distribution of their paper, and through deportation and other repressive means, the US government was able to greatly inhibit and weaken the tenacious radical and socialist wing of the Mexican Revolution.

After crossing the border, the PLM were surveilled and subjected to assault, their presses destroyed, and they were detained, kidnapped, deported, and prosecuted incessantly by the US agents at the behest of the Mexican government. Díaz himself personally offered a $20,000 reward for their capture.[8] At the outset, the federal government

allowed Díaz's operatives to conduct their campaign against the PLM on US soil un-
impeded. As a result, from the time they first crossed the national boundaries in 1904,
they were pursued from Laredo and San Antonio, Texas, to St. Louis, Missouri, where
they were jailed for two months as part of the cross-border repressive blowback for the
Cananea strike. After release, they fled across the border once more to Montreal, Canada, before clandestinely returning to San Francisco and finally settling in Los Angeles
in 1907. Through its consulates, the Díaz government tracked and hounded the PLM.

As the Porfirian regime gained more enemies in the first decade of the twentieth century, and as radical dissidents and disaffected exiles accumulated and
worked out of the southwestern borderlands, it began to place more interest in the
activities of Mexicanos *de afuera* (Mexicans in the US). The expansion of Mexican consulates throughout the Southwest occurred within this framework. It also
flowed within the parameters of US imperialism, which had no desire to see regime
change in Mexico or the interaction between radical political exiles and its sizeable
Mexican working class.

Therefore, starting with the administration of Theodore Roosevelt, the federal
government allowed the Mexican state to pursue and repress its own dissidents across
the US as it saw fit. As Michael Smith explains,

> Although regulations governing the role of consuls limited their official duties
> to encouraging trade and commerce, promoting friendly relations, and assist-
> ing compatriots, revolutionary conditions had transformed them into the key
> components of a network of bi-national clandestine operations . . . the Secret
> Service was not an independent intelligence agency but rather an appendage
> of the Mexican consular system. In the early 1900s, Enrique Creel, Don Por-
> firio's Minister of Foreign Relations, organized and directed an "international
> detective agency" to combat Ricardo Flores Magón and other members of the
> Partido Liberal Mexicano (PLM) seeking to overthrow the Díaz regime.[9]

These consular officials, in league with their US counterparts, constructed a
shadow network of agents, informants, spies, and other operatives. For instance, they
contracted with the Furlong Secret Service Company of St. Louis, which had pursued
the PLM leadership through the US, Canada, and back to Los Angeles, where along
with the LAPD they helped detain the group in mid-1907.[10] According to historian
W. Dirk Raat, efforts were escalated by various arms and branches of the US government, involving a wide variety of agencies to suppress the activities of the magonistas,
including

> US Army Intelligence officers, Secret Service agents of the Treasury Depart-
> ment, and . . . Bureau of Investigation agents . . . state governors, military com-
> manders, and federal authorities on both sides of the border.

Furthermore, at the regional and local level,

> federal attorneys and marshals, local sheriffs and police, city detectives,
> customs and immigration officials, territorial and state police (such as the

Arizona and Texas Rangers), and private citizens (for example, Colonel William Greene) who had the services of labor spies, lawyers, and manufacturers' associations.[11]

The federal post office participated, suppressing the circulation of *Regeneración* and other magonista-aligned papers in 1916 when they took public positions against World War I. This was accomplished by expanding existing "anti-obscenity" laws to include those that took antiwar positions.[12] For their part, the capitalist media also waged a campaign against the group, portraying them as a foreign threat and distorting or embellishing their actions. The scale of the repression belied the small size of the junta leadership, while at the same time serving as a testament to the influence of the group, the commitment of its adherents on both sides of the border, and its ability to operate even under the most adverse conditions.

The constant disruption of their efforts and sequestration of the leadership took a heavy toll on the morale of the membership. While in prison between 1908 and 1910, for instance, they suspended publication of *Revolución* until it was relaunched once more as *Regeneración* in 1910. These setbacks wore down the resolve of some of the group, with one junta leader, Manuel Sarabia, going into second exile in Europe. One regional partisan, Ascencio Soto, president of the Club Liberal de Gonzáles, Texas, expressed anguish in a letter when he stated that "the militants are becoming demoralized because of the arrests of the leadership."[13] Despite these odds, the group managed to build an organization that spread across the Southwest and included a core of organizers and a large base of adherents in the barrios, colonias, and work camps.

The Binational Evolution of Magonismo

While the primary objective of the exiled magonistas was to rally their fellow expatriates and exiles behind their revolutionary project in Mexico, their attention was also drawn to the plight of Mexican Americans and their migrant compatriots that formed a growing segment of the southwestern proletariat. They received a crash course in anti-Mexican racism and witnessed more directly the link between US economic imperialism in Mexico and the condition of migrant workers north of the border. Their efforts brought them into contact with the variants of Jim Crow in the Southwest. As Ricardo Flores Magón wrote in 1911:

> Mexicans have been abandoned to the forces of luck in this country—akin to the way they are treated in Mexico . . . excluded from hotels and restaurants . . . found guilty and sentenced in the twinkling of an eye; the penitentiaries are full of Mexicans who are absolutely innocent. In Texas, Louisiana, and in other states they live without hope.[14]

In other cases, would-be PLM leaders directly experienced workplace discrimination as a prelude to joining the PLM. Future leaders, such as Práxedis Guerrero and Francisco Manrique, for instance, joined the PLM after working in a Morenci, Arizona, mining camp for several months. They formed a union organizing committee called Obreros Libres and affiliated to the PLM after witnessing the Cananea strike.[15]

Historian W. Dirk Raat observes that PLM recruits typically represented the economic concerns of their regions (miners in southern Arizona and railroad workers in Los Angeles, for instance), and they often recruited the most experienced "agitators," who were already locally established strike leaders and militants.[16] Many had accumulated experience in previous labor conflicts in which combating racial discrimination was a fact of life.

Experiencing the racial stratification of American labor had a profound effect on the PLM leaders' outlook, as it dispelled the residual belief that American democracy had something fundamentally different to offer than repressive porfirismo. The stark class divides in Mexico were also present in the United States. What's more, racial segregation delineated and intensified those class divides, pushing the magonistas to increasingly identify with Mexican American workers and their important role in the revolutionary process. According to Juan Gomez-Quiñones,

> Flores Magón lived 18 years in the United States during a particular phase of US history, a fact that ideologically and politically had a major, if not decisive, effect on his personal development. As the reality around him affected him, he and the Partido Liberal Mexicano had an impact upon the Chicano community. The PLM propagandized, recruited, and organized among Chicanos and from within the Chicano community . . . across all the southwestern states from Tejas to California.[17]

Crossing the border changed the equation. No longer was the struggle a solely Mexican one. Poverty, land dispossession, exploitation, and the other forms of capitalist oppression so loathed by the magonistas had followed the Mexican experience into the US. The US recruits to the party brought these experiences into the fold of the PLM, effectively broadening out the international dimensions of its revolutionary outlook. The growth of radical political organization among mexicanos in the US at a time of revolutionary effervescence among mexicanos in Mexico proved too threatening for the US capitalist class. Like in Mexico, the PLM was repressed and its leaders chased and jailed as a means to crush the movement before it could reach a critical mass in the US. Despite facing relentless persecution, threats and assassination attempts, long jail stints, and in some cases deportation, Ricardo Flores Magón and the magonistas in the US were able to establish bases in several US cities across the Southwest that laid the foundation for the rise of a mexicano and Mexican American radical Left.

In the US the magonistas redoubled their efforts to activate opposition to Díaz, creating political clubs, unions, and other organizational structures to become the basis for a national uprising. They tried to connect with established radicals and labor leaders with track records in places like Laredo, Texas, Oxnard, California and Clifton-Morenci, Arizona. Their focus bifurcated. In order to recruit Mexicans in the US, they had to engage the people and issues that were immediate and relevant to them.

In 1906, 1908, and again in 1911, they spearheaded armed uprisings in different regions of Mexico. While that ultimately failed to generate the necessary force to topple

Díaz or induce social revolution, they consolidated a corps of radical cadre, created organizational infrastructure, and built relations with the US unions and radical groups across the Southwest that had a profound effect on the course of events on both sides of the border.

For instance, the infrastructure they created along the border and within Mexico was crucial to the initial successes of the Maderista uprising in 1911 that eventually toppled Díaz.[18] The PLM's base-building efforts in the Southwest also created the first organizational infrastructure to give impulse to the first generation of mexicano working-class struggle in the centers of magonista activity that had developed in Texas, Arizona, and California. PLM clubs were built from small groups of converts or from existing organizations that adhered to the party program and ranged from dozens to hundreds of members. From these locales, the first cadres of Mexican American radicals helped form and lead social movements for land reform, unionization, and against the various manifestations of Jim Crow racial discrimination. Their evolution and propagation of their self-styled anarchism-communism and indefatigable determination to advance the wheels of history eventually split the revolutionary movement between militant supporters of the PLM and others who became intransigent adversaries. Nevertheless, their radical political outlook sank deep roots in the popular memory of the Mexican working class on both sides of the border and informed the world view of a whole generation.

From Jacobin Radicalism to Anarchism-Communism (1906–1911)

The first comprehensive and highly influential program of the PLM, the Manifesto of 1906, can be best understood as a reformist document, as the social content was theoretically realizable within the framework of bourgeois, democratic capitalism. Nevertheless, the historian León Díaz Cárdenas describes the PLM radicals as a different breed than the old "anticlericals," branding them in the pre-1906 days "left liberals," representing the most socially advanced ideas that were possible for that day and age.[19] Armando Bartra states that their 1906 plan "formulated the social content of a radical bourgeois revolution, and from that political point of view proposed a democratic revolutionary path, founded not in legislative changes from above, but in the 'mass intervention of the people in determining the course of their own lives.'"[20]

At the same time, it can be contextualized as a transition; signifying the leftward-moving trajectory of a layer of radical intellectuals informed by revolutionary doctrine and inspired by a transnational landscape of industrial class struggle coming into focus, indigenous-led rural revolt, interaction with US-based radicals, and the terrain-shifting events of the Mexican Revolution. What began as a unified, cross-class alliance forming a singular block against a dictator, fragmented into competing revolutionary camps as class struggle intensified and reconfigured the component parts along their respective class lines. After crossing the border, the PLM underwent further splits and evolutions, now informed by an internationalist outlook and a steely opposition to capitalism, while they continued to describe their organization with the moniker of Liberal. As Flores Magón later explained, "If from the first we had called ourselves anarchists, no one, or not but a few, would have listened to us."[21]

Synthesis with US anarchists and socialists and their theoretical doctrines, and a cross-border perspective from the vantage point situated at the heart of the empire, enabled the junta to see the fatal contradictions of liberal capitalism, and to therefore analyze and conclude that the revolution in Mexico had to transcend its bourgeois limits. In fact, while the PLM leadership and especially Ricardo Flores Magón were labeled as rigid and dogmatic ideologues in their thinking by their critics, they were more committed to the realization of workers' revolution than any one sectarian doctrine, leading them to observe and draw lessons from world events. For instance, they celebrated all manifestations of the anticapitalist struggle, which reached its apogee with the victory of the Bolshevik Revolution of 1917. The events captured the imagination of the PLM, with Ricardo Flores Magón praising Lenin and the Bolsheviks, and identifying events in Russia as the opening shot of the "global worker's revolution."[22] In the pages of *Regeneración*, he proclaimed,

> The Bolsheviks are true internationalists . . . They have understood for some time that the revolution . . . has to spread across borders and racial distinctions, in order to overcome the opposing forces, because if it stays confined in one country . . . it will be suffocated by the capitalist and authoritarian states.[23]

By 1908, the PLM press began to articulate criticisms of capital and empire into its invective as its base of supporters became more coherently left wing and proletarian. As Ricardo Flores Magón wrote in 1908, "in reality, our secret liberal clubs are socialist."[24] For Flores Magón and the leadership of the PLM, their forced exile into the United States further validated an anticapitalist orientation. The racialized structure of the economy, with Mexican workers relegated to the bottom tier, underpinned by political marginalization, illustrated how US capitalism was dependent on subjugating the Mexican laboring classes on both sides of the border.

The magonista idea of revolution was based on the notion that Mexican workers on both sides of the border had the potential to be instruments of transformation through their own self-activity. While in Mexico they placed primacy on armed insurrection over struggle at the point of production, they moved beyond the singular figure of Díaz and toward an indictment of the international system that propped up his regime. In the US, working in different conditions, the junta gravitated toward the Anarcho-syndicalist principle that saw union organization as a prerequisite for concentrating class power at the point of production. This was aided by their integration into the US radical Left, especially the unification with the IWW (also referred to as Wobblies) and the collaboration with anarchists and left-wing Socialists whose organizations had the infrastructure to support the PLM.

As early as 1908, Ricardo Flores Magón began to theorize and imagine the character of the Anarchist-Communist transition in a revolutionary Mexico. From prison in Los Angeles, Ricardo Flores Magón wrote to Enrique Flores Magón and Práxedis Guerrero explaining that the pending revolution would have to be

> against the owning class and "ruling caste": the redistribution of the lands,

factories, and mines to the people will take place "in the course of the revolution," work will be no more than eight hours per day and for no less than one peso per hour. The redistribution of property would not be to individuals but to all "to avoid that the workers who benefit do not become a new bourgeoisie in place of the old, it will be prescribed that all who work within a workplace will have equal right to participate in all affairs. The same workers will also be the administrators of the workplaces [. . .] the land will be worked in common," and for that reason, both the lands and the industries should not be transferred.

To facilitate this, a state commission would need to be created to facilitate exchange between producers as

the workers would mutually exchange their products and surplus production and maintain the soldiers of the revolution. Besides that, it could advise the armed workers how to defend their revolution . . . from the soldiers of tyranny, and the likely attack which will come from the United States or some other nation.[25]

He then adds that "we would then cultivate international relations, not with government, but with workers' organizations from all nations that are already trade-unionist, whether Socialist or anarchist."[26]

In September of 1911, a newly configured PLM junta publicly revealed their commitment to socialist revolution in Mexico and adherence to the principles of anarchist communism.[27] That year, when the northern bourgeoisie entered the revolutionary field in November of 1911 against Díaz behind the banner of Madero, the PLM leadership joined in the call to arms by launching their own uprisings in Baja California and Chihuahua, but on a separate line of march and with fundamentally different intentions. These were spelled out in their anticapitalist Manifesto of the PLM, which characterized events in Mexico as one front in a global struggle against the capitalist system.[28] Like their counterparts taking shape in other parts of the world, being forged by revolutionary movements with the mass participation of the working classes, they declared they were in favor of socialist revolution and advocated for the laboring classes of Mexico to take the means of production and land directly into their own hands.

In the manifesto, they first targeted the three pillars of the system underpinning the Díaz government, "Capital, Authority, and the Church," as being responsible for conspiring to steal the "product of the toiler's sweat, of the blood of the tears and sacrifices of thousands of generations of workers," creating only "hell for those who, with muscle and intelligence, till the soil, set the machinery in motion, build the houses and transport the products." Between capital and labor, the document asserts,

there cannot exist any bond of friendship or fraternity, for the possessing class always seeks to perpetuate the existing economic, political and social system which guarantees it tranquil enjoyment of the fruits of its robberies, while the working class exerts itself to destroy the iniquitous system and institute one in which the land, the houses, the machinery of production and the means of transportation shall be for the common use.[29]

Secondly, they tore to shreds the idea that a bourgeois revolution can uproot the fundamental inequalities and privations rooted in capitalism and imperialism, and counterposed their rebellion to those of the bourgeoisie, organized as "Maderistas, Reyistas, Vazquistas, Científicos" so that "they may [continue to] do business without any consideration for the mass of Mexico's population [...] and protect the privileges of the capitalist class." They celebrated the first expropriations taking place by zapatistas and called for the process to be generalized:

> Expropriation must be pursued to the end, at all costs, as part of this great movement. This is what has been done and is being done by our brothers of Morelos, of Southern Puebla, of Michoacán, of Guerrero, Veracruz, of the northern portion of the State of Tamaulipas, of Durango, Sonora, Sinaloa, Jalisco, Chihuahua, Oaxaca, Yucatán, Quintana Roo, and parts of other States . . . The proletariat has taken possession of the land without waiting for a paternal government to have to do it on their behalf, for it knows that nothing good is to be expected of governments and that the emancipation of the workers must come from the workers themselves[...]
>
> These . . . acts of expropriation . . . must not be limited to taking possession of the land and the implements of agriculture alone. There must be determined expropriation of all the industries by those working in them, and done in a way that the lands, the mines, the factories, the workshops, the foundries, the railroads, the shipping, the warehouses of all kinds, and the houses shall be under the direct control of the people of Mexico, without distinction of sex [...] We liberals encourage you to take immediate possession of the land, the machinery, the means of transportation and the buildings, without waiting for anyone to give them to you and without waiting for any law to decree it.[30]

This final, major treatise of the PLM signified the final stage of their political evolution and initiated their first explicit call for socialist revolution reflected in their efforts in Baja California. It also punctuated the last significant split in the organization.

Revolution and the Second Major Split in the PLM

After Díaz stole the election in 1910 and attempted to suppress opposition, the combined action of the revolutionary forces led by Francisco Madero, Emiliano Zapata, and agents of the PLM toppled Díaz in armed rebellion in April of 1911 after four months of conflict. The defeat of the Díaz dictatorship, nearly twenty years in the making for the Liberals, proved to be bittersweet. While the revolutionaries coordinated efforts between November 1910 and May 1911, their political aims quickly diverged thereafter. With Díaz removed, the social questions moved to the fore, creating schisms and recalculations between the aligned forces that also played out within the PLM itself. By 1911, the US-based PLM junta split further into Anarchist-Communist and Socialist wings over the nature and progression of the revolution. This division led the Socialist wing of the group to join the ranks of the maderistas, while the regrouped anarchists led by Ricardo Flores Magón orchestrated their own insurrectionary campaign in Baja California.

The reconstitution of a liberal bourgeois opposition, united behind Francisco Madero, had mustered a regional coalition that proved capable of militarily defeating the enfeebled forces of Díaz. The capture of the strategic capital of Ciudad Juárez by Madero's troops, coinciding with the armed seizure of Cuautla, Morelos, by zapatistas, shifted the locus of the revolution away from the junta. The defeat of the federal army and the rapid dissolution of the state apparatus, as former loyalists abandoned the dictator in droves, led to a negotiated settlement that favored the limited, conservative aims of Madero over the radical agrarianism of Zapata. Nevertheless, the rise and assumption of power by an alliance of northern capitalists led by Francisco Madero required the active participation of popular forces.

This included the attainment of support from a coterie of middle-class landowning caciques from the north with the capacity to raise and lead armies of small and landless campesinos, unemployed workers, and other middling and proletarian elements into the field. With a program calling for democratic reform and national development, maderismo also appealed to intellectuals and socialists on both sides of the border that subscribed to the orthodox Socialist view of the day that

> Mexico was a backward country with only incipient industrialism and a largely "feudal" countryside. Socialism was not immediately attainable, but would need a long process of progressive economic development. Their aim, therefore, was to change the government and then engage in a protracted democratic struggle that would progress in tandem with industrialization.[31]

The dynamics of Magonismo thought, fractured and reconstituted within the interplay of class struggle, the cross-border experience, and the political and cultural exchange with US radical organizations, eventually underwent another political split within the group over this period. While sharing the proletarian orientation of the radical PLM, the Socialists within the ranks of the junta begin to diverge in their analysis of the character of the revolution. PLM leaders such as Antonio Villareal, Antonio Díaz Soto y Gama, and Juan and Manuel Sarabia, believed that the predominantly agricultural character of Mexican society and the small and politically underdeveloped industrial working class made the potential for the transition to socialism impossible under existing conditions.

This divergent class analysis that separated radicals into "reform" and "revolutionary" socialist camps was occurring internationally, pressurized under the weight of historic events. By 1911, the reform-oriented Socialists in the PLM aligned politically with the majority right wing of the US Socialist Party, the minority Menshevik wing of the Russian Social Democratic Party, and others.[32] Those that subscribed to the potential for the direct revolutionary transition to socialism, even in underdeveloped capitalist countries, also found themselves in international realignment. Ricardo Flores Magón and the Anarchist Communist wing of the PLM themselves shared a similar ideological outlook with the Industrial Workers of the World, which fully split from the US Socialist Party in 1912, and the Bolshevik wing of the Russian Social Democratic Party, which fully split from the Mensheviks in 1914.[33]

These splits had major implications for the direction of the Mexican Revolution. The Socialists parted ways with the junta and led their supporters into the ranks of the Maderistas, positioning themselves as the left flank of the new government. In general, they supported the notions of modernization embedded within Madero's platform, which called for the mitigation of the excesses of industrial capitalism, the prioritization of national capitalist development, some degree of subordination of foreign interests, the elimination of monopolies and all vestiges of the feudal past, the expansion of secular education, and the right to form unions.[34] Some, like Jesús Flores Magón, Juan Sarabia, and Camilo Arriaga, took official positions within the Madero government, while others found roles in the military or state government offices. Others, such as Antonio Soto y Gama, Manuel Sarabia, Santiago de la Vega, and Lázaro Gutiérrez, continued the work of organizing the working class, even relaunching a rival Liberal Party in Mexico City in an attempt to reclaim the mantel from their former comrades. They also played a role in creating the Casa del Obrero Mundial.[35] With the defeat of the final PLM-led insurrection in Baja California and Chihuahua, many rank-and-file magonistas on both sides of the border resigned themselves to joining or supporting the Madero efforts to topple Díaz.[36]

While the base of support for the group had shrunk considerably as a result of repression and ideological splits, the PLM merged its efforts with the Industrial Workers of the World in 1911. Together they jointly endeavored to lead explicitly anticapitalist insurrections across the border into Baja California and Chihuahua in 1911 and then again in Chihuahua in 1915. More significantly, they collaborated with the IWW and left-wing Socialists in the first comprehensive attempt to organize the Mexican and Mexican American working class into labor unions and revolutionary parties north of the border. In doing so, they fell victim to spasms of state and vigilante repression. During the coinciding events of World War I and the Mexican Revolution, the federal government declared open war on the radical Left on a national scale, while state and vigilante agents followed suit against Mexicans in the border region.

After the second split between the Socialists and Anarchist Communists, only the reconfigured politics of the PLM represented a continued threat to capitalism in Mexico. The breakaway factions aligned with Madero, and later Carranza, Obregón, and Calles; who eventually made accommodations with US capital that allowed for the continuity of US control over the key sectors of the national economy. This is one explanation as to why left-wing magonistas contributed to the creation of the next generation of reconfigured anarchist, Anarcho-syndicalist, and socialist organizations that claimed the PLM mantel, or continued or built on their ideology and traditions in some way.

Librado Rivera [left] – PLM leader and close collaborator of Ricardo Flores Magón who continued to pursue the revolutionary objectives of magonismo long after the group disbanded, with Enrique Flores Magón.

Decline of the PLM

While the 1906 Plan of the PLM served as the template for the 1917 Constitution, in-spired national uprisings, and cultivated a generation of revolutionaries on both sides of the border, Magonismo fell short of the socialist transformation to which it aspired. Three main factors contributed to its demise. While the junta's revolutionary exhorta-tions and bold initiatives were timely and inspired many to carry out heroic feats, the voluntary, secretive, and adventurist character of PLM actions meant that in practice they involved only small numbers and were quickly crushed by state repression. Many of the most capable magonistas were killed during these events.

The group's lack of emphasis on class struggle within the pillars of the capitalist economy, where the working classes are able to translate their collective power into forceful action, meant that they relied on a utopian conception of class consciousness where the moral will to act transcends material realities. As historian Javier Pares Tor-res Parés observes this phenomenon, the "volunteerism" embedded in Magonismo and its "utopian idealism" were not solely the result of ideological failure, but rather a reflexive characteristic of the insufficient development of the proletariat and its own self-consciousness.[37]

Second, the ideological character of the PLM allowed for different and eventually diametric ideological tendencies to persist well beyond their functionality. This led the group to repeatedly fracture into irreconcilable camps until it was whittled down to the point of irrelevance. Infighting and rupture consumed much of the group's resources, while layers of leadership were drawn into other camps and revolutionary groupings as events proceeded.

Lastly, repression took a devastating toll. The PLM leadership was relentlessly pursued across North America by an army of agents, which punctuated the continuity of leadership with long stints of incarceration.

By 1918, it had finally run its course as a lightning rod of the social revolution. Its leading revolutionaries had either been killed on the battlefield; co-opted into the reconfigured bourgeois governments of Madero, Carranza, and Obregón; drawn into the agrarian movement of Zapatismo; or, as in the case of Ricardo Flores Magón and his most consistent collaborators Librado Rivera, Anselmo L. Figueroa, and his brother Enrique Flores Magón, extinguished in North American prisons until death or deported after long sentences.[38] As a result, the group could no longer carry out basic functions. Ricardo Flores Magón himself died in Leavenworth Prison under controversial circumstances in 1922. Despite failure, the PLM's ongoing analysis of events and strategic assessments proved the most prescient, the revolutionary character of their ideological line the most consistent, the loyalty and dedication of its adherents the most selfless and unwavering, and their influence the most enduring. Additionally, their appeal for their supporters in the United States to join unions and radical organizations ushered in the first significant convergence of Mexican workers and the US Left.

The PLM cultivated a network of radical activists in the US involved in the struggle against Jim Crow capitalism, which is the starting point for understanding the birth of mexicano radicalism in the US. The PLM became openly anticapitalist, and the message emanating from the pages of *Regeneración* spoke more directly to the experiences and aspirations of the urban working class and agricultural proletariat. As one editorial proclaimed, "We need to take possession of the factories, the mines, the smelters . . . instead of abandoning our tools and crossing our arms . . . my brothers let's continue to work but not for the bosses but for ourselves and our families."[39] As Josef Barton concludes: "The movement's legacy—a model of ideology, a corps of leaders, and a resource of organization—bridged the activism of the early twentieth century and the rebirth of radicalism in the 1930s."[40] As a result of their role in this formative revolutionary period, they can best be understood as the progenitor of modern labor radicalism among Mexican workers on both sides of the border.

Chapter 10
The US Socialist Party, Race, and Immigration

"The chief boast of Socialism has been its brotherliness. It disregards national boundaries, pays very little attention to patriotism, insists upon class consciousness, proposes a war against private property in all quarters, and makes internationalism its basis."
—**"Socialists and Immigration," US newspaper editorial, 1910**

The founding of the Socialist Party in 1901 represented the unification of diverse tendencies within the Marxist tradition alongside other social-reform-oriented elements that coalesced into a national party to vie for leadership and influence within the US working class. Over the course of the next decade, the party fractured into different camps over the fundamental political questions of the day. A divergent range of opinion emerged over the party's position on racial oppression, labor immigration, and the character of colonialism. Different camps emerged at the extremes, with a more conservative Right favoring an electoral orientation toward white, native-born male workers in craft-based trade unions in the American Federation of Labor; and a radical Left looking to organizing the great masses of "unskilled" workers into industrial unions that transcended racial, national, and gender lines. These distinctions had significant implications for how Socialists viewed or related to Mexican workers in the Southwest.

As the exploitation of race and gender divisions and the manipulation of restrictive immigration policy became central features of class rule, majority sentiment within the Socialist Party leadership proved incapable or unwilling to stand against the rising tide of exclusion and subjugation structured into class relations. Nevertheless, the socialist movement was neither monolithic nor limited to purely electoral aspirations. Some affiliated unions, branches, and individual leaders took action independently and struck significant blows against the divides that inhibited industrial labor organization. The advent of the Mexican revolutionary process brought the issues of US imperialism, Mexican labor migration, and potential for international solidarity to the forefront of party discourse, which further solidified difference and contributed to splitting the Socialist Party into distinct reformist and revolutionary camps.

Early Socialist History on Race and Class
The launch of the First International Workingmen's Association (IWA) chapter in the US occurred when the German-led Communist Club of New York affiliated as the first branch of the England-based organization in 1867. The club was founded in 1857

by German working-class immigrants who were veterans of the defeated 1848 revolution and partisans of the principles of Karl Marx and Friedrich Engels' *Communist Manifesto*. As early as 1858, for instance, the Communist Club declared their support for all workers and stated that they recognized "no distinction as to nationality or race, caste or status, color or sex."[1]

Their efforts to build an international, anticapitalist working-class movement across borders mirrored the internationalization of capital and the recognition that workers needed radical ideological orientation and political coordination in the movement for socialism. Unlike the utopian socialist, who promoted socialism as an ideal attained through various stages of educational enlightenment, the first scientific socialists understood that it could only be attained through class struggle. An early Marxist periodical written in 1869 promoted scientific socialism to a US audience, explaining class struggle as follows:

> The struggle for mastery . . . is necessarily a class struggle, a struggle between the proprietary and the non-proprietary class. The interests between these two classes being diametrically opposed, a class struggle is inevitable. Nothing is so important as to keep clear the class character of the movement. When a laborer realizes that he can only permanently improve his condition by improving the condition of his class, and realizes what his class interests are and how they can be advanced, he is said to be class-conscious. When he becomes class-conscious, he recognizes the class struggle and takes his stand with the class of which he is a member. A recognition of this fact of class antagonisms on the part of the whole working class and a united political action would enable them to master the public powers and put an end to capitalistic exploitation.[2]

A second principle was internationalism. This stressed that workers had common cause against the capitalist class, which operated as an international class but asserted its own territorial domination by promoting "bourgeois nationalism." Acquiescence to this form of nationalism weakened class consciousness, as workers subsumed and confounded their own class interests with those of the capitalist through the abstraction of the "nation," i.e., the established rule of the bourgeoisie. "National consciousness" served to align the working class with the capitalist's wars abroad, which led the worker to kill other workers for the enrichment of the capitalist and to be susceptible to other divisive and destructive facets of bourgeois ideology, such as racism and chauvinism. The proletariat, it was argued, shared a similar international character that necessitated their unity across national, racial, and cultural boundaries. As the founding convention of the First International proclaimed:

> [T]he emancipation of labor is neither a local nor a national, but a social problem, embracing all countries in which modern society exists . . . this International Association and all societies and individuals adhering to it, will acknowledge truth, justice, and morality, as the basis for the conduct toward each other, and toward all men, without regard to color, creed, or nationality . . . This Association is established to afford . . . cooperation between working men's societies

existing in different countries, and aiming at the same end . . . the protection, advancement, and complete emancipation of the working classes.[3]

Class struggle and internationalism and were the unifying tendencies of the First International, which set out to establish socialist affiliates on a global scale.

The first Marxist socialists in the United States put the abolition of slavery at the forefront of their agitation.[4] Marx observed in the United States at the conclusion of the Civil War:

> The workers in North America have at last fully understood that white labor will never be emancipated so long as black labor is still stigmatized; and later repeated in *Capital* . . . every independent movement of the workers was paralyzed so long as slavery disfigured a part of the Republic. Labor cannot emancipate itself in the white skin when in the black it is branded.[5]

While the victory of the North in the Civil War led to the end of chattel slavery, it created a large, impoverished and dispossessed black proletariat. The rapprochement between Northern industrial capitalists and the Southern plantation owners and the subsequent demise of Reconstruction preserved, reconfigured, and reconsolidated white supremacist governance across the South. The legal framework of Jim Crow was reimposed through state-sanctioned racial violence and terrorism across the South from the 1870s to the 1930s.[6]

Racism persisted beyond slavery, as it served as the ruling ideological means to continue the social and political degradation of labor in order to maximize exploitation of a racially heterogeneous workforce. The black proletariat, subjugated as racially "inferior," meant in practice that black wages, living, and working conditions could be artificially suppressed, creating in turn a threshold by which to hold down the wages and living standards of white labor through direct competition.[7] Under conditions of economic crisis, inequality, labor militancy, and war, racism and existing state or employer-enforced structural divisions could be manipulated to prevent unionization, solidarity, and other forms of combination between different racial groups within the working class, to prevent their collective action.

In the western and southwestern United States, the black/white racial dichotomization of the labor force contextualized the further hierarchical substratification of indigenous, Asian, and Mexican labor.[8] For capital, this allowed the manipulation of one "race" against the other, to keep the class divided against itself, in competition, and thereby disorganized and less capable to engage class struggle. Racialization was further elaborated into national, cultural, and gender-based distinctions as women, immigrants, and diverse linguistic and national groups entered in larger numbers into the US working class.

In the United States, the IWA became the first agglomeration of groups with different trajectories and overlapping interests based on challenging the capitalist system. This included radical abolitionists agitating for full equality, integration, and land redistribution to uplift the black population in the aftermath of Civil War, immigrant German workers versed in Marxism with revolutionary experience in their homeland, and Irish workers with fresh memories of opposition to British colonialism and capitalist exploitation in Ireland. It also included northern trade unionists who had opposed slavery and advocated for expanding unions and labor's power nationwide alongside and in conflict with capitalist expansion into the south and west.[9]

Despite early attempts to unify the broad elements of the International Workingmen's Association in the US, the groups factionalized over the questions of race and gender. This occurred for two reasons. According to historian Philip Foner, after the victory of the union in the Civil War, early Marxists believed the rapid spread of industrialization would accelerate the revolutionary showdown between capital and labor. Since black workers were marginal to the industrial economy until World War I, their specific issues were considered secondary.[10]

The second and more significant factor involved the accommodation to the rightward political shift that occurred with the defeat of Reconstruction and the revitalization of white supremacy as a governing and social-economic sorting mechanism. Political persuasion and practice on the issue of racial unity varied between regions and locals of the IWA, akin to Left and Right tendencies, but the issue as a national priority receded into the background. Nevertheless, as Foner concludes, "the fact remains that American socialism emerged from the crucial years of Reconstruction without the semblance of a meaningful policy for black Americans and without providing any guidance on the Negro question for American socialism in the future."[11] The International suffered a series of splits internationally and nationally between 1872 and 1876 that led to its demise. In 1889, existing socialist and workers' parties took up the Marxist mantel, once again forming the Socialist International, also known as the Second International. By the turn of the twentieth century this produced a merger of smaller socialist parties into the Socialist Party of America.

The Socialist Party on Racism

The Socialist Party formed in 1901 in an attempt to unite different socialist groups into a genuine national, working-class party in line with the Marxist Second International. A broad range of political tendencies merged into the party at its inception, drawing in Marxists and non-Marxists alike, populists, reformers of all stripes, and revolutionaries.[12] Despite its heterogeneity, prominent radicals shaped its early character. One hundred delegates, representing 6,500 socialists gathered at the first convention in Indianapolis in 1901, launched the party and became the "first socialist organization to claim a clear majority of native-born members."[13]

At its first convention, the subject of racial oppression, particularly that of black workers in the South, was taken up in a way it hadn't been before. The proletarianization of ten million black people and the conscious ploy of capitalists to use race as a means to segregate workers, play groups against each other to prevent unions and break strikes, and foster competition between different racial groups pushed the issue into the center of socialist circles by the turn of century. The convention delegates agreed with the general premise that the capitalist class exploited the black working class for their own gain, but divided on the question of its centrality to the socialist cause. Thinking on the subject diverged into three general tendencies that stayed consistent through the party's first two decades of existence.

In debating the "Negro Question," the Left was represented by the three African American delegates: William Costley, a minister from San Francisco; and John W. Adams and Edward D. McKay, coal miners from Indiana. In the resolution, they argued that black workers held a "peculiar position" within the working class, that the capitalist class fostered "color prejudice and race hatred between the white worker and the black, so as to make their social and economic interests to appear to be separate and antagonistic." This included "the persecution of innocent members of the race, their severe punishment for trivial offenses, their lynching, burning and disfranchisement."

Furthermore, they resolved that the Socialist Party "assure our negro fellow worker of our sympathy with him in his subjection to lawlessness and oppression, and also assure him of the fellowship of the workers who suffer from the lawlessness and exploitation of capital in every nation." Lastly, the party resolved to "declare to the negro worker the identity of his interests and struggles with the interests and struggles of the workers of all lands, without regard to race or color or sectional lines" and to take special measures to "invite the negro to membership."[14]

Figures on the right wing of the party, such as founding member and later Socialist Party congressman Victor Berger, generally opposed the resolution on the basis of philosophical disagreement. Berger was well-known for his racist views, publishing articles in his paper, the *Social Democratic Herald*, extolling the virtues of white supremacist theory.[15] He opposed the resolution on the basis that it would alienate potential white voters in the US South, and emphasized an economistic approach compatible with racism. He and other white supremacists in the party were satisfied with the removal of the clause condemning racist persecution and lynching.

In the center of the debate were leading figures like Morris Hillquit, who posited that class struggle and worker emancipation were central, and that questions of race were secondary. As he stated, there is no reason "for singling out the negro race especially . . . than for singling out the Jews or Germans or any other nationality, race or creed here present."[16] Color blindness became the mantra of the party's center and the dominant position until 1912. During those years, leading members of the party continued to fight it out politically within the party and through its press.

Eugene Debs, for instance, saw racial oppression as an onerous and despicable feature of capitalism. In an article entitled "The Negro in the Class Struggle," he condemned the presence of racists within the Socialist Party, scathingly recounted and condemned the long and continued history of barbaric violence against black people as a "crime without a parallel," and concluded:

> Socialists should with pride proclaim their sympathy with and fealty to the Black race, and if any there be who hesitate to avow themselves in the face of ignorant and unreasoning prejudice, they lack the true spirit of the slavery-destroying revolutionary movement.

Nevertheless, within the same article he called for the revocation of the "Resolution of the Negro Question," claiming "we have nothing to offer the negro, and we cannot make separate appeals to all the races."[17] Racism, he surmised, existed as a byproduct of the class system that would only vanish after the transition to socialism. Still, other members like Hubert Harrison, W. E. B. Du Bois, A. Philip Randolph, and Caroline Pemberton argued eloquently against this position and fervently appealed to the party to prioritize the organization of black workers and to fight Jim Crowism, but they encountered intransigent opposition from the party's right wing and passive disinterest from its center.

The contradictory development of the Socialist Party inhibited its ability to take decisive action on the question of racism within the working class. In his exhaustive investigation into the ideological origins of the Socialist Party, Anthony Esposito identifies an amalgamation of "producer ideology" with elements espousing orthodox interpretations of Marxism as a doctrine of class-struggle Marxism.[18] Producer ideology was grounded in a populist variant of "American Exceptionalism," which believed US political institutions to be uniquely and inherently democratic and independent of the class conflict rooted in economic relations. According to the early socialist proponents of this view, the political system had been corrupted by monopoly capitalism but maintained the capacity to be restored to a previously harmonious state.

Grounded in romantic notions of a pre-industrial, egalitarian democracy driven by an active citizenry, this conservative element within the party maintained a single-minded focus on a purely electoral strategy to achieve state power. It took socialists to see the corruption wrought by capitalists, and to wage a tireless political struggle to wrest control of the economy from the band of barons who had hijacked it. Once the seat of power was gained by the party, monopoly capitalism could be dismantled in the interest of creating a cooperative and egalitarian socialist society, reminiscent of a pre-industrial golden era. Even as class struggle at the point of production increased during their first years of existence,

> The Socialist Party leadership . . . did not draw the conclusion that intensified industrial conflict heightened class consciousness or that unions could be a key source of socialism. Instead, it continued to endorse the theory that class consciousness arose from the political struggles of the party while unionism gave rise only to immediate economic demands or, at best, labor parties.[19]

The left wing of the Socialist Party did see industrial class struggle at the point of production as the fulcrum for class consciousness, and an epicenter for the battle for class supremacy as transcending the electoral arena. Those socialists inclined to this outlook tended to be labor organizers and workers in the heavy industries where the great masses of the "unskilled" were concentrated, and where black, Mexican, Asian, and Native American workers comprised a substantial part of the workforce. For these socialist union organizers and workers, the application of the Marxist principle of "workers of all countries unite" was not a rhetorical debate or purely philosophical exercise. It was the precondition for defeating the employers. Within the nexus of race and labor, the politics of immigration also divided the Socialist Party.

The Socialist Left crystallized politically and organizationally around a series of fundamental questions, which included the orientation toward black workers and, by extension, other groups of workers of color. In 1905, the Socialist Left played a leading role in the creation of the Industrial Workers of the World (IWW). The IWW took a bold approach to organizing all workers into industrial unions, effectively breaking out from and eventually counterposing itself to the racial ambiguity of the Socialist Party. As Ahmed Shawki describes,

> The IWW vigorously opposed racism in all of its publications, and its unflinching opposition to all forms of discrimination was not only verbal. Unlike some unions before and since, the IWW practiced what it preached, even in the southern states. The Wobblies, as IWW members called themselves, launched an impressive campaign to recruit Black workers in 1910, and at no time in its history did the IWW organize a segregated union.[20]

The black-white dichotomy of racism that employers used to regulate labor then carried over into the debate within the Socialist Party over labor migration.

Colonialism, Imperialism, and Immigration

Starting in the first decade of the twentieth century, the political representatives of the capitalist class constructed further racial categories as a means to control and determine the employment, movement, and settlement of different immigrant labor groups. They also learned to take advantage of the interplay between racism and the construction of labor migration as a threat, in order to sow conflict between different racial, national, and ethnic groups. For example, black migration was used to discourage white support for ending slavery. According to an article in the pro-slavery *New York Herald* on the eve of the Civil War,

> If Lincoln is elected today, you will have to compete with the labor of four million emancipated slaves. His election is but the forerunner of the ultimate dissolution of the Union. The North will be flooded with free negroes and the labor of the white man will be depreciated and degraded.[21]

Racial dynamics further fused with the immigration restriction of Chinese workers after 1882 and Japanese workers after 1907. The government's entanglement of race and immigration with labor posed a fundamental question to the Socialist Party, engendering a rift that shaped the party's approach to Mexican labor.

In the second half of the nineteenth century, immigration had been increasing in relation to the deeper penetration and expansion of capitalism on a global scale through the agency of colonialism and imperialism. Western European powers and the United States expanded their empires into Eastern Europe, Asia, and Latin America. The export of capital, the flood of imports and people, and the commoditization and privatization of land typically resulted in systematic dispossession, de-industrialization, and the disruption of local economies. Colonial "citizenship," the integration of transportation networks between imperialist centers and subject nations, and the increased demand for labor at the center incentivized the creation of formal and informal transnational operations to transfer colonial and subject populations and reconstruct them as labor armies. The immigrant workers then served as a "reserve army of labor" that satisfied demand for surplus labor during economic booms but was also used to pressure wages downward during periods of overproduction as native-born workers were forced to compete with migrant labor for fewer available jobs. As Karl Marx theorized,

> The main purpose of the bourgeois in relation to the worker is, of course, to have the commodity labor as cheaply as possible, which is only possible when the supply of this commodity is as large as possible in relation to the demand for it.[22]

Furthermore, racial, national, and cultural divisions were fostered by capitalists to prevent or break union organization.

By the outbreak of World War I, socialists were most heavily concentrated in the imperialist centers of Europe and North America, while most of Asia, Africa, and Latin America were either colonies or within the imperialist sphere of influence of Europe or the United States. Second International Socialists were hostile to capitalist imperialism, but they were divided on the question of the character of colonialism and imperialism in relation to nations and people where capitalism was underdeveloped. On this question, turn-of-the-century Marxists took their cue from the *Communist Manifesto*, which characterized capitalism as a destructive, yet modernizing force in the colonies, disrupting the pre-capitalist economic systems and ushering in the formation of the proletariat:

> The need of a constantly expanding market for its products chases the bourgeoisie over the entire surface of the globe. It must nestle everywhere, settle everywhere, establish connections everywhere . . . All old-established national industries have been destroyed or are daily being destroyed. They are dislodged by new industries, whose introduction becomes a life and death question for all civilized nations, by industries that no longer work up indigenous material, but raw material drawn from the remotest zones; industries whose products are consumed, not only at home, but in every quarter of the globe . . . The bourgeoisie, by the rapid improvement of all instruments of production, by the immensely facilitated means of communication, draws all, even the most barbarian, nations into civilization.[23]

Marx later modified his position on the character of imperialism in colonized and pre-capitalist countries. In his writings, observations, and activism, he came to understand colonial populations as indispensable allies of the proletariat in the imperialist nations, and revolt against colonialism and imperialism as inherently progressive steps strengthening the international revolutionary movement.[24] Nevertheless, this more advanced internationalist outlook toward the colonial struggle did not become widely embraced until the Bolshevik Revolution.[25] Until then, political attitudes toward colonized people were divided. In the US the dominant perspective within the Socialist

Party expounded upon the manifesto's earlier interpretation, which viewed immigrants from colonial or underdeveloped nations as "uncivilized," lacking in class consciousness, and immune to the basic precepts of scientific socialism and trade unionism.

Reflecting this position were nearly half of the delegates to the Second International's 1907 conference in Stuttgart, Germany, who signed on to a convention platform that supported the maintenance of colonies as necessary for the modern industrial capitalist system to sustain itself. They promoted colonialism as a progressive pathway to "civilization" in underdeveloped regions. The Left's position, which narrowly won, opposed "capitalist colonial policy" that "destroys the wealth" of colonized countries, while "enslaving and impoverishing the native peoples as well as waging murderous and devastating wars."[26] The left-wing Socialists at the conference were also successful at passing a resolution that called on all Socialist affiliates to oppose racial exclusions and restrictions on immigrants coming into their countries. While the right-wing-dominated leadership of the Socialist Party in the United States passed a resolution that same year to stand for equal civil rights for all, regardless of race or nationality, they chose to ignore the International's call and proceeded to support anti-Asian immigration restrictions.[27] This put them on closer footing with the AFL and, in varying degrees, with the mainstream of the two capitalist parties.

Left-wing Socialists like W. E. B. Du Bois, who soon left the party, criticized the accommodation to anti-immigrant and racist sentiment. In 1911, he linked anti-Asian racism vis-à-vis immigration policy to anti-black racism embodied in Jim Crow, stating that

> [t]he Negro race will not take kindly to Socialism so long as the International Socialist movement puts up bars against any race, whether it be yellow or black. If Socialism is to gain the confidence of the Negro and get him to join the Socialist Party, it will have to begin by changing its attitude toward the yellow races. The ban upon Asiatic labor . . . will have to be repealed.[28]

Left-wing Socialists like "Big" Bill Haywood, who was a mine labor organizer on the national executive leadership of the party, condemned all immigration restrictions on principle. Historian Joseph Conlin called him the "consummate internationalist" who opposed all forms of racial prejudice and "reinforced by his rudimentary Marxism . . . condemned war based on national differences and interests."[29] After he helped found the IWW, he frequently restated that the "Workers of the World" in the name meant all workers, including immigrants. As a labor organizer and mass leader with the IWW, Haywood and others put these principles into practice through their methods of organizing, including uniting different ethnic and national groups into common unions.

The more conservative forces within the party chose to focus on the American Federation of Labor, seeking to build a base for socialism among predominantly white craft workers. While Samuel Gompers had roots in the early socialist movement, he and the other like-minded elements in the federation had made a decisive break with radical politics and acclimated to working within a framework of capitalism. Under the mantra "pure-and-simple unionism," the AFL leadership rejected the idea of class struggle and employed a reformist outlook that built upon earlier "producerist" notions of "American exceptionalism" as well as a capitulation to institutionalized racism.

They maintained the idea that the state was inherently neutral and that the interests of the white craft unions could attain legitimacy by aligning with "national" interests; i.e., class collaboration with those aspects of domestic and foreign policy for which they could derive material benefit. This trajectory led the AFL leadership to move into alignment with the capitalist class in its virulent opposition to socialism, labor internationalism, and industrial unionism. The conservatizing AFL bureaucracy gradually carved out a "labor position" within the stream of bourgeois politics, which included support for racially exclusive immigration policy. While this alone did not garner unconditional support from the capitalist class, which continued to actively oppose all forms of unionization, it did lead them to temporarily tolerate AFL unions as a practical alternative to radical unions like the IWW when they got a foothold within their industries.

While AFL unions continued to grow in periods of explosive worker militancy, they were also able to benefit by assisting in efforts to break strikes by their radical rivals. Their position as a conservative union federation made them a more attractive option to employers when working-class radicalism gained momentum and could not be stopped by traditional means. This earned the AFL unions a recurring role and relevance in the cyclical upturns of class struggle, especially in the service of Democratic Party politicians as they sought out the electoral allegiance of white craft workers as a bulwark against the Left challenge from the Socialists.

The AFL's first signficant foray into politics transpired with the publication of the 1906 "Labor's Bill of Grievances," a letter that outlined a raft of policy proposals endorsed by 117 union representatives and signed by the AFL Executive Council.[30] Representing the AFL's first overt act of submission to bourgeois political strategy through lobbying, the letter articulated the possibility for far-reaching class collaboration in exchange for mild reform. Happening concurrently with the rise of radical unionism and the emergence of the IWW, it signaled to the US capitalist class the possibility for conservative labor partnership against a potential rising tide of labor struggle and the growth of the Socialist movement.

Furthermore, the AFL leadership officially endorsed the bourgeois conception of "white nationhood," an emerging notion that associated radicalism and anticapitalism with foreign and non-European workers. Endorsing the exclusion of Chinese immigrants, the AFL articulated the idea that both American workers and capitalists had a common interest in excluding the Chinese; in fact the letter called for more restrictive measures.[31] This approach earned the AFL executive leadership a hearing at the top levels of government, as they were granted audiences with Presdident Theodore Roosevelt, president of the Senate Joseph Frye, and House Speaker Joseph Cannon.

Within one year, the AFL had become a national champion of immigration restriction. The 1907 convention of the AFL conveyed the hardening attitude of nativism within the AFL leadership, now in line with US government policy. Resolution number 53 read:

American public sentiment against the immigration of Chinese labor, as expressed and crystallized in the enactment of the Chinese Exclusion Act, finds still stronger justification in demanding prompt and adequate measures of protection against the immigration of Japanese and Korean labor on the grounds (1) that the wage and living standard are dangerous to and must, if granted recognition in the United States, prove destructive of the American standards in these essential respects; (2) that a racial incompatibility, as between the people of the Orient and the United States, presents a problem of race preservation which it is our imperative duty to solve in our own favor, and which can only be thus solved by a policy of exclusion[.][32]

This coincided with the rise of an extremist anti-Asian movement, which linked support from the two bourgeois parties, middle-class associations such as the Japanese and Korean Exclusion League, and now the white craft unions of the AFL. Resolution 53 coincided with the "Gentlemen's Agreement" with Japan of 1907, a federal anti-Japanese initiative to further cut off all Asian migration across the Pacific.

By 1908, the dominant right wing of the Socialist Party was coalescing with the AFL on its policies of immigration restriction. Using the language of class struggle, the restrictionists blasted immigration as a tool of the bosses to undermine the union movement, as workers from "backward" countries were accustomed to less-developed material conditions and could be easily lured into breaking strikes and organizing drives. While voices on the Left of the party contested the nativism, they remained in a minority. The national organization remained divided on the issue until the 1910 convention, when it swung even more sharply to the right. By the 1910 convention, the divisions between majority nativist sentiment and the principled internationalists broke out into the open with the former gaining the upper hand. As Charles Leinenweber describes,

The committee report and the statements supporting it are prime examples of racism and nativism couched in left-wing rhetoric. Orientals should be excluded, the report stated, because their "backwardness" makes them "a menace to the progress of the most aggressive, militant and intelligent elements of our working class population." Oriental immigration would relegate "the class war to the rear . . ." by weakening labor organizations and increasing race conflict.[33]

Another resolution by Morris Hillquit skirted the issue of race but reiterated opposition to workers from poor countries based on the preconceived notion that they were ignorant pawns of the bosses. His resolution called for the prevention of the "immigration of strikebreakers and contract laborers, and the mass importation of workers from foreign countries, brought about by the employing classes for the purpose of weakening the organization of American labor, and of lowering the standard of life of American workers."[34] By avoiding discourse on race and focusing on national origin, the centrists assisted the right wing in moving the party into closer alignment with the AFL. This closed the party door on most immigrant and migrant workers and amplified white nationalism within the party. This led the national organization to largely ignore the condition and plight of Asian and Mexican workers in the West. As Ira Kipnis explains:

> They were not encouraged to join the party, and socialist agitation among them was carried on by independent [. . .] socialist organizations . . . And the immigration controversy which developed in 1907 and continued through 1912 indicated that a good proportion of the party, anxious to win the support of the A.F. of L. leaders, had no desire for immigrants in the country, much less in the party.[35]

This was aided by an initiative led by right and centrist elements after 1910 to expand party membership into the middle classes, or, as Morris Hillquit explained, to "transcend the interests of any one class . . . and attract large numbers of men and women from other classes." Among the new influx of middle-class supporters were reform-oriented "ministers, lawyers, editors" and professionals neither versed in Marxism nor interested in class struggle. As William Preston concludes, "large numbers of reform voters had joined the organization, and large numbers of radical working men had left it."[36]

While the Left continued to vie for leadership, the middle-class influx gave the right wing of the party the upper hand by 1912, which began the process of driving out the radical and revolutionary Left. Socialist leaders who were also members of the IWW, such as Big Bill Haywood, were expelled, or left on their own accord. Since this segment of the membership was the bastion of revolutionary internationalism, their gradual exodus enabled a further shift to the right on the question of immigration. The rightward shift also alienated the more radical immigrants in the party. When the thirty thousand members of the party's seven foreign-language federations refused to disavow and oppose the Bolshevik government of Russia, the party expelled them en masse in 1919.[37] Within just a few years, the Socialist Party began to slide into irreversible decline. Many on the left of the party migrated into more radical parties, beginning with the Industrial Workers of the World and later the Communist Party.

US Capital, Imperialism, and Mexican Labor

Mexican migration into the US in the early twentieth century corresponded with meteoric economic growth, especially with the establishment of the railroads, the integration of the Southwest into the national economy, and the influx of eastern and international capital into extractive industries. Modern corporations, legislated and adjudicated into existence in the late 1800s, were the midwives of expansive capitalist growth. They quickly established monopolization over whole industries and colonized state and local governments while still in their infancy. Between 1897 and 1904, for instance, 318 industrial trusts contained $7 billion in capital and consolidated control of over 5,300 industrial plants within every sector of production.[38] In southwestern industries Mexican labor was favored by the 1870s, and increased as immigration restrictions between 1882 and 1924 stemmed the flow of Asian and European labor.[39] Furthermore, Mexican labor was perceived as docile, pliable, and temporary, as the proximity to the border ensured that many migrants returned (or could be re-turned) and would not take up permanent residency. The perception of Mexicans in the United States began to change with the onset of the Mexican Revolution of 1910, as more workers began to take collective action and join radical movements.

While the importation of labor and industrial growth in the East and Midwest was reaching an equilibrium point, the far west economy encountered disruptive shortages of labor in the first decades of the twentieth century. This dichotomy led to tensions within the capitalist class over the question of immigration, with intentional and deliberate facets aiming to appease different segments of capital with different needs. This came to a head in 1917, when the first comprehensive, restrictive national legislation cut off Mexican migration, by then a lifeline of labor supply for southwest-ern industry.

Mexican migration into the United States was unregulated and flowed in rhythm with industrial demand for labor in the Southwest. Agricultural, railroad, and mining operators had found Mexican labor useful in the context of economic growth, and federal immigration authorities had overlooked them in their first attempts at com-prehensive regulation. The United States Immigration Commission (known as the Dillingham Commission) was formed in 1907 to study immigration and establish the guidelines for exclusion. With a million-dollar budget, forty-one volumes of research were produced after a four-year study. Mexicans were conspicuously ignored as their labor was considered essential.[40]

Despite their invisibility in immigration discourse, there were other factors in motion that functionally categorized Mexicans as a racially excluded population in practice. Increased Mexican migration occurred during the growing popularity of eu-genic ideology, a pseudo-scientific movement to establish biological white suprem-acy. This movement emanated from within the bourgeois ideological laboratories that were the early twentieth-century elite universities, and was widely embraced by industrial capitalists and won many converts across the political spectrum.[41] Racial heredity theory was first used to establish exclusion and segregation in the military and throughout the education system, and was gradually institutionalized across the public and private sectors of the economy. The popularity of using race theory to ex-clude or limit the citizenship rights of immigrants increased as these same workers gravitated toward radical working-class organizations in large numbers during the sec-ond decade of the twentieth century.

The Dillingham Commission applied eugenic race theory to immigration, which came to influence subsequent policy. A significant economic recession in 1907 sig-nified the slowing down of US industrial expansion, and the intensification of class struggle produced the first radical organizations looking to include Mexican workers in their ranks, especially the Industrial Workers of the World, after its inception in 1905. Between 1907 and 1924 federal policy-makers engineered a volte-face on im-migration, rapidly constructing strict and discriminatory policies of exclusion and ending more than a hundred years of overt inclusion through active recruitment and benign neglect.

The declining rate of northern and western European migration by the late nineteenth century, and an increase in Asian, Mediterranean, and eastern European migration, provided the pretext for elaborating a racial schematic for exclusion. Applying the pseudo-scientific race theories of eugenics to immigration, the Dillingham Commission developed racial categories as the primary basis for restriction. Lumping them together under the moniker of "new immigrants," the commission characterized these groups as racially and culturally defective, incapable of assimilation, and socially undesirable. The Immigration Act of 1917 contained a prohibition on contract labor, the exclusion of all Asian migration, a broad range of health exclusions, and the requirement that future immigrants pass a literacy test and pay a head tax. The result of the legislation was a steep decline in all labor immigration, including from Mexico. When Mexican migration fell by 40 percent within one year, southwestern capitalists immediately cried foul to their allies in Washington, DC. In response, Secretary of Labor William B. Wilson unilaterally issued a revision of the policy, effectively exempting Mexicans from the law's provisions.[42]

The ranks of Mexican workers grew as the exemption was extended through the major immigration acts of 1921 and 1924. During that period, they increased as a percentage of the workforce, becoming preferred by industrialists due to their mobility, availability, and now institutionalized lower "Mexican wage." Accounting for this apparent contradiction between the racialization of immigration restriction on the one hand, and the increasing Mexican composition of the workforce on the other, the congressional representatives of capital inverted racist logic to justify their actions. As the Dillingham Commission noted:

> The Mexican immigrants are providing a fairly acceptable supply of labor in a limited territory in which it is difficult to secure others . . . [T]heir incoming does not involve the same detriment to labor conditions as is involved in the immigration of other races who also work at comparatively low wages. While the Mexicans are not easily assimilated, this is not of very great importance as long as most of them return to their native land after a short time.[43]

In fact, it was widely believed that Mexicans' "inferior mental traits" made them ideal workers, as agricultural growers, cannery operators, mine operators, and other economic interests testifying before the Dillingham Commission asserted that Mexicans were akin to beasts of burden. In fact, a sociological study widely disseminated among the boosters of eugenics claimed that Mexican children did not intellectually develop past the age of twelve, thus making them ideally suited for manual labor.[44] Support for this approach was self-serving for their economic interests. They could keep the spigot of migrant labor from Mexico open, but also set the stage for later restriction or expulsion if and when necessary.

As long as Mexicans provided essential and cheap labor and returned to Mexico when not needed, they were not viewed as a substantive threat. The rate of migration accelerated during the Mexican Revolution of 1910–1920, as significant numbers crossed the border fleeing the conflict and economic displacement. The substantial increase in migration from Mexico altered the landscape of border politics. Among the thousands crossing the border were political exiles aligned with revolutionary factions, effectively carrying revolutionary sentiment across the border. The growth of radical mexicano political movements in Mexico, and the extension of that radicalism among Mexicans in the US evoked panic among the capitalist class, who now saw in Mexicans the specter of anticapitalism. In this regard, Mexican workers also captured the attention of the US Left for the first time, who were now witnessing a revolution unfolding on their southern doorstep.

The Employers' Offensive and Class War from Above

There was significant growth in AFL trade unions between the years 1898 and 1903, as the US industrial economy expanded rapidly and with it the demand for skilled labor. With their bargaining power enhanced, workers were able to compel the major sectors of industry through strikes to temporarily accept the presence of unions within their midst.[45] For instance, the number of strikes, primarily for union recognition, increased from 1,098 in 1898 to a pre–World War I high point of 3,648 in 1903.[46] Over the same period, the ranks of the AFL swelled from 278,000 in 1898 to 1,876,000 in 1904.[47] This explosive upsurge in struggle and growth didn't last, however. A confluence of factors shifted the initiative to the capitalist class, which set out to crush the unions and all forms of political resistance to the emerging industrial order.

Intensified one-sided class war exposed the limitations of exclusionary craft unionism, and government-led repression of the labor movement dispelled notions of a neutral state that could be harnessed through the election of socialists, which could then set out to peacefully dismantle capitalism. The intensity of class struggle, especially the significant advances among the western mine workers, showed that workplace struggle does indeed produce class consciousness and militant advocacy for socialism.

The AFL model of craft union organization and the gradualist reformism of the Socialist Party leadership became questioned and directly challenged. Militant sections of the working class and Socialist Left became frustrated by the failure to organize and wield the full spectrum of class power, especially in the face of employer opposition and state complicity. The language of class struggle itself began to change, with "republican producerist" notions of democratic reformism being replaced by the permanency of class and "wage slavery." As Anthony Esposito explains,

> The vision of the worker this ideology held most dear was that of the skilled and propertied producer exercising his independence at the ballot box to redeem himself from servitude. It was not an image that the industrial worker, mostly unskilled, propertyless, immigrant and non-voting, fit very neatly.[48]

As the party reached a crossroads, in either orienting toward the vast unorganized ranks of largely immigrant industrial workers or, for segments of the middle class, becoming disillusioned with the two capitalist parties, the leadership chose the latter much to the chagrin of the minority left wing. In this breach, left-wing socialists helped launch Industrial Workers of the World (IWW) in 1905 as a means to organize all workers across racial, national, and gender boundaries; along industrial lines, and against not just one employer, but the capitalist system as a whole. The IWW's official antiracist outlook broke with a long history of hostility or ambivalence toward immigrant and nonwhite workers, representing the US radical Left's first substantial effort at organizing Mexican workers.

By the turn of the century, the structures of the industrial economy changed relations of production, and the fusion of corporate capital and the state became more complete. As the power of the capitalist class increased, the inherent weaknesses of craft unionism became more apparent and self-defeating, as a large and more diverse "unskilled" workforce developed alongside a dwindling "skilled workforce." As industries expanded, employers implemented new techniques for mass production as a means to increase output and gradually grind down as much "skilled work" as possible, and also to grind down craft unions. When the economy began to slow down, with a downturn in 1903 and severe recession in 1907, employers were emboldened to go on the offensive, as skilled labor's negotiating power was greatly weakened.

Beginning as early as 1902, employers went on the offensive nationally, orchestrating a coordinated, no-holds-barred, and relentless drive to eliminate unions from industry. Known as the "open shop drive," employers formed 137 "employers' associations" between 1897 and 1932, through which unmitigated class war and the full power of capitalist America could be unleashed and brought to bear on the labor movement overtly and covertly.[49] The employers were eager to break the workplace control of the craft unions, reorganize production using mechanized, mass-production techniques requiring less-skilled workers, and combat the growth of radical, socialist ideas gaining ground among workers.

The employers' organizations, led by the Chamber of Commerce, the National Association of Manufacturers (NAM), and others relied on several tactics to advance their collective cause. As NAM president David Parry stated in his 1906 address to leading industrialists: "Only a few years ago trades unionism unrestrained and militant was rapidly forcing the industries of the country to a closed shop basis . . . but a change has come and the Association is largely responsible for it . . . What has brought these changes? The question can be answered in one word—Organization."[50] The broad vision of capitalist-class insurgence was to assert absolute control over the workplace, dismantle organization, and fragment class consciousness, which rose in tandem with class struggle. For this, the employers developed a multifaceted approach.

First and foremost was the introduction of new systems of "factory administration" and "scientific techniques" to replace skilled workers with unskilled labor as means to degrade the crafts. As a bulwark against worker-controlled unions, capitalists preempted organizing drives by forming management-controlled company unions. The pseudo-unions created the veneer of worker participation in determining workplace conditions, but in practice they were used to divide workers into individual units and prevent collective action. Typically, these "unions" prohibited strikes, assigned privileges to loyal workers, set up toothless grievance processes on an individual basis, and served as a bully pulpit for management diktats. Another tactic was the creation of a vast network of labor spies, with an estimated two hundred thousand in operation by 1928, and a central reserve system for the joint procurement of strikebreakers in the event of a strike.[51] Perhaps most significantly, corporate capital could increasingly rely on direct intervention from the state, which would be on their side, with the passage of a stream of anti-labor legislation. Easy access to judicial injunctions and other rulings became handy weapons for debilitating union action.

One key strategy of state-capitalist coordination developed through the use of immigration policy to serve the needs of capitalist enterprise. Immigration law became a malleable and often contradictory set of policies that has remained permanently nestled in the orbit of political economy. Immigrant workers were enticed into the US, while a web of race and class-based restrictions and exclusions was elaborated to determine the substance of citizenship once inside the country. Through the legal establishment of racial citizenship and immigrant exclusions, employers manipulated and differentiated workers in ways that increased profits directly and indirectly. The significant wealth accrued through the dual-labor segmentation of the workforce, leading to the substandard black, Mexican, immigrant, or woman's wage, was itself part of a larger cycle within the capitalist political economy.

Racial and immigration policies degraded the social value and limited the democratic rights of large segments of the workforce, who were then excluded from or marginalized within the labor unions (and political parties) of white skilled workers. To further fragment class unity and the potential for larger coordinated working-class action within a heterogeneous working class, employers used the same marginal groups to cross picket lines during strikes or to replace unionized workers. Furthermore, the proportional growth of the unskilled workforce became used in the same way, creating a highly fractured, sectional, internally divided, and politically dysfunctional working class.

By 1906, the leadership of the American Federation of Labor faced resolute capitalist opposition to the union movement. Corporate capital had consolidated its power on a national scale and had begun to wield its influence directly in steering various state and law-enforcement agencies against the labor movement. Within this orbit, a critical mass of middle-class organizations had turned against "class struggle" and was aligning with capital to crush strikes. Rather than embracing a strategy of resistance, the AFL sought accommodation. As Anthony Esposito explains:

> Sensing weakness beneath the growth of his own American Federation of Labor, Gompers sought to legitimize the demands of the craft segment of the working class and avoid the wrath of employers. He did this . . . by playing on the corporations' great desire to avoid unions in the mass production industries. The federation repudiated, through contract agreements with employers and the elimination of sympathy strikes, any further organizing of the larger, mostly new immigrant labor force.[52]

The AFL leadership was faced with an existential threat if it persisted with the same strategy of craft exclusionism and "republican producerism." It could either expand the

struggle to include the growing ranks of previously excluded groups, embrace industrial unionism, and build broad resistance at the point of production; or it could seek
further accommodation with capital. Between the years 1906 and 1908, Gompers and
the majority leadership chose the latter by positioning the labor federation as an official
ally for the Democratic Party, the wing of capital that most fervently embraced white
nationalism. Through this alliance, the labor federation shed any residual pretense of a
socialist orientation or independent class politics, and instead sought accommodation
to bourgeois capitalism in exchange for recognition and legitimacy.

In accommodating to corporate power instead of resisting it, they chose to manage their own subordination to the preeminence of capital. Shunning a class-struggle
orientation, they pursued class-collaborative positions based on the assumption of
shared interests between capital and labor. In doing so, they internalized capitalist
notions of anti-radicalism, racial citizenship, and immigrant exclusions, although
dressing up bourgeois ideology in the language of working-class interest. For its part,
the AFL leadership under Samuel Gompers offered his political guidance as a bulwark against growing radical influences within the labor movement, and maintained
its practice of excluding unskilled industrial workers, immigrants, workers of color,
and women. Despite the illusion of peace through class collaboration at the official
level, the rank-and-file members of the affiliated AFL unions continued to experience
unmitigated class war on the shop floor. By 1908 the number of strikes plummeted
to a low of 315.[53]

The conservative turn of the AFL leadership and general membership toward an
open embrace of class collaboration and national chauvinism had a debilitating effect
on the socialist Left. While many radical abolitionists and early immigrant Marxists
grasped the magnitude of the "race question" as inseparable from the question of class
in the United States, the rightward drift of labor politics pulled much of the Left along
with it. The Socialist Party, the largest Marxist organization in the country by the turn
of the twentieth century, illustrates this pattern. The failure of the first significant wave
of socialist organizing to break the lines of exclusion established by the rising capitalist
class meant that Mexican workers remained largely unorganized and marginalized,
even as their militancy increased significantly.

In the Southwest, the left wing of the socialist movement clarified its commitment to internationalism and antiracism within the context of class struggle alongside
Mexican workers and radical exiles. Left-wing socialists gravitated toward and supported efforts to organize Mexican workers into industrial unions, both within the
AFL where possible and the IWW, and witnessed the militancy and resolve of immigrant and migrant workers. This dismantled the common-held prejudices of their
inherent political backwardness. Furthermore, the observation and cross-fertilization
of political discourse with Mexican radicals who drew from their own distinct political traditions educated the socialist Left on Mexican peoples' traditions and culture,
organizational traditions, and political character. Lastly, the Mexican Revolution was
the first social revolution of the twentieth century, beginning what many believed to
be great ruptures of the international capitalist system. As the revolution proceeded,

the socialist Left in the United States, especially those based in the border states, paid closer attention. By 1907, Socialists had established contact with the PLM and their networks of adherents across the Southwest, laying the foundation for closer collaboration and joint action.

Chapter 11

The Partido Liberal Mexicano
and Socialists in Los Angeles

"[T]he Mexican worker deeply understands socialist doctrines, and for
this reason we are able to organize ourselves in societies of resistance
to confront capital that robs us, stupefies us, and kills us."
—**Libertad y Trabajo**

The arrest of the PLM junta in Los Angeles had international implications. The city's well-organized financial and industrial elite did not want to see a revolution succeed in Mexico, where they had high-stake investments underwritten by the Díaz regime. From the time of their arrival, the Mexican exiles were treated as personae non gratae by an international alliance of forces resolved to remove them from the picture. Despite constant persecution, the PLM established a base in Mexican working-class districts of Los Angeles and extended party branches throughout barrios and rural colonias throughout Southern California. The PLM painstakingly forged together a mass base of adherents through the production of an impressive, widely diffused media network and a tireless cadre of organizers working at all nodes of the transnational organization. From their base in Los Angeles, they had established access to one of the largest populations of Mexicans in the US, many with existing connections to Mexico.

In Los Angeles, they also came in contact with Mexican Socialists, which enabled them to form a relationship with the local, left-wing Socialist Party leadership, which already had some experience organizing Mexican workers into the union movement.[1] Other more practical motivations developed in the context of the realities faced by the exiled PLM leadership. As the US and Mexican governments colluded to silence the PLM leadership through persecution, arrest, and deportation, the PLM formed strategic alliances with their US counterparts on the radical Left for support. Secondly, when the US government threatened a full-scale invasion to defend US investments and to stifle the revolution, PLM leaders understood the urgent need to build a broad anti-intervention campaign through aligning with US anti-imperialist radicals.[2]

For the Socialist Left, Mexican labor militancy and pro-union tendencies demonstrated their potential value as allies for US workers and the radicals attempting to organize them into common unions. Socialists and the PLM also found common cause against US imperialism in Mexico. Not only did the US government prop up the Díaz regime and aid in the repression of revolutionaries, but the export of profits and natural resources ensured the continued outflow of impoverished workers and peasants leveraged by capital north of the border to lower wages.

The left-wing Socialists based in the city had significant local influence within the American Federation of Labor and national connections through the Socialist Party, which had emerged as the third party in US politics. Using their influence, Los Angeles-based Socialists built a national campaign of solidarity and support for the persecuted PLM leadership, which proved invaluable in preventing their deportation and execution in Mexico. The Mexican revolutionary process had a further effect on the US Left, as strikes and revolts in the first decade of the twentieth century culminated in the uprising that involved Mexico's laboring classes in 1910. These convulsions sent shockwaves across the border, not only radicalizing Mexicans and Mexican Americans in the US, but also capturing the imagination of US radicals who were witnessing a thoroughgoing revolution unfold on their doorstep.

Mexican Workers at the Intersection of Industry and Empire

Los Angeles, a one-time Spanish colonia founded by Mexican migrants in 1781, became a familiar destination for thousands of Mexicans moving north to look for work at the turn of the century. By 1900, between three and five thousand Mexican workers and their families had already lived or settled in the barrio Anglos called Sonoratown and the several smaller colonias situated across the city, while a separate, itinerant population lived in temporary urban and agricultural work camps on the outskirts. Further migration rapidly increased the population, more than tripling the barrio population, to about seventeen thousand, by 1916, and also growing the population of migrant and itinerant workers.[3] The population swelled as railroad companies and agricultural interests conducted significant labor recruitment from Mexico via El Paso, Texas. Los Angeles was transformed into a central transportation hub, exporting the region's agricultural production to national and international markets, while simultaneously importing a Mexican workforce to do the labor.

Los Angeles became an industrial upstart and seat of the growing Asian-Pacific US empire by the turn of the twentieth century. The metropolitan elite, a coterie of fiercely class-conscious capitalists, envisioned their city as one that set a new standard for industrial and commercial growth through heavy-handed labor management and unfettered international expansion. Their fortunes were bolstered through the purchase of Mexican land and natural resources, which they jealously guarded in becoming staunch defenders of Porfirio Díaz. To protect their interests, this core group cohered around an autocratic commitment to oppose labor unionism and political radicalism with an iron fist, especially pertaining to the organization or mobilization of the Mexican population. Tightly controlled political organization, free-handed police repression, racial discrimination and anti-immigrant demagoguery, and influence over the legal system were but some of their tools and techniques for waging the class war.

The chief administrator of capitalist class organization was Harrison Gray Otis, the publisher of the *Los Angeles Times*, the largest daily newspaper on the West Coast.

Otis had an extensive background in the service of empire and substantial investments in Mexico, and was a vocal white supremacist. He was a brigadier general in charge of volunteers who assisted in crushing the Filipino independence movement, and later joined in the land grab in Mexico enabled by the policies of Porfirio Díaz. He staunchly advocated for aggressive US interventionism abroad to protect "national interests," i.e., his own, while simultaneously denouncing Mexican and Asian immigration. For instance, the *Los Angeles Times* "cultivated in print the ominous image of Chinese, Japanese, and Mexicans blended into the 'Bronze Menace,' against which white Americans had to stand guard."[4]

Otis coalesced a general staff in the foundation of a fifteen-hundred-member Chamber of Commerce, which united the representatives of the various industrial and financial sectors to orchestrate and implement strategy while mitigating sectional differences and conflicts. Through the Chamber, Otis, with other notables, including railroad magnate Henry Huntington, founded and directed the Merchants and Manufacturers Association (known as M&M), which further subdivided the capitalist class into trade-based groupings that could act in unison.

Otis used the new organization to consolidate opposition to the closed shop. As a means of enforcing its orders, the M&M financed the organization of a right-wing coalition of the most resolute anti-union forces in the city into chapters of the Citizens' Alliance, whose membership of business owners and conservative middle-class people conducted boycotts of businesses and institutions that observed collective bargaining agreements. Seeking to get ahead of the union movement that was much stronger in other parts of the county, these consortia and their boosters formed the ranks of an aggressive, well-organized, and vigilant capitalist class.

On a citywide basis the open-shop coalition required all employers to sign on to the anti-union pledge or face the consequences. To publicize their campaign, media tycoons, led by Otis, formed a newspaper publishers' union between the four daily Los Angeles newspaper editors (from the *Times*, *Herald*, *Express*, and *Tribune*), which coordinated boycotts of those who refused to follow the anti-union pledge and provide mutual support against organized working-class action.

Their industrial ambitions mirrored the methods of the agricultural sector developing in California: to vertically and horizontally integrate the capitalist class in order to plan, manage, and expand industrial development. With quasi-religious fervor, they sought to convert Los Angeles into a model city of growth and rapid profit accumulation. To do this, they needed to attract national and international investors to their project. This vision was predicated on promoting Los Angeles as a union-free, open-shop city with a docile labor force, which ensured low wages and "labor flexibility."[5]

In 1890, the M&M began a campaign to stamp out existing unions, unilaterally imposing 20 percent wage cuts on the printers in his own press in order to provoke a strike and lock out his workers. Otis was able to secure strike replacements from rival, conservative craft printers from San Diego to effectively crush the AFL-affiliated International Typographical Union.[6] This set the stage for the rise of the M&M-led war in which existing union contracts across the city were cancelled following this model.

They fired and blacklisted known union sympathizers, employed strikebreakers to cross picket lines, formed or joined local and national anti-union organizations, became direct benefactors of law enforcement, and saturated the electoral process with their money and representatives. They shaped local, state, and regional politics in their own image, with the maintenance of a docile and compliant labor force as a centerpiece of their plan. If building their industrial empire was contingent on maximizing the exploitation of labor in the city, it was also interdependent with accumulation from their speculative ventures and mutual interests abroad.

Otis and his partners, son-in-law and heir apparent Harry Chandler, as well as multimillionaire speculators Moses H. Sherman and Otto Brant, purchased great swaths of land stretching from Baja California to the Imperial Valley in southeastern California. Their company, called the California-Mexican Land and Cattle Company, "made tremendous profits while enjoying the favor of Mexican President Porfirio Díaz . . . in exchange for favorable reports on the Díaz regime in the *Times*, Otis and his associates enjoyed unfettered business freedom in Baja California."[7] By 1910, for instance, Harrison Gray Otis had bought up over half a million acres in Baja California, William Randolph Hearst had acquired over two million acres of land in Chihuahua, and Harry Huntington was one of the chief investors that sat on the board of directors for the Cananea Copper Company.[8] Profits extracted from Mexican investments also had a secondary effect that worked to their advantage: displacement and labor migration into Los Angeles industries.

Maintaining a large and unorganized population of segregated Mexican workers was a central pillar of their labor control strategy. They could be maintained in the ranks of menial and low-wage labor, and be made to perform supporting tasks in the main industries but kept separate from the white, skilled workforce while always under white supervision. Their employment followed a pattern established by employers in the expanding urban centers across the Southwest, heavily concentrated in the most difficult and demanding labor aspects of construction and industrial agriculture. In construction, they were the hod carriers, wearing shoulder harnesses to move materials on construction sites, ditch diggers and trench diggers, road excavators, tracklayers, and dirt and gravel haulers. Due to the contingent and highly inconsistent nature of their employment, many urban Mexican male workers essentially functioned as temporary laborers, gathering in informal hiring centers to appeal for employment from contractors.[9] Mexican workers also tended to be concentrated in canning and packing, with women forming up to 90 percent of this workforce in California by the 1920s.[10]

Henry Huntington built on his inherited empire and became the largest employer in the city of Los Angeles in the first decade of the twentieth century, employing five thousand workers in rail-line construction, a power company, and in his real estate holdings. At the turn of the century, his pet project, along with other investors, became the establishment of an interurban rail system called the Pacific Electric Highway, which was to provide the primary means of transportation within the growing city.

Huntington had cut his teeth opposing the unionization of rail lines owned by his uncle, Collis Potter Huntington. In the 1894 Pullman strike, he urged his uncle not to negotiate. Instead, with the help of the federal government, the strike was broken after federal troops were sent in to break it under the pretext of ensuring mail delivery. As he gloated to his uncle in the aftermath, "[W]e have not taken an American Railway man [American Railway Union member] back without his first resigned and severing his connection with that organization."[11] Breaking the 1903 Pacific Electric strike was one of the first coordinated efforts of the open-shop movement.

Early Labor Militancy: Mexican Traqueros and the 1903 Pacific Electric Strike

In 1903, nine hundred Mexican laborers formed a AFL-affiliated federal union with the support of the Los Angeles Council of Labor. The council-affiliated Amalgamated Association of Street Car Employees had tried on two previous attempts to organize the Pacific Electric motormen and conductors, but these efforts were defeated by mass firings. As the Mexican construction workers were broadly united in their interest in unionization, council secretary Lemuel Biddle believed future efforts to organize the car men would be strengthened if coordinated strike action were necessary. The union signed up nine hundred workers, with its headquarters located in the Mexican barrio of Sonoratown, near the same central plaza that would become the PLM's base of operation four years later.

From its inauguration, the Unión Federal Mexicanos (Mexican Federal Union) opposed the racial exploitation of its members, who as construction workers were paid at the "Mexican wage" rate of $1–$1.25 per day compared to the $2–$2.50 a day for white workers, and $1.45–$1.75 for immigrant, Asian, and black workers.[12] Within one day of its inception, on April 23, 1903, it declared its intention to negotiate a contract with the rail company. Taking advantage of a forthcoming visit by President Theodore Roosevelt and the urgent pace of work needed to complete the line by his arrival, the Mexican workers demanded pay increases on par with the others. When Huntington personally stonewalled the union demand, seven hundred Mexican workers walked off the job. As Charles Wollenberg describes the context, "The strike occurred at a time when the first great wave of Mexican immigration was sweeping into the Southwest. Labor demands of American railroads were drawing thousands of Mexicans across the border, and el traque, as the immigrants called the railroad, was transporting Mexican workers throughout the country."[13]

In response to the strike, Huntington made arrangements with the local police to arrest Mexican picketers. The company promptly recruited white, black, and Asian workers as strike replacements. They were paid 22 cents an hour, more than what the strikers were demanding, and brought in under direct LAPD protection. Huntington consciously hired different ethnic and national groups, exploiting racial divides and fanning existing antagonisms in order to weaken the threat of unity or spontaneous outbreaks of solidarity. This became significant after a group of Mexican workers from other Huntington-owned lines was also brought in. On April 25, at least thirty Mexican women, primarily the wives of the strikers, "harangued the esquiroles [scabs] to join the fight and marched boldly onto the grade site and wrestled shovels, picks, and tamping irons away from the hands of the strikebreakers."[14] Many joined the strike or left the area. Two days later, another anti-scab procession was organized, this time led by Teresa Urrea (La Santa de Cabora), a popular Mexican spiritual figure and folk hero whose preaching had inspired several failed revolts against the Díaz regime. Invited by the union to encourage unity, she led a procession of thirty-eight women to the work sites, encouraging another fifty Mexican strikebreakers, who put down their tools and joined the strike, swelling the total number of Mexican strikers to fourteen hundred.[15] Despite these disruptions, all line operations were up and running with trucked-in replacement labor by April 27.

The Amalgamated Association of Street Car Employees saw the unity of the Mexican workers as a strategic opportunity to involve and win union recognition for the car operators. On April 29, they called on conductors and motormen to walk off the job and shut down the whole rail line. In the end, only 12 of the 764 workers walked off the job, effectively killing the strike. While the Mexican ranks held strong for several more days, most of the strikers drifted away or found other employment.

In 1910, after a strike by Mexican construction workers at Pacific Electric was defeated once again, Huntington sold the company to the Southern Pacific Transportation Company. The Southern Pacific was one of the largest railroad corporations at the time, with operations extending throughout the US and into Mexico. As the railroad conglomerate's operations in Mexico were supported and subsidized by the Díaz regime, its lobbyists in Washington were staunch defenders of the dictator.

Magonismo Takes Root in the Los Angeles Barrios

When the junta clandestinely resettled in California, they began developing a base of support in the large Mexican barrios of Los Angeles. Devra Weber estimates that at its peak, the PLM had as many as six thousand adherents and supporters in the Los Angeles area alone.[16] Through its press, ranks of adherents, and club structure it developed into the prototype of an international revolutionary party.

While not the only political influence in the Mexican community in the US, the radical ideas of the PLM sunk deep roots within the majority working-class element in this population. Many driven to migrate north as a result of the economic vagaries of the Díaz regime were receptive to the idea that the entrenched dictatorship needed to be deposed. They also saw their conditions of existence north of the border in more immediate terms. Through their propaganda networks, they recruited a second layer of leadership that had more explicit connections to the US, having roots or history in the region, having crossed the border to work in the Southwest, or having crossed the border and resettled. This group included such figures as Antonio P. Araujo, Primo Tapia, Anselmo Figueroa, Tomas Sarabia, Jesús Rangel, Fernando Palomares, and Práxedis Guerrero. Having shared experiences, or by becoming leaders and organizers in their own right, this group established organic relationships with the Mexican working class in the US. The basis of the growth and the spread of the PLM in the Southwest relied on their knowledge and understanding of the existing political culture and organizational forms common in the Mexican community, namely the universal presence of voluntary associations, or mutualistas. Throughout Southern

California, Mexicans had established these organizations to absorb and integrate new immigrants, host social and cultural events, provide forms of social welfare, and to serve as vehicles for communal action when needed. Voluntary associations and mutualistas also organized their own auxiliary schooling throughout Southern California, where children were taught Spanish, Mexican history, and Mexican geography.

For Mexican workers, voluntary associations could morph into unions during labor conflicts and strikes, becoming spaces for debate, the cultivation and selection of leadership, communication, and resource management and distribution. As many immigrant workers had experience with such organizations in their homeland, the mutualistas facilitated the integration of established residents with newcomers. They cropped up across the Southwest and into the Midwest, allowing for cultural and class-based bonds to be forged within reconstituted Mexican communities north of the border. Because of the working-class character of some mutualistas, they were the natural recruiting grounds for the PLM. When the magonistas launched the Organizing Junta of the Mexican Liberal Party from St. Louis, Missouri, in 1905, they had this audience in mind.

In their Manifesto to the Nation, they proclaimed that Mexicans on both sides of the border should form liberal clubs as the nuclei for the impending revolutionary uprising in Mexico to topple the "gang of exploiters, comprised of the government, the church, and their friends, a handful of national and international capitalists."[17] Appealing to mexicanos to join the PLM, they proclaimed:

> We need to become strong and in order to do this we must unite and organize ourselves. While we're divided and isolated, a powerful league of our enemies beats us down with ease, and will not let us advance one step. We are dispersed members of a party, the Liberal Party, and we only need to join together and we will be respected. Organize yourselves as part of us, so that men of liberal principles join together under the same banner so that we can all devote our energies, resources, and intellectual capacities toward strengthening the progress of the liberating party.[18]

The appeal goes on to lay out recommendations for how to organize meetings, keep abreast of political issues and developments, set up communication networks, raise funds, and form labor unions where possible.

In response, PLM clubs formed in Mexican barrios across the West over the next several years, especially in South Texas, Arizona, and throughout Southern California, with individual supporters scattered throughout the Midwest. Some early adherents in Mexico crossed the border as migrants or exiles and formed clubs, while others joined in the US. When the PLM moved their base of operations to Los Angeles in 1907, they lived and worked among the Mexican population crowded into a working-class barrio district in the downtown area in the eastern part of the city.

The Mexican barrio formed as the largest segment of a broader working-class population of separate and subdivided ethnic-national immigrant groups that lived clustered together in the industrial zone. Urban historian Raul Villa observed that turn-of-the-century city planners subordinated large-scale housing development, integration, and community input to the immediate needs of the business sector. As the urban zone expanded, the working-class districts faced increased isolation and long-term deterioration as resources and planning shifted to residential districts outside the inner city.[19]

The Mexican community (and other barrios in the region) was referred to colloquially as "Sonoratown," due to it being a link along a migration corridor from the northern border state. The barrio was situated around a historic, Spanish-era plaza and expanded in relation to the city's growing industrial core. Many barrio residents worked in the zone's factories, food processing plants, and small businesses.[20]

By the turn of the century, Mexican families, single migrant workers, and a variety of political exiles had settled in the area and brought their social and political traditions into their newly established communities. These traditions included the formation of mutualistas and other voluntary organizations, especially as they were denied support services by established charities, government agencies, and the city's main labor organizations. By the turn of the century, a small but significant core of Liberal exiles and sympathizers had made their residence in Los Angeles, some of whom began to follow the developments of the PLM, subscribe to *Regeneración*, and become promoters and proselytizers of the magonista cause within the barrio. Through these organic links, the PLM connected to an existing social base in the working class. As the *Los Angeles Herald* editors observed with concern in 1907, "The junta is a thoroughly well-organized one and has a membership of more than 20,000 Mexican laborers, self-styled patriots, who are employed in and near Los Angeles as laborers on railroads, canals and irrigation works, and in this city as section hands or street sweepers."[21]

While this number does not likely represent membership in the PLM, it may signify the population of Mexicans affiliated with organizations with at least some tangential relationship to the group.

Early PLM Leadership and Growth in Southern California

Early supporters in Los Angeles included a woman named María Brousse de Talavera and her daughter Lucía Talavera-Norman. Talavera's family moved from Zacatecas to Los Angeles at some point in the 1890s, and by 1905 she had joined the Socialist Party in Los Angeles. Through interactions with other Mexican Socialists in Los Angeles, she came into contact with PLM adherents. She became a supporter of the then St. Louis-based PLM, with records showing her in regular correspondence with the group and donating funds to their cause.[22] She also became Flores Magón's partner and confidant, tasked with communicating and coordinating with other supporters in the city.

When the junta was being hounded and threatened by US and Mexican government agents, Brousse de Talavera made arrangements for the PLM leadership to transfer their base of operations from St. Louis to Los Angeles (after temporarily hiding out in Canada). The group relocated to LA in 1907, settling into the Mexican barrio located in the Central Plaza district in the eastern part of the city. Ricardo Flores Magón took up residence in Maria's house, living clandestinely until his discovery and arrest by Los Angeles police officials working illicitly on behalf of the Mexican consul. After their first arrest, they had to rely on others to carry out organizational tasks.

While women leaders in the organization were theoretically subordinated to the males, the circumstances of incessant police harassment and recurring stints in prison led the machismo to break down in practice. When the junta leadership was incarcerated in 1907 in the aftermath of the failed uprising the year before, women like María Brousse de Talavera and Lucía Talavera-Norman, and Andrea and Teresa Villarreal rose to prominence in the organization by carrying out operational tasks. María Brousse de Talavera and Lucía Talavera-Norman became the backbone of the organization and maintained its essential functions behind the scenes. They became a communications liaison between Ricardo Flores Magón and the rest of the organization. María Brousse de Talavera, along with a Socialist named Ethel Duffy Turner, frequently smuggled communiqués from Ricardo Flores Magón out of the Los Angeles County Jail and delivered them to PLM contacts, including the plans for the 1908 insurrection.[23] Women's Liberal clubs were formed as auxiliaries to the men's, with the expectation that they perform various supporting and clerical tasks.

Mexican women affiliated with the PLM also took on other roles, including as gun and ammunition runners. Women smuggled weapons across the border in baby carriages, under long dresses, or in other creative ways to assist in the insurrections. According to a 1912 El Paso Herald article, for example, two Texas mexicanas, Maria Salls and Jofenia Santa Cruz, were arrested trying to bring 120 rounds of ammunition into Ciudad Juárez.[24] By ensuring that radical publications remained in circulation, agitational activities were coordinated, contact with various representatives was maintained, and public speaking and solidarity campaigns were arranged, women demonstrated in practice their capacity to lead. Furthermore, they were able to assert a stronger feminist analysis and criticism into the propaganda, transforming the character of the organization through their actions.

When in 1912 Ricardo Flores Magón, Librado Rivera, and Anselmo Figueroa were once again targeted by the US government for violating neutrality laws for their alleged role in the Baja insurrection, an outpouring of support emerged from the Mexican community. Magonista women, led by Flores Magón's stepdaughter, Lucía Norman, organized street demonstrations in front of the courthouse to protest the prosecution. They packed the courthouse during the trials, heckled hostile witnesses, and led marches and rallies. When the stacked court convicted the men on July 25, 1912, Lucía and Mercedes Figueroa (daughter of Anselmo), led a militant march through downtown Los Angeles of more than two thousand people including magonistas, socialists, Wobblies, anarchists, trade unionists, and sympathizers from the barrio. As one historian describes the scene,

> The police eventually called the occurrence a riot—which according to the Los Angeles Examiner was "one of the wildest riots witnessed on the streets of Los

Angeles" as "many of the women during the riot wielded hat pins with painful effect." The police beat many of the protesters as they resisted. At the end, the police arrested thirteen men and five women, including the "girl leader" Lucía.[25]

The repression and decimation of the male leadership through arrest, deportation, or death on the revolutionary battlefield created the conditions of necessity by which women like Lucía could challenge existing patriarchal norms within the organization and assert their leadership. Aside from support and solidarity campaigns, women began to write for the periodicals and became public speakers and organizational representatives. The higher profile of female leadership also coincides with a further evolution of the PLM from within an anarchist-communist identity. More radical notions of gender equality entered into their theoretical formulations, even while preserving some patriarchal preconceptions. In an article entitled "Protest," twenty women within the organization signed on to a call to Mexican men and women to take protest action in defense of the PLM:

> We are proletarian women that live from our labor that is exploited by the cursed bourgeoisie. We are Mexican women that have learned that the woman should struggle at the side of the man in order to break the chain of capital that has immiserated both of them. We are women, but we are ready for any sacrifice. We are women, but we are more brave than the men whom at this trying moment for our brothers in the Junta scatter and hide when they should speak out defiantly and disdainfully, or better yet, demand the immediate release of our comrades Ricardo and Enrique Flores-Magón, Librado Rivera, and Anselmo L. Figueroa.[26]

Historian David Adán Vázquez Valenzuela identifies three other Mexicans with long-standing roots in the Mexican barrio of Los Angeles who were some of the first promoters of Magonismo: a bookseller named Rafael López de Lara, a Socialist named Rafael Carmona, and railroad worker Federico Arismendez.[27] Arismendez, along with another sympathizer named Modesto Díaz, worked within local mutualistas to propagate and recruit to the magonista cause. Their efforts produced the first PLM-affiliated organization in Los Angeles in 1905, named El Club Liberal Justicia. The PLM grew through further recruitment efforts working within mutualistas across the city. Between 1910 and 1923 an estimated eighty voluntary associations existed in the Los Angeles area alone, with radical workers serving as the material for launching twelve more PLM clubs throughout the county.[28]

Mexicans on both sides of the border were being radicalized by the revolution in Mexico and the rise of class struggle in the US, leading to the growth and spread of the PLM. Another twenty-five branches were launched throughout the California counties of Orange, Ventura, San Diego, Riverside, San Bernardino, Imperial Valley, Kern, Tulare, Merced, and San Francisco over this period.[29] The urban centers contained the largest concentration of PLM groups, with branches fanning out along the rural migration routes with significant Mexican populations, including Santa Paula, Oxnard, San Gabriel, Chino, and Colton, California. This showed how Magonismo spread along the agricultural migratory corridors. Like other migrant workers, many

Mexicans resided in the cities in the off season and then cycled through the agricultural regions, picking grains, nuts, fruits, and vegetables. Over time, Mexican families established colonias along the agricultural route when permanent work and housing could be procured.[30]

The working-class character of the PLM is affirmed by an analysis of the regional adherents of the organization. In a survey of twenty-five PLM club organizers (based on Los Angeles and federal directories), twelve were listed as "common laborers," working in factories, agriculture, construction, as rail tracklayers, and in other manual labor jobs; while other types of work included food-service, painting, plumbing, bookselling, and street vending.[31] By 1908, the working-class character of the organization also reflected in its aligned press, both in the vernacular and the self-awareness of the intended audience. For example, early PLM supporter Lucía Talavera-Norman wrote for an early PLM-aligned independent Los Angeles newspaper called *Libertad y Trabajo*. In a June 1908 article, she penned an appeal to Mexican workers in Los Angeles as a class, at a time when some PLM organizers were actively recruiting among workers in the sugar beet and railroad sectors: "Workers, my brothers, I admire your sacrifice, I understand your efforts, I appreciate the importance of your mission. For me, you are the true authors of progress, the real giants that will someday smash the little [oppressors and tyrants]. I am with you in your struggle."[32]

The Los Angeles-based Wobbly-magonista newspaper *Libertad y Trabajo*, 1908

As the PLM oriented toward organizing Mexican workers, its Los Angeles organizers carefully studied local and regional economies and the significant role of Mexican labor in capitalist industries. For instance, PLM organizers observed the concentration of Mexican workers in the railroad industry, dominated by the Southern Pacific Railroad, and the sugar beet industry, which was dominated by the American Sugar Refining Company. Recent migrants with experience in Mexican industry witnessed and may have participated in the tumultuous strike that characterized the waning years of the Porfiriato. Some of these characteristics of class struggle in Mexico carried over into the United States with migrant workers.

By 1907 Mexican workers made up the majority of the railroad work crews on the California lines but were paid less than Greek and Japanese workers as a company standard.[33] Despite this norm, Mexican railroad workers had developed their own standards, echoing similar demands from their brethren in South Texas and in Mexico. One demand that resurfaced on several occasions was for Mexican workers to be paid the same as US workers doing the same work on the railroads; an end to the ubiquitous dual-wage system.[34] In 1908, 250 Mexican track-workers went on strike in Colton, California, a major railroad junction town east of Los Angeles in San Bernardino County. They demanded the removal of a despised white foreman. Instead of negotiating, representatives of the Southern Pacific Railroad, with the aid of local law enforcement, herded the workers onto trains and deported two hundred of the most recalcitrant strikers to El Paso.[35]

The ASR, also known as the Sugar Trust, operated as a virtual monopoly over sugar production and distribution, controlling 98 percent of sugar refining capacity by the turn of the century and relying heavily on Mexican labor in its California operations.[36] An agent working as a spy for the Díaz regime in Los Angeles observed the growing influence of the PLM among the betabeleros, stating:

> In Colton, 25 miles from Chino, there are around 500 [Mexican] workers . . .
> Three miles further in San Bernardino there are 300 or 400 Mexican workers
> employed in common labor. In discussing their presence and residence in the
> US, I have had the opportunity to talk to many of them about their apparent dis-
> content with conditions in Mexico . . . [and have learned that] in Colton there is
> a man that is actively involved in organizing the Mexicans in Liberal Clubs. This
> same man . . . has a great number of followers among the Mexicans that live in
> Colton and San Bernardino.[37]

While organizers were often political exiles who crisscrossed the border, the expanding base of the movement was drawn from the ranks of the working class. One method for directly reaching large numbers of workers with their propaganda was through soapbox rallies held within gathering spaces in working-class districts. In Los Angeles, representatives of the PLM would address gathered crowds of workers, the unemployed, radical groups, and political exiles. By the eve of the Mexican Revolution, a vast network of clubs, a cadre of capable leaders and organizers recruited from barrio and work camps across the Southwest, and a vibrant press allowed the junta to transmit its analyses and exhortations to thousands of partisans, adherents, and sympathizers.[38]

Radical Magonista Press

As clubs sprang up across the Southwest, the magonistas used their media to educate, organize, and coordinate their movement. The PLM's flagship paper, *Regeneración*, was widely diffused across the Southwest and throughout Mexico. By 1910, the print run reached twenty thousand, and by 1914 over ten thousand issues were sold in Los Angeles County alone. [39] There was also a proliferation of other PLM-aligned newspapers that reprinted articles from *Regeneración* alongside local stories, signifying the important role that media played in linking Mexican communities as well as connecting them to national and international developments. Historian Nicolás Kanellos has discovered the existence of over a hundred radical Spanish-language newspapers in the US between 1890 and 1940, mostly in the border region, while W. Dirk Raat has identified that at least thirty of those were affiliated or aligned with the revolutionary thinking of Magonismo during its existence. [40]

A main function of being a magonista was distribution of the party organ. Members sold the paper on street corners throughout the Mexican communities of Los Angeles, the outlying districts, and throughout barrios and colonias in the Southwest. The papers were read in individual homes, in discussion groups in club meetings, and wherever sympathetic groups of Mexican workers gathered. *Regeneración* and other aligned papers were also co-circulated on both sides of the border, creating a mass readership of PLM-affiliated press from the Southwest to Mexico City. They also reprinted each other's articles, cross-fertilizing radical discourse.

Radical and magonista papers were distributed on both sides of the border, but began to reach a wider audience among Mexicans and Mexican Americans in the US. Through a network of militants and PLM-affiliated clubs, the paper spread from Los Angeles to Texas, with subscriptions also scattered throughout the Midwest. Reflecting the coordination with the US Left and a widening orientation toward English-speaking workers, *Regeneración* included a page in English that had regular columns devoted to the analysis of issues and events affecting Mexicans in the US. The flourishing of the radical press signaled its expansive influence within the Mexican community. According to Juan Gómez-Quiñones,

> Between 1906 and 1912, members of the party made possible the distribution of various editions that each exceeded 20 thousand copies. Despite the police surveillance, newspapers were smuggled to several points throughout the US and Mexico. The militants of the PLM and their supporters, some of whom worked on the railroad, distributed the newspaper in the large population centers along the railroad lines. From there, they sent copies to the populations living in the outlying regions. The strategic infrastructure grew thanks to the establishment of a network of local affiliated publications, which were distributed in established Mexican communities across the United States. [41]

In efforts to build international solidarity, the PLM newspaper *Regeneración* began to show the common cause of Mexican and US peoples. This often took the form of polemics against the US media, which perpetuated the myth of "American exceptionalism" versus "Mexican backwardness," contesting "US journalistic portraits of Mexico as a backwater within the evolving world order," and asserting that "[t]he lumber camps of Louisiana, the mines of Colorado and West Virginia" were the "same as the hell-holes of Yucatán and the Valle Nacional." Furthermore, the PLM editors promoted the Mexican worker as being at the forefront of the international struggle against capitalism.[42]

The paper was used as a means to educate, organize, and make occasional calls to action, through regional transmission belts that included railroad workers, miners, small farmers, farmworkers, and sympathetic intellectuals. Through this expanding base of proletarian media, radical journalists began to not just focus on Mexican events, but to pay closer attention to the realities facing Mexicans in the US and the mechanics of US capitalism. As Ricardo Flores Magón identified in *Regeneración*:

> Thousands of Mexican families in the Southwest find themselves without housing, always on the road, spending the night sleeping in forests or under bridges, crowding into cow pastures, without a piece of bread, in the elements without hope, without solace . . . [These are the same] men that tend the rails, build the bridges, construct the houses, work the fields, move the foundations, and with their weathered hands produce the material well-being that they themselves do not enjoy.[43]

Women aligned with the PLM also took up leadership roles in creating and circulating their own press. In Texas, for example, where the junta had its largest base of support, the sisters Andrea and Teresa Villarreal rose to the occasion. From their base in San Antonio, they became the liaisons for the PLM and its various clubs, and wrote numerous articles for various magonista papers in Texas, condemning the arrest of their comrades and maintaining a scathing line of opposition to the Díaz regime in the junta's stead. In 1909, they founded the newspaper *El Obrero* and later in 1915 edited the first Socialist-feminist, PLM-linked newspaper, *La Mujer Moderna*, which among other features attempted to organize women's participation in the PLM.[44]

La Voz De La Mujer

● SEMANARIO LIBERAL DE COMBATE ●

Defensor de los Derechos del Pueblo y Enemigo de las Tiranías.

La mujer forma parte integrante de la gran familia humana; luego tiene el deber y el derecho de exigir y luchar por la Dignificación de su Patria

AÑO I.   EL PASO, TEXAS, SEPTIEMBRE 6 DE 1907.   NÚM. 9

LABOR DE FIGAROS.

El flagelo de nuestra fiesta sagrada los escamosos morrillos de la burguesía altanera. Nuestras rebeldías no han conocido valladar que contenga las justas iras emanadas contra el sistema atentatorio con que los impuros aseñan en reivindicar su historia de oprobio: por que, impotentes para combatir con razonamientos, son tenaces, también para reincidir, enfangados en el estercolero que les sirve de lecho.

Á nuestra mesa de redacción nos llegan distintas quejas de los atentados que cometen en la tinaja de los contrabandos los bandidos caciques investidos de autoridad.

El primer fustazo que nuestro semanario asestó al contrabandista en funciones de Jefe Político, Silvano Montemayor, lo hizo convertirse en réptil, se enronció, y dió un chillido, le robó a nuestro papelero unos ejemplares y lo amagó con hos pedarlo en el *hotel de su propiedad*, si volvía a vender "La Voz de la Mujer." Nuestra protesta cargó sobre el cacique vulgar, castigando su insolencia como lo merecía.

Un Castrado ascendido y cornamentado ha tomado a su ehcargo molestar a los abonados y repartidores de nuestro periódico, amagándolos con cárcel ¿Con qué derecho lo hace este Mesa?

¡Tales son los méritos de los bandidos de uniforme!

Hoy nos visita una nueva querella: Un paquidermo que representa de cobrador en el mercado de C. Juárez, y de eunuco de antesala, se opone a viva fuerza á que circule "La Voz de la Mujer," en la cafrería donde cree tener, en símil el derecho de usufructo. Este estulto cuadrúpedo no está conforme con andar en cuatro remos, sino que, persiste en encarbar con la trompa.

La impudicia de tales moluscos congestiona, padecen sonambulismo y sueñan en el exterminio de la prensa independiente. ¡Falsa creencia! para que los ideales mueran, se necesita destrozarnos, ya que odiados somos; sólo que ese odio nos eleva por que prueba nuestra honradez, desde el momento en que los tiranos no nos estiman. Por esto los flagelamos para despertar su encono, seguras de que al sucumbimos debe ser levantando ámpula; nuestra vacante será substituida con nuevas energías, con plumas viriles empapadas en luz febea.

Nuestros carácteres están enteramente trocados: nosotras, rebeldes, ellos serviles; nosotras honradas, ellos bandidos; nuestro medio no es el de ellos; el espíritu de rebeldía tonifica nuestros cerebros y es el talismán que nos hace prepotentes en los azares políticos, en la cruenta lucha que sostenemos con los burgueses; somos pobres y la pobreza es maga cuando va emparejada con honradez y abnegación; porque en los mayores infortunios, el porvenir nos sonríe, nos da fuerza y nos acaricia. Esto no pasa con los tiranos criminales: su existencia es mezquina y ruin; sus espíritus siempre están emponzoñados por el crimen y la maldad; son morbosos y enfermizos cerebros a diario se sienten atacados por la misma ruindad que los deprime; no tienen convicciones propias y viven en continuo asecho de víctimas que aseguran sus canonjías; sus almas siempre sermonean sólo piensan en el mal; jamás se preocupan por nada loable.

¡Horrible torcedor para los tiranos, pensar en día de las represalías! ¡La hora suena, inexorable y justiciera contra los autores de tanto crimen! ¡Oído, bien, tiranos y bandidos y si es que lo olvidáis, nosotras os lo recordaremos!

¡Vivid tranquilos!

DEFUNCION.

En San Antonio, Texas, rindió tributo á la Naturaleza el rebelde liberal Aurelio N. Flores, dejando un vacío en las filas liberales. ¡La muerte se engalanó al apoderarse de alma tan noble! El Partido Liberal perdió un valiente luchador. ¡Paz á sus restos! ¡Consuelo á sus deudos!

Texas-based feminist-magonista newspaper in Texas, *La Voz de la Mujer* (Woman's Voice), 1907.

Another radical newspaper, *La Pluma Roja* (The Red Pen), was founded in 1913 by Blanca Moncaleano. The paper aligned with the thinking of the magonistas, and reframed the struggle through a feminist lens. The paper rejected national borders as a myth, and envisioned a revolutionary struggle to free women (alongside men) from the oppression of the "state, religion, and capital." For revolution to be successful, they posited that a concurrent and parallel battle had to be waged against machismo (sexism), which they characterized this way: "consumed by their supposed superiority, conceited in their ignorance, men believe they can achieve the goal of human emancipation without the help of women."[45]

The evolution and growth of a radical Mexican press in the Southwest developed in tandem with the political awakening and self-activity of the working class. The appearance and broad appeal of *Regeneración* inspired replication among individuals and groups of radicals in different regions, which developed their own periodicals and affiliated to the PLM to assist both local and national organizing efforts.[46] As explicitly radical Spanish-language newspapers circulated through Mexican American barrios in the first decade of the twentieth century, concurrent with the rise of working-class militancy and union agitation on both sides of the border, so too did they attract the attention of the Los Angeles–based champions of transborder empire.

The PLM in the Crosshairs of Empire

By the time the PLM junta settled in Los Angeles in 1907, the transnational capitalist class based there had become familiar with the Mexican Liberal Party. They had carefully observed the events of the Cananea strike, the PLM-inspired uprising against foreign-owned properties in southern Veracruz and Yucatán, and elsewhere. They were also well aware of the disruptive strikes taking place in the Panama Canal Zone led by Spanish Anarchist clubs that were similar in character.[47] In their plans to turn Los Angeles into the imperial capital of the West, they needed to preserve the status quo.

The unbridled growth of industry, uninterrupted flow of profits, and growth of personal fortunes depended on the suppression of socialists, fiercely vying in the first decade of the twentieth century to crack the capitalists' grip over city politics by running their own candidates and organizing labor unions. When Mexican socialist "agitators" then tried to spread their message through the barrios, they also earned the enmity of the elites. The PLM were targeted, harassed, and persecuted by transnational state agents, and the hired guns of the capitalist autocrats teamed up to isolate and extinguish the threat.

When the junta leadership resurfaced in Los Angeles after the not-so-inconspicuous launch of their new paper, *Revolución*, they were arrested and detained. They were held in jail on trumped-up charges until representatives of the US Attorney's Office could formally consult the Díaz regime and concoct a legal scheme to get them extradited to Mexico.[48] The heavy-handed violation of fundamental habeas corpus was roundly condemned. Even the conservative *Los Angeles Herald* was incredulous, editorializing:

> This man [Ricardo Flores Magón] and his two compatriots have been held in Jail in Los Angeles on such ridiculous charges as "spitting on the streets of the City of Mexico"; on John Doe warrants for various alleged offenses, time and place not specified; on pretexts so flimsy that they would be laughed out of court if Americans were arrested on them and taken before our police magistrates.[49]

With massive public support, they were finally released, but only after spending eighteen months in prison, a recurring phenomenon in the Organizing Junta of the PLM's thirteen-year history in the United States. While the Los Angeles–based capitalist press had an ambiguous view toward the group between 1907 and 1909, the radicalization of the group, its agitation among Mexican workers, its open alliance with the socialist movement, and its vocal anti-imperialism turned them into an object of derision for the official press.[50]

The Otis-owned *Los Angeles Times*, for instance, railed against the PLM shortly after their arrest on its front page, intermixing accusations of labor rabble-rousing, with wild and baseless conspiratorial plots of assassination revealed in letters "found" by Díaz agents that also managed to implicate local socialists and labor unions:

> [The 1906] uprisings […]in Douglas, Arizona, and in Cananea and Juárez […
>] were all directed from these men arrested in Los Angeles. It is also shown that
> the revolutionists had a hot anarchist meeting in the open air in Los Angeles last
> July […] The letter seems to involve the Socialists; among the other documents
> is found a letter which carries the labor unions into the guilt […] the feature
> that seems to have aroused the I.W.W. unionists is [sic] the attack upon President
> Roosevelt […] One of their letters intimates that President Roosevelt is to be
> a victim equally with Díaz. All through their documents Roosevelt is alluded to
> with fearful hatred.[51]

After that edition, there was no further mention of the "assassination letters," although a year later they continued with the narrative of the PLM as terrorists after recovering alleged correspondence relating to plans for the 1908 insurrection. In an article supporting their long-term detention, they described the junta as having plans to "assassinate public officials, to dynamite customhouses and stores and loot banks wherever they went," continuing the false narrative of the PLM as terroristic.[52]

By 1911, the junta leadership articulated anti-imperialist editorials that began to identify the role of US empire in maintaining the framework that produced the contemporary Mexican condition. In an open letter addressed to US workers, Ricardo Flores Magón explained the dimensions of their common oppression:

> We are in revolt against unspeakably atrocious slavery, forced on us and supported by the American money power. The Standard Oil Co., the Guggenheims,
> the Southern Pacific Railway, the Sugar Trust—all that Wall Street autocracy
> against which you and the great masses of your nation are making such vigorous
> protest—are the powers against which we of Mexico are in revolt. They have
> dispossessed us of our lands and rendered us homeless by the hundreds of thousands; they have left us the choice of exile or imprisonment in such hells as the
> Valle National.[53]

The pronouncement of the PLM's call for an Anarchist-Communist revolution coincided in the same year as their third insurrectionary attempt. Armed magonistas, joined by members of the Socialist Party and the Industrial Workers of the World

(IWW), captured several Mexican border towns, threatening the investments and lucrative arrangements of the city's most prominent capitalists.[54]

Based on connections between the radicals in Mexico and the PLM, both real and perceived, the federal government saw the activities of the PLM as an international threat. In a 1913 congressional inquiry into revolutionary developments in Mexico, an assistant United States attorney for the southern district of California summarized why the federal government targeted the PLM. In confiscated correspondence, the agents found broad support for the efforts of the PLM.

> In looking through this [seized] correspondence we found that the junta had sent broadcasts throughout the country . . . the junta and the Magóns individually received replies from all over the United States . . . I became convinced that a great many very respectable people and a great many respectable women were responding to their requests for assistance in furthering the cause of the Mexican Liberal Party.[55]

By 1913, the revolution in Mexico was taking a radical turn. The zapatistas were carrying out revolutionary land expropriations across southern Mexico and threatened to take their efforts national, threatening the interests of US capital. The next year, the villista-dominated forces met in Aguascalientes, declaring for a radical program of nationalization. In 1914, the *agraristas* captured Mexico City, presenting the possibility of realizing foreign expropriation on a national scale, including the strategically important oil fields in Veracruz. This was too much for US capital and the Wilson administration, who intervened militarily to protect US oil interests. Simultaneously, federal and local governments unleashed a wave of repression against Mexican radicals in the US, triggering what has come to be called by historians the Brown Scare, a racist and anti-radical-induced panic that the Mexican Revolution could spread across the border.[56]

An example of the ruling classes' rabid paranoia was captured in a *Los Angeles Times* editorial entitled, "Magóns Outline Programme of Terrorization Here," claiming they had plans for

> [a] general uprising of the Mexican population of Southern California, the seizure and holding of the land by force of arms, following a programme of terrorization by pistol and bomb assassinations, looting and anarchistic demonstrations, together with wholesale jail deliveries . . . .the red program . . . is a part of a scheme of the Mexican revolutionists to take all of California and Texas.[57]

Showing the link between the PLM and radicals in the US, the agent observed that among the subscriptions and financial contributions were those made by "Socialistic and anarchistic organizations."[58] Local state agents and media watched the junta closely and perceived them as capable of influencing the local Mexican population, and so viewed the working class as suspect. After witnessing a speech by Ricardo Flores Magón at Italian Hall in East Los Angeles in 1914, one wrote that the PLM was "an organization of radical Mexicans who are striving to arouse interest in the Mexican

Revolution among the Mexicans here emphasizing the social and universal character of that revolution."[59]

Socialist Support for the PLM

Prior to the period of the Mexican Revolution, the experience of Mexicans in the United States garnered little national attention from the US Left with the exception of some Wobblies, anarchists, and left-wing socialists.[60] Nevertheless, Socialist Party organizers in the borderlands, especially in Southern California and South Texas, came into direct contact with significant Mexican working-class populations as well as radical co-thinkers operating in exile from Mexico.

While the national party paid scant attention to the specific plight of Mexican workers in the US, these regional branches developed their own perspectives by necessity. Applying Marxist notions of international solidarity to transnational realities, socialists in these regions paid close attention to Mexican affairs and developed local strategies for organizing Mexican workers. They viewed US capitalist investment in the economy and military intervention in the Mexican Revolution and World War I as "organic extensions of local class struggles," and tried to mobilize workers against imperialism.[61]

Through support for the PLM, radicals in the Socialist Party also found an ally against powerful corporate interests that dominated US electoral politics, as many of these capitalists had a hand in directing imperialist endeavors in Mexico. Through an extensive press, circulating 730,000 copies nationally by 1912, left-wing Socialists, especially those in Southern California, tried to turn public opinion against Díaz and the US corporate cabals that profited from his policies, while promoting solidarity with Mexican political exiles. For those on the party's left, their Mexican co-thinkers in the PLM served as a conduit for US radicals to work with the junta leadership and directly reach the Mexican American working-class population with the attempt to create Mexican branches of the Socialist Party. Because of their shared ideological affinities, several Mexican radicals later linked to the PLM had already joined the US Socialist Party and helped organize Spanish-speaking affiliates as early as 1905.

When the PLM exiles relocated their headquarters in Los Angeles and staged their 1906 and 1908 insurrectionary forays against the Díaz regime, prominent socialist commentators took notice and followed the events. For socialists based in Los Angeles, the connection between US capitalist interests in Mexico, the persecution of the PLM, and the bourgeois presses' rigorous defense of Porfirio Díaz became abundantly clear. The same capitalist oligarchs vigorously opposing their efforts in Los Angeles were simultaneously investing large sums of capital in Mexico while the business press touted the laurels of the Mexican capitalist model.[62] The *International Socialist Review* pointed out this contradiction, stating that

> No longer will [. . .] capitalist magazines tell of the atrocities being perpetrated in Mexico today, by the help of the United States Government, for the profits of American Capitalists. Today, on our southern border, United States troops are massed to prevent the escape of Mexican revolutionists who seek refuge in our Land of the Free (?). The work of suppressing information is making swift

headway [. . .] do not permit the American workingmen and women to be deceived in this matter. The Mexican Revolution is your revolution. If the capitalists are permitted to maintain slavery in Mexico, they can and will crush down American wage-workers to the Mexican level.[63]

The activities of the PLM invoked heavy-handed repression from the US government. For the socialist movement beginning to articulate an anticapitalist critique of US imperialism in the region, the role of the US state in repressing the PLM revealed its true class character.[64] As a result, the Socialist Party of Los Angeles became an early advocate and supporter of the Mexican Liberal exiles, providing crucial legal support, launching solidarity campaigns nationwide, and opening the pages of their press to take aim at US empire in Mexico and to publicize the radical cause of the PLM.

Early organizing activities in working-class Los Angeles had brought socialists into contact with Mexican radical and Liberal exiles, several of whom had joined the party in Los Angeles prior to the arrival of the PLM junta. Others joined the Socialist Party as part of a larger radicalization of the working class taking place by the 1910s. In his 1914 survey on Mexicans in Los Angeles, William Wilson McEuen claimed that most Mexicans able to do so voted for the Socialist Party. The California Socialist Party, for instance, grew to 7,600 registered members by 1912, of which a third were concentrated in Los Angeles.[65] Prominent figures that met the PLM through their membership in the Socialist Party included Lázaro Gutiérrez de Lara, Anselmo Figueroa, and Simon Berthold Chacón.

De Lara was a lawyer and writer based in Nuevo León, Mexico, who became an avowed socialist. In 1905 he moved to Cananea and, along with Esteban Baca, worked in coordination with the PLM leadership to organize among miners in Sonora. By 1906, the two had become the principal organizers of the Liberal clubs La Unión Liberal Humanidad and the Club Liberal Cananea. After the repression of the strike, de Lara fled into exile in the United States. Shortly after his arrival in Los Angeles, he made contact with other Mexican exiles and joined the Socialist Party soon thereafter.

Anselmo Figueroa, who later joined the junta leadership, was not an exile or migrant. Unlike his later compatriots, he was born in Yuma, Arizona, and worked there as a miner. By 1906, Figueroa had come in contact with US socialists there and joined the party. When the Socialist Party took a position in support of the Mexican Liberals, he moved to Los Angeles with his daughter Mercedes, where along with another socialist named Rafael R. Carmona, they formed the Mexican branch of the Los Angeles Socialist Party. Through his support work, he grew closer personally and politically to the PLM and served as part of the inner circle of leadership.

Anselmo L. Figueroa

Simón Berthold Chacón moved to Los Angeles from Guaymas, Sonora, in 1905 and joined the Liga Socialista (Socialist League), where he heard speeches given by Gutiérrez de Lara, which won him over to the PLM.[66] In 1906 he was sent to Ventura County, California, to set up Liberal clubs among the beet-sugar workers in Oxnard and other agricultural colonias in the county. In 1910 he was the lead PLM representative in the Baja insurrection, which saw the joint PLM and IWW expedition capture the northern border region of Baja California.

By 1910, Figueroa had become a member of the junta and an editor of *Regeneración*. Mexican Socialists like Brousse de Talavera, Gutiérrez de Lara, and Figueroa became important links between the US Left and the magonistas. For example, Job Harriman, a national leader of the Socialist Party based in Los Angeles, came into contact with the PLM through Figueroa and became a leading advocate of the PLM and a legal representative of the leadership when they were incarcerated. Harriman, a prominent lawyer and national figure within the party (and 1910 Socialist candidate for Los Angeles mayor), took up the legal defense. Socialist lawyers James H. Ryckman and Ernest E. Kirk also defended the PLM leadership as part of the Harriman team during their second trial and incarceration.

Harriman's relationship with Los Angeles Socialists connected to the PLM opened the door for fellow socialist John Kenneth Turner to collaborate with magonista intellectual Lázaro Gutiérrez de Lara in publishing the very successful series of journalistic accounts (made into the book *Barbarous Mexico*) that informed tens of thousands of US readers about the tyranny of Díaz, and the complicity of US capitalists in bolstering his regime. As historian James Sandos explains:

> Turner's exposé achieved its desired effects. American public opinion grew, the plight of Mexican refugees became a subject of popular concern, and Turner became famous… *Barbarous Mexico* became as important in molding public opinion as Harriet Beecher Stowe's *Uncle Tom's Cabin* had been in its time. Through Turner, the PLM had achieved an important victory over Díaz in the United States.[67]

The groundbreaking book became a bestseller, exposing the brutality of life for workers and peasants under the Díaz regime and the role of the United States government and capitalist class underwriting his perpetuation in power. De Lara served as a guide for Turner in an investigative tour through Díaz's Mexico, providing access, information, and his own journalistic skills (allegedly as a co-author). Turner also wrote incessantly in defense of the PLM, was a journalist who had a national readership that closely followed his criticism of US imperialism in Mexico, and wrote regular columns in spirited defense of the revolutionary process.

The relationship between the Mexican socialists and the local Socialist Party also brought the magonistas into contact with John Murray. Murray, a left-wing Socialist and journalist, had moved to Los Angeles to become editor of the Socialist Party's statewide paper, *The Socialist*. He later became affiliated with the Los Angeles Labor Council and had been a staunch advocate for the inclusion of Mexican workers into the AFL. He and other socialists within the council had been instrumental in supporting the 1903 Oxnard beet sugar strike. Through his position within the Socialist Party and the AFL, he was able to procure significant labor support and resources for the PLM through the Political Refugee Defense Fund, a national fundraising body that solicited funds through AFL unions and Socialist Party chapters to provide legal support

for immigrant and exiled radicals in the US facing state repression. From the socialist press, such as the *International Socialist Review*, through AFL-affiliated craft unions
across the country, such as the Brotherhood of Painters, Decorators, and Paperhangers
of America, Murray appealed for support and funds. Murray called on organizations to
form "Labor and Liberty Defense Committees" to raise money as part of the national
effort.[68] The support of socialists and unionists around the country provided critical
funding, publicity, and solidarity for the three imprisoned PLM leaders.

Other Los Angeles–based socialists, led by the writer and socialist revolutionary
Ethel Duffy Turner (John Kenneth Turner's wife), founded the short-lived magazine
The Border. This publication, launched in 1908, is the first known effort by US-based
radicals dedicated wholly to covering events in Mexico and defending Mexicans in the
US. Duffy Turner also helped fund other PLM newspapers and even served a stint as
the English-language columnist for *Regeneración*. She later became one of the group's
first English-language historians.

These figures bridged the activities of the two groups, which had significant secondary effects. Mexican socialists leveraged support for the PLM through the Socialist Party's national apparatus, which had a significant membership, connections to organized
labor, and numerous periodicals with a substantial readership. After the arrest of Ricardo
Flores Magón and other PLM leaders in 1908 on the charge of violating US neutrality
laws, the Socialist Party came to the Mexicans' defense.

> The Socialists of Los Angeles made the cause of these men their own and in-
> stituted a tremendous campaign of protest against this violation of law . . . The
> campaign spread rapidly to all parts of the United States, Canada, and Europe.
> Hundreds of mass meetings were held which passed unanimous resolutions
> expressing sympathy for the Mexican revolutionists and denunciation of the
> United States authorities. The American Federation of Labor, the Industrial
> Workers of the World, the Western Federation of Miners, the United Mine
> Workers of America, all officially declared themselves in sympathy with the Lib-
> eral junta and its revolutionary propaganda, and as strongly opposed to United
> States intervention in Mexico, backing up their declaration with substantial fi-
> nancial aid to the revolutionary cause.[69]

Support for the imprisoned exiles also came from the party's recognized national
leader, Eugene V. Debs. As part of his nationwide campaign for president in 1908 as the
Socialist Party candidate, Eugene Debs regularly denounced the Díaz government,
distributed informational pamphlets about the persecution of the PLM, and collected
donations. At a campaign stop in Los Angeles, he addressed a crowd of seven thousand at the Shriner's Auditorium, standing in front of a large portrait of Karl Marx. As
the *Los Angeles Herald* described:

> He made an eloquent plea for the alleged Mexican revolutionists now in the
> county jail, saying that they must not be handed over to death, seeing that their
> sole defense was the endeavoring to do in their country what all socialists were
> trying to do here, namely, to emancipate their fellow countrymen from slavery.[70]

Appeals for support and funds and even reprinted articles from the PLM press were published in socialist and labor journals when the three PLM political prisoners were shipped off to stand trial in the small Arizona border town of Tombstone in 1909 (where they were accused of launching the failed 1906 uprising).[71] With the intention of making the impending trial a cause célébré of the socialist project, Socialist Party sympathizers poured into the city. According to Mexican consul Arturo M. Elías, the spectacle was "the work of Socialist sympathizers and the determined protectors of the accused . . . [that] are speaking in favor of the defendants with everyone, in the streets, restaurants and public places."[72]

When the three junta leaders were released from prison and arrived in Los Angeles in 1910, they were greeted by three hundred enthusiastic supporters at the train station. Socialist Party members led by Job Harriman helped organize the homecoming and arranged a mass meeting that same night at the downtown labor temple before a crowd of two thousand supporters to gather funds to relaunch *Regeneración*.[73] Speakers included LA Socialists Job Harriman and John Kenneth Turner alongside Lázaro Gutiérrez de Lara, Librado Rivera, Antonio Villareal, and Ricardo Flores Magón, who addressed the audience in Spanish and English.[74] To assure his audience that prison did not in any way weaken his resolve, an "exhausted and sick Ricardo Flores Magón spoke briefly, leading rousing chants [of] ¡Viva la Revolución Social!"[75]

Chapter 12

The PLM and the Socialist Party in Texas

"The whole border line ... is in rebellion ... magonistas ...
are running like locusts through the chapparal."
—US newspaper editorial, 1911

The radical agrarianism of the Mexican Revolution carried over into Texas, where the Mexican and Mexican American population was also dispossessed and reduced to an impoverished agricultural proletariat. Texas towns like Laredo and San Antonio were already havens for PLM exiles and other regime opponents. Their ranks were increased by migrants crossing into Texas from Coahuila, who, influenced by the PLM, "brought with them their ideas about socioeconomic justice when they crossed the river."[1] The organizing activities of the PLM coincided with those of the Socialist Party, with the two groups of radicals coordinating in their efforts to agitate and recruit from among the large, south Texan Mexican population.

For Mexicans in Texas, unequal land distribution was compounded by attendant racial segregation, violence, and discrimination. This terrain proved fertile for agitation, especially as the agrarian revolutionaries were rising up across Mexico. South Texas Mexicans, who maintained a transnational connection through labor migration, kinship ties, and cultural and political affinities, were animated by the radicalizing effects of the Mexican Revolution and in some cases sought to spread it north of the Río Bravo. Both the PLM and the Socialist Party saw in Mexican agricultural workers in Texas a similar potential, and hoped to tap into that discontent as part of building their respective movements. Both groups in their own ways, and in conjunction, oriented toward the Mexican population as a catalyst for revolution.

The PLM in Texas

By the turn of the century Mexicans throughout the Texas borderlands were intimately bound up with events in Mexico, as many were migrants or exiles existing on the perimeter of their homeland. As a revitalized Liberal movement spread across the regions of Mexico, so too did many Texas expatriates approve of the scathing criticisms and radical stirrings of the Mexican Liberal Party, specifically its spokesman Ricardo Flores Magón. Beginning in 1904, the leaders of the PLM moved their base of operations briefly into Laredo and then into San Antonio, beginning a long and troubling odyssey to escape first Mexican and then US-state repression. A core of magonistas had been established in Laredo and San Antonio early on among local mexicano intelligentsia, some of whom had gone into exile years before. Journalists such as Sara

Estela Ramírez, Juana B. Gutiérrez de Mendoza, and Elisa Acuña y Rosete worked tirelessly to promote the magonista project through their newspapers. The latter two had fled Mexico to Texas with the other Mexican liberals after having spent several months languishing in Belem Prison for their part in publishing anti-Díaz press.[2] The regrouped intellectual radical press carried significant weight among Laredo's Mexican working-class population and circulated across the border as well.[3] Between 1907 and 1913 thirty-nine distinct PLM-aligned papers entered into circulation, and between 1911 and 1917 at least fifty-two branches of the PLM sprang up around the state, many led by women.[4] The largest number of subscriptions of *Regeneración* went to Texas by 1915, twice the number sold in California and Mexico combined.[5]

A history of class consciousness, labor struggle, and cross-border solidarity already existed among the small core of Mexican industrial workers in Texas. Mexican workers began to develop local unions, and a culture of solidarity emerged that allowed for regional networks to form, reinforced along ethnic lines in a racially segregated and polarized social environment. According to Josef Barton,

> Mexican surface workers in Colorado mines, drawn largely from the Mexican border, developed strong ties with agricultural workers and miners' unions in South Texas, for example. During the prolonged strikes in the southern Colorado coal fields, aid flowed from the Texas locals to the Colorado miners.[6]

These networks received a new "idiom of resistance" from the PLM and its affiliated radical organizations, which provided a vehicle to spread information, propagate anticapitalist theory in relation to the conditions of daily life, and coordinate activities on larger scale.[7] Rank-and-file members of El Unión de Mecánicos Mexicanos (the Railroad Mechanic's Union), which carried out one of the first major industrial strikes against the Díaz dictatorship in 1906, circulated radical newspapers through railroad hubs on both sides of the border. Their own newspapers, called *El Ferrocarrilero*, published photos, stories, and accounts of the PLM, referring to them as "brothers" and promoting their newspaper, *Regeneración*.[8]

The arrival of the exiled PLM leadership was an instrumental step in politicizing and drawing together Mexican radicals in Texas. Many within the early mutualistas were supporters of the PLM, either as migrants politically shaped by their experiences in Mexico under the Porfiriato, or as adherents to the PLM as it also adapted its critiques to US society. These radical networks expanded after 1906 as the PLM agitated aggressively within Mexican barrios in order to recruit participants for their insurrectional activities. Locally, they also provided the means for Mexicans in the US to coordinate labor organizing, host cultural events, and engage in political activity. For instance, between 1900 and 1920, mexicanos formed seventeen mutualistas in Texas, primarily in the south of the state.[9] In their efforts, the organizing work of PLM organizers intersected with that of US radicals, especially the Texas Socialist Party and the Industrial Workers of the World (IWW).

By the time the exiled Flores Magón brothers and other Liberal leaders arrived in Texas in 1904, they had a network of allies and supporters ready to get behind the efforts to regroup. By the turn of the century, Laredo and San Antonio, both situated near the border along a major international railroad junction, became a primary entry point, transitory corridor, and home base for radical Mexican exiles, akin to New York City for Caribbean revolutionaries at the turn of the century. The party's first US head-quarters were located in the home of Sara Estela Ramírez, a supporter and major in-tellectual proponent of the revolutionary cause. Like in other parts of the Southwest, Mexican Liberals worked through mutualistas as the recruiting bases for the growth and operational activities of the PLM. The base of the PLM in Texas broadened as a result of migration from Mexican border states, especially Coahuila and Chihuahua. Many migrants from these regions were already versed in class politics and influenced by Liberal and radical movements, bringing "with them their ideas about socioeco-nomic justice when they crossed the river."[10]

From there, they moved to St. Louis, beginning their clandestine odyssey across the continent, trying to stay one step ahead of a small army of agents and mercenaries on their trail. While the group remained in Texas for less than a year before moving on to St. Louis, their efforts to launch a revolutionary campaign against Díaz found a receptive audience. This was especially the case in the predominantly Mexican south-ern half of the state. Here, a large rural population of migratory farmworkers, tenant farmers, small ranchers, and ranch hands comprised a population similar in social composition to the revolutionary villista and zapatista armies south of the border.

For instance, one PLM club, Liberal Union de Farmworkers of Fentress, Texas, comprised agricultural workers.[11] Migratory workers crisscrossed the frontier region following the seasonal harvests, settling into their households in the crowded barrios of San Antonio in the off-season, while ranchers and tenant farmers lived in more sparsely populated agricultural counties at the southern rim of the state. A military intelligence official, charged with monitoring PLM activities in Texas, estimated that the group had a thousand supporters in San Antonio by 1908.[12]

The presence of a significant radical expat community and a vibrant political cul-ture within the Mexican working class was apparent to the bystander, with regular political meetings, soapbox speeches in the plazas, and visible literary culture. When Socialist John Murray visited the San Antonio barrio in 1915, he observed the presence of a radical bookshop selling the works of writers such as "Poe, Spencer, Darwin, Kro-potkin, and Marx [. . .] at affordable prices." He recalled a conversation with a Mex-ican working-class immigrant named Carlos Ruiz about the popularity of the radical bookstore, who told him,

> it is the Mexican in blue overalls, the labor leader, as you call him, that supports these libraries of world-wide knowledge and passes all that he learns to his brothers who may not be able to read. And more, those are the books read not only by Mexicans but by organized labor throughout Latin America.[13]

The reconfiguration of the PLM in the urban areas of Laredo and San Antonio also led to the first significant endeavors at Mexican feminist organization in that state. Radical intellectuals transplanted from Mexico City, alongside homegrown Tejanas, sought to assert their rights in the apertures produced by the Mexican Revolutionary process and in alignment with PLM radicals. Sara Estela Ramírez, a pioneering radical feminist, had developed her own newspaper called *La Corregidora* (in honor of a female hero of the Mexican independence movement) and was already taking critical positions against the conditions of Mexicans in Texas. She established communications with radical journalists in Mexico City and later joined the PLM in 1901. She championed efforts to build the organization through her paper and on the ground, and was part of a leading "group of women organizers who insisted that the women's question be integrated into the revolutionary struggle."[14]

Like the Villarreal sisters previously mentioned, Ramírez was a member of the local core of female leaders that assumed the public roles that other, more popular PLM leaders were unable to undertake. Harassment by local police, Pinkerton men, and Furlong detectives often forced the men to be less conspicuous and prompted the women to fulfill the more public roles of propagandizing and transmitting PLM policy.[15] Between the years 1911 and 1912, for instance, PLM-aligned women formed and led several feminist groups, including La Liga Feminil Mexicanista (the Mexican Feminist League), the Grupo Feminino Aspiraciones Libres (the Aspirations for Freedom Feminist Group), and the Grupo Regeneración "Prismas Anarquistas" (Regeneration Group: "Anarchist Prisms"). Jovita Idar, who led La Liga, explained the motivation for her agitation, stating that when "the obrera [woman worker] recognizes her rights, proudly raises her head and joins the struggle, the time of her degradation is over, she is no longer a slave sold for some coins, she is no longer a servant, but the equal of man."[16] Women leaders were prominent in the Texas movement, and their perspectives, sometimes even at odds with their own compañeros, reflected in the critique of patriarchal family structure, and more attention focused on the role of women workers in the workforce and in the struggle.[17]

The Socialist Party in Texas

The Texas Socialist Party formed in 1903 with the intention of spreading among the state's workers and farmers. In order to build a statewide party capable of challenging the two capitalist parties, the leadership recognized the need to develop a rural strategy to spread through the agricultural heartlands. They set out to organize farmers, sharecroppers, tenant farmers, and agricultural workers against a much-maligned class of capitalist landlords who had concentrated most of Texas's arable land into their own hands by the turn of the century. The state party drew from the tenets of the national organization's platform, pledging to end the capitalist system. They called for raising wages and shortening work hours, instituting workers' compensation and government-run pensions, abolishing child labor, and creating public ownership of transportation, communication, and exchange. To build a strong voting base they called for radical democratic reforms, including the abolition of the poll tax and universal adult suffrage.[18]

While the party had an urban orientation in other regions, most attention in Texas was given to the rural areas where nearly two-thirds of the population resided.

State party co-founder E. O. Meitzen, for instance, had a history of radical populism and carried this experience into the Socialist Party. He had been a member of the Grange (a farmers' mutual aid society), helped organize the Farmers' Alliance (an anti-corporate collective aligned with the Knights of Labor), and later joined the Populist Party, where he edited an affiliated newspaper during the 1890s.[19] The party recruitment strategy in the countryside setting used the encampment model. Drawing from populist and Christian revivalist traditions common in the region, these encampments brought together hundreds of farm families in the off-season to camp, play games, share food, and to hear speakers give rousing, revival-like sermons. In this case, instead of Christian gospel, they heard socialists preach of class struggle between capital and labor.

In rural Texas, the Socialists entered a terrain with a long tradition of agrarian organization and radicalism. Nevertheless, the forces of capitalism were winning the battle for supremacy. Huge tracts of land were awarded or sold on the cheap to financial speculators, railroad conglomerates, cattle companies, well-connected Washington insiders, and other rich and powerful interests in the immediate aftermath of the Civil War. By the turn of the century, industrial agriculture and land speculators backed by eastern finance capital were running rampant over small and middle-sized farming and ranching communities and penetrating deeper into the farthest reaches of the state. As Socialist leader Tom Hickey observed,

> In no place in the world can the trend of capitalism along the lines of agriculture be observed at first hand as it can in Texas. The great steam plows and mechanical cotton pickers on bonanza farms can be observed side by side with primitive methods of agriculture, that Potiphar's men might have used in Egypt. Of still greater benefit to the student of economic development is the fact that this tremendous area has been taken over, within the lives of men now living, by a few great capitalists who possess greater landed possessions than any landlord in Europe ever dreamed of.[20]

The introduction of industrial irrigation accelerated dispossession in the southern border counties, as investment soared and the value of farmland skyrocketed. In Cameron and Webb Counties, the value of farmland doubled, and in Hidalgo County it tripled.[21] As land was concentrated in fewer hands, a growing number of the dispossessed farmers turned to tenancy. Tenants grew as a class of land renters who worked on large farms in exchange for up to a third of all produce in a given harvest, as well as a range of other deductions that eroded the income of tenants to the level of subsistence. Tenancy was virtually nonexistent until 1870, when it increased to 5 percent. With the invasion of capital, it increased to 37.6 percent by 1880 and to over 52 percent in 1910, representing close to 220,000 tenants.[22] The growth of a class of white small and subsistent tenant farmers paralleled the experience of the Mexican tenants. In the southern region of the state, white, black, and Mexican tenants labored alongside each other, amid a larger population of Mexican itinerant workers. Particularly egregious for those without land was that much of the concentrated land was not under cultivation or used for productive purposes. According to historian Neil Foley, more than one hundred million acres of tillable land in Texas was held idle for speculation, amid a sea of small tenant farmers and landless agricultural workers.[23]

The party grew quickly in this environment, recruiting thousands of dues-paying members by 1910 and becoming the second-largest vote getter by 1912, second only to the Democrats.[24] The Socialist Party's main newspaper, The Rebel, rose in circulation to become the largest regional paper with a circulation of 25,000 at its height, and the third largest paper in the Socialist press nationally.[25] The growth of the party throughout the southern portion of the state brought it into direct contact with a large population of Mexican tenant farmers, landless laborers, and the PLM. Like their counterparts in Los Angeles, the Socialist Party of Texas formed an alliance with the magonistas and encouraged its organizers to recruit Mexicans and form Spanish-speaking branches, especially after the outbreak of the Mexican Revolution and the prospect of agrarian rebellion.

Despite an official platform that advocated for racial equality, the party initially accommodated to pervasive racial prejudice. Emerging from the populist movement, some party leaders internalized the racial contradictions that characterized the "People's Party" in its final years. At the height of its growth and influence, the populists supported multiracial organizing and opposed black lynching and disenfranchisement. After fusing with the Democrats in 1896, many party leaders, such as Tom Watson, abandoned notions of racial equality and accommodated to the Democratic Party's drive for racial segregation. Tom Hickey regularly pandered to racists within the party ranks, often publishing articles and letters that assailed black workers as inferior and incapable of being organized, and serving only as stooges for bosses against white and socialist tenant farmers.[26]

Unlike the Oklahoma Socialist Party, which actively opposed the disenfranchisement of African Americans, the Texas organization remained aloof from fighting the issue on racial terrain. While the party opposed the poll tax and organized fundraisers for branch members, its positions on the specifics of racial equality vacillated and were muddled. The Rebel, for instance, reflected an early accommodation to the volatile and contradictory characteristics of small, proprietary farmers. Early editions contained articles and published letters from white tenants akin to conservative craft labor's notion of Mexican immigration threatening white labor, which reflected how white landlords manipulated racial divisions to their advantage. When white tenants became "politically active," the landlords turned them out and replaced them with newly arrived Mexican migrants. Mexican socialists and PLM adherents were instrumental in pushing the Texas Socialist Party's position toward organizing the Mexican tenants.[27]

By 1908, Socialist leaders like Hickey tempered their anti-Mexican stance, following the national party's lead in openly supporting the Partido Liberal Mexicano and raising funds for the imprisoned leadership. This opened the door for more collaboration between Socialist Party operatives and the magonistas and their supporters and collaborators. The convergence of the socialist movement in Texas with mexicano revolutionaries led to a synthesis of outlook and objective. Like the PLM, the Socialist Party elaborated a critique of US imperialism and its deleterious effects on workers on both sides of the border, and both saw the need to recruit the Mexican laboring classes in order to win their cause. These and other commonalities provided a nexus point, with the PLM and Socialists working together in the Mexican barrios and camps and cross-promoting their respective causes. The PLM organizers had the contacts and networks, and understood the people, culture, and history. The socialists were able to provide organizational infrastructure and resources to mobilize Mexican workers as part of their struggle against a common class enemy in the capitalist landlords north of the border. Together, they created the potential for a mass movement of agricultural labor, tenants, and itinerant labor that could turn the tables on a landowning class deeply invested in Jim Crow racism as a means to preserve their wealth.

The outbreak of the revolution, and especially the onset of the radical agrarian phase with the zapatista uprising, inspired Texas socialists to envision the possibility for a similar revolt at home. The Plan de Ayala, for instance, called for a radical re-distribution of the land from the hacendados to the campesinos and Indian pueblos from whom it was taken through corrupt and unjust means. This fit the mold of the analysis of Texas, and the more radical elements looked upon the Mexicans in their own environs in a different light. The Socialist Party openly supported the organiza-tion of Mexican tenant farmers, and the pages of the *Rebel* moved sharply to the left as the Mexican Revolution progressed, heaping admiration for the revolutionary ardor of the Mexicans on both sides of the Río Grande. The first Socialist endeavor in this direction was the effort to recruit both white and Mexican tenant farmers and laborers into the same organization, the Land League.

The Renter's Union, the Land League, and the Mexican Tenant

Socialists in the Midwest looking at the land tenure question developed different points of view about how to address it. These divisions were aired at the 1912 national convention of the Socialist Party in Indianapolis. Left-wing positions advocated for a socialist model based on land collectivization, state ownership, and planned, collabo-rative production as a means to negate capitalist competition and tenancy. Delegates on the right of the party supported the retention of private landownership rights as a practical means to recruit small farmers, whom they characterized as potential allies, oppressed by large farmers. After a bruising debate, the idea of collectivization was defeated, and a modified proposal was passed. The new proposal supported a mixed public-private ownership model, in which private ownership was to be retained based on existing occupancy patterns.

As a concession to the Left, the platform contained a plan to end tenancy by converting publicly owned land into state-supported collective farms, and to place a progressive tax on landownership to militate against speculation and concentra-tion. This compromise allowed for the two wings of the party to coexist and grow in the short term, but it also set up longer-term problems as the appeal to proprietary farmers increased the ranks of middle-class landowners in the party. For instance, between 1910 and 1912, the state party increased its membership over 200 percent and added several additional newspapers.[28] Nevertheless, left-wing Socialists developed a campaign in 1911 called the Renter's Union (changed to the Land League in 1915), which aimed to organize the ranks of landless tenants and agricultural laborers into a common union.

For the socialists, highly unequal land distribution produced fertile terrain for making socialism relevant for a large, rural population. The Renter's Union was formed in Waco, Texas, in November of 1911, with 110 representatives of tenant groups coming together from 24 counties across the state. As a *Waco Morning News* commenter observed prior to the conference:

> [S]ome active minds among the tenant farmers have been doing some figuring based on that enormous acreage of idle raw land. They figure that, dividing the 130,000,000 [acres of idle land] by 219,000 the number of tenant farmers reported in the state of Texas by the 1910 census, would give each tenant 622 acres.[29]

The raucous conference proceeded under the slogan, "Landlordism must go!" and called for radical changes to defend renters. These included declaring the principle that use and occupancy were the only title to land, that a "confiscatory tax" be placed on idle land held in speculation, and that excessive and arbitrary taxes be eliminated. They pledged to organize a national renters' congress, to boycott parties at the polls who did not support their demands, and to use a "renter's strike" as a tool against the landlords. The next day's *Waco Morning News* made sure its readers were well aware of the role of socialists in the conference, remarking how it was "closing its session with the singing of a socialist hymn, adopting resolutions written by socialists and serving under officers who were socialists."[30]

On the question of organization, the convention declared that only bona fide tillers of the soil could be members, and only small renters who were producing for need. They also called for an independent, nonsectarian, and democratic organization inclusive of all renters. While broad in scope, Socialist Party members won the main leadership posts. In fact, the Renter's Union provided the main vehicle for the growth of the party in Texas.[31] While the exclusively white conference did not address explicitly the issue of multiracial organizing, Socialist Party members used its mandate to do just that with the assistance of the PLM. PLM members joined with Socialist Party members to organize large speaking engagements in San Antonio to recruit for the Renter's Union.

The Renter's Union focused on the challenges of previous efforts to combine small farmers and laborers in the same organization. The union declaration compared tenant farming to factory-like relations of production, with landowners imposing oppressive and inefficient production farming methods that essentially robbed the fruit of the tenant's labor:

> Landlords demand contracts that interfere with the individual and personal liberty of the tenant, as well as the manner in which he cultivates his crop. Through

this system of tenantry [*sic*] that is inherent in the capitalist system, overcrop-ping and single cropping is causing the soil to lose its fertility and thereby the present and future generations are robbed. The increase in land values has made it impossible for the tenant under ordinary conditions to buy and pay for land.[32]

Since the Mexican and Mexican American population were disproportionately concentrated in the ranks of tenant farmers and landless workers, they joined in sig-nificant numbers, bringing party workers into contact with this population and their existing organizations. The most militant of the Mexican workers and farmers joined the Socialist Party, and the more radical elements of the party encouraged the forma-tion of Mexican locals in Bridgeport and Matagorda Bay.[33]

Impressed with their interest in the party's efforts and Socialist program, the leadership hired Antonio Valdez in 1910 to build branches of the Renter's Union among the Spanish-speaking, Mexican population in the central and southern parts of the state. Valdez, a Tejano veteran of the PLM, organized Renter's Union gatherings in coordination with locally established PLM clubs or affiliated mutualistas.

According to *The Rebel*, Valdez was "the livest wire in the movement," organizing four Mexican locals: one in Gonzales County; one in Fentress (where a PLM club already existed) and another in Luling, both in Caldwell County; and a fourth lo-cal at Bluff Springs in Travis County.[34] One regional gathering of the Renter's Union brought over a thousand mostly Mexican delegates from across Central Texas to Uh-land, Texas.[35] Shortly after these successes, Valdez, like other Mexican radicals at the time, packed up and headed south to fight in the revolution.[36]

As a result of the success within the Mexican community, the Socialist leadership hired two more Mexican organizers, the brothers José Angel and F. A. Hernández. The Hernández brothers came to Houston around 1911 from Tepic, Nayarit, for work. They took jobs in construction and meatpacking and became socialists through reading Mex-ican socialist papers in Texas linked to the PLM.[37] In 1913, they were recruited into the Socialist Party, and José Hernández became a Spanish-speaking orator on behalf of the party. He continued to work alongside PLM organizers as well, at one point sharing a speaking platform with fellow Socialist and magonista Lázaro Gutiérrez de Lara, and two other Texas-based PLM activists named Lucio Luna and Donancio Hernández. The group, who also published their own joint newspaper, *Lucha de Clases* (Class Struggle), addressed a crowd of over a thousand Mexican tenants and laborers.[38] In his speech, he revealed the influence of magonista thought: "I said that I favored a free education of the masses, untrammeled by church or capitalistic rule, on the order of the Ferrer schools . . . I told my countrymen that the Land League was the best organization of the workers . . . [and to] vote the ticket of the working class, the Socialist Party."[39] José Angel Hernández was later arrested for his speech and charged with "inciting rebellion." It was the third time he had been arrested. As the editors of *The Rebel* explained:

> It was his advocacy for the Socialist City ticket, and his subsequent attempts to organize the farm workers in the country adjoining San Antonio that drew down on him the ire of interlocked parasites of Southwest Texas who could all the more persecute him and get away with it because he was a Mexican and because

of the disturbed conditions on the border . . . [He was] on the point of bringing thousands of Mexicans into the Land League, and from thence into the party of the working class.[40]

The brothers were hired on as organizers to continue the work of Valdez and the Renter's Union, which was renamed the Land League of America in 1915 and re-structured to allow small, proprietary farmers into the membership. The organizing efforts of the two brothers were well-received within the Mexican communities with the help of other PLM activists in the state, who helped publicize their campaigns through their press and through the coordination of speaking events in the Mexican communities. As Neil Foley observed, "the Land League derived much of its radical ideology and oppositional strategies from its Mexican membership and their ties to the PLM."[41] Over the course of one year, they successfully organized a total of twenty Mexican Land League locals in fourteen counties in the central and southern part of the state and traveled regularly through the Mexican communities speaking at rallies and meeting with league locals.[42] The efforts of the Land League occurred while Mex-ican revolutionaries were expropriating vast estates south of the border and the Plan of San Diego stirred major conflict on the border.

The radical agrarianism that motivated Zapatismo carried over into Texas, where the Mexican and Mexican American population was also dispossessed and reduced to an impoverished agricultural proletariat. Socialists in Texas like Tom Hickey became inspired by the Mexican Revolution and used it as an example to press for radical action north of the border. After learning of agrarian revolutionaries expropriating haciendas and implementing land reform at gunpoint, many left-wing socialists and Mexican laborers were radicalized, supporting the idea of replicating land expropria-tions in Texas. As Hickey proclaimed,

> Why should not the Mexican masses own the soil, where they were born, and which they till, and where their ancestors were born . . . [T]hings are rapidly shaping themselves for a similar revolution in Texas where four-fifths of the till-able land is held out of cultivation by . . . landlords who raise fake issues to dis-tract the minds of our people.[43]

The Rebel's editor even predicted the rise of a Zapata "north of the Río Grande" to settle accounts with the landowning oligarchy. The ensuing occupation of the state by thou-sands of federal troops and the persecution of the Hernández brothers showed that the US government also perceived this threat and moved to strangle it in its infancy.

When José Hernández was arrested and held on trumped-up federal charges (he was released January 1916), his brother F. A. was elected assistant state organizer of the league and continued his brother's work.[44] The Rebel claimed that by the end of 1915, over a thousand Mexicans had joined the Land League,

> furnishing an inspiration to the American renters and actual farmers who have less difficulties to overcome . . . than these strangers in a strange land, that certainly are of better metal than the poor fools that call them "greasers."[45]

For the landowners, repression was one of the antidotes for the growing ranks of a Socialist Party aligned with tenant rights, especially one uniting poor whites and Mexicans into the same organization. For instance, landowners circulated black-lists to exclude known members of the Renter's Union, and local sheriff's deputies hounded and harassed known socialist sympathizers at every turn. Violent methods of repression became more common after the Democratic Party officials, landowners, and law enforcement formed alliances through support for a rejuvenated, "new" Ku Klux Klan, which developed early on in East Texas in response to labor radicalism among black and white timber workers who formed an IWW union called the Broth-erhood of Timber Workers.[46] The other method to weaken the socialist movement was through racial co-optation.

Democrats, the state's dominant party of landowning capitalists and speculators, and the steward of promoting Jim Crow laws, had ignored the tenancy issue until the socialists came along. Beginning with the election of 1913, the Democratic Party can-didate James Ferguson ran on a platform that included a pledge to regulate land rental, explaining: "Take away the abuses of the present rent system and the Socialist would not have a leg to stand on."[47] Once in office, the Democrat pushed for a watered-down version of his pledge, which was quickly ruled unconstitutional by grower-aligned state courts. Nevertheless, this served as a pull for the middle-class farmer elements in the party, which shifted their support back to the Democratic Party and accommo-dated to the practice of Jim Crow and anti-immigrant sentiment.

The Rebel decried the opportunism of the Democrats, claiming that "the system-atic agitation of the Land League has brought to the front the plight of the tenant so that designing demagogues have been able to ride into office with fair promises on the wave of public sentiment created by this agitation."[48] By rhetorically taking on the issue while aggressively advocating against Mexican immigration, and fervently supporting racial segregation, the party tried to divide the fledgling movement. The success of this effort was aided by divisions within the Socialist Party, opening the door to its decline.

When cotton markets collapsed in 1915, class tensions intensified across the southeastern region of Texas. Bankers charged more excessive loan rates and cut off credit, landlords pushed up rents across the board, and tenants who spoke out or joined the Renter's Union were summarily evicted, blacklisted, and replaced with wage labor.[49] These efforts coincided with increased repression, as an alliance of state and private agents conducted campaigns of collective punishment of mexicano com-munities along the border. While no similar "army of liberation" emerged in Texas, revolutionary activity did spread across the border in the different manifestations of the Plan of San Diego.

The Plan of San Diego

The Socialist Party was much weaker in the southern border counties, although the PLM had a concentration of adherents, sympathizers, and readers of *Regeneración*. By 1915, the revolutionary movement had returned to the borderlands. The Plan of

San Diego was a call to arms to spread insurrection into South Texas, but in this case by appealing directly to the sensibilities of Mexicans living within the United States. The small town of San Diego, straddling the southern Texas borderline of Duval and Jim Wells Counties, served as the birthplace of the plan. A majority mexicano town, San Diego was a regional agricultural hub sitting along the Texas Mexican Railway line and had a history of PLM activity among railroad workers in the area. The plan was the culmination of simmering tensions building within the Mexican community in Texas, now coming to the surface as workers and campesinos across Mexico were rising up against the dictatorship in its backers. At the height of the Plan of San Diego rebellion, an estimated 1,000–3,000 Tejanos and Mexicanos had reportedly pledged to support the cause.[50]

By the turn of the century, Mexicans in South Texas had lived under the dominion of white landowners. The form and function of the Texas Rangers mirrored the social enforcement needs of this landowner class. Historically, the Rangers were used specifically to police the frontiers between the dominant whites and subordinate classes in their midst. They expelled the indigenous population, and were used to hunt and retrieve runaway slaves and to suppress acts of Mexican discontent following the Texas occupation and annexation. As the land became concentrated in the hands of large capitalist farmers and speculators and Mexicans filled the ranks of the agricultural proletariat and farm tenant class, the purview of Ranger enforcement expanded. As Jim Crow segregation was implemented to reproduce this class structure, the Rangers became part of the apparatus used to contain Mexicans in their communities and to suppress labor organizing and left-wing agitation.

By the outbreak of the Mexican Revolution, state violence and racial segregation were normalized features of life for most Mexicans. The magonista press monitored and condemned increasing instances of violence.

> In the state of Texas, Mexicans are not admitted in restaurants, inns or hotels used by whites, and many public schools exclude Mexican children. The so-called Courts of justice trample on the rights of Mexicans without a second thought, and it's the same with the police and other agents of authority. In this country "justice" is an expensive commodity rarely obtained by the disinherited.[51]

The first manifestation of the Plan of San Diego was attributed to a pair of recently arrived mexicanos who took up residence in the town, led by a Nuevo Laredo customs agent named Basilio Ramos and a former schoolteacher named Augustín Garza. The collaborators circulated the plan and conspired locally through kinship connections, acquiring a small cohort of followers. In the process of recruitment, Ramos was subsequently revealed to the police by a would-be adherent, arrested, and the plan revealed.

The original Plan of San Diego was modeled after recent Mexican revolutionary plans. It contained some radical agrarian characteristics of Zapata's Plan de Ayala, but focused wholly on Mexicans and their conditions in the Southwest of the United States. The plan called for the creation and armed uprising of a "Liberating Army of Races and Peoples" against the US government on February 20, 1915, and encouraged

Native Americans, Japanese, and African peoples to support the effort. The stated goal was the reclamation of Texas, New Mexico, Arizona, Colorado, and California as part of a new and racially egalitarian independent nation, free of "North American imperialism." The lands of native people were to be restored and six US states awarded to the black population to form their own nation. To accommodate this transfer, all Anglo males over sixteen years of age were to be executed. While the plan outlined the rudiments of a military structure that united a network of commanders under one central command, it appears that the effort was launched without any local infrastructure or a significant base of support within the community. Due to this disconnect, as well as the utopian and extreme character of its vision, the true origins and purpose of the plan remain unclear and debated by historians.[52] After the arrest of Ramos, Garza joined with a new group of participants that included individuals previously linked to PLM activity in South Texas.

After its abortive inauguration the idea of the plan later served as a rallying point for others attracted to the idea of taking direct action against the symbols of state violence and Anglo dominance in South Texas. A second manifestation of a revolutionary plan emerged, containing a focus and language of a more radical nature and reflecting convergence between the original conspirators and some magonistas. The PLM was active in South Texas when the Plan of San Diego was announced. Several clubs were active in the southern counties, with around 165 known magonistas active in Cameron and Hidalgo Counties alone.[53]

The PLM adherents in South Texas were active and organizing in different ways, like their comrades in other parts of the Southwest. A moderate wing led by Aniceto Pizaña focused on organizing PLM clubs, developing *Regeneración* reading groups and supporting local labor activity. Another wing led by a man named Luis de la Rosa, became more pronounced and coherent as the revolution progressed and radicalized Mexicans north of the border. After the pronouncement of the Plan of San Diego, this group became inspired by the possibilities for expanding the revolution into Texas. This was contrary to the wishes of the PLM leadership, which retained its focus on Mexico exclusively.[54]

Aniceto Pizaña was a migrant farmworker turned rancher in Cameron County who had become a devoted magonista after meeting the group in Laredo in 1904. He became an organizer for the PLM, forming a club in Brownsville. Through the club, he and others distributed copies of *Regeneración* and built up a base of supporters to prepare for the coming insurrections. His club, named Perpetual Solidarity, was linked to PLM cells across the border in Tamaulipas and provided material support for the abortive insurrections of 1906 and 1908. Despite his fervor and persistent support, Pizaña did not join the insurrections initially. He owned a small ranch, was married, and had several children. A racist incident drew him into the leadership of a subsequent armed campaign in Texas.

His rancho was raided by a squad that included the sheriff of Cameron County, several sheriff's deputies, a group of white vigilantes, and a detachment of ten army cavalry. The aim was to arrest local Mexican ranchers based on the false allegation of a resentful white rancher named Jeff Scrivener, who accused them of abetting cross-border raiders. Upon arrival, a shootout occurred, killing one soldier and wounding Pizaña's twelve-year-old son. Fearing execution if he was arrested, Pizaña fled. He perceived that Anglo landowners were using the conflict as a cover to carry out a coordinated campaign to dispossess Mexican ranchers like himself across the region. According to Rodolfo Rocha, "He concluded that the solution was to drive the Anglos out of the Valley. By September he had identified a sufficient number of like-minded Mexicans [likely PLM cohorts] in the area to initiate the Tejano revolt."[55] Under his leadership, thereafter began the second iteration of the Plan of San Diego.

The second manifestation had the fingerprints of PLM ideological influence. Declaring the impossibility of ignoring racial depredations against Mexicans in Texas, it was addressed to "Nuestros Compatriotas, Los Mexicanos en Texas" and declared itself the beginning of a "social revolution that would emancipate all peoples and races in the United States."[56] The trajectory of the new plan shows convergence with the tenants' movement and PLM campaigns for education reform. As historian James Sandos summarized its main tenets:

> The Plan of San Diego now enumerated specific clauses describing particular objectives. Clause IV called for delivery of cultivated land to the proletarians, with preference given to tenant farmers and those fighting for the movement. Absolute communization of the land might be proclaimed. Communal sharing and distribution of rural property, of access to communication media, and of supplies and tools—all without national distinction (VI, IX)—complemented the abolition of race hatred. To help build the new future, the Plan now called for creation of "Modern Schools where all children regardless of color and without class prejudice [might] prepare the future happiness of a Society whose acts would be governed by the norms of UNIVERSAL LOVE."[57]

While linked directly to the events of the Mexican Revolution, the second revolt was also a reaction to increased violence against Mexicans, especially through ranger and vigilante actions. The narrative of pro-Texan history has characterized the early border region as a lawless border region, characterized by "Mexican and Indian depredations." Texans deported Kickapoo Indians from their homelands in South Texas in 1839. Texas Rangers made incursions into Mexico to snatch and return escaped slaves.

Pizaña and de la Rosa coordinated groups of up to one hundred armed ranchers and workers to conduct targeted attacks that persisted from May to October 1915. One attack targeted Alfred Austin, a notoriously anti-Mexican landowner and member of a vigilante group called the Sebastian Law and Order League, notorious for the lynching of Mexicans. He and his adult son were killed in an attack on July 4. Other attacks targeted large ranchers and their properties, military personnel, Mexicans aligned with local power structures, vital points of transportation such as bridges and railroad trestles, and communications systems such as telephone and telegraph lines. All told, plan adherents organized about thirty attacks and raids over the course of eight weeks, involving on average around eighty participants.[58] Posters appeared and were circulated in greater frequency on both sides of the border and took on a more radical character. One called for "'Redemption of the Disinherited" through expropriation:

> The moment has come to shake off the iron yoke . . . let us destroy it but at the same time build . . . War to Capital, War to the Clergy, War to the State, [to] every-thing that smells of oppression. War without quarter to the *gringos*. ¡*Basta Ya*![59]

Another handbill appealed to the memory of the Chicago Haymarket martyrs, while another called for the destruction of "capitalistic society" and the implantation of a new society, forming one "universal family in which peace and justice may reign."

The pace and scale of the attacks increased over time, but remained scattered and isolated. Furthermore, they failed to spark wider involvement although they revealed the depth of socio-economic polarization and antagonism between poor Mexicans and the dominant Anglo establishment. The raids and attacks affected only small numbers in the countryside. According to official statistics, six civilians were killed and eight wounded, while eleven soldiers were killed and seventeen wounded.[60] Later historians calculate that it was closer to sixty-two civilians (including vigilan-tes) and sixty-four soldiers.[61] Nevertheless, a perceived fear of a general uprising of poor Mexicans spread among the white elites. A *San Antonio Express* article captures the paranoid histrionics:

> Practically every American citizen in the three southernmost counties of Texas, Cameron, Hidalgo, and Starr, is resting under arms tonight in fear that the over-whelming population of this section may break out in a racial fight . . . The dis-turbance today came out definitely in its true colors, an attempt to turn part of Texas back to Mexican control, a wild scheme backed partly by ignorant classes of Mexicans, helped by escaped convicts and fugitives from justice on the Amer-ican side, including some Mexican soldiers.[62]

Anglo landowners and their families moved into nearby towns, abandoning their properties and threatening the economy. The response from the state was to crush the disturbances with overwhelming power, which opened the door to wholesale vio-lence against the Mexican community.

In response to revolutionary events crossing the border in Texas, a villista raid into Columbus, New Mexico, and massive wartime strikes in Arizona mining, the federal government mobilized the military. Approximately fifty thousand regular troops were sent to the southern border region, which was designated a new military zone called the "Southern Department."[63] The troop movement included the redeployment of US forces then withdrawing from the US invasion and occupation of Veracruz. The largest portion of the troops were stationed in Texas, with a base of operations at Fort Sam Houston in San Antonio under the leadership of General Frederick Funston. Funston had a distinguished career in the US Army, working his way up to general through his participation in armies of colonial occupation in Cuba and the Philippines. He man-aged the occupation of Veracruz in 1914, and was now tasked with administering the

Southern Department, a military base of operations extending from South Texas to San Diego, California.

As a participant in the war against the Filipinos, he openly bragged of his bravado and disdain for basic human rights, stating that the war could be won quicker with the use of terror and violence:

> I personally strung up thirty-five Filipinos without trial, so what was all the fuss over ... 'dispatching' a few 'treacherous savages'? If there had been more [of such killings], the war would have been over long ago. Impromptu domestic hanging might also hasten the end of the war. For starters, all Americans who had recently petitioned Congress to sue for peace in the Philippines should be dragged out of their homes and lynched.[64]

His celebrated "war with no quarter" approach, tinged with racist disdain for the "savage" enemy, was determined by the chain of command to be the most suitable approach against Mexicans in South Texas. Military detachments were stationed across South Texas at fixed locations and in roving patrols. They rode on trains, guarded irrigation depots, and were posted near other strategic locations where attacks could occur.

Other high-ranking law enforcement officials involved in the operations were inclined toward violent suppression of the Mexican population in the direct interest of their own investments. William Mangum Hansen, for instance, rose from sheriff of Gonzales County to an investor in the San Antonio and Gulf Shore Railroad. In 1898, he received the appointment of United States marshal for the Western District of Texas, once again leaving law enforcement in 1906 to join the frenzy of investors speculating in Mexican oil and agricultural production. He became part owner and general manager of the Mexico Land Company, controlling approximately thirty thousand acres; the sole owner of a three-thousand-acre citrus farm; and president of the Mexico Gulf Coast Fruit Association, which was the largest citrus producer in the nation. He was also president of the Buena Vista Land and Irrigation Company controlling eight thousand acres; general manager of the Tamesi Petroleum and Asphalt Company; and general manager of the Standard Petroleum Company and architect of its endeavors in the Tampico oil fields.[65]

In protecting his substantial investments in the face of revolutionary instability, Hansen became a political partisan in aligning himself with counterrevolutionary efforts on both sides of the border. He used his personal hacienda in Mexico as a base of operations to spy on Mexican officials and report troop movements and other activities that might be of value to officials in Texas and Washington.[66] After being expelled from Mexico and nearly executed for his collaboration with the fallen Huerta regime, he returned to the US to seek a means to recover his losses. While back in Texas, he actively supported counterrevolutionary plots. In one instance, he helped arrange the provision of five million rounds of ammunition for Felix Díaz, nephew of the deposed dictator, raising funds and support from US investors eager to help him march his troops into battle and strangle the revolution once and for all.[67] By 1918, Hansen was appointed to the position of inspector of the Rangers, a sort of Internal Affairs chief, whose first task was to investigate a Ranger massacre of fifteen Mexicans in Porvenir, Texas. According to witnesses, a group of Rangers and white ranchers singled out fifteen Mexican men of this community, led them outside the village, and executed them: "The Rangers and ranchers shot the victims, in the body and the head, each skull hallowed by a bullet hole. The Rangers left the bodies in parallel lines, with no pretense of burying the bodies . . . then they and their accomplices whooped and hollered as they rode into the night."[68] Shortly thereafter, the remaining population of 140 people fled south, abandoning the village.[69]

The results of Hanson's "investigation" yielded no wrongdoing, and the investigation was concluded. The heinousness and scale of the crime led to a separate investigation by the army, which proceeded to make its results known directly to Hanson. Quietly, the Rangers involved were reassigned or dismissed from duty without further scrutiny of the rampant violence of the Rangers. With federal and state agents taking a tack toward widespread repression and impunity, the military operation opened the door for an even more violent campaign conducted by white terror organizations against the Mexican community.

For Ricardo Flores Magón and the Socialists, the scale of US military deployment, from the Gulf of Mexico to the Pacific Ocean, exposed the role of the US military as a counterrevolutionary bulwark. The Veracruz occupation and encirclement and threat of invasion served to temper the radical protagonists, while the suppression of the Mexicans on the border served to protect the transnational investments and pacify disaffected Mexicans. Under the cover of military occupation, localized violence was unleashed.

Vigilante and white terror organizations were already part of the fabric of white society as a means to enforce Jim Crow racism and oppose labor radicalism. These organizations reactivated en masse across the South to begin operations. Wealthy landowners formed their own "protective associations" and business groups applied pressure on the state and federal government to send in troops and artillery. When federal troops were stationed throughout the region, vigilante groups in league with the local power structure operated with impunity under their watch, carrying out widespread and systematic lynching. The organized groups unleashed a reign of terror against the whole Mexican population. Within the border counties, vagrancy laws were enacted to control the movement of Mexicans, social gatherings were prohibited, and homes in Mexican barrios were systematically searched, resulting in beatings and summary executions if guns were found.

White vigilante groups openly developed and circulated lists of Mexicans to target for execution, and the state governor announced in October 1915 a thousand-dollar bounty for the leaders of the revolt, "alive or dead."[70] The "open season" manner in which extralegal violence was meted out against whole populations regardless of their guilt or innocence allowed for unscrupulous white ranchers (like Jeff Scrivener) to target their Mexican rivals or to dispossess Mexican ranchers of the lands they coveted.[71] They also attacked communities in an arbitrary manner to instill fear and to weed out supporters and participants. White vigilante groups also burned down homes, forcibly entered residences to confiscate firearms, and ethnically cleansed whole communities as punishment for alleged sympathies with the rebels. The violence was so intense that one conservative historian even expressed dismay at the scale and lawlessness of the bloodletting:

Killing suspected captives "while attempting to escape" was widely practiced by rangers and local officials, and deliberate execution of other prisoners was so common that it created hardly a ripple of interest among newsmen. The number of men subject to such summary "justice" is unknown.[72]

Judges, local politicians, Rangers, and landowners engaged in or supported a campaign of terror within the Mexican community, assuming that all laboring Mexicans were in a state of insurgency, were supporters of their countrymen, or were at least indifferent to it. As the military commander of Brownsville casually stated, "Owing to race antagonism engendered the past few months in this section of the valley about fifty percent of the Mexican male population [is] disloyal in thought and possibly ten percent of these disloyal in action when opportunity offers."[73] One Anglo newspaper, the *Cameron Herald*, reveled in the lynch-frenzy and bloodletting, callously commenting, "Let's don't kill any more of these poor wretches than can be helped. The average Mexican down on the border would behave himself if he knew how."[74]

An estimated seven thousand Mexicans fled in terror across the border from the counties of Cameron and Hidalgo alone, leaving behind their homes, lands, and whatever they couldn't carry. The evaporation of the agricultural workforce further destabilized the regional economy, spreading panic among the state's economic interests. Since the violence was so widespread, unreported, and unaccounted for, the death statistics for the period are unknown. Historians estimate anywhere from 300 to 5,000 were killed.[75]

While the Socialist Party had no direct connection to the events on the border, some party leaders linked the repression of Mexicans to what their members were experiencing. After a 1915 Associated Press article carried by several South Texas dailies leveled a racist attack on Mexicans in South Texas, *The Rebel* came to their defense. The article claimed that wanton violence from Mexico was now cropping up in South Texas, as Mexicans were preparing to unleash a "reign of terror" to restore "to Mexico the lost state of Texas" because the "long existence of unhampered barbarous warfare has incited many ignorant greasers to deeds of violence."[76] Exposing the story as concocted, factually erroneous, and racist in nature, the editors mockingly explained the article's purpose in a hypothetical first-person narrative of the original writer:

> Let us in the interest of the landlord and moneylord stir up strife between the races. Let us pit the Texas worker against the Mexican worker and inflame the public mind by the pricks of our poisoned pens. Let us do this for the financial aggrandizement of the landlords and then mayhap we may get a few of the crumbs that may fall from his table, because we can show him that we can stop the organization into the Land League of the men whom they exploit regardless of which side of the line they were born on.[77]

While Mexican forces under the Constitutionalist banner engaged in some intrigue with the Texas revolt, the epicenter of the actual revolt was Texan in origin.[78] Carranza's faction in the Mexican Revolutionary process used the Texas insurgency to his advantage, allowing local commanders to engage in intrigue with cross-border raiding for their own reasons as part of a larger strategy to leverage US recognition of his regime.

When efforts moved more favorably in that direction, Carranza worked closely with the Wilson administration to squash the stirrings of revolt on the border, deploying a permanent force of over 100 rural police (rurales) to monitor eighteen separate common crossing areas along the border.[79] It also became part of a larger imperative for both ruling groups to suppress radicalism in the borderlands, as they increased their overall efforts to suppress radical labor movements in their own respective countries. Carranza launched a war to crush the Casa Del Mundo Obrero in Mexico, which began to organize nationwide strikes against the regime in 1916. For Wilson, a simultaneous war of elimination was directed toward the Left in the US, including the arrest and suppression of Socialist Party leaders (including in Texas as well as other parts of the country), PLM organizers, and Wobblies in the lead-up to US entry into World War I.[80]

By June of 1916, events took another turn. As the campaign to suppress low-intensity guerrilla warfare in South Texas was coming to a conclusion, a possible full-scale invasion into Mexico to protect profitable investments and to retain control of the nation's strategic resources seemed imminent. Regular troops were positioned for invasion, while 150,000 National Guard troops scrambled from 47 states and the District of Columbia fanned out across the border. In response to the *revoltoso* activity along the border and possible invasion of Mexico, Congress expeditiously passed the National Defense Act of 1916, allowing the president to move troops quickly to respond to "invasion, insurrection, or threat of invasion."[81]

Ricardo Flores Magón paid close attention to events unfolding in Texas. While he distanced himself from the original plan and downplayed the relationship of the uprisings to the Mexican Revolution, he characterized the events as a reflection of social and economic inequality and the participants as disinherited people "who found themselves in misery and saw the opportunity to gain bread through violence."[82]

He criticized how the bourgeois media made use of the rhetoric of the original Plan of San Diego to whip up anti-Mexican sentiment and lynch-mob violence, and then conflated it with the revolt led by Aniceto Pizaña and Luis de la Rosa. After these men and others took up arms in self-defense against vigilante lynch law, the media "continued insisting this was a race war whose principal objective was to kill Americans and to carry on the war until the recovery of the immense territory Mexico lost in 1847."[83] In the pages of *Regeneración*, he identified what was happening as an "authentic economic and social movement," and wholeheartedly condemned the "orgy of blood" that killed hundreds of innocent people. He concluded:

> Justice and not bullets, is what should be given to the revolutionaries of Texas. And from there, we should all demand an end to the persecution of innocent Mexicans, and, in respect to the revolutionaries, we should demand that they not be shot. Those who should be shot are the "rangers" and the mob of bandits that accompany them in their depredations.[84]

As the border became a zone of revolutionary conflict, so too did the Socialist Party become a battleground for the different tendencies now aligning with different factions.

Chapter 13
Socialists, the PLM, and the Mexican Revolution

*"During long years of talk dissensions necessarily arise; but when
action takes the place of talk; when at last the proletariat rises
to throw off its chains; these differences should vanish, and every
honest soul should feel that it is treason to stand aside."*
—**Appeal sent to US Socialist Party locals calling for
support of the PLM's revolutionary objectives**

y 1912, the Socialist Party became a formidable third force in US politics, coinciding with an upturn in labor militancy in the US and the growth of the
American Federation of Labor. In 1910, there were 2 million workers in unions,
of which about 1.5 million were AFL-affiliated craft workers heavily concentrated
in mining, transportation, building trades, and manufacturing. One million more
joined AFL-affiliated unions by 1916.[1] In 1914, there were 1204 strikes nationally,
more than quadrupling to 4,450 in 1917.[2] The explosive rise in class struggle coincided with active US interventionism in the Caribbean, Central America, Asia, and
Mexico.

The Socialist Party had 58,000 members in 1910, and more than doubled to
125,000 in 1912; with 1,039 Socialists elected to office nationally, including 18 state legislators, 2 state senators, 56 mayors, 160 city council members, and 145 aldermen.[3] As
the Socialist Party grew on a national scale, so too did its press. By 1912, it claimed 323
papers and periodicals, including 44 non-English editions, estimated to have reached
up to a million readers.[4] By the time of the Mexican Revolution, the party exercised
significant influence within the working class. Through its southwestern branches, the
party made contact with the clubs of the PLM.

The PLM's tireless actions against the Díaz regime, the relentless persecution of
its membership in the US, and a small but significant core of Mexican Socialists north
of the border focused the US Socialist movement's attention to the chain of events unfolding in Mexico. The same capitalists concentrating corporate power in the US, conducting war on unions through the open-shop movement, using state power to crush
significant labor advances, and influencing the state to manage their affairs through
imperial intervention in Asia, the Caribbean, and Mexico were also those most agitated by Mexican revolutionaries in their midst.

Socialists closely followed developments in Mexico and publicly defended and
aided the PLM exiles, and took positions in their press on the course of events in
the revolution. They attempted to cultivate working-class support for the revolution,

225

while fervently condemning the role of capital and the threat of US military intervention in Mexico. As the revolution entered into an internecine phase after the toppling of Díaz, with moderate and radical forces vying for state control in order to implement rival doctrines, so too did the unified support fragment along ideological lines. The polarization between left, right, and center also played out in unfolding phases of the Mexican Revolution. Left socialist revolutionaries supported (and even joined) the magonistas in their cause for socialist revolution. Right and centrist socialists limited their support to the bourgeois revolutionary leadership of Madero and Carranza, believing the Mexican working class to be too underdeveloped for socialism.

Socialists Defend the Mexican Revolution

Between 1907 and 1911, a diverse range of liberals, radicals, organized labor, socialists, and anarchists built intersecting and overlapping campaigns of support for the persecuted PLM junta leaders and rallied against US intervention in the revolution. Opponents included agrarian Socialists in Texas, transnational miners in Arizona, radical West Coast journalists such as John Kenneth Turner, John Reed, Jack London, and Lincoln Steffens; Socialist labor leaders such as Mary "Mother" Jones and prominent national party leaders such as Eugene Debs; direct action-oriented Wobblies such as "Big" Bill Haywood; and high-profile Anarchists such as Emma Goldman.

Through their presses they provided detailed coverage and analysis, while also petitioning readers for funds and announcing events and activities. Some, like small groups of Mexican socialists in Los Angeles, Arizona, and Texas, co-organized with or recruited for the PLM. At the height of the international moment of solidarity, the AFL leadership even briefly entertained the prospect of organizing Mexican workers in Los Angeles into a federal union. More enthusiastic co-thinkers, including members of the Industrial Workers of the World, crossed the border into Mexico to organize workers into IWW unions, and to participate in the PLM-led insurrection in Baja California in 1911.[5]

Militant opposition to US imperialist intrigue in Mexico, and to the threat of US intervention to preserve capitalist arrangements, manifested on both sides of the border before and during the revolution. The potential for the revolutionaries in Mexico to expropriate the land and key industrial facilities (such as oil) threatened a very profitable and geostrategic arrangement for US capital and military planners alike. Panicked US investors, who had substantial investment in the Mexican economy and in existing political arrangements, worked desperately through their channels to Washington, DC, to secure intervention. This included calls for a military invasion to protect their interests and to prop up the accommodating factions. The aggressive posturing, troop movements, interimperialist intrigue, and direct intervention of the federal government into the revolution drew strong opposition from the Socialists. *Appeal to Reason*, the largest of the papers with a half-million copies printed, began shedding light on the events in Mexico and the role of US capital in propping up the Díaz dictatorship:

> The Capitalist press is silent, for it does not want the truth known to the people. We on the other hand, must do everything in our power to turn on the light and to have the facts known ... [so that] this infamous conspiracy of capitalists against the wage slaves of both Mexico and the United States may be thwarted.[6]

Ad for *Barbarous Mexico* by Socialist John Kenneth Turner from the *International Socialist Review,* April 1916

In April of 1911, the National Executive Committee of the Socialist Party of

America issued a proclamation of opposition to the threat of US military intervention. In their statement, they characterized the military invasion of Mexico as the postscript of economic invasion.

> [Mexico] has been invaded by our Smelter Trust and Oil Trust, our Sugar Trust, Rubber Trust and Cordage Trust. The Wells-Fargo Express Company has acquired a monopoly of the Mexican express business, and the railroads, land and mines of the country are largely in the hands of American capitalists. The Rockefellers, Guggenheims and J. Pierpont Morgan, have vast holdings in Mexico; Henry W. Taft, brother of the President of the United States, is general counsel for the National Railways of Mexico, and hundreds of other American trust magnates are heavily interested in Mexican enterprises.[7]

The mission of the US troops, it concluded, was to save Díaz and crush the Mexican revolt. They called on socialists around the country to protest. Following the proclamation, Socialists joined coordinated rallies in different parts of the country. In April of 1911, for instance, a mass rally was held in San Francisco to oppose the placement of US troops along the border as a prelude to intervention. An estimated two thousand turned out to hear PLM leader Antonio Araujo, Socialist journalist John Kenneth Turner, and Wobbly Austin Lewis give speeches condemning US efforts to strangle the revolutionary process.[8]

The transnationalization of US capitalist exploitation had made socialists starkly aware of their potential ally in the Mexican radical, as they opposed the same robber barons on both sides of the border. Socialists began serious analysis of the character of the revolution through their party papers, developed a critique of US imperialist intervention, and refuted racist misconceptions about Mexico and its people in an attempt to foster solidarity from US workers. As *Appeal to Reason* explained:

> Their prejudice against their Mexican brethren, fostered in the interest of their masters, is disappearing as the truth dawns upon them that at bottom this struggle is an industrial struggle, and that Magón and his associates are [persecuted] only because they are leading an agitation which threatens the Díaz Administration, which is in fact the administration of the American trusts and corporation.[9]

The general accord against US imperialism in Mexico gave way to further theoretical divergence when analyzing the class character of the revolution itself.

Antonio de Pio Araujo 1908

Socialist Analyses of the Mexican Revolution

Most Socialists on the party's Right and Center viewed Mexico as a semi-feudal society with a small industrial proletariat, with a massive, underdeveloped peasantry
living in conditions of debt peonage or slavery. For them, following one traditional
interpretation of orthodox Marxism, Mexico had to go through a "bourgeois" revolution in order to shake off the semi-feudal social and religious traditions that prevented
democratization and capitalist modernization.[10] Furthermore, Mexico was locked into
backwardness by the dictator Díaz's Faustian pact with US imperialism, which kept it
subordinated to foreign capital as a colonial supplier of raw materials. As a result, this

arrangement kept most of the rural population steeped in backward, pre-capitalist social relations and traditions.

Accordingly, capitalism could play a liberating role in the "ancient," "feudal," and "Asiatic" societies underdeveloped by colonialism or isolated from the nodes of global capitalist development. As one *International Socialist Review* article surmised about the completion of the Panama Canal,

> it is commerce that has awakened the nations of the far East into a desire to adopt capitalistic methods of production. It is capitalistic production that produces a wage-working class of men and women. And it is these men and women who become the revolutionists that will one day arise to make the world a world of, for and by the workers themselves. The Isthmian Canal will be a great civilizer of the Eastern nations, and it is Civilization that produces socialists.[11]

While the conditions of debt peonage undoubtedly afflicted large swaths of the rural countryside, they co-existed alongside capitalist relations of production, which primarily served foreign capital. For many of these Socialists, the relatively small and isolated industrial proletariat, and the predominant scale and perceived backwardness of the indigenous and mestizo agricultural population, made it difficult for them to see their socialistic potential. In an article for the *International Socialist Review*, John Murray toured Mexico in 1909 with the support of the PLM. While one of the most stalwart supporters of the magonistas, he revealed his own biases against the working classes, and ignorance of the country's socioeconomic complexities. His report, titled "Mexico's Peon-Slaves Preparing for Revolution," metaphorically captures this gaze:

> I kept my face glued to the carriage window and asked myself this question: Mexico, Mexico, Mexico is—what? The answer seemed to rise from the passing throng of bent-backed human burden bearers, "Mexico is a land of cargadores" . . . In no other country in the world does the back so stagger under a dead weight as here in Mexico.[12]

Imperialism, economic underdevelopment, autocracy, and the reactionary hold of the Catholic Church terminally inhibited the development of Mexican society. For rightwing Socialists, this was conflated with already-existent notions of American exceptionalism and racial superiority, which were the dominant ideas of the US ruling class and the AFL by 1910.

The Right and Center defended the PLM of 1906–1911, whose plan contained the seeds of the bourgeois revolution that they believed Mexico needed. After the PLM's radical pronouncements of 1911, they broke with the magonistas and threw their support behind the bourgeois revolutionaries Madero and Carranza, who represented in earnest the bourgeois revolutionary promise of political democratization and unfettered capitalist development.

The left Socialist tendencies drew different conclusions. They agreed with the PLM's analysis of the class struggle, seeing the potential for a worker and peasant revolution and the direct transition to socialism. Left socialists also drew from a different aspect of Marxist thought. For instance, after Marx originally characterized the US-Mexico war as a progressive step toward stimulating capitalist development in feudal Mexico, later reexamination led him to change his views. After a thorough study of US westward expansion in the years prior to the Civil War, he characterized the Mexican American War as a calculated means by Southern planters and Northern bankers to profit off the spread of slavery into the northern territories of Mexico where slavery had been previously abolished. In other words, rather than a liberating force, capitalism had proven to be a retrogressive force preserving and expanding slavery and other forms of servitude for profit.[13]

Furthermore, in the early 1860s, Marx already observed how imperialism, as an international extension of the capitalist system, had stymied development in colonized countries and bred barbarism against the colonized. Marx also studied how colonized people resisted the imposition of capitalist relations of production through their own collective traditions of resistance, concluding that this made them natural allies of revolutionary workers in the imperialist countries. By 1865, he had fully changed his analysis of colonialism. Rather than seeing its demise as a consequence of the proletarian revolution, he now considered colonial revolution to be "a condition for the development of the workers movement" in the industrial, imperialist countries.[14] In other words, neither could be liberated unless both were. He also came to believe that pre-existing, pre-capitalist forms of socialist consciousness could enable people in the colonized world to transition to a modern socialist society without having to go through a complete "bourgeois capitalist stage of development."[15] The broad tent of the Socialist Party, with such divergent tendencies developing under the weight of world events, polarized over the socialist potential of the Mexican working class in the US.

Wilson Splits Labor and the Socialists
The influence of the Socialist Party press and the popularity of its main exponents contributed to the party's substantial influence within the working class, including within the AFL. Such a scale of support presented a challenge for the proponents of US intervention in Mexico in the period of the revolution. Anti-imperialist socialists had made a compelling case exposing the avaricious and deleterious effects of US capital south of the border and its nefarious role in propping up a venal and brutal dictatorship. Furthermore, the Socialists were able to demonstrate how labor on both sides of the border was exploited by the same financial interests and backed by Washington, DC.

When the Democrat Woodrow Wilson was elected in 1912, his rival, Socialist candidate Eugene Debs, received nearly a million votes.[16] The Socialists had made opposition to intervention in Mexico a rallying point. Along with a substantial bloc of pacifists, socialists and those on the labor left

> argued that the greatest threat to American security lay within American borders; the formidable block of military and business interests promoting

preparedness exercised significant influence in Washington, D.C., and sought to involve the country in perpetual wars—ranging from Europe, to Mexico, and other parts of Latin America.[17]

The radical turn in the revolution in 1914, when the Mexican Conventionalists (the zapatista-villista government) began their policies of land expropriation, coincided with increased labor struggle at home and the outbreak of World War I in Europe. The potential for the Socialist Left to turn public opinion against US intervention in Mexico, and later in World War I, had even further implications. Radicalized labor under the leadership of Socialists presented a grave threat to an ascendant capitalist class with global ambitions, namely, the ability to strike against intervention and war. According to Elizabeth McKillen, this palpable fear of the potential power of labor to disrupt the functioning of US empire led Woodrow Wilson to make unprecedented overtures to the AFL to divide organized labor from the Socialist Left, as "they anticipated the need for more militant campaigns to offset the influence of business groups over foreign policy in Washington, D.C."[18]

The United Mine Workers, which contained many Socialists and took positions that situated it on the left wing of labor, publicly opposed US intervention in Veracruz, Mexico, in 1914. The military invasion of the oil-rich state occurred at the same time that mine company guards were shooting down strikers in Ludlow, Colorado.[19] As UMW president John White proclaimed, "We have a war in Colorado that transcends in barbarity any contest south of the Rio Grande." Furthermore, the UMW "circulated a petition to its locals as well as municipal labor bodies such as the Seattle Labor Council that it then sent to the president and to Congress urging, For God's Sake . . . Leave Mexico Alone and Come into Colorado to Relieve These Miners Wives and Children Who Are Being Slaughtered by the Dozen by the Murderous Mine Guards."[20]

Beginning in 1914, the Wilson administration made overtures to Samuel Gompers, offering him a direct role in Wilson's administration in exchange for taming radicals within AFL unions, preventing alliance with the Socialists, and for supporting US intervention abroad. Gompers, already gravitating toward the Democratic Party as the best vehicle to promote the interests of craft unionism, accepted. Gompers became an advisor to Wilson on labor affairs through the newly established cabinet-level Department of Labor. The Wilson administration appointed representatives of the AFL to sit on the Commission on Industrial Relations, which was tasked with conducting a large-scale study of labor law and workplace relations and conditions, in order to make recommendations for how to promote "industrial democracy" and achieve "labor peace" by dividing labor and isolating Socialist influence.

Starting in 1914, Gompers spoke out publicly against radicalism in the Mexican Revolution and opposed land expropriations, while supporting the US interventions in 1914 and 1916. He was later tasked by the Wilson administration to coordinate with the Carranza government's efforts to contain the Casa del Obrero Mundial, relying on Right Socialists to serve as his liaison. When this failed and the Carranza government crushed the labor federation and repressed its leaders, he was enlisted to help rebuild a more conservative labor movement in Mexico modeled on the AFL. His efforts evolved into the ambitious attempt to launch the short-lived Pan-American Federation of Labor, an international federation linked to the AFL. This was done to preempt the growing influence of the Industrial Workers of the World and the regrouping of Anarcho-syndicalists in Mexico, and later, in a more urgent attempt, to counter the influence of the Communist International.[21] Gompers later secured an AFL endorsement for US entry into World War I over the heads of the national constituent unions, who were largely opposed to it.[22] He was later appointed to the Council of National Defense, which coordinated labor and resources in support of US entry into the war. The AFL's dramatic rightward shift into the Democratic Party had profound implications for the US labor movement, including for the PLM and Socialist Party.

The PLM and AFL Split

When the exiled Mexican Liberals first came into the US, they made a concerted effort to open lines of communication with organized labor. After the arrest of the PLM leadership in 1907, Gompers and the AFL executive council intervened on Ricardo Flores Magón's behalf to prevent extradition to Mexico, with Gompers personally delivering an appeal letter to Theodore Roosevelt during a meeting. At the 1908 national convention of the American Federation of Labor, Samuel Gompers got the highest delegated body of the AFL to endorse a call for the freedom of Ricardo Flores Magón, Librado Rivera, and Antonio Villareal. These overtures toward the Mexican exiles did not translate into significant support for Mexican workers in the US. Despite some scattered initiatives, the AFL abandoned any pretense toward immigrant inclusion after 1912 as it adopted pro-imperialist policies and ideologically entrenched itself in the Democratic Party.

Pre-revolutionary expressions of solidarity opened up space for collaboration on a local scale. In exchange for the Socialists' support for the persecuted Mexican Liberals, activists within the PLM's ranks attempted to organize Mexican workers into AFL unions. PLM writers made appeals to Mexicans to join AFL unions:

> The American Federation of Labor, the most powerful organization of labor in the world, counting some three million in members, has launched through the columns of our paper a call to the Mexicans to affiliate. In their own interest the Mexicans must hasten to heed that call in order to be placed in a position to demand within the shortest period possible better wages and better conditions. The American Federation of Labor with its enormous resources will give them support . . . in order to make and force the demand that they be paid at least the wages accorded to other races . . . Unionism will not only improve the standard of living of the Mexican, it will put a stop to the degrading humiliations and irritating outrages heaped upon our people.[23]

Between 1907 and 1912, some efforts were made by the AFL in Los Angeles to make links with the Mexican community. This included purchasing ad space and circulating appeals for Mexicans to join the AFL through the pages of the Spanish-language press, including *Regeneración*. A December 1910 edition, for instance, announced a mass meeting to be held in Los Angeles and conducted in Spanish and Italian for the purpose of uniting Mexican and Italian workers into a newly formed AFL Federal Union. The announcement, with the Spanglish title "Gran Meeting Internacional" stated that the meeting was to

> [j]oin together the Mexican [and Italian] laborers into the "United Laborers"... recently founded in the city, and now they are trying to spread the message among the Mexicans and to unionize the laborers of other races in order to establish among all . . . a strong and broad spirit of solidarity that will help all to obtain victory in their industrial disputes.[24]

The Los Angeles AFL's Central Labor Council also hired a Mexican organizer named Juan Ramírez to help create a laborers' union local for unskilled Mexican workers. On the eve of the Mexican Revolution in 1910, the United Laborers Federal Local 13097 was organized with the aid of PLM leaders Antonio Villareal, Librado Rivera, and Lázaro Gutiérrez de Lara, who encouraged their contacts, supporters, and affiliated workers to join.[25] The three also formed the union's first officers, and articles widely circulated through *Regeneración* made appeals and gave information for where to sign up.[26] With the help of the PLM, Juan Ramírez went on to organize seven AFL-affiliated locals throughout Los Angeles County, which included a total membership of over three thousand workers by October of 1911.[27] A coming out for this group occurred in the Labor Day Parade in 1911, in which a band of two thousand Mexicans marched in their own contingents and with their own union banners behind the big battalions of the city's organized workforce. As one Socialist publication observed of the striking contrast between the white craft workers and the Mexican contingent:

> The unions marched in the van with their crafts organization banners and the national flag at the head of each division. But what emblem could the unskilled workers carry? The fact, however, as usual produced its own expression and the Mexican workers paraded under the Marxian adjuration "Workers of the World Unite." The craft organizations expressed themselves in trade mottoes and national flags; the unskilled with their mass organization could find no other expression than a statement of solidarity which their condition demanded.[28]

Despite the promise of the new union, many Mexicans left the city to follow the harvests during picking seasons, leading to a turnover of membership not long after their establishment. The Mexican organizers recognized the need to form agricultural union locals in the farming towns to accommodate the cyclical movement of workers, but the AFL leadership balked. They did not see agriculture as a strategically important industry to organize. Furthermore, organizing on the farms necessitated the inclusion of Japanese workers, which the AFL prohibited. The AFL pulled support for the plan, and within one year, the locals folded and the AFL leadership walked away from the effort.

Despite initial acts of solidarity, the support of labor and some socialists was not wholly predicated on the principle of solidarity. The tepid support for Mexican inclusion was grounded in a form of pragmatic craft unionism, in which local leaders toyed with the model of creating separate federal unions as subordinate to the needs of the craft-based locals. The federals could be used to keep nonwhites separate, to prevent their use as strikebreakers, and to maintain them as low-wage support labor for skilled workers. The declining interest in organizing Mexican workers in Los Angeles coincided with the AFL leadership's increasing alienation from the restive PLM revolutionists.

After 1911, support for Ricardo Flores Magón waned as Samuel Gompers grew weary of the group's radical proclamations. In a final letter exchange between Ricardo Flores Magón and Samuel Gompers in 1911, Gompers made it known that further support would be contingent upon Flores Magón and the PLM making their true political ambitions clear. Flores Magón responded vaguely that they were "struggling for possession of the land, reduction of the hours of labor, and increased wages."[29] This exchange occurred while elements of the IWW and PLM joined forces in the Mexican revolutionary process by leading an insurrection in Baja California.[30] The AFL then distanced itself from the PLM and supported Madero. Gompers continued to oppose US intervention in Mexico until 1914, when the AFL leadership decided to work within the trajectory of US imperialism, rather than against it.

Gompers and his co-thinkers were won over by the idea that the extension of US empire, without the obligation of colonial management, could facilitate US access to raw materials necessary for industrial output and food products for consumption, and could be used to open up new markets to absorb growing exports. Furthermore, it was reasoned, this could lead to more jobs, and more opportunities for social mobility and advancement in skilled work and management positions at home and abroad.[31] As junior partners in the Democratic Party coalition, they also leveraged their influence to attain other types of benefits.

Beginning with the Wilson administration, for instance, the AFL was allowed to administer the reconstruction of organized labor in its own image, beginning in Mexico. In exchange for the repudiation and extrication of socialism and radicalism at home, the AFL had the opportunity to increase the material benefits for white skilled labor within the architecture of the expanding US empire. This began by working with Mexican labor leaders to eradicate radical influences, and to shore up a labor movement that worked in a similar manner to gain material benefits through collaboration with the postrevolutionary Mexican government. In the meantime, it was reasoned, the benefits of this trajectory were undermined by unfettered immigration into the US and corporate efforts to curtail unions through the manipulation of foreign labor.

If US capital succeeded in cultivating a workforce made docile under the aegis of dictatorship, then "cheap peon labor" could be used to undersell US labor, and white labor's living standards would go into decline. Opposition to Mexican migration had already hardened attitudes within some sectors of the Los Angeles AFL. In the context of the intense battle over the open shop, more conservative elements had prioritized immigration restriction and exclusion over socialist solidarity.[32] Nationally, the AFL embraced more restrictive policies, including the requirement that all immigrants pass a literacy test in which they demonstrated the capacity to speak and write in English.[33] Historian Lewis Lorwin asserts the AFL's support for the PLM was in part predicated on the notion that the impoverished and migratory state of Mexican labor was the result of Díaz's policies. With his ouster, these conditions that sent poor Mexican labor migrating north could potentially be reversed.[34]

While contradictory elements persisted in the AFL, the overall arc was toward more conservative stances as the revolution unfolded and Mexican immigration increased. Migration continued out of Mexico throughout the revolutionary period, especially as conservative forces around Venustiano Carranza (Constitutionalists) triumphed over those of the zapatistas and villistas, ensuring more radical labor and land policies were halted, tempered, or reversed. Los Angeles continued to receive waves of migrants as the Los Angeles economy slid into recession in 1916, fueling "intra-class segmentation" and fanning racial resentments from "native-born and old-immigrant skilled workers".[35] The AFL retreated from any substantial efforts to organize Mexican workers thereafter, and instead reaffirmed its opposition to Mexican immigration and the inclusion of Mexican workers in its ranks.

The AFL Opposes Mexican Immigration

White supremacist ideas became more widely disseminated through the native-born working class as a result of its integration into the Democratic Party, which served as the policy spearhead of Jim Crow segregation in the South and anti-Asian exclusion in the West. The popular diffusion of white supremacy also found amplification in the context of expansion abroad as well as within the workshops of capitalist production.

As displaced peoples circulated into the US through global capitalist nodes, employers used notions of race to arrange and stratify workforces, relying on the principle of white supremacy to bind the white segment to its own identity as a means to foster segregation. As class struggle emerged within the contradictory social differences located in white identity, forms of worker resistance emerged that utilized the notion of white privilege against capitalist violation of the same principle, such as hiring immigrants or workers of color, or using them to cross picket lines.

While this could serve white workers' interests in short-term situations, it could only work as long as the capitalists themselves respected the very rules they created, which they didn't. In fact, employers continued to resist unionization and to break strikes whether or not immigrants were involved. Furthermore, as capitalists controlled the commanding heights of the economy, and not the workers, they used their influence over the state to shape the larger trends within the political economy, which workers had limited means to influence or control.

For example, as capitalism globalized through the extension of corporations on an international scale, facilitated by state policy, so too did displacement. Alongside the repatriation of profits and economic growth, so too arrived displaced immigrants. As workers condemned the next wave of immigrants as a threat to their job security, their support for immigration controls and restrictions did not equate with the power to stop immigration; it only made them complicit in the discrimination and criminalization of those present, which allowed employers to degrade the value of their work. While white craft workers perceived restriction as an accomplishment preserving their national primacy, they also undermined their potential power to unite with other groups of workers collectively and withdraw their labor power as a form of real material counterpower that exists within the relations of production. By the late nineteenth century, employers were well aware of the benefits of creating nationally, ethnically, and linguistically mixed and hierarchically stratified work forces. By the second decade of the twentieth century, this became the rule, enabled by the AFL's reconciliation with US imperialism.

While the Socialist Party attempted to create a counternarrative to the racist characterization of colonized and immigrant workers, there was a growing consensus between the Democratic and Republican Parties, the AFL leadership, and a resurgent white supremacist movement for immigration restriction and exclusion by 1917. The AFL had been opposed to imperialism at the turn of the century as it brought no perceived gains for workers, only higher taxes, oligarchic rule, more immigrant labor, and the incessant demand for workers to put on uniforms and take up arms.[36] In opposition to the annexation of Cuba, the Philippines, and Puerto Rico after the Spanish-American War, it did so for practical reasons grounded in notions of white supremacy and the need for protectionism. At an 1898 AFL national conference on foreign policy, "most delegates . . . emphasized the danger of annexing lands populated by 'servile races' and a 'semi-barbaric population' as well as express concern about the influx of more cheaply produced goods that will 'remove our products from competition.'"[37]

The AFL, Socialists, and Mexican Immigrants in the United States

The outbreak of the revolution and subsequent rupture between the contending classes in Mexico reconfigured allegiances on the US radical Left based on divergent political doctrine and preconceived notions. As the first coherent iteration of a national political party based explicitly on the tenets of Marxian socialism, the Socialist Party was formed in 1901 as a fusion of various smaller reformist, social democratic, revolutionary groupings and tendencies. Socialists were in prominent positions of leadership within AFL trade unions, giving them influence within the organized working class in some geographical regions and within some industries.

Other Socialists and radical trade unionists (and anarchists) supported the organization of industrial unions that would include all workers regardless of race, gender, or nationality, launching the Industrial Workers of the World (IWW) in 1906. The IWW developed as an industrial union federation that served in an ancillary role to the Socialist Party until its formal separation into an independent entity in 1912.[38] Due to its attraction of those most committed to proletarian revolution and internationalism, its membership was a concentration of the party's most left-wing members.

By the second decade of its existence, the Socialist Party began to recruit broadly from the political expressions of the middle class moving to the left of the Democratic

Party and attracted to the reformist character of the Socialist Party.[39] This included the Progressive movement, farmers' organizations, and professional groups. By the 1910s, the party had a broad and heterogeneous character. In the face of complex world events, different quarters within the party articulated a spectrum of political positions. While there was a high degree of unity in opposition to US imperialism, in practice theoretical formulations and racial views broke the socialist movement into different camps, journals, and regions within the national party. Alongside the emerging differences over the class characterizations of the revolutionary process was the question of race and immigration, especially in relation to Mexico, which affected socialist attitudes toward the alliance with the AFL on one hand, and the priority of organizing Mexicans on the other.

The Socialist press rejected the normalized racial terminology used to characterize colonized people and immigrants in the mainstream press, and emphasized the crimes of capital over any failings of the people. Nevertheless, their analysis ran into theoretical problems, which hobbled their practice. They characterized Mexico (and Asia) as "uncivilized" and semi-feudal, and thus economic refugees from imperialist expansion into these nations were also considered socially and politically underdeveloped. This led to their characterization as "coolie" or "peon," and not as fellow workers, which in turn constructed them as lacking class-consciousness and rational thought, and therefore disinclined to American ways.[40] The elaboration of early socialist thinking tended to exclude a distinct analysis of race and racism as a factor of imperialism, which then impeded the possibility for genuine unity and solidarity with Mexican workers within national boundaries. The AFL's shift to the right into closer alignment with the foreign and domestic objectives of the Democratic Party also pulled the party's more conservative members along with it.

Socialists Divide on Mexican Immigration

The ossification of anti-immigration as official AFL policy coincided with the rise of the Progressive movement, a rising middle-class movement to remake US society in its own image. Beneath the rhetoric of populistic reform aimed at curtailing unchecked corporate power, urban poverty, and political corruption, progressivism as a social doctrine reinforced and consolidated notions of white supremacy already entrenched as official policy of the Democratic and Republican Parties.[41] This reflected the dual developments originating in the rising US capitalist empire: the consolidation of corporations and institutionalization of pseudo-scientific "social Darwinist" theories, and the acquisition of colonies and the internationalization of racialized doctrines. As historian Daniel Walden observed,

> after two decades of progressivism, the most stupendous problem of the twentieth century was still the problem of the color line. Roosevelt's New Freedom, muckraking, Wilson's New Nationalism—all had benefited the white community [...] and yet [...] had no more than scratched the surface of that ugly blot of racism here and colonialism abroad ... It must be faced in William Leuchtenburg's words, that "the Progressives were completely a part of American life,

accepting the traditional values and ideals, cherishing the aspirations of middle-class Americans, including the new sense of delight in the rise of the United States as a world power."[42]

These notions permeated the Right and centrist sections of the Socialist Party, especially conservative middle-class and craft-worker elements that adapted to the rightward drift of the AFL. This pattern included gradual accommodation to the growing chorus for comprehensive immigration restriction. The Right and Center segments of the Socialist Party did not make it a point of principle to challenge the racial politics of the AFL leadership, believing these issues were secondary to maintaining class unity with white craft workers and the AFL. When a Socialist Party Conventional Committee on Immigration proposed that the party support Asian exclusion in 1910, left-wing Socialists pushed back. Eugene Debs, for example, castigated the committee in an article published in the *International Socialist Review*. Pulling no punches, he fumed,

> The plea that certain races are to be excluded because of tactical expediency would be entirely consistent in a bourgeois convention of self-seekers, but should have no place in a proletariat gathering under the auspices of an international movement that is calling on the oppressed and exploited workers of all the world to unite for their emancipation.

Furthermore, he states:

> Let those desert us who will because we refuse to shut the international door in the faces of their own brethren; we will be none the weaker but all the stronger for their going, for they evidently have no clear conception of the international solidarity, are wholly lacking in the revolutionary spirit, and have no proper place in the Socialist movement while they entertain such aristocratic notions of their own assumed superiority.[43]

Nevertheless, the center-right captured the leadership in 1912, which was followed by a campaign of expulsion of the Left over the next few years.

Magonismo Versus Maderismo
The position of a centrist, majoritarian tendency of the party was clarified after the entrance of the bourgeoisie on the revolutionary stage in Mexico in 1911. This group included many long-standing supporters of the PLM, who broke with the magonistas to support Francisco Madero after the junta proclaimed an Anarchist-Communist outlook and commitment to socialist revolution. In line with its own outlook that socialism could only be attained at the ballot box, and only after the full maturation of the working class, they saw in Madero the embodiment of the first step in that direction for Mexico. After the coup against Madero, this tendency stayed consistent in supporting the bourgeois revolutionary forces, culminating in their virtually unqualified support for Venustiano Carranza after his defeat of the radical agraristas and the consolidation of bourgeois control.

Internationalists, revolutionary socialists, and anarchists took a different track, criticizing the "political socialists" that "relegated their revolutionary hopes to the ballot box."[44] They also rejected the undertones of American Exceptionalism within the Socialist camp that relegated Mexicans as unfit to liberate themselves. They continued to support the potential for a socialist revolution in Mexico, pushing them closer to the PLM's thinking, reflected in a polemical debate that played out through their respective party presses. As one article in *Regeneración* asserted:

> Do not be misled into supposing that the quarrel between Madero and ourselves is a quarrel between Mexicans, which Mexicans should be left to settle for themselves. It is not. It is the old inextinguishable quarrel between bourgeoisie and proletariat; between monopolist and disinherited; it is between those who wish to live peacefully under the existing system and those who know that under the present system there is no peace.[45]

Until their last efforts were defeated in 1915, the IWW supported PLM-led armed uprisings of Mexico.

This calculation was based on the perception that the Mexican Revolution signified the first great rupture in the global capitalist system of the twentieth century, and revealed the revolutionary potential of Mexican peasants and workers to achieve some form of socialism. Some of these radicals bolted south of the border to take part directly in the revolution. The revolution radicalized Mexicans in the US, who, aside from already supporting the PLM, also supported the IWW and Socialist-affiliated unions and organizations in substantial numbers between 1910 and 1917.

In 1908, Ricardo Flores Magón was optimistic about the prospects of aligning with US Socialists, seeing them not only as anticapitalist allies, but as people who took a stand against racism. As he stated in a letter to his partner and Socialist Maria Brousse de Talavera: "You see, my dear Maria, trends of our party are exactly the same as the International Socialist Party, with respect to racial aversion, an aversion that will end through education once we win freedom."[46] Nevertheless, support for the far-left radical vision of the PLM faded by 1911. After PLM-led revolts ended in failure and the forces scattered or were repressed, another wave of revolutionary leadership emerged in Mexico in 1910. Under a moderate banner of democratic reform, a new challenge manifested from disgruntled capitalists in the northern states, led by the scion of one of Mexico's richest families, Francisco Madero. Madero publicly broke with the PLM as a result of its avowed anticapitalist orientation.

When Madero managed to unite a broad alliance of class forces, including former magonistas, many socialists shifted support to his forces based on the moderate socialist conception that Mexico needed to pass through a bourgeois democratic revolution. Mirroring the broad splits taking place within socialist camps internationally, the right-wing majority of the Socialist Party withdrew support for the PLM while left-wing socialists and Wobblies became even more dedicated to the revolutionary cause. Wobblies took up arms alongside magonistas in Baja California and South Texas and made organizing forays directly into Mexico to spread the Wobbly gospel across the border.

The breach with the mainstream labor and socialist support was formalized by the publication of the second major PLM revolutionary pronouncement, the Manifesto of the Mexican Liberal Party of 1911. This document represented the evolution of the junta's radical formulations and served as the official coming out of the PLM as an explicit anticapitalist organization seeking to open a separate revolutionary socialist front in the Mexican Revolution, defining the revolution as proletarian and anti-imperialist in character.[47]

While the PLM moved left, US socialists developed a divergent range of conclusions. Socialists in general understood and criticized US imperialism, but differed on strategy. Left-wing revolutionary socialists supported organizing Mexican workers in US labor unions. When the Los Angeles Central Council of Labor was under the leadership of some left-leaning socialists, the council carved out independent positions on organizing Mexican immigrants that placed them at odds with national leadership. These elements also tended to join or support the IWW, and some even joined the Baja Revolution. While the left of the party exerted influence at various levels, it could not take the reins of power at the national level.

While the party membership was eclectic, transient, and loosely administered, the party majority tended to support moderate and conservative leadership positions. This trend became more pronounced as the party hewed more closely to the American Federation of Labor (AFL) and accommodated to its policies. For instance, after the AFL national leadership officially endorsed Asian exclusion, the California Socialist Party followed suit, making it the plank of its gubernatorial platform in 1906.[48] Through the same Los Angeles Council of Labor, they formed a chapter of the Asiatic Exclusion League in 1910. The anti-Asian platform had implications for views toward Mexicans. The racist substance behind the rejection of Chinese "coolie" labor as infantile, ignorant, and exploitable also informed the view of the Mexican as "peon." In a March 1909 article in *Appeal to Reason*, the author manages to cast aspersions on fourteen million Mexican people while admiring Flores Magón.

> The fourteen million half-naked, degenerate wretches employed at two-bits a
> day are employed in competition with American workers and this accounts in
> large part for the stagnation of industry and the great army of unemployed in
> the United States. Magon and the others are being vilified just as your own best
> leaders are—and for the same reason.[49]

Underdeveloped and feudalistic Mexico meant an infinite stream of cheap peon labor that lacked the social and political capacity to understand or appreciate the benefits of unionism, according to this strain of thought. Therefore, displaced migrants could be easily manipulated and used by employers against US workers.

This line of reasoning also assimilated the chauvinistic notion that workers' rights were arrayed on a hierarchy of racial and national significance, with the protection of white, skilled native-born labor at the pinnacle. While socialist articles framed their critiques of capitalism as oppressing workers on an international scale to extract a maximum "surplus value," their pronouncements had a chauvinistic tinge that pandered to resentment of the pliability and lack of agency of workers in colonized countries or pre-capitalist settings. An article in the *International Socialist Review* captures some of the sentiment that problematizes the internationalization of capital and its effort to exploit cheap labor, but it also conflates the rapacity of capitalism with the ignorance and culpability of Chinese workers.

> This then is the "yellow peril" that we workers of the older civilized world are getting up against, a peril which is now become very real. In the course of "developing" the East the capitalist class has discovered that the cost of production of labor power in Oriental countries is much less than in America or Europe . . . Millions of us are today idle because the masters cannot profitably employ us. Industry goes to China where more profit can be made. But tomorrow our condition will be even worse as the yellow man working in his own country—or rather his master's country—will compete and beat us.[50]

While the article concludes that for this reason "you and all workers white, black, yellow, red, without distinction, will have to revolt against capitalism," it completely ignores the way in which opportunistic employers and racist demagogues used a similar vernacular and oppressed and excluded Chinese workers within the US; and it offered no remedy for overcoming the racial divides.

With the rise of a bourgeois revolutionary front in 1910, many moderate socialists limited their support of revolutionary efforts in Mexico to those which could bring "democratic capitalism" to Mexico, with land reform and the introduction of plural democracy being the key to resolving the conditions of backwardness that created problems in the form of mass migration for US workers. Socialism was relegated to a future time, unattainable and utopian under current conditions.[51] Many of the moderate socialists ended up supporting Madero, and then Carranza, and eventually taking positions against the PLM, Casa del Mundo Obrero, and other left-wing elements of the revolution. The significance of these splits was captured by the US press, where even the capitalist press gave a platform to moderate socialists in order to widen the divides. When the Socialists in the PLM split with the junta, the *El Paso Herald* interviewed Jesús Flores Magón after his failed attempt on behalf of Francsico Madero to get his brothers to desist in their revolutionary efforts. In the interview, he reiterated the reform Socialist analysis:

> They asked impossible things. They hold to anarchistic ideas. They want all the land divided among the people of Mexico. I told them that is impossible at this time; that there are many ignorant persons in Mexico at this time and what they ask is not possible of achievement. I told them but they would not agree, that the first thing we must do is to educate the uneducated, but they would not listen to me and so they are still magonistas.[52]

Eugene Debs, who had previously championed the cause of the PLM, also publicly broke with the group. While characterizing Madero as a "landed aristocrat," he dispelled any notion that the conditions for the laboring classes would improve. Nevertheless, he also conformed to the belief that Mexican workers weren't capable of self-emancipation.

> First of all, the masses of Mexican workers and producers, like those of other countries, are ignorant, superstitious, unorganized and all but helpless in their slavish subjugation. In their present demoralized state economic emancipation is simply out of the question. They must first be reached and aroused, educated and organized, and until this work is accomplished to at least some extent all hope of successful revolution is doomed to disappointment.[53]

He then chided the PLM's "anarchistic attitude" and its revolutionary delusions:

> The battle-cry of the Mexican Liberal party is, "Land and Liberty," and its leaders declare that "the taking away of the land from the hands of the rich must be accomplished during the present insurrection." If the land can be taken from the rich in this insurrection so can also the mills, factories, mines, railroads, and the machinery of production, and the question is, what would the masses in their present ignorant and unorganized state do with them after having obtained them? It would simply add calamity to their calamities, granting that this impossible feat were capable of achievement.

He concludes with a warning that radical action will draw in the US military (echoing Samuel Gompers) and that a Madero government is preferred to open the door to "great industrial organization" and affiliation with the Socialist Party.[54] While Samuel Gompers did intervene to organize an AFL counterpart in Mexico, this was to prevent a genuine socialist orientation. Like the AFL, the break of the Socialist Party's Center and Right with the PLM signifies the end of the party's orientation toward the Mexican working class in the US. Concurrent with this rupture, the party's left wing moved into closer collaboration.

A minority of socialists and radicals influenced by the great upheavals of the Mexican revolutionary process moved further left, concluding that internationalist and transnational organization was needed to facilitate socialist revolution on a global scale. Socialists like John Murray and the others in the Los Angeles Council of Labor continued to promote the proletarian aspect of the revolution and caution others in their support for Madero. In a 1911 article entitled, "Why Mexican Workers Rebel," he detailed the history of the great strikes of 1906–1907 and the continued participation of workers in the revolutionary upheavals. John Kenneth Turner warned of the substantial differences between Madero and Magón.

> While, as always, the working class will do most of the fighting and endure most of the suffering, the movement is dominated by middle class interests. If Madero wins, his party will undoubtedly free the slaves, ameliorate the condition of the peons, pass a few labor laws, and establish free speech, free press and actual elections. The Liberal party would take immediate measures to break up the vast haciendas and give the lands back to the people. In my opinion the Mexican Liberal party is as

thoroughly a movement of the toilers as is the Socialist party of the United States.[55]

Some regional socialists that had the most direct contact with the PLM and the Mexican working class, such as in Texas and Los Angeles, maintained support, in some capacity, for the PLM's vision of social revolution. The most active radical supporters to rally around the far-left vision for social revolution in Mexico were the IWW.

Chapter 14

The PLM and IWW Join Forces

"Now what do we mean when we say revolutionary Socialist? We mean that the land shall belong to the landless, the tools to the toiler, and the products to the producers."
—Lucy Gonzalez Parsons at the founding conference
of the Industrial Workers of the World, 1905

B y 1903 radicals within the Western Federation of Miners were at the forefront of labor militancy in the US, rejecting the conservative AFL in favor of a more radical form of industrial unionism. With a significant Socialist membership and class-struggle orientation, they identified the corporate corruption and control of electoral politics and state complicity as a dead end for labor reform and socialism. Rather than capturing the state and transforming it from within, as was the dominant position of the Socialist Party, these radicals believed industrial workers had to fight to unite all workers at the point of production and compel capital to concede reform as "legislation through the strike."[1]

The defeat of the major strikes of the previous two decades were the result of a new reality in class relations. Corporate and state power had converged and deployed a strategy of using racism and immigration policy as a means to contain, divide, and conquer a powerful, multinational, and multiethnic working class. This changing configuration of ruling-class domination required radicals to respond in kind. They did so by creating a militant union organization capable of uniting all workers across racial, gender, and national lines, and regardless of trade or skill. In 1905, they, along with left-wing socialists and Anarcho-syndicalists, constituted the Industrial Workers of the World (IWW).

As the SP and AFL parted ways with the PLM, the Industrial Workers of the World drew closer. The IWW had developed at a critical juncture in US class politics where the left wing of the socialist movement was elaborating principles of internationalism, direct action, and class-struggle unionism. For the revolutionary socialists and Anarcho-syndicalists within the IWW, solidarity was interpreted not only through passive support, but through direct collaboration with other radicals. Ralph Chaplin, a longtime leader of the IWW, explained how Mexican radicals helped shape his own political identity: "The struggle in Mexico, like that of Russia, India, and Ireland, was becoming my struggle; Enrique and Ricardo Flores Magón were becoming my personal heroes, and Porfirio Díaz my personal enemy."[2]

The growth and spread of the IWW coincided with a rising tide of militant class struggle among the vast ranks of the unskilled and immigrant workforce. The flashpoints of independent and collective struggle among Mexican workers across the Southwest over the first decade of the century supports the thesis that they saw the IWW as the best vehicle for advancing their class interests.[3]

The IWW merged efforts and in some cases organizations with the PLM in the border states, developed and synthesized a more coherent internationalist doctrine and practice, and applied their thinking by joining with the PLM to launch a socialist insurrection in Baja California. Their efforts presented an existential threat to US imperialism in the region, leading the federal government to deploy the military to curtail the socialist movement, while concurrently enabling the success of the pro-capitalist campaign of Francisco Madero.

The Rise of the IWW

In the aftermath of the first convulsions of large-scale industrial action, leaders of the Western Federation of Miners in alliance with left-wing socialists launched the Industrial Workers of the World in 1905. The exigency for the creation of the IWW was the culmination of the experiences of the class war in the West and the diffusion of radical systems of thought that immigrant workers carried with them from their home countries and previous experiences. The organization was an effort to link together anticapitalists, militant unionists, and the vast unorganized masses of migratory, racially proscribed, and other excluded groups of workers.

The IWW was originally conceived of as an auxiliary vehicle of the Socialist Party that could provide the means for industrial unionism and coordinated workplace action as a complement to the party's primary focus on political action. It instead took on a life of its own, becoming the repository organization for leftward-moving elements promoting industrial unionism, interethnic and international organizing, militancy at the point of production, and variants of anarchism and revolutionary socialism.

It became a laboratory for new stratagem and tactics for waging class struggle, and developed the first significant vehicle for the advancement of revolutionary industrial unionism and internationalism, with the notion of "one big union" organizing all workers across racial, gender, and national boundaries. The rise and spread of the IWW brought it into direct contact with Mexican workers throughout the Southwest, and into direct alliance with the PLM and magonistas.

The first meeting to launch the IWW took place on January 2, 1905. Organized by prominent left-wing socialists of the day, the goal was to create a radical labor union along industrial and internationalist lines. From the outset, the founders wanted to be clear and unequivocal in their rejection of the exclusionism, chauvinism, and tepid reformism of the ossified AFL leadership. As the preamble to the first constitution proclaimed: "The working class and the employing class have nothing in common . . . between these two classes a struggle must go on until the workers of the world organize as a class, take possession of the earth and the machinery of production, and abolish the wage system." Industrial unionism would allow for the labor movement to recalibrate and reorient to the realities of Taylorist production that "deskilled" and homogenized the working class at the point of production.[4]

The twenty-three participants who attended were united only in the perception that a new organization was needed to transcend the entrenched conservatism of the AFL. According to its first manifesto, the emergent organization acknowledged the changing conditions of industrial society. This included the aligned and coordinated power of the corporate capitalist class to suppress unions; through its own national organizations, the two political parties, and the state; while the workers' movement was being routed based on the outdated and decrepit mode of craft unionism and elitist and chauvinistic exclusion.[5]

While Socialist Party members were instrumental in creating the IWW, its separate existence proved to be a portent for an eventual rupture within the socialist movement. As the Socialist Party tacked rightward by 1912, the IWW tacked left, creating a widening chasm between the two organizations and setting into motion the first discernible divide between reformist and revolutionary socialists. The period of 1908–1912 saw significant growth in the ranks of the Socialist Party, which coincided with its official alliance to the IWW and embrace of labor militancy. When the IWW became the leading force in organizing the great industrial strikes of the period, from miners in Goldfield, Nevada (1908), to textile workers in Lowell and Lawrence, Massachusetts (1912), Wobbly organizers recruited radicalizing workers to join and vote for the Socialist Party in droves. By 1912, the Socialist Party membership reached 150,000, and it could claim nearly 1,000 elected officials across the country, including 56 mayors.[6]

The party's growing electoral influence strengthened the resolve of the prominent reformist wing, which grew more eager to attract AFL votes by accommodating to its nationalistic, xenophobic, and white supremacist tendencies. As the Socialist Party leadership's position toward immigrants hardened, and as they neglected Mexican, black, and women workers, the IWW reached out to them. In an effort to break through to national prominence, the Socialist Party leadership sought to make the party more respectable to bourgeois critics by distancing itself from its radical roots and the revolutionaries within its ranks. Beginning in 1912, it jettisoned its revolutionary elements and rebranded itself as a reformist party, capable of reforming capitalism through legislation.

Conversely, the IWW oriented toward labor organizing at the point of production, direct action, and an unwavering commitment to anticapitalism and revolution. Rather than contest the terrain of skilled crafts, the IWW emphasized organizing the majority of unskilled and migratory workers being created in the shadows of industrial capitalism. This volatile population was breaking out in the 1910s and redefining the character of the labor movement. Between April 6, 1917, and November 11, 1918, for instance, there were 6,205 recorded strikes, taking on an outlaw quality since the AFL had taken a position against striking during the war effort with over one million workers winning significant on-the-job victories (such as the eight-hour day) through striking.[7]

Over this period, much of the radical Left and immigrant sections had been driven out or had voluntarily abandoned the Socialist Party and its electoral strategy for the IWW. The Wobblies had become a pole of attraction for an array of radical elements within the working class looking for an alternative to the stagnant reformism of the Socialist Party and the conservative rightward drift of the AFL. This included the most militant and class-conscious workers in the AFL unions, and left-wing Socialists drawing explicitly revolutionary conclusions about the future of the workers' movement. In shedding its radical orientation after 1912, the Socialist Party began its long decline, as its reformist political message was partially co-opted by the two capitalist parties, leaving their political identity indiscernible and ultimately marginal in the shadow of the Democrats.[8]

While aiming to achieve real material improvements in wages and working conditions, the Wobblies believed that gains were made only through ongoing class struggle in the form of strike action, boycotts, sabotage, and mass civil disobedience.[9] Furthermore, they asserted that gains remained only temporary under capitalist labor relations, as employers were in a state of constant class war to reclaim what they were forced to concede. Believing that organizational power and militancy determined the balance of class forces at the point of production, they shunned traditional union structures and rejected labor-management negotiations and collective bargaining agreements as "contracts" that generally prevented further strike action where it might be needed. While competing revolutionary doctrines co-existed within the IWW, the dominant ideology gravitated toward revolutionary syndicalism. As one early sympathetic historian noted:

> I.W.W. not only advocated revolutionary methods but emphasized in ever stronger terms its own conception of social evolution, according to which the industrial unions carried within themselves all the elements of the socialist society of the future. They minimized the importance of political organization and action and declared their faith in the economic organizations of the workmen, which at some future time would lock-out the capitalist class and assume the control and management of the industries of the country.[10]

To build the concentrated power necessary to challenge the corporate behemoths, the IWW looked to organize the vast armies of unskilled and ethnically heterogeneous majority of workers in the US into industrial unions.[11] They opted to build a new type of union: industrial, militant, and open to all. In doing this, the IWW redefined the very notion of class by broadening the categories of labor. The criteria for membership in the first constitution was anyone who worked for a wage, including:

> Itinerant labor . . . the unwaged, and precarious and illicit workers (it was the first American labor union to consider housework as work, and to organize chamber maids and prostitutes). . . . Later constitutions thus continue: "No unemployed or retired worker, no working class student, apprentice, or housewife, shall be excluded from membership."[12]

They also repudiated class collaboration in any form, extolling the irreconcilability of class interests between workers and owners of any stripe and criticizing those deemed "labor aristocrats," who favored collegiality with managers and owners, while viewing unskilled and immigrant workers with disdain. They rejected the narrow sectionalism that metastasized within the AFL-linked craft model, which saw workers willingly scab on other workers to protect their own interests. In the new organization, the veneer over the deep-seated class war raging in US society was to be ripped clean. Eugene Debs conveyed this sentiment at the first convention:

> The American Federation of Labor has members . . . but the capitalist class does not fear the American Federation of Labor; quite the contrary . . . There is something wrong in that form of unionism whose leaders are the lieutenants of capitalism; something wrong in that form of unionism that forms an alliance with such a capitalist combination as the Civic Federation, whose sole purpose is to chloroform the working class while the capitalist class go through their pockets.[13]

An uncompromising revolutionary orientation, democratic culture, and commitment to mass strike action led the IWW to become a laboratory for innovative strategies and tactics not known within the labor movement. New and unique forms of militancy emerged from creative experiment and practical need. IWW organizers went into industries among the unskilled and developed creative methods for organizing job actions at the point of production, including slowdowns, strikes, and even occupations. They emphasized building broad unity and solidarity and a culture of workers' power, discouraging formal contracts since these locked workers into long-term stasis that undercut their power to strike at will—which was the actual basis of workers' power according to Wobbly thought.

As explained by an early sympathizer, "In the case of unskilled working-men, a strike requires a swift and decisive move, a concerted attack all along the line, disorganizing the employers' plans and plants. The aim of a strike is realized as soon as the material demands are granted."[14] The Wobblies also experimented with new forms of workplace action. For instance, in 1906, IWW militants led the first known sit-down strike on record at a General Electric plant in Schenectady, New York.[15] Incidentally, the tactic of the sit-down strike was foreshadowed by IWW founder Lucy Gonzalez Parsons, who called this a more revolutionary (and pragmatic) form of strike, saying in 1905: "My conception of the strike of the future is not to strike and go out and starve, but to strike and remain in and take possession of the necessary property of production. If someone has to starve [. . .] let it be the capitalist class."[16]

As part of their analysis of the failed methods of the AFL, IWW leaders emphasized the centrality of organizing the unorganized. In the West, this included the vast ranks of the agricultural proletariat. While shunned by the AFL and disparaged as "hoboes" and "vagrants" by middle-class society, migratory labor was, in the IWW leadership's view, the lifeblood of western capitalism and a potential ally of the anticapitalist movement. At the second convention in 1906, the national leadership explained the strategic importance of migratory farmworkers in both practical and ideological terms:

> The organization of farm employes [sic] is therefore necessary, so that in the periods when the demand of laborers for the farm exceeds the possible supply,

such working conditions may be obtained for the farm laborer, as to enable him to see the necessity of co-operation with the workers in the city for the establishing of conditions, under which the private ownership of land and all the implements of production will be abolished and the exploitation by owners of factories or of farm land will cease.[17]

In elaborating an orientation toward the vast unskilled majority of the working class, it engaged ethnically and linguistically diverse populations. Drawing from its Marxist and internationalist roots, it became the first union to systematically oppose racism and chauvinism within the labor movement as a political principle of the first order, taking public stances against the anti-Chinese and anti-Japanese racism that prevailed in the labor movement and the Left. As David Brundage explains: "Not only did it welcome African Americans, Chicanos, and eastern and southern European immigrants to its ranks but it also opened its doors to Asian and Asian-American workers, breaking with a long and violent anti-Asian tradition in the American labor movement."[18]

The Wobblies took action in organizing the excluded and unorganized, waged a consistent propaganda struggle against racism and chauvinism within their press and pamphlets, and extended their struggle across borders. At its height, more than ninety newspapers and periodicals nationwide aligned with Wobbly thinking. Nineteen were published in languages other than English, including two in Spanish and Italian, and one each in French, Portuguese, Russian, Polish, Slavic, Lithuanian, Hungarian, Swedish, and Yiddish.[19]

In breaking with the racial conservativism of the AFL, the IWW threatened the order that maintained labor in a weakened state. Though small in numbers in its early years, the first strike successes revealed the shape of things to come. Corporations, long resistant to all forms of unionization, began to legitimate and even partner with conservative unions to stem the rising influence of the IWW within the working class.[20] Ultimately it took the full force of state power to quell the IWW, although its legacy carried on for many years to come.

Lucy Gonzalez Parsons, a co-founder of the Industrial Workers of the World

Lucy Gonzalez Parsons: Founding Figure of the IWW

One of the founders and ideological architects of the IWW was Lucy Gonzalez Parsons. Gonzalez Parsons was born in Texas in 1853, of mixed African, Mexican, and Native American ancestry. She identified her mother as Mexican and father as Native

American, making her a *mestiza* by custom in the US-Mexico borderlands.[21] Gonzalez Parsons lived through the Civil War and as a teenager witnessed the racial terrorism of the Ku Klux Klan and the promise of Reconstruction. Sometime in the early 1870s, she met and married Albert Parsons, a Confederate soldier turned Radical Republican and supporter of black suffrage. They moved to Chicago by 1874, likely fleeing the threat of racial violence and the prohibition of interracial marriage, and there began their involvement with the labor movement.[22] They joined the Workingman's Party and became journalists and activists in the Socialist Labor Party, and union organizers.

Albert became a prominent labor leader in the Chicago Typographical Union Local 16.[23] Lucy helped found the local branch of the Working Women's Union, which was the first attempt by the Marxist-led Workingman's Association to create unions for women workers.[24] The two worked with the Knights of Labor and later became founders and prominent leaders in the International Working People's Association (IWPA), a coalition of anarchists and socialists that rejected the reformism of the electoralism within the Socialist Labor Party (a forerunner of the Socialist Party), in favor of direct action for workers' rights as the strategy for social revolution.

As part of their national campaign for the eight-hour workday, the IWPA organized a general strike on May 1, 1886. During the strike, Lucy and Albert helped lead a march of eighty thousand workers and their families through downtown Chicago. Within two days, squads of police began attacking and firing on groups of strikers congregated nearby, killing at least two. The next day, three thousand workers gathered in a rally to protest police violence and were met by a group of nearly two hundred heavily armed police determined to smash the protest. In the ensuing melee, a bomb was thrown, killing seven policemen and untold numbers of workers. In the swift and indiscriminate repression of the Chicago Left that followed, many radical labor leaders were arrested, and four, including Albert Parsons, were executed.[25]

Lucy Gonzalez Parsons continued to be a tireless activist and working-class revolutionary, whose work as a journalist, organizer, and orator garnered her recognition as a national labor leader, feminist advocate, and antiracist militant. When Left Socialists, labor unionists, and Anarcho-syndicalists gathered in Chicago in 1905 to launch the IWW, she was asked to be a delegate and was at the forefront of shaping the character of the organization. From the floor, she made several interventions that affirmed the group's orientation. One was on the question of national borders:

And let me say to you brothers and sisters [...] remember that we are here as one brotherhood and one sisterhood, as one humanity, with a responsibility to the downtrodden and the oppressed of all humanity, it matters not under what flag or in what country they happened to be born.

She continued on the issue of gender equality:

We, the women of this country, have no ballot even if we wished to use it, and the only way that we can be represented is to take a man to represent us. You men have made such a mess of it in representing us that we have not much confidence in asking you; and I for one feel very backward in asking the men to represent me. We have no ballot, but we have our labor [. . .] we are exploited more ruthlessly than men. Wherever wages are to be reduced, the capitalist class use women to reduce them, and if there is anything that you men should do in the future it is to organize the women.

Finally, she spelled out the distinction between reformists and revolutionaries that clarified the rift taking place within the socialist movement:

> We say, "The tools belong to the toiler." They are owned by the capitalist class. Do you believe they will allow you to go into the halls of the legislature and simply say, "Be it enacted [. . .] the capitalist shall no longer own the tools, and the factories and the places of industry, the ships that plow the oceans and our lakes?" Do you believe they will submit? I do not . . . Hence, when you roll under your tongue the expression that you are revolutionists, remember what that word means. It means a revolution that shall turn all these things over to where they belong—to the wealth producers.[26]

IWW Militancy Crossing Racial and National Boundaries

The early years of the IWW were fraught with conflicts, as it underwent various splits, expulsions, and defections until a core of left-wing socialists converged around a revolutionary vision for the new organization. What emerged in 1907 was a radical union movement intent on organizing all workers under the banner of "an injury to one is the concern of all."[27] The new movement was led by a core of experienced radicals and veteran organizers, drawn especially from the committed ranks of socialists from the Western Federation of Miners. Their emergence represented a continuity of labor radicalism inherited from the previous generation. As early Wobbly James Cannon described its lineage:

> The IWW had its own forebears, for the revolutionary labor movement is an unbroken continuum. Behind the convention assembled in Chicago fifty years ago stood the Knights of Labor; the eight-hour movement led by the Haymarket martyrs; the great industrial union strike of the American Railway Union; the stormy battles of the Western Federation of Miners; and the two socialist political organizations—the old Socialist Labor Party and the newly-formed Socialist Party.[28]

Undoubtedly, the independent role of immigrants and workers of color in joining or supporting the great upsurges of labor struggle was embedded in the DNA of the IWW. Many immigrants entering the ranks of the working class between 1886 and 1910 came from countries with strong syndicalist movements.[29] Florecio Bazora, for instance, a Spanish émigré anarchist who worked closely with Ricardo Flores Magón and helped publish the PLM newspaper *Regeneración*, was present at the founding conference of the IWW. The participation of international revolutionaries and working-class leaders of color (such as Lucy Gonzalez Parsons) from the organization's inception likely added to the IWW's resolve to break racial and national boundaries. Furthermore, the IWW began to appeal to the more radical foreign-language federations of the Socialist

Party.[30] When, in 1917, these groups were driven out of the party for their sympathies with the left-wing socialist conception of class struggle and for their general enthusiasm for the Bolshevik Revolution in Russia, many joined the IWW.

A seasoned leadership congealed within the IWW that also identified the persistent and finely honed practice of employers to use racism to divide workers. In the West this took on special significance in relation to Chinese, Japanese, and Mexican workers. The discrimination and marginalization of these groups by organized labor made them ideal as reserve armies of highly exploitable labor for capital. Their vulnerable position made it easier for capitalists to use them strategically to leverage down wages, undermine union organization, and break strikes. For example, an IWW supporter observed in a 1910 edition of the *Industrial Worker* how the stoking of anti-Asian racism was being used to poison organizing efforts:

> It would seem that an effort is to be made to revive the old superstition of "race antagonism," based upon the assumed inferiority of the race which happens to be in the minority . . . Today we are witnessing an attempt to perpetuate this hoary folly under the alluring but deceptive claim of the inferiority of the Chinese and Japanese . . . The working class should be taught that it has only one enemy on this earth, and that enemy is the capitalist class and its comical defenders, those who teach that there is virtue in such shabby superstitions as "race antagonisms."[31]

While the IWW did not develop an orientation toward specific strategies of antiracist organizing, it did make great strides toward building working-class unity by emphasizing the inclusion of racially excluded groups. For example, delegates at the second convention called for IWW reception centers to be placed at US harbors to welcome immigrants, for all literature to be published in multiple languages, for bilingual branch meetings to be arranged, and, when desired, for foreign-language branches of union locals to be established.[32] Furthermore, the interaction of the Wobblies with Mexican revolutionary exiles opened the door to international collaboration and the growth of the IWW among Mexican workers on both sides of the border.

The IWW collaborated with Mexican radicals on various fronts. In what Salvatore Salerno refers to as "revolutionary pluralism," prior to 1915 the organization functioned as a loose association of chapters based on the "emotion of working class solidarity rather than doctrine, and a concern with agency rather than fixed organizational formation."[33] This early model afforded locals in different regions to take on characteristics adapted to local conditions. In Southern California, Arizona, and Texas, the magonistas had encouraged their core members to collaborate with the IWW. Where IWW locals were organized within Mexican communities, they served as points of convergence for joint action between Wobblies and magonistas. According to Norman Caulfield, Mexican workers were attracted to the IWW because of their shared traditions of anarcho-syndicalism and their anti-imperialist views. The IWW's critique of US empire in Mexico converged with their own radical and nationalist desires to reclaim their "natural resources, productive systems and economic infrastructure."[34]

Of primary importance for this group was breaking through the racial and national lines of class struggle. After the final exit of groups and individuals opposed to the radical trajectory laid out, the group identified the need to make it accessible to those vast ranks of unskilled and migratory laborers, and others marginalized by the AFL, especially "timber beasts, hobo harvesters, itinerant construction workers, exploited eastern and southern European immigrants, racially excluded [African Americans], Mexicans, and Asian Americans."[35]

Composed of a significant immigrant component from its inception, the IWW also emerged as a staunch internationalist organization. During the first convention in June of 1905, the delegates unanimously approved a resolution actively supporting the Russian revolution taking place at that moment in the form of an insurrectionary general strike of the workers. Attendee Lucy Gonzalez Parsons exhorted the crowd, saying "you men and women should be imbued with the spirit that is now displayed in far-off Russia."[36] The organization participated in an international day of support to raise funds for the workers. Internationalism was also practiced in organizing. The IWW appealed to all workers, making a conscious effort to build active solidarity between workers of different national origin and to promote unity amid diversity. Organizers were recruited and groomed from the different ethnic and linguistic groups for practical and ideological reasons, and newspaper articles made constant appeals to interethnic, international, and even interpersonal solidarity. The steps taken toward building racial solidarity from below went on to include the dissemination of IWW literature in different languages, interethnic and international organizing drives, and formal alliance with foreign-born radicals and organizations.

In the Southwest and border region, this meant most specifically with the Partido Liberal Mexicano. In this way, the IWW made the most significant advances toward building its ranks among immigrants and workers of color, including significant numbers of Mexicans in the Southwest. In its efforts to unite workers and extend organization and revolution across borders, many members of the IWW were drawn into international events. For those in the Southwest, this entailed active involvement in Mexican affairs, including active participation in the Mexican Revolution.

At the IWW's sixth convention in 1911, western organizer Frank Little spearheaded a resolution calling for resources to organize Mexican workers in the Southwest.[37] Spanish-language branches were established through the joint activities of magonistas, whose cadre were encouraged by the PLM leadership to merge efforts with the Wobblies. As the secretary of the San Diego IWW Local 13, Stanley Gue, asserted, "Active steps should be taken . . . to organize several hundred thousand Mexican workers in the Southwest. The Mexican Liberal Party and their organ 'Regeneración' has paved the way for a powerful I.W.W. movement among the Mexican workers, both in America and Mexico." He appealed to the national organization to take Mexican labor radicalism seriously, further identifying that "[t]here are several good Mexican I.W.W. speakers who, if they were given proper support, could do wonders in getting the Mexican workers in 'One Big Union' . . . and all would have support of [Phoenix-based PLM paper] 'La Union Industrial' and 'Regeneracion.'"[38]

Great effort was made to produce literature that connected radical theory, international events, and editorial commentary to the experiences of the working class. Over the course of its first two decades of existence, the IWW produced numerous affiliated or sympathetic periodicals that disseminated organizational analyses, aired strategic and philosophical debates, and gave forum to workers' perspectives. Through the pages of the Wobbly press one could find analysis of class struggle using the common vernacular and a constant reframing of the narrative of strikes to counter the dominant media and the tactics of the employers. In this regard, the IWW was the first to oppose racism and national chauvinism in a comprehensive way, identifying the role it played in undermining class unity.

For instance, during a 1912 IWW-led construction workers' strike in British Columbia, the *Industrial Worker* centered on ploys to divide and weaken the largely foreign-born workforce of seven thousand strikers representing sixteen different nationalities. The federal government had "relaxed its immigration regulations to allow contractors to procure strikebreakers" by bringing in different sets of immigrants to cross the lines.[39] Meanwhile newspapers attempted to whip up xenophobic sentiment, characterizing the strikers as racial outsiders who lacked moral and hygienic practices. For instance, according to *The Sun*, a Vancouver-based newspaper, "the whole movement represents an invasion of the most despicable scum of humanity . . . The government must show its strength and drive these people out of the country even if the use of force is required to do so."[40]

In responding to these lines of attack, IWW strike leader Floyd Hyde used the pages of the *Industrial Worker* to counter the racial and anti-immigrant narrative, stating:

> The strikers . . . have learned that there are only two nationalities, and that these nations are divided by class, and not by geographical lines. They realize that in one nation are the contractors, no matter where they are born, and in the other nation are the workers, no matter what country they happen to hail from.[41]

During another IWW-led strike in 1912, more than twenty thousand workers went on strike throughout the textile mills at Lawrence, Massachusetts. The strike involved women, men, and children representing fifty-one nationalities who were segregated by nationality and skill. The AFL organized small clusters of the largely native-born skilled workers, while ignoring the vast ranks of predominantly immigrant and unskilled women and men. These workers downed tools on the morning of January 11 in response to employers' efforts to resist state law mandating the reduction of hours for women and children from a maximum of fifty-six hours to fifty-four hours per week. They used the reduced hours as a justification to cut pay, pushing the already impoverished workers to the point of starvation.

As the IWW took over leadership of the strike, "they organized mass meetings in various localities of the different language groups and had them select a strike committee of men and women which represented every mill, every department, and every nationality."[42] Documenting the strike in the pages of the *International Socialist Review*, Socialist journalist and Wobbly partisan Mary Marcy transcribed a speech from

"Big" Bill Haywood:

> [Y]ou all come to America with the expectation of improving your conditions.
> You expected to find a land of the free, but you found we of America were but
> economic slaves as you were in your own home. I come to extend to you tonight
> the hand of brotherhood with no thought of nationality. There is no foreigner
> here except the capitalist and he will not be a foreigner long for we will make a
> worker of him. Do not let them divide you by sex, color, creed or nationality, for
> as you stand today you are invincible. The I.W.W. is composed of different na-
> tionalities and with such a fighting committee you can lick "Billy" Wood [police
> repression]. "Billy" Wood can lick one Pole, in fact he can lick all the Poles, but
> he cannot lick all the nationalities put together.[43]

Some IWW leaders even saw foreign-born workers as more potentially radical if organized effectively. In an article in the *Industrial Worker*, J. S. Biscay explained the complexities of organizing a multiethnic and multilingual workforce of immigrants:

> The foreign worker upon landing here is made to feel that he is inferior to the
> native product ... the foreigner naturally resents being treated thus. At the same
> time, he cannot prove his equality or superiority because of the lack of the dom-
> inating language. In [IWW] meetings the foreigner is at the same disadvantage
> and as a rule little attention is given him ... If the agitator does not actually feel
> that the foreigner is every bit as intelligent and revolutionary as the native, he
> had better not mingle with him. Yet the organizer who goes out of his way to
> make the foreign element at ease, finds that he is given more hearty support than
> the natives show.[44]

By 1911, antiracist action began to feature more prominently in the IWW, especially
when confronting Jim Crow segregation. Efforts were underway to organize black
timber workers in the South and Mexican agricultural workers and miners in the
Southwest. As one IWW organizing leaflet titled "To Colored Workmen and Work-
women" proclaimed:

> If you are a wage worker you are welcome in the I.W.W. halls, no matter what
> your color. By this you may see that the I.W.W. is not a white man's union, not a
> black man's union, not a red or yellow man's union, but a workingman's union.
> All of the working class in one big union.[45]

While most Mexican radicals were drawn into the revolution in Mexico, others
with more established roots north of the border turned to IWW-led unions for practical as well as ideological reasons. To find recruits for PLM-led uprisings, organizers
worked among the most militant Mexican workers in the border states. This drew
them into local organizing efforts as well, bringing them into contact with Wobblies in
California agriculture, Arizona mining, and other points of interface.

Furthermore, the incarceration of the leadership of the PLM led supporters to
immerse themselves in building a solidarity campaign to prevent deportation, raise

funds for the defense, and demonstrate public support and other forms of pressure
for their release. PLM and Wobbly orators jointly gave soapbox speeches in work
camps, barrio plazas, and other public spaces where Mexican workers congregated.
The Mexican PLM-IWW also built support for the Liberal Party, even launching
their own defense committee in Los Angeles in 1908, the Defense Committee of the
Imprisoned Mexican Liberals. The PLM-IWW paper *Libertad y Trabajo* announced
that they had raised eleven hundred dollars for the campaign, including donations
from IWW branches, the Western Federation of Miners, and the Journeyman Tai-
lor's International Union.[46] The PLM and IWW in Los Angeles also co-organized
bailes (dances) and other types of community fundraisers for the imprisoned junta
leadership.[47]

While the IWW relied on a coterie of cross-border Mexican radicals to agitate
in the Mexican barrios, it also recruited among the rooted Mexican population. For
instance, a California Commission of Immigration and Housing survey showed that
by 1919, 65 percent of the Mexican population in LA had resided there for more than
four years while 32 percent had been in the state for ten or more years.[48]

Mexican members affiliated with the IWW and sympathetic to the PLM spear-
headed efforts to formally merge the two organizations in 1919.[49] While it appears the
PLM leadership continued to focus on their role in fomenting social revolution in
Mexico and did not coalesce groups, the leadership of the PLM did encourage its ad-
herents to join the IWW where possible. In a 1910 edition of *Regeneración*, Antonio I.
Villarreal makes this case:

> It is indispensable that the workers organize in unions to struggle against the abuses
> of capital, to wrestle from the hands of capital concessions for the well-being of the
> producers of all wealth. These efforts toward the emancipation of labor take on the
> explicit character of internationalism. The crude race prejudices vanish in the light
> of the ever more universal recognition of the community of interests amongst the
> proletarians of all lands. The tendency towards uniting the workers of all races to
> beat the exploiters of all races, is a highly rational trend that will put humanity on
> the road to true emancipation.[50]

Efforts between the two groups to collaborate in organizing Mexicans occurred in
places like San Diego, where joint PLM-IWW efforts were behind two strikes in 1910.[51]
Also that year, the IWW took up a public campaign to support 150 Mexican workers
brought in from Mazatlán, Sinaloa, by US labor contractors working for the Southern
Pacific to develop the new line connecting San Diego to Arizona. The workers were
promised jobs in San Diego at two dollars a day, as well as good food and lodging for
their families. Instead, the company shipped them to Tijuana and forced them to cover
all of the costs of feeding and housing their families, reducing their pay to roughly twenty-five cents a day (or less) for ten to twelve hours of work. After organizing a protest,
they were driven from the railroad camp and dispersed. In response to the publicized
fiasco, the IWW launched a public campaign to support ninety of the workers and find
them jobs in San Diego through their local branch. As the *Industrial Worker* implored,

Mexican Fellow Workers, and workers of all tongues, do you stand for this kind of treatment to your class? Let every Spanish speaking worker organize in the Industrial Workers of the World and act with the workers in every land to gain our freedom.[52]

Like the PLM, Mexican Wobblies also used the printing press to reach the Spanish-speaking working class with their message and mission. Included in this range of publications were those linked to Mexican IWW locals in the Southwest: *Huelga General* and *El Rebelde* were two Los Angeles–based newspapers linked to Mexican Wobblies Aurelio Azuara and Fernando Velarde. *Libertad y Trabajo* was another short-lived Los Angeles–based journal edited by Fernando Palomares. It was the "official organ of the Club Tierra, Libertad, y Justicia," which functioned as a joint effort of the PLM and IWW. *El Proletario* and *Tradajadores y Trabajadoras de El Paso* were two IWW-linked papers in West Texas, and *La Union Industrial* was the official organ of the Phoenix Wobblies.[53]

Reflective of their hybrid PLM-IWW foundations and intended cross-border readership, these papers elaborated a radical analysis and critique of Díaz and US imperialism in Mexico and became scaffolding for local workers' struggles, organizing drives and transmitting international labor news. The pages of *Libertad y Trabajo* illustrate the cross-fertilization of revolutionary causes. The first page in its first May 1908 issue is adorned with a portrait honoring Ricardo Flores Magón. An author listed only as "Juan José" makes an appeal for support for the imprisoned leaders, proclaiming, "The Liberals have worked to initiate a revolution to get rid of the dictator; we believe it is their legitimate right, since 'every Mexican is obligated to take up arms to defend Mexico and its institutions.'"[54]

In an adjacent column, the Wobblies call on their working-class readership in Los Angeles to form unions and understand the class system, saying that in "Mexico and all other capitalist nations"

[t]he children of the workers die from hunger and cold in their miserable shacks ... [T]he remedy for this is in education and the organization of unions; read sufficiently and study to the best of your abilities your social condition: because the capitalist class is already organized in a unified way, and supported by the church and state.[55]

In a later issue, they published a direct appeal for Mexicans to join the IWW on behalf of the national organization, stating:

The IWW invites Mexicans to join its ranks, and there is no reason for you not to. In different regions of the US, Mexican branches already exist. We want to introduce you to our doctrines, so that Mexicans don't find themselves unorganized and defenseless when facing the endless abuses of the bosses.[56]

Between 1908 and 1910, Mexican radicals formed branches of the IWW or heeded the PLM in their appeal to join the IWW. Mexican branches were established in Los Angeles, San Diego, San Francisco, Redlands, and Holtville, California. PLM-aligned

Wobblies Fernando Velarde and Rosendo Dorame launched a Mexican chapter of
the IWW in Phoenix in 1908, and Fernando Palomares and Fernando Velarde then
helped found a multinational branch in Fresno, California, shortly thereafter. These
were initially successful because they were established in communities with a magonista presence or communities that had been centers of PLM organizing at some
previous point. Mexican workers also joined mixed locals in other regions where the
IWW existed. By 1910, an estimated 400 Mexican members joined the Wobblies in
the Los Angeles area, 100 had joined the San Diego branch, and 500 were active in the
Phoenix branch.[57] The addition of the Mexican locals in California especially helped
fuel overall growth of the IWW across the state, which grew from 500 in 1910 to 4,500
by 1915.[58] It is also estimated that as many as 200 Mexican smelter workers affiliated
with the IWW in El Paso in 1913.[59]

PLM Convergence with the Industrial Workers of the World
The practical efforts of the PLM intersected with Wobblies and other US socialists.
After 1910 the magonistas came into increasing contact with US radicals, especially
the Industrial Workers of the World and the Western Federation of Miners, who had
also begun to form links to radical Mexican workers as part of their union-organizing
efforts. From an ideological standpoint, the two groups gravitated toward an analysis
that social revolution, not just political revolution, was needed in Mexico and the US.
While the Wobblies and magonistas provided organizational and ideological structures for action on both sides of the border, this depended on unifying the Mexican
militants and organic labor leaders who had developed as a result of local struggles
and conditions. As Troy Robert Fuller summarizes about the crystallization of a radical Mexican leadership:

> Class divisions, exacerbated by the exploitive and racist conditions confronting
> Mexican immigrants, contributed to this militant attitude. The ideological ori-
> entation of Mexican workers, combined with the deft advertising of the PLM
> and the IWW, produced within the Mexican community a group of politically
> informed and motivated workers.[60]

These local radicals provided the bases for the growth of the PLM, while also
joining or following the IWW in their efforts to organize local unions at the point
of production. The internationalist approach of the IWW aided the efforts to recruit
Mexican workers as they expanded their efforts into the Southwest. The Wobbly leadership prioritized the recruitment and employment of Mexican and Spanish-speaking
Wobblies to organize among their paisanos and to publish Spanish-language newspapers, flyers, and handbills.

The political alignment of these organizations, a convergence of anticapitalist
and internationalist traditions, allowed for class-conscious Mexicans to see the value
of both. After 1908, the two groups focused more attention on Mexicans in the United
States in response to the turn of events. This included efforts to resist increased state-
led repression after the arrest of PLM leaders, meeting the practical needs of labor

organizing in the US, and what to do about the outbreak of revolution in Mexico and the threat of US intervention.

An example of how Mexican workers bridged the activities of the IWW and PLM are found in the activities of Simón Berthold Chacón and José María Leyva. Berthold Chacón was a Mexican migrant betabelero working in the Oxnard area at the turn of the century. By 1905, he had come into contact with the PLM and became a devoted magonista. He later moved to Los Angeles, where he became a truck driver and teamster. Through his labor activism and through social networks formed between Mexican workers, he came into contact with the IWW, where he became active in Local 12.[61] José María Leyva was a miner active in the PLM during the 1906 strike at Cananea. He later migrated to Los Angeles, where he became active in the short-lived, AFL-affiliated Hodcarriers Union. Like Berthold, he joined Local 12. The two Mexican radicals later teamed up to help spearhead the PLM-IWW uprising in Baja California in 1911, launched from the Spanish-speaking IWW hall in the California border town of Holtville.

Other Mexican Wobblies made inroads deeper into the Midwest and across the border through networks of Mexican migrants and PLM contacts:

> The journeys of other organizer-propagandists suggest the broad geographic expanse of PLM Wobbly organizing. Tomas Sarabia Labrada, for example, organized from 1907 to 1912 in Oklahoma and worked in Arizona, New Mexico, and Texas. Antonio Araujo traveled across Kansas, Oklahoma, Texas, Arizona, and New Mexico before being caught in the 1919 net of repression against the IWW. Eduardo Manzano . . . joined the IWW and organized Mexican miners in Arizona, Colorado, and the coal mines of Oklahoma.[62]

Furthermore, the press of the Mexican Wobblies in the US circulated across the border, reaching a Spanish-speaking audience, and in some cases Mexican organizers returned to Mexico and continued their efforts there.

Primo Tapia de la Cruz, a Purépecha from Michoacán who left his pueblo to work in the US, became a prominent figure that represents this trend. Like other Mexican migrants heading north at the time, Tapia migrated to the US Southwest in 1907 and remained north of the border for the next fourteen years. During that time, he worked in various jobs in agriculture, the railroads, and mining. He came into contact with radical miners and participated in strike activity, which may have contributed to his turn toward radical politics.[63] By 1908, he moved to the Mexican barrio in Los Angeles and eventually became an ardent magonista under the direct tutelage of Ricardo and his brother Enrique, where he vigorously studied anarchist and Communist texts. He became part of the PLM leadership but later became a migrant worker moving throughout the western and Rocky Mountain states taking jobs in the sugar beet fields, copper mines, and on the railroads after the PLM leadership was arrested in 1911.

Tapia likely joined the IWW Local 12 in Los Angeles as a magonista and somewhere along his sojourn became an active IWW organizer. By 1916, he was a bona fide Wobbly, organizing migrant harvest workers across the West and Midwest, by now accompanied by fellow migrant Purépechas from his hometown of Naranja, Michoacán. His fluency in both English and Spanish proved useful for Wobbly efforts to organize the growing Mexican migrant workforce alongside a host of other nationalities. In 1918, along with a coterie of fellow Naranjeños, he went to Bayard, Nebraska, where he set up an IWW local as a base to organize several hundred workers at a sugar refinery, a significant minority of whom were Mexican. Shortly after a failed strike to raise wages was launched in 1920, in which only Mexican workers walked off the job, he fled the area and ultimately left the United States for fear of government repression.[64] Tapia returned to Michoacán but did not leave his radicalism behind. He became a member of the Mexican Communist Party, a national agrarian leader in defense of indigenous land rights, and an armed rebel leader until his death at the hands of the state in 1929.[65]

Cross-border distribution of Spanish-language Wobbly material occurred through PLM-established networks, cross-border transit, and through collaboration with the Casa del Obrero Mundial. In 1916, the IWW and the Casa del Obrero Mundial collaborated to extend the IWW-affiliated Marine Transport Workers Union into Mexico, beginning with the large oil complexes in Tampico, Veracruz. To assist in on-the-ground operations, an Arizona-based Mexican Wobbly and labor organizer named Pedro Coria moved to the Gulf Coast. In January 1917, Coria helped establish the IWW-affiliated Marine Transport Workers Union 100 in Tampico.[66]

Experienced Mexican radicals like Palomares, Berthold Chacón, Leyva, Coria, Tapia, and others formed the ranks of an international revolutionary diaspora that forged the links between the PLM and IWW, moving across borders and between organizations. While in the US they became the proselytizers and organizers of a burgeoning revolutionary cause, now international in scope. They worked, organized, and lived within segregated Mexican barrios, but they also crossed paths with US radicals in the early stages of turning their attention toward these same communities.

The Baja Insurrection

The third attempt at revolutionary insurrection occurred in January 29, 1911, when a coalition of magonistas, Wobblies, maderistas, and others launched an armed insurrection seizing the towns of Mexicali, Algodones, Tecate, and Tijuana along the far northern rim of Baja California. The revolt took place in the context of Madero's call for an armed uprising to install himself as president, but it also reflects the emerging rupture between these two camps. It signified the radical turn of the magonistas, who saw the need to carry the revolution forward along explicitly anticapitalist lines. It also represents the highest level of convergence between the PLM and IWW in Southern California, and part of the larger IWW effort to spread into Mexico. Despite being poorly planned and executed, the Liberal forces controlled the border region for nearly six months before being defeated by a combination of Mexican and US troops. During the short experiment, the *insurrectos* attempted to catalyze a social revolution on an international scale.

With the actions in Baja, the PLM junta was publicly breaking ranks with Madero and the Plan de San Luis Potosí, while joining in and encouraging PLM *grupos* active across thirteen states in Mexico to join the uprising of November 20, 1910. Ricardo Flores Magón denounced the Madero plan as a bourgeois one, seeking to contain the revolution to the limits of electoral reform, while maintaining the capitalist system underwritten by imperialism and contingent upon the continued oppression of the working class.[67] In taking the rupture public in such terms, the events in Baja California fractured relations with reform Socialists, liberals, and the AFL. Nevertheless, the Baja insurrection was one piece of a larger uprising already taking place, as PLM cells were activating and joining the uprising so Baja could serve to provide the model for implementing revolutionary change in action.

Timed to coincide with Madero's call for revolution in 1910, PLM activists laid the groundwork by preparing *foco* groups on both sides of the border who would converge into a revolutionary army. The plan for insurrection emphasized collaboration with indigenous groups who were dispossessed from their ancestral lands as part of Porfirio Díaz's land-privatization policy. As an article in an edition of *Regeneración* concluded, "all of the indigenous tribes of Baja California . . . have been displaced from their lands by American adventurers, by the millionaires of this country, that have Mexico's wealth in their clutches. It's time to begin the revolutionary process and take possession of the land."[68] For this work, the PLM sent its own indigenous organizers with connections to the region and the peoples to prepare the groundwork and logistics and to organize among the indigenous communities.

Fernando Palomares and Pedro Ramírez Caule, along with Camilo Jiménez, a Tarahumara PLM adherent and leader among the Cucapá, arranged the logistics for the capture of Mexicali. The polyglot forces that took part in the Baja insurrection were a combination of US radicals, principally affiliated with the IWW, and a few Socialists. There were also Mexican magonistas, including small detachments of PLM-affiliated Native Mexican groups from the Kiliwas, Pa-ipais, and Cucupá, as well as others with different ideological motivations but a shared desire to see Díaz fall.[69] About thirty individuals joined the revolutionaries, attracted to the PLM's call for land restoration and indigenous self-determination. *Regeneración* made a public salute to the allies, as well as a general appeal to take up arms. As Flores Magón wrote in June of 1911,

> The Pimas, Papagos, Tarahumaras and all of the rest of the indigenous tribes should follow the example of the Yaquis and Cucapás. The Liberals will help you to reclaim your lands. But do not forget, Indian brothers, that it is necessary to arm yourselves to prevent becoming once again a victim of plunder. You can work your land and keep your gun close by. In each Indian pueblo our brothers will plant the red flag.[70]

Another small portion later joined government forces, while the majority of the different groups did not involve themselves in the events.

Historian Marco Antonio Samaniego explains that those indigenous who joined had preexisting reasons for aligning with the magonistas. This includes high poverty rates inflicted in the collapse of the local mining industry during the recession of 1907, as many of the males worked as miners. It also includes the increased presence of Anglo colonists, investors, and "tourists," who encroached on Indian land and introduced alcohol and prostitution into the indigenous areas, which was tacitly tolerated by local Mexican authorities. They also opposed the disruption of their water supply, facilitated by Anglo capitalists colonizing the Colorado water supply, which sustained indigenous hunting and farming in the region.[71]

Shortly before the insurrection, the Roosevelt administration invested two million dollars in irrigation projects in the valley of Mexicali on Mexican soil, directing water from the Colorado River to serve US-owned and operated and imperial farming complexes that stretched from the valley of Mexicali, to Sonora and down to the Gulf of California. The Colorado River Land Company controlled 850,000 acres of land on both sides of the border, and was owned by a consortium of investors that included Los Angeles–based capitalists Harrison Gray Otis, his son-in-law Harry Chandler, and George Hunt.[72]

The insurrectos targeted the border towns for several reasons: proximity to the US, as the PLM and IWW had a strong presence in the border region; the transborder smuggling of weapons could be more easily facilitated; a weak central government and the limited presence of federal forces; and because the zone had seen substantial tracts of land bought up by US capitalists that the revolutionaries intended to expropriate. As historian Agustín Cue Cánovas points out, Baja California was exceptional in the volume of land that was parceled out and sold cheaply by the Díaz regime to foreign capitalists: "A surface area of over 150,000 square kilometers was carved up from one extreme to the other and from sea to sea, including the concessions granted to foreigners, including the islands and the coast lines."[73] In an act that symbolized this consciousness, the revolutionaries made it a point to seize the San Ysidro Ranch in Tijuana, an estate owned by a consortium of Los Angeles–based capitalists invested in preserving the Díaz dictatorship. This group included Harrison Gray Otis, who was also the architect of the anti–organized labor movement in LA and an accomplice to the repression of the PLM.[74]

Samaniego points out that those newspapers affiliated with capitalist interests in the urban centers of San Diego, Los Angeles, and San Francisco took positions on the Baja insurrection that aligned with their economic interest. With substantial investments in Mexico under the Díaz regime, papers such as the *Los Angeles Times*, *San Francisco Call*, and *San Diego Union* watched the Baja insurrection with great distress. John D. Spreckels, owner of the latter, for instance, was eager to see his investments in the rail system currently under construction in Tijuana preserved. This group was most instrumental in soliciting military intervention on both sides of the border.

Conversely, other sets of capitalists had annexationist ambitions, and saw the Mexican Revolution as the opportunity to press the US government to lay claim to strategically valuable sections of Baja California. This included William Randolph Hearst, owner of the *Los Angeles Examiner* and *San Francisco Examiner*, whose transpacific ambitions envisioned an annexed Baja as the home for a new US port that could facilitate greater volumes of trade vis-à-vis the Panama Canal. The *San Diego Sun, Calexico Daily Chronicle*, and the *Imperial Valley Press* also expressed tacit support for the insurrection, believing that a Baja Peninsula independent of central authority would eventually lead to its absorption into the United States.[75]

The motives of the rival cliques led Ricardo Flores Magón to condemn the designs of the capitalists, affirming that the revolution would not aid their cause, but prevent it. As he argued, the Díaz regime had already conceded so much land to the capitalist annexationists, allowing them to lay claim without firing a shot:

> Well then: Baja California does not belong to Mexico, but to the United States, England, and France. The north of Baja California is in the hands of . . . Otis and other North American millionaires. All of the western coast belongs to a powerful English [. . .] company, and the region of Santa Rosalía belongs to a rich French company.[76]

The magonistas saw the intrigue and maneuvering over Baja California as a consequence of US imperialism, which, faced with a crumbling regime in Mexico City, ultimately threatened Mexico's territorial integrity in the far north. Its isolation from the rest of the country and the near-total foreign ownership of the land at that critical juncture made the peninsula a strategic starting point for the launch of their socialist revolution. The establishment of a revolutionary commune, it was surmised, could serve as a base for extending the revolution while also providing a pole of attraction for Mexicans north of the border eager to return to be part of the liberatory project.[77] This notion was further reinforced by a sense that the socialist uprising would be replicated across those regions in Mexico where magonista cadre were still in operation.[78]

On January 29, 1911, a team of sixteen PLM revolutionaries and one Wobbly under the direction of Fernando Palomares and José María Leyva captured Mexicali, a small border outpost of four hundred residents. One of the first acts of the movement was the freeing of the prisoners in the town jail, which included two Liberals, who promptly joined the group.[79] Since as many as a thousand adherents of the PLM in Mexico languished in Díaz's draconian prison system, liberating prisoners was one of the designated actions to be carried out by a foco group. After the capture of the Mexicali, the rebels opened up the town as a passage point for about two hundred Wobblies and some mercenary elements, who offered their services to the operation. The Wobbly contingents came through IWW locals based in Holtville, Redlands, and San Diego, California. By March 13, the revolutionaries captured Tecate, and on May 9 they captured Tijuana. To secure control of the peninsula, the revolutionaries aimed to capture Ensenada, the seat of commerce and government. This never came to pass, allowing for counterrevolutionary forces to use the port city as their base.

A structured military command in which officers were democratically elected was organized with an indigenous Canadian Wobbly named William Stanley leading the English-speaking contingent and Simón Berthold Chacón leading for the Spanish-speaking group. The training and experience of at least a dozen participants in the American Legion who were deserters from the US military, including IWW member and leader Jack Mosby, likely aided the revolutionaries in their battles and skirmishes.[80] While the group had only small arms to launch their campaign, they hoped their victories in the small towns would lay the basis for the capture of Ensenada, the largest town in Baja, with a military base and a substantial number of PLM adherents. After engaging and defeating a small scouting troop that crossed over from Ensenada, the group began its westward march. By February 21, revolutionaries captured the small town Algodones.

As the insurrectionaries took and held the towns, socialists in the United States supported them with arms and funds. John Kenneth Turner, for instance, made several trips to the border, smuggling guns to the combatants through the border crossing at Mexicali. The Socialist Party organized rallies in different cities in support of the revolution. The Socialist Party branch in San Diego, for instance, held regular mass meetings to show public support and to collect funds. On February 4, two thousand people gathered in the downtown area to discuss the latest news unfolding just below the border, to generate support and possibly participation, and to pledge opposition to US intervention.[81] Leading Socialists in San Diego E. E. Kirk and Kasper Bauer formed the San Diego Anti-Interference League, which lobbied the state and federal government to not intervene and represented members of the group in legal affairs. The participation of Socialists in the leadership, its public activities, and the strong anticapitalistic language expressed in their messaging "indicated that it was closely associated with Flores Magón and the Liberal Junta in Los Angeles."[82]

There was evidence of significant support for the revolutionaries' efforts. Letters of support and donations destined for the PLM office in Los Angeles were seized by federal agents, revealing the scope of interest. As one revealed, "there were . . . contributions sent from socialistic and anarchistic organizations. Apparently small bodies would hold receptions or entertainments or take collections among themselves and send them in to the Magóns for the purpose of helping along their work." A dozen retired military veterans, for instance, sent in five dollars "for the Mexicans to fight against beaurocrat-tyranny [sic]."[83] An Italian section of the Socialist Party in Connecticut and another in Cleveland sent in donations, as did a Socialist Party branch in Indianapolis, and two International Committees of the PLM based in Los Angeles and San Francisco sent $16.10 to purchase armaments and rail travel for volunteers. Two German socialists from Chicago offered their military skills for the revolution. A surgeon from New Mexico offered to be a field doctor. A weapons engineer from Northern California offered to make cheap gunpowder for use by the revolutionaries. A $4.25 donation came from Minneapolis, Minnesota, with requests for updates from the battlefield.

The San Francisco branch of the Socialist Party sent ten dollars plus a request for "300 copies of Regeneración at once" as "[t]he people of San Francisco are waking up to the real significance of the revolution." IWW halls across the Southwest sent urgent requests for bundles of *Regeneración*, seen as the best source for news and analysis of events in Baja, which were "selling like hotcakes." Urgent requests for papers also arrived from the Jerome Mining Union, while another letter from the IWW in Brawley, California, reported that "[a] number of young men of this place, principally members of the Industrial Workers of the World, are ready and willing to give their services and lives, if necessary, to the cause of the liberals and to freedom in Lower California." By late May they had collected ten thousand dollars from local Mexicans and supporters nationwide, and were arranging the deployment of volunteers to Ensenada.[84] These reports and many others give a sense of the enthusiasm generated by the revolution, and the way it fired the imagination of the radical Left in the US.[85]

Defeat of the Baja Insurrection

While the US federal government had turned a blind eye to the armed insurrection launched by the forces of Francisco Madero in November of 1910, they did not afford the magonistas the same treatment. President William Taft, in conjunction with the smaller-scale efforts of Porfirio Díaz, initiated a massive military mobilization to suppress the insurgency in Baja California. Furthermore, the failure of the magonista-led uprising to achieve any other significant victories in the country, to inspire significant support from the Mexican working classes, or to spread beyond the isolated northern frontier led to its fragmentation and decline. While the rebels held the Baja border region for six months, their defeat led magonista cells in other parts of the country to join Madero's forces. They then worked to permanently suppress the junta with the support of the US government.

Around the sixth of March, Taft and Díaz ordered troop movements to the region. Taft ordered 20,000 troops to occupy the full extent of the US-Mexico border, with 2,500 concentrated at the crossing points between the US and Mexican border towns of the Californias. Operations were coordinated from San Antonio, Galveston, Los Angeles, and San Diego. Fort Rosecrans, near downtown San Diego, was the command center for troops stationed to secure the San Diego-Tijuana region.[86] Of particular concern was the prospect of thousands of Mexicanos, especially those with radical leanings, returning to Mexico to join the magonista ranks.[87] The US Department of Defense moved significant military armaments to the border. The Oregon-based newspaper the *Daily Capital Journal* joyfully reported that the destroyer-class warship *Lawrence*, the transport ship *Buffalo*, with large stocks of arms, a supply ship, *Glacier*, with significant rations, and the cruisers *Cincinnati* and *Raleigh* were being prepped or were already en route to San Diego while troops were put on alert at forts along the Pacific Coast, from California to Alaska.[88]

The US navy also docked the gunboats US *Yorktown* and USS *Truxtom* in Ensenada, while the British patrolled the West Coast of the peninsula with its own gunboat, the HMS *Shearwater*. The ground troops sealed the border to prevent supplies and more revolutionaries from crossing it, while the gunboats blockaded the main port at Ensenada to prevent resupply via boat. Under the watch of the US navy

ships, the Mexican government landed five hundred federal troops of the Eighth Infantry Battalion, armed with machine guns and heavy artillery under the command
of Colonel Celso Vega. Their first objective was to establish a garrison to protect the
US-funded irrigation works near Mexicali, and then to eliminate the rebels. Despite
the blockade, superior firepower, and isolation, it took nearly six months for the Mexican army to prevail, as the rebels sustained themselves by taxing US commerce crossing the border and by expropriating resources from the large, US-owned farms and
ranches in the Mexicali Valley.[89]

Radicals on the US side appealed for direct action to prevent what was believed
to be an imminent US invasion. The San Diego branch of the IWW opposed the
buildup of US troops on the Mexican border in anticipation of a US military invasion
to suppress the PLM/Wobbly uprising in Baja California. In the April 27 issue of the
Industrial Worker, the secretary of the San Diego branch called on railroad workers to
strike in order to prevent the transfer of troops by rail, "[a]s a means to stop this hurl-
ing of one part of the working class against another part of the working class."[90] In the
end, the invasion didn't need to manifest, as the Mexican troops got the upper hand.

The Mexican troops had superior numbers and firepower, and with the failure to
capture Ensenada, Díaz could move in more troops by boat at will. Many of the most
capable rebel leaders, especially those with military training and those whose respect
commanded loyalty in battle, were killed in skirmishes and battles. This included the
popular leaders Simón Berthold, William Stanley, and Camilo Jiménez. Internal conflicts led the rebel force to divide, leading to many desertions. This was accompanied
by a growing number of US-based opportunists, spies, and other shady figures with
ulterior motives clandestinely crossing the border into rebel-held territory.

The appearance of more *norteamericanos* with no left-wing affiliation cast a pall of
confusion over the character of the revolution in the waning weeks of June, providing
fodder for detractors and opponents on both sides of the border and demoralizing its
supporters. Until the end, when the revolutionary leadership tried to expel or exile
these elements, they simply formed their own groups and goals and operated independently from IWW-PLM leadership. For instance, the *San Diego Union* observed
that Mexicans constituted 80 percent of the five hundred rebels that remained in the
field in early June.[91] As a result of the deterioration, some of the PLM-aligned figures,
such as José María Leyva, deserted and joined with the maderistas. Madero aided this
by offering to pay the last sixty holdouts six hundred dollars to lay down their weapons
and return across the border or join his forces.[92] After the defeat of the rebels in late
June, US military forces arrested all of those marched across the border in violation
of neutrality laws, and remained on the border until Madero assumed the presidency
on July 1 of that year.

Some historians contend that Madero's success had a lot to do with his larger
resource base as a representative of the richest class of capitalist landlords in Mexico.[93] In addition, support for the US government was also pivotal. While the stability of Díaz's regime was seen as a priority for US investors in Mexico, support was
withdrawn as the regime began to fall apart after 1908. Support for Madero widened

as Díaz faced revolt on all sides. The US enabled his ascent while concentrating its firepower on the magonistas to prevent a socialistic revolution from threatening to expropriate the vast US-owned economic interests of US capitalists.

While the PLM had a mass following through the press and a substantial core of revolutionary adherents on both sides of the border, their strategy for armed insurrection left the overwhelming majority of their supporters in the working class on the sidelines as nonparticipants. Rather than concentrate revolutionary efforts at the point of production, the magonistas believed that small groups of armed adherents would inspire mass action. The repression and elimination of the leadership of the PLM revealed the weakness of this strategy, as the base of supporters were left on the sidelines without an independent course of action.

After the collapse of the magonista-led wing of the insurrection, remaining PLM-affiliated groups around Mexico either integrated themselves into maderista forces, were arrested and disarmed by their successful rivals, or remained independent. The latter later joined in with the next phase of radical organizational efforts under Madero, including a regroupment in the Casa del Obrero Mundial, learning the importance of building power in the organization of the industrial working class.[94]

As a denouement of the Baja Revolution, the successful Madero sent a "peace delegation" composed of Magón's now-estranged brother and former collaborators-turned-maderistas, Jesús Flores Magón, José María Leyva, Juan Sarabia, and Jesus Gonzales Monroy; to meet with the Organizing Junta in Los Angeles on June 14, 1911. Madero's emissaries offered Ricardo Flores Magón the symbolic office of the vice-presidency of Mexico under Madero, but only if he ended his relentless campaign for socialist revolution. True to form, Flores Magón scornfully rejected their overture and sent them packing. The next day PLM representatives informed US federal agents that they intended to pursue their revolutionary operations against the government of Francisco Madero. This information was then used to file new charges against the junta for violating neutrality laws in their complicity in the Baja insurrection. With their ground forces neutralized and their leadership once again in prison, the PLM ceased to be a coherent political force within the Mexican revolutionary process.

Part 3

Chapter 15

Radicals in the Arizona Copper Mines (1907–1917)

"The problem with Mexicans… is that strike comes first and not last."
-Observation made by US Labor Department
representative in southern Arizona

The PLM had gained a following among Mexican miners in southern Arizona as early as 1905, and they became a sizeable component of the cross-border insurrections. The mining camps of the Arizona and Sonora border region were also convergence points between the PLM and US radicals, as Mexican workers became a larger share of the mining workforce. By 1907, more recent unskilled immigrant workers eclipsed the ranks of the US-born and older immigrant skilled workforce, with Mexicans becoming the majority.[1] The Western Federation of Miners, an industrial mineworkers' union, had helped to launch the IWW as a platform for joint industrial action and solidarity among industrial unionists and socialists. By 1908, political divides emerged within the WFM over the IWW, and the two groups formally split and became rivals in the southern Arizona mining camps. One of the dividing lines was that of racial inclusion and the organization of Mexicans and immigrant workers. Early Anglo settlement in southern Arizona carried with it the anti-Mexican prejudices of the post–Mexican-American War period, including racially justified dispossession and disenfranchisement. This included restrictive policies and legislation that deprived Mexican miners of the right to make claims, kept them from occupying skilled positions, and kept them spatially and socially segregated.

Despite established racial barriers and the primacy of racial subordination over class solidarity in most spheres of existence, miners did unite and overcome prejudice through coordinated and joint action at the point of production at key moments in the Arizona mining wars, especially the strikes at Miami-Globe, Ray, and Clifton-Morenci in 1915. These breakthroughs toward coordinated action allowed for miners to make great advances toward racially integrated industrial unionization, leading to the largest mining strike in the region in 1916–1917, which took on an anticapitalist character. Radical workers and revolutionary activists from the WFM, PLM, and the IWW were instrumental in providing ideas and leadership that helped overcome the crippling racism institutionalized and physically enforced by the copper companies, federal, state, and local officials, and various bodies of law enforcement, the media, and aligned civic and vigilante organizations. In the context of the radical phases of the Mexican Revolution of 1914, Mexican workers once again pushed the labor struggle forward with a near general strike in Arizona's copper mines in 1916. It took massive state repression and unprecedented vigilante violence to defeat the radical miners' movement in 1917, and even then it was only possible through the divisions in the labor leadership.

PLM Activity in Southern Arizona

During the period 1905–1909, political exiles affiliated with the Mexican Liberal Party had enlisted the aid of mexicanos in Arizona, conducted an extensive propaganda campaign, and launched insurrectionary forays. Moreover, a network of PLM-aligned Mexicans in Arizona coordinated the purchase and supply of arms and ammunition across the border to be used against the Díaz government.[2] As part of this work, PLM organizers working as miners had also built a substantial following in the Arizona mining camps and border towns. By 1905–1906 clubs had existed in the mining towns of Clifton, Morenci, and Metcalf. Notable magonistas that served as organizers and points of contact for the junta included Práxedis Guerrero in Morenci, Reinaldo Ornelas and Serapio Murillo in Clifton, Manuel Flores in Globe, Inés and Angel Salazar in Metcalf, along with Manuel and Melquíades Orozco, who participated in the IWW and WFM.[3]

The PLM saw southern Arizona and northern Sonora mining camps as one of its principle bases of operation for fomenting revolt in Mexico. A starting point for PLM activity in Arizona was in the border town of Douglas, where many of the PLM-aligned veterans of the Cananea strike relocated after it was crushed and which served as a base of operations for the group. One participant in the PLM-affiliated Club Libertad estimated that the group had upward of three hundred members in 1906.[4] After the failed uprising of 1906 and the arrest of many Douglas magonistas, focus shifted to a new round of recruitment in the mining camps.

PLM adherents crisscrossed the border between Sonora and Arizona smuggling arms and ammunition, and moving among Mexican migrant workers and through barrios and colonias as they conducted their organizing work. Perhaps no one illustrates this role more than Fernando Palomares, especially as it connected Mexican mining communities to PLM-inspired actions and revolutionary ideology. In 1904, a Mayo indigenous socialist named Fernando Palomares from Los Mochis, Sinaloa, affiliated with the Mexican Liberal movement, becoming an adherent and distributor of the Liberal papers El Hijo de Ahuizote and Excelsior across north Mexican border towns. In 1905, he moved to Tucson, Arizona, where he became a contact and organizer for the Organizing Junta of the PLM, then based in St. Louis. In Tucson he joined with another magonista named Juan Olivares to publish El Defensor del Pueblo. By late 1905, Palomares was an operative of the PLM regional network, joining with Manuel Sarabia, Práxedis Guerrero, Lázaro Gutiérrez de Lara, and entering into the mining camps across southern Arizona to distribute Regeneración and recruit to the PLM among Mexican miners for the coming insurrection.[5] He moved to Cananea in early 1906 and began recruiting for the PLM cause there.

Fernando Palomares, Mayo Indian, Wobbly, and dedicated magonista

The story of Práxedis Guerrero, a militant with the PLM, also captures this experience. Originally from a wealthy landowning family in Guanajuato, Guerrero underwent a political evolution beginning with his opposition to Díaz. He renounced his family wealth and journeyed north alongside other Mexican migrants to find work. After crossing in 1905, he found work as a miner in Denver, Colorado, then as a woodcutter in Northern California, then as a coal miner in Arizona, and later in the copper mines at Morenci, Arizona. In Arizona, he and his collaborator, Francisco Manríquez, formed a mutualista called La Sociedad Benito Juárez, uniting Mexican miners and small ranchers from the region. This mutualista affiliated with the PLM in 1906 as Guerrero had become radicalized through his experiences and exposure to *Regeneración* and their Plan of 1906. Furthermore, he made an independent effort to launch a Spanish-language socialist newspaper called *Alba Roja* (Red Dawn) when he was living in San Francisco in February of 1905.[6] His paper published original news, political analysis, and poetry.

In 1906, he became part of the junta leadership, helped edit *Revolución*, and became tasked with organizing and coordinating revolutionary cells along the border for the impending uprising. His initial efforts produced the formation of a mineworker group Obreros Libres in Morenci. Drawn from the most radical and class-conscious elements from La Sociedad, this group trained Mexican miners to carry the revolutionary message to mining camps throughout the border region. According to reports made by spies for the Mexican consul, "La Sociedad had between 40 and 50 members, all of which were Mexican workers from the states of Chihuahua . . . and Sonora, and

Yaqui Indians who were refugees from the war now working in the mines of Arizona."[7] Through this experience, many magonista miners likely came into contact with radicals from the IWW and Western Federation of Miners, providing an interface that would aid in the increasingly radical orientation of the PLM and the integration of the two groups in future endeavors.[8]

Práxedis G. Guerrero, PLM leader and revolutionary theorist and organizer

Abrán Salcido, Juan B. de la O, and Luis Mata, three of the leaders of the 1903 strike, had joined the PLM by 1906, perhaps through interactions with Palomares,

Guerrero, or others. Salcido, who served two years in the Yuma Prison as a result of the repression of the Clifton-Morenci and Metcalf strike, returned to Metcalf as an adherent of the PLM seeking to recruit Mexicans for the coming insurrection. On May 5, 1906, he spoke to a crowd of two thousand in Morenci and condemned Díaz. Shortly after this appearance, he was forced out of the district and joined efforts in Douglas to organize for the scheduled September 16 PLM uprising in Cananea. Up to a hundred other Mexicans left Morenci in a short period thereafter to join the insurrectionary call. This included many of the most experienced and radical elements affiliated with Magonismo.[9] After the uprisings failed, Salcido along with other participants were arrested, shortly thereafter deported to Mexico, and ended up in the notorious prison at San Juan de Ulúa, where he languished until the overthrow of Díaz.

PLM exiles continued to cross back into Arizona after the failed 1906 and 1908 insurrections. Juan Cabral and Salvador Alvarado were two examples. Cabral, a cashier at a lumberyard at Cananea, and Alvarado, a local vendor who frequented the mine company, were both activists who conspired to launch an uprising in coordination with the junta's call for June 19, 1906. After their efforts were betrayed, they fled on foot across the border, finding their way into the Ray work camp, where they later opened a guns and ammunition shop as a front to stockpile and smuggle weapons for the next phase.[10] The Díaz regime, with its extensive intelligence-gathering network, complained to Arizona and Washington officials that exiled revolutionists of all stripes were organizing in Arizona towns and mining camps, and that miner insurrectos were smuggling weapons across the border on a regular basis.[11] Mexican radicals and revolutionaries gathered in Tucson, Nogales, and Douglas, regularly speech-making to large crowds in the Mexican barrios and colonias.

Other PLM militants migrated or were recruited out of the mining camps and smelter towns of southern Arizona and northern Sonora. One Arizona recruit was Javier Buitimea, a Yaqui laborer who was part of a cell that moved to Cananea in 1906 to prepare the grounds for the uprising. In 1908, Buitimea, along with Fernando Palomares, was tasked with forming a guerrilla foco among the Yaqui and Mayo in the Sonora borderlands. Other members of this circle of revolutionists included those working in the mines, such as Lázaro Puente, Antonio de Pío Araujo, Tomás D. Espinosa, Luis A. Garcia, Bruno Treviño, Callis Humbert [of French origin], Leonardo Villareal, as well as a professor named Luis G. Monzón Teyatzin. They formed a core of PLM collaborators based in Douglas, Arizona, but operating out of Mowry, Metcalf, Clifton-Morenci, and Patagonia in Arizona, and at Cananea, Nacozari, Nogales, and Agua Prieta in Sonora.[12] According to a Buitimea communiqué, the PLM had one of its strongest bases of support in Clifton-Morenci-Metcalf, which was the site of one of the most significant strikes in Arizona history several years later. In fact, lists drawn up by labor spies noted and documented several dozen known organizers and sympathizers throughout the camps.[13]

Western Federation of Miners

Socialists were prominent within the ranks of the Western Federation of Miners. In contrast to the Socialist Party's "socialism," which meant electoral ambitions based on the belief of a neutral democratic state that could be harnessed by labor, the leadership of the WFM redefined their socialism as the battle for supremacy in the workplace. Illustrating this, WFM president Edward Boyce downplayed the value of participation in a rigged political system and openly declared in favor of direct action and armed self-defense for the labor movement. As he told the national WFM convention in 1897:

> Every union should have a rifle club. I strongly advise you to provide every member with the latest improved rifle . . . I entreat you to take action on this important question, so that in two years we can hear the inspiring music of the martial tread of 25,000 armed men in the ranks of labor.[14]

The leadership of the WFM, led by President Boyce, developed explicitly anticapitalist and revolutionary positions. At the 1901 convention, the delegated body approved a resolution promoting the divorce of the working class from the capitalist-dominated Democratic and Republican Parties and the formation of an independent political movement. Breaking out of the political orbit of capital, the leadership of the Western Federation of Miners also bolted from the AFL in 1897 for its conservatism and unwillingness to confront capital. Independently, the WFM union began seeking broader horizontal growth based on the principles of class struggle. In 1898 the WFM launched a rival labor federation to the AFL along industrial unionist lines called the Western Labor Union. The organization was renamed the American Labor Union in 1902, and finally relaunched as the Industrial Workers of the World (IWW) in 1905. This evolution in fits and starts charted the development of a new radical form of unionism and revolutionary socialism. This trajectory also led to a rupture with the Socialist Party, which after 1901 came to represent official socialism and in which many WFM leaders and rank and filers were already members. As Anthony Esposito describes it:

> The western labor movement's desire to get hold of industry, however, was not synonymous with the Socialist Party's program of state control of industry; rather the exigencies of the industrial struggle, in which the metal miners found themselves arrayed against mine owners, armed citizen groups and the state, propelled them consciously toward an industrial unionism whose objective was labor's direct control of the workplace. This in turn made socialism, with its commitment to solidarity, seem logical.[15]

By the turn of the century, the WFM leadership had aligned itself with the socialist movement, which coalesced to form the Socialist Party in 1901. Their convention resolutions and press emphasized the need to overthrow capitalist relations of production. For instance, a *Miner's Magazine* of the same year stated:

> We believe the time has arrived for all those who desire the emancipation of the toiler . . . to cease their cowardly supplications for the reformation of a government, the very foundation of which is crumbling into decay through the corruption and infamy of the self-constituted governing class, and demand a complete

revolution of present social and economic conditions to the end that justice may
be meted out to all people of the earth.[16]

While the leadership closely affiliated with socialist ideas, divides emerged within
the ranks over radical or conservative strategies and tactics for carrying out the class
struggle. Several concrete issues divided the body as a whole, which was even more
diverse politically than the leadership. One of these was over the question of immigration and the place for workers of color in the ranks. While the AFL and the socialist
organizations officially proclaimed for racial unity, in practice these principles were
applied unevenly or, in the case of the AFL, largely ignored and discarded. This same
quandary affected the WFM.

By 1904, two distinct camps emerged in the WFM with regard to the inclusion
of immigrant and nonwhite miners, which have been labeled by historians as inclusionists and exclusionists.[17] The exclusionists, who opposed the organization and
inclusion of Mexican and immigrant workers, dominated union leadership positions
from its inaugural attempts to organize in Arizona. The inclusionists, which favored
their inclusion and who tended to be socialists, Wobblies, and the most militant workers, gained more prominence at the local level in periods of rising class struggle. The
self-activity of Mexican miners in southern Arizona, in 1903 and again between 1914
and 1917, dispensed with the racial stereotype of Mexicans as "unorganizable." Furthermore, it showed in practice the possibility of using solidarity as the basis to unite
miners across racial divides, which was fundamental for wielding enough class power
to defeat a copper industry backed by the state. The leverage of the inclusionists was
also increased by the presence of PLM organizers in the mines, and by Mexican workers politicized and radicalized by the Mexican Revolution. This convergence of factors
culminated in the first significant strike victories in the southern Arizona mining industry between 1914 and 1917.

After the turn of the century, the WFM began a long-term campaign to organize miners in Arizona, primarily focused on white miners in the northern half of the
state. Entering into the political terrain of white supremacy that had already facilitated the racial segregation of mineworkers by occupation and settlement, Western
Federation exclusionists adapted to the anti-immigrant and anti-Mexican sentiment
already pervasive among most miners. Following the trajectory of the AFL, which the
WFM eventually rejoined in 1911, they supported restrictions on Mexican immigration, accepted the logic of segregation, supported their exclusion from white locals,
and supported disenfranchisement. They also sought alliances with local white middle classes, who opposed aspects of corporate capitalism that harmed their interests.

After encountering intense opposition from the big corporate firms to their
mine-organizing efforts, the union turned to an electoral strategy as white miners
composed a significant portion of the voting population. This trajectory encouraged
WFM strategists to seek political allies in other classes that had grievances with the
big operators. According to Melvin Dubofsky, while the WFM's official position was
for "class war,"

it was a most peculiar variety of class war, for in most mining communities local farmers, businessmen, and professionals allied with labor unionists; and public officials, including judges, elected by union votes, often supported labor's goals. Instead of class being pitted against class, local communities united in coalitions cutting across class lines to combat "foreign" capitalists.[18]

While some of the middle classes wanted to curb the excesses of the corporations, they were neither anticapitalist nor generally in favor of racial inclusion. In the course of crafting or supporting state legislation, they also promoted policies inimical to labor, making them erstwhile and capricious allies. Big corporations also learned to rely on federal connections and access as a counterweight, rendering this alliance of convenience less potent. One short-term area of convergence that was ultimately a poison pill for the growth of the WFM was immigration.

The exclusionist majority aligned the WFM with reactionary forces in the state on the issue of immigration restriction and was backed by newspapers aligned with the copper operators.[19] They supported the 1909 Literacy Law, which effectively disenfranchised most Mexican voters. During the Constitutional Convention, which preceded statehood in 1912, the WFM openly supported an anti-immigration proposal known as the Kinney-Claypool Law, which would have limited immigrant employment to 20 percent in any type of business in the state with more than five employees. In doing so, the WFM aligned themselves with the thoroughly pro-business convention composed mainly of "cattlemen, farmers, bankers, lawyers, and merchants."[20] This became the foundation of the Democratic Party, which dominated state politics between 1910 and 1916, backed by a large influx of southern migrants who gave the party a wide majority of voters.[21]

The first state governor elected in 1911 was George W. P. Hunt, who fashioned himself as a "pro-labor" Progressive Democrat. Like Southern-origin Democrats at the time, his labor populism was couched in the preservation of white primacy, with Anglo miners providing a significant base of support. He rhetorically chastised the mining corporations for meddling in politics and paying too-low taxes, while in practice he championed the cause of the corporations on their bread-and-butter issues. For instance, he campaigned for tariffs to protect Arizona's mines from foreign competition at their behest.[22] This was expressed by his fervent support and sponsorship of the Kinney-Claypool law, which failed to initially pass through the legislature. Mexican organizations across the state, especially the mutualistas, fervently opposed the legislation, which was crafted to target Mexicans in the mines.[23]

Ironically, only those delegates linked to the mining companies opposed it, effectively blocking its passage, recognizing the importance of maintaining access to Mexican labor in holding on to its racial labor hierarchy. Nevertheless, this same coalition won all of the major state offices in the 1912 and 1914 elections, and finally brought the proposal to fruition in 1914 through a popular referendum in which overwhelming support came from the mining districts. While federal courts struck it down within one year, it registered the effects of persistent anti-immigrant campaigning among white miners. Ironically, the same mining corporations that institutionalized segregation within its own structures to create, manage, and exploit divisions to prevent unions and defeat strikes positioned themselves vis-à-vis the WFM as the defenders of immigrants.

At the local level, fierce battles raged between the two camps. In some cases, mining companies colluded with exclusionists to prevent election of their rivals. When in 1909 upstart inclusionists were poised to take control of the local at Jerome, the United Verde Company appointed only exclusionists to administrative positions within the company, effectively giving them supervisorial positions to leverage against their rivals.

For those situated in the inclusionist camp, their opponents' strategy revealed major failings that spelled doom for their organizing efforts. They were acutely aware of the companies' strategy to employ racial tactics to divide and conquer organizing drives and strikes. The employers openly boasted about the usefulness of racialized work. One owner even stated that, "[t]he mixing of nationalities [was the] secret of his company in downing the unions . . . [because] the unions cannot hold peoples from different countries together into a solid mass."[24]

Unlike the prominent restrictionists who relied on political maneuvering and calculation, inclusionists were forged in practice, as they came to see solidarity and joint action at the point of production as the only way that labor could counter to the preponderant power of the capitalist class, the enforcement state, and a media stacked against them. When miners were confronted with state repression, this was even more apparent, revealing how far these forces would go in order to protect pro-business arrangements. Perhaps the most convincing contributing factor to the elevated class consciousness of this wing was the militancy of the Mexican miners themselves, which bolstered inclusionist trends in the WFM at these junctures. When the Mexican miners were at their most militant, the inclusionist leadership was most ascendant. When both parts were in synch, Arizona miners won their greatest victories.

Labor Radicalism of Mexican Miners

The Western Federation of Miners sent organizers into mining camps across the Southwest. Their efforts to organize the major copper camps of Arizona spilled over into Mexico. From their base in Bisbee, the WFM tried to organize the Consolidated Copper Company camps in Cananea and Santa Rosita in Sonora, Mexico. They initially organized the skilled white miners, helping to organize several job actions between 1899 and the general strike of 1906. As a company labor report produced in 1913 noted,

> [t]he Western Federation of Miners had at that time many members in Cananea, including a number of foremen who took advantage of the political and labor conditions to promote their own interests with an eye toward making this camp a branch of the Western Federation of Miners. To achieve this objective, they encouraged and promoted discontent and likely funded the revolutionaries [PLM members].[25]

A WFM-led strike for union recognition occurred in Bisbee, Arizona, in 1907, after the company went on a firing spree, laying off upward of sixteen hundred miners who were alleged to have union sympathies and threatening the rest that they would be "replaced by Mexicans" if they persisted. Over three thousand workers struck, although the company was able to unite most local merchants and bankers against extending credit to the strikers. The company brought in immigrant workers as strikebreakers, including many Mexicans, who having experienced the racial disdain and animosity from the WFM-affiliated workers had little reason to abstain from work. Nevertheless, the strike failed primarily because the white workers divided, with many skilled workers in craft positions, such as the mechanics, refusing to honor miner picket lines.

Despite its limited record in supporting Mexican miners, the WFM nationally and in Arizona came to the defense of the PLM after its principal leaders were arrested in the aftermath of the Cananea strike on the charge of violating US neutrality laws. When PLM leader Manuel Sarabia was kidnapped from Douglas, Arizona, by US agents and handed over to the Díaz regime in 1907, Socialist leader and labor organizer Mary "Mother" Jones and miners affiliated with the WFM organized an angry protest in front of the Mexican consulate. According to Ethel Duffy Turner, "The miners hung a rope, a noose, in front of the consul's office, with a sign: 'You are going to get this unless Manuel Sarabia is returned alive.'" After about ten days he came back. The United States authorities sent word that he was to be freed.[26]

As they did for others in the AFL, the Socialist Party, and the IWW, events in Mexico came into closer focus for the WFM leadership after Cananea. The WFM took a position against Díaz, and the collusion between his government and US capitalist speculators, a relationship "that wrenches profits from the soil and keeps Mexicans impoverished and produces destitute and desperate 'peons.'"[27] As the WFM's *Miner's Magazine* reported,

> The Mexican government, like all other governments that are upheld by the capitalist system, is pursuing to death three men who have raised their voice for human liberty. Antonio Villareal, Ricardo Flores Magón, and Librado Rivera have been marked for death . . . The lives of these three men are wanted by [Cananea mine operator] Col. Greene and his lieutenants. The wealth and prosperity of the Greenes of Mexico is more important to President Díaz than the happiness of a million subjects, who endure the pangs of poverty and bear the infamous wrongs of peonage.[28]

The common view of Mexican workers as debased and feeble peons contributed to the commonly construed notion that as unfree people, Mexican workers lacked the will or capacity to join, build, or sustain unions. They were dismissed as non-class-conscious workers who could be easily manipulated by bosses to undercut wages, break organizing drives, or cross picket lines. Nevertheless, this view began to gradually change for some as Mexicans proved not only willing unionists, but the militant vanguard of the mining workforce.

In July of 1907, about 140 non-unionized Mexican workers walked off the job at the Arizona Copper Company's smelter in Clifton for an increase in pay from $3 to $3.50, in parity with white workers, using their mutualista to facilitate organization.[29]

It failed soon after, as it occurred amid an oncoming recession and the collapse of copper prices, and also lacked support from Anglo workers and the WFM. Nevertheless, it kicked off a stint of strikes that showed that Mexican self-organization was decidedly pro-union and that in racially divided workplaces, unity was essential to victory.

That same year, 1907, the WFM had success in organizing twelve hundred smelter workers, of which the majority were Mexican. In an article discussing the important victory, the editors of *Miner's Magazine* mocked pro-immigration capitalists who now labeled "unionized" Mexicans as a social threat that would "throw the town into a state of anarchy." Revealing their own reasoning for organizing Mexicans, the article concludes, saying:

> Well, the Mexicans are being organized, this competition will be removed, and now the corporation newspapers say the Mexican laborers are "vicious." The organization of Arizona by the Western Federation of Miners is in full progress and nothing can check it. Every mining and smelting district will be invaded by organizers, and the Clifton-Morenci district will receive its full share of attention.[30]

Despite these ambitious proclamations, the zeal to organize Mexican workers was modest and punctuated; and still based on the extant regional and occupational racialization. A first step toward an inclusive approach occurred in 1907 (and later in 1912), when the WFM leadership hired at least three Mexican organizers to begin working in the Mexican sections of southern Arizona mining camps. Grounded more in practicality than ideology, the early efforts of Carmen Acosta and Fernando Velarde, and the later efforts of Julio Mancillas, were directed toward educating Mexican workers about the union, and soliciting solidarity and support when actions were taken on behalf of the underground Anglo miners. The union did not challenge the racial structures as they existed, but began to see the value of including the Mexican aboveground workforce involved in construction, maintenance, milling, smelting, and other tasks. Like early AFL efforts through the use of federal unions, Mexican organization was downplayed or viewed as an expediency to neutralize their use as strikebreakers in the course of organizing white miners, rather than a means to recruit them as equals or challenge racial segregation.[31]

By 1910, the Socialist Party made a concerted effort to establish branches and participate in elections across the state. With the support of the WFM, the party made gains, especially in the mining regions. In July 1910 for instance, Socialists captured two of the eight city council seats in Jerome, and lost many more by small vote margins. By 1912, the party "won many more offices throughout the state as the public mood turned anti-corporate."[32] The Socialist Party had branches throughout Arizona, including in the mining towns of Ray, Globe, Bisbee, Jerome, and others. Party members were subject to harassment in the mining towns and camps. In Ray, for instance, after Socialist Eugene Debs received more votes in the 1912 election than Republican William Taft, the sheriff deported known Socialists from the town.[33] Nevertheless, Socialists did not attempt to organize miners in any direct way, although many rank-and-file members of the WFM locals were members of the party and most likely were represented in the ranks of the inclusionists.[34]

WFM inclusionists did appreciate rising militancy among Mexican workers as evidence of their ability to organize themselves and their willingness to be unionized. As the editors of *Miner's Magazine* reasoned:

> Let it be said here, without fear or favor, that as a race, the Mexicans in the Clifton-Morenci district have shown more of a desire for economic independence and more fearlessness in avowing that desire than have the Americans . . . Being ground a little harder between the upper and nether millstones of capitalistic greed and capitalistic oppression than the white wage worker who draws a larger pittance and who is able to drink a few more bottles of beer a day, they see somewhat more plainly the necessity for organization.[35]

As part of the effort, the WFM inclusionists turned to the IWW to organize in the Mexican-majority mining camps of Clifton-Morenci, where Mexicans were confined to the "unskilled" positions, which typically indicated the most difficult work, including the most difficult aspects of underground mining. Frank Little and Fernando Velarde, both originally organizers for the WFM who gravitated toward the more radical IWW in 1906, were sent in to accomplish this task. Rather than challenge the racialized structures within the WFM itself, the IWW served as an auxiliary organization that could house the Mexicans in their own organization.

The economic recession that hit in late 1907 deflated the exuberance for organizing. Copper markets crashed as a result of aggressive speculation, creating a substantial bubble that burst and sent prices spiraling downward. For instance, the stock of one behemoth copper holding company dropped from sixty-two dollars a share on October 14, to fifteen dollars two days later.[36] Under these conditions, copper operators cut wages 10 percent across the board and carried out layoffs; workers were put on the defensive. By the time efforts were renewed in 1912, the population of Mexican miners increased in relation to Anglos and European immigrant miners. For instance, the advent of World War I increased copper demand while cutting off most European migration, thereby increasing the mine operators' reliance on Mexican out-migration, which was exacerbated by the revolution.

Between 1910 and 1920, the Mexican population grew substantially as a percentage of the total population. In 1910, Mexicans were 14 percent of the population and 63 percent of the foreign-born contingent, while in 1920, this increased to 18 percent and 77 percent respectively.[37] Many of the migrant workers of this period had experience with the revolutionary movements in Mexico, which added a higher degree of class consciousness and organizational experience among the Mexican workers during outbreaks of labor conflict. Nevertheless, the increase in migration renewed the central debate over political strategy regarding immigration. Small numbers claimed membership in the WFM, while exclusionists pushed the immigration restriction strategy through lobbying. The final breakthrough for inclusionism occurred with the great strikes of 1915 in Miami-Globe, Ray, and Clifton-Morenci.

Mexican Miners Strike at Ray and Clifton-Morenci-Metcalf in 1915

Increased copper demand, aided by the outbreak of war in Europe in 1914, led to rising prices and immense profits for Arizona's copper companies. For instance, the total estimated value of copper mined in Arizona rose from $40 million in 1910 to $95 million in 1915, and again doubled, to $200 million, by 1917.[38] Huge profit windfalls richly rewarded stockholders and boosted executive pay, while workers' wages stagnated and food costs increased as a result of rising wartime inflation, with low-paid Mexican households hit the hardest as a by-product of their racially imposed precarity.[39] As European immigration slowed to a trickle, the mining workforce gained more leverage to unionize as a means of driving up wages, as production levels increased and profits rolled in to the companies.

By the beginning of 1915, several years of relative labor stagnation gave way to a flurry of activity, as workers gained the confidence to take workplace actions. As labor demand increased, many recent migrants entered into the mines from revolutionary Mexico, playing a significant role in the strikes and shattering the exclusionist myths. Campaigns of solidarity, aided by the participation of the PLM and the radicalizing effects of the Mexican Revolution, encouraged Mexican miners to take large-scale co-ordinated strike action. From 1915 to 1917, Mexicans were at the forefront of the largest strike wave that Arizona copper operators had ever seen, culminating in the possibility of a general strike in Arizona copper production as the US entered into World War I.

By 1916, the WFM had extricated itself from the more radical IWW, shrunk significantly, reaffiliated to the more conservative AFL, and changed its name to the International Union of Mine, Mill, and Smelter Workers (IUMMSW). In the face of a renewed labor upsurge, the WFM was in an atrophic state. The IWW, building off significant successes and growth through the Agricultural Workers Organizing Committee, shifted away from free-speech fights toward direct organizing in the workplace. Western Wobblies turned their sights to Arizona and brought their doctrine of direct action, racial inclusion, and industrial unionism into the mining camps in order to supersede the perceived failures of the IUMMSW's sclerotic approach. As early as 1913, they had an operational local setup in the border mining town of Bisbee.

In January of 1915, six hundred AFL-affiliated smelter workers involved in the refinement stages of copper production from the four main copper companies in the Miami-Globe district walked off the job to protest the hiring of non-union labor, and for the restoration of the daily wage to $3.75, which had been reduced by 10 percent.[40] This effectively shut down all metal refinement in the district. Shortly thereafter, over fifteen hundred miners and mill men affiliated with the WFM and a Mexican-led strike committee called the Comité por Trabajadores en General (General Workers Committee) walked off in solidarity. Reflecting the mood, union locals in different parts of the state pledged support for the strike.

Most importantly, the unity between the white craft workers and the ethnically mixed miners held firm, and the companies assumed a conciliatory approach, since the disruption threatened substantial profit loss during a boom in production. The negotiations yielded wage-cut restoration and increases across the board for all classes of labor, creating a new wage threshold referred to thereafter as the Miami Scale, which tied wages to wholesale value of copper per the stock market. This raised wages to their highest point and reinvigorated the WFM organizing efforts. The strike launched the Globe Miners Union Local 60, whose contract now covered Mexican miners. Comprising one-third of the total mining workforce in Globe-Miami, Mexicans also benefitted through wage increases, even though the racial wage scale remained intact. Nevertheless, the significant victory sent shockwaves throughout the mining camps, and the Globe union set out to organize the majority-Mexican workforce at nearby Ray.

Ray, Arizona, a town of about eight to ten thousand, was a mining company town in the truest sense of the phrase. The large Ray Consolidated Mining Company owned all of the land and operated as a virtual dictatorship over the towns and surrounding mines. It retained sheriffs and local judges on the payroll and managed the political affairs of the town as an autocracy. A minority of white workers, merchants, and administrators (about 15 percent) lived separately from the majority of Mexican and, to a lesser extent, Spanish immigrant miners. Labor organizers were physically driven from town, blacklists of union sympathizers were maintained, strikers were evicted, and the company even determined acceptable voting patterns. This was the case when the WFM hired Mexican organizers E. J. Moreno and Julio Mancillas to try to organize the Mexican miners in Ray in 1914.

In July of the same year, the virtually complete body of a thousand Mexican miners at Ray walked out on strike, hoping to replicate the Miami-Globe gains, while only 10 of the 311 Anglo skilled workers walked out in solidarity. Miners called for equivalent wage increases, an eight-hour day, safer working conditions, an end of abuse by Anglo foremen, an end to labor contracting, and the right to unionize (in this case affiliating with the nearby Miami-Globe union). With local white skilled workers in opposition, the Ray Consolidated Company stonewalled negotiations and began evicting Mexican families. After two weeks of a unified Mexican strike and a company shutdown, the Anglo workers acted to end the strike. Without apparently consulting the Mexicans, they sent a delegation to negotiate a settlement with the company, one which gave all workers a sixty-cent daily wage increase with only Anglo workers receiving the eight-hour day and the right to affiliate with Miami-Globe.[41] The wave then spread to Clifton-Morenci, which was the center of Mexican labor activism, and a hotbed of PLM organizing, with a history of class solidarity.

The minimum-wage threshold of miners in Greenlee County, where Clifton-Morenci and Metcalf was situated, was the lowest in the state. By calling for the Miami Wage, the workers were effectively calling for an end to the racist dual-wage system, threatening the very foundation of the racialized class system. Between 70 percent and 80 percent of the workforce was Mexican American, Mexican, or Yaqui; representing the vast majority of the 6,000 men that eventually participated in the nineteen week strike.[42] The remainder were from different immigrant groups including Italians, Finns, Spaniards, Austrians, and Poles; Anglo workers filled the highest-paying jobs in the skilled trades. Mexican workers not only suffered from the lowest wages, but employers were also implementing the 20 percent Kinney-Claypool

Law and using it to lay off Mexican workers of their choosing, especially targeting known union sympathizers.[43]

In February, a delegation of leaders representing six thousand Mexican workers from Clifton, Morenci, and Metcalf began a formal protest at the state capitol opposing the anti-immigrant legislation, claiming that it was "drastic," "unjust," and would "throw out of employment many of the pioneers and up-builders of the state."[44] Despite the economic insecurity instilled by the law and the enabling of racial intolerance toward them, the Mexican workers prepared to take further action. In anticipation of job action, Mexican miners requested a WFM organizer, but found the union unable to provide resources. The Detroit Company, Arizona Copper Company, and Shannon Copper Company took their own countermeasures, uniting their efforts behind the Phelps-Dodge Corporation, owner of the Detroit Company.

In an effort to blunt worker militancy and further solidify racial hierarchy, Arizona Copper management in the Clifton-Morenci mines instituted a policy of increasing the ratio of white supervisors to Mexican workers by hiring a crew of "timbermen" to oversee operations. The racial implications of imposing white rule in an environment of increased tension encouraged arbitrary, abusive, and punitive behavior among the new supervisors. In a matter of months, the Clifton-Morenci workers conducted nineteen wildcat strikes in opposition to the heavy-handed tactics of the supervisors, and in one incident a timberman supervisor was killed.[45]

The official strike began on September 11, 1915, as Mexican workers in the Morenci smelter walked out, with all departments within every mine, mill, and smelter downing tools throughout the region in a domino effect, producing a general strike within twenty-four hours. Pickets were distributed across the mining complexes to shut down freight and close the warehouses, and company guards were ejected from the mines.[46] Through the support of WFM organizer Guy Miller, the Clifton, Morenci, and Metcalf miners were given charters to form locals of the WFM, although it had become clear to the Mexican miners by then that WFM support was going to be limited and that they would be largely left to their own devices.

As they had in 1903, the Mexican workers led the strike effort, preparing primarily through their mutualistas and selecting their own leadership as a committee of the regional workgroups. This leadership included Juan Guerra of Clifton, Carlos Carbajal of Metcalf, and Abrán Rico of Morenci. The latter was a member of the Partido Liberal Mexicano and used this connection to solicit support from former PLM leader and Socialist Party member Lázaro Gutiérrez de Lara. The WFM organizer, Guy Miller, who was also a Socialist, supported and advised the strike committee, and through his participation reported on the events and solicited support from the branches of the WFM. It is noted in press coverage and in some of his public statements that the WFM had no official role in the strike, and that his initial presence and support in organizing the strike may not have been officially sanctioned by the WFM leadership.[47]

At the ground level, Miller's participation represented the inclusionists' efforts to rally behind the cause while the official leadership remained aloof. The wave of victories at Miami-Globe and Ray, as well as the high level of unity between the Mexican workers, inspired radical WFM miners throughout the state, who raised funds through their locals and sent delegations of support. The Socialist press in Arizona gave favorable coverage to the strike and documented the acts of solidarity. Newspapers, distributed locally among the striking miners, were well-received.[48] Guy Miller, Lázaro Gutíerrez de Lara, and the strike committee leadership conducted the strike through daily mass meetings in the plazas of Clifton and Morenci, in which gatherings of striking workers discussed the course of events.

In response to the strike, the companies shuttered all of their operations and refused to negotiate, although the level of organization and support for the strike discouraged the mine operators from initially attempting a strikebreaking operation, although they did threaten to replace striking Mexican miners with Anglos. Instead, like in 1903, the mine operators and other "prominent citizens," including local elected officials, fled the city after miners protested outside their offices, claiming their lives were at risk by remaining in the region. In an unsuccessful ploy to divide popular support, representatives threatened to deport all Mexican strike leaders. The military occupation of the border region by US troops taking place at that time to suppress insurrecto activity was also used by opponents of the strike to foment anti-Mexican hysteria. A Tucson newspaper, for instance, alleged (without evidence) that the strike was a conspiratorial by-product of the Plan of San Diego and the PLM, and that it signaled the opening shot of a Mexican revolutionary uprising.[49] Despite the machinations, public opinion did not favor the companies' position, and the miners held firm. As an *Arizona Republican* article observed, "the general opinion is that the [wages] will be adjusted quickly. If they are not, the shutdown will be a long, drawn out affair working great hardship on the entire community."[50]

During the impasse of the four-month strike, the WFM, the PLM, IWW, and other organizations built solidarity campaigns for the Clifton-Morenci-Metcalf (CMM) strikers, raising money and holding rallies, speaking events, parades, and other activities to raise strike funds and moral support. The WFM got the AFL-chartered Arizona State Federation of Labor (ASFL) to endorse the strike, sending fundraising letters to all of its locals.[51] This was managed through the efforts of an inclusionist network of the WFM that was active inside the ASFL and that was committed to organizing all miners into one industrial union. Led by John L. Donnelly, this group of socialists and industrial unionists used their base within the ASFL to challenge Moyer's entrenched leadership faction in the WFM.

Nevertheless, consistent support from the WFM and the ASFL tapered off, and the strike became a test of wills between the strikers and mine operators. The contradictions of supporting the exclusion of Mexican workers while simultaneously backing a strike of the same workers may have contributed to vacillation and equivocation in fully investing in a strike victory. As one historian observes:

> [T]he electorate of Greenlee County [where the CMM mining camps were situated] had approved the [Mexican exclusion] law, 1,270 to 640, even though the mining companies in the Clifton area employed almost the converse of the proposed statute. More important, the Western Federation had been a leading

advocate of this so-called 80 percent law, which would have deprived jobs to almost all the workers it now proposed to organize.[52]

Workers and their families held regular marches through the town. In one march of fifteen hundred, sheriff's deputies had to be called in to save several known strike opponents from being run out of town. They were kept in the jailer's office for their protection.[53] Over the course of the strike, those who were publicly known to be in opposition were run out of town, hostile businesses were boycotted, and the strikers collectively decided to shut down the courts and other functions of local government when any legal cases were made against them.[54] Strikers also took over and ran the lighting plant in Clifton, which provided the electricity for streetlights in the three mining districts.

Violence also flared up as strikebreaking operations were later established at the nearby town of Duncan among workers who opposed the strike and fled the district. On one occasion a mine manager snuck back into town to entice individuals to re-group with others in Duncan. Once discovered, he was pelted with eggs by a group of strikers. He left town the next day after an unknown assailant shot a bullet through his home window.[55] In another case, a non-union worker shot and killed a striker in Morenci during a confrontation, but was rescued by police and delivered from the city for his protection.

Former PLM leader-turned-Socialist Party representative Lázaro Gutiérrez de Lara came to the Mexican mining camps to extend support and help conduct the strike. Charles Moyer, president of the WFM, also came to address the strikers. At the Fourth Annual Convention of the Western Federation of Miners, which was held in Miami, Arizona, during the strike, various resolutions were passed in support of the strike, in-cluding one calling for the state to "take over the mines in the Clifton-Morenci-Metcalf district and operate them for the benefit of the people."[56]

Unity between the strikers and support and solidarity from within the rank-and-file labor movement was so broad that even the governor, a passionate advocate for the reactionary anti-immigrant proposal to restrict Mexican employment to 20 percent, came out publicly in stammering support of the strikers as a necessary measure to try to end it.[57] He was even compelled to attend a rally of three thousand miners and their families to present himself as pro-strike. As the (anti-strike) *Copper Era and Morenci Leader* newspaper observed:

> This has been a unique strike in many ways . . . the men on strike and the offi-cials of the Western Federation of Miners . . . were to listen to speeches by the Governor and Attorney General of the state. Probably no similar scene was ever witnessed in an industrial crisis anywhere in the United States.[58]

In his speech, the governor conceded that the workers' demands were justified. He furthermore threatened to bring state troops into the area and arrest mine opera-tors if they did not negotiate, who in his terms "would be no different to me than the poorest Mexican he controls."[59] He later sent three hundred members of the Arizona National Guard and state militia into Clifton, but only after all of the mine operators had left.[60] Many of the militia and guardsmen were also union members, who fraternized with the strikers, and upon the governor's orders were sent to keep out strikebreakers.

Pressured by the persistence of the strikers and the broad support for them among his base on one side, and the opposition and recalcitrance of the operators on the other, Hunt was largely paralyzed. He asked for a federal mediator to be sent, but the mine operators stonewalled outside efforts. As a result of Hunt's unwillingness to take steps to break the strike, the copper mine operators turned on him, initiating a failed recall campaign against him through the Arizona press they owned. The operators turned to federal courts to file claims against the WFM and strike leaders. By the end of December, US marshals entered the area to serve subpoenas to the strike leadership. This was followed by a Tucson-based federal judge issuing an injunction against the strikers. This prevented them from interfering with the company's efforts to bring fifteen hundred strikebreakers back into the mines.[61] While the operators upped the ante in turning to the federal government to break the strike, the WFM maintained a marginal position.

The WFM leadership did not make the strike a priority, provided limited resources, and committed only one organizer to the three mining districts. The leadership failed to help raise funds to support the strikers and did not consider spreading the strike. The significance of the WFM for the success of the strike had declined significantly by January 1916, which gave the mine operators leverage to make the exclusion of the WFM a condition for negotiation. The mine operators' apprehension toward an industrial mining union in the region led them to draw the battle lines on that exact issue.[62] So when the WFM continued to publicly demur from the strike and support it only from the sidelines, the operators got the upper hand. This vacillation allowed the mine operators to gradually divide the strikers and the WFM, and instead allow AFL representatives linked to the Arizona State Federation of Labor to negotiate on their behalf.[63] When the operators finally agreed to negotiate with a strike committee that excluded the WFM, further weakening the prospect of unionization, the Clifton-Morenci-Metcalf workers agreed to the terms.

During this episode, Ricardo Flores Magón commented on the events in the pages of *Regeneración*. He criticized the timidity of the Western Federation of Miners in confronting the companies. He penned articles directly to the Mexican workers, calling on them to reject limited reforms and to expropriate the mines. Perhaps revealing the intensity of the times, with revolts now occurring on both sides of the border, he exuberantly declared:

> [F]or the workers to make real gains, it has to be directly against the system of private and individual property by declaring the land, the homes, the machinery, everything involved, should become the property of all men and women. For this to happen, you cannot wait, but continue working the mines and the foundries, but under your control. Only in this manner will you obtain the full product of your labor.[64]

While this did not come to pass, the unity among the strikers for a period of four months compelled company representatives to concede higher wages, although these were maintained within the dual-wage structure. By the end of February 1916, wages for Mexican miners increased to about $2.40 per day, about 80 percent of what white miners made in the same mines, and about 68 percent of what they made in other districts.[65] Collective bargaining procedures were negotiated, such as the creation of a grievance process, but the company refused to recognize any outside union body as a direct representative of the Mexican workers. Nevertheless, by the next year, the Clifton-Morenci-Metcalf and Ray-area miners had affiliated with the AFSL. The influx of radical miners' representatives into the AFSL induced a comprehensive reorganization of forces within miner unionism in Arizona, starting with the ascendancy of the inclusionists. As Philip Mellinger concludes from the 1915 strikes:

> Ethnic-racial inclusionists had become the WFM's majority at the big Globe-Miami locals in Arizona; and at both Ray and Clifton-Morenci in 1915 they seized power. Using their tactical control of these big mining districts, and also utilizing their solid State Federation of Labor connections with AFL crafts unionists, the Globe-Miami men briefly dominated the entire Arizona AFL. [They] achieved the goal to which Charles Moyer . . . had aspired in vain.[66]

The shift in orientation within the union leadership coincided with the entrance of the IWW into Arizona copper mining districts, and the continued militancy of the Mexican miners set the stage for another round of strikes in 1917.

The IWW and the Copper Strikes of 1917

The entrance of the United States into World War I on April 2, 1917, did not stem the tide of labor militancy in southern Arizona. In 1916, the IWW began a massive organizing drive through the camps, seeking to harness the militancy and channel it into one big miners' union called the Metal Mine Workers Industrial Union. The union leadership identified the convergence of factors that made a new round of strikes possible: growing militancy, increased demand for copper, and substantial working-class opposition to the war. Increased demand was fueled by the war effort, when in March of 1917 the federal government pledged to buy fifty-five million pounds of copper.[67] Labor militancy across the country, for instance, had skyrocketed. The number of strikes had nearly tripled between 1915 and 1916, from 1,246 to 3,678, and then increased again to 4,233 in 1917.[68] The IWW set out to build a third "camp" within southern Arizona copper mines, and in doing so were opposed by both the IUMMSW and the Donnelly faction within the AFSL.

At their national convention in 1916, the IWW came out publicly against the war in Europe, and called for workers to oppose US entry. In a widely distributed proclamation at their tenth national convention, the IWW national leadership declared:

> With the European war for conquest and exploitation raging and destroying the lives, class consciousness and unity of the workers, and the ever growing agitation for military preparedness clouding the main issues and delaying the

realization of our ultimate aim with patriotic and, therefore, capitalistic aspirations, we openly declare ourselves the determined opponents of all nationalistic
sectionalism, or patriotism, and the militarism preached and supported by our
one enemy, the capitalist class. We condemn all wars and, for the prevention of
such, we proclaim the anti-militarist propaganda in time of peace, thus promoting Class Solidarity among the workers of the entire world, and, in time of war,
the General Strike in all industries.[69]

At the same convention, the mine union delegates also identified Mexican miners as
the leading wedge of the general strike. As one delegate from Arizona commented,
"The Mexicans of that state who have always been discriminated against by working
men and bosses alike are showing pronounced activity in the organization, and will
become earnest members of the I.W.W."[70] This framed the push by the IWW to move
into the Arizona and Montana copper mines, where they intended to organize: in
Butte, Montana, and in the four copper-producing centers of Arizona, whose combined copper output amounted to nearly two-thirds of total national production.[71]
The convention delegates saw an opening to relate to the militant workers in the country at a time of labor radicalization. For instance, of the record four thousand strikes
in 1917, the mining industry accounted for 407 of the strikes, with 20 in Arizona that
year alone.[72]

The IWW launched their Arizona campaign by calling for a standardized $6 a day
for all miners, $5.50 for all surface workers, and a six-hour workday. They also included
rhetorical calls for better working conditions, an end to technologically induced unemployment, an end to speed-ups, and an end to autocratic company policies.[73] In
January 1917, IWW organizer Grover H. Perry organized the IWW-affiliated Metal
Mine Workers Industrial Union (MMWIU) in Phoenix, Arizona, as a base to organize active MMWIU locals in all of the state's mining camps. Wobblies Frank Little,
Pedro Coria, and Fernando Velarde were the most successful recruiters, the latter two
working among the Mexican miners. A military intelligence document reported on
the recruitment of IWW members as follows:

> The Mexicans are being organized and have been organized into the I.W.W. by
> paid organizers, Mexicans, who are aliens and are not citizens of the United
> States, most of these organizers are Magonistas, and cannot go into Mexico,
> they are of the Ricardo Flores Magón school of anarchists, most of the meet-
> ings for the organization of Mexicans into the I.W.W. are held under the guise
> of dances.[74]

The Wobblies reached out directly to Mexican workers using the IWW demands to
illustrate how the new union would abolish the dual-wage system and create racial
equality in working conditions and union rights.

By mid-1917, the IWW had grown rapidly, forming their own locals in Bisbee,
Miami, and Jerome in a direct attempt to gain influence and control in the WFM locals. The IWW quickly eclipsed the size and influence of the WFM by late 1916, now
renamed the International Union of Mine, Mill, and Smelter Workers (IUMMSW).

They did this by applying radical principles that fit the mood and the time. They unapologetically argued for one inclusive union that united all miners together and harnessed their collective power to defeat the operators' divide-and-conquer tactics. They also understood that the miners were willing to take the fight to the next level, aware of the tremendous wealth generated by their labor in the context of a war boom, and the fact that the war had diminished migration, creating labor shortages in industries like mining. Furthermore, labor conflict carried over from the 1915 strike, especially in the CMM mines, where the Mexican miners conducted another sixteen wildcat strikes between the resolution of their strike in January 1916 and June 1917.[75] With these factors taken together, the IWW calculated the situation was ripe for another strike call.

By early 1917, IWW organizers and sympathetic miners had gained influence within the Bisbee Miners' Union, switching to Metal Mineworkers Union branch in June, which became the epicenter for a statewide copper strike and the first site where different ethnic groups joined in the same union local. Within a month of its founding in Bisbee, for instance, the IWW leadership reported that 85 percent of the 350 Mexican surface workers had joined the IWW local.[76] IUMMSW president Charles Moyer promptly revoked the charter and disavowed the strike and the IWW.

The rivalry between the IWW and IUMMSW reached a climax with competing calls for strikes around different demands in early summer of 1917. As opposed to the more radical IWW demands, the IUMMSW demands included a call for a $1 per day wage increase across the board, company recognition of the grievance process, and reinstatement of fired union workers.[77] The companies, believing they now had sufficient support to crush the unions once and for all, refused to negotiate with either. On June 26, the IWW made a call for a strike in Bisbee and Globe-Miami. IUMMSW locals followed suit in making their own call but separate and opposed to the IWW, with about 8,000–10,000 workers walking out (or otherwise prevented from working) between the dueling union calls in the three mining districts. In CMM, the three AFSL-affiliated locals had already presented the management with a list of demands on July 19, with the central demand being a wage raise to the Miami Scale.[78] After the July 26 walkout in the other mining districts, smelter, mill, and mineworkers followed suit, with as many as 10,000 downing tools across the three districts. For the Mexican CMM workers, this was their nineteenth strike in two years. Jerome miners walked out a week later, although only about 250 miners joined the effort.

As a ploy to weaken the efforts of the IWW, Woodrow Wilson's secretary of labor, William B. Wilson, "relaxed" immigration restriction along the US-Mexico border to facilitate the mine operators' recruitment of strikebreakers from across the border. According to Michael Parrish,

> With Arizona in the grip of a statewide miners' strike, Wilson exempted from the $8 head tax and literacy test all immigrants who held certificates of future employment in agriculture, railroad maintenance, and mining. This incredible decision, demanded by the state's farmers and business interests, actually augmented the strength of the IWW, above all in the border areas of Bisbee and Ajo . . . The Mexicans did not become strikebreakers, much to the operators' disgust[.][79]

Rather than break the strike, they followed the lead of the radical Mexican leadership in the IWW. By July 6, at least 25,000 miners across the state were on strike, effectively bringing wartime copper production to a halt.[80]

Massive State Repression

The militant shutdown of copper production in Arizona was met with a wave of violent reaction at the federal, state, and local level. Nationally, the Wilson administration devised and conducted a nationwide campaign to repress and destroy the Industrial Workers of the World. The actions of the Democratic president were then amplified in Arizona by a Republican governor, Thomas Campbell, in 1917; a Democratic Party–controlled state legislature that included many Progressives; and mixed Republican and Democratic Party–controlled mining town administrations. As William Preston observes, "when political necessity or public hysteria required it, Progressives, Republicans, and Democrats were equally eager proponents of a repressive antiradicalism."[81] The strikes of 1917 were violently repressed with the exception of the CMM strike, which required a different treatment because of its significant size, militancy, and solidarity.

Using anti-radical immigration exclusions written into the national policy between 1903 and 1917, the federal government declared IWW was explicitly "antigovernment," which designated its immigrant membership as subject to deportation. To enable a carte blanche approach to mass deportation of radicals, Congress removed a statute of limitations of anti-radical exclusionism in 1916. This was handcrafted for the targeting of the IWW leadership and allowed any noncitizen to be deported regardless of how long they had lived in the United States. Furthermore, the War Department authorized military command centers around the country to be deployed to break local strikes, in open violation of federal laws stemming from the Posse Comitatus Act. As a result, US troops were deployed across the country to suppress strikes and to allow for federal, state, and local agents to identify and arrest known radicals. This included the deployment of troops to break the IWW copper strikes in Michigan and Arizona. As part of this operation, 64 IWW offices were raided, and 166 of the national leaders were arrested in one massive coordinated sweep in the summer of 1917.[82]

Twenty states and two territories passed criminal syndicalism laws between 1917 and 1919, including Arizona. These laws were specially designed to suppress industrial strikes, including language that made it a felony to advocate, teach, aid, or abet the commission of a crime, to commit sabotage, or to employ other "unlawful methods" as a means of "accomplishing a change in industrial ownership or control or affecting any change." Other wordings of the law warned against "effecting or *resisting* any industrial, economic, social or political change," while in Arizona the law also specified "the destruction of property" and "violating the Constitutional or statutory rights of another as a means of accomplishing industrial or political ends."[83] These laws were broadly designed to give employers and police carte blanche to break pickets, arrest radicals, and otherwise use violence as they saw fit to suppress a strike.

The national press, including the mining-operator-owned or -supported *Copper Era, Morenci Leader*, and *Bisbee Daily Review*, waged an incessant propaganda campaign against the IWW in line with the federal government's crackdown. Using hyperbolic jingoistic language and anti-immigrant and xenophobic characterizations, and leveling grossly inaccurate charges without any evidence, the media helped turn the US middle class violently against radical and immigrant workers. For instance, the IWW was commonly linked to phantasmal German espionage and sabotage. As the *Bisbee Daily Review* howled, "'Hands across the seas' has a new and most sinister meaning these troubled days. They are the hands of the rioter and striker and agitator and spy stretched forth to clasp hands with the Kaiser and his Junkers."[84]

The full-spectrum assault on the IWW encouraged and sanctioned vigilante and mob violence. For example, a prominent, Globe-based superior court judge named D. W. Shute publicly proclaimed his desire to go to the mines and "mow those sons of bitches down with a machine gun."[85] With unified support from the ruling class, mine owners and local police in the mining areas harnessed and organized hostile middle-class opponents to radicalism and unionism into their own proto-fascist militias to smash strikes, often under the watch of or with direct support from local police, state troopers, and the US military. This occurred in various forms in Globe-Miami, Jerome, and Bisbee; and later in CMM.

When overt violence or repression wasn't possible, as in CMM, the federal government used the tactic of "mediation" to erode the strikers' stamina before using the military to suppress it.

Within the first two weeks of the strike, the full force of this spectrum was brought to bear in Jerome, Globe, and Bisbee. In Jerome, where the strike had the least support, the mine companies agreed to pay all workers who crossed the picket line $5.15 per shift, 65 cents above the normal wage.[86] Within a few days, company-organized "loyalty leagues" were formed throughout the struck zones. These comprised "leading citizens," businessmen, and professionals who were deputized by the sheriff's department and served as armed enforcers for the companies. In Jerome, a squad of 250 of these deputized citizens arrested 65 IWW-affiliated miners and organizers. They were identified with the help of representatives of the IUMMSW, who provided information about known Wobblies in the town, although the vigilantes targeted all unionists regardless of affiliation.[87] They were threatened with lynching if they continued their strike, a statement that was satisfactorily reiterated in the state press.[88] They were then forcibly deported from the town by July 11.

In Globe, the loyalty league leadership included ex-military officers from Arizona who served in the occupation of the Mexican border region. They re-constituted as paramilitary strikebreakers at the behest of the companies, who funded their operations. The press assisted by playing up nationalist and xenophobic sentiments, labeling the strike as "treasonous," and the participants as distrustful foreigners whose leadership was described by the loyalty league chairman as "a flagless mob of foreign delinquents capable only of trouble and spending their days in uproar and idleness." Nevertheless, they were not sufficient in number and power to suppress the two thousand striking mine, mill, and smelter workers.[90]

Since the vigilantes could not do so on their own, US troops were used to break the strike. About five hundred US Army troops, including one machine-gun company, entered Globe. They set up their positions around the mine entrances and physically broke the picket lines and dispersed the workers. Local sheriffs proceeded to arrest IWW leaders, identified with the help of the IUMMSW officials. In Globe, for instance, a Mexican Wobbly named Jesus Lavendero and an Anglo Wobbly named John Smith were arrested on the spot and charged with rioting, although over a dozen witnesses testified they were merely guarding the mine entrance in an orderly way.[91] After the picket lines were broken, white unskilled workers were brought in from Texas as replacement workers, and the strike fell apart by the middle of August. Once again, the IUMMSW worked with company representatives to identify and remove known radicals affiliated with the IWW.[92]

The most brutal episode of repression occurred in Bisbee, where the IWW had its strongest base and where the IUMMSW denounced the strike. By the second week of the strike, the mine owners (Phelps-Dodge Corporation) used the isolation of the IWW to devise a scheme to completely eliminate all unionists and sympathizers from its midst. As Vernon Jensen explains,

> [C]arefully laid plans were made to carry out a mass deportation of the strikers. Early in the strike, it [was] reported, Sheriff Harry Wheeler was approached by officials of mining companies with the request that they be allowed to appoint men, who would be deputized by him, for the purpose of keeping strikers from trespassing on company property.[93]

Company men and the local liberty league worked out detailed plans to recruit over two thousand armed vigilantes (with no legal authority) from different towns in the area to carry out a mass deportation, in flagrant violation of the law and the basic rights of the workers and their families, as well as Bisbee townsfolk who sympathized with them. On the morning of July 12, everyone in the town affiliated with the strike, especially known IWW or IUMMSW leaders, including at least 250 Wobbly-affiliated Mexican miners, were rounded up and forcibly marched two miles to a baseball stadium outside of town. From there, the 1,186 people were then crammed into 24 cars of a Phelps-Dodge-owned freight train, where they began a slow 60-hour ordeal without food or water until they were deported into the New Mexico desert and dumped into a makeshift prison camp where they were held by US troops for two months.

On August 10, the federal government then took the extraordinary step to officially declare an end to all strikes in industries where government contracts existed and a purge of all labor radicals. Then President Woodrow Wilson ordered the Council of National Defense to appoint a labor Mediation Commission responsible for ending the labor conflicts by imposing binding arbitration and rooting out Wobbly radicals. For his commission, Wilson appointed two capitalists, Colonel J. L. Spangler, a coal mine operator and banker, and Verner Z. Reed, capitalist engaged in metal and petroleum mining. Alongside them, he included Samuel Gompers's appointed allies

John H. Walker, president of the Illinois State Federation of Labor; and E. P. Marsh, president of the Washington State Federation of Labor. The AFL helped coordinate the purge of the copper-mining workforce, preferring to rid the industry of the IWW and the inclusionist radicals of the IUMMSW in exchange for the preservation of the skilled AFL affiliates.[94] US troops were then stationed throughout the Arizona copper mines, including Clifton-Morenci-Metcalf, even though it had been spared much of the violence because of the strength and solidarity of the strike, which carried on for four months.

The commission ultimately worked to validate the breaking of the strikes, which had already occurred by October, with the exception of CMM. It rejected any wage increases, authorized the mass firings of suspected IWW members, and required all remaining strikers to return to work. Strikes were forbidden for the duration of the war, and any further labor grievances had to be conducted through a government-established arbitration board.[95] While the commission ruled the deportations illegal, no one was held accountable for the crimes committed. The CMM miners held out for four months, until the commission's ruling, when they were compelled to return to work or be arrested.

Chapter 16
From Casa del Obrero Mundial
to Communist International

"The rapid growth of the [Mexican] labor movement in the . . . twentieth century, influenced by the ideologies of Anarchism, Socialism, and Communism . . . [meant that] . . . labor had new demands which it wanted realized in a hurry; the workers were prone to listen to any voice which would promise fulfillment of their desires."
—*The Comintern in Mexico*

The toppling of Díaz, led by insurgent capitalist landowners in the north and fronted by Francisco Madero, fomented a significant split in the PLM. While moderates envisioned the possibility of economic reform and political democratization with the advance of bourgeois democracy, Ricardo Flores Magón and the radicals argued that the dismantling of the structures of capitalism required social revolution from below. Combining anarchist and Communist concepts, Donald Hodges summarizes the core of the PLM postrevolutionary vision:

> In no uncertain terms the PLM's September 1911 program called for a war to the death against private property, political authority, and the established church. Not only lands would be expropriated, but also agricultural implements and urban industries . . . As the manifesto spelled out the "egalitarian principles" of its final, or communist, solution to the social question.[1]

In 1912, eight veteran radicals convened in Mexico City to unify the working class into a nationwide organization undergirded by such principles. The meeting was initiated by the veteran organizer and Colombian anarchist émigré Juan Francisco Moncaleano. Moncaleano had embraced anarchism, fled military service in his homeland to Cuba, and later left with the wave of exiles to Veracruz, Mexico. From there, he found his way to Mexico City, where he eventually worked in conjunction with other like-minded radical intellectuals and labor activists, including Jacinto Huitrón, Rodolfo García Ramírez, Eloy Armenta, Pioquinto Roldán, Luis Méndez Ciro Z. Esquivel, and J. Trinidad Juárez. Together, they founded the Grupo Anarquista Luz in June of 1912. The group later attracted a membership representing a wider range of political tendencies, including former magonista Antonio Díaz Soto y Gama, and radical labor organizer Rosendo Salazar. It also included the Spanish Anarchist émigré and founder of the printers' union, Confederación Tipográfica Mexicana, Amadeo Ferrés. Furthermore, the group expanded to include Marxists, agrarian-oriented radicals, nationalists, and anarchists of every derivation; many of whom were officers or rank-and-file members of existing unions.[2]

Their first steps included the publication of a theoretical journal, *Luz*, which promoted magonista thought alongside its own theoretical formulations. They also oversaw the foundation of an *escuela racionalista* inspired by the pedagogy of Francisco Ferrer Guardía, which was dedicated to the rational and radical education of the urban working class. Classes taught ranged from physics, personal hygiene, and music, to ideological courses on "How to Organize Women Workers" and "Equality, Liberty, and Love."[3] They envisioned the school as serving as the collective memory of the class. They included international working-class histories as a feature of the curriculum and incorporated important labor anniversaries and benchmarks as part of their calendar. This included commemorations of the Paris Commune, the Haymarket Affair (as May Day), and great strikes such as those at Cananea and Río Blanco, among others.

Within a year they then turned toward union organizing, creating a labor federation organized along Anarcho-syndicalist lines that came to be known as Casa del Obrero Mundial (International Workers' Center; referred to hereafter by the Spanish abbreviation COM).[4] The COM served as an interface for collaboration between working-class-oriented radical individuals and groups, and as a central labor council for radical-led unions or as an organizing springboard for new unions and locals. While the first center developed in Mexico City, other COM subsidiary centers were developed in the major agro-industrial zones of Orizaba, Mérida, and Guadalajara, and interlinked through the locals of the major industrial unions of oil workers, electrical workers, dockworkers, and railroad workers. Alongside these, and in greater numbers, were more traditional mutualistas and artisanal workers that also affiliated to the centers, giving them their mixed and uneven character.
According to Anna Ribera Carbó,

> It was through this model that they exercised influence within the Mexican working class and among a small group of foreigners that participated in the modernization process; including the formation of unions, the dissemination of political ideology, and the promotion of cultural values.[5]

Radicals Turn to the Working Class

Bringing together representatives of different doctrines, the group took form around a shared commitment to worker organization while political debates among the leadership only partially clarified the ideological orientation. COM co-founder Rosendo Salazar attributes the turn to the working class as a result of a larger shift among radicals, who recognized the class power of labor to assert its independence, confront foreign and domestic capital, and shape the outcomes of the revolution in its own interests. This notion was bolstered by international events; most significantly by the experience of the Paris Commune, the rise of the International Workingmen's Association and the growing magnitude of the industrial working class and general increase in strikes nationally. In Mexico, for instance, there were forty significant strikes between January and September of 1912 alone.[6]

Mexican radicals were now collectively arcing toward working-class organization in both the artisanal and industrial sectors. Because of this shift, previous sectarian differences could be put aside, with distinct leaders and organizations now willing and able to converge in broader organization. This included the rise of working-class struggle, the diffusion and appeal of the PLM's 1911 anarchist-communist manifesto, and a new wave of union organizing taking place within industrial centers across the country.[7]

The turn to the working class occurred internationally, alongside the rise of a new organizational expression reflecting the theory and practice of anarcho-syndicalism. As José González Sierra describes its European expression:

> In late nineteenth-century France, Spain, and Italy, a new current of collective anarchism began to manifest: anarcho-syndicalism, which incubated in the process of re-combining classic elements of anarchist doctrine and adding others; from Marx they take the theory of class struggle, as general explanation and guide of proletarian action; from Blanqui, Bakunin and the French revolutionary tradition, they embrace the role of violence in revolutionary change. However, they diverge from classical anarchism by focusing on the working class as the subject of action, and not on individuals in the abstract, even though they take from Proudhon the fight against the authority and the State, and a refined consciousness that the emancipation of workers will have to be the work of the workers themselves.[8]

Similar developments were also crystallizing within North American radical circles, including with the Industrial Workers of the World in the United States, and with the constituent elements coming together to comprise the COM.

With a majority Anarcho-syndicalist presence, the founding pronouncements of the Casa oriented it on the potential power of the working class as the agent of anticapitalist transformation. Drawing eclectically from Marx and Engels, Peter Kropotkin, and a range of other anarchist thinkers from Europe and the Americas, they declared the COM in the tradition of the First International and the Paris Commune, and advocated for the use of the general strike as the means to bring about the end of capitalism.[9]

The COM also embraced anarchist social doctrine based on the full liberation of the individual, regardless of sex. They favored the elimination of the patriarchal institutions that engendered and enforced sexual and gender divisions and inequalities, including the Catholic Church, the state, and the capitalist mode of production. In organizing the working class, the COM saw this task as including the unionization and full integration of women workers within their ranks.

In their doctrinal formulations they rejected participation in electoral politics in favor of union organizing along revolutionary principles. Merging anarchist and socialist tenets with syndicalism, they set out to organize workers into labor unions while simultaneously constructing a national confederation that could build the capacity for a revolutionary general strike. As part of their effort to consolidate a national movement, they elaborated on the methods of "direct action" to be used in the class struggle:

It is adopted that direct action exclusively consists of the arrangements coming out of the struggle between labor and the bosses, without intermediaries, and achieved by the use of the weapons of revolutionary syndicalism, which are: the boycott, sabotage, the partial strike and the revolutionary general strike where appropriate.[10]

They saw the 1871 Paris Commune as a model for their efforts of combining a general strike with the revolutionary overthrow of the bourgeois political order. COM leader Jacinto Huitrón explained, the goal of the revolutionary strike was to "emancipate labor by taking full possession of the means of production and running them under direct workers' control."[11] Believing that a radical workers' movement was urgently needed, and that it was possible to organize rapidly in the context of a revolutionary crisis, COM adherents were sent to the major urban centers to set up offices, dispense revolutionary literature, and recruit to the cause. Their affiliated newspapers, with names such as *Lucha* (Struggle), *La Tribuna* (Tribune), *Emancipación Social* (Social Emancipation), and *Ariete* (Battering Ram), combined radical proclamations, excerpts from classical and popular literature, notices of strikes and solidarity actions, information on union activities, and stories covering everyday working class issues.[12]

The group congealed nationally amid a series of massive and debilitating strikes following the collapse of the Díaz regime, shutting down whole industries at a time. As Anna Ribera Carbó explains their meteoric rise:

The Casa del Obrero Mundial, founded at the moment of revolutionary effervescence in the country when it was perceived to be possible to transform the existing system . . . raised expectations, intensified struggle, and converted the organized workers movement of the capital into a determining factor of national political outcomes.[13]

In its first year of experience, the group organized unions and helped lead over seventy strikes nationwide.[14] The organization and magnitude of these strikes revealed the changing character of the working class, spreading along industrial lines and shutting down whole sectors simultaneously. For instance, there were over one hundred strikes in textile factories across the country between 1912 and 1913 alone.[15] In observing the radical networks and the new unions conducting this strike wave through the aegis of the COM, historian John Lear concludes:

These new organizations incorporated an unprecedented number of working people... and helped bring together workers who had historically been separated by skill, gender, and cultural traditions. This organizational transformation set the stage for more direct confrontation with employers and, eventually and inevitably, a reckoning with the leaders of the revolution[.][16]

The Madero regime initially allowed for the strikes and even intervened through the Department of Labor to support favorable outcomes, ultimately issuing a Law of Associations in 1913 to officially recognize the right for workers to unionize. For Mexico's capitalists, the growth and self-activity of the COM threatened to raise the specter of revolutionary class struggle in the cities, a prospect that led Madero to reverse his tolerance and initiate plans to suppress the COM shortly before he was toppled in a coup.

After the overthrow of Madero, Huerta temporarily tolerated the COM and even increased the budget of the Department of Labor. This was done in an effort to maintain political and economic stability in the industrial centers while his dictatorship worked to suppress the agrarian revolution roiling the countryside, a lesson not lost on the Constitutionalists once in power. While the COM leaders bided their time, they worked to build up their forces for an ultimate showdown with Huerta. On May 1, 1913, the COM called for a mass demonstration of workers in the capital, a national coming out for the working-class movement and an indirect challenge to Huerta amid the revolution. Among a sea of COM's red-and-black flags (*banderas rojinegras*), signs commemorating the "Martyrs of Chicago," and union and mutualista banners of every stripe, twenty-five thousand workers marched through the capital to the national palace, where maderista legislators joined the crowd taking a decidedly anti-Huerta turn. Like Madero, Huerta repressed the COM when it became clear that it could not be controlled, closed their offices, and conducted a campaign of arrests and deportation of its known foreign-born leaders.

Workers carry the banner of the Casa del Mundo Obrero

Constitutionalists and the Casa

The COM reemerged after the Constitutionalists deposed Huerta in the summer of 1914, and began to rebuild and redouble their efforts to unite the working class into a national labor federation founded along Anarcho-syndicalist lines. Their march forward was complicated by the dissolution of the revolutionary alliance, and the realignment of the armed groups along more clearly defined class lines. Within three months, the revolution transitioned into its next phase; with the radical agrarian villistas and zapatistas closing ranks against the bourgeois landlord Carranza and the urban middle-class forces aligned with his first general Álvaro Obregón. Within this shifting political landscape, the nascent COM attempted to accelerate their efforts to organize the working class on a national scale. Informed by its predominant Anarcho-syndicalist doctrine, the leadership charted a path toward the ultimate goal: transcending the bourgeois boundaries of the existing factions and carrying forward the socialist revolution. Along this course, they made the strategic decision to align with the capitalist faction of Venustiano Carranza, which had grave consequences for the revolutionary workers' movement.

After taking the capital in August of 1914, the Constitutionalists led by Carranza re-established the Maderista government. The fracturing of the revolutionary forces and their reconstitution into oppositional factions occurred at the Convention of Aguascalientes, where a new constitution of government was to be decided between the victors. A falling-out between the representatives quickly descended into the re-positioning for war. In a paramount calculation, the carrancistas extended the hand of friendship to the radical COM, recognizing the precariousness of the moment and the need to win over the urban working classes to prevail against their capable opponents. Through the aegis of Álvaro Obregón, a middle-class Constitutionalist general who became Carranza's minister of war and the navy, and the government's attaché on labor issues, the new regime offered funds to re-establish the COM. They opened up the pages of the Constitutionalist press to allow the COM to reach a wider population and intervened favorably in the first series of labor struggles that soon broke out in the capital among teachers, printers, streetcar workers, and restauarant and bakery workers.[17] The COM had emerged from the smoke of the revolution as a formidable class organization, with its proletarian adherents growing in self-consciouness by the day. By early 1915, it claimed a membership of 52,000 workers through twenty-three different affiliated unions in Mexico City alone, with thousands more in other urban centers around the country.[18]

The collapse of the Huerta regime and the fragmentation of the state created an opening for the COM to grow quickly and begin to settle accounts with the individual capitalists no longer shielded by the dictator. Within the first days after the fall of Huerta, the COM published an open appeal to the Constitutionalist forces that outlined a list of priorities for the working class, including an increase in the minimum wage, the establishment of the eight-hour workday, the abolition of piecework, and the imposition of price controls on basic goods to arrest skyrocketing inflation. In doing so, the COM established itself as an independent political force attempting to articulate the interests of the urban working class. Due to its own fragility, the carrancista factions that took over Mexico City were eager to appease, already calculating the strategic importance of enticing the radical-led union movement into an alliance ahead of the impending showdown with the agraristas.

Shortly after reconstituting a central government, the carrancistas issued a decree that reaffirmed the Madero-era Department of Labor nationally, expanding it in the states, cities, and industrial zones where the carrancista generals held sway. Among its new tasks was the charge to intervene in and conciliate labor disputes between owners and workers, and to serve as arbiter if both parties agreed. Through the Department of Labor, the carrancistas hoped to inaugurate a corporatist labor model that centered the state as the arbiter of labor disputes. This arrangement located in the state the power to regulate class conflict in a way that was purported to be mutually beneficial to both capital and labor.

This was counterposed to the model of the COM, which created independent unions as the primary vehicles of class struggle coupled with schools of revolutionary education. Not only were the unions to be completely independent of the state, but they would work toward the goal of *overthrowing the state* through general strikes and the resumption of the economy under workers' control. In these early stages of worker radicalization and self-activity at a time of political volatility, the weak carrancista government had to accommodate its own class enemy and posture in favor of workers. This was to both ingratiate itself with the workers' existing representative organization in the COM and aligned unions, and to begin a process of weakening labor's allegiance to anticapitalist organization by presenting itself as labor's ally. After consolidating its power, the capitalist foundation of the central government could shift more decisively in favor of developing the national economy by subordinating the working class.

The activist role of the government on behalf of labor occurred quickly. Within the first month of their rule, representatives of the Carranza government intervened in the strikes of streetcar and textile workers, hoping to demonstrate the regime's intention to administer justice on behalf of their interests. To further shore up working-class support in the impending showdown with the agraristas, Carranza's first general and secretary of war and navy, Álvaro Obregón, began to make direct overtures to the radicals in the COM. He organized the "Revolutionary Committee for the Relief of the Poor" which taxed the capitalists and the Catholic Church in order to raise money to feed the poor, he channeled money directly into the COM, gave public pronouncements of political support, including the procurement of the Palacio de los Azulejos as a headquarters; and provided the COM a direct line of communication via a Constitutionalist operative named Gerardo Murrillo (referred to within the labor movement by the moniker "Dr. Atl"). Through direct funding, political favors, and the allure of promotion within the ranks, the carrancistas also aimed to cultivate allies from the COM.

Through Murrillo, Obregón and the carrancistas were able to leverage his influence in the emerging labor movement in Mexico City, carefully cultivating a loyal, moderate, and more pliable faction within the leadership structures of the COM. In January of 1915, for instance, Murrillo helped arbitrate a strike of telephone workers at the Companía Telefónica y Telegráfica Mexicana. In this strike, the incipient Union of Mexican Electricians (SME by its Spanish initials) called for the eight-hour workday, wage increases, overtime pay, and the elimination of company guards. Acting as Obregón's agent, Murrillo was authorized to declare the company nationalized and placed under workers' self-management as a means to implement the workers' demands. After the event, Murrillo asserted his newfound authority to designate Luis N. Morones head of the SME. Morones then went on to become a loyal partisan, and later a hand-picked national union official, who remained closely aligned with the postrevolutionary, pro-capitalist objectives of Obregón and his successors. By inducing labor reforms and leadership realignments using state power, "[Obregón] was able to use these networks to win over the leadership of the anarchist association."[19]

While Carranza temporarily tolerated Obregón's strategy to co-opt the union movement for immediate aims, he was also an intransigent anti-socialist landlord. He fervently opposed the growth of a radical or independent labor movement, especially one that could oppose or complicate his vision of postrevolutionary capitalist development.[20] Both he and Obregón understood the fluidity of the situation differently, reflecting their class positions in relation to a radicalizing urban proletariat. Carranza wanted to deploy the working class to debilitate the bourgeoisie's immediate threats in the agrarian radicals, and to bolster his efforts to contain imperialist intervention.

Obregón, for his part, understood that real and significant concessions to the urban working class would be necessary to divide the radicals from the moderates over the question of the state and the function of unions in order to facilitate the labor control necessary to rebuild the national economy along capitalist lines.[21] Furthermore, the *obregonistas* represented the emerging radical middle class (or Jacobin) impulse when pushed by revolutionary activity and fervor from below that threatened to take independent form. These elements were compelled to eliminate the most recalcitrant elements of the ruling class to ensure the completion of the "bourgeois-democratic revolution," one that repositioned them as the new ruling class. This could only be achieved by leveraging the power of the laboring classes through concessions and strategic alliance, while containing it through co-optation to prevent it from articulating an independent anticapitalist vision for social reorganization.

Obregón's left-wing shift was accelerated after the Conventionalists drove the Constitutionalists from Mexico City in 1914 and threatened to rout them completely in Veracruz. Carranza created a Central Office of Revolutionary Propaganda under the Ministry of Government, issuing directives to its statewide representatives for how to use the rhetoric of reform to cultivate worker support. According to one:

> If the region is agricultural the theme of the discussion will be the resolution of the agrarian problem: improvements for the day worker or rural peon, division of the land, irrigation, etc. If the region is industrial, the themes relative to worker problems will be developed: implementation of the eight-hour day, formation of unions, protection of women and children who work in the workshops and the factories, laws for work-related accidents, sanitary conditions, and increases in wages, etc.[22]

Concurrent with the pro-worker reform campaign of the carrancistas, the COM intensified its radical worker education and union organizing campaign to prepare for what they believed to be the coming worker revolution. Crystallizing within the contours of a factionalizing revolution, the COM was not sufficiently developed, neither organizationally nor politically, to assert an independent class perspective that could unite the laboring classes into a revolutionary front.[23]

The COM leadership therefore made the tactical decision to align itself temporarily with the big bourgeois-led faction of the revolutionary forces. They believed its Jacobin, leftward moving lieutenants would come to dominate and create the democratic openings for the COM to grow and develop into the national class formation that could carry through a socialist revolution. While this internal class tension existed in the infancy of the relationship between the COM and the Constitutionalists, it was temporarily mitigated by the strategic alliance of convenience they formed against the agrarian revolutionaries. Led by the ex-Constitutionalist general Pancho Villa and Emiliano Zapata, these forces broke decisively with Carranza over the question of revolutionary land redistribution, after the northern-based capitalist landlord refused to endorse the Plan de Ayala.

The COM-Constitutionalist Pact and the End of the Revolution

When the agrarian forces of the convention (Conventionalists) broke from the carrancistas, and briefly captured and occupied Mexico City after the Constitutionalists fled ahead of their advance, the agrarian revolutionaries and the COM had their first significant encounter. While the agraristas did not ignore the urban working classes, they did not figure prominently in their initial revolutionary plans. During the discussion of labor at the Convention of Aguascalientes, for example, representatives of the zapatistas proposed a program that mirrored the operational ideas of the COM. They called for the right to unionize, strike, boycott, and even engage in sabotage. Representatives of the villistas supported mutualistas, but called for restrictions on revolutionary unionism and "violent tactics" that were associated with the COM.[24] More concretely, they did not prioritize the labor question when in a position to do so.

From December of 1914 until July of 1915, the Conventionalist armies controlled Mexico City and much of the country. During their occupation of Mexico City, the zapatista and villista forces did not dismantle or significantly restructure the Huerta-era government bureaucracy. Instead they focused on the implementation of their Plan de Ayala to restore their lands, installing a zapatista-aligned intellectual named Manuel Palafox as the minister of agriculture to begin land surveys.[25] While they implemented various stratagems to control prices of basic commodities, they did not address relations of production or see in COM a potential partner in socio-economic reorganization. Food shortages worsened and unemployment increased during the period of Conventionist rule, with the occupying forces incapable or disinterested in addressing fundamental questions of class relations of production and distribution in the city at a time of acute social crisis.

The forces that staffed the leadership of their armies reflected the provincial outlook of the radical campesinos in their ranks, and placed priority on rural questions. The few radical intellectuals from the COM that sided with the zapatista leadership, such as former magonista Antonio Díaz Soto y Gama, tried to form relations with the workers' movement, but it proved too insignificant or too late. During a

COM-led commemoration of the 1907 Río Blanco massacre in early 1915, Díaz Soto y Gama spoke in front of twenty thousand gathered workers to proclaim solidarity from the "campesinos from the South," but the symbolic act generated only fleeting appreciation. Díaz Soto y Gama was able to ensure a labor code was passed, but not until a few weeks before the Conventionalists were defeated and driven from the capital in July.

In doing so, they were perceived by the COM to be narrowly defining their revolutionary objectives to ones that offered no guarantees for labor, and by default leaving intact the class relations and structures of the Díaz era. From the point of view of the doctrinaire anarchists, the deeply held religious views of the campesinos also presented a serious problem. The campesino support for the Catholic Church, it was reasoned, reflected their cultural underdevelopment and made them beholden to a backward-looking world view that was hostile to the radical, progressive notions of the COM. While mobilized against a common enemy in the huertistas, they concluded that the trajectory of the peasant rebellion could be manipulated and redirected toward a reactionary direction by the clergy.

While the carrancistas were forced to retreat and establish their base in Veracruz and Tamaulipas, they continued to foster favorable relations with the COM. As opposed to the hands-off approach of the Conventionalists, Obregón took more radical measures to posture as the defender of labor. He issued a decree placing a tax on the various business transactions, luxury consumption, and other economic activities directed toward the wealthy. The funds raised were redistributed to meet the basic needs of the working classes behind Constitutionalist lines. During this time, debates emerged within the COM over the question of alignment in the conflict. The pro-Constitutionalist majority pointed to the ineffectiveness of the campesinos once they took over Mexico City. They were unable to form an independent government and did not attempt to meet the basic needs of workers facing high unemployment, food shortages, and deteriorating living conditions. A minority of the COM membership dissented or remained neutral.

For instance, PLM and COM co-founder and leading anarchist theorist Antonio Díaz Soto y Gama became an advisor and confidant of Zapata and the group's chief publicist until Zapata was assassinated in 1919.[26] Another leading socialist organizer and schoolteacher, Dolores Jiménez y Muro, had joined the zapatistas after publishing her own plan (the Social and Political Plan of 1911) for insurrection against the Díaz regime. After the plan was taken up by revolutionaries in several central states, their efforts were merged with the zapatistas, and Jiménez y Muro remained part of the Morelos movement until 1919.[27] Influenced by the anarchists in their ranks, the zapatistas incorporated the agrarian aspects of PLM ideology into their work, adopting as their own Flores Magón's call for the revolutionary expropriation of the land with the slogan "¡Tierra y Libertad!" ("Land and Liberty!"). Some affiliated unions, such as the railroad and oil workers' unions, opposed the idea of affiliation with either side in line with the principles of anarcho-syndicalism. Despite a dissenting position, the majority faction chose to align with the carrancistas. They decided to suspend their operations in Mexico City and commit themselves to the full victory of the Constitutionalist-led revolution by enjoining workers to enlist in COM-organized, proletarian "Red Battalions" that were integrated into the larger military structure of the carrancistas.

An estimated seven thousand workers based in Mexico City made the journey to Veracruz, where they were arranged into six of these battalions and integrated into the Constitutionalist forces in preparation for the imminent showdown. Under Carranza's direct orders, the six battalions were separated and dispersed to different regions to prevent the possibility for autonomous action along class lines. They were situated in expropriated convents and churches, and paid well for their service. The Red Battalions made significant contributions in the string of battlefield victories outside of Mexico City that culminated in the defeat of Pancho Villa's División del Norte in April of 1915.

In exchange for their support, the COM was granted the right to establish centers and committees to "agitate among the workers to join the Constitutionalist cause" in the territories occupied or taken by aligned forces.[28] To this effect, they sent twenty-two propaganda commissions comprised of 139 COM organizers and propagandists throughout the county to set up operations.[29] This proved to be a point of contention in practice, as the COM and the carrancistas (through the offices of the Department of Labor) jockeyed for leadership among the working class in the different regions.

In the large industrial textile factories of Orizaba, Veracruz, for example, COM organizers and carrancista agents of the Department of Labor engaged in a pitched battle of influence over the workers. On March 11, 1915, the COM gave a show of strength when it called for a march from Orizaba to the textile mills of nearby Río Blanco, to commemorate the bloody suppression of a textile strike by the Díaz regime in 1907 (discussion in chapter 8). In solidarity, over twenty thousand marched in Mexico City, with smaller actions taking place throughout the regions. A little over a week later, on March 22, Carranza gave his own display of power in response. In an effort to peel away growing support from the Anarcho-syndicalists, Carranza arranged a deal with the owners to grant a 35 percent wage increase, housing rights, child labor restrictions, and a raft of other reforms.[30]

The defeat of the Conventionalists reconfigured the Constitutionalist-COM alliance into a power struggle. The successful use of the organized working class by the bourgeois carrancistas to ensure the defeat of the armed campesinos was decisive. It signaled the beginning of the end of the military phase of the revolution, as the zapatistas who remained centered in their home territory of Morelos and were eventually encircled and defeated. Furthermore, it removed the possibility of the conflict developing into social revolution based on the potential for convergence between the rural and urban laboring classes against the reconsolidation of the bourgeoisie. Nevertheless, the COM leadership seized the opportunity to extend its influence and try to build the COM into a national force capable of matching and exceeding the power of the victorious carrancistas.

Between February of 1915 and January 1916, the COM grew considerably. The carrancistas had categorically legalized unions and decreed various reforms that

energized the working class and spurred on the COM. While individual capitalist enterprises resisted the efforts, the COM increased its militant activities and the
state remained on the sidelines. This included the launch of a new press reflecting its
militant advance, *Ariete* ("Battering Ram"). During this time the COM founded numerous unions and extended thirty-six branches in or throughout Veracruz, San Luis
Potosí, Mérida, Zacatecas, Yucatán, Jalisco, Michoacán, Guanajuato, Colima, Tabasco,
Monterrey, Tlaxcala, Mexico state, and Coahuila. By 1916, the national membership
of the COM reached its height at between 100,000 and 150,000.[31] Concomitant with
its growth across the country, the COM increased its rhetoric against capital, foreign
and domestic, the state, and the Catholic Church. In one issue of *Ariete*, the editors
proclaimed that the state was "the apparatus that oppresses, extorts, and crushes the
individual and suffocates all initiative and independence. Whichever type of government: imperialist, monarchy, republican [. . .] it will always be oppressive and will
always protect the vested interests of the privileged classes."[32]

In the last six months of 1915, after the reinstallation of carrancista forces in the
city, a series of strikes paralyzed Mexico City and other urban centers. Oil workers,
railroad workers, electrical workers, restaurant workers, bakers, typesetters, carpenters, tailors, textile workers, and other sectors went on strike in this period showing
the relative growth and strength of the COM still in its infancy. The strikes also began
to take on a political character, as the COM began to call for worker control of production, price controls, and pay scales. In response to increased militancy, Carranza began
to take targeted action. When railroad workers struck the railroads of Veracruz, he had
their leaders impressed into the military. A proto-intelligence service, the Confiden-
tial Agency, was tasked with collecting intelligence on the COM. By late December,
the Carranza government was orchestrating plans for the destruction of the COM,
sending directives to regional military and political officials, giving them the green
light to suppress COM branches. This plan received a further boost when the US government, also in the act of suppressing a radical labor movement in the IWW, officially
recognized the Carranza government and offered its political support by arranging for
the American Federation of Labor to send a mission to help replicate their model of
business unionism in Mexico.[33]

Simultaneous with the growth of the COM and the carrancista campaign of
repression in these pivotal months was the rapid deterioration of economic conditions. Through 1914 and 1915, food production declined dramatically amid the full-
scale war mobilization and associated dislocation. The new currency issued by the
Carranza government progressively de-valued, such that by the time the carrancistas
returned to Mexico City, inflation had increased the price of corn by 1500 percent,
beans by 700 percent, and rice by 800 percent in the capital. This disproportionately
affected the urban laboring classes. As a result, 9 percent of all deaths registered in
1915 were attributed to starvation.[34] This induced further crises. There was a significant out-migration of the urban poor, returning to ancestral pueblos in the countryside. Food protests, sometimes graduating into full-scale riots involving thousands,
were a common feature of the city's landscape. Veterans from the Red Battalions,

the putative heroes of the revolution, disbanded and disarmed and returned to the workforce with two months' severance pay. Within a short period, they became restive, beset by unemployment and hunger. Scarlet fever, typhus, and smallpox epidemics ravaged the poorer districts.

In response to the spiraling crisis, the COM began to make a series of demands on the government to take radical measures to alleviate the crisis, including that the government scrap the new currency and pay salaries in gold and at a 50 percent increased base pay to lift the working class from mass privation.[35] The carrancistas then withdrew all subsidies that were allocated for the COM and collaborated with the capitalist press to censor their activities. Over the first two months of 1916, regional governors and generals began to restrict the activities of the COM branches or close them altogether. In this environment, moderate leaders and allies affiliated with the COM, such as Luis Morones, began to publicly renounce the radical labor federation and pledge support to the new government.

On May 19, 1916, a railroad strike disrupted the rail lines in Mexico City. Machinists, firemen, metalworkers, and mechanics on the Constitutionalist-controlled railroad lines walked off the job in protest of deteriorating living conditions. Within forty-eight hours the strike was declared illegal and crushed after the leaders were arrested by Constitutionalist forces. It became clear that Carrancismo would not tolerate the emergence of an independent and radical labor movement. In an act of defiance, a week later city lighting, streetcar, and telephone services were brought to a halt by COM-affiliated unions. The strike was called off after Carranza threatened severe punishment of those "disrupting public services."

In order to bring the full force of the COM to bear against the Carranza government in the face of the existential threat he posed, plans for a general strike were hastily made. It was to be spearheaded by the SME and carried out on July 31, 1916. The planning occurred in secret, as the unionists were now aware of spying and infiltration. They formed three strike committees from the rank-and-file union leadership, to ensure that the strike continued if the established leaders or one or more committee was arrested. The committees comprised men and women, reflecting the character of the working class in the capital. On the day of the strike, around eighty-two thousand workers walked out, shutting down all water, electricity, streetcars, and telephones across Mexico City, with only limited effect in other parts of the country where the COM branches had been neutralized.

Incensed at the audacity of the COM, and confident he now had the upper hand, Carranza decreed the death penalty for anyone inciting, convoking, preparing for, or participating in the suspension of work "in factories or businesses intended to serve the public."[36] He then told the military to arrest all known COM leaders and to raid and shutter locals of the COM throughout the city. They also closed local union offices and halls affiliated to the COM-linked Union Federation of Mexican Workers, shut down the COM-affiliated press, declared martial law, broke up street meetings and prohibited gatherings, and organized military patrols throughout the city. The ferocity and swiftness of the repression effectively broke the strike, which failed to unite significant mass support spread beyond the capital. The COM was promptly declared illegal and disbanded by force throughout the country.

While the COM met its demise, closing with it the small window of possibility for socialist revolution, a radical labor movement continued in new forms. As was the course of the Mexican Revolution, even after the radicals were defeated, much of the content of their program was eventually implemented by the victors, as the rural and working classes remained a potent and volatile force into the next decade. The COM produced the cadre of working-class leaders that continued to shape Mexican politics over the next decade and beyond. Its ranks included a regroupment of many veterans of the PLM, the founders of the Communist Party and later anarchist groupings, the founders and leaders of later unions and union federations, and even state and federal politicians.[37] The defeat of the COM dealt a crushing blow to the nascent workers' movement, and signaled a gradual decline of the predominance of Anarchist doctrine in the Mexican working class. In the aftermath of the successful Russian Revolution of 1917, Marxist thought and practice eclipsed anarchism as the doctrine believed most capable of guiding the working class to socialist revolution.

Marxism in Mexico

Marxism was slow to enter into Mexico, but developed rapidly after 1917. By the time of the revolution, anarcho-syndicalism had become the dominant expression of radical doctrine within the Mexican labor movement, but had been unsuccessful at carrying the revolution beyond its bourgeois limits. The victory of the Bolsheviks in leading the first successful socialist revolution in history shifted the political center of gravity within the workers' movement, with many orienting toward Marxism after 1919.

Marxism, in its revolutionary form as expressed in Russia, offered the first example of a workers' victory over capitalism and imperialism at a time when Mexican workers were immersed in their own revolution. The Bolsheviks employed a different organizational model, one inspired by Vladimir Lenin's conception of a party composed of the revolutionary vanguard of the working class. Unlike the anarchist models, the Bolsheviks participated in both economic and political struggle, with the intention of uniting a critical mass of the most revolutionary elements of the working class into an organization capable of replacing bourgeois state power with workers' councils, abolishing capitalism, and administering the socialization of the means of production.[38]

On another level, Marxism also provided a system of analysis that helped the radical Left within the workers' movement overcome some of its historic weaknesses. This included an argument for working-class independence and self-emancipation, and a specific analysis of American imperialism's role in underdeveloping Mexico as a by-product of the global capitalist system. Marxists also aimed to bridge the ideological divide between industrial workers in the cities and agrarian workers in the countryside through propagation and agitation that unified urban and rural struggle against a common enemy in capitalism. As a result of these ideological advances, some leading anarchists of the revolutionary period later coalesced into the first Communist organizations.

Marxist antecedents in Mexico began with the first ephemeral Mexican Communist

Party, founded in 1878 but dissolved shortly thereafter. In 1884, the main labor federation of the period, El Gran Círculo de Obreros de México, published the Communist Manifesto in the pages of their newspaper, *El Socialista*. Nevertheless, according to Enrique Condés Lara, early Marxist ideas were "combined, even contradictorily, with mutualismo, *cooperativismo*, as well as anarchism and liberalism."[39] This was also the case later in 1911, when the small but influential Partido Obrero Socialista (Socialist Workers Party; also known as the POS) was founded along the principles of the Marxist mantra "the emancipation of the working class will have to come through self-emancipation." The small party developed an eclectic mix of reformist and radical politics, and combined Marxists and anarchists, with an orientation vacillating between electoral strategies and organizing class-struggle-oriented unions.[40]

The party was founded by German socialist immigrants Pablo Zierold and Juan Humboldt, who were inspired by the Spanish Socialist Party, or the Menshevik model of reform socialism, which favored union organization, participation in bourgeois elections, and a rigid commitment to the idea that capitalist modernization must precede the potential for socialism. In practice, they worked tirelessly distributing Marxist literature to workers across the country and agitating for unionization. After its first year, the group had built a small following in the industrial centers, which attracted an array of radical reformists, syndicalists, and committed Marxists. They also ran candidates in municipal elections, with limited success.

Historian Mario Gill credits the POS with organizing a generation of young workers that went on to become radical labor leaders in their respective regions.[41] This included a cadre of radicals including Jacinto Huitrón, Pioquinto Roldán, Luis Méndez, and Adolfo Santibañez, who were later instrumental in the formation of the COM, while the latter was also a founder of the Mexican Communist Party. This group gravitated leftward toward direct action–oriented anarcho-syndicalism, inducing a split in 1912 that led a minority to joining the syndicalist group Luz (and later the COM). Despite the split, the group continued on a trajectory of militant union agitation and rebuilt a nascent labor movement in the period after the defeat of the COM, which got a boost after the victorious workers' revolution in Russia.

In an environment energized by news of the workers' revolution in Russia, the POS embarked to organize a socialist labor union federation and enjoyed some success with the creation of the Gran Cuerpo Central de los Trabajadores. By 1919, this formation had grown into the largest labor federation in the Mexican Valley with twenty affiliated unions and nuclei forming in the provinces. The success of this federation was a result of yet another strike wave that developed in 1918–1919, involving railroad workers, flour factory workers, bakers, teachers, and oil workers. Militants within the Gran Cuerpo Central worked feverishly, building militant solidarity campaigns and directing their demands "against the bosses and Carranza government."[42] Concurrent with this new development, the remnants of the defeated Casa were also reorganizing.

The defeat of the Casa del Obrero Mundial in 1916 had led to a split in the ranks. The majority sentiment believed that the workers' movement should form a new federation, and held that their interests could be advanced through alignment with the stabilizing "revolutionary government," which, in its infantile weakness, continued its efforts to establish patronage links to worker organizations. The other, representing the accumulated lessons of past defeats and recommitting to the principles of class struggle, argued for the need for the complete independence of the working class and abstention from elections. The moderates of the first grouping went on to form La Confederación Regional Obrera Mexicano (CROM), while those of the second re-grouped into new anarchist formations outside of the confederation.[43]

The militant strikes of 1919 were brutally put down by the military, which jailed hundreds of militants and internally deported strike leaders and sympathetic mem-bers of the press; effectively breaking the Gran Cuerpo Central de los Trabajadores. In the aftermath of the defeat, the government felt compelled to promote a new labor federation that could be controlled while creating the illusion of it being pro-worker. Carranza and his advisors decided to embrace the fledgling CROM as the *oficialista* la-bor federation—sanctioned by the revolutionary government and incorporated into the patronage system in exchange for labor peace.

By 1917, many post-COM Anarcho-syndicalists regrouped. One group reformed around the journal *Luz*. The first editions of that same year contained a study and defense of the Russian Revolution, especially as the Mexican bourgeois press be-gan a campaign of slander against Bolshevism and its purported threat to Mexico.[44] Another group, Hermanos Rojos, developed another periodical that was named *El Bolcheviqui*, proclaiming itself the first *sovietista* newspaper in Mexico.[45] According to Barry Carr, some Mexican syndicalists were drawn to Marxian communism through the inspiration of what was happening in Russia in the first years of the revolution. The emergence of worker control over production in the form of Soviets, or workers' councils, became "the very epitome of direct action by the working class engaged in the destruction of the authoritarian state."[46] In fact, the convergence between anar-chists and early conceptions of Bolshevism go back even further.

According to Donald Hodges, the experience of Ricardo Flores Magón and the radical wing of the PLM mirrored that of the Russian Communist experience. Like Lenin and the Bolsheviks, the anarchists in the PLM split from the moderates on the basis of promoting revolutionary anticapitalism against reformism and compromise with the bourgeoisie. He states:

> Ricardo Flores Magón, the progenitor of Mexico's indigenous anarchism, be-lieved that capital is a form of theft and considered government and religion to be the allies of capital. Like Marx, he advocated a political organization of the proletariat and a policy of coalitions with both liberals and socialists. In this way, anarchists might unite with liberals to overthrow a tyrannical government and then with socialists to abolish capitalism. So it is understandable that, after Flores Magón's party was suppressed, some of his followers turned to the Com-munist Party.[47]

He then asserts that the latter PLM was essentially communistic, and even makes a comparison between Flores Magón's evolved positions on the revolutionary process as reaching conclusions similar to those of Russian Revolutionary Leon Trotsky in his work *Theory of Permanent Revolution*.[48] The PLM were also staunch defenders of the Russian Revolution, proclaiming that Lenin and the Bolsheviks were "at the front of the Great World Revolution."[49] Even after his break with Bolshevism, he continued to urge his anarchist comrades in Mexico to cooperate with "revolutionary Marxists."[50] Furthermore, former adherents of the PLM were instrumental in the growth and expansion of the socialist and Communist movements in Mexico after the revolution. The socialist movements in Yucatán and Michoacán are examples of this historical development.

Socialist Movements in the Regions of Mexico

In 1915, former Tucson-based PLM gunrunner Salvador Alvarado was appointed Military governor of Yucatán. Backed by 7,000 constitutionalist troops, he was sent into the region to carry out the revolutionary process in a state largely untouched by the revolution's first phases. The state economy reflected the worst elements of rural life in pre-revolutionary Mexico. It was dominated by 50,000 landowning elites, whose haciendas relied on the enslaved labor of 120,000 Maya, 8,000 Yaqui, and 3,000 Koreans.[51] For Alvarado and Carranza, the radical reconstruction of Yucatán's economy was necessary for the consolidation of the new state, as it was a major producer of henequen and other natural resources sold on the world market.

Furthermore, the small but concentrated working class had been unionizing at a rapid pace, under the influence of Anarcho-syndicalist doctrine. In 1913, for instance, a coalition of unions affiliated to the Casa del Obrero Mundial, veterans of the PLM, mutualistas, and renters'-rights groups initiated the first-known general strike for higher wages and better working conditions in the port city of Progreso on the Gulf Coast.[52] Another ten-day strike hit the capital city of Mérida in 1915. Restaurant, bakery, and cantina workers affiliated with the Union of Waiters, Cooks, and Servers shut down most food production in the city for ten days in 1915 demanding a 100 percent wage increase. The early stages of a militant labor movement, led by the railroad workers, were also a factor that compelled action on behalf of the governor to contain further worker radicalization.

Alvarado issued several hundred decrees that amounted to the partial liquidation of the landowning oligarchy. All debts held by indigenous indentures were cancelled, sweeping labor laws were introduced for men, women, and children; thousands of schools and libraries were built across the state, and land reform was introduced to redistribute land to the dispossessed. During his tenure, the governor closed the Catholic churches in response to their counterrevolutionary role and nationalized the railways. In this context, the radical movements grew quickly, with a socialist and labor press flourishing throughout the state.[53] As a loyal lieutenant of Carranza, Alvarado's measures were calculated to cultivate labor support for the Mexican state as it grappled with radical agrarian movements at home and the threat of US imperialism abroad. Despite its nationalist aims, the Alvarado period led to the convergence of a new Left in 1918 in the Socialist Party of the Southeast.[54] The shift to the left was further realized with the toppling of Carranza in 1920, ushering in a period of more radical change in Yucatán.

The Socialist Party of the Southeast was founded in 1917 by a coalition of radical Jacobin Constitutionalists and Socialists, led by the soon-to-be governor Felipe Carrillo Puerto. The party turned its sights to revolutionary restructuring of the Yucatecan countryside and the organization of the vast rural proletariat comprised of Maya-speaking peoples. The group recruited and trained a bilingual cadre of organizers (Spanish and Maya languages) and fanned out into the rural regions to organize the population. In a short time, they built a substantial social base among Maya campesinos that were organized into 425 Ligas de Resistencia (Leagues of Resistance). The party grew to 26,000 members by 1918, and won the governorship first under Socialist Manuel Berzunza (1921–1922) and then under former PLM supporter and self-proclaimed Marxist revolutionary Felipe Carrillo Puerto.

During this period, the Socialists had a brief window of power to carry out a radical transformation of the region. Using the base organization model of the *ligas* as shock troops, they dismantled the last of the notorious slaveholding haciendas, appropriated and redistributed nearly 600,000 hectares of land to over 104 pueblos, and attempted to unionize the entire agricultural workforce.[55] They built a universal socialist education system, infused with the pedagogy of class struggle and modeled on the Ferrerian Rational School and the newly established "revolutionary schools" of the Soviet Union. Socialist-feminist leaders in the party Elvia Carrillo and Rosa Torres led efforts that established forty-five *ligas feministas* (feminist leagues), which organized 55,000 working-class women throughout the state.[56] Through their campaigning, birth control was legalized, divorce on demand was made available for women as well as men, and sex education classes were offered for urban and rural women alike.

They established formal relations with revolutionary Russia, and while not formally joining the Communist International, they publicly praised its efforts. They openly opposed the Catholic Church as a reactionary instrument of the old regime. They encouraged their supporters to paint village churches red (as a symbol of the "new religion" of socialism) and to replace traditional religious hymns with the "Internationale." They encouraged the institutionalization of the Maya languages, funded the restoration of Maya archaeological sites, promoted the flourishing of indigenous art forms, and coordinated weekly mass events (called "Red Mondays") promoting cultural themes that attracted thousands at a time.[57]

Before they were overthrown in 1924 by the short-lived coup regime of Adolfo de la Huerta in league with the regional planter and merchant class, the Socialists began implementation of an ambitious plan to expropriate the large henequen plantations that dominated the export economy and to reorganize them under worker control. The coup cut this short, as the central layer of leadership of the party was executed, their party repressed, and much of their work undone.[58]

Another significant Socialist Party was founded in the state of Michoacán in 1917. El Partido Socialista Michoacana (PSM) brought together labor leaders, intellectuals, and students from around the state who were inspired by the events of the Russian

Revolution. As one participant later explained: "The example of the October Revolution in Russia, led by Lenin, stimulated those elements of the Left in Michoacán to organize themselves into the first class-based party."[59] Like other postrevolutionary Socialist groupings, the party had combined former Anarcho-syndicalists on its left and Jacobin nationalists on its Right.

Those on the left of the party included veterans of the COM and participants of the Battallion Melchor Ocampo, who served as volunteer resistance fighters who went to Veracruz to oppose the US invasion of that port city in 1914. After returning, they formed chapters of the COM in the state capital of Morelia.[60] They later participated in the Red Battalions and brought important lessons into the PSM about the counterrevolutionary nature of the bourgeois state after their experience in 1915–1916 with the Carranza government. The latter included initial support from a one-time magonista turned representative of the Constitutionalist forces named Francisco Múgica Velázquez. An early participant included Pedro Corria, who had a long history of working with the Partido Liberal Mexicano and the Industrial Workers of the World on both sides of the border. Another significant participant was the indigenous leader Primo Tapia. Tapia returned to his home state of Michoacán in 1919, after fleeing persecution in the United States for his participation with the PLM and the Wobblies. Tapia and the other revolutionaries were instrumental in leading PSM-affiliation to the Communist International in 1919.

The Communist International and the Communist Party of Mexico

Mexico's economic and social development had come up deficient, distorted, and periodically halted as a result of foreign conquest and exploitation. Revolutionary Marxists, especially the Russian Bolshevik leader Vladimir Lenin, developed a systemic analysis of imperialism explaining the inner workings of capitalism as it expanded on an international scale. Marxist thought had a significant impact on Mexican thinkers by describing the way in which imperialist intervention plays out within the marginalized nations, for instance dividing the ruling class between sections in league with foreign capital, acting as their domestic instruments, and a marginalized "nationalist bourgeoisie" seeking national development as the road to its own supremacy.[61]

Furthermore, Marxists elaborated an analysis of the internal effects of imperialism within nations in the imperial sphere. They exposed the limits of bourgeois nationalism and located the power to overthrow imperialism in the revolutionary potential of the working class. For example, Soviet thinkers posited that in countries subjugated by imperialism, bourgeois nationalist leadership

> such as the Mexican revolutionaries or the Chinese [...] could not change a
> country's economic and political structure because during the period of capitalist imperialism semi-colonial countries "constituted a link on the chain of world
> finance capital."[62]

These principles were embedded in the founding of the Third International, or Communist International. The Comintern, as it was known, was established by the Bolshevik government in 1919 to serve as an international gathering of revolutionaries to discuss and debate the project of spreading the Communist Revolution internationally. Representing an international reorganization of the international socialist movement, the first Congress brought together 218 delegates from 37 countries.[63] The Bolshevik Revolution had formalized the break with the reformism of the Second Socialist International, as well as its capitulation to nationalism and imperialism during World War I. As one historian observes, the Comintern "was engaged in a virtually unprecedented enterprise; for it was the […] claim of its leaders that the workers' organization which had preceded it, the Second International, had either ignored the colonial world or else had ranged itself openly on the side of the imperialist overlord."[64] By 1920, the subject of discussion shifted to spreading revolution into colonized countries as well as those under the domination of imperialist powers. This was apparent by the Second Congress of the Comintern's convocation of a special Congress of the Peoples of the East, held in Baku, Azerbaijan, in the fall of 1920. The conference was the "first attempt to appeal to the exploited and oppressed peoples in the colonial and semi-colonial countries to carry forward the revolutionary struggles under the banner of Marxism and with the support of workers in Russia and the advanced [capitalist] countries of the world."[65]

In 1921 the Comintern sent emissaries to Mexico to establish the American Agency, which consisted of Soviet advisors whose task was to help organize various Comintern-aligned groupings in Mexico into a singular Communist Party. They also sent representatives of the Pan-American Bureau of the Red International of Labor Unions with the goal of gaining the adherence of workers from Canada to Argentina to the Soviet-led labor international.[66]

The coalescence of Communist-oriented forces into what became the Communist Party of Mexico began in 1919. Convened as the first National Socialist Conference, it brought together delegates representing an array of political tendencies gravitating leftward: socialists, anarchists, militant unionists, and individual intellectuals. After several stages of splits and regroupment the Communist Party of Mexico went on to become the main radical organization of the Mexican working class.

Continuity of US Empire in Mexico

The defeat of the COM signified the end of urban, working-class radicalism as an independent current within the revolutionary process, the only potential force capable of overturning capitalism. The victory of a reconfigured bourgeoisie intent on rebuilding a nationalist capitalism ran into the harsh reality of a US-centered postwar reorganization of the global imperialist system. The US, an intact industrial powerhouse with global financial ambition, was eager to establish a new international economic order in its own image, and under its direct supervision, beginning in Mexico.[67]

Only after the most radical elements were suppressed could the US defenders of empire seek out a new and acceptable partner within the disparate middle-class revolutionaries that formed the new ruling group in Mexico. In these efforts, the Wilson administration found a willing partner in the leadership of the American Federation of Labor, who tied the fortunes of craft labor to the Democratic Party and their vision for empire-building in Latin America. After a tumultuous postrevolutionary decade, the US ruling class and its allies reasserted their primacy within the Mexican economy.

The Mexican Revolution accelerated the decline of European influence in Mexico, now supplanted by American imperialism.[68] According to historian Emilio Zebadúa:

> The outcome of the Great War left the US in a relatively strengthened geopolitical position. From 1914 to 1918 its gross national product increased 20 percent and the volume of manufacturing 26 percent. US bankers helped make New York a world center of capitalist accumulation and the United States a principle creditor nation with more than $3.3 billion worth of external loans in its possession; the European nations, on the other hand, left the war dependent on US credit for their reconstruction.[69]

In his analysis of global imperialism, Vladimir Lenin described this phenomenon as the imperialist redivision of the world market, stating that once the advanced capitalist nations have divided up the world among themselves, only repartition is possible through conflict: "For the first time the world is completely divided up, so that in the future *only* redivision is possible, i.e., territories can only pass from one 'owner' to another, instead of passing as ownerless territory to an 'owner.'"[70]

The bourgeois and middle-class elements that dominated the leadership of the *carrancista* forces, especially the radicalized Jacobin generals, cohered as a genuine leadership, squeezed between the divided sectors of the old bourgeoisie and the popular forces. In the final stages of the revolution, these forces, led by Álvaro Obregón, first toppled Carranza and the most conservative and unmovable elements of the anti-Díaz bourgeoisie. Then, they turned against the radical agraristas and the urban industrial workers, each in turn. While the Constitution of 1917 contained language that held out the promise of a radical restructuring of Mexican capitalism, it also represented the salvaging of Mexican capitalism for future restoration and expansion. Despite its bourgeois nationalist character, the Mexican revolution fell short of presenting a challenge to international capital. A continuity of imperialist intervention, now primarily from the US, took on new forms in Mexico's "reconstruction."[71]

After revolutionary forces toppled the coup government of Victoriano Huerta in 1914, the revolutionary governments that took control of Mexico City ceased paying the external debt. The revolutionary government in the hands of the zapatistas and villistas found itself isolated by international banks, completely cut off from access to credit. International capital was displeased with the radical turn in the course of the revolution, as Mexico was now perceived "in political circles and in the big financial centers as a discredited nationalist regime that imposes restrictions on private property."[72]

In the period after the revolution the bankers became determined to limit the scope of the revolution, to curtail radical and national sentiment, and to ensure capitalism was preserved. Post-revolutionary governments, after having availed themselves of the radical agrarian challenge on the one hand, and insurgent workers on the other, complied and affirmed their commitment to integrate Mexico into the world capitalist system.

To this end, foreign and domestic bankers convened a national conference in Mexico City in 1924, with the support of the US government and their European allies, to develop a consensus on the process of reintegration. In its larger scope, the conference was designed to accomplish two major objectives. The most immediate and practical was to reconcile the salvageable elements of the Porfirian bourgeoisie with the upstart middle-class elements now in control of the state.[73] The second objective was to extend credit to Mexico as a means to achieve solvency and reintegration into the international capitalist system, and to establish "financial discipline."[74] If Mexico were to reestablish as a capitalist economy, it would have to abide by the rules of financial capital or risk isolation. Beginning with Madero, and continuing with Carranza and the postrevolutionary presidents, Mexico's new ruling class demonstrated their reliability to the capitalist system by crushing the radical movements and then submitting to the diktats of the multinational banks. According to Thomas O'Brien,

> After 1917 the Americans clearly understood that the new [Mexican] elite required their assistance to stabilize conditions in Mexico and consolidate its power. The stabilization was an essential countermeasure to the continuing popular protest against the transformation of Mexican society by American corporate culture.[75]

The consolidation of a new ruling class acceptable to the world powers was an essential precondition. For full integration—to obtain emergency loans; establish lines of credit; and to reduce the risk of invasion, blockade, etc.—the new ruling group committed to paying back half a billion dollars (in 1925 dollars) in outstanding external debt to foreign creditors. They also agreed to allow US capital to continue to dominate Mexican oil and other key sectors of the economy into the next generation.[76] In this reconfiguration of Mexico's bourgeoisie, once again in the fold of the US imperial project, Mexico's laboring classes would continue to pay the price. The promise of revolution contained the possibility of breaking the debilitating shackles of imperialism. Failing to attain this, it ensured that underdevelopment and inequality would continue to plague Mexico into the next generation, leading to waves of out-migration to the United States.

Chapter 17
California Agriculture and Migrant Mexican Labor

*"Personally I believe that the Mexican laborers are the solution to our
common labor problems in this country. Many of the people live here, this
was once part of their country, and they can and they will do the work."*
—**Excerpt of letter from a cotton company executive
to President Woodrow Wilson, 1917**

By the 1920s Mexican migrants became the majority of field workers in California agriculture. They gradually replaced other migratory groups after federal and state governments engineered a series of racial exclusions on behalf of a rising grower class, which were designed to sustain white land-ownership primacy, ensure sufficient flow of controlled labor, prevent unionization, and guarantee high margins of profitability.[1] By 1910 an estimated 3.4 million migrant workers formed the ranks of a massive, mobile, and migratory proletariat whose labor sustained agricultural production on a national scale.[2] In California, which assumed the mantel of the largest agricultural commodity producer in the country, as many as two hundred thousand migratory workers circulated through the fields during the busy summer months.[3]

The Rise of Capitalist Agriculture

The development of capitalist agriculture in California coincided with the ascendancy of corporate power on a national scale over the second half of the nineteenth century. Through various machinations, a small class of large landowners acquired the land and intertwined with other sectors of capital to construct an economic model based on commodity production for international markets. Confronted with the need to accumulate on a vast scale to punch into national and international markets, growers formed vertically and horizontally integrated organization designed to coordinate and control all stages of production. The concentration of prime farm land in the hands of a powerful class of capitalists was complete by 1930, where 4 percent of "farmers" controlled 62 percent of California farmland, and 66 percent of all farmworkers in the state were employed by 7 percent of the largest landowners.[4]

Industrial agricultural growth was driven by a partnership between the state and capital, especially reflecting the growth and consolidation of corporate power at the turn of the century. For instance, congress passed the Federal Reclamation Act of 1902, which procured and allocated national funds toward the construction of a massive irrigation complex consisting of hundreds of miles of dams, canals, dykes, reservoirs, and wells across the Southwest.[5] In conjunction with the Homestead Acts of 1862–1916, water allocation was promoted as a populist project to allocate water resources to small farmers who had previously received land allotments at little or no cost from the federal government. This was touted as a means to populate and spur economic development in the West.[6] In practice, throughout the history of the laws, there was no effort to provide the necessary resources to relocate the masses of unemployed and impoverished workers in large US cities; or the landless laborers and subsistence sharecroppers and tenant farmers across the South.[7]

Furthermore, there was no enforcement framework to protect the few small producers who did acquire land, nor stringent requirements to retain the land. Land speculators dominated the process on all sides of the transaction—as homestead speculators, land agents, bankers, and the emerging land barons that purchased or acquired the deeds—and much of the land passed into the hands of the larger growers.[8] Actual homesteaded land distributed in smaller tracts was limited to an estimated 3.5 percent of all arable western land.[9]

As the immensely profitable enterprise of land speculation drew in all segments of the bourgeoisie, eager to invest, they merged into politics. As Paul Wallace Gates observed:

> To gain their objectives, the speculators were forced to enter politics. Whether from the East or West, they opposed a free homestead policy which, they feared, would reduce the value of their holdings. They favored grants for railroads and measures to make easier land-accumulation. They were influential in local and state governments, which they warped to suit their interests . . . These men opposed land reform, fought other agrarian legislation, championed protective tariff duties, and condemned monetary heresies. They represented the creditor, the large property owners, the railroads, and the rising industrialists . . . The successful land dealer of one generation became the banker, the local political oracle and office-holder, or the country squire of the next.[10]

The concentration of landownership proceeded quickly under these circumstances of class consolidation within the state apparatus. For instance, between the years 1860 and 1880, the number of US farms of between 500 and 1,000 acres grew from 20,000 to 76,000, while the number of farms over 1,000 acres had grown from less than 6,000 to nearly 29,000.[11] Capitalist farmers developed their farms into economies of scale engaged in commodity production throughout the West.[12] California was one of the primary beneficiaries, so that by 1930 irrigated megafarms were responsible for the consumption of 96 percent of the state's total water resources.[13]

The muscle of the growers' movement took shape with the development of the American Farm Labor Bureau, and its state and local subdivisions. This syndicate of elites crafted favorable policy or merged efforts to curtail, suspend or reshape opposing interests. They promoted their class interests through various direct and indirect links to governmental agencies, and through direct participation or vis-à-vis their representatives in the Democratic and Republican Parties. These organizations played an instrumental role in shaping various policy such as land and water use, immigration, and labor policy.

The fusion of agricultural capital and the state reached a point where the two became indistinguishable, where agriculture became the dominant form of capital investment and accumulation. According to the Department of Agriculture 70,000 of the biggest capitalist growers in 1,195 counties across 47 states sat on local, state, and federal committees to "develop agricultural plans, policies and programs for their counties" by the 1930s.[14] Another 200,000 farmers had direct access to local offices of the Department of Agriculture scattered throughout the country. The creation and population of the agricultural interfaces allowed for farmers to use state agencies, funds, and personnel to serve as guarantors for their industrial success. All stages of production were managed through the state including soil conservation, public purchase of surplus commodities, public funding for land development, crop insurance, flood control, forestry, farm tenancy, credit deficiencies, road construction, and more.

In California, growers formed trade associations representing the largest and most capitalized farms as a means to improve marketing techniques, coordinate efforts, and to otherwise strengthen their hand within state politics. Fruit, vegetable, and grain growers formed their own statewide organizations and began the process of vertical integration as early as 1913 with the establishment of county-level farm bureaus, culminating with the creation of the California Farm Bureau Federation in 1919.[15] These state-level federations then conjoined to form the American Farm Bureau Federation in 1920, representing a total membership of one million farmers, with California growers emerging as the driving force. As Ernesto Galarza observed the consolidation of agricultural interests within the state:

> The growth of these marketing organizations was remarkable: in 1900 there were sixty such associations, and by 1937 over 500 organizations represented California's specialized crops, such as cherries, olives, peaches, figs, asparagus, prunes, pears, avocados, apples, beans, onions, melons, rice, vegetables, and sweet potatoes.[16]

Highly capitalized and mechanized "bonanza farms" became the agricultural standard along the Pacific Coast, supplanting the family farm, and adapting industrial relations of production between worker and owner.[17]

While small and medium-sized farmers were members, the leadership of the California Farm Bureau Federation was more than just an average grower. They were the some of the richest and most powerfully placed capitalists in the state, vested in the major sectors of the economy. They were finance capitalists with diversified investment portfolios, of which ownership of vast quantities of land comprised only part of their wealth. A roll call of presidents includes directors of banks, the powerful marketing associations, and members of various boards of other major industrial organizations.[18] By the 1930s, a discernible oligarchy of the largest farm capitalists stood out from the pack in both the magnitude of operations and degree of control within the corridors of political power. As one study illustrated:

> 10 per cent of all farms in the state received 53 per cent of gross farm income; 9 per cent spent 65 per cent of the total wage bill; 7 per cent employed 66 per cent

of all farm workers and held 42 per cent of all crop lands harvested; and 4 per cent of all farms controlled 62 per cent of all farm land.[19]

These farming capitalists in California molded state political structures in their own image, such that the profitability of commodity production was of primary concern to office-holders big and small. They operated within the capitalist parties, either directly controlling offices or sponsoring their own candidates. They were instrumental in the adoption of a constitutional amendment that assigned state senatorial representation by county regardless of population size, giving rural regions disproportionate power (prior to 1968). They influenced the outcome of agriculture-related legislation and policy through various means: maintaining a coterie of beltway lawyers, lobbyists, and industry experts on the payroll. They financed departments at universities, enabling them to write legislative proposals and monitor and control the flow of information made accessible to the public.[20] They financed and controlled local elections, law enforcement, and other local and regional seats of power, leading agricultural counties to operate like their own fiefdoms. Essential to this arrangement was the procurement of sufficient pools of labor.

While federally funded land and water distribution didn't spur the development of a hypothetical yeoman class, the consolidation of a landowning capitalist class did create a need for a large pool of migrant workers. In this, the federal government played a supportive role once more, through financing railroad construction, facilitating labor recruitment, and ultimately utilizing immigration policy as a labor procurement instrument that could also function to deprive workers of basic civil and labor rights based on racial discrimination.[21]

The Racialization of Agricultural Labor

After the US acquired California, Native Americans formed the largest population of farmworkers in the state. Incoming speculators, settlers, and mercenary elements orchestrated spasms of violence to dislodge the estimated hundred thousand Native Americans from their lands, forcing into existence the first semblance of an agricultural proletariat.[22] International expansionism, from the acquisition of imperial possessions in the Caribbean and Asia following the Spanish-American War and the establishment of the "Open Door" in China, created further pathways for colonized people to be drawn into the corridors of migration to the US in proportion to economic growth.

As early as 1853, the US Navy asserted itself in Asia under Commodore Matthew C. Perry, establishing a military route linking several Pacific Islands all the way to Japan and China. US merchants and consulate offices followed suit, establishing the forward operating bases of US capitalist integration and territorial administration. The US, for instance, asserted its military power to force the opening of China and Japan to US trade. By 1898, the US annexed Hawaii and acquired the Philippines after defeating the decaying Spanish empire and seizing its colonial holdings. Resistance to the assertion of US power was met with brutal military action. Between 1898 and 1904, for instance, US Marines drowned a fledgling Filipino independence movement through a scorched-earth policy that saw over a million Filipinos killed.

Military power and the threat of war or colonization coerced economic integration on terms favorable to US economic interests, opening the door to the circulation of migrants as a source of labor power. As Edna Bonacich explains,

> As an imperial power in Asia, the United States could not only impose unequal treaties in terms of trade and tariffs, it could also impose unequal conditions on the flow of personnel, or labor power. United States and Hawaiian capital could send representatives to Asian countries to actively recruit labor, and could play an important, sometimes determinative role in setting the conditions under which the workers emigrated.[23]

In California, Chinese workers were drawn into mining, but gradually pushed out and into agriculture, comprising 15 percent of the workforce by 1870.[24]

The severe economic depression of 1873 saw swelling groups of unemployed white workers flood into California's rural regions. Government-supported recruitment programs also facilitated the mass transfer of poor whites and European immigrants from the East and South.[25] By the late nineteenth century, white laborers made up the majority of the itinerant workforce in the state.[26] Economic crisis, oversaturation of labor markets, and high unemployment encouraged segments of the urban capitalist classes concerned with economic instability and the class volatility that comes with unemployment to turn to racial scapegoating.

Anti-Chinese demagogues, especially in the state's Democratic Party, led an anti-immigrant movement that germinated across the West. Chinese were racially segregated in the cities and pushed out of the more lucrative mining jobs and into agriculture. An editorial from the *Marin Journal* exemplifies how grower-aligned newspapers fanned the flames of anti-Chinese sentiment, feigning sympathy for the white worker:

> [The Chinese laborer] is a slave, reduced to the lowest terms of beggarly economy, and is no fit competitor for an American freeman; that he herds in scores, lives in small dens, where a white man and wife could hardly breathe, and has none of the wants of a civilized white man. . . . That American men, women, and children cannot be what free people should be, and compete with such degraded creatures in the labor market.[27]

By 1882, the year Congress passed the Chinese Exclusion Act, an estimated 132,300 Chinese had entered the West Coast of the United States, dropping to 71,532 in 1910 as anti-Asian racism flared and this particular source of labor diminished in importance.[28]

Coinciding with the decline of Chinese immigration, tens of thousands of rural migrants exiting Japan were enticed to take their place. The accession of the Meiji Restoration government in Japan represented a revolution from above, in which urban capitalists liquidated the feudal rural structures as part of a coordinated campaign to accelerate industrialization. Eager to avoid China's fate, namely US and European colonization, the Japanese employed a form of economic shock treatment to integrate and centralize the economy in the hands of a new capitalist class. Displaced peasants and agricultural workers entered via indentured migration to the sugar plantations of Hawaii, where American and European private colonization companies were in great need of labor. Many of these migrants moved into California after 1898.[29]

By 1910, an estimated 72,157 Japanese had relocated in the US along the Pacific Coast, with 41,356 residing in California (about 1.7 percent of the state population).[30] While a small percent of the overall population, they were heavily concentrated in agriculture, making up an estimated 53 percent of the labor force.[31] Once they established their presence in the fields, Japanese workers enjoyed great success in asserting collective power through the formation of *keiyaku-nin*, or ethnic labor associations that functioned as labor unions. Over the course of the first decade of the twentieth century,

> Japanese field hands were the first to initiate and secure collective bargaining agreements systematically on a wide-scale basis, the first to establish functioning ethnic labor unions, and the first to be condemned by growers. . . . [T]hey capitalized on their solidarity, demanded and broke contracts, altered and improved working conditions, boycotted and confronted growers, engaged in organized slowdowns, withheld labor at key planting times, walked out during harvests, participated in interracial strikes, set minimum wages, and initiated the first efforts at large scale farm labor organization.[32]

Japanese labor militancy was so effective it threatened to break the monopoly of control that the large landowning class of growers exercised over their rural fiefdoms.[33] In response to an economic rival, exasperated white growers created their own associations. They organized the first California State Fruit Growers Convention in San Francisco in 1902. Out of this convention, they formed the California Employment Committee with the intention to organize a mass recruitment campaign of white workers from the Midwest to be used as a reserve army of labor against the Japanese keiyaku-nin.

Furthermore, growers around the Imperial Valley of southeastern California began to recruit and transport Mexicans from across the border to leverage them against Japanese workers. Growers also formed a strategic alliance with anti-immigration groups, including conservative trade unions, who began to agitate for immigration restriction, boycotts of Japanese goods, and racial segregation of Japanese people across the state. They also invested in university research to support their efforts. In 1904, they began to apply Taylorist methods, scientific management techniques to erode the element of training and skill that gave Japanese workers an advantage.

Through their efforts, large growers were instrumental in curbing Japanese migration and restricting their landownership. Between 1907 and 1913 federal and state governments passed a series of sweeping exclusionary laws that greatly reduced Japanese migration and disqualified Japanese migrants from landownership.[34] Following the California Alien Land Act of 1913, which disqualified landownership for those ineligible for citizenship, similar laws were passed in other western states: Oregon, Washington, Texas, Arizona, Utah, Idaho, Montana, and Wyoming. The Supreme Court sanctioned the discriminatory laws in 1923 and set the stage for an outright ban on

Asian immigration in 1924.[35]

The liquidation of the Japanese property-owning population and agricultural workforce aligned the state, capitalist growers, conservative AFL unionists, and white supremacists in support of policies that contributed to the maintenance of a permanent agricultural workforce deprived of labor and civil rights. Growers found the recruitment of foreign workers to be to their advantage, as a noncitizen and immigrant workforce could be disenfranchised, deprived of citizenship, or even deported.

The Making of a Mexican Migratory Workforce

Within the border region, Mexican migratory labor increased in importance during the first three decades of the twentieth century. The establishment of capital-intensive western agriculture coincided with the linkage of five major railroad systems from the Mexican interior to the US border (four in Texas and one in Arizona). Through these hubs, the US rail lines fanned out to the principal US border towns in Texas, New Mexico, Arizona, and California, and further and into Colorado.[36] By the second decade of the twentieth century, capitalist growers in the western states had sent out an army of recruiting agents across the Southwest transit hubs and deep into the interior of Mexico stocked with pamphlets in Spanish and promises of well-paying jobs.[37]

As a result of recruitment projects such as this, migration increased exponentially. The Mexican population in the US increased from 100,000 in 1900 to over 220,000 in 1910, 486,000 in 1920, and up to a million in 1930.[38] Migratory agricultural labor in the early twentieth century flowed into three primary economic corridors. Entering through El Paso, Mexican workers were densely concentrated in Texas cotton production. From there, others went into sugar beet production in Colorado and throughout the Midwest, and to grain, fruit, and vegetable harvesting in California. In the Pacific states, Mexican labor surpassed that of the Japanese by 1915.[39]

Mexican migratory workers were favored by agricultural employers because, as migrants set in motion by economic developments in Mexico, they could be obtained more easily without having to make great investments in transportation and without the necessity of resettlement. The railroad lines originally developed for commodity extraction within Mexico also served a dual purpose in distributing economically displaced workers among US farms. Furthermore, the circulation of a Mexican-origin workforce reduced some of the burden of production and reproduction of a yearly workforce. For instance, the social costs of workforce development were shifted onto the Mexican state and the Mexican workers themselves.

In particular, the costs of "producing" the Mexican migrant laborer, i.e. training, health services, education, etc., were borne out in Mexico; while the migrant family in the US had to provide its own transportation, housing, and other means of sustenance with limited or nonexisting state support.[40] The preference for migratory labor was contingent upon the idea that individual farmworkers or their families not take up permanent residence in the cities, as second-generation immigrants as citizens tended to strive for social mobility. The mechanisms used to constrict settlement and alternative employment opportunity were exercised through state power, such as austere forms of racial discrimination and manipulation of citizenship categories and policies.

The hardening structures of racial segregation and restrictive immigration policy provided the parameters by which growers could exploit their social and political vulnerability and limited mobility. Through their collective and accumulated experiences with the absence or weakening of rights for Native American, Chinese, and Japanese and other Asian workers, the most calculating of the growers understood that Mexicans could also be acquired when needed and be dismissed and encouraged to return to Mexico more easily when not needed. The advantage provided by this arrangement led others to follow suit to remain competitive.

The proximity to Mexico and the coordination between growers to stagger their operations made perpetual migration and cyclical return more likely than mass congregations of disgruntled unemployed and impoverished workers settling in local communities. This helped to construct a cyclical migration pattern that became celebrated as a model by agriculture's boosters in the government. A 1908 Department of Labor study shows how the agricultural interests working with and within the federal government began to promote this idea of Mexicans as a labor solution in cotton, beets, and grain while employing racist notions as a means to justify it. For example, in the section promoting the value of Mexican labor in cotton, the study states:

> Cotton picking suits the Mexican for several reasons: It requires nimble fingers rather than physical strength, in which he cannot compete with the white man or the Negro; it employs his whole family; he can follow it from place to place, living out of doors, which seems to suit the half-subdued nomadic instinct of a part of the Mexican race . . . So the man with 40 or 80 acres opening secures two or three families of Mexicans that migrate from the southward at this season, camp in an outhouse or in their canvas-topped cart, and pick the fields clean, then move on northward to where the crop is just maturing.[41]

The report goes on to conclude that while Mexicans are favorable as laborers, they are not favored as potential citizens, neighbors, or even as guests. Racial segregation spread through the Southwest, making it very difficult for Mexicans to obtain housing, employment, and other necessities. Validating racist views, the report assures growers that Mexicans will neither settle nor enjoy rights afforded to citizens:

> Mexicans are not likely to be employed the year round by small farmers because they are not entertained in the family like American, German, Scandinavian, or Irish laborers of the North. Yet they do not occupy a position analogous to that of the Negro in the South. They are not permanent, do not acquire land or establish themselves in little cabin homesteads, but remain nomadic and outside of American civilization.[42]

While growers were eager to maintain access to a steady flow of Mexican migrants, they were also determined to limit their mobility and control the conditions of their labor.

One way Mexican labor came to be controlled was through the creation of immigration policy that enabled migration while precluding or delimiting the substance of citizenship. This elaborated, through state mechanisms, a second form of segregation derived through the denial of full citizenship, mirroring the methods and consequences of racial segregation. Immigration policy and citizenship stipulations were used to regulate the flow, limit mobility, and curtail access to the means to change or challenge the conditions of labor.

When Congress passed the Immigration Act of 1917, it included the first broad and comprehensive restrictions on labor entry. A head tax and literacy test excluded poor migrants, reflecting a pattern of exclusion mirroring the practice of Jim Crow. While Asian and European migration slowed greatly as a result of the act, Mexican migration was also stanched. Nevertheless, the legislation contained a clause that allowed the labor secretary the flexibility to create exemptions on a temporary basis. When growers pressed for Mexican exemptions, the office of the labor secretary complied, creating a lever for southwestern capital to administer its own labor needs.[43] For example, one of the first uses of this exemption occurred in 1918 when the Department of Labor and Immigration and Naturalization Service approved the importation of thirty thousand Mexican nationals to work in southwestern industries.[44]

The specific character of Mexican labor status was further elaborated after the Exclusion Law of 1921 and National Quota Act of 1924, which together brought eastern European and Asian migration to a halt. In the official discussions to align these policies with economic imperatives, capitalists and key state institutions rallied on behalf of Mexican labor exceptionalism. While growers pleaded their case to keep the pipeline to Mexico open, "the Department of Agriculture asserted that Mexican labor was needed for reclamation projects; and the State Department contended that the application of the quota to the Western Hemisphere would adversely affect the efforts of Pan-Americanism."[45]

The opposition from racist critics of Mexican migration and organized labor was marginalized this time around, as the convergence of factors that produced consensus on Asian exclusion fell apart. Mexico had become a strategically important ally and valuable economic asset by the outbreak of World War I. The volatility of the Mexican Revolution had begun to subside by 1918, and the administration of Woodrow Wilson attempted to reassert control over its southern neighbor. The rising middle-class forces around Carranza and Obregón were consolidating their power in Mexico City against a more radical working-class movement, presenting the best opportunity for regional realignment. As US agricultural output continued to expand into the war period, with its concomitant shortages of labor, US growers and railroad magnates were in no mood for limiting Mexican labor access, at least at the moment.

While growers wanted no obstacles to labor migration from Mexico, it can also be observed that neither were they interested in workers attaining citizenship rights. While Mexicans were excluded from the quotas and restrictions embodied in the 1921–1924 acts, which exempted "Western Hemispheric nations," they were more stringently policed within the United States. To placate the most vocal critics of the Mexican exemption, the State Department vowed to crack down on unauthorized Mexicans already in the country. In 1924 the Border Patrol was created as a means to police Mexican communities along the border and in barrios throughout the South-west. This special armed force began to become a presence in and around Mexican communities, apprehending and deporting individuals in a seemingly arbitrary—but not comprehensive—pattern that began to intimidate and instill fear among the Mexican population. As Gilberto Cárdenas points out:

> By establishing a reign of terror over Mexicans already in the United States, either by intent or by accident, the Border Patrol proved its effectiveness. Reports during this period suggest that thousands of Mexicans in the United States fled to the border and sought permission to cross in fear of arrest.[46]

Those noncitizen Mexican workers that remained in the United States or came thereafter now had to endure the threat of deportation from a largely unrestrained police force that expanded its reach deeper into the interior of the country. This precluded civic involvement and isolated Mexicans, who were compelled to retreat further into their barrios and colonias to evade harassment, arrest, or deportation. The intensification of repression coincided with the potency of anti-immigrant groups driving the discourse by popularizing racist doctrine, which paralleled the interest of growers to limit Mexican access to citizenship, but not to work.

One of the groups that played an instrumental role in promoting anti-Japanese and Chinese discourse was the Asiatic Exclusion League. This cross-class alliance included the American Legion, segments of the AFL, and the Native Sons of the Golden West. The latter group was a bourgeois fraternal organization that included high-ranking military figures, politicians, and capitalists that fashioned themselves as the stewards of land, people, and policy in the West. One prominent member was Valentine Stuart McClatchy, a large land-owner and one-time president of the California State Reclamation Board, which oversaw the transfer of state wetlands to use for agriculture. He was also a prominent newspaper publisher who controlled several periodicals along the central coast of California, including the *Sacramento Bee*. In establishing the precedent of racial exclusions and quotas, the Asiatic Exclusion League repackaged itself as the California Joint Immigration Committee (CJIC). Between 1924 and 1946 this group set out to continue the project of racial engineering in the United States through the construction of restrictionist immigration policy.[47]

In terms of their anti-Mexican campaign, the CJIC pursued the same approach as with the Japanese, attempting to disqualify Mexicans from naturalization and citizenship. Over the course of the 1920s, this group constructed the multifaceted narrative of the Mexican threat, from their purported racial inferiority to their being the harbingers of great epidemics.[48] In a 1933 press statement, the CJIC proclaimed the rising threat of diseased Mexican migrants and the social costs of treating them, stating (without citation):

> Some years ago Los Angeles spent over a million dollars to eradicate the pneumonic plague introduced by Mexicans. In Orange County the death rate from tuberculosis is 9 times as great for Mexicans as for other races—355 per 100.000 as compared with 42—and Mexicans, constituting 10 percent of the population,

furnished 34 percent of clinical cases, occupied 34 percent of the total beds in
the county hospital, and 57 percent of the beds in the tubercular wards. Similar
conditions are to be found in other southern California Counties.[49]

A significant edifice of anti-Mexican sentiment was built into the anti-immigration movement and found multiple founts of expression within the political establishment. Like in previous epochs, racism proved a useful tool to fragment labor and
establish gradations of noncitizen segmentation that could be leveraged against US-
born workers. Within this terrain, support for immigration from growers was limited
only to access, but not for rights or citizenship, as this undermined their exploitability.
Most sectors of the AFL bought into the notion of native white primacy over foreign
labor, while small white farmers saw employment of Mexican agricultural workers as
giving further advantage to their corporate competitors.[50] In an atmosphere devoid of
labor solidarity to counter the narrative of the Mexican threat, the political landscape
could be shifted further to the right by demagogues and opportunistic politicians.
One Texas congressman named John Box refashioned himself the champion of anti-Mexican exclusion.

In 1926, Box called for amending the 1924 National Origins Act by including
Mexico in the list of nations subject to quota, effectively reducing legal Mexican migration to negligible numbers. The Texas Democrat sought to give voice to the disparate elements rumbling against Mexican migration. Drawing from the budding eugenics movement then gaining a foothold in elite circles, he applied racial theory against
Mexicans in demagogic and evangelistic fashion to animate the oppositional sentiments of small white farmers. Simultaneously he appropriated conservative labor's
arguments against migration, claiming Mexican workers were backward and easily
exploitable, lowering white workers' wages, or readily used to break strikes.[51]

Capitalist interests moved into open opposition to Box's bill, having formed the
Lower Río Grande Valley Association to protect their access to Mexican workers in the
Río Grande Valley. This group included representatives from the Texas Cattle Raisers
Association, Texas Citrus Fruit Growers Exchange, railroad interests, and energy and
power interests, among others. While they were successful in thwarting the Box Bill,
they strategically sought reconciliation with the aspirations of the anti-immigrant elements to limit Mexican access to settlement and citizenship. A statement made by a
spokesman for the Chamber of Commerce captures the synthesis of these two seemingly contradictory positions. While prefacing his comments by reiterating business's
need for unrestricted migrant labor, he added that "a rider should be attached to the
'Box Bill' to allow supervised Mexican workers to stay on farms" adding that "they
should be monitored."[52]

In what would become the pattern in large agricultural border states like California and Texas, conservative middle-class whites and the most powerful sectors
of organized labor lined up against Mexican immigration, while big business supported fluid migration but discouraged pathways to citizenship. While big business
constantly won the larger political battle of access, anti-immigrant forces suppressed
the social and political rights of migrants in the country through periodic spasms of

violence and by leveraging their electoral clout at the polls.

Nevertheless, many did permanently settle as the statistics previously mentioned bear out. For this reason, the favorability of Mexican workers was in the process of keeping them as migrants and limiting the prospects for permanent settlement or landownership. It was repeatedly emphasized that Mexicans did not want to settle, as a justification for increasing their temporary access. According to one report citing an official with the Mexican Central Railroad, over 50,000 migrant workers rode their trains to the US in 1907, while 37,000 repatriated the same year.[53] The notion of the perpetual Mexican migrant played to the dominant racist narrative among Southwest growers of the day: that Mexicans were not a threat to American culture since they did not settle; that they were intellectually incapable of advancing up the agricultural ladder and biologically pre-disposed to do "stoop labor," that they worked cheaply, and that their families did not need to be sustained using state resources.

Among growers and their allies, it served their interests to perpetuate the stereotype that Mexicans were disinterested or incapable of owning land and operating their own farms. This glossed over the actual functioning of a system to deprive Mexican migrants of the means to transcend their impoverished and vulnerable conditions. Mexican migrants learned early on that their prospects for landownership were indeed limited. In the Southwest, various practices marginalized Mexican and Mexican American farmworkers, so that landownership remained elusive.

There were deliberate ways Mexican migratory workers were denied pathways to landownership. For instance, agricultural companies tended to maintain Mexican workers segregated and concentrated in seasonal low-paying harvesting work, while European and US-born workers maintained a monopoly over the skilled and technical dimensions of agricultural production or in year-round field maintenance jobs. In Colorado, for instance, the National Sugar Company helped US-born and European immigrant farmworkers rent or purchase lands to become beet producers to supply the refinery with raw materials, while it was common practice to routinely dismiss Mexicans after each season.[54]

In another example, California sugar producers created a similarly stratified pattern. In testimony before a congressional committee, it was reported that:

> Of the total labor required in the industry, 10 percent was factory labor and chiefly white-American, and 90 per cent was field labor which was practically 100 per cent foreign labor . . . in Southern California it was 1/5 Japanese and 4/5 Mexicans."[55]

The manufacturing of corridors of migration from Mexico produced over time periodic influxes of migrant workers who were then drawn into a vicious cycle. The institutionalization of depressed wages for Mexican workers (the Mexican wage) made it difficult for individuals to accumulate significant savings, and the seasonal work kept them from establishing roots in local rural economies.[56] The elaboration of a regime of immigration controls and an expanding web of interior enforcement coupled with racial segregation followed Mexican workers into the urban centers, where many migrants resided in the off-season. Mexicans and Mexican Americans were confined to the economic margins there as well. As David Díaz explains:

> Barrio formation was tied to segregation patterns, and housing and infrastruc-
> ture within barrios were poor. In an era of dense urban form, barrios were on
> the immediate periphery of downtowns and manufacturing zones. Due to poor
> wages, home ownership patterns were low, and residential segregation was rig-
> idly enforced.[57]

The construction of a permanent, isolated, and cyclical reserve army of Mexican ag-
ricultural labor became the foundation for the agricultural capitalist economy in the
Southwest by the 1920s. A synthesis of this historical process is captured by Mario
Barrera:

> A racially segmented labor force allowed the employers greater control of the
> labor supply. A reserve labor force, for example, gave greater elasticity to the
> supply of labor. In addition, the system gave employers greater control of their
> workers in other ways. The reserve labor force was used as leverage to weaken
> the bargaining power of all workers. The use of minority workers as buffers
> served to pacify the non-minority workers in periods of excess labor. Perhaps
> most importantly, the fact of a segmented labor force created built-in divisions
> among the workers, and helped prevent the emergence of a class consciousness
> among them. Conflicts and antagonisms tended to be directed against other
> workers, rather than against employers. At the heart of the system, then, lay the
> interests of the employers as a class.[58]

The subjugation of the Mexican farm-working population in the US also made
them a volatile and potentially explosive segment of the agricultural proletariat, capable of joining or spearheading wider class struggle in the fields. As Paul S. Taylor
identified, "Mexican Americans have accepted the role of farm wage worker though
they have not been content with this role. Their record is one of protest in the form
of strikes, boycotts, and a succession of attempts to organize and bargain collectively
with their employers."[59] In other words, Mexican workers did not accept these conditions without a fight. Their agricultural militancy caught the attention of the Industrial Workers of the World, and later the Communist Party, which saw in the Mexican
workers an important ally in their efforts to rebuild a new labor movement along anticapitalist and internationalist lines.

Chapter 18

Wobblies and Mexican Farmworkers in Wheatland

*"There is one bright spot in that story—the superb solidarity shown
in the strike... when a motley crowd of Swedes, Mexicans, Japanese,
Syrians, Americans, and other nationalities, men, women, and children
stood as one man for decent human conditions and a living wage."*
—*International Socialist Review*, "The Wheatland Boys"

In their analysis of the agricultural proletariat, IWW strategists saw a volatile and potentially revolutionary force. The exploitation of migrant workers spread from the urban areas, where predatory farm employment agencies charged high rates and over-hired, to the fields themselves, where growers managed labor pools to their advantage to keep wages low and working conditions poor. Organizers grasped the magnitude of power vested in the hands of the growers and countered the narrative of the perpetually struggling farmer with an application of the Marxist labor theory of value. A July 1909 editorial in the *Industrial Worker* signaled a new orientation on agricultural workers:

> The farmer is a robber of labor, and the man who works in the harvest field is
> entitled to all he produces, but we must begin to take as much as possible every
> day, and always remember that although we are not able to take the farm—not
> yet—still we must keep this in view. The final aim of the IWW is revolution. But
> for the present let's see if we can't get a bed to sleep in, water enough to take a
> bath, and decent food to eat; then we will be ready for the next installment at the
> expense of the "poor farmer."[1]

The article then goes on to explain the potential power of farmworkers to exploit harvest vulnerabilities and existing divisions between the growers in order to get higher pay and shorter hours.

After 1909, the IWW concentrated efforts in organizing migratory agricultural workers in the West. Between 1907 and 1915 IWW organizers went into agricultural fields and camps across Washington, Iowa, Minnesota, Montana, the Dakotas, and California. The early strategy was to establish a base in cities like San Diego, Los Angeles, San Francisco, and Spokane, where the union could find large numbers of unemployed migrant workers that congregated in the cities during the agricultural off-season. IWW street meetings in plazas and squares, and on street corners were the means by which to recruit, educate, train, and then send worker-organizers to the migrant camps to agitate during harvesting time. Wobbly gatherings were repressed, as city governments had outlawed public speaking by Socialists beginning in 1903. In an attempt to curtail the activities of leftists, they required that all public events require permits, which were never forthcoming to socialists and Wobblies. The Wobblies challenged the ban by calling in hundreds of members and followers to flock into the city centers to protest, get arrested, and overfill the jails as a form of protest. This set in motion several years of grueling free-speech fights in cities along the Pacific Coast, which proved violent and costly, and with mixed results.[2]

By 1914, the IWW built the infrastructure for a statewide organization in California with the establishment of the Agricultural Workers Organization the following year. This new strategy, called the "job-delegate" system, saw the formation of permanent locals, with organizers then going directly into the fields to organize alongside workers while on the job, as well as in the camps along the migrant corridors. The union began to press for industrywide wage increases and improved working conditions, while organizers among the field hands helped orchestrate and direct strikes and slowdowns that began to yield concrete results. The AWO also attempted to create industrial locals, which included all workers interconnected to the agricultural economy, including lumberjacks, construction workers, and railroad workers. By 1914 forty locals were established throughout California with an estimated 5,000 members, primarily in agriculture.[3] By June of 1916, the AWO had a total membership of around 20,000 members across eleven states: Missouri, Iowa, Washington, Montana, Kansas, Nebraska, Minnesota, Wisconsin, Idaho, Oklahoma, and California.[4] It was through these mixed locals and the organizing efforts in the field that Mexican workers and the IWW first came into contact.

Prior to the outbreak of the Mexican Revolution, individual Mexican workers in the United States were joining the IWW or following its lead. Their opposition to the racist exclusionary policy of the AFL, their anti-imperialism, and their direct efforts to organize field workers attracted a significant following among Mexican workers. As previously mentioned, Mexican Wobblies in Los Angeles attracted a significant following within the barrios. Many Mexicans left their barrios to work in the fields during harvest season, moving as far north as the San Joaquin Valley and Sacramento valleys to pick cotton, nuts, grapes, citrus fruits, and other crops, including hops.

By 1909, IWW locals in Los Angeles, San Diego, and San Francisco had begun to actively recruit Mexican farmworkers, many of whom lived in the city but migrated across the state during harvest season.[5] Along the agricultural corridor, another multinational IWW local, 66, was established in Fresno in 1911 with the assistance of Wobbly-magonistas Fernando Palomares and Fernando Velarde. Local 66 was a gathering point for many IWW-aligned migrant workers, including many Mexican workers, who continued the trek to work in the large farms to the north, including the vast hop fields in Wheatland, California.[6] Furthermore, Wobbly organizers also met workers through the practice of campsite organizing, as migrants formed temporary camps along migrant routes. As Hyman Weintraub explains:

> [T]he influence of the organization was completely out of proportion to its membership. When migratory workers gathered for their social entertainments, they sang wobbly songs, when a group of farm laborers had special grievances to

present to the ranch foremen, the I.W.W. member on the farm would be spokesman for the group.[7]

One example is in what has come to be known as the Wheatland Hops Riot, while it
can be better understood as a strike that was violently repressed.

Mexicans were among the migrant farmworkers organizing with the IWW in Wheatland California in 1913

Wheatland

Hops production in the US grew in tandem with increased beer consumption. While
hops production was concentrated in the Midwest, growers in Northern California
adopted the crop in their rotation. One group of prominent growers, the Durst family,
grew the crop on their ranchlands in the town of Wheatland in Yuba County, California.[8] By 1878, Wheatland became a major agricultural hub in the region, shipping
out more than eighteen million pounds of wheat, hops, barley, potatoes, and other
agricultural products a year.[9] In 1876, Daniel Durst and his wife Rose Francis Haines
Durst purchased the first plots of what came to be known as Durst Ranch. Durst was
a wealthy doctor, and Rose the daughter of a rich farm equipment inventor and manu-
facturer in Illinois. The Durst family moved into the region as part of the larger speculative land rush of these years.

The massive 670-acre Durst ranch was inherited by Ralph and Jonathon Durst
from their father, and by 1913 it was the largest hop farm in the world and the single largest employer of migrant farmworkers in the state. As the largest growers, they
also set the standards for others, which included innovative techniques to squeeze as
much profit from their workers as possible. The Durst brothers had invested significant funds through various employment agencies throughout California, southern

Oregon, and western Nevada to attract a sizeable surplus of workers. A 1914 statewide survey of 897 large California farms revealed that of the 35,953 farmworkers housed at these camps, about 51 percent of were noncitizen immigrants (representing 40 nationalities), 49 percent were US-born or naturalized immigrants, 7 percent were women, and 4 percent were children, all of whom worked in the fields.[10] Of the estimated 2,800 workers that assembled at Durst Ranch on August 3, 1913, up to half were migrants, predominantly Mexican, but they also included Syrian, Italian, Puerto Rican, Polish, Indian, Japanese, and workers of twenty other nationalities.[11] Between eight hundred and a thousand were women and children.

Once in the camps, the workers found the conditions abysmal, symptomatic of the degraded conditions that growers normalized through minimal investment in health, sanitation, and hygiene. Farmworker housing amounted to rows of salvaged gunnysack tents and large piles of straw to use as makeshift beds. There were no toilets or bathing facilities, and only two water faucets served the whole camp; although the well they were drawn from dried out by midday. This occurred while temperatures climbed to over one hundred degrees on average during the height of the three-week summer harvest. Six latrines served the whole workforce, and were large open trenches covered with wood planks constructed in close proximity to the camps. Without sanitation systems, garbage removal, or running water, the sewage trenches also doubled as the camp trash dump. Industrial wastes, animal manure, and the offal of slaughtered animals made up the discarded refuse collecting in fetid pits. One observer described them as "swarming with blue flies" and being "alive with maggots," with sewage from the latrines draining into stagnant pools along the environs of the camp.[12] These conditions produced a breeding ground for dysentery and other bacterial infections.[13]

The Durst Ranch became a laboratory for new cost-cutting techniques, employing the latest trends in the industry, mirroring Taylorist scientific management in the factories. As part of their effort to cut costs and increase productivity, the Durst brothers introduced a number of speed-up techniques. They eliminated the position of "high-pole men," whose job it was to climb upward of 30 feet to detach sprawling vines from support fences for ease of picking, and afterward to pack, carry, and load hundred-pound sacks while farmworkers gathered the hops. Now the migratory field workers—men, women, and children—were required to complete all stages.

Furthermore, to compel the workers not to leave before the harvest was complete, they instituted a wage theft scheme misnamed the bonus system by which part of each week's wages was withheld until the end of the harvest. The fake bonus began with the suppression of wages by ten percent for the first week (90 cents per 100-pound bag; with $1 being the going wage in 1913), increasing 10 percent for the second week to $1, and then to $1.10 on the third week. It was estimated that the brothers profited to the tune of about $100–$150 per day in wage holdbacks forfeited by pickers who left before the third week, often because of the extreme conditions.[14] To create a scenario by which workers would be enticed to accept the wage scheme, the brothers overadvertised the number of positions. When nearly 3,000 turned out for 1,500 available jobs, a labor surplus could be used to divide the workers against each other. Those desperate enough would be hired and the rest turned away. In later testimony, workers stated that the difficulty of the work under the Durst system limited them to filling little more than one bag per day, ensuring that they typically made less than a dollar per day, while the average price of hops on the market was 20 cents per pound.[15] Meanwhile, hundreds of other workers unable to sustain work and stranded remained around the camp hoping for a slot to open up.

While the Durst brothers deprived their workers of basic necessities, they maintained a concession stand to sell fake lemonade (water and acetic acid) to the workers. The only source of food for the workers was a local grocer who was granted a monopoly by the Durst brothers in exchange for a share of the profits derived from inflated prices. In their later investigation of the Durst Ranch, the California Commission of Immigration and Housing concluded that these working conditions constituted an "aggravation of industrial warfare" and that similar conditions plagued migrant labor camps across the state. By the second day of the harvest, the bulk of the workers were incensed at the low wages and unbearable working conditions at the camp. Historian Woodrow C. Whitten identified that the specific conditions of agricultural production in Wheatland were symptomatic of class polarization reaching a breaking point: concentrated ownership, large-scale production, high capitalization, and repressed labor conditions that "combined to build up factory conditions of farming with a partly industrialized rural proletariat, and to construct a setting charged with 'social dynamite.'"[16] Once the IWW was able to launch organizing forays into this environment, even small numbers of seasoned radicals could give shape to large-scale coordinated action.

According to Carleton Parker, a state agent who studied California agricultural working conditions, as much as 8 percent of the migratory workforce at the time of the Wheatland riot and strike were active Wobblies, read IWW literature, or had some experience or interaction with the group.[17] This coincides with a major push to organize migratory farmworkers through the Agricultural Workers Organization. Nicholas Thoburn describes this as one of the most successful of the Wobbly unions in their capacity to adapt organizing techniques to the conditions of work.

> The AWO invented a system of recruitment—the "job delegate system"—based on migratory practices. Essentially, a group of mobile organizers would start in the early spring at the Mexican border, and end in late autumn in the Canadian provinces, recruiting new members, collecting dues, selling literature, passing on news and tactics, and organizing industrial action as they went.[18]

In his study of the IWW in California agriculture, Cletus Daniel also concludes,

> Between 1909 and 1917, the period of its greatest activity among farmworkers, the I.W.W. had a profound impact on agricultural labor relations in California . . . It is difficult to imagine that by 1917 there was anywhere in California, and indeed anywhere in the West, a group of farmworkers or employers who had not, either directly or indirectly, felt the influence of the I.W.W.[19]

A later state report estimated that about four hundred workers at Wheatland were familiar with the IWW while a smaller group of one hundred were card-carrying members. Some of these members organized a loosely formed local in the camp, of which about thirty Durst Ranch workers had joined.[20]

This background can explain how quickly the anger and frustration of the disgruntled workers at the Durst brothers' ranch could be turned into mass action. After the second day of the August 1913 harvest, an impromptu protest quickly grew into a mass meeting of several hundred to discuss the conditions of work. As George Bell describes the scene,

> Fathers and mothers of families full of indignation, laborers fired with the resentment of class consciousness, hoboes and revolutionaries keen for any demonstration or struggle—all collected, without orders or organization, in the summer twilight. Inflammatory speeches were made, and the living and wage conditions were denounced.[21]

Women workers were at the forefront of the upsurge. As Vincent DiGirolamo explains: "Women, to the degree that they took primary responsibility for cooking, cleaning, and caring for their families, were among the most distressed by the rampant and perhaps calculated deprivation."[22]

Within this quick turn of events, Wobblies took steps to channel the anger into a set of demands and the formation of a strike committee. The next morning, August 4, they held another mass meeting to determine a set of demands. After deliberation and mass voting, the workers determined that all workers be paid $1.25 per hundred-pound bag and that there should be an immediate improvement of camp conditions. The latter included the restoration of paid "high pole men," the service of real lemonade, ice water delivered twice a day to workers in the fields, mobile toilets made available for women in the field, and functioning toilet facilities in camp. The two most prominent leaders that emerged were Richard "Blackie" Ford, an ex-Wobbly, and Herman Suhr, an active job delegate.

At the conclusion of that meeting the elected strike committee presented their demands to Ralph Durst. In the face of such unity, he feigned a willingness to negotiate but became enraged, slapping Blackie Ford in the face with his glove and ordering him to leave his property. As Ford refused, he stormed off and returned with Wheatland town constable Lee Anderson to arrest and remove Ford on trespassing charges. When Anderson singled him out from the crowd with his gun drawn, he was surrounded by several women workers who physically blocked his path. They began taunting him and daring him to shoot. As he later testified, "a girl ran towards me shouting: 'Shoot me! Shoot me!'"[23] Other workers gathered around Durst and the constable and began cursing them. They quickly lost their nerve and fled the scene, with some throwing rocks at them as they scurried away.[24]

Among those that chased off Durst and the constable was Valores Barrera, a mexicana who later testified in court on behalf of the strikers, showing that women "attended mass meetings, spoke out in public, voted on demands, and physically confronted their bosses and local authorities" alongside the men.[25] From this experience, the Wobblies realized that they would need to defend their leaders and that the strike needed to move forward. For his part, Durst sent word to the Yuba County sheriff to form a posse of deputies and quickly mobilize by day's end to enforce the arrest of Ford and head off the strike.

By early evening, the IWW called for a mass meeting and rally to prepare for a strike. After singing popular Wobbly songs, the two thousand workers and their families that had gathered began listening to speeches by the strike committee that were then translated into seven languages, including Spanish, reflecting the presence of Mexican workers. When Durst and the sheriff's posse returned, eight men emerged from two cars: Yuba County sheriff George Voss, the local district attorney Edmund Manwell, and several armed deputies. As the men positioned themselves around the large crowd, the sheriff ordered the crowd to disperse and moved toward the stage with his gun pointed at Ford, followed by Durst, Anderson, Manwell, and one of the deputies. Three other deputies, including Deputy Henry Daken, stood on a nearby incline monitoring the situation with their guns pointed at the body of the crowd.

As Constable Anderson stepped onto the makeshift platform serving as a stage for the strike leaders, the added weight caused a plank to snap, sending the whole group tumbling forward. As that happened, Deputy Daken fired directly into the crowd, falsely claiming that "shots were fired [from] within crowd."[26] The attack on the crowd began what became mislabeled as the Wheatland Hop Riot.

After the shots were fired, men, women, and children scattered in all directions. Some workers physically grappled with the deputies, and a short but violent melee ensued. An unidentified Puerto Rican worker (described as a "Negro" in some papers) disarmed, shot, and killed a Deputy Reardon as well as the district attorney, Manwell, while Sheriff Voss was knocked unconscious by a blow to the head. Firing from a distance and from a vantage point above the farmworkers, Sheriff Daken then felled the Puerto Rican worker by shotgun blast. When the dust cleared, another young unidentified male worker of English origin was found shot, probably by the initial volley. The posse regrouped and quickly fled the scene.[27]

The Wheatland incident triggered a series of transformative events, starting with severe repression. Immediately after the event the governor dispatched six companies of National Guard troops, who surrounded the camp and worked with the company to arrest over a hundred of the purported "ringleaders."[28] Yuba County authorities turned the police operation over to the William J. Burns Detective Agency, and over a hundred of its private guards were deputized to assist with investigating and arresting accused IWW members and strike leaders. Eric Chester points out that those arrested were "held for weeks, even months, without charges being filed. They were refused access to attorneys, interrogated for long periods day after day, deprived of sleep . . . [and] were badly beaten when they refused to cooperate."[29] In the end four men were detained and charged with "conspiracy to murder" District Attorney Edward Manwell, even though there was not a shred of evidence to support the claim. These included Blackie Ford, Herman Suhr, Walter Bagan, and Walter Beck, the latter being described by the *San Francisco Call* as a "youthful Mexican."[30]

In a mockery of justice, the trial judge, the prosecutor, and a second state-appointed special prosecutor were all lifelong friends of the slain district attorney. The trial was conducted in the town of Marysville, close to Wheatland, where for months the local press railed against the IWW and the individual defendants, turning public opinion against them well in advance of the trial.[31] Just days after the shootings, the *San Francisco Call*, for instance, condemned the Wheatland workers as "anarchistic hoboes" that needed to be dealt with harshly by "order-loving elements of society [that] have learned the lesson which may be drawn from the tragedy, and [should] defend themselves against the worthless element who threaten their destruction."[32]

Furthermore, eight of the jurors were growers from the region, and another worked for the Manwell family. Bagan and Beck were acquitted, while Suhr and Ford were convicted to life in prison. A relentless statewide solidarity campaign soon followed, separately pursued by both the IWW and the California State Federation of Labor, including an attempted IWW-led general strike during the following season's hops harvest.[33] Nevertheless, the two remained in prison for over a decade.

The level of brutality and repression did not prevent the strike from happening, but succeeded in cutting it short. From Wheatland, a hops strike spread from Fresno to San Francisco and Sacramento, reducing the crop's total value by 10 percent before the strike collapsed due to repression and the collapse of organization.[34] While the Wheatland events unleashed a wave of state repression against the IWW and their attempts to organize farmworkers, it also had two secondary effects. The conditions of migratory labor were brought out into public light, contributing to the establishment of the California Commission on Immigration and Housing. This agency introduced the first labor reforms to affect conditions in the field, if only to preempt the growing influence of the Wobblies. The Wheatland strike also set the stage for the launch of the AWO 400, which demonstrated to migrant workers across the land that the IWW was ready and willing to take on the mighty growers.

The conditions of Mexican workers in agriculture during the first two decades of the twentieth century garnered little attention in the press of the time, except to condemn them for participating in IWW activities. As an article in the *Literary Digest* lamented in the standard tone of paternalistic racism of the day:

> Despite their good qualities, [Mexicans] are . . . illiterate and grossly misinformed about the United States. Accordingly . . . I.W.W. agitators find it comparatively easy to play upon their ignorance and to convince them the United States is a tyrannical country. We must remember that the only government of which they have any knowledge is one of license and misrule. The church missions working among the Mexicans throughout the Southwest are striving valiantly to combat this sinister propaganda, but the government should recognize the necessity for such efforts and tackle the problem on a big scale.[35]

Mexican agricultural workers increased as a percentage of the migratory workforce in California, while further efforts to organize unions in the fields were abandoned until the late 1920s.

Chapter 19
Socialists and Mexican Miners in Colorado

"If labor was united as it should be, there would be no state militia, armed with the most modern weapons of warfare, to create a reign of terror and to awe and intimidate men who are protesting against economic injustice."
—**"Industrial Solidarity Must Come,"** *Miner's Magazine*, 1914

ntensification of class conflict created the conditions for significant advances in class consciousness among industrial workers, which by the early twentieth century was developing in contradistinction to the dominant ideas of the working class at the time. The confluence of three factors led to a growing rejection of narrow craft exclusionism and electoral reformism: the defeats and severe weakening of craft unionism by aggressive industrial capitalists, unwilling to embrace the overtures of class collaboration by the AFL; the failure of the Socialist Party strategy of capturing state power through the electoral process; and the growth of radicalism among immigrant workers who brought their own political traditions, were marginalized by AFL, and were increasingly targeted by the state for persecution or removal. Furthermore, international events influenced the trajectory of political development. The Mexican Revolution brought the prospect of wide-scale revolt to the forefront of class consciousness, while the Russian Revolutions of 1905 and 1917 significantly altered conventional Socialist thought about the path to socialism. It is within this latter context that Mexican radicals and workers in the US changed the discourse of left-wing politics.

In response to capitalists' attempts to assert complete control over the conditions of work, the character of labor struggle at the point of production began to change. Labor historian David Montgomery describes a process of radicalization in which workers began to transcend the ideological limitations of the leadership in both the AFL and Socialist Party. As the AFL and Socialist Party moderates continued to focus electoral contests as the primary arena for working-class politics (vis-à-vis the Democratic or Socialist Party candidates), significant layers of workers began to reject a purely political strategy and shift the focus of struggle to the shop floor.

In resisting the employers' efforts to degrade skilled laborers' traditional control over working conditions, they began to engage in defensive "control strikes." This included a new array of forms of resistance, including enforcement of work rules, union recognition, discharge of unpopular foremen or retention of popular ones, regulation of layoffs or dismissals, and actions of sympathy with other groups of workers.[1] Significantly, the broadening of the class struggle also opened up a way for radicals to

develop new ideas for how to unite a vast, heterogeneous workforce composed of different racial, national, and ethnic groups.

Even more significant were the stirrings of industrial action and an ethnically
heterogeneous workforce in the mining industry. Railroads linked western boomtowns to national and international markets, also transporting and distributing workers across the map. By 1905, an estimated 595,000 miners across the country were
extracting the coal across thirty-one states to meet the growing needs of "railroads,
blast furnaces, rolling mills, shipyards, and homes across the country."[2] The role of
miners in producing the lifeblood of industrial capitalism gave them significant leverage against the operators, which they used to build the unions that served as the prototypes for point-of-production militancy and industrial unionism. Industrywide
strikes became common by the end of the nineteenth century, as unions attempted to
coordinate large-scale action as a form of symmetric power to counter armed power,
divide-and-conquer tactics, and the disproportionate influence and control that mine
operators wielded within local and state government. Coalfield-wide strikes in Colorado were launched in 1884–1885, 1894, 1901, 1903–1904, and 1913–1914.[3] While the
individual strikes produced mixed results, they compelled the state to intervene and
mitigate the most oppressive and antagonistic aspects of labor exploitation. The state
legislature created the Office of State Inspector of Coal Mines, the Bureau of Labor
Statistics, and the State Board of Arbitration. Furthermore,

> [t]he legislature also passed laws that allowed miners to hire check weigh-men,
> banned the use of scrip, eliminated screens when weighing coal, and instituted
> biweekly paydays; in 1899, the legislature rewarded workers with a law establish-
> ing an eight-hour workday for mine, mill, and smelter workers.[4]

Despite these reforms, the operators' influence and power over state politics worked
to limit the scope of enforcement.

The United Mine Workers (UMW) was formed in 1890 through the fusion of scattered Knights of Labor mining assemblies and the AFL-affiliated National Federation of
Miners and Mine Laborers.[5] In Colorado mining, the Western Federation of Miners had
already established its base in the predominantly white camps of the "hard-rock" miners in the north and east, when the UMWA attempted to organize the "soft-rock" coal
camps along the southern border where the mining workforce was nationally, ethnically,
and linguistically heterogeneous. This necessitated a strategy for establishing cross-cultural communication and collaboration. Through this process, miner's groups worked
and lived closely together, became interdependent, and established a culture of unity
more resilient to the chauvinism and other tactics used to divide and conquer strikes and
union drives. When one group of workers engaged in worksite stoppages or other forms
of job action, they understood their success was dependent on support from others. Because of this, these miners had come to embrace a more inclusive form of unionism in
order to build the critical mass necessary to wage large-scale, coordinated struggles.[6]

Furthermore, they saw the need to build a national union that could coordinate
strike activity on a regional and national scale and muster the resources necessary to

counter the immense power of the operators, whose influence, direct collaboration against unionization, and rising class consolidation at the national level reflected in more overt support and backing of local, state, and federal government.[7] Corporate power was further underwritten by the backing of dominant finance capital. Bankers repeatedly demonstrated their willingness to collaborate in support of other branches of capital when faced with debilitating labor conflict. The geographical spread and expansion of mining and the consolidation of capitalist power on a regional and national scale led to reinvigorated efforts to organize the mining camps extending through the South and Southwest. This required a substantive break with practices that reinforced the primacy of white and native-born miners if any progress was to be made by the union.

After 1900, the expansion of mining into the South and Southwest led the industries to construct workforces drawing from local sources of labor and migrant workers. In southerly states such as Alabama, Kentucky, Tennessee, Virginia, and West Virginia, this included a large number of black workers; while in the southwestern states such as Colorado, Utah, Arizona, Nevada, and New Mexico, this included Mexicans and mexicano migrants. These mining camps were developed outside of the range of the existing unions, and employers aimed to keep it this way. Due to the late nineteenth-century patterns of racial unionism, they were neglected by earlier union efforts, leading to their isolation and the development of the dual character of mining. The racial marginalization of black, Mexican, and Asian miners allowed for employers to stratify work, camps, and company towns along racial lines. During times of labor strife, they could manipulate these divides to undermine the unity and solidarity essential for strike or union drives to succeed.

While racial and national chauvinism proved a potent weapon against interracial and international union organizing, a new generation of union radicals influenced by socialism began to confront these self-defeating barriers. The UMW built on the Marxist framework inherited from the left wing of the Knights of Labor and put into action industrial methods based on organizing all who worked "'in and around the mines,' regardless of race, color, creed, or nationality."[8] Their efforts were aided by the particular geographic character of the mines, which created

> the special feeling of unity among all mine workers engendered by the isolation of the mining towns. Usually cut off from direct communication with the outside world, these communities rarely developed more than two classes: the "company," with its manager, mine guards, and all-pervasive authority on the one hand, and the workers, whether machinists, coal loaders, or whatnot, on the other.[9]

A new generation of miner leaders learned from the practices of the employers that the union efforts would fail if they accepted the "color line" drawn by the bosses. Bolstered by socialist tenets, which became more widely embraced within the working class in the first decade of the twentieth century, these leaders sought to include all workers in the union. They also developed the practice of appealing to those marginalized groups exploited as strikebreakers. In the process, they built up the ranks of a multiethnic mining workforce that proved resilient over time to the racialized divide-and-conquer strategies employed so adroitly by the operators in previous years.

Socialist Miners

By the turn of the twentieth century, corporate capital exercised effective control over the two political parties on a national scale, and came to dominate or influence electoral structures down to the local municipality. For many socialists, this dampened enthusiasm for the possibility of building workers' power through the ballot box. At the turn of the twentieth century, the leadership of the Western Federation of Miners had reoriented toward the ballot box. Miners formed a significant portion of the population in mining states. As Mark Wyman points out,

> [t]he 1900 Census reported that miners and quarrymen formed the following percentages of the gainfully employed in the major metal-mining states and territories: Montana 15.1 percent (17,387 miners and quarrymen); Arizona 14.9 percent (7,497); Nevada 13.8 percent (2,741); Colorado 13.7 percent (29,957); Idaho 11.7 percent (7,318); Utah 8.3 percent (7,028); New Mexico 6.8 percent (4,548); and California 4.2 percent (26,891). Relatives, merchants, and others dependent upon miners could swell these totals, adding to the miners' dominance of their own districts.[10]

Union locals across mining towns throughout the West had enjoyed success in putting miners and their allies into local office, raising the prospect of wielding working-class voting power to transform the state into a vehicle for labor power. Nevertheless, the miners discovered that this power was ephemeral. Acting through State Federations of Labor, miners' unions in Arizona, Colorado, and Utah were instrumental in promoting eight-hour workday legislation. In response, industrial capitalists began to organize opposition through the nationally dominant Republican and Democratic Parties.

In 1902 the Colorado labor movement led by the Western Federation of Miners succeeded in the passage of a popular referendum empowering the state legislature to enact an eight-hour law. Despite the overwhelming support, the legislature refused to act. The new Republican governor, James Peabody, was elected that year with the support of the mine operators, and spearheaded resistance to the eight-hour day and the WFM. Along with the "Citizens' Alliance," and local business-owner associations, the state began to act more aggressively on the side of capital through the use of the National Guard to discipline the WFM. With the legal path to the eight-hour day blocked, miners went out on strike across the mine camps owned by the Colorado Fuel and Iron Company (CF&I), beginning the Colorado Coal Wars in 1903–1904, and again in 1913–1914. These strikes took on a more combative form, in which miners and operators were fighting over control of the mines and conditions of work. The miners' strikes became touchstones for intense and bloody wars, going far beyond traditional work stoppages.

Through their experiences, the miners' unions had moved in an increasingly radical direction based on the exigencies of class struggle and open support for socialism. Under increasingly radical leadership, the WFM broke away from the craft unionism, nationalist politics, and class collaboration metastasizing in the AFL. The WFM acquired a class-war outlook through bitter lessons learned from defeats in the strikes of 1894–1897, as the state moved into open alliance with capital against labor. Miners shed the "producerist" conception of the state as inherently neutral and fundamentally democratic under capitalism. A burgeoning class-war outlook was also buoyed by the recurring use of the National Guard as the strikebreaker of last resort, the ranks of whom, especially the officers, were drawn heavily from the white middle and upper classes. For the largely immigrant workers, the direct manner by which mine operators could leverage their political connections to the statehouse to "send in the troops" became apparent. In fact, between 1879 and 1929, the Colorado National Guard was sent in to suppress coal field strikes on sixteen different occasions.[11]

Confronting disproportionate capitalist power within the corridors of electoral power, many union organizers and militants looked to socialist politics as a means to construct workers' power. By the mid-1890s, some union leaders developed a critique of rising industrial capital and moved toward socialist solutions, rejecting the Democratic and Republican Parties they traditionally backed. As early as 1894, the *United Mine Workers Journal* concluded in its electoral analysis: "It makes no difference to us working people whether the Democrats or Republicans are at bat, so long as Wall Street controls the game."[12] That year the UMW broke with the Democrats and endorsed the Populist Party. After the founding of the Socialist Party in 1901, many within the union hierarchy became active members. Reformists within the UMW leadership looked to the Socialist Party and its electoral strategy of improving the living conditions of workers through electoral gains, while more radical organizers at the local level drew from socialist principles to inform organizing and strike strategy. Socialist doctrine offered the most cogent organizing principles that could be applied in the coal fields.

Socialist organizers and prominent orators such as Eugene Debs gave speaking tours through the mining camps to popularize Marxist doctrine and built solidarity campaigns and raised funds during strikes. Prominent socialists were regular attendees and keynote speakers at UMW conventions. While the national leadership remained aloof from the rising Socialist Party, significant regions were led by active members and sympathizers. The Illinois, Indiana, and Pittsburgh district presidents, for instance, were members of the Socialist Party, representing about 150,000 members, or half the union's national total.[13] Members of the UMW wrote for the party press, published socialist tracts of their own, and were delegates to Socialist conventions. Socialists in the UMW played a key role in passing a resolution within the UMW Convention in 1909, which called for "the necessity of public ownership and democratic operation of the means of production and exchange . . . so that every man and woman willing to work . . . [could have] free access to the means of life and get the full social value of his product."[14]

Local UMW organizers in immigrant-majority coal regions, such as Colorado, were less focused on electoral campaigns than they were on applying the Marxist principles of class struggle and internationalist solidarity. As much as 75 percent of the population in bituminous coal-mining regions were racially segregated or immigrant (and mostly noncitizen), making the vote less relevant. Here union organizing along industrial lines, uniting diverse ethnic groups, and coordinating class struggle were more significant. This radicalism from below occurred even as the national leadership of the UMW and the conservative elements of the Socialist Party moved toward accommodation with the chauvinism and discriminatory orientation of the AFL. These two approaches help explain the popularity of socialism among the different groups of miners. They received significant electoral support in mining regions where the mining workforce was predominantly citizen and white; and ideological support in those areas where socialism translated into more effective strike strategy.[15]

Rejecting the SP's rightward-moving reformist notions hitched to the political outlook of conservative white craft workers and middle-class professionals, the miners began to look for allies elsewhere. Building a broad-based working-class organization that could contest power at the point of production now necessitated organizing the previously marginalized and excluded workers. In mining, Mexican workers were key to this strategy.

This shift in orientation was also influenced by the active participation and resolute militancy of Mexican and immigrant miners in the throes of insurrectionary class struggle across the West beginning in the 1890s. After the Mexican-led Clifton-Morenci strike of 1903 in Arizona and the participation of Mexican and immigrant miners in the Colorado labor wars, these mining unions began to actively embrace interethnic unionism. The strategy to actively organize and unite all workers based on the radical Knights of Labor mantra "an injury to one is the concern of all" was less a philosophical imperative, as it became an act of necessity for victory.

For labor radicals, the effort to unite the whole working class into a common organization was paramount. The outbreak of the Colorado Labor Wars of 1903–1904 was the first significant attempt to spread a strike throughout the industry. By the end of 1903, WFM-led union-recognition strikes of smelter workers in Colorado City, Denver, Durango, and Pueblo sparked sympathy strikes in the hard-rock mines of Cripple Creek. Simultaneously, strikes led by the UMW around various demands, including the eight-hour workday, spread throughout the collieries in the south of the state, including in Las Animas and Huerfano Counties. Miners in the coal mines in the northern part of the state also walked off the job. While the labor wars were ultimately defeated by a combination of factors including intense state repression, violence, and leadership treachery, they gave the first glimpses of the enormity of power miners could wield vis-à-vis the operators if unified in concerted action and solidarity across regional, racial, and ethnic lines.[16]

Mexican Displacement, Class Formation, and the Rise of Colorado Mining

After the Mexican-American and Civil Wars, industrial capitalists established their firm control over the nation-building project. Western and southern regions of the country were thrown open to accelerated capitalist speculation, led by eastern investors eager to establish mining, railroad, and agricultural empires. Unlike in the East, large-scale industrial developments did not evolve gradually, but were superimposed on largely pastoral and sparsely populated regions. Without a substantial autochthonous workforce, one had to be created artificially.

As with their compatriotas in Arizona and New Mexico, the initial formation of a mining workforce in Colorado included native Mexicans and mexicano immigrants. The history and experience of these miners became intertwined with the efforts to build the first miners' unions throughout the region. Like sedimentary rock, the industrial mine labor force was built in layers, with indigenous groups forming a core followed by later waves of migrants. Class formation in the mining regions of southern Colorado begins with the displacement of native peoples and Mexican landowners and the mass importation of migrant and immigrant labor.

Capitalist speculators into New Mexico and Colorado followed quickly on the heels of the US conquest and military occupation. Shortly after Colonel Stephen Watts Kearney and the "US Army of the West" captured Santa Fe in 1846, waves of Anglo merchants, investors, and schemers poured in as well. Congress refused to recognize Mexican and indigenous land-tenure relations in 1851, creating an expensive, labyrinthine, and corrupted process for retaining title, the most precious acreage and landholdings became targeted for expropriation. After the Civil War, displacement was expedited through various legal and semi-legal means.[17] For some, the inevitability of land loss led them to sell quickly and cheaply.

The most coveted regions for mining development were Mexican-era land grant zones spreading across the San Luis Valley straddling the New Mexico and Colorado Border. Distributed prior to the war to Mexican landowners between 1832 and 1843, these grants included the Tierra Amarilla, Conejos, Sangre de Cristo, Las Animas (Vigil and St. Vrain), Nolan, and the Beaubien-Miranda grant (later renamed the Maxwell Grant). The Maxwell Grant was one the largest and most prized regions, 1.7 million acres of land stretching from northern New Mexico across southern Colorado. This territory later fell into the hands of the CF&I mining company, the titan of western US coal production.[18]

When precious metals and coal were discovered in the region, capitalist investors moved in quickly. By 1867, at least fifteen mining companies had moved into the New Mexico and Colorado region, purchasing claim rights throughout the region of the Maxwell Grant. Railroad networks expanded, linking local agricultural regions to national and international markets. By the early 1870s, the Kansas Pacific Railway linked Colorado to the national rail grid while a series of connecting rail lines linked the southern coalfields to major economic centers throughout the Southwest. Aside from increasing coal production, it also catalyzed the rise of agricultural markets and increased competition, as land itself became commoditized and systematically taxed.

Maxwell used this shifting balance of power to cajole other Mexican landowners in the region, who lacked sufficient capital, technology, territorial and federal political connections, and access to banking credit to withstand pressure to relinquish their land in advance of aggressively expanding capitalist industry. By 1870, what became the Maxwell Grant had grown to a massive 1.7 million acres, for the paltry sum of about $50,000.[19] After the federal government officially recognized the grant, Maxwell sold the land to a syndicate of railroad investors linked to the New Mexico Santa Fe Ring for $1.3 million. This began a twenty-year process to evict over five hundred long-standing Mexican farmers, miners, and more recently arrived Anglo homesteaders who had moved onto the land.

The company sought to completely commoditize the land, parceling it out for railroad construction, mining, and other capital-intensive endeavors. The struggle over the land formally ended in 1894, when the Supreme Court affirmed the claims of capitalist investors, with many of the displaced mexicanos from the grant joining the growing ranks of mine labor in the region. In 1901, the Maxwell Grant Company then sold the northern portion of the grant to the Colorado Fuel and Iron Company (CF&I). The company became the largest employer and coal operator in Colorado, with its operations concentrated in the southeastern corner of the state in Los Animas and Huerfano Counties. These two mining counties were responsible for about half of Colorado's coal production by 1923 (5 million of 10 million tons) and contained the largest concentration of Mexican American and mexicano miners.[20]

Many of the southern coal fields in Colorado now owned by the CF&I were located in or near traditional Mexican pueblos that predated US expansion and economic colonization. These pastoral communities developed a regional farming and ranching network by the middle of the nineteenth century, and grew as a result of northward-moving migration from New Mexico. With the expansion of the mining industry and the discovery of vast coal deposits across the southern portion of the state, great amounts of capital investment accelerated the commoditization of land and the gradual displacement of Mexican and other truck farmers operating in the region.[21]

The coal industry continued to develop rapidly between 1885 and 1900, with production increasing from 110 million tons to 243 million tons and making the US the world's leading producer.[22] While most coal was extracted along a corridor stretching from Pennsylvania to Tennessee, Colorado became the largest coal-producing state in the West. Most of Colorado's coal deposits stretch out along a north-south axis; with northern fields concentrated in Boulder and Weld Counties, and southern fields concentrated in Huerfano and Los Animas counties. English miners from Cornwall and Wales were the initial migrants in the region in the 1860s, but more waves of migration would follow.

Mexican Americans moved into the southern Colorado coal camps from New Mexico as early as the 1870s and continued in a steady stream through the 1890s. Between 1900 and 1910, eleven thousand Nuevomexicanos moved into southern Colorado to mine or work in supporting industries.[23] Migrant workers from Sonora and Chihuahua also began to arrive in significant numbers by the turn of the century, joining with other groups arriving in rhythm with labor demand from southern and eastern Europe and Japan. After railroads established connections between Colorado to Northern Mexico, the migration of Mexican workers increased into the industrial and agricultural zones of the state. By the early 1920s, five thousand Mexican American and mexicano railroad workers lived and worked in the state, populating the region along the lines linking southern Colorado to Texas.[24]

Thousands migrated into the beet-sugar growing regions, while others moved into the coal camps along the southern border. It was in these coal camps where migrants joined autochthonous populations and successive waves of earlier migration to establish large Mexican communities and mining traditions. Due to the centrality of this mining workforce, especially in the counties Huerfano and Los Animas, less-intensive forms of segregation more characterized life in the mines on contrast to the "white man's camps" in other parts of the state.

For Mexicans, the higher wages paid in the coal fields, in parity with Europeans, was also an attractive alternative to the lower "Mexican wage," ubiquitous across the Southwest. While numbers fluctuated over time, an estimated total Mexican American and mexicano miners together comprised up to 15 percent of the total mining workforce in the CF&I coal mines of Las Animas County by 1915.[25] By August 1918, approximately 20 percent of all CF&I miners were Mexican or mexicano, and increasing to an estimated 33 percent (5,000) of all miners by 1924.[26] In neighboring Huerfano County, an estimated 60 percent (12,000) of the total population of 18,000 were Mexican American or mexicano, with this population comprising up to 30 percent of the population in the mining camps.[27]

Over the first decade of the twentieth century capital investment continued to pour into the region. The rapid rise of the Colorado coal industry was driven by increasing demand for its high-grade bituminous coal, essential for the production of the nation's expanding railroad networks, rapidly multiplying in the West. Led by the Rockefeller and Gould family empires, these investment cartels formed the largest coal-mining complex, CF&I, by 1903. CF&I, along with its smaller corporate counterparts that comprised the "coal operators" in the south, established near-absolute control over all aspects of coal production and the lives of the workforce; and further extending into coal towns, the press, and over local government. As historian F. Darrell Munsell describes:

> Coal operators in the southern coalfield did everything in their power to gain control over all local public officials, from county clerks to sheriffs and their deputies on up to judges. As allies of the coal operators, the sheriffs of the [southern coal counties] determined the jury lists for district courts. The same was true for coroners' juries, which, under the direction of coroners who had long played cheap politics, were part of the companies' political machine.[28]

In the great strikes of the early twentieth century, the miners had to go up against not only the companies and their despised private "mine guards," but also a quasi-corporate state that used every legal form of manipulation and physical form of repression in its vast arsenal.

Chapter 20

Mexican Miners in the Colorado Coal Wars

*"How many more women and children must die in order that John D.
Rockefeller may have peace to exploit the workers in Colorado and Mexico?"*
—*International Socialist Review,* "A Letter from the Front in Mexico"

Socialist UMW organizers and miners interested in winning strikes began to recalibrate their ideas toward race. This was aided by the militancy of Mexican, black, and immigrant workers themselves. At the margins of exclusion, they formed their own organizations, launched their own strikes, and demonstrated a willingness to forge cross-cultural bonds to coordinate action in resisting their common conditions of exploitation. For the radicals within the nascent mineworkers' unions seeking to counter the power and influence of the operators, the inclusion of Mexicans, blacks, and the diverse array of immigrants in southern and western mining became paramount for the future of the union.

The geographic isolation, sparse autochthonous population, and rapid growth of southern Colorado mining meant that the formation of a sufficient workforce relied heavily on labor importation through immigration. From 1880 to 1910 substantial economic investment necessitated labor recruitment in the eastern part of the US, Mexico, Europe, and Asia. Labor importation continued in other forms after initial class formation. One reason included the high turnover rate due to dangerous working conditions. Another, more conniving reason became the recruitment and installment of outside workers to undermine local union-organizing drives and break strikes. As a result of these infusions of migratory labor, no fewer than thirty nationalities comprised the ranks of the mining workforce by the turn of the twentieth century.[1]

The workforce was further divided by patchworks of racial segregation and exclusion. Like in Arizona, many camps throughout the northern region were "white only." In southern Colorado, there was more integration, especially in the areas with large Mexican populations. Even in these camps, varied forms of racial discrimination were built into labor relations to buttress local hierarchies. For instance, the company promoted white English speakers into foremen or other managerial positions and provided this group with more on-the-job privileges. Local law enforcement and mine guards, dependent on the company for their positions, were primarily white English speakers and repositories of the most virulent racism. The latter were also the primary enforcers of white supremacy and racial discrimination in the mines and in larger society. During strikes or organizing drives they attempted to inflame racial sentiments by appealing to white supremacy or singling out other ethnic groups for harsher treatment.[2] The realities of semi-integrated work and life in these camps provided the union a platform by which to urge solidarity against these practices.

In the small towns and mining camps in Las Animas and Huerfano County, for instance, the workers commonly lived, worked, and sent their kids to the same schoolhouses. In these camps there were higher rates of integration, with Mexican miners taking up leadership positions within the union and other rank-and-file organizations created during the course of strikes. In some cases, camp loyalties were more significant than racial or national loyalties. Campwide parties and dances were events where different groups would share food and music, and form social bonds. Nevertheless, it was still common that within some camps the families of Mexican, black, and Asian workers were excluded or internally segregated, and in some mining areas local Mexican Americans and mexicanos were not hired at all.[3] Various forms of racial discrimination were maintained through the racial division of labor and segmentation within the workplace, creating a highly contradictory and volatile environment where both racism and unity could co-exist depending on the temperature of class antagonism. Prejudice and discrimination tended to regulate behavior under static conditions, as the state, company, and racist organizations maintained primacy of place in capitalist society.

For instance, in 1913 Colorado state law mandated rigorous examinations for promotion within the industry, but the tests were conducted in highly technical English only, which was used as a pretext to deny promotion to Mexicans.[4] Mexicans were typically the first fired or transferred out to maintain the racial hierarchy that gave primacy to Anglo miners. In the steel mills, Mexicans were deprived of attaining "skilled positions" and shut out entirely from management. Segregation in all facets of mining life also carried into social spaces and was reinforced by the activities of the Ku Klux Klan, which had established branches throughout the region with the tacit support of the mine operators.[5] Ubiquitous norms of racial prejudice reinforced notions of privilege and superiority among many white miners, who could be turned against the others under normal conditions.

The production and maintenance of racial subdivisions within the mining workforce and segregation within the larger regional population served a useful function. It contributed to the development and maintenance of a reserve army of labor that could be manipulated by the mining companies to undermine worker unity during strikes or other job actions. Opposition to unionization and the rejection of strike solidarity also came from newly introduced European American workers who could be enticed to cross picket lines.[6] Despite being the norm under these conditions, the hegemony of structural racism was challenged by countervailing tendencies within the features of the work itself that created periodic crisis and waves of resistance.

For instance, the nuclei of organization and networks of solidarity were formed out of necessity by daily life on the job, aided by the need to resist the employer offensives to drive down wages (especially following periods of market collapse during capitalist crisis), and to develop point-of-production demands for better working conditions. Put in other terms, racism as a means to divide work groups was counterposed by the practical need for the same workers to collaborate and coordinate to send multiple moving parts forward in conjunction.

The boom and bust cycle in coal production made the industry unstable and subject to periods of great expansion followed by sharp recession. As historian Thomas Andrews explains, the eruption of strikes usually followed on the heels of recession and the attempt by employers to push the costs of failure onto the miners:

> Demand for coal increased exponentially between the 1870s and 1910s, yet industry fortunes nonetheless declined whenever hard-rock mining, railroad construction, and urban expansion veered from boom to bust. Coal companies reduced output and cut prices during economic downturns such as the panic of 1883–1884. Strikes ensued as operators, pressed by financial challenges of their own and emboldened by the ready availability of workers discharged from other industries, tried to cut labor costs.[7]

To sustain the practice of managing downturns, the employers turned to their own forms of collaboration to keep unions out of their camps. This included sharing information and resources, and standing together to prevent any strike or unionization victory from inspiring other camps across the state.

The dangerous conditions of mine work and the necessity for collaboration and mutual aid to ensure survival forged a countercurrent to the bosses' divisive racism. Death in the mines was a common occurrence, often due to company negligence. Between 1884 and 1912, 1,708 miners lost their lives in the south Colorado mines, which were considered the most dangerous in the nation.[8] For the mine operators, the unwillingness to invest in safety infrastructure in the mines, even after repeated disasters, was considered a factor for maintaining maximum profitability. Instead of costly investments in safety equipment and the implementation of work rules, which ate into profits derived from maximum exploitation, it was more cost effective for the management to invest in the infrastructure of local government. In the aftermath of accidents, law enforcement, local courts and judges, and even coroners would line up behind the company and absolve it of wrongdoing.[9]

Under these conditions, high rates of transience persisted. Those who did not drift away in search of safer work developed a variety of techniques to improve their conditions. To increase their chances for survival, miners learned and applied different techniques into their daily work routines involving forms of cooperation, safety practices, and collective vigilance. Nevertheless, the constant threat of gas poisoning, mine collapse, and respiratory disease took its toll, especially as the company managers constantly deployed new strategies to increase production. When tensions reached a tipping point, workers shut down production in protest, making strikes a regular feature of the mining industry. This practical urgency seeded the soil for interethnic unity and coordinated strike action, or as stated by Andrews, "[l]ike the coal dust that blackened white and brown skins alike, workscape dangers held the power to overcome race, ethnicity, and other distinctions."[10]

The Radical Roots of Interethnic Unionism

Strikes in Colorado coal are as old as the industry itself, as was the effort to divide workers along ethnic and racial lines to break them. As early as April 1881, Mexican "Penitente" miners at the Engleville mine in Los Animas County went on strike for two weeks after refusing to work during a religious holiday. This was followed by a string of walkouts throughout the month by Mexican laborers working within the mines who were inspired to follow suit to call for higher wages.[11] When the next wave of strikes hit mining in 1884, led by newly formed Knights of Labor chapters, the coal operators deployed racial antagonism as a strategy.

In the years before the big coal boom, mine operators were already honing their skills in divide-and-conquer tactics, such that the conscious employment of national and racial antagonism created a model of success for other capitalists by the turn of the century. Strikes in the 1860s by English immigrant workers were broken by the importation of Irish and US-born strikebreakers from other parts of the state. By the 1870s the expansion of the railroad hubs linking southern Colorado to a national and international grid made it even easier to bring in strikebreakers from different parts of the country and Mexico. A strike led by local Mexican miners in 1879 at a coal camp in Engleville had been broken when Mexican immigrants were brought in as strikebreakers.

Strikes organized by the Knights of Labor and led by Mexicans and Italians in southern mines in 1884–1885 were broken after the owners brought Italians from the East and African American workers from the South by train to cross the picket lines. By the late 1890s, newly arrived central, southern, and eastern Europeans were used against strikes throughout the state, and so on. Each cycle of conflict coincided with different ethnic or national groups being brought into the area to break or disrupt organizing drives, often without the incoming group having previous knowledge. Some strikebreakers refused to work upon learning of the strike, while others willfully participated. Once employed, these ethnically diverse groups of workers became part of the permanent workforce upon termination of the strike. In fact, strikebreakers from one era became the strikers of the next, and new strikebreakers were brought in.[12]

The structured fragmentation of the workforce became institutionalized by the coal operators. As Rick Clyne explains:

> The operators believed that such a diverse ethnic mix worked in their favor, for evidence indicates that they tried to manipulate ethnic and language differences to discourage worker solidarity. Lamont M. Bowers, CF&I's Colorado manager in the early 1900s, admitted that the company consciously mixed nationalities, so that "when too many of one nationality [got] into a given district . . . [CF&I] would go adjust their men so that no very large percent in any mine could communicate with the others."[13]

The manufacture of a workforce with multiple ethnic and linguistic differences was an investment against unions. As one government official explained, "The purpose was, of course, to produce in advance a condition of confusion of tongues, so that no tower upon which they might ascend the heavens could be erected."[14] In other words, ethnically and linguistically diverse groups were mixed down to the work crew so as to discourage discussion of even the smallest common grievance.

During the subsequent strikes of 1894, and 1903–1904, some Chinese and Japanese, large numbers of southern and eastern Europeans, and Mexican migrants were brought in to break strikes. When strikes were upended, the new groups were kept on, weaving in additional ethnic groups into a complex mosaic of nationalities and languages. By 1903, CF&I employed around 16,000 people in mining and steelmaking, of which two-thirds were immigrants.[15] Company census figures list total workforce demographics as:

> 3,700 "Americans," 3,500 Italians, 2,000 Austrians, 1,000 "Mexicans" (including local[s] . . . and recently arrived Mexican nationals), 900 Irish, 800 English, 600 Slavs, 600 "Colored," 400 Hungarians, 400 Welsh, 300 Scots, 300 Germans, 250 Swedes, 200 Poles, 200 Greeks, 150 French, 100 Swiss, 50 Belgians, 50 Finns, 25 Bohemians, and 25 Dutch.[16]

When workers managed to overcome these divides, or when mine unions made inroads, mine operators developed other tactics to break strikes and discipline the miners. With their expanding influence, for instance, they could martial the full force of local and state government, business and vigilante "citizen committee" groups, law enforcement agencies, and private guards against the miners. Under these conditions, the survival and growth of mine unions in the face of vicious repression led to ideological and organizational evolutionary divergences from the rest of organized labor.

Socialists and militants within the unions pressed for the need to unite all miners across racial and ethnic lines against more backward and conservative elements within their ranks. Accumulated experience of the need for unity, at the least to maintain unity on picket lines, created the fertile ground for these union organizers to take initiative. Many of those sent in as organizers had gained experience in previous strikes and were influenced by socialism and labor radicalism, which bolstered the impulses toward seeking higher forms of class unity. Ultimately, the unions began to hire organizers directly from the ranks of the different ethnic groups, opening the door for mass coordinated organizing and action.

In the face of significant opposition, the intense nature of the class conflict created the possibility for these unions with conservative and racist foundations to make significant antiracist advances in increments, and in relation to the lessons learned from previous defeats. This progress was aided by the radical traditions of the workers themselves, who drew from their own experiences and world views as a means to overcome divisions. This was also facilitated by the actions and ideas of the Mexican American, mexicano, and other immigrant mineworkers themselves.

Learning from Struggle: The Colorado Coal Wars

The successive defeats culminating in the strike of 1903 were a pivotal part of the mine unions' evolution on the questions of racial and ethnic unity and strike strategy. The companies, led by CF&I, were determined to keep the unions out of the mines at all costs, and used all means at their disposal to do so. For instance, between 1900 and 1903, the company discharged between six and eight thousand new recruits fingered by company spies as union sympathizers.[17]

Solidarity and creative militancy were the only way to overcome an alliance of corporations that operated with impunity. Union organizers acknowledged their incapacity to organize effective strikes without overcoming these divisions, and to resist the forceful strike-breaking methods of the companies. They developed forms of solidarity that undercut the tensions and nurtured forms of collaboration between miner groups. While miners lost the strike of 1903, the defeat crystallized a set of lessons that set the stage for the insurrectionary strike ten years later.

The UMWA led a campaign to unionize the coal mines in Las Animas and Huerfano Counties, designated as District 15, in late 1903. When over ten thousand miners shut down the southern Colorado coal mines on November 9 there was a high level of solidarity between the predominantly European, Anglo, and Mexican miners. The miners showed widespread support for the UMWA's strike call, whose demands centered around a 20 percent wage increase and compelling the companies to comply with existing state law. The operators, the former banker-turned-Republican governor, James Peabody, and a coalition of 3,000 Colorado capitalists invested in the mining industry called the Citizens' Alliance colluded to crush the strike with force. Peabody called in 400 state troopers and declared martial law, assisted by 115 deputized mine guards and company employees, who were armed with guns purchased by the company.

The Citizens' Alliance raised the necessary funds to pay for the National Guard troops and deputies. Once in operation, they identified and arrested and beat 160 strike leaders, and subsequently deported 97 of them from the town. To exploit racial tension, they brought in black, Japanese, Chinese, and southern and eastern European strikebreakers without informing them that a strike was underway. They blocked townspeople and miner reinforcements coming in from other areas. The troops and deputies then evicted the families of strikers from company housing, while the coal-operator-owned press ran anti-strike stories to turn public opinion against the union. As one historian concluded, "The anti-union forces now had all of the power of the state at their disposal in their effort to combat organized labor. Within a month, those forces were unleashed against strikers in the central and southern Colorado coalfields. As a result the strike was broken and the UMWA defeated."[18] The defeat of the strike left a lasting impression. As many as six thousand more workers were fired and blacklisted for their participation in the strike.[19] The employers reveled in the belief that they had rid themselves once and for all of the union, and continued to flout even the most basic labor codes over the next decade.

Because the miners maintained unity, the company came to depend more actively on local non-mining populations and outside groups against the miners. In Colorado after the turn of the century, the companies employed local non-mining Mexicans and migrant workers brought in from Mexico. In the strikes of 1903, for instance, CF&I offered money and other incentives to these groups to act as strikebreakers, relying on the fact that most Mexicans were still excluded in other regions from the unions and maintained no knowledge of or connection to the unions.[20]

A developing culture of solidarity in the mining camps made this strategy less effective. Many Mexican strikebreakers refused to cross the picket lines in 1903, due to a sense of solidarity or perhaps fear upon encountering the militant and well-organized miners. In his analysis of the strike, Victor S. Clark noted that Mexican strikebreakers "would join the union when urged, and remain faithful to the labor cause so long as they were paid strike benefits."[21] Company management learned from this as well, seeing that racial manipulation to foster strike-breaking alone was insufficient to undermine the union efforts.

As a result, the companies instead relied more on the state to deploy the law and armed bodies to repress them. During the four-month strike, the state militia was stationed throughout the mining camps, and a veritable shadow army of armed guards was assembled through the deputization of company foremen, private detective agency gunmen, and anti-labor zealots from within the professional middle class and business elite. The company also leaned heavily on the state political apparatus to line up against the strikers. Historian Scott Martelle describes,

> the overt co-optation of local legal authority by mine operators, which, combined with the deputizing of Baldwin-Felts gunmen and mine guards, cemented the miners' hard-to-refute belief that the local political structure had been corrupted against them.[22]

After the defeat, it became clear to the miners that the political system was rigged in favor of the operators, and that they could leverage local, state, and federal agencies of the state against them.

State opposition led the miners to appeal for broader unity to counter the power of the state-capitalist alliance. This meant a conscious break with the traditions of racial segregation and occupational segmentation. Under these conditions, diverse ethnic populations of miners had to learn to replace long-standing traditions of racial tension and animosity fanned by the mine companies with creative forms of community-building and collaboration. The miners' unions had to adapt their orientation if they were going to overcome the preponderant power of the mine companies.

Learning pragmatic lessons from strike defeats was a significant factor in building interethnic unionism. This was also aided by the radical political traditions of some of the immigrant workers themselves, whose own experiences made it easier for interethnic unity to develop. Many Irish immigrants coming into Colorado in the late 1800s, for instance, brought with them radical nationalist traditions and organizational methods derived from active participation in anti-British colonial movements in their homeland. One group of Irish nationalists rooted in the working class was known as the Fenian Brotherhood.

In its efforts to build solidarity for the Irish national struggle at home and in the US, it had developed an integrationist orientation toward other class struggles, based on the experience of having to overcome religious and sectarian divides within Ireland in order to unite secular, Catholic, and Protestant workers against the British empire.

The group demonstrated solidarity with other groups opposing forms of national oppression, including support for black suffrage, as a means of building support for their own cause. As they professed, "Fenians are not interested in where a man was born, nor what his religious principles were . . . provided he was willing to enter into the cause of liberation of that long oppressed and abused people of Erin."[23] These politics influenced the formation of the Knights of Labor, which in turn influenced the DNA of the UMW.

Other migrants came from different regions of the world with different histories, with some miners bringing traditions of class struggle, militant unionism, armed struggle, and ethnic or national solidarity, enabling the possibility for unity in struggle. As historian Thomas Andrews describes:

> A surprising number of coalfield migrants sought refuge in the American Southwest from conflict-ridden borderlands in the Tirol, northern Mexico, Crete, and elsewhere. Also seeking refuge were African-Americans terrorized by the violence and repression of the Jim Crow South, Christian Slavs seeking to evade partitions and Ottoman oppression, radicals exiled from many homelands, and blacklisted unionists.[24]

Mexicans in the southern borderlands of Colorado brought with them the traditions of mutualistas, or fraternal mutual-aid associations. These organizations provided forms of material mutual aid where none was otherwise provided by the state, and served as a nexus for political action and cultural self-preservation. One such mutualista, the Sociedad Protección Mutua de Trabajadores Unidos (Mutual Protection Society of United Workers), was founded in 1901 in the southern Colorado Mexican community of Antonito and spread into seventy chapters throughout Utah, southern Colorado, and New Mexico. While membership was socially and politically heterogeneous, local concilios (lodges) constituted near the coal mining regions or other industrial centers could be used by Mexican workers in lieu of a formal union to coordinate workplace action when necessary.[25]

Mexican migrants from regions in the northern mining provinces had established the practice of moving across the border into southwestern mining camps for work. The circular migration patterns meant that many miners had experience in the great strikes of previous years, such as the one at Cananea in 1906.[26] Others came into contact with the Partido Liberal Mexicano, while a significant number of Mexican miners had joined the ranks of the revolutionary armies that formed after 1910, in particular the villista army (División del Norte). These traditions influenced the spread of radical unionism among Mexican miners from Sonora to southern Colorado.

The experience of 1903 and the reconstitution of a mining workforce that included working-class migrants with traditions of radicalism, mutual aid, military experience, and a deep-seated resentment toward the exploitative mining corporations and the racist and thuggish mine guards given license to rule over the workers set the stage for the explosive and insurrectionary strike of 1913. The UMW set out to organize the southern coal mines after success in winning the first union contracts, covering miners at seventeen companies in the northern "hard-rock" mines in 1908. In response to the UMWA gains, the southern coal operators took it upon themselves to counsel their northern counterparts on how to break the union and provided material and political support for their efforts in succeeding years. This convinced the UMWA that they could only secure their gains in the north if the south were also unionized.

Mexican miners among the armed Ludlow strikers

The Colorado Labor War of 1913

On September 23, 1913, an estimated 13,000 miners (93 percent of the total workforce) shut down CF&I operations across Las Animas and Huerfano counties in Southern Colorado, effectively cutting off the steel supply at a time of heightened demand on the eve of World War I.[27] The strike was the culmination of an ongoing battle for union recognition and control over the conditions of work, with miners joining together across ethnic and national lines to push back against increasing company control over all aspects of daily life. Strikers called for the enforcement of existing labor law, and demanded a 10 percent wage increase, and an end to unfair and illegal company labor practices, the company guard system, and payment in scrip.[28] Over the course of the fifteen-month conflict the strike evolved into an insurrectionary war, involving whole communities in and around the coal mines in open battle against a private, company-funded militia and forces of the state National Guard. This also included the families of the miners, an estimated 4,000 women and 9,000 children that were active participants in all stages of the labor war.[29]

After the strike commenced, the company gave the orders to evict the miners and their families if they supported the walkout. In response, the United Mine Workers Association (UMWA) purchased supplies and helped workers organize the creation of eight tent colonies outside of company property. The eight strike camps were strategically constructed at sites near the access points to the CF&I-owned coal mines in order to intercept trucked-in strikebreakers.[30] One of the largest and most strategic of these encampments was called the Ludlow Camp, with about two hundred tents housing twelve hundred miners and their families. These camps developed into mutual-aid communes, with a high level of social organization, collaboration, and democratic participation.

With memories of the 1903 strike in mind, the union leader on the ground, John Lawson, organized the camps along military lines, with each camp having a chain of command, police force, and an appointed captain for each of the different ethnic and linguistic groups. The union purchased and distributed hundreds of Winchester rifles and thousands of rounds of ammunition to defend the camps and the picket lines from the mine guards. Mexican miners and their families had a sizeable presence within the camps, with Mexicans among the elected camp leaders at five camps, including Ludlow.[31]

While a gendered division of labor was universal within the mining families, with the men working in the mines and women confined to domestic labor, the strike and uprising evolved into a united front between the men and their families. Women had a stake in the strike. While not union members, they had developed a class consciousness shaped by their own unique experiences. The struggle opened up space for them to assume leadership roles, become organizers and fighters, and assert themselves in different ways. The conditions of daily life in the company towns were shaped by the contours of power between the mining company and the miners.

Within the gendered division of labor, women had to learn to make ends meet within the closed company towns notorious for their high costs. When miners were killed, the women were thrown into conditions of poverty and uncertainty. According to state records, 730 children were left fatherless because of mining accidents between the years 1909 and 1913, with at least 438 of those children in Los Animas County alone.[32] This became the reality for most widows, especially as company coroners consistently absolved the CF&I of wrongdoing and relinquished them from liability.

A company guard was created, consisting of a motley assortment of former strikebreakers, soldiers of fortune, ex-policemen, and army deserters that roamed the towns and carried out company orders like a quasi–police force.[33] Typically white and nativist, these guards regularly targeted vulnerable women as a form of punishment or to incite fear and terror, especially during times of strikes or union drives. Under these conditions, women commonly endured sexual harassment, assault, and also instances of rape when their husbands were away in the mines.

As historian Priscilla Long has identified, the centrality of the family unit in the miners' struggle reflected in the demands of the strike:

> Two of the seven strike demands—one for the abolition of the notorious and criminal guard system which has prevailed in the mining camps . . . and another for the "right to trade in any store we please, and the right to choose our own boarding place and our own doctor"—related directly to the community as a whole. Three other demands—those pertaining to the miners' standard of living—would also have a direct impact on the conditions in the home.[34]

Within the strike camps, the women became the chief organizers. Food distribution, medical care, guard duty, and the organization of roving pickets were part of the daily distribution of tasks that involved the women, men, and children. Because of the high level of unity between the strikers and their families, the miner operators tried to break the strike from the outside.

In an effort to weaken striker unity, the CF&I strategists relied on the strategy of recruiting non-mining Mexicans from outside the area as strikebreakers, deputized sheriffs, and militia members. In most cases, they dispersed when confronted with the large encampments and resolute opposition of the Mexican miners and their families in the strike camps. Nevertheless, the wider Mexican community did divide over the strike. Those with mining history or family ties to the miners lined up in support of the strike, while many from the surrounding farm communities were recruited into the National Guard units created to suppress it.[35]

In one instance, a Mexican strikebreaker was killed in a confrontation with strikers from the tent colony near the predominantly Mexican town of Aguilar. While the strikebreaker, Pedro Armijo, was visiting his family in the town, he was met by a group of Mexican strikers from the same community. When a confrontation ensued, Armijo was run out of town, where he was later found shot dead. Militia members arrested a striking miner named Francisco Gonzales, who allegedly confessed to killing Armijo.[36]

Despite these divides in the larger society, the high degree of unity and mutual support that developed within the strike camps led to the dissipation of racial tensions, and a new spirit of solidarity redefined social relations. The union developed various methods to build broader unity and solidarity between the different ethnic groups. The union integrated locals within the coal camps at the turn of the century and hired organizers able to communicate in the different languages of the workers. In 1902, the union hired Mexican organizer Julian Gomez, followed by Italian and Greek organizers and others thereafter. Mexican and other immigrant-led locals grew throughout the region in subsequent years; they had about two thousand card-carrying members among the larger striking population.[37]

In the camps, the union sponsored open-air dances and live musical performances to bring the groups together. As one music historian noted:

> [M]usic in mining camps came from many origins: Welsh, Scottish, Irish, English, African American, Italian, Mexican, Hispanic. "When they began to express their feelings . . . , the miners adapted the bardic and minstrel arts which were part of their racial heritage."[38]

As part of this performance, Mexican miners brought the *corrido* into the mix, a popular musical form used to tell stories and register protest and struggle against injustice. This musical form originated in Mexico, became widely popular as a form of information-sharing and storytelling during the revolution, and spread throughout the Mexicano Southwest as part of the great labor migration. One miner who participated in the strike, Elias Baca, recalled fighting with scabs, helping to organize the camps, and then performing corridos as a chronicle of the strike. Baca, in fact, was later hired by the United Mine Workers union as a traveling musician who performed in Mexican and mixed-ethnicity mining camps across the West in an effort to build support for the union. In the process, he created some of the earliest known pro-union songs in Spanish, and helped launch a tradition of using corridos to help spread pro-labor solidarity and awareness within the mexicano and Mexican American working class.[39]

The development of interethnic solidarity made the tactic of sowing racial animosity to break strikes less effective. When small groups of African American, Mexican, and Japanese workers were brought in over the duration of the strike, the miners tried to convince them to turn back or join the strike instead of engaging in racial abuse. As it became clear that the traditional method of suppressing worker militancy through divide and rule wasn't working, the operators turned to physical violence.

In response to the strike, the sitting governor, a Democrat named Elias M. Ammons, refused to call out the National Guard. Elected with the support of the miners, he was reluctant to openly side with the companies, but gave the company a free hand to carry out its own anti-strike operations. In response, the company organized its own militia comprising mine guards, local sheriffs, and volunteers from the business community and professional middle class. In a show of ruling-class solidarity, a collection of prominent Denver bankers had promised to provide all of the necessary funds to maintain the militia until the strike was broken, although the state was required to pay the banks back. The company also brought in over a hundred members of the notorious Baldwin-Felts Detective Agency, many of whom had previous experience suppressing coal strikes in Virginia, and purchased eight machine guns and other arms and munitions to equip their troops. The agency and the militia set out to physically break the strike using tactics designed to terrorize and ultimately provoke violent confrontation, which could be used to justify state intervention on the side of the mine operators. As Mark Walker explains:

> The harassment took the form of high powered searchlights playing over the colonies at night, murders, beatings, and the use of the "death special," an improvised armored car that would periodically spray selected colonies with machine-gun fire. The purpose of this harassment was to goad the strikers into violent action, which would provide a pretext for the Colorado governor to call out the National Guard, thus shifting a considerable financial burden from the operators to the state.[40]

Faced with violence and provocation, the women supported the strike effort by developing more militant tactics. They participated in roving groups that would harangue scabs and militia members along the roads to the mines. They organized blockades to stop trains attempting to bring in strikebreakers, and engaged in melees with company guards and private detectives when under attack. On one occasion, when a trainload of strikebreakers was to be brought in, "the women brandished baseball bats, clubs with spikes driven through them, or sharpened branches . . . [and were] cursing in violent fashion."[41] Confronted with the prospect of a mass melee, the strikebreakers were sent back on the same train.

On October 24, a group of mine guards and sheriff's deputies fired directly into a crowd of unarmed miners, women, and children who were protesting their presence near one tent colony in Walsenburg, killing three miners. Enraged at the cold-blooded killings, and believing that this signaled an aggressive turn against the tent colonies, the miners retaliated. In a concerted early morning attack four days later, about three hundred miners descended upon two mine guard encampments in the vicinity, killing ten of the guards and losing two of their own during a fierce firefight that lasted for several hours. Amid the intensifying violence between the strikers and the Baldwin-Felts agents and company guards, the governor sent in a detachment of a thousand National Guard troops shortly after the reprisals. When troops arrived in the region, union rail men refused to take them into the war zone, leading to the commandeering of the train by Baldwin-Felts agents.[42]

The group included soldiers recently recalled from service in the US troop buildup along the Southwest border, who had potentially participated in the invasion and occupation of Veracruz, Mexico. They were brought in under the command of Adjutant General John Chase, a veteran of suppressing earlier miners' strikes in the state, and a notorious opponent of the mine worker unions. Upon their arrival, a "military district" was declared allowing for arrests without warrant, and the miners were ordered disarmed. In response, the miners buried all of their rifles in the hills, turning in only old, rusted, and dysfunctional junk, which included a child's toy pop-gun, to show their noncompliance.

The guard troops were ordered to prevent strikebreakers from entering until both sides agreed to negotiate, which the companies refused, but the guard troops clearly sided with the companies. Mine guards and company men were then drafted into the militia to give them more power, including the most notorious and hated figures. Chase made it clear through these early actions that the Guard was there to help break the strike. Under the cover of martial law imposed on the strikers, mine guards, local sheriffs, and armed citizens' committee members engaged in a dirty war against the strikers over a period of six months that included abductions, arbitrary arrests, mass jailing, beatings, torture, and the systematic demolition of the tent camps.

Some of the National Guard officers and private militia leaders had direct military experience and employed this against the strikers and their families. One notorious figure, Colorado National Guard lieutenant Karl Linderfelt, had established a sanguine reputation for his service in US colonial expansion in Asia. He participated in the repression of Filipinos during the US war of colonization in 1899 and joined with US irregular troops to crush the Boxer Rebellion in China in 1901. Later he returned to ply his trade in the Colorado labor wars of 1903–1904 and then again in 1913. The miners, for their part, also had experienced soldiers in their ranks. Recently arrived Greek workers included skilled veterans of the Balkan Wars, who made up a fierce fighting group that led most of the field battles. The ranks of the workers also included US veterans from the Spanish-American War and Italian participants in colonial wars in North Africa.

Despite the campaign of violence, the strike encampments held strong. Tensions reached a boiling point after a group of women was brutally attacked by militiamen on horseback. When Mary "Mother" Jones was arrested and detained after coming into the area to rally the strikers, the women from the camps organized a march to where she was being detained. The group of over a thousand women and children was blocked and attacked by company militiamen with fixed bayonets on their rifles. A melee ensued and the women fought back with sticks and bottles.[43] The men on horseback charged the women, wounding three with their bayonets and eventually arresting over one hundred of them. Upon hearing the news of the attack, the livid miners organized for a final showdown in the form of a coordinated military attack on the concentrated forces of the private militia forces and mine guards. As F. Darrell Munsell describes it:

> The riot aroused the passions of coalminers throughout the state and revived support for the strike . . . Hundreds of angry strikers decided to annihilate the militiamen and mine guards . . . The plan called for an attack, in which the Greek fighters and other miners would close in on the militia from all sides and destroy them with one mighty blow. Other groups of miners . . . quietly slipped into [the town of] Trinidad and unobtrusively manned the rooftops of business buildings. A hundred sharpshooters took up sniping positions around General Chase's headquarters. Hidden in buildings were detachments of twenty-five to thirty men ready to spring into action when the signal was given.[44]

The attack was called off at the last minute, when news reached the camps that the US Congress had approved a comprehensive investigation of the strike and surrounding events. All but two hundred of the state National Guard troops were pulled out in the belief that a fragile peace would hold while the investigation was conducted.

Before the National Guard troops were withdrawn in April, over 150 mine guards and company men were formed into two separate company-funded militias under newly appointed Guard leader Karl Linderfelt. A third company was formed, comprising "the most hardened strike-breakers," who went to work in the mines with their guns and militia uniforms.[45] In Guard uniform, or under Guard leadership, the militias and the Felts-Baldwin agents continued the war. They were well-stocked with heavy weaponry and more determined than ever to bring the strike to an end by all means possible and before the conclusion of the investigation. They routinely assaulted strikers, fired randomly into the camps, and committed other acts of violence to provoke a showdown that would justify the destruction of the tent colonies and dispersal of the miners and their families.

Ludlow Massacre

On April 20, 1914, these militias went on a violent rampage at the Ludlow camp, spraying machine gun and rifle fire into the encampment for several hours and setting the tents on fire. During the attack, many miners, women, and children fled the camp into the hills or took cover in foxholes along the perimeter that had been dug as refuge from the recurring gun attacks. The men had also dug pits beneath the tents as emergency shelters during the barrages. As was the pattern when under attack, some women and children not able to flee sought cover in these bunkers. During the attack, the intense and relentless volley of gunfire was aiming to kill. The mine guards and militiamen continued their fire sporadically for several hours, preventing the miners, nurses, and Red Cross volunteers from tending to the fallen.

Over the course of the attack, several tents caught on fire and were quickly consumed. As Maria Chavez, one of the striking women hiding in a camp foxhole, later testified, the mine guards spread the fire from tent to tent to make sure all of the dwellings were destroyed. After the camp was fully leveled, they then picked through the rubble, looting salvageable goods, money, jewelry, and other valuables.[46] It was in this ignoble endeavor that the looters made a macabre discovery.

Since these tents were large-framed dwellings with various hanging objects, makeshift furniture, and other heavy objects, when they collapsed they buried the covered pits and filled them with toxic smoke. Below one of these collapsed tents the militia members discovered two women and eleven children who had suffocated to death. Based on the coroner's records, among those killed were Patricia Valdez and four of her children: Elvira, 3 months old; Mary, 7; Eulalia, 8; and Rudolph, 9.

Survivors of the Ludlow Massacre

Six miners were also killed in the attack, including Louis Tikas, a Greek camp leader who was captured, beaten badly, and executed after returning to the tents in an attempt to rescue the buried.[47] Even though the deaths were ruled homicides, no one was ever charged for the murders.[48] The only operating press in the region not tied to the operators, the *Rocky Mountain News*, claimed that the militia gunman shot Tikas fifty-one times.[49] John Lawson, the UMWA executive leadership representative for District 15 and leader of the strike, claimed that as many as fifty women and children in the camp were unaccounted for after the fires, believing that the second round of fires were intentionally lit to burn evidence of the massacre.[50]

The massacre at Ludlow set off several days of intense armed conflict between miners and enraged community members against state troops and company militias. Miners throughout the state were called to arms by the leaders of the Colorado State Federation of Labor, the WFM, and the UMWA, and joined by others. Socialist journalist John Reed reported that "After Ludlow, doctors, ministers, hack drivers, drug store clerks, and farmers joined the fighting strikers with guns in their hands."[51] A call was made in Denver for a mass meeting of unionists to form a Workers' Defense League. The convocation included a rousing condemnation of the coal capitalists, claiming:

> The money masters, realizing that we will not surrender as long as life lasts, are resolved upon a campaign of utter annihilation. Of all those who labor, whether in mine, mill, shop or store, not one is safe from capitalism's savage menace. It is the turn of the miners today. Oh, brothers in other callings, it may be yours tomorrow. It is not a handful of coal diggers that have been marked down for slaughter; it is the right of the worker to better his condition that they mean to destroy. If Ludlow shall go unanswered it will be the death knell of human hope and human aspiration.[52]

Out of the meeting, the unionists called for "the instant seizure of the coal mines by the state pending an agreement between the operators and the strikers" among other demands.

A circular was then created by the state UMWA leadership, the WFM, and the president of the AFL-affiliated State Federation of Labor, and distributed to unions across the state, and to UMWA affiliates nationwide, with this text:

A CALL TO REBELLION.

Denver, Colo., April 22, 1914.

Organize the men in your community in companies of volunteers to protect the workers of Colorado against the murder and cremation of men, women and children by armed assassins in the employ of coal corporations, serving under the guise of state militiamen.

Gather together for defensive purposes all arms and ammunition legally available. Send name of leader of your company and actual number of men enlisted at once by wire, phone or mail, to W. T. Hickey, Secretary of State Federation of Labor. Hold all companies subject to order. People having arms to spare for these defensive measures are requested to furnish same to local companies, and, where no company exists, send them to the State Federation of Labor.

The State is furnishing us no protection and we must protect ourselves, our wives and children from these murderous assassins. We seek no quarrel with the State and we expect to break no law; we intend to exercise our lawful right as citizens to defend our homes and our constitutional rights.[53]

Throngs of miners and local townspeople descended into the region and formed into irregular military units to protect the remaining camps and to engage in guerrilla warfare against the militia, in an episode that became known as the Ten Days' War. The governor of the state, Elias Ammons, put out an emergency call for 600 militiamen to report to duty; only 25 percent showed and proved no match for the enraged miners.[54]

By April 22, armed miners had assumed effective authoritative control over all of the camps throughout CF&I territory, laying waste to company property across the two counties. On April 29, three hundred miners from Camp San Rafael, a newly constructed tent city established by refugees from Ludlow, marched on the nearby town of Forbes to disperse a militia encampment that had garrisoned there along with a group of strikebreakers. The group, consisting of Italian, Slavic, and Mexican miners, routed the company guards and armed strikebreakers, killing ten of them in the ensuing shootout, amid shouts of "Remember Ludlow!"[55] All told, the insurgent miners laid waste to two company towns and destroyed six of the most notorious mines. In effect, the miners were in total control of the southern Colorado coal-mining region as the last vestiges of state control had been dispersed. By the end of the ten-day war, a total of thirty-three mine guards and twenty-four miners had been killed. With the miners in a state of open insurrection, the federal government stepped in to quell the uprising.

To stave off the spread of the uprising and to prevent further radicalization, Woodrow Wilson sent in federal troops from Fort Leavenworth, Kansas, which arrived on April 30. Wilson asserted the neutrality of the troops and rationalized the occupation as a means to establish an environment for equitable conflict resolution mediated under the watch of the federal government. After much debate, the miners decided to stand down. Recognizing the seriousness and volatility of the situation, as well as broad support among the working class, Wilson made gestures toward the miners, claiming the intervention to be on their behalf. He established a national grievance commission (referred to as the Low Commission after commission chairman and former New York City mayor Seth Low), proposing it as a means to mediate the major labor conflicts of the day. In response, the UMW called off the strike on December 14 in good faith.

In practice, the use of troops and invention of the commission broke the momentum of the miner revolt. More significantly, it provided the pretext for US Army troops to disarm and disperse the striking miners, who had seized much of the mining company's property and held it under workers' control. Once disarmed, law enforcement regrouped and, supported by the state and federal government, unleashed a massive campaign of retribution against the miners. Over the next several months, a total of 369 murder charges, 191 charges of arson, and 100 charges of assault with the intent to kill were levied against striking miners.[56]

Despite the strike defeats, tangible and intangible gains were registered over time, and the lessons of interethnic organizing became institutionalized. By 1922 the UNMA grew to 484,468 members, becoming the most unionized sector in the economy. Seventy-five percent of membership was bituminous coal miners, who were the highest-paid industrial workers in the nation, with average wage levels 82 percent greater than those in the manufacturing sector.[57] This population was also one of the most ethnically diverse working groups, whose rising power reflected in their willingness to go on strike and a level of unity and solidarity on a scale unprecedented in the US labor movement. Coal miners typically went on strike twice as often as workers in other industries and had a higher rate of unity in action. For example, a typical coal strike saw 94 percent of workers walking off the job, compared with an average of only 58 percent of workers participating in coordinated strike action in other industries.[58] Even where strikes or union-organizing efforts failed, coal workers that engaged in collective strike action (such as in Colorado), had higher wages than industry averages.[59] Coal workers' strike action and solidarity also forced the coal operators to change their strategy. In response to the perpetual class warfare, the employers turned to even more elaborate schemes to control labor, generalizing the use of the contained company town, introducing welfare capitalism to alleviate the most extreme conditions of exploitation and the "company union" to create the illusion of grievance management.[60]

The interethnic organizing efforts of the UMW had a significant impact on the future of the labor movement. The Colorado Labor Wars of 1913–1914 provided a powerful counternarrative of working-class solidarity to the exclusion and chauvinism of the AFL. As the US working class became more international and multiethnic, the capitalists more aggressive, and the nature of work large-scale and industrial, unifying all workers together in a common union presented a clear path forward for labor. This took socialist initiative within the unions and the self-activity and solidarity of a multiethnic and multinational workforce to confront and defeat the most powerful corporations in the country, who were backed by the full force of the state.

Chapter 21
The State, Mexican Immigration, and Labor Control

"Where land is very cheap and all men are free, where everyone who
pleases can easily obtain a piece of land for himself, not only is labour
very dear . . . but the difficulty is to obtain labor at any price."
—Edward Gibbon Wakefield, British capitalist and politician
advocating for labor-control policies in the western United States

The post–World War I years saw a significant transition in the US Left. Between 1917 and 1918, the federal government unleashed a wave of savage repression that decimated the ranks of the IWW and the Socialist Party. The third arrest of the PLM leadership in 1918, followed by the death of Ricardo Flores Magón in 1922 in Leavenworth Prison and the deportation of other key leaders shortly thereafter, dealt a final, fatal blow to the PLM. The crippling of the Left set back efforts to overcome the racial divides in the US working class, until events in Russia transformed the international political landscape and inspired regroupment.

This period also saw the first victorious socialist revolution. The world-shaking events of the Russian Revolution, when workers under the leadership of the Bolshevik Party seized power in Russia and created the first tangible workers' state in history, led to the formation of Communist Parties around the world. This included the United States, where left-wing socialists and Wobblies merged into a unified Communist Party in 1921, bringing with them the radical traditions forged over the previous decade.

Over the course of the 1920s, the party lumbered through a series of debilitating splits, mergers, and purges. By 1932 it remained small, sclerotic, and confined to the margins of the US working class. This changed with the outset of the Great Depression, where Communists emerged as a leading force within a working-class upsurge.

The onset of the Great Depression in 1929 produced an unprecedented crisis of capitalism on a global scale. Between 1929 and 1932, world trade decreased by approximately 61 percent. The Gross National Product decreased by 46 percent, 85,000 businesses shuttered, 5,000 US banks failed, the total value of stock on Wall Street dropped by over 70 percent, and unemployment reached 15 million, or a quarter of the total national workforce by 1932.[1] Agriculture was the hardest hit, triggering a wave of farm foreclosures that displaced over four million people by midcentury, many of whom migrated to California.[2]

The rapid consolidation of an industrial agricultural sector, geared toward national and international markets, changed the labor structure and composition during the 1920s. Mega-harvests necessitated large migratory bodies of workers, which were legislated into formation through the manipulation of immigration policy. The onset of existential capitalist crisis led to an unprecedented era of aggressive state intervention to preserve existing relations of production.

The near collapse of the capitalist economy induced an unprecedented shift in the federal government toward direct intervention. In 1933, the Roosevelt administration passed the National Industrial Recovery Act (NIRA) and the Agricultural Adjustment Act (AAA), bold attempts to stabilize the economy and restore growth and profitability. The National Recovery Administration, a regulatory agency produced by the NIRA, oversaw the establishment of industrial codes that regulated price, production levels, and employment levels. For the first time, federal legislation included Section 7a, which afforded workers the right to collectively bargain through unions. In essence, the NRA introduced the state as the regulator of the economy: to rationalize production, increase consumption through improved labor conditions, and to minimize competition. Despite the promise of labor rights, the provisions of the NRA (and later the National Labor Relations Act, or NLRA) excluded farmworkers from its union provisions. In practice, the NRA failed to introduce workers' rights. In practice, there were no mechanisms put in place to enforce labor rights, leaving it to the different industries to determine how to apply the laws to their own advantage.

According to Kenneth Finegold and Theda Skocpol, "Prices, output, GNP, and money supply increased . . . unemployment and bank failures went down . . . The NRA did raise nominal wages for a minority of workers. But because the NRA also raised prices, it produced no increase in real wages and thus no increase in purchasing power."[3] On the contrary, government intervention in the economy tended to strengthen the hand of employers over the workers. Despite the passage of NRA, the period witnessed a spike in anti-union repression. According to Art Preis, "at no time has there been such widespread violations of workers' rights by injunctions, troops, private police, deputy sheriffs, labor spies and vigilantes."[4]

A similar outcome occurred with the passage of the AAA. With agriculture facing a substantial crisis of overproduction, the government established a subsidy system to pay farmers to produce less. Oriented toward the largest-scale capitalist growers, the provisions of the AAA excluded farm tenants and sharecroppers, who were gradually transformed into wage labor. Cash payments and price stabilization programs to growers functioned as an economic bailout, greatly aiding in the restoration of profits, while farmworkers were denied the right to collectively bargain. This policy also aided in the formation of a national coalition of growers, Dixiecrats in the South, and Republicans in the West. Their hands were strengthened by federal policies designed to squelch labor organization in agriculture, especially among the most militant sections: black workers in the South and Mexicans in the Southwest. This broke out into violent bursts of open class war in the early 1930s, as the Communist Party made the strategic decision to unionize the agricultural working class against an array of powerful land-owning oligarchs, various echelons of the state, and vigilante shock troops. Labor radicalism and militant mass strikes became a feature of the landscape, intertwined with the rise the Communist Party. During the period of 1930 to 1939, there were 275 strikes in agriculture spread out over 28 states, involving 177,788 workers. Fifty of these strikes involved over 1,000 workers, reflecting the industrial scale and factory-like conditions of agriculture, which reached its apex in California.[5] At least 141 strikes were recorded in California, involving 127,000 workers.[6] At the forefront of this labor upsurge in the Golden State were Mexican Americans and Mexican migrants. Through political networks derived from the experience with the PLM, Socialists, and Wobblies, or through participation in the Mexican Revolution, they formed the radical ranks of farmworkers that joined with the Communist-led unions in the fields.

State Capitalism and Agriculture in California

Agriculture is the cornerstone of modern industrial economy and provides the foundation for other forms of production. Under capitalism, large-scale, food-commodity production developed for profit based on the privatization and commoditization of land. In the western United States, especially in California, agricultural capitalism developed in tandem with other capitalist institutions. The growth and success of the industry also shaped the fortunes of other sectors of capital. Railroads linked productive centers with distant markets, banks financed land speculation, merchants purchased products for retail, and other capitalists invested directly or indirectly in the industry as part of the cross-fertilization of capitalist investments characteristic of the early twentieth century.

The centrality of agricultural production to the incipient development of industrial capitalism and its dependence on large armies of labor made it vulnerable to class conflict and union organization, and made it a staging ground for extreme forms of labor control. The class intersection of politicians and landholders was direct. Many prominent politicians, judges, and other government agents were landowners, investors, or speculators, giving them a direct interest in sustaining capitalist profitability. Beyond this favorable placement, large landowners developed a variety of cutting-edge techniques to influence state policy to protect and expand their profits, including techniques to subdue working-class organization using violent methods, such so that some historians have likened the scale of repression to European fascism.[7]

Despite the proliferation of capitalist initiative and government support, early endeavors to build agricultural infrastructure in California were marked by failure, fiasco, corruption, and bankruptcy; inevitably relying on state intervention, land and water allocation, and other public resources to ensure success.[8] In the Imperial and San Joaquin Valleys, for instance, federal and state initiative helped to create a powerful class of cotton growers through the establishment of a monopoly that favored industrial production for international markets.[9] Rather than a pioneering class of capitalists "taming the land" and the natural extension of "free markets," the growth of western agricultural economies of scale was managed through direct state intervention.

Capitalist agriculture was interwoven with the state through a complex webbing of bureaucracies that directly or indirectly served the growers, and also by individual bureaucrats throughout all levels of government with a stake in agricultural well-being.

As one historian observed, "These agribusiness elites handpicked and directed judges and police to do their bidding, all in the quest for commercial farming domination over nature and fieldworkers."[10] In another example, Border Patrol agents tended to wind down patrols, arrests, and deportations during harvest time to ensure a steady labor supply for growers.[11]

Besides the most overt sympathies among the local, state, and federal echelons of law enforcement, other less obvious connections ran throughout the avenues of government. The Department of Agriculture helped fund employment agencies to recruit labor in farm towns. The founder of the desert town of El Centro and the Imperial Irrigation District, for instance, was an absentee grower from Los Angeles. Furthermore, relief agencies in rural areas pegged relief payments to the lowest prevailing wages in agriculture to keep workers in the fields.

Grower money also funded grants for scientific research that aided agricultural production. One of the larger agricultural interests in the state, the Bank of America, created the Giannini Foundation (named after the bank's founder, A. P. Giannini), which specialized in farm economics and the management of farming as a profit-making enterprise. The Giannini Foundation helped found an agricultural economics institute at the University of California, Berkeley, which regularly produced studies geared toward the technical and political needs of the growers.[12] Armed with a well-paid staff of university researchers and corporate lobbyists, growers produced their own legislative proposals through their aligned representatives.[13]

Devra Weber illustrates the interconnected webbing of the agricultural industrial complex and a staff that moved seamlessly between state and capitalist organization, looking at the career of one prominent agricultural representative named Parker Frisselle:

> Parker Frisselle was the influential manager of the experimental 500-acre Kearney farm near Fresno that was operated by the University of California. A leading member of the state Chamber of Commerce . . . he was active in attempts to organize the agricultural industry. In 1917, he had formed the Valley Fruit Growers. By 1926, he chaired the agricultural committee of the Fresno County Chamber of Commerce, and in 1932 he became chairman of the state-wide Agricultural Committee of the Chamber of Commerce. He was a founding member of the Agricultural Labor Bureau.[14]

Large growers turned on and disciplined recalcitrant farmers who did not sign on to their efforts, while supporting each other when in alignment. Bankers favored land concentration and consolidation over small farms. Bankers preferred to finance only large capitalist production, and played a significant role in engineering land concentration. Repossessed farms accumulated by the Bank of America, for instance, were sold to the large growers. By 1929, farms with 1,000 or more acres constituted only 3.8 percent of growers, but controlled 63.6 percent of all of the farmland in the state.[15] The value of the income from agricultural production in California had become the highest in the nation, comprising 30 percent (about $760 million in 1935 dollars) of the state's total income from production, $2.6 billion.[16]

Situated between the grower and the worker in the rural communities were an assortment of small and medium-sized financial and commercial interests, whose economic well-being was tied directly to industrial agricultural production. This includes local insurance, banking, processing, real estate, and machine tool interests. This smaller capitalist class

> represents the effective agents and mobilizing forces of big business and finance capital in its attacks on small farmers, agricultural workers and the rural proletariat. Concentrated in the towns and dominating the towns, this class invariably plays a leading role in all maneuvers and attacks against the struggles for organization of the rural proletariat and the small farmers.[17]

At the base of the agricultural system lay the local police, which in rural areas were funded, staffed, and politically validated through local grower associations. In exchange for their sanction, they functioned as private gendarmes used to smash labor organization. When the scale of agricultural strikes and labor radicalism in the 1930s rendered local police forces impotent to stop them, it was common for local sheriffs to deputize the growers and their management staff. During these strikes, the growers used the office of "deputy" to unleash reigns of violence and terror against typically unarmed strikers.

Through economic power, vested interrelations with other capitalists, and preponderant influence and control over all echelons of government, grower organizations in western states rose to wield immense power within the capitalist class. The food commodity industry became a profitable webbing that was bound up with investments in other major industries such as transportation, commerce, retail, and finance. They created vertically and horizontally integrated organization at the national, regional, and local level. Grower influence extended into the universities, where whole departments devoted research to serve the industry. Through these nodes of power, elite growers could shape congressional behavior at the federal level while also mobilizing forces at the local level (elected officials, small growers, farm management staff, sheriffs, etc.) to take action on their behalf. When official forces proved incapable of taking the necessary action to prevent workers' organization, the growers were able to assemble their own private vigilante militias and assert their will though mob violence.

If growers could not prevent significant social and political changes that had implications for their interests, they could resist, reshape, and neutralize their effects. The introduction of labor policy codified in the NRA, and then into the National Labor Relations Act of 1935 as a part of the New Deal, is an example. In the early 1930s, great explosions of class struggle shifted the balance of class power as the Depression drove capitalists to drastically cut wages and the standard of living of workers as a means to staunch the crisis. An upsurge in class consciousness, union organizing, strikes, and an attendant breakdown of faith in the capitalist system among large segments of the working class produced significant splits in the political system. While the corporate alignments backing Roosevelt conceded the right for labor to join unions, grower interests in both the Republican and Democratic Parties blocked the extension of the right for agricultural workers, beginning the partition that has greatly weakened labor unionism in agriculture up to the present.

The framework for denying labor rights to farmworkers developed in the context of maintaining racial segregation, especially in the Southern states. Black workers comprised the majority of farmworkers, whose condition as highly exploited wage labor was maintained through Jim Crow laws and state and Klan violence. Jim Crow laws disenfranchised black workers, and denied them access to finance, education, and other fundamental means to improve their condition. The reforms of the New Deal threatened the arrangement. If farmworkers formed unions, they could raise wages, establish labor codes, and appeal for government relief or protections (such as Social Security, child welfare, etc.). Any such disruption of the conditions of isolation and subordination enshrined in the white supremacist, capitalist power structure, would upend the profitable arrangement built on black super-exploitation. As historian Juan Perea concludes:

> Racism ran rampant against blacks during the New Deal ... Congress accommodated and preserved this racism through the systematic, intentional exclusion of blacks from all the major enactments of the New Deal ... [including] ... the National Industrial Recovery Act, the Agricultural Adjustment Act, the Social Security Act, and the Fair Labor Standards Act. Congress excluded blacks by proxy through occupational exclusions and by allowing southerners to discriminate against blacks through local, rather than federal, administration of benefits. By excluding agricultural and domestic workers ... from federal protections, southern representatives guaranteed that the New Deal posed little or no threat to the Jim Crow South.[18]

Southern Democrats were intent on maintaining their totalitarian control over black farm labor. Many Southern landowners migrated into California's farming regions, especially as part of the expansion of cotton production. They brought their racist paradigms with them and transposed these views onto Mexicans. This racial strategy to control labor resonated congenially with the dominant Republican-aligned landowning class in California, who shared a desire to maintain their Mexican workers in similar conditions of control.[19]

Deportation as Labor Control

Another significant form of state aid has been in the form of labor control. Growers have relied on the state apparatus to procure labor when needed, and to help temper and suppress it as well. For example, grower organizations have leveraged their power and influence at the state and federal level to align immigration policy with their interests.

As migration served the labor needs of growers, they invested their efforts in manipulating state power to regulate the flow of immigrants. They also attempted to mobilize public sentiment in their favor. This included preaching the virtues of controlled labor in the case of Mexicans, while turning on a dime to ignite and inflame anti-immigrant sentiment when these same workers went on strike or joined unions. Constructing immigration policy as a system for labor procurement grew in tandem with the racial policing of immigrants as a form of labor control.

By the turn of the twentieth century, the US did not regulate Mexican migration as it was not a significant phenomenon worthy of special study. By the second decade of the century, Mexicans were entering in larger numbers and filling the ranks of the growing agricultural workforce. As previously mentioned, growers' organizations through their elected representatives got Mexicans exempted from restrictions embedded in the Immigration Act of 1917. Mexicans received a special waiver designating them as registered temporary workers, whose wages would be partially withheld to assure their return to Mexico. Even with this overt concession, growers complained that the bureaucratic process was a hindrance and advocated for the elimination of all restrictions on Mexican labor. The champion of this cause was none other than president-to-be Herbert Hoover. In 1917, Hoover was appointed by Woodrow Wilson to head the US Food Administration. He promptly staffed the agency with representatives of the agricultural industry and crafted policy to increase production and profits for growers during and after World War I. In 1918, he preached the doctrine of free Mexican migration, only to become the executor of mass deportation of Mexicans a decade later. According to Mark Reisler:

> The growers' foremost champion and lobbyist in Washington was Food Administrator Herbert Hoover. At the behest of farmers, Hoover asked the Secretary of Labor to waive the head tax on all Mexican immigrants . . . He [then] contended that all time limits be done away with. He favored elimination of wage withholding as a guarantee that Mexican workers would return to Mexico because "we do not want him to return."[20]

Hoover then took several more direct steps toward eliminating obstacles: he called for Mexicans to be free to work in all industries, that no records be kept to track them, and that Food Administration offices be set up on the border to directly assist in their placement on farms and other industries. Most of these concessions were granted directly or in modified form.[21] The passage of the Immigration Act of 1924, also known as the Johnson-Reed Act, enacted racially informed immigration quotas but exempted immigration from countries in the Western Hemisphere, allowing a loophole for Mexicans to enter unabated. According to Natalia Molina, this "made possible . . . an unprecedented expansion in large-scale industry and agriculture" by maintaining a large reserve army of cheap labor that could be more easily controlled.[22]

While Mexicans could cross the border with little inconvenience, increased movements of people across the border during the revolutionary period and an exponential growth in cross-border smuggling led government officials to establish the US Border Patrol as a regulatory presence in 1924. These agents staffed border processing stations that regulated the flow of migrant workers in the first efforts to synch economic patterns with an algorithm of enforcement.

When self-structured access to the flow of Mexican labor was threatened by pressure from racial exclusionists in state and federal government, capitalist growers flexed their muscle to carve out exceptions in their corner of the economy. As an example, the Western Growers and Shippers' Protective Committee was formed in 1925 in an effort to unite fruit and lettuce growers in Southern California around their immediate labor needs. One of their first efforts was to prevent the inclusion of Mexican workers on the growing immigration quota list.[23] Migration regulation developed less as a mechanism for restriction than as a means to align movements of labor with the ebbs and flows of capitalist production. As Balderrama and Rodríguez explain:

> The Border Patrol and the Immigration Service exercised their extensive powers selectively. This was done to serve the needs of influential growers and industrialists. Regulations were loosely enforced when Mexican workers were needed to harvest crops or increase production in the mines or on the assembly lines. Conversely, the strict letter of the law was applied when Mexican labor exceeded the seasonal demand.[24]

Growers relied on armed immigration agents to threaten, arrest, or deport noncitizen workers at their behest. For instance,

> [d]eportation raids at the worksite, usually before payday became common occurrences. The raids were sometimes conducted at the request of unscrupulous employers. The Border Patrol and the Immigration Service were often assisted in their roundups by local police and sheriff's deputies.[25]

With the Border Patrol serving as labor regulators, growers began to call for their own farmworkers to be deported when they tried to unionize. In the farming community of San Bernardino County, California, a coalition of peach, grape, citrus, and apricot growers faced a spreading strike among Mexican field workers in 1933. Led by the Communist-affiliated Cannery and Agricultural Workers Industrial Union (CAWIU), they called for a 20 cent wage increase per hour. In response, the grower coalition, assisted by the representative of the county relief association, called on all Mexican workers to be removed and replaced with "white American men and women to avail themselves of the opportunity offered by the strike."[26]

The selective and targeted enforcement of immigration exclusion that reflected the growers' preponderant position within the economy to shield Mexican workers gave way to full-scale removal with the onset of the Great Depression in 1929. Amid the economic crisis, the clamor for deportation to reduce the Mexican population was taken up by broad segments of society, from then president Herbert Hoover, racist demagogues within the Democratic and Republican Parties, to the AFL and a broad array of right-wing nativist organizations. As the economy crashed, politicians and bureaucrats across the country braced for destabilizing social effects, and swung quickly behind the idea of targeting immigrants as a prelude to a likely upsurge in riots and rebellions. Under these conditions, agricultural capital's privileged niches for unfettered Mexican labor and glutted labor markets were constrained but not closed entirely.

Between 1929 and 1939 an estimated one million Mexican nationals were driven out of the country by a coordinated effort between federal, state, and local law enforcement agencies. Barrios across the country, from Los Angeles to Chicago, were terrorized by mass sweeps and arrests, without the right to counsel, judicial proceedings, or even the ability to prove citizenship in some cases. It was not uncommon for individuals to be snatched from the streets and shuttled south of the border before their families were made aware of their disappearance. Others fled in advance of the raids, while some hid out or left willingly. Because transportation was provided by the US government, they referred to the mass expulsion using the euphemism of "repatriation." Despite the official pronouncements that these deportations were to open up jobs for citizens, the patterns of removal guarded essential labor for agriculture.

The Immigration Service was housed at that time in the Department of Labor, suggesting that immigration was seen as a vital means to staff the economy with necessary workers. When the economy began to experience profound recession and near-collapse, the Department of Labor moved to eject foreign-born workers, although the evidence suggests that this was more for political reasons than economic rationalization. In fact, targeted deportations were carried out in urban areas and largely bypassed rural regions, although the Border Patrol monitored and targeted Mexican workers during strikes as per the directives of Secretary of Labor William Doak. To placate business interests,

> Doak concocted the brilliant idea of monitoring strikes involving foreigners. Strike leaders and picketers would be arrested, charged with being illegal aliens or engaging in illegal activities, and thus be subject to arbitrary deportation. This insidious scheme assumed the proportions of national policy and became a widely implemented tactic. In California and elsewhere, many agrarian strikes were broken up by arresting and deporting leaders who were of Mexican origin.[27]

Rendered vulnerable by discriminatory immigration policy, Mexicans who were targeted en masse were those who were not working, unable to work, or receiving relief. Mexican immigrants who had entered the US through legal channels before 1924 were eligible for different forms of welfare relief. Those who were technically ineligible by law, but who applied for and received relief, became a soft target for deportation after 1929, as immigration agents cross-checked immigration records and relief rolls. Furthermore, an existing immigration stipulation that disqualified immigrants "likely to become a public charge" (in other words, those who were not able-bodied workers) from citizenship was seized upon and became widely enforced during the Depression. Immigration agents, therefore, became an instrument for clearing out segments of the "non-productive" Mexican population.

This became an expediency, especially as welfare payments surpassed the average wage in agriculture, which was substantially cut after the onset of the Depression. By 1933, 1.6 of the state's 6 million people were on relief, with majorities in the farming regions receiving some form of aid. Many farmworkers rationally opted to not return to the fields to perform intense labor for the same pittance they could receive from aid agencies. Growers and their associates, who had valued government subsidization of low wages in the 1920s, now resented the same government "intervention."[28] In response, all major growers' organizations intervened to limit the dispersal of aid.

To inflame sentiment against the Mexican workers' access to welfare, grower representatives railed against government aid as a factor driving the agricultural strike movement, ostensibly because it afforded them some stability, and therefore options. George P. Clements, head of the Agricultural Department of the Los Angeles Chamber of Commerce, proclaimed, "The Mexican on relief is being unionized and is being used to foment strikes among the few still loyal Mexican workers. The Mexican casual laborer is lost to the California farmer unless immediate action is taken to get him off relief."[29] These efforts ultimately succeeded in getting relief agencies, from the State Emergency Relief Administration to the Works Progress Administration, to drop unemployed agricultural workers from their rolls if they refused to take jobs on the farms.[30] As many as 70,000 were released from the rolls, primarily Mexicans, and compelled to return to agriculture in order to avoid potential deportation.

Further measures were implemented after state and local bureaucracies took their lead from the Hoover administration. Another anti-Mexican and anti-immigrant measure taken by the Hoover administration required all federal contractors to employ US citizens only. This gave the green light for state and local governments to also pass laws restricting the employment of noncitizen workers. Theoretically, punishment for noncompliance included up to six months in jail for employers who hired nonresident workers. While there is no evidence that any punishments were meted out to employers, this encouraged the layoffs of expendable noncitizen workers, increased unemployment, and augmented the power employers had over vulnerable workforces. These factors contributed to the deterioration of wages and working conditions in agriculture and industry and increased unemployment in the barrios across the Southwest, leading many to seek relief from state agencies. It was precisely the rolls of the hastily crafted emergency relief programs that federal, state, and local agencies used to identify and target Mexican families for apprehension and removal.

The state-orchestrated assault on the Mexican community opened the door for other forms of violence. The Ku Klux Klan revived and grew rapidly in the shadows of the racist anti-immigrant reaction that accompanied the repression of the burgeoning labor movement. Alongside the deportation of cross-sections of the Mexican working class, Klan terror operated openly and simultaneously with the immigration raids occurring across the country. As historian Carlos Larralde describes, the Klan

> conducted nighttime raids along the Mexican border. They lynched Mexicans and . . . even used them for target practice . . . [I]n the mornings, disfigured bodies lay along dusty roads. In remote farms, skeletons and corpses surfaced. Some were beyond recognition due to the long exposure to the elements while buzzards circled in the sky.[31]

Bert Corona, a labor organizer who experienced this violence firsthand, concluded, "In a way, US border authorities saw the Klan's deeds as a form of Mexican repatriation in the 1930s."[32]

Klan forces were also ingrained within the grower class and their auxiliaries and allies that ruled over their domains. During the strike wave of the 1930s, Klan tactics were used to sow fear among the Mexican, Filipino, and Japanese workers especially. Klansmen burned crosses near strike camps and outside of jails when workers were arrested as part of the ritual of terror.[33]

The Making and Controlling of a Mexican Agricultural Workforce

The top echelon of the grower class comprised financiers and investors from Los Angeles and San Francisco who were seasoned veterans of the class war in the fields. In transforming the agricultural farm belts of California into vast industrial landscapes, they needed armies of labor. Building on tried and true tactics honed in the cities, they used racial and national differences to divide and segment production. Between 1900 and 1920, grower organizations brought Chinese, Japanese, South Asian, Filipino, African American, white, and Mexican laborers into the farms. Over this period Japanese, Indians, and whites increased as a percentage of smallholders, renters, and tenant farmers as large growers subdivided their growing holdings as a means to generate revenue streams. Mexicans, Filipinos, and African Americans, on the other hand, found the door closed to upward mobility and were disproportionately concentrated among the ranks of farm labor for both the growers and their tenants. This hierarchy was codified into law through the use of racial discrimination and periodically reinforced through acts of violence. Migration from the Mexican countryside into the United States continued into the postrevolutionary period, as the economy was severely damaged by over a decade of war, the new regimes curtailed radical land redistribution, and the US economy expanded significantly in the 1920s and was in need of new infusions of labor.

By 1920, Japanese, Indian, and, to a lesser extent, Chinese and whites constituted 49 percent of the Imperial Valley's tenant farmers, while an estimated 85 percent of the titleholders were absentee landowners living in cities along the California coast.[34] Despite the success of the Alien Land Act of 1913 in wiping out significant Japanese landholdings, many farmers persisted and thrived as tenants, or found a legal loophole by forming corporations to bypass the restrictions on individual ownership. The prominence of Japanese tenantry and their persistence as commercial competition led the AFL, the Farm Bureau, and the state's Democratic Party to pursue further Japanese restriction. This coalition engineered the passage of the Alien Land Law of 1920, which prohibited the further occurrence of noncitizen Asian tenancy and forbade Asian-controlled corporations from purchasing farmlands.

As a result of the law, the tenant class was obliterated. This enabled another round of land consolidation while increasing dependence on migratory labor. Mexican migration filled the ranks of the mobile mass of pickers and field workers, as access to land faded in post-revolutionary Mexico. Despite the promise of social investment and land redistribution enshrined in the Constitution, the economy was in tatters. The new government was eager to consolidate its power and accommodated to US

imperialism to establish credit and receive loans. In exchange, it ceased land expropriations, smashed independent unionism, and declared war on the Mexican Communist Party, which attempted to organize rural workers. There was a rapprochement
between the new ruling group and the adaptive elements of the oligarchy and state
contingent upon the desire to grow a modern capitalist economy. Since this depended
on stanching the radical redistributive aspects of the Constitution, keeping land concentrated and oriented toward export, and keeping wages low to maximize the extraction of surplus value, migration continued and even increased.

In 1910, 17,760 people emigrated from Mexico to the US, a number that multiplied annually reaching 51,042 in 1920 and 87,648 in 1924.[35] Many of these migrant
workers settled in the towns of the Imperial Valley and the San Joaquin Valley, the two
largest agricultural belts in the state. By 1925, for instance, 35,000 pickers, including an
estimated 12,000 migrants, were needed for the fall cotton harvest in the San Joaquin
Valley alone.[36]

By 1928, Mexican migrant workers comprised 84 percent of the migratory workforce, working in the fields of Southern California in the first half of the year and then
trekking north to work in the later cotton harvest. Between 1924 and 1930, an estimated 58,000 Mexican workers moved from the southern border counties to the San
Joaquin Valley to work the cotton harvest. By 1930, many had settled in permanent
residences in the US and followed this cycle each year but were joined by migrants
from Mexico.[37]

As other streams of migrant workers diminished due to immigration restriction
after the racial quota system was first established in 1921, growers developed an appreciation for Mexican labor due to its availability and productivity. Mexican migrants
came from Southern California cities and towns composed of earlier migrants who
had planted roots in the Southwest. A smaller portion were from Mexico, including
displaced subsistence farmers, off-season miners, and those with other labor experience, but very few had knowledge or experience of industrial farming. A portion
of these were skilled pickers from the cotton-growing regions in central and western
Mexico who followed the harvest north. Because of immigration enforcement the
portal for legal immigration narrowed; an estimated 85 percent of Mexicans inside
the country were undocumented. While growers viewed Mexicans as essential labor,
they also viewed them with racial disdain, relegating them to "stoop labor, to work as
cotton pickers or grape pickers, to prune vines or pick peaches."[38]

They preferred Mexicans as permanent laborers, a caste that they perceived could
be reproduced without social mobility. Racial discrimination and structural segregation crippled the economic opportunities for Mexican workers to achieve social mobility. It was common for workers to send their earnings as remittances to Mexico to
sustain families or rebuild homes and farms after the revolution. These factors combined to inhibit the rise of a Mexican landowning class, and conditioned growers to
see them as willing, perpetual labor.

While many migrants from Mexico saw their stay as temporary, by the mid-1920s
an increasing number left the sojourner lifestyle behind and settled permanently in the

United States as job opportunities remained elusive or prospects to acquire redistributed land in Mexico faded. This usually occurred in waves at the end of the peak harvest cycle, from July to October. In the off-season, most of the harvest workers were left unemployed and were shunted out of the farming towns, while small numbers were able to settle permanently after finding work in farm maintenance or other auxiliary industries.[39]

While most returned to Mexico, growing streams trailed into urban areas to look for work. In large cities like Los Angeles, Mexican workers found job prospects limited as racial segregation relegated them to unskilled menial work that was unstable and low paying. These workers increasingly joined the ranks of the reserve army of labor, relying on relief to sustain them during periods of cyclical unemployment. In 1926, for instance, Mexican workers made up 7 percent of the workforce, while comprising 27 percent of those on relief.[40] The onset of the Great Depression in 1929 led growers to cut wages to maintain profits, with agricultural wages dropping by half by 1933. Furthermore, the amount of work declined, with the average rate of work dropping from 33 weeks to 29 weeks between 1928 and 1929, and 1934 and 1935, so that by 1933 Mexican agricultural workers were at a crisis point as a return to Mexico offered no relief.[41]

As previously mentioned, the Mexican population was reduced through deportation, although this was done through a pattern that left a significant workforce available for agriculture. For instance, while an estimated 150,000 Mexicans were deported or repatriated from California by 1936, they still comprised 93 percent of farmworkers in Southern California that same year.[42] As more Mexican migrants continued to settle permanently with the intention of acquiring better wages and their own land, this thwarted the growers' vision. Furthermore, as migration increased from Mexico during the 1920s, the character of the population changed. A larger percentage of migrants in this period were shaped by the experiences of the revolution, with many having had experience resisting land theft from the government and hacendados, having "joined rural uprisings, labor unions, and armed forces of the Mexican revolution."[43]

As one form of response to the instability and uncertainty, Mexicans formed or reactivated mutual aid societies. These societies once again formed the de facto labor organization for Mexicans throughout the Southwest in the urban barrios and along the agricultural corridors. By 1919, for instance, a mutualista was organized in El Centro and several more were created in smaller towns in the Imperial Valley in subsequent years. In the San Joaquin Valley, thirty-five mutualistas, patriotic societies, and worker organizations were founded.[44] Like in other locales in the United States, these mutualistas provided the organizational infrastructure for Mexican workers to coordinate labor action. They were often the staging grounds for participation in union drives, leadership coordination in strikes, and collaboration with other groups, especially Filipinos.[45] Like the Mexican workers, Filipinos also brought labor and political traditions with them that led many to join unions and the Communist Party.[46]

As in other industries, growers maintained ethnic divides in their workforces to preempt labor organizing. As a California Department of Industrial Relations "Fact Sheet" on Filipino migration observed:

Laborers speaking different languages and accustomed to diverse standards of living and habits are not as likely to arrive at a mutual understanding which would lead to strikes or other labor troubles during harvesting seasons, when work interruptions would result in serious financial losses to the growers.[47]

Like other Asian migrant workers, Filipinos were characterized as a social threat by the business press and middle-class "patriotic" associations, even while they were enticed to come in droves to tend the California crops. Historian Mae Ngai describes the context in the following terms: "By the 1920s, anti-Asiatic politics had fully matured on the West Coast, especially in California, where exclusion had become a staple of the urban and middle class Progressivist strain of the Democratic Party."[48] They were also excluded from AFL unions. Paul Scharrenberg, president of the California State Federation of Labor, wrote several widely circulated articles about the threat they posed to white workers, mostly reiterating the racist notions then circulating among nativists that characterized the Filipinos as the worst of the "yellow peril."[49]

As part of their turn toward organizing farmworkers, the Communist Party publicly protested in the major cities of California and throughout the pages of its press against the cropping up of racial violence in the early 1930s. After the anti-Filipino riot at Watsonville in 1930, the Communist Party organized protests in San Francisco, Oakland, and Los Angeles. They condemned racial violence and called for the complete independence of the Philippines from the US, while attempting to build agricultural organization that oriented toward Filipinos in the fields.

According to the *Daily Worker*, these types of actions led Filipinos to join the Communist-led, agricultural union Cannery and Agricultural Workers Industrial Union (CAWIU), and the most militant and class-conscious workers to join the party itself. Party organizers also confronted white workers over the poisonous results of racism, maintaining its principled position that all workers would have to unite to overcome grower unity and their facile exploitation of racial tension to prevent unionization. As one *Western Worker* article urged, "the solution of the situation from a worker's viewpoint, rests in the organization of white and Filipino organizations for the development of struggle against the bosses' attempt to use one race against another."[50]

Part 4

Chapter 22
Communists in the California Fields

"The Imperial Valley was a corridor of radicalism. Exploited workers,
political radicals, labor organizers, social dissenters, and veterans of the
Mexican Revolution entered from the four cardinal directions."
—**Benny J. Andrés, Jr.,** *Power and Control in the Imperial Valley*

At the Second Congress of the Communist International in 1920, the delegates encouraged constituent members to organize the "agricultural proletariat." Large rural working populations became an urgent subject for Communists internationally, who, inspired by the Bolshevik Revolution in Russia, attempted to develop a revolutionary strategy that assigned a role for the agricultural proletariat in their respective countries. In the US context, this referenced the dense pockets of migrant agricultural workers, tenant farmers and sharecroppers, and small and subsistence farmers in the Midwest, South, and Southwest. The Comintern's strategy called for Communists to work within established unions to achieve their objectives, but the AFL had abandoned attempts to organize farmworkers; moreover, they had fervently opposed the inclusion of Mexicans in their unions.

By 1928, Comintern directives had changed during its "Third Period." The Comintern fashioned its own international Communist union federation named the Red International of Labor Unions (RILU) and invoked party affiliates in different countries to launch "red unions" to rival the established ones or to create them from scratch where they didn't yet exist. With this policy shift, the Communist Party aimed to fill the void in southwestern agriculture by creating their own farmworker unions.

The Communist Party and the Third Period (1928–1935)

The early Communist movement in the US took shape through splits and mergers that informed and launched a new party aligned with the Bolshevik Revolution. This allegiance continued through the internal power struggles within the Russian Communist leadership, the outcome of which was the rise of Stalin and a fundamental shift in direction for the international Communist movement. This began with the Comintern's declaration of the Third Period in 1928.

This formulation, generated in 1928 as a geo-strategic calculation of a new regime consolidating as the base of the soon-to-be dictatorship of Josef Stalin, proclaimed a new period of capitalist instability and potential revolutionary transformation.[1] The practical application of this sweeping, ultra-left declaration was for Communists to denounce the reformist leadership that restrained the working class, and to build revolutionary organization as an alternative. For those in the United States, this included the rejection of the "boring from within" strategy of working within AFL unions, and the urgency to launch rival unions directly under Communist Party control and leadership.[2]

Party activists were directed to denounce and oppose Socialists, Trotskyists, and AFL unionists as "social fascists." This position held that liberals and reformists worked in parallel with right-wing fascism to prevent socialist revolution. Based on the misguided belief that workers in capitalist countries had achieved revolutionary consciousness, it was then prescribed that the reformist trade union leadership and other political influences within the working class conspired to suppress, restrain, and suffocate revolutionary yearnings. This sectarian approach served to alienate Communists from workers in most instances, and to undermine the possibility for joint action. The actions of the Communists during the third period generally failed to make inroads into existing unions or peel away significant numbers into their ranks; albeit with some exceptions.

The commitment, dedication, and fortitude of rank-and-file party organizers could make significant gains among those sections of the working class where AFL unions were absent.[3] As Bert Cochran explains:

> The Communist Party resembled the prewar IWW to the extent that it supplied leadership for workers abandoned or ignored by AFL officials. These groups of workers, isolated and without finances, forced into hopeless strikes against superior forces, were not in a position to choose their allies, and because of their desolate state, were impervious to the usual anti-Communist tirades.[4]

This was significantly aided by the presence of Mexican radicals and existing organizational structures and political traditions that made it possible for the party to help ignite conditions already ripe for struggle. The Communist Party–supported and led strikes in the California fields represented a glimpse of potential success for even small groups of radicals to organize mass strike action in the heart of California's vast agricultural complexes.

Nevertheless, the gains were often lost as fast as they were won, or otherwise came at debilitating cost. Local, state, and federal governments aligned with landowner associations and fascistic vigilante forces to violently repress strikes and eliminate the Communist leadership through the application of the criminal syndicalism laws. The Party's alienation from the rest of the Left and the AFL labor unions rendered it even more isolated and vulnerable, and their gains more fragile amid constant attack. Additionally, the party's mischaracterization of the period as "revolutionary" created a dissonance between them and the vast majority of the farmworkers. While there was the presence of radicals and revolutionaries in their ranks, the party failed to build strong organization, instead seeing the strikes as part of a revolutionary process that alone would win the masses to the party.

While the party failed to recruit large numbers of farmworkers, or establish a sustainable union presence in the fields, it was the first successful effort to organize California's migrant agricultural workforce into unions capable of winning strikes. A surge of militancy and wildcat actions among Mexican and Filipino farmworkers began in 1928, drawing the party into its tailwinds. In 1930, the party launched the Agricultural Workers Industrial League (AWIL; soon renamed Cannery and Agricultural Workers Industrial Union, CAWIU). Through the CAWIU, a small group of untrained yet wholly dedicated cadre found themselves in the leadership of the most extensive agricultural strike wave in history. The CAWIU, which lasted until 1935, had its origins in the mutating formulations of the Comintern, which began with the creation of the Trade Union Unity League in 1929.

The Trade Union Unity League

Beginning in 1920, radical unionists within the AFL formed the Trade Union Education League (TUEL) to unite left-wing, socialist unionists within the AFL around a common strategy to challenge the conservative leadership, advance class-struggle politics in US labor, and merge the crafts into industrial unions.[5] The shift to the Third Period approach led Communists in the United States to abandon the "boring from within" project in favor of "dual unionism." At its fourth conference in Cleveland in 1929, the TUEL voted to repudiate the conservative reformism of the AFL and retool itself as the Trade Union Unity League (TUUL). The TUUL became the industrial union umbrella organization of the Communist Party, and affiliated to the RILU.

Through the TUUL, it was reasoned, workers could be won over to break with AFL unions through militant practice and by demonstrating the potency of industrial unionism in class struggle. In the industries where AFL craft unions maintained exclusively white skilled members, the TUUL afforded the opportunity to organize the ranks of unskilled workers, women, immigrants, and workers of color. This took on a special urgency as the Comintern began to encourage its US affiliate to make it a priority.[6] Not only was the TUUL a springboard for unionizing the vast, marginalized sectors of the working class, it also emphasized involving workers in the leadership and decision-making processes so as to cultivate worker-militants able to conduct mass action at the point of production. As historian Edward P. Johanningsmeier concludes:

> Dual unionism and the Third Period helped measure the limits of Communist unionism in America, and represented an opportunity to begin learning how to organize the kind of workers that the AFL (and American Communists) had largely ignored in the 1920s . . . [and it] . . . represented an important transitional phase in the CPUSA's reorientation toward a more inclusive, mass-based unionism during the Great Depression.[7]

Across the country, the TUUL had set up or incorporated dual unions in coal, textile, needle, food, tobacco, furniture, office and building, marine, metal, and steel industries, with an estimated 125,000 members at its height in 1933.[8] The TUUL also incorporated some local agricultural unions, such as the Asociación de Betabeleros (Beet Workers' Association) of Colorado in 1929, making it the first national union in agriculture since the IWW. Many of the these radical betabeleros who joined the Communist-led CAWIU were former Wobblies who attempted to organize a failed general strike of eighteen thousand in the beet fields of southern Colorado in 1932 to call for higher wages. Like what was to come for its counterparts in California, the strike was smashed through the use of state-aligned grower terror.[9]

For Communists in California the centrality of industrialized agriculture to the regional capitalist economy was an ideal backdrop for a TUUL organizing effort, which began in earnest in 1930. Preliminary connections had been established with groups of agricultural workers, organizing directly in racially segregated communities through Communist Party members of the same nationality, especially the Japanese, Mexican, and Filipino communities.[10] This work of small groups or individuals was a precursory step to aligning the different ethnic groups into one industrial union.

Communists in the Trade Union Educational League (TUEL) in Los Angeles, for example, helped Japanese radicals establish the Japanese Agricultural Workers Organizing Committee (JAWOC) in 1926. This group affiliated with the TUEL and agitated for organization among Japanese farmworkers. Similar work occurred among Mexican workers, the most militant of whom formed the left wing of the Los Angeles-based Confederación de Uniones de Obreros Mexicanos (Confederation of Unions of Mexican Workers; CUOM by its Spanish acronym). Communists had also made inroads among Mexican sugar beet workers in Colorado, whose local union had affiliated to the TUEL in 1928. Japanese and Mexican radicals in the TUEL sent delegations to the founding conference of the TUUL in Cleveland. After these groups returned from the Cleveland conference in 1929, they eagerly constituted the first Communist farmworkers' union, the Agricultural Workers' Industrial League.[11] In a 1928 issue of the TUEL's publication, *Labor Unity*, an article titled "For a Real Fight on Imperialism" called on radicals to organize Mexicans into common unions, proclaiming:

> We must understand clearly and act unequivocally, on the fact that "our own" struggles are only a part of one greater struggle involving the exploited classes of Latin-America in defense of the common daily, material interests of the toilers of both north and south. The fact must be forcefully brought home to us, and realities will awaken us if we remain unaware, that there are a number of Latin-American workers, estimated at 4,000,000, within the United States itself, unorganized, as long as we allow them to remain so it is our fault if they are used against the native born and other foreign-born workers in wage struggles. Most of these Latins are from Mexico.[12]

Communists and Mexican Farmworkers

Growers' organizations originally discouraged the recruitment of Mexican farm labor during the revolution, concerned that experience with revolutionary activity or radical sympathies would make them less prone to accept low wages and working conditions and more susceptible to labor unionism.[13] Their attitude changed as restrictive immigration policy developed between 1917 and 1924 and gave employers significant power to police immigrant workforces.

Even with the threat of deportation hanging over their heads, Mexican field workers began to organize binationally in the Mexicali and Imperial Valleys in 1922.

Both sides of the Imperial-Mexicali region were dominated by US growers. To meet their labor needs, the landowners coordinated staggered production schedules to allow for access to the same body of migrants as they moved northward along California's agricultural corridor. This "superstructure of agro-industrial labor control" induced migration northward as growers evicted farmers after harvest completion sending them off to the next farms.[14] By 1922, workers trekked across the border annually, following a route that extended all the way to the Sacramento Valley.

In May of 1922, farmworkers in the Mexicali and Imperial Valleys formed clandestine union committees with the intention of taking collective action in the upcoming harvests. Leaders of the effort were radical veterans of the revolution who had returned to the region to work among the farm laborers, bringing their experiences and skills and into farm labor organization. In Mexicali, local workers had grown impatient as the promise of land redistribution failed to materialize after the revolution. There, workers called for a strike on the US-owned cotton farms that quickly escalated to a wave of land occupations. The strikers not only stopped work but seized and occupied large swaths of land on US-owned farms, many of whose owners actively aided the counterrevolution in the region and continued to retain their land as the government stalled on land reform measures.[15] Commenting warily on the situation, one concerned company representative remarked, "[t]here is quite a lot of regular Bolshevikis in and around Mexicali that are getting quite strong and they are claiming these lots and profess that they will take any lots they want."[16]

In response, the Mexican government under Álvaro Obregón, then consolidating his presidency and rapprochement with his US counterparts, instructed local auxiliaries to end the occupations by force. The Mexicali mayor declared martial law and sent in loyal federal troops to round up and imprison the leaders, expel the squatters, and restore the lands to US owners. During mop-up operations, the Calexico police closed the border on the US side to prevent their escape and regroupment in the Imperial Valley where a concurrent strike was taking place among cantaloupe pickers.[17] Mexican troops were maintained in the region to guard farms and ranches and arranged for Chinese and Filipino workers to be brought in to replace the strikers.

North of the border, representatives of two thousand migrant workers coming into the Imperial Valley from Baja California announced their refusal to work the thirty-one thousand acres of bonanza cantaloupe (with an estimated value of $13 million) unless growers raised their pay rate from twelve cents per crate to sixteen cents per crate.[18] Weakened by the arrest and repression of the Mexicali-based collaborators and the fear of similar reprisals, the strike fell apart quickly after growers arranged for two thousand Japanese and Filipino workers to be brought in as replacements. In September, there were also unsuccessful efforts by Mexican migrants to form an independent union among grape pickers in Fresno, followed by a strike for higher wages.[19] Even though these early strikes failed, they showed a glimpse of the labor struggle to come.

By the mid-1920s grower organizations continued to hone their craft at controlling their labor supply and suppressing unionization. In the San Joaquin Valley of California, for instance, a consortium of farm bureaus, chambers of commerce, and various growers' associations coalesced to form the Agricultural Labor Bureau. This body expanded the efficiency and regional capacity of agribusiness on a wider regional scale by coordinating the procurement of labor and timing harvests so as to eliminate competition, regulate the movement of workers, and minimize the efforts of union organizing. One effective strategy used through the bureau was a labor contracting system in which the growers set wage scales and distributed worker pay through labor contractors.

Since state law did not regulate or enforce contract labor law, it allowed for growers to use the system to their advantage. Growers could "avoid the arduous task of recruiting, paying, feeding, transporting, overseeing, and paying the medical bills and workman's compensation of laborers."[20] Instead, labor contractors arranged and assigned labor, withheld up to 25 percent of total pay until the harvest was complete, and subtracted a commission from each worker's total earnings. This system developed as a means to create a buffer between growers and labor, to preempt collective bargaining, and to keep wages low.

By the late 1920s, Mexican immigrant labor was the majority in California agriculture. As an immigrant workforce, many returned to Mexico in the off-season, diminishing the potential for unionization. For this reason, they were highly favored by employers as tractable and compliant, based on the false perception of labor peace, as no significant strikes occurred amid sustained agricultural growth between 1924 and 1927.[21] Meanwhile, no significant land redistribution occurred in Mexico during this period and the Cristero Revolt wracked whole swaths of the Mexican countryside with violence and war between 1926 and 1929.[22]

This led many thousands of migrants to cross the border and not return; instead taking up permanent residence in southwestern farming towns. With a larger, more stable Mexican population working in agriculture, Mexicans began to look to collective action and unionization to address deteriorating conditions. In a study by farm labor historian Paul Taylor in 1937, abject poverty among Mexican farmworker families had severe effects on their well-being. His study found that few children had access to schooling, 27 percent of children of farmworkers suffered from malnutrition, families had no access to medical care, and due to residency requirements few families qualified for government relief.[23] Racial segregation, discrimination, and social and political neglect assured that the second generation of Mexicans born in the US would experience the same conditions as their parents and do the same type of work.

The Confederation of Unions of Mexican Workers (CUOM)
Preeminent grower control of the rural economy was the most formidable obstacle for farmworker organization. With the retreat of the AFL from organizing Mexicans and with the decline of the IWW, they took inspiration from developments in their homeland and from their own traditions. In 1927, representatives of several mutualistas in Los Angeles convened a meeting for the purpose of forming a new labor

organization. In Mexico, a government-aligned labor body called the Regional Labor Confederation of Mexico had taken on national dimensions by the late 1920s, claiming a membership of a million workers. Working through the mutual aid societies in Los Angeles, Mexican workers were eager to replicate efforts north of the border. In 1928, they launched the Confederación de Uniones de Obreros Mexicanos (CUOM) with twenty-two affiliated locals and three thousand members within a year. Organizers of this effort included veterans of the PLM, who helped shape the orientation of the new group, drawing from the principles of the PLM and IWW. There were also a small number of Communists, who attended the founding conference of the party-led Trade Union Unity League. As the new organization proclaimed in March 1928,

> That the exploited class, the greater part of which is made up of manual labor, is right in establishing a class struggle in order to affect an economic and moral betterment of its condition, and at last its complete freedom from capitalist tyranny . . . That the corporations, possessors of the natural and social wealth, being integral parts of the international association of industry, commerce and banking, the disinherited class must also integrate by means of its federation and confederation into a single union all the labor of the world.[24]

The group was originally envisioned as a cross-border worker alliance, with the direct support of Mexican president Plutarco Calles. Post-revolutionary governments walked a fine line, needing to present themselves as "friends of labor" to co-opt a labor movement still infused with revolutionary aspirations, while marginalizing revolutionaries. As part of this strategy, the Calles government sought to incorporate Mexican workers into the state-controlled Confederación Regional Obrera Mexicana (CROM). Through his consuls, Calles also considered affiliating Mexican workers in the US to the CROM for the same purpose, as US Communists began vying for influence among Mexican workers. Containing and taming Mexican labor on both sides of the border was also part of a strategy to show that the Mexican government could once again be a reliable partner for the US government, and to encourage more foreign investment.

While it was not uncommon for the Mexican government to rhetorically support its citizens north of the border, this sentiment was dispensed with when labor militancy reared its head. The Calles government was in the process of fostering the growth of the CROM as a tame and controlled labor organization that worked within the corporatist structures of the new state. The ascendant bourgeois class consolidated its power after the elimination of its enemies on the far left and right, and was eager to extinguish residual revolutionary sentiment lingering within the working class. In order to achieve a modus vivendi with its northern neighbor, its primary creditor, trade partner, and potential military threat, the Calles government took a direct role in administering its migrant policy vis-à-vis its consuls. By 1928, the million Mexican workers in the US posed a potential problem. On the one hand, their economic stability and well-being benefitted the fledgling state by providing an outlet for displaced and impoverished workers. If they were compelled to return in large numbers as a result of repressive or exceptionally exploitative policies, they could become a volatile and explosive factor. On the other hand, labor radicalism among Mexican workers in the US threatened to spill across the border, jeopardize newfound stable relations, and even threaten more US intervention.

The active involvement of the Mexican government helped to cultivate a conservative wing of the group, although it still deployed residual revolutionary language in its dealings with Mexican labor. Through this wing, the Mexican government worked through its consular channels to control the CUOM, and to align it with its own efforts to consolidate and reach rapprochement with US capital. While the consuls supported worker organization, they did so tepidly and as a means to counteract a revival of radicalism and labor conflict. Nevertheless, radicals played a role in swinging CUOM-affiliated workers into alliance with the Communist Party during the union's first affiliated strike in 1928.

The goal of the CUOM was to inspire Mexican working-class associations, primarily mutualistas, to constitute unions and affiliate. To encourage broad participation, the organizers laid out principles thought to appeal to the sensibilities of Mexicans ready to take collective action around a number of issues affecting the working class. Included in its organizing principles was the aim to unite all Mexican workers in one union along syndicalist lines, to fight for equal rights between immigrants and native-born citizens, to preserve Mexican culture and identity, to build up educational and welfare systems for Mexican families, and to defend Mexicans persecuted and detained in US jails.[25] The call was heeded especially where workers with organizing experience and class consciousness could be found. The first general convention took place from May 5 to May 7, 1928, in Los Angeles. Delegates were seated from twenty-one cities and towns throughout Southern California. Within a month, the new confederation voted to affiliate with the Central Labor Council of Los Angeles and adhere to the principles of the American Federation of Labor.

One union that formed and affiliated to the CUOM involved agricultural workers in the Imperial Valley in southeastern California. In the Imperial Valley, Mexican farmworkers comprised 90 percent of the field labor force and about one third of the total population (about 20,000 people).[26] Most were farmworkers, but there was also a small business community, which as a more stable population featured prominently in local affairs. This cross-class character within the Mexican community was also present in the mutualistas that operated in the Imperial Valley. In 1928, in the weeks before the advent of cantaloupe-picking season in May of 1928, organizers with the union held mass meetings throughout the region to recruit members primarily through the mutualistas. The mutual-aid structure carried over into the new union. Under the supervision of the consul, the union recruited among the different Mexican groups—farmworkers, merchants, and even labor contractors—with the intention of creating a conservative organization that limited its aims to petitioning for modest improvements in the living conditions of the Mexican community as a whole.

The representatives focused on raising wages but also presented the union as an alternative to the notorious labor contracting system. Through this system, growers secured farm labor through brokers who recruited labor gangs for the farms. Instead of having to negotiate wages with workers directly, the growers gave a lump sum to the contractors, who then paid the workers after jobs were complete and took a cut for themselves. California courts had consistently ruled that the labor contracting system absolved growers of responsibility for labor camp and work conditions.[27] Because contractors were not regulated, this system bred abject corruption, with contractors frequently skimming, underpaying, or simply skipping town without paying after the job was complete.

Growers also found reasons to deduct or disqualify pay, making it precarious for the workers. This system, with some exceptions, set up cozy relations between growers and contractors, who both profited in one way or another from the exploitation of the farmworkers.[28] An estimated twelve hundred Mexican workers joined La Unión de Trabajadores del Valle Imperial (Union of Imperial Valley Workers) by the time the harvest began in 1928, with hundreds more ready to follow its lead. Despite its growth, as an ethnic-based union, La Unión did not allow Filipino workers to join, which allowed the growers to exploit the racial divisions that emerged during the strike.

Under the direction of the Mexican consul in Calexico, Carlos Arizu, the newly formed union leadership sent a delegation to leading cantaloupe farmers in the region with the intention of establishing a minimum standard of 15–20 cents per crate for the workers, depending on the specific characteristics of the work. They also called for readily available ice water and for building materials to make storage sheds and outhouses for the workers in the fields. When growers stonewalled any form of collective bargaining and held fast to the 14-cent rate, the union leadership under Filemón González balked, and a series of wildcat strikes were launched. Rebellious Mexican workers took action independent of the union, beginning with a walkout at the Sears Brothers ranch in Brawley on Monday, May 7. Similar walkouts occurred at other farms over the next two days as the workers defied the union and sought to spread the strike themselves. By Wednesday an estimated 2,000–3,000 Mexican workers were on strike, while the Filipino and white workers remained on the job, undermining the effectiveness of the walkout. In its opposition to the strike, the local media blamed it on "radicals" and played up the class divides within the Mexican community. As the editor of the *Imperial Valley Press* hissed, "It is unfortunate that a few radicals within the ranks are likely to subject all the Mexican laborers in Imperial Valley to criticism and censure." He further concluded that the strike was not supported by "the better class of Mexican people."[29]

Caught off-guard by the worker militancy, the leadership of the union attempted to take control of the strike by arranging negotiations. Refusing to meet, the growers instead colluded and used local government to crush the strike before it could be spread throughout the region. Repression was swift. After the initial walkouts, the grower-aligned Imperial Valley County Board of Supervisors instructed the sheriff to deputize growers, foremen, vigilantes, and other sympathizers, and dispatched at least forty of these armed men to break up "all meetings of the workers" and to "arrest agitators wherever found."[30] Growers circulated flyers throughout the region warning strikers that they would face deportation unless they returned to work. Meanwhile, the *Los Angeles Times* and local media began a concerted campaign to discredit the strike, calling it the work of "outside agitators" affiliated with the IWW, who were threatening violence against workers if they did not strike.[31] This was belied by evidence that showed broad support for the strike, which can explain why the growers relied on police violence to break it.

Union leaders began organizing mass meetings to conduct the strike, attracting crowds of thousands. At one gathering outside a Mexican pool hall in Westmoreland, a cantaloupe-growing region just west of Brawley, a thousand Mexican farmworkers gathered to hear union activists announce the details of the strike. When a deputy advised the group to disperse, he was driven out of the area. Shortly thereafter, reinforcements were called in and a squad of heavily armed sheriff's deputies charged into the crowd, arrested several attendees, and declared the gathering illegal.

Within twenty-four hours of the initial walkouts, fifty Mexicans were arrested, including organizers and strike sympathizers, and charged with vagrancy, disturbing the peace, and resisting arrest, although no actual laws were broken.[32] The secretary of the union, Refugio Rio, was singled out and held incommunicado for an extensive period as a means to weaken the fledgling union.[33] To prevent the trial episode from distracting from the harvest, the presiding judge delayed it until July, when the harvest was over.

After the arrests, the sheriff's deputies set up roving patrols to prevent any further organizing or job actions. They closed the union office and shut down four pool halls where workers commonly gathered in an overwhelming show of force against the strikers. The *Los Angeles Times* triumphantly announced the failure of the strike in its May 12 edition.[34] During the strike, the consul, Arizu, was dumped in favor of a more conservative figure as a gesture to the growers in the region. Despite defeating the strike, growers implemented some of the strike demands to head off future unrest. Most significantly, the practice of withholding wages was abolished, standardized pay periods were established, and the growers assumed full responsibility for paying farmworkers instead of the contractors.[35]

The Cannery and Agricultural Workers Industrial Union

In 1920 the Second Congress of the Communist International had outlined a strategy for Communist parties in the advanced capitalist countries to organize the large populations of rural laborers oppressed by capitalist landowners. Characterizing the unity between urban and rural workers as a "fundamental task" in order to create the basis for revolutionary transformation, the Comintern used the Bolshevik model to show how rural workers, tenants, and subsistence farmers stood to

> [g]ain everything by the victory of the proletariat, which brings with it: a) liberation from the payment of rent or of a part of the crops . . . to the owners of large estates; b) the abolition of all mortgages; c) abolition of many forms of pressure and of dependence on the owners of large estates (forests and their use, etc.); d) immediate help from the proletarian state for farm work (permitting use . . . of the agricultural implements . . . on the big capitalist estates expropriated by

the proletariat, the immediate transformation . . . of all rural cooperatives and agricultural companies . . . into institutions primarily for the support of the poor peasantry, that is to say, the proletarians, semi-proletarians, small farmers, etc.).[36]

They further identified the oppression of agricultural workers by capitalist landlords as particularly brutal, establishing semi-feudal political systems of control that kept large populations of workers in abject poverty and materially underdeveloped. According to western Communists, the condition of workers on farms in California matched this analysis.

By 1930, 2,892 large capitalist farm operations had come to dominate a large statewide agricultural economy, which intersected with financial, transport, and commercial capital. While only 2 percent of total farms, they produced 28.5 percent of total agricultural output.[37] These farms, concentrated in San Joaquin, Kern, Monterey, and Imperial Counties, resembled, as Carey McWilliams described them, "factories in the fields." They employed thousands of workers subdivided into different aspects of production, and used industrial equipment and machinery and scientific labor management techniques.

By 1930, the Imperial Valley earned its name in terms of landownership, as fifty-one growers came to control 83 percent of all farmland, most of whom were absentee owners.[38] Their preponderance of influence over the design of city polity allowed for them to run the valley as their personal fiefdom. The concentration of these great landholdings in regional clusters brought into proximity and contact large numbers of migrant workers. They shared similar experiences, using the same migratory routes, working the same fields, and receiving similar wages and working conditions.

Growers drastically lowered wages and downsized production during the Great Depression, pushing workers to absorb the most immediate and acute effects of the economic crisis. As a result, average agricultural wages in 1933 plummeted to 12.5 cents an hour, less than half of the 30 cents per hour earned thirteen years earlier. That same year, the State Relief Agency reported that there was a surplus of around eight to nine farmworkers for every job available, with the practice of maintaining a large reserve army of labor exacerbated by economic crisis.[39] The resulting wage cuts across the board, unemployment, and underemployment threw tens of thousands of workers and their families into destitution and abject poverty. Workers had little to lose going on strike, and much to gain.

Another wave of wildcat strikes occurred in first week of January of 1930 during the lettuce harvest, after growers began to employ white migrant workers and pay them at a higher rate. Faced with an unjust and discriminatory racial wage structure, former members of the union and Filipino work crews coalesced around the need to demand equal wages. With the separate camps, leadership was selected and the two groups decided to present the growers with unified demands in what amounted to an ad-hoc union. When grower representatives refused to negotiate, several hundred Mexican and Filipino lettuce workers in the Imperial Valley walked off the farms in a unified wildcat strike. Learning from the failure of the 1928 strike, Mexican and Filipino workers had made an agreement to collaborate in any job action to prevent the growers from exploiting racial divisions or granting concessions to one group to weaken the other. The newly installed Mexican consul, Hermolao Torres, for his part, disavowed the strike and did not provide any form of support.

Much like the 1928 strike, local government and the sheriff's department began to break up meetings, arrest those identified as militants, and keep the media out of the area. Without the CUOM to help organize the strike, Mexican workers appealed to the leadership of a local mutualista. The Mexican Mutual Aid Society, dominated by leadership drawn from merchants and small businessmen with ties to the local Chamber of Commerce, limited their efforts to an offer to negotiate with the Western Growers. When the entreaties were rejected, they refused to support a strike and abdicated leadership, while the consul also opposed the strike.

It was during this wildcat strike that the Communist Party caught wind of the moment and made its first effort to apply the TUUL strategy to agriculture. Party members in Los Angeles were following events in the press and, identifying an opening for radical leadership, decided to test the organizing skills. Three organizers sent from Los Angeles, Frank Waldron, Harry Harvey, and Tetsuji Horiuchi, were tasked by the party to go into the Mexican barrios in the towns to organize and provide leadership for the strike through the newly created Agricultural Workers Industrial League (AWIL). Without any farm work experience or direct contacts with the workers, the three made their way into the Imperial Valley.

Due to the apparent scale of repression, the three organizers quickly decided to take their efforts underground. They established their base in Brawley and worked clandestinely for several days among the Mexican and Filipino workers to build strike organization. As Harry Harvey later described:

> We had to keep ourselves under cover as much as possible . . . after dark we would immediately scoot around the shacks and hovels of the workers who were always glad to see us. They warned us against the stool pigeons, gave us information, and let us know the temperature of the workers in the various fields . . . toward the strike. The workers we visited would arrange little meetings of the strongest union elements among the workers and out of these we would set up committees . . . In talking to these splendid rank and file representatives of the working class one was heartened. No sacrifice, in the matter of getting them better living and working conditions, seemed too great to make.[40]

The organizers were able to remain unknown within the barrios, which were segregated and squalid shanties located outside the well-kept, modern towns where the white inhabitants lived. To make life habitable for the growers and their families, who spent non-summer months living in the valley and tending to their businesses, they turned arid desert into pockets of air-conditioned modernity and shaded comfort that even attracted tourism. Mexicans and other farmworkers were not part of the design, so they formed their own homesteads in the surrounding environment without any amenities. As Kathryn Olmsted describes:

The men and women who harvested the crops lived outside the towns in fetid, crowded colonies. Mostly from Mexico, these migrants in the shanty towns drank water from the irrigation ditches, and as a consequence sometimes watched their babies die of typhoid fever. During the summer months, the children swatted away the swarms of flies and flopped down under the tents to seek relief from the temperatures, which soared up to 125 degrees.[41]

After several days of networking, identifying a core of trustworthy militants, and developing strategy, the AWIL organizers went public with their strike demands. The twelve-point plan they circulated throughout the region called for more than doubling the hourly wage to 50 cents for all workers, guaranteed four-hour minimum pay each shift and a maximum eight-hour day with overtime and double time for Sundays and holidays; an end to child labor, no discrimination based on race or sex, employer-provided housing, abolition of the labor contracting system, and for recognition of the union and a closed shop in which the AWIL exercised the exclusive right to hire workers through its own hiring hall.[42] The strike demands were broadly taken up by the Mexican and Filipino strikers, who aligned with the AWIL leadership and their strategy, rejecting the passive subversion of the Mexican Mutual Aid organization. In response to the AWIL's success, their own anti-Communist sentiment, and the desire to redeem their standing with local growers, the society turned against the strike.

As the strike pressed into its third week, the growers implemented further tactics beyond overt violence to break the strike. Working through the office of Imperial County District Attorney Elmer Heald, growers were able to repress the strike leadership through the enforcement of California's Criminal Syndicalism Act. This anti-radical law, largely crafted to repress the socialist and labor movement, allowed for the arrest of labor activists who purportedly advocated for crime, sabotage, violence, or any other unlawful method as part of conducting a strike. In practice, they were purposefully vague to allow for broad interpretation and carte blanche application at the local level. As one historian points out,

> The "red hysteria" or anti-radical feeling thus created made itself felt in the political organs of the community, the legislature, the executive, and the courts. By various methods . . . criminal syndicalism bills [were] designed to put a stop to the activities, doctrines, practices, or existence of the radical groups . . . any measure associated with opposition to [radicalism] was practically assured of passage with only slight examination.[43]

Furthermore, the deployment of violence and the suspension of fundamental civil and human rights carried out in "accordance" with this law assured that no one would be held accountable for whatever occurred as a consequence. The suspension of bourgeois law became the means by which the capitalists maintained their autocratic rule over the farmworkers.

With the assistance of Captain William Francis Hynes, the head of the Los Angeles Police Department's notorious anti-Communist "Red Squad," labor spies were integrated into the ranks of the strike committee to gather intelligence on the composition of the leadership. These spies were then later used as hostile witnesses against those arrested, claiming that the AWIL-led strike included a secret call to bomb lettuce sheds and use violence to intimidate strikebreakers despite the lack of any evidence or corroboration.[44] This story, taken up by the grower-friendly media, then allowed the local governing apparatus to bring its full weight to bear on the strike leaders.[45]

Using the law, sheriff's deputies sought out and arrested the three AWIL organizers, holding them incommunicado for several days. When the Reverend Clinton Taft, the head of the Los Angeles chapter of the American Civil Liberties Union, made a special trip to appeal for the release of the men, the sheriff physically assaulted him and threatened his safety if he did not leave town. During that time, growers worked with the Mexican consul and Mexican Mutual Aid Society to divide the Mexicans from the Filipinos. The consul encouraged Mexican strikers to repatriate to Mexico under the false pretense that they would be resettled and given land, while the Mexican Mutual Aid Society warned Mexicans that if they did not separate from the Filipinos and return to work, they would be deported. Lastly, when a smaller group of white shed workers walked out on strike in February, reinvigorating the field strikes and potentially uniting workers across the racial and occupational lines, the growers eagerly granted wage increases to the white workers. The threat of a general strike threatened not only the power of the growers and their allies to rely on physical repression, but it also threatened the whole racial labor system that underwrote the spectacular growth and profitability of industrial agriculture in the first place. The majority of white shed workers refused to unite their efforts with Mexican and Filipino workers and a Communist-led organization. They chose to return to work and to prevent a unified strike among all groups of workers.[46]

Soon many Mexicans gradually left the area, returned to Mexico, or begrudgingly returned to work. While small groups held out alongside the remaining Filipino workers, the AWIL recognized the defeat and called it off on January 23. Consul Torres, with grower support, used the opportunity to help foster the organization of conservative mutualista groups as a bulwark against the AWIL and radicalism. The growers, now acutely aware of the AWIL's efforts to spread the union, went into war footing. Rallying to their side were federal and state officials weary of the Communist Party's growing influence. Charles T. Connell, a Department of Labor official sent into the area during the strike, reported to his bosses in Washington that more strikes were likely, concluding that the Communist organizers were "bound to stir up trouble . . . the pickers are Mexicans [and] are easy subjects for the Communistic organizers, then there are several thousand Filipinos in the Valley who are tainted with the propaganda of the Communists. It is a dangerous situation and serious trouble is feared, as if the Mexicans walk out in May [sic], the shippers are due to lose large profits."[47] In a sign of things to come, Connell worked in league with the growers and endorsed the conclusion that the radical threat needed to be eliminated at all costs by using whatever means necessary.

The next potential opportunity to organize discontent into organization and action was the June cantaloupe harvest in the Imperial Valley. In April of 1930, a month before the harvest was set to begin, the Communist Party planned a farmworker conference for April 20 in order to identify and organize farmworker militants that could become the network of strike committees for the coming actions. In response to the conference, the farm-aligned state apparatus in Imperial Valley unleashed another round of violent repression throughout the county under the criminal syndicalism statute. Four days before the conference a mob led by the Imperial County sheriff orchestrated massive roundups of Communists and union-aligned workers. AWIL offices were raided and meetings were broken up. At one meeting at a workers' hall in El Centro, the whole group, including AWIL organizers alongside 114 Mexican, Filipino, African American, Japanese, and white workers, were arrested en masse.[48] Over the course of two months workers with citizenship were gradually released in small groups at a time, although the Mexicans and some Japanese organizers were deported.

Seven members of the group were identified as leaders based solely on the testimony of three undercover infiltrators from the Bowling Detective Agency. The case was presided over by a judge who was an active member of the American Legion, and sentenced by a jury of grower-allied men. The seven were sentenced to between three and forty-two years in prison, although they were paroled after two years. This group included a Japanese TUUL organizer Tetsuji Horiuchi; Los Angeles District organizer Carl Sklar; Oscar Erickson, national secretary of the AWIL; Lawrence Emory of the TUUL-affiliated Marine Workers Industrial Union; Frank Spector of the International Labor Defense; Danny Roxas, a Filipino worker and secretary of the AWIL; and Eduardo Herrera and Braulio Orozco, both Mexican workers and supporters of the AWIL.[49] Orozco and Herrera were veteran supporters of the PLM and were some of the first and most committed organizers in league with the AWIL.[50] The men were sent off to either Folsom or San Quentin Prison, where they served two-year terms before being paroled. Horiuchi and Sklar were subsequently deported to the Soviet Union.

The smashing of the 1930 strike occurred as part of an ascendant nationwide alignment of anti-Communist forces reacting to the threat of rising worker militancy. That year the House of Representatives of the Seventy-First Congress conducted a national investigation against Communist activities, amounting to the opening shots of a second aggressive ruling-class offensive against the stirrings of labor radicalism and anticapitalist politics. Highly dramatized hearings were conducted across the country with handpicked witnesses giving scripted testimony about the deep infiltration of communism. Reports were compiled and widely published through the media that outlined the need for a coordinated and heavy-handed response from capital; agents of the local, state, and federal government; and non-governmental "patriotic" societies such as the American Legion.[51] In California, this brought growers together with an array of anti-Communist politicians, police officials, judges, and other segments of the state bureaucracy, who trained their sights on the farmworker movement. The Mexican government, for its own reasons, also joined the coalition through its US consulates. As Gilbert González observes,

> The subject of communism brought agreement among the growers, the Department of Labor, the National Labor Board, the Federal Imperial Valley

Commission, and the Mexican consul. They divided into two camps: those who favored any action, legal or illegal, to oust CAWIU, and those who favored more subtle, indirect, but generally legal, action.[52]

As the Communists observed this active alignment of forces, they concluded that "the entire fascist apparatus of the State has been mobilized" against their efforts through the Trade Union Unity League and the CAWIU.[53] Alongside repressive criminal syndicalism laws, which gave the state carte blanche to arrest Communists, striking workers, and anyone in their path; the federal-led efforts also merged immigration enforcement and deportation to break the labor movement.

The Federal Immigration Act of 1917 had nestled the exclusion of political radicals firmly in immigration policy, and this became a hammer against the large segment of the foreign-born workforce who were at the forefront of the industrial union movement.[54] In California, weaponized immigration policy became a means to cut the head off of the agricultural union movement, led by Mexican workers. A representative of the San Francisco Waterfront Employers' Association explained the value of the policy during the anti-Communist hearings in Washington, when he affirmed the efficacy of the collaboration between business, the police, and immigration officials to identify and target foreign-born Communist and immigrant union organizers working on the docks: "It has only been by the closest cooperation of the police and Immigration Department and Department of Justice here that they have been able to handle this situation here at all."[55]

Even with the setbacks and gathering forces of reaction extending their reach, the CAWIU settled into the valley for the long haul, demonstrating a courageous tenacity to build farmworker organization in the face of extreme hostility and state-sanctioned vigilante terror and violence. As a result, some Mexican and Filipino workers especially either joined the union or looked to it for leadership. Committed to the task, party leaders sent more organizers from Los Angeles and San Francisco, opening up several regional offices and trying out new tactics to build the foundations for future strikes in the Imperial Valley through the recruitment of the most militant workers from ranches, farms, and sheds that could in turn become organizers in the fields. The vision, driven by political analysis and a palpable and organic militancy among the advanced sections apparently chomping at the bit for organization, led the Communist organizers to foresee the rapid development of a nationwide industrial farmworker union under the aegis of the party. A resolution from the June 1930 convention of District 13 (covering California, Arizona, and Nevada) read:

> The Imperial Valley strikes, where the Communist Party and the Trades Union Unity League obtained increasing influence over the workers, is of special significance, embracing Mexican and Filipino workers as well as Americans, and are an important link in the anti-imperialist struggle. The crisis in agriculture, sharpening the attack on the agricultural workers, puts upon this district the need of actively working, as is stated in the draft thesis for the national convention, among the farmer migratory workers who have been transformed into a

semi-industrial agricultural worker . . . We are closer now than ever to the task of winning the majority of the workers for the Communist Party.[56]

While their optimism was undoubtedly overblown, the party did establish itself early on as the only vehicle able and willing to fight the growers. After the defeat of strike efforts in early 1930, the farmworker movement was weakened and confidence receded. Over the next two years only nine more strikes were attempted in California, without success. At this time, the party changed its strategy to focus more heavily on the organization of the unemployed in the urban areas. This included the organization and recruitment of unemployed farmworkers congregated in the cities, who could then become the vanguard of subsequent organizing efforts thereafter as these recruits returned to the harvest. Despite the retreat, the CAWIU kept a presence in the field, sending organizers out to respond to walkouts and wildcat actions, often assuming leadership such as during the Santa Clara cannery strike in 1931, the pea workers' strike at Half Moon Bay in 1932, and an orchard pruners' strike in Solano County in 1932. A combination of weak organization, poor planning, and severe repression by police and vigilantes contributed to the defeat of these strikes.

When workers took initiative to strike for better wages and conditions in 1933, the CAWIU was more prepared. In the coastal cities, federal and state relief became more adequately distributed and there were signals of economic recovery, leading unemployed workers to food security or back to employment. The same was not the case in the countryside, where conditions continued to deteriorate. The Communist Party and the CAWIU anticipated the possibility for renewed struggle in agriculture as first indications confirmed that growers refused to offer higher wages, even as they were rising in urban work.

Rising inflation and low wages, even as some markets like cotton were stabilizing, led workers to begin taking action. In doing so, they turned to the CAWIU for leadership and joined in CAWIU-led strikes by the thousands. In 1933, for instance, Mexican and Filipino pea pickers sent their own representatives to CAWIU headquarters in Los Angeles to request organizers, after efforts through the revived La Union de Trabajadores del Valle Imperial and the Mexican consul failed to produce results. By the outbreak of the strike wave of 1933, the CAWIU had learned some practical lessons from previous failures and developed new strategies and tactics to overcome the disproportionate advantages of the growers.

Chapter 23

The CAWIU and the Strike Wave of 1933

"If there is no strike in the San Joaquin Valley now,
there will be one when we get there."
—**Striking El Monte Berry Picker, 1933**

T hrough their efforts, the Communist-led CAWIU became the largest farmworker union in history. A core of militant workers provided the organizational
backbone for CAWIU strikes, serving on strike committees as picket captains.
Some of the Mexican workers who passed through the union would make contact
with the union to solicit support for local strikes. Through their intimate interactions,
Communists also recruited some farmworkers to the party. While many historians
have reiterated the presumptive idea that the farmworkers were only interested in effective organization and not radical politics, their analyses lack a fundamental understanding of two things: how the aspect of organization and politics interrelated, and
how some of the Mexican farmworkers had *their own* radical politics that did not have
to be taught by Communists, but rather were compatible.

The Communist-led CAWIU organized their union along radical, class-struggle
principles. This included the primacy of building multiracial unity, the mass involvement of whole farming communities in democratic decision-making, building solidarity
campaigns between different working-class groups, and bases of support linking rural
and urban areas. They also understood the disproportionate class power of their rivals,
which gave them an unwavering focus on the worker's capacity to disrupt capitalist production as the only means to win, and the discipline to resist state repression. The lack
of this class struggle-orientation rendered their chief rivals in the AFL impotent and
irrelevant to the farmworkers, whereas the Communists won the workers over to their
politics in organizational practice. Not only did their experienced members become
mass leaders, the party itself grew significantly in this period, including among Mexican
workers in Southern California. In constructing their political framework, they once
again took their lead from the Communist International.

The Communist International was instrumental in outlining a policy identifying
the intersection of racism and imperialism and the way employers used national chauvinism and exploited racial tensions among different groups of workers to their own advantage. On the question of national oppression, the Communist movement nationally
took as its starting point the writings of Marx, Engels, and Lenin on the subject. This
included the principle of the "rights of oppressed nations to self-determination." The
Communist International also paid close attention to the racial oppression of African

Americans in the United States.

At its Sixth World Congress, the Communist International developed its thesis on the revolutionary movement in the colonies, which informed the world view of the Communist Party cadre that entered the fields of central and Southern California. This thesis began with the condemnation of the destructive role of US imperialism in the colonies and nations under imperialist spheres of influence, including Mexico:

> The growing economic and military expansion of North American imperialism in the countries of Latin America is transforming this continent into one of the most important meeting places of the antagonisms of the whole imperialist colonial system. The influence of Great Britain . . . is being replaced by the United States . . . North American imperialism is conquering the commanding positions in the economy of these countries, subordinating their governments to its financial control . . . [and] is taking on a character of undisguised violence.[1]

The anti-imperialist analysis identified the destabilizing role that capital played in these countries, extracting primary resources, cultivating compliant regimes, and retarding or reversing industrialization.

> *This is the essence . . . [of the] function of colonial enslavement*: the colonial country is compelled to sacrifice the interests of its independent development and to play the part of an economic (agrarian-raw material) appendage to foreign capitalism, which at the expense of the laboring classes of the colonial country, strengthens the economic and political power of the imperialist bourgeoisie in order to perpetuate the monopoly of the latter in the colonies and to increase its expansion as compared with the rest of the world.[2]

As a function of imperialism, the underdevelopment of colonial economies assured the increased impoverishment and marginalization of the laboring classes. This led to displacement and the potential for revolt on the one hand, and out-migration on the other. The 1928 Platform of the Workers (Communist) Party (forerunner of the CP) identified:

> The *immigration laws* which restrict the freedom of movement of the foreign-born workers and discriminate against the peoples of Asia are part and parcel of the system of American imperialism . . . The newest demand of the bosses . . . is to give full authority to the President to regulate, restrict, or enlarge the immigration quotas according to the needs of the different industries.[3]

Framing racism toward immigrants as a means of capitalist control of labor in the context of imperialism abroad, the party developed a more elaborate strategy to combat anti-immigrant racism directly, rejecting the Socialist Party's tendency to subsume the distinct experience of racial oppression to class struggle.

Taking a public stand against the racial discrimination embedded in immigration policy, the party took an unequivocal stance against national chauvinism and racialized immigration restriction. Its official demands called for the abolition of all immigration restrictions and discriminatory laws, an active campaign to "uproot" prejudices fostered by the employers between workers, the need to integrate immigrant workers into the political life of the country (whether or not they could vote), and the call for equal pay for equal work between foreign and native-born workers. For Mexican workers specifically, the party developed a message of cross-border working-class unity and solidarity. This was aided by the growth and influence of the Communist Party in Mexico, especially among farmworkers. Some of those with experience with the party in Mexico also worked seasonally in the Imperial Valley, Los Angeles County, and the San Joaquin Valley. Building on these connections, a July 1930 edition of the *Daily Worker*, the Communist Party's main newspaper, appealed to Mexican farmworkers with an internationalist approach:

> Fellow workers, the Communist Parties of the United States and Mexico, sections of the Communist International, appeal to all exploited by imperialism and the bourgeoisie of Mexico and the United States to struggle together against their common enemy. The Communist Parties of Mexico and the United States fight in their respective countries for the betterment of the conditions of the working class and to overthrow the respective exploiting classes and to establish a government of the workers—that is, to establish a government such as in the Union of Socialist Soviet Republics, where the workers and poor peasants exercise power and are the bosses of their own lands and factories. The Communist Parties of Mexico and the United States don't wage the struggle separately within the national boundaries of their respective countries. On the contrary, their struggle is an international one, forming and reinforcing the most intimate alliance against the bourgeoisie and imperialism and for the victory of communism the world over.[4]

Acting on these principles, the TUUL incorporated into their public pronouncements opposition to the targeting of foreign-born workers. They held protests across the Southwest through the 1930s to oppose the deportation of Mexicans and others, achieving some success in curtailing anti-immigrant legislation.[5]

California Communists applied their antiracist principles to their analysis of the Filipino and Mexican farmworkers that were prominent segments of the agricultural workforce in that state.[6] After the anti-Filipino riots, the Communist Party and its auxiliary organizations defended Filipinos as others closed ranks against them. As Stuart Jamieson describes,

> Representatives of the Workers International Relief and International Labor Defense were sent to Watsonville to help Filipinos who had been arrested and beaten during the disturbances. Protest meetings to agitate against race discrimination were organized in San Francisco, Los Angeles, and Oakland. Mexican and Filipino beet workers and asparagus cutters were reported attending organization meetings called by the Agricultural Workers Industrial League in Sacramento County during the spring of 1930. Joint meetings of local unemployed councils and branches of the A.W.I.L. were also held in Stockton and other central California towns.[7]

The party relied on recruiting Japanese, Mexican, and Filipino workers, who became indispensable as organizers, bridging party work directly to these communities. Party leaders also learned that success relied on making connections to existing organizations within these communities. When in response to the racism and exclusion experienced by Mexicans and Filipinos they formed ethnic-based unions, Communists angled to work with them in united fronts under the CAWIU umbrella.[8] They observed that ethnic unionism was an advance toward industrial unionism, but their exclusiveness tended to undermine the efficacy of strike efforts as growers could exploit racial and national divisions to turn different groups against each other. They also criticized the racial chauvinism of the AFL leadership, which clung to its craft orientation and persisted in opposition to immigrant inclusion. In the face of these challenges, party-led CAWIU organizing efforts prioritized the building of class solidarity between the Mexican and Filipino leadership as a prerequisite for any successful strike action, especially as these two groups formed the majority of the migratory pickers in the early 1930s.

After welding together the basis for joint action between the two groups, the Communists proceeded with a call for a renewed strike in the cantaloupe fields in 1930. The Communist-led breakthrough toward multiracial organization demonstrated for the first time the organizational capacity to mobilize sufficient labor power to effectively bring total production to a halt. Racial unity took from the growers their primary means to keep unions out of the fields. Facing the threat of a unified workforce going on strike together in common cause led the growers to turn to more violent and extralegal methods to repress and defeat the threat.[9]

In attempting to build a party of the most militant workers recruited from their organizing endeavors, the Communist Party also applied their theories of racial unity to their internal structures. The Communist Party rejected the separation of immigrant workers into ethnic branches, instead creating fully integrated branches. Like their IWW forerunners, they also realized the importance of recruiting and training organizers who could speak the languages of the workers and understand the cultural nuances of the workers. They also learned through experience the need for flexibility and adaptability when organizing among Mexicans, who had their own traditions and organizational models. For instance, the successes of the CAWIU increased when they turned to worker-led organizing that utilized existing relationships:

> The union utilized inherent organization among workers. Union organizers depended on social and familial networks among workers. Day to day leadership arose from these networks. The earlier affiliation with the Partido Liberal Mexicano and the Industrial Workers of the World set a precedent for transethnic cooperation among progressives and laid the basis for a particular openness to the CAWIU.[10]

As part of the strategy to counter the growers' tendency to activate racial tensions by playing ethnic groups against each other, the CAWIU inserted into all of their demands a provision that growers not discriminate against any group of workers based on race or sex.

The CAWIU organizing strategy also involved mass democratic participation. While organized working-class leadership was sought out, the union organizers politicized involvement using a number of tactics. All members who joined the union were expected to become organizers, rejecting the rigid bureaucratic chain-of-command structure of AFL unions that often bypassed the workers in decision-making. Strike leaders and field organizers were voted on by the workers, and strike demands were constructed in close consultation with workers themselves. During strikes, strike committees held mass meetings in different work camps and colonias to involve the people in every stage of decision-making. Issues of the day were debated and voted upon in large gatherings that often included family members. Through this mass process, the creativity and ingenuity of the workers was a factor that allowed improvisation, flexibility, and innovative tactics that could outflank their opponents. For instance, during the cotton strike, the workers invented the tactic of "guerrilla picketing," in which caravans of strikers were moved across a large area where they used bugles and drums to call out workers to join the strike.[11]

By politicizing and leading the great class struggles of the period, the Communist Party grew significantly, from 25,000 in 1934 to 75,000 in 1938. Dorothy Healy, a party leader and CAWIU organizer, estimated in her memoir that the party had 3,000 members in Los Angeles, with a significant number of this total being Mexican and Mexican American.[12] As part of its direct confrontation with racial segregation and discrimination, the party ran Mexican, Asian, and African American party members for California office. One such member, John Díaz, was a Mexican American farmworker who ran for San Francisco supervisor in November of 1933, as the strike wave rolled across the state. The party used the platform to connect their ongoing political causes, but Díaz's statement of intent alludes to the class struggles raging in the fields at the moment:

> Inasmuch as the city government, through its police force and courts, attacks workers, employed and unemployed, in their struggles for the right to live, I pledge myself to fight against all police terror, all anti-labor legislation, for the abolition of all vagrancy laws, repeal of the Criminal Syndicalism Law . . . I militantly oppose discrimination and Jim-Crowing of Negro workers, and the deportation of foreign-born workers; will fight for the release of . . . political prisoners. I endorse the Communist Party platform for improving conditions.[13]

As part of their campaign strategy, the party's five candidates for supervisor ran to replace the existing elected body for neglecting the needs of the poor and unemployed. The group led a "hunger march" of unemployed workers on the office of the Board of Supervisors every Monday leading up to the day of the election.[14]

The different forms of propaganda, agitation, and direct organizing won many recruits among the Mexican workers, especially among those who already had developed their own radical world views through experience. As Dorothy Healy paraphrased her political interactions with one group of veteran radicals during a Party meeting of farmworkers:

> I spoke in English about Communism and someone translated my words for the two dozen or so workers who were crammed into this tiny room. The response of the Mexican workers was essentially, "Of course we're for the revolution. When the barricades are ready, we'll be there with you, but don't bother us with meetings all the time. We know what to do, we know who the enemy is!" They were part of the generation of Mexican workers who had come out of the Revolution: very anticlerical, very sophisticated politically, and very Anarcho-syndicalist in orientation. "Just tell us when the revolution is ready, we'll be there."[15]

While it is not clear how many Mexican farmworkers joined the party in this period, there were seven predominantly Mexican branches formed along the agricultural corridor. According to anecdotal evidence drawn from interviews, this included over twenty members forming a chapter of the Young Communist League in Tulare (San Joaquin Valley), and fifteen to twenty-five members of a party branch in Brawley (Imperial Valley). Several Mexican workers who became lead organizers in the CAWIU also joined the party, including José Gomez, Francisco Medina, John Díaz, and Miguel Gutiérrez.[16]

The CAWIU and the Strike Wave of 1933

Growers reacted to the Depression by scaling back production as markets shrank. This, in turn, produced higher unemployment and gave the growers leverage to drastically reduce farm wages. Rapidly deteriorating conditions sapped worker confidence, which was further affected by mass roundups and deportations. The situation changed dramatically in 1933, as the AAA's subsidies helped growers become profitable again. Profits from the California cotton harvest, for instance, increased from 5 million in 1932 to 12.4 million the next year, a 150 percent increase.[17] Nevertheless, the growers kept wages suppressed in order to recoup lost profits from the previous years as well. The workers were well aware of this turn of events, and the CAWIU zeroed in on this frustration. Federal government bailouts doled out while workers were facing subsistence wages intensified the strike movement. One federal researcher took note, stating that "the crops in which strikes were most extreme were those crops which benefitted most by government efforts."[18]

In 1933, an estimated 56,800 workers participated in about 61 agricultural strikes across 17 different states across the country.[19] This explosive year ushered in the first generalized uprising of agricultural labor in United States history. The most militant edge of this upsurge took place in California. Having lived through several failed spontaneous strikes and sanguine repression, workers looked increasingly to organize in advance. The CAWIU, learning from its experiences, set out to build effective strike organization in the farm regions. Over the next year, the Communist Party-led CAWIU and predominantly Mexican workers rose up to challenge the most powerful grower organizations in the country, striking in succession across the most important sectors of agriculture at peak harvest time.

The façade of labor peace of the 1920s came to an end, and class tensions began
to break out into the open. This was driven by a decline in agricultural wages, which
stagnated between 1927 and 1929 despite economic growth, followed by a substantial
drop in wages between 1929 and 1932 with the onset of the Great Depression.[20] Beginning in 1928, Mexican farmworkers in Southern California took the first steps toward
unionization, meeting vicious employer resistance and opening up a sanguinary decade of intense class struggle that raged across the fields and farms. Mexican workers
led a mass strike wave that disrupted the whole industry and threatened to bring the
highly organized and well-connected class of growers to their knees.

Between 1933 and 1939 there were 180 strikes in California agriculture, of which
150 were fought out in bloody battles in the fields and orchards from the Imperial
Valley to the San Joaquin Valley.[21] These strikes fanned out over 34 of California's 58
counties, involving over 60,000 workers and consisting primarily of Mexicans and Filipinos.[22] In 1933 alone, there were 37 significant strikes in California involving 45,575
workers, of which 24 strikes involving 37,550 people (or 79 percent of the total) were
organized and led directly by the CAWIU.[23] All told, twenty-one of the CAWIU-led
strikes won wage gains for 32,800 workers, while only four ended in defeat, affecting
4,750 workers.[24] The year 1936 saw the second-largest number of strikes at twenty-four
and involving 13,500 workers.[25]

While the seeds of militancy germinated in the dramatic deterioration of conditions for farmworkers, the CAWIU political orientation and its organizational
capacity-building were crucial for the success of the strikes. Building on a foundation
of political analysis, accumulated experiences, flexibility and adaptability to changing conditions, and a broad support network that could help break the isolation of
the farmworker movement that favored the growers, the CAWIU was instrumental
for the advances in unionization in agriculture.

The organizational run of the CAWIU at the front end of this strike wave was
ephemeral but forceful. The combination of rapidly deteriorating conditions in the
fields with the onset of the Depression, a militant body of workers drawing from previous experiences and political traditions to lead others in wildcat strikes, and the
leadership of a courageous and determined core of Communist Party cadre made for
a highly combustible moment. In January of 1933, amid the deepening crisis in agriculture, the outbreak of a new round of wildcat strikes drew the CAWIU back into
the fields. By 1933, the state Communist Party was in a better position to now move
resources into the project, including tested and devoted party cadre and a statewide
apparatus with auxiliary support organizations that could attempt to counter the preponderance of the growers and their arsenal. Most significantly, Mexican farmworkers
took the initiative in launching wildcat strikes across the fields beginning in early 1933,
propelling forward the diametrically opposed forces into the epochal agricultural class
struggles of the period.

Leadership of these strikes by Communist Party–led organization was achieved
through the careful work of organizers who learned to integrate their efforts into
the existing social and political dimensions that they encountered. This began with

a careful study of the conditions of farmworkers throughout the state. Communists understood the tensions being created by diverging urban/rural wage scales influenced by the National Recovery Act, and the expectations that labor reform would eventually extend to the farms. They built on the rising expectations while also understanding the forces of opposition arrayed against them would produce the conditions for radicalization and the need to fight back. They also recognized the impact of labor struggle in the cities on the agricultural workforce, especially the San Francisco general strike. The CAWIU brought this analysis into their organizing, which by 1933 produced a general set of demands that could be the rallying point for strike action from El Centro to Santa Clara.

This strategy included winning over the militant vanguard of farmworkers from the pseudo-unions formed by Mexican consulate personnel to co-opt Mexican workers and thwart labor radicalism. The building of a network of CAWIU locals throughout the agricultural heartland of the state enabled organizers to agitate within the farmworker colonias, often beginning with door-knocking campaigns in the evening to meet the workers and identify the first layer of militants and sympathizers.

The CAWIU learned through experience to develop bottom-up strike strategies in which the workers themselves became instrumental in planning and executing strike strategy and developing impromptu tactics to respond to the growers' offensives. Dorothy Healy claimed that its organizers "followed the dictates of the Mexicans who better understood the community" while "decisions were made by Mexicans in large strike meetings."[26] The Communists came to appreciate the militancy, experiences, and political traditions of the workers, and jettisoned their preconceived or top-down notions in favor of mass democratic action. After the failure of the hastily organized strikes of the 1930s, the CAWIU took painstaking steps to build solid strike organization in 1933. This included the organization of strike committees to link farms, mass meetings to discuss and debate strike strategy and tactics, the utilization of whole families in strike operations, the creation of flying pickets to call workers out of the fields and prevent the maneuvers of strikebreakers, and community patrols to protect against vigilante violence.

While men were the primary workers in the fields, their wives and children were included in the strikes in various ways. In one of the 1933 strikes, involving betabeleros (sugar beet workers) in Oxnard, the local newspaper remarked that women and girls were central to the success of the picketing operations by forming roving brigades that sealed off every tangible entrance point into the environs of the struck field. As the *Oxnard Courier* reported, "Reinforced by their women, the strike of Mexican field laborers today continued on its fourth successive day . . . Groups of women and girls in addition to men, picketed every entrance of the local [beet sugar] factory, adobe house, and every exit from Oxnard."[27]

The CAWIU also used the industrial union model in their approach to organizing. Not only did they seek to overcome and transcend racial divisions, they also aimed to unite all segmentally structured and segregated forms of agricultural labor into one industrial union. This included organizing field workers alongside cannery, packing, and food processing workers. Industrial unionism was augmented by the creation of auxiliary organizations and campaigns to bridge support for farmworkers from urban areas, where the large Mexican barrios could provide forms of aid and support and where labor solidarity efforts could be spearheaded.

The party organized unemployed workers in the cities, which included large numbers of farmworkers in the off-season. They also procured and mobilized other forms of human and material resources in service to support workers in struggle and to defend them from repression. This included backing strikers with legal support in the form of the American Civil Liberties Union, raising strike funds, food, and other support through the International Labor Defense committee, and opposing political persecutions and deportations of immigrants through the National Committee for the Defense of Political Prisoners.

The Communist Party and its affiliated organizations such as the TUUL saw the strategic significance of organizing the broadening ranks of unemployed workers. The economic crisis hit agriculture even more severely, leaving throngs of migratory workers bottle-necked in towns and cities as growers cut back on hiring. For the difficult task of organizing an unstable and transient migrant workforce, these unemployed councils gave the party the opportunity to propagandize among farmworkers during the off-season, when thousands of migrants moved in droves into the larger cities of San Diego, Los Angeles, and San Francisco; or remained idle in smaller rural towns where even higher rates of unemployment afflicted the agricultural workforce. When the CAWIU organized strikes in rural areas, the unemployed councils served as transmission belts to mobilize support and aid.

The first conference of the Red International in 1921 proclaimed that the existence of unemployment could be used by capitalists to "pit the unemployed against their comrades who are still employed, and those who are still working against the unemployed."[28] By 1925, the party began to refine its orientation toward the unemployed, announcing the development of a national organization comprised of unemployed councils across the country. Despite the heady goals of the program, it floundered with little effect until the onset of the Great Depression in 1929, when the unemployed council movement was relaunched through the aegis of the TUUL.

When millions of workers were idled during the collapse, the party found traction around their demands for immediate relief, unemployment insurance, the seven-hour workday (to create more jobs), social insurance, and other demands that resonated with the downtrodden.[29] The party organized marches of unemployed workers to local city halls to press for immediate relief, often encountering armies of police who attacked the crowds unsparingly with clubs, blackjacks, and brass knuckles; and targeted Communists for arrest. The number of councils spread across the country rapidly, culminating in a national conference in New York in July 1930. The national gathering brought together 215 delegates representing 13 states. That same year, the party called a national day of action on March 6, declaring it "international unemployment day," and brought tens of thousands out in marches across the country. This included 35,000 in New York, 5,000 in Chicago, 2,000 in San Francisco, and several thousand more in Detroit, Washington, DC, and Boston.[30]

The Communist Party also built support for farmworker struggle by providing other forms of resources. The International Labor Defense Fund provided legal support for farmworkers, especially when facing arrest, deportation, or incarceration under the criminal syndicalism law. The Workers International Relief Fund established and utilized a fundraising network that worked through party branches and allies to raise money for food relief for unemployed or striking workers. While these organizations were no legal or financial match for the growers, they provided crucial support when no other resources were available.

The rise of the Communist-led farmworker movement in California showed the greatest potential to date to break grower hegemony over agriculture and to align urban and rural labor in terms of wages and union rights. The decline of the movement can be attributed to several factors: deep alliances of state and capital (on both sides of the border) to crush rural labor organization, rapidly shifting and disorienting policy diktats from the party hierarchy, and the vulnerability of agricultural labor.

Between April and December of 1933, thirty-seven strikes spread from the south northward, following harvests and migrant workers through the Imperial, San Joaquin, San Gabriel, and Santa Clara Valleys, as well as Los Angeles and Ventura Counties. Twenty-one of these strikes were led by the CAWIU. The CAWIU had established contacts among farmworkers in the Mexican community during the 1930 lettuce strike, the stillborn melon strike, as well as during the efforts to organize unemployed workers in the two subsequent years. Intent on leading the agricultural proletariat into the formation of an industrial union, handfuls of organizers were dispatched to different regions with only their political training and faith in the class as their guides.

El Monte Berry Strike

One of the first strikes to be lead directly by the CAWIU occurred in eastern Los Angeles County. Mexican berry pickers in the small truck-farming community of El Monte, located in the San Gabriel Valley, kicked off a strike that lasted twenty-seven days and spread to involve up to 7,000 workers. Here, Japanese berry growers relied on about fifteen hundred Mexican, Filipino, and some Anglo and Japanese farmworkers to harvest the annual crop, with the lion's share of workers comprising Mexican families including children.

Although Japanese landownership and tenant farming was restricted, white landowners ignored the laws when it was profitable, and enforcement was selective. Japanese growers also operated throughout other parts of Los Angeles County in a similar manner. On June 1, 1933, eight hundred workers walked off out of the raspberry fields of El Monte on strike, pitting mostly Mexican workers against Japanese growers. The strike was timed with a vulnerable harvest, which had to be picked quickly to avoid spoilage. As pay rates had declined to between 9 and 15 cents per hour, and 20–40 per crate depending on the berry, the workers demanded 25 cents per hour or 65 cents per crate across the board. In seeking an increased standard wage rate for adults, they also demanded an end to child labor, where growers paid children as little as six cents per hour to work alongside their parents.[31]

When growers rejected the demand, the strike went forward as did social polarization and the alignment of opposing classes. The countywide strike became the largest agricultural shutdown in history up to that point, and drew in a constellation of federal, state, and local government forces intent on ending it. It was also the first time that the Mexican government (through its consulate) intervened directly to suppress labor radicalism among Mexican Americans and Mexican immigrants, beginning a trend that continued throughout the 1930s.

CAIWU organizers had been active in the area for at least a month before the strike and organizers operated in the Hicks farmworker camp, the largest of three Mexican farmworker colonias located outside of the center of El Monte. As a result of their preliminary efforts, organizers built a base of support among the farmworkers through the recruitment of some militant workers. They held nightly mass meetings among Mexican workers to discuss wages, conditions, and demands, and circulated a petition calling on growers to meet CAWIU demands. On the morning of June 1, a mass meeting of 500 that included CAWIU organizers voted unanimously to strike, and a total of 1,500 workers stayed away from the fields that day. The next day, a strike committee was formed from 60 representatives from the different camps in the region, including mostly Mexicans, but also Filipinos and Japanese workers. Among the strike committee leadership were Lino Chacón and J. Ruiz, two farmworkers who had become party members and CAWIU organizers. With the strike organization in place, pickets were planned, relief distribution systems arranged, and organizers sent out to reach surrounding camps. As Ronald López describes,

> Women and children were actively involved in the picketing and in the distribution of leaflets. The leaflets were printed in Spanish, Japanese, and English and were distributed in thirteen of the surrounding communities.[32]

Mexican workers organized flying pickets to call workers out of the fields in the neighboring farm regions. Beyond extending pickets, CAWIU organizers encouraged workers to publicize their strike and try to build support. Through the Communist media, the unemployed councils, International Labor Defense (the legal wing of the party), and a network of other groups, the CAWIU was able to garner national attention to the strike. Mexican workers, for their part, spread word in the Mexican barrios and the Spanish-language press throughout Los Angeles County. Through kinship networks and the Spanish-language media, and through the various outlets of the Communist, CAWIU, and TUUL aligned-press, solidarity committees sprang into action. News of the strike led other groups of Mexican workers in the county to walk off of farms, with some sending delegations to El Monte to coordinate. Immediately following the strike declaration on raspberry farms in El Monte, strikes spread to strawberry, potato, and celery fields as well. By the second day of the strike, about 1,500 workers, estimated as 90 percent of the total workforce in the San Gabriel Valley, had left the fields. As the CAWIU dispatched representatives to the nearby fields, the strike continued to spread quickly over the next five days. According to Charles Wollenberg,

> Meetings were held in many barrios, and residents not only responded with moral and material support for the San Gabriel Valley strike, but also with strike action of their own. On June 7 the Spanish-language daily, La Opinion reported that 2,000 Mexican farm workers were striking against Japanese employers throughout the Los Angeles Area. Within a week, La Opinion had raised the figure to 7,000 and was treating the combined walkouts as a general strike of Mexican workers against Japanese growers.[33]

Melquiades Fernandez asserts that the rapid spread of the strike and solidarity actions relied on the existing networks established by veteran magonistas, who had organized a PLM club in the town of El Monte in the 1910s, and remained active in the workforce and labor movement through the 1930s.[34] Many of these experienced radical workers formed the ranks of a militant vanguard within the Mexican working class, and formed strike committees that comprised the nucleus of a new union. The spread of the strike created the conditions for regional coordination and mass action. Hicks Camp become the base of operations for a chain of other camps spread through at least a dozen other towns in the county.[35] Strike organization developed so effectively and there was such broad support that there was virtually no scabbing, leading the growers to have to look elsewhere to commence strikebreaking operations. Whole families, led by the five hundred Mexican families in Hicks Camp, took part in the strike. As the Western Worker reported: "Scores of youth, boys, and girls, and children, are on the road and in the field, helping on the picking line. These militant pickets have brought in workers who wanted to scab and made them join the Cannery Agricultural Workers Union. They are fearless."[36] Amid the growth of the strike, the same paper claimed that 350 workers joined the CAWIU, and Mexican youth formed a chapter of the Young Communist League in El Monte.

Japanese growers, who were organized into their own associations, also worked through business and civic networks such as the Japanese American Citizens League and kinship connections throughout the county. They mobilized support for the growers by providing temporary workers for the harvest for the duration of the strike, including the procurement of Japanese schoolchildren and youth in El Monte to help with the harvest.[37] White landowners and the white business establishment also rallied support. While formally disdaining the Japanese, white landowners feared that a successful strike might spread across farms and affect their profits, which led them into an uneasy defense of the Japanese and to arrange political support and maneuvers behind the scenes. Through the white business community, primarily the Los Angeles Chamber of Commerce, state and federal efforts were procured to halt the strike as soon as possible. Frank Clements, manager of the Los Angeles Chamber's Agricultural Department, expressed the dual concern of growers at the time: that unionization would hurt profits and that racist reaction might lead to increased deportations in the countryside. Representing the mindset of white growers, he asserted in the coded language of the day: "Our particular interest is, of course, maintaining the integrity of our Mexican labor supply."[38]

The growth and spread of the strike also attracted the attention of other elements within the Mexican community who intervened for their own reasons. By June 10, the CAWIU-led call for strike solidarity soon produced a rival committee of strike supporters formed under the leadership of Armando Flores, a veteran of the CUOM who attempted to organize Mexican farmworkers in 1928. In the years following the failed 1928 strike, he retreated from labor organizing and accommodated himself to the conservatism of the Mexican state, and became a conduit for the Mexican state to maintain direct contact with Los Angeles Mexicans as a means to promote its interests abroad.

By 1933, Flores had opened and operated a print shop in Los Angeles, maintaining his CUOM connections by providing print material for the Mexican labor activities in the city. In exchange for official treatment as a liaison between Mexican workers and the Los Angeles consular officials, Flores became a useful tool in the Mexican government's attempts to stamp out Communist Party influence among Mexican workers on both sides of the border. Through him, the Los Angeles consular Alejandro Martinez and his vice consul, Ricardo Hill, helped organize a conservative Mexican support committee to serve as an alternative and rival to the CAWIU, and in effect it aligned itself indirectly with the growers.

This group, known as the Comité Pro-Huelga, deployed militant rhetoric but attempted to confine Mexican labor struggle and limit efforts to conservative goals. As Gilbert González describes, after the postrevolutionary government consolidated its position, it moved to the right to squash labor radicalism in favor of a rhetorically radical, yet deeply conservative nationalism.

> The Los Angeles consulate had long cultivated a tradition of Mexicanismo, a Mexican conservative political consciousness consonant with the ruling party. Hill and Flores were well schooled to carry the conservative banner that had been passed to them. In attempting to subvert leftist tendencies and build a conservative union movement, the two men invoked a narrow nationalistic Mexicanismo that was antithetical to the Marxist principles of class politics espoused by the CAWIU. This conservative consulate perspective . . . stopped far short of the working-class politics that formed the bread and butter of the CAWIU.[39]

While battling the radical Left elements of labor within Mexico, these new governing forces represented a rapprochement of old-guard Porfiristas with the new government. What was most important at the moment for the new state was to squelch revolutionary inertia at home and wield control over mexicanos de afuera to use as leverage in part of a larger strategy of reaccommodation with US capital.[40]

The Mexican consul and his vice consul inserted themselves into the strike under the direction of the Mexican president, Abelardo Rodriguez, and other high-ranking officials, who ordered "a powerful offensive against leftist organizations [CAWIU] involved in the El Monte Strike."[41] The consulate also collaborated with California's Republican governor, James Rolph, who agreed to dispatch state labor mediators to help reach an agreement.[42] This began a collaboration of mutual benefit; where the Mexican Consulate could serve as a bulwark against labor radicalism in exchange for modest reforms. The consul spent the remainder of the thirties intervening in strike activity by Mexican workers as a means to marginalize radical elements and to contain and suppress labor militancy. They aggressively organized an operation designed to unite Mexican strikers against the CAWIU through the reactivation of an agricultural affiliate to the CUOM, with direct Mexican government support, and to present themselves as a safe alternative to the growers.

In light of the involvement of the CAWIU, the growers in alignment with the sheriff's department of El Monte arranged to collaborate with the Comité in order to peel the workers away from the Communists as their primary objective. In these efforts, they had the backing of the anti-union business establishment in LA and the media who saw in the CAWIU a menace to their hegemony. The Comité, local officials, and the growers formed a strategic alliance to oust the CAWIU. In an effort to present a viable alternative to the CAWIU, which was the only force in the fields, Flores was encouraged to regroup the CUOM, rename it, and reframe it as an extension of the Mexican government–controlled union, the Confederación Regional Obrero Mexicano (CROM). In this way, the new union could have some leverage among workers and against the CAWIU, as it had not even existed until after the strike had begun.

Under false pretenses of inviting the CAWIU as a bargaining representative to settle the strike, the sheriff of El Monte lured the leadership of the Hicks Camp strike committee to the police station, where they were detained. The detained workers were compelled to meet with Flores and Martinez, who roundly denounced the CAWIU as "reds" who were merely using Mexicans for their own gain. Along with Flores, the two quickly announced the creation of a new union, La Union de Campesinos y Obreros Mexicanos (CUCOM), which was put forth as the bargaining unit as an alternative to the CAWIU. To encourage the workers to join the new union, and lure support away from the shoestring operation of the CAWIU, they were promised thousands of dollars from the Mexican government and the state-affiliated CROM. They were also given sympathetic coverage and support from local Mexican media, along with other blandishments. These proved irresistible to the consul-aligned strike leadership.

The next day, CAWIU organizers called for a mass meeting in the camp to discuss and debate the agreement to allow the CUCOM to take over the strike, an accord dubiously reached through the chicanery of the consul-sheriff alliance. According to the *Western Worker*, in the open and democratic debates that ensued, the CAWIU retook the initiative and rallied workers back to their side. In light of this information filtering back through spies, the next day a group of deputy sheriffs and throngs of armed vigilantes surrounded Hicks Camp and arrested the seven CAWIU organizers present at the makeshift union hall, including worker-leaders Chacón and Ruiz. The seven were arrested on vagrancy charges, thrown into the county jail, and displaced from the strike for the duration. This opened up space for the CUCOM to move into action.

From that moment on, the Comité went into overdrive, exploiting its reach to create a parallel solidarity campaign to the CAWIU and eventually marginalize it.

After the arrests, Consul Hill, in league with the local police, held a meeting in Hicks Camp. He encouraged the workers to "run the agitators [Communists] out" and hastily arranged the expulsion of the CAWIU members from the strike committee.[43] In exchange for ridding the strike of the Communists, he pledged major financial and political support. As part of this effort, he encouraged the workers to return to work and allow the CUCOM to resolve the grievances from there on out. This was categorically rejected, but leadership did by default pass to the consulate, and strike meetings were moved away from Hicks Camp to an office rented by the consul.

Despite this setback for the CAWIU, loyalties in the camp remained divided for the remainder of the strike. The consul feverishly worked to bring an end to the strike and coordinated efforts with the Los Angeles Chamber of Commerce, the State Bureau of Industrial Relations, and representatives of the Department of Labor to work with the growers to negotiate a settlement. The Los Angeles "Red Squad" also began an intelligence-gathering and infiltration operation in secret alliance with the Mexican consulate to eliminate the CAWIU. When the CUCOM took over the strike, the consul now walked a fine line between needing to win the strike, while simultaneously preventing it from spiraling any further out of control, and limiting the scope of the demands.

By the second week of the strike, it had spread to several more cities and towns in the county, including vegetable pickers in Santa Monica and Culver City. As more workers went on strike and affiliated their efforts with the strike center at El Monte, the growers panicked and the berry-pickers began to understand the larger dimensions of conflict. On the third day of the strike, the growers offered modest wage increases of 15 cents per hour, or 40 cents per crate. Three weeks later, with an international corps of negotiators working in concert against the strike, a second offer by the growers was made to increase wages to 20 cents per hour and 45 cents per crate. The offer was rejected again. This was for two reasons: the El Monte workers demanded it be still higher and generalized to all striking workers, which was rejected, with the Mexican farmworkers refusing to budge and demonstrating their independence from the CUCOM.

While the newly launched CUCOM exercised some control over the strike by this time, CAWIU organizers remained active on the margins of the strike, using their paper, leaflets, and loyal supporters in an attempt to expose the conservative intentions of the consulate and the new union, and to criticize their quickness to agree with grower propositions and sell out the original demands of the strike. According to later assessments, they played a role in persuading workers to reject the second offer, which they later criticized as a tactical mistake.[44]

By the end of June, the strike continued to hold strong, despite creative ploys by the growers to break the strike. On June 29, they decided to encourage thousands of families to come pick berries for a penny a basket, choosing to take a significant loss rather than concede to the strikers.[45] Truckloads of deputized sheriffs were brought in to keep the fields open. While this helped alleviate the urgency of the harvest, various state and business institutions had now intervened in an attempt to end the strike as it had spread throughout the region.

Through these various channels, a settlement between the CUCOM and the growers was reached on July 6, raising wages to $1.50 a day for "permanent workers," 20 cents per hour for temporary workers, and no reprisals and the immediate rehiring of strikers. According to Gilbert González, this was initiated by the Mexican government, which was impatient with the stubbornness of the strikers and ready to shelve its public overtures of solidarity in favor of labor peace.[46] The consul pushed it through over the heads of the workers with the support of the growers and their brokers, as the final negotiated settlement was less than the previous offer.

Originally, the accord was to cover all striking workers in the berry and vegetable fields. Later, after the Japanese growers reconstituted a replacement workforce capable of finishing the remainder of the harvest, the representatives of the Bureau of Industrial Relations who participated in the negotiations revoked its application to the berry workers. This left the original strikers based at Hicks Camp and the surrounding environs out of the contract. The strikers were not rehired, and effectively mass-fired and left to languish in the camps without work or food until some relief was provided to stave off further protest.

The divide-and-conquer strategy left Mexican farmworkers incensed. This experience informed later action, as they assessed the value of state intervention and the role of the various factions in advancing or retarding the strike effort. As one of the San Gabriel Valley workers announced en route to the next harvest further north, "If there is no strike in the San Joaquin Valley now, there will be one when we get there."[47] The role of the state and business interests laid bare the power arrangements in the capitalist system. The white capitalist class that linked growers to urban industrialists and financiers showed its depth and breadth in its ability to muster the forces to bring labor conflict to an end and preserve existing class relations. It also gave a glimpse of state antipathy toward independent unionism and the efforts of Communists to politicize class relations. The scale of the El Monte strike showed the volatility of the class struggle in agriculture. The CAWIU redoubled its efforts to organize an industrial union, and the alignment of capital and state agencies made plans to strangle these efforts in their cradle.

The San Joaquin Valley Cotton Strike

In preparation for the upcoming cotton harvest, the CAWIU began organizing throughout the San Joaquin Valley, forming locals as part of their organizing drive. The cotton farms in this region were the largest in the nation, with an average of seventy acres per farm, and they were largely uniform in growing one single strain of cotton called Alcala for world markets. The high level of coordination in marketing and scientific production facilitated the centralization of labor policy and the funding of political activities.[48] The cotton growers were highly organized, determined to keep unions out of their fields and keep wages low, claiming that Depression conditions and reduced cotton prices made higher wages an economic impossibility. But as Lawrence I. Hughes, the regional director of the Farm Security Administration, later testified, the low wage threshold maintained by the growers was the result of them being "more powerful and organized . . . than the workers who were 'practically defenseless.'"[49]

In anticipation of a contentious fall harvest, they prepared themselves. The grower-organized Agricultural Labor Bureau held its annual conference in Fresno in September of 1933. With support through AAA programs, cotton prices had been rising. Nevertheless, they reasoned, losses over previous years could only be recouped by holding down wages. The gathering of the largest landowners and investors determined the picking rate for the coming harvest, setting it at 60 cents per hundred-weight, nearly half of what it had been in 1929. According to Donald Fearis, "The determination of the ginning corporations and their allies to hold the line against field worker demands virtually assured conflict as the processors' word was law in the burgeoning San Joaquin cotton industry."[50] The growers' steely determination to compel workers to accept wages below the subsistence level sparked animosity among arriving migrants, many of whom who had just experienced recent strike action in Salinas, San Jose, Lodi, Visalia, Oxnard, Fresno, and El Monte.[51] Their resolve to raise wages was equally ironclad. The CAWIU had got in front of this showdown, agitating throughout the summer to recruit workers for the inevitable strike action. Their initial plan was to start the strike in the south rim of the county, and roll it north as the cotton ripened.

By early September, they had established twenty-five locals throughout the region, which became the organizing hubs designed to turn out large numbers in the advent of a strike. They also recruited a "militant nucleus" of Mexican, black, and white worker-organizers who had joined the ranks out of previous CAWIU-led strikes and who coalesced together for the cotton harvest.[52] On September 17, the union organized a convention in Tulare to prepare for the upcoming harvest. The conference brought together sixty delegates representing more than seven thousand aligned workers from the different locals.[53] The delegates determined the strike demands that would unify the workers throughout the region: a $1.00 wage per 100 pounds of cotton picked, recognition of the CAWIU and a hiring hall, the abolition of the labor contracting system, and no racial discrimination. The wage increase resonated with the workers, as their wages had dramatically declined from $1.50 per 100 pounds in 1928 to 40 cents in 1932.[54] The union intended to present their demands to a rival conference of grower-financiers taking place in the days that followed. In the two weeks leading up to the strike, the CAWIU led numerous parades, rallies, and other actions of farmworkers to demonstrate their strength. As some observers later commented of these actions:

> The excitement of the parades, the fiery talks, the cheering, appealed to the Mexicans particularly, and race discrimination, poor housing, and low pay, especially the latter, were rallying cries which appealed to a class of workers with adequate personal experience to vivify the charges hurled by Communist leaders and rendered exposition of the theories of Karl Marx superfluous.[55]

The Agricultural Labor Bureau was a bosses' association that brought together the largest farmers, the gin operators (cotton-processing plants whose owners were also typically large growers or investors), and smaller farmers. This group of capitalists had achieved the organizational authority to set and enforce wage rates across the faming landscape. While some smaller farmers occasionally broke ranks from the large operators on one or another policy, the majority tended to go along with the diktats of the largest growers. This is due to the fact that bureau members, especially ginners, helped finance the smaller farmers and monopolized seed distribution and cotton gin production in the region. Through this economic stranglehold, capitalists held together a heterogeneous array of farmers, and directed them like generals on the battlefield. Of primary importance was the ability to maintain a united front and prevent labor militancy from dividing the farmers over wage increases and collective bargaining rights.

On October 4, 1933, the strike began with several thousand pickers walking out of the fields and reached its peak of about 18,000 farmworkers as flying pickets in cars and on motorcycles drew workers out of the fields across the cotton farms of the San Joaquin Valley. As one organizer-picker, Lillian Dunne, described her forays into the fields alongside a young Mexican translator:

> I began to go with them around the fields and there was a little Mexican girl . . . she would tell me what to say because the people in the field were mostly Mexicans. She taught me to say, "Huelga Piscadores, Pickers Strike,"—I had a loud voice and I would get the people out of the fields . . . I began to help get the people out of the fields. Then the authorities began to say that I was an agitator and they called me the worst red-headed agitator in Tulare County because I could really get the people out of the fields.[56]

The strike quickly spread over 100 miles, affected 2,000 ranches, and idled cotton cultivation on over 100,000 acres; effectively bringing the $50 million cotton harvest to a standstill for a period of 27 days. The strike engulfed farms situated across Merced, Fresno, King, Tulare, Kern, San Joaquin, and Stanislaus counties. An estimated 75 percent of the workers were Mexican, with the remainder Filipino and smaller numbers of black and white workers. Large-scale strike organization and solidarity was built through innovative strike strategy derived from the particular conditions of the strike, antiracist concepts derived from Communist theory, and the organic experiences generalized by workers engaged in struggle.

Work crews, the basic unit of production among farmworkers, had multiple overlapping intersections that facilitated joint strike organization. These included the collaborative solidarity of working side-by-side, mutual-aid connections, familial links, ethnic or regional connections, and shared or common experiences. As Devra Weber explains,

> Overlapping familial, social, and community networks formed the structural basis for Mexicans' lives in California . . . Through these networks Mexicans partially transferred their social relations from Mexico to the fields of California. These networks helped define relations among workers and between workers and contractors, and they helped workers adapt to the larger transformations in social relations.[57]

The ability to utilize these connections was aided by actions of the growers, which co-ordinated a mass eviction campaign after the onset of the strike, kicking thousands of workers and their families out of the ramshackle housing units maintained on grower property. This allowed different groups of workers to convene in larger spaces to co-ordinate and continue the strike. Large tent colonies were organized by the strikers and their families, which regrouped in fields or rented lots in Corcoran, McFarland, Porterville, Tulare, and Wasco. These makeshift colonies were quickly organized, with mass meetings held daily to discuss strike strategy, assemble picketing schedules, ar-range collectivized cooking and cleaning teams, and do other forms of planning con-ducted between the strike camps to coordinate strike operations across the breadth of the valley.

A central camp was established in Corcoran on a piece of land rented by the CAWIU, which served as the command center. As many as five thousand mostly Mex-ican workers and their families settled into the camp, naming streets after Mexican pueblos and revolutionary heroes. This development coincided with the Communist Party's changed strategy after the failure of the berry strike. The top-down leadership model had inhibited mass participation, and so the CAWIU reoriented toward mass mobilization and the democratization of leadership.[58] This included bringing unem-ployed workers, women, youth, and children into the life of the strike. The CAWIU also employed its learned strategy to organize striking workers along racial lines, which utilized the existing organizational structures among Mexican, Filipino, and white workers. Each group elected its own leadership, which coordinated jointly with the others, ultimately forming a committee of thirty worker representatives to coor-dinate strike activity.

The camps were well-organized and modeled the Communists' goal of full racial integration. While racial prejudice was deeply entrenched within the white farmwork-ers, the Communists understood that these attitudes could be challenged and changed under conditions of collective struggle.[59] Caroline Decker, CP strike organizer, claimed "even the capitalist press had to admit our solidarity—Mexicans, whites, and colored workers, living, eating, picketing, and going to jail together—forgetting racial prejudice."[60] Amid this all-out class war, even the most deeply ingrained racial animos-ities gave way to a spirit of solidarity. One incredulous group of journalists remarked that "Mexican, Negroes, and whites picked together, cooked, were beaten and went to jail together. Southern white workers would say to Negroes, 'comrade would you do this?', 'Comrade, you're elected to that committee.'"[61]

Jointly, the workers created a camp that was the antithesis of the racially segre-gated society outside its perimeter. The Mexican, Filipino, black, and white workers organized integrated schools for the children, and integrated nightly entertainment events for the adults. When local officials cut off all forms of aid, and the nearest hospital refused to treat strikers or their families, the workers developed their own sanitation services, medical facilities, and food preparation systems. Mexican workers played a key role in coordinating security, developing a quasi-military organization to defend the camp from assault by police or vigilantes, relying on training acquired through participation in the revolution. In interviews with strike participants, Devra Weber observed that some had experience in (or living memories of) rural rebellions against land expropriations by large landowners before and during the revolutionary period. This instilled a profound class consciousness among the Mexican workers, who understood the underlying nature of the growers, and the need for strong organization and militancy to win.[62]

Striking Mexican farmworkers in a roving picket line. The sign says "Disarm the rich farmer or arm the worker for self-defense."

Despite strong organization, poor sanitary conditions developed from lack of potable water and food scarcity, especially as the growers had publicly united around a strategy to seal off, lay siege, and starve them out of the camps. As was reported in the *San Francisco Chronicle*, "county supervisors, District Attorney and sheriff, a chief of police and 'other officials' sat in on a plan to 'starve out' the cotton field strikers."[63] They agreed in principle to neither sell nor donate any food to the camp. Under these deteriorating conditions, typhoid, dysentery, pinkeye, and diphtheria broke out.[64] One of the camp guards, identified only as "Gomez," lamented that as many as nine people, mostly infants, starved to death while the "farmers have burned wilted vegetables rather than give them to the strikers. . . . Dairymen have fed excess milk and cream to hogs before they would give it to the hungry children of strikers."[65]

Through the Workers International Relief and fundraising activities through the CAWIU and Communist Party districts, necessities were finally brought through to the camps from the outside. Federal emergency aid agencies, working through their state counterparts, resumed the distribution of food aid to the strikers against the wishes of the growers, representing the divergence of strategy for ending the strike. The distribution of food aid was used as a device to end the strike, as it would only be granted to those who returned to work at the previous rate. Nevertheless, this clause was temporarily suspended after the workers universally refused this condition without a wage increase. As local area hospitals refused to treat the strikers despite the deteriorating health conditions, the federal government directly intervened, made arrangements to cover costs, and ordered local hospitals to provide care.

The fact that the strikers held their ground in the camp and continued to coordinate and conduct the strike over a large geographical area sowed panic among the growers. In response, they turned to a variety of tactics to break the strike by other means. These included the launching of an anti-Communist media campaign, the use of vigilante violence, and eventually the use of the Mexican consul to create a rival union drive to divide the workers and weaken the CAWIU.

By October 10, the strike had spread and consolidated into a unified front. Unable to stop the strike from spreading, the growers' vigilante shock troops then moved into action. In absence of any legitimate means of stopping the strike other than negotiation, they turned to their most potent option: state repression and vigilante terror. Across the region, local chapters of the farm bureaus and Chambers of Commerce formed "protective associations," which combined public opposition to the strike condemnation of the CAWIU, with the formation of secretive armed vigilante squads. Local sheriff's deputies arrested strike leaders and workers when and wherever possible. They were given carte-blanche authority under the criminal syndicalism laws to target whomever they deemed Communist. The State Highway Patrol was brought in to control the roads, break pickets, and to prepare for an assault on the camp.

Then, the grower-vigilantes went after the CAWIU leadership. On the afternoon of October 10, an armed group of eleven grower-vigilantes rode into the farming town of Pixley (in Tulare County), where they were ushered past posted sheriff's deputies to where about five hundred workers had gathered to hear a report from the lead organizer of the CAWIU, a former Wobbly organizer named Pat Chambers. Several minutes into the speech, Chambers sensed the impending threat and attempted to beat a hasty retreat into the hall. As the workers retreated, the vigilantes drew their weapons and fired. As an eyewitness reported:

> The farmers began shooting across the highway and into the strikers' hall. When the shooting began there were still some men out on the street. The Mexican Consul and another man tried to wrestle the guns away from the farmers and were shot and killed. The farmers shot eight people running from them into the strikers' hall.[66]

After the volley of shots into the unarmed crowd, two people, Delfino Davila, a representative of the Mexican consul, and Dolores Hernandez, a cotton picker, lay dead on the ground. Nine others were wounded. The attackers then fled the scene unhindered.

Shortly after the first attack, a second group of armed ranchers drove into Arvin, another strike headquarters in Kern County. One striker, named Pedro Subia, was shot dead and six were wounded. In this second case, the enraged farmworkers fought back, overcoming the armed men and severely beating several before the police intervened to rescue the vigilantes.

While the Pixley killers were eventually identified and arrested, the local, grower-loyal government apparatus refused to prosecute. Instead they went through a charade of a trial. According to Lillian Dunn, an eyewitness who attempted to testify:

> Of course, there was a trial for these farmers which was a mock trial. They didn't try to find out what they had done. They arrested Pat Chambers and Caroline Decker and nine others and I think there were nineteen of them who were called Communists. They had witnesses at the trial which was held in Sacramento who lied about them. These so-called Communists were sentenced to ten years in prison . . . claim[ing] that he had incited a riot . . . [T]hey wouldn't let me testify even though I was sitting with the Mexican Consul in his car when Pat Chambers gave his speech. I know what he said. But they never let me testify because they knew I would tell the truth and that I wasn't afraid to tell the truth.[67]

In the Arvin case, the local police, in collusion with the grower, clumsily attempted to blame the strikers for shooting their own men. This story was picked up by the *Los Angeles Times* and the *San Francisco Examiner*, which dutifully proclaimed the killings as resulting from pitched battles where the strikers felled their own. The *Examiner* asserted, according to the vigilantes, that the shot was fired "by a striker stationed as a sniper in a nearby tree."[68] The *Times* followed in line, claiming that Subia was killed "by a charge of buckshot . . . intended for one of the officers."[69] Nine strikers were held for murder, while the alleged shooter, ostensibly a CAWIU leader who was a possible intended target for the attack in the first place, was not even present in Arvin at the time.

In a massive show of solidarity, over 2,000 workers marched in Pedro Subia's funeral procession, while another mass protest outside the jail holding the wrongfully accused strikers drew an angry crowd of 6,000 strikers.[70] In the immediate aftermath of the killing, the sheriff's department arrested Pat Chambers on criminal syndicalism charges. The presiding judge at the Superior Court of Tulare County denied his release for the remainder of the strike. Even as various forces were at play to weaken the strike, it progressed and began to significantly affect production. One study identified that gin operators were processing 38 percent less cotton at that point in the harvest than the previous year.[71]

When these tactics failed, the growers tried other avenues. They requested that the California Department of Industrial Relations conduct health inspections on the camp at Corcoran. Much to the dismay of the growers and their local government representatives, the inspection team sent in to investigate camp conditions deemed the camp "better than the average temporary camp in the state." Despite the reports of collective solidarity, unity, and high levels of organization, and a positive approval by state officials, the media reported a different tale. The editors of the *Los Angeles Times* chose to run a hysterical rant by a hostile journalist, who conjured up a concentration camp-like hellscape of sickness, sex, and violence:

> The camp is the danger spot . . . there are no sanitary precautions, no water for
> bathing, not much for drinking. Three or four shallow latrines for nearly 4,000
> persons. Long lines of misery-marked humanity await their turn . . . there is
> grave danger of epidemic. Promiscuity is unlimited . . . At the main entrance,
> and at various gaps in the barbed wire fence Mexicans armed with clubs keep
> people out or in. Inmates are practically prisoners . . . and at night picked crews
> are loaded onto trucks and started on their raids of sabotage and violence.[72]

Perhaps most ludicrous in this report is the claim that fifty police had surrounded
the camp to "protect the 'civil rights' of the herd within." When inspections failed,
the Mexican consul from San Francisco, Enrique Bravo, was called in to appeal to the
Mexicans to cease. Using his position as a representative of the Mexican government,
he warned of "grave international complications" and repatriation if the strike continued. His convoluted appeals to nationalism and subtle threat fell upon deaf ears, and
he was ultimately shouted down by a cacophony of boos.[73]

When violence and repression began to turn public opinion against the growers, some growers beckoned state and federal intervention. The successful resistance
began to fracture the unity of the growers, with some preferring concessions over the
total loss of the whole harvest, and others calling for the iron heel. The Roosevelt
administration sent in George Creel, regional coordinator of the Federal Emergency
Relief Administration in California. He was sent to conduct a fact-finding mission and
to bring about a resolution to the strike. In coordination with the governor, he set up
a committee to investigate conditions in the cotton fields.

When grower violence produced a backlash and public sympathies shifted toward the strikers, the most reactionary growers were not hesitant to threaten their
own communities. In Tulare, the growers harangued residents and threatened to relocate their farms elsewhere, declaring:

> Notice! To the citizens of Tulare. We the farmers of your community, whom you
> depend upon for support, feel that you have nursed too long the Viper that is at
> our door. These Communist Agitators must be driven from town by you, and
> your harboring them further will prove to us your non-cooperation with us, and
> make it necessary for us to give our support and trade to another town that will
> support and cooperate with us. Farmers' Protective Association.[74]

These were not empty threats. As one vigilante lamented his participation in violent
activities, "I'd like to be out of this mess, but what can I do? If I don't line up my business will be ruined."[75]

As the strike entered into its third week, the federal government took a more
aggressive role in overriding the intransigence of the cotton growers. Understanding
the scale and volatility of the class struggle exploding on a national scale, especially
its possible contagion through industrial agriculture, federal officials took action to
head off further spread of the strike beyond the San Joaquin Valley. The growth of the
CAWIU and the Communist Party was also of paramount concern. Amid capitalism's
most profound crisis, the Roosevelt administration understood the stakes and took a

more active interventionist role when required to inhibit the growth of the workers' movement through negotiation and co-optation. Temporary concessions were superior to revolution, it was reasoned.

By the fourth week of the strike, Governor James Rolph, himself a landowner, was compelled to agree to support the fact-finding committee headed by University of California labor historian Ira B. Cross. Revealing the dramatic shift of opinion against the growers, the committee condemned the violence against the strikers and the widespread violation of civil rights. They suggested a compromise wage increase of 75 cents. When the Agricultural Labor Board dragged its feet, reflecting widening divisions among the growers, federal and state officials compelled them. According to Stuart Jamieson,

> Acceptance of the committee's recommended 75-cent rate was in effect made mandatory by various Federal and State agencies. The Federal Intermediate Credit Bank exerted pressure on growers to accept the terms. Grower-employers met in a valley-wide conference in Fresno at the office of the Agricultural Labor Bureau of the San Joaquin Valley. After some opposition they voted to accept the 75-cent scale "in the interests of good American citizenship, law and order, and in order to forestall the spread of communism and radicalism and to protect the harvesting of other crops."[76]

The workers were initially divided. Growers also split, as some had broken ranks and agreed to pay $1 per hundred pounds and recognize the union. The state then turned on the workers. All forms of relief were cut off for those that did not accept the compromise. The State Highway Patrol was reinforced and positioned throughout the region, empowered to arrest workers who urged a no vote. The CAWIU union leadership reluctantly agreed to the new term, perhaps recognizing in the moment the best possible outcome given the impending balance of forces to contend with. They were able to claim victory in raising wages but fell short of union recognition. While the workers were voting to improve the wage gain, the forces of reaction were already moving into position. Growers bided their time, circulating blacklists, and waiting out the end of the season. The Highway Patrol dismantled the strike camps, and the workers migrated to the next harvest and, in some instances, on to the next strike. The conclusion of the strike did not end the persecution of the CAWIU leadership, which faced arrests, a whole new round of repression, and severe jail terms in the aftermath of the showdown in San Joaquin.

A total of eighteen leaders of the CAWIU were rounded up and arrested on criminal syndicalism charges in a mass sweep fueled by anti-Communist hysteria after the San Francisco general strike of 1934, effectively decapitating the most experienced leadership from the organization.[77]

Nevertheless, the victory of the great cotton strike inspired farmworkers to join the CAWIU in large numbers. By the end of the year, historians Linda and Theo Majka estimate that the membership in the CAWIU rose to over 20,000, with about 1,000 of these farmworkers joining or aligning with Communist Party ideology.[78] Kate

Bronfenbrenner states that average farmworker wages rose from about 16 cents to 25 cents per hour as a result of successive strike victories in the late summer harvest.[79] The following cotton harvest saw wages reach the $1 per hundred-pound threshold, as growers nervously increased wages to head off another potential strike.

Despite the gains, the union went into decline shortly after reaching this peak. The leadership of the CAWIU was drawn into lengthy and costly court battles to attain their freedom, most of the locals evaporated as migrants moved on to the next harvest, and the lack of solidarity and support from other labor organizations left the CAWIU isolated. Most significantly, the Communist Party itself made an abrupt break with the policies that produced the CAWIU. In 1934, the party followed Comintern diktats and shed its Third Period policies in favor of the Popular Front. After ditching dual unionism, many of the experienced party leaders of the CAWIU then merged into the United Cannery, Agricultural, Packing, and Allied Workers of America (UCAPAWA), which later affiliated with the Congress of Industrial Organizations (CIO).

For their part the growers and other capitalists vested in agriculture coalesced into their own united front, the Associated Farmers, who, along with forces of the state, unleashed a reign of terror against any semblance of farmworker organization. The Associated Farmers formed amid the largest agricultural strike wave in US history and codified and generalized the strategies culled from their efforts to crush the CAWIU. The vanguard of agribusiness at that time, the Western Growers, then merged with panicked capitalist interests across the state. This included bankers, investors, shippers, regional grower associations, canners, retailers, paper producers, sugar producers, livestock associations, and insurance companies. These powerful entities mobilized their networks of local and state judges, representatives, and bureaucrats, who oversaw their interests in the state capital as the legal, legislative, and administrative arm of the bloc.

They also rallied to their banner reactionary anti-Communist and anti-union zealots and shock troops drawn from the middle classes, such as those in the American Legion. The legion, a national federally chartered corporation of military veterans, became a bastion of anti-communism and anti-labor radicalism. Its internal organization mirrored a military command, with its high-ranking officers comprised of military veterans who now steered the capitalist economy. Below them was a chain of command of middle-class lieutenants who could muster chapters across the country to suppress meetings, rallies, and strikes when called to do so. In 1923, a prominent commander in the American Legion likened their efforts to crush communism to the rise of Italian fascism, stating:

> If ever needed, the American Legion stands ready to protect our country's institutions and ideals as the Fascisti dealt with the destructionists who menaced Italy! . . . The American Legion is fighting every element that threatens our democratic government—Soviets, anarchists, IWW, revolutionary socialists and every other red . . . . Do not forget that the Fascisti are to Italy what the American Legion is to the United States.[80]

Even staunch anti-Communists were appalled by the level of extralegal violence. After breaking a strike in Imperial Valley in 1934, federal government mediator Pelham D. Glassford concluded that "the Valley is governed by a small group, which in advertising a war against communism is sponsoring terrorism, intimidation and injustice."[81] Before departing, he concluded that "a group of growers have exploited a Communist hysteria for the advancement of their own interests; that they have welcomed labor agitation, which they could brand as 'red,' as a means of sustaining supremacy by mob rule, thereby preserving what is so essential to their profits—cheap labor." He also stressed that county officials were "the principal tools of their machine."[82]

The Associated Farmers maintained its own investigative operation against the Communist Party through the 1930s. They enlisted the services of a former army intelligence officer, General Rolph Van Deman, to compile information on Communists and labor radicals throughout the state. Van Deman was in charge of the Division of Military Information during the campaign to suppress the Filipino nationalist insurgency during the US occupation of that nation from 1899 to 1902. According to Kathryn Olmsted, he "invented new procedures for cataloging and indexing information on the enemy . . . [and after] [r]eturning to the United States, Van Deman lobbied to transfer the lessons of empire to the war on subversives[.]"[83] With this intelligence, along with surveillance conducted by American Legion departments throughout the state, the Associated Farmers identified over a thousand radicals who they targeted to be neutralized.[84]

AF representatives then lobbied state agencies for their prosecution under the criminal syndicalism law. Law enforcement agents then worked to identify, apprehend, and "eliminate" Communist organizers, deport Mexican organizers and strikers, and prosecute labor organizers under the Criminal Syndicalism Act. They asked that relief agencies be "directed" to give relief only to what they called the "involuntary idle" . . . and urged that jurisdiction over labor disputes be removed from the National Recovery Administration and turned over to the more amenable Agricultural Adjustment Administration.[85]

The growers and their supporters in the state, local government, law enforcement, and ad-hoc vigilante organizations defeated the strike wave of the 1930s that tried to unionize farmworkers. In California, the growers emerged stronger and more committed to maintaining a pliant migratory workforce that was conditioned to accept substandard wages and working conditions. Relying on their preponderant influence over immigration policy, they turned their gaze south to Mexico. In 1941, the American Farm Bureau requested that the US Employment Service import eighteen thousand Mexican workers as "braceros." The Bracero Program was crafted to reflect the ideal terms of labor to subsidize substantial grower profits in the form of a new reserve army of labor. Braceros were temporary contract workers beholden to growers for employment, they were proscribed from joining or forming unions, and they remained disenfranchised noncitizen residents, exclusively isolated from the rest of the working class. The Border Patrol assisted by policing the margins of the fields in places like California and Arizona, commonly detaining and deporting those who refused to return to Mexico after the harvest.

The alliance of capitalists and the state destroyed farm labor unionism for a generation. Their crowning achievement was to work through their legislative representatives to get farmworkers excluded from the labor provisions of the New Deal, including the 1933 National Industrial Recovery Act, the 1935 Social Security Act, and the 1935 Wagner Act.

Chapter 24
Mexican Workers in Depression-Era San Antonio

*"Simultaneously the large employers contrived to maintain the labor reservoir
at a high level. It paid to keep the Mexicans both numerous and hungry."*
—"The Mexican Return," *Nation* magazine

The influx of Mexican migrants into Texas and a secondary migration into urban centers like San Antonio was fueled by continued economic turmoil in Mexico.[1] Over the course of the 1920s, migration became an escape valve for the regime, deflecting away the urban poor, displaced agricultural proletariat, and the unintegrated remains of the revolutionary armies.[2] These different groups entering into Texas filtered into a racially structured system that used them as a disenfranchised reserve army of labor. Between 1920 and 1930, the Mexican population in Texas nearly doubled, growing from 388,075 to 683,681.[3] By 1930, 70,000 Mexicans lived in San Antonio (about 30 percent of the total population).[4] Eight years later, that number climbed to over 100,000, and another 250,000 resided in the outlying regions around the city hub, making it the second-largest concentration of Mexicans in the US after Los Angeles.[5] About 65,000 of the Mexican population lived in a four-square-mile barrio on the west side of the city.

The majority of the Mexican population in San Antonio worked in agriculture, with large numbers migrating to work the fields of central Texas and as far away as Michigan, Colorado, New Mexico, and Arizona. Many men, women, and sometimes whole families entered the harvest routes from March to October, and then returned to shell pecans the remainder of the year. A smaller, more sedentary population worked in cigar-making, construction, textiles, and other manual labor jobs within San Antonio. It was these Mexican-concentrated industries in San Antonio that would witness an upsurge of labor militancy between 1934 and 1940. At the forefront of this strike movement were mexicanas and Mexican American women, who made up 16 percent of the labor force in San Antonio by 1930.[6]

Concurrently in the United States, mass unemployment and generalized poverty in the early 1930s foreshadowed the emergence of radical and combative working-class militancy as well. In Texas, these factors contextualized the greatest uprising of Mexican and Mexican American labor in that state's history, and intersected class struggle in the workplace with the first significant mass actions for civil rights. Key to this qualitative advance in combining class and race demands was the leadership of Communists such as Emma Tenayuca, whose political training, organic leadership skills, and deep roots in the Mexican working-class experience enabled her to emerge as a lightning rod of mass collective action.

Agricultural Displacement and Migration to the Cities

By the mid-1920s, agricultural capital became the economic powerhouse of Texas, and by 1930 Texas boasted the largest capitalist farms in the nation. Absentee growers who lived in the large cities exercised political influence at the state and municipal level through their leverage within the dominant Democratic Party. The leadership of the AFL-affiliated Texas State Federation of Labor moved to the right in this period, aligning itself with the Democratic Party and the Ku Klux Klan on issues of racial exclusion and immigration restriction.[7] By the mid-1920s, it had ceased any efforts at organizing Mexican workers in the state, a neglect that continued into the late 1930s and the arrival of the CIO. The decline of living conditions for Mexicans in Texas was further aided by a political changing of the guard over the decade of the 1920s that saw both Democrats and Republicans close ranks behind the racial disenfranchisement of Mexican labor. This began with the rigid implementation of racial segregation in rural farming communities by the landowners in order to isolate, dominate, and maintain as subservient local concentrations of Mexican labor.

Segregation was reinforced and undergirded by a complex system of labor controls used to keep workers tethered to the farms during harvest time. The expanded presence of the Border Patrol on the perimeter of the fields ensured migrants didn't leave the farm regions during the season or face deportation. On the farm, workers commonly fell into debt, as the growers monopolized the provision of necessities, and became bound to employers through debt peonage. To prevent flight from debt, a pass system was established between the growers to prevent the workers' movement without prior consent. Furthermore, fleeing workers faced arrest by local sheriff's deputies. Those arrested for "vagrancy" for not paying their debts were then returned to the same grower as "convict labor." Once back in the fields, those caught carried out their work under the watchful eye of armed guards.[8] According to John Weber, the racial stratification in the countryside provided the template for intensified racial segregation of the cities by the late 1920s.[9]

By 1930, an estimated 50 percent of the Mexican population, roughly 600,000 workers, engaged in agricultural work, with about two-thirds of this population comprised of migrant laborers and the remainder small tenant farmers.[10] Mexican migrants comprised 85 percent of the total migratory workforce in the state, and virtually the whole workforce in the central and southern half of the state.[11] Most Mexican migrants followed the cotton harvest from the Río Grande Valley to the High Plains, while a smaller percentage with the means to do so headed for the sugar beet harvest in the Great Lakes region. After the harvest, migrants commonly took up temporary residence in San Antonio until the next agricultural cycle, using it as what one municipal report described as "a farm labor camp during the winter months since it [was] the largest recruiting center for [Mexican] farm labor in the country."[12]

Many also entered pecan production in these off months to survive until spring work was available, joining the larger settled population of pecan shellers, primarily women, that formed the majority of the workforce. Over time, more migrants and their families settled permanently in San Antonio. From the west-side barrio, men and boys often continued migratory harvest work during the peak season, while many women and young girls worked shelling pecans from October through May.

The onset of the Depression severely affected Mexicans working in agriculture. The largest proportion of laborers and tenants worked in cotton. When cotton prices collapsed in 1930 due to the global slump, large landowners scaled back production and laid off surplus labor. Federal intervention on behalf of large growers triggered a reorganization of agriculture, which led to the displacement of tens of thousands of Mexicans. Many were repatriated back to Mexico while others moved to urban areas in search of jobs and relief.

In an effort to stanch the substantial overproduction of cotton, the state legislature introduced the Texas Cotton Acreage Control Law of September 1931, which required that over half of all land dedicated to cotton cultivation be withdrawn or shifted to an alternative crop by the next harvest (approximately 7 million acres). Even though the law was declared unconstitutional a year later, growers acted accordingly with the provisions of the law and evicted tenants and sent migrant workers away. Thousands left for Mexico or moved into towns to find work. *La Prensa* newspaper captured the plight of the displaced, calling on the Mexican community to rally transportation and funds to help relocate 4,000 unemployed workers and landless tenants and their families across the border to Mexico.[13]

The displacement continued after 1933, when the federal government initiated the acreage-reduction program of the Agricultural Adjustment Act. The program was so broadly embraced in Texas that 40 percent of all cotton production on the largest plantations was halted or plowed under by 1940, an estimated 4,351,000 acres.[14] To take advantage of the cash payments for themselves, the landowners commonly terminated contracts with their tenants and reclassified them as laborers or simply evicted them.

Thousands of tenants then poured into cities seeking jobs and relief. As the *Texas Business Review* observed, "Thousands of agricultural laborers, especially Negro and Mexican cotton choppers and pickers, will be forced immediately on relief rolls and will stay there until a comprehensive plan of rehabilitation can be worked out."[15] Many of these farmers and their families moved to San Antonio and sought work in the large pecan-shelling industry, swelling the Mexican population there from about 82,000 in 1930 to an estimated 100,000 by 1938.[16]

Whether descendants of long-standing Tejano families, second-generation immigrants, or recent migrant arrivals, working-class Mexicans experienced the different facets of Jim Crow segregation in San Antonio. These included exclusion from "Anglo" jobs, disenfranchisement through the "white primary," racial zoning laws, low wages, little or no access to health services and education, lack of infrastructure, and neglect from white officeholders. These conditions inflicted severe poverty throughout the Mexican quarter of the city. There were few paved roads, no sidewalks or public parks, and no available public transit.

As a result of this enforced poverty, living conditions in the Mexican quarter of

San Antonio were squalid. Despite city mandates requiring basic standards for hous-ing, codes were not enforced. Only 9 percent of workers had inside plumbing and toi-lets (necessitating outhouses), 25 percent had electricity, and 12 percent had running water. Lack of clean running water and basic sanitation compounded health problems, contributing to one of the highest infant mortality rates in the nation.[17] The *San An-tonio Light* reported that 90 percent of children who were checked into health clinics in the barrio suffered from malnutrition, while dietary-related diseases such as scurvy and pellagra were widespread.

The education system was also segregated, with an estimated 90 percent of Mex-ican children attending poorly funded and underequipped "Mexican schools." Pov-erty ensured most workers dropped out of school by the fifth grade to subsidize the family wage. Even when children attended school, they typically went to the pecan sheds after classes and on weekends to work. The dysfunctional education system reflected the social reproduction needs of city capitalists, who desired to maintain a large population of manual laborers for the economy they created. Sex work was also widespread among women, as poverty drove an inordinate number into the practice to supplement incomes, also contributing to high rates of venereal disease. High un-employment, malnutrition, and the attendant cycles of sickness and disease became even more rampant in the Depression years.

The local police, tied to the Democratic Party machine that controlled the city, targeted the barrio for heavy-handed repression based on the notion that the barrio was a breeding ground for crime. The notorious anti-Mexican police chief, Owen Kilday, organized his department like an army of occupation within the community, alleging that "disorganization and deprivation meant more delinquency and prostitu-tion in the barrios." The focus on "Mexican crime" led to the targeting of Mexicans, especially young men. Mexican American youth filled the juvenile detention system with a 55 percent incarceration rate in 1938, despite the fact that the overall arrest rate for Mexicans (14 percent) was lower than that of whites (25 percent).[18]

The economic and political conditions produced by the Depression not only affected the Mexican working class, but it also affected the small bourgeois and middle-class ele-ments. San Antonio's Mexican merchant class shrunk by over 500 percent between 1924 and 1939. Local growers and industrialists benefitted from these conditions, using racial logic as a justification for maintaining wages as low as possible. Most Mexicans resided in the ranks of a vast reserve army of labor that became viewed as a growth engine and source of rapid capital accumulation for those willing to invest. Illustrating this view, the San Antonio Chamber of Commerce advertised cheap and exploitable Mexican labor in business magazines to lure investors from across the country. In one ad, they praised the racial features of Mexican labor that made them prone to low wages:

> [L]ong nimble fingers and. . . [their] natural taste and personal aptitude [*sic*] that were characteristic of all the Latin races were no doubt responsible for the beautiful work [done] by these industrious [Mexican] people in San Antonio in-dustries. They are willing and efficient workers, peaceful, and easy to handle . . . and slow to respond to agitation and elements of discord.[19]

Utilizing this pool of labor and local industry, agricultural capitalists converted San Antonio's pecan-shelling industry into one of the largest in the nation. In fact, the abundance of cheap labor led pecan capitalists to demechanize production. When the highly capitalized firm the Southern Pecan Shelling Company opened in San Antonio in 1926, relying completely on hand labor, the other producers jettisoned their machinery in favor of hand-shelling as well, which accrued them higher profit margins. The move to hand shelling allowed for the advent of home production, leading to the growth of a contracting system as a means to distribute and collect product over a larger geographical area.

Individual contractors delivered pecans to different shelling sheds, as well as to individual homes, with shelling taking place during the harvest and carrying over into the remainder of the year. Low wages in San Antonio also led other piecework industries to move into the labor market, including cut garments sent from as far away as New York to be sewn into the final products. The maintenance of artificially low wages was reinforced by the investors' constant threat of moving piecework from San Antonio to Puerto Rico if the workers demanded higher wages. The colonial status of Puerto Rico allowed US economic interests to operate outside the norms of US labor policy, in effect using it as a laboratory for experimental methods of labor exploitation.

Employers also policed their immigrant workers using the threat of deportation to quiet restiveness. In practice, Mexican "deportability" subsumed the previous notion that migrants from south of the border "were likely to return to Mexico" and therefore posed no significant threat for establishing citizenship and its attendant claims to rights and higher wages. To further ensure this, migrant workers denied federal food aid for lack of residency requirements.[20]

Deportation Sweeps in Texas

Like in other parts of the country, the deportation of Mexicans from Texas was ramped up as part of the federal government's effort to link the economic crisis with the presence of Mexican workers after the Depression-induced mass unemployment. The reserve labor army, so carefully constructed by southwestern capitalists as a feature of labor control, now served as a release valve for federal policy-makers eager to shift attention from capitalist crisis to cross-border migration, and to leverage white supremacy over potential worker solidarity. While some Mexicans did leave Texas of their own volition due to lack of work, most were expelled or fled in advance of deportation. Raids, detentions, and expulsions began across the Lower Río Grande Valley in 1928, and intensified over the course of the following year. By 1930, operations were taking place across the state, with people being plucked from streets, roads, plazas, and other public places where people gathered, worked, or conducted daily affairs. Between December 1930 and September 1931 an estimated 15,000 Mexicans were deported.[21] Preceding and concurrent with increased deportation of Mexican workers from Texas was a paralleled increase of women migrating to reunite with husbands who had become rooted north of the border over the previous several years.[22]

Raids through Mexican colonias and barrios had a terrifying effect on the people across the South Texas border region. Fear and uncertainty, especially in a region with a recent history of brutal state violence, lynching, and collective punishment, drove many families to flee ahead of the operations. As the *Hidalgo County Independent* newspaper reported:

> Arrests by agents have terrified the Mexicans, the immigration officials acting in accord with orders from Washington to deport every deportable alien. It is obvious only a small fraction of the number returning to Mexico would be deportable, but ignorance of the law and fear of arrest has added to the movement across the border.[23]

The roundups of Mexicans were carried out in a haphazard way, with little respect for due process, civil rights, or constitutional guarantees. The primary legal justification, like in other parts of the country, was to target Mexican nationals without legal authorization who were "likely to become a public charge." Able-bodied employed workers, essential to low-wage industries, were mostly bypassed in favor of the unemployed, young, aged, infirm, and nonproductive populations. People were arrested without warrants, detained in local jails, without the ability to consult legal representation, and not given fair trials pending their removal. Whole families were caught up in raids and dragnets.

Over 3,000 Mexican children under the age of fifteen, many presumably born in the US, were among those deported from Texas in 1930–1931 along with their parents, after immigration officials conducted targeted raids in public schools in El Paso.[24] Others were deported after living in the United States for decades, some were veterans of World War I. Families were separated, and hospitals, clinics, and homes for the mentally disabled were also emptied out of their deportable inhabitants. So many were expelled without prior transitional arrangements with the Mexican government that large makeshift refugee camps had to be hastily constructed in Ciudad Juárez until the deportees could be resettled throughout the country.

The abrupt displacement of so many people left them little time to make arrangements and handle their affairs. Thousands of families lost their homes, properties, other belongings, and unpaid wages, which were forfeited after deportation, abandoned or sold cheaply as people fled south ahead of arrest. An *El Paso Evening Post* article noted that some people fled, leaving up to two years of back wages unpaid.[25] While the largest operations were conducted in 1930–1931, periodic operations continued throughout the decade. The scope of deportable offenses was expanded to include participation in unions, strikes, and radical political organization, especially as working-class militancy and mobilization increased among Mexican and Mexican American workers after 1933. All told, the Mexican-born population was reduced from 266,046 to 159,266 between 1930 and 1940.[26]

Mutualistas

Social and political marginalization, and neglect by AFL unions, left Mexicans to their own devices when it came to organization and advocacy. Drawing from their own class and cultural traditions, the people in the west-side barrio of San Antonio created about twenty-five mutualistas between the years 1915 and 1930, which included up to 8 percent of the total male population in the membership, primarily skilled and manual laborers. Like other mutualistas, these performed several important functions, including the provision of health insurance and burial services and the organization of cultural celebrations and Mexican holidays. They also provided other services, building libraries and offering classes and social events.

While mostly female-exclusive, women formed at least one mutual aid society, and five were eventually opened up to female membership. For the exclusionary ones, women commonly formed auxiliary organizations. The most significant was the Cruz Azul, which began as a ladies' auxiliary of the Comisión Honorífica in San Antonio in 1920 and spawned an independent organization in 1923 that spread to fifty-two chapters throughout Texas by 1930.[27] Like other mutualistas, the Cruz Azul included both Mexicans and Mexican Americans, provided basic welfare and food relief to migrant agricultural workers, assisted families affected by deportation, helped build community clinics and vocational schools, raised money for the legal defense of Mexicans ensnared in the Jim Crow legal system, and sponsored "Mexicanization" cultural programs to teach Mexican history and Spanish to counter the discriminatory "Americanization" programs sponsored by Anglo-led Christian and philanthropic organizations.[28]

Other forms of intra-class collaboration further cemented cultural, community, and familial relations. This included efforts to commemorate important holidays and cultural events, from Dia de los Muertos to Mexican Independence Day. These parades, processions, and other ceremonies required organization and collaboration on a communitywide basis, and were designed to positively reinforce a public Mexican identity that was otherwise socially and institutionally degraded. As one historian noted, such events "heightened the Mexican workers' sense of community, their sense of Mexicanness, and provided a consciousness of joy in a life of toil, misery, and depression."[29] *Compradazgo,* or co-parenting, also bound families, friends, and neighbors together through the ritualized extension of relationships designed for mutual support and benefit.

While most mutualistas and their auxiliaries were cross-class institutions, combining workers and the small-business and professional middle class together, others were more strictly groupings of the working class. These labor mutualistas primarily grouped the working class together and became remarkably adaptable in response to class needs, converting into quasi–labor unions and strike organizers under conditions of class struggle. Labor mutualistas also tended to be the only active supporters of strikes within the Mexican community, opening their halls for meetings, joining pickets, and supporting campaigns.

The radical Left traditions within working-class Mexican San Antonio, dating back to the era of the magonista movement, the Socialists, and Wobblies, were part of the living legacy of these mutualistas. For instance, labor mutualistas were at the center of campaigns to abolish labor contracting and support the organization of farmworkers in negotiating with cotton growers in the early 1930s. They also hosted regular political gatherings that included radical labor groups. One such group, Claridad, trained workers in the principles of labor organizing, holding courses in public speaking, negotiating, and teaching other skills relevant for building class solidarity and labor unions. While there was a small middle and political professional class that vied for political leadership over the community, one contemporary observer concluded that "the vast majority of the Mexican people have more esteem for the radicals."[30]

Another crucial function of the labor mutualistas was to allow for migrant and US-born Mexican Americans to work together. A Julie Leininger Pycior observed:

> While native-born and immigrant mexicanos might be pitted against each other for jobs or housing, they often cooperated in the mutualist sphere. This comradeship reminded them that in the world of work, employers tried to distinguish between immigrants and Mexican-Texans, paying the former lower wages. Out of this realization came the labor mutualistas.[31]

One of these mutualistas, Sociedad de la Unión, counted 58 percent of its membership as Mexican-born and 38 percent as Texan-born. The closeness to the border and parallel experiences led citizen and immigrant workers to understand the value of collaboration in the labor mutualistas, contrary to the sharp distinction encouraged by middle-class organizations like the League of United Latin American Citizens (LULAC).

South Texas mutualistas were also geographically located in proximity of the border, allowing for cross-border interaction and exchange with Mexican mutualistas and labor organizations. San Antonio–based groups hosted speakers from south of the border discussing the workers' movement, social and political developments, and other topics. They also provided workshops and presentations on workers' rights and other relevant class-based themes for their membership. Cross-border links served to strengthen cultural identity in a racially hostile environment, as well as connect workers in the US to draw inspiration and ideological influence from the radical labor movement in Mexico. Beginning in the early 1930s, there was an upsurge in Mexican working-class militancy that led to an increase in strikes and a radicalization that altered the political landscape of that nation. Mutual aid societies were the first to take to the field against racial discrimination, condemning lynchings and opposing exclusion from swimming clubs, theaters, and cemeteries, and protesting school segregation and police brutality.

Mutualistas reached their height of organization by the late 1920s, but many collapsed or disappeared during the Depression. The outbreak of militant strikes led by Mexican and Mexican American women between 1934 and 1938 beckoned for union organization, transcending the limits of mutualism as class struggle intensified at the point of production. This process was furthered by the rise of the New Deal–era welfare state, in which state-provided aid and services gradually supplanted their self-help function. Nevertheless, the nodes and networks established throughout the community by the mutualista served as the basis for mobilizing community support and solidarity for the labor movement. They also formed a bulwark of support for the Communist-led movement of the unemployed that directly confronted Jim Crow exclusions in the distribution of jobs and relief.

The Communist Party and the Popular Front

By the Seventh Congress of the Comintern in Moscow in 1935, a distinct new state had emerged in Russia that centralized power and control around the dictatorship of Joseph Stalin. The bureaucratic class that shouldered Stalin's rise to power did so by purging or eliminating all internal opposition within the Bolshevik Party, and by suppressing the last vestiges of Soviet democracy that persisted since the October Revolution of 1917. In doing so, it also charted a different course internationally through its control and influence within a restaffed and repurposed Communist International. Instead of fomenting international revolution, as its original architects envisioned, the new Soviet state used the Comintern as a transmitter of its own foreign policy objectives based on the immediate and urgent impulse of self-preservation.[32]

The Comintern lamented the sectarian failures of the Third Period and carried out a polar shift to the Right. The rise to power of the Nazi party in Germany and its subsequent rearmament after 1933 threatened the survival of the newly reconstituted Soviet regime under the direct rule of Joseph Stalin. The new shift was premised on uniting all sections of the working class into a "united proletarian front" alongside other "progressive classes" (middle class, farmers, liberal capitalists), bringing them together into an international "anti-fascist front."[33] The Soviet government sought rapprochement with western European capitalists also concerned about resurgent German power. In place of struggle against their respective bourgeoisies, Communist parties around the world were encouraged to align with progressive capitalists as part of a popular front against the threat of fascism. In doing so, national Communist Parties began to seek alignment with liberal bourgeoisies against local manifestations of fascism.

This abrupt abandonment of the policies of the Third Period had significant implications for Communists in the United States, leading to an about-face on several fundamental positions. As part of the realignment with potential "anti-fascist allies," the Communist Party shifted their stance of active opposition to the Roosevelt administration, from one of guarded rapprochement to stalwart support of the New Deal and the progressive wing of the Democratic Party. This was characterized as capitalists who saw their own class interests best advanced by preserving Democracy. As leading Communist William Foster explained:

> Roosevelt, born and reared in upper class circles, believes in capitalism. But he is opposed to the fascist course being pursued by the big monopoly capitalist groups. He believes that capitalism, that private ownership, private profit, private initiative, can best be advanced by preserving democracy, by carrying through a limited reform of those most marked abuses which threaten to arouse the people against capitalism. This has brought him into sharp conflict with the representatives of monopoly interests in politics and has compelled him to rely more and more on the masses of the people for support.[34]

Ultimately, this led the Communist Party to gravitate toward the New Deal Coalition as the arena for progressive realignment to build broad working-class unity and an anti-fascist front. In scrapping their revolutionary aims, they found a more receptive welcome into the orbit of the Democratic Party and the CIO. The fervor and organizational skills of the party's rank and file was harnessed and put to use for the larger aims of capitalist restructuring.

Dual unionism was unceremoniously ditched in favor of working within the established unions, and revolutionary rhetoric was gradually muted as party units within the industries sought to ingratiate themselves with their fellow workers by being the most dedicated unionists. Active party-building was submerged in favor of coalescing with liberals and the Socialists, or by creating new groups aligned with the reformist wing of the Democratic Party while hewing religiously to the need for urgent defense of the Soviet Union. Bridging all activity to a defense of the Soviet Union was paramount, which led the party to eventually drop its principled opposition to "capitalist war" and become fervent supporters of war against the Axis powers.

The threat of fascism embodied in the rise of Hitler and Nazi Germany's impending pivot to Russia was further theorized as an international phenomenon applicable in all countries, including the United States. This compelled Communist Parties to seek allies in the bourgeoisies of those countries positioned against the rise of Germany. In the United States, the rise of Germany was seen as detrimental to US long-term capitalist interests, which led FDR to gradually position US support behind England and France as the European states inched closer to war. For the Comintern (and US Communist Party), this warranted support for the "progressive character" of the US ruling faction. This form of support was couched as an existential necessity internationally, as a means to prevent the further slide of liberal democracy under the march of fascism supported by the "reactionary bourgeoisies" of global capitalism. The US section dutifully applied the Comintern's model onto the US, even if it didn't easily fit.

In applying the Popular Front theory to conditions in the United States in a way that could justify fusion with the Democratic Party under the banner of the New Deal, the CP located a nascent fascist threat in the Republican Party. According to party chairman Earl Browder, who was tasked with transplanting Russian formulations to US soil, fascist movements mirroring the rise of Hitler and Mussolini were taking shape internationally and in the US by 1935:

> In every capitalist country its forces are organizing, backed and inspired by the monopolists of finance capital, and, where not already in power, are preparing with all energy, ruthlessness, and demagogy, to seize control of government. In the United States, this camp is headed by the dominant leadership of the Republican Party, with its allies of the Liberty League, Black Legion, Ku Klux Klan, Coughlin, and others.[35]

The gradual alignment with Democrats was justified using a conservatizing formula while retaining a radical veneer in order to obscure the party's right turn. The central role of the Communist Party in defeating the fascist threat internationally, as the driving force of an alliance nominally led by vacillating and inconsistent liberal capitalists in the Democratic Party hemmed in by their reactionary Southern brethren, could strengthen the hand of the party and win over the population to the party and its program. In effect, the party leadership obediently abandoned any remaining revolutionary ambitions and shed all pretenses of autonomy. It firmly ensconced itself in the task of tailing the foreign policy directives of Stalinist Russia, which now shifted erratically in the quickening pace of world events. According to Max Shachtman:

> It was now for the League of Nations, for collective security, for nonaggression pacts, and for the defense of democracy. It was toning down or abandoning the disruptive utopia of world revolution, and subordinating its Communist dogmas to the preservation of world peace and democracy. It was ready to unite with all other democracies, despite their capitalist character.[36]

The party also saw this new alignment as a means to carry out a democratic revolution by moving its membership into the CIO and leading efforts to organize the unorganized: industrial workers, women, and the black and Latino working class. Through leadership in this open field, the party could emerge as champion of a new industrial union movement and extend democratic and civil rights as part of its goal of a "united proletarian front." Building on their ongoing work against racism, the party seized upon the convergence to reframe the continuity of Jim Crow as a form of "Hitlerism" in the United States. As William Z. Foster explained in a 1939 pamphlet,

> From the day the Communist Party was organized it has fought for equality of the Negro people with all other people of this country. We demand equal right to jobs, equal pay for equal work, the full right to organize, to vote, to serve on juries and to hold public office. We demand abolition of the poll tax. These rights are inseparable from the right of complete social equality, including the right of intermarriage. It is about time that a stop is put to the reactionaries who, with their Hitler-like theories of racial superiority, slander the dignity and standing of the Negroes by branding them as an inferior people.[37]

Along these lines the party leadership hushed direct criticism of the Roosevelt administration, moved away from its long-held position on the need for a revolutionary party of labor, and limited its objectives to achieving radical reform within the political architecture of the New Deal coalition. It worked with the emerging Left of the AFL to launch the CIO, partnering with the same progressive forces that it had previously denounced in no uncertain terms. In sum, the growth of the party under these conditions would allow quantity to turn into quality, in which a stronger party could revisit the question of revolution and socialism at a later date under more suitable conditions. As Earl Browder concluded:

> [T]he direct issue of the 1936 elections is not socialism or capitalism, but rather democracy or fascism. At the same time we emphasize, and will always

emphasize, that consistent struggle for democracy and progress leads inevitably, and in the not distant future, to the socialist revolution.[38]

These perspectives also led them back into the AFL and into alliances with former nemeses. John Lewis, who fiercely opposed CP-led TUUL efforts to organize miners in the 1920s, now turned to the experienced and dedicated CP trade-union cadre as the shock troops of the mass-organizing drives of the CIO. After all, even with their limited success with the TUUL, several thousand Communists "already had fought for years trying to organize independent unions and had won a reputation in several industries as militant partisans of industrial unionism and workers' rights."[39] Earl Browder estimates that about one-quarter to one-third of CP members were "experienced union organizers trained in a tough school when organizing was a kind of guerrilla warfare."[40] Since the Communists had now shed their revolutionary aims, and largely hid their party membership and worked dutifully within the framework of the New Deal, Lewis tolerated them in leadership positions so long as their actions served the CIO and could be controlled.

By the end of the decade, they wielded leadership in unions that represented about a third of all workers in CIO unions, and maintained some influence in another third.[41]

> The Communist Party was clearly the tail on the New Deal kite operating more and more as a pressure group within the president's coalition: its political position gradually reduced itself to support of the CIO and certain domestic New Deal objectives (never completely fulfilled) as well as the increasingly pressing demand for an antifascist foreign policy based on collective security and collaboration with the Soviet Union.[42]

During the period of 1936 to 1939 the party achieved its greatest period of growth, from 26,000 members in 1934 to 85,000 by 1939, as well as hundreds of thousands of supporters and fellow travelers.[43] Despite this flurry of growth, the party also experienced a high turnover rate as party building and member development was subordinated to the priorities of the Peoples' Front. The party was later terminally weakened after the end of the war, as the US and the USSR turned from allies to enemies in their scramble to administer the former colonies of the defeated Axis powers. The US capitalist class, including the representatives of the New Deal coalition, reconciled and closed ranks against the Soviet Union and aligned parties to launch the Cold War abroad and anti-Communist witch-hunts at home.

Nevertheless, the party did make significant strides in leading mass working-class movements as part of their efforts in organizing the unemployed, building CIO unions, and directly confronting Jim Crow racism in the South and Southwest. The latter included organizing significant strikes and civil rights campaigns among Mexican workers in Texas and California. Historian Mark Naison asserts that the antiracist actions of the party during the Popular Front period had the most significant and long-term impact. Speaking of the party's effects on the black working class, he concludes that Communists marshaled substantial resources, forged broad networks of solidarity, and targeted mass direct action against racial discrimination in employment, voting, and the legal system; and in favor of full integration and equality in education, the arts, sports, and public and private cultural spheres.[44]

A similar historical experience also took place between the party and Mexicans and Mexican Americans. While the years 1935–1939 saw the party converted into the "most single-minded, practical reform party that America ever produced," its radical theoretical foundations and direct practical organizing against racism positioned it to lead the first substantial Mexican working-class civil rights struggles in US history.[45]

Chapter 25

Mexican Women at the Forefront of Labor Militancy

"Anticipating a fierce assault from hostile sheriff's deputies accustomed to roughing up 'Meskins,' the Tejana strikers placed one hundred of their most militant and fearless union members on the picket line."
—Zaragosa Vargas, *Labor Rights Are Civil Rights: Mexican American Workers in Twentieth-Century America*

The gendered division of labor in the US economy relegated women's work as supplemental to men's (especially if married) and to a narrow range of occupations. For Mexican and black women, this was limited to domestic service, part-time and seasonal work, canning, and other agricultural tasks. The gendered sectors of the economy were excluded from all major labor, benefits, and work-relief-related legislation. They were proscribed from Social Security benefits, the collective-bargaining and wage provisions of the National Labor Relations Act, and most women were excluded from Works Progress Administration projects. NRA and WPA wage codes assigned and standardized lower wages for women, mirroring the private sector's devaluation of their labor. Furthermore, thousands of women were laid off from their jobs as a result of a piece of Depression-era legislation that established that only one married spouse could work for the federal government at the same time, meaning women had to go.

Similar to the deportation of Mexican workers as a performance of "government action" to prioritize white employment amid capitalist crisis, Section 213 of the Economy Act of 1932 was a measure that called for women in federal public-sector jobs to be laid off if their husbands were also employed by the government. The provision, a bipartisan measure supported by the Roosevelt administration, stayed on the books until 1937. While an estimated few thousand women were laid off, state legislatures, municipal governments, and private employers across the country followed suit, passing legislation or instituting policy in the same vein. Various manifestations of these laws barred married women from the job market, set income caps for eligible women, or established other limits for women's employment. Even after the law was overturned, the official devaluation of women's labor spread through society in various ways. An economic survey of the period captures the law's effects, stating that

> the national mood concerning married women being employed in both public and private positions did not change. In 1938 the National Educational Association surveyed 291 cities across the United States. More than three-quarters of

the city administrations reported that they would not hire married women as teachers. A National Industrial Conference Board study the next year, moreover, reported that more than 50 percent of banks, insurance companies, and public utilities across the United States would not hire married women.[1]

The degradation of women's labor occurred in a period when an estimated twelve percent of working-class women in the national labor force were the sole providers for their families.[2]

While Mexican women in San Antonio were already racially excluded from federal, state, and local government jobs, they were still affected by generalized sexist ideas that affected all women, where their employment opportunities were the most limited and their labor the least valued. Married women were generally the least employed outside the home, and were limited to doing home piecework in textiles, cigar rolling, and pecan shelling alongside domestic tasks.[3] The majority of female workers employed in San Antonio were young and single, and primarily confined to low-wage, manual labor jobs in pecan-shelling, garment production, laundries, domestic service, and cigar manufacturing; with a smaller percentage working in meat-packing plants and in cement factories.[4] While the small employment numbers of married Mexican women are often attributed to "patriarchal features" of the traditional Mexican family structure, we can see that these views were also common among the Anglo population, at the highest levels of government and among the capitalist class.

Women—black, Mexican, and white—were at the forefront of union organizing in San Antonio in the 1930s within the industries in which they formed the ranks of the workforce. They created the first garment workers local, united into the National Federation of Telephone Workers, attempted to organize cigar rollers, and launched a chapter of UCAPAWA in 1938. Mexican women especially were instrumental in forging a militant labor movement during the Depression decade. As many men followed the harvests in the fields, women more typically remained behind and worked to maintain their households.

The upsurge of working-class militancy among Mexican women in Texas occurred in the context of a surge in labor movement activity in other parts of the country as well as across the border in Mexico.[5] It also occurred as the Communist Party was growing in size and influence within the working class. In the US, women led militant strikes in the early 1930s from within the industries in which they were concentrated. Between 1933 and 1937, they participated in strikes in the textile, garment-making, hotel service, and department store industries, and as clerks and other service workers across the country. When a wave of sit-down strikes swept across various industrial centers in 1937, women sewers, clerical workers, restaurant servers, retail workers, and others also participated in job actions in conjunction with their male counterparts in the same industries. A similar labor radicalization was occurring in Mexico.

The participation of large numbers of women in the revolution was followed by a reaction against incipient feminism in the counterrevolutionary consolidation of the late 1920s, as a newly stabilizing capitalist state sought to suppress independent labor radicalism. An upsurge of feminist organizing took place in the early 1930s as part of the social mobilizations of the period. A significant wing of this campaign involved working-class women participating through the aegis of radical political parties.[6]

An example was through the formation of the Congreso Nacional de Mujeres Obreras y Campesinas, whose members were socialist and Communist women who held a series of conferences between 1931 and 1935. Events in Mexico carried over the border and were regularly reported through the Spanish-language press. The election of Lázaro Cárdenas, buoyed by a revived radical labor movement, inspired a surge of revolutionary nationalism that carried across the border.[7] This combined with the rooted historical traditions of Magonismo and socialism in San Antonio to help cohere an ideological orientation toward class struggle and ethnic solidarity under Depression conditions. The radicalization of a new generation of the working class in San Antonio, women especially, provided the basis for Communists to send organizers to the Lone Star State.

When Communist organizers moved into Texas in 1930, they oriented their efforts toward this growing population of women workers, organizing them in the Trade Union Unity League, the Unemployed Leagues, and the Workers Alliance. The party also encouraged organizers to address birth control, childcare, housework, unequal pay, and maternity insurance, although party work fell short of organizing "working-class women's new consciousness and militance into a feminist position."[8] Most significantly, the party offered a vehicle for Mexican working-class women to develop as leaders and organizers where machismo had wholly excluded or limited their participation in most mutualistas, the AFL, and even the CIO.

The 1934–1935 strikes occurred within a context of political isolation for the Mexican working-class women against a unified ruling class. As Irene Ledesma explains, "The companies . . . had newspapers, city officials, and other government officials, speaking in their favor."[9] Despite the adversity, Mexican workers forged networks of solidarity and collaboration that were built over the course of the period, especially through the aegis of the Communist-led Unemployed Councils and the Workers Alliance. Striking against this powerful confluence of forces, the Mexican working class in San Antonio needed to confront racial oppression alongside economic super-exploitation. In doing so, they drew from their own recent revolutionary traditions, which fostered an openness toward the radical class analyses of the Communist Party that enabled them to build broad class solidarity.

Bound up in the 1934–1938 labor upsurge of Mexican working-class women was not only a confrontation with the powerful heads of industry, but also a violent and reactionary political structure whose very design and longevity was predicated on the submission, marginalization, and underdevelopment of the Mexican population. In fighting for basic improvement in working conditions, the economic struggle grew into a full-scale war for civil rights. As Communist and pecan sheller strike leader Manuela Solís Sager concludes:

> One of the first groups of organized workers that I remember were women and it is with them that we saw the beginning of the breakup of the type of political organization that existed in San Antonio . . . In both the Finck Cigar and pecan shelling

strikes there was a desire to keep the Mexican population, the Mexican workers, as a reserve labor pool which could be used in case of strikes . . . I believe that what was done there and what had to be done was confronting the power structure.[10]

Cigar Workers

On August 4, 1933, eight hundred women who worked at the Finck Cigar Company walked out on a wildcat strike for union rights and higher wages, with about 350 of these predominantly Mexican women carrying out a hard-fought three-week strike.[11] The action kicked off a protracted two-year struggle that culminated in a total of three strikes by 1935. The first strike began after one Mexican American worker, Sra. W. H. "Refugio" Ernst, was fired for trying to organize her co-workers into an independent union. Ernst formed a crew of collaborators to help conduct a strike, including Adela Hernandez, Modesta Herrera, and Mrs. E. J. Padilla. They exhorted their co-workers to walk out to protest unsanitary working conditions and the lowest wages in the cigar industry.

Other grievances boiling over among the workers included wage theft, being required to pay for work clothes and implements with high interest rates on loans, docked pay for "substandard" cigars, bathroom breaks limited to five minutes for a whole shift, and the practice of being locked inside the factory until closing time, even if their cigar quota was met.[12] Beyond these, the workers also faced sexual harassment and humiliating practices such as the use of company doctors to conduct routine physical examinations of the women at their expense along with occasional firings of women deemed too unhealthy to work.[13]

Under the leadership of these women, the strikers heeded the call for a coordinated walkout and the formation of pickets at the entrance to the cigar factory. Following the work stoppage, the whole lot were subsequently fired by Finck. Nevertheless, the organizers and most committed strikers maintained their pickets and encouraged others to eventually join the strike. The original strike committee managed pickets, which were maintained with regularity for the duration. When the San Antonio police attempted to shepherd strikebreakers into the factory, they were physically blocked by the strikers. According to the El Paso Herald-Post, "of the several policemen who had been summoned to clear a path through the strikers to the plant entrance, three were disarmed and driven back. They also suffered severe scratches and bruises . . . [and after,] the picketing resumed."[14]

The strike committee also raised money for the strike fund through door-to-door solicitations and community carnivals. To facilitate decision-making without a union organization in place, the strike leadership held mass community meetings on a regular basis. Through these meetings, strike strategy was hammered out and appeals were made for solidarity. The AFL-affiliated International Cigar Makers' Union expressed some support, with members attending rallies, picketing, and speaking at hearings, and helping them form their own local, which added resources and organizational support to their efforts.

The strike committee raised money for a lawyer to conduct a legal defense campaign and appealed to the Mexican consul to intervene. When direct appeals to

Finck were ignored, the committee announced its daily communiqués to the media, attended city council meetings, and appealed directly to the mayor to compel intervention by the local city government. When the mayor called on Finck to submit to arbitration, it seemed the strike might be won. In discussion with the mayor, Finck allegedly agreed to rehire the fired striking workers, and to address all of the other demands. Despite returning to work triumphant a month after walking out, the workers quickly observed that nothing had changed and that the mayor's words rang hollow. While strikers were rehired, the strike leaders were not, and the company reneged on its promise to address the work practices and conditions. Instead, the company used its "medical inspections" to gradually lay off recalcitrant strikers, who were dubiously deemed medically unfit to work. Either through collusion or by Finck's duplicity, the agreement evaporated and Finck dug in his heels.

In response, a second strike was launched in early 1934. Going over the head of the mayor, the leadership of the local took their case before the newly inaugurated National Labor Relations Board. During the hearings, the workers complained of wages well below NRA code and their long list of other grievances. Federal mediators interviewed all parties, scrutinized all of the claims, and gave the impression that federal intervention would finally rectify the situation. Seemingly assured that justice would prevail, the strikers returned to work pending an outcome to the investigation.

When the regional labor board eventually ruled in favor of the women, it seemed as though the strike had finally been won. Showing the weakness of implementation under the NRA, the Finck management flouted the ruling, refused to rehire any of the fired strikers, and trucked in more strikebreakers. When workers went out on their third strike, Finck turned to the local Democratic Party establishment to break the strike, allying with virulent anti-labor party boss and police chief Owen Kilday and County sheriff Albert West. These two officials took a hardline stance against labor activism, threatening the strikers with violence, arrest, and deportation. As W. H. Ernst described, "The deputies went to the girls' homes and told them if they didn't go to work they would be sent back to Mexico."[15]

With the NLRB ruling on their side, the strikers changed tactics and began to physically block strikebreakers from entering the establishment. According to Julia Kirk Blackwelder, "disorder broke out in which clothes were torn, hair was pulled, and strikebreakers were pelted with lumps of coal."[16] For their part, the police shepherded strikebreakers into the plant and even tried to force reluctant strikebreakers through the pickets. When altercations and brawls broke out between the two sides, the police used this as a justification to arrest twenty-one of the strike leaders, and thirty-six supporters.[17]

Because of the police heavy-handedness, the strikers changed their tactics. They waited for strikebreakers to leave the factory and followed them home to shame and confront them. They encountered them in different parts of town and publicly stripped them of their clothes as a form of humiliation and retaliation. On other occasions they showered strikebreakers with stones as they entered the plant.[18] Soon company management and the police encouraged strikebreakers to retaliate, and full-blown melees broke out periodically in front of the cigar factory. Groups of strikers, strikebreakers, and even the police were wounded in the intense battles. The strike ultimately went down in defeat, followed by another short-lived strike that was defeated the following year.

Garment Workers

From 1932 to 1936, garment workers across the country launched a total of 311 strikes involving 239,744 workers.[19] One of these labor actions was a twenty-two-day general strike for union recognition that spread across thirteen states, shaking the whole industry.[20] The strike wave then spread through the small garment industry in Texas, centered around Dallas, Houston, and San Antonio. Texas was a state notorious for anti-union employers and local governments aggressively opposed to the "closed shop." Like other gender-segregated industries, working conditions and wages in the predominantly female textile workforce set the low-end threshold nationally. The abundance of low-wage workers in Texas attracted northeastern and midwestern capitalists eager to relocate away from the garment districts of New York, Chicago, and Philadelphia. At its peak, San Antonio's four main garment factories employed 7,000 Mexican and Mexican American women workers, including those working in shops and as homeworkers.[21]

Beginning in 1921, a strike wave swept the apparel industries in Texas, and by the end of the decade the Amalgamated Clothing Workers of America and the International Ladies' Garment Workers' Union (ILGWU) became firmly established, setting the ceiling for wages and working conditions.[22] By 1935, for instance, 220,000 of the nation's 260,000 garment workers were already members of the ILGWU, with the largest contingent of the non-union workforce located in the South.[23] Capital flight and runaway shops took off to the South, with the number of apparel shops increasing 435 percent between 1937 and 1945.[24] Much of the industry shifted production to Texas, where low wages were underwritten by a virulent anti-union business alliance called the Texas Open-Shop Association, which also relied on gender and racial discrimination as tools to divide and weaken the workforce. In Dallas, the base of operations for TOSA, the group pressured all employers to join and punished any who hired a card-carrying union member by fining them $3,000 per offense.[25]

Garment workers made about half of what their counterparts in the East made, earning an average of $6 a week and working between 44 and 54 hours.[26] White women made between 50 and 65 percent of what white men made, and Mexican women and African American women were paid less than white women.[27] Although NRA-mandated codes had been established in 1934 limiting hours to forty a week and raising pay as high $14 a week (depending on the dress material used), employers ignored them, exploited loopholes to evade the codes, or simply paid less than the scales prescribed, a practice that lured more investment into the region.

After the passage of the National Industrial Recovery Act in 1933, there were attempts by women workers in Dallas to establish an independent garment workers' union. A core of twelve workers who met in secret at night in each other's homes were openly organizing in the shops. The group contacted the ILGWU, which was poised to move south in tow of the runaway shops. The union sent three organizers to Dallas, assisting this core of organizers in forming the nucleus that chartered Locals 121 and 204 with the International Ladies' Garment Workers' Union in late 1933.

After several months of tireless organizing, the employers clamped down on the union effort. Collaborating through the Texas Dress Manufacturers' Association, which was an anti-union combination of all thirteen garment factories, they were able to identify and fire eight of the twelve known leaders. ILGWU organizers then crafted the first set of demands for union recognition along with the demand for reinstatement of the fired workers. In January of 1935, the locals threatened to strike if the employers didn't increase wages and provide more job guarantees for full- and part-time workers. While the negotiation was underway, a small group of workers incensed that their co-workers had not been rehired forced the issue by walking out in early February 1935. By March, workers at thirteen of the fifteen garment factories had walked out on strike. The Dallas Dressmakers' War, which would rage for nearly a year, was on.

The eleven-month strike was gradually defeated as the whole city establishment closed ranks behind the garment factory owners. They secured anti-picketing injunctions, which the police then used to engage in mass arrests and intimidation of strikers, gradually weakening the picket lines. Despite the tenacity of the workers, the strike eroded as those fired or arrested were blacklisted and unable to find work as the strike fund was gradually depleted.

Although the strike ended in defeat, its effects reverberated through the region, signaling the opening shots of a larger struggle.[28] The resolve of the women and the threat of a replay of the costly strike led the main dress factories in Houston to band together and recognize ILGWU Local 214 a few months later. By 1935, workers in Houston's five garment companies secured a contract that saw their wages rise from between $6 and $8 a week to $12 a week, and their workweek reduced from forty-eight to fifty-four hours to forty hours.[29] By 1937, most of the Dallas garment employers had relented, formally recognizing the two predominantly Anglo ILGWU locals.

In 1934, garment worker militancy also spread to San Antonio, where the majority of the workers were mexicana and Mexican American women. Like in Dallas, a core of union-minded workers sent a request to the ILGWU for support. President David Dubinsky enlisted the help of a young tejana radical named Emma Tenayuca in organizing two Spanish-speaking locals.[30] After three failed union drives, organizers targeted the Dorothy Frocks Company in 1936, winning the ability for a majority of workers to sign cards with Local 123. While the owner of the company expressed a willingness to negotiate, he abruptly passed away. His widow took over the company reins, reneged on the agreement, and refused to negotiate with the workers for a union contract. The workers walked out on strike in May of 1936. The company responded by promptly shutting its doors and subcontracting production at another shop across town, with the strikers quickly relocating to the new location.

Like in Dallas, the San Antonio establishment secured anti-picketing injunctions, which the police then used to engage in mass arrests and intimidation of strikers, especially as strikers became more militant and confrontational against scabs. Strikers commonly tore and ripped the dresses of strikebreakers using seamstresses' pin hooks. These "stripping parties" were carried out to discourage other Mexican American and Anglo women from crossing the picket lines. To avoid arrest, they followed scabs home, publicly serenading them along the way with corridos that heaped shame and scorn upon them for their actions. They also confronted them and defrocked them in other public spaces including at a street parade.

The tactic became so effective at discouraging their return that the police began to escort strikebreakers to their homes and back to work, and a local judge even issued an injunction prohibiting the strikers from being "loud or insulting" toward the scabs.[31] These and other creative efforts showed how the workers evolved and expanded tactics in the face of preponderant adversity from an alliance of city government and local capitalists. Nevertheless, in an atmosphere of legal vigilantism, where the veneer of equal protection under the law was suspended for the strikers, the police began to arrest union leaders after every incident in a quid pro quo. The brazen corruption even led Texas senator Morris Shepherd and Representative Maury Maverick to publicly call for an investigation into the role of the police. When repression alone did not kill the strike, the company closed entirely and moved operations to Dallas, effectively killing the strike. Nevertheless, the ILGWU clandestinely sent laid-off strikers to Dallas to get into the new garment factory, where they orchestrated another walkout at the new plant two months after it opened. The company was forced to sign a contract with the union in November of 1936.

The defeat at Dorothy Frocks was followed by a second strike against the Shirlee Frock Company in 1937, a producer of infant and children's wear that depended on in-factory production as well as home workers. Factory workers could earn up to 60 cents an hour while home workers were paid as little as 5 cents an hour.[32] The union worked on both fronts, successfully bringing out home workers to walk the picket lines when the factory workers shut down operations. When the anti-union mayor, Charles K. Quin, declared the home workers' picket line illegal at the behest of the company's owner, his political ally, Police Commissioner Phil Wright, then declared open season. Over eighty picketers were arrested, released, and in some cases rearrested on the same day as they quickly returned upon release.[33] The company finally caved after four months on August 4. The strikers had won an injunction against the mayor and commissioner after Texas State Representative and New Dealer Maury Maverick intervened, threatening a full National Labor Relations Board investigation of the police actions. More importantly, the heavy-handed repression of the police failed to weaken the workers' resolve or break the picket lines. According to historian Melissa Hield,

> Not only did the [ILGWU] win the strike, but also they succeeded in eliminating the worst abuse of the home work system for these workers—low wages. The union won a wage increase to 20 cents per hour and a five-day, 40-hour work week, which doubled their former pay with a five-hour decrease in their work week. In addition, 18 strikers were reinstated in their jobs and scabs were given 60 days to either join the union or leave the shop.[34]

ILGWU Local 180, a second Spanish-language local, grew out of this strike.

Less than a year later, the strike wave spread to a third shop, with mexicanas and Mexican American women shutting down the Texas Infants' Dress Company. They also called for wage increases, a decrease in the workweek, the abolition of piecework, and the decertification of a company union in favor of the ILGWU. While they were unsuccessful in their main demands, they did reach an agreement to scrap the company union and designate ILGWU as the sole representative. The victorious (or partially successful) strikes at Shirlee and Texas Infants' led another producer, the Juvenile Manufacturing Company, to avert a strike by agreeing to a twenty-cent minimum wage and recognition of the ILGWU. By 1940, a third local was established and over a thousand women were working under union contract in three locals.[35]

Chapter 26
Communists and the Workers Alliance in Texas

*"In the absence of economic power or social prestige, organization among
destitute and unemployed persons has made its imprint on public policy largely
through mass mobilization and the tactics of pressure and demonstration."*
—**Report by the American Public Welfare Association, 1937**

Mass unemployment as a persistent feature of capitalist crisis during the 1930s destroyed the economic stability of millions of workers. The total economic loss between 1930 and 1934 is estimated to be equal to the cost of World War I, between $100 billion and $120 billion (in 1913 dollars), with unemployment disproportionately hitting the young, immigrant, African American, and female sections of the working class in the highest proportions.[1] When the AFL scoffed at the idea of organizing the unemployed, radicals stepped in. Between 1930 and 1937, they created mass unemployed organizations nationwide that were instrumental in yielding significant concessions. In the case of Texas, the Workers Alliance of America also initiated one of the first great struggles for Mexican American civil rights.

The loss of income, the evaporation of accumulated wealth, and the absence of significant welfare infrastructure destabilized the working class. Hunger, starvation, and illness emerged on a large scale as families lost access to food, housing, and medical services. Homeless camps and shantytowns sprang up across the country on the margins of urban centers, as destitute families faced systematic eviction. Local, state, and federal government negligence of a rapidly widening population of destitute workers fired class consciousness and anger, sparking action.

The situation reached a crisis point by 1932, inducing spontaneous and semi-organized forms of protest. In cities across the country, throngs of unemployed workers began to protest outside of city government offices and engage in what historian Irving Bernstein refers to as "illegal self-help." This included spontaneous and sometimes organized operations to take food and other necessities from markets, delivery trucks, retail outlets, and former places of employment without paying.[2] Eviction resistance and rent strikes also took on spontaneous and organized forms, with Communists and Socialists scrambling to organize and lead the surging self-activity of the working class.

The Communist Party's first orientation toward unemployed workers took place through the TUUL and involved party members in the unions linking demands of the unemployed with the employed. This emphasized demands centered around increasing job security, including resistance to wage cuts, the seven-hour day and five-day week, free rent, immediate relief, and unemployment insurance. It also intersected with opposition to imperialism, with the slogan "Not one cent for armaments, all funds for the unemployed."[3] The party then turned to the direct task of organizing unemployed workers through the creation of "Unemployed Workers Councils." As Irene North explains,

> This work took on the form of gathering and disbursing food, organizing and maintaining close contact with new unemployment committees and councils, organizing rent eviction, mortgage foreclosure, and gas and light resistance, demanding free lunch service in the schools, registering the unemployed in trade unions . . . The Councils took pains to especially defend the interests of minority races, as they suffered the worst because of discrimination.[4]

Neighborhood unemployed councils were formed from New York, to Chicago, to Los Angeles. They organized marches, occupations, and anti-eviction community defense mobilizations. Party organizers in the Bronx, New York, for instance, helped to coordinate a rent strike to demand a citywide 15 percent rent reduction in 1932 after people refused to be evicted.[5] They called for a citywide moratorium on evictions and formed rapid-response committees to gather people in neighborhoods for home-defense campaigns when cops were sent in to turn families out.[6] The unemployed workers' movement even occupied state legislatures in Colorado and New Jersey to protest the lack of relief funding, and in both cases increased support was forthcoming. In San Antonio, party members established their presence in the city in early 1930. In April, they organized an unemployed march to City Hall, which, according to a newspaper account, included "approximately 1,200 men and women, the majority of whom were Mexicans."[7]

These community actions often brought brutal repression by local police, who functioned as the last line of defense for private property amid widespread direct action that outgrew the constraints of capitalism. Between 1930 and 1934, at least fourteen unemployed workers were killed by police, and thousands more were beaten, arrested, or jailed for participating in the unemployed relief movement.[8] For example, historian Franklin Folsom points out that at any one moment in 1934 it is estimated that three thousand people were in jail across the country for striking or taking part in an unemployed protest, or had been arrested as political radicals.[9]

Nevertheless, organizers were tenacious and community support widespread.[10] Roy Rosenzweig, a historian of the unemployed workers' movement, estimates that as many as two million workers took part in some form of this direct action over the Depression decade, winning thousands of local victories or successful resistance campaigns across the country.[11] Some of these occurred in the state of Texas, where in 1930 local chapters of the TUUL began to launch branches of the Unemployed Councils, which were organized on a neighborhood, block, and citywide basis under the slogans "Don't starve—Fight!" and "Work or Wages."[12]

Radicals Merge into the Workers Alliance of America

By 1933, the Communist-led Unemployed Councils claimed a national membership of 150,000.[13] The Trotskyist-influenced Unemployed Citizens' Leagues claimed a membership across several states of about 200,000, while the Socialist Party's Unemployed Leagues had forged a national network of branches that claimed 450,000 adherents.[14] The rapid growth of the tripartite movement did not lead to its mergence, as sectarian divides hindered the process, especially the Communist Party's adherence to the ultra-left opposition to Socialists as "social fascist." In 1934, the Socialist Party spearheaded the largest coordinated action on a national scale. The protest actions were launched as part of National Unemployment Day and mobilized an estimated 350,000 workers in twenty-two states.[15] The magnitude of the event led the Socialist leaders to embark on a campaign to unite all groups (with the exception of their nemeses in the Communist Party) under their umbrella. The trajectory of this effort was aided by the fact that local, state, and even the federal government was shifting resources toward the unemployed.

The election of Roosevelt signified the first shift in federal policy influenced by the unemployed workers' movement. Within his first year in office, FDR launched three federal campaigns to address unemployment: the Civilian Conservation Corps, as an effort to get unemployed youth into government-sponsored public works; the Federal Emergency Relief Administration to directly distribute relief; and the Works Project Administration to directly employ unemployed workers in federally funded jobs. For the first time in history, the federal government directly aided displaced workers; being pulled in tow by an unprecedented upsurge in mass action led by radical and anticapitalist parties during the greatest crisis of capitalism in the nation's history.

As Fox and Piven conclude from this significant shift toward socialized relief: "It had taken protest and the ensuing electoral disturbances to produce federal relief legislation, and it took continued protest to get the legislation implemented . . . And during 1933, 1934, and 1935, groups of the unemployed continued to agitate, and were at least partly responsible for the fact that many states and localities participated in federal emergency relief programs at all."[16] Local relief funds rose across the country, from $71 million in 1929 to $171 million in 1931. After federal grants were allocated through the passage of the Federal Emergency Relief Act in 1932, total expenditures rose to $794 million in 1933, $1.4 billion in 1934, and $1.8 billion in 1935.[17]

The Communist Party's abandonment of its Third Period ultra-leftism in 1935 created the opening for collaboration between the separate unemployed movements. Radicals in the Communist Party, the Socialist Party, the Trotskyist Workers' Party, and smaller unaffiliated groups immersed themselves in this struggle of the unemployed and had witnessed the effects on government policy. Under these circumstances, and in line with the Communist Party's conciliatory Popular Front approach, rival Socialist and Communist camps agreed to merge efforts to have an even greater impact. After nominally merging in early 1935, they created the Workers Alliance of America. In April of 1936, a delegated body of 900 people representing unemployed workers' organizations from 36 states (including the Unemployed Council from San Antonio, Texas) convened in Washington, DC. From their efforts emerged a nationwide organization with 1,600 locals representing a membership of 600,000.[18] By 1938, the Communist Party had 27,000 active members working within the Workers Alliance chapters across the nation, including in San Antonio.[19]

Combating Racial, National, and Gender Discrimination

While particular industries, communities, and sectors of the economy were impacted more severely than others, the most devastated were Mexican and black workers, whose labor was concentrated in a narrow range of occupations that were most vulnerable to capitalist instability. In industrial centers, Mexican unemployment rates ranged from 20 percent to as high as 75 percent in the first three years of the Great Depression.[20] Mexicans were often fired first, and were disproportionately concentrated in fewer, low-wage occupations. Another study estimates that only 28 percent of Mexican families had more than one gainfully employed member, typically the male, as women were laid off in higher proportion.[21] Furthermore, wages dropped precipitously for those who could find work. This was a trend illustrated by the example in Los Angeles, where the value of wages in the early 1930s plummeted to about 35–40 percent of what they had been during the previous decade.[22]

While all of the involved political tendencies pledged support for national, racial, and gender unity as part of their organizing efforts, it was the Communist Party that made the greatest strides toward putting this into action. The party emphasized the need to organize in black and Mexican communities as well as the need for the inclusion and support of the demands of immigrants and foreign nationals. They built into their organizing efforts opposition to all forms of discrimination in distribution of relief, hiring, wage scales, and the devolution of policy implementation to Jim Crow oppositionist forces in southern states. As a 1931 party pamphlet exhorted the reader:

> It is absolutely necessary that the Unemployed Councils, organized on the basis of full equality of all races and of native and foreign-born workers, shall vigorously take up and resist the fiendish measures now being taken by the capitalist . . . The Unemployed Councils must resist the special persecution of the Negroes, must resist the continuation of segregation and Jim Crowism [. . .] The Unemployed Councils must take up the struggle for protection of the foreign-born workers against . . . persecution through police agents of the Department of Labor to punish every foreign born worker for loyalty to the working class, and thus to weaken the strength of the workers' movement, especially in the heavy industries where foreign-born workers form a large proportion of those employed and unemployed.[23]

Racial exclusions across the economy already made unemployment a feature of daily life, only to be exacerbated by contractions in the vulnerable markets in which their labor was contingent. The Communist Party's antiracist approach, and its understanding of the volatility within working-class communities of color, led them to select these areas for their organizing campaigns. These included African American workers in Harlem, Atlanta, Richmond, and Birmingham; and Mexicans in San Antonio and

Los Angeles. The party also prioritized the cultivation of unemployed worker-leaders from within the ranks of these communities, leading to the recruitment of individuals with influence and direct ties to the local populations. The stated support for noncitizens was given special focus within Communist-led or influenced organizations especially as the opponents of the New Deal–era reformism began to conflate immigration with welfare. By 1933, for instance, twenty-three states had passed laws prohibiting noncitizen employment in public service or had enacted "Americans first" provisions that led to mass firings of immigrant workers.[24] Private industries followed suit. Following the government's actions, they were given license to fire expendable workers, those considered undesirable, and especially known supporters of unionism.[25]

While the advent of federal relief fired the hopes of San Antonio's disproportionately high population of unemployed workers, government assistance was not forthcoming. The city offered no aid to displaced workers, and the state coalesced around opposition to any federal efforts to intercede into the affairs of labor. The post-Reconstruction-era Texas constitution was explicitly designed to deny state aid to the poor, a preemptive effort to preclude the possibility for state intervention between poor black workers and white landowners. By the 1930s, the state and local government administrations also sought to block or bottleneck the distribution of federal unemployment benefits to prevent Mexican workers from accessing relief as an alternative to the extremely low agricultural wages. As a result, San Antonio had the lowest median income in the nation, when compared to other cities of its size.[26]

Anti-immigrant Southern Democrats in Congress and in state legislatures where the Mexican working class was most essential to interests of agricultural capital, as both a workforce and reserve army of labor, were the most restrictive of Mexican participation in New Deal policies of relief. In the first three months of 1935, for instance, 107 bills were introduced into Congress, establishing more grounds for deportation and for an array of increased restrictions and discriminatory exclusions of the foreign-born in employment and access to social services.[27] Democratic Texas congressmen such as Martin Dies and Fritz Garland Lanham were among the most vociferous opponents of extending relief to Mexican-born workers.[28] For the same reason—keeping Mexican workers isolated from both rights and relief—they were also among the most hostile anti-Communists in Congress.

Myriad racial exclusions were wired into the legislation or grafted onto the legislation once implemented by the Texas state government, rendering much of the New Deal an illusion for Mexican workers. For instance, participation in the Works Progress Administration (WPA) was limited to US citizens, after Texas representative Fritz Garland Lanham introduced an amendment requiring states purge their rolls of those who had not previously applied for naturalization or without updated and correct documents. This clause was used broadly by the Texas Relief Commission (TRC) to systematically exclude Mexicans, as well as Mexican Americans, who were denied, disqualified, or removed systematically from the rolls.[29]

One common loophole was to disqualify anyone who did not reside in the city for the duration of the previous year. This excluded thousands of San Antonio–based migratory agricultural workers that left the city at least part of the year to follow the cotton harvest through Texas or the beet harvest up through Michigan.[30] Another common practice was to use an English-speaking requirement as a means to reject Mexican American applicants, even if they spoke the language fluently.

Since the government of San Antonio refused to provide relief to unemployed workers, those in need had to turn to the limited resources available from private sources. For instance, a survey of 512 pecan-shelling families reported that 88 percent relied on emergency food aid from churches, soup kitchens, and other charity since they were paid less than they needed to survive. When federal aid did reach the state, the TRC instructed relief offices throughout the state to limit Mexican American access, and to direct them and their families to seasonal agricultural work based on the needs of the large landowners.

Building the Workers Alliance in San Antonio

In was in this context that Workers Alliance organizers in San Antonio tried to establish an organizing base among the Mexican workers. The Communist Party's Unemployed Councils already had a presence in the city going back to 1930. In April of that year, the Communists led a march against unemployment through the streets of San Antonio, consisting of "approximately 1200 men and women, the majority of whom were Mexicans."[31] By 1936, the Councils then merged with local Socialists to relaunch a united Workers Alliance of America in 1936. Emma Tenayuca, a young Mexican American radical, became a lightning rod for the growth of the movement. She first joined the West Side Unemployed Council through her support for striking cigar workers. She began to support efforts to get relief for those who were fired and blacklisted, and through this work joined the Communist Party's West Side Unemployed Council, becoming its secretary. She was part of the merger that brought the different unemployed rights groups together and quickly became a prominent organizer within the group, along with Manuela Solís Sager. Solís Sager and her husband, James Sager, both Communist Party members, had come to San Antonio shortly after they helped organize the South Texas Agricultural Workers Union as a legacy of the TUUL's efforts to organize Texas farmworkers, as the CAWIU had in California. They relocated to San Antonio to help spearhead efforts to organize the vast ranks of Mexican workers into the Alliance, and later the CIO-affiliated Pecan Sheller's Union.

Under her leadership, the San Antonio chapter of the Workers Alliance grew exponentially. The Alliance was transformed into a multifaceted organization to serve the needs of the Mexican working class, with an emphasis on facilitating self-activity and organization within the community and building the notion of civil rights for Mexicans into labor struggle. The Workers Alliance had a dual function. It built neighborhood campaigns to compel the city government to meet the needs of the community. They successfully advocated for the construction of low-income housing projects, and for the creation of jobs through the Works Project Administration, which sponsored a restoration and revitalization campaign of run-down and abandoned buildings in the Mexican barrio.[32]

Another function of the group was to confront Jim Crow segregation and other forms of racial violence through direct action. The group agitated to extend relief to fired and unemployed workers and to oppose deportation. Furthermore, they protested to overturn racial exclusion of Mexicans from WPA jobs, for wage parity, and for the provision of legal and educational services. The Workers Alliance also functioned as a union to organize strikes. Through the day-to-day efforts of methodical and tireless organizing, the Alliance grew to represent over 10,000 members spread across fifteen locals throughout the city, making it one of the largest centers of Workers Alliance activity in the nation. Tenayuca was essential to the growth of the ten locals built across the West Side, which included at least 3,000 Mexican workers, most of whom were underemployed pecan shellers.[33] She became general secretary of these branches, which had been built through family, workplace, and mutualista networks.

Life inside the organization for Mexicans was inclusive, democratic, and integrated. While racial segregation characterized life in the city, the Workers Alliance established racially integrated locals and pledged to fight "vigorously any attempt to encroach upon the Democratic rights of the unemployed, whether they be native or foreign-born, Negro or white."[34] The emphasis on integration within the organization, largely adapted from the practice of the Communist Party, was welcomed by many on the West Side. Emma Tenayuca, herself of a product of that community and acutely aware of the racial dimensions, strove to create an organizational culture that reflected the community and made it a priority to help foster a Mexican leadership that could act in its own self-interest.[35]

One strategy for growing the ranks of the Alliance was through outreach to the mutual aid societies, whose memberships were often comprised of workers in the local industries. Through the pages of *La Prensa*, the Alliance built on the traditions of the Mexican Left and held mass gatherings in the plazas where families gathered on weekends. They held these assemblies to recruit and appeal to *sociedades mutualistas* and workers in general to join the Alliance, and to solicit affiliation in their respective organizations.[36] The work of Emma Tenayuca as a community organizer was key to building support and affiliation from the labor mutualistas, whose members actively joined the Alliance's actions, especially as they produced results. The Alliance also organized communities block by block, offering basic social services in the absence of city relief. Built along the radical line that mass action and disruption could force negotiation and concession, the organization regularly organized mass marches to carry protest to the centers of power. Sit-ins, occupations, and picket lines became a regularly deployed tactic to confront and disrupt power, especially where it served to reinforce practices of racial segregation.

Mass Action against Discrimination

One of the first actions of the Workers Alliance, beginning in 1935, was to organize a protest of the city's exclusion of Mexican families from its relief roll. The substantial expansion of federal relief programs between 1932 and 1934 reached about 45 million people, or nearly one-third of the population in some way. Beginning in 1935, the Roosevelt administration began to restructure relief distribution as a means to downsize and ostensibly dismantle federal relief programs under the mantra "the government must and shall quit the business of relief." Federal cuts working through the system were seized upon by Texas administrators of federal relief to begin purges of Mexican Americans.

The city government wanted to either deport them or compel them to work on farms. It was common practice for workers to be cut from relief rolls during harvest season. They would then be rounded up in sweeps by police, arrested, and charged with vagrancy. To avoid jail, these workers and their families were then impressed into agricultural labor.[37]

The Alliance seized on the failure of city government to meet the needs of the unemployed, organizing regular marches and demonstrations outside the offices of the mayor and other officials who directly oversaw various New Deal relief policies. Workers Alliance organizers led those denied aid in rallies, which put pressure on city officials to act.[38] In early March of 1937, the Alliance launched a campaign to demand resources for unemployed and disabled workers, increased funding for works projects, higher wages and union rights for WPA workers, and equal pay for Mexican workers.[39] In their publicity for the march, which included a mass meeting at Cassiano Park, they called on support and participation from all workers throughout the city "regardless of race, color, creed, or political affiliation."[40] A march of over fifteen hundred winded through the city. As a reporter from *La Prensa* described:

> The majority of the protesters were Mexicans, those registered on relief rolls, independent workers, and others affiliated with the nine branches of the Workers' Alliance; a workers' society from New Braunfels, the Sons of Texas Society, Circulo Social Mutualista, the Union of Nut Workers, and other labor groupings.[41]

The march also featured the Workers Alliance youth wing wearing Alliance uniforms and matching caps, showcasing the broad base-building the organization conducted over the previous year. On the steps of the mayor's office, Emma Tenayuca gave a speech in which she condemned the local government for blocking implementation of New Deal relief programs and called for the Mexican community to take militant action. As *La Prensa* transcribed segments of her speech, including her closing statement:

> The time is now for the workers to organize . . . we can no longer wait for better days without fighting for those better days . . . the organization of the working class is paving the way forward."[42]

Following the speeches, a delegation entered the building to present their demands to the mayor.

Another focus for the Alliance was to organize against deportation. Deportation accelerated in Texas during the first years of the Depression, which led the nation in expulsion of Mexicans, resulting in more than 70 percent of the over 345,000

Mexicans being driven out of the country by 1931.[43] The Alliance held a 5,000-strong mass march against deportation and racial discrimination, and for jobs and justice for Mexican workers in 1937.[44] As the Workers Alliance positioned itself as a defender of immigrant workers, cases of misconduct and brutality at the hands of immigration agents were brought to the group by those seeking protection and redress. The Alliance sponsored workshops and community meetings to explain US immigration laws in a "know your rights" format. These meetings also became action-oriented, planning meetings against state violence against immigrants.

The Alliance began to take public actions against these cases of violence, organizing protests in front of immigration offices to denounce mistreatment. In one case, covered in *El Heraldo de Brownsville*, around 175 members of the Workers Alliance "stormed the immigration office in the federal building" to protest several incidents of brutality, and took their protest directly into the offices of the mayor and local immigration officials.[45] These protests attracted national attention and led to federal inquiries into local operations, especially when local police detectives began to target and arrest Workers Alliance leaders and turn them over to immigration agents with the threat of deportation. Alliance members organized three protests and occupations of the mayor's office in one week in late February to protest the intimidation tactics.[46]

The Workers Alliance provided an important educational and organizational platform for the region's workers. Weekly meetings were held by the branches, countywide assemblies were periodically convened, and large public rallies were commonplace in the West Side plazas. For instance, one countywide assembly was organized to support the thousands of seasonal migratory cotton pickers that lived in San Antonio. At the August 1936 assembly, the Alliance strategized and planned protests against unscrupulous cotton contractors who often lured workers to cotton fields promising higher wages than they were willing to pay.[47] On another occasion, the Workers Alliance tried to obtain a permit for a May 1 march through San Antonio. When the mayor refused it, two hundred Alliance members occupied the office of Mayor C. K. Quinn, declaring a sit-in until the permit was granted. It took the mustering of over fifty police agents to finally dislodge the occupation.[48]

As part of a new national strategy, the Workers Alliance began to directly organize workers employed through the WPA. Tenayuca and the Alliance took a public position against the exclusion of Mexican workers from the WPA, demanding full inclusion and equal pay. They criticized the fact that only 2 million of the estimated 15 million unemployed nationally were actually employed through the program at its peak, only about 1 in every 4 unemployed workers.[49] More anti-immigrant laws and amendments were passed nationally, including the Hamilton Fish Amendment to the Relief Appropriation Act of 1936, which disqualified over a million noncitizen workers from WPA employment. Undocumented workers were excluded outright, and state administrators of the program in Texas widely discriminated against Mexican Americans in hiring, regardless of their status. Beginning in 1936, the San Antonio branches of the Alliance held weekly meetings to attract WPA workers to their educational presentations and to recruit them into the Alliance to work on their behalf as union representatives.

The Workers Alliance advocated for all WPA workers to be able to have full citizenship rights through service, including the right to form public workers' unions and achieve wage parity with the private sector, and to prevent the government from converting the program into one of controlled or forced labor in the service of capital.[50] Tenayuca applied this principal of labor rights being linked to citizenship, expressing that undocumented Mexican workers should also receive citizenship through labor service. The Alliance also opposed the WPA's acceptance of racial and gender wage differentials, which accommodated especially to Jim Crow state governments who established and maintained racial disparities in the service of local capital.

When the Roosevelt administration began defunding of the Works Progress Administration, effectively laying off an estimated six hundred thousand workers, this led to a second wave of Workers Alliance–led mass protests across the country in 1936–1937. After local plan administrators in San Antonio laid off thirty-six Mexican American WPA workers, the Alliance took direct action, storming the offices and launching a sit-in at the San Antonio office of the Public Works Administration. This Alliance then began to regularly use the tactic of the mass sit-in to protest and disrupt the various government offices as part of their campaign.

The effectiveness of the Workers Alliance at confronting and disrupting the functioning of government produced a backlash of police violence. In June of 1937, the police raided and sacked the offices of the Workers Alliance, disrupted a meeting, and beat and detained those present. They methodically destroyed furniture, literature, a piano, and typewriters, seized all records, and arrested four identified leaders, including state organizer Robert Williams, San Antonio organizer Juan Mendoza, San Antonio general secretary Emma Tenayuca, and members Anastasio García, A. Fernando Moreno, and José Alfaro. Charges against the group included organizing illegal assemblies, inciting public disturbances, and assaulting a police officer.[51]

In response to the arrests, according to the Texas ACLU, "thousands of people swarmed around the city jail and demanded that Emma Tenayucca [sic] be released . . . [and] telegrams of protest poured in from around the country."[52] While the protest vigils continued, hearings were conducted to determine if Tenayuca would be charged. According to La Prensa, multiple eyewitnesses were able to expose the police accusations as fabricated, and all of the charges were dropped.[53] While the attempt to crush the Workers Alliance with brute repression backfired, provoking an overwhelming outpouring of public support, police violence continued to intensify against the Workers Alliance. This became the case especially after its members organized and participated in a strike in the pecan sheds in early 1938.

At its height, the Workers Alliance was able to stitch together a broad coalition of the working class in the barrio of westside San Antonio. Under the leadership of Communists like Emma Tenayuca, the Alliance became the repository of the decade's labor militancy through its recruitment and organization of veteran strikers, union organizers, and those radicalized by persistent and racially structured unemployment.

Through mass direct-action campaigns, the Alliance mobilized a previously inconceivable mass power that disrupted and debilitated the functioning of the Jim Crow power structure. As they won concrete gains, even more workers flocked to their banners.

When the economy took another downturn in 1938, pushing unemployment up to 29 percent among Mexican workers, the branches of the Alliance swelled. Among those that joined the Workers Alliance were *nueceros* (pecan shellers), the largest and poorest section of the working class. The organizing experience, the interface with broad community alliances, and class-struggle training gained by the pecan workers through their participation in the actions of the Workers Alliance created the basis for a network of militants to lead the largest strike in San Antonio history. In doing so, the Workers Alliance morphed into a union capable of producing and activating trained leaders, and mobilizing mass action to win one of the most significant strike victories in Texas history.

Chapter 27
The Pecan Shellers Strike of 1938

"We learned a whole lot ... [W]e learned how to ... defend ourselves more ...
[W]e forgot the fear that we had. ... Afterwards it was entirely different."
—**Reflections of a participant in the 1938 pecan strike**

The convergence of Communists, the Workers Alliance, and mass discontent among the city's largest workforce in pecan shelling produced the biggest and most militant strike in San Antonio history. On January 31, 1938, an estimated 6,000 to 8,000 pecan shellers walked out of about 170 workshops (referred to locally as "sheds"). Within days, leaders of the Workers Alliance and United Cannery, Agricultural, Packing, and Allied Workers (UCAPAWA) Local 172 representatives and rank-and-file strikers went shed to shed, calling out more workers until the strike ranks grew to 12,000 shellers, effectively closing down up to 120 sheds. In an intense 37-day strike, 40 percent of the nation's pecan production was shut down. What began as a walkout quickly evolved into a citywide battle between Mexican workers, community members, and youth on one side, and the police, strikebreakers, and the local political and business establishment on the other. The strike also divided the Mexican community, primarily along class lines, as middle-class organizations such as the League of United Latin American Citizens (LULAC) and Catholic Church–affiliated groups opposed the strike or condemned its radical leadership.

The locus for the strike action did not originate from existing union organization, but rather it was a wildcat strike called forth by networks of workers affiliated with the Workers Alliance. The strike occurred at the convergence point of several significant factors, which gave it the characteristics of a mass uprising of Mexican labor on the West Side. It was the culmination of four years of intense labor struggle in the city, over the course of which the Mexican working class learned important lessons about the nature of the system they were up against. They built broad solidarity networks through class, familial, and cultural connections. While neglected by AFL unions in the city, they were welcomed by the radicals in the Workers Alliance, where very capable organizers like Emma Tenayuca understood the potential power of mass action.

The radicalization of Mexican workers was influenced by the national and international dimensions of global capitalist crisis and upturns in class struggle not seen since the period of World War I. Labor militancy surged within the major industries of US capitalism, in some cases achieving the magnitude of citywide general strikes. From 1930 to 1937 there were over 4,700 strikes, reaching a high point in 1936–1937 when almost half a million workers engaged in militant "sit-down" strikes, driving the divide within the AFL and producing the industrial union movement called the Congress of Industrial Organizations (CIO).[1] The crisis of capitalism and the upsurge of class struggle pushed national politics to the left. Liberal New Deal Democrats were achieving sizeable gains at the polls, revealing a palpable pro-labor and anti-corporate mood that had spread through much of the nation as capitalist crisis lumbered on and unions and the labor movement began to win big victories. The incoming Congress in January 1935 represented this trend with a substantial margin of victory for left-wing reformists, increasing Democratic control of the House to 322 seats (74 percent of seats), and further expanding its ranks to 334 in 1937 (77 percent of seats).[2]

The "Liberal Bloc," as this group was called, included Maury Maverick, who was elected as a representative of the region that included San Antonio. Maverick, a former Bexar County tax collector, built a personal reputation and career opposing corrupt machine politics in San Antonio. He also took a public stance against the Klan and lynching as early as the 1920s, setting himself apart from other Southern Democrats.[3] He campaigned in 1934 on pushing New Deal reforms forward, building a coalition that included those who supported "clean" government, workers who wanted more funding and support for federal relief and jobs programs, and local capitalists eager to overcome local opposition to receiving New Deal dollars. He was joined by another liberal New Dealer, James Allred, who was elected governor of the state in 1935.[4] In office, the Liberal Bloc program included more funding for relief, realization of the Fair Labor Standards Act, full employment, greater civil liberties, and neutrality in the impending European war. Its members, like Maverick, also aligned themselves with the CIO breakaway faction within the AFL.

Across the border, an emerging labor movement in Mexico influenced by the Communist Party was growing in militancy. The number of strikes rose from around 70 nationally in 1934 to 642 in 1935 and 674 in 1936, a nearly tenfold increase in two years.[5] In 1936, agricultural workers across the border in the La Laguna region of Coahuila launched a general strike, with 15,000 workers shutting down the profitable cotton harvest. Amid the rise of class struggle, several smaller labor federations gathered at the first Congreso de la Unificación de Trabajadores Mexicanos in 1935, and later merged into the Confederación de Trabajadores Mexicanos in 1936, which included Communists figuring prominently in the leadership. The CTM emerged as the largest labor federation in Mexico, now dominated by self-identified Marxists, bringing together into a unified body "nearly 3,000 unions, guilds, syndicates, local, regional, and national organizations, with approximately 600,000 members who constitute over 90 percent of the organized workers of the country."[6]

The explosion of class struggles finalized the widening rifts within the AFL over the question of industrial unionism and multiracial inclusion. For Mexican workers in Texas, a similar process was unfolding across the border among the industrial working class, taking shape in the formation of a new industrial union movement. On both sides the border, the Communist Parties were instrumental in the splits and strikes, and were catalysts in the creation of the new industrial union federations.

Southern Pecan Shelling Company

By 1938, half of the national market in pecans was controlled by one company based in San Antonio, the Southern Pecan Shelling Company, owned and operated by Julius Seligmann and his junior partner Joe Freeman. Seligmann inherited a large landed estate from his father and converted it to pecan growing, which had been established in the mid-nineteenth century due to the proliferation of the pecan tree throughout Texas. Seligmann calculated that the abundance of vulnerable and politically marginalized Mexican labor could help his operation undercut his rivals and create a more profitable model. By 1926, the industry had largely mechanized and relied on factory-like workshops and wage labor, which was governed by minimal labor protections, by the passage of the NRA in 1933. Seligmann broke away from other pecan shellers, ignoring NRA codes and driving wages down to the lowest possible point.

Seligmann concocted a plan to deindustrialize the process by devolving it into a contract system that allowed for the skirting of existing wage laws and the maximization of "family labor." This occurred in two forms. The whole nuts were sold in bulk to contractors, who bought the product, procured buildings to group together workers to crack and extract the nuts, and paid them piece rates that allowed them to go below established wage thresholds. Contractors also distributed the nuts to workers in their homes, a process that commonly involved the whole family, including grandparents and young children. The contractor, who was often handpicked by the grower, then sold the shelled nuts back to the company to be distributed to domestic and international markets. Seligmann controlled his own small army of 120 contractors, which managed ten thousand people, or about 50 percent of the total shelling workforce.

This system generated a large, diffuse system of production, spread out across over 120 "sheds" and an untold number of homes by the mid-1930s. Most of the hastily arranged work sheds lacked ventilation, windows, adequate lighting, bathrooms, and other sanitary necessities. This strategy proved highly profitable, eventually leading to systematic demechanization of the industry in San Antonio and the dissolution of most of Seligmann's competitors by 1929.[7] Other pecan growers followed suit to remain competitive.

By 1935, the Southern Pecan Shelling Company had morphed into a regional commodities speculator, purchasing surplus pecans from around the country for local production, and turning an average annual profit of half a million dollars. While profitable, the ongoing success of this setup was contingent upon the maintenance of racial discrimination and the social and political marginalization of Mexican workers.

Racial segregation and poverty concentrated San Antonio's sixty-five thousand Mexican workers in a four-square-mile barrio area in the poorer, western part of the city. Male workers were confined to low-wage agricultural employment. Mexican women and girls were excluded from the gendered occupations reserved for white women, such as sales and clerical work, and instead concentrated in agriculture, cigar-rolling, and garments; while white women who worked alongside Mexican women were paid higher wages for the same work.[8]

The expansion of the pecan-shelling industry drew in the largest numbers of Mexican workers. A gendered division of labor was created where men were paid a higher piece rate to crack the pecans and women were paid less to do the shelling. Women comprised 80 percent of the peak 20,000-strong pecan-shelling workforce, some as young as eleven years of age. They worked up to ten hours a day during the October-through-May season. Since many women could not leave households behind to follow the summer harvests, and since other occupations were closed to Mexican women, they experienced stints of unemployment until the next season came around. Furthermore, pecan operations were kept racially segregated, with Mexicans, blacks, and whites working in separate sheds as part of the Jim Crow social structure.[9]

In a study conducted by the Texas American Civil Liberties Union, the average weekly income for pecan shellers ranged between $10 and $12 prior to the Depression.[10] The deindustrialization of pecan shelling and the reintroduction of contracting and home work, coupled with the effects of the economic crisis, led wages to drop precipitously over the course of the 1930s. By 1938, weekly pay bottomed out at $2.73, paying less than farm work. The average annual combined family income of a family of 4.6 people in 1938 amounted to $251, making it the lowest-paying job in San Antonio, and among the lowest-paying occupations in the nation.[11] Contractors were also squeezed under these conditions, as monopoly-like conditions allowed Seligmann to leverage down piece rates by refusing to sell or buy from contractors or by cutting off lines of credit.

The ranks of home shellers, which comprised about 4,000 primarily single and married women in 1935, expanded dramatically to up to 20,000 by 1937 as economic instability continued to push more Mexican families into poverty.[12] The unregulated home worker labor market grew to include whole families, family elders, and young children as families struggled to stay fed. As one study observed of the deteriorating conditions: "Thousands of human beings living in decrepit wooden shacks or in crowded corrals, breathlessly shelled pecans in a race with starvation."[13] The conditions and pay rate for homeworkers was even lower, which made this population more vulnerable and volatile when the shop workers took action.

When an agreement was hashed out through the National Recovery Act in October 1934 to nearly triple the minimum weekly wage for women to $6.60, and for men to nearly $11 (enshrining gender inequality in NRA wage scales) it was ignored by state and local governments at the behest of the pecan growers.[14] As a WPA report on pecan shellers explained:

> [It was] almost completely ineffective. The principal reason for its failure, according to an official NRA report, was that adherence to the code was voluntary, enabling dissenters to nullify its effect. The report also pointed out that until the contracting system and home shelling of pecans at low piecework rates were done away with, little could be done to raise the wage standards in the industry.[15]

In the face of compliance among pecan growers in the north and west of the country, Seligmann broke ranks from the National Pecan Shellers Association and formed his Southwestern Pecan Shellers Association, establishing a separate labor code for workers in Texas.

In testimony explaining his rationale for reforming a whole trade association around low wages, Seligmann appealed to a brand of racial paternalism that viewed Mexicans as less intelligent beings with simple needs: "Mexican pecan-shellers eat a good many pecans, and five cents a day is enough to support them in addition to what they eat when they work." As another shelling operator similarly explained: "The Mexicans don't want much money . . . Compared to those shanties they live in, the pecan shelleries are fine. They can be warm while their [sic] shelling pecans, they can talk to their friends while they are working, their kids can come in and play . . . because it is better than going home."[16]

Government recognition of the super-exploitative conditions maintained for Mexican workers did little to change them, as no resources were allocated for enforcement. This served as the backdrop for the series of wage cuts carried out by the Southern Pecan Shelling Company between 1934 and 1938, triggering strike action by nueceras. By the end of January 1938, for instance, wages were cut down to an all-time low average of $1.65 a week.[17]

Radical Nueceras and the Mass Strike

The pecan-shelling workforce ballooned to over 20,000 (including home workers) by 1938 as recession and high unemployment rates pushed more men and whole families into shelling.[18] High unemployment led a larger share of men to work alongside women, children, and seniors, although a majority of 80 percent of the total workforce remained women. About three thousand members of this workforce were also members of the Workers Alliance, which provided the leadership and organizational structure to initiate the walkout. Zaragosa Vargas contends that the leadership within the ranks of the pecan shellers' movement included workers who were former magonistas, socialists, and Communists, like Emma Tenayuca and Homer Brooks.[19] Some had been participants in or supporters of two earlier pecan strikes as well as those in garments and cigar-rolling, gaining invaluable experience and training that would serve them well this time around. Others had experience with unions as part of their sojourns to the beet sugar fields in Michigan, Minnesota, Colorado, and other areas.

Participants in the strike and strike solidarity also had experience as beet sugar workers, where they were exposed to union organizing in the Great Lakes region because of the proximity to industrial unionism in Detroit, and in Colorado, where the IWW organized a 1927 beet sugar strike.[20] UCAPAWA organizing among beet sugar workers in these regions preceded their efforts in Texas. As historian Dennis Nodín Valdés observed,

> At its peak this Communist-led union [UCAPAWA] claimed between 18,000 and 20,000 settled and migratory dues-paying members in the Great Plains states. The membership was estimated at 60 percent Mexican born and 40 percent United States born, proportions probably representative of the composition of the adult beet labor force in the region.[21]

Another contributing factor was the success of the Funsten nut strike four years earlier, which created a template for efforts in San Antonio. On April 24, 1933, an estimated 1,200 pecan and walnut shellers at the four plants of the Funsten Nut Company in St. Louis, Missouri, went on strike, shutting down the industry. Led by black women, who comprised about 90 percent of the workforce, the shellers went on strike against a series of successive wage cuts that decimated their pay alongside already poor working conditions between 1931 and 1933. White shellers were making an average of $2.75 a week, while black workers made $1.80 (3 cents per pound for halves and 2 cents for pieces).[22] The majority of the black workers walked out, with a smaller portion of eastern European immigrant women following suit in solidarity on the second day.

Led by a Communist, Trade Union Unity League–affiliated union called the Food Workers Industrial Union, the workers demanded wage increases and equal pay, as well as union recognition. In the year before the strike, the party did preliminary work among the unemployed, launching an Unemployed Council and organizing primarily among black workers. Through this effort, they recruited militant workers who later helped organize and lead the strike. Despite over a hundred arrests as a result of police repression, strikers fought successfully to keep the picket lines intact and to prevent strikebreakers from gaining a foothold. After nearly one month of a unified strike, the company folded, increasing all wages to 8 cents for halves, and 4 cents for pieces, amounting to a civil rights victory and nearly 100 percent wage increase.[23]

Despite the rabid anti-communism that framed the San Antonio establishment's strategy to divide and weaken support for the pecan shellers, the effort failed to internally weaken the strike. Racial segregation and a Jim Crow culture of racial ignorance and disdain already limited support from San Antonio's white middle class. The Mexican middle class, for its part, divided along political, religious, and class affiliation. The Mexican working class was not threatened by the presence of Communists in their midst, as they were already familiar with the basic tenets of radicalism and class struggle echoing the radical traditions of revolutionary Mexico and the surging labor movement on both sides of the border in the 1930s. Rather than being repulsed, they flocked to the movement.

The first two pecan sheller strikes took place in 1934 and 1935. The first occurred when the Pecan Shelling Workers' Union, a company union, was organized under the direction of Magdaleno Rodríguez, a political opportunist with a checkered past linked to the local Democratic Party machine. Rodríguez worked under the auspices of Seligmann in order to impose Southern's wage standards across the industry. Seligmann funded organizing efforts with a duplicitous intention, as Rodríguez focused on organizing drives among competitors and threatened to strike if they attempted to undercut Southern's wage scale. At the same time, the union openly opposed the higher NRA wage scales and discouraged genuine organizing efforts, taking public positions against the actions of the Workers Alliance. Workers saw through the double-dealings of Rodríguez and the union dissolved. Nevertheless, Rodríguez and repackaged versions of the "union" reentered the scene when actual organizing drives took place on the West Side, as a means to confuse and divide workers. When this failed, Rodríguez and his paid staff ditched the façade and hired themselves to the companies as paid muscle to provoke and attack picket lines in order to help break the strike.

Without formal union leadership, pecan shellers launched an early strike of 2,000 in 1934 (of a total workforce of 8,000) that collapsed after three weeks as the pecan growers and labor contractors coordinated an effective scabbing operation and the AFL refused to endorse or support the strike. A second strike was carried out in 1935, winning only a modest wage increase. The lack of resources, a broad base of organized support, and experienced leadership led both strikes to fail or fall short of winning the goal of union recognition and significant improvements in working conditions.

In the aftermath of the two strikes, new efforts to develop a genuine union began, with several independent organizing efforts taking place simultaneously. One of these was spearheaded by a Mexican American Communist Party organizer named Albert Gonsen, who was sent by the party from New Mexico to organize and agitate among the pecan shellers in anticipation of affiliating to the rapidly rising UCAPAWA. His effort merged with the small, legitimate remnants of Rodríguez's group, as well as with another short-lived independent union of 4,000 called El Nogal (The Walnut Tree), founded by a worker named Lilia Caballero. This group then merged again into the efforts of the CIO, which sent three Mexican organizers, Minnie Rendón, Leandro Ávila, and Willie Garcia to lead the organizing drive.

The joint efforts produced the Texas Pecan Shelling Workers Union, which was chartered by UCAPAWA in 1937 as the Pecan Workers Local 172. After winning a federal lawsuit designating nut shellers as industrial workers and not agricultural workers, the pecan shellers became covered by the provisions of the Wagner Act. After 1937, the union began to turn its attention and move resources to the region. The president of UCAPAWA, Donald Henderson, was also the Communist Party's chief theorist on organizing agricultural workers and was likely kept apprised of the situation through reports from the party members in the Workers Alliance. Despite the intervention of the national union in San Antonio, it was the Workers Alliance, led by two local Communists, that assumed the organic leadership of the strike.

The third strike was triggered after the Southern Pecan Company reduced the pay rate by a penny for shellers (to 6 cents per pound for whole pieces and 5 cents for halves); and 10 cents per 100 pounds for crackers (to 40 cents). Wages sunk so low, to an average of about $1.65 per week, that some workers accepted foodstuffs as payment instead of wages. Despite its spontaneous character, the strike was the culmination of the workers learning from the earlier failures as well as several years of direct community organizing and base-building by the Workers Alliance. The undisputed leadership of the Workers Alliance in the third strike was reflected in the election of its leadership. At the first mass meeting after the walkout, Emma Tenayuca was unanimously elected as strike leader. As historian Irene Ledesma asserts, "It would have been strange for the pecan shelling strikers in 1938 not to have chosen her as their leader."[24] Other leaders of the Alliance, including Juana Sánchez and fellow party-member Manuela Solís Sager, formed part of the first strike organizing committee. Showing their connection to the CIO and their intention to help facilitate its transition into leadership, they also incorporated Minnie

Rendón and Leandro Ávila from Pecan Workers Local 172 into the first strike commit-tee. The first challenge for this leadership was to keep itself out of jail.

Within twenty-four hours of the walkout, Emma Tenayuca, her husband Homer Brooks, Minnie Rendón, and Liandro Ávila were tracked down and arrested. The po-lice chief released the latter two but held Tenayuca and Brooks, claiming that he re-fused to let "reds get involved in the strike." The strikers immediately organized to get them out. As reported in *La Prensa*, several hundred striking pecan shellers concluded their first mass meeting with a march to police headquarters to demand the release of the leaders. A crowd of three hundred marched to the station, led by a delegation of strike leaders that included "Juana Sánchez, Francisco Alvarez, Ms. Mela Solís, Eulalio López, Ms. Catarina Díaz, Ms. Amelia de la Rosa, and Alberto Fuentes."[25] The quick and decisive show of solidarity sent an immediate message to the establishment that the strike would not be defeated by arresting individual leaders, as a core of trained leaders and organizers were ready to step into their place.

The first few days of the strike were a marvel of collective self-organization. From the first day of the strike, mass meetings were held each evening in vacant lots on the West Side to assess the day's events and discuss strike strategy. These gatherings ranged in size and sometimes reached crowds of several thousand strikers and other community members, standing shoulder to shoulder.[26] Occasionally multiple meet-ings were organized at different strategic points simultaneously to accommodate the crowds. Strikers organized roving picket squads, ranging from a handful to several hundred, that targeted the larger sheds where significant scabbing operations were being organized.

With limited funds and infrastructure, the Workers Alliance maximized its hu-man resources to meet the immediate needs of an estimated 5,000 hungry picketers, supporters, and other strikers actively participating in some way.[27] Three communal kitchens were established in proximity to the main bodies of picketers to prepare and distribute food to the strikers and their families. Volunteers helped prepare beans, tor-tillas, and tacos in makeshift kitchens. As one striker observed, "Different people, who they were, where they came from, where they got the food, I don't know. But what little they had, they would share. There was always something to eat."[28]

Jim Crow and Anti-Communism Unites the Opposition

The magnitude of the strike, which quickly took on characteristics of a mass move-ment, began to mobilize the community on a scale never before witnessed. From the vantage point of the local Democratic Party machine, the big investors who profited from subdued Mexican labor, and the racist defenders of Jim Crow, this threatened to grow beyond limited economic demands. The white supremacist capitalist system itself, already challenged directly by five years of strikes, protests, and direct actions by the Mexican working class, was now being targeted directly by a mass movement led by Communists. When the strike could not be weakened by scabbing operations aided by the police, the order was given to beat, arrest, and deport strikers to over-whelm its participants. The actions of the police were tacitly abetted by the local newspapers, the Catholic Church, the Chamber of Commerce, Mexican middle-class organizations, and others that opposed the strike by echoing the condemnation of Communist participation.

Upon taking office in 1933, Mayor Charles K. Quin took hold of a political machine grounded in abetting patronage, vice, and graft as part of the ruling tradition in San Antonio. Through his efforts, he extended control over much of city and county government through the aegis of the preponderant Jim Crow wing of the Democratic Party. The ability to concentrate power in his hands and run the city in a feudal manner was rooted in the nature of the city charter. As described in the *Handbook of Texas*:

> [The] city charter . . . concentrated power in the hands of the mayor and four
> city commissioners. In addition to making policy decisions, each commissioner
> headed one of the city's main departments (i.e., health and sanitation, parks and
> recreation, police and fire, and public works). With these departments came
> huge patronage resources that helped assure the commissioners' reelection.[29]

Since much of the Anglo voting population lived outside of city limits, the machine relied upon the votes of the white middle class and the business community (including those overseeing gambling, prostitution, and other illicit operations). Through a system of patronage, Quin doled out an array of government jobs to white allies in exchange for votes, while maintaining direct connections with the KKK and the right-wing American Legion, whose affiliated members often held posts within the city and county government.

Ironically, the machine also relied on the votes of people of color. Quin's administration worked through well-placed middlemen in the black community that mobilized a substantial number of votes in exchange for material concessions.[30] Mexican Americans were largely unorganized politically and marginalized as a disenfranchised reserve army of labor by the machine. Nevertheless, the machine procured a small percentage of the Mexican vote through vote-buying and collaboration with employers that compelled Mexican workers to vote for Quin as a condition of employment. The strike movement of the 1930s began to break Mexicans out of this subordinated position, which is why the machine directed its full fire against the Mexican community when it threatened to upset the system.

Opposition quickly materialized around an array of institutions. The mayor promptly denied the existence of a strike. Maintaining this line for much of the strike, the mayor and the police intended to dispense with any idea that the right to form a union and strike, as guaranteed by the federal Wagner Act, existed in San Antonio. Instead, they justified repression of the strike by declaring the strike an attempted "revolution," provoked by outside "reds." Following the lead of the mayor's office, the city bureaucratic apparatus, from judges to health officials to immigration agents, was used to break up the strike. Since the mayor "signed the checks" of all officials, he was able to use the offices for political ends.

Conservative business and religious institutions also condemned the pecan shellers, including the San Antonio Mexican Chamber of Commerce, the US Chamber of

Commerce, LULAC, the Catholic Church, and the San Antonio Ministerial Association. Showing the emerging split in labor, representatives of AFL unions came out against the strike, most significantly Rebecca Taylor, president of the International Ladies Garment Workers Union, who worked with the police to single out suspected Communists and sympathizers. The largest and most influential opponent was the Catholic archdiocese of San Antonio.

While 90 percent of the pecan shellers were Catholic, the hierarchy of the archdiocese was firmly opposed to their strike, drawing a sharp polarization between and within the different church constituencies. There were an estimated 100,000 Catholics in the city, mostly from the Mexican West Side. Despite comprising the largest segment of the Church, the conservative archbishop, Arthur Droessarts, ordered that Mexicans be segregated into their own churches and that the mainly Spanish priests combine Catholic instruction with intensive Americanization education that brought them into "civilization," believing that Mexicans clung steadfastly to their "pagan indigenous" ways.[31]

Contempt for Mexican labor activism within the church hierarchy began at the top, where Droessarts gave public support to fellow Catholic Bill Finck and his cigar company against his largely female Mexican workforce in 1933. Class divides in the church played out during these strikes, as some of the white and typically wealthier Catholics looked upon the working-class Mexicans with contempt and disdain. Historian David Badillo points out that even within the church, Mexicans experienced the "prevailing patterns of labor exploitation and a pervasive anti-Mexican racial animus."[32] Taking special aim at Mexican Communists like Emma Tenayuca, the Catholic hierarchy encouraged the editors of its newspaper, *La Voz*, to attack the moral character of the leadership. In one article, the columnist appears so stricken with contempt for Tenayuca, that he is barely coherent through rage:

> In the midst of this community exists a woman by the name of Emma Tenayuca who wants to spread disorder and hatred . . . . Mrs. Teneyuca [sic] de Brooks is not a Mexican, she is a Rusofile, sold out to Russia, communist. If she was a Mexican, she should not be doing that type of work.[33]

Even when some local clergy attempted to intervene on behalf of their striking constituents, such as Father Juan Lopez of the National Catholic Welfare Council, they became more fixated on rooting out Communists than aiding the strike.[34] For their part, Protestant ministers who did take a public stance on the strike also denounced it. The participation of radicals in the leadership even brought the otherwise rival Catholic and Protestant hierarchies together in their revulsion of Communists leading their respective flocks.

In their efforts against the strike, the city government was wholeheartedly backed by the local press. While news of the strike spread across the major national press, the local Texas press took a hardline anti-strike position. The Texas newspaper industry was generally anti-union, and often anti-Mexican as part of its standard narrative. A study of the Texas media conducted a few years after the strike showed how lopsided its reporting had been. In an analysis of editorials on the subject of unions and labor activism in the ten Texas newspapers with the highest circulations (reaching over a million readers), the study identified 381 references to labor over a four-month period. According to the findings, 295 were hostile to labor's demands and only 4 sympathetic, while 82 took no discernable position.[35]

The two main San Antonio newspapers, the *San Antonio Light* and the *San Antonio Express*, were two of the most hostile toward labor. The *San Antonio Express* was one of nineteen William Randolph Hearst–owned newspapers, notorious for their anti-union reporting. Both papers were unabashedly opposed to the strike, aligning closely with the Southern Pecan Shelling Company, the mayor, and the police. They repeated the line that none of the sheds were affected, and that the strike was faltering from the very beginning. They commonly described the actions of police as justifiable, brave, and decisive; while referring to the actions of strikers as incompetent, confused, and violent. Revealing of the shoddy journalism, the paper often published as true incriminating and bombastic statements attributed to strikers or their supporters as merely being "overheard" by unknown persons or police. For instance, the *San Antonio Light* published the testimony of police sergeant William Christoph, who had claimed that the strikers intended to commit violence against churches. He testified that a "Mexican woman who lived [near] a policeman's house told the officers' [sic] wife, who in turn told the officer, who told Christoph that . . . 'they're going to tear down the churches and kill the priests.'"[36]

The strike polarized the Mexican community along class lines, with elements within the small middle class using the opportunity to publicly distance itself from the multitudes of poor workers and ingratiate themselves to the local machine by condemning Communist involvement. Other middle-class segments, especially those aligned with the League of United Latin Americans, remained neutral or opposed the strike so long as Communists were involved. At the height of the strike, LULAC tried to organize counter-rallies in the barrio to inveigh against the "Communist-led" strike. To their dismay, and revealing of the limits of their influence and leverage within the community, these rallies fell flat and Mexican workers stayed away. The efforts by these institutions to divide the workers from the radicals had failed. Another group, the League of Loyal Americans, which was affiliated with the Mexican Chamber of Commerce, circulated affidavits among Mexican strikers also proclaiming their opposition to "Communists" in the strike. As president of the group Pablo Meza explained: "Our main object is to protect our people from being branded as Communists."[37]

When political intervention failed, the mayor unleashed the police. The mobilization of the forces of repression was immense. The chief of police, Owen Kilday, mustered 150 police from across San Antonio and on loan from nearby cities, and later swore in 50 "special officers," which included local firemen.[38] The police were also supported by members of the Vigilance Committee, a special appointed body that oversaw the distribution of city permits. This group aided the mayor's efforts to prevent any strike-related activity from operating in a legal way. The Jim Crow establishment, from the mayor to the police, equated communism with civil rights, which reflected how they viewed the participation of the party in the Mexican community. Any threat to white supremacy became described in revolutionary terms, which was then used as a justification for extralegal violence. For instance, as his proclamation of war against the strike, Kilday declared: "It is my duty to interfere with revolution, and communism is revolution."[39]

The police were organized in paramilitary fashion, with riot gear and tear gas guns, and stationed throughout the barrio in proximity to the struck sheds like a foreign occupying army. Their principal objective was to keep the sheds in operation. They escorted and protected strikebreakers who crossed the lines, they dispersed, beat, or arrested picketers or "loiterers," and they tried to prevent supporters from delivering food and other forms of aid to the striking workers and their families that congregated near the sheds and joined pickets. Picketers were commonly arrested on sight, although when large groups congregated, the police fired tear gas directly into crowds to disperse them. In such violent episodes, strike leaders and picket captains were chased down, beaten, and arrested. In one case, a striker named Felix Ferdín testified that forty workers were detained and lined up alongside the wall of one of the sheds when a cop fired tear gas indiscriminately into the group.[40] The police also abetted occasional episodes of violence by shed owners against strikers. In one case an owner pulled a gun and threatened to shoot a striker in the presence of the police, who did nothing to stop the intimidation.[41] They raided homes where strike leaders lived, confiscating flyers, signs, and other picketing material.[42] Over the duration of the strike, the police arrested over a thousand women, men, and children. When San Antonio police were required to attend a hearing on the possible use of "excessive force" in San Antonio's 45th District Court, the presiding judge, a Kilday ally named S. G. Tayloe, had already written up his decision of "not guilty," even before all of the evidence was presented.[43] As one striker observed early on: "The establishment and the community were quite frightened. They had been exploiting these people and here was an uprising. The Chief of Police was reacting as a frightened man—totally senseless arrests were made."[44] In one massive show of force against a picket of three hundred, police and deputies encircled and then swarmed into the crowd, swinging clubs and savagely beating the assembled picketers and then arresting the whole group down to a person. Known radicals and CIO unions were singled out for the most vicious treatment. Through a regular flow of specious injunctions against picketing from machine-aligned judges, the police were empowered to arrest strikers for a host of fictitious crimes, including blocking sidewalks (where no sidewalks existed), disturbing the peace, and vagrancy, and they even resurrected a long-abolished ordinance against the use of "unlawful display signs for advertising" for holding CIO picket signs, which were confiscated and destroyed by police.

The police served as the labor regulators for the companies, offering amnesty to jailed workers if they pledged to quit the strike, renounce the union, and return to work. When this didn't occur, the jails overflowed. Both the men's and women's cells were overstuffed with people, well over the designed capacity. When strikers sang corridos and other songs of solidarity to maintain morale in the cells, the police turned high-pressured fire hoses on the workers. When the jails could hold no more, the county immigration inspector, W. W. Knopp, worked with the police to identify and threaten Mexican strikers with deportation. Acting on this threat, the police began rounding up picketers and driving them outside city limits and dumping them on the side of the road, effectively deporting them out of the city.

With the help of Quin machine–aligned health officials, the police tried to shut down the food kitchens in an attempt to starve the workers away from the sheds. One focus of police harassment was the Women's Peace and Freedom League, which set up a makeshift kitchen and distributed food to nearly two thousand people per day.[45] With support from machine-aligned officials in the health department and the Vigilance Committee, the police were able to shut the kitchens down. City officials threatened to find any reason to shut down any Mexican-owned businesses that offered aid or assistance to the strikers.[46]

Emma Tenayuca after being released from prison in 1938

Despite the intense repression, the strikers adapted their tactics accordingly. Nightly mass meetings changed locations, pickets became more fluid, and picketing tactics more creative with the wider community being drawn into participation. The decentralized, bottom-up community-organizing model meant that arrests and repression could not disable the strike movement even if known leaders were constantly harassed and arrested. By the second week, the strike "took on the character of a mass uprising of hundreds/thousands of people, whether or not they worked with pecans: support committees, mass meetings, community pickets across the barrio."[47]

One participant, CIO organizer George Lambert, described how people with no direct connection to the pecan industry plugged into the campaign in different ways:

> I remember one guy by the name of Cisneros who had a large family, and he worked the beet fields in Michigan every summer, but he had several good years; he had a big car [and] his family didn't have to work during the winter. They had no connection at all with the pecan shelling industry . . . He was taking a most active part transporting people and providing protection. He was a tough-looking *hombre*—big scar on his face and a big man, providing protection for Emma Tenayucca [*sic*].[48]

As the strike and repression gained wider attention, it began to evoke public support. Sympathetic small-business owners allowed picketers to stand inside their storefronts with their signs to avoid being arrested or having their signs confiscated and destroyed. Money donations flowed into the union headquarters, and there was an outpouring of local and national support. The strike brought large swaths of the working class into active support. Whole families came out to the picket lines and thousands who were not directly involved participated in some way to support the pecan shellers, demonstrating in practice an advanced level of class consciousness in which they understood their own well-being to be intimately bound up with the outcome of the strike. The largest mutualista, Sociedad de la Unión, supported Tenayuca, the CIO, and UCAPAWA, allowing them to use their hall and donating food and other resources to the strike.[49] Beet sugar workers back in town during the off-winter months participated in strike solidarity campaigns, joining pickets and providing security.

UCAPAWA Takes Over

On the fifth day of the strike the president of UCAPAWA, Donald Henderson, arrived in San Antonio to take over the coordination of the effort. He was joined by CIO leaders, including Regional Director Barney Eagan, CIO organizer J. Austin Beasley, and later Luisa Moreno. Upon his arrival, Henderson addressed a mass meeting of strikers, pledging the full support of UCAPAWA and the CIO. Emma Tenayuca played a key role in easing the CIO into the leadership of the strike, calling on the workers (citizen or not) to sign cards for UCAPAWA Local 172. They signed up by the thousands in response to her appeals. All told, over ten thousand workers joined the union during the strike.

While the strike unity and organization held firm, the leadership of the CIO turned against itself over the leadership of the strike by known Communists. This was initiated by Red-baiting and repression by the police, which framed the strike as a Communist-inspired insurgency from the outset. Upon arrival, for instance, Donald Henderson was immediately made the subject of a grand jury investigation for being a Communist.

Despite the high level of unity, especially between the Communist Party members who were now at the head of a mass strike, the application of Popular Front

politics in this context began to reveal its intrinsic weaknesses in the face of an anti-Communist campaign. When faced with a coordinated campaign of Red-baiting,
the union could have either asserted their Communist affiliation and relied on the
unity and solidarity of the workers, the effectiveness of strike strategy rooted in class
struggle and mass mobilization; or they could hide their identities, conceal their politics, abdicate leadership, and concede ground to their right-wing opponents in the
name of maintaining "broad unity" with erstwhile middle-class supporters like LU-
LAC. Emma Tenayuca chose the former, while the Communists in the CIO-UCAP-
AWA adhered to the latter.

They suspended efforts to recruit into the Communist Party, hewed very closely
to the reformist trade-union politics of the CIO, and remained silent or defensive in
the face of their opponents' campaign. This passive approach did little to deflect the
anti-Communist thrust against them by the state, and only encouraged the intensification of the strategy. The majority of the workers, who proved they were not susceptible to anti-Communist Red-baiting by following open Communist leadership, did not
factor as much into the strategy as did the attempt to maintain unity with the liberal
Democratic establishment, which also opposed communism.

The CIO, on the other hand, was further divided within. Regional Director Barry
Egan, for instance, was part of the anti-Communist opposition within the CIO and declared that he and others in the statewide leadership would abstain from supporting the
strike so long as it was led by Communists. Caving to the anti-Communists, Henderson
conceded his leadership and called for strike leaders to make public anti-Communist
pledges. The vacillation and ambivalence of the Communists encouraged conservatives
to call for the removal of Emma Tenayuca from the strike leadership, even as she enjoyed
the confidence of thousands of striking workers and proved the most capable leader.
Pressed on all sides, the party leadership acceded to the Red-baiting, withdrew from the
visible positions of leadership, and tried to remove Tenayuca to the background. She
later criticized the "top-down approach" of the UCAPAWA organizers that she felt weakened the strike.[50]

In testimony in front of the State Labor Commission, Donald Henderson denied
being a Communist and claimed that he had removed Tenayuca, Solís Sager, and Homer Brooks because their strategy was leading the strike toward failure since the police had smashed their picket lines.[51] Henderson replaced the strike leader in favor of
J. Austin Beasley, a known Democrat, with background support from Luisa Moreno, a
founder of UCAPAWA and a California CIO state representative who had experience
working with Spanish-speaking cannery workers.

J. Austin Beasley assumed the role of strike organizer, effectively removing the
women leaders that were so instrumental in the development, organization, and
unity of the strike movement from its beginning. Put off by the capitulation to anti-
communism and top-down imposition, Tenayuca originally called for a vote of the
workers themselves to remove her, but ultimately submitted to party discipline.[52] She
concluded that this weakened the movement's trajectory and stifled the development
of organic working-class leadership. Nevertheless, she continued to organize support

for the strike behind the scenes and played a pivotal role in encouraging the strikers to join UCAPAWA Local 172. By the conclusion of the strike, an estimated ten thousand pecan shellers joined the union, with the workforce signing up en masse at the daily mass-meetings occurring throughout the strike.

While the Popular Front approach may have afforded short-term peace, it also led to the weakening of the strike as its most capable leaders were sidelined. Nevertheless, the intervention of the CIO brought a committed willingness to organize Mexican workers, resources and skilled organizers, lawyers, a national support network, and channels to political support. It is through these channels that direct lines of communication were established with New Deal–aligned Democrats at the local, state, and federal level. By concealing and submerging their politics, they had achieved a temporary alliance within the CIO and New Deal coalitions, so long as there were mutual benefits to be gained from their tireless and dedicated organizing efforts. Under these conditions, a window of opportunity was opened for the party to exert significant influence within the labor movement, even if the radical edge of Marxist politics was blunted.

Communists within the CIO were gaining positions within the CIO at the state level and even took over the leadership of the Texas branch of the CIO, the Texas State Industrial Unions Council, in 1938. They tried to push a radical antiracist agenda, including the abolition of racially segregated locals, and the establishment of an affirmative-action rule requiring CIO state vice-presidents to be "Latin-American" or black, and for CIO unions to prohibit any patronage of segregated businesses as part of any official duties.[53] Their ascendancy coincided with the rise of class struggle throughout the state, including the wave of strikes in San Antonio that brought ten thousand pecan shellers into UCAPAWA that year. As Texas historians George Norris Green and Michael R. Botson, Jr., explain,

> A pent-up class antagonism was unleashed among Texas workers that had not been seen since the rise of the Populist Party in the 1890s. Against this backdrop, the Texas Communist Party enjoyed a measure of toleration for championing such liberal/left causes as a minimum wage, an eight-hour day, an old-age pension system, low-interest state loans to landless farmers and agricultural workers, protection of farmworkers under the Wagner Act, a state income tax, abolition of the poll tax and white primary, and civil rights for blacks and Mexican Americans.[54]

State Intervention and Victory

After nearly a month, the strikers gained the upper hand. They significantly reduced pecan production and maintained strike coordination and unity in the face of intense repression and a coordinated Red-baiting campaign. Lawyers with the CIO filed unfair labor practice grievances with the National Labor Relations Board, while others sent delegations to protest police violence at the state capital. Still other supporters appealed to the Roosevelt administration. The resilience of the strikers supported by the CIO had garnered public sympathy, national and international attention, and ultimately led to government intervention, producing a victory that changed the face of the industry and local politics in San Antonio. Like in other cases of mass strike activity, New Deal politicians intervened only after strike movements led by Communists galvanized mass support and threatened to destabilize local ruling structures.

The CIO legal and media outreach campaign worked on various fronts. The most immediate was through Maury Maverick, the New Deal Texas congressman who represented Bexar County. Maverick had cast his lot with the New Deal realignment taking place nationally amid a significant rise in class struggle. As one historian explains:

> Maverick's support for the strikers was not merely rhetorical or theoretical. Rather, it was at Maverick's urging that Governor Allred asked the state industrial commission to hold a hearing on the strike. Maverick also opened the door for a union delegation led by organizer George Lambert and rank and file leader Santos Vásquez that traveled to Austin to meet with the governor and seek assistance from members of the state legislature. Such interventions quickly led to the settlement of the strike.[55]

In response to the appeals to Governor James Allred by CIO representatives and CIO officials, Maverick summoned union representatives, city leaders, and pecan growers to Austin for an emergency meeting about the strike. At this meeting he expressed support for the strikers and arranged to send in the Texas Industrial Commission to conduct hearings. At the conclusion of the meeting Chief of Police Kilday ordered the police to stop using tear gas against the strikers.[56]

The largely symbolic hearings conducted by the state Industrial Commission in San Antonio contained no actual enforcement power but gave a public forum for workers to describe their experiences. Everett Looney, the assistant state district attorney, presided over the reports from men, women, and youth who were brutally beaten or arrested without formal charge.[57] The hearings publicized in the local press concluded with a condemnation of police violence and an implicit warning that the state would intervene more directly if the mayor did not negotiate for a reasonable settlement.

Another public form of protest took place through the Citizens Labor Aid Committee. This group of prominent San Antonio liberals appealed to Secretary of Labor Frances Perkins to intervene in the strike on behalf of the pecan shellers. The group, comprised of prominent women, tried to counter the narrative of the newspapers, affirming police violence and calling for an end to "tear gassing, police brutality, and the complete denial of civil rights."[58] The Mexican consul also intervened to protest the treatment of Mexican nationals, at least three of whom were arrested for picketing. This revealed the more interventionist posture on behalf of Mexican government in the US during the presidency of Lázaro Cárdenas, who was also facing a significant uptick in class struggle south of the border. Lastly, the Mexican Workers Confederation, or CTM by its Spanish acronym, also sent representatives and resources in solidarity with the strike.[59]

As a result of the intervention, a humbled mayor, restrained police, and economically weakened growers agreed to arbitration. A three-member board was created, one arbiter selected by the union, one by the growers, and a third selected by consensus of the other two. The final agreement included an increase of all wages to $4 a week, recognition of the Pecan Shellers Union Local 172 (UCAPAWA) as the sole bargaining agent for the whole pecan workforce; guarantees of no reprisals against union members; and all charges against picketers dropped and all remaining prisoners released.[60]

The victory of the strike was announced at a mass meeting in front of city hall on the night of March 22. In an enormous outpouring of support and joy, an estimated twenty-five thousand people flowed into the streets to celebrate the victory. As the *Daily Worker* described the scene,

> [M]en, women, and children wanted to dance gaily . . . in victory celebration of the end of the six weeks' strike of pecan shellers. But so tightly did they pack City Hall Plaza from rim to rim that they had to be content to stand for hours, listening to the Mexican orchestra and to the reports of their leaders. Under banners proclaiming, "Viva CIO," the huge throng, [the] largest San Antonio ever saw, on any occasion, and one of the greatest labor demonstrations in the history of the South, heard J. Austin Beasley . . . tell of the terms of the strike settlement and how [they defied] . . . the reactionary city administration.[61]

Rally attendants then broke out in song, singing corridos that mocked the defeated city administration. The success of the strike had significant repercussions, including the formation of a strong pecan sheller UCAPAWA local. It also contributed directly to the defeat of the Jim Crow Democratic machine of C. K. Quin in 1939, initiating a hard-fought campaign for civil rights that would continue into the next decade.

Chapter 28
Emma Tenayuca and the Mexican Question

"According to the informants interviewed, the vast majority of the Mexican people have more esteem for the radicals . . . they feel that their big need is aid in fighting discrimination . . . there is more likelihood that the radicals will take effective action."
—Results of a sociological survey conducted within
the working-class barrios of San Antonio

By 1937, there were an estimated one thousand members of the Communist Party of Texas, of which a significant number in San Antonio were Mexican.[1] While a small number in scope, party members were able to engage and lead thousands of Mexican workers in San Antonio in the 1930s. Two factors were key to this convergence: The radical traditions of Magonismo were kept alive in the daily class struggles of Mexican workers who had experience with the PLM in Texas or participated in revolutionary activity in Mexico. This, coupled with the rigorous institutionalization of the strictures of Jim Crow through the state and the economic turmoil of the Great Depression, led to explosive episodes of mass struggle in the 1930s. These signaled the opening shots in a generational struggle for supremacy between capital and labor as well as a civil rights movement to overturn racial segregation.

Key to the mass mobilizations of Mexican workers was base-building through party organization, especially the work combating workplace discrimination and unemployment through the Workers Alliance. It also relied fundamentally on the ability to recruit organic working-class leaders and intellectuals within the Mexican community. These figures became conduits for the party to reach a larger population within the barrios, and also brought into the party fold capable thinkers who could provide analyses, sensitivities, and crucial insights as part of organizing efforts. The most towering of these figures in San Antonio was Emma Tenayuca, referred to by her admirers as "La Pasionaria de Texas" and by her detractors as "Red Emma." Tenayuca's prowess as a mass leader with deep roots in the community, as an astute and confident organizer, and as a budding Marxist theoretician able to convey the historical experiences of Mexicans as part of the framework of class struggle, earned her public enemy number one status among the ruling cliques of San Antonio.

The evolution of Emma Tenayuca began as a child growing up in a working-class family in San Antonio's West Side. Her mother's family had roots in San Antonio going back to the period of Spanish colonization and her father was an *indio* from South Texas. Members of her family were involved in local party politics, and from a young age she was keenly aware of important issues being discussed and debated in her community. The presence of mutualistas led her to observe and appreciate a model of working-class organization that brought citizens and immigrants together in common cause.

480

Emma learned from a young age the effects of racism on the Mexican community. She learned from her parents and grandparents of the threat of the Ku Klux Klan, which targeted the black and Mexican communities and served as the enforcer of racial segregation. She even saw that her mother's extended family looked down on her indigenous father, which led her to repudiate and reject middle-class notions of racial differentiation and upward mobility within the Mexican community.[2] She herself directly experienced the effects of Jim Crow segregation in school, and by the time she was a teenager she became cognizant of its larger effects on the Mexican population. She had learned of the massacres of Mexicans by Texas Rangers and white supremacist vigilantes, and witnessed state violence against Mexicans and Mexican Americans through the mass deportations at the onset of the Depression.

Throughout her youth, she was also made acutely aware of social and political developments in Mexico. As San Antonio served as a crossroads of migration between the US and Mexico, the westside barrio where she grew up became the home for waves of incoming migrants or a way station for those passing through. Each wave coincided with each stage of the revolutionary and counterrevolutionary process, educating her on the intricacies and oppositional forces in Mexican politics. The revolution and subsequent events in Mexico animated Mexicans through Texas, contributing to a highly politicized culture among the working class at the time.

The Spanish-language press proliferated through Texas, with many papers orienting on events in Mexico. In the plazas on the west side, there were regular rallies, speeches, and other political events attracting families and large crowds. Working-class people gathered in groups to hear a volunteer read aloud the latest edition of a newspaper. Emma's grandfather, Francisco Zepeda, who had been particularly interested in attending political events, often took her along to rallies at the Plaza del Zacate, which featured some of the largest gatherings every Sunday. During these Sunday outings, she recalled seeing magonista papers and other press being circulated and read aloud and hearing radicals of all stripes addressing throngs of Mexican workers and families that would gather to listen:

> There was the plaza in front of the Santa Rosa Hospital on Milam Square. You could go there on Sundays . . . And you could hear anarchists. I started going to the plaza and political rallies when I was only 6 or 7 years old . . . I learned the anarchist words to the Marseillaise. You had the influence of the Flores Magón brothers . . . [and] . . . we had the Wobblies . . . San Antonio was [also] buzzing with the influence of Carrancistas, Villistas, and Maderistas, etc. And if you . . . knew Spanish, well, all you had to do was go there on a Sunday at any time.[3]

The harsh conditions created by the Great Depression for her family and for the Mexican American population as a whole had further politicized her. The difficulties of raising eleven children in abject poverty led her parents to send her to live with her maternal grandparents. She observed how Mexicans, already economically marginalized, were plunged even further into desperation and destitution with no recourse during economic crisis. From where she was situated, anti-Mexican racism and capitalist crisis led Mexican Americans and Mexican migrants to share a similar fate and to languish in the same conditions at the nadir of the social order. As Gabriela González concludes, "she took note of how the group victimized by capitalism was the same on both sides of the border: dark-skinned peasants and working-class people."[4] Her exposure to radical political culture in San Antonio occurred at a young age in the plazas and provided the backdrop for her experiences as a teenager. The presence of radicals with deep roots in the community and a familiar history of political activism likely facilitated Emma Tenayuca's transition toward activism at a young age.

Tenayuca's personal odyssey toward radical politics occurred when she was in her first year of high school. She became acutely aware of the mechanisms of racial segregation that undermined Mexican students. As her first political act, she joined the League of United Latin American Citizens (LULAC), the predominant Mexican American middle class organization in San Antonio, in 1932 at the age of fifteen. Her experience in LULAC led her to become disillusioned, leaving the group a year later while repudiating their call for Mexicans to "Americanize."[5] She came to reject the fundamental tenets espoused by the organization as the only entry point to US society: accommodation to anti-Mexican racism, the exclusion of immigrants as a means to extoll the value of citizenship and demonstrate loyalty, the exclusion of women from leadership positions, and disdain toward labor activism. As she explained, the middle-class accommodationist mentality "succeeded in dividing the Mexican population of Texas, leaving all who were residents without representation . . . Few of the many who were citizens could afford the poll tax, and many refused to deny their language or cultural heritage."[6]

She joined a student study circle and began reading radical texts, including the writings of Karl Marx, Charles Darwin, and radical US historians such as Charles Beard.[7] By the time she was a senior in high school, she was attending protests, including a statewide march for unemployed relief in the capital city of Austin. She became interested in the Wobblies and loosely identified with anarchist thought. Upon leaving high school, she joined the ranks of the working class. She worked as an elevator operator for three months, but refused to return after facing sexual harassment from a manager. She learned firsthand the normalized forms of sexual violence and gender discrimination experienced and endured by Mexican women in the matrix of power and powerlessness within the racialized caste labor system in San Antonio. Her attraction to Marxism was also infused with a feminist fist, something that played out in her orientation toward unionizing women workers and paying close attention to training militant leaders as part of the process. Emma Tenayuca inspired and facilitated other mexicanas to become leaders in line with the Marxist dictum that most served her motivation: "That the emancipation of the working classes must be conquered by the working classes themselves."[8]

She was first drawn into class politics by the strike that broke out at the Finck cigar factory in 1933, witnessing firsthand how marginalized Mexican working-class women like herself were able shut down one of the largest industries in the city. She observed how city and state officials attempted to break the resolve of the women by threatening arrest and deportation and by police provocation and violence. The strike polarized the Mexican community along class lines, with the middle-class organizations and the Catholic Church opposing the cigar workers.

When the second strike occurred a year later, she joined the picket lines at the gates of the factory after the school day ended. When the police began violently attacking pickets, she was not spared, and was arrested alongside the striking women. Amid the social polarization that occurred during the strike, she experienced a significant shift in consciousness. She came to see the justice system as rigged in favor of the owners of industry, the Catholic Church as complicit in keeping Mexicans acquiescent and accepting of their class conditions, and middle-class Mexican organizations (such as LULAC) that ignored or denounced the strikes as bankrupt.[9]

She then looked to radical organizations for answers, first attending Socialist Party meetings and later joining the Young Communist League in 1935. Through her affiliation with the party, she began organizing Mexicans and Mexican workers into the Communist-led Unemployed Councils, and later officially joined the Communist Party in 1937 after becoming a leader in the Workers Alliance. Due to its antiracist and anti-sexist principles, the Communist Party offered a path to leadership that the liberal organizations like LULAC did not. As she forthrightly stated in a later interview, the "Communists were at the forefront of the struggles."[10] Furthermore, she was inspired by the Communist Party in Mexico. The party's role in organizing the CTM and leading a nationwide strike movement significantly improved the living conditions of the working class, challenged US imperialism, and practiced internationalism.[11] Emma Tenayuca and Manuela Solís Sager even went to Mexico City to attend the CTM's "Worker University." La Universidad Obrera was founded to provide workers a radical model of education, designed to develop class consciousness through the teaching of the "origin of the world, the origin of life, an understanding of mankind, the basis of human society and social development, the material character of all material phenomenon, and the laws of dialectical materialism."[12]

Emma devoted herself to supporting the class struggle after her experience in the Finck strike. Through her involvement she met different labor activists, who valued her potential as an organizer. She also met Communists who saw in her a militant looking for an understanding of how to defeat Jim Crow. She was recruited into various organizing drives and solidarity campaigns and played a vital role as a liaison between unions and Spanish-speaking workers. She also helped organize unemployed workers within the Mexican community to obtain relief.[13] Through this period she moved closer to the Communist Party, studied labor history, and developed her own understanding of effective strike strategy, leadership development, and community organization. She was drawn into alignment with Communist principles based on the political conclusions she reached through her experiences. This included the desire to organize Mexican workers regardless of race, citizenship status, and sex, and to smash the barriers to full civil rights and equality for all Mexican workers.

Her tireless efforts, militant demeanor, and accrued organizing skills propelled her into the leadership of the unemployed movement, first as a volunteer and then as secretary for the Communist-led West Side Unemployed Council in 1935. In 1936 this group merged into the Workers Alliance of America, in which Tenayuca become the secretary and lead organizer in San Antonio and a member of the National Executive Council. Tenayuca helped build the Workers Alliance as a citywide organization of over 10,000 workers, including 3,000 Mexicans in ten chapters based on the West Side. Through the organization of Mexican workers in WPA jobs into unions, Emma Tenayuca envisioned a new approach that would negate the regime of deportation. She argued that through performing productive work that contributed to the social good, undocumented workers should attain legal naturalization.

The Mexican Question

In close contact to a militant working-class upsurge and radical circles, she gained organizing experience and an understanding of labor politics. Along the way, she began to develop an independent analysis and criticism of the limited knowledge that both labor organizers and radicals had of the Mexican community, beginning with the inability to speak Spanish, flawed organizing strategies, and ignorance of familial, ethnic, and political networks. Tenayuca had an intimate understanding of both the cultural and political needs of the Mexican working people, and used the resources and infrastructure of the organizations she joined to address the direct needs of the Mexican working class.

Many historians and commentators de-emphasized her commitment to Marxism. According to George Lambert, a contemporary who worked alongside her in San Antonio: "The only reason that [Tenayuca] identified herself as a Communist was because as far as she could see there was nobody else in this country who were [sic] in the least interested in doing anything about the economic situation on the West Side of San Antonio or among the Mexican Americans in those days . . . [H]er interests were with the people there."[14] While it is undoubtedly true that environment influences one's political development, her dedication to reading and studying Marxist theory in conjunction with her street-level organizing led her to produce the first and most influential comprehensive radical analysis of the Mexican working class in the United States.[15]

Her experiences over the years 1934 to 1938, combined with her Marxist training, inspired her to develop a theoretical framework to explain the history and condition of the Mexican worker. "The Mexican Question," co-authored with her husband Homer Brooks, was an in-depth essay written for the party's main theoretical journal, *The Communist*. The essay was the first Marxist analysis of the racial and class dynamics governing the subjugation of Mexican workers in the United States, and advanced a theory for how to defeat Jim Crow. With the essay, the two Texas-based Communists intended to make a push within the party ranks for an orientation toward the Mexican working class, and to also recruit Mexican workers directly into the party, a theoretical contribution to complement the party's extensive work for black liberation.

The essay lays out a sweeping description of Mexican history in the US and an indictment of the social, economic, and cultural oppression experienced by Mexican workers as a function of Jim Crow capitalism. The authors lay out the way in which the tenets of anti-black racism were reshaped and applied to Mexicans in southern Texas, and how they, along with Anglo workers, had a shared material interest in defeating white supremacy as it propped up the most reactionary defenders of capitalism that opposed all worker organization.

In condemning Jim Crow, the essay calls for the abolition of all forms of "Jim-Crowism" including "segregation in living quarters, schools, parks, hotels, restaurants . . . [and that] this struggle must be linked with the Negro people."[16] The authors call for the elimination of all voting restrictions, such as the poll tax, residency, and language requirements, and appeal for a return to provisions of the Texas Constitution that allowed noncitizens to vote until they were suspended in 1921. They also called for the elimination of the racist structures within the economy that kept Mexicans from attaining skilled, professional, and white-collar jobs.

The authors also identify the intersection of racism and imperialism in Latin America, where as the notions of white supremacy that justify military intervention and "Wall Street's imperialistic exploitation of Latin America" carry over into the treatment of Mexicans within the United States. This included an analysis of state oppression of immigrants to prevent civil rights and unionization through the use of deportation and immigration restriction. They called for full equality for Mexican immigrants in the United States, educational opportunities for their children, and the need for their inclusion into unions as a primary form of working-class self-defense.

In articulating a vision for the requisite forms of class struggle necessary to overturn Jim Crow capitalism, the authors diverge from the Stalinist notions of "oppressed nations," common in the party at the time, that supported the idea of black workers constituting a "separate nation."[17] Tenayuca and Brooks identified Mexican Americans not as a distinct "oppressed nation" but as a population with a common condition and shared experience with the Mexican immigrant within the United States.

> Historically, the Mexican people in the Southwest have evolved in a series of bordering, though separated, communities, their economic life inextricably connecting them, not only to one another but with the Anglo-American population in each of these separated communities. Therefore, their economic (and hence, their political) interests are welded to those of the Anglo-American people of the Southwest.[18]

Lastly, the authors link the gains of the class struggle to a confidence to fight for cultural rights. Through the Spanish-speaking workers in UCAPAWA locals in South Texas, for example, workers first demanded that union literature be published bilingually, and then carried this effort into community campaigns to compel local schools to create bilingual education programs for their children. Anticipating the Chicano/a civil rights movement, the essay built on this demand for language rights, linking the class struggle to the idea of "cultural democracy." Cultural democracy necessitated the abolition of segregated schools, the implementation of bilingual education programs in public schools and universities, and the granting of equal status of Spanish to English where Mexican people formed a significant part of the population.[19]

"The Mexican Question" became a living document of the radical experience in the barrio, drawing from earlier Mexican working-class traditions and influences that carried over into a new epoch in the form of Mexican American Communists being fired in the kiln of class struggle. As Gabriela González observes, Tenayuca's analyses "seem remarkably similar to the analysis of the Mexican condition offered by Ricardo Flores Magón a generation or two earlier."[20] The analysis of the Mexican and Mexican American working-class condition detailed in "The Mexican Question" built on the established principles, ideals, and conclusions of previous Mexican radicals. Emma Tenayuca added her uniquely perceptive insights and proposed solutions for the liberation of Mexicans in the seminal tract, which influenced and informed the generation of radicals that followed.

Chapter 29

North American Communists
and the "Good Neighbor Policy"

*"[T]he 'Good Neighbor' policy was integral to the general
diplomacy pursued by Roosevelt ... to extend American economic,
political, and strategic interests on a global scale."*
—**Michael J. Hogan**, *Paths to Power*

The growth and influence of the Communist Party also took place within the barrios of Los Angeles. Like in Texas, it took place in the context of worker radicalism and cross-border agitation in Mexico, the rise of the CIO, and the guiding role that Communists played within its structures. The Comintern's shift to the Popular Front proceeded with the defense of the Soviet Union from Nazi aggression first and foremost in mind. In the US, it coincided with favorable conditions for the expansion of the Communist Party: emerging rifts in the US capitalist class resulting from the Depression and working-class struggle, the rise of Roosevelt and the New Deal, and the splits in the AFL leading to the birth of the CIO and industrial unionism. This changing landscape allowed the party to find a much larger audience for its class doctrines, especially as it opened the door for Communists to play a direct role in the new organizational expressions of the period.

Skilled and tested Communist organizers and unionists were strategically useful for the CIO leadership to help break the grip of AFL opposition, and at various points in serving as the shock troops for Roosevelt's policies. In this capacity, the party leadership raised its sights on its ability to shape the course of events, gradually moving away from an emphasis on shop-floor class struggle toward the electoral arena. In California, for example, Communist Party members flocked into the CIO's political formation, the Labor's Non-Partisan League (LNPL), a political action committee that was partisan in support of the New Deal wing of the Democratic Party. Citing a CIO official, Robert Cherny estimates that the staff of the Northern California wing of the LNPL was about "90 percent Party members."[1]

Their attempt to acquire, wield, and deploy political power in alignment with the New Deal of the Democratic Party produced mixed results. While they reached their highest point of influence when they buttressed Roosevelt's positions, they also fell victim to a coordinated bipartisan campaign of reaction when they were no longer useful. Nevertheless, building the broad Democratic front for these purposes did strengthen the party's commitment to racial unity and justice.

Party members in higher positions within the architecture of the CIO and New

Deal used these offices in a dualistic manner. These party members or close allies, especially Mexican Americans, were able to shepherd resources, influence, and human power, and otherwise turn the larger wheels to organize the Mexican working class around the issues specific to their own experiences. While great strides were made by Mexican radicals working within this process, the contradictions of the party's approach and the heavy hand of McCarthyist repression weakened the efforts.

The Communist Party began to fracture amid the tensions of world events, straining between its own efforts to ingrain itself in the class struggles of the US working class, and adapting to the erratic diktats of the Stalinist regime. As Maurice Isserman describes:

> [The Communist Party] delivered many and conflicting messages over the years—in opposition to and in support of Roosevelt's New Deal, in favor of an anti-fascist Popular Front, in opposition to the "Second Imperialist War" and, since the Nazi invasion of Russia in June 1941, in support of the Grand Alliance of the United States, Great Britain, and the Soviet Union.[2]

The party reached its high point of influence after the Nazi invasion of the Soviet Union brought it back in alignment with the Allied powers and Roosevelt, especially after the US entered the war in 1942. The convergence of the anti-Nazi allied forces temporarily diminished anti-Communist persecution. The histrionic pro-war fervor of the Communist Party in its defense of the Soviet and now uncritical support for Roosevelt's war drive allowed the party to reach its highest watermark of support, albeit at significant long-term cost.

During this period, party activities unceremoniously pulled the tent-stakes on all activities that were critical of US policy and all domestic projects not related to the war drive. This included, most shamefully, support for Franklin Delano Roosevelt's Executive Order 9066, which compelled the forced relocation of 125,000 Japanese immigrants and citizens into sixteen concentration camps in 1942. Antiracist organizing in this period shifted focus, now determined to increase access and participation of Mexican Americans and African Americans in industries supporting the war effort and in the military.

The Chicano generation in Los Angeles was composed of younger, working-class Mexican Americans who came of age in the 1930s. Unlike San Antonio, there was a smaller US-born middle-class; which was less capable of influencing this generation. As a result, the revolutionary generation of migrants that settled in Los Angeles conveyed their Mexico-oriented class politics, which were heavily influenced by Magonismo, to the next generation, which was now facing capitalist Depression, a resurgence of cross-border activism, and radical unionism, especially within the CIO.[3]

The party built a sizeable base among the Mexican working class in Los Angeles, with many intersections with the PLM clubs that persisted in the city. For instance, a coalition of CP-affiliated groups led by the Unemployed Councils led a Hunger March on October 2, 1933, in which the party press claimed between 40,000 and 50,000 marched, including "15 units of the Mexican Liberal Club."[4] The PLM had also experienced resurgence in the early years of the Depression, as veterans revived their dormant traditions with the onset of capitalist crisis.

The national leadership took up the mantel of opposing Jim Crow, but focused scant attention on the "Mexican Question." In the Southwest regions where the party had a significant presence, Communist organizers were much more in tune with the condition and activity of the Mexican working class. Following the lead of a core of dynamic and skillful Mexican leaders, the party made organizing inroads into the Mexican barrios in Los Angeles and in the mining camps of New Mexico, especially through the aegis of the CIO. Nevertheless, the party's overall lack of engagement with Mexican history, political traditions, and cultural identity limited the scope and scale of base-building within the Mexican working class.

Despite the shortcomings, the intensification of class struggle emanating from the barrios changed the circumstances of neglect, allowing for Mexican and Latina radical leadership to set the wheels in motion. Over the course of the 1930s, the Communist Party's local leadership incorporated the Mexican working class into the CIO, the Popular Front, and the party itself. As Douglas Monroy observes, "The CP fought for the right of Mexican workers to organize themselves, and later in the 1930s assisted in the organization of Mexicans into independent as well as CIO unions."[5] From the point of production, the fight was then carried into the larger society. With the political and organizational support of the Communist Party and its leverage within the CIO, the course of events produced the first comprehensive Mexican civil rights movement, emerging from within the Mexican working class itself and at the junctures of labor militancy.

Collaboration through the Good Neighbor Policy

FDR's pledge to abate the aggressive interventionism of previous administrations under the mantra of the Good Neighbor policy was grounded in strategic calculation. He wanted to increase the volume of trade and investment in Latin American as other markets closed, and to strengthen the US geo-political military position in the lead-up to World War II. The US sought allies in Latin America to shore up support against Axis powers. A longer-term strategy was to cultivate the oppositional forces necessary to counter the economic nationalism percolating throughout the region before the war's end. Nevertheless, it was presented as a genuine volte-face in long-standing asymmetrical relations in the interest of democracy and equality. It created the political space for cross-border collaboration between US-Mexican labor and the Left.

During this period the Communist Party of Mexico mirrored its counterparts north of the border, playing an active role in organizing industrial unions as a secondary leadership of the CTM and with the approval of Vicente Lombardo Toledano. In both cases, the Communists rationalized subservience to bourgeois leadership in the context of the reformist turn during the Popular Front period. The US party jettisoned revolutionary politics and sidelined class struggle in favor of class collaboration with the "progressive bourgeoisie" as the best means to ensure the survival of the Soviet Union. In Mexico, the Communists (and Lombardo Toledano) applied Stalin and the

Soviet state's "stages" policy of socialist revolution. Believing Mexico needed to pass through a completed "national-democratic revolution" before a socialist revolution could occur, the Mexican Communist Party aligned with the "nationalist bourgeoisie" in the form of the administration of Lázaro Cárdenas and the PRM (Partido Revolucionario Mexicano).[6] In their 1936 proclamation aligning with the Popular Front turn, the party announced a significant shift in this direction:

> The Communist Party had not understood that the PNR (Partido Nacional Revolucionario; forerunner to the PRI) was not only a party of landlords and millionaires that served imperialism and imperialist corporations, but also contains sectors of the commercial and industrial bourgeoisie whose interests are opposed to imperialism and who struggle for economic independence of the country and to develop our own national economy.[7]

Applying a "common enemy" framework, the CTM leadership projected its politics north of the border. Lombardo Toledano and the CTM sought allies in its attempt to weaken US imperialist influence in Mexico in order to strengthen national development through a coordination of interests aligning the CTM with domestic Mexican capital on the one hand, and the CIO vis-à-vis the Mexican American working class and Communist Party on the other.[8] In these efforts, the leadership hoped to partner with the CIO to develop a common, mutually supportive strategy to organize Mexican workers. Communist organizers within the CIO served as the main liaison, especially Mexican Americans and those organizing them, who saw in the CTM a powerful benefactor that could leverage its influence in aiding in the unionization of the vast ranks of Mexican workers in Texas. As Zaragosa Vargas observes:

> This marked a significant new phase in the labor movement's basic character. Mexican American workers were making international labor solidarity a priority, since assistance in the form of guidance and organizers now came from Mexico's newly formed [CTM]. In solidarity with the CIO in its organizing drives in Texas and the rest of the Southwest and Midwest, the CTM would make use of the willingness of Mexican Americans to assist in its promotion of a "CTM del Norte" (A CTM of the North).[9]

The high point of cross-border collaboration occurred in support for the nationalization of Mexican oil companies. Between 1937 and 1942, Communists also organized an array of other joint actions:

> In 1937 5000 workers marched to the bridge in Laredo during an onion strike in the Río Grande Valley. The major working class organizations of the border states were present—the Congreso de Trabajo, the railroad union and the Mexican Communist Party. Vicente Lombardo Toledano came from Mexico City to speak . . . Together with grassroots unions organized by left-wing workers on the US side, the groups cooperated in setting up the Asociacion de Jornaleros (the Agricultural Workers Union) in Laredo, Texas. In the following years, Mexican unions increased their organizing activity in Texas. The CTM held

Conventions of Mexican Workers in Dallas in 1938, in San Antonio in 1940, and in Austin in 1941.[10]

Other acts of solidarity included the attempt to create a transnational labor federation,[11] transborder strike support,[12] and the transborder circulation of organizers and newspapers.

Vicente Lombardo Toledano and the CTM established a direct line of communication to labor unionists in the US through the publication of the *Mexico Labor News* (MLN), an English-language publication designed to communicate the perspectives of the CTM directly to a US audience. Three thousand copies of each weekly newsletter were sent to the US. They were distributed by Communist Party members and allies through the arterial networks flowing from the CIO through Popular Front organizations. These included Mexican American militants organizing within the Mexican working-class communities and CIO locals, who understood the significance of the cross-border alliance as a mechanism for relating to a large expat Mexican community with revolutionary memory and sympathy for *cardenismo.*

The newsletter focused on the role of US imperialism in Mexico while emphasizing how transnational US capital exploited labor on both sides of the border, distinguishing between Roosevelt-aligned Good Neighbor progressive capital and "fascist-enabling" reactionary capital tied to Wall Street.[13] For instance, during a strike showdown between the oil workers' union and US-owned oil companies, the MLN noted:

> What's known as the "petroleum controversy" between the Mexican Government and the companies is, in reality, nothing but one chapter more in the gigantic struggle of the powerful world petroleum monopoly to drain at its own pleasure the oil deposits of the entire world . . . The oil trusts, naturally the enemy of all democratic regimes, are equally interested in fighting both Roosevelt and Cárdenas . . . the objectives of which are, in the United States, to defeat Roosevelt in the coming elections, and in Mexico to weaken the position of Cárdenas and . . . [will] aid in the victory of an opposition which . . . will rectify the Cárdenas policies with respect to expropriations.[14]

The crowning achievement of the labor movement in Mexico occurred with the oil nationalization in 1938. The CTM organized the twenty-one different petroleum workers' unions into one powerful industrial union, the National Petroleum Workers Federation, which launched an industrywide strike in June 1937. Prolonged resistance by the oil companies to recognize the union, negotiate demands, or even recognize any of the legal pronouncements of the Mexican state led the Cárdenas government to nationalize US and British holdings in March of 1938. Production then resumed under the control of a government-appointed petroleum board, which included representatives of the CTM.

The CTM-led strikes and social mobilizations during the *sexenio* of Lázaro Cárdenas inspired class consciousness and confidence among the Mexican working class on both sides of the border. Commenting on the northward flow of Mexican revolutionary ideals to even the "lowest strata" of Mexican ethnics in the United

States, a consular official lamented that new attitudes of "social freedom . . . spread like wildfire and . . . inspir[ed] Mexicans to demand a better status wherever they may be found."[15] The Mexican government and the CTM had transformed their society and commanded "respect for the laboring classes and their strong organizations." Latino organizations in the US had "sprung up with the same views in mind."[16]

The Mexican Communist Party and the CTM used these cross-border channels to support the CPUSA's efforts to appeal to Mexicans and Mexican Americans in the north. Beginning in 1937, they distributed their newspaper, *El Machete*, to contacts in the Southwest, even introducing an English-language column for a bilingual readership. Earl Browder proclaimed to the comrades in Mexico that the US party would "help secure for your paper its rightful circulation among US citizens of Latin American origin, to whom both languages are common, especially among the second generation."[17]

The use of the paper as part of daily organizing tasks emerges from within internal party literature. In one report on recruitment in East Los Angeles, a party member discussed organizing with Mexican agricultural workers during a strike:

> As an organizer of my unit, I decided that it was my duty to go among the strikers and help them in every possible way. So we attended every strike meeting held . . . and collected about $150 for them . . . got clothing, investigated families, etc. The first time I appeared at their strike meeting I told them I was a member of the Communist Party and brought in the *Western Worker* and *El Machete* to every meeting . . . As a result we recruited six or seven agricultural workers, and were able . . . to build a local of the Workers Alliance, and at our last meeting there were 50 workers present.[18]

The member enthusiastically concludes:

> There is no end to recruiting among the agricultural workers and . . . Workers Alliance, because they are the most exploited people. These people are not afraid of us. They elected me their financial secretary. At the rate we are going, we will soon have them all recruited to the party.

El Machete received financial contributions from mutualistas and other sympathetic organizations across the US where sizeable barrios and Communist Party branches existed in proximity, including Comités Pro-Machete in Chicago, St. Louis, Los Angeles, and New York City. The Texas and Oklahoma branches of the Communist Party held special fundraising events for the production and distribution of *El Machete*, which received accolades in the pages of the newspaper.[19] With a Mexican readership now based among the Mexican working class north of the border, the paper included more coverage of US issues.

The potential for large-scale action and organizing was enormous during the Good Neighbor period, opening the door for unprecedented transnational collaboration. Nevertheless, the subordination of the Communist Party to the foreign-policy objectives of their respective ruling bourgeois parties subverted their efforts. This was initiated by the Soviet government in Russia, which ordered their party affiliates worldwide to unite with the "progressive bourgeoisie" against fascism. Submerging party program to interests of the liberal wings of the capitalist class was to be conducted in order to defend Stalin's Russia at all costs against the fascist threat. Both parties jettisoned revolutionary rhetoric and framed their own alliance with their respective bourgeoisies as within the framework of their respective constitutions.[20] Both parties jettisoned revolutionary rhetoric in favor of nationalism, and aligned with their respective bourgeoisies in the name of defending the constitutional order:

> I will consider my visit here of importance . . . as a symbol of the growing unity of the masses of Mexico and the US, in the fight against our common enemy [. . .] The presidents of both countries, alike in being progressive men [. . .] are attacked with the most vicious abuse and slander by the reactionary and fascist forces [. . .] It is with great joy to us in the United States to witness the Mexican people . . . more and more realizing the great objectives of the national revolution set up in your Constitution.[21]

Cárdenas, like FDR, relied on the support of organized labor to weaken his enemies at home and channel working-class support behind their efforts to defend the interests of the capitalist class. Neither leader wanted to see the Communist Party survive and succeed within their nations, and their ruling parties turned on them when they were no longer needed.[22]

Chapter 30

Communists, the Popular Front, and the New Deal in California

"The Party was active not only in organizing workers, but also in community issues: working for school desegregation, opposing segregation in public facilities such as swimming pools and houses, protesting police abuse, obtaining relief aid, and preventing the deportation of Mexicans during the 1930s."
—Bert Corona, union organizer and participant in multiple "Popular Front" organizations in the 1930s and 1940s

The Communist Party built its second-largest statewide presence in California (after New York) during the Depression years, making its first comprehensive efforts to organize the Mexican working class on a mass basis. Through their union-organizing efforts in agriculture with the CAWIU, Communist organizers helped coordinate or lead strikes of tens of thousands of Mexican farmworkers. Through the Unemployed Councils and Workers Alliance, the CP experienced exponential growth in numbers and influence, including within the urban barrios. Because the Mexican population was the most impoverished and unemployed segment of the working class, they turned to the Alliance for support.

The CP-led Alliance organized the unemployed together, regardless of race, actively petitioned for increases in federal and state relief budgets, opposed the exclusion of noncitizens, filed grievances, provided lawyers, and opposed attempts by relief agencies to use unemployed workers as strikebreakers in agriculture. Through tenacious campaigning, the Alliance became a powerful force in the state, attracting a broad membership that saw its work as crucial to their well-being. By 1939, for instance, the Workers Alliance had 186 locals, 12,000 dues payers, and 42,000 affiliated members overall throughout the state, of which party members were a significant organized minority.[1] Through its International Workers Order, the party also provided low-income workers with health and life insurance, medical and dental clinics, and funds to support local publications, and to sponsor cultural and educational activities. Through these interactions in the Mexican barrio, the Communist Party actively recruited a new generation of Mexican radicals as part of its overall growth in the period. This generation of radicals had roots or connections in the barrios, from the workplaces to the community organizations.

Nationally, the CP grew from 7,500 in 1930, to 26,000 in 1934, to 85,000 by 1939, with another 20,000 youth members in the Young Communist League.[2] In California, CP membership reached 5,000, and the state party's newspaper, the *People's World*,

reached a circulation of 25,000 by the outbreak of World War II.[3] While accurate recruitment data is scarce, it was noted in party records that about eleven percent of the
nearly 2,000 members recruited to the party in 1936–1937 were "Spanish and Mexican
workers." This included the "Benito Juárez" branch in Los Angeles, a "Nueva Vida"
Club, and a No Pasarán branch of the Young Communist League.[4] The growth of the
radical Left was the cause of great consternation among the capitalist class, uniting
the anti–New Deal and anti-Communist forces within both parties. With the police,
courts, and news media in their hands, the US Right regrouped with the intention to
crush radicalism through the aegis of the Cold War.

The Communist Party achieved its greatest influence in California politics within
the New Deal wing of the Democratic Party in the Popular Front period. By 1938,
California was the second-largest base of membership for the Communist Party, especially in San Francisco and Los Angeles. Firmly rooted in the CIO, party members occupied leadership positions within different unions and within internal organizations
such as Labor's Non-Partisan League, the CIO's electoral lobbying apparatus. Their
strategic position and coordinated orientation allowed them to leverage resources and
an army of trained organizers to mobilize large sections of the working class during
elections. The sharp reformist turns during the Popular Front period led the party
to become the most cohesive and disciplined force now housed on the left flank of
the Democratic Party. In the pages of the party press, California party chair William
Schneiderman described the role that the party played in creating a substantial electoral organization behind the New Deal candidates. On the eve of the 1938 statewide
elections, he blithely noted:

> We Communists are keenly aware of the responsibility we bear to bring about
> this unity. We have become an important factor and a recognized force in the
> labor and progressive movement, and the progressive forces are beginning to
> appreciate and understand the role we are playing in the building of the dem-
> ocratic front.[5]

The pinnacle of influence was reached during the governorship of Culbert Olson
(1939–1943), a liberal Democratic state senator representing Los Angeles who joined
the New Deal electoral realignment cohering within the party. Olson, who previously
backed Socialist Upton Sinclair's gubernatorial campaign predicated on "Ending Poverty in California" (EPIC),[6] rode the momentum of popular support for the New Deal
all the way into the governor's mansion, with a groundswell of support coming from
the party-driven, left-wing unions of the CIO. As a result of the CIO/CP role, Communists and those aligned with the party were awarded leadership positions in the
State Relief Administration and other government posts. Until a rift developed between the CIO/CP and Olson over the implications of the Hitler-Stalin Pact, Olson
could be counted on to give symbolic support for the endeavors of the Popular Front
as they pertained to support for racial equality.

Burke and Cherny both emphasize that the Popular Front approach, union den-
sity and militancy coming out of the San Francisco general strike, and confident radical

pushback against the right-wing anti-Communist crusade in California allowed the state government to move to the left during the 1938 election, bucking the general rightward trend nationwide.[7] As a nod to the role of the CIO and CP in mobilizing support for Olson, party members and co-thinkers were appointed to posts within the administration. For instance, Carey McWilliams, a radical Popular Front lawyer closely aligned with the CP and an advocate for Mexican civil rights, was appointed as state director of Immigration and Housing.

In the first few months of 1939, a raft of social and labor reform legislation was introduced: state-funded health insurance for low-income workers, the right to picket and limits placed on court injunctions, improvements in unemployment compensation, housing for migrant workers, repeal of the criminal syndicalism law, the disbandment of the notorious anti-labor Red Squad in Los Angeles, the freeing of political prisoner Tom Mooney, and the establishment of statewide minimum wages and maximum hours.[8] At the height of the left-wing mood, party influence reached its apex. New Deal Democrats in the legislature introduced bills compelling desegregation of publicly funded institutions and services, representing the first overture toward statewide comprehensive desegregation in the nation. While most of these efforts failed, they opened up space for radical initiatives to be undertaken at the local level, which manifested as the working-class roots of the civil rights movement.

Communists and the CIO

By 1940 there were an estimated twenty million industrial workers clustered in burgeoning industries that were mostly unorganized. This included steel and other metals, auto, electrical appliances, rubber, textiles, garments, agriculture, transport, retail, and construction. Mexican workers were scattered throughout this industrial workforce, from auto plants in Detroit, to steel mills in Kansas, and meatpacking plants in Chicago.[9] They were most concentrated in the industries throughout the Southwest, especially in mining, agricultural industries, and textiles. The single largest grouping was located in Los Angeles, the fifth most populated city in the pre-WWII US, with about 250,000 of the city's 2.7 million inhabitants being Mexican.

By 1934, the Communist Party had established a substantial network of party members assembled into shop "nuclei" spread through the crafts and industries nationally. In a 1934 membership report, the party reported 338 shop nuclei, of which 154 were in basic industries. Total party membership amounted to 2,355, with 1,323 in basic industries. Furthermore, they calculated that a total of 350,000 workers total were in the plants where shop nuclei were located and 36,000 were in trade unions divided between TUUL "red" unions (9,579), independent unions (5,427), and AFL unions (21,823).[10] The CPUSA estimated that over one million workers had struck since the beginning of 1933, with the TUUL-affiliated unions leading about 20 percent of the workers.[11] Some of these nuclei were present in the garment, canning, and furniture workers' unions in the Los Angeles area.

During the period of the Popular Front, the number of party units in shops increased significantly, as the Communist Party liquidated its TUUL unions in favor of merging into the AFL. The transition was swift and impactful. By 1936, the party revealed that nearly 30 percent of its members were active in AFL unions, with 460 shop nuclei and 5,243 members active in the nuclei.[12] By 1938, the number of shop and industrial units increased again, with 582 encompassing over 18,000 party members.[13] The party noted a total of 27,000 members active in trade unions nationally. Communist labor organizers played a pivotal role in the shop floor leadership of the labor movement during the radicalization of the Depression years, especially during the New Deal period when they congregated en masse in CIO industrial unions. Total union membership exploded during this period, from 2.9 million in 1933 to 15 million by 1946.[14]

In California, the party claimed to have 226 total units in the state: 55 industrial units, 9 shop units, and 167 street units and branches. There were 1,500 members in unions, with 1,203 members working in the industrial and shop units, primarily light industry, where a larger share of the Mexican working class was concentrated.[15]

By the onset of the Great Depression, Los Angeles had rapidly become a burgeoning industrial center, with the country's ninth-largest industrial economy, based in manufacturing, construction, petroleum, agriculture, and service industries.[16] An alliance of the local political establishment, the Chamber of Commerce, and various media outlets maintained a united front against unions, which made the city a pole of attraction for capital investment desired by city planners. The maintenance of a large, tractable, non-unionized workforce was key to this arrangement. While the AFL had a presence in the city, the leadership made only symbolic gestures toward organizing Mexican workers in the 1920s. What's more, the long-standing anti-immigrant and anti-Mexican sentiment of the AFL crafts resurfaced with the economic downturn. The AFL's main publication, *The Citizen*, called for immigration restrictions and the economic exclusion of Mexican laborers already in the country, while the Central Labor Council advocated for the passage of a city ordinance barring immigrant labor from employment on public projects.[17] The AFL also supported the deportation campaign, which uprooted thousands of Angeleños, ensuring that Mexican workers remained largely unorganized and alienated from the existing union presence in the city.

The role of Communists in organizing the abortive TUUL-aligned unions, Unemployed Councils and the Workers Alliance, and other party-aligned groups enabled them to lay the groundwork for organizing the largely unorganized Mexican working class. In the transition to the Popular Front and in the abandonment of dual unionism, a phalanx of trained and experienced union organizers moved into the AFL. Having cut their teeth under the most difficult and adversarial conditions, they brought an array of talents, resolve, and discipline into the ranks that made an immediate impact. With an antiracist and industrial union orientation, the party was well placed to be an intermediary agent and the influential left-wing in the breakaway CIO. The opportunity was made even more amenable for the growth of the CIO within the largely organized barrios of Los Angeles by the pro-union sentiment of the Mexican working class and the outbreak of militant strikes. While the field was largely open to organizing, the AFL still remained an obstacle determined to sabotage any and all CIO efforts.

The CIO leadership's program of breakaway industrial unionism needed a big boost of support if it was going to survive a separation from the AFL. They also had to overcome entrenched employer resistance bolstered by allies in local government, police, and the courts. They also had to compete with a company union movement, funded by employer associations and the Chamber of Commerce, and staffed by conservative and reactionary middle-class civic organizations with campaign names like "The Neutral Thousands," "Truth Not Terror," "Women of the Pacific," and "Southern Californians, Inc."[18] This strategy sought to preempt CIO unionization efforts after the passage of the NLRA by establishing phony company unions.

Furthermore, the trajectory of the CIO toward anti-fascism and civil rights organizing among the multiracial workforce required coalition with progressive liberals affiliated with the Democratic Party, especially against deeply rooted conservative forces defending Jim Crow segregation as a mechanism to keep workers divided and the black and Latino working class subjugated. Communists had already joined the federation en masse, and this convergence of interests allowed a window to be opened for the CP to rise in the ranks and wield political influence among the rank and file and over organizing strategy.

By 1946, party members comprised less than one percent of the CIO but were concentrated in strategic leadership positions. Of a total 38 CIO-affiliated unions, Communists were active directly in the leadership of 14 unions with a combined membership of 1.4 million, or wielded some influence within another 11 unions representing 1.6 million members.[19] The CIO's base was expanded greatly through organizing the vast ranks of the "unskilled" unorganized industrial workforce in places like Los Angeles, where Mexican workers formed a significant and militant minority of the region's working class. It took militancy and resilience from below to break through the anti-union business alliance that held sway over local government through the mid-1930s. As a result of their efforts to organize the unorganized, including hundreds of thousands of black and Mexican workers, the unionized workforce expanded from 22 percent in 1937 to 35.5 percent of the total workforce in 1946.[20]

In 1938, national CIO leaders John L. Lewis and John Brophy called on West Coast director Harry Bridges to form a statewide CIO federation to unite the countywide affiliates taking shape. To coordinate this process, more than 400 delegates representing 60,000 unionists gathered to elect top federation officials. Those elected included leading Communist and Los Angeles labor activist Philip "Slim" Connelly as the first president of the California CIO Council, which oversaw the coordination between CIO affiliates across the state. By late 1938, the LA Industrial Union Council claimed to have 50,000 union members through its affiliates.[21] There was such a presence of Communists in the architecture of the LA CIO that party leaders saw it as an important outpost for national operations. In Southern California, where Mexican Communists were the most concentrated in leadership positions (especially in Los Angeles County), an estimated 15,000 Mexican Americans and mexicanos were members of CIO-affiliated unions. The federation also claimed 65 Mexican/Mexican American full-time representatives, business agents, union officials, and shop stewards among the leadership.[22]

Frank López, veteran of the furniture workers' movement and an active party member, was promoted to the post of vice president of the LA-CIO Council, illustrating the rise of a radical Mexican labor leadership forged out of local class struggle.

As a result, the LA-CIO Council served as the vanguard for civil rights advocacy on behalf of the Mexican working class. The leadership sought to integrate racially segregated industries, negotiating the first nondiscrimination clauses in union contracts in the city.[23] They also built the prototype model of social movement unionism, actively spearheading or supporting progressive causes that benefitted the whole working class. For instance, it endorsed and participated in Workers Alliance–led marches against cuts in unemployment relief. Like their position nationally, Communists and aligned radicals in Los Angeles were concentrated in leadership positions within the state CIO, which gave them influence over tens of thousands of workers, which came to include the substantial Mexican working class concentrated in Los Angeles.

Communist Party Perspectives on Defeating Racism

From its very inception, the Communist Party elaborated antiracism as a theoretical pillar of its program. Rooted in the Marxist principles of the rights of oppressed nations to self-determination and the exigency of working-class unity as a precondition for social revolution, the party added substance to their appeals to racial unity when they began to actively organize working-class communities of color. Direct political engagement with communities experiencing state repression, institutional discrimination, and vigilante violence on account of their skin color or nationality pressed the party to articulate more refined criticism and specific forms of organization to proffer resistance. While applied inconsistently, unevenly, and at times opportunistically, Communist Party efforts to confront and defeat racism initiated the first comprehensive campaigns for Mexican American civil rights. The recruitment of Mexican and Mexican American radicals into the party and their direct leadership added cultural, linguistic, and historical insights and understanding to the organizing efforts. This convergence of organic Mexican radicals with the politics, resources, and networks of the Communist Party opened the door to the first significant mass-organizing campaigns in the major Mexican population centers of San Antonio and Los Angeles.

By the early 1930s, the party's efforts to create the dual unions of the Trade Union Unity League and to organize the Unemployed Councils led to the first substantial efforts at multiracial organizing. In their efforts in the Southwest, party workers came into the contact with the specific obstacles that Mexicans faced. In the countryside, grower-led vigilante violence functioned as the rule of law; in the cities police brutality, criminalization of youth, and targeted and systematic deportation punctuated daily life and shaped the contours of resistance within the barrios. The defense of cultural rights, embedded within the internationalist model of class unity articulated by the Partido Liberal Mexicano, was carried through the next generation of Mexican radicals drawn into the Communist Party. Here, these ideas interacted with other theoretical models generating within the party experience.

In the early 1930s, party ideologues identified racism in the US as a reactionary byproduct of colonialism and imperialism, and an intractable impediment to class unity as long as it persisted unchallenged in institutional form. During the Popular Front period, they linked Jim Crow racism to rising Nazism, characterizing it as a tool that reactionary capitalists used to leverage their rise to power akin to Hitler exploiting anti-Semitism. After the Nazi invasion of the Soviet Union, they then identified racist movements as a fifth column, an internal enemy attempting to polarize society in the service of the Axis powers. In a 1944 party pamphlet titled "Smash the Secret Weapon: How to Fight the Fifth Column," International Workers Order president William Weiner connects the attacks by sailors on Mexican Americans in Los Angeles to other forms of racist hate crimes in other parts of the county as manifestations of the Axis enemy within:

> Let us never forget for a moment that it will do us little good to win the war and lose the peace. And that is now the objective of the treacherous fifth column in the United States—to disrupt national unity, to turn one American group against another, to plunge the country into the hell of Fascism. For the truth of the matter is that these attacks against Negroes, Mexicans, Jews and other minority groups, constitute the enemy's invasion of the United States. They make up Hitler's counter-second front on the soil of the United States.[24]

During the period of the war, the party dismantled or suspended their campaigns against Jim Crow racism for the sake of creating "national unity," watchwords for uncritical support of the US war effort. Party leaders reconfigured their approach to fighting Jim Crow, now calling on racially oppressed people to join the war effort to oppose racism in the form of military exclusion. As expressed in the pages of *The Communist*:

> The only course that is to the benefit of the Negro people is the course of entering the war effort fully, completely, making it their war effort, making their demands for unity in the war effort, making their demands in the first place against these measures of brutality, of the Jim-Crow system, that prevent their participation in the war effort.[25]

Support for Latin American self-determination was also muted, in favor of hemispheric unity to prevent penetration and influence of the Axis powers and to tacitly support the restructured Good Neighbor policy of strengthening US access and control over Latin American natural resource markets to increase the production of war materials.

While the Communist Party's application of antiracist politics at any given moment was subject to abrupt turns and reinterpretations in light of Comintern policy, party intellectuals and co-thinkers developed their own schools of thought in an attempt to deepen the party's understanding and commitment to the issue. The Mexican Question introduced by Emma Tenayuca and Homer Brooks intellectually informed the contemporary generation of Mexican and Latino radicals acting for Mexican working-class self-determination in the US.[26]

Concurrently other strains of thought circulated, intersected, or overlapped within Communist circles as the "race question" pertained to the specific experiences of immigrants, Mexicans, and indigenous peoples. The Yugoslavian immigrant writer and later party member Louis Adamic wrote extensively on the experience of immigrants, with his work informing the party's campaign against deportation and the racialized criminalization of the foreign-born. Carey McWilliams, a close ally and supporter of the party, wrote widely distributed tracts appealing to the white working class to understand, integrate, and unite with the Mexican working class in the US. Adamic and McWilliams formulated a "distinctive antifascism . . . that constituted an early version of multicul-turalism, that is, an antiracist sentiment focused on Mexican Americans, Asian Amer-icans, and Native Americans as well as African Americans."[27] They promoted the idea that unionization would foster "proletarian Americanization" by integrating all work-ers, regardless of race, nationality, etc., into common CIO unions. The heterogeneous working class could be integrated through class consciousness, shared class experience, and multinational and multiracial solidarity. On the Mexican side of the border, Vicente Lombardo Toledano also made contributions on the subject, articulating an antiracist analysis of the Mexican experience that could inspire and empower cross-border unity.[28]

While Communists were at the forefront of fighting racism of the 1930s, their consistency was compromised by their abrupt and polar shifts in activity in adherence to party directives emanating from Moscow. When, for instance, winning World War II became the singular area of concern for the party, they collapsed their civil rights organizing so as not to challenge or criticize the US government in any way. For the party, "total unity to win the war" included the abandonment of secondary principles in the name of a singular cause.

The CIO, Class Struggle, and Civil Rights

The symbiosis between the Communist and liberal wings of the CIO was abetted by several factors. The party's Popular Front turn saw the leadership encourage the abandonment of revolutionary rhetoric in favor of "unity" with liberal reformists. By de-emphasizing recruitment and Marxist politicization, they found an easier path into the AFL. Second, an experienced core of trained and disciplined unionists and organizers was now at the disposal of the CIO industrial wing, which was essential for the fledgling industrial union federation to overcome great obstacles looming over its survival. The most immediate key to the growth of the CIO was class struggle, which was provided on a national scale throughout the thirties and again during World War II. From 1942 to 1945, for instance, nearly 7 million workers took part in over 14,000 strikes, despite a surge of right-wing patriotism that discouraged labor militancy.[29] The convergence of the Communist Party's antiracist orientation with the CIO's drive to organized the unorganized, which included the vast populations of workers of color, found expression in the establishment of the labor federation. At its inaugural conven-tion in 1938, the CIO set forth a declaration of its "uncompromising opposition to any form of discrimination, whether political or economic, based on race, color, creed, or nationality."[30]

If the CIO was going to organize the unorganized industrial working class, which included large clusters of black, Latino, and Asian workers, they would need to confront the formidable structures of Jim Crow racism that underpinned their racial subjugation. This included state actors such as elected officials, the police, and the courts, as well as non-state actors in the form of reactionary business groups and associations, "patriotic" organizations, vigilante movements, and racist and fascist organizations. Beyond that, they also faced a hostile AFL leadership determined to strangle the CIO in its cradle. Born into a hostile environment, even the anti-Communist right of the CIO understood the need for militancy to gain a foothold, although for some the justification was also framed as a necessary step to preempt the rapid growth of communism.[31]

The first efforts to fight racial oppression occurred at the base of the class struggle among Mexican and Latina/o workers in Southern California. After the great repatriation, US-born Mexican Americans raised in the communities felt compelled to fight for more economic security and opportunity, felt vested enough to demand that their rights be protected, and saw unions and the radical Left and Popular Front groups as the only organizations willing to breach the color lines and actualize their sentiments.[32] A significant minority of mexicanos and Mexican Americans was animated by left-wing sentiments, having direct memory of past experience with radicalism or that of their parents.

Mexican workers led, joined, or participated in the first great strikes of the 1930s, including those of the garment workers, furniture workers, and cannery workers. These strikes had to confront racism directly to achieve their aims, from the notorious "Mexican wage," to segregated job placement, to outright hiring exclusions. Radical Socialists and Communists (and would-be Communists) were an integral part of building and supporting these strike movements, and they helped organize and train a new generation of leaders and rank-and-file militants. They developed creative tactics to win the strikes bolstered by radical notions of class struggle, relying on mass mobilization, interethnic solidarity, and industrial unionism.

Furthermore, some non-Mexican party activists engaged in direct organizing of Mexican workers and, within the barrios, made an effort to understand the culture and history, and overcame the physical and psychological barriers imposed by racial and cultural segregation. In doing so, they recruited small but significant layers of Mexican working-class leaders, who in turn were able to communicate directly how the party applied antiracism, transnational class unity, and class power to local conditions. This second layer of leaders coming directly from the barrios then took these notions of class struggle, racial justice, and liberation and turned them into a concrete strategy. Their efforts were bolstered by the developments at the national level, where even the liberal and conservative wings of the CIO understood the need for radical approaches to break the many-headed resistance to industrial unionism.

To confront racism on a national level, the national CIO leadership characterized racial discrimination as a domestic variant of "Hitlerism." Internal organizations were formed with the task of advocating from within and outside the organization for racial equity. The Committee Against Racial Discrimination (CARD) was an example. Despite formal efforts at the top, commitment to fighting racism was uneven across the organization, from the regional to the local level. The national leadership did not directly intervene in race relations, but encouraged regional and local affiliates to establish their own CARD committees. Over a hundred committees were formed nationally, and were strongest and most active in those CIO unions and locals with the largest percentage of Communists and people of color, such as Los Angeles.

There, these antiracist initiatives were given greater impetus and more resources, as the CIO/CP militants were more intimately aware of the need to combine the political struggle for civil rights with economic demands in order to confront more directly the strictures of racial segregation.[33] As a result of the national direction and local efforts, hundreds of thousands of black and Mexican workers were incorporated into integrated CIO locals. The Left-led and Communist Party–influenced locals with higher densities of black workers in the South and Mexican workers in the Southwest were those that linked economic struggle to the need for civil rights issues and promoted leadership from within the ranks.

This included confronting forms of on-the-job racism, actively cultivating and promoting leadership among black and mexicana/o workers, and educating white workers of their own class interests in opposing racism. The conservative tendencies in the predominantly white sectors of the union tended to downplay racial equity, from rejecting it outright to adhering to antiquated Socialist Party notions that racism was a secondary issue that would become subsumed by the larger class struggle. Nevertheless, in the context of heightened class struggle, white workers could be won to unified action that included antiracism, a factor that made the CIO potentially the most powerful instrument for dismantling racial discrimination and segregation.

The convergence of factors allowed for concerted action against the most vulnerable links of racism in the context of union organizing, under the strategic leadership and direction of Communists. A core of Mexican and Mexican American working-class militants and Communists cultivated from CIO-led class struggles pushed this process forward. They built on Mexican working-class cultures and traditions, utilizing kinship networks, fostering interethnic cooperation, and centering class unity and internationalism. Through their interface within the party and CIO structures, they envisioned, developed, and acted on a strategy to wield the power of class organization to smash Jim Crow racism.

Mexican and Latina/o Communists within the infrastructure of the CIO built a network of like-minded individuals to build on the trajectory of the strike movement to expand and deepen organizing efforts for civil rights in tandem with union organizing. Many of these individuals were instrumental in leading their locals into the CIO and beyond into the party and its front groups. The most significant of the CIO/CP-led grouping was El Congreso, a broad-based Mexican American civil rights campaign that was the convergence of the work of this new leadership, especially Luisa Moreno of UCAPAW, Bert Corona of the ILWU, and others in leadership positions distributed through the various CIO unions intersecting through the Mexican working class. While the Congress was short-lived, the commitment and the networks carried over through various efforts and organizational manifestations from 1938 to 1954.

Under the statewide CIO leadership of Harry Bridges, Philip Connelly, and Luisa Moreno, antiracist organization was elevated and coordinated through its regional councils. By the 1943 CIO convention, antiracist organizing became a prominent and mainstay feature in the Minorities Committee, which expressed its mission to "rally our CIO movement for the establishment of the Four Freedoms for all nations, minority groups and colonial people now as a vital part of total victory."[34] Statewide campaigns were spearheaded, assessed, and refined; and then given charge through the regional and local affiliates. Actions were given coverage through the state CIO's newspaper, the *Labor Herald*.

Chapter 31
Mexican Labor Militancy in 1930s California

"The Mexican girls and women, who were by far the majority
[of the strikers], acted almost like seasoned unionists."
—**Rose Pesotta, garment union organizer in Los Angeles**

The political leadership and economic conditions within the Mexican community went through a transformation during the Depression years. Repatriation led to the removal of tens of thousands of established community members and with them many of their relationships, organizations, and social arrangements. One casualty was the predominance of a Mexico-oriented political leadership routed through to the Mexican consulate and ingrained in the Mexican transnational population. In its place stepped the next generation of younger, US-born working-class leadership, reflecting the demographic shift to US-born majority within the barrios.

Despite their claim to citizenship and partial assimilation into the mainstream culture, pervasive racial discrimination confined them to the same social and economic positions as their parents. The racially segmented structure of the labor market in Los Angeles concentrated Mexicans in the lower echelons of industrial production, accounting for 70 percent of the manual labor workforce compared to just 6 percent of white male workers.[1] Mexican workers were most densely concentrated in agriculture, the garment industry, and furniture manufacturing. Key to the profitability of these sectors was the maintenance of national, racial, and gender subdivisions, which kept Mexicans socially and politically isolated from the rest of the working class.

Furthermore, Mexican women were further subdivided by gender. By 1930, 22 percent of all US women over the age of ten worked for wages, while the percentage of working Chicanas was 15 percent. Of this population 85 percent of mexicanas worked in agriculture, manufacturing and mechanical industries, as well as domestic and personal services.[2] In Los Angeles, Mexican women were a significant part of the new industrial working class, especially in garment work and agriculture, reinforced by the gendered notions of labor that women's work was an extension of their "domestic skills and duties," which were then transferred to the paid workforce. These notions changed once World War II got underway, when women were desperately needed to fill shortages in heavy industry. In some sectors, such as war production, Mexican and Mexican American women in Los Angeles comprised up to 80 percent of the workforce. By 1943, women were nearly 27 percent of the workforce in all manufacturing.

Because they were shunned by the AFL craft unions and concentrated in the low-wage, "unskilled" industrial occupations, Mexican workers in Los Angeles were mostly unorganized. Through the foundation of the TUUL-affiliated unions and the Unemployed Leagues, the Communist Party was the only significant political force that attempted to organize and welcome Mexican workers into its ranks before 1933. As a report in the *Party Organizer* pointed out:

> The great majority of the newly organized workers had never been in the A.F. of L. before. Coming mostly from basic industries, a large number of these militant workers had participated in some struggles led by the Unemployed Councils, or by other unemployed organizations and by the T.U.U.L. unions.[3]

Before the party dismantled the TUUL nationally in 1935, it had organized over 125,000 workers into its different industrial locals.[4] The core of party militants and loyal workers forged from the labor battles of the TUUL period played a pivotal role in the party's strategic reintegration into the AFL after the shift to the Popular Front. The surge in class struggle after 1933, in conjunction with the migration of a substantial Communist labor cadre into the craft locals, led to a strategic gambit within Los Angeles AFL unions to create industrial affiliates with an eye toward organizing the Mexican workforce.

Militancy among the Mexican working class was an integral part of a general upsurge in class struggle beginning in 1933 at the depths of the Depression. From mid-1933 through 1934, about 2.5 million workers went on strike, through their contact with hastily organized independent unions, Communist-affiliated TUUL unions, and existing AFL unions.[5] A catalyst for the surge in union-organizing was the passage of the National Industrial Recovery Act (NIRA) in 1933. The NIRA created the National Recovery Administration (to regulate wages and prices) and established the National Labor Board (NLB) which administered the labor provisions of NIRA, including Section 7(a) which established the right of union organization.[6] The passage of the NIRA was followed by the passage of the California Industrial Recovery Act (the state's version of the NIRA) in June of 1933. Almost instantly, there was an explosion of over two hundred strikes per month by summer, the highest rate in a decade. Because this upsurge took place in the larger industrial mass-production facilities, the AFL leadership was compelled to become more amenable to industrial unionism, forming the Committee for Industrial Organization in 1935.

These industrial affiliates, also known as "federal locals," allowed for diverse mass-production facilities to be brought into the federation, albeit as appendages to the crafts. The drive to organize the unorganized bore fruit where the federation had been in decline. Nationally, the total membership of the AFL had fallen from 4 million to 2.1 million in 1933, rising to over 3 million by 1934 due to the influx of industrial workers. This ancillary membership entered the ranks of the AFL primarily through the aegis of federal locals, which grew to number over 1,400 nationally.[7] In Los Angeles, efforts to unionize the workshops and factories ran up against different types of racial subdivisions, divide-and-conquer techniques, and institutionalized discriminatory practices used by employers. Where racial unity was achieved, significant gains were made.

In Los Angeles an estimated 15,000 new workers entered AFL unions by the fall of 1933, with a significant surge coming from Mexican women in the garment industry. The Los Angeles Federation of Labor claimed a total membership of 70,000 members spread over 152 locals and 14 women's auxiliaries by the end of 1933.[8] The promise of this militancy among industrial workers inspired the Left and industrial-union-oriented elements to the possibilities for growth, but also produced a backlash from the craft protectionists and racial exclusionists.

The gains were limited by internal opposition within the AFL. Much of the leadership, rooted in the dominant unions and including federation president William Green, remained committed to the primacy of skilled craft unionism, the principle of exclusion, and white national unity as the keys to stability, power, and longevity for organized labor. Their refusal to loosen the purse strings and support the efforts of industrial unionism led to a showdown and eventual split. The expulsion of the CIO from the AFL in 1937 ushered in an enthusiastic wave of industrial organizing in Los Angeles. Mexican workers were part of the incipient labor struggles that pushed the industrial union movement to grow within the AFL's Committee on Industrial Organizations, which grew to over a hundred locals in operation by the end of 1937. They were then the militant disciples of the CIO, and some of its most loyal adherents when it parted ways with the AFL. This pattern can be observed through the first major labor struggles in Los Angeles in the 1930s, which include the strikes and union drives of workers in the garment, cannery, and furniture industries.

Garment Worker Strikes

By 1930, mexicanas became the majority workforce of the dressmaking segment of the garment industry (called La Costura), which comprised 221 plants employing 6,302 workers.[9] By 1933, the number of workers rose to over 7,000, 75 percent of whom were Mexican women and girls, working alongside Jewish, black, and European workers clustered throughout the garment district in the heart of downtown Los Angeles. About 750 workers were members of the AFL-affiliated International Ladies Garment Workers Union (ILGWU), but the companies refused to negotiate as the open-shop movement extended into the growing dressmaking sector.

By the late 1920s ILGWU organizers had effectively written off the Mexican segment of the workforce, instead focusing on the white and Jewish workers as the base for the new Los Angeles Local 52.[10] Due to their own incapacity to communicate and unwillingness to learn Spanish or appreciate the cultural norms necessary to form relationships with the women, the white monolingual English-speaking male organizers had concluded that the Mexican women were impossible to organize.[11]

The Communist Party, which operated its own separate TUUL-aligned "red" union, the Needle Trades Workers Industrial Union (NTWIU), did not have the same racial bias. Party members in the garment industry had been an important part of the ILGWU's growth and militancy on the East Coast, and were an active part of the membership of Los Angeles Local 52. After Communists won leadership of the predominantly Jewish local, the Socialist Party's national leadership revoked its charter, dissolved it, and relaunched a new Local 65 under its own appointed leadership. This stoked long-standing antagonism that would handicap the garment workers' union-organizing efforts.

In 1928, when the party ditched the union to construct a dual union to compete with the ILGWU, both were significantly weakened. Furthermore, the CP-led NTWIU had fewer resources on the West Coast, and its sectarian opposition to the ILGWU limited its effectiveness to make inroads. The fledgling local also had to confront a preponderant opposition in the city's anti-union ruling class, determined to maintain the City of Angels as the model of the open shop. The 1933 dressmakers' strike signified the opening shot in the decades-long class struggle to break the open-shop movement, led by mexicanas. The emergence of a labor vanguard rooted among Mexican garment workers resulted from several convergent historical factors.

Between 1900 and 1930 the economy of Los Angeles grew exponentially, especially the completion of the Panama Canal in 1914 increased the volume of trade with Asia and Europe. LA emerged as a major center of shipping, production, and distribution.[12] The garment industry was one of the fastest-growing industries in Los Angeles by 1930, estimated to have annual revenues of $3 million per production season, and increasing output and adding to the workforce amid an economic depression. Workers were employed on the basis of piecework, and the availability was inconsistent from day to day.

This method rendered the women vulnerable to the whims of the managers. They were made to compete for jobs, which gradually degenerated into a kickback payment system in which women forfeited part of their wages in exchange for work. In other cases, women were encouraged to take their work home and complete it there. Through these procedures, owners were able to speed up productivity while suppressing wages. Moreover, employers kept their workers separated by race within the factories to inhibit unionization. Under these arrangements, conditions were abysmal. According to one study:

> The garment industry's growth at the height of the Depression . . . was in part a function of the industry's severe exploitation of its female labor force. The companies' profits were made at the expense of the labor force, and the industry minimized its labor costs. The industry's workers labored in unsafe, unsanitary, poorly ventilated, congested, and crowded work places.[13]

The conditions of mexicanas were made even worse by the racial discrimination that they faced, including the occurrence of raids and deportations by immigration agents. As Clementina Durón explains, "Employers threatened to report outspoken employees to the immigration authorities and have them 'sent back' if they joined the union. The ILGWU assured the dressmakers that the union and its attorneys would fight such tactics."[14]

Women also experienced sexual harassment by foremen and management, while those individuals who complained were fired and blacklisted. Under these conditions, wages fell from $23 in the late twenties, to a bottom threshold of $8 in the early 1930s, and reaching only $13-17 per week in 1935, when the NRA minimum-wage code was set at $18.90.[15] An outbreak of garment worker strikes on a national scale began to turn this around, especially after the passage of the NIRA and rising expectations that the perceived pro-union provisions now authorized collective action.[16] In Los Angeles, however, the open-shop alliance organized through the Merchant and Manufacturers Association (M&M) strategically blocked local implementation of NIRA reforms, staffing the NRA and NLB boards with allies who stymied all efforts to implement adherence to wage codes and facilitate collective bargaining rights. Led by the predominantly mexicana workforce, the ILGWU in Los Angeles kicked off a contentious industrywide garment strike on October 12, 1933, after it became apparent that the employers would block all efforts at reform.

Despite the obstinate resistance by a determined coalition of garment factory owners, the women workers had some recent experience with organizing. In 1930, the then fledgling ILGWU Local 56 (with 300 members) launched a failed strike for collective bargaining rights and the 40-hour work week. The limited membership and resources, the failure to rally the majority of workers to walk out, and the lack of public support led it to collapse in the face of coordinated employer opposition. Many of the women had also participated in the large and often militant Socialist Party and Communist Party–led unemployed marches in the first years of the Depression. By October of 1933, the moment was ripe for collective action. Key to the ability to overcome the ethnic and sectional divides was a new organizing strategy oriented toward the Mexican working class.

Rose Pesotta was the newly assigned ILGWU organizer sent to help build Los Angeles Local 65 in anticipation of organizing the industry nationwide after the passage of the NRA.[17] Unlike her predecessors, she took a different approach. Pesotta, a self-described anarchist, recognized the need to connect with the workers directly and on terms that respected, understood, and appreciated their culture, identity, and customs. She immediately recognized the need to publish union materials in Spanish. Union handbills were published in both English and Spanish, and a bilingual, four-page, semi-weekly newspaper called *The Organizer* was printed and distributed to the membership. As more Mexican workers joined the union, meetings became bilingual. Under her leadership, the local also tried to launch a weekly bilingual radio program to communicate to the workers during the strike. When this failed, mexicanas within the union took initiative and arranged to move the broadcast to a sympathetic radio station in Tijuana called El Eco de México. The new leadership also organized mass meetings to involve the rank and file in strategic decision-making.

Pesotta also relied on a network of militants among the mexicanas, who became avid organizers that carried out much of the legwork. As historian George Sánchez describes, these radical organizers were key in

> redefining the oppositional culture of Mexican organized workers during the
> 1930s. Building on histories of Mexican cooperative organizations and memo-
> ries of radicalism on both sides of the border, these organizers placed this his-
> tory within a context of current labor struggles and encouraged workers to see

themselves living out an important American tradition of radicalism . . . as workers participated in activism that placed them side-by-side with fellow workers
of other nationalities, a reformulated notion of radicalism bonded individuals
of different ethnicities together, creating new definitions of American political
activity.[18]

Showing their historical memory of previous labor struggles, the women sang Wobbly
songs on their picket lines. When the strike approached, they worked through community relationships, kinship networks, and other cultural associations to build support.

After weeks of outreach to the Mexican workers, their community-based organizations, and the Central Labor Council, the ILGWU leadership put the question of an
industrywide strike to the membership. To test support, they called for a ninety-minute
work stoppage on the afternoon of September 25 to hold a mass meeting at Walker's
Orange Grove Auditorium, in which several hundred cloak-makers attended and authorized a strike. Two days later, over 1,500 dressmakers, mostly mexicanas but also some
eastern European immigrants and Anglos, followed suit and voted enthusiastically to
strike.[19] The demands hammered out at the meeting included union recognition, a
35-hour/5-day workweek, a guaranteed minimum wage in compliance with NRA industry codes, set regular shifts (8:30 a.m.–4:30 p.m.), a lunch break, no work taken home, a
joint labor-management grievance committee, the election by workers of management
representation on the shop floor, and an impartial price committee.

To implement a coordinated strategy, a strike organization of two hundred that
included the rank-and-file mexicanas was formed to divide up the essential tasks necessary to maintain the strike, including food preparation and distribution, legal support, setting pickets, and community outreach. Captains were appointed to fan out to
all of the shops on the morning of the strike to encourage the workers to walk out. On
October 12 at five a.m., the walkout began. Within days, over 3,000 (of the estimated
7,000) cloak-makers and dressmakers were on strike, affecting 80 factories. By the end
of the first day of the strike, 3,011 strikers had signed with the union, including male
cloak- and suit-makers, and an additional 1,132 had come out in support.[20] The influx
of workers, especially Mexican dressmakers, led the union to establish a new local
(96), of which 6 members of the 19-person executive board were Mexican women.

In anticipation of the strike, the city government and employers' associations
also sprang into action to undermine it. For their part, the Merchants and Manufacturers Association worked through their NRA staff to stall any kind of recognition
or support from the state or federal authorities. The M&M had helped the garment
shop owners affiliated to the Southern California Garment Manufacturers Association to build a united front against unionization. They arranged emergency meetings
to counsel the garment factory owners on breaking the strike, encouraging them to
fire union sympathizers wholesale to discourage the remaining workers from walking
out and to blacklist known militants. In those shops where there was majority support
for the union, they were encouraged to lock out all of the workers. They then tried a
divide-and-conquer approach, agreeing to settle with the male cloak-makers but not
the women dressmakers.

The Los Angeles Police Department (LAPD) forcefully escorted strikebreakers across the picket lines and into the factories once the strike began. Over a hundred police were reassigned to guard the factories, which were located in close proximity within the garment district. Melees broke out in front of the factories as police and strikebreakers attempted to break through picket lines. At the first significant confrontation at the Paramount Dress Company on October 17, the picketers succeeded in turning away forty-five strikebreakers, frustrating police shepherding efforts. Violence ensued when the cops and some strikebreakers attacked the lines to try to disperse them to no avail.[21] Seven strikers were arrested for disturbing the peace, while one picketer, Frances Nuñez, was struck by a police vehicle.[22] As a result of the incident, the M&M-aligned garment factory owners turned to the state. Within twenty-four hours, they were able to get an aligned judge to issue an anti-picketing injunction and twenty-two more police assigned to break the strike.

The injunction allowed for the police to declare open season on the workers. By the end of the day, they'd arrested as many picketers as possible, holding them in jail overnight to intimidate them.

With the changing circumstance, the strikers changed tactics and flouted the injunction. They organized "strike patrols" and used other means to keep the factories from resuming operations. Some strikers, for instance, began throwing tacks in the roads near factories in order to prevent the police vehicles from easily moving between shops. Strikers also threw projectiles at known scab cars when they approached a work site. Like in Texas, strikers attempted to strip scabs of their clothing when they tried to cross the lines.

They organized on different street corners within the district and quickly formed "flash" pickets to block shop entrances in groups large enough to prevent arrest and discourage strikebreakers. In one confrontation, a striker named Josephine Ramirez was arrested for throwing salt in the eyes of a scab trying to enter the factory, while three others, Beatrixce Wilds, Theresa Planannell, and Rose Kartiloff, were arrested for pulling one out of a car while trying to flee. Three other strikers, Hazel Crane, Lucía Hernández, and María Hinojas, were also arrested for allegedly "pummeling" strikebreakers.[23] In another instance, María Rodríguez, Josephine Riolo, Josephine Messina, Luna Hernández, and María Herrojos were arrested for assaulting or using scissors to cut the dresses off of women crossing the picket lines.[24] These picket-line battles raged over the course of the strike.

To try to weaken the leadership, the notorious Red Squad of the LAPD was called in to target, beat, and arrest those most militant after being supplied with employer blacklists. Over the course of the three-week strike, approximately fifty targeted leaders and militants were arrested. Charges against them included "disturbing the peace," using "profane" language, unlawful picketing, and battery. In response to the skirmishes, the *Los Angeles Times* gave Captain Hynes of the Red Squad free rein in their newspaper columns to develop the narrative of the strike over its duration, downplaying support for the strike and painting the women as violent. Despite the repression, the strike held strong.

After three weeks, NRA officials in Washington intervened over the heads of local representatives. Like in other instances, the Roosevelt administration took an active role in diffusing class conflict through mediated arbitration when it became clear that workers might prevail or an employer's repression might backfire, spreading labor militancy on a local, regional, or national scale. When both sides agreed to arbitration, the workers went back to work on October 12 while the arbitration carried on until December 6. The results were mixed. All strikers were reinstated, wages were brought on par with prevailing NRA codes, a 35-hour workweek was instituted, a grievance procedure was initiated, and the ILGWU was given access to all shops without the union being officially recognized as a bargaining agent, effectively maintaining the "open shop." Sixty of the shops and the three locals (65, 84, and 96) recognized and signed off on the ruling.[25] The partial victory set the stage for further organizing, which included veteran Communists of the NTWIU, which had disbanded and joined the ranks of the ILGWU during the transition to the Popular Front.

The ILGWU continued its organizing drive, focusing on the 7,000 dressmakers. By 1934, the ILGWU had organized the whole industry, establishing a fourth and fifth local (97, 236) along the way. By 1935, the total dues-paying membership increased to 2,460, with an influx following the successful strikes. The fastest-growing segment of the membership of the ILGWU came from mexicanas, who comprised three-fourths of the total ILGWU membership in Los Angeles.[26] In 1936, they launched efforts to unionize the underwear and pajama manufacturers, leading a strike in eleven shops and obtaining agreements that extended the 35-hour week and higher, union-scale wages. These victories culminated in a general strike of dressmakers on July 1, 1936, which was led by the mexicanas of Local 96. Three thousand workers faced similar conditions but won after only a few days, as a high level of organization and coordination led the dress shop owners to concede. Fifty-six firms representing 2,650 workers signed contracts, conceding the closed shop, wage gains, and the thirty-five hour workweek.[27]

Despite the mixed gains of the strike movement and the limited cultivation of a Mexican leadership within the ILGWU, the 1933 strike and subsequent organizing efforts resulted in another tangible outcome. According to Clementina Durón,

> It did . . . give many women, particularly Mexican women, their first experience in union organizing. In addition to developing organizing skills, many of the women learned for the first time to confront employers, the police, and local officials . . . Their collective action is even more courageous in light of the red-baiting, anti-union, and deportation activities that were rampant at the time.[28]

ILGWU Spanish-speaking branch on a parade float, 1938

Cannery Workers

By 1930, Mexican women were a sizeable component of California's workforce. An estimated 50 percent of married women worked outside of the home, while 25 percent of women overall were employed in industry, contributing about 20 percent of the family wage.[29] Single Mexican women comprised 75 percent of all workers in California's numerous canneries, gravitating toward this type of work because of racial restrictions, proximity to agricultural zones, as well as "seasonal schedules and extended family networks."[30] Besides their efficiency, Mexican women were favored by cannery owners who perceived that they could be paid a lower wage than both Mexican men and white women, be more handily exploited due to their gender, and be dispensed with more easily when they were no longer needed. While women cannery workers made one-half to two-thirds of what men made, their contribution helped sustain the family wage, especially facing the destabilizing factors of the day, including poverty wages, higher rates of unemployment, and family disruption through deportation. Women's wages helped sustain housing, care of elders, and other family necessities.

Labor militancy among mexicana cannery workers in California began with a CAWIU-led wildcat strike in 1931 among cannery workers in San Jose in the Santa Clara Valley, the most important center of production of canned goods in the US between 1930 and 1950.[31] After the demise of the CAWIU, rural organizing continued slowly on two tracks: a core of Communist veterans set out on their own in the form of the National Committee for Unity of Agriculture and Rural Workers (NCUARW) and through AFL federal charters.

In 1935, Communist veterans and organizational remnants of TUUL-affiliated agricultural unions gathered to regroup and reframe their efforts in the context of the Popular Front. Rather than create a dual union, they intended to continue the work of bringing industrial unionism to the masses in the countryside with the goal of winning a charter with the AFL. With a new paper, *The Rural Worker*, NCUARW began its work constituting 23 mixed-occupation locals and 8 agricultural locals across seven states (California, Florida, Washington, Arizona, Michigan, Ohio, and New Jersey) in its first few months, growing to a total of 72 locals by the end of 1936. During this time, the union led eighteen strikes to build its base of 13,500 members.[32] When the fledgling union appealed for a charter at the 1936 convention, its petition was sidelined as a result of the running battles taking place between the CIO and AFL. Communist labor leader Donald Henderson and his cohorts would soon find a welcome home in the CIO emerging as the industrial wing of the AFL. Support for building a multiracial industrial agricultural union, aided by the passage of the Wagner Act in 1935, was crucial for a breakthrough against the overwhelming opposition from the growers.

When unions did attempt to organize in the fields and canneries, they were met with terror and violent resistance from police, private militias, and statewide official backers. Coming on the heels of two years of protracted war against the CAWIU, and its eventual demise, agricultural interests dug in and formed a new industrywide syndicate to block the effort. The California Processors and Growers Association formed as an affiliate of the Associated Farmers in 1936, and dedicated itself to keeping unions out of the Pacific Coast fields, canneries, and packinghouses. As Henderson understood:

> These farmers, the big landlords in the cotton industry in the south, the big absentee land companies, the big packing houses, the big canneries in California, the big citrus concerns in Florida, the Great Western Sugar Company . . . this type of so-called farmer we regard as our enemy, and they regard us as their enemies.[33]

The growers dug in against any and every unionizing effort, intertwining racism and physical violence into their larger strategy to smash labor militancy. As one Associated Grower seethed, "We do not propose to sit idly by and see the fruits of our labors destroyed by a bunch of Indian ignoramuses from the jungles."[34]

On the Pacific Coast, the California AFL issued federal union charters to cannery workers beginning in 1935, with these efforts largely led by Communists and radicals transitioning into AFL organizers during the Popular Front period. These federal labor unions formed through mergers with independent unions of Mexicans and Filipinos. By September 1935, there were sixteen such AFL local organizations of field, cannery, and packing-house workers in California. The AFL's State Federation of Labor then sponsored a conference of agricultural workers in San Francisco in February of 1937. Delegates represented fourteen local or federal labor unions chartered by the AFL, fifteen locals of the Mexican CUCOM, four branches of the Filipino Labor Union, and the Japanese Agricultural Workers Association of Southern California. When the state executive council refused to finance the organization of a statewide agricultural union, contending that cannery and field workers should maintain separate unions, the project faltered.

When food-processing workers did take initiative, the rival International Longshoremen's Union and Teamsters Union competed for jurisdiction. This represented a widening political rift between the two unions. Some successful coordination of efforts did occur with the warehousemen's division of the International Longshoremen's Association, which aimed to expand horizontally and create industrywide unionization and wage scales. Despite the creation of scattered locals, the attempts at industrywide unionization stalled, undermined by the lack of support, resources, and commitment from the AFL to predominantly unskilled Mexican women workers. As Donald Henderson, the Communist Party–affiliated president of the United Cannery, Agricultural, Packing, and Allied Workers of American (UCAPAWA), remarked at the founding convention of the union:

> The people here ... are, in a large part, the result of a slow, steady, painful growth over a period of the last four or five years ... In large part, we have built this up literally with our own bare hands ... Nationally ... not one penny has ever been taken out of the treasury of the American Federation of Labor to finance an agriculture or cannery workers organization.[35]

Following the lead of the ILA/ILWU, now under the lead of Harry Bridges, CIO-oriented elements rooted in the locals formed their own counter-effort. As Stuart Jamieson describes the process,

> The insurgents called another convention of agricultural field and processing workers in April. Delegates from 18 federal labor unions and independent organizations, claiming to represent a total membership of 15,000, met in Bakersfield and established the California Federation of Agricultural and Cannery Unions. The executive board elected to direct this organization represented the left-wing element in the agricultural labor movement including [Communist and cannery organizer from San Francisco] George Woolf; Dudley Sargent, secretary of Agricultural Workers Union No. 20221 of Stockton; Marcella Ryan, organizer of Cannery Workers Union 20099 of Oakland; C. W. Johnson, organizer of Agricultural Workers Union No. 20289 of Bakersfield; C. D. Mensalves, secretary, Filipino Labor Union; and Bernard Lucero, secretary, Mexican Confederation of Agricultural Workers.[36]

A significant divergence occurred in the trajectory of organizing the rural workforce with the passage of the Wagner Act in 1935. Bowing to the requests of landlords and growers, the act excluded agricultural workers from the right to collective bargaining, while allowing for it among food-processing workers. While further attempts to organize farmworkers ran into the same obstacles, the UCAPAWA made a breakthrough among cannery workers. An understanding of the strategic position of the canning industry was first analyzed by Marxist theoreticians of the agricultural economy.

Communists and the Rural Proletariat

Donald Henderson was a one-time Columbia University professor of economics and Communist Party member who specialized in the agricultural economy. After being driven out of Columbia for his politics, he applied his political and academic studies as an organizer for the CAWIU. Looking at the Bolshevik model and following the Communist International's call for an orientation toward the populations in the countryside and small towns, he adapted his studies into a class analysis and organizing plan for the party to relate to the "rural proletariat." He identified the rapid industrialization of agriculture, the concentration of ownership of the means of production, and the role of finance capital in underwriting the national and international integration through transportation, communication, and other intersecting industries. As he explained:

> This indicates one aspect of the penetration and domination of American agriculture by finance capital. The effect of the world crisis showed earlier in American agriculture than in American industry, and the consequent collapse of agriculture contributed to the collapse of industry in 1929 precisely because of the close integration of capitalist agriculture and capitalist industry; the crisis in agriculture was in turn intensified by this collapse of industry and finance.[37]

This transformation of rural production, he surmised, restructured the nature of work by eroding small production, proletarianizing farmers, and necessitating the creation of a large and diverse workforce to provide the requisite labor from production to distribution. Completely integrated vertical unions were necessary to counter the bargaining power of employers. This included differentiating segments of permanent, semi-permanent, and seasonal labor. The interconnected and interdependent industries, from agricultural work to canning and packing; from the railroads to the docks, created a vast and horizontally integrated rural proletariat. Finance capital, through its elaboration of these nodes of production on a regional, national, and international scale, now linked the rural to the urban proletariat in the cities. What's more, they experienced class exploitation and conducted class struggle in relation to the same market forces. In essence, Henderson was a co-thinker of Harry Bridges in the concept of an industrial union that organized workers along nodes of food production linking the country to the city. The idea of one big union, embodied in the ILWU's ambitious all-inclusive industrial organizing campaign referred to as the "March Inland," found its counterpart in Henderson's vision for rural unionism running from field to factory, railroad to warehouse, and from truck to store or to the docks.[38] One important link in this chain was the food-processing industry, which was a stable and semi-permanent base of workers that developed across belts of small towns situated between the fields and urban centers.

His experiences were borne out during his leadership of a successful 1934 strike at the large industrial farming complex at Seabrook Farms in Cumberland County, New

Jersey. After owner Charles Seabrook cut recently raised wages, the workers went on strike. An interracial rank-and-file strike committee was formed of black and Italian workers, elected by the workforce, and the strike organization brought together the different sections of the workforce including women. One account described a scene from the strike:

> For two weeks, black and white striking workers did battle with the local po-
> lice force, as well as with vigilantes and members of the Ku Klux Klan whom
> Seabrook enlisted to break the strike. In one incident that received national and
> international attention, a group of approximately 250 workers tried to prevent a
> fleet of tractors from harvesting beets, which local sheriffs, intervening on be-
> half of the company, dispersed with teargas. When a group of women strikers
> hopped on the tractors and began throwing bushels of beets back into the field,
> they were attacked with blackjacks, revolver butts, and billy clubs ... Despite the
> forces arrayed against them, "the strike idea was born in all defiance of South
> Jersey public attitudes, in all defiance of Klan threats, in all defiance of the tra-
> ditional belief that Negroes will not strike and that Negroes and whites cannot
> organize together successfully."[39]

As one black organizer named J. A. Ingalls told a mass rally of strikers during the third week: "In the eyes of Seabrook, we are either yellow or red. I would far rather be classified as the latter, fighting for my rights, than to be suppressed and live at starvation wages."[40] Not only did the workers demand their wages restored, they also called for the end of racially discriminatory policies against black workers including a first-out policy when picking season slowed. While the strike was only partially successful, restoring wages, ending some discriminatory practices, etc., it provided Donald Henderson a template for UCAPAWA. Among other factors, he recognized that all workers—agricultural, cannery, and packing shed workers alike—should be brought into one union. Secondly, rank-and-file leadership, gender, and interracial solidarity had to be cultivated between the different ethnic groups to prevent growers from exploiting racial and gender divi-sions. Lastly, the unemployed had to be organized alongside the strikers to petition for relief and to prevent them from crossing the picket lines.[41] These principles were the key to building UCAPAWA, which grew to become the seventh-largest union in the CIO and the union with the largest Mexican membership, including in leadership.

UCAPAWA and Civil Rights

UCAPAWA held its first convention in Denver, Colorado, in 1937, on the cusp of the break with the AFL. The delegated body represented a gathering of delegates from twenty-four states including those long excluded or written off by the AFL unions: Mexican, black, Filipino, Chinese, and Japanese agricultural workers, fruit pickers, dairy workers, sharecroppers, small and subsistence farmers, and what would become the backbone of the union: cannery and packinghouse workers.[42] The convention pledged to organize all agricultural and rural workers into integrated, industrial unions. Due to the influence of the Communist Party and its diverse ranks, UCAPAWA took

a militant, pro-civil-rights approach from its inception. The union front-loaded strategies of solidarity and interdependence to overcome the commonly employed racial
and national divide-and-conquer strategies they encountered.

Resolutions passed at the first convention showed the civil rights trajectory of
the union and its alignment with party-affiliated campaigns. These included a resolution against racial discrimination and child labor, a resolution for the rights of
Mexican migrant workers to join unions, a condemnation of police violence, a resolution for cooperation with the Workers Alliance to organize the unemployed to
support strike efforts, and a statement against war and fascism.[43] The intent of the
convention was to empower and direct the new organization to build a foundation
around a new set of politics that best prepared a fight from below against the entrenched power and reactionary anti-union tactics of the agricultural capitalists and
their attendant henchmen.

The resolution against racial discrimination identified racism in class terms, as
a tool "designed to separate the people of the world, and thus subject [workers] to
continuous exploitation and subjugation by the employers." It recognized and condemned the long-practiced employer technique of fostering and maintaining racial
and national divisions within their work crews, and consciously using different racial
and ethnic groups as "scabs" against others. The convention promoted the antidote
of antiracism and internationalism. The convention directed their locals to unite all
workers into the same local and to fight for contracts establishing equal wage scales,
working conditions, job opportunities, and benefits. They called for full democratic
rights for African Americans, opposed the use of deportation against migrants and
immigrants, and advocated for all workers to have access to government benefits and
relief, regardless of national status.[44]

The spirit of interracial, ethnic, and international unity coming out of the convention was embodied in the adoption of the Knights of Labor/Wobblies slogan: "An
injury to one is an injury to all." The bottom-up organizing strategies, leadership development, and social-justice orientation led many within its ranks to see their fight
as one on behalf of the interests of the whole working class, not just rural workers.
The pages of *UCAPAWA News* regularly ran stories of interracial unity during strikes
and organizing drives.[45] They also condemned the deportation of Mexicans and the
exclusion of Filipinos from citizenship.[46]

To demonstrate its commitment to fighting racism within its own ranks, the
union established a grievance procedure and disciplinary protocol to respond to any
acts of discrimination. One such case was published in the union newspaper, where
two white members in a Houston local were fined and put on probation for petitioning for segregated branches. As the article reported, efforts to expel them from the
local were blocked only after the black members of the local "expressed their desire to
give the two men another chance . . . They thought the offenders should have another
opportunity to become good union workers."[47]

The union also responded to worker needs by publishing its press in a bilingual
format. Luisa Moreno set up and edited the Spanish-language *Noticias de UCAPAWA*

to deliver the national bulletin in the first language of a significant base of its membership. Furthermore, the union negotiated language provisions into contracts, where employers were required to publish company bulletins, employee paperwork, and contracts in Spanish.[48] In this, UCAPAWA became a model for integrating civil rights demands into economic struggles, and also reflected changing gender dynamics as women became more central to the life of the locals.

While its first executive board was all-male, it included mexicanos and African American males. While CIO unions were typically born with the patriarchal birthmarks of the AFL, the role of Communist organizers and leadership and the increase in women membership led to qualitative changes over time. The gains of women through the union occurred in an industrywide context of gender and discrimination in position and promotion, rampant sexual harassment, and less job security.

By the second annual convention, women were elected to the national leadership, including the Communists Dorothy Ray Healey and Luisa Moreno. The influx of women workers into the organization and the conscious efforts to cultivate and promote women into the leadership bore fruit at the local, regional, and national level. Mexicanas quickly assumed leadership positions, rising from their ranks based on their organic capabilities. This included women such as Monica Tafoya, a Colorado beet worker, Angie González, a Florida cigar roller, and Emma Tenayuca, leader of the pecan sheller strike.[49] One mexicana named Julia Luna Mount worked at the Cal San cannery during a strike in 1939, where she joined the party and organized a chapter of the Workers Alliance to support the strike. Julia Luna Mount later participated in the Spanish-Speaking People's Congress, a Communist Party–led, Mexican American civil rights organization, as a representative of the Workers Alliance. In 1947, Luna Mount was a co-chair of the Mexican American Civil Rights Congress in Los Angeles, which campaigned against police brutality and racial discrimination toward the Mexican and Mexican American community.

Luisa Moreno played a leading role in many of the organizing drives among Mexican workers. She facilitated communication between English and Spanish speakers, development of local leadership, rank-and-file training of members as organizers, and democratic decision-making. She pioneered a model for creating "womens' auxiliaries" among the predominantly male segments of the agricultural workforce that was widely replicated throughout the union. As she explained in the union press,

> [O]rganizing the wives, mothers, daughters and sisters of union members . . . [will] strengthen every step the locals take, whether the goal is toward a better contract, an unavoidable strike, campaigns for needs-based legislation, or to save labor laws that are being furiously attacked by the representatives of big business.[50]

In the canneries, which were female-dominated, Moreno encouraged the development of new organizing strategies coming from the rank and file. This included the practice of rank-and-file women organizing other women workers in adjacent canneries. As Patricia Zavella has analyzed, Chicana cannery workers built kinship and friendship "sisterhoods" in which camaraderie and solidarity facilitated the creation

of collaborative networks. These work-based networks laid the basis for political con-
sciousness-raising and collective action. Once set in motion during a strike or organizing drive, "women's political involvement even takes precedence over relations with
their own families," breaking down traditional patriarchal relationships.[51] Furthermore, sometimes these intergenerational networks included "daughter, mother, and
grandmother" working together in the same cannery.[52]

The political culture also shifted, with contracts including more benefits specific
to the needs of working-class women. Working-class feminism became a strong current through the organization. As Dorothy Healey explained,

> Even though I was not in any conscious sense a feminist in the 1930s, I was still
> somewhat nonplussed when the women's liberation movement came along in
> the sixties and spoke as if it had invented the "liberated woman." I didn't see
> anything all that new in what they were advocating. That's how many of us lived
> our lives all along. It would never have occurred to me in the 1930s or afterward
> to subordinate what I was doing to what any male companion wanted.[53]

Using these bottom-up strategies, UCAPAWA grew rapidly thanks to the organizing model and leadership: 371 affiliates and 124,000 members by 1938.[54] In California cannery locals, Mexican women were able to attain leadership positions such
as officers and executive board members, and negotiating teams regularly included
mexicanas in their ranks. The different elements of UCAPAWA's strength came to the
fore in the 1939 Cal San strike.

Cal San Strike

After careful and consistent outreach and recruitment at the factory gates, and methodical base-building through networks of home meetings, Mexican cannery workers led the first major victorious strike that shut down production at the California
Sanitary Canning Company (Cal San). Cal San was one of the largest canning facilities
in Los Angeles County, located in the southern port city of Long Beach and employing 430 workers, primarily mexicanas and a smaller group of Russian Jewish immigrants. The strike was timed to begin on the eve of peach-canning season, as trucks
were scheduled to deliver their cargos from the orchards. On August 31, 1939, over
416 of the 430 workers at the plant walked out, bringing production to a halt. The
strike lasted for three months and achieved significant gains that represented a turning
point in labor history and the Mexican working class. It served as a touchstone for a
decade-long struggle to organize the California statewide expansion of the canning industry. The contracts that emerged from this intense campaign of women worker-led
class struggle produced some of the greatest gains for the working class in history.

The strike occurred as a result of the stubborn anti-union position of the owners,
George and Joseph Shapiro, who stonewalled attempted negotiations to raise wages and
improve working conditions for over a month with no intention to budge. UCAPAWA
organizers held meetings in the striking workers' homes, where union cards were signed,
collected, and then further disseminated throughout the community through family and

friend networks. Where ethnic or familial connections didn't exist, the workers built along other lines. As Vicki Ruiz explains:

> At Cal San many Mexican and Jewish workers shared another bond—neighbor-hood. Both groups lived in Boyle Heights, an East Los Angeles working-class community. Although Mexican and Jewish women lived on different blocks, they congregated at street car stops during the early morning hours. Sometimes friendships developed across ethnic lines. These women, if not friends, were at least passing acquaintances. Later, as UCAPAWA members, they would become mutual allies.[55]

Brought together by class and gender under the conditions of class struggle, they forged a unified movement. Discussion of demands, picket schedules, and other aspects of strike strategy were discussed. One worker who joined the party, Julia Luna Mount, become an organizer for the Workers Alliance. The initial organizing within the first few weeks of the strike led to the establishment of the new Local 75 of UCAPAWA.

The strikers and their family and community supporters formed a solid and consistent 24/7 picket line around the factory. Strike demands included union recognition, the closed shop, elimination of a piece rate system, wage increases, and the dismissal of abusive supervisorial staff. Revealing the antiracist current of the union, they also called for the hiring of black workers, which was prohibited by the racist Shapiro brothers. Dorothy Healy formed a Food Committee to solicit donations through a network of sympathetic East LA grocers formed by El Congreso. This committee provided a lifeline of supplies to keep striking families fed for the duration of the strike. They then utilized this network to organize a secondary boycott of scab Cal San products at the same grocers.

Even though the International Brotherhood of Teamsters pledged not to cross picket lines, this declaration proved hollow and unenforced. Upon understanding this duplicity, strikers began to confront Teamsters directly. At one confrontation, "Mexican women union members became so incensed by the sight of several Teamsters unloading their trucks that they climbed onto the loading platform and quickly 'de-pantsed' a group of surprised and embarrassed Teamsters."[56] After a two-and-a-half-month strike impasse, the union local employed more militant tactics that had been improvised by Communists and militant workers in previous strikes. They deployed the tactic of the home picket, setting up a protest directly in front of the homes of the Shapiro brothers. The *UCAPAWA News* reported that forty wholesale groceries refused to stock Cal San products on their shelves.[57] These efforts broke the resistance of the brothers, who conceded to the demands of the young and militant local.

UCAPAWA Gains

Prior to the existence of UCAPAWA, 20–50 percent wage differentials existed between Anglos and Mexicans in canning and packing, and further divides existed between men and women. UCAPAWA's growth and civil rights orientation began to dismantle

the Mexican and gender differentials, as well as the subordination of women within
the union locals. Industrywide scales built into contracts negated the racial and gendered rates. Luisa Moreno encouraged the institutionalization of women leadership
and their successful tactics into the practice of the union. From Local 75, for instance,
the veteran strikers of Cal San were tasked to create an organizing committee to replicate their efforts to organize nearby canneries. The first fruit of their labor was the
establishment of Local 3, another predominantly mexicana workforce.

Mexican women assumed 11 of the 15 executive board positions in Local 3, and
were responsible for negotiating the strongest contracts in industrial agriculture, comparable to the most advanced urban industries. These included stipulations that provided health care and free legal counsel. In other UCAPAWA locals, such as Local
64 in San Diego, Mexican women won the highest wages in the whole tuna-canning
industry.

During the period of the self-imposed no-strike pledge within CIO unions,
UCAPAWA nevertheless won thirty-one NLRB elections across rural counties in
Southern California during an eighteen-month period from late 1943 to early 1945.[58]
Working through family networks, using rank-and-file worker committees to organize nearby canneries, and with other innovative tactics, Mexican workers were key
to the spread and growth of the union. Unlike other CIO unions, which continued to
exclude Mexicans from the leadership, the UCAPAWA under the leadership of Communists broke the mold. Spanish-surnamed women assumed 21 percent of national
leadership positions, 46 percent of executive board and trustee positions, 28 percent
of negotiation committee membership, and 43 percent of shop steward positions
within the union.[59]

When World War II ended, the union led a whirlwind organizing drive of
food-processing workers under the leadership of Vice President Luisa Moreno and
with the collaboration of the ILWU. Beginning in August of 1945, UCAPAWA locals
were formed from Modesto to Sacramento to San Jose under her leadership. The
ILWU supported the drive by providing picketers and security, primarily against
Teamsters and other AFL affiliates that attempted to break the drive by stepping in
to arrange "sweetheart deals" with management. By affiliating with the AFL, it was
posited, they could keep out the CIO for collaboration with a more amenable AFL.
Dockworkers and warehousemen also provided security for the cannery workers, as
the Teamsters had a long track record of using violence to intimidate or disperse their
opponents. Within two months 14,000 were signed up. By 1946, 66 percent of contracts had equal pay for equal work clauses, and 75 percent had provisions that allowed
for maternity leave or leave of absence without loss of seniority. Some contracts included provisions for management-financed childcare. The victories of UCAPAWA
generated a high level of enthusiasm for working-class women to join, which allowed
for rapid membership bursts and a high level of solidarity and militancy to defend
gains made. As one Cal San striker named Carmen Bernal Escobar reflected on her
participation forty years later, "UCAPAWA was the greatest thing that ever happened
to the workers at Cal San. It changed everything and everybody."[60]

Furniture Workers

Furniture manufacturing was another industry that relied on "unskilled" Mexican labor to bolster its growth in Los Angeles. By the onset of the Great Depression, most Mexican workers remained unorganized, as the AFL craft unions excluded Mexican and unskilled labor, and as the bosses' open-shop movement resisted all attempts for the union movement to advance. The organizing efforts of the AFL's craft union in furniture manufacturing, the Upholsterer's International Union (UIU), focused on the "skilled" white upholsterers and seamstresses, but otherwise excluded the various "unskilled" subdivided tasks within the same industry, including many secondary and supporting positions filled by Mexican workers.

The expansion of industry in LA in the twenties created more opportunities for white workers, who shifted to higher-paying industries. In response, furniture manufacturers turned to the growing population of Mexican workers in the city, who comprised an estimated 13 percent of the furniture workforce by 1928, primarily in the racially segregated roles of "helpers" and finishers in the different subcategories of production.[61] Over time, an increasing number of Mexican workers were being trained for skilled positions, while being paid as helpers. As Luis Arroyo describes:

> Hired as helpers, the employers nevertheless encouraged the Mexicans to learn and perform skilled labor. Soon many Mexicans were performing mechanic's work, while paid helper's wages. The employers profited from this situation, while the skilled white workers found their demands for higher wages dampened, and their jobs endangered by a growing pool of Mexicans who were mechanics in every aspect, except name and remuneration.[62]

The AFL craft union leadership hewed to the position that the "unskilled" Mexican presented a threat that must be contained, which was aided on the shop floor by an influx of Southern white migrants into the industry in the early years of the Depression. They maintained the belief that labor-management cooperative negotiation and white solidarity and mutual interest won greater concession than industrial conflict. The Communists and the workers they influenced called for industrial organization and equal pay for equal work, agitating against the employers' ability to exploit the racial tension.

Communists active in the union attempted to change the course of the AFL to include Mexican and unskilled workers in its ranks. Through the 1920s, the Communist Party's Trade Union Educational League approach of "boring from within" saw Communist workers form caucuses and win leadership positions across the country, including within the Los Angeles–based AFL UIU Local 15. Their strategy of pushing for all-inclusive industrial unionism to organize all workers within a factory, regardless of race, proved unsuccessful due to internal resistance. At the height of the party's Third Period in 1931, Communists and their allies broke away to form a dual union through the aegis of the Trade Union Unity League. Efforts to launch a national union saw activity in all the major production zones, from Boston to Los Angeles. By 1934, the CP-led, TUUL-aligned Furniture Workers' Industrial Union claimed ten thousand members nationwide, including a chapter in Los Angeles.[63]

Former members of the UIU established the Furniture Workers' Industrial Union in 1931 as an industrial alternative to the racially exclusive, fragmented, and sclerotic craft unions. This led to the creation of FWIU Local 10 in Los Angeles in 1933, claiming more than three hundred members by the end of the year.[64] In contrast to the AFL, FWIU leaders attempted to found the local on a more democratic and inclusive basis, declaring in its charter the pledge "to unite all workers in the furniture industry irrespective of craft, skill, color, nationality, age, sex, religion, or political affiliation into an industrial union."[65] The Communist Party also gained a significant foothold in UIU 15, forming a unified caucus linking the two unions in advance of increased labor militancy in 1934 after the first phase of recovery from the Depression. Lastly, left-wing Socialists interested in an industrial furniture workers' union independent of the Communists and the AFL leadership formed the Independent Furniture Workers Union Local 1 (IFWU), which claimed 750 members by July of 1934.

The first two years of the Depression devastated the furniture industry, with an estimated one- to two-thirds of all manufacturers going out of business and wages dropping by over 60 percent.[66] By 1933, there was recovery in the industry, with 126 firms in Los Angeles generating $10.2 million in revenue. By 1934, there was confidence among the workers to reclaim their lost wages through union recognition. One of the first efforts was led by the FWIU against wage cuts.

The strike began after the Sterling Furniture Company tried to cut wages in two of its subdepartments. The cuts of 30 percent for the fabric workers and 15 percent for the spring installers disproportionately affected Mexican workers, reflecting the racial segmentation and unequal pay corresponding to associated "skill" levels. The fifty-one registered members of the FWIU led over a hundred workers from the different departments to down their tools after the owner, Harry Hartstein, refused to rescind the cuts. When the owner saw the white upholsterers join with the Mexican workers, he chided them, saying: "What are you fellows fighting for those Mexican and unskilled workers for? We're not bothering your wages." According to the *Western Worker*, the white FWIU committeemen responded that "their conditions are our conditions, and we'll all fight together against any cut."[67] The wage cuts were rescinded and the union added twelve new members to their ranks.

After the growth of IFWU 1, the socialist leadership of John Murray, Al Walker, George Walker, Ernest Marsh, and Frank López (the latter two members of the Communist Party) led their first attempted strike of 250 furniture workers in August of 1934. The strike came in response to threatened wage cuts by the large and politically dominant Gillespie Furniture Company. While the strike was called off after a couple of weeks, it wasn't fully defeated despite the small size, limited resources, and police repression of pickets. Ten firms agreed to arbitration and ultimately reemployed all of the strikers without retaliation. The ability of the fledgling industrial union to stand up to the largest company signified a new mood of confidence and the appeal of industrial unionism. IFWU was eventually brought into the AFL's Carpenter's Union Local 1561 as an industrial affiliate. Independent industrial unions like IFWU, led by socialists and other radicals, began to spring up in other California and West Coast cities where socialists had a presence, and affiliate in a similar manner.

On October 8, 1934, upholsterers in five locals spread along the West Coast (San Francisco, Seattle, Portland, Tacoma, and Los Angeles) walked out over the protests of their regional leadership. The Communist-led, coastwide strike involved over 3,000 workers, including 1,500 in Los Angeles, and shut down 35 furniture factories. The workers demanded union recognition, a $1 minimum wage, and the 35-hour week. The strike lasted over three weeks until October 28, despite police arrests and beatings of picketers, and the targeted detention of known Communist leaders by the notorious Red Squad. The repression of the Communists allowed the AFL leadership to regain control, demobilize the strike, and accept only modest gains in wages and without union recognition. One result of the strike was the increased influence of the Communists, which paved the way for a merger when the party shifted its orientation to the Popular Front. After a second joint strike in September 1935, the two locals amalgamated under the UIU banner with the stipulation that the AFL leadership be retained, and that it operate as an industrial union.

The 1935 Industrywide Furniture Workers' Strike

The continuing recovery of the furniture industry created the conditions for consolidation of the two antagonistic forces moving toward an industrywide showdown. In league with the Merchants and Manufacturing Association, the furniture companies merged into the Furniture Manufacturers' Association and presided over the fourth-largest furniture manufacturing center in the nation. For their part, the different unions put aside their sectional and political differences to coordinate action. In March of 1935, all of the furniture locals held a summit to discuss an industrywide action. They came up with a list of demands, including an industrywide standard of 75 cents for skilled work and 50 cents per hour for unskilled labor, to be presented on behalf of 2,000 workers at more than 60 plants. After a blanket refusal by the Manufacturers' Association, the unions coordinated a full walkout on April 29, 1935.

Like in previous strikes, the employers' associations, directed by the Merchants and Manufacturers' Association, deployed their stratagem to break the strike. Strikebreakers were recruited at the rate of $1.50 an hour, more than two-thirds more than what the strikers had made. The Gillespie Company formed a unified front of ten shops that pledged to give no quarter to the unions, with each putting forth a thousand-dollar bond that would be forfeited in the event that they entered into negotiations. The Chamber of Commerce funded recruitment efforts, while the LAPD and Red Squad herded scabs into the struck factories.

Under the leadership of Frank López, the workers at Local 1561 used innovative techniques to conduct the strike under such adverse conditions. They organized flying picket squads that went from factory to factory, calling out the workers, while also showing the owners their capability to mobilize hundreds at a time to shut down a whole factory. They also developed the strategy to divide manufacturers and retailers by calling on the latter to agree to not purchase furniture made by strikebreakers.

They sent delegations of picketers to retailers who bought from the struck factories throughout Los Angeles and as far away as San Diego and San Francisco. In San Francisco, for instance, the delegation targeted fifty-nine retail outlets. Fearing the loss of profit from the newly recovering markets, most retailers signed on to the boycott or faced disruptive pickets.

Over the course of eight months, the workers reached agreements with nineteen companies. Ten companies signed closed-shop agreements and nine agreed to pay union-scale wages.[68] The remaining Gillespie-aligned shops held firm, especially emboldened by the Supreme Court's abrogation of the National Industrial Recovery Act in 1935, including the provision on industry wage standards. To continue the fight, Local 1561 called off the strike at those locations, instead expanding the secondary boycott movement to other unions through the Central Labor Council in 1936. While the AFL leadership balked at such a radical and disruptive tactic, other AFL affiliates, especially those aligned with the Committee of Industrial Organizations, supported the effort. The period of 1936 was a high point of industrial class struggle in Los Angeles, and different industrial unions began to follow the lead of the furniture workers in carrying out secondary boycotts as part of strike strategy.

In April of 1936, one year into the strike, more than forty union leaders met at Local 1561 to pledge support for a union-led, citywide boycott of all retailers that continued to sell scab furniture. The boycott also served as a vehicle to organize the different groups of workers affiliated with the retailers that sided with the furniture manufacturers, from truck drivers to garment workers. In a show of force, pickets of up to a thousand-strong were organized in front of retailers across the city over the course of the next two months. By June, sixty retailers capitulated and signed on to the boycott, with one company conceding union affiliation for its drivers and clerks.[69] By August, the number of closed-shop agreements increased to fourteen with large firms and twenty-six with small workshops. The remaining anti-union factories and some that moved back into the fold had dug in and reconstituted as a new front named the Furniture Manufacturers Open Shop League.

Over twelve hundred furniture workers were now covered by union contracts and received union-scale wages. Because the workforce included Mexicans, the union was sure to stipulate in the contracts that all workers were to be paid the same wage, regardless of race. The new union wage threshold even surpassed the old NRA wage codes the manufacturers so vehemently opposed. The militant movement led to the toppling of the old craft leadership in favor of one oriented toward industrial unionism. The Communists, socialists, and other pro-industrial unionists within the UIU Local 15 and Carpenter's Union Local 1561 then lead majorities of their respective local memberships into a new furniture workers' industrial union in the CIO, which was constituted in early 1938 as the United Furniture Workers of America Local 576.[70] Demonstrating the leading role of the Carpenters' Union Local 1561 in the furniture workers' movement, about half of the membership and three of the ten elected leaders were Mexican.

Jack Estrada, Julius Dávila, and Communist Party member Frank López sat on the board of officers for the new union. Shortly thereafter, a Mexican unionist named

Manuel García Jiménez became president of the local. While the AFL leadership declared war on the fledgling union from its inception, the UFWA-CIO became the dominant union among furniture workers by 1940. What's more, the UFWA worked to equalize pay and benefits on a national scale, overcoming racial and regional segmentation. By 1944, for instance, the UFWA had established an industrywide, employer-financed health insurance and life insurance plan, three-fourths of UFWA contracts contained closed-shop provisions, over half had gained paid vacation, and many contained paid holidays.

The organizing drives and strikes of the Mexican garment, furniture, and cannery workers fit into the larger mosaic of class struggle in Los Angeles that defeated the seemingly invincible open-shop movement. The rise of the Mexican working class also shifted politics locally, as they filed into the breakaway industrial union movement of the CIO by the thousands. The efforts of the Communist Party to organize and recruit Mexican militants into its ranks, and by extension into leading roles of the CIO, helped push the political arena to the left as the CIO became a vehicle for conducting the first mass fight against Jim Crow racism alongside the struggle for better working conditions. Mexican workers also brought new and innovative techniques into the local strike movement, including the use of the secondary boycott, mass community mobilization in support of strikes, and the inclusion of political demands for civil rights into bargaining agreements. By 1939, the nails were hammered into the coffin of the "open-shop league" as 50 percent of the Los Angeles workforce was unionized and wages rose higher than the national average.[71] By 1944, the number of manufacturing workers doubled in the city. What's more, the period of struggle produced an organic Mexican working-class leadership that set in motion the first stage of mass struggle for civil rights.

Chapter 32
Radicals Build the CIO in the Barrios

"Onward fellow workers
Let's fight like lions
don't make any excuses and join the Union."
—**From the union song "La Escuela de Betabeleros,"**
honoring Luisa Moreno, Communist and CIO leader

The Communist Party worked through its shop and community units to make antiracism a focal point of its work in places like Los Angeles. A goal of their recruitment efforts was to identify the most militant workers and bring them into leadership, as well as to identify and recruit "mass leaders." The latter referred to the natural and organic leadership already situated in relation to the rest of the class in each locale that "clearly expressed the sentiments of a growing section of the working class."[1] Through building the CIO and party organizations in the barrios of Los Angeles, the Communists came into contact with and recruited some of these militant workers and mass leaders, who were able to further operate from their vantage points. Having shared culture, language, historical experiences, and traditions, these individuals began to aggregate within party and CIO structures, and created the basis for independent action derived from the guiding principles.

While working within the meandering and often erratic shifts of the party and internal tensions of the CIO, these working-class leaders carved out their own history. Occurring simultaneously in other parts of the Southwest, they set into motion the first mass struggles for civil rights for Mexicans. Through the organization of class power through antiracist industrial unionism, they fused civil and labor rights organizing through the mobilization of class struggle to win contracts that guaranteed equality for all workers within a factory or shop. In doing so, they achieved the first great victories against the anti-Mexican variant of Jim Crow in California and framed the battles of the larger civil rights era to follow.

Communists in the CIO leadership not only pushed local affiliates to organize Mexican workers into their respective locals, but also to cultivate a Mexican leadership. Party members in the shop units and street units also followed suit. Inter-Union Council president Philip Connelly, for instance, ordered affiliated unions to increase membership among the cities' black and Mexican working classes within the respective industries in which they were concentrated. To achieve this for the Mexican workforce, the council and the locals allocated more funding to hire Mexican, Spanish-speaking organizers, often directly from the ranks of the workforce being organized.

528

They also produced union and party literature in Spanish, recognizing the need to communicate directly in the language of the people. This form of affirmative action was further buttressed by other Communist officers and rank-and-file members in the locals who provided political and moral support.[2] As part of organizing campaigns, the CP-led IUC also directed the affiliated unions to organize protests against employers who openly discriminated against black and Mexican workers.[3] The approach was to use protest action as a tool to politicize union drives and cultivate community support and participation, pioneering the concept of social justice unionism.

The Communist Party also made efforts to implant organizational activity in the barrios. They produced literature in Spanish and cultivated Spanish-speaking members and leaders. Through the newspaper *Western Worker*, the California party announced the launch of the Spanish-language *Lucha Obrera*. To build support for the press, and to raise awareness and support for "Spanish and Cuban revolutionary workers," a Chicano Communist named Pete Garcia conducted a statewide tour of Mexican barrio communities. The tour passed through at least nineteen cities over the first few months of that year to raise funds and build support for the new paper.[4] Party members spent countless hours selling the paper, giving speeches, and agitating in Placita Olvera, the traditional gathering spot for Mexican working-class families in East Los Angeles. Party-led or affiliated organizations like the International Workers Order, the Workers Alliance, and CIO union representatives also set up shop and conducted their work in similar avenues.[5]

One major inroad into the barrio was the work on unemployment relief, for unemployed Mexican Americans as well as for Mexican migrant workers. The story of Jesús Cruz captures how some Mexican workers entered into the orbit of the party. Jesús Cruz came from the Mexican state of Guanajuato, where he migrated to work on the railroads, eventually settling in Los Angeles. After being laid off during the Depression, he found work in the orange groves, where Communists in the CAWIU were attempting to organize the pickers. After joining the picket lines, the growers called in the LAPD Red Squad to break up the pickets and arrest the leaders. Cruz was beaten so badly by the police that it "made a Communist out of him."[6] After joining the party, he was later tasked with organizing a branch of the Workers Alliance in his barrio, where he helped organize sit-ins at the WPA office, rent strikes, and eviction defense campaigns.

During the Popular Front period, the party and its affiliates also pursued electoral goals through their contacts in the barrios. This is reflected in how the CP/CIO organized Mexican voters to support Culbert Olson, who had included a "Spanish-American" outreach division as part of the campaign. Olson's recognition of the significance of the Mexican community's support went back to the campaign of Socialist Upton Sinclair in 1934, whose campaign paid local Democratic Party broker Eduardo Quevedo, a later participant in the CP-led El Congreso, five dollars for each speech he gave to audiences on behalf of his campaign in the barrios of Los Angeles.[7]

By 1938, the party recruited a layer of working-class militants that became a conduit for mass recruitment of Mexican workers into CIO unions. Whether actual party members or not, these militants were influenced by previous experience with party-affiliated organizations, attracted to the party's perspectives toward antiracism, and inspired by the ability to wield and mobilize class power through the CIO to achieve their aims. According to historian Luis Arroyo, a discernable cadre began to coalesce around specific actions to fight for the civil rights of Mexican workers alongside economic demands. One of the first independent actions of this group was to form a "Committee to Aid Mexican Workers," which included:

> Bert Corona, president of Warehouse Local 1-26, was the chairman of the committee whose members included: Albert Rentería; William Taylor [a Chicano born in Arizona]; Frank Gómez and William Trujillo of Warehouse Local 1-26; Carmen Castro, Frank López and Luisa Moreno of UCAPAWA; business agent Armando Dávila and Eddie Valles of UFWA Local 576; Robert Rivas and Marshall Lechuga of United Steelworkers of America (USA) Local 2172; Jess Armenta of the Transport Workers' Union; and Rosendo Rivera of the Electrical Workers who was also president of the Spanish-Speaking People's Congress. All were members of the Congress.[8]

These and other individuals formed the core of an organic radical Mexican working-class leadership that carried the fight for civil rights into the shops, factories, docks, fields, and barrios.

Bert Corona and the ILWU

Bert Corona was one of the pioneering Mexican radicals of Los Angles, whose family history represents his orientation to Communist Party–led class struggle in the barrios. His father was a PLM member in Chihuahua, part of the Junta Revolucionaria Mexicana headed by Abrán González. His family later left the region and settled in El Paso, Texas. Corona embodied features of the second-generation Mexicans raised in the United States with parents with direct connections to the Mexican Revolution, especially with Magonismo. He was raised in an environment where family members and friends regularly discussed radical ideas and analyzed and debated world events. He learned about notions of class struggle, racial oppression, US imperialism, and the idea of *transfronterismo*—the right for people to cross borders.

He was raised to be proud of his culture and to assert his identity as a means to resist racism. As he explained his outlook, "We felt even more American because of our Indian heritage, in contrast to the Anglos, who were Europeans—and relative newcomers, at that."[9] Throughout his life, Corona contended that "America" referred to the whole continent and its inhabitants, not just Anglos. This framed his ideas about immigration, which coincided with the transnationalism of the magonista movement, the antiracist theoretical formulations of the Communist Party, and the notion that citizenship and the border under capitalism served only to divide and control the working class. He was especially influenced by Emma Tenayuca's observations in "The Mexican Question." Unlike the conservative, accommodationist politics of middle-class Mexican organizations like LULAC, which called on Mexicans to assimilate and distinguish themselves from immigrants in order to be accepted by whites, he embraced her assertion that "the Spanish-speaking people of the Southwest, both the American-born and the foreign-born, are one people."[10]

In his high school years during the Depression in El Paso, Corona was politicized by increased inequality, especially as it impacted Mexican youth. He helped organize protests against racist school officials. From his early activist days, Corona was drawn into a radical study circle which included in-depth discussions of socialism (including works by writers such as Upton Sinclair, Lincoln Steffens, and others), the Russian Revolution, and the origins of fascism.[11]

His political trajectory led him to join the Sociedad Anarcho-Sindicalista, a small grouping of local supporters seeking to continue the legacy of the PLM and Ricardo Flores Magón. Corona later moved to Los Angeles to attend college at the University of Southern California.[12] Through his interaction with radical students, likely including members of the youth wing of the Communist Party, Corona was again drawn into left-wing political circles on campus. Through these campus networks, Corona learned of the efforts of the International Longshoreman's Association (ILA; which joined the CIO as the International Longshore and Warehouse Union in 1937) and its efforts to organize the unorganized. In 1937, while working as a stocker in a drug warehouse, he joined the ILA as a volunteer officer and attempted to organize his workplace.

Known as the "March Inland," the ILA embarked on a bold campaign to organize all secondary industries affiliated with maritime commerce, spanning from the ports to the interstate highways. Between 1934 and 1937, the ILA organized the longshoremen, and then moved on to organize 400 warehouses covering the majority of the 8,500 workers in the Bay Area.[13] Between 1934 and 1936, the ILA engaged in 353 "quickie" strikes to enforce contract rules and 117 sympathy strikes in support of the unionization of warehouse workers. They had to overcome intensive opposition from the Industrial Association Committee, an alliance of the Chamber of Commerce, ship-owners, warehouse owners, manufacturers, growers, and various other industrialists with a stake in the fight. They were joined by AFL unions, especially the Teamsters, who asserted a jurisdictional right against the ILA, and then blanket opposition when the ILA left the AFL and joined the CIO. Despite coordinated efforts, including the selective firing of union sympathizers and organizers, the deployment of Pinkerton Security guards, the use of labor spies, and the deployment of Teamsters to break ILWU pickets, the ILA-ILWU prevailed.

ILA-ILWU president Harry Bridges envisioned the incorporation of all unions linked to port-based commerce as a "Maritime Federation" that would function as one single industrial union. Party militants in the union pushed to include canning and agricultural workers in the federation, incorporating the large agricultural sector that relied on long-range distribution across the nation and overseas. The great agricultural strikes led by Communist Party organizers also inspired the militant longshoremen to see them as natural allies. As the ILWU's *Waterfront Worker* newspaper commented about the San Joaquin Valley cotton strike,

> This the money powers of California do not want to see, nor will they permit it without a terrific fight—UNITY between the agricultural workers and the maritime workers the two chief industries of California. Didn't the vigilante hordes

just railroad eight innocent, but courageous workers to jail because they dared
organize and lead the agricultural workers in some of the most bitterest [sic]
fought strike struggles that ever swept the State?[14]

Unemployed or itinerant agricultural workers who gathered in cities in the off-season,
for instance, were often recruited as strikebreakers.[15] If they were unionized at the
point of production, it was reasoned, they would have more job security and be less
likely to scab.

The effort grew out of the 1934 longshoremen-led general strike, in which the
ILA handily forged a broad coalition of nearly thirty-five thousand maritime workers
to bring all commerce through the city of San Francisco to a virtual halt. One of the
key lessons of the strike for the leadership was the necessity to expand the union horizontally into all affiliated industries to prevent the divide-and-conquer tactics of the
employers, especially using non-union labor as strikebreakers. In the previous wave
of longshore strikes in 1916 and 1919, the port owners used the racial exclusions of the
AFL against them, consciously hiring black and Mexican workers as strikebreakers.
To carry out the painstaking tasks of tenacious union-building from the ground up,
Bridges and the ILWU leadership promoted Communist organizers.

The role of Communists in the efforts was critical, as they brought their antiracist focus into the forefront of the union drive. Unlike their AFL counterparts, which
maintained racial exclusions within their various trades associations, the ILA forbade
discrimination in their hiring halls. The ILWU's *Waterfront Worker* featured regular
commentary opposing Jim Crow racism and emphasizing examples of interracial
unity. One 1935 issue, for instance, featured the condemnation of a state execution
of a nineteen-year-old black man named Rush Griffin, falsely accused of murder and
hanged. As the author reported,

> The framing of innocent men will continue, and the hanging of innocent Negroes
> will go on and on UNTIL WE THE WORKING CLASS STOP IT! There is no
> justice in the courts for the workers, the courts are the machinery used by the
> ruling class to suppress, stifle and railroad innocent but militant workers to jail . . .
> we must smash the class character of the capitalist courts. This can be done by all
> workers organizing and fighting together . . . regardless of race or color.[16]

This was followed by a story covering a strike of relief workers in Dallas, where "Negro,
Mexican and white workers stood shoulder to shoulder."[17] The *Waterfront Worker* and
the *Voice of the Federation* (the official publication of the ILWU-led Maritime Federation of the Pacific), devoted significant space to educating white workers on issues
of race and racism. CIO delegates at the 1943 convention went so far as to pledge to
drive known racists from their ranks, expelling them from the union and banishing
them from the hiring hall. As one delegate at the convention declared, "If any union
member thinks Negroes and Mexicans shouldn't live in the house next door to him . . .
the union has failed."[18] At the end of the war, the CIO condemned a rash of violence
against Japanese Americans after their return from the concentration camps and called
for full naturalization of Filipinos and for the Chinese Exclusion Act to be rescinded.[19]

The approach was grounded in the Communist notion that worker solidarity broadened the chances of union victory and strike success, and that by incorporating all workers into one industrial union the employers would be unable to use excluded groups as anti-union bulwarks and strikebreakers. For this reason, the ILA employed African American and Mexican organizers to launch efforts into the racially segmented warehouse districts, and among the separate clusters of ship-builders, cooks, firemen, fishermen, boilermakers, machinists, and other waterfront workers along the major West Coast port cities from Seattle to San Pedro. The union also aimed to expand its influence internationally.

A strong sense of internationalism led Harry Bridges and the ILA leadership (including Bert Corona) to establish formal contacts with the CTM in Mexico. Cooperation between ILU/ILWU and CTM-affiliated dockworkers eventually led to the establishment of a short-lived Pan-American Maritime Workers Federation, uniting the Maritime Committee of the CIO, the CTM, a Cuban federation, and the National Maritime Union (NMU), an East Coast union with significant Communist membership and a 25 percent Mexican/Latino workforce.[20] During strikes, both groups of dockworkers refused to unload scab ships.[21] The ILWU then publicly supported the nationalization of Mexican oil in 1938, providing crucial solidarity at a time when US oil companies were pushing for US intervention. The dockworkers of the ILA (which became the ILWU after affiliating with the CIO in 1937) brought their internationalist values into the formation of the California State CIO, which the ILWU launched in 1938 with Harry Bridges as the first director. The ascension of a left-wing leadership, staffed with numerous Communist militants throughout the organization, then kicked off the ILWU's ambitious March Inland.

As part of the March Inland in Los Angeles, the ILWU recruited Mexican organizers to expand into the warehouses in the Mexican barrio, where a Communist organizer with the ILWU named Lloyd Seeliger met Bert Corona and took him under his wing. During his participation with the ILWU, Corona was immersed in the political world of the Communist Party and its various front groups, which intersected with the CIO, the New Deal wing of the Democratic Party, and the CTM and *cardenista* government in Mexico. Integration into these circles was transformative for Corona, who saw the potential for wielding these resources to organize within the barrios of LA. As he later reflected on this period:

> I was further attracted to socialist ideas because of my sense that socialism could solve many of the problems created by capitalism. The Communist Party always stressed the example of the Soviet Union and the significant progress there since the Bolshevik Revolution. Closer to home, we had the example of the cardenistas in Mexico, where President Lázaro Cárdenas in the 1930s had brought about agrarian reform under a quasi-socialist system and had nationalized the oil industry.[22]

Corona became a full-time organizer with the CIO in Los Angeles. Along with others, he began to organize Mexican workers in waste-material removal, shoe industry, war industries, transportation, smelting, construction, and in electrical plants. All together twenty-six separate union contracts were signed under his tenure as ILWU/CIO organizer, which included nondiscrimination clauses. Corona was instrumental in marshaling the efforts of the CIO into the Mexican barrios, understanding the potential of a long-neglected segment of the working class. His own political background and understanding of the Mexican working-class traditions led him to break through the residual racial attitude within labor that perceived Mexicans as passive or incapable of being organized. He also understood the cultural dimensions of the Mexican working-class traditions, utilizing the existing communal and familial networks as levers to mobilize the class struggle.

Corona came up with the strategy of recruiting Chicano youth to join the picket lines when organizing CIO unions in the barrios. Youth clubs, sometimes operating as self-defense gangs against rival groups, racial violence, and police repression, formed throughout the barrios on a community-by-community basis. These youth, commonly racially profiled and targeted by police, were the sons and daughters of the Mexican industrial working class, and sometimes took on jobs in the same workplaces. The CIO held community dances to bring out the youth and use the opportunity to discuss how they could support their parents and neighbors in their efforts to unionize. As Corona explains:

> The gangs agreed to assist us, and large numbers of their members came out to picket the plants . . . A real alliance was formed, and youths proved invaluable because of their courage and commitment. Some of them actually had jobs in these industries and participated in the strikes. We developed an official relationship with some of the gangs.[23]

The hands-on efforts of Corona in building the CIO in the barrios of East Los Angeles led him to come into direct contact with the many facets of racial discrimination faced by Mexican workers on the job and by extension in the community. Instead of unionization being the antidote to racial discrimination, Corona understood that racism itself created the practical barriers to unionization. In realizing this, he began to identify the need for more concerted action directly against the configurations of Jim Crow. In reaching these conclusions, he found a strong ally and co-thinker in Luisa Moreno.

With the support of CIO director Harry Bridges and Vice President Luisa Moreno, Bert Corona launched the Committee to Aid Mexican Workers (CAMW) in 1939 as a working group within ILWU Local 26. The goal of the CAMW was to attend to the specific needs of Mexican workers as part of integrating them into CIO-affiliated unions. The focus included the abolition of the dual-wage system (the "Mexican wage" and gender-based differentials) by guaranteeing equal pay for equal work clauses in contracts for both men and women workers. They also included anti-discrimination clauses in hiring and promotion, ending the customary exclusion of Mexican workers from "skilled" positions and war industries, and opposing the many acculturated forms of discrimination against Mexicans in society.[24] The CAMW regularly organized mass protests involving the community as part of their strikes and contract negotiations.

In 1941, Bert Corona was elected president of ILWU 26. Under Corona's leadership, the local took action against housing discrimination as part of their community-based organizing drives. Mexicans were segregated into barrios, where neglect by the city government and private investment fueled structural and economic underdevelopment, and cramped and unsanitary living conditions. They set up pickets in front of the Los Angeles Housing Authority to demand more housing and inclusion of noncitizens in war housing projects designated for veterans.[25] As a result of their tenant organizing, housing projects were opened up to Mexican families across the city.[26] By forging a relationship with the community through the advocacy of the CAMW, the ILWU took on the role as representative of the interests of the whole class, expanding the scope of its work. The success of the committee's work led the LA-CIO leadership to expand the model.

The CAMW was expanded in 1941, becoming a standing committee of the Los Angeles Inter-Union Council working through all affiliated unions, with Bert Corona still at the helm. The committee worked with CIO unions to produce bulletins and other relevant documents in Spanish, and to conduct meetings in Spanish or bilingually where Mexican workers were the majority. The committee also arranged a staff of lawyers to provide their services to help members attain citizenship or to defend them if they were victimized by employers because of their status.[27] When the war drive induced the proliferation of government contracts with defense contractors in Los Angeles, the CAMW advocated for the placement of Mexican workers in those industries in compliance with Executive Order 8802, which forbade discrimination in the war industries in 1941. The committee also responded to urgent issues as they arose. By 1942, the new focus was opposing a campaign of criminalization of Mexican youth by the police, media, and city officials.

During a citywide campaign of persecution of working-class Mexican youth spearheaded by the police and local media during the repression of the "Zoot-Suiters" and the "Sleepy Lagoon" trials, Mexican warehouse workers circulated petitions through the barrios calling for an increase in funding for recreational facilities for barrio youth to counter the chorus of racist criminalization. The effectiveness of the CAMW to bring to public attention the grievances of the Mexican community and mobilize resources to conduct campaigns in the workplace and in the community led it to be expanded through the LA-CIO Inter-Union Council to provide organizing and strike support for Mexican workers on a regional basis. The committee supported agricultural strikes in Orange, Riverside, Ventura, and San Joaquin Counties; miner strikes in Arizona, and railroad track-workers throughout the region. While Bert Corona and the ILWU were blazing a path from the docks and warehouses of Los Angeles, Luisa Moreno was leading a similar whirlwind effort through the canneries across California.

Luisa Moreno

Luisa Moreno was born Blanca Rosa Rodríguez López in 1907 into an elite landowning family in Guatemala. Due to a radical transformation at a young age, she later changed her name as part of her rejection of her bourgeois background and entrance into the working class. In various interviews, Luisa Moreno identified the key markers of experience that nurtured her incipient radicalism. At the age of eight, she was sent to a Convent of the Holy Names in Oakland where she encountered her first taste of the inequality and racism that she later devoted her life to fighting. Her white classmates degraded her mestiza background and the nuns hoarded food while the children lacked nutrition. After finishing and subsequently rejecting her religious schooling, she returned to Guatemala to continue her educa-

Luisa Moreno, ca. 1940.

tion. After completing secondary school, she was denied entrance into the university, even with her privileged background. This led her to start a proto-feminist club, La Sociedad Gabriela Mistral, dedicated to agitating for universal education for women. Their efforts led to the first openings for elite women to attend university, an opportunity she helped create but never realized as she began to undergo a politicization that led her to flee her family.

Increasingly sickened and constrained by the insulated and racialized class privilege and pomp that surrounded her, she absconded to Mexico City in search of something different. There, at the age of nineteen, she became a journalist and writer and fell in with the artist community. She met and soon married an artist and Guatemalan expatriate named Miguel Angel de León, who brought her into radical Left cultural circles that included people like Frida Kahlo and Diego Rivera. It was here that the future lifelong radical labor leader came into contact with Marxist ideas and the Mexican Communist Party. In 1928 at the age of twenty-three, she left with her husband to resettle in New York City and the couple found themselves in destitution and with child in tenement housing in Spanish Harlem by the Wall Street crash. To support her child and unemployed artist husband, Moreno entered into the ranks of the working class as a seamstress alongside other Latinas in the garment district.

She became a seamstress in New York City, where she met Puerto Rican socialists in the factories. By 1930, an estimated 45,000 Puerto Ricans lived in New York City; many came after the restrictive Immigration Act of 1924 closed the door to labor migration from Europe. US business interests then turned to Mexicans on the West Coast and Puerto Ricans on the East Coast. Another transfer occurred during the Depression, which hit the island nation's garment industry particularly hard, which functioned as an outsource of production for US markets. The disproportionate effects on the weakened economy produced more labor displacement, including from among the nation's 70,000 seamstresses, who then migrated to New York to find work in the garment production center.[28]

Working in the garment district of New York City, Moreno came into direct contact with the lives of working-class Latinas. Accustomed to comfort, she underwent a radical transformation in living and working conditions, which also induced an attendant political radicalization. She was appalled by the horrid living conditions in the workers' tenements, which were not maintained and were crowded and rat-infested.[29] This triggered her first attempt in the US to apply her organizing experience to help unionize her co-workers. She joined a leftist workers-rights collective called the Centro Obrero de Habla Española and with support tried to launch an independent union called Liga de Costureras. The liga then affiliated with the Communist Party's TUUL-aligned Needle Trade Workers Industrial Union, and later the ILGWU when the TUUL disbanded.

Through these efforts, she came into contact and worked with Puerto Rican women who were affiliated with the Puerto Rican Socialist Party. Some Socialist Party leaders in New York had either become members of the Communist Party, established working relationships, or joined their efforts.[30] The interethnic unity and antiracist actions of the party also inspired Moreno. New York branches of the Communist Party, for example, led by a Mexican party member named Gonzalo Gónzales, organized a protest and picket line in front of a theater showing the Hollywood film *Under a Texas Moon*, which depicted Mexicans, using racist stereotypes, as simple-minded and violent. Pickets were regularly attended by Latinos, African Americans, Anglo, and European immigrant party members. Party gatherings were regularly attacked by police, and party members defended each other and fought back collectively.[31]

After the beating death of an African American Communist named Alfred "Levy" Luro at the hands of the police, a contingent of thirty Latino/a party members led by Gonzalo Gónzales led a protest march through the Spanish-speaking section of Harlem with signs and banners in Spanish calling for justice for their slain comrade. The march was cut short when police attempted to suppress it, shooting the unarmed Gónzales down in the street and arresting five other Latino workers.[32] In protest of the police killings, the party led over 2,500 through the streets of Harlem in an angry march. As one speaker declared:

> The murder of the Communist Gónzales three days after the beating death of the young Negro Alfred Luro, at the hands of police, constitutes the consistent policy of bloody brutality followed by the United States Government and city officials throughout the country in a new wave of historical Red hunting, suppression and persecution against all working-class expression.[33]

The acts of antiracist solidarity and unity inspired Luisa Moreno to join the Communist Party and dedicate herself to organizing Latino workers as part of a

multiracial fight for economic and social justice. After organizing La Liga and sep-
arating from her husband, she was hired to became a full-time organizer for the IL-
GWU to start other locals. When that work led her away from organizing Latina/o
workers, whom, she believed, evinced little interest from the ILGWU leadership,
she moved on to other possibilities to continue her pursuits. She first joined the
AFL and then the CIO, tirelessly organizing agricultural workers across the country.
While she left the Communist Party in 1935, she did not discard Communist politics.
She immersed herself into a lifelong commitment to organizing Latino workers as
part of the great struggle. Signifying the final rupture with her bourgeois past, she
began referring to herself as Luisa Moreno. With the *Moreno* (dark) negating the
Blanca (white) in her birth-name, it was an act of solidarity with the class of people
with whom she now identified.

  She was hired to organize Latino, African American, and Italian cigar workers in
plants at Ybor City, Lakeland, and Jacksonville, Florida, producing a union and contract covering thirteen thousand workers.[34] She also organized sugarcane workers in
Louisiana, cotton pickers and pecan shellers in Texas, and sugar beet workers in Colorado. Along the way, she gained valuable insights into the nature of the class struggle
specific to the experience of Latinas and Latinos. She became aware of and criticized
the AFL's superficial interest in Mexican and Latino workers and their willingness to
sell them out if it served their interests. She experienced racist Klan violence, and how
it served as a violent and divisive extension of anti-unionism that occasionally worked
hand in glove with employers. She also learned the significance of mutualistas and
other forms of worker self-organization, and the role that cultural, kinship, and gender
networks played in building solidarity.[35]

  Through the Communist Party, she met other union organizers, militants, and
theorists committed to organizing the "rural proletariat" along industrial union lines.
This included UCAPWA president Donald Henderson, who saw in Moreno a dynamic and highly skilled organizer capable of bringing together the diverse groups of
workers in California's sprawling food-processing zones into an industrial union. Like
her comrades in the party, she joined the exodus into the CIO once it was expelled
by the AFL, becoming an organizer and then vice president of UCAPAWA, the first
Latina/o to achieve a top leadership position in the AFL and CIO.

  In 1937 Luisa Moreno moved to San Diego to begin her work. With local party
member and union activist Robert Galván, she spearheaded UCAPAWA drives that
led to the formation of Local 64, which covered hundreds of fish cannery workers at
five different regional waterfront factories.[36] She was then brought to Texas to organize Mexican farmworkers in the south of the state and then to San Antonio to support the pecan shellers. As Vicki Ruiz explains of Moreno's contribution to the effort,
she helped to "move the UCAPAWA affiliate from street demonstrations to a functioning trade union . . . Moreno organized the strikers into a united, disciplined force
that employers could no longer ignore."[37] While there was alleged friction between
Luisa Moreno and Emma Tenayuca over the question of strategy and leadership, the
two shared similar ideas, analyses, and goals toward the Mexican/Latino working

class, and the cross-fertilizations of experience and thought contributed to the later formation of the first mass movement for Mexican/Latino civil rights in the form of El Congreso del Pueblo de Habla Española.

Living in the US-Mexico border region, Luisa Moreno began to understand and see the effects of anti-Mexican and anti-immigrant racism, and understand both its political and cultural consequences. The Ku Klux Klan, for instance, conducted armed patrols in the desert regions east of San Diego and terrorized and killed Mexican workers moving through the area. Through their downtown UCAPAWA office, she and Galván

> regularly received reports of the horrors faced by those who attempted to cross the treacherous Mojave and Colorado deserts into California. One pregnant woman trying to avoid the Klan's border patrol gave birth under a bush, screaming in pain. A compassionate man struggled to cut the baby's umbilical cord with a pocketknife, but both woman and child died. Some families were abandoned in the desert by their Coyote (smuggler) and left to their own fate. Women caught by the Klan in remote regions were brutally raped and assaulted, while some were murdered, their skeletons discovered in rural areas.[38]

When they later launched a chapter of the civil rights organization El Congreso del Pueblo de Habla Española, which attempted to mobilize public opposition to the anti-Mexican activities of the Klan, the group made an attempt on their lives. UCAPAWA's office was fire-bombed, leading to the death of a Congreso supporter. On another occasion they attempted to wire Galván's car to explode by dynamite. Both the San Diego and Los Angeles police refused to investigate the acts of terrorism. As a result, Congreso supporters began to carry guns.

Luisa Moreno began to see racial violence and cultural oppression as intrinsic features of class domination, deployed to marginalize, isolate, and subjugate the Mexican working class in order to perfect their class exploitation. Anti-immigration campaigns, deportation, and citizenship restrictions were the starting point for understanding the social, cultural, and political persecution of all Mexicans, regardless of birthplace. Their isolation made it more difficult to organize, and their victimization rendered them less confident to resist. Furthermore, the institutionalization and popularization of anti-Mexican racism eroded the potential for interracial unity.

For this reason, she drew the conclusion that Mexican immigrants and Chicano/a workers should organize together within a broader multiracial movement. Challenging the effects of anti-immigrant nationalism, internalized within the Mexican American population, could strengthen the necessary unity within the largest section of the unorganized working class in the Southwest to lay the basis for breaking out of isolation. Furthermore, as she and other Mexican-Latino/a Communists understood, class militancy from these most oppressed sectors could provide the basis for Anglo workers to see them as potential allies, thereby uprooting the AFL prejudice that the Mexicans served the employers as cheap labor and willing strikebreakers.

In ideological terms, Moreno began to fiercely advocate for the rights of immigrants. Through her speeches and pronouncements, she directly challenged the dominant narratives of immigration restriction, which characterized immigrants as a "public charge." Reframing their social contributions in class terms, she stated:

> These people are not aliens. They have contributed their endurance, sacrifices, youth, and labor to the southwest. Indirectly, they have paid more taxes than all the stockholders of California's industrialized agriculture, the sugar beet companies, and the large cotton interests that operate or have operated with the labor of Mexican workers.[39]

She and her co-thinkers opposed all border and immigration restrictions, and advocated for equal access to all rights, services, and privileges as citizens. Since unions were the primary vehicle for advancing class interests as a whole, she advocated for unions to organize immigrants into the same unions as citizens. She also applied Marxist principles to her analysis of cultural oppression. She asserted that the Mexicans and other ethnic and national minorities should have democratic cultural rights. Specifically, for the Mexican working class, this included the right to speak and learn in Spanish, and to have bilingual access in regards to official documents and education.

In practical terms, these concepts became realized through their inclusion in UCAPAWA union contracts and the publication of a Spanish-language bulletin within the union called *Noticias de UCAPAWA* to ensure the full inclusion of Spanish speakers in union affairs. Moreno also took care to nurture a culture of collective democracy and gender equality as central features of her organizing strategy. She understood the significance of the work of others and generalized it. For instance, she was instrumental in supporting Bert Corona in his efforts to organize the Mexican working class in Los Angeles, and led the charge to replicate these feats in other cities and at the state level. Working through the CIO, Luisa Morena tirelessly spearheaded various antiracist struggles, developed and disseminated educational materials in Spanish, launched membership drives in different barrios, and welded together an organizational framework to mobilize the Mexican community behind the CIO and CP-led popular front campaigns.

Luisa Moreno used these guiding principles to inform her work, from UCAPAWA to El Congreso to her position as a vice president of the state CIO. She unified, coordinated, and centralized the concentric networks of collaborators and co-thinkers necessary to orchestrate action on a higher plane. She procured the resources and personnel, and cultivated the political will among others to build the infrastructure that could unite the fight for civil and labor rights, from the Committee to Aid Mexican Workers, to El Congreso, to the Minorities Committee of the state CIO.

Chapter 33
El Congreso del Pueblo de Habla Española (1939–1942)

"The fight against discrimination and deportation, for economic liberty, for equal representation in government, for the building of a better world for our youth—this is our Congress's answer."
-Josefina Fierro, in an interview with the Communist Party newspaper *People's World*

When El Congreso del Pueblo de Habla Española (Congress of Spanish-Speaking Peoples, or El Congreso) organized its inaugural national conference on April 28, 1939, it represented the first coordinated attempt by Mexican and Latino radicals to build a comprehensive and combative fight for labor and civil rights within the nation's barrios. The congreso was the result of a convergence of factors intersecting through the Communist Party's Popular Front. First and foremost, it was the result of the Pan-Latino vision of the Communist and national labor leader Luisa Moreno, who through her tireless efforts as vice president of UCAPAWA cultivated a national network of unionists, intellectuals, prominent liberals, New Deal–aligned políticos, and popular organizations in Mexican and Caribbean working-class barrios. For the Mexican and Central American radicals, El Congreso was the manifestation of the realization that labor organizing could not advance without a parallel effort to mobilize mass opposition to racism and sexism, and for civil rights.

Second, the upsurge in class struggle in both Mexico and in the barrios of the US over the course of the 1930s provided the backdrop for elevating the class struggle from the point of production to all social and political spheres. Third, the election of New Deal Democrat Culbert Olson as governor in 1938 created a sense of opening, as his administration pledged to support efforts against racial segregation in the state. Fourth, the Communist Party's cultivation of a small but significant network of mexicano and Latino working-class leaders could organize and coordinate within and across barrios from Texas to Denver to Los Angeles. This provided the impetus, intellectual and cultural capacity, and skills for the effort. Lastly, the infrastructure and resources of the CIO were essential to realize the effort. Taken together, the aspirants of the congreso envisioned a radical transformation of the "Mexican Question" by fighting for civil rights on the economic, social, and cultural front.

In the year preceding the first conference of El Congreso, Luisa Moreno took a leave of absence and traveled extensively across the country to lay the groundwork for a mass mobilization to the first congress. She used $500 of her own money to organize

El Congreso based on her experience that Mexican workers could not be organized without confronting Jim Crow racism and all of its violent manifestations. As she commonly stated, "You cannot organize workers facing violence and terror." Working through UCAPAWA chapters that had cultivated local relations with labor, community, and progressive religious institutions, she mobilized sentiment, raised funds, and assembled delegations. Support was also solicited from the CTM, with Vicente Lombardo Toledano sending representatives and resources to assist, publicize, and participate in the base-building effort. Through Moreno's tireless efforts, supported by the left-wing leadership of the CIO and developed through a network of mexicano/latino radicals, El Congreso emerged as a potentially powerful civil rights force within the configurations of the Popular Front.

While national in scope, the organizing efforts of the Mexican and Hispano-American Congress (later renamed the Congress of Spanish-Speaking Peoples) radiated from Los Angeles, where at least ten different committees were established in different Mexican barrios. The first regional conference occurred on December 4, 1938 at the Music Art Hall in downtown Los Angeles. Representatives of 158 regional organizations gathered to hear opening speeches by Mexican consul and Cárdenas emissary Victor Pasqueira, Governor-elect Culbert Olson, LA mayor Fletcher Bowen, and others.[1]

Congreso chapters were then built in other parts of California and throughout the Southwest, but they were strongest where the CIO-affiliated unions already had a presence. In California, for instance, the CIO-affiliated United Electrical Workers (UE) played a supporting role in some chapters, such that Rosendo Rivera, an organizer with the UE, was elected president of the statewide congress committee. In Texas and Colorado, the UCAPAWA-organized locals of pecan shellers and beet sugar workers respectively, launched congress committees. Representatives from the International Union of Mine, Mill, and Smelter Workers from New Mexico and Arizona were instrumental in the establishment of El Congreso in those regions. Locals with a presence of CP-led organizations were also vital to the launch of the congress. For instance, committees were formed with the support and input of the Workers Alliance chapters in New Mexico, Colorado, Texas, Arizona, and California.[2]

Beyond the radical and union core, El Congreso drew in liberal organizations such as LULAC, Latino Democratic organizations, mutual aid societies and Mexican patriotic associations, local New Deal políticos, individual Socialists, and sympathetic artists and celebrities who were part of the Hollywood Left. One key player was well-known and connected Mexican liberal Democrat Eduardo Quevedo. Quevedo was an experienced local-level party broker and organizer, a key liaison to the statewide Democratic New Deal Coalition. Anglo, black, and Jewish civic leaders were also present at the event, showing the broad, multiethnic coalition being assembled in the city by the CIO/Popular Front alliance.

While the congreso was constructed as a broad alliance of left and liberal forces, Communist Party ideology, strategy, and tactics remained the dominant current. This included adherence to the party's main positions on both domestic and international questions, an emphasis on disruptive and combative protest tactics, and the centrality of organized labor as the muscle to confront deeply entrenched racism. These emphases found their strongest resonance from within a mexicano Left with historic connections and popular memory linking to the magonista movement. It also brought along sections of the mexicano working class that had experience working with the Communist Party's previous organizing efforts in the TUUL unions (especially the CAWIU), Unemployed Councils, Workers Alliance, International Labor Defense, and the Left-led CIO unions.

The centrality of radical thought came out in the crafting of the platform of El Congreso, which was articulated in the two preliminary gathering of California delegates in Los Angeles. The framework spelled out a comprehensive plan of radical reform that foreshadowed the full scope of the civil rights movement: a nationwide campaign against racial segregation; for full and constitutionally guaranteed workers' rights at the point of production; for the desegregation, expansion, and subsidization of housing; for integration of schools and the incorporation of ethnic studies and bilingualism; for access to government-subsidized health care, unemployment benefits regardless of citizenship status, and the multiracial, multiethnic, and pan-Latin-American unification of workers and the Left into one fully integrated movement.[3]

From its very inception, El Congreso was attacked from all sides. The presence of Communists throughout the leadership, the radical antiracist program espoused (which hewed closely to the analysis laid out in Emma Tenayuca and Homer Brooks's treatise on the "Mexican Question"), and the potential scale of the mobilization behind it threatened the very foundations of Jim-Crow-era capitalism. As such a threat, the bipartisan torchbearers of anti-communism gathering in the architecture of government made it a prime target, beginning in New Mexico. When the First National Congress was scheduled to be held at the University of New Mexico in Albuquerque in March of 1939, the Democratic governor, John Miles, applied pressure on the university administration and supporting professors to have it cancelled. As a result, it was relocated back to Los Angeles a month later, where a more accommodating political environment and supportive population allowed the gathering to proceed.[4]

First National Congress

On April 29, 1939, El Congreso held its first international conference at the New Mexico-Arizona Club in downtown Los Angeles. Over a thousand people filled the hall, including 137 delegates representing 105 registered organizations, which, including CIO unions, represented over half a million people.[5] A survey of the attendees revealed the proletarian base of the Mexican population and the popular character of the event. According to Congress Secretary Josefina Fierro, besides trade unionists, those present at the opening plenary included "migrant workers, teachers, organizers, social workers, housewives, and youth leaders." There was a penetrating sense of solidarity that filled the packed venue. Historian Kenneth Burt captures the diverse range of attendees, the radical civil rights themes, and the electrified urgency of the campaign:

> Refugees . . . from the Mexican Revolution, their [US]-born children, immigrants from Central and South America, and descendants of 17th-century

Spanish settlers. Roughly one thousand women and men had arrived by train, streetcar, and automobile. Colorful banners captured the objectives of El Congreso: "Let Us Form a Committee for the Congress in Each Town," "In Youth is the Future," "We Ask for Justice for the Latin Race," "Citizens and Non-Citizens Unite Our Strength," "In Defense of Our Homes, Let Us Fight Deportations," and "Let's Unite for Progress."[6]

As Fierro noted, "the delegates were united solidly over discrimination, that curse of an unfulfilled democracy which damns the beet-picker of Colorado, the school teacher of New Mexico, the Texas pecan-sheller, and the Los Angeles railway worker alike."[7]

The opening plenary was addressed by Eduardo Quevedo, who read a congratulatory letter from Governor Culbert Olson. Keynote speakers included Lieutenant Governor Ellis Patterson, who opened his address by stating: "I cannot welcome you here, because when my ancestors came here your ancestors were already here to welcome them" and concluded by stating that "we should fight for the ideals of Presidents Cárdenas and Roosevelt."[8] He was followed by a delegation of representatives from the CTM and the Cárdenas administration, led by CTM official Adolfo Uribe de Alva. He spoke of the great advances of the Mexican people since the revolution, reviewing a recent history of class struggle in Mexico and attributing the success to the leadership of Cárdenas and Vicente Lombardo Toledano.

He was followed by Carey McWilliams, an early radical supporter of Mexican civil rights who through his long-standing work as a migrant farmworker advocate and Popular Front affiliation was appointed chief of California's Division of Immigration and Housing. Speakers also included a representative from the Mexican government's Secretary of Relations, who sent greetings and support on behalf of President Lázaro Cárdenas. A range of liberal, Democratic Party–aligned functionaries and politicians who also presented at the first congress included Frederick Oliphant of the Pan-American Fellowship, and member of the Los Angeles City County Board of Supervisors John Anson Ford. Delegations arrived from throughout California, Texas, Colorado, Arizona, New Mexico, and from as far away as the Midwest, Florida, and New York.

For the next two days, conference-goers attended dozens of different workshops, conducted in both Spanish and English, thematically designed to craft a plan of action for the coming year. These covered the subjects of labor and union organizing, relief and immigration, civil rights, health, housing, and women's and youth issues. As historian David Gutiérrez contends, "What was radical about the [Congreso] was not merely that these activists and organizers demanded full civil rights for Mexican American and Mexican immigrant workers but also that they insisted on the recognition and extension of full cultural rights for ethnic Mexican residents as well."[9] The panel workshops were structured as campaign working groups, with established leaders and organizations speaking on their specific areas of expertise with the intention of recruiting more people into their particular area of work.[10]

Over the course of its three years of existence, the Congress of Spanish-Speaking Peoples served as a tribune for the Mexican and Latino communities, hosting regular public forums and town halls to dialogue and mobilize around important issues.

The Congreso then mobilized its base to take direct action as a means to advance the cause of civil rights, with chapters established throughout California. Chapters were also present in Phoenix, Arizona; El Paso, San Antonio; and Brownsville, Texas; and in Florida, New York City, Pittsburgh, and Kansas City. Affiliated organizations and individual supporters spread across other states as well. With a national base, institutional support, and resources, El Congreso inaugurated the largest undertaking in history to smash the anti-Mexican variant of Jim Crow segregation. The forces set in motion by a small core of Mexicano-Latino Communists in 1939 continued as an oppositional force in different forms and expressions over the succeeding two decades. These forces, driven by working-class people from within the barrios, contributed the early victories and suffered from devastating setbacks that informed the next generation of struggle.

Josefina Fierro

Women were at the forefront in the development and leadership of the congress. Their role was primarily facilitated by membership in the left-wing unions of the CIO, especially UCAPAWA. Luisa Moreno enlisted the help of Josefina Fierro, a mexicana and Communist with deep roots in Los Angeles, to manage the day-to-day operations of El Congreso. Furthermore, about 30 percent were women, whose participation and leadership brought multiple facets of gender discrimination to the fore of El Congreso: equal wages, and social, economic, and civil liberties.

Josefina Fierro, who assumed the position of secretary of the congress, was a skillful organizer whose gravitation toward the efforts of the Communist Party was rooted in her family history. As a child in Mexicali, Sonora, she was born into the Mexican Revolution through the actions of her parents, who were both partisans of the PLM and the magonista movement. Her father was an aide to Flores Magón while her mother helped smuggle weapons across the border, occasionally tucked into Josefina's stroller, to assist in the armed insurrections. Their family, like many magonistas, was driven into exile north of the border, taking up residence in San Diego. When her parents separated with her father leaving to later join the forces of Pancho Villa, her mother took her to resettle in Los Angeles.

From there, Josefina worked alongside her mother in the agricultural fields as a *bordera*, an attendant providing basic necessities to migratory workers from San Diego to the San Joaquin Valley. This included legal support, translation, food, and other miscellaneous support for farmworkers for a low fee. From this experience, she learned from a young age how Mexican workers experienced various forms of racial discrimination, including the deportation of relatives back to Mexicali. She also saw firsthand the militant strikes carried out by "reds" and Mexican migrants. Before long, her mother, Josefina Amador, joined the IWW and attended the meetings of the Mexican branch. She later joined the Communist Party.[11]

In high school in Los Angeles, Josefina excelled, becoming captain of the girls' basketball team and editor of the school newspaper. Nevertheless, she began to experience racial discrimination and question the failures of capitalism to meet the basic needs of the working class. After debating her Economics teacher on the subject, she was told

that she was thinking like a "red."
When she discussed this with her
mother, she began "recalling Flores
Magón and the many passionate
harangues of her husband from
the days of Pancho Villa, Señora
Fierro talked about the two classes
in society—the landlords and the
workers. Those who protested
against this division of things were
'reds,' those who did something
about it were persecuted."[12]

Like Bert Corona, she was
one of a very small percentage of
Mexicans to gain access to college
after completing high school. She
went to UCLA to study to become
a doctor, but dropped out after a
short time. A clever thinker, astute

Josefina Fierro de Bright, ca. 1940.

mathematician—and from her experiences as a bordera, skilled at the art of making
money from very little—she became intrigued by the vagaries of Wall Street and dab-
bled in investing. She also became fascinated by music and art, and through a family
connection worked part time at a "Latin" piano bar in Los Angeles frequented by the
artistic community and Hollywood figures. As she moved through bohemian circles,
she encountered political and cultural radicals, many of whom were members or in the
orbit of the Communist Party.[13] She soon fell into the Hollywood scene, interacting
with a wide range of writers, actors, and artists. Through these circles she met Hollywood screenwriter and future husband John Bright. Bright was one of the ten founders
of the Screen Writers Guild, and one of the original "Gang of Four" that established the
Hollywood branch of the Communist Party.[14]

Through Bright and her own charismatic personality, Fierro made contact with
wealthy and high-profile celebrities with left-wing sympathies. They became part of
an important network that supported and financed the causes that she led. Her move
to the left and into the party was facilitated by her husband and interactions with
other radical artists in the party circles, but was driven by her experiences navigating
into other social spaces. According to an interview with Fierro, she revealed that she

> never forgot the plight of field workers who were prevented from joining labor
> unions and who were accused of being Communists. Those who demonstrated
> against meager wages or substandard housing or questioned the authority of the
> Associated Farmers of California were spied upon by vigilante groups through-
> out the 1930s, especially by the Ku Klux Klan in the Imperial Valley.[15]

A complex person, Josefina lived in comfort, interacted with the Hollywood elite, invested in numerous money-making schemes, and rejected conservative sexual norms; all while devoting herself tirelessly to the popular struggle she saw developing around her. This became her goal after entering the Communist Party.[16]

As an activist, Fierro began organizing against racial discrimination in the barrio while still a teenager. With other mexicano radicals, she helped coordinate community boycotts of establishments that discriminated against Mexicans. Her Hollywood contacts, including Anthony Quinn, Dolores del Río, and Orson Welles, helped her raise funds and establish a Spanish-language radio program to inform the community about important political issues, boycotts, and other campaigns. Through her activism in the barrios of Los Angeles, Fierro came into contact with Luisa Moreno. Moreno was so impressed with her vision, commitment, and range of contacts that she encouraged her to become executive secretary of El Congreso. Women played a central role in the establishment of the civil rights organization and helped develop the constellation of chapters throughout the Southwest.

The congress had a special focus on cultivating female leadership. Out of the conference, a Comité de Damas del Congreso (Women's Committee) was tasked with recruiting and organizing women into the ranks of the congress committees. During the regular meetings of the Women's Committee, working-class women who worked in factories or at home could bring their grievances to be discussed and acted upon. The role of women as organizers and activists was also illustrated by incidents of violence directed at them, especially in the rural chapters.

> The Damas also faced victimization by the KKK. Galvan wept when he heard that Margarita Flores had been brutally beaten by the Klan near Brawley. She lost her right eye and several teeth. Later, [Celia] Rodriguez also was beaten by the Klan and left along a road in Anaheim. A few Damas disappeared and were never seen again. One informer claimed that they were buried alive somewhere in the Imperial Valley.[17]

With strong leadership from people like Bert Corona, Luisa Moreno, and Josefina Fierro, El Congreso set out to establish a platform for taking the Mexican and Latino civil rights struggle national. Among the comprehensive range of topics discussed at the founding conference were immigration, housing, police brutality, education, and union organizing.

El Congreso Confronts Racism

A galvanizing aspect of the Congreso platform was the goal of unifying citizens and immigrants in the fight for civil rights. As one conference attendee told La Opinión, "The main goal that the Mexican and Hispano-American Congress follows is the unification of Mexican-Americans and Mexican nationals, and through them bringing closer the people of the US and Mexico."[18] As part of their platform, the attendees emphasized the need to take action to defend and support the immigrant and migrant working class. Carey McWilliams, then head of the state Department of Immigration and Housing, expressed the urgency to resist anti-immigrant sentiment pervading national politics and implored mobilization to defeat them. As he cautioned:

> There are now 27 bills aimed at the "alien" pending in Washington ... These bills
> however, are not directed at "aliens," but at the democratic institutions of Amer-
> ica. Take these bills, substitute the term "Jew" or "non-Aryan," and you have the
> laws of Nazi Germany. Please give these matters your urgent attention.[19]

The conference resolutions included advocating for the removal of all barriers to citizenship (based on race, political viewpoints, etc.) and a quick, easy, and low-cost
method to attain citizenship status. They also stood for the full and equal right to work
and receive benefits regardless of immigration status, arguing that the contribution
of labor warrants equal status. Lastly, they opposed deportation and the general enforcement of immigration policy, seeing the Immigration Service and Border Patrol as
instruments of political repression that tore apart families only to increase profits for
the employers through the subjugation of labor. Over the next three years of its existence, the congress acted on its platform using the strategy of mass mobilization and a
range of tactics including lobbying, protest, and other forms of direct political action.
They provided legal services for those applying for citizenship and worked through
the National Lawyers Guild to defend those being victimized. El Congreso also called
for the abolition of immigration fees, and opposed requirements for English-language
fluency and educational completion as conditions to attain citizenship.

One of these campaigns was in opposition to a bill (SB 470) sponsored by a
right-wing state senator named Ralph H. Swing, which if made law would have denied
relief or any state-appropriated funds for those who could not document their legal
status or who did not pursue citizenship once in the country with legal authorization. El Congreso organized community meetings and protests against the bill, and
lobbied their political allies to try to block its passage. When these efforts failed and
it proceeded to pass both houses of the legislature, Fierro and other congresistas organized a mass mobilization to the capitol to pressure Governor Olson to veto the bill.
According to Fierro, "We got hold of trucks, of cars, of trains, buses, any way we could
to get to Sacramento." The caravan gathered people from San Diego to Los Angeles
and from other cities and towns along the way, until a mass protest of twenty thousand
people converged on the statehouse steps to demand a veto. The protest was so effective that Governor Culbert Olson joined the rally after personally meeting with Fierro
and announced the veto, symbolically tearing it up in front of the cheering crowd.[20]

For the chapters closer to the border, opposition to Klan activities became a primary focus. Housing reform was also a major civil rights focus for El Congreso. As
Josefina Fierro explained,

> Housing conditions among the Mexican people ... [are] the worst in the state of
> California and throughout the Southwest of the United States ... Yet ... no at-
> tempt has been made ... to alleviate these terrible conditions ... We must start a
> real drive to make the housing authorities see the need of treating our problem.[21]

Most Mexicans lived in segregated barrios within the eastern section of the downtown

area or in colonias located on the unincorporated outskirts. The lack of decent affordable housing, and neglect by local government, contributed to poor health and sanitation, and overcrowding. The political culture of neglect was reinforced by federal
policy. El Congreso lobbied against the practices of the federal Home Owners' Loan
Corporation, a New Deal–era institution set up in 1933 to allocate low-interest federal
loans for families to purchase homes. Despite its benevolent aim, the program legitimized and enabled the continuation of "red-lining," now at a national level.

Through its implementation in Los Angeles, program administrators created a
grid system that elaborated a favorability rating for loan distribution based on features
of the different communities. In an overtly racist manner, the grid system administrators automatically designated low-income black and Mexican communities at the
lowest rating, assuring that they would be off-limits to home loans. The creation of the
FHA the following year, which provided insurance to the banks that made loans to
developers and construction companies, further enshrined racist practices by allowing these companies to incorporate "restrictive covenants" in their housing projects.
These covenants allowed the triad of bankers, developers, and real estate agencies to
designate new developments as "white only," which facilitated the racial segregation
of the expanding suburbs. El Congreso supporters led protests against segregated
housing and petitioned for all-new developments open to all community members,
regardless of race, nationality, or immigration status.

The Congress of Spanish-Speaking Peoples organized working-class people and built popular mobilizations for
civil rights.

They also organized public meetings to involve community members in city planning discussions that otherwise bypassed or excluded the Mexican population. In one situation, city officials were using eminent domain to tear down homes in the Mexican barrio of Maravilla in order to open up space for new housing development. Congreso activists organized a town hall for the community and compelled representatives from the housing authority to attend in order to ask questions. Several hundred community members turned out and shared grievances with the startled the officials, who were unaccustomed to "dialogue" with Mexicans. As a result of the event, the government representatives agreed to negotiate higher prices for their soon-to-be demolished homes, and to ensure Mexican families would also have access.

Police brutality was identified as a major concern for the Mexican community. Police routinely harassed, beat, and occasionally killed Mexican youth. Congreso activists built an emergency response network to respond to police violence. After the killing of a Mexican youth named Florentino Sanchez, El Congreso organized two thousand people to participate in a funeral march and silent protest. After another killing of two Mexican youth by LAPD, El Congreso mobilized several hundred angry community members to march to the police station to call for the officers involved to be charged with murder.

The group also raised funds and provided legal resources for the defense of Mexican people unjustly arrested and incarcerated. Through their relationship with Culbert Olson, the group was able to get him to set up an official commission led by Eduardo Quevado and Josefina Fierro to conduct an investigation into conditions in juvenile centers after several Mexican youths were found dead under suspicious conditions.[22] They organized public protests against sexual harassment of Mexican women by police, and against the common practice of the cops arresting working-class mexicanas on false charges of prostitution. They also provided support to people in prison, which included offering legal services and help with letter-writing for illiterate detainees.

In its embrace of "cultural democracy," El Congreso rejected the premise of Anglo assimilation as a manifestation of racism that harmed the social development of the youth. They held up the ideal of the US as multicultural and criticized how the racial discrimination corrupted that notion by devaluing non-European culture. Furthermore, they believed that the contributions of mexicanos and Latinos to the US were ignored and that the people of the US "owe an enormous cultural and physical debt to the Spanish-speaking people."[23]

In their educational program, they called for a sweeping set of reforms to dismantle racial practices and cultural norms that stunted the positive self-development of Mexican children. Foreshadowing the later demands of the Chicana/o student movement, this included the call for the hiring of more Mexican American teachers and administrators and classes and programs that taught children about Latin American history and culture and the contributions made by Mexican Americans to US history and society. They believed that bilingual education was necessary through to the eighth grade, in order to socially validate the language for Mexican children and to aid monolingual Spanish speakers in English-language acquisition.

Since education was key to socialization, they believed that in order to realize the goal of interracial unity, all children should be immersed in an education that was antiracist and multicultural in outlook. They also advocated for culturally relevant arts programs, cultural centers in the communities, and publicly funded and supported art expositions. They called for increased funding of recreational facilities for youth and protested segregated swimming pools. Lastly, they also promoted the "formation of departments in colleges and universities that will deal exclusively with the study of the social, economic, educational, and political development of the Spanish-speaking people."[24]

CIO unions with substantial Mexican memberships were a driving force of El Congreso and formed its core. Union staff and members from UCAPAWA, ILWU, IUMMSW, UFWA, and UE helped organized and attend the conferences and workshops, and were the most disciplined force to lead campaigns and attend rallies, protests, and community meetings, etc., for the duration of its existence. A primary CIO objective in the SSPC was to build community support for its organizing drives and its efforts to overthrow the "Mexican wage." El Congreso emphasized the importance of union officials learning, understanding, and valuing the culture of the Mexican working class. As Mario Gárcia explains,

> The union movement could succeed with Spanish-speaking workers . . . only if it kept in mind the cultural and language differences between Mexican and Anglo workers. Union meetings had to be conducted in both Spanish and English and information disseminated in Spanish through either the press or the radio. Only through all these efforts could Spanish-speaking workers and the US labor movement come together.[25]

Over its duration, El Congreso became a central organizing hub for the CIO to address issues specific to the Mexican population. Special conferences on the experiences and needs of "Latin-American workers" were attended by CIO-affiliated unionists and personnel that allowed them to interface with the community.

El Congreso also became a useful network to bring together solidarity campaigns to support striking workers or union drives. In 1939, for instance, three chapters in the San Joaquin Valley (Tulare, Shafter, and Bakersfield) created a solidarity committee to provide material aid to a cotton pickers strike in Madera in 1939. Other chapters worked to raise funds and supplies that were then centralized and distributed. Over its short existence, El Congreso assisted union efforts among longshoremen, electrical workers, packinghouse workers, garment workers, and farmworkers.

The SSPC also conducted lobbying campaigns, petitions, and letter-writing campaigns. One such effort was to petition the NLRB to include farmworkers and domestic workers in the purview of labor protections. They also tried to intervene in the negotiations over the Bracero Program, a contract labor system with Mexico outlining their own plan which called for organized labor on both sides of the border to be part of negotiations.[26]

When the war drive was underway, with massive infusions of federal dollars into the LA defense industry, El Congreso created the Hispanic Committee on Defense Jobs to petition for the inclusion of Mexican and Latino workers. After the creation of the Fair Employment Practices Committee (FEPC), El Congreso worked with the representatives of the federal government to conduct a survey within the Mexican communities to determine eligibility for defense jobs; they registered 50,000 and directly assisted 8,000 to work in war industries. They also participated in international events, including providing support for events in Mexico. In 1939 they led a march of over 8,000 in support of the Mexican oil nationalization and publicly denounced calls for US intervention.[27]

From El Congreso to the CIO Minorities Committee

After the Soviet Union began to inflict significant defeats on Nazi Germany, Stalin's regime was rehabilitated as a positive ally against the Axis powers in US political circles. From high-ranking US officials to the editors of the *New York Times*, Stalin was called on to ditch his support for Communist Parties operating throughout the West as an overture toward reconciliation and mutual support in the war.[28] Seeking to "restore" the Soviet Union to the "community of nations," Stalin was ready to make concessions to the US government to accommodate the process.

To appease anti-Communists in the US ruling class, Stalin dissolved the Comintern in 1943. The CPUSA, responding to this next significant shift, became the loudest and most persistent supporter of US intervention into the war. The party rebranded itself as a "loyal American" institution capable of peaceful co-existence within the new Anglo-Soviet order. In order to prove their makeover was non-threatening to US institutions, the party dismantled their various front organizations, including the Spanish-Speaking People's Congress, beginning in 1943. By 1944, the party went one step further in "liquidating" itself and reforming as the nebulous "Communist Political Association." Despite the demise of El Congreso, Mexican radicals continued their work through the CIO's Minorities Committee.

At the Sixth Annual State Convention of the CIO, Luisa Moreno was elected as a vice president of the federation, overseeing the newly created Minorities Committee, which brought together twenty-three local and union representatives divided into northern and southern California divisions. Five of the original delegates were mexicanos or Latinos, including three from Southern California: Armando Dávila from the Furniture Workers, Jaime González of the Steel Workers Organizing Committee, and Luisa Moreno from UCAPAWA. The statewide committee attempted to integrate all ethnic groups into its purview, represented in the ethnic diversity of the delegates.

While the new statewide approach continued to conceptualize, conduct, and generalize different campaigns and coordinated action for civil rights at the statewide level, it also worked within the context of the new pro-war positions. The inner shift toward war mobilization taking place within the Communist Party and the CIO apparatus now intertwined the struggle against racism with full support for war. Strikes were banned to encourage the increase of war production, and racial discrimination was condemned as undermining national unity at an urgent moment of need. When the federal government pumped $11 billion into Los Angeles as part of a massive defense spending campaign, nearly 500 new factories sprang into production, creating a massive labor need.[29] The Communist Party and the CIO focused their antiracist efforts on opening up these industries to local Mexican and incoming black workers, largely bypassed in favor of midwestern and southern Anglo-Americans also pouring into the region.

One function of the committee included the full mobilization of "minority" workers into defense industries, setting up regional Anti-Discrimination Committees (ADC) to ensure black and Mexican participation. For instance, the LA-ADC called for an emergency committee meeting and citywide conference to oppose the exclusion of Mexican noncitizens from defense jobs, in conjunction with the Spanish-Speaking People's Congress.[30] While no such clause existed within the War Department guidelines, employers used it as a tactic to target and remove Mexican workers, especially those in unions. The committee assembled a team of lawyers and publicly called for reports of such abuses.[31] The CIO (and Communist Party's) commitment to antiracism in war industries was fraught with contradictions, as they accepted the exclusion of "enemy aliens" from defense jobs and ultimately supported Japanese internment.[32]

ADC committees partnered with the Labor Supply Division of the War Production Board to survey, procure, register, and train qualified black and Mexican recruits for defense industries. They set up training centers in the barrios that also included government-sponsored workshops for how to attain citizenship; and called for defense jobs to be open to women and that "Negro and Mexican teachers, advisors, field workers, clerks, etc., be hired to help integrate the minority groups in defense training."[33] Furthermore, an office of the US Employment Service was established with the collaboration of the CIO to set up and facilitate a grievance process. While great leaps were made by the CIO to usher in the inclusion of Mexican and black workers in the rapidly expanding war industries, the government side of the process was slow and inadequate, driven by what the ADC identified as the persistence of Jim Crow and "prejudice as usual."[34]

The report of the Minorities Committee captured the various types of work engaged in at the local level across the state. This included reports from the CIO-led Northern California Conference on Racial and National Unity in Wartime. This conference brought together 1,200 people from 109 organizations, and 657 registered delegates from trade unions (CIO and AFL), civic, fraternal, municipal, county, and state bodies to discuss issues, including how to follow expand their own pro-war, anti-discrimination efforts.[35]

The convention also called for the expansion of federal nondiscrimination policy, including the immediate implementation of nondiscrimination policy directives in housing, planning, welfare, educational, and other agencies of the state government. Also, they called for the prohibition of restrictive covenants in property deeds based upon racial considerations."[36] They also called for civil rights legislation banning discrimination in employment, and for the state government to exclude businesses that discriminated when contracting with the private sector. For the duration of its existence, the CIO Minorities Committee continued to frame its work as within the "win the war" Good Neighbor policy framework in order to build unity with Latin Americans and integrate them as a means to support the war effort.

The abrupt abandonment of civil rights organizing by the Communist Party led to a fragmentation of the groups involved in El Congreso, and the party's submergence of antiracism into the narrow construct of "supporting the war effort" had limited impact on the institutional character of racism in US capitalism. Nevertheless, some significant civil rights victories did occur, as party members working in the barrios dedicated themselves to defending the Mexican community from state violence. This principled and enduring support is illustrated in the party's defense against the legal lynching of Mexican youth in the Sleepy Lagoon case and the anti-Mexican sailor's riots in wartime Los Angeles.

Chapter 34
Sleepy Lagoon: Communists, the CIO, and Civil Rights

"I believe that the federal government should concern itself with the problem of improving the living and working conditions among the 3,500,000 Spanish-speaking people resident in the United States."
—**Carey McWilliams of the Sleepy Lagoon Defense Committee, countering the public clamor for the persecution of Mexican youth, 1942**

The arrest, show trial, and false conviction of twenty-one Mexican youth for murder in Los Angeles in late 1942, followed six months later by a ten-day orgy of anti-Mexican violence that raged throughout the city, capped a period of intense racial targeting of the Mexican working class. The war intensified an already combustible admixture of regional factors that led the local and state government, the media, the police, and the FBI to socially and politically categorize the Mexican population as a threat. In the context of heightened CIO-led class struggle, the advent of Communist Party–linked militant civil rights organization and activism, and the weakening of the ideological hegemony of Jim Crow in maintaining a passive and compliant labor force, the targeting of the primarily US-born youth for wholesale criminalization was an attempt to reimpose marginality by force. This is the framework that led the Communists and their liberal allies, through El Congreso, the International Labor Defense, and other aligned organizations and unions to mobilize against the crusade.

The Sleepy Lagoon case signaled an intensification of the criminalization of Mexican working-class youth in wartime Los Angeles, generally identified as "pachucos" and "pachucas." *Pachuquismo* came to refer to a working-class youth culture that developed in the barrio, infused with African American–inspired "zoot" style, and verbalized through a syncretic Spanish-origin street slang (Caló). It represented a cultural phenomenon that was increasingly characterized as "deviant" by conservative social forces because it implied a repudiation of the aggressive model of assimilation imposed on Mexican youth in the schools, through the media and law enforcement, and through other private, public, and official interactions. This form of assimilation conditioned Mexicans to passively accept unequal relationships, to stay within their barrios, and to reject their own Mexican culture as backward and inferior in relation to that of the Anglo. The zoot suit phenomenon, crystallizing self-determined identity, and the assertive attitude that accompanied it represented a rupture with Jim Crow–imposed peace in an environment that was even more racially polarized at a time of war.[1]

Pachucas and Pachucos in the Working Class

As the children of workers, or workers themselves, the social presence of *pachucas* and *pachucos* expanded in relation to their growing economic and political power; as exercised through their participation or interaction with the CIO-affiliated unions active in the barrios, and the Communist Party front groups organizing protest actions at the production points of racial, class, and gender discrimination. As a component of the working class, the younger generation also experienced the class consciousness, self-awareness, and confident assertiveness that is an outgrowth of collective struggle and resistance.

Many Mexican youths in the barrios of Los Angeles worked in the same occupations as their parents, either as migrant farmworkers or after leaving high school, once settled in the city. While a minority completed high school, most dropped out in order to work and support their families, since a single or even double household income based on the lower "Mexican wage" was insufficient to sustain a whole family. Others dropped out because of mistreatment or difficulty with rigid assimilationist practices.[2] Once they entered into the workforce, they experienced a different range of influences, while still maintaining a connection to the youth cultures of their community and social networks. The fact that individuals of this generation could afford cars and expensive tailored suits exhibits their status as wage workers. José Díaz, the young pachuco killed after a fight at the Sleepy Lagoon, exemplifies this experience.

José Díaz came with his family at a young age from Durango, Mexico, where they entered into the migratory agricultural workforce that supplied the fruits, nuts, and vegetables that fed much of the western US population. They followed the crops for five years, before permanently settling in Los Angeles in 1928, living in a bunkhouse on a ranch-land barrio that developed on the outskirts of the city. Alongside his parents, Díaz transitioned in the off-season from farmworker to packinghouse worker, where he found employment at the Sunny Sally vegetable-packing plant near his colonia on the unincorporated outskirts of 1942 LA. At twenty-two years old, he worked to support his family, with whom he still lived and had a close relationship. He enlisted in the army in the summer of 1942 and was set to ship out to boot camp before his life was cut short at Sleepy Lagoon.[3] Díaz worked in the same plant as two other pachucos charged with his murder, while most of their parents worked in the same canneries, packinghouses, or factories and attended the same churches and social functions.

When the defense industry expanded to build the armaments of the US military, many Mexican workers left the canneries, garment factories, and other low-wage jobs to find more lucrative work in defense jobs. As the CIO-led efforts against discrimination leveraged more opportunities for Mexican workers, significant numbers transitioned in. This was especially the case for Mexican women, as significant numbers of male workers and youth were being drawn or drafted into war.

Douglas Aircraft, for instance, one of the largest aviation manufacturers in the country in the World War II period, increased its total workforce from 13,300 workers in 1939 to 228,400 in 1943. Of this number, 12,000 were Mexican workers, of which 80 percent were women of all ages.[4] The aviation industry, which was completely organized by the CIO-affiliated United Automobile Workers by the end of the war, included equal-pay clauses that negated the traditional race and gender differentials on the assembly lines. As Elizabeth Escobedo noted, "many young Mexican American women worked in war jobs and wore coveralls by day, only to jitterbug dressed to the nines in Pachuca attire by night."[5]

The Criminalization of Mexican Youth: From Sleepy Lagoon to the Sailor Riots

The visibility of this generation, through their clothing, cars, and assertiveness, permeated into social spaces long exclusive to whites only, which was deemed problematic by law enforcement, the media, and the representatives of the capitalist class. A chorus of disaffection began to resonate, as Mexican working-class youth were transcending the physical boundaries of the barrio and the passive resignation of the assimilated. Furthermore, for some, this outlook actively carried over into the participation in a radical-led labor movement that inspired the feeling of confidence that it was possible to resist the racial discrimination that had previously scarred all aspects of their social experience. Under the inflated urgency of war, the normalized racism that had underpinned the structures of racial segregation was intensified and unleashed against this upstart segment of the Mexican working class. It also paved the way for the criminalization of the radical working-class leadership, which fell victim to the rise of anti-Communist persecution in the years that followed.

The Sleepy Lagoon case broke on August 1, 1942, when 22 Mexican youth, 17 males and 5 females, were arrested and indicted for the alleged murder of José Díaz in the largest "mass trial" in history. The police conducted raids throughout the city following the murder, carrying out the mass arrest of 300 "known" pachucos, regardless of their having any direct connection to the events. The death of Díaz occurred in a small rural barrio located in the vicinity of the Sleepy Lagoon Reservoir beside the Los Angeles River. After a small group of youth from the Thirty-Eighth Street barrio were attacked near the lagoon, they regrouped their friends, returned, and retaliated against a nearby group of partygoers they mistook for the assailants. In the ensuing melee, Díaz was wounded and later died en route to the hospital. The event, not exceptional in and of itself, occurred in a climate where racial tensions had been increasing, and the pachuco youth culture was being monitored and stigmatized as a distinct form of criminal delinquency.

After a three-month trial, seventeen of the youth were found guilty and convicted on charges ranging from first-degree murder to assault. Twelve of the boys, ranging from 16 to 22, were convicted of murder and sent to San Quentin Prison. The remaining five saw their charges reduced to assault, and they were sent to the Los Angeles County jail. Five young women present at the scene refused to testify against their brothers and boyfriends and were sent to the Ventura School for Girls, at the time the only reformatory for girls in the state, designed for "wayward" and "sexually promiscuous" young women. While the males ultimately had their charges dropped on appeal, the young women, ranging in age from 16 to 20, did not. Lorena Encinas, Frances Silva, Josephine and Juanita Gonzales, and Dora Barrios were forced to languish behind bars at the notoriously oppressive institution until they reached twenty-one years of age.[6] Encinas was separated from her newborn child for over a year as a result of the detention.

No credible or tangible evidence was presented that could adequately determine the guilt of the youth. The youth were not allowed to consult their lawyers during the trial and were prevented from changing, shaving, or showering, to fit the stereotype of unkempt street youth. Instead of using typical evidence-based procedures, the prosecution and city officials decided to make the case a public spectacle to put the whole Mexican "race" on trial. During the ensuing grand jury investigation, a barrage of anti-Mexican testimony, "research," and "statistics" were showcased to support the prosecution. High-ranking police agents, Captain Vernon Rasmussen of the LAPD, Chief Clement B. Horrall, and Sheriff Lieutenant Edward Duran Ayres, were given free rein to construct a narrative of Mexican biological inferiority and predisposition toward criminality.

Ayres argued crude eugenics and linked Mexicans to the maligned Japanese enemy languishing in concentration camps, painting Mexicans as an indigenous subgroup descended from "Orientals" who conveyed an "utter disregard for the value of life." He then characterized them as descendants of Aztecs, restating fallacious claims of mass human sacrifice and bloodlust. Further arguments purported Mexicans as ignorant immigrants who could not understand or control their children, and as a group that refused to assimilate, tolerated substandards of living, and was prone to criminal behavior.[7]

The three concluded that because of these biological and cultural factors, Mexicans needed to be systematically and severely punished and generally kept under control. In Los Angeles County Superior Court judge Charles "San Quentin" Fricke, notorious for sending more people to prison than any other sitting judge, they found a sympathetic ear. While these testimonies were conducted behind closed doors, they revealed the outlook of LA's "criminal justice system." They were given a public platform through the pages of the Los Angeles Times, which ran lurid stories that played on the racial fears of conservative whites.

The condemnation of the people as inherently inferior and prone to violence served to legitimize the segregation, heavy-handed policing, and ultimately the criminalization and incarceration of a whole generation. A convergence of several factors, including the prominence of racist ideas among the white population, the outbreak of World War II and Japanese internment, and the desire by capitalists to arrest and reverse the scale of racial integration to maintain a subservient labor force contributed to the explosion of racism and state violence that followed in the wake of the Sleepy Lagoon incident up to the sailor riots of 1943.

By 1942, the Anglo population of Los Angeles had developed through several waves of migration, with the most recent component of the 2.6 million whites coming from the Midwest and South during the late 1920s through the 1930s to work in the expanding manufacturing and defense industries. The 1920s had witnessed a resurgence of the Ku Klux Klan nationally, as eugenics and scientific racism reached its highest level of institutional support through government and institutions of higher education, and among the elite. Many of the migrants brought with them established racial predispositions. As one historian of the period has written, by 1942, "Nativism ran strong among whites in Southern California, to the extent that many Angelenos openly supported the Ku Klux Klan."[8]

Furthermore, white migrants had entered a welcoming city layout in which housing and employment segregation patterns were already established to ensure white dominance. Exclusive zoning ordinances, restrictive covenants, and planning commissions worked in tandem with the customary habits of the employers to ensure economic marginalization of Mexican workers and underdevelopment of the barrios. As Mark Weitz asserts, the goal of city planners in the 1920s was to establish a white-majority city, and migration recruitment, employment, and settlement aided the effort to further "whiten" the city.[9] This became a concern after the sizeable growth of Mexican and black populations at the margins, anchored to the lowest-wage sectors of the economy. Therefore, the large influx of whites accustomed to rigid norms of segregation found their sensibilities disturbed by being in closer social proximity to populations of young Mexicans who did not adhere to their expectations of strict separation.

Pachuquismo also flouted the social conventions that discouraged racial intermixing. White segregationists throughout the state had succeeded in broadening the state's anti-miscegenation laws, when the 1872 California Civil Code, Section 60 banned the intermarriage of "whites" with "negroes" or "mulattoes." In 1941 the scope was expanded to prohibit and criminalize marriage between whites and "Negroes, Mongolians, members of the Malay race, or mulattoes."[10] The pachuco-zoot culture rejected these lines of separation. Community dances, house parties, and other gatherings became zones of racial integration, with working-class blacks, Mexicans, Filipinos, and whites intermixing and cross-influencing each other.

The Japanese attack on Pearl Harbor in December of 1941 initiated a series of events that contributed to the climate of racial polarization, beginning with Japanese internment. Since February of 1942, the Justice Department had conducted sweeps and raids to round up Japanese families after Roosevelt issued Executive Order 9066, authorizing the internment of over 125,000 Japanese Americans in a patchwork of western concentration camps.

In this environment, latent anti-Mexican attitudes became inflamed, especially as pachuco identity transgressed white patriotic ideals of how nonwhite people should conduct themselves, which through a racist lens projected the expectation of Mexican social invisibility, servility, and deference to whites. As a result, when they crossed established social boundaries they experienced a spectrum of discriminatory practices, from the egregious to the trivial. This included the general assertion to the right of free movement, use of public space, and equal application of citizenship rights; it also assumed the equal right of access and opportunity to employment as whites. As Luisa Moreno observed, "The hysteria against the Sleepy Lagoon defendants and the Pachucos over all was the outward manifestation of a complex fear in Southern California that Mexicans were moving more into the essential industries like agriculture, the food-processing commerce, the garment commerce, construction and other businesses."[11]

This was also an irritant to capitalists, long accustomed to the ability to control and exploit Mexican workers as they saw fit. As this generation began to assert itself as a class through unions and radical political organization identifying and tearing at the foundations of segregation, the capitalist class and its attendant organizations sought to put the upstart generation back into the barrios. As historian of the period Mark Weitz explained, the campaign of denigration occurred precisely at the time that Mexican Americans engaged in militant actions for social change, including "boycotts, embargoes, strikes, slowdowns, and the effective use of voluntary organizations . . . to improve basic conditions and gain fundamental rights."[12]

The shock troops of this effort were members of the Los Angeles Police Department, backed by a political class and justice system that closed ranks against the first significant generation of the Mexican American working class. The police began to ramp up their targeting of Mexican youth. In order to instill fear, compliance, and resignation in the face of racial inequality, the LAPD routinely harassed, detained, and beat Mexican working-class youth on the social boundaries of the barrios. As Eduardo Obregón Pagán describes, from a young age they learned

> the harsh realities of being born poor and deemed "Mexican" in Los Angeles. Where they were lucky enough to find a restaurant that would serve them, people of color often encountered rude service and dirty utensils or silverware. And in the name of law and order, members of the Los Angeles Police routinely raided parties in East Los Angeles, broke up outdoor games and gatherings and chased young people out of the parks after sundown. It was common for young people . . . to be arrested for loitering and then beaten while in custody until they confessed their guilt.[13]

Through regimented policing, frequent incarceration, and an ongoing media narrative of inherent Mexican delinquency, groups of youth who shared the class and cultural characteristics of pachuquismo were officially designated as bona fide gangs. As a result, youth crime and delinquency increased in proportion to the "policing" directed toward Mexican and black communities.[14] Increased institutional violence against Mexicans, now broadly legitimized in the eyes of the public, then manifested in racist mob violence.

State-Sanctioned Mob Violence against Mexicans

The sensationalized trial of the Mexican youth, which rested upon histrionic proclamations of Mexican racial savagery and treachery, triggered racist reactions from within the Anglo population. For many white residents of Los Angeles, the spurious conviction of the seventeen youth in January of 1943 confirmed and inflamed their existing fears and animosities. Furthermore, these tensions increased even more as at least seven million soldiers and sailors, with many from the US South, were moved to the West Coast in anticipation of protracted war in the Pacific against Japan. Large contingents of sailors were packed into naval bases and stations in Los Angeles and San Diego, putting them into already densely populated areas, where they interacted and moved through the same spaces as the civilian population. Racial animosity culminated in an outbreak of violence on June 3, 1943, as white sailors, police, and Anglo civilians attacked Mexicans in the streets of Los Angeles for ten straight days. Orchestrated attacks on Mexicans (and black zoot-suiters) then spread to San Diego, Oakland, Delano, San Jose, Chicago, Philadelphia, Detroit, and New York City.

Tension and conflict between military personnel and the civilian population had already broken out into the open before the attacks. In the last two weeks of May alone there were eighteen reported incidents of violence involving sailors and civilians, seven of which resulted in death.[15] The war further heightened existing racial divisions by creating racial paranoia, as the patriotism of marginalized peoples was called into question based on preconceived notions of difference. Historian Mauricio Mazón identifies another contextual explanation for the advent of the sailor riots: a temporary release valve for controlled violence at a time when support for the war effort was deteriorating. CIO leader John L. Lewis effectively broke the "no-strike pledge" when he led the United Mine Workers out on strike on May 1, 1943. Furthermore, this occurred at a time of "public criticism over rationing, the cost of living, [and] wage controls, and as adverse working conditions increased, there was a corresponding decrease in the propaganda value of media exposure to the heroism and sacrifices of men at war."[16] As a counter to the social deterioration, the federal government began to conduct high-profile sweeps looking for "draft dodgers" while the Los Angeles Times began publishing articles playing up the potential for Japanese and other "enemy aliens" to carry out elaborate acts of subversion and terrorism.[17] When the sailors began to attack Mexicans, ostensibly because of spurious articles in the Los Angeles Times and Hearst's Los Angeles Examiner alleging that gangs of Mexican youth were assaulting sailors and white women, the local establishment encouraged and abetted the rampage.

For ten days, gangs of sailors were allowed to leave their bases to clear the streets of Mexican pachucos. They roved through the downtown areas and into the Mexican barrios, accosting and beating any Mexican they encountered. Amid the orgy of violence, the black and Asian youth were also targeted, revealing the profound racial character of the violence. People were pulled off trolley cars, dragged out of storefronts and movie theaters, or nabbed walking down the street only to be beaten and stripped of their clothes in public. Those identified as pachucos were routinely stripped and beaten, and had their hair shorn off. Police were spotted joining with the servicemen, or holding back and arresting the victims as the gangs of sailors moved on. Police arrested and imprisoned an estimated six hundred Mexican youth, and not the sailors, over the course of the ten days.[18]

After the first night, the Los Angeles Times began to gleefully report on the violence, while also abetting it. The paper "leaked" times and locations for sailor actions in advance, which informed and encouraged thousands of angry whites to converge as a mob and join with the sailors and police in the beatings. An estimated five thousand white Los Angeles residents took part in the violence. Furthermore, amid the free-for-all, the city council hastily organized a council session on June 9 to formally announce a "ban" on the zoot suit, giving the vigilante mobs more confidence to carry out their attacks. Only after nearly two weeks of incessant attacks, conducted all the way into the Mexican barrios, did the Roosevelt administration instruct the military leadership to restrain the sailors.

Mexican radicals and the Communist Party played a leading role in the Sleepy Lagoon Defense Committee

Citizens Committee for the Defense of Mexican American Youth

In the wake of the Sleepy Lagoon arrests, the Communist Party–led International Labor Defense, the Spanish-Speaking People's Congress, and the CIO took actions to defend the youth. This included the provision of legal and monetary support alongside the mass mobilization of public opinion and protest against the actions of the police, city government, and the capitalist media. Furthermore, the coalition of forces constructed a counternarrative to the racism that permeated society over the course of the trial, going against the reactionary tide of local politics. The campaign on behalf of the Sleepy Lagoon defendants was pivotal for the overturning of the murder charges and securing the eventual release of the young men. By turning the indictment back onto the justice system itself, radicals within the defense campaign also initiated and framed the opposition to the nascent incarceration complex taking shape as a statewide solution to the "Mexican problem." Instead, they identified institutional racism and structural underdevelopment of the barrios as the underlying problem.

The International Labor Defense (ILD), the legal apparatus of the Communist Party, also committed early on to support the incarcerated youth. Since its inception in 1925 as the US section of the Comintern's International Red Aid network, the organization set out to

> defend all workers who are being persecuted by the capitalist government and various other agencies of the employing class, for their participation in the class struggle, by rendering legal aid, moral and financial support to these workers and their dependents, by wide publicity, organizing mass demonstrations of support and protest, both here and abroad.[19]

The ILD gained international acclaim for its role in defending the Scottsboro Boys, nine black teenagers falsely accused of rape in Alabama in 1931. When the Los Angeles party began to organize Mexican workers in early 1930s, ILD executive director LaRue McCormick and other radical lawyers frequented the courtrooms and jails of Southern and central California. They aided agricultural workers, party members, union members, and black, Mexican, Japanese, and other people of color targeted by police, typically for their participation in strikes or party activity. The LA chapter of the ILD also had some historical connections with the Mexican community, having supported protests and legal action against the placement of Spanish-speaking children in special education classes. They routinely monitored court reports to identify cases that fit their purview.

Upon becoming aware of the Sleepy Lagoon case, McCormick and the ILD formed its own ad hoc committee called the Citizens' Committee for the Defense of Mexican American Youth (CCDMAY). They assembled a legal team of allied veteran left-wing lawyers, and then organized a meeting to launch a solidarity campaign. McCormick sent out 200–300 telegrams to invite all interested groups to join the campaign and present the details of the case, and charted a course for action.[20] While the CCDMAY fought in the courts, the Sleepy Lagoon Defense Committee, as it came to be known, mobilized a grassroots-oriented campaign. The two wings of the defense campaign became integrated over time, with the organizational leadership developing out of El Congreso.

Since the ILD was affiliated to the Congress of Spanish-Speaking Peoples, it was the logical place to organize a broad, community-based defense coalition. This was especially apparent when it became clear to the activists that support would be coming from no other quarters.[21] El Congreso organized an investigation into the death of Benny Moreno, a Mexican youth who died under suspicious circumstances in the notorious Whittier School reformatory. El Congreso made it a priority to investigate and build public protest campaigns against state brutality toward Mexican youths, establishing committee infrastructure to defend incarcerated youth and to articulate various criticisms of corruption and bias within the legal system.[22]

Josefina Fierro, Luisa Moreno, Bert Corona, and Carey McWilliams worked with LaRue McCormick to develop a strategy to begin work through the Sleepy Lagoon

Defense Committee (SLDC). One of the first actions was to coalesce involvement from affiliated and aligned Popular Front organizations, solicit funding and public support from prominent Hollywood backers through the networks of Josefina Fierro, and to activate the various chapters of the congress as part of the campaign. Fierro made arrangements for a speaking tour through El Congreso chapters across the Southwest in order to raise publicity for the events outside of Los Angeles as well as raise funds to support the legal defense.

In short order the committee expanded to include a growing list of supporters that included the International Workers Order, the ILWU, the Council for Pan-American Democracy, the Office Employees Guild, American Newspaper Guild, Screen Actors Guild, National Lawyers Guild, the Los Angeles and California CIO councils, the Amalgamated Clothing Workers of America, the National Maritime Union, numerous Hollywood actors, and individual Communists from various branches assigned to work behind the scenes in building the campaign in various capacities. Local left-wing press outlets supported the committee and countered the narrative of the *Los Angeles Times*, including Charlotta Bass of the African American *California Eagle* and Al Waxman of the *Eastside Journal*. Since one of the incarcerated youths was a Mexican national, the SSPC was able to secure the support of the Mexican consulate, which provided a lawyer as part of the team.

The CIO turned its central wheels in alignment with the campaign. The national CIO passed a resolution in support of the youth at its sixth convention. In August 1942, the LA Inter-Union Council–sponsored Mexican Workers' Trade Union conference was organized to coordinate a plan for labor to participate in the defense of the Mexican youth.

> They came up with a plan: a call to the Mexican government to intervene, CIO endorsement for the defense committee, protest against the racist press, the District Attorney to drop the charges, that police stop rounding up Mexican youth, and the hiring of Mexican organizers to recruit Mexican workers into the various CIO unions.[23]

The LA-CIO leadership appointed Bert Corona to be its official liaison to the committee (and later Luisa Moreno when Bert Corona went into the military), and he began a three-pronged campaign to publicize the Sleepy Lagoon case and create a communitywide committee to support the youth, to organize meetings within union locals to integrate Mexican workers into union and community activity, and to lobby county officials to create more affordable housing for Mexican workers crowded into segregated barrios. Other CIO union activists affiliated with the party such as Frank López and Roberto Galván also contributed time and energy.

The CIO leadership also provided important resources. Philip Connelly, for instance, arranged for national labor attorney Abraham Isserman to join the defense team. The Los Angeles CIO's Anti-Discrimination Committee, chaired by Revels Clayton and Luisa Moreno, became another vehicle for building labor support for the Sleepy Lagoon youth. At the state level, the CIO Minorities Committee held a conference on racial unity after the sailor riots and condemned racial discrimination and induced poverty as the root of the problem (as opposed to "delinquency"). The CIO Minorities Committee also petitioned the state attorney general, Robert Kenney, to investigate in the aftermath, which he reluctantly did.

Intellectuals and artists aligned with the party also played a key role. Carey McWilliams, for instance, assumed leadership of the Sleepy Lagoon Defense Committee during the appeal process. His participation as a former state official (leaving his post in November 1942) gave the campaign a widely recognized and respected voice with knowledge of the system and numerous connections. He helped with the Special Committee on the Problems of Mexican Youth, which collected information and testimonies that were delivered to the grand jury to counter the racist narrative of the police. McWilliams and Luisa Moreno later spearheaded an investigation into military violence against Mexicans in San Diego. Communist Party member, novelist, and Hollywood screenwriter Guy Endore penned a novel based on the events called *The Sleepy Lagoon Mystery*, which was used to popularize and raise funds to support the defense campaign. Over the course of the defense campaign, upward of fifty thousand copies were sold, reaching people and communities far beyond Los Angeles.

At the forefront of the campaign were the families of the victims and Spanish-speaking Mexican radicals with roots in the communities, who did the important legwork of holding fundraising parties and gatherings, and doing outreach to mutualistas, patriotic societies, churches, and other community-based organizations. The family members of two defendants facing the longest jail terms, Henry "Hank" Leyvas and Robert Telles, were tireless campaigners. As Frank Barajas explains

> Spanish-speaking activists and labor organizers such as Bert Corona, Frank Corona (a youth member of the ILD), Lupe Leyvas (the daughter of Mrs. Leyvas and younger sister of Hank), and [Robert's mother] Margaret Telles informed people in and out of the Mexican community about the central issue of the case—the denial of legal justice to the boys.[24]

Mexicans south of the border followed the Sleepy Lagoon case closely. The administration of Manuel Ávila Camacho also got involved, although treading lightly and working primarily through his secretary of the exterior, Alfredo Elias Calles. As Richard Griswold del Castillo has noted, the US and Mexico government had moved closer into political alignment after the conclusion of the Cardenás sexenio. US capital was beginning to pour back into the Mexican economy, especially agriculture.

The Camacho administration had just signed the accord to send bracero contract laborers from Mexico to work in US fields, which exported large swaths of Mexico's economically displaced rural population and allowed them to send lucrative remittances back into the Mexican economy. The US was absorbing a high quantity of Mexico's exports for the war effort, while the infusions of labor also freed up Mexican American farmworkers to be drafted by the tens of thousands without jeopardizing grower profits resulting from a labor shortage.[25] The administration was not interested in strained public relations but provided modest support through its consulate, including the provision of a lawyer for one youth that was a Mexican national.

Other Mexicans were more vocal. Left-wing college students in Mexico City organized a solidarity protest against racism against Mexicans in the US and formed a Committee for the Defense of Mexicans Abroad (Comité de Defensa de los Mexicanos de Afuera), whose goal "was to protest the mistreatment of Pachucos as well as the race riot against African Americans in Detroit, Michigan and to protest the actions of the Mexican government that exhibited 'a lack of patriotism.'"[26] Despite the best efforts of both the Mexican and US governments to downplay the events, the anti-Mexican violence and persecution were presented in the Latin American press as proof of the racial prejudice of Americans toward people with indigenous, African, or mestizo ancestry. Despite the popular discontent, the CTM and Mexican Communist Party condemned the protest as counterproductive to North American unity against the Axis powers.

Through the tireless work of hundreds of individuals and organizations, the defense campaign built the broadest left-wing coalition and reached the largest audience nationally and internationally since the Sacco and Vanzetti and Scottsboro cases. The Communist Party saw the plight of Mexican youth as an opportunity to challenge deeply entrenched racism by relating it to the enemy ideology of Nazism and utilizing pro-war fervor to the opposite effect of the reactionaries' intent on fortifying the boundaries of racial segregation. They painted multiracial unity as a precondition to the mustering of forces necessary to win the war.

Communist Party Politics, Strategy, and Tactics

The Sleepy Lagoon case occurred in the aftermath of the US entrance into World War II. The Communist Party retuned its political tone once again. When the Nazis invaded the Soviet Union, nullifying the Hitler-Stalin Pact, it moved away from its previous line of opposition to US involvement in the European war and began pleading ad nauseum for a "second front" to save Russia.[27] With the US now in the war, the party swung even further into an uncritical position of US policy in the name of national unity. Each abrupt turn had immediate implications for how to conduct party work, leading to the emergence of divisions especially when it came to fighting for civil rights. The advent of the Sleepy Lagoon Defense Campaign on the heels of the entrance of the US into World War II allowed for the party to reactivate a version of its earlier Popular Front and pull together a broad coalition of forces to defend Mexican working-class youth.

In the context of "winning the war" the party reframed racial discrimination in the Mexican barrios as a destructive toxin that poisoned national unity. These divisions aided the enemy and opened the door for fascistic elements in the Mexican community (sinarquistas) to exploit anti-US sentiment and weaken support for the defeat of the Axis powers. Pro-war sentiment against the Axis powers therefore framed the struggle for civil rights for the duration of the war, without grounding it as an intrinsic function of the capitalist system. While this allowed for a higher level of collaboration with non-radical pro-war forces, such as in the Sleepy Lagoon case, it also weakened the party's approach to resisting the anti-Communist reaction intensifying within both parties as a result of the convergence between a rising industrial labor movement and working-class communities of color. Despite the inherent long-term weaknesses of its politics, the party, the CIO, and its Popular Front organizations and allies were able to mobilize significant forces to win a battle against significantly larger adversaries.

Through the communiqués of the defense committees, the writings of aligned intellectuals, and the pages of the CP/CIO press, the ideological orientation of the campaign posited racism as part of a concerted effort by reactionaries with Axis sympathies to debilitate the war effort. It was therefore reasoned that the state had an interest in using its power to obliterate the obstacles to its full military capacity. This included the role of corrupt officials, unpatriotic capitalists, and others that benefitted from the direct oppression of national minorities that inhibited the development of national unity and its full potential. Furthermore, the structural underdevelopment of Mexican barrios blocked the development of productive workers, loyal soldiers, and positive transnational relations with Mexican allies. As one CCDMAY circular explained:

> Hitler, too, began his attack against the people of Germany by first attacking the minorities. It wasn't long after his success in whipping up disunity among the various groups that he was able to destroy them all. We have seen Hitler work too often in too many places not to recognize the vicious fascist rattle when we hear it in our own midst. Nor indeed, was it just by chance that the axis radio harped upon the outcome of this trial for days on end as an example of "democratic justice" and our "Good Neighbor Policy."[28]

The party further played up the links to fascism by attributing a cause of racial tension and instability to the actions of the sinarquistas. This group was established as the Mexican branch of the Spanish Falange (a fascist movement led by Francisco Franco) and favored an alliance with the Axis powers, with a purported membership of half a million members. In a public letter written by Josefina Fierro, she claimed that sinarquista branches had been established in all of the major Mexican population centers and were actively subverting the war effort.[29] The effort to explain racial violence by refracting it through the alleged actions of Mexican "fifth column" subversives did not resonate very broadly and revealed the weakness of the religious-like pro-war fervor of the party. This was especially the case as investigative reports revealed the presence of sinarquistas in the Southwest was limited, isolated, and irrelevant in the Mexican community. Perhaps less ideologically inflated, Luisa Moreno concluded that "the Sleepy Lagoon Case is a reflection of the general reactionary drive against organized labor and minority problems. This case now sows all sorts of division amongst the racial, national, and religious groups among the workers."[30] More significant than the nuanced differences was how the defense campaign presented solutions to the crisis, which rejected criminalization and favored significant investment in Mexican barrios and the elimination of all vestiges of racial segregation.

In November of 1942, at the height of racial tensions provoked by the ongoing trial and media campaign, the LA-CIO Industrial Union Council convened a meeting of "Mexican workers in CIO shops" and prominent officials to "bring the program of the CIO into the Mexican community." The nine-point program that was adopted from the meeting was presented as the strategy for defending the Sleepy Lagoon 22, including: a direct appeal to the Mexican government to condemn the police violence; for the CIO to actively endorse and help fund the SDLC; for the police to cease their racial profiling, round-ups, and harassment of Mexican youth; for the firing of racist sheriff's lieutenant Edward Duran Ayres; for the district attorney to drop the charges; for the CIO to join protests against the *Los Angeles Times* and *Los Angeles Examiner*; for the sale of liquor and marijuana to be prohibited and strictly enforced; and for a permanent "Mexican Committee" to be established in the LA Inter-Union Council that would continue active organizing in the Mexican barrios.

Furthermore, the CP/CIO began to call for massive state-funded direct investment in the Mexican barrios to expand job training, end discriminatory hiring practices, improve housing, improve recreational facilities for youth, eliminate the threat of sinarquismo, and hire more capable officials without racial prejudice who could administer to the Mexican communities' needs.[32] They identified the lack of affordable, integrated housing as a contributing factor to the underdevelopment of the barrios. They cited an example of city planners developing new housing projects, and in some cases demolishing Mexican colonias to make way for the new units, only to then exclude Mexican families from moving into the homes.[33] The CP/CIO also applied this line to the anti-Mexican riots of June 1943.

Philip Connelly connected the violence of the sailors back to the racial climate created by the police crackdown on pachucos, claiming, "The Sleepy Lagoon prosecution with its gestapo tactics was the experiment of the forces of reaction to see what they could get away with in the way of persecution of minorities."[34]

The SDLC raised money for the legal defense, circulated petitions, had union resolutions passed, and organized rallies, pickets, and protests. They attempted to turn the case into a trial against the same system persecuting the youth, as McCormick explained the party's approach through the ILD:

> That's what we did—turn the courtroom into a classroom. Don't let them get away with this. Do it in such a way that you will educate the greatest number of people. And, of course, we filled the courtroom to capacity. We kept picket lines going if we could. We did all of the things that you possibly could to direct attention at what kinds of things were going on. Sometimes they decided that it would be best not to have a case.[35]

After several days of unchecked sailor violence, Josefina Fierro flew to Washington and asked Vice President Henry Wallace to declare all of Los Angeles out of bounds for the servicemen. Wallace called the War Department and demanded that all Mexican communities be declared off-limits. Finally, on June 9, 1943, the navy declared all Los Angeles out of bounds to military personnel on leave.

The SLDC and its historic social mobilization led to the acquittal and release of the youth and struck a blow against the rampant and unchecked violence of the Los

Angeles Police Department.[36] The inroads made by the Communist Party into the CIO, and by the CIO into the Mexican working class, threatened the long-standing economic arrangements of the region's powerful agricultural and industrial interests. As an interracial, class-based movement for civil rights materialized and mobilized, the traditional means of containing the barrios began to weaken. From within this juncture emerged a new coordinated campaign against the threat of communism in the form of the California Committee on Un-American Activities, referred to as the Tenney Committee, named after its stalwart anti-Communist chairman. The Tenney Committee was a state counterpart to the federal House Committee on Un-American Activities Committee (HUAC), also known as the Dies Committee after its fervent anti-Communist chair, Texas Democrat Martin Dies. In 1938, the federal HUAC began to investigate and identify Communists in the CIO, publicly identifying 248 CIO officials and organizers affiliated with the party as the opening shots of a generational campaign to drive radicals out of the unions.[37]

Jack Tenney, a California New Deal Democrat, represented growers opposed to Communist organizing of Mexican farmworkers. Tenney promoted anti-communism to weaken radical efforts against racism and to maintain segregation and anti-miscegenation as official doctrines designed to keep Mexican workers marginalized. While the SLDC conducted its campaign to expose anti-Mexican racism as a threat to wartime unity and the work of reactionary elements serving Axis aims, the Tenney Committee simultaneously targeted the SDLC as a "subversive plot" to stir up the Mexican working class toward the same ends.

In its formative stage, the Tenney investigations represented the incipient role of anti-communism as an instrument of repression to divide the radical Left and the Mexican working class. Red-baiting was also used to weaken the resolve of liberal allies of the Communist Party, who through public association and investigation could face repercussions that would make them "more cautious in opening their purses or lending their names to [Communist] organizations."[38] To cultivate public support for his crusade, Tenney published reports and made regular pronouncements to the media. A common refrain by anti-Communists and white supremacists alike was the allegation that the party stoked racial consciousness and antipathy where it didn't already exist; that Mexicans were content with their condition. Communist civil rights organizing, Tenney claimed, resulted only in the "accentuation, stimulation, and furtherance of the 'class struggle,'" by making "the Mexicans of southern California" aware of their "minority status."[39]

Chapter 35
Communist Miners and Cold War Civil Rights

*"The attack on the foreign-born is not an isolated matter. It is part of the whole
cold war drive. It is part of the Taft-Hartley Slave Act which was instituted
against labor. It is part of the drive against the living standards of all labor."*
—**Louise Pettibone Smith, American Committee
for the Protection of the Foreign-Born**

On August 23, 1939, the representatives of the Soviet and Nazi governments announced an unexpected "non-aggression pact" pledging non-intervention and
peaceful coexistence. The announcement of the Non-Aggression Pact was devastating for many radicals and rank-and-file Communists in the United States. They
saw in the Soviet Union the principled bastion of Communist internationalism that
represented the only force willing and capable of defeating fascism and Nazism. The
pact also undermined one of the organizing principles of the antiracist efforts of the
Communist Party in the South and Southwest, that Jim Crow racism was a US variant
of international fascism. When that proved hollow, and the Stalinist regime proved
more interested in self-preservation, many either left the party or adjusted accordingly.

The shift in policy led to an abrupt about-face by the Communists. For the next
twenty-two months they revived their characterization of the impending war as having imperialist, anti-USSR aims. The notion that the US and its western European
allies comprised a "Democratic Front against fascism" was discarded, and they now
opposed a British- and French-led war as a machination employed to ultimately crush
the Soviet Union. As a result, they called on the US government to cut off all aid to
the British and French. Domestically, they refocused their opposition to Roosevelt
and the US bourgeoisie, decrying its inexorable march into the "belligerent camp"
by aligning with the allies in their push for war. Furthermore, they believed, a mobilization toward war would lead to repression of unions and the Left.[1] By implication
of this shift, they now supported an intensification of workplace militancy and other
direct challenges to weaken the ruling class and its institutions.

As a result of its abrupt abandonment of several years of principled anti-fascist
organizing, thousands of supporters and members left the party and aligned front
groups. Concurrently, the new perspective opened the door for the revival of domestic struggle as criticism of Roosevelt and the ruling institutions was back on order.
In the interstices of these policy shifts, a grouping of Mexican/Latina Communists
and liberal allies formed the Spanish-Speaking People's Congress. At the forefront of
these efforts were Luisa Moreno, Bert Corona, and others previously mentioned. The

short-lived efforts of El Congreso came to an end when the pact ended with the full-scale Nazi invasion of Russia.

When on June 22, 1941, the Nazis invaded the Soviet Union, the Non-Aggression Pact was nullified, and the Communist Party engineered yet another 180-degree turn in its orientation. Complete and utter defense of the Soviet Union, including the abandonment of any projects that focused on domestic policies unrelated or contrary to full war mobilization, was the new and singular operational mantra of the party. The party became an uncritical supporter of the war effort, calling for full invasion. All criticisms of FDR were once again halted in the name of "wartime unity," as the party lurched to the right in its duty to align with the "progressive bourgeoisie" in its war against fascism. This led the party to support Japanese internment, while also fervently opposing strikes and any other attempt to halt total war mobilization. The party's full capitulation to war patriotism, including its own liquidation and reformation into a "political association" in 1944 to placate anti-Communists in the name of national unity, was conducted in line with the Stalinist regime's diktats and the leadership's unwavering loyalty. The intoxicating fervor of temporary convergence with pro-war and nationalistic capitalist forces in the United States and the diminishment of fervent anti-communism led party leaders into the delusion of long-standing postwar US-Soviet détente.

While the Allied victory in World War II brought an end to the war overseas and the illusion of class peace, the greatest strike wave in US history broke out on the home front. Wartime productivity had increased while employment decreased, and the prospect of mass unemployment with the end of the war loomed. As labor historian Art Preis explains, "through the steady rise of unauthorized strikes in 1944 and 1945, the American workers had been serving notice that the end of the war would bring a reckoning." Between January 1 and May 30, 1945, over half a million workers led primarily by CIO affiliates voted to authorize strikes, touching off a decade of class struggle that saw 43,279 strikes and over 26 million strikers.[2] By war's end, over 15 million workers had poured into unions. The rapid growth of unions and the prospect of another decade of mass labor militancy, this time with significant Communist leadership and influence, sowed panic within ruling circles.

The capitalist class's momentary toleration for Communists in the unions lasted until the end of the war and the onset of renewed labor militancy. Beginning in 1945, the ruling parties, led by the majority Democratic establishment, set out to eliminate the Communist Party once and for all. They used the state at all levels to implement a barrage of draconian laws designed to identify and root out Communists and their sympathizers from unions, government agencies, and throughout the private sector, where employers gladly aided in ousting union leaders and sympathizers. In alliance with the business class, Southern segregationists, and middle-class conservative organizations, the US government set out to destroy the operations of the Communist Party by merging the Cold War with the class war.

For the Mexican and Mexican American radicals the repression was carried out through the construction and deployment of immigration policy and enforcement.

As a form of labor control amid an immigrant and immigrant-descendant working class, repression through the manipulation of citizenship provided the now tested extra-constitutional means to suspend the most basic rights of people and eject them from the country. The Communist Party and its allies waged a two-front battle against the repression of Mexicans and other immigrant groups targeted by the state, both in the streets as well as in the courts. From 1933 until its gradual dismantling in the late 1970s, the American Committee for the Protection of the Foreign Born campaigned against police violence, political deportation, Operation Wetback, and other manifestations of state violence against radicals, unionists, and the Mexican working class as a whole.

From World War to Cold War

By the late 1930s, efforts were initiated by anti-Communists in Congress to begin isolating and repressing the Communist Party. The House Un-American Activities Committee (HUAC) was formed in 1938 to investigate disloyalty and "subversive activities." Originally known as the Dies Committee, the HUAC represented the Democratic Party–led effort to squash the Communist Party, drive it from the unions, and push it out of the barrios. While the Democrats began sharpening their knives to rid themselves of the Communists once and for all, the party leadership remained unwavering in its commitment to a united front with its executioners as part of the "win the war" effort. HUAC-led legislative efforts to suppress labor radicalism commenced with the Voorhis Act. This law, led by California Democrat Jerry Voorhis, required political organizations alleged to be "controlled by a foreign power" to register with the Justice Department, establishing the Communist Party as a "foreign entity."[3]

This was followed by the passage of the Smith Act of 1940. The act, championed by Virginia Democrat Howard Smith, criminalized membership in any organization "advocating the violent overthrow of the government." The Smith Act also contained provisions that required the registration of all "aliens" in the US, and reestablished and bolstered a 1918 provision that excluded immigrants from entry into the US if they were known to be affiliated with political radicalism. Like other anti-radical emergency measures, the wording was purposefully vague in order to allow for selective interpretation and the strategic targeting of left-wing groups.[4] The act enabled the deportation of any immigrant who joined or participated in the activities of any radical group since entering the country, regardless of length of residency. Over five million immigrants and noncitizens registered under the law, which allowed for the HUAC investigators to identify and target immigrant radicals, workers, trade unionists, and others deemed "undesirable" by the government.

By the late 1940s, state repression of the Communist Party and aligned organizations intensified. The Cold War with the Soviet Union offered the US ruling class the pretext for destroying the Communist Party, much as World War I served the same purpose in smashing the IWW. Both instances required the suspension of constitutional rights, the suppression of their press, the coordinated mass production of anti-radical propaganda associating the actions of the Left with supporting the enemy, and the mass arrest and deportation of those on the Left who were noncitizens. The state governments followed suit with their own anti-Communist restrictions, and the federal and state courts typically affirmed them or refused to hear legal challenges. By the mid-1940s, for example, sixteen states passed legislation to suppress all public activity of "subversive" groups and individuals.[5] The California Subversive Organization Registration Law of 1941, for instance, required the registration of organizations that advocated "overthrow of our government by force" or were "subject to foreign control."[6] Furthermore, state action against radicals encouraged private action. Employers willfully terminated radicals, landlords evicted them, and vigilantes who targeted them with violence or intimidation were given tacit approval without repercussion.

In 1947 the Truman administration opened a pathway for the suppression of the Communist Party and the CIO when it issued Executive Order 9835.[1] The order required loyalty oaths by all federal employees, but was more broadly worded and enforced to allow for the dismissal of a wide array of liberal and left-leaning officials. Shortly after that, a coalition of Republicans and Southern Democrats coalesced behind the passage of the Taft-Hartley Act in 1947, which expanded the purview of anti-Communist loyalty oaths into the labor movement. This opened the door for the attack on the union movement, as it contained a clause that required union officers to file an affidavit with the federal government declaring whether or not they were members of the party.

The Truman administration's move against Communists in the unions opened the door for a frontal assault on CIO unions most influenced by their interracial radicalism and class struggle militancy. In 1949–1950, the emboldened right wing of the CIO, supported by the federal government's offensive, led the charge to expel eleven unions from its ranks. These unions, including the International Union of Mine, Mill, and Smelter Workers (now commonly referred to as Mine Mill), represented over a million members, comprising about 20 percent of the CIO's total membership. These unions were also the most multiracial, representing the more recently organized industries that included significant numbers of Mexican, black, and women workers. As historian James Lorence describes, these unions were the "embodiment of labor force diversity in 1950s America, gender-integrated and multiracial."[7] Furthermore, they also contained a significant number of immigrant workers from Mexico, who were then further persecuted through a raft of intersecting anti-immigrant policies designed to further suppress the surge of left-wing organized labor.

The Internal Security Act of 1950, also called the McCarran Act after its chief sponsor, Democratic senator Pat McCarran of Nevada, introduced a series of sweeping police powers for the federal government to investigate, arrest, and deport "subversives" residing in the country.

> It shall be unlawful for any person knowingly to combine, conspire, or agree with any other person to perform any act which would substantially contribute to the establishment within the United States of a totalitarian dictatorship, as defined in paragraph (15) of section 3 of this title, the direction and control of which is to be vested in, or exercised by or under the domination or control of, any foreign government, foreign organization, or foreign individual.[8]

The congressional forces behind the law purposefully created a broad legal framework to ensnare radicals whether or not they broke any law. They claimed that communism was an international movement whose adherents were fanatically loyal to Russia over their own nation. As communism aimed to conquer foreign governments, mere association with the party or its ideals was enough to be implicated as a spy, an agent of a foreign government, or supportive of a totalitarian form of government.[9]

According to the law, "Communists" could not take government employment, obtain passports, or send publications through the US mail. The law set up a Subversive Activities Control Board to identify, investigate, and monitor alleged Communists. Organizations deemed Communist or Communist fronts by the board had to register with the federal government and provide names and addresses of the membership. These registers were made public, allowing for employers to have access to the political status of their workers.

The language of the law linked immigration with subversive activity, claiming, "There are, under our present immigration laws, numerous aliens who have been found to be deportable, many of whom are in the subversive, criminal, or immoral classes who are free to roam the country at will without supervision or control."[10] It revoked legal status of any foreign-born person in the US, regardless of length of residency, who was an anarchist or affiliated with the Communist Party or an organization designated as a Communist front. It required annual registration and the revocation of citizenship of those charged if they had held citizenship for less than five years. Furthermore, the law also targeted those foreign-born residents who were shown to be in agreement with radical principles or distributed any form of literature based on these principles, whether or not there was proof of membership. Any citizen that aided a known, excludable "alien" could be charged with a felony and up to five years in prison.

Two years later, McCarran teamed up with fellow Democrat and congressman from Pennsylvania Francis Walter to lead the passage of the Walter-McCarran Act, or the Immigration and Nationality Act of 1952. This act gave the attorney general near-dictatorial powers to administer over immigration and repress immigrant radicals. Immigrants could be arrested without warrant, denied citizenship, indefinitely detained without bail, and deported without due process, constitutional protections, proof of evidence, or the ability to appeal. No stipulations or oversight mechanisms were built into the act, which translated into the ability of employers to single out and fire immigrant workers (typically unionists and strikers) based on the assertion that their actions were in violation of the act. Furthermore, the law removed all statutes of limitations for application against those suspected of radical activities even in the distant past. It established the first links between the CIA and FBI to cross-check the political activities of immigrants. The act further reaffirmed racial exclusion via general immigration quotas and created the legal basis for mass deportation of undocumented Mexican laborers, which began in earnest in 1953.

The "War on Communism" and the immigrant Left empowered bureaucrats and cops to target these groups more aggressively, while one clause even allowed for the arrest and indefinite detention of registered Communists based on "emergency powers" delegated to the attorney general. The capitalist class was unified in its will to smash the Communist Party's influence within the labor movement, especially within those unions that modeled multiracial civil rights activism. This was apparent within both national political parties, which closed ranks behind an FBI campaign to internally disrupt and dismantle the Communist Party as a domestic component of the Cold War. For its part, the Communist Party characterized the repression as emerging fascism and moved its operations underground in 1950. This action greatly weakened its ability to maintain a national organization, with many people going into hiding or publicly distancing themselves from the party. Party members in the CIO unions, on the other hand, publicly renounced their memberships to stay in their position and, in the case of the Mine-Mill, carried on with their work under increasingly adverse and difficult conditions.

Communists, Mine Mill, and Civil Rights Unionism

Members of the Southern California branches of the Communist Party paid much closer attention to the "Mexican Question" in the aftermath of the anti-Mexican violence of 1942–1943. According to party leader Dorothy Healey, debates emerged over the national character of the population, with some advocating that Mexicans constituted an "oppressed nation" along Stalin's formulation, and not just a "national minority."[11] These debates played out in the late 1940s as state repression against the Mexican population intensified. At the Communist Party's 1948 convention, delegates from the Southwest branches of the party appealed to the national leadership to make the "Mexican Question" a central feature of party work.

In the document submitted to the convention, the delegates engaged in a much deeper analysis of the Mexican working class of the time. This started with a recognition of the independent political traditions of the Mexican working class in the United States:

> The effect of the Mexican revolutionary movement upon the Mexican Americans is very deep. The Mexican anarchist Flores Magón, who inspired the great peasant leaders Zapate [sic], came to California, set up headquarters in Los Angeles, and issued a newspaper, Regeneracion, which reflected the intense suffering of the Mexican people and their militant fight to better conditions. It sympathized with the Mexican Revolution and defended it against the imperialist attacks and maneuverings of the US government. He was imprisoned by the US government for rallying the Mexican Americans against participation in World War I [...] The effect of his thinking on the more advanced sections is still apparent.[12]

Furthermore, they likened the opposition of Mexicans in the US to assimilation to their resistance to US imperialism, which further laid the theoretical basis for incorporating the fight for cultural rights into the class struggle.

The group called on the national leadership to study the condition of Mexican people in the US "with the object of arriving at a scientific formulation of this question." They proposed the publication of party materials in Spanish, the holding of "cadre training schools" in Mexican barrios, a party platform on the question of agricultural work, including a minimum wage for field workers and their inclusion in the National Labor Relations Act, unemployment insurance coverage, and Social Security programs. They also proposed that they "increase our activities in the struggles for civil rights, including the fight against police brutality, deportations, and all other violations of the Bill of Rights."[13]

The authors also highlighted the international characteristics of the "Mexican Question," claiming that the perpetuation of racial oppression served as the "internal manifestation of American imperialism's predatory attitude toward Latin America [...] Yankee imperialism happening within our own border." Furthermore, they stated:

> In order to fully aid the oppressed people of Latin America, and to discharge the responsibilities incumbent upon us as the Communist Party of an oppressing nation, a more consistent struggle must be conducted on this question. The national liberation struggles of the Latin-American people against their American imperialist exploiters makes of them powerful allies of the American working class.[14]

While it does not appear that the national leadership was moved to change its orientation, the efforts of the southwestern Communists to agitate around Mexican civil rights did appear to resonate on a regional basis. Working through unions like Mine Mill, Communist Party members and the leadership of the southwestern locals took these concepts to heart. They formed the Popular/Democratic Front actions against discrimination through the Fair Employment Practices Committee, and the rank-and-file organizing and strike activity such as that in New Mexico in the late forties and early fifties.

Before the end of World War II, the CIO anti-discrimination committees worked in conjunction with Executive Order 8802, in which FDR compelled the defense industries with federal government contracts to desegregate their workforces. Showing the working-class beginnings of a left-led civil rights campaign, the order was given to preempt a call for a mass civil rights march on Washington, DC. A. Philip Randolph, a Socialist and founder of the Brotherhood of Sleeping Car Porters union, promised to turn out a hundred thousand workers to take over the capital if desegregation didn't occur. This led to the outlawing of racial discrimination in defense industry and government jobs, and reflected an opening for the CP/CIO to fight for the inclusion of Mexican workers from the defense industries in Los Angeles. It was also made into a fight within other strategic industries where labor was vital, including mining. As Clete Daniel explains:

> The labor of Chicanos had long been indispensable to the profitable operation of agriculture and industry alike in the border regions of the Southwest, but with only rare exceptions their exertions earned them neither equal standing in the society they helped to sustain nor a fair share of the material prosperity they helped to create ... Chicanos in the Southwest, whether native born citizens or recent immigrants, shared at the beginning of World War II a collective status

that had remained essentially unchanged in the nearly one hundred years since the end of the Mexican-American War.[15]

Efforts to implement FEPC measures were strongest in the southwestern mining regions, where Mexicans remained a majority of the workforce in copper and other operations crucial to the war effort.

While the FEPC was designed as a gesture and not an actual disruptive policy intent on challenging structural racism, Communists and CIO militants in Mine Mill attempted to fight to make it real in order to break down the wage and occupational differentials that continued to be enforced by the mine operators in Arizona, New Mexico, and Texas. Mexican radicals in the Mine Mill pushed policy enforcement forward through the aegis of the Good Neighbor policy, by appealing directly to the Office of the Coordinator of Inter-American Affairs. This was a recently created agency housed in the Department of Commerce that was headed by Nelson Rockefeller. During the war years, the federal government felt pressure to ameliorate anti-American sentiment in Latin America, concerned that discontent could ignite protest and "pro-Axis" sentiment. The deep poverty and structural poverty that persisted among Mexicans in the Southwest served as an area of concern, especially as CIO unionists, Communists, and other radicals made it a focus of their propaganda.

The Office of War Information worried that widespread attention to discrimination against Mexicans in the American Southwest undermined continental strategy. US racism was "a constant irritant in hemispheric relations, [making] a mockery of the Good Neighbor Policy, [providing] an open invitation to Axis propagandists to depict us as hypocrites to South and Central America and, above all, [was] a serious waste of potential manpower. . . . As one Roosevelt Administration official proclaimed, The Spanish-speaking people who live in the United States, both citizens and noncitizens, are a link between the country and Mexico and all of Latin America. If discrimination exists against them in this country, the other Americas are aware of it."[16]

The Mexican government opposed the actions of the Mexican workers in the Mine Mill to force hearings on racial discrimination in mining, believing that they would torpedo negotiations over the Bracero Program. Southern Democrats vehemently objected to hearings, concerned that FEPC expansion into the South would bring attention and energize opposition to Jim Crow. The actions were also opposed by white miners who were recruited from southern states including Texas and Arkansas. They perceived the campaign for equality as a threat, and organized "hate strikes" to oppose the inclusion of Mexican workers and preserve their racial status.

Copper companies wanted to bring braceros into the mines, which was vehemently opposed by the Mine Mill, who raised the issue of racial discrimination as a reason for Mexican public opposition. The Mine Mill formed its own Southwestern Industrial Union Council, comprised of forty locals from Arizona, New Mexico, and West Texas to collect data and investigate instances of racial discrimination on the job. They found that they were denied promotions, excluded from skilled work and management, paid lower wages for the same work, and given arbitrary work assignments. It was also common for Mexican workers to train Anglos while receiving lower wages than the trainees. Also housing, recreational facilities, and medical offices were segregated and inferior.

In the end, efforts to expose racism within the mining industry were sabotaged by the employers, AFL craft unionists, and from within the FDR administration, whose sentiment ranged from grudging tolerance to thinly veiled contempt. The investigations were restricted, stonewalled by employers, and derailed by politicians. Ernest Trimble, the lead investigator in charge of the El Paso office of the FEPC, concluded that collusion between oppositional forces doomed the effort, while Reid Robinson, president of the Mine, Mill, and Smelter Workers Union concluded that "it is unfortunate that the [FEPC] was prevailed upon by vested interests and by old-time politicians in the State Department to call off its announced hearings . . . The failure of this committee to carry out its commitments is a victory for the reactionary forces of the Southwest."[17]

Nevertheless, the Mexican government abandoned efforts to expand the Bracero Program into the copper mines out of fear of protest and homegrown opposition from the CTM. Meanwhile, it found more political support for the agricultural Bracero Program as the Camacho government began winding down land redistribution and the PRI made rapprochement with US capital. When FEPC failed to challenge racial discrimination in the workplace, the fight for equality moved to the point of production. The Mine Mill Union then conducted strikes in an effort to eliminate the "southwest differential" racial wage structure. As part of this effort, the union helped create La Asociación Nacional Mexicana-Americana to cultivate political support, while they relied on the Mexican Miners' Union to discourage Mexican miners from crossing the border to cross picket lines.

Mine Mill Local 890

Communists in the Mine-Mill led the initial efforts to organize Mexican and Anglo miners into integrated locals in New Mexico in the 1930s. The growth of the union on a national scale during and after World War II was intertwined with its commitment to class-struggle unionism, facilitated by a radical layer of members and officers cultivated by the Communist Party, and trained by the great class battles of the 1930s. For instance, the preamble to Mine Mill's constitution defined the union in Marxist terms (reminiscent of the IWW):

> We hold that there is a class struggle in society, and that this struggle is caused by economic conditions. We affirm the economic condition of the producer to be that he is exploited of the wealth that he produces, being allowed to retain [a portion] barely sufficient for his elementary necessities [. . .] We hold that the class struggle will continue until the producer is recognized as the sole master of his product. We assert that the working class, and it alone, can and must achieve its own emancipation. We hold that an industrial union and the concerted political action of all wage workers is the only method of attaining this end. An injury to one is an injury to all.[18]

This generation of union leaders was also committed to antiracism as a strategy of organizing racially oppressed workers, through direct confrontation with racial discrimination at the point of production and through the incorporation of racial equity clauses in negotiated contracts. These two features of radical unionism converged to form Mine Mill Local 890 in Grant County, New Mexico, and one of the most fiercely fought strikes of the period, which had direct implications for the eventual defeat of Jim Crow racism in mining.

Mining camps in New Mexico had changed little in the way of racial structures by the end of World War II. Work in mining towns like those in Grant County remained divided between Anglo and Mexican occupations and wage scales. Communities were further segregated, with hotels, restaurants, movie theaters, swimming pools, and other public facilities having separate sections for Mexicans or excluding them outright. Racial segregation persisted even though Mexicans were the majority of the population, and about 90 percent of the unionized mining workforce in the county, and 85 percent of total Mine Mill membership in New Mexico, Texas, and Arizona by 1950.[19]

Wages were historically lower for miners in Arizona and New Mexico than in the northern regions because mine operators exploited racial segregation to pay Mexicans less than whites, pulling down wages for whites as well as weakening union efforts. According to Jack Cargill,

> Separate payroll lines, washrooms, toilet facilities, and housing for Mexican Americans were still commonplace in the mines of Grant County during the early 1950s [. . .] Wage rates for laborers, muckers, and miners (jobs usually performed by Mexican Americans in the Southwest) were much lower in Arizona and New Mexico than in Utah, Nevada, or Montana where Anglos worked in these jobs [. . .] Miners in Arizona and New Mexico had won wage increases equal to those gained at other mines in the West during the postwar period, but industry bargainers had refused to eliminate the area differentials and thereby had perpetuated the discriminatory rate structure.[20]

Mexicans were singled out and denied secondary forms of pay, including the practice of paying underground workers for time traveled to and from the surface (referred to as "collar-to-collar" pay). They were also customarily denied access to better-paid "skilled" work.

In the 1940s, the Mine-Mill in the Southwest made opposition to racial discrimination against Mexicans a central feature of its organizing. The union deployed skilled Mexican American organizers, many of whom were also members of the Communist Party or sympathized with its civil rights orientation within CIO-affiliated unions. This coincided with the ascendancy of Communist leadership nationally within CIO unions, the need to overcome the employers use of racial antagonisms, and the practical necessities of organizing among a substantial Mexican workforce. Mine Mill launched a national organizing drive, establishing uniform standards for all work, which in effect challenged regional variations based on racial discrimination.

In 1942, for instance, Mine-Mill locals in New Mexico led by Mexican workers won a contract with the Kennecott Copper Company that struck a significant blow against racial segregation. The negotiated contract contained an article stating that the company would not "discriminate against any employee ... because of union membership ... or ... race, creed, color, or national origin."[21] This set a precedent for the union to equalize wages and working conditions in future contracts. As Ellen Baker explains, "National bargaining helped secure better wages, and especially important to Grant County, an equalization of wages: it guaranteed fewer regional differences in wages, and companies could not as easily insist on 'local custom' to justify a discriminatory dual-wage system."[22] Furthermore, seniority rights were built into contract language, which protected Mexican workers who tended to be targeted first for layoffs, considered last for rehire, and bypassed for consideration for promotion. This confrontation with employer-enforced racial discrimination led to the significant expansion of Mine Mill in New Mexico. Between 1941 and 1944, for instance, Mine-Mill membership nationally had nearly doubled, from 50,000 to 97,000, with a significant portion of this growth occurring in New Mexico.[23] Mexican workers began to have access to "skilled" work alongside Anglos.

The 1950 Empire Zinc Strike

Mine Mill Local 890 in Grant County was a majority-Mexican local, which reflected these trends within the union: Communist Party leadership and influence, integrated membership, and an active orientation against racial discrimination. Clinton and Virginia Jencks were sent to Grant County as part of the Mine Mill International's efforts to rebuild and strengthen the locals by building roots in the Mexican mining barrios. They lived and worked among the Mexican community and made it a priority as part of the reorganization. The Jencks, with the support of left-wing Mexican unionists, merged the five existing locals throughout the county into one big industrial local in 1946, representing about five thousand workers at six different mines.

While maintaining jurisdiction over the whole of Grant County, Mine Mill 890 conducted its early business in a tavern and at a local mutualista hall in the Mexican barrio of Hurley. They later located their permanent headquarters in Bayard, New Mexico, in close proximity to several of the region's Mexican residential communities. Union documents, publicity, and negotiated contracts were published in Spanish as well as English. Mine Mill union officials introduced new strategies for cross-ethnic organizing in its New Mexican locals, and built on local traditions, history, and leadership. In Grant County, this included bilingual training schools and the cultivation of a layer of Mexican stewards, organizers, and union officers. They also operated a local radio station, in which pro-union programming was transmitted in both Spanish and English.

Meanwhile, a small but significant percentage of Anglo miners in the district who valued higher wages, better working conditions, and democratic decision-making structures over maintaining racial segregation joined or stuck with the union through this transition into a fully integrated union with a civil rights orientation. As one Mine Mill organizer explained, "It didn't take a man working in the mine or a mill or a smelter long to find out that his problems were the same as the Mexican-Americans, and vice-versa."[24]

Bending to the right-wing shift in the Democratic Party and its aggressive clamoring for the suppression of Communists in the unions, the national leadership of the CIO retreated from its principled opposition to the Taft-Hartley Act, especially its anti-Communist tenets. Instead, the CIO leadership punted on the issue in 1948, allowing constituent unions to determine their own policy. Mine Mill leaders were among the last holdouts, refusing to sign anti-Communist affidavits. Metal corporations initially refused to negotiate with "Communist" unions like Local 890, and actively aided decertification campaigns against them. Hostile CIO unions like the United Steelworkers raided the Mine Mill, while the National Labor Relations Board worked expeditiously to recertify "non-communist" unions.[25]

Despite the opposition, Local 890 carried out militant actions on the job to demonstrate their power to disrupt production and unity in their ranks. This militancy rendered the anti-Communist posturing impotent and compelled the mining companies to eventually sign contracts with the local. Furthermore, raiding attempts were also beaten back, as Mine Mill had won profound loyalty from its Mexican workers, who fiercely defended their union. Many of the local Mexican miners, especially leaders like Juan and Virginia Chacón, the former being president of Local 890, joined the party even as it was being persecuted on all sides. As Virginia Chacón explained, communism was part of strong trade unionism, "part of getting us to learn and walk further and see things the way they are happening. As far as we were concerned, Juan and I . . . didn't think anything of the Communist Party. We just joined it because we wanted to be in it." Another member, Anita Torres, proclaimed that she joined the party after realizing, "If this is what they are gonna call communist, fine: Let's all be communists then! Because we're fighting for our *rights!*"[26] Her husband, a miner named Lorenzo, further explained that he began to get interested in communism because the press called the most active and militant people communist: "I began to get curious and I used to invite them to a bar, for example, after a meeting. And I would ask them, 'Well, why is it that they're calling you a communist?,' And they would relate their experience in the union . . . how they handled grievances, how they built the union, how they had eliminated discrimination. Well, for me, that was the way it was supposed to be."[27]

The Mine Mill leadership and party affiliates eventually conceded in an effort to placate the right wing within its own ranks, remain in the CIO and stop the hostile raiding attempts by other unions, and seek protection from the NLRB. Prominent Mine Mill leaders throughout the organization who were known members of the Communist Party publicly resigned from the party in 1949 to hold on to their positions. Despite the capitulation, this did not stop the attacks. Eventually, Mine Mill was expelled from the CIO in February of 1950. The reactionary assault on the Left and civil rights set the context for Local 890's strike against Empire Zinc.

Mexican and Mexican American miners in the mining town of Hanover, New Mexico, went on strike against the Empire Zinc Company, a subsidiary of the multinational New Jersey Zinc Company. The strike lasted for nearly a year and a half, from October 1950 until January 1952, in a brutal fight that arrayed the government, media, mine companies, other unions, and a reactionary political climate against 150 mostly Mexican miners organized in Local 890. Despite every possible trick, maneuver, and act of violence against the strikers, the miners beat the company in a mass strike that in the end relied primarily on the leadership, tenacity, and the solidarity of the strikers' wives.

The main demands of the strike centered around equality for the Mexican workforce. In the predominantly white mines, workers were paid for time spent in transit between the surface and mine depths and received more paid holidays. Injecting a civil rights perspective into the contract negotiations, Local 890 called for full equalization for Mexican workers on these issues. The employers stonewalled on these matters as racial discrimination was integral to its profitability, spending over $1 million (in 1950 dollars) to break the strike. In fact, Empire Zinc made prior arrangements with the other companies—Kennecott, American Smelter and Refinery Company, and Phelps-Dodge—to work together to win the strike and effectively break the union. They agreed in advance to the sharing of profits with Empire Zinc to offset losses incurred during a prolonged work stoppage.[28] Further support for the company's efforts to break the Mine-Mill picket lines came from the local government. District judges, the district attorney, and the sheriff's department aligned to break the strike however possible. As a result, there were several turning points that occurred during the strike that threatened its continuation.

Local 890 mobilized the strikers into fixed and roving pickets to prevent the entrance of strikebreakers. They blocked the entrance and back roads into the mining complex, holding the lines intact for the first six months. In response to the strong support for the strike, the company financed the hiring of an additional twenty-four "special deputies," which were drawn from the ranks of strikebreakers, mine foremen, property owners from non-mining communities, and others predisposed to be against the union and the strike. Despite the overt buildup, the local was able to rally miners and millers from other locals when the sheriff's deputies attempted to break the lines. When the pro-company district attorney authorized arrests of Local 890's strike captains on charges of blocking a public thoroughfare, reinforcements were called in to hold the lines. For the first six months of the strike, the company could not get strikebreakers through the lines.

Union strategy during this time relied on the high level of solidarity between the Mexican workers to maintain the lines, as well as other tactics that allowed the miners and their families to persevere without paychecks. They successfully appealed to unions countywide to not cross their picket lines, including railroad workers and AFL crafts. The union built up a strike fund to financially support the striking families for the duration of the strike. Various methods were used to maintain the fund, including the release of some strikers from picket duty to find work elsewhere, especially those with large families. Those who found work were required to return 25 percent of their paychecks into the strike fund.

The union also relied on support from other locals within the Mine Mill International and those still sympathetic within the CIO. Through these other unions and locals, fundraising efforts extended into barrios across the Southwest, which served to publicize the strike. The strike fund was also maintained through the efforts of the Ladies' Auxiliary, a support organization of the miners' wives, who regularly organized fundraisers and public events to appeal to the larger public for material support.

In 1936, the national convention of the International Union of Mine, Mill, and Smelter Workers affirmed the establishment of a national auxiliary organization, in which women in miner union families organized to support strikes, pay dues, and have a say in union affairs. Grant County union women formed the Ladies' Auxiliary Number 209 in 1948, which came to play a pivotal role in the outcome of the Empire Zinc strike. Not only did they raise money, print leaflets, organize food production and distribution, and help maintain the radio program, but they eventually took over the picket lines in June of 1951 until the strike's conclusion seven months later.

This transition occurred after the company was able to secure an injunction from a sympathetic federal district judge in Silver City, who was now empowered by a Taft-Hartley provision to issue injunctions against union activity determined to be an "unfair labor practice." Taking the company's side, the judge permanently prohibited any picketers from blocking entry points into the mining complex. The two dozen deputies, paid for by the company, were now a fixture at the picket lines, along with vehicles at the ready to haul away any picketers who defied the order. The union membership, divided over how to proceed, remained in a holding pattern.

In June of 1951 their hand was forced when the company announced its intention to reopen the mines, trucking in a caravan of strikebreakers from out of town. Between June 5 and June 12, sheriff's deputies arrested over a dozen unionists for failure to observe the injunction. They were aided by the local, company-aligned (and often company-funded) media. Local newspapers such as the *Silver City Daily Press* and the *Daily Press* regularly attacked the Mine Mill, infusing anti-communism and allegations that its members were spies, industry saboteurs, and the like, with overt racial contempt against Mexicans challenging racial boundaries.[29] Their problems were further compounded in August, when the United Steelworkers of America (USWA) launched an "anti-Communist" raid on the Mine-Mill local in the middle of the strike. Despite its failure, as the Mexican American miners remained fiercely loyal to Local 890, the USWA maintained a presence in the region, trying to undermine the Mine Mill Union across the county for years thereafter.[30]

Under these deteriorating conditions, women in the auxiliary supported by Communist Party members in the union pitched the idea that women should take over the strike. After an intense debate at the union hall, the women prevailed, invoking a union clause that allowed the local leadership to extend to the women's auxiliary the right to vote in union affairs. This change inspired women from other non-striking locals to participate, greatly increasing the numbers far beyond the original strikers. The dynamics of the strike changed dramatically, as the company, deputies, and strikebreakers now had to deal with a new type of resistance for which they were initially unprepared. Believing the women would last only a few days, they were taken aback by their resolute militancy and ultimately relied on the same tactics of repression as used against the men.

Within the first month of the pickets, the sheriffs tried to use tear gas to scatter the pickets, drove their cars recklessly into the lines, and carried out mass arrests. But the women held the lines and fought back fiercely. After one battle for control of a picket line, six women were charged with assault and battery on scabs, but women picketers blocked the police car sent to arrest them. While some women were hurt in the melees, they organized a strategy of resistance that relied on their numbers and changing tactics that kept their opponents off-balance. This included systematically bombarding the cars with rocks to break their windshields, throwing chile powder into the eyes of the police when they approached, sending teams to sabotage parked cars by ripping out wiring, and a number of other measures. They also took the fight to the sheriff's deputies. After one particularly violent episode of police brutality, they led a march of families that surrounded the sheriff's office in Hanover demanding that the district attorney fire the two deputies involved.

In another case, the deputies arrested forty-five women and seventeen children and transferred them to the local jail. When the sheriff informed them that they would only be released if they relinquished participation in the strike, the women pledged to stay together and refused to sign. After several days, the sheriff was forced to release them after it became impossible to house and feed such a sizeable group. To accelerate this process, the women sang labor songs, chanted relentlessly, and turned their incarceration into a mass action of protest and disruption. After it became apparent that the ladies' picket line could not be broken, and that the local strike movement was intensifying beyond the control of the sheriff's office, the governor sent in state troops. Strikers and their wives spent the equivalent of 1,100 workdays in jail, but nevertheless maintained the picket lines throughout.

Negotiations were gradually reconvened, and in January of 1952, at the height of the anti-Communist and anti-immigrant onslaught, the union families claimed victory and won their demands. As Anita Torrez explained, "Finally, the company called the union and proposed a settlement. Most of the demands were met. There would be equality in housing, sanitation. After the strike, the company put in running water to our houses. The pool and the theater were desegregated. Segregation was done away with."[31]

La Asociación Nacional México-Americana

Mexican and Mexican American radicals within CIO unions in the Southwest formed the civil rights organization La Asociación Nacional México-Americana (ANMA) amid a rising tide of police violence, deportation, and other forms of state repression against the Left. Mexican Communist Party members and supporters in CIO unions, especially in those unions with the largest concentrations of Mexican membership, such as the Mine Mill, the ILWU, and the Furniture Workers, convened a gathering in February of 1949 in Phoenix, Arizona, to build a union-led civil rights campaign.

The ANMA continued the trend of earlier Communist-led civil rights efforts, which characterized the Mexican population in the US, whether citizen or immigrant, as "one people" and called for political as well as cultural rights. The ANMA's membership requirements reflected its broad character, whose welcoming of immigrants, Communists, and other racial groups cut against the retrenchment of Jim Crowism and its attendant anti-immigration sentiment and anti-communism. The founding convention established that the ANMA was open to all who supported the progress of the pueblo Mexicano "regardless of nationality, race, citizenship, sex, or political affiliation." ANMA chapters also functioned as cultural centers akin to mutualistas, holding community dances, Mexican holiday celebrations, Spanish-language classes, and other events.

Fifty delegates from thirty CIO union locals from California, Texas, Colorado, New Mexico, and Arizona represented a membership of four thousand union members across the Southwest. Membership drives were conducted where CIO locals served as a base of operations to reach into southwestern Mexican barrios, and as far away as Detroit, Chicago, and New York City. The Mine Mill Union provided the organizational infrastructure of the ANMA, with the national headquarters of the ANMA established in the Mexican barrio of Boyle Heights in East Los Angeles. In Grant County, New Mexico, for instance, the leadership comprised Local 890's *mesa directiva*, or executive board.

The group was founded as a "national association for the protection of the civil, economic, and political rights of the Mexican people in the United States, as well as for the expansion of their education, culture, and progress."[32] The ANMA represented the last effort by CP/CIO to wield class power to break the hold of Jim Crow racism over the structures of the southwestern economy, building on the gains of the 1950 zinc strike and the militant activism of El Congreso.[33]

In practice, the ANMA functioned more as a self-defense organization, as the political climate shifted starkly to the right as the government began a scorched-earth campaign to uproot and liquidate the Communist Party. For its three years of existence, the ANMA focused primarily on opposing state violence, including the detention and deportation of immigrant unionists and radicals. As one edition of the ANMA's paper *Progreso* proclaimed: "[T]he Mexican people are objects of an accelerated program of discrimination, deportations, physical assaults, police brutality, and at times, murder."[34]

In the face of rising violence, the Mexican leadership within the CIO, including Bert Corona, Alfred Montoya, and others, believed that only mass organization of the Mexican people in unions and civil rights and self-defense committees could prevent the emboldened Right from rolling back the union and civil rights gains to date. Showing the influence of the party on the ideological framework of ANMA, the perspective documents and press emphasized the characterization of Mexicans as a "conquered people" whose condition of extreme class subjugation under capitalism began with US expansion and occupation of Mexico, and was maintained by the structural violence and segregation of Jim Crow racism.

Like El Congreso, the ANMA incorporated the concept of "cultural democracy" framework into their antiracism program, including the defense of language rights for Mexicans. Because of this fundamental role of racism in dividing workers in US capitalism, the ANMA stressed that Mexican and African American unity had to be the basis for coordinated action. They stressed the need for social expressions of culture and multinationality to counter "Anglo chauvinism," which was characterized as a by-product of American imperialism.[35] Furthermore, the promotion and celebration of Mexican cultural identity was a frontal challenge to the stifling racist conformity embedded within anti-communism. As McCarthyism converged seamlessly with Southern racism, opposition to Communist-led "multiculturalism" and "race-mixing" was encoded in the DNA of anti-communism.

ANMA provided support for workers facing deportation after Mexican deportation increased in the early 1950s, culminating in Operation Wetback. They joined in coalition with the American Committee for the Protection of the Foreign Born, a Popular Front immigrant rights organization, helped organize mass meetings and protests, and raised and distributed funds to support legal efforts to block deportations.

In some locales, the ANMA also formed the ranks of a proto-labor party, promoting union-aligned Mexican working-class political candidates under the Progressive Party against reactionary incumbents for local office. They also worked with party-affiliated lawyers to oppose various Jim Crow practices. The Grant County chapter publicized, protested, and brought legal suits against the racial segregation of Mexican schoolchildren and the use of restrictive covenants to enforce residential segregation.

After the onset of the Korean War, the group took a public stance against the war, calling attention to the disproportionately high Mexican casualty rate, and how pro-war patriotism led police to be more violent against the Left, and how it provided jingoistic cover for more anti-Communist persecution. Because of their antiwar position, anti-Communists all the way to arch-reactionary Republican senator Joseph McCarthy publicly alleged that Communists in the unions, especially in the mining sector, like the one in Grant County, were a threat to the production of war materials.

By 1950, the emboldened right wing within the CIO had gained the upper hand and expelled Mine Mill and ten other "Communist-led" unions from the union federation. This opened the door to the CIO leadership then sponsoring or tolerating raiding operations by other unions in order to wreck the left-wing unions and salvage what was left over. Targeted by both the government and their own fellow unionists, employers declared open season on alleged Communist-led unions, firing leaders and organizers and violating contracts.

The ANMA was declared a subversive organization by the federal government in 1954, and the group soon dissolved under the weight of repression, with the arrest or deportation of members and leaders of the group, and the increased threat of physical violence by vigilantes, the KKK, and other racial terror groups. The KKK was revived and experienced substantial growth under the conditions of anti-Communist reaction. They made anti-communism and anti-immigration their guiding principles to align with federal, state, and local government efforts, especially as radical and Communist-led unionism had led to the growth of mass interracial centers of union power in the Southwest.

The American Committee for the Protection of the Foreign Born (ACPFB)

The campaigns of Mexican mass deportation coincided with the anti-Communist crackdown after the end of World War II. In 1948, over two hundred thousand Mexican people were deported, over half a million were deported in 1951, and over one million were deported in 1954.[36] Beginning with the passage of the McCarran Act of 1950, the federal government then went after the Communists. A campaign of mass deportation was unleashed on Mexican and Latino CIO leaders, Communist Party members, and those associated with the party through their participation or support in designated "front organizations." The party and its allies had long understood the role of deportation as a tool for breaking unions and left-wing political parties. In 1933, members of the party, their supporters, and principled liberal allies created what became known as the American Committee for the Protection of the Foreign Born, to serve as a legal defense network and political lobbying vehicle to support the rights of immigrants in the United States.

The ACPFB opposed all deportations and other forms of victimization of the foreign-born over its three decades of existence. It called for the opening of the US to refugees from fascist Italy and Nazi Germany, and opposed all restrictions on immigrants receiving relief and other forms of government assistance. They campaigned against the exclusion of noncitizens from employment, linking anti-immigrant discrimination to the low wages and poor working conditions of the native-born. Reflecting its ideological alignment with the Communist Party, the intellectual leadership analyzed the oppression of immigrants through the politics of class.

According to its foundational thinking, the repression of immigrants and tightening political control of immigration flows was bound up with the leading role of foreign-born workers in left-wing political parties, in union organizing, and in civil rights causes. Furthermore, the ideological attack on the immigrant section of the unemployed was used as a pretext to cut funding for relief. Co-founder Dwight C. Morgan explained this in the literature of the ACPFB:

> In the attempt to rid themselves of the foreign-born workers most active in the trade unions and working class political organizations, the employers fostered the system of laws to expel the most militant from the country. Thus while some workers were excluded because it was said that they lowered the standard of living, others who fought to raise it were deported. These laws were amended to meet new situations as they arose in the class struggle [...] In this period of decline of the present economic system, reactionary forces are striving more desperately than ever before to pit the native against the foreign born in order to

reduce the wages and cut the relief of all the workers [...] Almost every struggle for higher wages and better working conditions has been classed by reactionaries as the attempt of "foreign agitators" to "undermine" American institutions.[37]

Party supporters and liberal co-thinkers identified the political nature of immigration politics in the patterns of repression of labor unionism in the 1930s. The Immigration Act of 1918 contained a provision that allowed for the deportation of immigrants if they entered while espousing anarchist or antigovernment philosophy. This provision was revived alongside the rise in class struggle in the 1930s. During a strike led by Mexican miners in Gallup, New Mexico, over a hundred Mexican workers were rounded up and deported. In another case, nearly four hundred "alien radicals" were rounded up in the aftermath of the San Francisco general strike. The ILWU leader during the strike, Harry Bridges, himself an immigrant, faced attempts at deportation for over two decades following the strike. In 1940, the 1918 act was made more punitive, stating that any noncitizen who espoused radical or antigovernment doctrine "at any time after entry" was subject to deportation.[38] While the crackdown on the immigrant Left had long roots in US history, it intensified after the end of World War II when labor militancy was once again on the rise.

Truman appointed Thomas Campbell Clark as attorney general in 1945. Clark was a zealous anti-radical whose singular focus was to root out and eliminate Communists. As attorney general, he told a gathering of federal attorneys in 1946, "If any alien in your district engages in Communist Party activity, there is no place for him in the United States." In his first year in office, the Justice Department identified over 4,000 suspected radicals, of whom 482 were being investigated and 228 were identified as "Communists" and fast-tracked for deportation. This included a number of union leaders around the country, those named as party members, and those known to have participated in strikes at some point over the previous decade.[39]

One of these was Humberto Silex, a Nicaraguan-born Mine-Mill union organizer who successfully organized the first CIO locals in El Paso, Texas, including the creation of Local 509 among Mexican smelter workers. Silex had entered the US with legal authorization and had lived in the US for twenty-five years, was married, and had US-born children. His prominence as a CIO organizer and his success in building locals that comprised Spanish-speaking Mexican workers made him a threat to the American Smelting and Refining Company. When his local went on strike in 1945, the INS was called in. After searching for any possible violation that could stick, they charged him with making an unauthorized crossing into Mexico (on an occasion when he crossed for lunch). When this wasn't sufficient, they declared him ineligible for citizenship as a so-called "undesirable." This was based on a recent incident in which he was arrested after a fight with an abusive, anti-union company foreman who tried to physically eject him from the company after an unlawful firing in 1942. Even though he received a direct pardon from the governor of Texas absolving him of any crime, and was ordered reinstated to his job by a federal appeals court, the incident was still used against him.[40] His arrest and attempted deportation under such contrived circumstances reflected how the corporations were becoming enabled by the punitive provisions of the anti-Communist laws to single out, report, and have removed labor leaders who were noncitizens. The Texas State Industrial Union Council opposed his deportation, passing a resolution that condemned the underlying motive to break the union:

> Powerful corporations and other forces in El Paso have demonstrated repeatedly that they are willing to go to any lengths to destroy the CIO organization in the community [and] …the deportation of Silex would be calculated to intimidate these prospective citizens and deter them from participation in the CIO.[41]

In response to the repression, the ACPFB and its allied organizations organized a national campaign of protest and lobbying. Thousands of protesters picketed the Immigration and Naturalization headquarters in New York, a mass picket was set up in front of the White House, and similar protests took place simultaneously in Chicago, San Francisco, Detroit, Los Angeles, Cleveland, and other cities. As a result of mass opposition, a federal judge responded to a request for an injunction by ACPFB lawyers and blocked the deportations in 1948. Despite the setback, the anti-Communist campaign gained more momentum and broad support within the ruling parties, which closed ranks to pass more sweeping national legislation.

After the political defeat, Clark made a public campaign against the ACPFB, placed it on the list of federally designated "subversive organizations," and went after its leadership and membership. Abner Green, the ACPFB national executive secretary, was sentenced to a year in prison in 1950 after he refused to turn over the names and addresses of the membership and financial contributors. Rose Chernin, who was part of the founding of the ACPFB in Los Angeles, was also arrested. Congress then passed the Internal Security Act of 1950, which allowed for the indefinite detention of "alien radicals." It passed Congress by an overwhelming majority, which then overrode a veto by Harry Truman, after his own Democratic allies and appointees revolted against him.[42] To facilitate "indefinite detention," immigrant concentration camps were established at Ellis Island in New York, and Terminal Island in San Pedro, California.

Los Angeles Committee for the Protection of the Foreign Born (LACPFB)

Even as a blacklisted and targeted organization, the ACPFB persevered. With the increased threat of deportations, the committee established a case system by which it developed a multipronged defense that included legal support, lobbying, and protest. At its 1947 annual convention in Cleveland, Ohio, the national organization turned its attention to the increasing repression and deportation of Mexican and Latino radicals in the Southwest. That same year, the party-linked Civil Rights Congress in Los Angeles formed a subcommittee called the Mexican-American Civil Rights Committee to oppose racial discrimination. In their archives, the group's documents discuss the types of cases handled by the committee, mainly the provision of support for Mexican youth and workers targeted by police and the INS and systematically ensnared in the criminal justice system or turned over to immigration officials for deportation.[43] Documents reveal that police routinely harassed, arrested, and occasionally killed young Mexicans. Cases on file describe police beatings, frame-ups, and regular harassment of young people. In one record, they describe a "reign of terror" in the Boyle Heights-Belvedere community "to break up and intimidate meetings of trade unions, progressive and minority organizations."[44]

As a committee flier circulated in the community appealed:

> Police Brutality and discrimination against the Mexican and Negro People. Police blockades which terrorize the Negro and Mexican communities. Police practices of arrest and search without warrant, beatings and lawless disregard of basic civil rights is a daily diet of the Mexican and Negro people . . . You can help stop these illegal police practices. Report all violation of civil rights, unwarranted searches and arrests and mistreatment at police blockades to the Mexican Civil Rights Committee.[45]

In 1949, the Los Angeles Police Department colluded with immigration agents to comb through the barrios and round up "deportable" Mexicans. They set up roadblocks, interrogated Mexican Americans on street corners, burst into homes without warrants, raided shops and factories, and hunted "deportable" Mexicans in train depots and bus stations. The INS estimated that it deported 50,000 Mexican nationals from Los Angeles (293,000 nationally) and supposedly freed up jobs for "citizens and veterans."[46]

In 1950, this committee spun off to form the Los Angeles Committee for the Protection of the Foreign Born (LACPFB), now devoted entirely to defending a growing number of foreign-born, mostly Mexican, radicals and unionists facing deportation. After the first year, the group reported:

> 1951 demonstrated the need to develop a fight to stop the mass deportation of Mexican workers and leaders of the Mexican community. We made the first attempts to align ourselves with the fighters of the Mexican people, and successfully halt some of the deportations . . . In 1952, we will enlarge our program of activities, broaden our work to repel coming attacks on the foreign born, and gather strength to defeat the deportation drive. We will strengthen friendly relations with our allies among the national groups, the Negro and Mexican people, the trade unions, and seek to extend our influence by reaching new sections of the people.[47]

The Los Angeles Committee for the Protection for the Foreign Born was launched as a joint effort by the Civil Rights Congress, the International Union of Mine, Mill and Smelter Workers, the International Longshore and Warehouse Union, La Asociación Nacional Mexicana-Americana, United Furniture Workers Local 576 and others. The executive secretary was Rose Chernin, a leading member of the Communist Party, who focused on building the committee as a broad-based community organization. To do this, the LACPFB set up community chapters, usually centered around the families of those directly affected by police violence or those facing deportation.

The intensification of state repression following the passage of the Internal Security Act in 1950 led the LACPFB to be consumed with the organization of defense campaigns for those targeted for deportation. The group defended Mexican radicals targeted for their affiliation to the Communist Party or its aligned organizations, zealously pursued by state agents empowered by the two McCarran Acts. They also supported various cases of Mexicans targeted for removal for other reasons unrelated to politics. In one case, a party member named Mike Ortiz was detained by police for his political activities and held under the provisions of the McCarran Act. The LACPFB organized an emergency meeting to raise money to bail him out before his case was to be handed over to the attorney general for review. They sent a delegation to meet with the district director of the Department of Immigration and activated fundraising efforts. As one press release for the fundraiser stated, "Unless we can raise bail money at once, there is a grave danger that in the future no bail whatsoever will be set."[48] When bail became customarily denied for those held for deportation, the committee organized weekly protests at the offices of the Department of Immigration. In one instance, a picket of two hundred was organized to demand bail for a group of detainees held under the McCarran Act.[49]

The LACPFB took on thirty cases of targeted political deportation against Mexican radicals and labor unionists over the course of the 1950s. Cases ranged from those active in the party to others who were determined to have some affiliation with the party in the past. The case of Agapito Gómez illustrates the former. Gómez, a steelworker, union activist in the United Steelworkers of America, and Communist Party member, was detained and ordered to be deported in 1952, after being identified and targeted by INS officials. The LACPFB provided a lawyer for legal representation, organized delegations of protest, and sent letters to various officials. They had previously set up the Political Prisoners Welfare Committee, which raised funds to support his wife and US-born children while he was detained. The LACPFB waged a nine-year legal battle and finally succeeded in overturning Gómez's deportation order and securing his release from federal prison in 1962.[50]

In other cases, long-standing residents were charged retroactively for having had some kind of connection to a group designated as "subversive" by the attorney general. Such was the case of Eusebio Mejia, who had resided for thirty-six years in the United States and was "named" for having been present at a meeting of an organization subsequently designated as a Communist front. The LACPFB also developed the infrastructure to support Mexican residents in the broader Los Angeles community who were snagged for and scheduled for removal according to the various criminal provisions of the Walter-McCarran Act. While working with finite resources, they took on controversial cases with the hope that they could set legal precedent and protect untold numbers that might otherwise be brought into the system and deported in a virtually anonymous way. They also called attention to the burden and trauma that deportation imposed on children, including the thousands of US-born children deported alongside their parents over the course of the decade.

The LACPFB engaged in various activities designed to build solidarity between immigrant communities and to counter the stifling forces of assimilation and conformity embedded in the racialized anti-communism of the period. This included organizing public events that promoted multicultural diversity and valuation at a time when right-wing elements were linking "foreignness" to the propensity for radicalism. This included a mass celebration of culture in the Festival of Nationalities, an annual gathering of communities to watch cultural performances, experience different foods, see displays of national dress, and learn about other aspects of the distinct nationalities and cultures in Los Angeles. As Jeffrey M. Garcilazo explains, "The festival reflected the committee's pluralistic ideology and served to create and reinforce solidarity between ethnic groups, deportees, committee organizations, and the Left community in general."[51]

Through these larger gatherings, sometimes bringing out thousands from the community, mostly Mexicans, but also other ethnic communities affected by state repression, the specific defense cases were showcased and the attendees encouraged to join one of the various campaign committees to support those detained and their families. These community mobilizations served as a direct challenge to the police and immigration authorities, whose expectations for immigrant communities to be submissive and afraid were confuted. The effectiveness of counter-mobilization earned the LACPFB special scrutiny from the LAPD and the California Committee on Un-American Activities, which publicly designated the group a "Communist-front organization" engaging in "racial agitation," which equated the idea of communism with racial equality.

By the end of the 1950s, the level of repression had taken a toll. In 1941, 6,082 people were deported. By 1944, this increased to 29,176 people being deported, and the numbers continued to rise over the next decade:

Year	Deportations
1946	101,478
1947	199,282
1948	203,945
1949	293,000
1950	480,000
1951	509,040
1952	528,815
1953	885,587

Source: US Border Patrol[52]

Furthermore, important labor leaders and radicals from within the Mexican community were targeted for removal. These included Luisa Moreno of UCAPAWA, Josefina Fierro of the Spanish-Speaking People's Congress, Refugio Martínez of the United Packinghouse Workers of America and La Asociación Nacional Mexicana-Americana; Tony Salgado of the Laborers Union Local 300; Frank Corona of the ILWU; and Armando Dávila from the United Furniture Workers of America Local 576 and ANMA.

To facilitate the mass roundups and deportations, the INS built makeshift concentration camps. One of these was a barbed-wire-enclosed detention center in Elysian Park, in proximity to the Mexican barrios in downtown Los Angeles. The center was rapidly constructed and housed upward of a thousand men, women, and children, before they were shipped to the border. Most deportees were transported in trucks, although in other locales within the operation they were sent by boat, airlifted, or loaded onto trains.

Mass deportation of Mexican workers and the selective targeting of the Mexican Left in the US led the ACPFB to appeal to the international community for support, specifically through the United Nations. They petitioned for the Human Rights Commission of the United Nations Social and Economic Council to conduct an investigation into the "widespread violations of the human rights of more than five million men and women of Mexican origin or descent who live in the United States."[53] The ACPFB proclaimed that the United States government was in violation of all of the major tenets inscribed in existing UN human rights conventions in its repression, detention, and deportation of Mexicans in the US. Since the United Nations as an international body was dominated by the US and its allies on the Security Council, it proved incapable of holding the US accountable in any meaningful way. Nevertheless, the platform brought international attention to the plight of Mexicans in the US and, alongside the experience of black people, exposed to the world the violence and discrimination underpinning American Democracy.[54]

Operation Wetback and State Suppression of Mexican Labor Radicalism

The launch of the unabashedly racist mass deportation campaign called Operation Wetback was carried out in 1954. The wholesale attack on the Mexican working class was the culmination of a decade of direct attacks on the left wing of the union movement, the Communist Party, and the radical leadership networks that had developed within the Mexican communities and the collective memory of class struggle. It was a reaction against the labor radicalism of the previous two decades, representing a convergence of forces that enabled a dramatic shift to the right in US politics. This included fervent consensus and resolve in both political parties to smash the left wing of labor in the CIO, particularly the Communist Party, as well as the black and Mexican civil rights radical networks that had been forged in class struggle and were redirecting labor power against Jim Crow racism. The success of the state's efforts to unravel the gains of labor was aided by divisions within labor itself, represented by the mass expulsion of Left unions and radical labor leaders, and the resulting fusion of the AFL and CIO on the basis of anti-communism and anti-radicalism.

Since state repression of immigrants was predicated on the amplification of long-standing racial animus, anti-communism became a welcome home for the aggressive Southern segregationist wing of the Democratic Party and their shock troops in vigilante movements and racial terror groups such as the Ku Klux Klan. Despite the Communist Party leadership's turn toward ultra-nationalism during World War II, rank-and-file unionists in the Southwest continued to push for labor and civil rights for the Mexican working class. Along with their black counterparts, they arranged themselves in opposition to Jim Crow capitalism, and thus represented an existential threat to its future existence. The growth of organizational capacity and larger-scale participation by workers of color in labor and civil activism weakened the traditional deployment of state and vigilante violence as a means to repression; deportation through the agency of the federal government became the legally sanctioned alternative.

The strategy of selective and mass deportation, and the consequential terrorization of millions of others, served to dismantle the organizational and social gains of the Mexican population, effectively pushing them back into the conditions of segregation and marginalization. The operation began by concentrating a mass of agents throughout the southwestern states with the aim of expelling undocumented Mexican nationals and US non-citizen residents. In practice, this was a "surge," or an intensification, of an existing buildup of agents and deportation efforts, now possible on such a scale as labor resistance was greatly reduced and anti-immigrant alarmism became official political and media discourse. At the local level, police and sheriff's departments allocated officers to assist in the operations.

The regional deployment of operations across the Southwest coincided with those sectors of industry with the highest concentration of Mexican workers, union organization, and recent history of labor struggle. This included factory districts in Los Angeles, the agricultural zones within the San Joaquin and Imperial Valleys, and along the perimeters of the mining towns of southern Colorado and southern Arizona.[55] The Labor Department requested that the roundups extend into the cities to apprehend migrant workers employed in different industries. Raids and deportation sweeps were therefore conducted in industrial zones outside of the rural Southwest, including San Francisco, Chicago, Detroit, Kansas City, and Seattle. Of the 620,207 workers detained and deported between July 1953 and 1954, most were agricultural workers while 18,245 worked in urban industries.[56] While there were smaller numbers of urban workers deported, they were targeted in union-dense sectors such as foundries, railroads, waste disposal, brick-making, fertilizer companies, processing plants, meatpacking, and auto repair. The deportations dealt a heavy blow to the unions, while the public spectacle of swarms of agents raiding and snatching people served to instill terror among the general population. As one account described:

> Flying squads of United States deputies swept out through fields, factories, and communities to ferret out, capture, and herd over the border Mexican laborers. Private homes were invaded in the middle of the night; men, women, and children were routed from their beds; business places were raided; street cars and buses were halted; planes swooped down upon fields trying to pick out Mexican workers.[57]

Also significantly, people were targeted in the public sphere, pulled from public transportation, restaurants, movie theaters, and markets. Those bypassed by the raids were those that remained hidden or in the shadows. The permanent implementation of immigration enforcement after 1954 was designed to maintain this social and spatial divide, making a contingent labor force available so long as it remained socially and politically invisible.

The convergence of anti-communism and anti-immigrant sentiment, especially its historically recurring variant directed explicitly at Mexican migrant workers, was then taken up dutifully by the capitalist media. According to Juan Ramon García,

> Journals, magazines, newspapers, reports, and radio programs ran countless articles and programs on the accompanying evils of this so-called invasion. The majority of the information dealt with the negative aspects of such immigration and attributed increased problems in health, disease, crime, narcotics, soaring welfare costs, and infiltration by subversives to the mass influx of "illegals"[...]
> [S]eemingly overnight, the public was flooded with a mass of articles and feature stories concerning undocumented workers [...] The media generally used terms such as "horde," "tide," "invasion," and "illegal"... causing many people to see them in unfavorable terms.[58]

These newspapers repeated verbatim allegations of the threat of "Communist subversion" linked with the Mexican communities, no matter how outlandish or unsubstantiated. One Texas newspaper quoted an unnamed immigration official stating, "Up to 100 Communists are crossing the Mexican border into Texas every day in the El Paso area alone ... They come disguised as wetbacks, but they are not unlearned farmworkers ... They are Communists taking advantage of the 'open border.'"[59]

The most intensively targeted areas tended to correspond with both recent and remembered labor and union activity. In agricultural regions, the deportations coincided with the increased use of workers contracted through the Bracero Program. In the San Joaquin Valley, for instance, where some of the most intense strikes of the 1930s took place, the deportation of the existing workforce was followed by their replacement with braceros. Unlike migrant workers, contract workers were proscribed from joining unions, seeking permanent residence, or legal recourse to address substandard wages and working conditions.[60] The advent of this transition from "migratory" to explicitly "noncitizen" labor represented a significant shift in the balance of forces in the fields.

Since migrant workers from Mexico had not been formally regulated in the 1930s by a permanent army of immigration enforcers, they were more likely to engage in strikes and militant activity. The elaboration of restrictions on their entry and movement, backed by a growing and permanent armed force, provided growers and employers an unprecedented control over migrant workers who were now labeled "illegal." This designation made workers vulnerable to targeted removal, giving employers an immense power to utilize these laws to temper, threaten, and pacify their workers. As the state consistently deported a percentage of workers each year, this served as a constant warning and threat that significantly shifted the balance of power in the workplace from labor to the employers.

Operation Wetback as an attack on the Mexican working class in the United States was greatly enabled by the complicity of labor, especially the AFL. George Weber, the AFL organizer of the Southwest, called undocumented workers "the number one enemy of organized labor at the border."[61] CIO regional leaders in the Southwest, now purged of their Communist leadership, also voiced public support for the deportations. AFL and CIO leaders, whose organizations were reunited in 1955 after the Communist expulsions, closed ranks behind the narrative that open borders exposed the nation to Communist infiltration and subversion. In a joint study of the Texas Federation of Labor and the American G.I. Forum titled "What Price Wetbacks?", representatives of the AFL and the liberal, middle-class Mexican American veterans group joined the chorus of condemnation of undocumented workers, repeating the racist characterizations now being amplified by anti-Communists. According to the document,

> The vast majority of wetbacks are plain agricultural workers including women and children, mostly from the peasant class in Mexico. They are humble, amenable, easily dominated and controlled, and accept exploitation with the fatalism characteristic of their class [. . .] He accepts good or bad treatment, starvation wages, diarrhea and other sickness for his children from contaminated drinking water and unsanitary living conditions—all this he accepts stolidly and philosophically. He does not think in terms of native labor displacement, lowering of economic standards and the socio-economic effects of his presence in the US. Ideologies are beyond his comprehension. He understands only his way of life: to work, to suffer, and to pray to the Virgen de Guadalupe for a better life in the hereafter.[62]

While they refrained from linking immigration to communism, the document did echo the allegations of criminality, stating that "the wetback Pachucos subdivide roughly into two classes. In one are found the criminals, the marijuana peddlers and users, the falsifiers of identity documents, the smugglers, the prostitutes and the homosexuals."[63] LULAC also supported the deportations, and assisted the federal government's efforts in Texas while appealing to US-born Mexicans to cooperate with Border Patrol operations. Furthermore, the AFL-CIO began to exclude those identified as "Communists" or "subversives," aiding in the isolation of the Left within their state and local federations.[64]

The operation also provided the field staff to carry out the selective targeting of the immigrant Left, working in conjunction with and implementing the provisions of the Walter-McCarran Act. According to testimony by Immigration Commissioner Joseph Swing, 5,574 "alien subversives" were investigated in 1954, and 8,224 were investigated in 1955.[65] At one point, he claimed that 30 percent of the "investigative force" was being applied to "criminal" and "subversive" cases.[66] The suppression of labor unionism and radicalism combined the targeting of the intellectual and organizational leadership with the systemic repression of whole communities, especially those located at or near these epicenters of recent class struggle. Coordinated round-ups and raids throughout the barrios of the Southwest were designed to strike terror in the population as a whole, in an attempt to dismantle the organizational centers of class power and political organization. As historian Jeffery Garcilazo explains about its effects in Los Angeles:

> Anticommunism and anti-Mexican hysteria permeated the everyday lives of the Mexican Americans living in Los Angeles between 1950 and 1954. Combined with the anticommunist climate, the occurrence of mass raids on so-called "wetbacks" had a chilling effect on virtually all people of Mexican background. And while the government conducted mass raids and deportations of Mexican workers, the xenophobia of the McCarthy period reached its high point in 1954 with the largest INS assault on the Mexican community in history.[67]

Despite a relentless campaign of mass protest by the ACPFB and their allies in the unions, religious groups, and liberal organizations against the deportations, they were incapable of stopping the machinery of repression. Their allies in the Democratic Party had turned against them or remained silent, while the regrouped AFL-CIO national leadership applauded the dismemberment of the radical Left and the expulsion of undocumented labor. By the conclusion of Operation Wetback at the end of 1954, 1,101,228 people had been victimized by the single-largest mass deportation in US history up to that point.[68]

After 1954, the federal government made permanent the apparatus of immigration "enforcement" by doubling the INS budget between 1954 and 1956 to over $3 million annually, and steadily increasing funding and the number of enforcement agents each year thereafter.[69] Fixed INS centers and Border Patrol stations were established along the US-Mexican border to shift the locus of political "illegalization" to future border-crossers, who would now carry the stigma of deportability wherever they worked in the United States. State-led repression of the Communist Party as a means to suppress labor militancy and radicalism also crossed the southern border.[70] Aggressive US military and political intervention to counter radical labor and political movements abroad marked the demise of the Good Neighbor policy, which was unceremoniously ditched as official foreign policy doctrine with the onset of the Cold War. Beginning with the CIA-supported overthrow of the democratically elected government of Jacobo Arbenz in Guatemala in 1954, the successive US government pursued a three-decades-long strategy to suppress Communist, socialist, and nationalist movements across the Americas.[71] The year 1954 also witnessed the beginning of the next phase of the civil rights movement, in which struggle shifted away from the point of production with Communists no longer the driving force.

ACKNOWLEDGMENTS

I would like to thank Norell Martínez for the invaluable help, support, and patience while completing this book. I would also like to thank others for providing assistance in ways that made the completion of the manuscript possible. This includes Anthony Arnove, Lance Selfa, Luis López Resendiz, Héctor Rivera, Miguel Castañeda, Shawn England, and Mike Corwin. Thanks to Rachel Cohen, Lindsey Alexander, and Eric Kerl for the editing, design, and production.

Notes

Introduction

"Recognition of Carranza Will Mark Beginning Instead of End of Revolution, Declares Villa," *El Paso Morning Times*, October 9, 1915; 2.

1. For a full discussion of this analysis see Adam David Morton, *Revolution and State in Modern Mexico: The Political Economy of Uneven Development* (New York: Rowman and Littlefield, 2013).

2. See Ted Nace, *Gangs of America: The Rise of Corporations and the Disabling of Democracy* (San Francisco: Berrett-Koehler Publishers, 2003), for a description of the historical legislative process.

3. Abdiel Onate, "La batalla por El Banco Central: Las negociaciones de México con Los Banqueros Internacionales, 1920–25," *Historia Mexicana* 49, no. 4 (April–June 2000): 634.

4. Frederick Howe, *Why War?* (New York: Charles Scribner's Sons, 1916), 72.

5. Stephen Haber, Armando Razo, and Noel Maurer, *The Politics of Property Rights: Political Instability, Credible Commitments, and Economic Growth in Mexico, 1876-1929* (New York: Cambridge University Press, 2003), 84.

6. Vladimir Lenin, "Imperialism: The Highest Stage of Capitalism" in *Lenin: Selected Works in One Volume* (New York: International Publishers, 1943), 215.

7. For a description of how these cross-border capitalist partnerships formed and operated, see Mark Wasserman, "Foreign Investment in Mexico, 1876–1910: A Case Study of the Role of Regional Elites," *The Americas* 36, no. 1 (July 1979): 3–21. Also see: John Skirius, "Railroad, Oil and Other Foreign Interests in the Mexican Revolution, 1911–1914," *Journal of Latin American Studies* 35, no. 1 (February 2003): 25–51.

8. Dan La Botz, *Edward Doheny: Petroleum, Power and Politics in the United States and Mexico* (New York: Praeger, 1991), 32.

9. See Justo Sierra, *The Political Evolution of the Mexican People*, trans. Charles Ramsdell, (Austin: University of Texas Press, 1979), 359.

10. Jorge Basurto, *El Proletariado Industrial en México 1850–1930* (México: Universidad Nacional Autónoma de México, 1975), 143.

11. Jonathon C. Brown, *Oil and Revolution in Mexico* (Berkeley: University of California Press, 1993), 84.

12. William K. Meyers, "Politics, Vested Rights, and Economic Growth in Porfirian Mexico: The Company Tlahualilo in the Comarca Lagunera, 1885–1911," *The Hispanic American Historical Review* 57, no. 3 (August 1977): 425.

13. Within the United States, John Mason Hart identifies four main financial centers of Mexican investment activity: New York, Philadelphia, Boston, and South Texas. See John Mason Hart, *Empire and Revolution: The Americans in Mexico Since the Civil War* (Berkeley: University of California Press, 2002), chapter 2, especially page 54.

14. John Mason Hart, *Empire and Revolution: The Americans in Mexico Since the Civil War*, 91.

15. Gene Z. Hanrahan, *The Bad Yankee-El Peligro Yankee: American Entrepreneurs and Financiers in Mexico*, 132–35.

16. James D. Cockcroft, *Intellectual Precursors of the Mexican Revolution, 1900-1913* (Austin: University of Texas Press, 1968), 18.

17. Gastón García Cantú, *Las Invasiones Norteamericanas en México* (México: Fondo de Cultura Económica, 1996), 225; and Francie R. Chassen-López, *From Liberal to*

601

Revolutionary Oaxaca: The View from the South, Mexico 1867–1911 (University Park: Pennsylvania State University Press, 2004), 44.

18. Jose Luis Ceseña, *Mexico en la Orbita Imperial* (D.F., Mexico: Ediciones "El Caballito," 1970), 54–61. On the US and stealth ownership of the rail lines, see John Mason Hart, *Empire and Revolution: The Americans in Mexico Since the Civil War*, 127–28.

19. Gilbert M. Joseph and Alan Wells, "Corporate Control of a Monocrop Economy: International Harvester and Yucatán's Henequen Industry during the Porfiriato," *Latin American Research Review* 17, no. 1 (1982): 69; Samuel Kaplan and Enrique Flores Magón, *Peleamos Contra la Injusticia* (Mexico: Libro Mex Editores, 1960), 333.

20. Jorge Basurto, *El Proletariado Industrial en México (1850–1930)*, 18; P. Harvey Middleton, *Industrial Mexico: 1919 Facts and Figures* (New York: Dodd and Co., 1919), 10–13.

21. John Skirius, "Railroad, Oil and Other Foreign Interests in the Mexican Revolution, 1911–1914," *Journal of Latin American Studies* 35, no. 1 (February 2003): 25.

22. See Teresa M. Van Hoy, "La Marcha Violenta? Railroads and Land in 19th-Century Mexico," *Bulletin of Latin American Research* 19, no. 1 (January 2000): 34. While the author emphasizes a lack of research showing the scope in which this led to successful displacement by the railroad operators, other historians such as John Coatsworth have used such factors such as the frequency of agrarian protest in proximity to railroad expansion as a form of evidence. This source citation is included primarily as a measure of how government policy privileged foreign capitalists and investment.

23. Gene Z. Hanrahan, *The Bad Yankee-El Peligro Yankee: American Entrepreneurs and Financiers in Mexico*, 5–6.

24. Jonathon C. Brown, *Oil and Revolution in Mexico*, 123, 319. Historian Gene Hanrahan suggests that as many as ten thousand American workers and speculators lived in the Tampico region alone at this time. See Gene Z. Hanrahan, *The Bad Yankee-El Peligro Yankee: American Entrepreneurs and Financiers in Mexico*, 17.

25. Dennis J. O'Brien, "Petróleo e intervención: Relaciones entre los estados Unidos y México 1917–1918," *Historia Mexicana* 27, no. 1 (July–September 1977): 109–10.

26. For a comprehensive historical overview, see Aurora Gómez-Galvarriato, *Industry and Revolution: Social and Economic Change in the Orizaba Valley, Mexico* (Cambridge: Harvard University Press, 2013), 22–23; 36; see also Jeffrey Bortz, *Revolution Within the Revolution: Cotton Textile Workers and the Mexican Labor Regime, 1910–1923* (Stanford: Stanford University Press, 2008).

27. Raymond Vernon, *The Dilemma of Mexico's Development* (Cambridge: Harvard University Press, 1963), 43.

28. Aurora Gomez-Galvarriato, "The Transformation of the Mexican Banking System from the Porfiriato to 1925," paper presented at the World Business History Conference, March 17, 2014, Frankfurt, Germany; available online at http://www.worldbhc.org/files/full%20program/A4_B4_TheTransformationoftheMexicanBankingSystemfromthePorfiriatoto1925.pdf, 6.

29. John Mason Hart, *Empire and Revolution: The Americans in Mexico since the Civil War*, 91.

30. Aurora Gomez-Galvarriato, "The Transformation of the Mexican Banking System from the Porfiriato to 1925," 33.

31. Clarence W. Barron, *The Mexican Problem* (Boston and New York: Houghton Mifflin, 1917), 14.

32. Gilbert Gonzalez and Raul Fernandez, *A Century of Chicano History: Empire, Nations, and Migration* (New York: Routledge, 2003), 68.

33. Gilbert G. Gonzalez and Richard Kluger, "Richard Kluger's 'Simple Justice': Race, Class, and United States Imperialism," *History of Education Quarterly* 44, no. 1 (Spring 2004): 143.
34. Gene Z. Hanrahan, *The Bad Yankee-El Peligro Yankee: American Entrepreneurs and Financiers in Mexico,* 116.
35. Jonathon C. Brown, *Oil and Revolution in Mexico,* 87–88.
36. Gene Z. Hanrahan, *The Bad Yankee-El Peligro Yankee: American Entrepreneurs and Financiers in Mexico,* 77.
37. Jonathon C. Brown, *Oil and Revolution in Mexico,* 329.
38. T. G. Powell, "Mexican Intellectuals and the Indian Question, 1876–1911," *The Hispanic American Historical Review* 48, no. 1 (February 1968): 21.
39. Cited in Greg Gilson and Irving Levinson, *Latin American Positivism: New Historical and Philosophical Essays* (Lanham, MD: Lexington Books, 2013), 49–50; 57.
40. Roger D. Hansen, *The Politics of Mexican Development* (Baltimore: Johns Hopkins University Press, 1971), 20; Rodney Anderson, *Outcasts in Their Own Land: Mexican Industrial Workers, 1906–1911* (Dekalb: Northern Illinois University Press, 1976), 29.
41. Gastón García Cantú, *Las Invasiones Norteamericanas en México* (México: Fondo de Cultura Económica, 1996), 225.
42. Gene Z. Hanrahan, *The Bad Yankee-El Peligro Yankee: American Entrepreneurs and Financiers in Mexico.* See chapters 1–4.
43. Jonathon C. Brown, *Oil and Revolution in Mexico,* 105.
44. Cockcroft, *Intellectual Precursors of the Mexican Revolution, 1900–1913,* 22.
45. Chassen-Lopez, *From Liberal to Revolutionary Oaxaca: The View from the South, Mexico 1867–1911* (University Park: Pennsylvania State University Press, 2004), 46.
46. Friedrich Katz, *The Secret War in Mexico: Europe, the United States, and the Mexican Revolution* (Chicago: University of Chicago Press, 1981), 26.
47. Jonathon C. Brown, *Oil and Revolution in Mexico,* 18.
48. Raymond Vernon, *The Dilemma of Mexico's Development* (Cambridge: Harvard University Press, 1963), 77.
49. P. Harvey Middleton, *Industrial Mexico: 1919 Facts and Figures* (New York: Dodd and Co., 1919), x.
50. Lawrence A. Cardoso, *Mexican Emigration to the United States, 1897–1931* (Tucson: University of Arizona Press, 1980), 6–7.
51. Ibid., 1, 38.
52. Statistics cited in Emory Bogardus, *The Mexican in the United States* (Los Angeles: University of Southern California Press, 1934), 16.
53. Paul Ganster and David E. Lorey, *The U.S.-Mexico Border into the Twenty-First Century* (Lanham: Rowman & Littlefield Publishing Group, 2008), 69.
54. Arthur F. Corwin and Lawrence A. Cardoso, "Vamos el Norte: Causes of Mass Mexican Migration to the United States," in *Immigrants—and Immgirants: Perspectives on Mexican Labor Migration to the United States,* ed. Arthur Corwin (Westport: Greenwood Press, 1978), 46.
55. As Friedrich Katz observed, Díaz believed substantial European investments, backed by their own militaries, would serve as an effective counterweight. Achieving a semblance of interimperialist equilibrium could also discourage aggressive Yankee interventionism should problems arise. In oil, which would prove to be the most lucrative of Mexico's natural resources, the Porfiristas helped form the British-Mexican

El Aguila Oil Company, which controlled 58 percent of the country's oil production by 1910. They also formed a rival railroad company that favored British interests. The Mexican National Railways, brought into existence in 1907–1908, gave control over the majority of the nation's rail lines to the Mexican government. See Friedrich Katz, *The Secret War in Mexico: Europe, the United States, and the Mexican Revolution*, 23–25.

56. John Coatsworth, "Railroads, Landholding, and Agrarian Protest in the Early Porfiriato," *The Hispanic American Historical Review* 54, no. 1 (February 1974): 49.

57. Jorge Basurto, *El Proletariado Industrial en México 1850–1930*, 39.

58. Ibid., 48.

59. Aurora Gómez-Galvarriato, "The Evolution of Prices and Real Wages in Mexico from the Porfiriato to the Revolution," in *Latin America and the World Economy since 1800*, eds. John Coatsworth and Alan Taylor (Cambridge: David Rockefeller Center for Latin American Studies, 1998), 351.

60. Oscar Diego Bautista, "La deuda externa en la historia de México," *Revista Iberoamericana de Administración Pública* 11 (July 2003): 13–14.

61. For a full discussion of this process, see Paul Ganster and David E. Lorey, *The U.S.-Mexico Border into the Twenty-First Century*, chapter 2; Juan Mora-Torres, *The Making of the Mexican Border: The State, Capitalism, and Society in Nuevo Leónm 1848–1910* (Austin: University of Texas Press, 2001), chapter 7; and Paul Garner, *British Lions and Mexican Eagles: Business, Politics, and Empire in the Career of Weetman Pearson in Mexico, 1899–1919* (Stanford: University of Stanford Press, 2011), chapter 1. For another example, see William K. Myers, *Forge of Progress, Crucible of Revolt: The Origins of the Mexican Revolution in La Comarca Lagunera, 1880–1911* (Albuquerque: University of New Mexico Press, 1994), 173.

62. Madero entered statewide politics as early as 1904. He advocated for reforms that stemmed the growing power of foreign capital, especially as foreign investment companies proliferated in the border states and threatened the regional hegemony of Mexican capitalist landowners. See William K. Myers, *Forge of Progress, Crucible of Revolt: The Origins of the Mexican Revolution in La Comarca Lagunera, 1880-1911*, 5–6.

63. Madero legalized unions and the right to strike, and created a "Department of Labor" that attempted to establish standardized wages and working conditions, believing this would curb the radicalism of the industrial working classes.

64. Francisco Madero, *La Sucesion Presidencial en 1910* (Mexico: Libreria de Educación de Baldomero de la Prida, 1909), 163.

65. In his effort to promote democracy while containing social revolution, his campaign became a rallying point for northern capitalists who were enriched as a result of policies and partnerships forged during the Porfiriato, but who felt more capable to rule. According to William K. Myers, "the Laguna elite emerged as a powerful new interest group within Porfirian Mexico. Many new fortunes began here after 1900 and joined with those of established families that further diversified and increased through regional investments" (97). By promising universal suffrage and an end to Porfirian cronyism and corruption, he also drew middle-class professionals, members of the agrarian middle class, and intellectuals into his camp. For instance, he maintained a base of advisors and supporters called *los renovadores* ("the renovators") who were part of his staff, political allies in the legislature, and later within the state bureaucracy. They served as the liberal flank of maderismo that desired to see democratic reforms through to their completion.

66. During his electoral campaign, he and over five thousand of his supporters were

arrested in a massive federal campaign to suppress the opposition. Able to escape from a minimally guarded prison in San Luis Potosí, he was quickly smuggled across the border to San Antonio, Texas. Here, he set up his government in exile, and announced his "Plan de San Luis Potosí," which called for an armed revolution to begin on November 20, 1910. The insurrection showed significant promise, as armed rebel groups formed and rallied across the nation and flocked to the maderista banner.

67. John Mason Hart, *Empire and Revolution: The Americans in Mexico since the Civil War*, 83–84.

68. For a description of the revolt in Mexico City, including a massive march on Diaz's personal residence, see John Lear, *Workers, Neighbors, and Citizens: The Revolution in Mexico City* (Lincoln: University of Nebraska Press, 2001), 140.

69. Greg Andrews, *Shoulder to Shoulder: The American Federation of Labor, the United States, and the Mexican Revolution 1910–1924* (Berkeley: University of California Press, 1991), 28.

70. Alan Knight, *The Mexican Revolution: Counter-Revolution and Reconstruction* (Lincoln: University of Nebraska Press, 1990), 69.

71. The Wilson administration used the arrival of the German steamer *Ypiranga* to legitimize the invasion and full occupation of the city and its key institutions, under the pretext that it was delivering German arms to potentially be used by Germans in Mexico against the United States at the advent of the war. While the ship was indeed a German-registered vehicle, it was delivering American-made weapons purchased through an American agent working as an adviser to Huerta, who was helped into power with US support. The circuitous route from New York to Germany and back to Mexico was only a ploy to skirt the arms embargo imposed by Wilson on Mexico. The German shipping company, Hamburg-American-Lines (HAPAG), was contracted because it offered the only direct line to Mexico. See Thomas Baecker, "The Arms of the Ypiranga: The German Side," *The Americas* 30, no. 1 (July 1973): 1–17.

72. By November 1914, the more radical nationalist factions led by Pancho Villa and Emiliano Zapata were gaining ground and espousing nationalization of the oil fields.

73. The pretext for the third intervention came in the form of a border skirmish in March of 1916. Several hundred Mexican rebels linked to the forces of Pancho Villa had crossed the border and sacked the town of Columbus, New Mexico. Following a battle, US forces mustered, and with the green light from Wilson, a pursuit of Pancho Villa's main forces ensued. By April 1, 6,675 US soldiers, increasing to over 11,635 by June, had crossed 350 miles into Mexico. While the "Pershing Expedition" proved fruitless in its attempt to capture Villa, the rationale quickly morphed into the larger strategic objective: an imposing military occupation designed to intimidate Mexicans into submission. According to Michael Tate, "This then became the new mission of Pershing's Expedition—to remain in Mexico until adequate defense of foreigners could be assured and until Carranza relaxed his revenue decrees." See Michael L. Tate, "Pershing's Punitive Expedition: Pursuer of Bandits or Presidential Panacea?" *The Americas* 32, no. 1 (July 1975): 46–71.

74. For an overview of the stages of the Mexican Revolution, see Adolfo Gilly, *The Mexican Revolution* (New York: New Press, 2005).

75. For a full discussion of these developments, see Sidney Lens, *The Forging of the American Empire, From the Revolution to Vietnam: A History of US Imperialism* (Chicago: Haymarket Books, 2003); and Walter La Feber, *The New Empire: An Interpretation of American Expansion 1860–1898* (Ithaca: Cornell University Press, 1998).

76. Henry W. Berger, "Unions and Empire: Organized Labor and American Corporations Abroad," *Peace and Change* 3, no. 4 (April 1976): 36.

77. Jack Scott, *Yankee Unions Go Home: How the AFL Helped the US Build an Empire in Latin America* (Vancouver: New Star Books, 1978), 93, 106.

78. Ibid., 95–96.

79. Ibid., 73.

80. Ibid., 153.

81. The "racial" status of Mexicans has changed over time and varied across localities, ranging from their classification as "white" to attempts to designate them as "Indian." Despite the variation, Mexicans in the Southwest generally experienced a form of racial segregation and oppression within the socio-economic framework already established for the subjugation of African Americans.

82. James N. Gregory, *The Southern Diaspora: How the Great Migrations of Black and White Southerners Transformed America* (Chapel Hill: University of North Carolina Press, 2005), 12–13.

83. See Charles C. Alexander, *The Ku Klux Klan in the Southwest* (Norman: University of Oklahoma Press, 1995), chapter 3; and Kenneth T. Jackson, *The Ku Klux Klan in the City, 1915–1930* (Chicago: Ivan R. Dee, 1992), chapter 2.

84. For a full discussion, see Reginald Horsman, *Race and Manifest Destiny: The Origins of American Racial Anglo-Saxonism* (Cambridge: Harvard University Press, 1981); and Mario Barrera, *Race and Class in the Southwest: A Theory of Racial Inequality* (Notre Dame: University of Notre Dame Press, 1979).

85. For a full discussion of this process, see Andrés E. Jiménez, "The Political Formation of a Mexican Working Class in the Arizona Copper Industry, 1870–1917," *Review* (Fernand Braudel Center) 4, no. 3 (Winter 1981).

86. For a full discussion, see Ellen W. Schrecker, *No Ivory Tower: McCarthyism and the Universities* (New York: Oxford University Press, 1986).

87. Cited in Mario T. García, "Mexican American Labor and the Left: The Asociación Nacional México-Americana, 1949–1954," in *The Chicano Struggle: Analyses of Past and Present Efforts*, eds, John A. García, Theresa Córdova, and Juan R. García (New York: Bilingual Press, 1984), 65.

88. Early exceptions include Ernesto Galarza, Carey McWilliams.

Chapter 1: The Mexican Working Classes

A note on terminology: I will use the identity terms "Mexican" and "*mexicano*" to describe both Mexican nationals and Mexican immigrants and migrants in the United States for most of the text. This is largely due to the fact that Mexicans in the United States were not treated as citizens by the state, nor did many Mexicans see themselves as part of US society, or necessarily believe their residence to be permanent. The use of the term "Mexican American" will begin to appear in discussion of the 1930s and beyond, as the first significant population of US-born descendants of mexicanos came of age during that period and began to use the term to describe themselves.
Cited in "Why Mexican Peons Rebel," *The Inter Ocean*, August 13, 1913: 6.

1. Rodney Anderson, "Mexican Workers and the Politics of Revolution," *The Hispanic American Historical Review* 54, no. 1 (February 1974), 95.

2. John Mason Hart, "Latin American Working-Class History: The Case of the Mexican

Revolution," *International Labor and Working-Class History*, no. 10 (November 1976): 15.

3. Anna Ribera Carbó, "Ferrer Guardia en la Revolución Mexicana," *Educació i Història: Revista d'Història de l'Educació*, no. 16 (July–December 2010): 37.

4. Jaime Tamayo and Patricia Valles, *Anarquismo, Socialismo, y Sindicalismo en Las Regiones* (Jalisco: Editorial Universidad de Guadalajara, 1993), 9.

5. John Lear states that 66 percent of Mexico City's population in 1900 had been born outside of the city. See *Workers, Neighbors, and Citizens: The Revolution in Mexico City* (Lincoln: University of Nebraska Press, 2001), 53.

6. While the vast majority of workers in Mexico have historically engaged in agriculture, the nuclei of an urban and industrial working class began to develop. This occured in the mines, cottage production, among pre-industrial labor apprentices, and among craftsmen and artisans displaced from their means of production through competition with an incipient factory system integrated into the expanding global capitalist system in the nineteenth century. For a full discussion, see Enrique Semo, *The History of Capitalism in Mexico: Its Origins, 1521–1763* (Austin: University of Texas Press, 1992); and Rodney Anderson, *Outcasts in their Own Land: Mexican Industrial Workers, 1906–1911* (Dekalb: Northern Illinois University Press, 1976).

7. William D. Raat, "Ideas and Society in Don Porfirio's Mexico," *The Americas* 30, no. 1 (July 1973): 32–33.

8. Alan Knight, "The Working Class and the Mexican Revolution, c. 1900–1920," *Journal of Latin American Studies* 16, no. 1 (May 1984): 61; Rodney Anderson, *Outcasts in their Own Land*, 43.

9. John Mason Hart, *Border Crossings, Mexican and Mexican-American Workers* (Wilmington, DE: Scholarly Resources, 1998), 10.

10. Rodney Anderson, *Outcasts in their Own Land*, 40–41; 92.

11. Jonathon Brown, "Foreign and Native-Born Workers in Porfirian Mexico," *The American Historical Review* 98, no. 3 (June 1993): 79; Ramón Eduardo Ruiz, *Labor and the Ambivalent Revolutionaries* (Baltimore: Johns Hopkins University Press, 1976), 5.

12. Jean-Pierre Bastian, "La estructura social en México a fines del siglo XIX y principios del XX," *Revista Mexicana de Sociología* 51, no. 2 (April–June 1989): 413–42.

13. Jeffrey Bortz, *Revolution Within the Revolution—Cotton Textile Workers and the Mexican Labor Regime: 1910–1923* (Stanford: Stanford University Press, 2008), 36.

14. Anna Macias, *Against All Odds: The Feminist Movement in Mexico to 1940* (Westport, CT: Greenwood Press, 1982), 31.

15. See Carmen Ramos-Escandón, "Mujeres trabajadoras en el México porfiriano: Género e ideología del trabajo femenino 1876–1911," *Revista Europea de Estudios Latinoamericanos y del Caribe / European Review of Latin American and Caribbean Studies*, no. 48 (June 1990): 30–31.

16. John Lear, *Workers, Neighbors, and Citizens: The Revolution in Mexico City* (Lincoln: University of Nebraska Press, 2001), 73–77.

17. Ibid., 32.

18. Anna Macias, *Against All Odds*, 31–32.

19. Luis González y González, "El agrarismo liberal," *Historia Mexicana* 7, no. 4 (April–June 1958): 486.

20. This early colonization project was nullified when the US speculators refused to comply with the Mexican stipulations. See Luis González y González, "El agrarismo liberal," 484.

21. The population had grown 50 percent between the years 1875 and 1910, but the structural underdevelopment and displacement of the Porfiriato meant that most of this population of six million was funneled into the growing subsistence economy and landless population. See Lawrence A. Cardoso, *Mexican Immigration to the United States 1897–1931* (Tucson: University of Arizona Press, 1980), 9.

22. See Jean Meyer, "Los obreros en la Revolución mexicana: Los 'Batallones Rojos,'" *Historia Mexicana* 21, no. 1 (July–September 1971): 3; and Héctor Mora Zebadúa, Victor Palacio Muñoz, and Omar M. Guzmán Navarro, *Un Siglo del Programa del Proletariado en México (Partido Liberal Mexicano 1906)* (Chapingo: Universidad Autónoma de Chapingo; Centro de Investigaciones Económicas, 2008), 44.

23. David W. Walker, "Homegrown Revolution: The Hacienda Santa Catalina del Alamo y Anexas and Agrarian Protest in Eastern Durango, Mexico, 1897–1913," *The Hispanic American Historical Review* 72, no. 2 (May 1992): 255.

24. William Bluestein, "The Class Relations of the Hacienda and the Village in Prerevolutionary Morelos" *Latin American Perspectives* 9, no. 3 (Summer 1982), 21.

25. Ibid., 26.

26. John Kenneth Turner, *Barbarous Mexico* (Austin: University of Texas Press, 1969), 224.

27. For a detailed and exhaustive description of how each of these processes unfolded, see David W. Walker, "Homegrown Revolution: The Hacienda Santa Catalina del Alamo y Anexas and Agrarian Protest in Eastern Durango, Mexico, 1897–1913," 241.

28. Merrill Rippy, "Land Tenure and Land Reform in Modern Mexico," *Agricultural History* 27, no. 2 (April 1953): 56.

29. Ibid., 56–57.

30. Robert Holden, "Priorities of the State in the Survey of the Public Land in Mexico, 1876–1911," *The Hispanic American Historical Review* 70, no. 4 (November 1990): 579.

31. Paul Friedrich, *Agrarian Revolt in a Mexican Village* (Chicago: University of Chicago Press, 1977), 3.

32. Gene Z. Hanrahan, *The Bad Yankee-El Peligro Yankee: American Entrepreneurs and Financiers in Mexico* (Chapel Hill: Documentary Publications, 1985), 133.

33. Rodney Anderson, *Outcasts in their Own Land*, 38.

34. See Sonia Hernández, *Working Women into the Borderlands* (College Station: Texas A&M University Press, 2014), 25.

35. Michael Foley, "Privatizing the Countryside: The Mexican Peasant Movement and Neoliberal Reform," *Latin American Perspectives* 22, no. 1 (Winter 1995): 59; also see Merrill Rippy, "Land Tenure and Land Reform in Modern Mexico," *Agricultural History* 27, no. 2 (April 1953): 57.

36. Raymond Vernon, *The Dilemma of Mexico's Development* (Cambridge: Harvard University Press, 1963), 54.

37. Luis González y González, "El agrarismo liberal," 489.

38. Paul Friedrich, *Agrarian Revolt in a Mexican Village*, 3.

39. Friedrich Katz, "Labor Conditions on Haciendas in Porfirian Mexico: Some Trends and Tendencies," *The Hispanic American Historical Review* 54, no. 1 (February 1974): 45–46.

40. Ibid.

41. Quote cited Daniel Nugent, ed., *Rural Revolt in Mexico: US Intervention and the Domain of Subaltern Politics* (Durham: Duke University Press, 1998), 68.

42. William K. Myers, *Forge of Progress, Crucible of Revolt: The Origins of the Mexican*

Revolution in La Comarca Lagunera, 1880–1911 (Albuquerque: University of New Mexico Press, 1994), 133.

43. The US invasion and occupation intervened in some regions where class struggle between peasants and landowners were at an advanced stage, opening up a three-sided conflict. Amid this crisis, the central government became unwilling to arm peasants. The foundering of the central government and the collapse of formal opposition devolved opposition to a popular guerrilla movement (along with growing protests in urban centers) that developed and spread across southern Mexico. At its cellular structure, the campaign united irregular bands of peasants and contingents of soldiers under a fragmented military command that engaged in asymmetrical warfare against the US military, ultimately pushing the United States to pull out from southern regions that could not be held without great cost. In the power vacuum created, peasant revolts against the landed oligarchy increased, culminating in an attempt to create a national movement combining anti-occupation revolt with radical land reform emanating from the state of Veracruz, ground zero of the US occupation. As historian Paul Foos illustrates, "In January 1848, peasant leader Juan Nepomuceno Llorente issued the plan de Tantoyuca, calling nationally for an alliance of the agrarian rebels. In Veracruz this meant the establishment of local governments sympathetic to peasant rights and the war effort, which would be authorized to collect levies according to the means of individuals to pay. The plan called for a national suspension of rents on all hacienda lands." Under these circumstances, the US brass and Mexican elites expedited efforts to generate a treaty to end the war and permit the re-establishment of Mexican authority in the renegade regions. As Foos concludes, while these peasant-centered revolts and guerrilla campaigns were contributing factors to the withdrawal of the US and later French occupations, they failed to radically alter patterns of traditional land tenure and later capitalist development in the countryside until 1910. See Paul Foos, *A Short, Offhand, Killing Affair: Soldiers and Social Conflict during the Mexican-American War* (Chapel Hill: University of North Carolina Press, 2002), 135–7.

44. William D. Raat, "Ideas and Society in Don Porfirio's Mexico," *The Americas* 30, no. 1 (July 1973): 38.

45. In Daniel Nugent, ed., *Rural Revolt in Mexico: US Intervention and the Domain of Subaltern Politics*, 90.

46. Ibid., 98.

47. Ibid., 107. The PLM will be discussed in more detail in succeeding chapters.

48. David W. Walker, "Homegrown Revolution: The Hacienda Santa Catalina del Alamo y Anexas and Agrarian Protest in Eastern Durango, Mexico, 1897–1913," 241.

49. Ibid., 259.

50. Roger Bartra, "Peasants and Political Power in Mexico," *Social Scientist* 4, no. 3 (October 1975): 19.

51. Adolfo Gilly, *A People's History of the Mexican Revolution* (New York: New Press, 2005), 242.

52. The short-lived government and its proclamations were largely symbolic, since the two revolutionary groups wielded limited influence outside their bases in Morelos and Chihuahua.

53. Adolfo Gilly, *A People's History of the Mexican Revolution*, 252.

54. This process is described in detail in Juan Felipe Leal, *Del Mutualismo al Sindicalismo en México: 1843–1911* (México: Juan Pablos Editor, 2012).

55. Claudio Lomnitz, *The Return of Comrade Ricardo Flores Magón* (New York: Zone Books, 2014), 98.

56. Douglas Richmond, "Nationalism and Class Conflict in Mexico, 1910–1920" *The Americas* 43, no. 3 (January 1987): 282.

57. John Mason Hart, *Border Crossings: Mexican and Mexican-American Workers*, 12.

58. R. Th. J. Buve, "Protestas de obreros y campesinos durante el Porfiriato: Unas Consideraciónes sobre su desarollo, e interrelaciones en el este de México central," *Boletín de Estudios Latinoamericanos*, no. 13 (December 1972): 5.

59. Another liberal-led organization developed within the working class, the Radical Convention, maintained that political participation was the only route for workers and that strikes were harmful to workers. See Georgina Limones Ceniceros, "Review: Del Mutualismo al Sindicalismo en México: 1843–1910 by Juan Felipe Leal y Fernández," *Historia Mexicana* 43, no. 1 (July–September 1993): 171.

60. Ibid.

61. John Lear, *Workers, Neighbors, and Citizens: The Revolution in Mexico City*, 108.

62. Juan Felipe Leal, *Del Mutualismo al Sindicalismo: 1843–1911*, 116.

63. Marjorie Ruth Clark, *La Organización Obrera en México* (Mexico: Ediciones Era, 1934), 13.

64. John Lear, *Workers, Neighbors, and Citizens: The Revolution in Mexico City*, 113.

65. See Juan Gómez-Quiñones, *Mexican American Labor, 1790–1990* (Albuquerque: University of New Mexico Press, 1994), 54; and Javier Torres Parés, *La Revolución Sin Fronteras* (Mexico: UNAM, 1990), 38.

66. Ramón Eduardo Ruiz, *Labor and the Ambivalent Revolutionaries: Mexico, 1911–1923* (Baltimore: Johns Hopkins University Press, 1976), 18.

67. For example, see León Díaz Cárdenas, *Cananea: Primer Brote del Sindicalismo en Mexico* (Mexico: Centro de Estudios Históricos del Movimiento Obrero Mexicano, 1976).

68. Sonia Hernández, *Working Women into the Borderlands*, 80–81.

69. Ibid.

70. Jorge Basurto, *El Proletariado Industrial en México 1850–1930*, 86.

71. Rodney Anderson, *Outcasts in their Own Land*, 90.

72. Richard Ulric Miller, "American Railroad Unions and the National Railways of Mexico: An Exercise in Nineteenth-Century Proletarian Manifest Destiny," *Labor History* 15, no. 2 (1974): 243.

73. James D. Cockcroft, *Intellectual Precursors of the Mexican Revolution 1900–1913* (Austin: University of Texas Press, 1968), 141.

74. Ibid., 142.

75. Charles D. Ameringer, *The Socialist Impulse: Latin America in the Twentieth Century* (Gainesville: University of Florida Press, 2009), 57.

76. Silva de la Cerda, *El Movimiento Obrero en México* (D.F., Mexico: Instituto de Investigaciones Sociales, 1961), 104.

77. Ibid., 97.

78. R. Th. J. Buve, "Protesta de obreros y campesinos durante el Porfiriato: Unas consideraciones sobre su desarrollo e interrelaciones en el este de México central," 11.

79. Jeffrey Bortz, *Revolution Within the Revolution—Cotton Textile Workers and the Mexican Labor Regime: 1910–1923*, 152.

80. Karl B. Koth, "Not a Mutiny, but a Revolution: The Río Blanco Labour Dispute, 1906–7," *Canadian Journal of Latin American and Caribbean Studies / Revue canadienne*

desétudes latino-américaines et caraïbes 18, no. 35 (1993): 42.

81. David W. Walker, "Porfirian Labor Politics: Working Class Organizations in Mexico City and Porfirio Díaz, 1876–1902" *The Americas* 37, no. 3 (January 1981): 281.

82. Karl Koth, *Waking the Dictator: Veracruz, the Struggle for Federalism and the Mexican Revolution, 1870-1927* (Calgary: University of Calgary Press, 2002), 59.

83. Moisés Gonzalez Navarro, "Las huelgas textiles en el Porfiriato," *Historia Mexicana* 6, no. 2 (October–December 1956): 202.

84. This included: making workers pay the costs for defectively made textiles and prohibiting visitors in workers' homes since they were on company property. See Karl B. Koth, "Not a Mutiny, but a Revolution: The Río Blanco Labour Dispute, 1906–7," 49.

85. Moisés Gonzalez Navarro, "Huelga de Río Blanco," *Historia Mexicana* 6, no. 4 (April–June 1957): 510–12.

86. Ibid., 510, 513–14.

87. Ibid., 510–16; 519.

88. For a timeline of revolutionary events and the leadership/participation of women, see Adelina Zendejas, "Ellas y la vida: Lucha y conquista de los derechos femeninos," *Debate Feminista* 8 (September 1993): 401–13.

89. Angeles Mendieta Alatorre, *La Mujer en La Revolución Mexicana* (Mexico: Biblioteca del Instituto Nacional de Estudios Historicos de la Revolución Mexicana, 1961), 48.

90. Moisés Gonzalez Navarro, "Huelga de Río Blanco," 510–16; 519.

91. For a more thorough discussion of the continuation of the GCOL after Río Blanco, see R. Th. J. Buve, "Protesta de obreros y campesinos durante el porfiriato: Unas consideraciones sobre su desarrollo e interrelaciones en el este de México central," 13.

92. Carmen Ramos-Escandón, "La política obrera del Estado Mexicano: De Díaz a Madero el caso de los trabajadores textiles," *Mexican Studies/Estudios Mexicanos* 3, no. 1 (Winter 1987): 37.

Chapter 2: Mexican Workers: From Liberalism to Anticapitalism

Rosendo Salazar, *Las Pugnas de la Gleba* (Mexico: SEI, S. A., 1974), 16.

1. Ricardo Pozas Horcasitas, "La evolución de la política laboral Mexicana (1857–1920)," *Revista Mexicana de Sociología* 38, no. 1 (January–March 1976): 90.

2. Ibid., 87

3. Rodney Anderson, *Outcasts in their Own Land*, 37.

4. Manuel Reyna, Laura Palomares, and Guadalupe Cortez, "El control del movimiento obrero como una necesidad del estado de Mexico (1917–1936)," *Revista Mexicana de Sociología* 34, no. 3/4 (July–December 1972): 785–6.

5. As one historian of the period commented, beside personal political styles, "it is difficult to determine any significant differences between the Porfirists, Juarists and Lerdists [rivals within the liberal factions]." See Frank Falcone, "Benito Juárez versus the Díaz Brothers: Politics in Oaxaca, 1867–1871," *The Americas* 33, no. 4 (April 1977): 631.

6. John Mason Hart describes how US capital moved increasingly in favor of Díaz against Juarez and Lerdo. *Empire and Revolution: The Americans in Mexico Since the Civil War* (Berkeley: University of California Press, 2002), chapter 2.

7. Raymond Vernon, *The Dilemma of Mexico's Development* (Cambridge: Harvard University Press, 1963), 48–49.

8. He describes the particular development of Mexican liberalism in this direction as

"organic liberalism." William D. Raat, "Ideas and Society in Don Porfirio's Mexico," *The Americas* 30, no. 1 (July 1973): 47.

9.   Douglas Richmond,"Nationalism and Class Conflict in Mexico, 1910–1920," *The Americas* 43, no. 3 (January 1987): 283.

10. David W. Walker, "Porfirian Labor Politics: Working-Class Organizations in Mexico City and Porfirio Díaz, 1876–1902," *The Americas* 37, no. 3 (January 1981): 258.

11. John Mason Hart, *Anarchism & the Mexican Working Class, 1860–1931* (Austin: University of Texas Press, 1987), 52–53.

12. Gastón García Cantú, *Idea de Mexico II: El Socialismo* (Mexico: Fondo de Cultural Económica, 1991), 116–17.

13. Jorge Sayeg Helu, *Las Huelgas de Cananea y Río Blanco* (Mexico: Biblioteca del Instituto Naciónal de Estudios Historicos de la Revolución Mexicana, 1980), 36.

14. John Mason Hart, "The Urban Working Class and the Mexican Revolution: The Case of the Casa del Obrero Mundial," *Hispanic American Historical Review* 58, no. 1 (February 1978).

15. José C. Valadés, "*Cartilla Socialista* de Plotino C. Rhodakanaty. Noticia sobre el socialismo en México durante el siglo XIX," *Estudios de Historia Moderna y Contemporánea de México* 3 (1970): 48. For a full exposition of how his ideas evolved, see Carlos Illiades, *Las Otras Ideas: El Primer Socialismo en México* (Mexico: Universidad Autónoma Metropolitana-Cuajimalpa, 2008), chapter 4.

16. R. Th. J. Buve, "Protesta de obreros y campesinos durante el Porfiriato: Unas consideraciones sobre su desarrollo e interrelaciones en el este de México central," *Boletín de Estudios Latinoamericanos*, no. 13 (December 1972): 4.

17. For a full discussion of this history, see Carlos Illiades, *Rhodakanaty y La Formación del Pensamiento Socialista en México* (México: Anthropos Editorial, 2002), chapter 2.

18. Gastón García Cantú, *Idea de Mexico II: El Socialismo*, 63.

19. R. Th. J. Buve, "Protesta de obreros y campesinos durante el Porfiriato: Unas consideraciones sobre su desarrollo e interrelaciones en el este de México central," 4.

20. Carlos Illiades, *Rhodakanaty y La Formación del Pensamiento Socialista en México* (México: Anthropos Editorial, 2002), 119–27.

21. For a detailed discussion of the international context for the development of anarchist politics in Mexico, see Clara E. Lida and Carlos Illades, "El anarquismo europeo y sus primeras influencias en México después de la Comuna de París: 1871–1881," *Historia Mexicana* 51, no. 1 (July–September 2001): 103–49.

22. Luis González y González, "La unión hace la huelga (1867–1876)," *El Trimestre Económico* 24, no. 93(1) (January–March 1957): 23.

23. John M. Hart, *Anarchism and the Mexican Working Class 1860–1931* (Austin: University of Texas Press, 1987), 21.

24. John Mason Hart, *Border Crossings: Mexican and Mexican-American Workers*, 9.

25. Gastón García Cantú, *Idea de Mexico II: El Socialismo* (Mexico: Fondo de Cultural Económica, 1991), 166.

26. Manuel Reyna, Laura Palomares, and Guadalupe Cortez, "El control del movimiento obrero como una necesidad del estado de Mexico (1917–1936)," (Wilmington: Scholarly Resources Press, 1998), 786.

27. David W. Walker, "Porfirian Labor Politics: Working Class Organizations in Mexico City and Porfirio Díaz, 1876–1902," *The Americas* 37, no. 3 (January 1981): 261.

28. Luis González y González, "La unión hace la huelga (1867–1876)," 23.

29. John M. Hart, *Anarchism and the Mexican Working Class 1860–1931*, 50.
30. Jorge Basurto, *El Proletariado Industrial en México 1850–1930* (México: Universidad Nacional Autónoma de México, 1975), 92.
31. John Mason Hart, *Anarchism and the Mexican Working Class 1860–1931*, 54.
32. Robert Graham, *We Do Not Fear Anarchy, We Invoke It: The First International and the Origins of the Anarchist Movement* (Oakland: AK Press, 2015), 254.
33. Jorge Basurto, *El Proletariado Industrial en México 1850–1930*, 94.
34. Ibid., 153.
35. Ibid., 100.
36. Carl Levy, "Social Histories of Anarchism," *Journal for the Study of Radicalism* 4, no. 2 (Fall 2010): 16.
37. Julie Greene, "Spaniards on the Silver Roll: Labor Troubles and Liminality in the Panama Canal Zone, 1904–1914," *International Labor and Working-Class History*, no. 66 (Fall 2004): 91–92.
38. Elbert Jay Benton, *International Law and Diplomacy of the Spanish-American War.* (Baltimore: Johns Hopkins Press, 1908), 194–95.
39. Steven Hirsch and Lucien Van der Walt, *Anarchism and Syndicalism in the Colonial and Postcolonial World: The Praxis of National Liberation, Internationalism, and Social Revolution* (Boston: Brill Publishing, 2010), 286.
40. Kirwin R. Shaffer, "Contesting Internationalists: Transnational Anarchism, Anti-Imperialism and US Expansion in the Caribbean, 1890s–1920s," *Estudios Interdisciplinarios de América Latina y el Caribe* 22, no. 2 (2011): 12–13.
41. Steven Hirsch and Lucien Van der Walt, *Anarchism and Syndicalism in the Colonial and Postcolonial World: The Praxis of National Liberation, Internationalism, and Social Revolution*, 286.
42. John Lear, *Workers, Neighbors, and Citizens: The Revolution in Mexico City* (Lincoln: University of Nebraska Press, 2001), 117.

Chapter 3: Los Caballeros de Labor

Quoted from Juan José Herrera, "Defenza y Respuesta: Los Injustificables Ataques de la Revista Católica de Las Vaega, N.M. Contra La Orden de Caballeros de Labor," *El Defensor del Pueblo*, July 11, 1891; 1.

1. The Knights' vision of racial unity did not generally extend to Chinese workers. For a full discussion of the contradictory positions taken by the Knights, see: Rob Weir, "Blind in One Eye Only: Western and Eastern Knights of Labor View the Chinese Question," *Labor History* 41, no. 4 (2000): 421–36.
2. Carroll D. Wright, "An Historical Sketch of the Knights of Labor," *The Quarterly Journal of Economics* 1, no. 2 (January 1887): 141.
3. José A. Rivera, *La Sociedad: Guardians of Hispanic Culture along the Río Grande* (Albuquerque: University of New Mexico Press, 2010), 10.
4. Carroll D. Wright, "An Historical Sketch of the Knights of Labor."
5. For instance, "From the formation of the General Assembly in 1878 up to 1883 there was a strong element in the Order in favor of supporting strikes, and strike funds were raised by a tax on the members. Meanwhile, the more advanced thinkers in the Order, led by Mr. Powderly, were trying to educate the members to use other means for the settlement of labor difficulties, and so far succeeded that at the Cincinnati session, in 1883, the strike laws were made so rigid that they practically amounted to

a prohibition of strikes, so far as the support of the Order was concerned." Carroll D. Wright, "An Historical Sketch of the Knights of Labor," 166.

6. It is important to note that in southern states, the Knights organized separate black and white local assemblies, capitulating to southern white racist sensibilities. Despite this, they organized integrated district, state, and national assemblies. See Theresa Case, "The Radical Potential of the Knights' Biracialism: The 1885–1886 Gould System Strikes and Their Aftermath," *Labor: Studies in Working-Class History of the Americas* 4, no. 4 (2007): 95.

7. Philip S. Foner et al., "The Knights of Labor," *The Journal of Negro History* 53, no. 1 (January 1968): 70.

8. For a good historical overview of this process, see Martin J. Sklar, *The Corporate Reconstruction of American Capitalism, 1890-1916: The Market, the Law, and Politics* (New York: Cambridge University Press, 1988).

9. Donald L. Kemmerer and Edward D. Wickersham, "Reasons for the Growth of the Knights of Labor in 1885–1886," *Industrial and Labor Relations Review* 3, no. 2 (January 1950): 213. Kemmerer and Wickersham estimate 700,000. Jonathon Garlock's more methodical study asserts the membership at 750,000. See Jonathon Garlock, *Guide to the Local Assemblies of the Knights of Labor* (Westport, CT: Greenwood Press, 1982), xii.

10. Michael Biggs, "Strikes as Sequences of Interaction: The American Strike Wave of 1886," *Social Science History* 26, no. 3 (Fall 2002): 585.

11. Ibid., 592.

12. This despite the formal position of its national leader, Terrance Powderly, to actively oppose strikes.

13. Ruth Allen, *The Great Southwest Strike* (Austin: University of Texas, 1942), 12.

14. Theresa Case, "The Radical Potential of the Knights' Biracialism: The 1885–1886 Gould System Strikes and Their Aftermath," 90.

15. Ibid., 91.

16. Frederick Merk, *Manifest Destiny and Mission in American History: A Reinterpretation* (Boston: Harvard University Press, 1995), 159.

17. Charles Montgomery, "Becoming 'Spanish-American': Race and Rhetoric in New Mexico Politics, 1880–1928," *Journal of American Ethnic History* 20, no. 4 (Summer 2001): 60.

18. On the eve of the Mexican-American War in 1845, fourteen land grants had been established that supported ten thousand people in New Mexico. See Robert J. Rosenbaum, *Mexicano Resistance in the Southwest: "The Sacred Right of Self-Preservation"* (Austin: University of Texas Press, 1981), 113.

19. David Correia, "'Retribution Will Be Their Reward': New Mexico's Las Gorras Blancas and the Fight for the Las Vegas Land Grant Commons," *Radical History Review* 2010, no. 108 (Fall 2010): 55.

20. Ibid.

21. Ibid.

22. Charles Montgomery discusses how the New Mexican elite attempted to recast themselves as "Spanish" during this period to fit more ably into the racist, Anglo society. Charles Montgomery, "Becoming 'Spanish-American': Race and Rhetoric in New Mexico Politics, 1880–1928," 59–84.

23. Miguel Otero, *My Life on the Frontier, 1864–1882* (New York: Press of the Pioneers, 1939), 228.

24. Phillip B. Gonzales, "Struggle for Survival: The Hispanic Land Grants of New Mexico, 1848–2001," *Agricultural History* 77, no. 2 (Spring 2003): 302.

25. Ibid., 303.

26. David Correia, "'Retribution Will Be Their Reward': New Mexico's Las Gorras Blancas and the Fight for the Las Vegas Land Grant Commons," 56.

27. Mary Romero, "Class Struggle and Resistance against the Transformation of Land Ownership and Usage in Northern New Mexico: The Case of Las Gorras Blancas," *Chicana/o-Latina/o Law Review* 26, no. 1 (Spring 2006): 87–110.

28. Ibid., 26, 94.

29. Robert J. Rosenbaum, *Mexicano Resistance in the Southwest: "The Sacred Right of Self-Preservation,"* 118.

30. David Brundage, *The Making of Western Labor Radicalism* (Chicago: University of Illinois Press, 1994), 156.

31. Joseph P. Buchanan, *The Story of a Labor Agitator* (New York: Outlook Publishers, 1903), 134–5.

32. Erlinda Gonzales-Berry and David Maciel, *The Contested Homeland: A Chicano History of New Mexico* (Albuquerque: New Mexico, 2000), 59.

33. Robert W. Larson, "The White Caps of New Mexico: A Study of Ethnic Militancy in the Southwest," *Pacific Historical Review* 44, no. 2 (May 1975): 178.

34. Robert J. Rosenbaum, *Mexicano Resistance in the Southwest: "The Sacred Right of Self-Preservation"* (Austin: University of Texas Press, 1981), 121; Jonathon Garlock, *Guide to the Local Assemblies of the Knights of Labor* (Westport, CT: Greenwood Press, 1982), 295–6.

35. Robert Kern, *Labor in New Mexico: Unions, Strikes, and Social History Since 1881* (Albuquerque: University of New Mexico Press, 1983), 37.

36. David Correia, "'Retribution Will Be Their Reward': New Mexico's Las Gorras Blancas and the Fight for the Las Vegas Land Grant Commons," 49.

37. Tobias Duran, "Francisco Chávez, Thomas B. Catron, and Organized Political Violence in Santa Fe in the 1890s," *New Mexico Historical Review* 59, vol. 3 (July 1, 1984): 293.

38. Robert J. Rosenbaum, *Mexicano Resistance in the Southwest: "The Sacred Right of Self-Preservation,"* 121.

39. Anthony Gabriel Meléndez, *Spanish-Language Newspapers in New Mexico, 1834–1958* (Tucson: University of Arizona Press, 2005), 83.

40. David Correia, "'Retribution Will Be Their Reward': New Mexico's Las Gorras Blancas and the Fight for the Las Vegas Land Grant Commons," 54.

41. Erlinda Gonzales-Berry and David Maciel, *The Contested Homeland: A Chicano History of New Mexico* (Albuquerque: New Mexico, 2000), 69.

42. "The White Caps," *Las Vegas Daily Optic*, March 20, 1891; 2.

43. Robert J. Rosenbaum, *Mexicano Resistance in the Southwest: "The Sacred Right of Self-Preservation,"* 109.

44. This outraged Anglos, who were not accustomed to Mexicans challenging their power, leading to widespread claims that this was the beginning of a race war or separatist movement. Throughout US-Mexico border history, there is a perpetual and irrational fear that Mexican people will rise up in the United States to "reconquer" the land taken from Mexico after the Mexican-American War. In reality, this notion is only heard from segments of the US population when faced with the idea of Mexican people attaining democratic rights. It is therefore used as a rallying cry to reaffirm that Mexicans should

not be "Americans" and therefore to subjugate them and relegate them into second-class or "alien" status.

45. "Told the Result in Bed," *Las Vegas Daily Optic*, November 3, 1890; 6.

46. See "Llamada para la Convención del Partido del Pueblo," *La Voz del Pueblo*, September 10, 1892; 1.

47. "On the Defensive, *Las Vegas Daily Optic*, April 4, 1891; 6.

48. David Correia, "'Retribution Will Be Their Reward': New Mexico's Las Gorras Blancas and the Fight for the Las Vegas Land Grant Commons," 65.

49. Phillip B. Gonzales, "Struggle for Survival: The Hispanic Land Grants of New Mexico, 1848–2001" *Agricultural History* 77, no. 2 (Spring 2003): 308.

Chapter 4: The Japanese Mexican Labor Association

John Murray, "A Foretaste of the Orient," *International Socialist Review* IV, no. 3 (August 1903): 79.

1. The Foreign Miners Tax Acts imposed restrictive taxes on foreign-born miners, effectively driving thousands out of the mines. The "Greaser Act" of 1855 was an anti-vagrancy law that targeted and characterized Mexicans as a crime-prone population, thereby sanctioning policies of social exclusion, restricting freedom of movement, political disenfranchisement, repressive policing methods, and vigilante violence.

2. Richard Steven Street, *Beasts of the Field: A Narrative History of California Farmworkers, 1769–1913* (Stanford: Stanford University Press, 2004), 440.

3. Abner E. Woodruff, *Evolution of American Agriculture*, Agricultural Workers Industrial Union no. 400, IWW, 1919. 46–53.

4. Frank Barajas, "Work and Leisure in La Colonia: Class, Generation, and Interethnic Alliances among Mexicanos in Oxnard, California, 1890–1945" (dissertation, Doctor of Philosophy, Claremont University, 2001), 35.

5. Tomás Almaguer, *Racial Fault Lines: The Historical Origins of White Supremacy in California* (Berkeley: University of California Press, 1994), 86.

6. Louie Herrera Moreno III, "Labor, Migration, and Activism: A History of Mexican Workers on the Oxnard Plain 1930–1980" (dissertation, Doctor of Philosophy, Michigan State University, 2012), 21.

7. Ibid., 18–21.

8. Frank Barajas, "Work and Leisure in La Colonia: Class, Generation, and Interethnic Alliances among Mexicanos in Oxnard, California, 1890–1945," 80–81.

9. A. Philip Draycott, *Sugar Beet* (Ames, IA: Blackwell Publishing, 2006), 19.

10. Juan Gómez-Quiñones, "The First Steps: Chicano Labor Conflict and Organizing 1900–1920," *Aztlán: A Journal of Chicano Studies* 3, no. 1 (1972): 22–23.

11. Tomás Almaguer, *Racial Fault Lines*, 98.

12. Tomás Almaguer, "Racial Domination and Class Conflict in Capitalist Agriculture: The Oxnard Sugar Beet Workers' Strike of 1903," *Labor History* 25, no. 3 (1984): 325–6.

13. David J. O'Brien and Stephen S. Fugita, *The Japanese American Experience* (Bloomington: Indiana University Press, 1991), 20.

14. Ibid.

15. This practice was especially effective for the Japanese workers whose ethnic-based worker organizations also served as vehicles for collective action. As early as the late 1800s, some Japanese Socialists migrated to the US via San Francisco, and others joined socialist clubs after arrival. While there has been some speculation that

socialists may have been among the JMLA organizers, it is only speculation at this point. For more on Japanese Socialist history in the US see Yuji Ichioka, "A Buried Past: Early Issei Socialists and the Japanese Community," *Amerasia* 1 (1971): 1–25.

16. John Murray, "A Foretaste of the Orient," 79.

17. "The Japs and Mexicans: Combined to Defeat American Contractors," *Oxnard Courier*, March 7, 1905; 5.

18. "Western Agricultural Contracting Company," *Oxnard Courier*, February 23, 1903; 5.

19. "Undesirable Immigrants Said to Be Coming to Southern California," *Oxnard Courier* April 4, 1903; 7.

20. Eric Arnesen, *Encyclopedia of US Labor and Working-Class History, Volume 1* (New York: Routledge, Taylor and Francis Group, 2007), 1051.

21. Editorial, *Oxnard Courier*, March 7, 1903; 4.

22. Tomás Almaguer, "Racial Domination and Class Conflict in Capitalist Agriculture: The Oxnard Sugar Beet Workers' Strike of 1903," *Labor History* 25, no. 3 (1984): 332.

23. Frank Barajas, *Curious Unions: Mexican American Workers and Resistance in Oxnard, California, 1898–1961* (Omaha: University of Nebraska Press, 2012), 235.

24. "The Japs and Mexicans: Combined to Defeat American Contractors," *Oxnard Courier*, March 7, 1903; 5.

25. Richard Steven Street, *Beasts of the Field*, 455.

26. "Large Acreage of Beets: Now Planted and Small Acreage Thinned," *Oxnard Courier*, March 21, 1903; 8.

27. "Climax in Labor Troubles," *Oxnard Courier*, March 28, 1903; 3.

28. For a hostile yet colorful account, see "Singular Outrages Allowed in Oxnard: Sugar Town in Hands of Armed Union Gang," *Los Angeles Times*, March 29, 1903; B8.

29. "Communication from the Union," *Oxnard Courier*, March 28, 1903; 1.

30. "Peace and Work Once More," *Oxnard Courier*, April 4, 1903; 1.

31. For example, see "War at Oxnard Between Unions," *San Bernardino County Sun*, March 25, 1903, 1; and "Bloody Union Rioting and Hail of Bullets," *Los Angeles Times*, March 24, 1903; 11.

32. This occurred with some exceptions, see Tomás Almaguer, "Racial Domination and Class Conflict in Capitalist Agriculture: The Oxnard Sugar Beet Workers' Strike of 1903," 343.

33. John Murray, "A Foretaste of the Orient," 77.

34. "Indorsed Rioting: Resolutions Adopted by the Council of Labor with Regard to Oxnard," *Los Angeles Times*, March 26, 1903; 10.

35. For a full discussion of how the Japanese exclusion movement came from within the California landowning elite, see chapter 22.

36. Yuji Ichioka, *The Issei: The World of the First Generation Japanese Immigrants, 1885–1924* (New York: Free Press, 1988), 100.

37. See "Socialists in Control," *Los Angeles Times*, September 21, 1902; 6.

38. John Murray, "A Foretaste of the Orient," 73.

39. Ibid., 73–74.

40. Tomás Almaguer, "Racial Domination and Class Conflict in Capitalist Agriculture: The Oxnard Sugar Beet Workers' Strike of 1903," 346–7.

41. John Murray, "A Foretaste of the Orient," 78.

42. "Gompers Slaps Japs: Cannot Enter Federation," *Los Angeles Times*, May 24, 1903; 8.

43. Within a month, the JMLA was already in decline as the company refused to honor

the terms of the March agreement and members began to leave the region to look for work elsewhere. This is mentioned in the *Oxnard Courier*, "Work of Japanese Labor Association," April 18, 1903.

Chapter 5: Mexican Miners in Arizona

Linda Gordon, *The Great Arizona Orphan Abduction* (Cambridge: Harvard University Press, 1999), 220.

1. See F. H. Hatch, "The World Production of Copper, Historically and Actually," *The Economic World* 106 (October 23, 1920): 583–5, and "Mineral Production of Arizona, California, 1903–1906," *Mining Reporter* 55 (January 18, 1907): 55.
2. James R. Kluger, *The Clifton-Morenci Strike: Labor Difficulty in Arizona, 1915–1916* (Tucson: University of Arizona Press), 24.
3. D. Wilson Eldred, "Early Mining in Arizona," *Kiva* 11, no. 4 (May 1946): 39.
4. Ibid., 44.
5. Thomas Sheridan, *Arizona: A History* (Tucson: University of Arizona Press, 1995), 70–71.
6. Thomas Sheridan, *Los Tucsonenses: The Mexican Community in Tucson, 1854–1941* (Tucson: University of Arizona Press, 1986), 36.
7. Anglo miners opposed the presence of foreign-born miners, mainly Mexican and Chinese, making claims to what they believed was theirs. In the decade following the conquest of California, white mobs routinely drove Mexicans from the mines during a period in which Mexicans were being displaced from the land and disenfranchised from the political system based on race.
8. Ken Gonzales-Day, *Lynching in the West: 1850–1935* (Durham: Duke University Press, 2006), 26.
9. Hubert Howe Bancroft, *In These Latter Days* (Chicago: Blakely-Oswald Publishers, 1917), 244.
10. Orick Jackson, *The White Conquest of Arizona: The History of the Pioneers* (Los Angeles: Grafton Co., 1908), 19–20; and Kathleen P. Chamberlain, *Victorio: Apache Warrior and Chief* (Norman, OK: University of Oklahoma Press, 2007), 107–8.
11. "There were 1300 Blacks in Arizona by 1890, while Mexicans were the single largest population." See Andrea Yvette Hugginie, "Strikitos: Race, Class, and Work in the Arizona Copper Industry, 1870–1920" (doctoral dissertation, Yale University, 1991), 42–43.
12. Linda Gordon, *The Great Arizona Orphan Abduction*, 24.
13. Samuel Truett, *Fugitive Landscapes: The Forgotten History of the US-Mexico Borderlands* (New Haven: Yale University Press, 2006), 42–43.
14. Manuel P. Servín and Robert L. Spude, "Historical Conditions of Early Mexican Labor in the United States: Arizona—A Neglected Story," *Journal of Mexican American History* 5 (1975): 44.
15. Phylis Cancilla Martinelli, *Undermining Race: Ethnic Identities in Arizona Copper Camps, 1880–1920* (Tucson: University of Arizona Press, 2009), 135.
16. Joseph F. Park, "The 1903 'Mexican Affair' at Clifton," *The Journal of Arizona History* 18, no. 2 (Summer 1977), 121.
17. Manuel P. Servín and Robert L. Spude, "Historical Conditions of Early Mexican Labor in the United States: Arizona—A Neglected Story," 44.
18. Joseph F. Park, "The 1903 'Mexican Affair' at Clifton," 131.

19. Andrés E. Jiménez, "The Political Formation of a Mexican Working Class in the Arizona Copper Industry, 1870–1917," *Review* (Fernand Braudel Center) 4, no. 3 (Winter 1981): 559.

20. James R. Kluger, *The Clifton-Morenci Strike: Labor Difficulty in Arizona, 1915–1916*, 23.

21. While "white" and "nonwhite" racial categories were somewhat rigid, how individual miners were categorized or how criteria were determined in different districts could be more fluid. For instance, while Mexicans were technically categorized as "white" by federal policy, they could be categorized as white, immigrant, or "Indian." Other types of ambiguities, prejudices, and arbitrary designations commonly occurred based on different circumstances. See Phylis Cancilla Martinelli, *Undermining Race: Ethnic Identities in Arizona Copper Camps, 1880–1920*; and Katherine Benton-Cohen, *Borderline Americans: Racial Division and Labor War in the Arizona Borderlands* (Cambridge: Harvard University Press, 2009), chapter 3, for fuller a discussion of this phenomenon.

22. Katherine Benton-Cohen, *Borderline Americans: Racial Division and Labor War in the Arizona Borderlands*, 82.

23. Ibid., 84–85.

24. Andrea Yvette Hugginie, "Strikitos: Race, Class, and Work in the Arizona Copper Industry, 1870–1920" (doctoral dissertation, Yale University, 1991), 52.

25. For instance, the first use of law enforcement to crush a strike occurred in Globe in 1896. See James Ward Byrkit, "Life and Labor In Arizona, 1901–1921: With Particular Reference to the Deportations Of 1917" (doctoral dissertation, Claremont Graduate School, 1972), 88.

26. Terry Boswell and John Brueggemann, "Labor Market Segmentation and the Cultural Division of Labor in the Copper Mining Industry, 1880–1920," *Research in Social Movements, Conflicts, and Change* 22 (2000): 193–217. Cited in Phylis Cancilla Martinelli, *Undermining Race: Ethnic Identities in Arizona Copper Camps*, 7.

27. Linda Gordon, *The Great Arizona Orphan Abduction*, 214.

28. Joseph Park cites one mine owner who expresses this sentiment openly. See Joseph F. Park, "The 1903 'Mexican Affair' at Clifton," *The Journal of Arizona History* 18, no. 2 (Summer 1977): 135.

29. Phylis Cancilla Martinelli, *Undermining Race: Ethnic Identities in Arizona Copper Camps, 1880–1920*, 5.

30. Linda Gordon, *The Great Arizona Orphan Abduction* (Cambridge: Harvard University Press, 1999), 217.

31. For instance, Phil Mellinger points out how after a strike of predominantly Mexican miners at Ray, Arizona, in 1900, the mine operator claimed that "hereafter . . . white miners will be employed exclusively." Other examples are also described. See "'The Men Have Become Organizers': Labor Conflict and Unionization in the Mexican Mining Communities of Arizona, 1900–1915," *The Western Historical Quarterly* 23, no. 3 (August 1992): 326–7.

32. José Amaro Hernandez, *Mutual Aid for Survival: The Case of the Mexican American* (Malabar, FL: Robert E. Krieger Publishing Company, 1983), 40.

33. Michael Casillas, "Mexicans, Labor, and Strife in Arizona, 1896–1917" (Master's Thesis, History, University of New Mexico, Albuquerque, 1979), 8–9.

34. James R. Kluger, *The Clifton-Morenci Strike: Labor Difficulty in Arizona, 1915–1916*, 26.

35. Andrés E. Jiménez, "The Political Formation of a Mexican Working Class in the Arizona Copper Industry, 1870–1917," 554.

36. James R. Kluger, *The Clifton-Morenci Strike: Labor Difficulty in Arizona, 1915–1916*, 20.

37. J. D. Porteous, "The Nature of the Company Town," *Transactions of the Institute of British Geographers*, no. 51 (November 1970): 132.

38. James Byrkit, "Life and Labor in Arizona, 1901–1921: With Particular Reference to the Deportations of 1917," 83.

39. For a full discussion of the Western Federation of Miners' political evolution, see Eric L. Clements, "Pragmatic Revolutionaries?: Tactics, Ideologies, and the Western Federation of Miners in the Progressive Era," *The Western Historical Quarterly* 40, no. 4 (Winter 2009), 449.

40. Phil Mellinger, "'The Men Have Become Organizers': Labor Conflict and Unionization in the Mexican Mining Communities of Arizona, 1900–1915," 327.

41. Linda Gordon, *The Great Arizona Orphan Abduction*, 241; and Michael Casillas, "Mexicans, Labor, and Strife in Arizona, 1896–1917," 21.

42. Discussed in more detail in chapter 8. See also Linda Gordon, *The Great Arizona Orphan Abduction*, chapter 6.

43. David R. Berman, *Politics, Labor, and the War on Big Business: The Path of Reform in Arizona* (Boulder: University Press of Colorado, 2012), 75.

44. José Amaro Hernandez, *Mutual Aid for Survival: The Case of the Mexican American*, 33.

45. Marcella Bencivenni, *Italian Immigrant Radical Culture: The Idealism of the Sovversivi in the United States, 1890–1940* (New York: New York University Press, 2011), 11.

46. Ibid., 13.

47. "Condition Not Changed: The Clifton-Morenci Strike is Almost Entirely Composed of Mexicans—Making Demonstrations," *Bisbee Daily Review,* June 5, 1903; 1.

48. "A Big Strike Now: Mines, Smelters, and Concentrators Closed Down," *The Copper Era and Morenci Leader*, June 4, 1903; 3.

49. Linda Gordon, *The Great Arizona Orphan Abduction*, 220.

50. Donald Garate, "Wenceslao (Three-Fingered Jack) Loustaunau: Blacksmith with a Cause," *The Journal of Arizona History* 48, no. 2 (Summer 2007): 116.

51. Phil Mellinger, "'The Men Have Become Organizers': Labor Conflict and Unionization in the Mexican Mining Communities of Arizona, 1900–1915," 331.

52. Linda Gordon, *The Great Arizona Orphan Abduction*, 226.

53. Donald Garate, "Wenceslao (Three-Fingered Jack) Loustaunau: Blacksmith with a Cause," 115–116.

54. Jennie Parks Ringgold, *Frontier Days in the Southwest: Pioneer Days in Old Arizona* (San Antonio: Naylor Publishing, 1952), 165–6.

55. Linda Gordon, *The Great Arizona Orphan Abduction*, 222.

56. Phil Mellinger, "'The Men Have Become Organizers': Labor Conflict and Unionization in the Mexican Mining Communities of Arizona, 1900–1915," 329.

57. Donald Garate, "Wenceslao (Three-Fingered Jack) Loustaunau: Blacksmith with a Cause," 120.

58. As Linda Gordon explains, the role of women and family support were vital for the success of the strike, although "not a single newspaper account, reminiscence, or legal document of the 1903 strike mentioned any women." See Linda Gordon, *The Great Arizona Orphan Abduction*, 244.

59. Jennie Parks Ringgold, *Frontier Days in the Southwest: Pioneer Days in Old Arizona*, 169.

60. "Condition not Changed: The Clifton-Morenci Strike is Almost Entirely Composed of Mexicans—Making Demonstrations," 1903; 1.

61. "Federal Troops are at Morenci," *Bisbee Daily Review*, June 11, 1903; 1.
62. Linda Gordon, *The Great Arizona Orphan Abduction*, 238.
63. "Morenci at Mercy of Armed Foreigners," *Bisbee Daily Review*, June 11, 1903; 1.
64. Samuel Truett, *Fugitive Landscapes: The Forgotten History of the US-Mexico Borderlands*, 138.
65. Joseph F. Park, "The 1903 'Mexican Affair' at Clifton," 119–48.
66. "Strike Situation Now Very Grave," *Bisbee Daily Review*, June 10, 1903; 1.
67. "Critical Moment Passed," *The Copper Era and Morenci Leader*, June 11, 1903; 3.
68. Donald Garate, "Wenceslao (Three-Fingered Jack) Loustaunau: Blacksmith with a Cause," 120.
69. Several historians believe the storm was what broke the strike, as many miners broke ranks to deal with the emergency situation. See "Aftermath of the Flood," *The Copper Era and Morenci Leader*, June 18, 1903; 3.
70. Cited in Joseph F. Park, "The 1903 'Mexican Affair' at Clifton," 145.
71. "Place Blame Where it Belongs," *The Copper Era and Morenci Leader*, June 18, 1903; 2.
72. The racist newspaper article that named them points out sarcastically that none are "American" names and claims that they caused a "reign of terror in Eastern Arizona." See "The Names of Them," *Arizona Republic*, June 15, 1903; 2.
73. "A Mexican Rebel Leader is Deported," *The Topeka Daily Capital*, September 15, 1906; 2.
74. Rodolfo F. Acuña, *Corridors of Migration: The Odyssey of Mexican Laborers, 1600–1933*, (Tucson: University of Arizona Press, 2007), 173. The US press at the time wrongfully reported his death. See "Abraham Salcido [*sic*] Reported Killed," *Tombstone Weekly Epitaph*, October 7, 1906; 2.
75. Andrés E. Jiménez, "The Political Formation of a Mexican Working Class in the Arizona Copper Industry, 1870–1917," 560.

Chapter 6: Early Mexican Labor Radicalism in Texas

"Como nació la huelga," *El Defensor del Obrero*, April 7, 1907; 303.

1. Richard Griswold del Castillo, *The Treaty of Guadalupe Hidalgo: A Legacy of Conflict* (Norman: University of Oklahoma Press, 1990), 86.
2. For an in-depth discussion of this period of conflict, see Kathleen P. Chamberlain, *Victorio: Apache Warrior and Chief* (Norman: University of Oklahoma Press, 2007); Jerry Thompson, *Cortina: Defending the Mexican Name in Texas* (College Station: Texas A&M University Press, 2007); Mary Romero, "El Paso Salt War: Mob Action or Political Struggle?" *Aztlán* 16, no. 1–2 (1985): 119–38; Paul Cool, *Salt Warriors: Insurgency on the Río Grande* (College Station: Texas A&M University Press, 2008); and Elliot Young, *Catarino Garza's Revolution on the Texas-Mexico Border* (Durham, NC: Duke University Press, 2004). John Mason Hart adds that court battles over displacement have persisted into the present. See *Empire and Revolution: The Americans in Mexico Since the Civil War* (Berkeley: University of California Press, 2002), 23.
3. José A. Cobas, Jorge Duany, and Joe R. Feagin, *How the United States Racializes Latinos: White Hegemony and its Consequences* (Boulder: Paradigm Press, 2009), 70–73.
4. David Montejano, *Anglos and Mexicans: The Making of Texas, 1836–1986* (Austin: University of Texas Press, 1987), 86.
5. See Henry D. McCallum, "Barbed Wire in Texas," *The Southwestern Historical Quarterly* 61, no. 2 (October 1957): 207–19.
6. David Montejano (citing Eric Wolf), *Anglos and Mexicans: The Making of Texas, 1836–1986*, 104.

7. See Randall H. McGuire and Paul Reckner, "The Unromantic West: Labor, Capital, and Struggle," *Historical Archaeology* 36, no. 3 (September 2002): 44–58.

8. For a full discussion of this "racialization" process see Reginald Horsman, *Race and Manifest Destiny: The Origins of Racial Anglo-Saxonism* (Cambridge: Harvard University Press, 1981), and Mario Barrera, *Race and Class in the Southwest: A Theory of Racial Inequality* (Notre Dame: University of Notre Dame Press, 1979).

9. David Montejano (citing Eric Wolf), *Anglos and Mexicans: The Making of Texas, 1836–1986*, 113.

10. See David Montejano, *Anglos and Mexicans: The Making of Texas, 1836–1986*, 126–7.

11. Benjamin Heber Johnson, *Revolution in Texas: How a Forgotten Rebellion and Its Bloody Suppression Turned Mexicans into Americans* (New Haven: Yale University Press, 2003), 19–20.

12. Ibid., 34.

13. For an early critical analysis, see Robert Wendell Hainsworth, "The Negro and the Texas Primaries," *The Journal of Negro History* 18, no. 4 (October 1933): 426–50.

14. Michael G. Webster, "Texan Manifest Destiny and the Mexican Border Conflict, 1865–1880" (Doctoral Thesis in Philosophy, Department of History, Indiana University, 1972), 303.

15. Ibid., 304.

16. Rodolfo F. Acuña, *Corridors of Migration: The Odyssey of Mexican Laborers, 1600–1933* (Tucson: University of Arizona Press, 2007), 39–40.

17. Jaime Tamayo and Patricia Valles, *Anarquismo, Socialismo Y Sindicalismo En Las Regiones* (Guadalajara: Editorial, Universidad de Guadalajara, 1993), 190.

18. William K. Meyers, *Forge of Progress, Crucible of Revolt: The Origins of the Mexican Revolution in La Comarca Lagunera, 1880–1911*, (Albuquerque: University of New Mexico Press, 1994), 7.

19. Arnoldo De León, ed., *War along the Border: The Mexican Revolution and Tejano Communities* (College Station: Texas A&M University Press, 2012),15.

20. Richard A. García, "The Making of the Mexican-American Mind, San Antonio Texas, 1929–1941: A Social and Intellectual History of an Ethnic Community" (doctoral dissertation, University of California, Irvine, 1980), 80.

21. Sonia Hernández, *Working Women into the Borderlands* (College Station: Texas A&M University Press, 2014), 109.

22. Juan L. Gonzalez, Jr., *Mexican and Mexican American Farm Workers: The California Agricultural Industry* (New York: Praeger, 1985), 7–8.

23. Emilio Zamora, *The World of the Mexican Worker in Texas* (College Station: Texas A&M University Press, 1993), 56.

24. Emilio Zamora, Cynthia, Orozco, and Rodolfo Rocha, *Mexican Americans in Texas History* (Austin: Texas State Historical Association, 2000), 68.

25. Barry Carr, "The Mexican Communist Party and Agrarian Mobilization in the Laguna, 1920–1940: A Worker-Peasant Alliance?" *The Hispanic American Historical Review* 67, no. 3 (August 1987): 376.

26. For a full discussion of the La Laguna economy, see William K. Meyers, "Seasons of Rebellion: Nature, Organisation of Cotton Production and the Dynamics of Revolution in La Laguna, Mexico, 1910–1916," *Journal of Latin American Studies* 30, no. 1 (February 1998): 63–94.

27. The character and diversity of these organizations are described in great detail in

Emilio Zamora, *The World of the Mexican Worker in Texas*, 56.

28. Elliot Young explains how Anglo racism could unite Mexicans of different classes and ideologies within the mutualistas and fraternal organizations, giving them a nationalist character; but those class cleavages came to the fore and divided the groups when some members formed or joined unions, went on strike, and promoted opposition to capitalism. See Elliot Young, "Deconstructing La Raza: Identifying the *Gente Decente* of Laredo, 1904–1911," *The Southwestern Historical Quarterly* 98, no. 2 (October 1994): 227–59.

29. Emilio Zamora, *The World of the Mexican Worker in Texas*, 114–5.

30. See Elliot Young, "Deconstructing La Raza: Identifying the *Gente Decente* of Laredo, 1904–1911," 238.

31. Emilio Zamora, "Chicano Socialist Labor Activity in Texas, 1900–1920," *Aztlán* 6, no. 2 (Summer 1975): 222.

32. An example of the distance between the local and the national AFL is evident in the "Report of Proceedings of the Twenty-Seventh Annual Convention of the American Federation of Labor" (November 11–23): 107. Despite FLU no. 11953 having participated in a significant strike the previous year, there is no mention of the event in the proceedings, only a brief reference to membership and a reimbursement (69).

33. For example, see Charles Romney, *Rights Delayed: The American State and the Defeat of Progressive Unions* (New York: Oxford University Press), 2016.

34. While industrial in character, the model called for organizing individual craft unions after reaching a critical mass.

35. Cited in Elliot Young, "Deconstructing La Raza: Identifying the *Gente Decente* of Laredo, 1904–1911," 227.

36. "Chisporroteos: Trabaja," *El Defensor del Obrero*, September 2, 1906; 76.

37. "Chisporroteos," *El Defensor del Obrero*, July 22, 1906; 30.

38. Editorial, *El Defensor del Obrero*, September 22, 1906; 104.

39. "Mazazos," *El Defensor del Obrero*, July 29, 1906; 33.

40. "Obreros, Accionemos," *El Defensor del Obrero*, September 2, 1906; 79.

41. Vicki L. Ruiz and Virginia Sánchez Korrol, *Latinas in the United States: A Historical Encyclopedia* (Bloomington: University of Indiana Press, 2006), 368.

42. Emilio Zamora, *The World of the Mexican Worker in Texas*, 118.

43. "El Trabajo es La Fuerza," *El Defensor del Obrero*, January 13, 1907; 219.

44. "Odios de Raza," *El Defensor del Obrero*, January 20, 1907; 225.

45. The strike of 1906 has also been identified as a key part of an industrial strike wave that contributed to the downfall of Porfirio Díaz (see James Cockcroft, *Intellectual Precursors of the Mexican Revolution 1900–1913*). For an overview of the strikes mentioned, see Francisco Javier Gorostiza, *Los Ferrocarriles en la Revolucion Mexicana* (Mexico, D.F.: Siglo XXI Editores, 2010), 46–48.

46. Mexican railroads were largely built with European and US capital, with investment groups often incorporated in their own home countries and according their own laws. Rail lines were later sold or transferred to the Mexican government. See Fred Wilbur Powell, *The Railroads of Mexico* (Boston: Stratford Co., 1921).

47. Emilio Zamora, "Chicano Socialist Labor Activity in Texas, 1900–1920," 224.

48. "La Huelga," *El Defensor del Obrero*, November 18, 1906; 168.

49. "Circular," *El Defensor del Obrero*, January 6, 1907; 211.

50. "Comunicado," *El Defensor del Obrero*, January 13, 1907; 224.

51. This action prefigured the increasingly common practice of businesses relocating or shifting production across borders in order to break unions throughout the twentieth century.

52. In English, one translation would be "The First Congress of Pro-Mexican Organizations."

53. José Limón, "El Primer Congreso Mexicanista de 1911: A Precursor to Contemporary Chicanismo," *Aztlán* 5, no. 1–2 (Spring and Fall 1974): 86.

54. Ibid., 89.

55. "The Strike of the Workers: Our Opinon," *El Democrata Fronterizo*, December 15, 1906, 1.

56. Their principles were outlined in Idar's paper. See "El Primer Congreso Mexicanista de Texas," *La Crónica*, February 2, 1911; 3.

57. José "Limón, "El Primer Congreso Mexicanista de 1911: A Precursor to Contemporary Chicanismo," 95.

Chapter 7: Ricardo Flores Magón and the Rise of the PLM

Quoted in Donald C. Hodges, *Mexican Anarchism After the Revolution* (Austin: University of Texas Press, 1995), 12.

1. For instance, an otherwise groundbreaking and influential text includes this characterization: James D. Cockcroft, *Intellectual Precursors of the Mexican Revolution: 1900–1913* (Austin: University of Texas Press, 1968).

2. Claudio Lomnitz, *The Return of Comrade Ricardo Flores Magón* (New York: Zone Books, 2014), xiv.

3. Flores Magón referred to his doctrine as "Anarcho-Communism," discussed later in the chapter.

4. See Hilario Topete Lara, "Los Flores Magón y su circunstancia," *Contribuciones desde Coatepec* no. 8, (January–June, 2005): 73, note number 3.

5. Francisco Camero Rodriguez claims that he was awarded three haciendas for his service to the liberals against the French, but that he rejected the offer since the haciendas were situated on indigenous communal land. See *Ricardo Flores Magón: El Prometeo de los Trabajadores Mexicanos* (Mexico: Distribuciones Fontamara, 2005), 18.

6. The broad idea of "Mexican liberalism" actually encompassed various strains of thought, regional interpretations and alliances, evolving and even contradictory notions and interpretations. For a discussion of the complexities of Mexican liberalism see Alan Knight, "El liberalismo mexicano desde la Reforma hasta la Revolución (una interpretación)," *Historia Mexicana* 35, no. 1 (July–September 1985): 59–91.

7. Paul Friedrich, *Agrarian Revolt in a Mexican Village* (Chicago: University of Chicago Press, 1970), 65.

8. Pedro Maria Anaya Ibarra, *Precursores de La Revolución Mexicana* (Mexico: Secretaria de Educación Publica, 1955), 15.

9. Genaro Amezcua, *¿Quien es Flores Magón y Cuál es Su Obra?* (Mexico, D.F.: Editoriales Avance, 1953), 20–21.

10. Ibid., 16.

11. A fuller discussion of the other Flores Magón brothers, Enrique and Jesús, is beyond the scope of this work. For a discussion of their roles in the movement, see Samuel Kaplan, *Peleamos contra la injusticia: Enrique Flores Magón, precursor de la Revolución Mexicana, cuenta su historia a Samuel Kaplan* (Mexico, D.F.: Libros Mex Editores, 1960).

12. José C. Valadés, *El Joven Ricardo Flores Magón* (Mexico: Editorial Extemporáneos, 1983), 18.

13. Flores Magón assisted in the production of, wrote for, or established his own newspapers over this period that engaged in social criticism or took direct positions against the Díaz regime. These included *El Demócrata*, *El Universal*, *El Ideal*, *Al Azote*, *Regeneración*, *El Hijo de el Ahuizote*, *El Nieto del Ahuizote*, and *El Bisnieto del Ahuizote*.

14. Jean-Pierre Bastian, "Jacobinismo y ruptura revolucionaria durante el porfiriato," *Mexican Studies/Estudios Mexicanos* 7, no. 1 (Winter 1991): 6.

15. Full text available online at: http://www.antorcha.net/biblioteca_virtual/historia/programa/21.html

16. Florencio Barrera Fuentes, *Historia de La Revolución Mexicana: La Etapa Precursora* (Mexico, D.F.: Biblioteca del Instituto Nacional de Estudios Historicos de La Revolución Mexicana, 1955), 20–21.

17. José C. Valadés, *El Joven Ricardo Flores Magón*, 27–32.

18. Armando Bartra believes that this is the result of the editorial influence of Jesús Flores Magón, who was a moderate liberal. He and Ricardo soon split over ideology, strategy, and tactics, and remained politically alienated from each other for the rest of Ricardo's life. See *Regeneración 1900–1918, La Corriente más Radical del la Revolución Mexicana de 1910 a través de su Periódico de Combate* (Mexico: Ediciones Era, 1977), 21–22.

19. Diego Abad de Santillán cited in J. Eduardo Vazquez Carrillo, *El Partido Liberal Mexicano* (Mexico: Talleres de B. Costa-Amic, 1970), 67–68.

20. José C. Valadés, *El Joven Ricardo Flores Magón*, 43–44.

21. Armando List Arzubide, *Apuntes Sobre la Prehistoria de la Revolución* (Mexico: Publisher not determined, 1958), 73.

22. Abelardo Ojeda and Carlos Mallen, *Ricardo Flores Magón* (Mexico, D.F.: Secretaría de Educación Pública, 1967), 19.

23. See Stanley Ross, "La protesta de los intelectuales ante México y su revolución," *Historia Mexicana* 26, no. 3 (January–March 1977): 396–437.

24. Colin M. Maclachlan, *Anarchism and the Mexican Revolution: The Political Trials of Ricardo Flores Magón in the United States* (Berkeley: University of California Press, 1991), 2.

25. Héctor Mora Zebadúa, Victor Palacio Muñoz, and Omar M. Guzmán Navarro, *Un Siglo del Programa del Proletariado en México (Partido Liberal Mexicano 1906)* (Chapingo: Universidad Autónoma de Chapingo; Centro de Investigaciones Económicas, 2008), 17.

26. Launched under his editorial control in 1901.

27. Lyle Brown, *The Mexican Liberals and their Struggle Against the Díaz Dictatorship, 1900–1906* (Mexico: Mexico City College Press, 1956), 318.

28. Armando Bartra, *Regeneración 1900–1918, La Corriente más Radical del la Revolución Mexicana de 1910 a través de su Periódico de Combate* (Mexico: Ediciones Era, 1977), 23.

29. Héctor Mora Zebadúa et al., *Un Siglo del Programa del Proletariado en México*, 29.

30. Chantal Lopez and Omar Cortés, *El Partido Liberal Mexicano (1906–8)* (Mexico, D.F.: Ediciones Antorcha, 1986),103.

31. James D. Cockcroft, *Intellectual Precursors of the Mexican Revolution: 1900–1913*, 94; and Samuel Kaplan, *Peleamos contra la injusticia*, 76.

32. For a good description of Porfirian centralization, see Stuart Easterling, *The Mexican Revolution: A Short History 1910–1920* (Chicago: Haymarket Books, 2012).

33. Pedro Maria Anaya Ibarra, *Precursores de La Revolución Mexicana*, 22.

34. Jean-Pierre Bastian, "Jacobinismo y ruptura revolucionaria durante el porfiriato," 41.

35. Armando Liszt Arzubide, *Apuntes sobre La Prehistoriade la Revolución* (Mexico:

Publisher not determined, 1958), 39.

36. Anna Macias, *Against All Odds: The Feminist Movement in Mexico to 1940* (Westport, CT: Greenwood Press, 1982), 26.

37. Angeles Mendieta Alatorre, *La Mujer en La Revolución Mexicana* (Mexico: Biblioteca del Instituto Nacional de Estudios Historicos de la Revolución Mexicana, 1961), 30–31.

38. José C. Valadés, *El Joven Ricardo Flores Magón*, 24.

39. Ángeles Mendieta Alatorre, *La Mujer en La Revolución Mexicana*, 38–41.

40. Ibid., 40.

41. Ana Lau and Carmen Ramos, *Mujeres y Revolución* (Mexico, D.F.: Instituto Nacional de Antropología e Historia, 1993), 24.

42. "El Deber de la Mujer," *Revolución*, July 6, 1907; 1.

43. Ibid.

44. J. Eduardo Vazquez Carrillo, *El Partido Liberal Mexicano*, 141; and Armando Bartra, *Regeneración 1900–1918*, 28.

45. Discussed in chapter 8.

46. Ricardo Cuahtémoc Esparza Valdivia. *El Fenómeno Magonista en México y en Estados Unidos (1905–1908)* (Zacatecas: Centro de Investigaciones Históricas, 2000), 170.

47. Armando Bartra, *Regeneración 1900–1918*, 42.

48. Ricardo Cuahtémoc Esparza Valdivia, *El Fenómeno Magonista en México y en Estados Unidos (1905–1908)*, 40–41.

49. William D. Raat's *Revoltosos* is the best source to understand how the binational campaign against the PLM was orchestrated.

Chapter 8: The PLM Turns to the Working Classes

José Revueltas, *Ensayo Sobre un Proletariado sin Cabeza* (Mexico, D. F.: 1962), 201.

1. John M. Hart, *Anarchism and the Mexican Working Class 1860–1931* (Austin: University of Texas Press, 1987), 44.

2. Ellen Howell Myers, "The Mexican Liberal Party: 1903–1910" (dissertation, University of Virginia, 1970), 360.

3. For an example of this, see Casey Harison, "The Paris Commune of 1871, the Russian Revolution of 1905, and the Shifting of the Revolutionary Tradition," *History and Memory* 19, no. 2 (Fall/Winter 2007): 6–7.

4. Angeles Mendieta Alatorre, *La Mujer en La Revolución Mexicana* (Mexico: Biblioteca del Instituto Nacional de Estudios Historicos de la Revolución Mexicana, 1961), 45.

5. Ibid., 47.

6. Arnaldo Córdova, *La Ideología de la Revolución Mexicana* (Mexico, D.F.: Ediciones Era S.A. , 1977), 175.

7. Héctor Mora Zebadúa et al., *Un Siglo del Programa del Proletariado en México*, 52.

8. James D. Cockcroft, *Intellectual Precursors of the Mexican Revolution: 1900–1913*, 134–43.

9. Juan Gomez-Quiñones, "The First Steps: Chicano Labor Conflict and Organizing 1900–1920," *Aztlán* 3, no. 1, (October 1972): 20.

10. Ward Albro, *Always a Rebel: Ricardo Flores Magón and the Mexican Revolution* (College Station: Texas A&M University Press, 1992), 30.

11. Leon Díaz Cárdenas, *Cananea: Primer Brote del Sindicalismo en Mexico*, 16.

12. J. Eduardo Vazquez Carrillo, *El Partido Liberal Mexicano* (Mexico: Talleres de S. Consta-Amic, 1970), 28.

13. Ricardo Flores Magón, *Land and Liberty: Anarchist Influences in the Mexican Revolution* (Montreal: Black Rose Books, 1977), 128.

14. Francois-Xavier Guerra estimates 250,000 in his work *México: del Antiguo Régimen a la Revolución, Tomo II* (Mexico: Fondo de Cultura Económica, 1988), 50; while William D. Raat estimates 750,000 in *Los Revoltosos: Rebeldes Mexicanos en los Estados Unidos 1903–1923* (Mexico: Fondo de Cultura Económica, 1988), 36.

15. Leon Díaz Cárdenas, *Cananea: Primer Brote del Sindicalismo en Mexico*, 19.

16. Héctor Mora Zebadúa et al., *Un Siglo del Programa del Proletariado en México*, 19.

17. Alfonso Torúa Cienfuegos, *Magonismo en Sonora (1906–1908): Historia de una Persecución* (México, D.F.: Hormiga Libertaria, 2010), 35.

18. Javier Torres Parés, *La Revolución Sin Fronteras: El partido Liberal Mexicano y las relaciones entre el movimiento obrero de México y el de Estados Unidos, 1900–1923* (Mexico: Ediciones y Distribuciones Hispánicas, 1990), 30.

19. Ibid., 53–54.

20. The Río Blanco Strike is discussed in more detail in chapter 1.

21. Samuel Truett, *Fugitive Landscapes: The Forgotten History of the US-Mexico Borderlands*, 92.

22. Ibid., 99.

23. Herbert Brayer, "The Cananea Incident," *New Mexico Historical Review* 13, no. 4 (October 1, 1938): 388. See also John Mason Hart, *Empire and Revolution: The Americans in Mexico Since the Civil War* (Berkeley: University of California Press, 2002), 147.

24. Philip Mellinger, *Race and Labor in Western Copper: The Fight for Equality, 1896–1918* (Tucson: University of Arizona Press, 1995), 2.

25. Ibid., 10.

26. Salvador Hernandez Padilla, *El Magonismo: Un Historia de Una Pasión Libertaria* (Mexico, D.F.: Ediciones Era, 1984), 33. (Translated by author.)

27. Herbert Brayer, "The Cananea Incident," 390–1.

28. Juan Gomez-Quiñones, *Sembradores: Ricardo Flores-Magón y el Partido Liberal Mexicano: A Eulogy and Critique* (Los Angeles: Aztlán Publications, 1973), 30.

29. Philip Mellinger, *Race and Labor in Western Copper: The Fight for Equality, 1896–1918*, 24–27.

30. Ibid., 36.

31. Joseph Park, "The 1903 'Mexican Affair' at Clifton," *Journal of Arizona History*, no. 18 (Summer 1977): 119–48.

32. Armando Bartra, *Regeneración 1900–1918*, 18.

33. Ward Albro, "Always a Rebel," 38.

34. Manuel Aguirre, *Cananea: Las Garras del Imperialismo en las Entrañas de México* (Mexico: Libro Mex, 1958), 51.

35. Ellen Howell Myers, "The Mexican Liberal Party," 64.

36. Eduardo Ruiz, Ramón, *Labor and the Ambivalent Revolutionaries: Mexico, 1911–1923* (Baltimore: Johns Hopkins University Press, 1976), 15.

37. Devra Weber, "Keeping Community, Challenging Borders . . . " in *Mexico and Mexicans in the Making of the United States* (Austin: University of Texas Press, 2012), 219.

38. Esteban Baca Calderón, *Juicio sobre la Guerra del Yaqui y Génesis de la Huelga de Cananea* (México: Centro de Estudios Históricos del Movimiento Obrero Mexicano, 1975), 28–31.

39. Arnaldo Córdova, *La Ideología de la Revolución Mexicana* (Mexico, D.F.: Ediciones Era S.A., 1977), 95.

40. Leon Díaz Cárdenas, *Cananea: Primer Brote del Sindicalismo en Mexico*, 17.
41. Salvador Hernández Padilla, *El Magonismo: Un Historia de Una Pasión Libertaria*, 31.
42. Ramón Eduardo Ruiz, *Labor and the Ambivalent Revolutionaries: Mexico, 1911–1923* (Baltimore: Johns Hopkins University Press, 1976), 24.
43. See Albro, 37–38, for a more in-depth description.
44. Manuel Aguirre, *Cananea: Las Garras del Imperialismo en las Entrañas de México* (Mexico: Libro Mex, 1958), 90–91.
45. Ibid., 102.
46. Ibid., 125–7.
47. Samuel Truett, *Fugitive Landscapes: The Forgotten History of the US-Mexico Borderlands*, 146.
48. "¡Cananea!" *Libertad y Trabajo*, May 30, 1908; 2.
49. Samuel Truett, *Fugitive Landscapes: The Forgotten History of the US-Mexico Borderlands*, 149.
50. Ward Albro, "Always a Rebel," 35.
51. Salvador Hernández Padilla, *El Magonismo: Un Historia de Una Pasión Libertaria*," 48–49.
52. Esteban Baca Calderón, *Juicio sobre la Guerra del Yaqui y Génesis de la Huelga de Cananea* (México: Centro de Estudios Históricos del Movimiento Obrero Mexicano, 1975), 115–7.
53. For the estimate of 200, see Florencio Barrera Fuentes, *Historia de La Revolución Mexicana: La Etapa Precursora* (Mexico, D.F.: Biblioteca del Instituto Nacional de Estudios Historicos de La Revolución Mexicana, 1955), 152. For the estimate of 350, see Colin M. Maclachlan, *Anarchism and the Mexican Revolution*, 18.
54. Jeffrey Bortz, *Revolution within the Revolution: Cotton Textile Workers and the Mexican Labor Regime* (Stanford: Stanford University Press, 2008), 94.
55. Jeffrey Bortz and Marcos Aguila, "Earning a Living: A History of Real Wage Studies in Twentieth-Century Mexico," *Latin American Research Review* 41, no. 2 (2006): 115–6.
56. Jeffrey Bortz, *Revolution within the Revolution* 114–22.
57. Discussed in further detail in chapter 16.
58. For instance, after Mexican independence, the Yaqui had temporarily driven the extant colonizers and military detachments out of what is today the Arizona/Sonora region, after forming a military alliance with other tribes in the region. After 1832, the population was subdued by the Mexican army, and an uneasy peace remained until the wars of La Reforma and French colonization, where the Yaquis and their allies reasserted their autonomy. In the intervening years, the Yaqui pursued strategic alliances with external forces based on calculations that could ensure their independence. As Evelyn Hu-Dehart explains it: "Thus they were found fighting alongside the Federalists, the Centralists, the Liberals and even the French Imperialists. Although they were merely used by these various political factions as a fighting force, their active participation contributed to the instability and impotency of the state government. For most of this period the Yaquis enjoyed a de facto independence, and were able to keep incursion into the Yaqui territory at a minimum." See Evelyn Hu-Dehart, "Development and Rural Rebellion: Pacification of the Yaquis in the Late Porfiriato," *The Hispanic American Historical Review* 54, no. 1 (February 1974): 74. Furthermore, in 1866 during the final wars of the French occupation, a northern army composed primarily of Yaquis, Mayos, Seris, and Pimas was instrumental in defeating a pro-French imperialist force composed of French troops, American Confederates, and Mexican conservatives at a decisive battle at San

Gertrudís, Tamaulipas. The indigenous troops were neither fans of the Juaristas and the Constitution of 1857 (which opened the door to their displacement) nor of the French imperialists and their allies. Their outlook toward such conflicts tended to be one in which they placed their own autonomy ahead of external loyalties, and made strategic decisions that supported these ends. See Frank Hillary, "Cajeme, and the Mexico of His Time," *The Journal of Arizona History* 8, no. 2 (Summer 1967): 130.

59. Myers, 24.

60. While the PLM's organizational model contained elements of a revolutionary party alongside anarchistic "propaganda of the deed" methods, the essay "Anarchist Communism" by Peter Kropotkin provides a postrevolutionary conception of social organization that appears to be the main influence on magonista thought. See Peter Kropotkin, *Anarchism: A Collection of Revolutionary Writings*, Roger Baldwin, ed. (Minneola: Dover Publications, 2002), 44–78.

61. For a full discussion of this philosophical arrangement, see Greg Gilson and Irving Levinson, *Latin American Positivism: New Historical and Philosophic Essays* (Lanham: Lexington Books, 2013), chapters 1, 4, and 6.

62. Claudio Lomnitz, *The Return of Comrade Ricardo Flores Magón* (New York: Zone Books, 2014), 40.

63. Héctor Mora Zebadúa et al., *Un Siglo del Programa del Proletariado en México (Partido Liberal Mexicano 1906)*, 41.

64. Francie Chassen-López, *From Liberal to Revolutionary Oaxaca: The View from the South, Mexico 1867–1911* (University Park: Pennsylvania State University Press, 2004), 73.

65. Ibid., 74.

66. Ibid., 92–93. Chassen-López discusses examples of armed uprising as well as more nuanced forms of resistance, including indigenous farmers recollectivizing labor systems even after land privatizations attempt to transform them into small-holders.

67. Moisés González Navarro, "Agonía del porfiriato," *Historia Mexicana* 57, no. 4 (April–June 2008): 1286.

68. Héctor Mora Zebadúa et al., *Un Siglo del Programa del Proletariado en México (Partido Liberal Mexicano 1906)*, 45.

69. Juan Carlos Beas, Manuel Ballesteros, and Benjamín Maldonado, *Magonismo Y Movimiento Indígena en México* (Mexico, D.F.: Taller de la Gráfica Popular, 1997), 41–42.

70. The Yaquis had a long history of resistance to colonization. For example, Mexicans and Anglo speculators backed by the central government began to despoil or lay claim to Yaqui land in the early 1870s. Concurrent with efforts to open up Sonora to agricultural development, the United States was launching wars of extermination against the Apache north of the border to open up Arizona to mining development. This provoked another uprising of Yaquis, who rose up in 1873 under the military leadership of a man named José María Leyva Cajame. Cajame had been a "Mexicanized" Yaqui, or *torrocoyorim* (in Yaqui), who had abandoned his position in the Mexican military to reintegrate among his people and lead them against his former comrades-in-arms, declaring "Yaqui autonomy" in 1873. According to Frank Hillary, "With his proclamation of Yaqui autonomy, thousands of warriors arose to his aid. Supposedly tame vaqueros left their ranches and appeared as yelling Yaqui cavalry. Miners left their jobs with the excuse that they were going to attend a relative's funeral, and were next tunneling to undermine fortifications, or throwing homemade bombs

into a beleaguered town. Maidservants, faithful for years, disappeared in the night carrying the master's gold away to swell Cajeme's treasury, or perhaps they carried away the master's infant sons to be raised as Yaquis and later fight their own kind. Hard working brown sailors murdered their captains, sold the cargo and returned to the Yaqui country with the necessities of war for Cajeme." See Frank Hillary, "Cajeme, and the Mexico of His Time," 133. Furthermore, between 1875 and 1886 the Yaqui maintained their "state within a state" in the Yaqui River Valley, protected through the development of an indigenous army of over three thousand soldiers, mainly Yaqui and Mayo, trained in both fixed-position and irregular warfare. After several years of maintaining their independence, the lack of military resources and personnel took their toll against a much larger, better equipped, and relentless Mexican army. The last stages of resistance collapsed into guerrilla warfare in the Sierra de Bacatete region, with holdouts maintaining their opposition until the outbreak of revolution. See Evelyn Hu-Dehart, "Development and Rural Rebellion," 72–93.

71. Gastón García Cantú, *Idea de Mexico II: El Socialismo* (Mexico: Fondo de Cultural Económica, 1991): 140.

72. Ricardo Ham, *De Anenecuilco a Huirivis Pueblos indígenas en la Revolución Mexicana* (Mexico, D.F.: Samsara, 2010), 37–38.

73. See Alfonso Torúa Cienfuegos, *Magonismo en Sonora (1906–1908) : Historia de una Persecución* (Mexico, D. F.: Ediciones Hormigas Libertarios, 2010), chapters 3 and 4. Tapia will be described more in chapters 11 and 14.

74. Jacques Chevalier and Daniel A. Buckles, *Land without Gods: Process Theory, Maldevelopment, and the Mexican Nahuas* (Halifax: Zed Books, 1995), 22.

75. For a full discussion of the event, see C. D. Padua, *Movimiento Revolucionario 1906 en Veracruz: Relacion Cronologica de las Actividades del P. L. M. en los Ex-Cantones de Acayucan. Minatltlan: San Andres Tuxtla Y Centro del Pais.* Publisher not listed. (Tlalpan, D.F., 1941). Available online at: http://archivomagon.net/wp-content/uploads/2014/01 /paduacandido_donato_movimiento_revolucionario_en_veracruz.pdf

76. There were only small groups of participants, and to some degree they were divided over the issue, although the historian seems to take great liberties interpreting the indigenous participants' intentions and seems oblivious to how indigenous responses long after the event might have been shaped by posterior events such as retribution, repression, etc., or fear or suspicions of the interviewer's intentions. See Roger C. Owen, "Indians and Revolution: The 1911 Invasion of Baja California, Mexico," *Ethnohistory* 10, no. 4 (Autumn 1963): 373–95 for a discussion of this episode.

Chapter 9: The PLM and Borderland Internationalism

Eugenio Martínez Nuñez, *La Vida Heroica De Práxedis G. Guerrero* (Mexico: Biblioteca del Instituto Nacional de Estudios Históricos de la Revolución Mexicana, 1960), 190.

1. Devra Anne Weber, "Wobblies of the Partido Liberal Mexicano: Revisioning Internationalist and Transnational Movements through Mexican Lenses," *Pacific Historical Review* 85, no. 2 (May 2016): 199.

2. Elizabeth McKillen, "Ethnicity, Class, and Wilsonian Internationalism Reconsidered: The Mexican-American and Irish-American Immigrant Left and US Foreign Relations 1914–1922," *Diplomatic History* 25, no. 4 (Fall 2001): 553–87.

3. Marc Rodriguez, ed., *Repositioning North American Migrant History: New Directions in Modern Continental Migration, Citizenship, and Community* (Rochester: University of

Rochester Press, 2004), 161.

4. Mario Barrera, *Race and Class in the Southwest: A Theory of Racial Inequality* (Notre Dame: University of Notre Dame Press, 1979), 47.

5. Juan Gomez-Quiñones, *Sembradores: Ricardo Flores-Magón y el Partido Liberal Mexicano*, 23.

6. Carlos Larralde, *Mexican-American: Movements and Leaders* (Los Alamitos: Hwong Publishing, 1976), 114.

7. While radicals like the magonistas were repressed, bourgeois exiles like Madero had the support of US backers. In 1911, for instance, he was able to proceed with his revolution from Texas unhindered while under the watchful eye of federal and state agents.

8. "Discover Junta at Los Angeles: Alleged Mexican Revolutionists Captured in California," *Tombstone Telegraph*, August 25, 1907; 1.

9. Michael M. Smith, "The Mexican Secret Service in the United States, 1910–1920," *The Americas* 59, no. 1 (July 2002): 66.

10. John. W. Sherman, "Revolution on Trial: The 1909 Tombstone Proceedings against Ricardo Flores Magón, Antonio Villarreal, and Librado Rivera," *The Journal of Arizona History* 32, no. 2 (Summer 1991): 174.

11. William Dirk Raat, "The Diplomacy of Suppression: Los Revoltosos, Mexico, and the United States, 1906–1911," *The Hispanic American Historical Review* 56, no. 4 (November 1976): 532–3.

12. *United States Compiled Statutes, Annotated, 1916, Volume 2* (St. Paul: West Publishing Co., 1920), 2374.

13. Cited in Ricardo Cuahtémoc Esparza Valdivia and Ricardo Cuahtémoc, *El Fenómeno Magonista en México y en Estados Unidos (1905–1908)* (Zacatecas: Centro de Investigaciones Históricas, 2000), 103.

14. Colin M. Maclachlan, *Anarchism and the Mexican Revolution*, 9.

15. Ellen Howard Myers, "The Mexican Liberal Party, 1903–1910" (doctoral dissertation, University of Virginia, 1970), 107–8.

16. William Dirk Raat, *Revoltosos: Mexico's Rebels in the United States, 1903–1923* (College Station: Texas A&M University Press, 1981), 28, 94.

17. Juan Gomez-Quiñones, *Sembradores: Ricardo Flores-Magón y el Partido Liberal Mexicano*, 2.

18. Héctor Mora Zebadúa et al., *Un Siglo del Programa del Proletariado en México (Partido Liberal Mexicano 1906)*, 51.

19. León Díaz Cárdenas, *Cananea: Primer Brote del Sindicalismo en Mexico*, 1976.

20. Armando Bartra, *Regeneración*, 25.

21. Cited in Ward S. Albro, *To Die on Your Feet: The Life, Times, and Writings of Práxedis G. Guerrero* (Fort Worth: Texas Christian University Press, 1996), 105.

22. Ibid., 35.

23. Ricardo Flores Magón, "La Revolución Rusa," *Regeneración*, March 16, 1918; 1.

24. Juan Gomez-Quiñones, *Sembradores: Ricardo Flores-Magón y el Partido Liberal Mexicano*, 24.

25. Cited in Ricardo Cuahtémoc Esparza Valdivia, *El Fenómeno Magonista en México y en Estados Unidos (1905–1908)*, 139–40.

26. Letter from Ricardo Flores Magón to Enrique Flores Magón and Práxedis G. Guerrero from the Los Angeles County Jail, June 13, 1908. Available online at http://archivomagon.net/category/obras-completas/correspondencia-1899-1922/c-1908/page/3/.

27. Some interesting commentary exists about the exact political character of the magonistas. Ellen Myers asserts that Flores Magón was already considered a "socialist"

by 1900, and that the terms "socialist" and "anarchist" were used interchangeably in the early 1900s. Donald Hodges states that later magonistas were more communist than anarchist due to their agitation for the total expropriation of the means of production.

28. Colin M. Maclachlan, *Anarchism and the Mexican Revolution*, 35.

29. Full text of the manifesto online at: http://www.antorcha.net/biblioteca_virtual/politica/ap1912/49.html

30. Ibid.

31. Claudio Lomnitz, *The Return of Comrade Ricardo Flores Magón* (New York: Zone Books, 2014), 256.

32. The political divergence between reformists and revolutionaries in this period is best captured and conceptualized by Rosa Luxemburg in her work *Reform or Revolution*, in Helen Scott, ed., *The Essential Works of Rosa Luxemburg* (Chicago: Haymarket Books, 2008).

33. For an example of this process, see Philip S. Foner, *History of the Labor Movement in the United States, Volume 4: The Industrial Workers of the World 1905–1917* (New York: International Publishers, 1965); and Tony Cliff, *Building the Party: Lenin 1893–1914* (Chicago: Haymarket Books, 2002).

34. For a full look at Madero's positions in practice, see John Lear, *Workers, Neighbors, and Citizens: The Revolution in Mexico City* (Lincoln: University of Nebraska Press, 2001), chapter 4.

35. Most of the radicals that aligned with Madero eventually fell out with the new president, especially as his reform agenda stalled and land reform failed to materialize. After Victoriano Huerta toppled and killed Madero in 1913, some, like Antonio Soto y Gama joined the forces of Emiliano Zapata. Others, such as Antonio Villareal, joined the Carranza faction and later was promoted to brigadier general and state governor of Nuevo León.

36. Cited in Ricardo Cuahtémoc Esparza Valdivia, *El Fenómeno Magonista en México y en Estados Unidos (1905–1908)*, 177.

37. Javier Torres Parés, *La Revolución Sin Fronteras* (Mexico: UNAM, 1990), 171.

38. Librado Rivera served five years in prison, from 1918 to 1923, after which he was deported to Mexico, staying true to the political ideals of the PLM until his death in 1932. Anselmo Figueroa was imprisoned from 1911 to January 1914, and died shortly after his release due to complications from his traumatic prison experience. Enrique Flores Magón was incarcerated in 1918 and later deported to Mexico in 1923. He was also committed to continuing the revolution along PLM lines as a leader and organizer in several capacities. He died in 1954.

39. Arnoldo de León, ed., *War along the Border: The Mexican Revolution and Tejano Communities* (College Station: Texas A&M University Press, 2012), 180.

40. Cited in Marc Rodriguez, ed., *Repositioning North American Migrant History*, 174.

Chapter 10: The US Socialist Party, Race, and Immigration

"Socialists and Immigration," *Post-Standard*, Syracuse, New York, May 20, 1910; 4. The purpose of the quote was the basis for a sarcastic commentary on how the recent Socialist Party convention voted in favor of immigration restrictions.

1. Timothy Messer-Kruse, *The Yankee International: Marxism and the American Reform Tradition 1848–1876* (Chapel Hill: University of North Carolina Press, 1998), 188.

2. John Martin, "Socialism and Class War," *The Quarterly Journal of Economics* 23, no. 3

(May 1909): 512.

3. David Fernbach, ed., *Karl Marx: The First International and After, Political Writings Volume III, Including Documents of the First International and other Writings: 1864–1883* (New York: Vintage Books, 1974), 82–83.

4. See Philip Foner, *American Socialism and Black Americans: From the Age of Jackson to World War II* (Westport: Greenwood Press, 1977), chapter 1.

5. Cited in Massimiliano Tomba, *Marx's Temporalities* (Chicago: Haymarket Books, 2014), 150.

6. For a complete overview of this period, see Douglas Blackmon, *Slavery by Another Name: The Re-enslavement of Black Americans from the Civil War to World War II*, (New York: Doubleday, 2008).

7. For an overview of this historical process, see Michael Keith Honey, *Black Workers Remember: An Oral History of Segregation, Unionism, and the Freedom Struggle* (Berkeley: University of California Press, 1999).

8. For a full exploration of the racist discourse in which Mexican racial identity was constructed, see Reginald Horsman, *Manifest Destiny: The Origins of American Racial Anglo-Saxonism* (Cambridge: Harvard University Press, 1981).

9. For a thorough discussion of the convergence of interests between abolitionists and industrial workers, see Timothy Messer-Kruse, *The Yankee International: Marxism and the American Reform Tradition 1848–1876*, chapter 1. Also see David Montgomery, *Beyond Equality: Labor and the Radical Republicans* (Chicago: University of Illinois Press, 1967), especially chapters 3 and 4. For a concise discussion of how the radical and anti-colonial traditions of Irish working-class immigrants influenced the US Socialist left, see David Brundage, *The Making of Western Labor Radicalism: Denver's Organized Workers* (Chicago: University of Illinois Press, 1994); David Brundage, *Irish Nationalists in America: The Politics of Exile, 1798–1998* (New York: Oxford University Press, 2016); as well as Elizabeth McKillen, "Ethnicity, Class, and Wilsonian Internationalism Reconsidered: The Mexican-American and Irish-American Immigrant Left and US Foreign Relations, 1914–1922," *Diplomatic History* 25, no. 4 (2002): 553–87.

10. Philip Foner speculates that this is the reason that Marx devoted such little attention to the question of Reconstruction in the early 1870s. See Philip Foner, *American Socialism and Black Americans: From the Age of Jackson to World War II* (Westport: Greenwood Press, 1977), 40.

11. Philip Foner speculates that this is the reason that Marx devoted such little attention to the question of Reconstruction in the early 1870s. See Philip Foner, *American Socialism and Black Americans: From the Age of Jackson to World War II*, 44.

12. For a full discussion of the broad character of Socialist Party membership and regional variations, see David A. Shannon, *The Socialist Party of America* (Chicago: Quadrangle Books, 1955), chapter 1.

13. Anthony V. Esposito, *The Ideology of the Socialist Party of America: 1901–1917* (New York: Garland Publishing, 1997), 61.

14. Cited in R. Laurence Moore, "Flawed Fraternity—American Socialist Response to the Negro, 1901–1912," *The Historian* 32, no. 1 (November 1969): 2. Josh Honn, "Coming to Consciousness: Eugene Debs, American Socialism and the 'Negro Question'" (Master's Thesis, Lehigh University, 2002), 13.

15. For instance, he was quoted as saying, "There can be no doubt that the Negroes and

Mulattoes constitute a lower race . . . " See chapter 5 in Manning Marable, *W. E. B. Du Bois: Black Radical Democrat* (New York: Paradigm Publishers, 2016).

16. Philip Foner, *History of the Labor Movement in the United States* (New York: International Publishers, 1975), 402.

17. Eugene Debs, "The Negro in the Class Struggle," *International Socialist Review* IV (November 1903): 257. Debs' views were inconsistent, shifting from tacit accommodation in some circumstances to active opposition in others. For a full discussion of this see Philip Foner, *American Socialism and Black Americans: From the Age of Jackson to World War II*, especially page 110–15.

18. Anthony V. Esposito, *The Ideology of the Socialist Party of America: 1901–1917* (New York: Garland Publishing, 1997), 47–54.

19. Ibid., 75.

20. Ahmed Shawki, *Black Liberation and Socialism* (Chicago: Haymarket Books, 2006), 125.

21. Cited in Philip Foner, *American Socialism and Black Americans: From the Age of Jackson to World War II*, 28.

22. From "Wages," *Collected Works of Karl Marx*, vol. 6; 415. Available online at https://marxists.architexturez.net/archive/marx/works/1847/12/31.htm.

23. For a full, annotated version of the Communist Manifesto, see Phil Gaspar, ed., *The Communist Manifesto: A Roadmap to History's Most Important Political Document* (Chicago: Haymarket Books, 2005).

24. For a full discussion of Marx's evolving views on the subject of colonialism, see Kevin Anderson, *Marx at the Margins: On Nationalism, Ethnicity, and Non-Western Societies* (Chicago: University of Chicago Press, 2010).

25. The question of working-class internationalism and solidarity between workers in the imperialist centers and the colonial and semi-colonial countries was a central issue for the Russian Marxists. See V. I. Lenin, *On the National Question and Proletarian Internationalism* (Moscow: Novosti Press Agency, 1970). This discussion will be explored in further detail in chapter 9 of this text.

26. Citation from Richard B. Day and Daniel Gaido, *Discovering Imperialism: Social Democracy to World War I* (Boston: Brill Publishers, 2012), 28.

27. Cited in R. Laurence Moore, "Flawed Fraternity—American Socialist Response to the Negro, 1901–1912," 7.

28. Cited in Richard Iton, *Solidarity Blues: Race, Culture, and the American Left* (Durham: Duke University Press, 2000), 110.

29. See Joseph Robert Conlin, *Big Bill Haywood and the Radical Labor Movement* (Syracuse: Syracuse University Press, 1969), 175.

30. Marc Karson, *American Labor Unions and Politics, 1900–1918*, (Boston: Beacon Press, 2010), 42

31. See the letter at the Samuel Gompers papers at the University of Maryland—College Park, online at http://www.gompers.umd.edu/Bill percent20of percent20Grievances percent201906.htm

32. Report of Proceedings of the Twenty-Seventh Annual Convention of the American Federation of Labor, Norfolk, Virginia, November 11–23, 1907, Washington, DC: The National Tribune Company, 123.

33. Charles Leinenweber, "The American Socialist Party and 'New' Immigrants," *Science & Society* 32, no. 1 (Winter 1968): 8.

34. Ibid., 10.

35. Ira Kipnis, *The American Socialist Movement 1897–1912* (Chicago: Haymarket Books, 2005), 130.

36. William Preston, Jr., *Aliens and Dissenters: Federal Suppression of Radicals, 1903–1933* (Chicago: University of Illinois Press, 1963), 47.

37. Charles Leinenweber, "The American Socialist Party and 'New' Immigrants," *Science & Society*, 22.

38. Melvyn Dubofsky, *We Shall Be All: A History of the Industrial Workers of the World* (Chicago: University of Illinois Press, 1968), 6.

39. See Kevin Johnson, *The "Huddled Masses" Myth: Immigration and Civil Rights* (Philadelphia: Temple University Press, 2004).

40. Katherine Benton-Cohen, "Other Immigrants: Mexicans and the Dillingham Commission of 1907–1911," *Journal of American Ethnic History* 30, no. 2 (Winter 2011): 33–57.

41. For a full discussion of the elite channels by which Eugenics spread in popularity, see Lynne M. Getz, "Biological Determinism in the Making of Immigration Policy in the 1920s," *International Social Science Review* 70, no. 1/2 (1995): 26–33.

42. Katherine Benton-Cohen, "Other Immigrants: Mexicans and the Dillingham Commission of 1907–1911," 37.

43. Ibid., 38.

44. Lynne M. Getz, "Biological Determinism in the Making of Immigration Policy in the 1920s," 31.

45. David Montgomery identifies General Electric, United States Steel, International Harvester, major mining interests, meatpacking, the building trades, machine tool industry, boot and shoe manufacturers, and northern textiles, among others. See "The 'New Unionism' and the Transformation of Workers' Consciousness in America, 1909–22," *Journal of Social History* 7, no. 4 (Summer 1974): 510.

46. Florence Peterson, *Strikes in the United States, 1880–1936*, Bureau of Labor Statistics, Bulletin no. 651. Washington, US Govt. print. off., 1938, 29.

47. Anthony V. Esposito, *The Ideology of the Socialist Party of America: 1901–1917*, 62.

48. Ibid., 77.

49. Larry J. Griffin, Michael E. Wallace, and Beth A. Rubin, "Capitalist Resistance to the Organization of Labor Before the New Deal: Why? How? Success?" *American Sociological Review* 51, no. 2 (April 1986): 156.

50. Ibid., 161.

51. Ibid., 160.

52. Anthony V. Esposito, *The Ideology of the Socialist Party of America: 1901–1917*, 122.

53. David Montgomery, "The 'New Unionism' and the Transformation of Workers' Consciousness in America, 1909–22," 513.

Chapter 11: The Partido Liberal Mexicano and Socialists in Los Angeles

Blas Lara, "La Voz de un Esclavo," *Libertad y Trabajo,* June 13, 1908; 1.

1. See chapter 4.

2. See chapter 2 of Troy Robert Fuller, "'Our Cause is Your Cause': The Relationship between the Industrial Workers of the World and the Partido Liberal Mexicano, 1905–1911" (Master's Thesis, Department of History, University of Calgary, August 1997).

3. Douglas Monroy, *Rebirth: Mexican Los Angeles from the Great Migration to the Great*

Depression (Berkeley: University of California Press, 1999),15, 23.

4.   David Montgomery, "Workers Movements in the United States Confront Imperialism: The Progressive Era Experience," *The Journal of the Gilded Age and Progressive Era* 7, no. 1, (2008): 3.

5.   The backers of this strategy believed that future growth had to be on the basis of attracting capital investment away from San Francisco, which had become the largest industrial economy in the state by the turn of the century. The means to undercut, they believed, was to stamp out unions, unite forces against striking workers, and drive out radicals, so as to exercise complete control over labor and keep wages stunted and substantially lower than their unionized counterparts in San Francisco. In this effort, the employers were successful. Between 1890 and 1910, average wages were between 20 percent and as much as 40 percent lower than their northern counterparts. See Douglas Monroy, *Rebirth: Mexican Los Angeles from the Great Migration to the Great Depression*, 116.

6.   Grace Heilman Stimson, *Rise of the Labor Movement in Los Angeles* (Berkeley: University of California Press, 1955), chapter 9.

7.   William David Estrada, *The Los Angeles Plaza: Sacred and Contested Space* (Austin: University of Texas Press, 2008), 139.

8.   Claudio Lomnitz, *The Return of Comrade Ricardo Flores Magón* (New York: Zone Books, 2014), 210.

9.   For an in-depth exploration of the historical and structural development of day laboring within the Mexican community, see Abel Valenzuela, Jr., "Controlling Day Labor: Government, Community and Worker Responses," Center for the Study of Urban Poverty University of California, Los Angeles, Working Paper Series, 2000, 3.

10.   See Douglas Monroy, *Rebirth: Mexican Los Angeles from the Great Migration to the Great Depression*, 120. This will be discussed in more detail in chapter 8.

11.   William B. Friedricks, "Capital and Labor in Los Angeles: Henry E. Huntington vs. Organized Labor, 1900–1920," *Pacific Historical Review* 59, no. 3 (August 1990): 377–8.

12.   Ibid., 383.

13.   Charles Wollenberg, "Working on El Traque: The Pacific Electric Strike of 1903," *Pacific Historical Review* 42, no. 3 (August 1973): 359.

14.   Jeffrey Marcos Garcilazo, *Traqueros: Mexican Railroad Workers in the United States, 1870–1930* (Denton: University of North Texas Press, 1995), 83.

15.   Ibid., 99.

16.   Devra Weber, "Keeping Community, Challenging Borders . . . ," in *Mexico and Mexicans in the Making of the United States* (Austin: University of Texas Press, 2012), 220.

17.   "Manifiesto: La Junta Organizadora del Partido Liberal Mexicano, a la Nación," *Regeneración*, September 30, 1905; 3.

18.   Ibid.

19.   Mike Hill and Warren Montag, eds., *Masses, Classes, and the Public Sphere* (New York: Verso Press, 2000), 47.

20.   Jeffrey Stansbury, *Organized Workers and the Making of Los Angeles: 1890–1915* (dissertation, University of California, Los Angeles, 2008), 282.

21.   "Plan Mexican Revolt Here," *Los Angeles Herald*, August 9, 1907; 1.

22.   Nathan Ellstrand Kahn, "Las Anarquistas: The History of Two Women of the Partido Liberal Mexicano in Early 20th Century Los Angeles" (Master's Thesis, Latin

American Studies, University of California, San Diego, 2011), 24.

23. Ethel Duffy Turner, *Writers and Revolutionists: An Interview Conducted by Ruth Teiser* (Berkeley: University of California, Bancroft Library, Regional Oral History Office, 1967), 12.

24. It is possible that the names are misspelled. See "Mexican Women Caught with Ammunition at Bridge," *El Paso Herald*, June 24, 1912; 3.

25. Nathan Ellstrand Kahn, "Las Anarquistas: The History of Two Women of the Partido Liberal Mexicano in Early 20th Century Los Angeles," 35.

26. "Protesta," *Regeneración*, July 1, 1911.

27. David Adán Vázquez Valenzuela, "Mirando atrás: la comunidad mexicana y mexicoamericana de Los Ángeles ante la revolución mexicana. Su participación en el floresmagonismo, 1905–1911" (Master's Thesis, Instituto de Investigacion Dr. Jose Maria Luis Mora, 2013), 98–101.

28. Nelson Pichardo, "The Establishment and Development of Chicano Voluntary Associations in California, 1910–1930," *Aztlán: A Journal of Chicano Studies* 19, no. 2 (Fall 1988): 111.

29. Nelson Pichardo, "The Establishment and Development of Chicano Voluntary Associations in California, 1910–1930," 117–21.

30. Stephanie Lethwaite, "Race, Paternalism, and 'California Pastoral': Rural Rehabilitation and Mexican Labor in Greater Los Angeles," *Agricultural History* 81, no. 1 (Winter 2007): 7–8.

31. David Adán Vázquez Valenzuela, "Mirando atrás: la comunidad mexicana y mexicoamericana de Los Ángeles ante la revolución mexicana. Su participación en el floresmagonismo1905–1911," 155–8.

32. "Los Verdaderos Grandes," *Libertad y Trabajo*, June 6, 1908; 1.

33. Victor S. Clark, "Mexican Labor in the United States," *Bulletin of the United States Bureau of Labor Statistics*, issue 78 (1908): 479.

34. Ibid., 516.

35. Jeffrey Marcos Garcilazo, *Traqueros: Mexican Railroad Workers in the United States, 1870–1930*, 92.

36. John A. Shields, *Federal Courts and Practice* (New York: Banks Law Publishing Company, 1912), 31.

37. David Adán Vázquez Valenzuela, "Mirando atrás: la comunidad mexicana y mexicoamericana de Los Ángeles ante la revolución mexicana. Su participación en el floresmagonismo1905–1911," 109–10.

38. While the precise number of self-identified Liberals or *magonistas* may be impossible to ascertain at any given point in this history, it is possible to estimate between ten and twenty thousand based on number of affiliated clubs and mutual aid societies and papers in circulation.

39. Nicolás T. Bernal, *Memorias* (México: Centro de Estudios Históricos del Movimiento Obrero Mexicano, 1982), 86.

40. James L. Baughman, Jennifer Ratner-Rosenhagen, and James P. Danky, *Protest on the Page: Essays on Print and the Culture of Dissent Since 1865* (Madison: University of Wisconsin Press, 2015), 60. See also, William D. Raat, *Revoltosos: Mexico's Rebels in the United States, 1903–1923*, 38.

41. Juan Gómez-Quiñones, "Sin Frontera, Sin Cuartel: Los Anarcocomunistas del PLM, 1900–1930," *Tzintzun. Revista de Estudios Históricos*, no. 47 (January–June 2008): 174.

42. Elizabeth McKillen, "Ethnicity, Class, and Wilsonian Internationalism Reconsidered: The Mexican-American and Irish-American Immigrant Left and US Foreign Relations 1914–1922," *Diplomatic History* 25, no. 4 (Fall 2001): 565.

43. Ricardo Flores-Magón, "Los Expropiadores," *Regeneración*, November 28, 1914 (translated by author).

44. Joel Bollinger Pouwels, *Political Journalism by Mexican Women During the Age of Revolution, 1876–1940* (Lewiston: Edwin Mellen Press, 2006), 58–59.

45. Blanca was also the partner of the Colombian anarchist José Moncaleano. They were PLM partisans in Mexico during the first stage of the revolution. They were deported to Los Angeles by Francisco Madero for their role in founding the Casa del Obrero Mundial. See Clara Lomas, "Transborder Discourse: The Articulation of Gender in the Borderlands in the Early Twentieth Century," *Frontiers: A Journal of Women Studies* 24, no. 2/3 (2003): 61–62.

46. William D. Raat, *Revoltosos: Mexico's Rebels in the United States, 1903–1923*, 37.

47. See Julie Greene, "Spaniards on the Silver Roll: Labor Troubles and Liminality in the Panama Canal Zone, 1904–1914," *International Labor and Working-Class History*, no. 66, New Approaches to Global Labor History (Fall 2004): 92.

48. John. W. Sherman, "Revolution on Trial: The 1909 Tombstone Proceedings Against Ricardo Flores Magón, Antonio Villarreal, and Librado Rivera," *The Journal of Arizona History* 32, no. 2 (Summer 1991): 174–5.

49. "Political Prisoners," *Los Angeles Herald*, October 11, 1908; 4.

50. While the Hearst-owned *Los Angeles Herald* provided more grounded coverage of their trial proceedings, for instance, the Otis-owned *Los Angeles Times* was hostile and vitriolic from the start.

51. "Murder-Plotting Letters Found on the Mexican Revolutionists," *Los Angeles Times*, September 19, 1907; 1, 14.

52. "Reds Tell Peons to Vote for Bryan," *Los Angeles Times*, October 29, 1908; 1, 10.

53. Ricardo Flores Magón, "The Appeal of Mexico to American Labor," in *Mother Earth* 4, no. 2 (April 1911).

54. Discussed in detail in chapter 14.

55. "Preliminary Report and Hearings of the Committee on Foreign Relations: United States Senate," Washington: Government Printing Office, 1920; 2497.

56. For a full discussion of this period, see Ricardo Romo, *East Los Angeles: History of a Barrio* (Austin: University of Texas Press, 1983), especially chapter 5.

57. "Planned Uprising of Mexicans: Magóns Outline Programme of Terrorization Here," *Los Angeles Times*, September 20, 1915; 3.

58. Sixty-Second Congress, Second Session. "Hearing before a Subcommittee of the Committee on Foreign Relations United States Senate," Washington: Government Printing Office, 1913; 189.

59. Ricardo Romo, *History of a Barrio: East Los Angeles* (Austin: University of Texas Press, 1977), 99.

60. Various US-based anarchists were longtime supporters and defenders of Ricardo Flores Magón and the PLM. These included Emma Goldman, Alexander Berkman, William Owen, and many others. Since this work does not focus explicitly on anarchists, see Paul Avrich, *Anarchist Portraits* (Princeton: Princeton University Press, 1988) for an introduction to Anarchist history, thought, and practice.

61. For an in-depth analysis of this phenomenon, see Elizabeth McKillen, "Hybrid

Visions: Working-Class Internationalism in the Mexican Borderlands, Seattle, and Chicago, 1910–1920," *Labor: Studies in Working-Class History of the Americas* 2, no. 1 (2005): 78.

62. *The International Socialist Review* published articles by Manuel Sarabia, a Socialist Party member in the PLM. He wrote about the role of capitalists from the US in Mexico. See "The Situation in Mexico," in *International Socialist Review*, no. 14 (June 1914): 732.

63. Advertisement for the ISR, page unlisted, *International Socialist Review*, March 1911.

64. Cited in Devra Weber, "The Organizing of Mexican Agricultural Workers: Imperial Valley, and Los Angeles, 1928–34, an Oral History Approach," *Aztlán* 3, no. 2 (1972): 311.

65. Ralph Edward Schafer, "Radicalism in California: 1869–1929" (Doctoral Thesis in Modern History, University of California, Berkeley, 1962), 193.

66. Guillermo Medina Amor, *No Fue Filibusterismo: La Revolution Magonista en La Baja California* (Mexicali: Ediciones 'Amor', 1956): 41.

67. James A. Sandos, *Rebellion in the Borderlands: Anarchism and the Plan of San Diego, 1904–1923* (Norman: University of Oklahoma Press, 1992), 16.

68. See "Political Refugee Defense Fund," *The Painter and Decorator; Journal of the Brotherhood of Painters, Decorators, and Paperhangers of America* 13, no. 6 (June 1909): 372.

69. L. Gutiérrez de Lara and Edgcomb Pinchon, *The Mexican People: Their Struggle for Freedom* (New York: Doubleday, Page and Co., 1914), 343.

70. "Debs Talks to Immense House," *Los Angeles Herald*, September 11, 1908; 3.

71. For example, see John Murray, "The Mexican Political Prisoners," *International Socialist Review* 9 (May 1909): 865.

72. John W. Sherman, "Revolution on Trial: The 1909 Tombstone Proceedings Against Ricardo Flores Magón, Antonio Villarreal, and Librado Rivera," *The Journal of Arizona History* 32, no. 2 (Summer 1991): 178.

73. "To Renew Fight on Díaz' Regime," *Los Angeles Herald*, August 5, 1910; 9.

74. "Audience Tosses Coin to Liberals," *Los Angeles Herald*, August 8, 1910; 2.

75. Chaz Bufe and Mitchell Cowen Verter, eds., *Dreams of Freedom: A Ricardo Flores Magón Reader* (Oakland: A.K. Press, 2005), 73.

Chapter 12: The PLM and the Socialist Party in Texas

"Armed Mexicans Raiding in Texas," *Arkansas Gazette*, September 19, 1911; 1.

1. Arnoldo De León, ed., *War Along the Border: The Mexican Revolution and Tejano Communities* (College Station: Texas A&M University Press, 2012), 180.

2. "Mexican Women Political Prisoners," *Minneapolis Journal*, December 5, 1903; 5.

3. Emilio Zamora, *The World of the Mexican Worker in Texas* (College Station: Texas A&M University Press, 1993), 114–15.

4. Arnoldo De León, ed., *War Along the Border: The Mexican Revolution and Tejano Communities*, 181; Marc Rodriguez, ed., *Repositioning North American Migrant History: New Directions in Modern Continental Migration, Citizenship, and Community* (Rochester: University of Rochester Press, 2004), 174.

5. Benjamin Heber Johnson, *Revolution in Texas: How a Forgotten Rebellion and Its Bloody Suppression Turned Mexicans into Americans* (New Haven: Yale University Press, 2003), 61.

6. Marc Rodriguez, ed., *Repositioning North American Migrant History: New Directions in Modern Continental Migration, Citizenship, and Community*, 172.

7. Ibid., 172.

8.   Enrique Canudas, *Las Venas de Plata en La Historia de México: Síntesis Historia Económica Siglo XIX* (Editorial Utopia: Universidad Juárez Autónoma de Tabasco, 2005), 1690.

9.   The character and diversity of these organizations are described in great detail in Emilio Zamora, *The World of the Mexican Worker in Texas*, 56.

10. Arnoldo De León, ed., *War Along the Border: The Mexican Revolution and Tejano Communities*, 180

11. Ricardo Cuahtémoc Esparza Valdivia, *El Fenómeno Magonista en México y en Estados Unidos (1905–1908)* (Zacatecas: Centro de Investigaciones Históricas, 2000), 93.

12. Ibid., 142.

13. Discussion cited in Emilio Zamora, Cynthia Orozco, and Rodolfo Rocha, *Mexican Americans in Texas History* (Austin: Texas State Historical Association, 2000), 87.

14. Inés Hernandez, "Sara Estela Ramírez: Sembradora," *Legacy* 6, no. 1, Western Women Writers (Spring 1989): 18.

15. Emilio Zamora, "Sara Estela Ramírez: Una Rosa Roja en El Movimiento," in Magdalena Mora and Adelaida Del Castillo, eds., "Mexican Women in the United States: Struggles Past and Present," Occasional Paper no. 2, Chicano Studies Research Center Publications, University of California, Los Angeles, 165.

16. Arnoldo De León, ed., *War Along the Border: The Mexican Revolution and Tejano Communities*, 181–3.

17. For a feminist analysis of pre-1910 PLM positions on gender, see Emma Pérez, "'A la Mujer': A Critique of the Partido Liberal Mexicano's Gender Ideology on Women," in *Between Borders: Essays on Mexicana/Chicana History*, ed. Adelaida Del Castillo (Encino: Floricanto Press, 1990), 459–82.

18. David O'Donald Cullen and Kyle G. Wilkison, eds., *The Texas Left: The Radical Roots of Lone Star Liberalism* (College Station: Texas A&M University Press, 2010), 77–78.

19. F. Ray Marshall, *Labor in the South* (Cambridge: Harvard University Press, 1967), 92.

20. Tom Hickey, "The Land Renters Union in Texas," *International Socialist Review* (September 12, 1912): 240.

21. James A. Sandos, *Rebellion in the Borderlands: Anarchism and the Plan of San Diego, 1904–1923* (Norman: University of Oklahoma Press, 1992), 69.

22. James Green, *Grass-Roots Socialism: Radical Movements in the Southwest 1895–1943* (Baton Rouge: Louisiana State University Press, 1978), 135; Tom Hickey, "The Land Renters Union in Texas," 243.

23. Neil Foley, *White Scourge: Mexicans, Blacks, and Poor Whites in Texas Cotton Culture* (Berkeley: University of California Press, 1997), 92.

24. David O'Donald Cullen and Kyle G. Wilkison, eds., *The Texas Left: The Radical Roots of Lone Star Liberalism*, 82.

25. By the entry point of World War I. For an overview of the growth of the Socialist press, see James Green, *Grass-Roots Socialism: Radical Movements in the Southwest 1895–1943*, chapter 4.

26. For an example, see "Rented Out for Talking Truth," *The Rebel*, November 22, 1913; 2.

27. Neil Foley, *White Scourge: Mexicans, Blacks, and Poor Whites in Texas Cotton Culture*, 113.

28. Kyle G. Wilkison, *Yeomen, Sharecroppers, and Socialists: Plain Folk Protest in Texas, 1870–1914* (College Station: Texas A&M University Press, 2008), 188–89.

29. "'Plan of the Farm Renters': State Convention at Waco," *Waco Morning News*, October 19, 1911; 10.

30. "Renters Take Steps to Relieve Conditions," *Waco Morning News,* November 5, 1911; 5.
31. Tom Hickey, "The Land Renters Union in Texas," 243–4.
32. Cited in Kyle G. Wilkison, *Yeomen, Sharecroppers, and Socialists: Plain Folk Protest in Texas, 1870–1914,* 189.
33. Benjamin Heber Johnson, *Revolution in Texas: How a Forgotten Rebellion and Its Bloody Suppression Turned Mexicans into Americans,* 65.
34. "Renters Union," *The Rebel,* August 31, 1912; 1; "Renters Union," *The Rebel,* May 11, 1912; 4.
35. Benjamin Heber Johnson, *Revolution in Texas: How a Forgotten Rebellion and Its Bloody Suppression Turned Mexicans into Americans,* 66.
36. E. R. Meitzen, "Renters Union," *The Rebel,* April 5, 1913; 3.
37. See "J. A. Hernández y Compañeros," *Regeneración,* October 9, 1915; 3.
38. E. R. Meitzen, and W. S. Noble, "Land League Organizer Arrested," *The Rebel,* October 23, 1915; 1.
39. Ibid.
40. Ibid.
41. Neil Foley, *White Scourge: Mexicans, Blacks, and Poor Whites in Texas Cotton Culture,* 105.
42. Benjamin Heber Johnson, *Revolution in Texas: How a Forgotten Rebellion and Its Bloody Suppression Turned Mexicans into Americans,* 66; Neil Foley, *White Scourge: Mexicans, Blacks, and Poor Whites in Texas Cotton Culture,* 249–50, note 88.
43. Benjamin Heber Johnson, *Revolution in Texas: How a Forgotten Rebellion and Its Bloody Suppression Turned Mexicans into Americans,* 65.
44. "Executive Committee Sets Convention Date," *Waco Morning News,* November 15, 1915; 10.
45. While definitely not "strangers in a strange land," this article shows the evolution of the Socialist Party though toward the Mexican radicals. E. R. Meitzen, and W. S. Noble, "Land League Organizer Arrested," 1.
46. James Green, *Grass-Roots Socialism: Radical Movements in the Southwest 1895–1943,* 274.
47. David O'Donald Cullen and Kyle G. Wilkison, eds., *The Texas Left: The Radical Roots of Lone Star Liberalism,* 83.
48. "Land League Convention," *The Rebel,* December 4, 1915; 2.
49. James Green, *Grass-Roots Socialism: Radical Movements in the Southwest 1895–1943,* 305–6.
50. David Montejano, *Anglos and Mexicans: The Making of Texas, 1836–1986* (Austin: University of Texas Press, 1987), 125.
51. Antonio I. Villarreal, "La Conquista del Bienestar," *Regeneración,* November 19, 1910, 1.
52. Ricardo Flores Magón and Benjamin Heber Johnson best capture the uncertainty of the forces at work. See "Los Levantimientos en Texas," *Regeneración,* October 30, 1915; 2; and *Revolution in Texas: How a Forgotten Rebellion and Its Bloody Suppression Turned Mexicans into Americans* (New Haven: Yale University Press, 2003).
53. James A. Sandos, *Rebellion in the Borderlands: Anarchism and the Plan of San Diego, 1904–1923* (Norman: University of Oklahoma Press, 1992), 77.
54. According to a testimony cited in Arnoldo De León, ed., *War Along the Border: The Mexican Revolution and Tejano Communities,* 113.
55. Emilio Zamora, Cynthia Orozco, and Rodolfo Rocha, *Mexican Americans in Texas History* (Austin: Texas State Historical Association, 2000), 111.

56.   James A. Sandos, *Rebellion in the Borderlands: Anarchism and the Plan of San Diego, 1904–1923*, 83.

57.   Ibid.

58.   Benjamin Heber Johnson, *Revolution in Texas: How a Forgotten Rebellion and Its Bloody Suppression Turned Mexicans into Americans*, 97.

59.   James A. Sandos, *Rebellion in the Borderlands: Anarchism and the Plan of San Diego, 1904–1923*, 69.

60.   Charles H. Harris III and Louis R. Sadler, "The Plan of San Diego and the Mexican-United States War Crisis of 1916: A Reexamination," *The Hispanic American Historical Review* 58, no. 3 (August 1978): 390.

61.   David Montejano, *Anglos and Mexicans: The Making of Texas, 1836–1986*, 125.

62.   "Lawlessness Widespread," *San Antonio Express*, August 12, 1915; 1.

63.   David Montejano, *Anglos and Mexicans: The Making of Texas, 1836–1986*, 123.

64.   Quoted in the *New York Sun*, March 10, 1902, cited in Spencer Jones and Peter Tsouras, eds., *Over the Top: Alternative Histories of the First World War* (London: Frontline Books, 2014), 83.

65.   Francis White Johnson, *A History of Texas and Texans: Volume III* (New York: American Historical Society, 1916), 1229.

66.   Sonia Hernández, *Working Women into the Borderlands* (College Station: Texas A&M University Press, 2014), Chapter 5.

67.   Arnoldo De León, ed., *War Along the Border: The Mexican Revolution and Tejano Communities*, 63.

68.   Ibid., 83.

69.   William D. Carrigan and Clive Webb, *Forgotten Dead: Mob Violence Against Mexicans in the United States, 1848–1928* (New York: Oxford University Press, 2013), 64.

70.   "Las Cabezas de Pizano y de la Rosa Puestas a Precio," *El Paso Morning Times*, October 28, 1915.

71.   Benjamin Heber Johnson argues that this was a widespread and systematic practice within the repression. He also argues that it intensified racial segregation. See *Revolution in Texas: How a Forgotten Rebellion and Its Bloody Suppression Turned Mexicans into Americans*, 70.

72.   Charles Cumberland, "Border Raids in the Lower Río Grande Valley, 1915," *The Southwestern Historical Quarterly* 57, no. 3 (January 1954): 301.

73.   Cited in James A. Sandos, *Rebellion in the Borderlands: Anarchism and the Plan of San Diego, 1904–1923*, 105.

74.   *Cameron Herald*, August 26, 1915; 4.

75.   Benjamin Heber Johnson, "Sedition and Citizenship in South Texas, 1900–1930," (dissertation, Yale University, 2000), 178.

76.   "The Newspaper Liars," *The Rebel*, June 5, 1915; 3.

77.   Ibid., 3.

78.   For a full analysis of the evidence, see James A. Sandos, *Rebellion in the Borderlands: Anarchism and the Plan of San Diego, 1904–1923*, chapter 6.

79.   Rodolfo Rocha, "The Influence of the Mexican Revolution on the Mexico-Texas Border, 1910–1916" (dissertation, Texas Tech University, 1981), 272.

80.   For a full discussion, see William Preston, *Aliens and Dissenters: Federal Suppression of Radicals, 1903–1933* (Chicago: University of Illinois Press, 1994).

81.   Brent A. Orr, "Borderline Failure: National Guard on the Mexican Border, 1916–

1917," School of Advanced Military Studies, United States Army Command and General Staff College, Fort Leavenworth, Kansas, 2011, 13–14.

82. "Los Levantimientos en Texas," *Regeneración*, October 30, 1915; 2.
83. Ibid.
84. Ibid., 1–2.

Chapter 13: Socialists, the PLM, and the Mexican Revolution

"Americans Awake! Do not Let Latin Races Put You to Shame," *Regeneración*, April 29, 1911; 4.

1. Elizabeth Sanders, *Roots of Reform: Farmers, Workers, and the American State* (Chicago: University of Chicago Press, 1999), 80.
2. *Historical Statistics of the United States, 1789–1945*, Bureau of the Census, Washington: Government Printing Office, 1949, 73.
3. Donald Drew Egbert and Stow Persons, *Socialism in American Life* (New Jersey: Princeton, 1953), 283–4.
4. Ira Kipnis, *The American Socialist Movement, 1897–1912*, 247–8.
5. The specific role of the IWW in relation to the PLM and Mexican Revolution will be discussed in chapter 14.
6. "The Rising Tide," *Appeal to Reason*, May 8, 1909; 4.
7. "Withdraw the Troops," *International Socialist Review* 11, no. 19 (April 1911): 586.
8. "Big Meeting," *Regeneración*, April 8, 1911; 4.
9. "The Rising Tide," *Appeal to Reason*, May 8, 1909; 4.
10. See Karl Marx, Frederick Engels, and Phil Gasper, eds., *The Communist Manifesto: A Road Map to History's Most Important Political Document* (Chicago: Haymarket Books, 2005).
11. "The Isthmian Canal Today," *International Socialist Review* (July 1910): 13.
12. John Murray, "Mexico's Peon-Slaves Preparing for Revolution," *International Socialist Review* (March 1909): 641–59.
13. See Karl Marx, "The Civil War in the United States (1861)." Print version in *Marx and Engels in the United States* (Moscow: Progress Publishers, 1979), 84–92. See also his article "The Intervention in Mexico," *New York Daily Tribune*, November 23, 1861. Available online at https://www.marxists.org/archive/marx/works/1861/11/23.htm.
14. For a full discussion of this evolution in his thinking, see Kevin Anderson, *Marx at the Margins: On Nationalism, Ethnicity, and Non-Western Societies* (Chicago: University of Chicago Press, 2010), chapter 1. Quote on page 71.
15. Ibid., chapter 5.
16. Eugene Debs received nearly 1 million votes for president in 1912 and again in 1920.
17. Elizabeth McKillen, *Making the World Safe for Democracy: Labor, the Left, and Wilsonian Internationalism* (Chicago: University of Illinois Press, 2013), 54.
18. Ibid., 27.
19. Discussed in detail in chapter 20.
20. Elizabeth McKillen, *Making the World Safe for Democracy: Labor, the Left, and Wilsonian Internationalism*, 40.
21. Discussed in chapter 16.
22. Elizabeth McKillen, *Making the World Safe for Democracy: Labor, the Left, and Wilsonian Internationalism*, 116–21.
23. Antonio I. Villarreal, "La Conquista del Bienestar," *Regeneración*, November 19, 1910; 4. The article is an English transliteration of a Spanish article in the same edition,

attributed to the same author.

24. "Gran Meeting Internacional," *Regeneración,* December 10, 1910; 3.

25. Jeffrey Stansbury, *Organized Workers and the Making of Los Angeles: 1890–1915* (dissertation: University of California, Los Angeles, 2008), 283.

26. See "La Organización Obrera," *Regeneración,* December 24, 1910; 2.

27. David Struthers, "'The Boss Has No Color Line': Race, Solidarity, and a Culture of Affinity in Los Angeles and the Borderlands, 1907–1915," *Journal for the Study of Radicalism* 7, no. 2 (Fall 2013): 75–6.

28. Austin Lewis, "The Basis of Solidarity," *New Review,* August 15, 1915, 185.

29. Samuel Gompers, *The Samuel Gompers Papers: Progress and Reaction in the Age of Reform, 1909–1913* (Champaign: University of Illinois Press, 2001), 192–93.

30. Discussed in chapter 14.

31. David Montgomery, *Workers Movements in the United States Confront Imperialism: The Progressive Era Experience,* 4.

32. Luis Leobardo Arroyo, "Mexican Workers and American Unions: The Los Angeles AFL 1890–1933," Working Paper, Chicano Political Economy Collective, University of California, Berkeley, 1981, 6.

33. A. T. Lane "American Trade Unions, Mass Immigration and The Literacy Test: 1900–1917," *Labor History* 25, vol. 1 (1984): 5–25.

34. Cited in Robert Jackson Alexander and Eldon M. Parker, *International Labor Organizations and Organized Labor in Latin America and the Caribbean* (Santa Barbara: Greenwood Press, 2009), 12.

35. Daniel Jon Johnson, "A Serpent in the Garden: Institutions, Ideology, and Class in Los Angeles Politics, 1901–1911" (doctoral dissertation, Department of History, University of California, Los Angeles, 1996), 520.

36. David Montgomery, *Workers Movements in the United States Confront Imperialism: The Progressive Era Experience,* 4.

37. Ibid., 3.

38. Discussed in more detail in chapter 17.

39. See Ira Kipnis, *The American Socialist Movement 1897–1912* (Chicago: Haymarket Books, 2004), chapter 11.

40. Socialist perspectives toward immigration are discussed in more detail in chapter 10.

41. For a good overview of this analysis, see Thomas C. Leonard, *Illiberal Reformers: Race, Eugenics, and American Economics in the Progressive Era* (Princeton: Princeton University Press, 2016); and Gabriel Kolko, *The Triumph of Conservatism: A Reinterpretation of American History, 1900–1916* (New York: Free Press, 1963).

42. Daniel Walden, "Race and Imperialism: The Achilles Heel of the Progressives," *Science & Society* 31, no. 2 (Spring 1967): 232.

43. Eugene V. Debs, "A Letter from Debs on Immigration." *International Socialist Review* (July 1910): 16–17.

44. For example of this criticism, see Helen Marot, "Federal Interference in Colorado," *New Review,* December 1914; 690.

45. "Americans Awake! Do not Let Latin Races Put You to Shame," *Regeneración,* April 29, 1911; 4.

46. Letter to Maria Brousse de Talavera, 1908 (date unknown). Available online at http://archivomagon.net/obras-completas/correspondencia-1899-1922/c-1908/cor281/.

47. See Colin MacLachlan, *Anarchism and the Mexican Revolution: The Political Trials of*

Ricardo Flores Magón in the United States (Berkeley: University of California Press, 1991), xii.

48. The vote dropped in that election cycle, and the party membership repealed the plank by referendum after the election. See Ralph Edward Schafer, "Radicalism in California: 1869–1929" (Doctoral Thesis in Modern History, University of California, Berkeley, 1962), 162.

49. Cited in Diana Chrisopulos, "American Radicals and the Mexican Revolution" (doctoral dissertation, Departments of Philosophy and History; Graduate School of the State University of New York, Binghamton, 1980), 89–90.

50. Roscoe A. Fillmore, "The Great Awakening," *International Socialist Review* 11, no. 10 (April 1911): 598–9.

51. Diana Chrisopulos, "American Radicals and the Mexican Revolution," 490.

52. "Magonistas Ask Impossibilities," *El Paso Herald,* June 20, 1911; 2.

53. Eugene V. Debs, "The Crisis in Mexico," *International Socialist Review,* July 1911; 22.

54. Ibid., 23.

55. John Kenneth Turner, "The Revolution in Mexico," *International Socialist Review* 11, no. 7, (January 1911): 421–2.

Chapter 14: The PLM and IWW Join Forces

Cited in Gale Ahrens, *Lucy Parsons, Freedom, Equality, and Solidarity: Writings and Speeches, 1878–1937* (Chicago: Charles Kerr, 2004), 81.

1. David Brundage, *The Making of Western Labor Radicalism: Denver's Organized Workers 1878–1905,* 150–1.

2. Ralph Chaplin, *Wobbly: The Rough and Tumble Story of an American Radical* (Chicago: University of Chicago Press, 1948), 106.

3. Troy Robert Fuller, "'Our Cause is Your Cause': The Relationship between the Industrial Workers of the World and the Partido Liberal Mexicano, 1905–1911" (Master's Thesis, Department of History, University of Calgary, August 1997), 17.

4. For a good overview of scientific management and class struggle, see David Montgomery, *The Fall of the House of Labor* (New York: Cambridge University Press, 1987).

5. Philip S. Foner, *History of the Labor Movement of the United States Vol. 4: The Industrial Workers of the World 1905–1917* (New York: International Publishers, 1997), 17–18.

6. See Joseph Conlin, "The I.W.W. and the Socialist Party," *Science & Society* 31, no. 1 (Winter 1967): 22–36; and Michael Nash, *Conflict and Accommodation: Coal Miners, Steel Workers, and Socialism 1890–1920* (Westport: Greenwood Press, 1982), chapter 4.

7. David, Montgomery, "The 'New Unionism' and the Transformation of Workers' Consciousness in America, 1909–22," 514.

8. For a full explanation of how this played out, see Conlin, Joseph "The I.W.W. and the Socialist Party" *Science & Society* 31, no. 1 (Winter 1967): 22–36.

9. Sabotage generally referred to "soldiering on the job, playing dumb, tampering with machines without destroying them—in short simply harassing to the point of granting his workers' demands." See Melvyn Dubofsky, *We Shall Be All: A History of the Industrial Workers of the World* (Chicago: University of Illinois Press, 1968), 93.

10. Louis Levine, "The Development of Syndicalism in America", *Political Science Quarterly* 28, no. 3 (September 1913): 473.

11. There was considerable debate over the question of working within the AFL unions or

organizing the unorganized. For a thorough discussion, see Foner, chapter 18.

12. Nicholas Thoburn, "The Hobo Anomalous: Class, Minorities and Political Invention in the Industrial Workers of the World," *Social Movement Studies: Journal of Social, Cultural, and Political Protest* 2, no. 1 (2003): 65

13. Philip S. Foner, *History of the Labor Movement of the United States Vol. 4: The Industrial Workers of the World 1905–1917*, 33.

14. Louis Levine, "The Development of Syndicalism in America," 472

15. Melvyn Dubofsky, *We Shall Be All: A History of the Industrial Workers of the World*, 126.

16. Gale Ahrens, *Lucy Parsons, Freedom, Equality, and Solidarity: Writings and Speeches, 1878–1937* (Chicago: Charles Kerr, 2004), 83.

17. Industrial Workers of the World, *Proceedings: Second Annual Convention of the Industrial Workers of the World, Held at Chicago, Illinois from September 17th to October 3rd, 1906;* Chicago: IWW, 1906, 65.

18. David Brundage, *The Making of Western Labor Radicalism: Denver's Organized Workers 1878–1905*, 4.

19. Vincent St. John, *The I.W.W.: Its History, Structure, and Methods* (Cincinnati: Red Dawn Press, 2000), 10. First published 1917 by IWW Publishing Bureau. Also see "IWW Newspapers," IWW History Project, University of Washington. Available online at http://depts.washington.edu/iww/newspapers.shtml.

20. Robert L. Bach, "Mexican Immigration and the American State," *International Migration Review* 12, no. 4, Special Issue: Illegal Mexican Immigrants to the United States (Winter 1978): 544.

21. For an in-depth exploration of Lucy Gonzalez Parsons's ethnicity, see Michelle Diane Wright, "Confounding Identity: Exploring the Life and Discourse of Lucy E. Parsons," Berkshire Conference of Women Historians, Workshop Paper, 2011. Available online at http://scholarworks.umass.edu/berksconference/Workshops/183/1/.

22. Carolyn Ashbaugh, *Lucy Parsons: American Revolutionary* (Chicago, IL: Charles H. Kerr Publishing Company, 1976), 15.

23. Background information from Gale Ahrens, *Lucy Parsons, Freedom, Equality, and Solidarity: Writings and Speeches, 1878–1937*, 4–5.

24. For background information, see "The Working Women's Union: Preliminary Meeting of Female Operatives to Form as Protective Association," *New York Times*, November 19, 1863. Available online at http://www.nytimes.com/1863/11/19/news/working-women-s-union-preliminary-meeting-female-operatives-form-protective.html.

25. For a full account from Lucy's point of view of the events, see Lucy E. Parsons, *Life of Albert R. Parsons, With Brief History of the Labor Movement in America* (Chicago: Self-Published, 1889). Reprint.

26. Speeches cited in Gale Ahrens, *Lucy Parsons, Freedom, Equality, and Solidarity: Writings and Speeches, 1878–1937*, 78–81.

27. The IWW slogan is an adaption from the earlier Knights of Labor slogan "An injury to one is the concern of all."

28. James Cannon, *The I.W.W.* (1955), Marxist Internet Archives, available online at https://www.marxists.org/archive/cannon/works/1955/iww.htm.

29. Salvatore Salerno, *Red November, Black November: Culture and Community in the Industrial Workers of the World* (Albany: State University of New York Press, 1989), 48.

30. David Montgomery, "The 'New Unionism' and the Transformation of Workers' Consciousness in America, 1909–22," 522.

31. David Burgess, "Workers and Racial Hate," *Industrial Worker*, June 4, 1910; 4.
32. Convention report described and cited in Paul Frederick Brissenden, *The I.W.W.: A Study of American Syndicalism* (doctoral dissertation, Colombia University, 1919), 159–60.
33. Salvatore Salerno, *Red November, Black November: Culture and Community in the Industrial Workers of the World*, 6.
34. Norman Caulfield, "Wobblies and Mexican Workers in Mining and Petroleum, 1905–1924," *International Review of Social History* 40 (1995): 52.
35. Melvyn Dubofsky, *We Shall Be All: A History of the Industrial Workers of the World*, 148.
36. Cited in Philip S. Foner, *History of the Labor Movement of the United States Vol. 4: The Industrial Workers of the World 1905–1917*, 36.
37. Hyman Weintraub, *The I.W.W. in California: 1905–1941* (Master's Thesis, February 1947, University of California, Los Angeles), 117.
38. Stanley M. Gue, "Organize the Mexican Workers," *Industrial Worker*, September 7, 1911; 3.
39. A. Ross McCormack, *Reformers, Rebels, and Revolutionaries: The Western Canadian Radical Movement 1899–1919* (Toronto: University of Toronto Press, 1977), 108.
40. Ibid., 108.
41. Floyd Hyde, "No Foreigner but the Boss," *Industrial Worker*, May 30, 1912.
42. Elizabeth Gurley Flynn, *The Rebel Girl: My First Life (1906–26), An Autobiography* (New York: International Publishers, 1955), 128.
43. Mary Marcy, "The Battle for Bread at Lawrence," *International Socialist Review* XII (March 1912): 538.
44. J. S. Biscay, "How to Organize," *Industrial Worker*, June 6, 1912.
45. Cited in Philip S. Foner, *History of the Labor Movement of the United States Vol. 4: The Industrial Workers of the World 1905–1917*, 125–6.
46. *Libertad y Trabajo*, May 16, 1908; 3.
47. It was advertised that enchiladas and tamales were served. See "Give Dance for Mexicans," *Los Angeles Herald*, February 23, 1908; 28.
48. Nelson Pichardo, "The Establishment and Development of Chicano Voluntary Associations in California, 1910–1930," *Aztlán: A Journal of Chicano Studies* 19, no. 2 (Fall 1988): 93–116.
49. "California Notes," *Industrial Worker*, September 17, 1910; 3.
50. Antonio I. Villarreal, "La Conquista del Bienestar," *Regeneración*, November 19, 1910; 1.
51. One was against the Barber Asphalt Company in September of that year, while the other was a strike at the San Diego Consolidated Gas and Electric Company. See "Mexican I.W.W.s on Strike at San Diego," *Industrial Worker*, August 20th, 1910; 1; and "San Diego on the I.W.W. Map," *Industrial Worker*, August 27th, 1910; 4.
52. "Capitalism International," *Industrial Worker*, September 17, 1910.
53. Marc S. Rodriguez, ed., *Repositioning North American Migration History: New Directions in Modern Continental Migration, Citizenship, and History* (Rochester: University of Rochester Press, 2004), n. 201.
54. Juan José, "Luchador Caido," *Libertad y Trabajo*, May 9, 1908; 1.
55. Mamíe Shea, "A Nuestro Hermanos y Hermanas los Trabajadores Mexicanos," *Libertad y Trabajo*, May 9, 1908; 1.
56. "Union Internacional. Trabajadores Industriales del Mundo," *Libertad y Trabajo*, May 23, 1908; 4.

57. George Sánchez, *Becoming Mexican American: Ethnicity, Culture and Identity in Chicano Los Angeles: 1900–1945* (New York: Oxford University Press), 230; Devra Anne Weber, "Wobblies of the Partido Liberal Mexicano: Revisioning Internationalist and Transnational Movements through Mexican Lenses," 194. The membership statistics for the other branches was not discovered.

58. Ralph Edward Schafer, "Radicalism in California: 1869–1929," (Doctoral Thesis in Modern History, University of California, Berkeley, 1962), 235.

59. Based on observations cited in the *El Paso Herald*. See "Blame Strike at Smelter on IWW," *El Paso Herald,* April 23, 1913; 1.

60. Troy Robert Fuller, "'Our Cause is Your Cause': The Relationship between the Industrial Workers of the World and the Partido Liberal Mexicano, 1905–1911," 61.

61. Frank Barajas, *Curious Unions*, 142.

62. Devra Anne Weber, "Wobblies of the Partido Liberal Mexicano: Revisioning Internationalist and Transnational Movements through Mexican Lenses," 222.

63. Alicia Castellanos Guerrero and Gilberto López y Rivas, *Primo Tapia de La Cruz, un Hijo del Pueblo* (Mexico: Centro de Estudios Históricos del Agrarismo en México, 1991), 32.

64. Wobblies and other radicals were being rounded up across the nation, deported, and even killed as a result of a government-led crackdown and vigilante terror campaign. Because of these repressions, many Wobblies (possibly including Primo Tapia), passed over into the Communist Party after 1918. See Paul Friedrich, *Agrarian Revolt in a Mexican Village*, 69–70.

65. For more on Tapia de la Cruz, see Verónica Oikión Solano, "De la Revolución mexicana a la Revolución mundial. Actores políticos, michoacanos y la Internacional Comunista en México," *Signos Históricos,* no. 21 (January–June 2009): 60–103; Apolinar Martínez Múgica, *Primo Tapia: semblanza de un revolucionario [michoacano]* (Mexico: El Libro Perfecto, 1946); and Castellanos Guerrero, Alicia y Gilberto López Rivas, *Primo Tapia de la Cruz, un hijo del pueblo* (México, D.F.: Centro de Estudios Históricos del Agrarismo en México / Confederación Nacional Campesina, 1991).

66. For a full historical account, see Norman Caulfield, "Wobblies and Mexican Workers in Mining and Petroleum, 1905–1924," 51–76.

67. "Degeneración," *Regeneración,* August 19, 1911, 1.

68. Ricardo Flores Magón, "A Hacer Obra Revolucionaria," *Regeneración,* May 27 1911; 1.

69. Marco Antonio Samaniego López, "La revolución mexicana en baja California: maderismo, magonismo, filibusterismo y la pequeña revuelta local," *Historia Mexicana* LVI, no. 4 (2007): 1202, 1201–62.

70. Ricardo Flores Magón, "La Verdadera Obra Revolucionaria," *Regeneración,* June 2, 1911; 1.

71. Marco Antonio Samaniego, *Nacionalismo y Revolución: Los Acontecimientos de 1911 en Baja California* (Tijuana: Centro Cultural de Tijuana y Universidad Autónoma de California, 2008), 60–133.

72. For a detailed history of the company, see Dorothy Pierson Kerig, *El valle de Mexicali y la Colorado River Land Company, 1902–1946* (Mexicali: Universidad Autónoma de Baja California, 2001), chapter 2, "Organización de Una Empresa Terrateniente," 61–112.

73. Agustín Cue Cánovas, *Ricardo Flores Magón, La Baja California, y Los Estados Unidos* (Mexico, D.F.: Libro Mex Editores, 1957), 48.

74. Colin MacLachlan, *Anarchism and the Mexican Revolution: The Political Trials of Ricardo*

Flores Magón in the United States (Berkeley: University of California Press, 1991), xii.

75. See Marco Antonio Samaniego, *Nacionalismo y Revolución: Los Acontecimientos de 1911 en Baja California*, 158–73.

76. Cited in Everardo Garduño, *La Dispute por la Tierra . . . La Disputa por la Voz* (Mexicali: Universidad Autónoma de Baja California, 2004), 30.

77. Augustín Cue Cánovas, *Ricardo Flores Magón, La Baja California, y Los Estados Unidos*, 30–31.

78. For an example of this view, see "Madero Vacillates, but the Revolution is on the March," *Regeneración*, April 29, 1911.

79. Pablo Martinez, *A History of Lower California (The Only Complete and Reliable One)* (Mexico, D.F.: Av. Escuela Industrial, 1960), 468.

80. Richard Pourade, *Gold in the Sun* (San Diego: Union Tribune Pub. Co., 1966), chapter 8. Available online at http://www.sandiegohistory.org/archives/books/gold/.

81. Marco Antonio Samaniego, *Nacionalismo y Revolución: Los Acontecimientos de 1911 en Baja California*, 239.

82. Margaret A. Secor, "San Diego Looks at the Maderista Revolution in Mexico 1910–1911," *Journal of San Diego History* 18, no. 3 (Summer 1972). Available online at http://www.sandiegohistory.org/journal/1972/july/maderista/.

83. "Revolutions in Mexico: Hearings before a Subcommittee of the Committee on Foreign Relations, United States Senate." (Washington: Government Printing Office, 1913), 189-191.

84. Richard Griswold del Castillo, "The Discredited Revolution: The Magonista Capture of Tijuana in 1911," *The Journal of San Diego History* 26, no. 4 (Fall 1980). Available online at http://www.sandiegohistory.org/journal/1980/october/revolution/.

85. "Revolutions in Mexico: Hearing Before a Subcommittee of the Committee on Foreign Relations, United States Senate," Washington: Government Printing Office, 1913, 189–201.

86. Ricardo Romo, *History of a Barrio: East Los Angeles* (Austin: University of Texas Press, 1977), 43.

87. Richard Griswold del Castillo, "The Discredited Revolution: The Magonista Capture of Tijuana in 1911."

88. "Some Details of the Mobilization," *Daily Capital Journal* (Salem, Oregon), March 10, 1911; 6.

89. For example, see "Rebels in Tijuana Collect Customs; Prepare Town's Defenses," *San Diego Union*, May 17, 1911, 5.

90. Stanley Gue, "Resolution," *Industrial Worker*, April 27, 1911; 3.

91. "Junta Officials to Run Tijuana Affairs," *San Diego Union*, June 3, 1911; 5.

92. "Price of Peace," *Arizona Republican*, June 18, 1911; 1.

93. See Lawrence D. Taylor, "The Magonista Revolt in Baja California," *Journal of San Diego History* 45 no. 1 (Winter 1999); and William D. Raat, *Revoltosos: Mexico's Rebels in the United States, 1903–1923*, 224.

94. See chapters 9 and 10.

Chapter 15: Radicals in the Arizona Copper Mines (1907–1917)

Michael E. Parrish, *Mexican Workers, Progressives, and Copper: The Failure of Industrial Democracy in Arizona during the Wilson Years* (La Jolla: Chicano Research Publications, University of California, San Diego, 1979), 6.

1.   Philip J. Mellinger, *Race and Labor in Western Copper: The Fight for Equality, 1896–1918* (Tucson: University of Arizona Press, 1995), 88.

2.   Anne Pace, "Mexican Refugees in Arizona 1910–1911," *Arizona and the West* 16, no. 1 (Spring 1974): 10.

3.   Cited in Ricardo Cuahtémoc Esparza Valdivia, *El Fenómeno Magonista en México y en Estados Unidos (1905–1908)* (Zacatecas: Centro de Investigaciones Históricas, 2000), 158.

4.   Javier Torres Parés, *La Revolución Sin Frontera: El Partido Liberal Mexicano y Las Relaciones Entre el Movimiento Obrero de Mexico y el de Estados Unidos, 1900–1923* (Mexico, D.F.: Ediciones y Distribuciones Hispánicas, 1990), 78.

5.   Alfonso Torúa Cienfuegos, *Magonismo en Sonora (1906–1908): Historia de una Persecución* (México, D.F.: Hormiga Libertaria, 2010), 57.

6.   Práxedis Guerrero was a central figure in the PLM leadership before his death on the revolutionary battlefield. For more on his life, writings, and revolutionary ideas, see Práxedis Guerrero, *Articulos de Combate* (Mexico: Ediciones Antorcha, 1977); Ward Albo, *To Die on Your Feet: The Life, Times, and Writings of Práxedis G. Guerrero* (Fort Worth: Texas Christian University Press, 1996); and Dave Poole, *Anarchists and the Mexican Revolution: Práxedis G. Guerrero (1882–1910)* (Orkney: Cienfuegos Press, 1977), 1–2.

7.   Jane-Dale Lloyd, "La sotolería, el canto y la lectura en voz alta: espacios y formas de socialización de una ideología radical, 1905–1911," *Historia y Grafía*, no. 27 (2006): 83.

8.   Jane-Dale Lloyd, *Cinco Ensayos Sobre Cultura Material de Rancheros y Medieros del Noroeste de Chihuahua, 1886–1910* (Mexico: Universidad Iberoamericana, A.C., 2001), 74–75.

9.   Philip J. Mellinger, *Race and Labor in Western Copper: The Fight for Equality, 1896–1918*, 71.

10.   Both Cabral and Alvarado went on the become Constitutionalist generals, and in the case of Alvarado, governor of the state of Yucatán.

11.   Anne Pace, "Mexican Refugees in Arizona, 1910–11," *Arizona and the West* 16, no. 1 (Spring, 1974): 7–10.

12.   Alfonso Torúa Cienfuegos, *Magonismo en Sonora (1906–1908): Historia de una Persecución*, 84–86.

13.   Ibid., 109–111.

14.   George G. Suggs, Jr., *Colorado's War on Militant Unionism: James H. Peabody and the Western Federation of Miners* (University of Oklahoma Press, Norman: University of Oklahoma Press, 1991), 23–4.

15.   Anthony V. Esposito, *The Ideology of the Socialist Party of America: 1901–1917* (New York: Garland Publishing, 1997), 109.

16.   Cited in Vernon H. Jensen, *Heritage of Conflict: Labor Relations in the Nonferrous Metals Industry up to 1930* (New York: Greenwood Publishers, 1968), 67.

17.   See David Brundage, *The Making of Western Labor Radicalism: Denver's Organized Workers, 1878–1905* (Urbana: University of Illinois Press, 1994), and Philip J. Mellinger, *Race and Labor in Western Copper: The Fight for Equality, 1896–1918*.

18.   Melvyn Dubofsky, *We Shall Be All: A History of the Industrial Workers of the World*, 37.

19.   For an example of one newspaper's opposition to interracial unionism, see Philip J. Mellinger, *Race and Labor in Western Copper: The Fight for Equality, 1896–1918*, 78.

20.   The measure lost by a small vote because a coalition of delegates aligned with mining companies opposed it. See Mellinger, *Race and Labor in Western Copper: The Fight for*

Equality, 1896–1918, 86.

21. David R. Berman, *Arizona Politics and Government: The Quest for Autonomy, Democracy, and Development* (Lincoln: University of Nebraska, 1998), 45.

22. Cited in an article that otherwise portrays him as a labor messiah. See Marjorie Haines Wilson, "Governor Hunt, the 'Beast' and the Miners," *The Journal of Arizona History* 15, no. 2 (Summer 1974): 121.

23. Thomas Sheridan, *Los Tucsonenses: The Mexican Community in Tucson, 1854–1941* (Tucson: University of Arizona Press, 1986), 169–72.

24. Philip J. Mellinger, *Race and Labor in Western Copper: The Fight for Equality, 1896–1918,* 6.

25. Juan Luis Sariego Rodriguez, *Enclaves y minerales en el norte de Mexico: Historia social de los mineros de Cananea y Nueva Rosita, 1900–1970* (Mexico: Centro de Investigaciones y Estudios Superiores en Antropologia Social, 1988), 132.

26. Ethel Duffy Turner, *Writers and Revolutionists: An Interview Conducted by Ruth Teiser* (Berkeley: University of California, Bancroft Library, Regional Oral History Office, 1967), 20–21.

27. "History Repeating Itself," *Miner's Magazine,* October 3, 1907 [microfilm].

28. Ibid.

29. "Clifton Smeltermen Out on Strike," *Tombstone Weekly Epitaph,* July 28, 1907; 4.

30. "The W.F.M. at Douglas," *Miner's Magazine,* July 25, 1907 [microfilm].

31. See examples in chapters 7 and 11.

32. James Byrkit, *Forging the Copper Collar: Arizona's Labor Management war of 1901–1921* (Tucson: University of Arizona Press, 1982), 50–51.

33. Andrea Yvette Hugginie, "Strikitos: Race, Class, and Work in the Arizona Copper Industry, 1870–1920" (doctoral dissertation, Yale University, 1991), 178.

34. Although his article (like so many from this Arizona-based journal) is hostile to socialists, Robert Reill apparently worked in the mines and identifies 300 miners who were socialists in Globe prior to the strike.See Robert Reill, "The 1917 Copper Strike at Globe, Arizona," *The Journal of Arizona History* 18, no. 2 (Summer 1977): 185–96.

35. "Arizona Labor Conditions," *Miner's Magazine,* February 21, 1907 [microfilm].

36. "Panic of 1907," Publication of the Federal Reserve Bank of Boston, n.d., 3.

37. Andrea Yvette Hugginie, "Strikitos: Race, Class, and Work in the Arizona Copper Industry, 1870–1920," 104.

38. James Byrkit, *Forging the Copper Collar: Arizona's Labor Management war of 1901–1921,* 69.

39. For an example of how racial economic subordination had a disproportionately negative impact, see Zaragosa Vargas, *Proletarians of the North: A History of Mexican Industrial Workers in Detroit and the Midwest, 1917–1933* (Berkeley: University of California Press, 1993), 63–68.

40. "Prospect Bright for Settlement of Miami Strike," *Arizona Republic,* January 22, 1915; 1.

41. Although the Mexicans could affiliate with the Arizona Federation of Labor, it was a largely symbolic gesture. Andrea Yvette Hugginie, "Strikitos: Race, Class, and Work in the Arizona Copper Industry, 1870–1920," 272–3.

42. Marjorie Haines Wilson, "Governor Hunt, the 'Beast' and the Miners," 275.

43. The firing of union sympathizers is mentioned in "End of Labor Trouble is Not Yet in Sight," *The Copper Era and Morenci Leader,* September 24, 1915; 1.

44. "Plea for Employment by Spanish Americans," *Arizona Republican,* February 12, 1915; 2.

45. Andrea Yvette Hugginie, "Strikitos: Race, Class, and Work in the Arizona Copper Industry, 1870–1920," 150.

46. "5,000 Strike in Clifton-Morenci Mining District," *The Copper Era and Morenci Leader*, September 17, 1915; 1.

47. This illustrates that inclusionists like Miller took matters into his own hands, perhaps against the wishes of Moyer and the Denver-based WFM leadership. For example, see "Guy Miller Had No Authority to Call Clifton Men from Work," *Arizona Republican*, January 25, 1916; 1.

48. David. R. Berman, *Politics, Labor, and the War on Big Business: The Path of Reform in Arizona, 1890–1920*.

49. Philip J. Mellinger, *Race and Labor in Western Copper: The Fight for Equality, 1896–1918*, 157.

50. "Recognition of Federation to be Waived," *Arizona Republican*, September 23, 1915; 1–2. This same newspaper ran an article (nearly directly below) with the dubious headline "Incites Insurrection Against the United States is the Charge," with a vague and spurious claim (without evidence other than a found letter) that unknown Mexicans were planning an uprising.

51. "Federation Gets Behind W.F.M. Campaign," *Arizona Daily Star*, October 5, 1915; 1.

52. James R. Kluger, *The Clifton-Morenci Strike* (Tucson: University of Arizona Press, 1970), 26.

53. "Efforts Being Made for Conference; Joint Committee Debating Proposition," *The Copper Era and Morenci Leader*, October 8, 1915; 1.

54. "Organizer Guy Miller Returns to District," *The Copper Era and Morenci Leader*, November 5, 1915; 1.

55. "Morenci Man Shot at by Unknown Assailant," *The Copper Era and Morenci Leader*, November 26, 1915; 1.

56. "Clifton Strike is Endorsed by Federation," *The Copper Era and Morenci Leader*, October 8, 1915; 1.

57. The elected governor was a representative of the so-called "Progressive" upsurge, which reflected a temporary alliance between labor and the middle classes to support political reform. Hunt, a former supporter of the WFM, represented a break with the previous administrations in towing the company's line, but his support was contingent on his own political calculations, and this "support" quickly evaporated during the repression of the Bisbee strike in 1917. For more on the governor, see Marjorie Haines Wilson, "Governor Hunt, the 'Beast' and the Miners," 119–138.

58. "Deadlock Continues in Clifton Labor Trouble," *The Copper Era and Morenci Leader*, October 1, 1915; 1.

59. Ibid.

60. "National Guard in Clifton Well Situated," *The Copper Era and Morenci Leader*, October 22, 1915; 1.

61. "Injunction Issued Restraining Strikers," *The Copper Era and Morenci Leader*, December 31, 1915; 1.

62. "End of Labor Trouble is Not Yet in Sight," *The Copper Era and Morenci Leader*, September 24, 1915; 1.

63. "Western Federation Eliminated in District," *The Copper Era and Morenci Leader*, January 14, 1916; 1.

64. Ricardo Flores Magón, "Las Huelgas," *Regeneración*, October 9, 1915; 3.

65. See "Wage Scale is Settled in Conference," *The Copper Era and Morenci Leader*, February 25, 1916, 1; and Thomas Sheridan, *Arizona: A History* (Tucson: University of Arizona

Press, 1995), 180.

66. Philip J. Mellinger, *Race and Labor in Western Copper: The Fight for Equality, 1896–1918*, 172–3.

67. Michael E. Parrish, *Mexican Workers, Progressives, and Copper: The Failure of Industrial Democracy in Arizona during the Wilson Years* (La Jolla: Chicano Research Publications, University of California, San Diego, 1979), 18.

68. Alexander Bing, *War-Time Strikes and Their Adjustment* (New York: E. Dutton and Co., 1921), 292.

69. Industrial Workers of the World: Proceedings, Tenth Convention, 1916, Chicago Illinois, 138.

70. Ibid., 38.

71. See Paul F. Brissenden, "The Butte Miners and the Rustling Card," *American Economic Review* 10, no. 4 (December 1920): 755; and William Preston, Jr., *Aliens and Dissenters: Federal Suppression of Radicals, 1903–1933* (Chicago: University of Illinois Press, 1963), 93.

72. James Byrkit, "Life and Labor in Arizona, 1901–1921: With Particular Reference to the Deportations of 1917" (doctoral dissertation, Claremont Graduate School, 1972), 288.

73. Andrea Yvette Hugginie, "Strikitos: Race, Class, and Work in the Arizona Copper Industry, 1870–1920," 301.

74. Ibid., 332.

75. Ibid., 310.

76. Terry Boswell and Diane Mitsch Bush, "Labor Force Composition and Union Organizing in the Arizona Copper Industry: A Comment on Jiménez," *Review* (Fernand Braudel Center) 8, no. 1 (Summer 1984): 146.

77. See "65 percent of Men Now Back In Mines . . .," *Arizona Daily Star,* June 30, 1917; 1.

78. "District Committee Refuses Request for any Further Delay," *The Copper Era and Morenci Leader,* June 29, 1917; 1.

79. Michael E. Parrish, *Mexican Workers, Progressives, and Copper: The Failure of Industrial Democracy in Arizona during the Wilson Years,* 18–19.

80. Andrea Yvette Hugginie, "Strikitos: Race, Class, and Work in the Arizona Copper Industry, 1870–1920," 304.

81. William Preston, Jr., *Aliens and Dissenters: Federal Suppression of Radicals, 1903–1933,* 50.

82. Ibid., 119–23.

83. Eldridge Foster Dowell, *A History of Criminal Syndicalism Legislation in the United States* (Baltimore: Johns Hopkins Press, 1939), 17–20.

84. *Bisbee Daily Review,* July 7, 1917; 4.

85. Michael E. Parrish, *Mexican Workers, Progressives, and Copper: The Failure of Industrial Democracy in Arizona during the Wilson Years,* 22.

86. Daphne Overstreet, "ON STRIKE! The 1917 Walkout at Globe, Arizona," *The Journal of Arizona History* 18, no. 2 (Summer 1977): 214.

87. Vernon H. Jensen, *Heritage of Conflict: Labor Relations in the Nonferrous Metals Industry up to 1930,* 400.

88. "Kingman Disperses Jerome I.W.W.s," *Weekly Journal-Miner,* July 18, 1917; 3.

89. Robert Reill, "The 1917 Copper Strike At Globe, Arizona," 189.

90. The author appears to approve of this characterization. See Daphne Overstreet, "ON STRIKE! The 1917 Walkout at Globe, Arizona," 209.

Radicals in the Barrio

91. "Women give Testimony in Globe Strike Trials," *Arizona Daily Star,* October 16, 1917; 1.

92. This is according to an anti-union company paymaster. Robert Reill, "The 1917 Copper Strike At Globe, Arizona," 189, 194.

93. Vernon H. Jensen, *Heritage of Conflict: Labor Relations in the Nonferrous Metals Industry up to 1930,* 404.

94. Michael E. Parrish, *Mexican Workers, Progressives, and Copper: The Failure of Industrial Democracy in Arizona during the Wilson Years,* 27–29.

95. Meyer H. Fishbein, "The President's Mediation Commission and the Arizona Copper Strike, 1917," *The Southwestern Social Science Quarterly* 30, no. 3 (December 1949): 175–82.

Chapter 16: From Casa del Obrero Mundial to Communist International

Donald L. Herman, *The Comintern in Mexico* (Washington, DC: Public Affairs Press), 36.

1. Donald Clark Hodges, *Mexican Anarchism after the Revolution* (Austin: University of Texas Press, 1995), 11.

2. For an overview of the diverse membership, see Gerardo Peláez Ramos, "En el centenario de la Casa del Obrero Mundial," *La Haine,* June 2012, 2-4. Available online at: http://www.lahaine.org/b2-img12/pelaez_com.pdf.

3. Anna Ribera Carbó, "Ferrer Guardia en la Revolución Mexicana," *Educació i Història: Revista d'Història de l'Educació* no. 16 (July–December 2010): 146.

4. For a full discussion of the formation of Grupo Luz, see chapters 14 and 15 of Jacinto Huitrón, *Orígenes e Historia del Movimiento Obrero en México* (México, D.F.: Editores Mexicanos Unidos, S.A., 1974).

5. Anna Ribera Carbó, *La Casa del Obrero Mundial: Anarcosindicalismo y Revolución en México* (Mexico: Instituto Nacional de Antropología e Historia, 2010), 19–20.

6. Ibid., 36.

7. Rosendo Salazar, *Las Pugnas de la Gleba* (Mexico: Comisión Nacional Editorial del PRI, 1972), 36–37.

8. José González Sierra, "Anarquismo y el Movimiento Sindical en México, 1843–1910," *Primer Anuario,* Centro de Estudios Históricos, Facultad de Humanidades, Universidad Veracruzana, 1977, 131.

9. John M. Hart, "Nineteenth Century Urban Labor Precursors of the Mexican Revolution: The Development of an Ideology," *The Americas* 30, no. 3 (January 1974): 318.

10. Cited in Anna Ribera Carbó, Anna. *La Casa del Obrero Mundial: Anarcosindicalismo y Revolución en México.* Mexico: Instituto Nacional de Antropología e Historia, 2010, 90.

11. Jacinto Huitrón, *Orígenes e Historia del Movimiento Obrero en México* (Mexico, D.F.: Editores Mexicanos Unidos, S.A., 1974), 215.

12. John Lear. *Workers, Neighbors, and Citizens: The Revolution in Mexico City* (Lincoln: University of Nebraska Press, 2001), 174.

13. Cited in Miguel Orduña and Alejandro de la Torre, eds., *Cultura Política de los Trabajadores (Siglos XIX y XX)* (Mexico: Universidad Nacional Autónoma de México, 2008), 141.

14. Anna Ribera Carbó, *La Casa del Obrero Mundial: Anarcosindicalismo y Revolución en México,* 53.

15. John Lear, *Workers, Neighbors, and Citizens: The Revolution in Mexico City* (Lincoln: University of Nebraska Press, 2001), 212.

16. Ibid., 191.
17. Ibid., 218-227.
18. Ibid., 179.
19. Enrique Condés Lara, *Atropellado Amanecer: El Comunismo en el Tiempo de la Revolución Mexicana* (Puebla: Benemérita Universidad Autónima de Puebla, 2015), 284.
20. See Steven E. Sanderson, *Agrarian Populism and the Mexican State: The Struggle for Land in Sonora* (Berkeley: University of California Press, 1981), chapters 4 and 5.
21. See Marcial E. Ocasio Meléndez, *Capitalism and Development: Tampico, Mexico, 1876–1924* (New York: Peter Lang, 1998), especially 191–93.
22. Heather Fowler-Salamini, "Women Coffee Sorters Confront the Mill Owners and the Veracruz Revolutionary State, 1915–1918" *Journal of Women's History* 14, no. 1 (Spring 2002): 40–41.
23. The eclectic political model, based loosely on the principles of "anarcho-syndicalism," combined with the heterogeneous artisanal and industrial character of the urban working class, contrasts with the Leninist model used to achieve success in the Russian Revolution, which was happening almost simultaneously. For an in-depth study of "Leninism" and the Russian Revolution, see Paul Le Blanc, *Lenin and the Revolutionary Party* (Chicago: Haymarket Books, 2015).
24. Several members of the COM had joined the Zapatista leadership, even becoming direct representatives of Zapata himself, which may explain why the Morelos-based group was more farsighted on the labor question than the villistas. The pro-union views likely represented the perspectives of these individuals, whether or not they were widely held or considered among the larger population of zapatistas. See Anna Ribera Carbó, *La Casa del Obrero Mundial: Anarcosindicalismo y Revolución en México*, 176.
25. See Susan R. Walsh Sanderson, *Land Reform in Mexico: 1910—1980* (Orlando: Academic Press, Inc., 1984), 28.
26. Jeffrey Lukas, "Antonio Díaz Soto y Gama and Changing Mexico: a Twentieth-Century Political Journey," *International Social Science Review* 83, no. 3/4 (2008): 132–57.
27. Anna Macias, *Against All Odds: The Feminist Movement in Mexico to 1940* (Westport: Greenwood Press, 1982), 29–30.
28. Anna Ribera Carbó, *La Casa del Obrero Mundial: Anarcosindicalismo y Revolución en México*, 129.
29. John Lear, *Workers, Neighbors, and Citizens*, 289.
30. Anna Ribera Carbó, *La Casa del Obrero Mundial*, 155.
31. According to Marcel van der Linden and Wayne Thorpe, "Auge y Decadencia del Sindicalismo Revolucionario," *Historia Social*, no. 12 (Winter 1992): 9.
32. Anna Ribera Carbó, *La Casa del Obrero Mundial: Anarcosindicalismo y Revolución en México*, 192.
33. For an in-depth study of this history, see Gregg Andrews, *Shoulder to Shoulder?: The American Federation of Labor, the United States, and the Mexican Revolution, 1910–1924* (Berkeley: University of California Press, 1991).
34. Jorge Basurto, *La Crisis Económica En La Revolución Mexicana Y Sus Repercusiones Sociales, 1913–1917* (Mexico, D.F.: Instituto de Investigaciones Sociales, Universidad Nacional Autónoma De México, 2010), 247.
35. Ibid., 256.
36. Enrique Condés Lara, *Atropellado Amanecer: El Comunismo en el Tiempo de la Revolución Mexicana* (Puebla: Benemérita Universidad Autónima de Puebla, 2015), 105.

37. Ibid., 277.

38. For a thorough study on the Bolshevik model, see Paul Le Blanc, *Lenin and the Revolutionary Party* (Chicago: Haymarket Books, 2015).

39. Enrique Condés Lara, *Atropellado Amanecer: El Comunismo en el Tiempo de la Revolución Mexicana*, 237.

40. Barry Carr asserts that anarchism continued to be a lingering influence, alongside reform socialism. See his "Marxism and Anarchism in the Formation of the Mexican Communist Party, 1910–19," *The Hispanic American Historical Review* 63, no. 2 (May 1983): 286, for a full description of the eclectic political character of the party.

41. Mario Gill, "Veracruz: Revolucion y Extremism," *Historia Mexicana* 2, no. 4 (April–June 1953): 619.

42. Paco Taibo, *Los Bolshevikis: historia narrativa de los origenes del comunismo en México, 1919–1925* (Mexico: Editorial Joaquín Mortiz, 1986), chapter 1.

43. For a more in-depth study of the CROM in this period, see Rocío Guardarrama, *Los Sindicatos y la Política en México: La CROM 1918–1928* (México: Ediciones Era, 1981).

44. Ibid., 30–31.

45. Ibid., 31.

46. Barry Carr, *Anarchism and Communism in Twentieth Century Mexico*, *The Hispanic American Historical Review* 63, no. 2 (May 1983): 290.

47. Donald C. Hodges, *Mexican Anarchism after the Revolution* (Austin: University of Texas Press, 1995), 4. See also Leon Trotsky, *The Permanent Revolution and Results and Prospects* (New York: Merit Publishers, 1969).

48. Ibid., 11.

49. Ibid., 16.

50. The break occurred over the Bolshevik government's suppression of the Kronstadt revolt in 1921. See Paul Avrich, "Prison Letters of Ricardo Flores Magón to Lilly Sarnoff," *International Review of Social History* 22, no. 3 (December 1977): 403. For the Bolshevik perspective on Kronstadt, see Vladimir I. Lenin and Leon Trotsky, *Kronstadt* (New York: Pathfinder Press, 1979).

51. John Kenneth Turner, *Barbarous Mexico* (Austin: University of Texas Press, 1969), 12–13.

52. Guillermo Boils Morales, "El Movimiento de los Trabajadores en Yucatán Durante la Gubernatura de Salvador Alvarado (1915–1917)," *Revista Mexicana de Sociología* 41, no. 3 (July–September 1979): 625–32.

53. Ibid.

54. Similar processes occurred in Campeche and Tabasco, although not as successful as in Yucatán. See Carlos Martínez Assad, "Del fin del porfiriato a la Revolución en el sur-sureste de México," *Historia Mexicana* 43, no. 3, Yucatán: una peculiaridad no desmentida (January–March 1994): 487–504.

55. Gilbert Joseph, *Revolution from Without: Yucatán, Mexico, and the United States, 1880–1924* (Durham: Duke University Press, 1988), 217–8.

56. Ibid.

57. Ibid., 221–2.

58. Several factors contributed to the party's downfall. While the party identified itself as Marxist, it failed to make inroads into the industrial working class, especially the independent, Anarcho-syndicalist unions of the railroad workers and dockworkers. In a replay of the divisions between the rural and urban proletariat in 1914 between the

Casa del Mundo Obrero and zapatistas and villistas, the Socialist Party alienated itself from the industrial working class by neglecting urban working-class interests in favor of the countryside. When counterrevolutionary forces in the federal army closed in on the Socialists, the industrial working class in the cities remained on the sidelines. Furthermore, while the ligas comprised a popular base in the agricultural proletariat, they retained the cacique leadership structure. With this model, local political bosses functioned as middlemen between the party and the rural proletarian base. Their loyalty was not fundamentally ideological, but based on retaining power and privilege. This top-down model prevented the development of a popular democratic leadership that could operate as an alternative base of support to the caciques. This failure allowed for many caciques to switch sides and neutralize organized opposition when the forces of the federal army moved into the state. Lastly, the Socialist leadership believed it could lead a "revolution from above" by using legislative methods that introduced socialist reforms incrementally. By pledging their loyalty to the national revolutionary leadership, they believed they could count on the support of powerful backers and leverage their support against regional bourgeois forces seeing their power wane and control diminish. In the end, this top-down, gradualist path to socialism failed. For a full treatment of these issues, see Gilbert Joseph, *Revolution from Without: Yucatán, Mexico, and the United States, 1880–1924*, chapter 9.

59. Verónica Oikión Solano, "De la Revolución Mexicana a la Revolución Mundial: Actores Políticos Michoacanos y la Internacional Comunista en México," *Signos Históricos*, no. 21 (January–June 2009), 65.

60. Gerardo Sánchez Díaz, "Los pasos al socialismo en la lucha agraria y sindical en Michoacán 1917–1938," *Tzintzun, Revista de Estudios Historicos*, no. 11 (2015): 109.

61. See Gastón García Cantú, *Idea de Mexico II: El Socialismo* (Mexico: Fondo de Cultural Económica, 1991), chapter 9.

62. Daniela Spenser, *The Impossible Triangle: Mexico, Soviet Russia, and the United States in the 1920s* (Durham: Duke University Press, 1999), 35.

63. Daniela Spenser, *Stumbling its Way Through Mexico: The Early Years of the Communist International* (Tuscaloosa: University of Alabama Press, 2011), 15.

64. Stephen White, "Colonial Revolution and the Communist International, 1919–1924," *Science & Society* 40, no. 2 (Summer 1976): 174.

65. See Brian Pearce, *Baku: Congress of the Peoples of the East, Baku, September 1920. A Stenographic Report* (New York: New Park Publications, 1977), ix.

66. For a full discussion of this history, see Daniela Spenser, *Stumbling Its Way Through Mexico: The Early Years of the Communist International*, 92.

67. Amid global trade dislocation and economic instability induced by the First World War, the administration of Woodrow Wilson took steps to aggressively extend US influence throughout the hemisphere. The confluence of revolution in Mexico, the breakdown of European and Latin American trade relations, and the global realignment of belligerent forces and interimperialist redivision of territorial control and influence led the US government to act on its assumptions of hemispheric authority in order to further strengthen its position. This included the effort to unite the region behind US war aims, extend "free trade" into those territories previously dominated by its European rivals, and reconstruct postwar governments and labor movements along lines more favorable to US capitalism. For further discussion, see Emily S. Rosenberg, "World War I and 'Continental Solidarity,'" *Americas* 31, no.

3 (January 1975): 321; and Abdiel Onate, "La Batalla por El Banco Central: Las Negociaciones de México con Los Banqueros Internacionales, 1920–25," *Historia Mexicana* 49, no. 4 (April–June 2000): 649.

68. Lorenzo Meyer, "El ocaso británico en México. De las causas profundas a los errores políticos," *Mexican Studies/Estudios Mexicanos* 11, no. 1 (Winter 1995): 25–43.

69. Emilio Zebadúa, *Banqueros y Revolucionarios: La Soberanía Financiera de México, 1914–1929* (México: El Colegio de México, 1994), 26.

70. Vladimir Lenin, "Imperialism: The Highest Stage of Capitalism," in *Lenin: Selected Works in One Volume* (New York: International Publishers, 1968), 223–4.

71. For a good overview of this history, see Dan La Botz, *Democracy in Mexico: Peasant Rebellion and Political Reform* (Cambridge: South End Press, 1995) and Josefina Zoraida Vázquez and Lorenzo Meyer, *México frente a Estados Unidos. Un ensayo histórico 1776-2000* (Mexico: Fondo de Cultura Económica, 1989).

72. Abdiel Onate, "La Batalla por El Banco Central: Las Negociaciones de México con Los Banqueros Internacionales, 1920–25," 635.

73. Ibid., 647.

74. Emilio Zebadúa refers to this as establishing the "limits of Mexico's sovereignty." See *Banqueros y Revolucionarios: La Soberanía Financiera de México, 1914–1929* (Mexico: El Colegio de Mexico, 1994), 24.

75. Thomas O'Brien, *The Revolutionary Mission: American Enterprise in Latin America, 1900–1945* (Cambridge: University of Cambridge, 1996), 252.

76. For instance: foreign direct investment continued to expand until 1930. See *Banqueros y Revolucionarios: La Soberanía Financiera de México, 1914–1929*, 26–27.

Chapter 17: California Agriculture and Migrant Mexican Labor

Cited in Paul Ganster and David E. Lorey, *The U.S.-Mexican Border Today: Conflict and Cooperation in Historical Perspective* (Lanham: Rowman and Littlefield, 2016), 71.

1. This included Native Americans, African Americans, Chinese, Japanese, Indians, Filipinos, Puerto Ricans, and Mexicans, among others. See Mark Wyman, *Hoboes: Bindlestiffs, Fruit Tramps, and the Harvesting of the West* (New York: Hill and Wang, 2010), 6.

2. Out of a total of farm labor (including family labor) of 13.5 million. See John Chala Elac, "The Employment of Mexican Workers in US Agriculture, 1900–1960: A Binational Economic Analysis," dissertation, University of California, Los Angeles (May 1961), 52.

3. Clarke A. Chambers, *California Farm Organizations: A Historical Study of the Grange, the Farm Bureau, and the Associated Farmers, 1929–1941* (Berkeley: University of California Press, 1952), 3.

4. Ibid., 5.

5. Juan L. Gonzalez, Jr., *Mexican and Mexican American Farm workers: The California Agricultural Industry* (New York: Praeger, 1985), 4.

6. These land allotments expanded over time, from 160 acres to 640, and required residency.

7. For a full discussion of this idea, see Fred Shannon, "The Homestead Act and the Labor Surplus," cited in Vernon Carstensen, *The Public Lands: Studies in the History of the Public Domain* (Madison: University of Wisconsin Press, 1968), 297–313.

8. Land speculators edged out small farmers to acquire great tracts of federally controlled

land through various tricks and schemes. One notorious land speculator, William S. Chapman, worked closely with "'land officers, judges, local legislators, officials in the Department of the Interior, and even higher dignitaries'" employing "'fraud, bribery, false swearing, forgery, and other crimes'" to amass one million acres of arable land also exempted from the Homestead Acts. See Allen G. Bogue and Margaret Beattie Bogue, "'Profits' and the Frontier Land Speculator," in Vernon Carstensen, *The Public Lands: Studies in the History of the Public Domain*, 369–84. While they conclude that many speculators made little or no profit, the process itself helped to concentrate land for those who did. Furthermore, see Carey McWilliams, *California: The Great Exception* (Berkeley: University of California Press, 1999), 94.

9.   Fred Shannon, "The Homestead Act and the Labor Surplus," cited in Vernon Carstensen, *The Public Lands: Studies in the History of the Public Domain* (Madison: University of Wisconsin Press, 1963), 298.

10. Paul Wallace Gates, "The Role of the Land Speculator in Western Development" cited in Vernon Carstensen, *The Public Lands: Studies in the History of the Public Domain*, 364.

11. Fred Shannon, "The Homestead Act and the Labor Surplus," cited in Vernon Carstensen, *The Public Lands: Studies in the History of the Public Domain*, 306.

12. The federal government brought the Transcontinental Railroad into existence to link emerging commodities production to global markets vis-à-vis eastern capitalist speculators. To accomplish this, Congress passed the Pacific Railroad Acts between 1862 and 1866, which set up a system by which private rail companies were paid to lay track under the aegis of government. As part of a generous compensation package, railroad companies were subsidized at the rate of $16,000 for each mile of track laid across level land, $48,000 per mile through mountain ranges, and $32,000 for areas in between (in 1862 dollars). Furthermore, they were awarded 6,400 acres of land adjacent to each mile of track laid. Between the years 1910 and 1919, for instance, the total national value of agricultural commodities grew from 9 to 24 billion. See John Moody, *The Railroad Builders: A Chronicle of the Welding of the States* (New Haven: Yale University Press, 1921), 123; and Greg Hall, *Harvest Wobblies: The Industrial Workers of the World and Agricultural Laborers in the American West, 1905–1930* (Corvallis: Oregon State University, 2001), 11.

13. Nelson Pichardo Almanzar, *American Fascism and the New Deal: The Associated Farmers of California and the Pro-Industrial Movement* (Lanham: Lexington Books, 2013), 37.

14. USDA, "Land Use Planning Under Way." Report prepared by the Bureau of Agricultural Economics in cooperation with the Extension Service, Farm Security Administration, Soil Conservation Service, Agricultural Adjustment Administration, and Forest Service, United States Department of Agriculture, July, 1940, 1.

15. Joon K. Kim, "California Agribusiness and the Farm Labor Question," *Aztlán: A Journal of Chicano Studies* 37, no. 2 (Fall 2012): 51.

16. Cited in Joon K. Kim, "California Agribusiness and the Farm Labor Question," 51.

17. By 1929, total income from agriculture production amounted to over $800 million, representing 30 percent of the state income. Furthermore, other sectors of capital servicing industrial agricultural, such as finance, transportation, energy, processing, packaging, refrigeration, and multiple smaller subsidiary industries became virtually dependent on its prosperity and well-being. See Clarke A. Chambers, *California Farm Organizations: A Historical Study of the Grange, the Farm Bureau, and the Associated Farmers, 1929–1941* (Berkeley: University of California Press, 1952), 5.

18. Ibid., 29–30.
19. Ibid., 5.
20. See Nelson Pichardo Almanzar, *American Fascism and the New Deal: The Associated Farmers of California and the Pro-Industrial Movement*, 41–42.
21. To break into the markets dominated by eastern and European capital, labor costs had to be kept low. To achieve this, labor control became an urgent matter for growers. The establishment of a large pool of cheap, pliable, and disposable workers was essential for accumulation to occur at a level that would enable western agriculture to compete and ultimately outproduce and undersell rivals in national and international fruit and vegetable markets. See Lucie Cheng and Edna Bonacich, *Labor Immigration Under Capitalism: Asian Workers in the United States Before World War II* (Berkeley: University of California Press, 1984), 141.
22. The profitable institution of slavery had informed the labor practices of early California settlers, many of whom were of Southern origin. They helped to "assure that the California natives would become a new class of slaves in the new state through the economic necessity of a laboring class. Indenture laws and other 'civilized' means legitimized the new society." from "When the Great Spirit Died" by William Secrest; Various state-sponsored strategies also served to proletarianize Native people, such as the sponsorship of schools of assimilation with vocational training for Indian youth designed to prepare a controllable labor force for growers. See Meriam Lewis, "The Problem of Indian Administration. Report of a Survey Made at the Request of Honorable Hubert Work, Secretary of the Interior, and Submitted to Him, February 21, 1928." Report prepared for the Department of the Interior by the Brookings Institution, Washington, D.C. 1928; 384–91. Furthermore, farm settlements expanded through the state in proximity to Indian rancherias, resettled Indian communities located on the margins of Spanish and later Mexican communities used as repositories of labor for agriculture and ranching. California's postwar military dictatorship was keen to maintain this system for use in the new Anglo capitalist system. By the late 1860s the rate of commodity production outstripped existing labor supply.
23. Lucie Cheng and Edna Bonacich, *Labor Immigration under Capitalism: Asian Workers in the United States before World War II*, 160.
24. Chinese migration greatly accelerated after 1868, when the US and Chinese governments signed the Burlingame Treaty, which legalized Chinese migration to the US, opening the door to hundreds of thousands of migrants. A colonial labor distribution system emerged in these years, as thousands of Chinese were drawn into unregulated trafficking operations that served as brokers for capitalist plantations.
25. To ensure the steady availability of labor, western farmers turned to the state for support. Alliances of rail, mine, and agricultural investors exerted immense political influence within federal government channels to act on migration and immigration. Using this power, they arranged for federal agencies to facilitate, coordinate, and regulate mass migration to serve the labor needs of western farms. By the second decade of the twentieth century, the federal government became a labor procurement agency to meet the needs of capitalist farming. In 1914, the United States Bureau of Labor began a campaign to allocate labor to key wheat-producing regions across the West. A request process was created and information circulated through area newspapers explaining how farmers could petition the government for how many and what type of workers were needed, the duration required, and how much they were

willing to pay. This job information was then mass published through newspapers, government, and labor recruiting agencies. In rural counties, farm bureau agents opened up offices as liaisons to create labor exchanges, and local draft boards "deferred classification of persons engaged in agriculture and the approval of applications for temporary furlough to engage in agricultural production." Through these mechanisms, the state induced and managed waves of migration. See Ted Grossardt, "Hoboes: The Production of Labor Organization through the Wheat Harvest," *Agricultural History* 70, no. 2, Twentieth Century Farm Policies (Spring 1996): 289, 297.

26. European American and European immigrants made up the majority of migratory farmworkers prior to the turn of the twentieth century, but this began to significantly change over the next two decades. Despite the agrarian ideal that envisioned the emergence of a white small-landowning class, organized capitalist farmers concentrated land and power in their own hands, inhibiting the significant development of a small and middle-sized farming class. As better jobs abounded in an expanding urban industry, or war demanded mass induction of workers into the military, white and native-born workers left the fields in droves. In desperation for labor, agricultural capitalists in the West turned to recruiting in all directions, especially south of the border.

27. Richard Steven Street, *Beasts of the Field: A Narrative History of California Farmworkers, 1769–1913* (Stanford: Stanford University Press, 2004), 281.

28. Edwin E. Ferguson, "The California Alien Land Law and the Fourteenth Amendment," *California Law Review* 35, no. 1 (March 1947): 63.

29. The US annexation of Hawaii in 1898 opened the way for tens of thousands of Japanese plantation workers to cross more easily to the mainland by steamship and into California agriculture. The incorporation of the Hawaiian Islands into the US economy and the growing presence of labor recruiters operating throughout the South Pacific promising well-paying jobs contributed to this migration. See Edwin E. Ferguson, "The California Alien Land Law and the Fourteenth Amendment," 64.

30. Lucie Cheng and Edna Bonacich, *Labor Immigration under Capitalism: Asian Workers in the United States before World War II*, 62; Edwin E. Ferguson, "The California Alien Land Law and the Fourteenth Amendment," 77.

31. Lucie Cheng and Edna Bonacich, *Labor Immigration under Capitalism: Asian Workers in the United States before World War II*, 70.

32. Richard Steven Street, *Beasts of the Field: A Narrative History of California Farmworkers, 1769–1913*, 409–10. See also Gilbert G. González, *Labor and Community: Mexican Citrus Worker Villages in a Southern California County, 1900–1950* (Chicago: University of Illinois Press, 1994), 27.

33. Wages had indeed increased across the board, from $1 for eleven hours in 1889 to around $1.50 for ten hours in 1903 and as high as $3 a day in 1906; making them the highest-paid farm labor in the nation. Furthermore, a small but significant number of Japanese workers had leveraged their increased incomes to purchase landholdings. In doing so, this presented a secondary challenge. Mobility from worker to farmer undermined the maintenance of a stable and permanent landless agricultural proletariat that could be kept marginal to urban industry. What's more, the emergence of a class of Japanese and Japanese American growers signified emerging competition for market share. Land ownership, for instance, had increased from 29 farms consisting of nearly 5,000 acres in 1900, to 1,816 farms comprising

nearly 100,000 acres by 1910. It is estimated that including land leased, sharecropped, and rented pushed the total land use to nearly 200,000 acres, or about 5 percent of total land, making the Japanese a threat to the hegemony of white landownership; See Richard Steven Street, *Beasts of the Field: A Narrative History of California Farmworkers, 1769–1913*, 474, 478, 517; and Edwin E. Ferguson, "The California Alien Land Law and the Fourteenth Amendment," 67.

34. For a full picture of this period, see Roger Daniels, *The Politics of Prejudice: The Anti-Japanese Movement in California, and the Struggle for Japanese Exclusion* (Berkeley: University of California Press, 1962).

35. By the 1930s, two generations of an established and Japanese landowning class had been dismantled. Virulent racist campaigns intensified with the onset of interimperialist tensions between the United States and Japan in Asia, paving the way for the mass arrest and internment of the Japanese Issei and Nisei populations into sixteen concentration camps strewn across the interior of the western states. The strategic alignment of public opinion against the Japanese reflected a plurality of interests converging behind US imperial interests in Asia. Public opinion was calibrated against the Japanese as US military planners were gearing up toward war with Japan over control of Asia.

36. Juan L. Gonzalez, Jr., *Mexican and Mexican American Farm workers: The California Agricultural Industry* (New York: Praeger, 1985), 6.

37. Manuel García y Griego, "The Importation of Mexican Contract Laborers to the United States, 1942–1964: Antecedents, Operations, and Legacy," Working Paper in US-Mexican Studies, University of California, San Diego, 1980, 6–7.

38. Ibid., 3.

39. Gilbert G. González, "Labor and Community: The Camps of Mexican Citrus Pickers in Southern California," *The Western Historical Quarterly* 22, no. 3 (August 1991): 294.

40. For a fuller discussion of this analysis of migratory labor, see Michael Burawoy, "The Functions and Reproduction of Migrant Labor: Comparative Material from Southern Africa and the United States," *American Journal of Sociology* 81, no. 5 (March 1976): 1067–8.

41. Department of Commerce and Labor, Bulletin of the Bureau of Labor Volume XVII-1908, Washington: Government Printing Office, 1909; 482.

42. Ibid., 485.

43. Robert L. Bach, "Mexican Immigration and the American State," *International Migration Review* 12, no. 4, Special Issue: Illegal Mexican Immigrants to the United States (Winter 1978): 547.

44. Gilberto Cárdenas, "United States Immigration Policy toward Mexico: An Historical Perspective," *Chicana/o Latina/o Law Review* 2 (1975): 66.

45. Ibid., 69.

46. Ibid., 74.

47. These groups were successful in shaping the discourse of immigrant exclusion around racist doctrines and attempted to build on the exclusion of Asians in the 1924 act by targeting Filipinos and Mexicans for exclusion, and later for the internment of the Japanese during World War II.

48. See Natalie Molina, "'In a Race All Their Own': The Quest to Make Mexicans Ineligible for US Citizenship," *Pacific Historical Review* 79, no. 2 (May 2010): 184–5.

49. California Joint Immigration Committee, "Increase of Mexican Population." Press

release. Sacramento, CA. June 20, 1933.

50. For examples of how organized labor in South Texas framed their opposition to Mexican migration, see Marshall Roderick, "The 'Box Bill': Public Policy, Ethnicity, and Economic Exploitation in Texas" (master's thesis, Texas State University, San Marcos, Texas, December, 2011), 29–30.

51. Examples of these arguments are well documented in Marshall Roderick, "The 'Box Bill': Public Policy, Ethnicity, and Economic Exploitation in Texas," 33–38.

52. Ibid., 47.

53. John Chala Elac, "The Employment of Mexican Workers in US Agriculture, 1900–1960: A Binational Economic Analysis," 12.

54. Mark Wyman, *Hoboes: Bindlestiffs, Fruit Tramps, and the Harvesting of the West*, 190.

55. Mario Barrera, *Race and Class in the Southwest: A Theory of Racial Inequality* (Notre Dame: University of Notre Dame Press, 1979), 44–45.

56. For example, it was common practice for local law enforcement to prevent migratory labor from moving into local towns through the selective use of anti-vagrancy law. During harvest time, the presence of migrants was tolerated. When completed, the police vigorously enforced local vagrancy statutes in which those found to be unemployed nonresidents were arrested, driven out of town, or placed into bonded labor. See Mark Wyman, *Hoboes: Bindlestiffs, Fruit Tramps and the Harvesting of the West*, 51.

57. David R. Díaz, *Barrio Urbanism: Chicanos, Planning, and American Cities* (New York: Routledge, 2005), 31.

58. Mario Barrera, *Race and Class in the Southwest: A Theory of Racial Inequality*, 50. By 1970, after more than six decades of forming the labor backbone of western agriculture, only 4.3 percent of the Mexican-born agricultural workforce in the US had become farm owners, and only 6.7 percent of those born in the US of Mexican parents. See Paul S. Taylor, "Mexican Migration and the 160-Acre Water Limit," *California Law Review* 63, no. 3 (May, 1975): 740.

59. Despite this important contribution, Paul Taylor fails to account for the role that racial discrimination, segregation, and violence played in the disenfranchisement and marginalization of Mexican workers in the US. Instead he contradicts himself, stating that cyclical migration between the US and Mexico "retarded Mexican assimilation" and that Mexicans themselves remained ignorant and aloof from the benefits of citizenship as a pathway to social mobility. See Paul S. Taylor, "Mexican Migration and the 160-Acre Water Limit," 741–2 for these contradictory claims.

Chapter 18: Wobblies and Mexican Farmworkers in Wheatland

Unsigned, "The Wheatland Boys," *International Socialist Review* 14 (January 1914): 442.

1. "Industrial Union for Harvest Hands," *Industrial Worker*, July 1, 1909; 3.

2. For background history and an overview of the major California free speech fights, see Ralph Edward Schaffer, "Radicalism in California, 1869–1929" (doctoral dissertation, History, University of California, Berkeley, 1962), chapter 10.

3. Greg Hall, *Harvest Wobblies: The Industrial Workers of the World and Agricultural Laborers in the American West, 1905–1930* (Corvallis: Oregon State University, 2001), 54.

4. E. (Walter Nef) Workman, "'History of 400': A.W.O. The One Big Union Idea in Action." Pamphlet. New York: One Big Union Club, 1939.

5. "Industrial Union for Harvest Hands," *Industrial Worker*, July 1, 1909; 3. The San Francisco local was founded when the whole Mexican section of the San Francisco

Socialist Party voted to affiliate to the IWW and form a new local. "A New Local," *Industrial Worker* September 7, 1911; 3.

6.   Historian Charles LeWarne identifies a significant number of Mexican farmworkers affiliated with the Local. If there weren't Mexican Wobblies among the farmworkers in Wheatland, they likely had contact with them and were aware of their role as radicals and organizers. See Charles LeWarne, "On the Wobbly Train to Fresno," *Labor History* 14, no. 2 (1973): 264–89.

7.   Hyman Weintraub, *The I.W.W. in California: 1905–1941*, 67.

8.   Wheatland had been built atop the land of the Marti indigenous people. When, in 1844, a Mexican field hand named Pablo Gutiérrez discovered gold near modern-day Bear River, he petitioned for and was awarded a 22,000-acre land grant by the Mexican governor Manuel Micheltoreno. When Gutiérrez was killed in an uprising of Anglo filibusters known as the "Bear Flag Revolt," his Rancho de Pablo passed into the hands of Anglo land speculators in 1849 after the US annexed the territory. The first order of business for the military detachment in the region (the 2nd US infantry) was to clear out the Native peoples. By 1851, the local native peoples were pushed out of the area and onto a nearby reservation in order to open up the area for Anglo colonization, while maintaining the indigenous population for labor needs. Located at the foothills of an eastern migrant corridor, the land was intersected by the Oregon and California Railroad in 1866, parceled out, sold, and ultimately converted into the farming community of Wheatland by 1874. See Wheatland Historical Society, *Images of America: Wheatland* (San Francisco: Arcadia Publishing, 2009), 7; City of Wheatland, "Archaeological and Historical Resources: Johnson Rancho and Hop farm Annexation" 4, no. 7, June 2011, 4. Available online at: http://www.wheatland.ca.gov/userfiles/file/4_7_Archaeological percent20& percent20Historical percent20Resources.pdf.

9.   Wheatland Historical Society, *Images of America: Wheatland*, 8.

10.   First Annual Report of the Commission of Immigration and Housing of California, January 2, 1915, 30.

11.   Ibid., 18. Other historians claim the number of Mexicans was closer to half or more. For example, see Carey McWilliams *Factories in the Field: The Story of Migratory Farm Labor in California* (Berkeley: University of California Press, 2000), 158.

12.   Ibid., 18.

13.   Ibid., 19.

14.   David A. Kulczyk, "Hops of Wrath: 1913's Bloody Wheatland Hop Riot Eventually Led to Better Conditions for Workers. Too Bad It Was Only Temporary," *Sacramento News and Review*, August 30, 2007. Available online at http://www.newsreview.com/sacramento/hops-of-wrath/content?oid=455416. See also David F. Selvin, *Sky Full of Storm: A Brief History of California Labor* (Berkeley: University of California, 1966), 33.

15.   Andy Barber, "Truth about Wheatland," *Industrial Worker*, August 21, 1913.

16.   Woodrow C. Whitten, "The Wheatland Episode," *Pacific Historical Review* 17, no. 1. (February 1948): 37.

17.   Carleton H. Parker, "The Casual Laborer and other Essays" (New York: Harcourt, Brace, and Howe, 1920), 72. Parker was tasked with producing a report and recommendations for reform, primarily as a means to minimize the influence of the IWW as they began to organize farmworkers. While presented as a reluctant sympathizer with the IWW, his writings subtly perpetuate the stereotypes and

caricatures of the IWW as a terrorist organization. In the vein of the group's liberal critics, he characterized the IWW as an unfortunate product of the excesses of capitalism.

18. Nicholas Thoburn, "The Hobo Anomalous: Class, Minorities, and Political Invention in the Industrial Workers of the World," 76.

19. Cletus E. Daniel, "Radicals on the Farm in California," *Agricultural History* 49, no. 4 (October 1975): 636.

20. Cited in Carey McWilliams, *Factories in the Field: The Story of Migratory Farm Labor in California*, 160.

21. George Bell, "The Wheatland Hop Fields Riot," *Outlook* 107, no. 3 (May 1914): 121.

22. Vincent DiGirolamo, "The Women of Wheatland: Female Consciousness and the 1913 Wheatland Hop Strike," *Labor History* 34, no. 2–3 (1993): 240.

23. Testimony cited in "Confession of Suhr is Introduced," *Daily Capital Journal* (Salem, Oregon) January 22, 1914; 4.

24. Eric Chester, *The Wobblies in their Heyday: The Rise and Destruction of the Industrial Workers of the World During the World War I Era* (Santa Barbara: Praeger, 2014), 5.

25. Vincent DiGirolamo, "The Women of Wheatland: Female Consciousness and the 1913 Wheatland Hop Strike," 246.

26. Testimony cited in "Confession of Suhr is Introduced," *Daily Capital Journal*, 4.

27. In wildly inaccurate and shoddy reporting, the *San Francisco Chronicle* alleged that "some excitable person in the mob of Mexicans fired a shot at random" setting off the shootout. See "Officers Slain in Riot at Wheatland," *San Francisco Chronicle*, Monday, August 4, 1913; 1. The article goes on, reaching a point of absurdity by reporting that after the shooting "it is said that many of the men have secured liquor and are drinking heavily."

28. "Troops Likely to Leave Hops Fields Today," *San Francisco Call*, August 5, 1913; 1.

29. Eric Chester, *The Wobblies in their Heyday: The Rise and Destruction of the Industrial Workers of the World During the World War I Era*, 10.

30. "Troops Likely to Leave Hops Fields Today," *San Francisco Call*; 1.

31. Cletus Daniel, "In Defense of the Wheatland Wobblies: A Critical Analysis of the IWW in California," *Labor History* 19 (1978): 494.

32. "The Wheatland Riots," *San Francisco Chronicle*, August 6, 1913; 6.

33. For an exhaustive account of the efforts to free Suhr and Ford, see Cletus Daniel, "In Defense of the Wheatland Wobblies: A Critical Analysis of the IWW in California," *Labor History* 19 (1978): 485–509.

34. Arnold Stead, *Always on Strike: Frank Little and the Western Wobblies* (Chicago: Haymarket Books, 2014), 57.

35. *Literary Digest*, July 17, 1920; 54.

Chapter 19: Socialists and Mexican Miners in Colorado

"Industrial Solidarity Must Come," *Miner's Magazine* 14, no. 551 (January 15, 1914), 5.

1. David Montgomery, "The 'New Unionism' and the Transformation of Workers' Consciousness in America, 1909–22," *Journal of Social History* 7, no. 4 (Summer 1974): 515.

2. Data from Frank Julian Warne, *The Coal-Mine Workers: A Study in Labor Organization* (New York: Longmans, Green, and Co., 1905), 1. Quote from Stephen Burnett Brier, "'The Most Persistent Unionists': Class Formation and Class Conflict in the Fields and the Emergence of Interracial and Interethnic Unionism, 1880–1904" (dissertation,

University of California, Los Angeles, 1992), 11.

3.   For a discussion of these strikes, see George G. Suggs, Jr., *Colorado's War on Militant Unionism: James H. Peabody and the Western Federation of Miners* (Norman: University of Oklahoma Press, 1990).

4.   F. Darrell Munsell, *From Redstone to Ludlow: John Cleveland Osgood's Struggle against the United Mine Workers* (Boulder: University Press of Colorado, 2009), 122–3.

5.   The history of the merger discussed in detail in chapter 8 of A. F. Hinrichs, "The United Mineworkers of America and the Non-Union Coalfields" (dissertation, Columbia University, 1923).

6.   Stephen Burnett Brier, "'The Most Persistent Unionists': Class Formation and Class Conflict in the Fields and the Emergence of Interracial and Interethnic Unionism, 1880–1904," 40.

7.   For discussion of how coal capitalists consolidated power, see John R. Bowman, *Capitalist Collective Action: Competition, Cooperation, and Conflict in the Coal Industry* (New York: Cambridge University Press, 1989).

8.   Herbert Northrup, "The Negro and the United Mine Workers of America," *Southern Economic Journal* 9, no. 4 (April 1943): 318.

9.   Ibid.

10.   Mark Wyman, *Hard Rock Epic: Western Miners and the Industrial Revolution 1860–1910* (Berkeley: University of California Press, 1979), 202.

11.   Scott Martelle, *Blood Passion: The Ludlow Massacre and Class War in the American West* (New Brunswick: Rutgers University Press, 2007), 20.

12.   Cited in Michael Nash, *Conflict and Accommodation: Coal Miners, Steel Workers, and Socialism 1890–1920* (Westport: Greenwood Press, 1982), 53.

13.   Ibid., 87.

14.   Ibid., 87–88.

15.   Ibid., chapters 3 and 4.

16.   Thomas Andrews, *Killing for Coal: America's Deadliest Labor War* (Cambridge: Harvard University Press, 2008), chapter 7. The outcomes of these strikes are thoroughly discussed in 242–3.

17.   For a discussion of this historical process in New Mexico, see Roxanne Dunbar-Ortiz, *Roots of Resistance: A History of Land Tenure in New Mexico* (Norman: University of Oklahoma Press, 2007).

18.   The Maxwell Grant had originally been parceled out and controlled by two wealthy Mexican landowners, Carlos Beaubien and Guadalupe Miranda. They had been granted the land by the Mexican government in 1841, after significant gains had been made in forcibly expelling the majority of the original Jicarilla Apache inhabitants. Despite formal ownership by the Mexican elites, hundreds of Mexican farmers and Jicarilla Apaches continued to live within its territorial boundaries, the former with reciprocal farming arrangements with the owners and the latter as scattered bands of resistors of dispossession. After the Mexican-American War, Miranda abandoned his land and relocated to Mexico, while Beaubien tried his luck within the US system. Adapting like so many other ricos of the period, he aimed for his daughters to marry Anglo Americans as a means of maintaining aristocratic family position and privilege through intermixing with the new rulers. One of his daughters, thirteen-year-old María de la Luz Beaubien, was married to Lucien Maxwell, who soon leveraged this relationship into taking total ownership of the massive grant. Maxwell, an adventurer,

filibusterer, and Indian slave-owner with high-level connections, had settled in the region with the intention of building a fortune in the aftermath of war. Intermarrying into the wealthy regional families was the quickest route into the dominant circles, but he also understood the nature of American capitalism, the US legal system, and the inevitable decline of the mexicanos. When Carlos Beaubien died, his land passed to his daughters, who under Mexican law were entitled to ownership. Since US law did not recognize female landownership under the feudal Anglo doctrine of "coverture," Maxwell convinced the remaining landowning female beneficiaries of the Beaubien family estate to sell cheaply to him before Anglo law disinherited them. Described in detail in María E. Montoya, *Translating Property: The Maxwell Land Grant and the Conflict over Land in the American West, 1840–1900* (Berkeley: University of California Press, 2002), chapter 2.

19. Ibid., 62.
20. Robert N. McLean and Charles A. Thompson, *Spanish and Mexican in Colorado: A Survey of the Spanish-Americans in the State of Colorado* (New York: Board of National Missions of the Presbyterian Church in the USA, 1924), 6.
21. The company cleared the lands, leveled much of the old pueblo structures, and fenced off its properties erasing the former land grants. The disruption of the existing economy compelled more farmers and ranchers and their offspring throughout the region to join the ranks of the expanding industrial workforce by the 1880s.
22. Rick J. Clyne, *Coal People: Life in Southern Colorado's Company Towns, 1890–1930* (Denver: Colorado Historical Society, 1999), 2.
23. Ibid., 50.
24. Primarily the line called the Denver and Río Grande Western. See Robert N. McLean and Charles A. Thompson, *Spanish and Mexican in Colorado: A Survey of the Spanish-Americans in the State of Colorado*, 26.
25. Rick J. Clyne, *Coal People: Life in Southern Colorado's Company Towns, 1890–1930*, 46.
26. See Jonathan Rees, *Representation and Rebellion: The Rockefeller Plan at the Colorado Fuel and Iron Company, 1914–1942* (Boulder: University Press of Colorado, 2010), 90; and Robert N. McLean and Charles A. Thompson, *Spanish and Mexican in Colorado: A Survey of the Spanish-Americans in the State of Colorado*, 2.
27. Robert N. McLean and Charles A. Thompson, *Spanish and Mexican in Colorado: A Survey of the Spanish-Americans in the State of Colorado*, 3–4.
28. F. Darrell Munsell, *From Redstone to Ludlow: John Cleveland Osgood's Struggle against the United Mine Workers* (Boulder: University Press of Colorado, 2009), 129–30.

Chapter 20: Mexican Miners in the Colorado Coal Wars

I.D. (initials only),"More Murdered Children! A Letter from the Front in Mexico," *International Socialist Review* 14, (June 1914): 731.
1. Stephen Burnett Brier, "'The Most Persistent Unionists': Class Formation and Class Conflict in the Fields and the Emergence of Interracial and Interethnic Unionism, 1880–1904," 231.
2. For class analysis of the Klan, including its fierce opposition to socialism and industrial unionism, see Nancy K. MacLean, *Behind the Mask of Chivalry: The Making of the Second Ku Klux Klan* (Oxford: Oxford University Press, 1995).
3. See John Tutino, ed., *Mexico and Mexicans in the Making of the United States* (Austin: University of Texas Press, 2012), 185.

4. Jonathon Rees, *Representation and Rebellion: The Rockefeller Plan at the Colorado Fuel and Iron Company, 1914–1942*, 93.

5. One example of Klan activities and collusion with mine operators is described in Rick J. Clyne, *Coal People: Life in Southern Colorado's Company Towns, 1890–1930* (Denver: Colorado Historical Society, 1999), 49.

6. Rick J. Clyne, *Coal People: Life in Southern Colorado's Company Towns, 1890–1930*, 9.

7. Thomas G. Andrews, *Killing for Coal: America's Deadliest Labor War* (Cambridge, Harvard University Press, 2008), 161.

8. Ibid., 138.

9. Ibid., 216.

10. Ibid., 172.

11. Ibid., 94.

12. According to Eric Homberger, many of the strikebreakers in 1903–1904 became the strikers in 1913–1914 after being integrated into the harsh realities of mining. See his book *John Reed* (New York: Manchester University Press: 1990), 75–76.

13. Rick J. Clyne, *Coal People: Life in Southern Colorado's Company Towns, 1890–1930*, 46.

14. Scott Martelle, *Blood Passion: The Ludlow Massacre and Class War in the American West*, 26.

15. Ibid., 26.

16. Thomas G. Andrews, *Killing for Coal: America's Deadliest Labor War*, 104.

17. Ibid, 85.

18. Ibid., 84–97.

19. Walter H. Fink, *The Ludlow Massacre* (Denver: Williamson-Haffner, 1914), 71.

20. Sarah Deutsch, *No Separate Refuge: Culture, Class, and Gender on an Anglo-Hispanic Frontier in the American Southwest, 1880–1940* (New York: Oxford University Press, 1987), 94.

21. Clark concluded, using racist logic, that it was because they preferred "a small income without work" to a "large income with work." See Victor S. Clark, "Mexican Labor in the United States," *Bulletin of the United States Bureau of Labor Statistics* 78 (1908): 516.

22. Scott Martelle, *Blood Passion: The Ludlow Massacre and Class War in the American West*, 95.

23. David Brundage, *The Making of Western Labor Radicalism: Denver's Organized Workers 1878–1905*, 42.

24. Thomas G. Andrews, *Killing for Coal: America's Deadliest Labor War*, 106.

25. For a discussion of the labor intersections within the mutualista movement, see Julie Leininger Pycior, *Democratic Renewal and the Mutual Aid Legacy of US Mexicans* (College Station: Texas A & M University Press, 2014), chapter 6.

26. Discussed in chapter 8. For a further overview, see Hector Aguilar Camín, *La Frontera Nómada: Sonora Y La Revolucíon Mexicana* (México: Siglo Viente Editores, S.A., 1981), 110–24.

27. Sarah M. Rudd, "Harmonizing Corrido and Union Song at the Ludlow Massacre," *Western Folklore* 61, no. 1 (Spring 2002): 22.

28. See Sarah Deutsch, *No Separate Refuge: Culture, Class, and Gender on an Anglo-Hispanic Frontier in the American Southwest, 1880–1940* (New York: Oxford University Press, 1987), 103; and Mark Walker, "The Ludlow Massacre: Class, Warfare, and Historical Memory in Southern Colorado," *Historical Archaeology* 37, no. 3, Remembering Landscapes of Conflict (2003): 68.

29. Priscilla Long, "The Women of the Colorado Fuel and Iron Strike, 1913–14," in *Women, Work and Protest: A Century of US Women's Labor History*, ed. Ruth Milkman

(New York: Routledge, 2013), 63.

30. Mark Walker, "The Ludlow Massacre: Class, Warfare, and Historical Memory in Southern Colorado," 68.

31. See Sarah Deutsch, *No Separate Refuge: Culture, Class, and Gender on an Anglo-Hispanic Frontier in the American Southwest, 1880–1940*, 104.

32. Commission on Industrial Relations, *Industrial Relations: Final Report and Testimony Submitted to Congress by the Commission on Industrial Relations Vol. VIII.* Washington: Government Printing Office, 1916, 7388–9.

33. John Reed, *The Education of John Reed: Selected Writings* (New York: International Publishers, 1955), 93.

34. Priscilla Long, "The Women of the Colorado Fuel and Iron Strike, 1913–14," 71.

35. Sarah Deutsch, *No Separate Refuge: Culture, Class, and Gender on an Anglo-Hispanic Frontier in the American Southwest, 1880–1940*, 104.

36. "Confessions of Strikers," *Herald Democrat* (Leadville, Colorado), November 11, 1913; 1.

37. Stephen Burnett Brier, "'The Most Persistent Unionists': Class Formation and Class Conflict in the Fields and the Emergence of Interracial and Interethnic Unionism, 1880–1904," 253–4.

38. Cited in Sarah M. Rudd, "Harmonizing Corrido and Union Song at the Ludlow Massacre" *Western Folklore* 61, no. 1 (Spring 2002): 24.

39. Ibid., 31.

40. Mark Walker, "The Ludlow Massacre: Class, Warfare, and Historical Memory in Southern Colorado," 68.

41. F. Darrell Munsell, *From Redstone to Ludlow: John Cleveland Osgood's Struggle against the United Mine Workers*, 217.

42. Mentioned in a local paper. See "War Breaks out Anew," *Montrose Daily Press*, April 27, 1914; 1.

43. Priscilla Long, "The Women of the Colorado Fuel and Iron Strike, 1913–14," 76.

44. F. Darrell Munsell, *From Redstone to Ludlow: John Cleveland Osgood's Struggle against the United Mine Workers*, 220.

45. John Reed, *The Education of John Reed: Selected Writings*, 113.

46. Testimony. Senate Documents, volume 26, Sixty-Fourth Congress, 1st Session, December 6, 1915–September 8, 1916. Washington: Government Printing Office, 1916. 7386.

47. Sarah Deutsch, *No Separate Refuge: Culture, Class, and Gender on an Anglo-Hispanic Frontier in the American Southwest, 1880–1940*, 105.

48. For instance, a local newspaper at the time points out that charges were filed but never pursued. "Ludlow Fire Horror," *Blue Valley Times* (Dillon, Colorado) May 9, 1914; 6.

49. Walter H. Fink, *The Ludlow Massacre*, 91.

50. Cited in a union-produced account of the events. Walter H. Fink, *The Ludlow Massacre*, 16.

51. John Reed, *The Education of John Reed: Selected Writings* (New York: International Publishers, 1955), 118.

52. Cited in Walter H. Fink, *The Ludlow Massacre*, 58.

53. Cited in an anti-strike pamphlet distributed on behalf of the companies titled, "Facts Concerning the Struggle in Colorado for Industrial Freedom." Issued by the Coal Mine Managers, J. F. Welborn and John C. Osgood, 12.

54. Vincent C. de Baca, ed., *La Gente: Hispano History and Life in Colorado* (Denver: Colorado Historical Society, 1998), 97.

55. Thomas, Andrews, *Killing for Coal: America's Deadliest Labor War*, 11–13.

56. Ibid., 14.

57. Price V. Fishback, *Soft Coal, Hard Choices: The Economic Welfare of Bituminous Coal Miners,1890–1930* (New York: Oxford University Press, 1992), 80–1.

58. Ibid., 199.

59. Ibid., 94.

60. Examples of welfare capitalism include improved housing, health care, recreational facilities, better schools, and the hiring of welfare workers and staff. See Price V. Fishback, *Soft Coal, Hard Choices: The Economic Welfare of Bituminous Coal Miners, 1890–1930*, 161. For a detailed description of the company union, see Jonathan Rees, *Representation and Rebellion: The Rockefeller Plan at the Colorado Fuel and Iron Company, 1914–1942*.

Chapter 21: The State, Mexican Immigration, and Labor Control

Cited in Raul E. Fernández and Gilbert G. González, *A Century of Chicano History: Empire, Nations and Migration* (New York: Routledge, 2003), 124.

1. Rhonda Levine, *Class Struggle and the New Deal: Industrial Labor, Industrial Capital, and the State* (Lawrence: University of Kansas Press, 1988), 49.

2. James M. Gregory, *American Exodus: The Dust Bowl Migration and Okie Culture in California*, Oxford: Oxford University Press, 1991), 6.

3. Kenneth Finegold and Theda Skocpol, *State and Party in America's New Deal* (Madison: University of Wisconsin Press, 1995), 11.

4. Art Preis, *Labor's Giant Step: The First Twenty Years of the CIO: 1936–55* (New York: Pathfinder Press, 1994), 17.

5. Strike information taken from Stuart Marshall Jamieson, *Labor Unionism in Agriculture, Bulletin #836*, 30.

6. Stuart Marshall Jamieson, *Labor Unionism in Agriculture, Bulletin #836*, 7.

7. See Carey McWilliams, *Factories in the Field: The Story of Migratory Farm Labor in California* (Berkeley: University of California Press, 1999), chapter 14.

8. For instance, the first group of entrepreneurs seeking to turn the eastern border region of southern California into a farming oasis by harnessing the southern delta of the Colorado River for a growing population of settlers formed the California Development Company in 1896. Their efforts to develop irrigation infrastructure through the formation of water distribution companies throughout the region failed due to incompetence. By 1911, the operation had failed and they went bankrupt. The state government of California took over the task of developing adequate water distribution systems for growers with the passage of the California Irrigation District Act, which produced the Imperial County–administered Imperial Irrigation District. This publicly funded agency came to acquire and administer all of the CDC's water companies in the region and was empowered to issue bonds, raise taxes, conduct surveys, employ eminent domain, and to buy out private competitors. Finally, in 1928, Congress passed the Boulder Dam Project Act, which publicly funded the construction of the Hoover Dam, the Imperial Dam, and the All-American Canal to procure the water needs for growers in the valley for generations to come. As historian Benny J. Andrés concluded: "Private enterprise had failed, and the settlers turned to public ownership of the water system, creating the Imperial Irrigation District in 1911. The IID's improbable success . . . was due to shrewd, tenacious leaders, public

ownership of the water system, governmental assistance, a media blitz promoting irrigated agriculture and the subjugation of nature . . . the IID was instrumental in persuading Congress to pass the Boulder Canyon Project Act . . . [which] quenched the thirst of Imperial Valley's agribusiness empire." A detailed description of the failure is documented in Benny J. Andrés, Jr., *Power and Control in the Imperial Valley: Nature, Agribusiness and Workers on the California Borderland, 1900–1940* (College Station: Texas University Press, 2015), chapter 1. Quote is on 38–39.

9.   In 1925, for instance, the United States Department of Agriculture helped to fund cotton operation expansion through the establishment of a regional office in Kern County. This office created a seed-breeding station, which developed and produced a cotton seed strain deemed most productive, uniform, and profitable. In response, the California state government, which was fervently pro-grower, passed the One-Variety Law banning all other cotton varieties except the Alcala strand. The law established a grower-led governing board that held a monopoly over seed distribution in the region so that all growers in cotton production, small and large, had to adapt the seed. Furthermore, the largest growers operated the cotton gins and denied access to non-Alcala cotton. This aided in the consolidation of large cotton growers and ginners across six counties: Fresno, Kern, Kings, Madera, Merced, and Tulare. The One-Variety Law of 1925 stayed in place for fifty years, leading to the consolidation of vast cotton farms that produced 95 percent of all cotton production in California (which is second in the nation) by the time the law was changed in 1978. See John H. Constantine, Julian M. Alston, and Vincent H Smith, "Economic Impacts of the California One-Variety Cotton Law," *The Journal of Political Economy* 102, no. 5 (October 1994): 953.

10. Benny J. Andrés, Jr., *Power and Control in the Imperial Valley: Nature, Agribusiness and Workers on the California Borderland, 1900–1940*, 47.

11. For an example of this, see Frank Barajas, "Resistance, Radicalism, and Repression on the Oxnard Plain: The Social Context of the Betabelero Strike of 1933," *The Western Historical Quarterly* 35, no. 1 (Spring 2004): 51.

12. For example, one study conducted at the height of a 1933 strike wave produced the conclusion that ethnic unionism was a front for communism and posed a grave threat to agriculture. See Don Mitchell, *The Lie of the Land: Migrant Workers and the California Landscape* (Minneapolis: University of Minnesota Press, 1996), 114.

13. Devra Weber, *Dark Sweat, White Gold: California Farm Workers, Cotton, and the New Deal* (Berkeley: University of California Press, 1994), 28.

14. Ibid., 30.

15. Don Mitchell, *The Lie of the Land: Migrant Workers and the California Landscape*, 116.

16. Hearings Before the Committee on Labor, House of Representatives, March–April 1935, 346.

17. Donald Henderson, "The Rural Masses and the Work of Our Party," *The Communist*, September 1935; 873.

18. Juan F. Perea, "The Echoes of Slavery: Recognizing the Racist Origins of the Agricultural and Domestic Worker Exclusion from the National Labor Relations Act," *Ohio State Law Journal* 72 no. 1, (2011): 104.

19. State support and class consciousness in the face of labor revolt led to higher levels of collaboration and integration into what became known as "agribusiness." Over the course of the 1920s and 1930s, they integrated production, pooled and controlled resources, and vertically integrated labor procurement, shipping, marketing, and financing.

20. Mark Reisler, *By the Sweat of Their Brow: Mexican Immigrant Labor in the United States, 1900–1940* (Westport: Greenwood Press, 1976), 30–31.

21. Ibid., 31–34.

22. Natalia Molina, "'In a Race All Their Own': The Quest to Make Mexicans Ineligible for US Citizenship," *Pacific Historical Review* 79, no. 2 (May 2010): 175.

23. Mexicans were excluded from quotas against consistent attempts by racial exclusionists throughout the 1920s. Benny J. Andrés Jr., *Power and Control in the Imperial Valley: Nature, Agribusiness and Workers on the California Borderland, 1900–1940*, 92.

24. Francisco E. Balderrama and Raymond Rodríguez, *Decade of Betrayal: Mexican Repatriation in the 1930s* (Albuquerque: University of New Mexico Press, 1995), 9.

25. Ibid.

26. "Hire American Fruit Pickers: County Urges," *The San Bernardino County Sun*, September 6, 1933; 11.

27. Francisco E. Balderrama and Raymond Rodríguez, *Decade of Betrayal: Mexican Repatriation in the 1930s*, 59.

28. Donald L. Zelman, "Mexican Migrants and Relief in Depression California," *Journal of Mexican American History* V (1975): 7.

29. Stuart Marshall Jamieson, *Labor Unionism in Agriculture, Bulletin #836*, 118.

30. Donald L. Zelman, "Mexican Migrants and Relief in Depression California," 10.

31. Carlos M. Larralde, "El Congreso in San Diego: An Endeavor for Civil Rights," *Journal of San Diego History* 50, no. 1–2 (Winter/Spring 2004): 19.

32. Ibid.

33. Sam Kushner, *Long Road to Delano* (New York: International Publishers, 1975), 75.

34. Benny J. Andrés, Jr., *Power and Control in the Imperial Valley: Nature, Agribusiness and Workers on the California Borderland, 1900–1940*, 83.

35. Devra Weber, *Dark Sweat, White Gold*, 52.

36. Ibid., 34.

37. Ramón D. Chacón, "Labor Unrest and Industrialized Agriculture in California: The Case of the 1933 San Joaquin Valley Cotton Strike," *Social Science Quarterly* 65, no. 2 (June 1984): 345.

38. Ibid., 347.

39. Due to the dependence on Mexican labor, especially as farmworkers established families, the growers were forced to begin building family housing. See Gilbert G. González, *Labor and Community: Mexican Citrus Worker Villages in a Southern California County, 1900–1950*, chapter 1.

40. Donald L. Zelman, "Mexican Migrants and Relief in Depression California," *Journal of Mexican American History* V (1975): 2.

41. Ibid., 3.

42. Ibid., 5.

43. Devra Weber, *Dark Sweat, White Gold*, 49.

44. Ibid., 68.

45. Filipino workers began to enter into California in the early 1920s, while their country remained an occupied colony of the United States. Under colonial rule, US capitalist investors were able to take command of the economy, privatize and accumulate large tracts of land, and reorient domestic food production toward export markets. As historian Erika Lee explains, "American companies and owners bought farmland to use for export crops, including sugar, and by the twentieth century the Philippines was

exporting so many of its agricultural products and natural resources that it could no longer feed itself. Even basic necessities ... had to be imported, and economic policies that kept the Philippines an unindustrialized export economy led to dislocation and inequalities ... Tenancy, landlessness, poverty, and migration followed." Erika Lee, *The Making of Asian America: A History* (New York: Simon & Schuster, 2015), 176. Furthermore, between 1906 and 1920, the Hawaiian Sugar Planters' Association brought over 33,000 Filipinos to the Hawaiian Islands to work in sugar plantations, with many, like the Japanese before them, moving into California. Filipinos were considered US nationals during the period of colonial occupation, and therefore able to enter the country freely after the passage of the Immigration Act of 1917. This act excluded Filipinos from the provisions barring Asian migration. Filipino recruitment into California agriculture became an expedient for growers by the late 1920s, as the impending deportation of Mexicans presented growers with potential labor shortage. Despite their access, Filipinos encountered a rigidly structured and enforced racial labor system, in which they were expected to work, not integrate into white society, and definitely not join unions. Racially segregated communities referred to as "Little Manilas" formed on the social margins in Los Angeles, Stockton, and San Francisco. They were proscribed in California from intermarrying with whites, were racially segregated in the cities, and were subjected to episodic spasms of racial violence in the farming towns. Racial violence against Filipinos amounted to at least thirty documented riots, assaults, firebombings, and other incidents by white mobs between 1929 and 1930. The concerted violence developed in the aftermath of increased Filipino labor agitation. See Maria Tria Kerkvliet, "Pablo Manlapit's Fight for Justice," *Social Process in Hawaii* 33 (1991): 154; and Mae Ngai, *Impossible Subjects: Illegal Aliens and the Making of Modern California* (Princeton: Princeton University Press, 2004), 108.

46. For example, many migratory Filipinos entered first to Hawaii, where they formed part of the ranks of the sugar plantation workforce, purposefully constructed as a polyglot of different nationalities to prevent unionization. When Filipino workers moved to the forefront of labor organizing in the early 1920s, they became the target of a widespread campaign by growers (the Hawaiian Sugar Planters Association, HSPA) to smash their efforts, creating the template for union suppression that would be replicated in California a decade later.

   Planters used information collected by spies to blacklist union supporters, often barring them from working or living on plantation property. Labor organizers faced relentless persecution from territorial authorities, who enacted a series of anti-union measures, such as criminal syndicalism statutes and anti-picketing ordinances, making it difficult to carry out organizing campaigns. In addition, the HSPA hired private mercenaries to assail strikers when the legal system proved inadequate. A prolonged multi-island strike in 1924 prompted a violent response from authorities culminating in the infamous Hanapepe massacre on the island of Kauai, where police sharpshooters killed sixteen Filipino strikers when they refused orders to disperse.

47. State of California, Department of Industrial Relations, Special Bulletin no. 3: Facts About Filipino Immigration into California. San Francisco, 1930, 60–61.

48. Mae Ngai, *Impossible Subjects: Illegal Aliens and the Making of Modern California* (Princeton: Princeton University Press, 2004), 109. In timeless fashion, they were publicly derided as prone to violence and disease, lustful for white women, and unwilling or unable to assimilate. For example, the president of the University of

California Berkeley, David T. Barrows, testified before a House of Representatives Committee on Immigration and Naturalization in 1930 that white disdain and violence against Filipinos was "primarily due to aroused sexual passion and a natural tendency for vice and crime." See Howard De Witt, *Violence in the Fields: California Filipino Farm Labor Unionization During the Great Depression* (Saratoga: Century Twenty One Publishing, 1980), 9.

49. For instance, at the 1927 Convention of the California State Federation of Labor, the body passed a resolution calling for Filipino exclusion, with other Pacific Coast states following suit. The Washington State Federation of Labor adopted a resolution condemning Filipinos, and even justifying race riots against them on the merit of the supposed threat they posed: "First, because they represent cheap and irresponsible labor of a type that cannot be assimilated, and as such they threaten American standards of wages and living conditions. Second, because they have given serious offense to communities in which they have congregated because of their moral conduct, with the result that in one community in Washington the citizens became so aroused that they organized and forcibly evicted the Filipinos. We feel sure that it is not good for labor nor for American institutions and standards to permit the free and unrestricted influx of these people, and we endorse the position of the California State Federation of Labor in asking for their exclusion, and instruct the officers of this Federation to assist in securing the legislation necessary to accomplish this end." Paul Scharrenberg, "The Philippine Problem: Attitude of American Labor Toward Filipino Immigration and Philippine Independence," *Pacific Affairs* 2, no. 2 (February 1929): 52.

50. "Canneries Try to Beat Down Women's Wages," *Western Worker*, June 15, 1932; 2.

Chapter 22: Communists in the California Fields

Benny J. Andrés, Jr., *Power and Control in the Imperial Valley: Nature, Agribusiness and Workers on the California Borderland, 1900–1940* (College Station: Texas A&M University Press, 2015), 127.

1. The Stalinist periodization was declared post hoc as the following: 1) the First Period was that of the revolutionary breakdown of capitalism during the First World War, in which a revolutionary upsurge produced the Bolshevik Revolution but several decisive defeats for the international working class; 2) the Second Period, which witnessed the stabilization, consolidation, and expansion of capitalism during the 1920s. For a thorough discussion of the Communist International, and its relationship to the Communist Party of the US, see Jacob A. Zumoff, *The Communist International and US Communism, 1919–1929,* (Chicago: Haymarket, 2014).

2. For many former Wobblies that joined or aligned with the Communist Party, this was reminiscent of IWW policy, especially when the national party trained its efforts on the agricultural proletariat. For instance, prominent party leaders previously in the IWW included Elizabeth Gurley Flynn, Big Bill Haywood, Lucy Gonzalez Parsons, William Z. Foster, James Cannon, and others joined, or, in the case of Lucy Gonzalez Parsons, supported the party.

3. This occurred with an earlier Comintern directive that was compatible with the Third Period turn. In 1925 they encouraged the party to "bore from within" but also encouraged them to set up unions where none existed.

4. Bert Cochran, *Labor and Communism: The Conflict That Shaped American Unions* (Princeton: Princeton University Press, 1977), 31.

5. See William Z. Foster, "The Principles and Program of the Trade Union Educational League," *The Labor Herald* (Chicago), March 1922. Reprinted as a four-page leaflet by TUEL. Available online at https://www.marxists.org/archive/foster/1922/principles.htm.

6. While early TUUL history organizing women and African Americans is mixed, some gains were made. This perhaps contributed to California and Texas Communists who were organizing in agriculture to study more closely the Mexican condition as part of TUUL organizing. For a description of early efforts to organize African American and women workers, see Edward P. Johanningsmeier, "The Trade Union Unity League: American Communists and the Transition to Industrial Unionism: 1928–1934," *Labor History* 42, no. 2 (2001): 173–6.

7. Edward P. Johanningsmeier, "The Trade Union Unity League: American Communists and the Transition to Industrial Unionism: 1928–1934," 176.

8. The breadth and depth of organizational strength was uneven and in most cases fragile or marginal. Nevertheless, the organization made some significant inroads. See Victor G. Devinatz, "A Reevaluation of the Trade Union Unity League, 1929–1934," *Science & Society* 71, no. 1 (January 2007): 42.

9. For a discussion of the strike see Zaragosa Vargas, *Labor Rights are Civil Rights: Mexican-American Workers in Twentieth-Century America* (Princeton: Princeton University Press, 2008), 73.

10. Sam Kushner, *Long Road to Delano* (New York: International Publishers, 1975), 57.

11. See Dennis Nodín Valdés, "Settlers, Sojourners, and Proletarians: Social Formation in the Great Plains Sugar Beet Industry, 1890–1940," *Great Plains Quarterly*, paper 418, 119; and F. Arturo Rosales, *Testimonio: A Documentary History of the Mexican American Struggle for Civil Rights* (Houston: Arte Publico Press, 2000), 246.

12. Harrison George, "For a Real Fight on Imperialism," *Labor Unity,* December 1928; 10.

13. Cletus Daniel, *Bitter Harvest: A History of California Farmworkers, 1871–1941* (Ithaca: Cornell University Press, 1981), 67.

14. Quoted from Benny J. Andrés, Jr., *Power and Control in the Imperial Valley: Nature, Agribusiness and Workers on the California Borderland, 1900–1940,* 104.

15. For example, even though land distribution was written into the Mexican Constitution of 1917 as Article 27, it was largely ignored after the revolution, and when done it was limited and not designed to solve the rampant and persistent landlessness. Rather, "property was redistributed predominantly for political reasons: namely, to hasten state formation by placating campesino discontent, placating the countryside, and establishing federal-regional alliances." John J. Dwyer, *The Agrarian Dispute: The Expropriation of American-Owned Rural Land in Post-Revolutionary Mexico* (Durham: Duke University Press, 2008), 19–20.

16. Quoted in Benny J. Andrés, Jr., *Power and Control in the Imperial Valley: Nature, Agribusiness and Workers on the California Borderland, 1900–1940,* 131.

17. The ardently anti-union *Los Angeles Times* claimed that the strike effort failed after its "red" leaders were arrested. See "Arrests Break up Strike of Melon Pickers," May 27, 1922; 16.

18. See "Strike Perils Cantaloupes in Valley," *Santa Ana Register,* May 25, 1922; 1; and Arch W. Anderson, "Pacific-Southwest Review," *Los Angeles Times* May 8, 1922; 3.

19. They chose September 16, Mexican Independence Day, to attempt their rally for action. See "Report Mexicans as Forming Union," *Los Angeles Times,* September 16, 1922; 8.

20. Benny J. Andrés, Jr., *Power and Control in the Imperial Valley: Nature, Agribusiness and Workers on the California Borderland, 1900–1940*, 113.

21. While labor actions likely occurred, there were no official attempts to organize farmworkers into unions during this period. Without organization, any actions were likely unknown or ignored by the press. In 1922 the American Federation of Labor chartered a short-lived international union under the name National Agricultural Workers Union, but there was no attempt made to organize farmworkers or affiliate any farmworker groups, and the charter was withdrawn shortly thereafter. The brutal repression of the Wobblies and other Socialists' efforts to support migrant farmworkers shifted the balance of labor power back in the growers' direction for several years.

22. See Julia Young, *Mexican Exodus: Emigrants, Exiles, and Refugees of the Cristero War* (New York: Oxford University Press, 2015), 5–10.

23. Paul S. Taylor, "Migratory Agricultural Workers on the Pacific Coast," *American Sociological Review* 3, no. 2 (April 1938): 229–31.

24. Douglas Monroy, *Rebirth: Mexican Los Angeles from the Great Migration to the Great Depression* (Berkeley: University of California Press, 1999), 223.

25. *Mexicans in California: Report of Governor C. C. Young's Mexican Fact-Finding Committee*, State of California, San Francisco, 1930, 125–6.

26. Charles Wollenberg, "Huelga, 1928 Style: The Imperial Valley Cantaloupe Workers' Strike," *Pacific Historical Review* 38, no. 1 (February 1969): 47.

27. Don Mitchell, *The Lie of the Land: Migrant Workers and the California Landscape* (Minneapolis: University of Minnesota Press, 1996), 119.

28. One of the major complaints made by Mexican farmworkers, cited in *Mexicans in California: Report of Governor C. C. Young's Mexican Fact-Finding Committee*, State of California, San Francisco, 1930, 130–1.

29. Cited in Gilbert González, "Company Unions, the Mexican Consulate, and the Imperial Valley Agricultural Strikes, 1928–1934," *The Western Historical Quarterly* 27, no. 1 (Spring 1996): 57.

30. "News Of Southern Counties: Melon Pickers Launch Strike," *Los Angeles Times*, May 9, 1928; A–10.

31. "Officers Curb Labor Leaders," *Los Angeles Times*, May 10, 1928; A–10.

32. After originally arresting forty-eight, two more were subsequently arrested the following day. See "Mexican Agitators Arrested," *Los Angeles Times*, May 11, 1928; A–10.

33. While no record can be found for the outcome of his detention, it is likely that Rio and the others were deported from the region.

34. "Strike in Melon Area is Failure," *Los Angeles Times*, May 12, 1928; A–10.

35. Stuart Marshall Jamieson, *Labor Unionism in Agriculture, Bulletin #836*, 77.

36. John Barnett, "Thesis on the Agrarian Question Adopted by the Second Congress of the Communist International," *The Communist* 10, no. 11 (December 1931): 1047.

37. Merle Weiner, "Cheap Food, Cheap Labor: California Agriculture in the 1930s," *Insurgent Sociologist* 8, no. 2 (Fall 1978): 185.

38. Howard DeWitt, *Violence in the Fields: California Filipino Farm Labor Unionization During the Great Depression* (Saratoga: Century Twenty One Publishing, 1980), 51–52.

39. Charles Wollenberg, "Race and Class in Rural California: The El Monte Berry Strike of 1933," *California Historical Quarterly* 51, no. 2 (Summer 1972): 157.

40. Cletus Daniel, *Bitter Harvest, a History of California Farmworkers, 1870–1941* (Berkeley:

University of California Press, 1981), 113.

41. Kathryn Olmsted, *Right Out of California: The 1930s and the Big Business Roots of Modern Conservatism* (New York: New Press, 2015), 111.

42. Cletus Daniel, *Bitter Harvest, a History of California Farmworkers, 1870–1941*, 114.

43. Eldridge Foster Dowell, *A History of Criminal Syndicalism Legislation in the United States* (Baltimore: Johns Hopkins Press, 1939), 46–47.

44. For a full discussion of the Red Squad phenomenon, see Frank Donner, *Protectors of Privilege: Red Squads and Police Repression in Urban America* (Berkeley: University of California Press, 1990).

45. "Congressmen End Red Quiz," *Los Angeles Times,* October 10, 1930; A–1.

46. "Deadlock on Wages at End," *Los Angeles Times,* March 1, 1930; 4.

47. Cited in Gilbert González, "Company Unions, the Mexican Consulate, and the Imperial Valley Agricultural Strikes, 1928–1934," *The Western Historical Quarterly* 27, no. 1 (Spring 1996): 58–59.

48. See "Asserted Reds Held for Trial," *Los Angeles Times,* April 17, 1930; 14.

49. This information was contained in a pamphlet written by Frank Spector while he was incarcerated in San Quentin Prison. "Story of the Imperial Valley," International Labor Defense Pamphlet #3, 1931, 6.

50. Devra Anne Weber, "The Organizing of Mexican Agricultural Workers: Imperial Valley, and Los Angeles, 1928–34, an Oral History Approach," *Aztlán,* 3, no. 2 (1972): 320.

51. For example, see "Congressmen End Red Quiz," *Los Angeles Times,* October 19, 1930; 1.

52. Gilbert González, "Company Unions, the Mexican Consulate, and the Imperial Valley Agricultural Strikes, 1928–1934," 64.

53. Convention document cited verbatim in "Investigation of Communist Propaganda: Hearings before a Special Committee to Investigate the Communist Activities in the United States, Part V, Volume Number One," House of Representatives, Seventy First Congress. Washington: US Government Printing Office, 1930, 55.

54. For a full discussion of how immigration policy came to exclude radicals, see Kristofer Allerfeldt and Jeremy Black, *Race, Radicalism, Religion, and Restriction: Immigration in the Pacific Northwest, 1890–1924* (Westport: Praeger, 2003), chapter 3.

55. "Investigation of Communist Propaganda: Hearings before a Special Committee to Investigate the Communist Activities in the United States, Part V, Volume Number Two." House of Representatives, Seventy-First Congress. Washington, US Government Printing Office, 1930, 4.

56. Convention document cited verbatim in "Investigation of Communist Propaganda: Hearings before a Special Committee to Investigate the Communist Activities in the United States, Part V, Volume Number One." House of Representatives, Seventy-First Congress. Washington, US Government Printing Office, 1930, 55.

Chapter 23: The CAWIU and the Strike Wave of 1933

Devra Weber, *Dark Sweat, White Gold: California Farm Workers, Cotton, and the New Deal* (Berkeley: University of California Press, 1994), 80.

1. "The Revolutionary Movement in the Colonies," Sixth World Congress of the Communist International, 1928, 6. Box 22, Folder 27 American Left Ephemera Collection, 1894–2008, AIS.2007.11, Archives Service Center, University of Pittsburgh.

2. Ibid., 14–15.

3.   "The Platform of the Class Struggle," National Platform of the Workers (Communist) Party, 1928, 53–54. Box 3, Folder 1, American Left Ephemera Collection, 1894–2008, AIS.2007.11, Archives Service Center, University of Pittsburgh.

4.   *Daily Worker,* July 31, 1930; 6.

5.   See Francisco E. Balderrama and Raymond Rodríguez, *Decade of Betrayal: Mexican Repatriation in the 1930s* (Albuquerque: University of New Mexico Press, 1995), 95–96.

6.   Concurrent with the AFL's racist prohibitions, the Communist Party was making its first international links to Filipinos, with their participation in the Pan-Pacific Trade Union Congress (PPTC). Under Comintern guidance, the PPTC was an effort to bring together Communist-aligned union leaders within Pacific nations, including representatives from China, Japan, the Philippines, New Zealand, Australia, and the US. The purpose of PPTC congress was to build solidarity, and to develop and integrate a set of regional objectives and principles into labor work. At the 1928 conference, these included the struggle against war, colonial independence, building peasant-worker organizations, international trade union unity, and the defense of immigrants. See "Pan Pacific Trade Union Congress Meets in Vladivostok in August," *Labor Unity,* December 28, 1929; 8.

7.   Stuart Marshall Jamieson, *Labor Unionism in Agriculture, Bulletin #836,* 84.

8.   Aside from the Mexican CUOM, for instance, Filipinos also formed their own unions. As early as 1928, the first-known labor organization was created in the San Joaquin Valley, known as the Sons of the Farm, which functioned as a fraternal order that linked work crews who recognized the need for larger coordinated organization as a counterweight to the growers. In this transition, some contractors began to get in front of the most militant work crews and convert their operations into the formation of unions. By 1935, there were seven distinct Filipino agricultural unions in operation. After experiencing neglect or rejection by the AFL, these union formations began in earnest to operate in the fields. The most significant of these efforts was the creation of the Filipino Labor Union (FLU) in 1933, after organizing efforts produced a membership of 4,000 within one year. The FLU led its first strike of lettuce workers in Salinas, California, in August 1933. Seven hundred Filipinos walked off the job, about 40 percent of the mixed workforce, to call for higher wages. When the growers brought in Mexicans, East Indians, and Asian workers to replace them, the strike quickly folded. The failure of the strike produced a violent anti-Filipino reaction, with growers and their allies staging anti-Filipino protests and attacks in several towns. See Howard DeWitt, "The Filipino Labor Union: The Salinas lettuce Strike of 1934," *Amerasia* 5, no. 2 (1978): 4–5.

9.   Don Mitchell, *The Lie of the Land: Migrant Workers and the California Landscape* (Minneapolis, University of Minnesota Press, 1996), 127–8.

10. Devra Weber, *Dark Sweat, White Gold: California Farmworkers, Cotton, and the New Deal* (Berkeley: University of California Press, 1994), 205.

11. Donald Friend Fearis, "The California Farm Worker: 1930–1942" (dissertation, History, Cornell University, 1955), 97.

12. Dorothy Ray Healy and Maurice Isserman, *California Red: A Life in the American Communist Party* (Chicago: University of Illinois Press, 1993), 59.

13. "Declarations of Candidacy: Including Statements of Qualifications for Candidates." General Election Voter Guide, San Francisco, General Municipal Election, November 7, 1933, 10.

14. "SF Red Candidates Lead Jobless in Hunger March," *Western Worker*, November 6, 1933; 1.

15. Dorothy Ray Healy and Maurice Isserman, *California Red: A Life in the American Communist Party*, 45–46.

16. Devra Weber, *Dark Sweat, White Gold: California Farmworkers, Cotton, and the New Deal*, 87; 262n.

17. Kathryn S. Olmsted, *Right Out of California: The 1930s and the Big Business Roots of Modern Conservatism* (New York: New Press, 2015), 79.

18. Donald Friend Fearis, "The California Farm Worker: 1930–1942," 87.

19. Stuart Marshall Jamieson, *Labor Unionism in Agriculture, Bulletin #836*, 16.

20. Sidney Sufrin, "Labor Organization in Agricultural America, 1930–35," *American Journal of Sociology* 43, no. 4 (January 1938): 552.

21. Merle Weiner, "Cheap Food, Cheap Labor: California Agriculture in the 1930s," *Insurgent Sociologist* 8, no. 2 (Fall 1978): 185.

22. Benny J. Andrés, Jr., *Power and Control in the Imperial Valley: Nature, Agribusiness and Workers on the California Borderland, 1900–1940*, 142.

23. Hearings Before the Committee on Labor, House of Representatives, March–April 1935, 345.

24. Ibid.

25. Don Mitchell, *The Lie of the Land: Migrant Workers and the California Landscape*, 134.

26. Devra Anne Weber, "The Organizing of Mexican Agricultural Workers: Imperial Valley, and Los Angeles, 1928–34, an Oral History Approach," *Aztlán* 3, no. 2 (1972): 324.

27. Frank Barajas, "Resistance, Radicalism, and Repression on the Oxnard Plain: The Social Context of the Betabelero Strike of 1933," *The Western Historical Quarterly* 35, no. 1 (Spring 2004): 39.

28. "Resolutions and Decisions of the First International Congress of Revolutionary Trade and Industrial Unions." *Voice of Labor,* American Labor Union Educational Society, November 1921; 82.

29. Karl G. Yoneda, *Ganbatte: Sixty-Year Struggle of a Kibei Worker* (Los Angeles: University of California, Los Angeles, Asian American Studies Center, 1983), 37.

30. Daniel J. Leab, "'United We Eat': The Creation and Organization of the Unemployed Councils in 1930," *Labor History* 8, no. 3 (1967): 306–7.

31. "Farm Strikers to Start Drive," *Los Angeles Times*, June 25, 1933; 14.

32. Ronald López, "The El Monte Berry Strike of 1933," *Aztlán* (1970): 104.

33. Charles Wollenberg, "Race and Class in Rural California: The El Monte Berry Strike of 1933," *California Historical Quarterly* 51, no. 2 (Summer 1972): 158.

34. Melquiades Fernandez, "Bittersweet Fruit: El Monte's Berry Strike of 1933," KCET, April 7, 2015. Available online at http://www.kcet.org/socal/departures/columns/east-of-east/el-monte-berry-strike-of-1933.html.

35. "Raspberry and Potato Pickers Answer Union Call," *Western Worker*, San Francisco, June 12, 1933; 1.

36. Gene Gordon, "Impressions of the Strike in San Gabriel Valley," *Western Worker*, June 19, 1933; 2.

37. "El Monte Berry Crop Threatened By Strike," *Los Angeles Times*, June 7, 1933; A16.

38. Charles Wollenberg, "Race and Class in Rural California: The El Monte Berry Strike of 1933," 161.

39. Gilbert G. González, "The 1933 Los Angeles County Farm Workers Strike," *New Political Science* 20, no. 4 (1998): 444.

40. See Gilbert González, *Mexican Consuls and Labor Organizing: Imperial Politics in the American* (Austin: University of Texas Press, 1999), chapters 2 and 3.

41. Gilbert González, "The 1933 Los Angeles County Farm Workers Strike," *New Political Science* 20, no. 4 (1998): 444.

42. "Action To End Strike Begun," *Los Angeles Times*, July 1, 1933; A12.

43. "Berry Strike gets Violent," *Los Angeles Times*, June 10, 1933; A6.

44. Lawrence Ross, "Lessons from the Southern California Strike," *Western Worker*, August 7, 1933; 3.

45. "Officers Watch Picketing Army," *Los Angeles Times*, June 30, 1933; 8.

46. Gilbert González, "The 1933 Los Angeles County Farm Workers Strike," *New Political Science* 20, no. 4 (1998): 455–6.

47. Charles Wollenberg, "Race and Class in Rural California: The El Monte Berry Strike of 1933," 163.

48. Ramón D. Chacón, "Labor Unrest and Industrialized Agriculture in California: The Case of the 1933 San Joaquin Valley Cotton Strike," *Social Science Quarterly* 65, no. 2 (June 1984): 340.

49. Ibid., 345.

50. Donald Friend Fearis, "The California Farm Worker: 1930–1942," 99.

51. Ramón D. Chacón, "Labor Unrest and Industrialized Agriculture in California: The Case of the 1933 San Joaquin Valley Cotton Strike," 350.

52. Stuart Marshall Jamieson, *Labor Unionism in Agriculture, Bulletin #836*, 101.

53. "Cotton Pickers Prepare to Strike," *Western Worker*, September 25, 1933.

54. Raymond Barry, *A Documentary History of Migratory Farm Labor in California*, "The California Cotton Pickers Strike–1933," Federal Writers' Project, Oakland, California, 1938, 2. Available online at http://content.cdlib. org/view?docId=hb88700929;NAAN=13030&doc.view=frames&chunk. id=div00022&toc.depth=1&toc.id=div00022&brand=calisphere.

55. Stuart Marshall Jamieson, *Labor Unionism in Agriculture, Bulletin #836*, 101.

56. Judith Gannon, "California Odyssey: The 1930s Migration to the Southern San Joaquin Valley, Oral History Program. Interview with Lillie Ruth Ann Counts Dunn," Bakersfield California, 1981, 9.

57. Devra Weber, *Dark Sweat, White Gold: California Farmworkers, Cotton, and the New Deal* (Berkeley: University of California Press, 1994), 10.

58. Dorothy Rae Healy claims that the party organizers in the field largely developed their own methods based on adaptation to experiences and actual conditions on the ground, as opposed to party principles or top-down diktats. See Dorothy Healey and Maurice Isserman, *California Red: A Life in the American Communist Party* (Chicago: University of Illinois Press, 1993), chapter 3.

59. Kathryn S. Olmsted, *Right Out of California: The 1930s and the Big Business Roots of Modern Conservatism* (New York: New Press, 2015), 53.

60. Don Mitchell, *The Lie of the Land: Migrant Workers and the California Landscape*, 144.

61. From a report cited in Donald Friend Fearis, "The California Farm Worker: 1930–1942" (dissertation, History, Cornell University, 1955), 95.

62. Devra Weber, *Dark Sweat, White Gold: California Farmworkers, Cotton, and the New Deal*, 53.

63. Anne Loftis, *Witnesses to the Struggle: Imaging the 1930s California Labor Movement*

(Reno: University of Nevada Press, 1998), 29.

64. Miriam Allen de Ford, "Blood-Stained Cotton in California," *Nation,* December 20, 1933; 705.

65. Federal Writers' Project, *Monographs Prepared for A Documentary History of Migratory Farm Labor in California,* 1938. The Bancroft Library, University of California, Berkeley, 40–41. Available online at http://content.cdlib.org/view?docId=hb88700929&chunk. id=div00022&br.

66. Judith Gannon, "California Odyssey: The 1930s Migration to the Southern San Joaquin Valley," Oral History Program. Interview with Lillie Ruth Ann Counts Dunn, Bakersfield California, California State College, Bakersfield, 1981, 9.

67. Ibid., 10.

68. Cited in Porter M. Chafee, *A History of the Cannery and Agricultural Workers Industrial Union* (University of California, Berkeley: Federal Writers' Project, 193–?). Page numbers unlisted. [microfilm]

69. "Four Dead and Scores Hurt In Cotton: Two Pitched Battles Result," *Los Angeles Times,* October 11, 1933; 1.

70. Porter M. Chafee, *A History of the Cannery and Agricultural Workers Industrial Union* University of California, Berkeley: Federal Writers' Project, 193–?. Page numbers unlisted [microfilm].

71. Donald Friend Fearis, "The California Farm Worker: 1930–1942," 108.

72. "Cotton Growers Accept Proposal to End Strike," *Los Angeles Times* October 26, 1933; 1.

73. Sam Kushner, *Long Road to Delano,* 69.

74. Clark Kerr and Paul Taylor, "Uprisings on the Farms," *Survey Graphic* 24, 1 (January 1935): 22.

75. Ibid., 44.

76. Stuart Marshall Jamieson, *Labor Unionism in Agriculture, Bulletin #836,* 104.

77. The 1934 San Francisco general strike will be discussed in more detail in chapter 32.

78. Linda C. Majka and Theo J. Majka, *Farm Workers, Agribusiness, and the State* (Philadelphia: Temple University Press, 1982), 82.

79. Kate Bronfenbrenner, "California Farmworkers' Strikes of 1933," Cornell University, ILR School, 1990. Available online at http://digitalcommons.ilr.cornell.edu/cgi/ viewcontent.cgi?article=1561&context=articles.

80. Cited in Diane E. Davis and Anthony Pereira, eds., *Irregular Armed Forces and their Role in Politics and State Formation* (New York: Cambridge University Press, 2003), 110. The authors point out that the leadership of the American Legion even invited Mussolini to speak at their convention in 1930.

81. Irving Bernstein, *The Turbulent Years: A History of the American Worker, 1933–1941* (Chicago: Haymarket Books, 2010), 168.

82. Benny J. Andrés, Jr., *Power and Control in the Imperial Valley: Nature, Agribusiness and Workers on the California Borderland, 1900–1940* (College Station: Texas University Press, 2015), 152.

83. Kathryn S. Olmsted, *Right Out of California: The 1930s and the Big Business Roots of Modern Conservatism,* 152–3.

84. Robert Justin Goldstein, *Little Red Scares, Anti-Communism and Political Repression in the United States, 1921–1946* (Burlington: Ashgate Publishing, 2014), 58–59.

85. Devra Weber, *Dark Sweat, White Gold,* 120.

Chapter 24: Mexican Workers in Depression-Era San Antonio

"The Mexican Return," *Nation* 135, no. 3503, August 24, 1932; 166.

1. The Mexican economy was wrecked after ten years of revolutionary war, and despite the radical character of the Constitution of 1917, land redistribution to the vast ranks of dispossessed agricultural workers did not materialize on a significant scale. The post-revolutionary government, representative of an ascendant middle class, was eager to stabilize its rule and integrate itself into the lifelines of international capital. In exchange for loans, legitimacy, and peace, the government of Álvaro Obregón stalled on major land reforms and engaged in rapprochement with elements of the Díaz regime.

2. These waves of migrants also included conservative Catholic peasants fleeing the repercussions of the defeated Cristero Revolt, who moved into the same fields and barrios as former revolutionaries and economic refugees.

3. Selden C. Menefee and Orin C. Cassmore, "The Pecan Shellers of San Antonio: The Problem of Underpaid and Unemployed Mexican Labor," Works Project Administration, Division of Research. Washington: United States Government Printing Office, 1940, 3.

4. Julie Leininger Pycior, "La Raza Organizes: Mexican American Life in San Antonio, 1915–1930 as Reflected in Mutualista Activities" (dissertation, University of Notre Dame, Doctor of Philosophy, 1979), 17.

5. Richard García, "The Making of the Mexican-American Mind, San Antonio, Texas, 1929–1941: A Social and Intellectual History of an Ethnic Community," 96, 350.

6. Julie Leininger Pycior, "La Raza Organizes: Mexican American Life in San Antonio, 1915–1930 as Reflected in Mutualista Activities," 77.

7. For a description of this process, see Irene Ledesma, "Texas Newspapers and Chicana Workers' Activism," *The Western Historical Quarterly* 26, no. 3. (Autumn 1995): 316–7.

8. John Weber, *From South Texas to the Nation: The Exploitation of Mexican Labor in the Twentieth Century* (Chapel Hill: University of North Carolina Press, 2015), 94–95.

9. Through the state apparatus, growers supported strengthening racial segregation and the construction of legal labor control through immigration. The largest capitalist growers converged their political efforts into the Republican Party at the state level, while the Democratic Party consolidated an alliance of large, small, and middle-sized farmers, craft unions, and local party machines that contested for power at the county and municipal level. See John Weber, *From South Texas to the Nation: The Exploitation of Mexican Labor in the Twentieth Century*, especially chapter 3.

10. R. Reynolds McKay, "Texas Mexican Repatriation During the Great Depression" (dissertation, Doctor of Philosophy, University of Oklahoma at Norman, 1982), 163.

11. Selden C. Menefee and Orin C. Cassmore, "The Pecan Shellers of San Antonio: The Problem of Underpaid and Unemployed Mexican Labor," 26–27.

12. Cited in Matthew Jerrid Keyworth, "Poverty, Solidarity, and Opportunity: The 1938 San Antonio Pecan Shellers' Strike" (Master's Thesis, Texas A&M University, 2007), 18.

13. "Se Encuentran en Situación Desesperada," *La Prensa*, September 27, 1931; 1.

14. R. Reynolds McKay, "Texas Mexican Repatriation During the Great Depression," 177.

15. Cited in R. Reynolds McKay, "Texas Mexican Repatriation During the Great Depression," 184.

16. Selden C. Menefee and Orin C. Cassmore, "The Pecan Shellers of San Antonio: The Problem of Underpaid and Unemployed Mexican Labor," 3.

17. Ibid., 44.

18. Ramiro Martínez, *Latino Homicide: Immigration, Violence, and Community* (New York: Routledge, 2015), 93.

19. Richard García, "The Making of the Mexican-American Mind, San Antonio, Texas, 1929–1941: A Social and Intellectual History of an Ethnic Community," 63.

20. John Weber, *From South Texas to the Nation: The Exploitation of Mexican Labor in the Twentieth Century*, 143.

21. "15,000 Mexicanos Repatriados en Diez Meses," *La Prensa*, September 28, 1931; 1.

22. For examples see Vicki Ruíz and John R. Chávez, *Memories and Migrations: Mapping Boricua and Chicana Histories* (Chicago: University of Illinois Press, 2008), chapter 4.

23. Cited in R. Reynolds McKay, "Texas Mexican Repatriation During the Great Depression," 112.

24. Ibid., 133.

25. Ibid., 139.

26. Irene Ledesma, "Unlikely Strikers: Mexican American Women in Strike Activity in Texas 1919–1974" (dissertation, Ohio State University, 1992), 28.

27. Adriana Ayala, "Negotiating Race Relations Through Activism: Women Activists and Women's Organizations in San Antonio, Texas during the 1920s" (dissertation, Doctor of Philosophy, University of Texas at Austin, 2005), 105.

28. Ibid., chapter 4.

29. Cited in Matthew Jerrid Keyworth, "Poverty, Solidarity, And Opportunity: The 1938 San Antonio Pecan Shellers' Strike," 75.

30. Francis Jerome Woods, "Mexican Ethnic Leadership in San Antonio, Texas" (dissertation, School of Social Science, Catholic University of America, 1949), 78.

31. Julie Leininger Pycior, "La Raza Organizes: Mexican American Life in San Antonio, 1915–1930 as Reflected in Mutualista Activities," 34.

32. For a full discussion of the evolution of the Comintern under Stalin, see Duncan Hallas, *The Comintern* (Chicago: Haymarket, 2008).

33. As explained by Communist International General Secretary Georgi Dimitroff at the Seventh World Congress of the Communist International, August 13, 1935. Published in Georgi Dimitroff, *The United Front: The Struggle Against Fascism and War* (San Francisco: Proletarian Publishers, 1975), 101.

34. William Z. Foster, *Your Questions Answered: On Politics, Peace, Economics, Fascism, Anti-Semitism, Race Prejudice, Religion, Trade Unionism, Americanism, Democracy, Socialism, Communism* (New York: Workers Library Publishers, 1939), 17.

35. Earl Browder, *The People's Front* (New York: International Publishers, 1938), 19.

36. Cited in Rita James Simon, ed., *As We Saw the Thirties: Essays on Social and Political Movements of a Decade* (Urbana: University of Illinois Press, 1967), 36.

37. William Z. Foster, *Your Questions Answered: On Politics, Peace, Economics, Fascism, Anti-Semitism, Race Prejudice, Religion, Trade Unionism, Americanism, Democracy, Socialism, Communism*, 85.

38. Earl Browder, *The People's Front*, 32.

39. Cited in Judith Stepan-Norris and Maurice Zeitlin, "'Who Gets the Bird?' or How the Communists Won Power and Trust in America's Unions: The Relative Autonomy of Intraclass Political Struggles," *American Sociological Review* 54, no. 4 (August 1989): 509.

40. Cited in Rita James Simon, ed., *As We Saw the Thirties: Essays on Social and Political Movements of a Decade*, 230.

41. Ibid., 231.
42. Malcolm Sylvers, "American Communists in the Popular Front Period: Reorganization or Disorganization?" *Journal of American Studies* 23, no. 3 (December 1989): 392.
43. Michael E. Brown, Randy Martin, and Frank Rosengarten, *New Studies in The Politics And Culture of US Communism* (New York: Monthly Review Press, 1993), 45, 47.
44. Ibid., 60–61.
45. Cited in Rita James Simon, ed., *As We Saw the Thirties: Essays on Social and Political Movements of a Decade*, 237.

Chapter 25: Mexican Women at the Forefront of Labor Militancy

Zaragosa Vargas, *Labor Rights Are Civil Rights: Mexican American Workers in Twentieth-Century America* (Princeton: Princeton University Press, 2005), 81.

1. John Thomas McGuire, "'The Most Unjust Piece of Legislation': Section 213 of the Economy Act of 1932 and Feminism During the New Deal," *Journal of Policy History* 20, no. 4 (October 2008): 534.
2. Mary Elizabeth Pidgeon, "Women in the Economy of the United States of America: A Summary Report" (Washington: US Government Printing Office, 1937), 78–79.
3. See Richard A. García, *Rise of the Mexican American Middle Class: San Antonio, 1929–1941* (College Station: Texas A&M University Press, 1991), 124.
4. Selden C. Menefee and Orin C. Cassmore, "The Pecan Shellers of San Antonio: The Problem of Underpaid and Unemployed Mexican Labor," Works Project Administration, Division of Research. Washington: United States Government Printing Office, 1940, 31.
5. For instance, in the Laguna region of Coahuila and Durango, the Communist Party had built a significant presence among agricultural wage workers. They formed 135 cells with an estimated 1,761 members and led an agricultural general strike that spread to 150 haciendas throughout La Laguna in 1936, winning significant wage increases. See Barry Carr, *Marxism and Communism in Twentieth-Century Mexico* (Lincoln: University of Nebraska Press, 1992), 100–2.
6. For an in-depth discussion, see María Teresa Fernández Aceves, *Mujeres en el Cambio Social en el Siglo XX Mexicano* (Mexico: Siglo Veinteuno Editores, 2014).
7. Geoffrey Rips, "Living History: Emma Tenayuca Tells Her Story," *The Texas Observer*, October 28, 1983; 8.
8. Communists at the time viewed feminism as "bourgeois reformism" and believed gender inequality would be overcome only through Communist revolution. Sharon Hartman Strom, "Challenging 'Woman's Place': Feminism, the Left, and Industrial Unionism in the 1930s," *Feminist Studies* 9, no. 2 (Summer 1983): 366–8.
9. Irene Ledesma, "Unlikely Strikers: Mexican American Women in Strike Activity in Texas 1919–1974" (dissertation, Ohio State University, 1992), 229.
10. Roberto Calderón and Emilio Zamora, "Manuela Solis Sager and Emma Tenayuca: A Tribute." National Association for Chicana and Chicano Studies Annual Conference, Austin Texas, 1984, 39–40. San Jose State Scholarly Works, available online at http://scholarworks.sjsu.edu/cgi/viewcontent.cgi?article=1098&context=naccs.
11. The 800 figure was reported in the *Cigar Makers' Official Journal* 58–61, no. 12 (Chicago: Cigar Makers' International Union). The 350 number is cited in Irene Ledesma, "Unlikely Strikers: Mexican American Women in Strike Activity in Texas

1919–1974," (dissertation, Ohio State University, 1992), 65.

12. The company reported it was in compliance with NRA wage codes, reporting the weekly average pay as twelve dollars. In practice, it was paying only $2 to $7 per week. See "Police Beaten by Texas Girls in Strike Riot," *El Paso Herald*, August 23, 1933; 1.

13. Teresa Palomo Acosta and Ruthe Winegarten, *Las Tejanas: 300 Years of History* (Austin: University of Texas Press, 2004), and Julia Kirk Blackwelder, *Now Hiring: The Feminization of Work in the United States, 1900–1995* (College Station: Texas A&M University Press, 1997), 134–5; John Weber, *From South Texas to the Nation: The Exploitation of Mexican Labor in the Twentieth Century* (Chapel Hill: University of North Carolina Press, 2015), 165.

14. "Police Beaten by Texas Girls in Strike Riot," *El Paso Herald*, August 23, 1933; 1.

15. Cited in Victor B. Nelson-Cisneros, "La clase trabajadora en Tejas, 1920-1940," *Aztlán* 6, no. 2 (Summer 1975): 256.

16. Julia Kirk Blackwelder, *Now Hiring: The Feminization of Work in the United States, 1900–1995*, 134.

17. Teresa Palomo Acosta and Ruthe Winegarten, *Las Tejanas: 300 Years of History*.

18. Irene Ledesma, "Unlikely Strikers: Mexican American Women in Strike Activity in Texas 1919–1974," 99.

19. Robert S. Shelton, "Yankee Devils in Paradise? Unionizing Efforts Among Dallas Garment Workers, 1933–1935," *Legacies: A History Journal for Dallas and North Central Texas* 6, no. 2 (Fall 1994): 14. Available online at http://texashistory.unt.edu/ark:/67531/metapth35113/m1/14/sizes/l/.

20. For an overview, see Melissa Hield et al., "'Union-Minded': Women in the Texas ILGWU, 1933–50," *Frontiers: A Journal of Women Studies* 4, no. 2 (Summer 1979): 59–70.

21. Irene Ledesma, "Unlikely Strikers: Mexican American Women in Strike Activity in Texas 1919–1974," 45.

22. Michelle Haberland, *Striking Beauties: Women Apparel Workers in the US South, 1930–2000* (Athens: University of Georgia Press, 2015), 22–23.

23. Robert S. Shelton, "Yankee Devils in Paradise? Unionizing Efforts Among Dallas Garment Workers, 1933–1935," 12.

24. Michelle Haberland, *Striking Beauties: Women Apparel Workers in the US South, 1930–2000*, 23.

25. Maximilian Krochmal, "Labor, Civil Rights, and the Struggle for Democracy in Mid-Twentieth-Century Texas" (dissertation, Department of History, Duke University, 2011), 29.

26. Judith N. McArthur and Harold L. Smith, *Texas Through Women's Eyes: The Twentieth-Century Experience* (Austin: University of Texas Press, 2010), 84.

27. Melissa Hield and Richard Croxdale, *Women in the Texas Workforce: Yesterday and Today* (Austin: People's History in Texas, Inc., 1979), 2.

28. For a full discussion of the factors arrayed against the strike, see Robert S. Shelton, "Yankee Devils in Paradise? Unionizing Efforts Among Dallas Garment Workers, 1933–1935," 12–19.

29. Judith N. McArthur and Harold L. Smith, *Texas Through Women's Eyes: The Twentieth-Century Experience*, 85.

30. Language-based locals were allowed within the ILGWU so that workers could organize in their own language without the cumbersome and unnecessary use of translation.

See Educational Department, "Structure and Functioning of the International Ladies' Garment Workers' Union" (New York: Abco Press, 1934), 9.

31. Irene Ledesma, "Unlikely Strikers: Mexican American Women in Strike Activity in Texas 1919–1974," 69–70.

32. Julia Kirk Blackwelder, *Now Hiring: The Feminization of Work in the United States, 1900–1995*, 102.

33. Melissa Hield and Richard Croxdale, *Women in the Texas Workforce: Yesterday and Today*, 9.

34. Ibid., 10.

35. "International Ladies' Garment Workers' Union." Texas State Historical Association. Available online at https://tshaonline.org/handbook/online/articles/oci02.

Chapter 26: Communists and the Workers Alliance in Texas

Helen Seymour, *When Clients Organize* (Chicago: American Public Welfare Association, 1937), 33.

1. John Garraty, "Unemployment During the Great Depression," *Labor History,* 17, no. 2 (1976): 134.

2. Irving Bernstein, *The Lean Years: A History of the American Worker, 1920–1933* (Chicago: Haymarket Books, 2010), 421–5.

3. Irena North, "Communist Party Theory and Practice Among the Unemployed, 1930–1938," *Theoretical Review,* no. 21 (March–April 1981). Available online at https://www.marxists.org/history/erol/ncm-8/north.htm.

4. Ibid.

5. "Reds Fight Police in Bronx Evictions," *New York Times*, February 2, 1932; 6.

6. "Reds Ask O'Brien to End Evictions: Mayor Explains City Is Doing Its . . . ," *New York Times,* June 1, 1933; 21.

7. Quoted from "Moody Asked to Curb Communists," *Denton Record-Chronicle*, April 7, 1930; 1.

8. American Civil Liberties Union, "What Rights for the Unemployed? A Summary of the Attacks on the Rights of the Unemployed to Organize, Demonstrate and Petition." Pamphlet, February 1935, 4.

9. Franklin Folsom, *America Before Welfare* (New York: New York University Press, 1996), 382.

10. After the police would disperse a protest or some other action against eviction, people would return to finish the task, such as restoring furniture and belongings to the vacated homes. Activists within the movement even learned how to reconnect gas, electricity, water, and other services that were disconnected for inability to pay. An estimated 77,000 of over 185,000 evicted families were returned to their dwellings in New York City through these efforts. In another example, 107 of 196 demands raised by the Communist Party–led Unemployed Councils in New York City were granted by groups carrying out protests, sit-ins, and mass pickets in front of district relief offices. See Frances Fox Piven and Richard A. Cloward, *Poor People's Movements: How they Succeed, How They Fail* (New York: Vintage Books, 1978), 67; and Richard O. Boyer and Herbert M. Morais, *Labor's Untold Story: The Adventure Story of the Battles, Betrayals and Victories of American Working Men and Women* (New York: United Electrical, Radio, and Machine Workers of America [UE], 1971), chapter 9.

11. Roy Rosenzweig, "Socialism in Our Time: The Socialist Party and the Unemployed,

1929–1936," *Labor History* 20, no. 4 (1979): 486.

12. Donald W. Whisenhunt, *The Human Tradition in America between the Wars, 1920–1945* (Wilmington: Scholarly Resources, 2002), 170–1.

13. Franklin Folsom, *Impatient Armies of the Poor: The Story of Collective Action of the Unemployed, 1808–1942* (Niwot: University Press of Colorado, 1991), 274.

14. Roy Rosenzweig, "Socialism in Our Time: The Socialist Party and the Unemployed, 1929–1936," *Labor History* 20, no. 4 (1979): 499, and Roy Rosenzweig, "Radicals and the Jobless: The Musteites and the Unemployed Leagues, 1932–1936," *Labor History* 16, no. 1 (1975): 52–77.

15. Roy Rosenzweig, "Socialism in Our Time: The Socialist Party and the Unemployed, 1929–1936," 501.

16. Frances Fox Piven and Richard A. Cloward, *Poor People's Movements: How they Succeed, How They Fail*, 66.

17. Ibid., 60, 66.

18. Ibid., 75–76.

19. "The January 1938 Registration—An Analysis and Conclusion," *Party Organizer* XI, no. 6 (June 1938): 3. Reprinted in New York: Greenwood Reprint Corporation, 1968.

20. Charles A. Gallagher and Cameron D. Lippard, *Race and Racism in the United States: An Encyclopedia of the American Mosaic* (Santa Barbara: Greenwood Publishing, 2014), 783.

21. Teresa Amott and Julie A. Mathaei, *Race, Gender, and Work: A Multi-Cultural Economic History of Women in the United States* (Boston: South End Press, 1996), 77.

22. Edward J. Escobar, *Race, Police, and the Making of a Political Identity: Mexican Americans and The Los Angeles Police Department, 1900–1945* (Berkeley: University of California Press, 1999), 79.

23. "Unemployment Relief and Social Insurance: The Communist Party Program Against the Capitalist Program of Starvation," *Daily Worker Pamphlet*, New York, 1931; 28–29.

24. Louise Pettibone Smith, *Torch of Liberty: Twenty-Five Years in the Life of the Foreign Born in the USA* (New York: King Publishers, 1959), 37.

25. The CIO openly opposed the firing of immigrants, although it did not appear to take much specific action to oppose the practice. See Louise Pettibone Smith, *Torch of Liberty: Twenty-Five Years in the Life of the Foreign Born in the USA*, 94–95.

26. Harold A. Shapiro, "The Pecan Shellers of San Antonio, Texas," *The Southwestern Social Science Quarterly* 32, no. 4 (March 1952): 234.

27. Louise Pettibone Smith, *Torch of Liberty: Twenty-Five Years in the Life of the Foreign Born in the USA*, 38.

28. Cybelle Fox, *Three Worlds of Relief: Race, Immigration, and the American Welfare State from the Progressive Era to the New Deal* (Princeton: Princeton University Press, 2012), 237.

29. Ibid., 237–49.

30. See John Weber, *From South Texas to the Nation: The Exploitation of Mexican Labor in the Twentieth Century* (Chapel Hill: University of North Carolina Press, 2015), 56.

31. "Moody Asked to Curb Communists," *Denton Record-Chronicle*, April 7, 1930; 1.

32. Transcript of interview with Emma Tenayuca by Jerry Poyo at her home in San Antonio. Institute of Texan Cultures. February 21, 1987, 31.

33. Zaragosa Vargas, *Labor Rights Are Civil Rights*, 132.

34. Chad Alan Goldberg, *Citizens and Paupers: Relief, Rights, and Race, from the Freedman's Bureau to Workfare* (Chicago: University of Chicago Press, 2007), 127.

35. Dedra McDonald, "Chicanas at the Forefront of Labor Organization: A Look at Emma

Tenayuca's Role as an Activist." Paper presented at Texas Lutheran College, July 26, 1990; 14.

36. For example, see "Sociedades y Clubes de Nuestra Colonia: Asamblea de la Unión de Trabajadores de WPA," *La Prensa*, August 2, 1937; 2.

37. Julia Kirk Blackwelder, *Now Hiring: The Feminization of Work in the United States, 1900–1995*, 177.

38. "La Alianza Obrera Sigue en Grandes Actividades," *La Prensa*, July 16, 1936; 2.

39. For instance, Mexican American pay averaged $21 while whites earned as much as $75. See Zaragosa Vargas, *Labor Rights Are Civil Rights: Mexican American Workers in Twentieth-Century America*, 130.

40. "Manifestación de los Desocupados," *La Prensa*, March 2, 1937; 1.

41. "Gran Manifestación: Participaron mas de 1,500 Mexicanos," *La Prensa*, March 9, 1937; 1.

42. Ibid.

43. Zaragosa Vargas, *Labor Rights Are Civil Rights: Mexican American Workers in Twentieth-Century America*, 218.

44. Dedra McDonald, "Chicanas at the Forefront of Labor Organization: A Look at Emma Tenayuca's Role as an Activist." Paper presented at Texas Lutheran College, July 26, 1990; 8.

45. See "Group Storms Alien Office: Workers Demonstrate at San Antonio," *El Heraldo de Brownsville*, February 24, 1937; 6.

46. "Otra Protesta del Grupo Sin Trabajo," *La Prensa*, February 20, 1937; 8.

47. "Una Asemblea de la Alianza Obrera de America," *La Prensa*, August 19, 1936; 8.

48. "La Policia de San Antonio en Accion: Desajolaron a Unos Individuos de un Edificio en Esa Ciudad Ayer," *El Heraldo de Brownsville*, April 27, 1937.

49. Frances Fox Piven and Richard A. Cloward, *Poor People's Movements: How they Succeed, How They Fail*, 83.

50. Chad Alan Goldberg, "Contesting the Status of Relief Workers during the New Deal: The Workers Alliance of America and the Works Progress Administration, 1935–1941," *Social Science History* 29, no. 3 (Fall 2005): 350.

51. "Dos Lideres de la Alianza en Libertad," *La Prensa*, July 2, 1937; 1.

52. Texas Civil Liberties Union, "San Antonio: The Cradle of Texas Liberty and Its Coffin?" Pamphlet. Austin: Texas Civil Liberties Union, 1938, 5.

53. "Emma Tenayuca Absuelta," *La Prensa*, July 15, 1937; 1.

Chapter 27: The Pecan Shellers Strike of 1938

Cited in Max Krochmal, *Blue Texas: The Making of a Multiracial Democratic Coalition in the Civil Rights Era* (Chapel Hill: University of North Carolina Press, 2016), 29.

1. Rita James Simon, ed., *As We Saw the Thirties: Essays on Social and Political Movements of a Decade* (Urbana: University of Illinois Press, 1967), 3.

2. So many leftward-moving liberals were produced by social discontent and elected with the intention of pushing radical reforms, leading party leaders to panic at the possibility of losing control of the national party. Conservative Democratic leaders in the House even tried to block the actions of the freshman group through bureaucratic measures. Ultimately, the turn to the right by the Roosevelt administration, and the onset of rabid anti-communism led many of these left-liberals to be voted out by decade's end. See Stuart L. Weiss, "Maury Maverick and the Liberal Bloc," *The Journal*

of American History 57, no. 4 (March 1971): 882.

3. Nevertheless, he tacitly endorsed local white supremacist party politics by not advocating for full voting rights for African Americans. For a description of his support for "white primaries" see Judith Kaaz Doyle, "Maury Maverick and Racial Politics in San Antonio, Texas, 1938–1941," *The Journal of Southern History* 53, no. 2 (May 1987): 198–202.

4. He also publicly aligned himself with the New Deal as part of his successful run for the governorship in 1935. In office, he took an active stance against the Klan and supported the implementation of New Deal–aligned programs within Texas, even as conservative Democrat and Republican municipalities opposed this at the state level. Both Maverick and Allred were drawn into the pecan shellers' strike in 1938, providing moral support and a national platform to expose attempts by the local government to crush the strike through violent police repression.

5. Merrill Rippy, *Oil and the Mexican Revolution* (Leiden: Brill Publishers, 1972), 181.

6. "Mexican Workers Achieve Unity The Confederation Of Mexican Workers," *Mexico Labor News,* July 1, 1936; 2.

7. Selden C. Menefee and Orin C. Cassmore, "The Pecan Shellers of San Antonio: The Problem of Underpaid and Unemployed Mexican Labor," Works Project Administration, Division of Research. Washington: United States Government Printing Office, 1940, 7–8.

8. Julia Kirk Blackwelder, *Now Hiring: The Feminization of Work in the United States, 1900–1995,* 90–91.

9. Mary Loretta Sullivan and Bertha Blair, *Women in Texas Industries : Hours, Wages, Working Conditions and Home Work* (Washington, DC: Government Printing Office, 1936), 58.

10. Texas Civil Liberties Union, "San Antonio: The Cradle of Texas Liberty and its Coffin?" 3.

11. Roger C. Barnes and James W. Donovan, "The Southern Pecan Shelling Company: A Window to Depression-Era San Antonio," 50–51. Selden C. Menefee and Orin C. Cassmore, "The Pecan Shellers of San Antonio: The Problem of Underpaid and Unemployed Mexican Labor," XVII.

12. See Eileen Boris and Cynthia R. Daniels, eds., *Homework: Historical and Contemporary Perspectives on Paid Labor at Home* (Chicago: University of Illinois Press, 1989), 75.

13. Irene Ledesma, "Unlikely Strikers: Mexican American Women in Strike Activity in Texas 1919–1974," 69–70.

14. Patricia E. Gower, "Unintended Consequences: The San Antonio Pecan Shellers Strike of 1938," *Journal of the Life and Culture of San Antonio.* Available online at http://www. uiw.edu/sanantonio/gower.html.

15. Selden C. Menefee and Orin C. Cassmore, "The Pecan Shellers of San Antonio: The Problem of Underpaid and Unemployed Mexican Labor," 16.

16. John Weber, *From South Texas to the Nation: The Exploitation of Mexican Labor in the Twentieth Century* (Chapel Hill: University of North Carolina Press, 2015): 173–4.

17. "S.A. Pecan Shellers to Arbitrate Trouble," *The Weekly Dispatch,* March 18, 1938; 1.

18. Because the homeworking population was difficult to quantify, historians can only rely on estimates. Robert Garland Landoldt estimates that by 1936 the total number of shed workers was 12,000, and homeworkers as high as 8,000, totaling 20,000. Julia Kirk Blackwelder estimates that by 1937, a total of 15,000–20,000 homeworkers were employed by pecan and garment companies in San Antonio alone, without specifying

proportions. See Robert Garland Landoldt, "The Mexican-American Workers of San Antonio Texas" (doctoral dissertation, University of Texas, Austin, 1965), 227, 232; and Eileen Boris and Cynthia R. Daniel, ed., *Homework: Historical and Contemporary Perspectives on Paid Labor at Home*, 75.

19. Donald W. Whisenhunt, *The Human Tradition in America between the Wars, 1920–1945* (Wilmington: Scholarly Resources, 2002), 176.

20. The IWW worked with and supported La Liga Obrera de Habla Española to conduct the strike. La Liga influenced migratory Mexican workers throughout Colorado and northern New Mexico. See Zaragosa Vargas, *Proletarians of the North: A History of Mexican Industrial Workers in Detroit and the Midwest* (Berkeley: University of California Press, 1993), 156.

21. Dennis Nodín Valdés, "Settlers, Sojourners, and Proletarians: Social Formation in the Great Plains Sugar Beet Industry, 1890–1940," *Great Plains Quarterly* (Spring 1990): 119.

22. Myrna Fichtenbaum, *The Funsten Nut Strike* (New York: International Publishers, 1992), 20.

23. Ibid., 34.

24. Irene Ledesma, "Unlikely Strikers: Mexican American Women in Strike Activity in Texas 1919–1974" (dissertation, Ohio State University, 1992), 107.

25. "Siguen Firmes Los Nueceros," *La Prensa*, February 1, 1938; 1.

26. Texas Civil Liberties Union, "San Antonio—The Cradle of Texas Liberty and its Coffin?" Pamphlet. Austin: Texas Civil Liberties Union, 1938, 7.

27. Five thousand was the estimate by Emma Tenayuca, who would have been the person in the best position to see the big picture of involvement. Cited in "Pecan Plant Workers Strike," *San Antonio Light,* January 31, 1938; 1.

28. Richard Croxdale, "The 1938 San Antonio Pecan Shellers' Strike," *Houston Breakthrough,* July 1979–August 1979; 29.

29. *Handbook of Texas*, "Quin, Charles Kennon." Texas State Historical Association. Available online at https://tshaonline.org/handbook/online/articles/fqu15.

30. See Judith Kaaz Doyle, "Maury Maverick and Racial Politics in San Antonio, Texas, 1938–1941," *The Journal of Southern History* 53, no. 2 (May 1987): 194–224.

31. Christopher D. Cantwell, Heath W. Carter, and Janine Giordano Drake, *The Pew and the Picket Line: Christianity and the American Working Class* (Champaign: University of Illinois Press, 2016), 159–60.

32. David A. Badillo, "Between Alienation and Ethnicity: The Evolution of Mexican-American Catholicism in San Antonio, 1910–1940," *Journal of American Ethnic History* 16, no. 4 (Summer 1997): 69.

33. Cited in Zaragosa Vargas, *Labor Rights Are Civil Rights: Mexican American Workers in Twentieth-Century America,* 138.

34. Christopher D. Cantwell, Heath W. Carter, and Janine Giordano Drake, *The Pew and the Picket Line: Christianity and the American Working Class,* 159.

35. Milton Gabel and Hortense Gabel, "Texas Newspaper Opinion: I," *The Public Opinion Quarterly* 10, no. 1 (Spring 1946): 61.

36. Cited in "S.A. Strikers Tell Police Beatings," *San Antonio Light*, February 15, 1938; 1.

37. Ibid.

38. "Chief Kilday Calls Out Reserve Force," *San Antonio Light,* February 7, 1938; 1, 5.

39. Patricia E. Gower, "Unintended Consequences: The San Antonio Pecan Shellers Strike of 1938."

40. "S.A. Strikers Tell Police Beatings," *San Antonio Light*, February 15, 1938; 1.

41. Ibid.

42. "Una Escuela de Comunismo en Esta Cuidad," *La Prensa*, February 16, 1938; 1.

43. "Beasley Tells Court 6,000 on Strike," *San Antonio Light*, February 24, 1938; 7A.

44. Richard Croxdale, "The 1938 San Antonio Pecan Shellers' Strike." 28.

45. "First Violence in S.A. Pecan Strike," *San Antonio Light*, February 4, 1938; 4A.

46. "Background," *La Voz de Esperanza* 12, issue 7 (September 1999). Benson Latin American Collection University of Texas at Austin.

47. John Weber, *From South Texas to the Nation: The Exploitation of Mexican Labor in the Twentieth Century*, 176.

48. Cited in Maximilian Krochmal, "Labor, Civil Rights, and the Struggle for Democracy in Mid-Twentieth-Century Texas," 43.

49. Julie Leininger Pycior, *LBJ and Mexican Americans: The Paradox of Power* (Austin: University of Texas Press, 1997).

50. Dedra McDonald, "Chicanas at the Forefront of Labor Organization: A Look at Emma Tenayuca's Role as an Activist." Paper presented at Texas Lutheran College, July 26, 1990; 14.

51. "Henderson Niega Ser Comunista," *La Prensa*, February 16, 1938; 1.

52. "Pecan Strike Heads Offer to Quit," *San Antonio Light*, February 3, 1938.

53. While the article takes an anti-Communist position, it contains a description of the influence of Communists within the CIO. See Murray E. Polakoff, "Internal Pressures on the Texas State C.I.O. Council, 1937–1955," *Industrial and Labor Relations Review* 12, no. 2 (January 1959): 227–42.

54. Cited in David O'Donald Cullen and Kyle G. Wilkison, eds., *The Texas Left: The Radical Roots of Lone Star Liberalism*, 118–9.

55. Maximilian Krochmal, "Labor, Civil Rights, and the Struggle for Democracy in Mid-Twentieth-Century Texas," 48.

56. "Allred Told Arbitration Stalled," *San Antonio Light*, March 4, 1938; 10.

57. See Texas Civil Liberties Union, "San Antonio—The Cradle of Texas Liberty and its Coffin?" Pamphlet. Austin: Texas Civil Liberties Union, 1938, 11–12.

58. Letter to Mrs. Frances Perkins. Document 16a: Mrs. Charles Britton, Secretary, Citizens Labor Aid Committee, to Mrs. Frances Perkins, Secretary of Labor, March 11, 1938. Cited in Thomas Dublin, Taina DelValle, and Rosalyn Perez, *How Did Mexican Working Women Assert Their Labor and Constitutional Rights in the 1938 San Antonio Pecan Shellers Strike?* (New York: State University of New York, 1999).

59. The CTM had attempted to establish links with unions and radical labor groups in Texas in previous years. For instance, in 1936, the CTM sent a delegation to New York to commemorate a May 1, International Workers Day celebration alongside representatives of some AFL unions and the Communist and Socialist Parties. The commission then toured across the country, arranging meetings with unionists and labor radicals throughout major industrial centers across the Northeast, Midwest, and West Coast. One of these stops was in San Antonio, Texas, which became a focal point for CTM leaders seeking to establish official relations with US labor representatives and to advocate on behalf of the plight of Mexican workers. At a 1936 conference held at the Labor Temple in San Antonio, state representatives from the AFL and a delegation from the CTM discussed formal collaboration to support the organization of Mexican farmworkers. The CTM representatives appealed to the AFL to support the

organization of Mexican labor, offering to block the recruitment of strikebreakers from the Mexican side of the border in the advent of strikes. AFL president William Green, who was not present, later disavowed the meeting. See "Desautorizan Los Arreglos Con La CTM. Pláticas entre la A.F.L. y Representantes de CTM en San Antonio," *La Prensa,* January 5, 1937; 1.

60.   "S. A. Pecan Shellers to Arbitrate Trouble," *The Weekly Dispatch,* March 18, 1938; 1.

61.   Pecan Shellers Dance in Street on Victory," *Daily Worker,* March 23, 1938; 3.

Chapter 28: Emma Tenayuca and the Mexican Question

Sister Frances Jerome Woods, "Mexican Ethnic Leadership in San Antonio, Texas" (dissertation, Catholic University of America, 1949), 78–79.

1.   David O'Donald Cullen and Kyle G. Wilkison, eds., *The Texas Left: The Radical Roots of Lone Star Liberalism,* 119.

2.   Dedra McDonald, "Chicanas at the Forefront of Labor Organization: A Look at Emma Tenayuca's Role as an Activist." Paper presented at Texas Lutheran College, July 26, 1990; 2.

3.   Geoffrey Rips, "Living History: Emma Tenayuca Tells Her Story," *The Texas Observer,* October 28, 1983; 8.

4.   Gabriela González, "Carolina Munguía and Emma Tenayuca: The Politics of Benevolence and Radical Reform," *Frontiers: A Journal of Women Studies* 24, no. 2/3, Gender on the Borderlands (2003): 209.

5.   Jaclyn Hise, "Radical Women of Texas During the Great Depression: An Overview of Communism and Labor Union Activities" (Master's Thesis, Department of History and Government, Texas Woman's University), 2013, 9.

6.   Cynthia E. Orozco, *No Mexicans, Women, or Dogs Allowed: The Rise of the Mexican American Civil Rights Movement* (Austin: University of Texas Press, 2010), 214.

7.   Marina Pisano, "Organizer Remembered for Passion, Controversy," *San Antonio Express-News,* July 24, 1999, A1. Also see Donald W. Whisenhunt, *The Human Tradition in America between the Wars, 1920–1945* (Wilmington: Scholarly Resources, 2002), 172.

8.   Marxist Internet Archives, "Provisional Rules of the Association, in the General Council of the First International; Minutes, 1864–66 [v.1], 288." Available online at https://www.marxists.org/history/international/iwma/documents/minutes/preface.htm.

9.   Geoffrey Rips, "Living History: Emma Tenayuca Tells Her Story," 9. Also see David J. Leonard and Carmen R. Lugo-Lugo, *Latino History and Culture: An Encyclopedia Volumes 1–2* (New York: Routledge, 2015), 531.

10.   Geoffrey Rips, "Living History: Emma Tenayuca Tells Her Story", 13.

11.   See Carlos Larralde, *Mexican American Movements and Leaders* (Los Alamitos: Hwong Publishing, 1976), 163. On the question of anti-imperialism, a national CTM-led oil strike of 1937 led to the expropriation of foreign oil holdings in Mexico. A massive strike was launched by CTM-member Sindicato de Trabajadores Petroleros de la República Mexicana (Union of Mexican Oil Workers) in 1937 that quickly spread across all sectors of oil extraction, processing, and shipping. For nearly two weeks, much of the national economy was paralyzed by the lack of petroleum. Originally the workers demanded union recognition and a closed shop, higher wages, overtime, hazard pay, health benefits, paid maternity leave, and a 40-hour work week. When the companies balked after eight months of arbitration, Cárdenas carried out the

expropriation and nationalization of the foreign-dominated oil industry. The act dislodged the Anglo-Netherlands-owned Royal Dutch Shell Company and the US-based Standard Oil Company, which had ruled over Mexico's oil fields like feudal barons since the beginning of the twentieth century.

12. Alicia Hernández Chávez and Manuel Miño Grijalva, *Cincuenta años de historia en México, Volume 1* (Mexico: El Colegio de México, 1991), 173.

13. For instance, after graduating high school she helped the International Ladies Garment Workers Union form two locals consisting of Mexican workers.

14. Maximilian Krochmal, "Labor, Civil Rights, and the Struggle for Democracy in Mid-Twentieth Century Texas," 42.

15. She was still promoting the achievement of socialism as an ideal to strive for toward the end of her life. See Jerry Poyo, "Interview with Emma Tenayuca." The Institute of Texan Cultures, Oral History Office. Audio transcript. Conducted in her home, February 21, 1987.

16. Emma Tenayuca and Homer Brooks, "The Mexican Question in the Southwest," 264.

17. For a full treatment of Stalin's theoretical formulation on "oppressed nations," see Joseph Stalin, *Joseph Stalin: Marxism and the National Question, Selected Writings and Speeches* (New York: International Publishers, 1942). On the "Black Belt Theory," see Hosea Hudson and Nell Irvin Painter, *The Narrative of Hosea Hudson: The Life and Times of a Black Radical* (New York: Norton, 1994), introduction.

18. Emma Tenayuca and Homer Brooks, "The Mexican Question in the Southwest," 262.

19. Ibid., 264.

20. Gabriela González, "Two Flags Intertwined: Transborder Activists and the Politics of Race, Ethnicity, Class, and Gender in South Texas 1900–1950" (dissertation, Department of History, Stanford University, 2004), 296.

Chapter 29: North American Communists and the "Good Neighbor Policy"

Michael J. Hogan, ed., *Paths to Power: The Historiography of American Foreign Relations to 1941* (Cambridge: Cambridge University Press, 2000), 212.

1. Robert W. Cherny, "The Communist Party in California, 1935–1940: From the Political Margins to the Mainstream and Back," *American Communist History* 9, no. 1 (2010): 18.

2. Maurice Isserman, *Which Side Were You On? The American Communist Party During the Second World War* (Middletown: Wesleyan University Press, 1982), 2.

3. The observations pertaining to the marginal influence of a more conservative, US-born middle class in Los Angeles are attributed to historian George Sánchez, *Becoming Mexican-American: Ethnicity, Culture, and Identity in Chicano Los Angeles, 1900–1945* (New York: Oxford University Press, 1993), 228–9.

4. Douglas Monroy, "Anarquismo y Comunismo: Mexican Radicalism and the Communist Party in Los Angeles during the 1930s," *Labor History* 24, vol. 1 (1983): 36.

5. Douglas Monroy, "Anarquismo y Comunismo: Mexican Radicalism and the Communist Party in Los Angeles during the 1930s," 42.

6. For a full exposition of Stalin's thought on the question, see "Marxism and the National Question." Available online at https://www.marxists.org/reference/archive/stalin/works/1913/03a.htm#s1.

7. Hernán Laborde, José Revueltas, and Miguel A. Velasco, *La Nueva Political del Partido*

Comunista de México (Mexico: Ediciones Frente Cultura, 1936), 6.

8. When the CIO-affiliated unions began their separation and exodus from the AFL, the president of the CTM, Vicente Lombardo Toledano openly sided with its emerging leader, John Lewis.

9. Zaragosa Vargas, *Labor Rights are Civil Rights: Mexican-American Workers in Twentieth-Century America*, 119.

10. David Bacon, "Building a Culture of Cross-Border Solidarity," Institute for Transnational Social Change, May 2011. Available online at http://escholarship.org/uc/item/05f6g6s7#page-1.

11. Vicente Lombardo Toledano and his co-thinkers also believed the Good Neighbor policy created the conditions and political space for expanding a new anti-imperialist labor alignment across the continent. Under the aegis of a US Good Neighbor détente in interventionism in Mexican affairs, and in tacit alliance with Lázaro Cárdenas, the CTM took the initiative to launch an internationalist labor federation under its political direction. Vicente Lombardo Toledano envisioned the Confederacion de Trabajadores de America Latina (CTAL) as an effort to build a hemisphere-wide labor organization that could confront reactionary oligarchies and the political-military forces that bolster them, while at the same time countering the forces of US imperialism. Swimming within the stream of the US-initiated Good Neighbor policy, the left-leading elements of the labor movements across Latin America forged a united front against fascism that could placate the US State Department, while also disavowing the idea that capitalism led to democracy or prosperity. Following the Stalinist formula, they saw in the CTAL the Popular Front elevated to a regionwide dimension, uniting labor and the popular classes with the "anti-imperialist bourgeoisie" to create a National Anti-Imperialist Front in every Latin American nation. Looking toward the Soviet Union, they prescribed state economic planning and controls on capital, especially foreign investments, as key to the next "stage" of the Democratic revolution as a precursor to socialism. In doing so, they proclaimed against fascism with the intention to work laterally against US imperialism to create a mutually beneficial organizational infrastructure to provide material and political support for reformist and nationalist projects across Latin America. Central to this effort from the Mexican perspective was reaching out directly to mexicanos de afuera in the United States. In publications, speeches, and other media, the lombardistas emphasized three intersections between Mexican and US workers: shared historical struggles, the same allies, and common enemies. Through delegations, publications, and forms of solidarity and support, the CTM worked to illustrate symmetry in the labor movements and reformist governments of both countries. See John V. Kofas, *The Struggle for Legitimacy: Latin American Labor and the United States, 1930–1960* (Tempe: Arizona State University, Center for Latin American Studies, 1992).

12. In one case, the CTM gave money to support striking beet-sugar workers. See "2 Million Pesos Go to Beet Workers," *UCAPAWA News*, October 9, 1939; 9.

13. Concurrently, the CTM leveraged anti-imperialist politics for its own domestic purposes, as a discernable left/right split emerged within the post-revolutionary ruling group in Mexico. To project its influence, the CTM took a lead in condemning the persistent alliance between foreign capital and the emerging anti-Communist right wing of the new ruling PRI. Fanning anti-imperialist sentiment in Mexico, the

CTM condemned the ways US interventionism was reasserting itself through various channels. For instance, the AFL worked with the US State Department to revive its idea for a Pan-American Labor Federation, which the CTM condemned as another tentacle of US empire probing post-revolutionary Mexico for easy access points. In the domestic power struggle, Vicente Lombardo Toledano, the CTM, and the left wing of the ruling party also saw the Mexican working class north of the border as an ally, attempting to push an unsuccessful reform to the electoral law to allow mexicanos de afuera to vote in Mexican national elections in 1940. See "Avanza el Proyecto En La Cámara," *La Opinión*, April 4, 1939; 1.

14. "Mexico Still Ready To Negotiate, Government Says," *Mexico Labor News*, August 17, 1939; 3–4.
15. Gigi Peterson, "Grassroots Good Neighbors: Connections Between Mexican and US Labor and Civil Rights Activists, 1936–1945" (dissertation, University of Washington, 1998), 12.
16. Ibid., 60.
17. Ibid., 100.
18. "Personal Experiences in Party Building," *Party Organizer* 10, no.5 (May 1937): 11; New York: Greenwood Reprint Corporation, 1968.
19. "Los Comunistas de Estados Unidos Saludan al Pueblo Todo de Mexico," *El Machete*, May 30, 1936; 1.
20. Cárdenas, for instance, was a representative of a fragile state still consolidating after revolution and weakened by the Depression. He was pressed from the left by a Communist movement finding its legs and a restive industrial working class. On the right, international capital and their local affiliates sought to reimpose its pre-revolutionary hegemony over the economy. In his role as president, he had to "recapture" the revolutionary masses, especially labor, and use this class's power to leverage their control vis-à-vis international capital over strategic sectors of the economy like oil. The national bourgeoisie under the Cárdenas administration emerged stronger vis-à-vis international capital externally and the popular classes at home, because of the role of labor. The Soviet-aligned politics of the PCM and Vicente Lombardo Toledano dovetailed with the aims of Cárdenas and the national bourgeoisie, albeit for very different purposes. Like in the US, the usefulness of the Communists as shepherds of the working class created an opening that allowed the party to reach a much larger audience. Like their counterparts in the US, the CTM and the PCM adhered to a no-strike policy once the war broke out. The CTM was therefore firmly incorporated into the corporate architecture of the ruling Revolutionary Institutional Party (PRI). Communist Party members were even awarded government posts as a reward for their service. With the end of the war, the demobilization of the CTM, and the emergence of the US as the preponderant world power, the ruling party in Mexico moved to the right.
21. Earl Browder, *The People's Front*, 243.
22. The degree of immersion of the Communist Party into support for their respective governments led them to oppose strikes and support strikebreaking during World War II. After the war, both parties faced a vicious campaign of repression as part of the larger Cold War, from which they never recovered.

Chapter 30: Communists, the Popular Front, and the New Deal in California

Cited in Mario T. García, *Memories of Chicano History: The Life and Narrative of Bert Corona* (Berkeley: University of California Press, 1994), 126.

1. Robert E. Burke, *Olson's New Deal for California* (Westport: Greenwood Press, 1982), 82.

2. See "Facts and Material on Organizational Status, Problems, and Organizational Tasks of the Party," *Party Organizer* 7, no. 5–6 (May–June 1934): 6; New York: Greenwood Reprint Corporation, 1968; and Mark Naison, "Remaking America," in Michael E. Brown, *New Studies in the Politics and Culture of U.S. Communism* (New York: Monthly Review Press, 1993), 45–73; and "Building the Mass Communist Party," *Party Organizer* 11, no. 7 (July 1938): 1; New York: Greenwood Reprint Corporation, 1968.

3. Steve Murdock, "California Communists—Their Years of Power," *Science & Society* 34, no. 4, American Radical History (Winter 1970): 484, 486.

4. See Douglas Monroy, "Anarquismo y Comunismo: Mexican Radicalism and the Communist Party in Los Angeles during the 1930s," 53; also see "Building the Party in California," *Party Organizer* 10, no. 3–4 (March–April 1937): 19; New York: Greenwood Reprint Corporation, 1968.

5. William Schneiderman, "The Democratic Front in California," *The Communist*, July 1938; 663.

6. For a full history of the EPIC campaign, see Upton Sinclair, *I, Candidate for Governor: And How I Got Licked* (Berkeley: University of California Press, 1994). The campaign is also discussed elsewhere in this book.

7. See Robert E. Burke, *Olson's New Deal for California*; and Robert W. Cherny, "The Communist Party in California, 1935–1940: From the Political Margins to the Mainstream and Back."

8. Robert W. Cherny, "The Communist Party in California, 1935–1940: From the Political Margins to the Mainstream and Back," 26.

9. See Zaragosa Vargas, *Proletarians of the North: A History of Mexican Industrial Workers in Detroit and the Midwest.*

10. "Facts and Material on Organizational Status, Problems, and Organizational Tasks of the Party," *Party Organizer* 7, no. 5–6 (May–June 1934): 7; New York: Greenwood Reprint Corporation, 1968.

11. Victor G. Devinatz, "A Reevaluation of the Trade Union Unity League, 1929–1934," *Science & Society* 71, no. 1 (January 2007): 44.

12. "New Forms of Party Organization Help us to Win the Masses," *Party Organizer* 9, no. 7–8, (July–August, 1936): 9; Reprinted in New York: Greenwood Reprint Corporation, 1968.

13. "The January 1938 Registration—An Analysis and Conclusion," *Party Organizer* XI, no. 6 (June 1938): 1. Reprinted in New York: Greenwood Reprint Corporation, 1968.

14. Kathryn S. Olmsted, *Right Out of California: The 1930s and the Big Business Roots of Modern Conservatism* (New York: New Press, 2015), 321.

15. "Party Organization in California," *Party Organizer* X, no. 7 (July 1937): 6–7. Reprinted in New York: Greenwood Reprint Corporation, 1968.

16. Luis Leobardo Arroyo, "Mexican Workers and American Unions: The Los Angeles AFL, 1890–1933." Working Paper, Chicano Political Economy Collective, University of California, Berkeley, 1981, 4.

17. Luis Leobardo Arroyo, "Mexican Workers and American Unions: The Los Angeles

AFL, 1890–1933," 23–24.

18. For a fuller discussion, see Louis B. Perry and Richard S. Perry, *A History of the Los Angeles Labor Movement, 1911–1941* (Berkeley: University of California Press, 1963), chapter 7.

19. Robert H. Zeiger, *The CIO: 1935–55* (Chapel Hill: University of North Carolina Press: 1995), 254.

20. Daniel B. Cornfield, *Becoming a Mighty Voice: Conflict and Change in the United Furniture Workers of America* (New York: Russell Sage, 1989), 23.

21. Louis B. Perry and Richard S. Perry, *A History of the Los Angeles Labor Movement, 1911–1941* (Berkeley: University of California Press, 1963), 421, 424.

22. "End Mexican Boy Gangs with Better Life–CIO," *Labor Herald*, Friday, October 9, 1942; 4.

23. Shelton Stormuist, ed., *Labor's Cold War: Local Politics in a Global Context* (Chicago: University of Illinois Press, 2008), 82.

24. "Smash the Secret Weapon: How to Fight the Fifth Column," International Workers Order, Issued by City Central Committee, 1944, 19–20.

25. Robert Minor, "The Nation and the War," *Communist*, January 1942; 53.

26. See the full discussion of this position in chapter 29.

27. Daniel Geary, "Carey McWilliams and Antifascism, 1934–1943," *The Journal of American History* 90, no. 3 (December 2003): 915.

28. Vicente Lombardo Toledano delved deeply into developing a Marxist, materialist analysis of racism, seeing it as an intractable obstacle to the advance of class unity. Much of his critique was directed at the racism bound up in the imperialist system, especially racial ideologies that flourished in Nazi Germany and the United States. His writings on the subject were widely disseminated through the CTM, the Universidad Obrera, and other means. In one of his tracts entitled, "Jews and Mexicans: Inferior Races?" he traces the roots of scientific racism through a lineage of European philosophers to the founding fathers of the US-based eugenics movement. With a rising Nazi state and anti-Semitism serving as the fulcrum of an international fascist movement, he took direct aim at its ideological roots. To counter the biological bases for racism he located the rise of virulent anti-Semitism with the consolidating power and concentrating wealth of finance capital in the capitalist centers. Their representatives, he posited, falsely promoted the idea that stateless and "orphaned" Jews controlled the economy and hoarded all of the wealth in order to distract attention away from their direct role in driving inequality on a previously unforeseen scale. He connects the experience of the Jews to the experience of mexicanos, a people colonized by Spanish Europeans. The ideologues of the conquest characterized the indigenous inhabitants as subhuman and irrational to justify the colonization and exploitation of their land and labor. The hegemonic idea of Indian inferiority, he posited, still infected the minds of Mexicans who internalize the inferiority of their own indigeneity. What's more, the "mestizo," neither Spanish or indigenous, remain an "orphan people" that under the shadow of colonialism continue to be victimized as inferior even within their own country. Nevertheless, he claims Mexico's revolutionary heritage shows that the Indians and mestizos comprise volatile classes prone to rise against the source of their oppression. He locates the progenitor of racism in class society: "There are no inferior or superior races in history . . . there are historical regimes that deprive the people, social systems that prevent their well-being, and

conditions of life that obstruct their happiness . . . forces that work together within a nation and internationally to benefit some groups of people over others." He furthermore contrasts Nazism with Jim Crow: "It would be absurd to combat the Nazi regime because it aims at establishing the hegemony of the German race, if at the same time among our own people there exist discriminatory sentiments with respect to Indians, negroes, and mestizos, if people continue to be classified according to their color. No man in America can or should call himself anti-fascist or democratic if he considers negroes, Indians, or mestizos to be inferior. In this hour, all discrimination is a boost to fascism." See Vicente Lombardo Toledano, "Judios y Mexicanos: Razas Inferiores?" (Mexico City: Universidad Obrera de Mexico, 1942).

29. Robert H. Zeiger, *The CIO: 1935–55*, 150–1.
30. Cited in Paul Leblanc, *A Short History of the US Working Class: From Colonial Times to the Twenty-First Century* (Chicago: Haymarket Books, 2016), 96.
31. Robert H. Zeiger, *The CIO: 1935–55*, 23, 25, 26.
32. George Sánchez, *Becoming Mexican American: Ethnicity, Culture and Identity in Chicano Los Angeles: 1900–1945*, 228.
33. Robert H. Zeiger, *The CIO: 1935–55*, 154, 157.
34. California CIO Council, "Report of the Executive Board: Sixth Annual Convention," Fresno, CA, October 21–23, 1943, 23.

Chapter 31: Mexican Labor Militancy in 1930s California

See Rose Pesotta, *Bread Upon the Waters* (Ithaca: Cornell University Press, 1987), 40.
1. Clementina Durón, "Mexican Women and Labor Conflict in Los Angeles: The ILGWU Dressmakers' Strike of 1933," *Aztlán: A Journal of Chicano Studies* 15, vol. 1 (1984): 148.
2. Ibid., 149.
3. "Build the Party in the Trade Unions," *Party Organizer* 8, no. 5 (May 1935): 4. Reprinted in New York: Greenwood Reprint Corporation, 1968.
4. Priscilla Murolo and A. B. Chitty, *From the Folks Who Brought You the Weekend: A Short, Illustrated History of Labor in the United States* (New York: New Press, 2001), 195.
5. Ibid., 193.
6. Historian Raymond Hogler points out the ambiguity of whether or not the intended scope of Section 7(a) of NIRA was to guarantee independent worker-controlled unions or also to allow for top-down company-managed unions which were also in existence at the time. See *The End of American Labor Unions: The Right-to-Work Movement and the Erosion of Collective Bargaining* (Santa Barbara: Praeger, 2015), 11.
7. Priscilla Murolo and A. B. Chitty, *From the Folks Who Brought You the Weekend*, 195.
8. Louis B. Perry and Richard S. Perry, *A History of the Los Angeles Labor Movement, 1911–1941*, 243, 266.
9. George Sánchez, *Becoming Mexican American: Ethnicity, Culture and Identity in Chicano Los Angeles: 1900–1945*, 232.
10. Founding members, leading organizers, and many rank-and-file members of the International Ladies Garment Workers Union were Socialists, especially Jewish workers from Russia who were part of the socialist movement there. As they formed the backbone of the union members in New York, the organizers sent to Los Angeles also saw them as the most likely prospect to support the union. See John Laslett and Mary

Tyler, *The ILGWU in Los Angeles, 1907–1988* (Inglewood: Ten Star Press, 1989), 22.

11. Ibid., 20.

12. See Eileen V. Wallis, *Earning Power: Women and Work in Los Angeles, 1880–1930*, (Reno: University of Nevada Press, 2010), 68–73.

13. Jose Pitti, Antonia Castañeda, and Carlos Cortes, "A History of Mexican Americans in California," in *Five Views* (Sacramento: Office of Historic Preservation, 1988), 232.

14. Clementina Durón, "Mexican Women and Labor Conflict in Los Angeles: The ILGWU Dressmakers' Strike of 1933," 152.

15. See John Laslett and Mary Tyler, *The ILGWU in Los Angeles, 1907–1988*, 28–29; also Vicki L. Ruiz and Virginia Sánchez Korrol, *Latinas in the United States: A Historical Encyclopedia*, 408.

16. This sentiment is captured in the quotes from union representatives in "Strike Clouds Hang Over City," *Los Angeles Times*, October 7, 1933; A3.

17. For a full account of her perspective on this period, see Rose Pesotta, *Bread Upon the Waters* (New York: Cornell University Press, 1987).

18. George Sánchez, *Becoming Mexican American: Ethnicity, Culture and Identity in Chicano Los Angeles: 1900–1945*, 239.

19. The theater was technically named the "Actor's Theater." Louis B. Perry and Richard S. Perry, *A History of the Los Angeles Labor Movement, 1911–1941*, 252.

20. John Laslett and Mary Tyler, *The ILGWU in Los Angeles, 1907–1988* 35.

21. "Writ Prohibits Strike Attacks," *Los Angeles Times*, October 18, 1933; A1.

22. "Police Change Strike Tactics," *Los Angeles Times*, October 19, 1933; A1.

23. "Strikers Beat Three Women," *Los Angeles Times*, October 21, 1933; A1.

24. "Police to Halt Brawls in Dressmaking Strike," *Los Angeles Times*, October 26, 1933; A1; also "Police Arrest Strike Group," *Los Angeles Times*, November 1, 1933; A1.

25. Louis B. Perry and Richard S. Perry, *A History of the Los Angeles Labor Movement, 1911–1941*, 257.

26. For a full discussion of membership, growth, and composition, see Isaias James McCaffery, "Organizing las Costureras: Life, Labor and Unionization Among Mexicana Garment Workers in Two Borderlands Cities—Los Angeles and San Antonio, 1933–1941" (dissertation, University of Kansas, History, 1999).

27. Louis B. Perry and Richard S. Perry, *A History of the Los Angeles Labor Movement, 1911–1941*, 415.

28. Clementina Durón, "Mexican Women and Labor Conflict in Los Angeles: The ILGWU Dressmakers' Strike of 1933," 159.

29. Vicki L. Ruiz, *Cannery Women, Cannery Lives: Mexican Women, Unionization, and the California Food Processing Industry, 1930–1950* (Albuquerque: University of New Mexico Press, 1999), 14, 15.

30. Ibid., xvii–xviii.

31. Patricia Zavalla, *Womens' Work and Chicano Families: Cannery Workers of the Santa Clara Valley* (Ithaca: Cornell University Press, 1987), 44.

32. Lowell K. Dyson, *Red Harvest: The Communist Party and American Farmers* (Lincoln: University of Nebraska Press, 1982), 97.

33. Official Proceedings, First National Convention of United Cannery, Agricultural, Packing and Allied Workers of America, Denver Colorado, July 9–12, 1937. Printed at Washington, DC: International Headquarters, 1937, 15.

34. Vicki L. Ruiz, *Cannery Women, Cannery Lives: Mexican Women, Unionization, and the*

700 Radicals in the Barrio

California Food Processing Industry, 1930–1950, 52.
35. Official Proceedings, First National Convention of United Cannery, Agricultural, Packing and Allied Workers of America, Denver Colorado, July 9–12, 1937. Printed at Washington, DC: International Headquarters, 1937, 19.
36. Stuart Marshall Jamieson, Labor Unionism in Agriculture, Bulletin #836, 141–7.
37. Donald Henderson, "The Rural Masses and the Work of Our Party: Speech Delivered at the Meeting of the Central Committee of the C.P.USA., May 25–27, 1935," The Communist, September 1935; 871–2.
38. Ibid., 867–9.
39. "Invisible Restraints: Life and Labor at Seabrook Farms." Exhibition detail, available online at https://rucore.libraries.rutgers.edu/rutgers-lib/49432/record/.
40. Cindy Hahamovitch, The Fruits of Their Labor: Atlantic Coast Farmworkers and the Making of Migrant Poverty, 1870–1945 (Chapel Hill: University of North Carolina Press, 1997), 144.
41. For a full discussion, see Victor B. Nelson-Cisneros, "UCAPAWA and Chicanos in California: The Farm Worker Period, 1937-1940," Aztlán, International Journal of Chicano Studies Research 7 (Fall 1976): 453–77.
42. Sophia Z. Lee, The Workplace Constitution from the New Deal to the New Right (New York: Cambridge University Press, 2014), 37–38.
43. Official Proceedings, First National Convention of United Cannery, Agricultural, Packing and Allied Workers of America, Denver Colorado, July 9th–12th, 1937. Printed at Washington, DC: International Headquarters, 1937, 39.
44. Official Proceedings, First National Convention of United Cannery, Agricultural, Packing and Allied Workers of America, Denver Colorado, July 9–12, 1937. Printed at Washington, DC: International Headquarters, 1937, 59.
45. For instance see "Get Together: A True Story About the CIO Agricultural Workers Union," UCAPAWA News, August 13, 1939; 13.
46. See "Mexican Workers" and "Citizenship for Filipinos," UCAPAWA News, December 4, 1939.
47. "Local Punishes Members Who Acted Anti-Negro," UCAPAWA News, July 1942; 2.
48. For instance, see Clyde Johnson, "$27 Contract Rate Proposed by UCAPAWA," UCAPAWA News, February 1940; 8.
49. Vicki L. Ruiz, Cannery Women, Cannery Lives: Mexican Women, Unionization, and the California Food Processing Industry, 1930–1950, 45.
50. Luisa Moreno, "Organizing the Women Folk," UCAPAWA News, October 9, 1939; 9.
51. Patricia Zavella, "'Abnormal Intimacy': The Varying Work Networks of Chicana Cannery Workers," Feminist Studies 11, no. 3 (Autumn 1985): 553–4.
52. Vicki L. Ruiz and Virginia Sánchez Korrol, Latinas in the United States: A Historical Encyclopedia, 110.
53. Dorothy Ray Healy and Maurice Isserman, California Red: A Life in the American Communist Party, 66.
54. Vicki L. Ruiz, Cannery Women, Cannery Lives: Mexican Women, Unionization, and the California Food Processing Industry, 1930–1950, 45–46.
55. Daniel Cornford, ed., Working People of California (Berkeley: University of California Press, 1995), 270.
56. Vicki L. Ruiz, Cannery Women, Cannery Lives: Mexican Women, Unionization, and the California Food Processing Industry, 1930–1950, 76.

57. "400 Cannery Workers Walk Out in Los Angeles Strike," *UCAPAWA News*, October Edition, 10.

58. Vicki L. Ruiz, *Cannery Women, Cannery Lives: Mexican Women, Unionization, and the California Food Processing Industry, 1930–1950*, 82.

59. Ibid., 84–85.

60. Vicki L. Ruiz and Virginia Sánchez Korrol, *Latinas in the United States: A Historical Encyclopedia*, 111.

61. Ibid.

62. Luis Leobardo Arroyo, "Industrial Unionism and the Los Angeles Furniture Industry, 1918–1954" (dissertation, UCLA, 1979), 69.

63. "The Revolutionary Unions in the New York District," *Party Organizer* 7, no. 5–6 (May–June 1934): 40. Reprinted in New York: Greenwood Reprint Corporation, 1968.

64. "300 L.A. Furniture Workers Drawing Up Wage Code," *Western Worker*, September 25, 1933; 3.

65. Daniel B. Cornfield, *Becoming a Mighty Voice: Conflict and Change in the United Furniture Workers of America*, 69.

66. Luis Leobardo Arroyo, "Industrial Unionism and the Los Angeles Furniture Industry, 1918–1954," 41–42.

67. "L.A. Furniture Workers Strike, Stop Wage Cuts in Sterling Shop," *Western Worker*, June 4, 1934; 4.

68. Luis Leobardo Arroyo, "Industrial Unionism and the Los Angeles Furniture Industry, 1918–1954," 87.

69. Ibid., 94.

70. See Daniel B. Cornfield, *Becoming a Mighty Voice: Conflict and Change in the United Furniture Workers of America*, 66, 76, 83.

71. Louis B. Perry and Richard S. Perry, *A History of the Los Angeles Labor Movement, 1911–1941*, 531, 537.

Chapter 32: Radicals Build the CIO in the Barrios

Cited in F. Arturo Rosales, *Testimonio: A Documentary History of the Mexican-American Struggle for Civil Rights* (Houston: Arte Público Press, 2000), 258.

1. See "The Most Active Workers Must Be Brought into Leadership," *Party Organizer* 7, no. 4 (April 1934): 28–30; and "Win Mass Leaders for the Party," *Party Organizer* 8, no. 12 (December 1935): 7.

2. Kenneth C. Burt, "The Birth of Latino Politics and Bipartisanship in California," *California State Library Foundation Bulletin*, no. 88, 2007, 34.

3. For example, the CIO led protests against the Kress department store in South Central Los Angeles, which reserved better-paying jobs for whites only. See Errol Wayne Stevens, *Radical L.A.: From Coxey's Army to the Watts Riots, 1895—1965* (Norman: University of Oklahoma Press, 2009), 267.

4. "Lucha Obrera Tour to Help Spanish Revolutionists," *Western Worker*, January 9, 1935; 4.

5. Stephanie Lewthwaite, *Race, Place, and Reform in Mexican Los Angeles: A Transnational Perspective* (Tucson: University of Arizona Press, 2009), 164.

6. Enrique Meza Buelna, "Resistance from the Margins: Mexican American Radical Activism in Los Angeles, 1930–1970" (dissertation, University of California, Irvine, 2007), 44.

7. Kenneth C. Burt, "The Birth of Latino Politics and Bipartisanship in California," 14.
8. Luis Leobardo Arroyo, "Chicano Participation in Organized Labor; The CIO in Los Angeles, 1938–1950. An Extended Research Note," in *Latino Employment, Labor Organizations, and Immigration*, ed. Antoinette Sedillo López (New York: Garland Publishing, 1995), 290.
9. Mario T. García, *Memories of Chicano History: The Life and Narrative of Bert Corona* (Berkeley: University of California Press, 1994), 73.
10. Emma Tenayuca and Homer Brooks, "The Mexican Question in the Southwest," 257–68. Bert Corona is credited with being the first to coin the phrase "No one is illegal."
11. Mario T. García, *Memories of Chicano History: The Life and Narrative of Bert Corona*, 65.
12. Corona was one of four Mexicans enrolled at USC in 1936. Mexicans were largely excluded from higher education, with some exceptions based on athletic ability or having backing from prominent white benefactors. See Mario T. García, *Memories of Chicano History: The Life and Narrative of Bert Corona*, 77–78.
13. Harvey Schwartz, *The March Inland: Origins of the ILWU Warehouse Division: 1934–1938* (San Francisco: International Longshore and Warehouse Union, 2000), 8, 98.
14. "Marine Federation Spreads," *Waterfront Worker*, April 15, 1935; 1–2.
15. According to an interview with Harry Bridges, published in Bruce Minton, "The Waterfront Marches Inland," *New Masses*, September 22, 1936; 6.
16. "State Executes Innocent Negro 'Hanged by Mistake,' Says Warden," *Waterfront Worker*, April 22, 1935; 5.
17. "Dallas Workers Unite, Win Strike Victory," *Waterfront Worker*, April 22, 1935; 5.
18. Sally M. Miller and Daniel A. Cornford, eds., *American Labor in the Era of World War II* (Westport: Praeger, 1995), 209.
19. See Congress of Industrial Organizations, National Policy Committee, "National Policy Reports, Issues 10–38," 1943, 72.
20. Enrique Meza Buelna, "Resistance from the Margins: Mexican American Radical Activism in Los Angeles, 1930–1970," 69.
21. "Mexican Labor Boycotts American Ships," *Mexican Labor News* 1, nos. 12 and 13 (November 25–December 25, 1936): 2.
22. Mario T. García, *Memories of Chicano History: The Life and Narrative of Bert Corona*, 96.
23. Ibid., 104.
24. Sally M. Miller and Daniel A. Cornford, eds, *American Labor in the Era of World War II*, 202.
25. "Urge Housing for Mexicans," *Labor Herald*, October 16, 1942; 1.
26. Sally M. Miller and Daniel A. Cornford, eds., *American Labor in the Era of World War II*, 207.
27. "Act to Improve Status of Mexicans," *Labor Herald*, November 7, 1941; 4.
28. For a full discussion, see Altagracia Ortiz, *Puerto Rican Women and Work: Bridges in Transnational Labor: Bridges in Transnational Labor* (Philadelphia: Temple University Press, 1996), chapter 1.
29. See Vicki L. Ruiz, and Virginia Sánchez Korrol, *Latina Legacies: Identity, Biography, and Community* (New York: Oxford University Press, 2005), 178.
30. For example, Communist Party leader Jésus Colón joined the party and became an electoral candidate. See Juan Flores, *Divided Borders: Essays on Puerto Rican Identity* (Houston: Arte Público Press, 1993), 136.
31. "Funeral for Red Today: Police Ready to Avert Outbreak at Services in Harlem," *New*

York Times, July 4, 1930, 30. The party then renamed the branch in Spanish Harlem after Gónzales to honor his memory.

32. See the pathetically written *New York Times* article, which constructs a pulp-fiction-like tale in its attempt to justify the killing: "Policeman, Beaten by Red Paraders, Kills The Leader," July 1, 1930; 1.

33. "2,000 Reds March in Harlem Funeral," *New York Times,* July 2, 1930; 21.

34. See Vicki L. Ruiz and Virginia Sánchez Korrol, *Latina Legacies: Identity, Biography, and Community,* 181.

35. For background information, see Jerrell H. Shofner, "Communists, Klansmen, and the CIO in The Florida Citrus Industry," *Florida Historical Quarterly* 71, no. 3 (January 1993): 300–309; and Patricia Zavella, "'Abnormal Intimacy': The Varying Work Networks of Chicana Cannery Workers," *Feminist Studies* 11, no. 3 (Autumn 1985): 541–57.

36. Carlos M. Larralde and Richard Griswold del Castillo, "Luisa Moreno and the Beginnings of the Mexican American Civil Rights Movement in San Diego," *Journal of San Diego History,* (Summer 1997). Available online at www.sandiegohistory.org /journal/97summer/moreno.htm.

37. See Vicki L. Ruiz and Virginia Sánchez Korrol, *Latina Legacies: Identity, Biography, and Community,* 182.

38. Carlos Larralde, "Roberto Galvan: A Latino Leader of the 1940s," *Journal of San Diego History* 52, no. 3–4 (March 2006): 154. Available online at https://www. sandiegohistory.org/journal/v52-3/pdf/2006-3_galvan.pdf.

39. David Gutiérrez, *Between Two Worlds: Mexican Immigrants in the United States* (Wilmington: Scholarly Resources, 1996), 122.

Chapter 33: El Congreso del Pueblo de Habla Española (1939–1942)

Cited in Paul Buhle and Dan Georgakas, eds., *The Immigrant Left in the United States* (Albany: State University of New York, 1996), 31.

1. "El Congreso Mexicano Será Hoy a las 10 A.M.," *La Opinión,* December 4, 1939; 3, 8.

2. David G. Gutiérrez, *Walls and Mirrors: Mexican Americans, Mexican Immigrants, and the Politics of Ethnicity* (Berkeley: University of California Press, 1995), 111.

3. See "El Segundo Congreso Mexicano Sera Celebrado Hoy en Los Angeles," *La Opinión,* February 26, 1939; 3.

4. "La Convención Nacional no Será en Nuevo México," *La Opinión,* March 5, 1939; 3.

5. Shana Bernstein, *Bridges of Reform: Interracial Civil Rights Activism in Twentieth-Century Los Angeles* (New York: Oxford University Press, 2011), 28.

6. Kenneth C. Burt, *The Search for a Civic Voice: California Latino Politics* (Claremont: Regina Books, 2007), 7–8.

7. Mario T. García, *Mexican Americans: Leadership, Ideology, and Identity, 1930–1960* (New Haven: Yale University Press, 1989), 151.

8. "Dia Principio El Congreso H. Americano," *La Opinión,* April 29, 1939; 8.

9. David G. Gutiérrez, *Walls and Mirrors: Mexican Americans, Mexican Immigrants, and the Politics of Ethnicity,* 116.

10. "US Latins Open 3-Day Congress," *People's World,* April 28, 1939; 3.

11. Devra Anne Weber, "Wobblies of the Partido Liberal Mexicano: Revisioning Internationalist and Transnational Movements through Mexican Lenses," 190.

12. Myra Page, "Mexican Girl," *People's World,* February 25, 1939; 7.

13. See Daniel Hurewitz, *Bohemian Los Angeles and the Making of Modern Politics* (Berkeley: University of California Press, 2007).

14. John Bright, *Worms in the Wine Cup: A Memoir* (Lanham: Scarecrow Press, 2002), xiii.

15. Carlos Larralde, "Josefina Fierro and the Sleepy Lagoon Crusade, 1942–1945," *Southern California Quarterly* 92, no. 2 (Summer 2010): 125.

16. For a full discussion of her complex life, see ibid., 117–60.

17. Carlos Larralde, "Roberto Galvan: A Latino Leader of the 1940s," *Journal of San Diego History* 52, no. 3–4 (March 2006): 157. Available online at https://www.sandiegohistory.org/journal/v52-3/pdf/2006-3_galvan.pdf.

18. "Discusión de Problemas de los Mexicanos," *La Opinión*, February 26, 1939; 8.

19. "US Latins Map Defense of Democracy," *People's World*, May 1, 1939; 3.

20. Mario T. García, *Mexican Americans: Leadership, Ideology, and Identity, 1930–1960*, 159–60.

21. Stephanie Lewthwaite, *Race, Place, and Reform in Mexican Los Angeles: A Transnational Perspective* (Tucson: University of Arizona Press, 2009), 205.

22. See Jennifer Uhlmann, "Communists and the Early Movement for Mexican-American Civil Rights: The Benjamin Moreno Inquiry and its Aftermath," *American Communist History* 9, no. 2 (2010): 111–39.

23. David G. Gutiérrez, *Walls and Mirrors: Mexican Americans, Mexican Immigrants, and the Politics of Ethnicity*, 113.

24. Digest of First Proceedings cited in Kenneth C. Burt, *The Search for a Civic Voice: California Latino Politics*, 15.

25. Mario T. García, *Mexican Americans: Leadership, Ideology, and Identity, 1930–1960*, 164.

26. For an in-depth critical study of the Bracero Program by a Congreso supporter, see Ernesto Galraza, *Merchants of Labor: The Mexican Bracero Story* (Santa Barbara: McNally & Loftin, 1964).

27. For a discussion of these events, see Jonathan Brown, *Workers' Control in Latin America, 1930–1979* (Chapel Hill: University of California Press, 1997), chapter 2.

28. Maurice Isserman, *Which Side Were You On? The American Communist Party During the Second World War*, 177–8.

29. Elizabeth Escobedo, *From Coveralls to Zoot Suits: The Lives of Mexican American Women on the World War II Home Front* (Chapel Hill: University of North Carolina Press, 2013), 7.

30. "Locals Urged to Join Conference on Plight of Spanish-Americans," *Labor Herald*, November 28, 1941; 4.

31. "Employers' War on Aliens to be Aired," *Labor Herald*, January 16, 1942; 6.

32. See "Alien Controls Accepted by CIO, Race-Baiting Hit," *Labor Herald*, February 27, 1942; 1.

33. See "Anti-Discrimination Group Sets Training, Job Program," *Labor Herald*, February 27, 1942; 5; and "CIO Asks for Minority Training Program," *Labor Herald*, May 1, 1942; 4.

34. "Race Bias Held Vital War Issue," *Labor Herald*, August 7, 1942; 6.

35. California CIO Council, "Report of the Executive Board: Sixth Annual Convention," Fresno, CA, October 21–23, 1943, 23.

36. Ibid., 24

Chapter 34: Sleepy Lagoon: Communists, the CIO, and Civil Rights

Passages from "Papers Read in Meeting Held October 8, 1942, Called by Special Mexican Relations Committee of the Los Angeles County Grand Jury." Cited in "The Pertinence of the 'Sleepy Lagoon' Case," *The Journal of Mexican American History*, no. 4 (1974): 76.

1. Observers at the time estimated that only 3–5 percent of Mexican working youth were actually part of the *pachuco* subculture in 1942 Los Angeles. Nevertheless, this identity was seized upon by the ruling class as representative of the "inherent threat" posed by Mexican youth to wider, Anglo society. See Eduardo Obregón Pagán, *Murder at the Sleepy Lagoon: Zoot Suits, Race & Riot in Wartime L.A.* (Chapel Hill: University of North Carolina Press, 2003), 39.

2. For a full examination, see Gilbert G. González, *Chicano Education in the Era of Segregation* (Denton: University of North Texas Press, 1990).

3. See "American Experience: People & Events: José Gallardo Díaz (1919–1942)," KPBS. Available online at http://www.pbs.org/wgbh/amex/zoot/eng_peopleevents/p_ Díaz.html.

4. Elizabeth Escobedo, *From Coveralls to Zoot Suits: The Lives of Mexican American Women on the World War II Home Front*, 74–75.

5. Ibid., 44.

6. Mirosalva Chavez-García, *States of Delinquency: Race and Science in the Making of California's Juvenile Justice System* (Berkeley: University of California Press, 2012), 2.

7. Mark A. Weitz, *The Sleepy Lagoon Murder Case: Race Discrimination and Mexican-American Rights* (Lawrence: University of Kansas Press, 2010), 32–34.

8. Eduardo Obregón Pagán, *Murder at the Sleepy Lagoon: Zoot Suits, Race & Riot in Wartime L.A.*, 24.

9. Mark A. Weitz, *The Sleepy Lagoon Murder Case: Race Discrimination and Mexican-American Rights*, 12.

10. Irving G. Tragen, "Statutory Prohibitions against Interracial Marriage," *California Law Review* 32, no. 3 (September 1944), 272.

11. Carlos M. Larralde and Richard Griswold del Castillo, "Luisa Moreno and the Beginnings of the Mexican American Civil Rights Movement in San Diego."

12. Mark A. Weitz, *The Sleepy Lagoon Murder Case: Race Discrimination and Mexican-American Rights*, 20.

13. Eduardo Obregón Pagán, *Murder at the Sleepy Lagoon: Zoot Suits, Race & Riot in Wartime L.A.*, 49.

14. Ibid., 94–95.

15. Mauricio Mazón, *The Zoot-Suit Riots: The Psychology of Symbolic Annihilation* (Austin: University of Texas Press, 2005), 59.

16. Ibid., 56.

17. For example, see "Supreme Court to Review Alien Curfew Litigation," *Los Angeles Times*, April 6, 1943: 1; and "High Court Upholds Jap Curb: Gen. DeWitt's Curfew Held Constitutional in Unanimous Ruling," *Los Angeles Times*, June 22, 1943; 1.

18. From an eyewitness account by Carey McWilliams, *North from Mexico: The Spanish-Speaking People of the United States* (New York: Praeger, 1990), 249.

19. "The International Labor Defense, Its Constitution and Organization Resolution; Adopted by the Fourth National Convention held in Pittsburgh, Pa., Dec. 29–31, 1929," New York: International Labor Defense, 10.

20. "LaRue McCormick, Activist in The Radical Movement, 1930–1960; The

International Labor Defense, the Communist Party," Women in Politics Oral History Project. An Interview Conducted by Malca Chall in 1976. Regional Oral History Office, The Bancroft Library, University of California, Berkeley, 69.

21. Frank Barajas quotes McCormick as saying: "They [the Sleepy Lagoon defendants] were all charged with first-degree murder. We waited around thinking that somebody was going to come to their defense. But they didn't. So I finally called a conference and we had several hundred people turn out to it and set up a Sleepy Lagoon Defense Committee." See Frank Barajas, "The Defense Committees of Sleepy Lagoon: A Convergent Struggle against Fascism, 1942–1944," *Aztlán* 31, no. 1 (Spring 2006): 40.

22. See Jennifer Uhlmann, "Communists and the Early Movement for Mexican-American Civil Rights: The Benjamin Moreno Inquiry and its Aftermath," 111–39.

23. Luis Leobardo Arroyo, "Chicano Participation in Organized Labor; The CIO in Los Angeles, 1938–1950. An Extended Research Note."

24. Frank Barajas, "The Defense Committees of Sleepy Lagoon: A Convergent Struggle against Fascism, 1942–1944," 44.

25. Richard Griswold del Castillo, "The Los Angeles 'Zoot Suit Riots' Revisited: Mexican and Latin American Perspectives," *Mexican Studies/Estudios Mexicanos* 16, no. 2 (Summer 2000): 372.

26. Ibid.

27. For example, see "May Day Manifesto of the Communist Party," *The Communist*, May 1943; 387–93, where the editors repeatedly make their case.

28. Cited in Frank Barajas, "The Defense Committees of Sleepy Lagoon: A Convergent Struggle against Fascism, 1942–1944," 45.

29. Josefina Fierro de Bright, National Secretary, Spanish Speaking People's Congress, Sleepy Lagoon Defense Committee Records (Collection 107). UCLA Library Special Collections, Charles E. Young Research Library, UCLA.

30. Carlos M. Larralde and Richard Griswold del Castillo, "Luisa Moreno and the Beginnings of the Mexican American Civil Rights Movement in San Diego."

31. "CIO Offers Plan to Put Mexicans Behind the War," *Labor Herald*, November 6, 1942; 6.

32. "End Mexican Boy Gangs with Better Life—CIO," *Labor Herald,* October 9, 1942; 4.

33. "L.A. Council Committee Meets to Tackle Mexican Discrimination," *Labor Herald*, November 20, 1942; 3.

34. "Plan 'Partnership' of Mexicans and CIO to Fight Race Bias," *Labor Herald,* June 25, 1943; 5.

35. "LaRue McCormick, Activist in The Radical Movement, 1930–1960; The International Labor Defense, The Communist Party," 45.

36. While the murder convictions of the Sleepy Lagoon youth were overturned in October of 1944, the persecution of working-class Mexican youth continued. In the aftermath of the anti-Mexican violence in August 1943, the state government activated the California Youth Authority Act (passed in 1941 with virtually no opposition from either party) and established a division for "delinquency prevention" in August 1943. The period of 1941–1943 saw the Mexican population in the US become a national subject of concern for state agents. The events of the period spurred more sociological evaluation of the population, more federal attention to its political structures, and focus on strategic policing and control of the population. Conversely, the racial violence, collective denial of basic human and civil rights, and the systematic targeting and persecution of individuals and leaders that began with Sleepy Lagoon led the

Communist Party/CIO civil rights infrastructure to champion the resistance to the state-led repression of the Mexican community.

37. Michael Wilson and Deborah Silverton Rosenfelt, *Salt of the Earth* (New York: Feminist Press, 1978), 97.

38. Lawrence A. Harper, "Legislative Investigation of Un-American Activities Exhibit A: The Tenney Committee," *California Law Review* 39, no. 4 (December 1951): 504.

39. Mauricio Mazón, *The Zoot-Suit Riots: The Psychology of Symbolic Annihilation*, 98–99.

Chapter 35: Communist Miners and Cold War Civil Rights

Louise Pettibone Smith, *Torch of Liberty: Twenty-Five Years in the Life of the Foreign Born in the USA*, 236.

1. Perhaps supporting their argument, albeit inverting their intention, Congress and the Roosevelt administration did intensify the repression of the Communist Party during this period for *opposing* the war effort. See Maurice Isserman, *Which Side Were You On?* chapter 4 for a full discussion of how this unfolded.

2. Art Preis, *Labor's Giant Step: The First Twenty Years of the CIO: 1936–55*, xv, 257–58.

3. Hearings on Proposed Legislation to Curb or Control the Communist Party of the United States, Committee on Un-American Activities (Washington: US Government Printing Office, 1948), 482.

4. Between 1940 and 1957, when it was curtailed by the Supreme Court, the Smith Act was primarily applied to Socialists and Communists.

5. "Control of Communist Activities," *Stanford Law Review* 1, no. 1 (November 1948): 90.

6. Ibid., 95.

7. James Lorence, *The Suppression of Salt of the Earth: How Hollywood, Big Labor, and Politicians Blacklisted a Movie in Cold War America* (Albuquerque: University of New Mexico Press, 1999), 20.

8. From page 991 of the text of the Internal Security Act of 1950. Available online at http://legisworks.org/congress/81/publaw-831.pdf.

9. This latter point was supposed to also implicate "fascists," although the law was used only against Communists.

10. From page 989 of the text of the Internal Security Act of 1950. Available online at http://legisworks.org/congress/81/publaw-831.pdf.

11. See Dorothy Healey and Maurice Isserman, *Dorothy Healey Remembers a Life in the American Communist Party* (New York: Oxford University Press, 1990), 70.

12. Communist Party Convention Bulletin, "The Mexican People of the Southwest," August 3, 1948, Box 4, Folder 114 American Left Ephemera Collection, 1894–2008, AIS.2007.11, Archives Service Center, University of Pittsburgh, 11.

13. Ibid., 1.

14. Ibid., 2–3.

15. Clete Daniel, *Chicano Workers and the Politics of Fairness: The FEPC in the Southwest, 1941–1945* (Austin: University of Texas Press, 1991), 4.

16. Ibid., 21, 147.

17. Ibid., 85, 89.

18. Ellen R. Baker, *On Strike and On Film: Mexican American Families and Blacklisted Filmmakers in Cold War America* (Chapel Hill: University of North Carolina Press, 2007), 76.

19. James Lorence, *Palomino: Clinton Jencks and Mexican-American Unionism in the American Southwest* (Champaign: University of Illinois Press, 2013), 47.

20. Jack Cargill, "Empire and Opposition: 'The Salt of the Earth Strike,'" in *Labor in New Mexico: Unions, Strikes, and Social History since 1881*, ed. Robert Kern (Albuquerque: University of New Mexico Press, 1983), 194.

21. Christopher J. Huggard and Terrence J. Humble, *Santa Rita del Cobre: A Copper Mining Community in New Mexico* (Boulder: University of Colorado Press, 2012), 100.

22. Ellen R. Baker, *On Strike and On Film: Mexican American Families and Blacklisted Filmmakers in Cold War America*, 69.

23. Zaragosa Vargas, *Labor Rights are Civil Rights: Mexican-American Workers in Twentieth-Century America*, 167.

24. James Lorence, *The Suppression of Salt of the Earth: How Hollywood, Big Labor, and Politicians Blacklisted a Movie in Cold War America*, 24.

25. See Laurie Mercier, "'Instead of Fighting the Common Enemy': Mine Mill versus the Steelworkers in Montana, 1950–1967," *Labor History* 40, no. 4 (1999): 459–80.

26. Ellen R. Baker, *On Strike and On Film: Mexican American Families and Blacklisted Filmmakers in Cold War America*, 80.

27. Ibid., 81.

28. Michael Wilson and Deborah Silverton Rosenfelt, *Salt of the Earth*, 116.

29. For example, see Jack Cargill, "Empire and Opposition: 'The Salt of the Earth Strike,'" 213–4.

30. Mine Mill locals nationally folded into the USWA in 1967.

31. Interview with Anita and Lorenzo Torrez, cited in "History-makers reflect on Salt of the Earth: Even more relevant now," *People's World,* October 31, 2003. Available online at http://www.peoplesworld.org/article/history-makers-reflect-on-salt-of-the-earth-even-more-relevant-now/.

32. Liliana Urrutia, "Research Note: An Offspring of Discontent: The Asociación Nacional México-Americana, 1949–1954," *Aztlán: A Journal of Chicano Studies* 15, no. 1 (1984), 178.

33. Mario T. García, *Memories of Chicano History: The Life and Narrative of Bert Corona*, 168

34. Cited in Mario García, "Mexican American Labor and the Left: The Asociación Nacional México-Americana, 1949–1954," 68.

35. Ellen R. Baker, *On Strike and On Film: Mexican American Families and Blacklisted Filmmakers in Cold War America*, 106.

36. See Communist Party Convention Bulletin, "The Mexican People of the Southwest," August 3 1948, Box 4, Folder 114 American Left Ephemera Collection, 1894–2008, AIS.2007.11, Archives Service Center, University of Pittsburgh, 8. Also see Juan Ramon García, *Operation Wetback: The Mass Deportation of Mexican Undocumented Workers in 1954* (Westport: Greenwood Press, 1980), 236.

37. Dwight C. Morgan, "The Foreign Born in the United States" Pamphlet, American Committee for the Protection of the Foreign Born, 1936, 50–51.

38. Abner Green, "The Deportation Terror: A Weapon to Gag America," cited in *Immigrant Rights in the Shadow of Citizenship*, ed. Rachel Ida Buff (New York: New York University Press, 2008), 366.

39. See Louise Pettibone Smith, *Torch of Liberty: Twenty-Five Years in the Life of the Foreign Born in the USA*, chapter 17.

40. He was later reinstated. See "Smelter Ordered to Reinstate Employee," *El Paso Herald-*

Post, May 28, 1942; 8.

41. Cited in "Union Opposes Deportation," *El Paso Herald-Post*, October 21, 1946; 9.

42. See Francis H. Thompson, *The Frustration of Politics: Truman, Congress, and the Loyalty Issue, 1945–1953* (Madison: Fairleigh Dickinson University Press, 1979).

43. "Cases Handled by the Civil Rights Congress," n.d. Los Angeles Committee for Protection of Foreign Born Records, collection no. MSS 080, Southern California Library for Social Studies and Research, Los Angeles, California.

44. Letter of Appeal for an Emergency Meeting, Civil Rights Congress, September 26, 1947, signed by William Bidner, Oscar Castro, and Ralph Cuaron. Southern California. Los Angeles Committee for Protection of Foreign Born Records, collection no. MSS 080, Southern California Library for Social Studies and Research, Los Angeles, California.

45. "No Gestapo in Los Angeles," flier issued by the Mexican Civil Rights Committee and the National Negro Congress. n.d. Los Angeles Committee for Protection of Foreign Born Records, collection no. MSS 080, Southern California Library for Social Studies and Research, Los Angeles, California.

46. Jeffrey M. Garcilazo, "McCarthyism, Mexican Americans, and the Los Angeles Committee for Protection of the Foreign-Born, 1950–1954," *Western Historical Quarterly* 32, no. 3 (Autumn 2001): 277.

47. "Greet the New Year with the L.A. Committee for Protection of Foreign Born," *Los Angeles Committee for the Protection of the Foreign Born.* Box 2, Folder 34 American Left Ephemera Collection, 1894–2008, AIS.2007.11, Archives Service Center, University of Pittsburgh.

48. Fundraising appeal letter, Los Angeles Committee for the Protection of the Foreign Born, July 3, 1952. Los Angeles Committee for Protection of Foreign Born Records, collection no. MSS 080, Southern California Library for Social Studies and Research, Los Angeles, California.

49. "Report to American Committee for Protection of Foreign Born Submitted by Delphine Murphy Smith, Executive Secretary, Los Angeles Committee for Protection of Foreign Born, October 1950 n.d. Los Angeles Committee for Protection of Foreign Born Records, collection no. MSS 080, Southern California Library for Social Studies and Research, Los Angeles, California.

50. Jeffrey M. Garcilazo, "McCarthyism, Mexican Americans, and the Los Angeles Committee for Protection of the Foreign-Born, 1950–1954," 286–8.

51. Ibid., 284.

52. Ernesto Galarza, *Merchants of Labor: The Mexican Bracero Story* (Santa Barbara: McNally & Loftin Publishers, 1964), 59.

53. "Our Badge of Infamy: A Petition to the United Nations on the Treatment of the Mexican Immigrant." Pamphlet produced by the American Committee for the Protection of the Foreign Born, New York, April 1959; 5.

54. In 1951, the Communist Party–aligned Civil Rights Congress initiated this approach to the United Nations in their publication of the document "We Charge Genocide," which asserted that the systematic lynching and other forms of Jim Crow violence against black people in the United States constituted a form of genocide.

55. For example, see "South Colorado Site Sought for Wetback Drive," *Greeley Daily Tribune*, April 17, 1954; 9; and "'Wetback Drive' Very Successful," *Tucson Daily Citizen* June 18, 1954; 4.

56. Juan Ramon García, *Operation Wetback: The Mass Deportation of Mexican Undocumented Workers in 1954*, 192.

57. "Our Badge of Infamy: A Petition to the United Nations on the Treatment of the Mexican Immigrant." Pamphlet produced by the American Committee for the Protection of the Foreign Born, New York, April 1959; 34.

58. Juan Ramon García, *Operation Wetback: The Mass Deportation of Mexican Undocumented Workers in 1954*, 123, 143–4.

59. See "Yarborough Blasts Shivers for 'Exploitation' of Wetback Issue," *Lubbock Morning Avalanche*, February 17, 1954; 27.

60. For a full exposition on the failures of the Bracero Program, see Ernesto Galarza, *Merchants of Labor: The Mexican Bracero Story* (Santa Barbara: McNally & Loftin Publishers, 1964).

61. Juan Ramon García, *Operation Wetback: The Mass Deportation of Mexican Undocumented Workers in 1954*, 122.

62. "What Price Wetbacks?" Pamphlet produced by the American G.I. Forum of Texas and the Texas State Federation of Labor, 1953, 6.

63. Cited in Eleanor Hadley, "A Critical Analysis of the Wetback Problem," *Law and Contemporary Problems* 21, no. 2, Immigration (Spring 1956): 335.

64. For example, Tony Salgado was denied a seat at the 1954 Convention of the California State Federation of Labor. See Phillip Taft, *Labor Politics American Style: The California State Federation of Labor* (New York: Oxford University Press, 1968), 202.

65. "Success of 'Operation Wetback' Sparked Subversive Alien Drive," *The San Bernardino County Sun*, July 22, 1955; 6.

66. "Wetback Roundup Cuts Crime, Says Immigration Chief," *El Paso Herald-Post*, July 20, 1955; 13.

67. Jeffrey M. Garcilazo, "McCarthyism, Mexican Americans, and the Los Angeles Committee for Protection of the Foreign-Born, 1950–1954," 291–2.

68. "Our Badge of Infamy: A Petition to the United Nations on the Treatment of the Mexican Immigrant." Pamphlet produced by the American Committee for the Protection of the Foreign Born, New York, April 1959; 35.

69. For example, see "Immigration and Naturalization Service Budget 1975—2003." Department of Justice, 2002. Available online at https://www.justice.gov/archive/jmd/1975_2002/2002/html/page104–108.htm.

70. As a national security doctrine elaborated by then secretary of state George F. Kennan in 1947, containment entailed the "long-term, patient but firm and vigilant containment of Russian expansive tendencies." Containment strategy sought to arrest the spread of Soviet power in two dimensions. "Strongpoint Defense" called for the concentration of military force and power at strategic geopolitical locations abroad where US interests were threatened, and "perimeter defense" called for securing of the "rim of the heartland" from enemy penetration. This latter component of the doctrine was institutionalized throughout the Cold War and influenced national policies in all forms, including border policy. See John Lewis Gaddis, *Strategies of Containment: A Critical Appraisal of Postwar American National Security Policy* (New York: Oxford University Press, 1982), 58–61.

71. Cold War ideology carried over into US funding and support for anticommunist movements in Central America, which became a strategic region during the Cold War in places like Guatemala. In 1954 a US-supported military coup toppled the reformist

government of Jacobo Arbenz. This was due to its alleged socialistic ambitions in pursuing land nationalization at the expense of the US-based United Fruit Company, a multinational corporation that controlled much of that country's arable land. Central American Cold War flashpoints, in the eyes of then president Dwight D. Eisenhower, placed the threat of a "possible Communist outpost on this continent" and within striking distance of America's southern border. This initiated a long period of US interventionism throughout the hemisphere against left-wing Socialist and radical nationalist governments and movements, a practice that persists to the present. For an historical analysis of the coup in Guatemala, see Stephen C. Schlesinger and Stephen Kinzer, *Bitter Fruit: The Story of the American Coup in Guatemala* (Cambridge: Harvard University Press, 2005).

Index

Page numbers in italics refer to illustrations.

About Haymarket Books

Haymarket Books is a radical, independent, nonprofit book publisher based in Chicago.

Our mission is to publish books that contribute to struggles for social and economic justice. We strive to make our books a vibrant and organic part of social movements and the education and development of a critical, engaged, international left.

We take inspiration and courage from our namesakes, the Haymarket martyrs, who gave their lives fighting for a better world. Their 1886 struggle for the eight-hour day—which gave us May Day, the international workers' holiday—reminds workers around the world that ordinary people can organize and struggle for their own liberation. These struggles continue today across the globe—struggles against oppression, exploitation, poverty, and war.

Since our founding in 2001, Haymarket Books has published more than five hundred titles. Radically independent, we seek to drive a wedge into the risk-averse world of corporate book publishing. Our authors include Noam Chomsky, Arundhati Roy, Rebecca Solnit, Angela Y. Davis, Howard Zinn, Amy Goodman, Wallace Shawn, Mike Davis, Winona LaDuke, Ilan Pappé, Richard Wolff, Dave Zirin, Keeanga-Yamahtta Taylor, Nick Turse, Dahr Jamail, David Barsamian, Elizabeth Laird, Amira Hass, Mark Steel, Avi Lewis, Naomi Klein, and Neil Davidson. We are also the trade publishers of the acclaimed Historical Materialism Book Series and of Dispatch Books.